CASES AND MATERIALS ON

CORPORATIONS

INCLUDING PARTNERSHIPS AND LIMITED LIABILITY COMPANIES

Tenth Edition

By

Robert W. Hamilton

Minerva House Drysdale Regents
Chair in Law, Emeritus
The University of Texas at Austin

Jonathan R. Macey

Sam Harris Professor of Corporate Law,
Corporate Finance and Securities Law,
Yale Law School

AMERICAN CASEBOOK SERIES®

Mat # 40603130

American Casebook Series and West Group are trademarks registered in the U.S. Patent and Trademark Office.

COPYRIGHT © 1976, 1981, 1986, 1990, 1994 WEST PUBLISHING CO.
© West, a Thomson business, 1998, 2001, 2003, 2005
© 2007 Thomson/West
      610 Opperman Drive
      P.O. Box 64526
      St. Paul, MN 55164–0526
      1–800–328–9352
Printed in the United States of America

ISBN 978–0–314–18074–2

 TEXT IS PRINTED ON 10% POST CONSUMER RECYCLED PAPER

Preface

This book is designed for introductory courses in the law of business associations or corporations. With a minimum of adjustment it may be used in courses covering anywhere from three to six semester hours. It is not designed for use in advanced courses such as securities regulation, mergers and acquisitions, or corporation finance. While it contains materials on agency and unincorporated business forms, including general partnerships, limited partnerships, and limited liability companies, it is not primarily designed for use in an introductory course devoted exclusively to these topics.

The popularity of unincorporated business forms, particularly the limited liability company and the limited liability partnership, continues to grow. These business forms provide essentially the same protection against personal liability as provided by corporations, and in addition sometimes have advantages over corporations in terms of income tax treatment, cost of formation and operation, and internal flexibility of management.

If one is to provide a rounded and accurate picture of modern business forms today to students in their first business-related law school course, consideration must be given to unincorporated business forms.

We are strongly of the view that the modern law of business associations can be most effectively taught only in the context of a specific set of statutes. The Statutory Supplement contains the full texts of the Uniform Partnership Act (1914), the Revised Uniform Partnership of 1994 (with amendments through 2000), the Uniform Limited Liability Company Act of 1995, and the Model Business Corporation Act of 1984 (with amendments through 2000). The Statutory Supplement also contains the financial provisions of the 1969 Model Business Corporation Act so that the mysteries of par value and legal capital may be explored if the teacher wishes. The Statutory Supplement to the 10th edition also contains the provision of the Delaware General Corporation Law pertaining to the capacity of partners and members of partnerships and LLC's to "opt-out" of their fiduciary duties. These statutes are abbreviated "UPA (1914)", "UPA (1997)", "ULLCA," "MBCA," and "MBCA (1969)" throughout the text.

We encourage students to become familiar with these statutes by the practice of referring to, but not quoting, the relevant provisions of these statutes throughout the casebook. Where significant amendments have been made to statutory provisions, as for example in MBCA § 8.30, the original statutory language is set forth in the casebook itself.

In the preparation of this book, numerous citations and footnotes have been omitted without specification. All footnotes have been renumbered in each chapter, though the original numbering of famous footnotes is referred to where appropriate. In a few instances the location of footnotes taken from original sources have been changed. In order to identify the source of footnotes, the bracketed phrases "[By the Court]" or "[By the Author]" appear at the beginning of footnotes that appear in the original source while footnotes beginning "[By the Editors]" were prepared by the undersigned.

Ellipses ("* * *") may indicate the omission of single words in a paragraph or entire paragraphs.

Finally, we would like to thank Judy Dodson, Professor Hamilton's patient secretary, who prepared the original text of this book. We also want to acknowledge the able research assistance of Allison Harlow, Cornell Law School class of 2001, Jeff Hanson and Rudy Koch, Cornell Law School class of 2003, and Christine Harlow, Cornell Law School class of 2004, Eric Rosenstock, Yale Law School class of 2005, Mark Cho, Sabrina Glaser and Robin Preussell, Yale Law School class of 2006 and Stephanie Biederman and Johanna Spellman, Yale Law School class of 2007, and Zoë Klusman, University of Pennsylvania Law School class of 2009, who performed able research, recorded innumerable changes, ensured consistency of form throughout, and checked galleys and page proofs.

Acknowledgements

Permission to use copyrighted materials is gratefully acknowledged from Albany Law Review, American Business Law Journal, American Business Law Journal, American Enterprise Institute, American Law Institute, Annual Survey of American Law, Arizona Law Review, Brooklyn Law Review, Bureau of National Affairs, Inc., Cardozo Law Review, Case Western Reserve Law Review, Catholic University Law Review, CBIZ Valuation Group, Inc., University of Chicago Law Review, University of Chicago Press, Cincinnati Law Review, Cleveland State Law Review, Columbia Law Review, Cornell Law Review, Delaware Journal of Corporate Law, Directors of the Columbia Law Review, Duke Law Journal, Fordham Law Review, George Mason Law Review, Georgetown Law Journal, Georgia Law Review, The Hartford Courant, Harvard Business School Publishing Corporation, Harvard Law Review, Harvard University Press, University of Illinois Law Review, Journal of Corporate Finance, Journal of Corporation Law, Journal of Small and Emerging Business Law, University of Miami Law Review, University of Michigan Journal of Law Reform, Michigan Law Review, Minnesota Law Review, National Association for Law Placement, National Law Journal, NCUSL, New York Stock Exchange, New York Times, North Carolina Law Review, Oklahoma City University Law Review, Penguin, USA, University of Pennsylvania Law Review, Practical Accountant, Prentice Hall Law and Business, Stanford Law Review, Texas Law Review, Vanderbilt Law Review, Wake Forest Law Review, Wall Street Journal, West Publishing, Wisconsin Law Review, Yale Law Journal, Barbara Aldave, Chancellor William T. Allen, Norwood P. Beveridge, Bernard S. Black, Margaret M. Blair, Dennis J. Block, Richard A. Booth, Douglas M. Branson, James R. Burkhard, William J. Carney, Pat K. Chew, John C. Coffee, Jr., Frank H. Easterbrook, Melvin A. Eisenberg, Richard A. Epstein, Edward A. Fallone, Allen Ferrell, Daniel R. Fischel, Geoffrey D. Genz, David D. Haddock, Susan Pace Hamill, James J. Hanks, Jr., Charles Hansen, Henry Hansmann, Harry J. Haynsworth, Allan Ickowitz, Dennis S. Karjala, Edmund W. Kitch, Richard H. Koppes, Reinier Kraakman, Jake Krocheski, James G. Leyden, Jr., Bayless Manning, Lawrence E. Mitchell, Joseph P. Monteleone, Stephen Norman, Adam C. Pritchard, Larry E. Ribstein, Roberta Romano, G. Santangelo, A. A. Sommer, Jr., Lynn A. Stout, E. Norman Veasey.

ROBERT W. HAMILTON
JONATHAN R. MACEY

Summary of Contents

*

Table of Contents

Page

*

Table of Cases

The principal cases are in bold type. Cases cited or discussed in the text are roman type. References are to pages. Cases cited in principal cases and within other quoted materials are not included.

CASES AND MATERIALS ON
CORPORATIONS
INCLUDING PARTNERSHIPS AND LIMITED LIABILITY COMPANIES

Tenth Edition

*

Chapter One

INTRODUCTION

A. THE SUBJECT IN GENERAL

The subject of this book is the means and devices by which business in the United States is conducted either by a single individual or cooperatively by a few or many individuals. "Business" is a broad term describing all kinds of profit-making activity. As so defined, the subject covers an extremely broad range of activities. At one extreme is the summer lemonade stand opened for one afternoon by a twelve-year-old. At the other is the Wal–Mart Corporation, which in 2006 had net sales of $312.4 billion and net income of $11.2 billion, with more than 6700 stores in 14 countries and 1.8 million employees.

This subject may be broken down in different ways for analysis and classification. A very traditional classification is by legal form. The lemonade stand is an example of a *sole proprietorship*, a business owned by a single person. Wal–Mart is a *corporation*. Other traditional forms of business are the *general partnership* and the *limited partnership*. In the 1990s, new forms of business were created with names confusingly similar to the limited partnership: the *limited liability company,* the *limited liability partnership,* and in some states, the *limited liability limited partnership*. While the names are similar, one should not be misled into thinking that the differences between these new business forms are insignificant. These new business forms are introduced in this chapter and discussed in detail in chapters 2, 3, and 4.

Classification by business form naturally breaks into two categories: (1) *corporations* and (2) *unincorporated associations*, e.g., proprietorships, partnerships, limited partnerships, etc.

A different method of classification, and the one basically followed in this book, is to divide business firms on the basis of whether they are *closely held*, that is, whether they have one or a few owners, or *publicly held*, with hundreds or thousands of owners. The fundamental dividing line between "closely held" and "publicly held" is not some arbitrary number of owners but whether a public market exists for ownership interests in the business.[1] A major advantage of this approach is that it permits a comparative examination of alternative business forms for closely held firms.

---

1. [By the Editors] Useful guidelines for this distinction are whether the firm has registered the sale of an issue of securities under the Securities Act of 1933, 15 U.S.C. § 77a, et seq., or whether it is itself required to register under the Securities Exchange Act of 1934, 15 U.S.C. § 78(a), et seq. These federal statutes are discussed in Chapters 8, 10 and 13.

Unincorporated firms are usually closely held. The new business forms developed in the 1990s currently are suitable only for firms that do not have publicly traded securities, although many closely held firms elect to be corporations. On the other hand, virtually all publicly held firms are corporations, and the problems of management, control, finance, and public regulation and oversight, as well as legal requirements specifically imposed on them, have little in common with closely held firms. However, closely held firms that are organized as corporations are similar in formal respects to publicly held corporations.

The closely held/publicly held classification does have disadvantages: It ignores the fact that in the real world there is a continuum of business size, complexity, and ownership, and it treats the world of business as polar rather than continuous. There are many corporations that are "publicly held" under the test described above even though they have many of the characteristics of closely held firms. Also, this classification tends to hide the fact that closely and publicly held firms draw from a common reservoir of principles and tradition, particularly with respect to the use of the corporate form, and each therefore to some extent influences the other.

Developments during the last two decades have greatly increased the attractiveness of unincorporated forms for closely held firms. The most important developments are (1) the creation of new unincorporated business forms that grant the advantage of limited liability for all owners of the business, and (2) changes in the regulations promulgated under the Internal Revenue Code that give unincorporated firms and their owners considerable freedom in electing how their income is to be taxed. The net result undoubtedly is to encourage firms with a few owners to use unincorporated business forms.

Trends in the modern law of business associations can be understood only if one has passing familiarity with the modern federal income tax structure. Chapter Three of this casebook includes a basic introduction to this subject.

B. THE STATUTES

Unlike subjects such as property and torts, the subject of business associations is largely governed by statute. This is true not only in the large commercial states such as California, New York, and Texas, but in the smaller states as well. Answers to many questions must be found in the statutes and cannot be answered solely on the basis of common sense or prior judicial decision. In this respect, the law of business associations is similar to many other areas of law in the modern commercial and government-oriented society.

An experienced attorney does not attempt to memorize the detailed provisions of the numerous complex statutes or regulations with which he or she must be familiar. Rather, the attorney becomes generally familiar with the provisions and keeps copies of them available for easy reference. Each student should follow approximately the same process. Accordingly, the materials that follow refer to but do not quote the basic statutory materials.[2]

2. [By the Editors] This statement refers to the basic statutory codification of the model and uniform statutes set forth in the Supplement. Relevant federal statutes and individual

Statutory references should be looked up in the Supplement, since the materials cannot be fully understood without doing so.

The Supplement to this book contains the text of the following statutes:

(1) The Uniform Partnership Act (1914) ["UPA (1914)"];

(2) The Uniform Partnership Act (1997) ["UPA (1997)"];[3]

(3) The Uniform Limited Liability Company Act of 1996 ["ULLCA"];

(4) The Model Business Corporation Act as amended through December, 31, 2002 [MBCA];[4] and

(5) The financial provisions of the Model Business Corporation Act of 1969 [MBCA (1969)].[5]

This book may be used either with the uniform and model statutes in the Supplement or with the statutes of a particular state. If the latter are assigned, it will be necessary to master the numeration of the specific statutes and to locate the most analogous provisions to the model or uniform statutes cited in the following materials.

Federal statutes and regulations relating to both publicly held and closely held corporations or firms appear in the text of the casebook itself.

The statutes in most jurisdictions today are modern and drawn from the common core of the model and uniform statutes. However, one should not assume that statutes always clarify and simplify. In specific circumstances, statutory language may appear to require an unjust or unreasonable result. This is more likely to be true in jurisdictions that have not drawn from the common core of the model and uniform statutes, but it is also true in some circumstances under these statutes as well.

C. THE ROLE OF AGENCY LAW IN BUSINESS ASSOCIATIONS

Many problems that arise in connection with business associations involve agency principles. Therefore, exposure to basic agency principles in the basic business course is essential for an understanding of personal relationships within the business context.

statutes of specific states discussed in the text that differ from the uniform or model statutes in the Supplement are quoted in the casebook itself.

3. [By the Editors] This statute is based closely on the "Revised Uniform Partnership Act" that was promulgated in 1994. In some academic commentary, this statute continues to be referred to as "RUPA." See Donald J. Weidner and John W. Larson, The Revised Uniform Partnership Act: The Reporters' Overview, 49 Bus. Law. 1 (1993).

4. [By the Editors] Following the major revision of this statute in 1984, it was briefly referred to as the "Revised Model Business Corporation Act" (or "RMBCA") and then renamed the "Model Business Corporation Act

(1984)." It may continue to be referred to as the RMBCA in some academic literature. The date of 1984 has been dropped because of the numerous amendments that have been made to the Model Act since 1984.

5. [By the Editors] Earlier versions of the Model Business Corporation Act are referred to by following "MBCA" with the date of the edition, e.g. "MBCA (1950)."

The Supplement briefly describes the background of each of these statutes and gives an indication of the extent of uniformity actually achieved by them. In the Sixth and earlier versions of this Supplement, the Uniform Limited Partnership Act was included; the reason for omission of this statute is discussed, infra, p. 10–13.

RESTATEMENT OF THE LAW THIRD—AGENCY[6]

§ 1.01 Agency Defined

Agency is the fiduciary relationship that arises when one person (a "principal") manifests assent to another person (an "agent") that the agent shall act on the principal's behalf and subject to the principal's control, and the agent manifests assent or otherwise consents so to act.

§ 1.02 Parties' Labeling and Popular Usage Not Controlling

An agency relationship arises only when the elements stated in § 1.01 are present. Whether a relationship is characterized as agency in an agreement between parties or in the context of industry or popular usage is not controlling.

§ 1.03 Manifestation

A person manifests assent or intention through written or spoken words or other conduct.

§ 1.04 Terminology

(1) *Co-agents.* Co-agents have agency relationships with the same principal. A co-agent may be appointed by the principal or by another agent actually or apparently authorized by the principal to do so.

(2) *Disclosed, undisclosed, and unidentified principals.*

(a) *Disclosed principal.* A principal is disclosed if, when an agent and a third party interact, the third party has notice that the agent is acting for a principal and has notice of the principal's identity.

(b) *Undisclosed principal.* A principal is undisclosed if, when an agent and a third party interact, the third party has no notice that the agent is acting for a principal.

(c) *Unidentified principal.* A principal is unidentified if, when an agent and a third party interact, the third party has notice that the agent is acting for a principal but does not have notice of the principal's identity.

(3) *Dual agent; joint principals.* A dual agent acts on behalf of more than one principal with regard to the same transaction. Such principals are joint principals.

* * *

(5) *Notice.* A person has notice of a fact if the person knows the fact, has reason to know the fact, has received an effective notification of the fact, or should know the fact to fulfill a duty owed to another person. Notice of a fact that an agent knows or has reason to know is imputed to the principal as stated in §§ 5.03 and 5.04. A notification given to an agent is effective as notice to the principal as stated in § 5.02(1).

(6) *Person.* A person is (a) an individual; (b) an organization or association that has legal capacity to possess rights and incur obligations; (c) a government, political subdivision, or instrumentality or entity created by government; or (d) any other entity that has legal capacity to possess rights and incur obligations.

* * *

§ 2.01 Actual Authority

An agent acts with actual authority when, at the time of taking action that has legal consequences for the principal, the agent reasonably believes, in accordance with the principal's manifestations to the agent, that the principal wishes the agent so to act.

§ 2.02 Scope of Actual Authority

(1) An agent has actual authority to take action designated or implied in the principal's manifestations and acts necessary or incidental to achieving the principal's objectives, as the agent reasonably understands them when the agent determines how to act.

(2) An agent's interpretation of the principal's manifestations is reasonable if it reflects any meaning known by the agent to be ascribed by the principal and, in the absence of any meaning known to the agent, as a reasonable person in the agent's position would interpret the manifestations in light of the context, including circumstances of which the agent has notice and the agent's fiduciary duty to the principal.

(3) An agent's understanding of the principal's objectives is reasonable if it accords with the principal's manifestations and the inferences that a reasonable person in the agent's position would draw from the circumstances creating the agency.

* * *

§ 2.03 Apparent Authority

Apparent authority is the power held by an agent or other actor to affect a principal's legal relations with third parties when a third party reasonably believes the actor has authority to act on behalf of the principal and that belief is traceable to the principal's manifestations.

§ 2.04 Respondeat Superior

An employer is liable for torts committed by employees while acting in the scope of their employment.

§ 2.05 Estoppel to Deny Existence of Agency Relationship

A person who has not made a manifestation that an actor has authority as an agent and who is not otherwise liable as a party to a transaction purportedly done by the actor on that person's account is liable to a third party who justifiably is induced to make a detrimental change in position because the transaction is believed to be on the person's account, if

(1) the person intentionally or carelessly caused such belief, or

(2) having notice of such belief and that it might induce others to change their positions, the person did not take reasonable steps to notify them of the facts.

§ 2.06 Estoppel of Undisclosed Principal

An undisclosed principal may not rely on instructions given an agent that qualify or reduce the agent's authority to less than the authority a third party would reasonably believe the agent to have under the same circumstances if the principal had been disclosed.

§ 2.07 Restitution of Benefit

A principal who is unjustly enriched by the action of an agent or a person who appears to be an agent must make restitution.[7]

§ 3.10 Manifestation Terminating Actual Authority

(1) Notwithstanding any agreement between principal and agent, an agent's actual authority terminates if the agent renounces it by a manifestation to the principal, or if the principal revokes the agent's actual authority by a manifestation to the agent. A revocation or a renunciation is effective when the other party has notice of it. * * *

§ 3.11 Termination of Apparent Authority

(1) The termination of actual authority does not by itself end any apparent authority held by the agent.

(2) Apparent authority ends when it is no longer reasonable for the third party with whom the agent deals to believe that the agent continues to act with actual authority.

Note

Among the more visible changes made by Tentative Draft No. 1 is the modernization of language. Earlier Restatements defined a "master" to be "a principal who employs an agent to perform service in his affairs and who controls or has the right to control the physical conduct of the other in the performance of the service" and a "servant" to be "an agent employed by a master to perform service in his affairs whose physical conduct in the performance of the service is controlled or is subject to the right to control by the master." References to "masters" and "servants" inevitably brings to mind domestic or household employees; the Tentative Draft uses "employer" and "employee." Also, to eliminate gendered terms, "workmen" is replaced by "workers."

* * *

With this background (and the aid of the statutes in the Statutory Supplement), consider the following simple situation:

---

7. [By the Reporter] Illustration: A is the head of procurement for P, a subdivision of the federal government. A's superiors within P have limited A's authority to purchase goods to a specified dollar amount. A contracts with T to buy goods in an amount that exceeds the limit imposed on A. T delivers the goods and all are put to use within P. T has a claim in restitution against P.

Problem

A and B are planning to go into the business of selling computer software. A will invest $100,000 while B will make no cash contributions but will operate the store and maintain the store's website on a day-to-day basis. A desires first, assurance that he will not be called upon to increase his investment and second, a veto power over basic decisions made by B in order to protect his investment. Profits are to be divided equally after B is paid a "salary" of $5,000 per month. The name of the new business is to be called the "AB Software Store." After some discussion and without consulting a lawyer, A and B shake hands on the deal, A gives B a check for $100,000, and B proceeds to obtain a domain name, rent a store, buy computer equipment and software to sell and commence business.

Questions

(1) In this relationship, can B be considered an "employee" and A his "employer?" What elements present in the relationship between A and B are missing in the usual relationship between employer and employee? For example, assume that B has operated the AB Software Store for a few months and A drops by to see how things are going. A is unhappy about the design of the webpage, the layout of the store, and the way the software is displayed. He orders B to make changes. Can B simply say, "No, I like things this way?" Can A then fire B for insubordination?

(2) In this relationship, can B be considered an "agent" and A his "principal?" If B is not A's agent, can B be viewed as an "independent contractor?" Section 2(3) of the 1958 Restatement states that an independent contractor "may or may not be an agent." Is that helpful?

(3) Is the relationship between A and B that of creditor and debtor? Did A lend B $100,000? Is there, for example, a promise to repay and a repayment date (the two most obvious aspects of a loan)? Most loan transactions also involve the payment of interest by the borrower. However, the parties can agree to an interest-free loan if they so desire. Many intra-family loans are made on an interest-free basis.

(4) Did A and B create a partnership? Consider UPA (1914) §§ 6(1), 7; UPA (1997) § 202(c)(3). If so, when they shook hands on their relationship did A and B inadvertently create a new "legal person" that is in some sense different from either A or B? See UPA (1997) § 201(a). Are A and B both agents of that legal person? Does it matter that neither A nor B may have been aware that they were creating a partnership or that A does not expect to be active in the business?

(5) Is the agreement that A will not be called upon to increase his investment consistent with a general partnership? See UPA (1914) § 15; UPA (1997) § 306. What about the provision that A is to have veto power over "basic decisions?" See UPA (1914) § 18; UPA (1997) § 103.

(6) When one is starting a new business, it is natural to assume that the business will be profitable. That was the case with A and B, who agreed to a division of the profits but did not consider that the software store might fail. Assuming that a partnership relation exists, what happens if B spends the $100,000 but the business never becomes profitable and A and B decide to close it down, leaving $30,000 in debts outstanding? If A and B are both solvent, who will have to discharge these debts? Assuming that B is without assets, is A liable for the entire $30,000? See UPA (1914) § 18(a); UPA (1997) § 306(a).

(7) Assume that after a few months, B decides that it is necessary to hire a third person, C, to assist him in running the store and maintaining the website. One of C's principal duties is to be the salesperson in charge of operations when B cannot be present. C also is to be a software installer, truck driver, and so forth. C is paid a weekly salary. Is C a partner? An agent? An employee? Is there any difference? Assuming that he is an agent, who is his principal? A? B? The AB Software Store? See particularly, UPA (1997) § 201.[8]

(8) The scope of C's actual or apparent authority as an employee is obviously critical in answering these questions. Usually the authority of an employee in a simple organization such as the AB Software Store will be reasonably clear or can be made reasonably clear with minimal effort. When the organization is a large artificial entity, however, there may be considerable uncertainty about the precise scope of authority of senior employees.

D. INTRODUCTION TO BUSINESS FORMS

Before the proliferation of new business forms during the last two decades, a two-person business such as the AB Software Store could be formed only as a general partnership, a limited partnership, or a corporation. The most significant, defining difference between these three traditional business forms is the scope of liability of A and B as individuals for the debts and obligations of the business.

1. THE PROPRIETORSHIP

A business owned by a single individual is called a sole proprietorship. The owner of a proprietorship is personally liable for all business obligations since there is no legal separation between the owner and the business. The risks that accompany a sole proprietorship tend to grow as the business grows, but the owner can minimize his personal exposure by transferring the business to a wholly owned corporation or limited liability company. This may be done simply by creating the new entity and transferring the business to it. The former owner's role then changes: He becomes a director, shareholder, and officer of the corporation or the manager of the LLC. In that way, it is unlikely that the proprietor's personal assets will be available to creditors whose claims arise after the transfer takes place. The former owner, however, remains personally liable for claims arising or liabilities created before the transfer to the new entity.

2. THE GENERAL PARTNERSHIP

The general partnership is the default form for businesses that are owned by more than one person. If two or more persons create a co-owned business without any explicit agreement about their relationship, then a partnership is formed. Co-ownership, further, need not be expressly created. An oral agree-

---

8. [By the Editors] It may be noted that UPA (1914) does not contain a provision similar to UPA (1997) § 201. Earlier this century, most courts viewed a partnership as an aggregate of the individual partners and not as an entity in its own right. However, recent cases arising under the 1914 Act generally view the partnership as a separate entity from its members. Admittedly, at first blush, it may be difficult to conceptualize an informal, hand-shake partnership such as the AB Software Store as an entity distinct from the individual partners. However, if one examines carefully the provisions of UPA (1914) it is apparent that there are many entity concepts embodied in that statute. See e.g. UPA (1914) § 18(b) [*"the partnership* must indemnify *every partner"*]; § 9(1) [each partner is an "agent of *the partnership"*].

ment to share profits may be sufficient to establish the existence of a general partnership even though initial financial contributions are unequal. Of course, many general partnerships are carefully-planned, formal affairs with a professionally-drafted written partnership agreement detailing most aspects of the relationship, but the business form does not require this formality.

Consider any of the liability scenarios described above in connection with the AB Software Store. Assume for the moment that you represent a person with a large potential claim against the Store. Who do you sue? A? B? The AB Software Store? All three of them? If B is judgment proof, and the assets of the AB Software Store are inconsequential, can you simply sue A?

For answers to these questions, consider again UPA (1914) § 15; UPA (1997) §§ 201, 306, 307. Is it clear that A, a general partner, is liable to the injured customer, the defrauded buyer, or the unpaid general creditor even though (1) he was not involved in any of the actions that gave rise to liability, and (2) he received little or no direct personal benefit or enrichment from any of them? By following appropriate procedures a plaintiff with a significant claim against the AB Software Store may recover from A's personal assets without limitation. What about B's promise that A will not be called upon to increase his investment in the business? Does that promise limit B's exposure to liability? If not, what does it do?

A general partnership is also fragile. Under the 1914 Act, a partner may dissolve it at any time simply by a statement of his or her express will. UPA (1914) § 31. Although the 1997 Act is considerably more complicated than its predecessor, it allows a partner to leave the partnership at any time ("dissociation" is the modern statutory term used; see UPA (1997) §§ 601–807).

Disputes among partners may be resolved by dissolution or dissociation if all else fails.

3. THE LIMITED LIABILITY PARTNERSHIP ("LLP")

Part D of Chapter Two discusses a modern variation of the general partnership, the "limited liability partnership" or "LLP." An LLP is a general partnership in all respects except that by statute the partners have no personal liability for obligations that exceed the assets of the general partnership. There is an exception: partners in an LLP have full personal liability for claims arising from their own misconduct. The LLP has been particularly popular with law and accounting firms, but has not been widely used by commercial businesses. See UPA (1997) §§ 1001–1003, 306(c), 101(5).

The LLP is a recent innovation, and the "shield of limited liability" it provides has not been directly tested as of 2006. However, fallen accounting firm Arthur Andersen operated in the LLP form, and the numerous claims pending against its individual members will likely challenge this shield.

4.   THE TRADITIONAL LIMITED PARTNERSHIP

ROBERT W. HAMILTON, BUSINESS ORGANIZATIONS: UNINCORPORATED BUSINESSES AND CLOSELY HELD CORPORATIONS (1997)
Pages 102–104 (1997).

* * * The history of limited partnerships may be traced back to medieval Europe where a *society comandita* was developed primarily to permit the nobility and the Church to quietly invest their wealth in mercantile enterprises. In England and the United States, limited partnerships were first authorized by statute in the late Nineteenth and early Twentieth centuries. Today, the limited partnership form of business is exclusively a creature of statute; in the absence of statute (or the failure to comply with the mandatory provisions of the applicable statute), all partners are general partners no matter what their private understanding is or how they are designated in the partnership agreement or held out to the public. Thus, there is no general common law of limited partnerships as there is a common law of general partnerships, and limited partnerships are not a default form of business.

During most of the Twentieth Century the law of limited partnership [in the United States] was based on the Uniform Limited Partnership Act of 1916,[9] which, like the Uniform Partnership Act of 1914, achieved virtually universal acceptance. * * * There are internal indications that ULPA (1916) was prepared on the assumption that the traditional limited partnership was a small local business that desired to raise capital from local risk-adverse investors.[10] What comes to mind is a local hardware store in a small town with two general partners and two or three limited partners, perhaps bankers or other persons of substance in the community, who are willing to invest the necessary capital for the hardware store to operate in exchange for a share of its profits but who are unwilling to assume the risk of personal liability for the hardware store's debts. A major emphasis of ULPA (1916) was to ensure that creditors of the hardware store not be misled as to who was responsible for partnership obligations.[11]

Notes

(1) Section 201(b) of the 1976 Limited Partnership Act provides that "a limited partnership is formed at the time of the filing of the certificate of limited partnership * * *." What if the person with responsibility to make this filing is over-anxious and business commences before the certificate is filed? What if the

---

9. [By the Editors] The 1916 Act is abbreviated here as "ULPA (1916)."

10. [By the Author] For example, ULPA makes no reference at all to the possibility that a limited partnership might conduct a business in more than one state.

11. [By the Author] * * * ULPA (1916) prohibited limited partners from providing services as their capital contribution to the limited partnership, prohibited the limited partnership from adopting a name that included the

name of a limited partner, and provided that a limited partner who participated in the conduct of the business became a general partner. Many states adopting this older statute provided that limited partnership certificates had to be filed in the county or city in which the limited partnership conducted its business. Multiple filings in each locality in which the limited partnership conducted business might be required. Also, no provision was made for the possibility that a limited partnership might engage in business in more than one state.

filing is ineffective because the document is filed in the wrong county? Or because it contains a minor technical defect and the filing authority refuses to file it? While filing is usually a simple formality, any mistake or delay creates serious risk that all partners are general partners and no limited partnership was created. Depending on the language of the statute, a person who inadvertently becomes a general partner in this way may avoid liability either by causing an appropriate certificate of limited partnership to be filed or by filing a certificate withdrawing from future equity participation in the enterprise.[12] See Continental Waste System, Inc. v. Zoso Partners, 727 F.Supp. 1143 (N.D. Ill.1989).

(2) At first blush, the limited partnership may seem to be an ideal business form for small businesses such as the AB Software Store enterprise. For example, A might be the limited partner and B the general partner. Undoubtedly many small businesses were created in this fashion in the past, but the limited partnership was rarely the business form selected by sophisticated attorneys. The basic problem was that A, the capital-contributing limited partner, could lose his shield of limited liability in the manner described below, and inadvertently become a general partner with full liability for all partnership obligations.

(3) Section 7 of ULPA (1916) provided, "A limited partner shall not become liable as a general partner unless, in addition to the exercise of his rights and powers as a limited partner, he takes part in the control of the business." So suppose B incurs debts and as a result the AB Software Store faces the risk of collapse and bankruptcy. A, the limited partner, then faces the unpleasant choice of (a) intervening in the business in an effort to save it, thereby taking part in the control of the business and becoming personally liable for all of the Software Store's obligations, or (b) remaining on the sideline, quietly watching the business and his $100,000 investment go down the drain. Under ULPA § 7, does A's mere possession of the power to veto important decisions constitute taking part in the control of the business? What if A exercises this veto power only once or twice?

(4) In an effort to make the limited partnership more attractive and less of a trap for the unwary partner, the present version of the Uniform Limited Partnership Act amended these rules. ULPA (1976) § 303 now provides:

(a) Except as provided in subsection (d), a limited partner is not liable for the obligations of a limited partnership unless he is also a general partner or, in addition to the exercise of his rights and powers as a limited partner, he participates in the control of the business. However, if the limited partner participates in the control of the business, he is liable only to persons who transact business with the limited partnership reasonably believing, based upon the limited partner's conduct, that the limited partner is a general partner. * * *

(d) A limited partner who knowingly permits his name to be used in the name of the limited partnership * * * is liable to creditors who extend credit to the limited partnership without actual knowledge that the limited partner is not a general partner.

Under the second sentence of § 303(a), can a partner participate in the business of the limited partnership and yet avoid liability by wearing a T-shirt that prominently says "I am only a limited partner; don't rely on me!"?

---

12. [By the Editors] Uniform Limited Partnership Act (1976) with the 1985 Amendments, § 304, provides that the certificate must be filed "on ascertaining the mistake."

5. THE LIMITED PARTNERSHIP WITH A CORPORATE GENERAL PARTNER

While the limited partnership is a traditional business form, it has evolved in the modern era. The most important change involves the use of a corporation as the sole general partner of a limited partnership. Courts have not only accepted this novel combination of business forms but have also permitted individuals and entities to be limited partners even though they are also officers, directors, or shareholders of the corporate general partner. If the corporate general partner has nominal assets, the limited partnership becomes a de facto limited liability entity that is similar to a corporation.

The limited partnership with a corporate general partner is adaptable to both publicly held and closely held enterprises. Many publicly held limited partnerships of this type have been created. There may be hundreds or thousands of limited partners, and an active market may exist for limited partnership interests. However, federal income tax laws now require limited partnerships with publicly traded ownership interests to be taxed as corporations.

A limited liability company may be substituted for the corporation in this business form.

6. THE LIMITED LIABILITY LIMITED PARTNERSHIP

Slightly fewer than half of the states have enacted legislation to create a new variation on the limited partnership, a "limited liability limited partnership," or "LLLP." An LLLP is a limited partnership with both general and limited partners, but the general partners have the protection of the LLP election.[13]

For tax reasons, publicly held limited partnerships and LLLPs are now used in only certain relatively narrow situations.

7. LIMITED LIABILITY COMPANIES ("LLCS")

As described in chapter 4, the limited liability company (or "LLC") is a relatively new business form. It provides limited liability for all participants, whether or not they are active in the management of the business, and permits total flexibility in internal management. In short, it provides the benefits of incorporation without the limitations and rules applied to corporations. The first LLC statute was enacted in Wyoming in 1977. Its survival depended on obtaining a favorable ruling from the Internal Revenue Service that the LLC was eligible for partnership taxation despite the fact that no participant was personally liable for firm obligations. On September 2, 1988, the IRS approved of the LLC. Rev.Rul. 88–76. By 1996, all 50 states had adopted such statutes. See Susan Pace Hamill, The Origins Behind the

---

13. [By the Editors] General partners with LLP protection may take part in the control of the business while limited partners usually have no right to participate. Neither type of partner has personal responsibility for debts of the limited partnership. One troublesome aspect of LLLPs is that it is quite possible that a limited partner may participate in control of the business in some minor way and therefore become liable for all partnership obligations, but a general partner who takes part extensively in control of the business is apparently fully protected against liability by the LLLP election. In other words, in an LLLP, limited partners may have narrower shields against liability than general partners. Problems of this type appear to be so intractable that NCCUSL in 1997 began the development of a revised ULPA (1976) initially called ReRulpa and now named RULPA (2001).

Limited Liability Company, 59 Ohio St.L.J. 1459 (1998). The use of the LLC form has increased exponentially since the 1990s.

Assume that A and B decide to form a limited liability company for their software enterprise. See ULLCA § 112. Like a traditional limited partnership or a corporation, an LLC is formed by filing a document with a state official. See ULLCA §§ 202, 203. Should the "AB Software Store, LLC" be "member managed" (limited liability, operated like a partnership) or "manager managed" (limited liability, operated like a corporation)? See ULLCA §§ 203(a)(6), 301, 404.

Studies indicate that the LLC is primarily replacing general and limited partnerships, and closely held partnerships to a much lesser extent. The LLC also can be used to hold non-business assets, such as a family mountain cabin or beach-front property, in a spendthrift trust type relationship. See Chapter 4.

Notes

(1) Why has the American legal system recently felt compelled to develop new business forms? Aren't they overlapping, repetitious, and redundant? Here are some possible explanations:

(a) The proliferation of overlapping business forms is a recent development. The full impact of these developments on older business is still taking place. It is not clear that all of the business forms described in this chapter will be in use a decade or two from now.

(b) The development of new unincorporated business forms reflects significant dissatisfaction with the limited choices provided by traditional business forms. Aspects of this dissatisfaction are discussed in Chapter 3; they arise in a variety of different areas: application of federal income tax rules, state income and franchise tax rules, state filing fees, differences in managerial rules applicable to various business forms, unlimited personal liability, and the ethical rules that states impose on lawyers, physicians, and other professionals. Also contributing are tax and accounting rules that have traditionally made it difficult and expensive to convert an ongoing business from one business form to another.

(2) There is a great deal of law relating to closely held corporations that might apply by analogy to unincorporated business forms, particularly those laws that (a) provide limited liability for all owners and (b) centralize the power to manage in specific individuals. The best-known example is the "piercing the corporate veil" doctrine discussed in Chapter 7. In deciding whether to pierce the "shield of limited liability" and hold the partners responsible, courts have looked to corporate law governing "piercing the veil." See Ditty v. CheckRite, Ltd., Inc., 973 F.Supp. 1320 (D. Utah 1997); Filo Am., Inc. v. Olhoss Trading Co., L.L.C., 321 F.Supp.2d 1266 (M.D. Ala. 2004). Another important doctrine, discussed in Chapter 9, imposes fiduciary duties on controlling shareholders who act in a way that the court perceives as unfair to minority interests.

8. THE CORPORATION

With the AB Software Store, can A obtain the structure he desires through the device of a corporation? The answer is clearly "yes," though there may be disadvantages in two areas: (1) federal income taxation, and (2) mandatory procedural requirements that may increase the cost of operation.

A corporation is formed by following the relatively simple procedures set forth in the corporation statute. See MBCA §§ 2.01–2.03, 2.05. Section 2.03 states that the "corporate existence" begins upon the filing of articles of incorporation.[14] This phrase recognizes the long-accepted theory that incorporation results in the creation of a new legal entity, a fictitious person with sole responsibility for its own obligations. Unlike general or limited partnerships, a corporation provides limited liability for all investors and participants, whether active or passive.

The notion that a corporation is an entity independent of its shareholders is deeply ingrained. The corporate business is conducted in the corporation's name. The corporation itself enters into contracts, borrows money, sues and may be sued in its own name, and otherwise conducts its business much as though it were a real person. It may own real estate in its own name free and clear of claims of the creditors of shareholders. However, the assets of the corporation are subject to seizure by corporate creditors and the shares of stock of the corporation are subject to seizure by personal creditors of A and B.

A useful classification of corporations is between "closely held" and "publicly held." "Publicly held" means that the corporation has shares that are traded on public securities markets subject to federal regulation. Virtually all publicly held businesses are conducted in corporate form.[15] Corporations that do not have publicly traded shares are described as "closely held."

In economic terms, the corporation dwarfs in importance many times over all other business forms combined.

Notes

(1) Theoretically, a corporation consists of three layers or tiers: (1) the shareholders who are traditionally viewed as the ultimate owners of the enterprise, (2) the board of directors, composed of the managers of the corporation's affairs (see MBCA § 8.01(b)), and (3) the officers, who act for the corporation to implement the decisions of the directors (see MBCA § 8.41). A single individual may simultaneously act as an officer, a director, and a shareholder. In the AB Software Store, Inc., A and B could each own 50 percent of the shares and be the sole directors of the corporation.[16] In addition, A may be president of the corporation with power to approve or disapprove all expenditures, while B may be vice president, secretary, "general manager," and whatever other office the parties desire to create. In this way, profits may be shared in the form of dividends and/or salary while A has the veto power he desires.

(2) Only the corporation is liable for corporate obligations. However, in a closely held corporation, it is relatively easy for a director, officer or shareholder to

---

14. [By the Editors] As in the case of limited partnerships, a premature commencement of business by a "corporation" before its articles of incorporation are filed might create personal liability on the part of corporate shareholders, directors, or officers. This issue is discussed in Chapter 6.

15. [By the Editors] The other principal business form for publicly held businesses is the real estate investment trust or "REIT."

16. [By the Editors] If this ownership structure is adopted, the inequality of initial contributions would have to be addressed in some manner. The simplest solution would be for A to loan the AB Software Store, Inc., $100,000 for the working capital, and issue shares to A and B in equal amounts for a nominal price. On dissolution of the corporation (assuming its operation was successful) A would first receive back his initial contribution before any liquidating distributions could be made on account of the shares of stock.

incur personal liability. If, for example, B engages in fraudulent or negligent conduct he will become personally liable to third persons who are injured by that conduct even though he is a director, officer, or shareholder. He is himself a tortfeasor and both he and the corporation are liable for the injury caused. In addition, sophisticated creditors understand the concept of limited liability in small corporations or other entities. For example, a supplier of inventory for the AB Software Store, Inc. or the AB Software Store, LLC might well refuse to extend credit to the corporation or LLC unless A personally guarantees the payment of all debts owed to the supplier.

(3) If B does not engage in negligent or fraudulent conduct but simply is an ineffective manager of the business and as a result the corporation or LLC ultimately fails, usually neither A nor B will be personally liable for the losses that may be suffered by creditors. There is, however, a well-established principle in corporation law, called "piercing the corporate veil," that permits creditors of closely held corporations in limited circumstances to recover directly from directors, officers, or shareholders.

(4) Even though a corporation appears to "solve" most liability problems, it may not be the most desirable business form for a small business in terms of income taxation, internal decision-making, mandatory formalities, and long term planning. An LLC may be an attractive alternative.

* * *

The "true nature" of a corporation has been the subject of a great deal of modern academic debate. Historically, a corporation has been treated as an entity separate and distinct from its owners for centuries. In England, this concept long antedates the development of limited liability for shareholders, which occurred in the middle of the nineteenth century.[17] It is a short step from the acceptance of the corporation as an "entity" in its own right to its further reification as an "artificial person," with many of the rights, privileges, and constitutional protections of individuals. As described by former Supreme Court Justice Sandra Day O'Connor:

> In the words of Chief Justice Marshall, a corporation is "an artificial being, invisible, intangible, and existing only in contemplation of law." Dartmouth College v. Woodward, 4 Wheat. 518, 636, 4 L.Ed. 629 (1819). As such, it is not entitled to "'purely personal' guarantees" whose "'historic function' * * * has been limited to the protection of individuals." First National Bank of Boston v. Bellotti, 435 U.S. 765, 779, n. 14, 98 S.Ct. 1407, 1417, n. 14, 55 L.Ed.2d 707 (1978). Thus, a corporation has no Fifth Amendment privilege against self-incrimination or right of privacy. On the other hand, a corporation has a First Amendment right to freedom of speech and cannot have its property taken without just compensation. A corporation is also protected from unreasonable searches and seizures, and can plead former jeopardy as a bar to a prosecution. Furthermore, a corporation is entitled to due process, and equal protection, of law.

> Whether a particular constitutional guarantee applies to corporations "depends on the nature, history, and purpose" of the guarantee. First National Bank, 435 U.S., at 779, n. 14, 98 S.Ct., at 1417, n. 14. * * *[18]

---

17. Consult Phillip I. Blumberg, The Law of Corporate Groups: Procedural Law 1–2 (1983).

18. See also Elizabeth S. Warren, The Case for Applying the Eighth Amendment to Corporations, 49 Vand.L.Rev. 1313 (1996); Charles D. Watts, Jr., Corporate Legal Theory Under

Consider also W. Hohfeld, Fundamental Legal Conceptions 197 (1923):

Strangely enough, it has not always been perceived with perfect clearness that transacting business under the forms, methods, and procedure pertaining to so-called corporations is simply another mode by which *individuals* or *natural persons* can enjoy their property and engage in business. Just as several individuals may transact business collectively as partners, so they may as members of a corporation—the corporation being nothing more than an association of such individuals. * * *

Hohfeld represented the "realist" approach toward law that was popular before World War II. Despite the general recognition and usefulness of the entity theory, we should recognize the fictional nature of this approach.

Many modern commentators have speculated on the proper way to analyze corporations. "[W]hat is the nature of a corporation?" Professor Alfred Conard has asked. "Is it a fund of property, a band of investors, a crew of workers, a place, an entry in official records, or a mere figment of legislative and judicial imaginations? What principle of justice grants it the same capacities to sue and be sued, to convey and to receive conveyances, to promise and receive promises, to trespass and be trespassed against, as a free and mature human individual?"[19] Professor Larry Soderquist suggests that a corporation should be viewed "as a constellation of relationships having a varied and varying hierarchical structure."[20]

STEPHEN M. BAINBRIDGE, BOOK REVIEW: COMMUNITY AND STATISM: A CONSERVATIVE CONTRACTARIAN CRITIQUE OF PROGRESSIVE CORPORATE LAW SCHOLARSHIP
82 Cornell L. Rev. 856, 859–70 (1997).

* * * Most law and economics scholars embrace a model of business organizations known as the "nexus-of-contracts theory of the firm." These so-called "contractarians" model the firm not as a single entity, but as an aggregate of various inputs acting together with the common goal of producing goods or services. Employees provide labor. Creditors provide debt capital. Shareholders provide equity capital, bear the risk of losses, and monitor the performance of management.[21] Management monitors the performance of

the First Amendment: Bellotti and Austin, 46 U.Miami L.Rev. 317 (1991). Browning–Ferris Industries of Vermont, Inc. v. Kelco Disposal, Inc., 492 U.S. 257, 284–85, 109 S.Ct. 2909, 2925, 106 L.Ed.2d 219, 244 (1989) (concurring in part and dissenting in part). Wilson v. United States, 221 U.S. 361, 31 S.Ct. 538, 55 L.Ed. 771 (1911); United States v. Morton Salt Co., 338 U.S. 632, 70 S.Ct. 357, 94 L.Ed. 401 (1950); Virginia Pharmacy Bd. v. Virginia Citizens Consumer Council, Inc., 425 U.S. 748, 96 S.Ct. 1817, 48 L.Ed.2d 346 (1976); Penn Central Transportation Co. v. New York City, 438 U.S. 104, 98 S.Ct. 2646, 57 L.Ed.2d 631 (1978); Marshall v. Barlow's, Inc., 436 U.S. 307, 98 S.Ct. 1816, 56 L.Ed.2d 305 (1978); United States v. Martin Linen Supply Co., 430 U.S. 564, 97 S.Ct. 1349, 51 L.Ed.2d 642 (1977); Helicopteros Nacionales de Colombia v. Hall,

466 U.S. 408, 104 S.Ct. 1868, 80 L.Ed.2d 404 (1984); Metropolitan Life Ins. Co. v. Ward, 470 U.S. 869, 105 S.Ct. 1676, 84 L.Ed.2d 751 (1985).

19. Alfred F. Conard, Corporations in Perspective 416 (1976).

20. Larry Soderquist, Theory of the Firm: What a Corporation Is, 25 J.Corp.Law 376 (2000).

21. [By the Editors] * * * [N]exus-of-contracts theory rejects traditional entity-based theories. Because shareholders are simply one of the inputs bound together by the web of voluntary agreements, ownership should not be a particularly meaningful concept in nexus-of-contracts theory. Someone owns each input, but no one owns the totality. Instead, the corporation is an aggregation of people bound

employees and coordinates the activities of all the firm's inputs. The firm is simply a legal fiction representing the complex set of contractual relationships between these inputs. * * *

The nexus of contracts model has important implications for a range of corporate law topics, the most obvious of which is the debate over the proper role of mandatory legal rules. Contractarians contend that corporate law is generally comprised of default rules, from which shareholders are free to depart, rather than mandatory rules. As a normative matter, contractarians argue that this is just as it should be.[22]

* * * Douglas Branson rejects this contractarian view and argues instead that mandatory rules pervade corporate law.[23] This attack is far from fatal. In the first instance, most contractarians probably regard the theory's normative claim as being the more important of the two. As such, we cheerfully concede the existence of mandatory rules, while deploring that unfortunate fact. In the second, as Bernard Black persuasively argues, many mandatory corporate law rules are trivial in nature.[24] Finally, nontrivial mandatory rules are often subject to evasion by choice of form and jurisdiction. Thus, the progressives' focus on mandatory legal rules is little more than a red herring.[25] * * *

* * * William Bratton's essay[26] * * * [argues] that the nexus-of-contracts model "has a significant shortcoming" in that it "gives us ex ante contracts across-the-board and thereby makes corporate governance entirely contractual without providing a description of the process by which corporate actors make contracts." Here we confront the distinction between actual and hypothetical bargaining. Contractarians concede, or at least should concede, that actual bargaining over rules such as limited liability is precluded by transaction cost barriers, but they contend that this is precisely why corporate statutes provide a set of off-the-rack rules amounting to a standard-form contract.

If transaction costs are zero, the substantive content of a corporate law rule does not matter greatly. If, for example, the law imposed full personal liability on shareholders, but limited liability is the efficient rule, shareholders

together by a complex web of contractual relationships. The contractarian account thus rests not on an out-moded reification of the corporation, but on the presumption of validity a free market society accords voluntary contracts. [This footnote has been moved from another portion of Professor Bainbridge's text.]

22. [By the Author] See, e.g., Frank H. Easterbrook & Daniel R. Fischel, The Economic Structure of Corporate Law 15 (1991); Larry E. Ribstein, The Mandatory Nature of the ALI Code, 61 Geo. Wash. L. Rev. 984, 989–91 (1993).

23. [By the Author] Douglas M. Branson, The Death of Contractarianism and the Vindication of Structure and Authority in Corporate Governance and Corporate Law, published in Progressive Corporate Law (Lawrence E. Mitchell ed., 1995) 94–5.

24. [By the Author] Bernard S. Black, Is Corporate Law Trivial?: A Political and Economic Analysis, 84 Nw. U. L. Rev. 542 passim (1990). The triviality argument provides a par-

tial response to William Bratton's observation that most contractarian scholars do not propose a sweeping repeal of mandatory fiduciary duties. Bratton attributes this failure to "doubts about both contractarian assumptions and their underlying ethical presuppositions." William W. Bratton, Game Theory and the Restoration of Honor to Corporate Law's Duty of Loyalty, in Progressive Corporate Law, supra note 13, at 139, 152. Yet, the contractarian position on mandatory fiduciary duties may simply indicate a belief that such rules are subject to evasion through choice of form or, to the extent that some duties appear across the spectrum of possible organizational forms, that they are trivial in the sense that they embody rules virtually everyone would demand in the event of actual bargaining. * * *

25. [By the Editors].

26. [By the Editors] William W. Bratton, Game Theory and the Restoration of Honor to Corporate Law's Duty of Loyalty, in Progressive Corporate Law, supra at 139, 152.

and creditors would contract around the rule through private bargaining. In the face of transaction costs, however, the rule's substantive content begins to matter very much. Indeed, if transaction costs are high, bargaining around the rule becomes wholly impractical, forcing the parties to live with an inefficient rule. Because the public corporation setting gives rise to prohibitively high transaction costs, parties cannot depend on private contracting to achieve efficient outcomes. Instead, a legally-imposed rule must function as a substitute for private bargaining. Identifying the party for whom getting one's way has the highest value thus becomes the critical question. In effect, corporate legal scholars ask: "If the parties could costlessly bargain over the question, which rule would they adopt?"[27] By imposing a rule to which parties would agree if they could bargain, society facilitates private ordering. * * *

Contractarians treat the corporation's organic rules as if they arose through the trading of rights and duties among the corporation's various constituencies and, accordingly, treat those rules as though they represent a bargain in which claims on the corporation were sold to their highest-valuing user. The bargains struck will vary from firm to firm, depending on a variety of factors, including the risk preferences of each of the firm's constituencies and the thickness of the markets in which the bargain is struck. Because the various contracts making up the firm differ little from contracts created through voluntary exchange, they enjoy a presumption in their favor, and ought to be enforced in the same way other mutually beneficial contracts are enforced.

Lawrence Mitchell rejects the contractarian account because the corporation's constituencies do not and cannot bargain:

> The idea that the bylaws of a public corporation were somehow bargained for by the stockholders in a manner that can be said to give rise to intent is troubling. In the first place, most public corporation stockholders have never read the corporation's bylaws, if they even are aware of their existence. While it is possible to argue that the stockholders should have read the bylaws to which they became bound by their purchasing stock, this in no way suggests any sort of bargaining process that gives rise to mutual intent. At best they can be said to have accepted the bylaws as one characteristic of the entire corporation, within the context of corporate laws holding that directors are fiduciaries of the corporation and its stockholders.[28]

This argument fundamentally misconceives the contractarian project by ignoring the distinction between outcome and process bargaining. A bargain can be understood in two distinct ways: as a process, which is how Mitchell appears to understand it, or as an outcome. As Mitchell correctly notes, there is no bargaining process between a shareholder and the public corporations in which he invests. But there is an outcome—the set of organic rules contained in the articles and bylaws as drafted by the corporation's founders or directors—that can fairly be described as a bargain. A bargain involving only

---

27. [By the Author] * * * As I have argued elsewhere, a rule of limited liability plausibly emerges from this hypothetical bargaining process.

28. [By the Author] * * * Lawrence E. Mitchell, Trust, Contract, Process, in Progressive Corporate Law, note 15, supra at 185, 186–187.

an outcome is just as much a contract as a bargain involving both a process and an outcome. * * *

Note

Corporation statutes are studded with provisions that are mandatory and cannot be modified by contract among the participants. As Professor Black argues, many of them are trivial, but some are not. See, for example, MBCA §§ 8.03(b), 16.02(d); John A. MacKerron, A Taxonomy of the Revised Model Business Corporation Act, 61 U.M.K.C.L.Rev. 663 (1993). Further, the federal securities laws, and particularly the regulations promulgated by the Securities and Exchange Commission under them, contain literally thousands of significant mandatory rules with respect to disclosure, insider trading, proxy solicitations, and other subjects. Economic theorists may of course respond that such mandatory provisions are archaic and should be eliminated. However, some may accept the idea that some mandatory regulation may be necessary even under the "nexus of contracts" approach. The latter appears to be the position taken in Frank H. Easterbrook and Daniel R. Fischel, The Corporate Contract, 89 Colum. L. Rev. 1416 (1989), though it is unlikely that those authors would accept the types of mandatory regulation currently being imposed. A revised version of this article appears as chapter 1 of Frank H. Easterbrook and Daniel R. Fischel, The Economic Structure of Corporate Law (1991). See generally Symposium, Contractual Freedom in Corporate Law, 89 Colum. L. Rev. 1395 (1989); William W. Bratton, The "Nexus of Contracts" Corporation: A Critical Appraisal, 74 Cornell L. Rev. 407 (1989).

Henry Butler elaborates on contractual corporate theory:

HENRY N. BUTLER, THE CONTRACTUAL THEORY OF THE CORPORATION
11 Geo. Mason L. Rev. 99, 100–23 (Summer 1989).

The contractual theory of the corporation is in stark contrast to the legal concept of the corporation as an entity created by the state. The entity theory of the corporation supports state intervention—in the form of either direct regulation or the facilitation of shareholder litigation—in the corporation on the ground that the state created the corporation by granting it a charter. The contractual theory views the corporation as founded in private contract, where the role of the state is limited to enforcing contracts. In this regard, a state charter merely recognizes the existence of a "nexus of contracts" called a corporation. Each contract in the "nexus of contracts" warrants the same legal and constitutional protections as other legally enforceable contracts. Moreover, freedom of contract requires that parties to the "nexus of contracts" must be allowed to structure their relations as they desire.

The contractual theory of the corporation should be of practical as well as academic interest. * * * Recently, corporation law scholars antagonistic to the contractual theory have adopted the methodology and terminology of the contractual theory, but have misapplied it in a way that reaches contrary policy positions. * * * [T]hese mistakes might be due to something other than a mere misunderstanding of the contractual theory[.] * * *

It is reasonable to assume that the parties to the nexus of contracts that form a firm anticipate the numerous problems associated with specialization, delegation, team production, and agency relationships. Freedom of contract allows the parties to structure their relations in a manner that ameliorates most of the agency problems inherent in the large corporation. * * *

[T]he contractual theory of the corporation offers a new [free market] perspective on the corporation and the role of corporation law. The corporation is in no sense a ward of the state; it is, rather, the product of contracts among the owners and others. Once this point is fully recognized by the state legislators and legal commentators, the corporate form may finally be free of unnecessary and intrusive legal chains.

Notes

(1) Consider an investor who purchases 100 shares of General Motors Co. common stock in a transaction executed on the New York Stock Exchange. In what sense has that investor entered into a contract with General Motors in order to become part of that "nexus of contracts?" If "contract" is understood in its normal legal sense, it seems that she has not. See Victor Brudney, Corporate Governance, Agency Costs, and The Rhetoric Of Contract, 85 Colum.L.Rev. 1403, 1412 (1985):

> It stretches the concept "contract" beyond recognition to use it to describe either the process of bargaining or the arrangements between investors of publicly held corporations and either theoretical owners first going public or corporate management. Scattered stockholders cannot, and do not, negotiate with owners who go public (or with management—either executives or directors) over hiring managers, over the terms of their employment, or over their retention.[29]

(2) See Melvin A. Eisenberg, The Conception that the Corporation Is a Nexus of Contracts, and the Dual Nature of the Firm, 24 J.Corp.L. 819, 822–23 (1999):

> Before proceeding further, it is necessary to clarify the meaning of the nexus-of-contracts conception. The conception neither can nor does mean what it literally says. In ordinary language, the term contract means an agreement. In law, the term means a legally enforceable promise. Pretty clearly, however, the nexus-of-contracts conception does not mean either that the corporation is a nexus of agreements or that it is a nexus of legally enforceable promises. Instead, the conception means that the corporation is a nexus of reciprocal arrangements. But then why is the term contracts, rather than the term reciprocal arrangements, used in the nexus-of-contracts conception?

> One possible explanation is that the term nexus of contracts was coined by economists, and "[e]conomists tend to view contracts as relationships characterized by reciprocal expectations and behavior." It also seems relevant, however, that the term contracts connotes markets, and conceiving the corporation as a nexus of contracts therefore connotes that a corporation is simply the product of market forces. As stated by David Campbell, "the central feature of [the nexus-of-contracts conception] is that the determinate empirical features of the company as a legitimately non-market institution are eroded to allow the purely hypothetical market to govern the company, from

29. This article originally appeared at 85 Colum.L.Rev. 1403 (1985). Reprinted by permission.

which, indeed, it cannot be distinguished."[30] Thus the inaccurate term nexus of contracts may have persisted, even among legal academics, because it carries connotations that nexus-of-contracts theorists find normatively or strategically appealing.

(3) As should be evident from the tenor of Professor Butler's analysis, proponents of the "nexus of contracts" analysis are strong believers in *laissez faire*. As such, they dismiss as unproblematic the concern that some parties to these contracts may lack full cognition and volition about risks and benefits, or that the relationships within a large corporation may not successfully prevent self-aggrandizing behavior by managers. See Henry N. Butler, The Contractual Theory of the Corporation, 11 Geo. Mason L. Rev. 99, 100 (Summer 1989). Good examples of articles reaching a contrary policy position are Marleen O'Connor, Restructuring the Corporation's Nexus of Contracts: Recognizing a Fiduciary Duty to Protect Displaced Workers, 69 N.C.L.Rev. 1189 (1991); Marleen O'Connor, The Human Capital Era: Reconceptualizing Corporate Law to Facilitate Labor–Management Cooperation, 79 Cornell L.Rev. 899 (1993).

(4) For a critical appraisal of the usefulness of the "nexus of contracts" theory as a basis for determining public policy, see Robert W. Hamilton, Business Organizations: Unincorporated Businesses and Close Corporations, § 8.6 (1997). For an application to the importance of worker involvement in management, see Stephen M. Bainbridge, Participatory Management Within a Theory of the Firm, 21 J.Corp.L. 857 (1996). For criticisms of the theory within the context of "law and economics," see Michael Klausner, Corporations, Corporate Law, and Networks of Contracts, 81 Va.L.Rev. 757 (1995); G.T. Garvey and P.L. Swan, The Economics of Corporate Governance: Beyond the Marshallian Firm, 1 J.Corp.Fin. 139 (1994).

(5) The notion of a corporation as essentially contractual in nature is not new. The corporate charter was viewed as a "contract" between the state and the corporation in the famous Dartmouth College case in 1819. By the middle of the Twentieth Century this "contract" analysis had been modified into a tripartite analysis: the corporate charter was not only a contract between the corporation and the state but also a contract between the corporation and its shareholders and a contract among the shareholders themselves. These modifications of "contract" theory arose because of the general recognition that many rights of shareholders may be modified by agreement, traditionally embodied in provisions in articles of incorporation.

MARGARET M. BLAIR AND LYNN A. STOUT, TEAM PRODUCTION IN BUSINESS ORGANIZATIONS: AN INTRODUCTION
24 J.Corp. L. 743 (1999).

For nearly two decades, legal and economics scholars who study business organizations have tended to view those organizations through the lens of a principal-agent model of the firm. This model rests on the assumption that the equity holders in a business (for example, the shareholders in a corporation) are the firm's residual claimants, entitled to all profits left over after the firm's contractual obligations have been paid. Thus the equity holders are in a sense the ultimate owners of the firm. * * *

30. [By the Author] David Campbell, The Role of Monitoring and Morality in Corporate Law, A Criticism of the Direction of Present Regulation, 7 Austl.J.Corp.L. 343, 361 (1997). (Trustees of Dartmouth College v. Woodward, 17 U.S. (4 Wheat.) 518, 4 L.Ed. 629 (1819)).

* * * Because the principal-agent approach assumes that the corporation is the shareholder's "property," it implies that corporate officers' and directors' primary duty is to generate wealth for shareholders. Yet in a publicly-held corporation with widely-dispersed share ownership, it can be difficult for shareholders to monitor managers and ensure that they run the firm in a fashion that serves the shareholders' interests. The resulting separation of ownership from control has led many corporate scholars who adopt the principal-agent approach to assume that the central economic problem to be faced in a public corporation is the "agency cost" problem of monitoring managers and motivating them to act as faithful agents. Not surprisingly, the solutions that come out of principal-agent analysis often involve strengthening shareholders' control rights and ability to negotiate contractual restraints on manager opportunism. * * *

* * * Team production problems arise in situations where three conditions are met. The first condition is that economic production requires a team. In other words, production requires the combined inputs (of time, money, or other valuable resources) of two or more individuals. The second condition is that at least some of the resources the team members must invest to produce are "team-specific," meaning they have a significantly higher value when used in the team than in their next best use. The third condition is that the gains resulting from team production—the economic "rents"—are joint or nonseparable, making it difficult to attribute any particular portion of the gains to any single team member's contribution.

Business organizations provide classic examples of team production. Successful businesses often require inputs from large numbers of individuals, including shareholders, creditors, managers, and rank-and-file employees. Many of the resources these "team members" invest are team-specific * * * [F]inancial investors' contribution also often becomes team-specific, as investors cannot easily recover the full value of their money after it has been spent on specialized equipment and salaries. * * *

Participants in team production * * * [often find that] [e]ach has made an essential contribution of resources. None can recover the full value of that contribution outside the team * * * [and they may] find themselves exposed to the opportunistic behavior of other team members. * * *

[W]e argue that a public corporation is best understood as a nexus of team-specific assets invested by shareholders, managers, employees, and others who hope to profit from team production. Property rights over these assets are held by a legal entity—the corporation—that is separate from any of the participants. And control over that entity rests not with the shareholders, but with a board of directors that serves as a trustee for the firm as a whole. While the board is nominally elected by the shareholders and in practice often heavily influenced by management, as a matter of law, it remains insulated from * * * direct command and control * * *.

MARGARET M. BLAIR AND LYNN A. STOUT, A TEAM PRODUCTION THEORY OF CORPORATE LAW

85 Va. L. Rev. 247 (1999).

* * * [W]e believe * * * [team production problems] may represent a more appropriate basis for understanding the unique economic and legal functions served by the public corporation. * * * We argue that public corporation law * * * [provides a] solution to team production problems * * * [through a] "mediating hierarchy" [that] * * * requires the team members to give up important rights * * * to a legal entity created by the act of incorporation. In other words, corporate assets belong not to shareholders but to the corporation itself. Within the corporation, control over those assets is exercised by an internal hierarchy whose job is to coordinate the activities of the team members, allocate the resulting production, and mediate disputes among team members over that allocation. At the peak of this hierarchy sits a board of directors whose authority over the use of corporate assets is virtually absolute and whose independence from individual team members * * * is protected by law.

The team production model of the public corporation both highlights and explains the essential economic function served by that otherwise puzzling institution, the board of directors. The notion that responsibility for governing a publicly held corporation ultimately rests in the hands of its directors is a defining feature of American corporate law; indeed, in a sense, an independent board is what makes a public corporation a public corporation. Yet while the board of directors is central to public corporation law, it raises troubling questions under the principal-agent model. Shareholders' rights and powers over directors in publicly held companies are remarkably limited both in theory and in practice, and as a result directors of public firms enjoy an extraordinary degree of discretion to pursue other agendas and to favor other constituencies, especially management, at shareholders' expense. * * *

The team production model provides an alternative answer to the question of why corporate law grants directors of public corporations so much leeway. In particular, it suggests that the legal requirement that public corporations be managed under the supervision of a board of directors has evolved not to reduce agency costs—indeed, such a requirement may exacerbate them—but to encourage the firm–specific investment essential to certain forms of team production. In other words, boards exist not to protect shareholders per se, but to protect the enterprise-specific investments of all the members of the corporate "team." * * *

Thus we argue that the mediating hierarchy interpretation of corporations is more consistent with the way a corporation actually works than are prominent contractarian interpretations of corporate law that focus on the principal-agent problem. * * *

Notes

(1) Internal issues that arise within any hierarchical bureaucratic structure are typically resolved within the structure by a process similar to the "mediating hierarchy" proposed by the authors. Typically, resolution occurs within the structure without involving the highest levels of the hierarchy, though basic or

fundamental issues may have to be resolved at the highest level. Within a public corporation the "highest level" may be the chief executive officer rather than the board of directors. Boards typically meet relatively infrequently (six or eight times a year is not uncommon) to deal with issues that are non-controversial and whose resolution may occur without real discussion. Does this fact cut against the "mediating hierarchy" approach?

(2) Peter C. Konstant, Exit, Voice and Loyalty in the Course of Corporate Governance and Counsel's Changing Role, The Journal of Socio–Economics 28 (1999) 203, 222–23:

> Perhaps the most exciting theoretical work attempting to explain the public corporation is the new Team Production Model of Blair and Stout. * * * The Team Production Model is helpful in explaining numerous anomalies in corporate law that are difficult to reconcile with the old agency model. These anomalies include why shareholders of public corporations give up so much control over their property to a board of directors who need not own any interest in the corporation; why public shareholders accept that they cannot direct or control management; and why shareholders accept such feeble protections as their largely meaningless voting power and the tenuous right to bring derivative suits on behalf of the corporation. The authors explain that all stakeholders are prepared to surrender power and make firm specific investments to achieve the enormous benefit of team production, and accept that an independent mediating hierarch will protect them in situations for which they cannot expressly contract in advance.

(3) David Millon's article New Game Plan or Business as Usual? A Critique of the Team Production Model of Corporate Law suggests that "corporate law does not currently reflect" the team production model's "idea of an independent board acting as mediator among the claims and interests of all team members. [The Model] therefore is better seen as a normative project. As such, it presents an impressive argument for rejecting the dominant shareholder primacy understanding of corporate law's purpose, which is reflected in the principal-agent model of the board's relation to shareholders." 86 Va.L.Rev., 1001, 1042–43 (2000).

(4) The "nexus of contracts" and "team production" models are competing theories that attempt to provide a basis for making policy judgments about large, publicly held corporations. Both begin with the same premise: the goal of all participants in the corporation is to maximize the wealth of the corporation. Private negotiation (nexus of contracts theory) or the allocation of wealth among corporate components by the board of directors (team production model) are the devices to allocate the wealth among corporate participants. According to the *laissez faire* vision the role of government should be strictly limited to enforcing the private contracts or arrangements created within the corporation.

(5) This *laissez faire* vision of the corporation was tested by events of 2001 and 2002, when more than a dozen publicly held corporations announced that their books had been manipulated to overstate current earnings, and that available capital had been diverted to enrich corporate directors and officers rather than paid as dividends to shareholders or reinvested in the corporation. Do these announcements cast serious doubt on the usefulness of both the "nexus of contracts" and the "team production model" as explanations of current corporate behavior?

Chapter Two

THE PARTNERSHIP

A. THE NEED FOR A WRITTEN AGREEMENT

Returning to the AB Software Store partnership discussed in Chapter 1, let us assume that the business is a general partnership. It is not necessary for A and B to enter into a written agreement, but, is it desirable for them to do so?

One major advantage of having a written agreement is that it may avoid future disagreements over what the arrangement actually was. It avoids litigation similar to that involved in, for example, Fulbright v. Culbertson, 429 S.W.2d 179, 182 (Tex.Civ.App.1968).

More generally, in the absence of a written agreement, the relationship between the partners will be governed by the provisions of the applicable state partnership statute. It is unlikely that the provisions of this statute will reflect all of the expectations and understandings among the partners.

A partner may also wish to lend rather than contribute specific property to a partnership. A written agreement clearly identifying which property is contributed and which is loaned is critical to protect the partner's interest in the loaned property.

Where real estate is to be contributed as partnership property or the agreement includes a term of more than one year, a written agreement may be necessary to comply with the statute of frauds. In Gano v. Jamail, 678 S.W.2d 152 (Tex.App.1984), for example, Gano claimed that he was made a partner by oral agreement in Jamail's one-person law practice in 1969 on a fifty percent participation basis, after which the firm was known as "Jamail and Gano." In 1978, Jamail terminated the arrangement, and Gano brought suit on the alleged partnership agreement. Gano lost because of the one-year provision of the statute of frauds. The court accepted the argument that the firm "was involved almost exclusively in a personal injury practice in which cases were based on contingent fee contracts, and almost always took more than a year to conclude," and the agreement contemplated that the partnership was to last until all of the cases signed up during the partnership were resolved. 678 S.W.2d, at 154.

A written partnership agreement is also advantageous to the attorney: not only may it justify a somewhat higher fee but also it places suggestions and advice in concrete form so as a safeguard against misunderstanding. The advantages of a written agreement are so substantial that lawyers who do not advise their clients to at least *consider* a written agreement before entering into a partnership risk a malpractice suit.

B. SHARING OF PROFITS AND LOSSES

In the absence of an explicit agreement, how are profits and losses shared? See UPA (1914) § 18(a); UPA (1997) § 401(b). Does it make any difference if the partners contributed unequal amounts of capital? In a word, "no"; see Dunn v. Summerville, 669 S.W.2d 319 (Tex.1984).

Profits of a business may be divided by agreement in numerous possible ways:

(a) The partners may share on a flat percentage basis without regard to any other factor. Profit sharing ratios for each partner may be established in the partnership agreement itself. They may also be established by issuing "partnership units" to each partner and determining the profit- or loss-sharing ratio for each partner by dividing the number of units owned by that partner by the total number of units outstanding. In this way, if new partners are added, dilution of existing interests occurs automatically without any need to amend the agreement; if old partners depart without new ones being added, the remaining interests are also automatically concentrated. Partnership units also permit the creation of incentive options or unit appreciation rights that permit successful partners to increase their percentage interest in the firm.

(b) Partners may be entitled to a fixed weekly or monthly "salary." This payment may be treated as a "cost" and subtracted before the "profit" is computed for division on some other basis, or it may be considered an advance to be credited against the amount the partner is otherwise entitled to after division of the profit. In the latter case, the agreement should consider the responsibility of the partner receiving a "salary" if the "salary" exceeds the actual profit allocable to him or her during any period.

(c) The partners may share on a percentage basis, with the percentages recomputed each year on the basis of the average amount invested in the business during the year by each partner. This type of arrangement is appropriate where the business is largely dependent on capital for income generation.

(d) The partners may share on a percentage basis, with the percentages recomputed each year on the basis of total income, the sales or billings by each partner, time devoted to the business, or on the basis of some other factor.

(e) In large partnerships, each partner may be entitled to a fixed percentage applied against perhaps 80 percent of the income. A committee of senior partners will allocate the remaining 20 percent among the junior partners as a form of incentive compensation on the basis of productivity, billings, or some other factor. Usually committee members are not themselves eligible to share in the "incentive pie."

(f) The agreement may be intentionally silent on the division of profits, so that each year the partners can work out the division of profits by agreement on a mutual acceptable basis. In larger firms, a committee or a single managing partner may have the responsibility of making the division of profits.

In what types of business would the various ways of sharing profits described above be most appropriate?

Turning to the unfortunate situation where the venture does not prove to be profitable, who is responsible for losses? Consider first UPA (1914) § 18(a), compared with UPA §§ 13–15. Why is § 18 modified by the phrase "subject to any agreement between them," while §§ 13–15 are not? Is it clear that an individual partner may be held personally liable on a partnership obligation even if the partnership is solvent and able to satisfy all its obligations? If so, why might a creditor elect to sue an individual partner and ignore a solvent partnership? May a creditor sue an individual partner even if the partner had nothing to do with the creation of the obligation and indeed was unaware that it was created? If so, and one partner is compelled to pay an entire claim, how does the Act contemplate the financial relations among the partners so that the resulting losses or reduction of profit are allocated as provided by the partnership agreement? Consider UPA (1914) §§ 18(b), 40(d); compare UPA (1997) §§ 401(a)-(e), 807(c)-(d).

With respect to a partner's liability for a partnership obligation, consider UPA (1997) §§ 305–307. UPA (1997) makes one radical, and three important, substantive changes from UPA (1914): (1) § 306(c) is the radical change; it reverses the general rule of individual partner responsibility for most partnership debts if the partnership has elected to be a "limited liability partnership," a status that is obtained by following the relatively simple procedural requirements set forth in §§ 1001 through 1004; (2) § 306(a) makes all liability joint and several and eliminates the old reference to partners being "jointly" liable for contract and related claims; (3) § 307(d) provides that a judgment creditor is first required to exhaust partnership assets (with certain exceptions) before proceeding directly against one or more partners individually; and (4) §§ 307(a), (b) and (c) set forth rules about the naming of partnerships and partners in lawsuits. Each of these developments deserves a brief description:

(1) A limited liability partnership (LLP) is still a partnership despite the fact that it has limited liability: It must be organized for profit, it must have two or more members, and it is subject to dissolution or dissociation as any other general partnership. Its unique feature is that by electing LLP status, partners may avoid *personal* liability for partnership claims that exceed partnership assets. The assets they have invested in the partnership remain at risk, and there is always some possibility that partners may become liable to third persons because of their own conduct. Nevertheless, the virtual elimination of personal liability of partners from firm obligations is a radical change. The court test of the extent to which the LLP business form protects partners from liability in cases of negligence or malfeasance will come in the case of the accounting firm Arthur Andersen, LLP, which had almost 2,000 partners at the time its largest client, Enron, collapsed in a wave of accounting scandals. The firm faces claims of over $1 billion.

(2) "Joint" liability, as contemplated by UPA (1914) § 15(b) required joinder of all partners as defendants in litigation. This joinder requirement

may create serious practical enforcement problems where process cannot readily be served on some partners. "Joint and several" liability permits suit to be brought against one or more of the partners without suing them all. Presumably, in 1914, most partnerships were small and local in character, and had joint liability. As partnerships grew, practical problems faced by plaintiffs seeking to sue large firms became more serious. For example, in 1990, the accounting firm of Laventhol & Horwath, with 360 partners in the U.S. and eight other countries, filed for protection from its creditors under Chapter 11 of the Bankruptcy Code. About 15 individual partners also filed bankruptcy petitions. The creditors' claims against Laventhol & Horwath were far greater than the value of the firm's assets. The ultimate settlement required individual partners to contribute amounts ranging between $4,000 and $450,000, depending on a number of factors, mostly seniority and whether the partner had management responsibility. Interestingly, the settlement did not attempt to differentiate between partners involved in the audits that led to the malpractice claims and those that were not involved in those audits. Can you think of why?

(3) The requirement that judgment creditors should first exhaust partnership assets before proceeding directly against the assets of one or more partners is an important change that was suggested by an ABA committee in 1986. The Committee stated that the new rule "would respect the concept of the partnership as an entity and would provide that the partners are more in the nature of guarantors than principal debtors on every partnership debt. We believe that this result would be most consistent with general business expectations today." UPA Revision Subcommittee of the Committee on Partnerships and Unincorporated Business Organizations, Should the Uniform Partnership Act Be Revised?, 43 Bus. Law. 121, 143 (1987).

(4) Paragraphs (a), (b) and (c) of UPA (1997) § 307 dealing with procedural requirements for suits brought by or against partnerships also clearly strengthen the view that a partnership is an entity separate from the original partners. UPA (1914) did not address how partnerships should sue or be sued. Many states evolved rules quite similar to those set forth in § 307, so that these changes are largely consistent with modern practice.

It is not uncommon in informal ventures for the parties to agree on a sharing of the profits but not discuss the sharing of losses. There is often some judicial sympathy for the unfortunate investor who is unexpectedly caught in a losing venture with the threat of personal liability for the venture's obligations incurred by others. In these cases, a court may accept the argument that the absence of an express agreement to share losses indicates that no partnership was ever created in the first place.[1] Many cases, however, recognize that an express agreement to share losses is not essential for the existence of a partnership, a result consistent with the language of UPA (1914) § 7 and UPA (1997) § 202(c)(3).[2]

---

1. See, e.g., In re Tingle, 34 B.R. 676 (Bankr.S.D.Fla.1983); Grimmett v. Higginbotham, 907 S.W.2d 1 (Tex.App.1994); FDIC v. Claycomb, 945 F.2d 853 (5th Cir. 1991).

2. See, e.g., Parks v. Riverside Ins. Co., 308 F.2d 175 (10th Cir.1962).

Notes

(1) In the AB Software Store, can A obtain protection against possible future liabilities by requiring B to execute a written agreement that provides: "It is understood and agreed that the parties hereto are not partners and that no partnership is formed by this agreement"? See UPA (1997) § 202(a), last clause. What about a clause that states that A will not be liable for any losses incurred in the business in excess of A's $100,000 investment? Would such an agreement have any legal effect at all? If so, what?

(2) Assume that the XYZ Real Estate Company is formed in a state that has adopted § 307 of UPA (1997). XYZ owns seven different rental properties. Although each property is subject to one or more separate mortgages, the fair market value of each property is somewhat greater than the sum of the outstanding balances owed on the mortgages applicable to that property. Your client, a bank, is considering making a loan to XYZ to permit it to do substantial repair and renovation work on its properties. Your client knows that X, a partner in XYZ, is independently wealthy and is relying on X to pay off the loan if XYZ is not able to do so. What provisions should you include in the loan agreements to ensure that your client is able to collect directly and immediately from X in the event of a default? See UPA (1997), §§ 307(c), 307(d)(3). Indeed, while you are at it, would it not be a good idea to revise the bank's form loan documents to include such provisions whenever a partnership is the borrower?

(3) In the AB Software Store, could A obtain the desired protection by being a "silent" partner? For example, the store might be known as B Software Store; A might advance the money but never appear in the store or participate in any public way in the management of the store. Assuming that creditors extend credit without knowing of A's interest in the business, can A escape liability? Should a negative inference be drawn from UPA (1914) § 35(2), a provision applicable only "after dissolution," or UPA (1997) § 703(b)(1), a provision applicable after "dissociation"? How might a creditor learn that A is a silent partner?

RICHERT v. HANDLY

Supreme Court of Washington, 1957.
50 Wash.2d 356, 311 P.2d 417.

ROSELLINI, JUSTICE.

This is an action for an accounting, wherein the plaintiff alleged that he entered into a partnership agreement with the defendant husband (hereafter referred to as the defendant), under the terms of which he, the plaintiff, was to purchase a stand of timber and the defendant was to log it, using his equipment, and the two were to share equally in the profits or losses resulting from the venture. He further alleged that the undertaking was unsuccessful; that after the payment of all operating expenses, the partnership suffered a loss of $9,825.12; that he had advanced $26,842 but had been repaid only $10,000 for his advances; and that he was entitled to $16,842 less $4,912.56 (one half of the net loss), or $11,929.44. In his amended answer, the defendant admitted that the parties had contracted with each other, but alleged that "there was no settled agreement between the partners as to recovery by the plaintiff for loss upon his capital contribution, nor as to the priority of any right to recover upon his capital contribution." In addition, he claimed certain offsets and asked that the complaint be dismissed.

The cause was tried to the court, which found in favor of the defendant in the amount of $1,494.51, plus costs. * * *

The facts found by the trial court are as follows:

"I That defendants C.C. Handly and Mildred Handly are husband and wife constituting a marital community resident in Mason County, Washington.

"II During the month of April 1953 plaintiff Richert advised defendant Handly that he had available for purchase, according to his cruise, 1,700,000 feet of timber in the State of Oregon, that he, Richert proposed to purchase said timber with his funds and requested Handly to log said timber on the basis that the two of them would share the profit or loss on the transaction.

"III Prior to the purchase of the timber by the plaintiff the parties inspected the same and defendant Handly advised Richert that there was no more than approximately 1,000,000 feet of timber on the tract in question, and that the cruise was in error.

"IV The plaintiff Richert purchased the timber for a price of $24,300.00 after the parties had inspected it as aforesaid, and Handly proceeded to log the same under an oral working agreement. The essential elements of this agreement were as follows: Handly was to furnish a tractor for which he was to be paid rental at the rate of $13.00 per hour and was to haul the logs on his trucks at the rate of $8.00 per thousand. He was also to manage the operation, keep the records and handle and account for the funds received and expended during the course of the same. The profit or loss resulting from this single logging venture was to be borne equally. There was no requirement that Handly contribute to Richert for the purchase price of the timber in the event of loss.

"V The tract involved yielded between 800,000 and 900,000 feet of timber and the transaction resulted in a loss, the loss being caused by the deficiency in timber.

* * *

"VII The gross receipts of the venture amounted to $41,629.83. These funds were banked and accounted for by Handly. There was no concealment nor unlawful withholding or conversion of any of the funds.

"VIII Handly drew from the proceeds of the sale of the timber the sum of $7,016.88. Richert received from the proceeds of the sale of the timber the sum of $10,000.00.

"IX There was no agreement express or implied on the part of Handly to repay Richert for his investment in the timber.

"X A partnership income tax was prepared for the year 1953 by Elliott B. Spring, accountant in Shelton, Washington. This return was signed by Handly after he protested the accounting shown thereon. The accounting appearing on said return was set up on the basis of Spring's understanding and opinion as to what the legal relationship of the parties was with reference to this single logging transaction.

"XI The $10,000.00 received by Richert and the $7,016.88 drawn by Handly are unexpended gross revenues of the undertaking."

Upon these facts, the court entered the following conclusions of law:

"I The arrangement of the parties hereto with reference to the single transaction involved constitutes a joint venture.

"II The defendant Handly is in no way responsible for plaintiff's loss on the purchase of the timber involved.

"III Of the total amount of $17,016.88 heretofore identified as unexpended gross revenue of the undertaking, each party hereto is entitled to $8,508.44. Richert has been overpaid in the amount of $1491.56, and Handly is entitled to judgment against him in the amount of $1491.56.

"IV Plaintiff is entitled to take nothing by his complaint. * * * "

Although the plaintiff maintains that the court erred in holding the undertaking to be a "joint venture" rather than a "partnership," we think the distinction is immaterial in this action. Deciding whether the relationship between the parties was that of partners or joint venturers does not determine their rights and duties under their contract or the status of their account. We will disregard, therefore, the conclusion of law that the arrangement constituted a joint venture.

On the other hand, it is manifest that the findings are inadequate to support the judgment entered, or any other judgment. There is a finding that the parties to the contract had agreed to share the profits or losses equally, but there is a further finding that the defendant had not agreed to contribute to the plaintiff for his investment in the timber in the event of loss; in other words, that they had not agreed to share the losses equally. Aside from the finding that the profit or loss was to be borne equally, which is inconsistent with the further finding that the defendant was not to contribute to the plaintiff for the purchase price of the timber in the event of loss, the findings are silent as to the basis on which the profit or loss was to be shared, whether proportionately to the contribution of each party, or otherwise. The mere fact that the defendant was not to be personally liable to the plaintiff for his losses does not mean that the plaintiff was not to be reimbursed out of the proceeds of the venture.

The findings also fail to reveal whether there was an understanding that the defendant was to be compensated for his services in managing the operation, apart from his share in the profits, and if so, in what amount. The only allegation contained in the amended answer pertaining to an agreement to reimburse the defendant for his services, was that he was owed $400 for maintaining fire watch and $25 for running property lines; and yet inherent in the court's disposition of the matter is a finding that these services were worth the full amount of the plaintiff's investment, or $26,842; for the court treated all of the "unexpended gross revenues" as profits and divided them equally between the parties, one of whom had lost nothing (unless his claimed offsets in the total amount of $4,800 were valid), while the other had lost an investment of $26,842.

The court appears to have lost sight of the fact that there could be no profits until the expenses of the operation were paid, including the cost of the timber. The conclusion that all of the "unexpended gross revenues" were to be divided equally between the parties could only be reached if it had been agreed that the plaintiff would not be reimbursed for his contribution. Such an intention cannot be inferred from any of the findings entered.

Since the findings are inadequate to support the conclusions and judgment, or any judgment on the matter in question, the cause must be remanded with directions to make findings regarding the basis on which the parties agreed that the losses were to be shared and whether the claims of one partner were to take priority over the claims of the other; the amount contributed by each (including cost of timber, and equipment rental, and also including services if there was an agreement that the defendant was to be compensated for his services, in addition to his share in the profits, if any); the total receipts and the authorized disbursements; the amount which each of the parties has received to date; and the amount due each on the basis of their agreement.

The judgment is reversed and the cause is remanded with directions to enter findings on the matters indicated above, conclusions, and judgment based thereon. * * *

RICHERT v. HANDLY

Supreme Court of Washington, 1958.
53 Wash.2d 121, 330 P.2d 1079.

HUNTER, JUSTICE. * * *

At the hearing on this matter pursuant to the remittitur, counsel for the respective parties agreed that no additional proof would be produced. Therefore, the trial court, after hearing argument of counsel, entered the following additional findings of fact in compliance with the remittitur:

"XII. The parties *did not agree upon or specify the basis* upon which losses were to be shared, nor whether the claims of *one partner* were to take priority over the claims of *the other.*

"XIII. Richert [appellant] contributed a total of $26,842 for cost of timber and incidental advancements. Handly [respondent husband] used his own equipment to haul logs, as agreed by the parties, and was paid $8,673.84 for this service. Handly used his own tractor, as agreed by the parties, and was paid $9,240 for this service. *There was no agreement that Handly was to be compensated for his services, in addition to his share in the profits, if any, (and except for the equipment and tractor services as last hereinbefore stated), and the accounting between the parties does not disclose any such compensation.*

"XIV. The gross receipts from the sale of logs were $41,629.83. The disbursements were hauling (as per Finding XIII), $8,673.84; falling and bucking, $3,474.21; tractor (as per Finding XIII), $9,240.00; payroll and taxes, $4,786.56; cruising, $35.00; right of way, $200.00; commission, $500.00; paid to Richert, $10,000.00; withdrawn by Handly, $7,016.88; Total $43,926.49.

"XV. *There was no agreement* of the parties as to how a loss of the capital contributed by Richert in the amount of $26,842.00 was to be borne, and *accordingly it cannot be determined the amount due each on the basis of their agreement."* (Italics ours.)

On the basis of such findings, the court concluded neither party was entitled to judgment against the other, that the complaint should be dismissed, and that the costs should abide the ultimate outcome of the case as provided by remittitur.

Mr. Richert has again appealed to this court from the judgment entered.

Since the trial court found that the parties had not agreed upon or specified the basis upon which losses were to be shared, or whether the claims of *one partner* were to take priority over the claims of the *other,* the provisions of the uniform partnership act are controlling. [The court quotes UPA (1914) §§ 18(a), 18(f).]

Therefore, applying the statute to the additional facts found by the trial court, to which no error was assigned, we find the following account established:

Capital Contribution:

Appellant Richert	$26,842.00
Respondent Handly	None
Gross Receipts From Sale of Timber	41,629.83

Expenses:

Tractor	9,240.00
Hauling	8,673.84
Falling & Bucking	3,474.21
Payroll & Taxes	4,786.56
Cruising	35.00
Right of Way	200.00
Commission	500.00
	$26,909.61

Gross Receipts	41,629.83
Less Expenses	26,909.61
Net Receipts	$14,720.22
Appellant's Capital Contribution	26,842.00
Less Net Receipts	14,720.22
Net Loss	$12,121.78
Appellant has received $10,000 from the venture leaving a balance due on his Capital Contribution of	$16,842.00
Less ½ of net loss ($12,121.78)	6,060.89
Amount respondent must reimburse appellant for loss resulting from logging venture	$10,781.11

It follows that the judgment of the trial court is incorrect, as a matter of law, under the facts found. Therefore, the judgment is reversed, and the cause remanded with directions to enter judgment in favor of the appellant in accordance with the views expressed herein.

Notes

(1) What was the theory adopted by the trial court in its first judgment?

(2) What was the theory adopted by the Supreme Court of Washington in its second opinion? Is this conclusion logically and irresistibly compelled by UPA (1914)? Not all cases accept the result of *Richert*; the leading case rejecting this approach is Kovacik v. Reed, 49 Cal.2d 166, 169, 315 P.2d 314, 316 (1957):

The rationale of this rule * * * is that where one party contributes money and the other contributes services, then in the event of a loss each would lose his own capital—the one his money and the other his labor. Another view would be that in such a situation the parties have, by their agreement to share equally in profits, agreed that the value of their contributions—the money on one hand and the labor on the other—were likewise equal; it would follow that upon the loss * * * of both money and labor, the parties have shared equally in the losses.

Academic commentators disagree as to the desirability of the result reached in *Kovacik*. See Randy E. Barnett, The Sound of Silence: Default Rules and Contractual Consent, 78 Va.L.Rev. 821, 884–5 (1992) (the rule set forth in § 18 "defies common sense"). But see Stephen M. Bainbridge, Contractarianism in the Business Associations Classroom: *Kovacik v. Reed* and the Allocation of Capital Losses in Service Partnerships, 34 Ga.L.Rev. 631, 668 (2000).

(3) The problem in *Richert* potentially arises whenever partners make unequal contributions of capital and services and decide precisely how they will split the profits but do not consider the possibility that the venture will result in a loss. UPA (1914) § 18(a) provides a rule of thumb for such situations that seems inconsistent with the parties' probable intention where one person is providing only capital and the other only services.

(4) During the course of development of UPA (1997), the Reporter suggested adding a provision that a court might award compensation "in other appropriate circumstances" to address the problem of *Richert* and *Kovacik* but the Committee rejected this language on the ground that it was an invitation to litigation. Consequently, UPA (1997) does not squarely address the issue. See UPA (1997) §§ 401, 807(b).

C. LAW FIRM PARTNERSHIPS

Assume that in ABC Law Firm, A is responsible for bringing 70% of the year's business to the firm. As the principal business-getter (or "rainmaker"), A spends most of his time entertaining potential clients on the local golf course so that his office time billed to clients constitutes only 10% of the total. B brings 30% of the business and her time billings constitute 35% of the total. C brought no business to the firm, but handled the bulk (55%) of the actual legal work. What formula might be used to divide the year's profits? Or might it be better not to have a fixed formula, and negotiate the division of the pie each year?

DENIS ORME, PAYING PARTNERS FOR NEW BUSINESS: AN EQUITABLE LAW FIRM PARTNER COMPENSATION SCHEME
70 A.B.A.J. 60 (Dec. 1984).[3]

In recent years, possibly because of economic pressure, law firms have begun to swing away from lock-step systems of partner compensation. Less emphasis is being placed on tenure and seniority, and more consideration is being given to merit performance and attraction of new business.

In a true partnership all income derived from the practice of law goes first to the firm and then is divided among the members on the basis of

---

3. Reprinted with permission from the ABA Journal, The Lawyer's Magazine.

individual performance, which is a measure of the individual's contribution to the prosperity of the firm. A generally accepted principle is that not all partners are equal in income distribution.

An equitable partner compensation system should divide profits primarily according to a partner's percentage of equity ownership in the firm, but it also should set apart a portion of profits into a "bonus pool" to be distributed according to new business brought in.

Compensation Factors

Among the various compensation schemes several factors govern the size of individual allocations. The following are perhaps the most common:

● **Productivity and billable hours.** Given that all partners achieve a threshold level of performance, special recognition should be given to those who regularly contribute the most billed and collected hours.

● **New business.** If a partner's activities produce new business for the firm, the compensation scheme should give that partner credit. This credit usually is a percentage of the total fees generated by the new business. The credit continues for a predetermined time period.

● **Client liaison.** Recognition should be given to efforts to retain the larger clients, although those efforts may not produce discernible, tangible results.

● **Practice economics.** Credit should be given to such efforts as client matter planning and control, prompt billing, accounts receivable follow-up and cash collection, fees received from clients, other fees directly resulting from partners' work, profitability by type of law, avoiding write-offs and overhead control.

● **Management, administration, training and supervision.** Recognition should be given for effective work delegation, supervision and good staff relations. Those contributions are hard to quantify, but they are essential to a true partnership.

● **Marketing advancement.** This includes firm promotion, enhancement of the firm's public and professional image and the pursuit of specific marketing opportunities.

A starting point in choosing a compensation scheme is to decide which factors to use and their relative weight. Regardless of which method is chosen, the goal is to arrive at a plan that will enable the partners to deal fairly with each other and to let them work together without friction.

Note

A survey, conducted by the Institute of Management and Administration, Inc. ("Law Firm Management Survey, 2000") in May 2000, reported that annual compensation calculations for partners were most influenced by business origination (59%), billable hours (48%), marketing and client development (46%), associate development (28%), and heading a practice group (26%). About 84% of gross revenue of all reporting firms was derived from hourly billing in 1999.

1. THE TRADITIONAL LAW FIRM OF THE 1960s[4]

In 1960, the traditional law firm was a general partnership in which all partners shared the benefits and burdens of the law practice. Under well-established partnership principles, each partner was personally liable for all obligations of the partnership contracts. However, malpractice was not a major concern; lawyers were rarely sued for malpractice, and many firms did not even bother to carry malpractice insurance, which was then incredibly inexpensive in contrast to present premiums.

By modern standards, traditional law firms of the 1950s and 1960s were small. A large firm might have 20 or so partners and ten or fifteen associates; a medium size firm was one with perhaps twelve or fifteen partners and associates combined. Firms usually had only a single office (although some firms had small branch offices in other cities, particularly if a major client had offices in that city). All the partners in a firm knew each other personally and typically prided themselves on acting civilly and with respect toward each other. The firm structure was usually informal; many firms did not have written partnership agreements, and most decisions were made through a committee, by a trusted senior partner, or by some form of consensus of all partners. When partnership decisions needed to be made, all the firm's partners could sit around a single table. When the decision involved who should be promoted from associate to partner, all the existing partners would have had at least some contact with and personal knowledge about the ability of each of the candidates.

Law firms during this period were entirely male. There were very few female law school graduates to begin with, but as a matter of policy most firms simply declined to interview or hire female lawyers, believing that their clients would refuse to accept a female lawyer in a professional relationship.

In this era, there was stability in firm membership. There was relatively little lateral movement by lawyers from one firm to another, and a person elected to be a partner in an established partnership could expect to spend his entire productive career with that firm. So long as the partner was reasonably productive, he could expect to receive a fair share of the partnership income; if his billings temporarily declined, for example because of ill health, the firm might carry him until he recovered.

In these traditional firms there was a fair amount of specialization among lawyers. The country lawyer or lawyer in general practice who did not hesitate to represent clients no matter what area of law was involved had largely disappeared from major law firms by World War II. Most lawyers had areas of specialization, although it was not uncommon for an individual lawyer to feel comfortable representing clients with problems in several quite different legal areas, for example, taxation, antitrust, and securities law. As the legal system became more complex during this period, however, lawyers generally found it increasingly difficult to retain proficiency in several different areas and therefore there was a trend toward narrowing individual areas of practice and increasing the degree of specialization of individual lawyers.

---

4. The discussion in this and the following sections are drawn from Robert W. Hamilton and Richard Booth, Business Basics for Law Students: Essential Concepts and Applications, 3d Ed. (2002), pages 480–97, and the earlier editions of this book.

Firms generally had established relationships with specific clients that were carefully cultivated. These relationships were often of long standing and based upon a lawyer also serving as the general counsel of the business. Where a single business relied upon more than one law firm, the areas of responsibility of each firm were generally clear-cut and there was little or no competition among the firms. These relationships were usually based on a handshake or on oral understandings.

Billing arrangements were usually flexible. The firm typically did not commit in advance to a price for its services on a specific matter; a new client might be advised of each lawyer's normal billing rate, but the amount of time to be spent was not normally estimated or established in advance. The amount actually billed after the work was completed was decided by the firm and the lawyer with responsibility for the matter. The bill typically stated that it was "for services rendered" without any itemization of costs, charges, or identification of who actually performed the work. The size of the bill might be based on the amount of time spent but more subjective factors also were common: the lawyer's assessment of the result achieved, the complexity of the matter, and what fee the matter would bear. Billing disputes of course occurred from time to time, but they were not common, and when they did occur, they were usually negotiated out as both firm and client recognized the importance of the continuing relationship. Lawyers were encouraged to keep time records, but sometimes these important records were skeletal or fragmentary.

2. THE TRANSITION TO TODAY

The very large law firm of today bears little resemblance to the typical firm of the 1960s. For example, Baker & McKenzie Global Services LLC, the largest American firm, in 2006 had 672 partners and 2,685 associates. It had a total of 3,357 lawyers, with its principal office in Chicago and nine offices in other American cities, plus 54 foreign offices.

The dramatic changes in law firms and the roles of lawyers from the 1960s to the 1990s were a result of fundamental changes in the practice of law. The volume of law business grew rapidly in the late 1960s and over the next two decades. As the demand for legal services grew, firms responded by both raising fees and hiring additional associates and attracting partners from smaller firms. Competition for high quality associates became particularly intense, and salaries increased to previously unheard-of levels—virtually doubling to as much as $85,000 per year in the largest firms—by the 1980s. Firms also opened branch offices in order to provide services to clients with multiple offices or outlets. Finally, there was a strong merger movement among the more successful law firms.

During this boom period, it was profitable to grow by increasing the number of associates. The salary of new associates could be multiplied three-fold and passed on to clients without objection—one-third for the associate, one third for administrative costs, and one-third to be divided as additional profits among the partners. Under this regime, the ratio of associates to partners increased rapidly, from 1:1 (or lower) in the traditional firm of the 1960s to 3:1 or 4:1, and even higher in many instances. Growth in the number of associates simply meant greater profits for the firm and its partners. Firms thus had every incentive to grow rapidly by increasing the number of associates relative to the number of partners, a process known as leveraging.

As word spread about the salaries new lawyers were commanding in the 1980s, the law schools began to receive a flood of additional applications for admission. At about the same time jobs were tightening in many traditional academic areas and many with master's or doctoral degrees changed their career plans and applied to law school. Law schools responded by increasing both standards for admission and the number of students admitted to law school. Tuition increased and several new law schools were opened during this period. While the number of law school graduates rose, jobs were plentiful and the cycle of growth continued. The government developed guaranteed student loan programs that enabled law students to finance virtually their entire legal education through loans on which principal payments began only after graduation. The booming market for young lawyers alleviated any concern about repayment of these loans and many law students took advantage of these generous programs.

In short, in the late 1980s, legal services were a major growth industry. The balloon was punctured by a brief recession that occurred in the late 1980s. The demand for legal services abruptly and unexpectedly failed to continue to grow; some law firms found themselves overstocked with lawyers and expensive office space. Some firms laid off new associates or refused to honor oral commitments to employ individual law graduates. Some firms paid new associates and summer interns a bonus not to accept previous employment offers. Virtually overnight, the market for legal services had changed from a seller's market to a buyer's market.

Notes

(1) The enormous economic changes that have rocked law firms * * * [since 1988] have resulted in a dramatic reversal of * * * one of the most fundamental elements of large law firm structure—partner leverage—according to data from The National Law Journal's annual surveys of the nation's 250 largest law firms.

Joel A. Rose, Firms Rethink Partners' Pay, The National Law Journal, February 15, 1993, p. 24, col. 1.

It is well-known that during the past several years, many of the largest law firms have increased their partnership ranks and decreased their number of associates. Some firms that once had a 2–to–1 associate-to-partner ratio now have more partners than associates. A few large firms now have twice as many, or even three times as many, partners as associates. * * * [T]he benefits once derived from leveraging associates has dried up. This is due to the declining volume of associate-intensive work, such as exhaustive research that a partner wouldn't normally do. As a result, the value of leveraging associates has decreased, as associates who once might have been considered 'profit centers' by their firms have become cost centers.

(2) Decline in leverage in large law firms was the most important single contributor to this tightening since it directly reduced the number of job offers being made to new lawyers for several years. Other factors, however, also contributed: (a) the movement of legal work away from outside law firms and to "inside" counsel of major companies; (b) the decline of certain areas of corporate practice, particularly takeover, merger, and public capital raising, that are ex-

tremely labor-intensive from the legal standpoint; (c) the elimination of the traditional "up or out" approach toward retaining associates and; (d) to a lesser extent, the use of "contract" or temporary lawyers ("temps") rather than hiring permanent associates because of overstaffing concerns.

(3) The decline in leverage also had significant effects on the compensation of some partners. Leverage hid the fact that some individual partners were not paying their own way. Compensation committees were forced to widen the spread of compensation within the firm between the most productive and least productive partners. Traditionally, the compensation ratio between the highest-and lowest-paid law firm partners was in the range of 2–1 to 3–1, with the most junior partners naturally in the lowest ranges and the most senior in the highest ranges. In some firms, the ratio in the mid–1990s was closer to 5–1 (or even higher) and seniority declined as a major factor in determining compensation.

(4) Increased competitiveness within law firms during the early 1990s meant that partners had considerably less security than they had in an earlier era. In the 1960s, an associate who "made" partner could expect to spend the rest of his productive career with the firm so long as he continued to be reasonably productive. In the 1990s, if a partner was not a substantial producer he was usually asked to leave.

JAKE KROCHESKI AND CHARLES J. SANTANGELO, TWO–TIERED PARTNERSHIPS PROLIFERATE[5]

Nat'l L. J., July 5, 1993, at p. 36, col. 1.

Many law firms have had to rethink their strategy of how and when—or even if—to promote associates to partners. The downswing in the economy has caused law firms increasingly to adopt two-tiered partnerships.

A two-tiered structure consists of income partners and equity partners. Income partners are paid a salary that is not contingent on their firms' profits. Equity partners are owners of their firms and share in the profits.

Many law firms are finding that a two-tiered structure is an alternative to terminating talented, well-regarded associates simply because they do not meet all of the criteria for becoming full equity partners. As partners find themselves challenged by a growing range of responsibilities—including management, business development and training—it can be unrealistic for firms to expect their associates to develop strengths in all these areas while improving their legal skills.

Income partners are entitled to many of the same benefits as equity partners, but there are differences. Income partners attain partnership status without assuming any risk. Typically, their privileges include:

- The right to attend firm meetings, except on specific topics that are overseen only by equity partners.
- The right to serve on most firm committees, except the compensation and management committees.
- The right to receive paid benefits—which equity partners typically have to pay for themselves.

5. Reprinted with the permission of the New York Law Publishing Company. National Law Journal, copyright 1993. The

● The right to see the firm's financial picture.

A law firm may promote some individuals to income partner as an interim step.[6] Others may remain at this level because of lifestyle decisions or an inability to meet all the expectations required of equity partners.

Notes

(1) Should "income partners" be viewed as partners if they are paid a fixed salary plus discretionary bonus? Or are they merely employees with a fancy title? In general partnerships, each partner is jointly (or jointly and severally) liable for the actions of all partners. Krocheski and Santangelo state that in a two-tiered firm, equity (or capital) partners "are liable for the debts of the firm, whereas income partners normally are indemnified." *Id.* at col. 2. Is a promise to indemnify income partners—presumably by the partnership—an indication that they are truly partners? If so, does indemnification provide adequate protection from the standpoint of income partners?

(2) In some firms, income and equity partners have essentially the same responsibility toward clients, except that an "equity" partner is expected to be a rainmaker while an income partner is not. In many law firms, a management committee and a managing partner make most decisions on behalf of the firm with other partners entitled to vote only on limited matters. In other law firms, the partner in charge of office management (e.g. hiring and firing of support staff, ordering of supplies, keeping the books) is designated the "managing partner" and the true managers of the firm are a committee of lawyers, typically the "rain makers."

(3) As part of the process of delaying promotion to full partner, some firms created classes of associates as well as classes of partners. Titles for the more senior associates may be "of counsel," "senior counsel," "senior attorney," "participating associate," "staff attorney," or some similar phrase. An associate might be promoted to senior attorney and then face the partnership decision several years later or might remain permanently in the senior attorney status. Thus, some firms created several steps between entering associate and full-scale partner and at the same time created permanent jobs for associates who, for one reason or another, did not "make" partner but were valuable to the firm. Many law firms thus abandoned the traditional "up or out" approach for associates who do not "make" partner.

(4) Even though partners have joint (or joint and several) liability for firm obligations, it was long assumed that the personal risk for individual lawyers in large law firms was entirely theoretical. The major risk, malpractice, could be insured. In the early 1990s, however, there were at least three widely-publicized failures of major law firms. For example, in 1992, the Office of Thrift Supervision sued New York's Kaye, Scholer, Fierman, Hays and Handler for $275 million based on its earlier representation of Lincoln Savings & Loan Association, and at the same time imposed a limited freeze on the law firm's assets. The freeze threatened the continued existence of Kaye Scholer since clients questioned the ability of the law firm to continue to function under the freeze. The parties

---

6. [By the Editors] In Winston & Strawn v. Nosal, 279 Ill.App.3d 231, 664 N.E.2d 239 (1996), for example, Nosal began as an associate with Winston & Strawn in 1970, was promoted to income partner in 1977, and became a capital partner in 1984. In 1992, he received notice that he was being "outplaced" or discharged by the firm, an action which he challenged in the courts.

reached a prompt settlement under which Kaye Scholer agreed to pay $41 million with an immediate payment of $25 million and the balance payable at the rate of $4 million per year for the next four years. Malpractice insurance covered only $21.5 million of this settlement, and therefore the balance was the responsibility of present and former partners. In 1993, another nationally known law firm, Jones, Day, Reavis & Pogue, settled claims also arising out of the Lincoln collapse for $51 million, $19.5 million of which was to be paid by the Jones Day partners over six years. These well-publicized events spurred efforts to develop forms of business that (hopefully) shield partners from massive malpractice claims.

(5) Relatively little publicity is given to the fact that personal liability for law firm obligations is not uncommon in smaller firms. A typical liability that haunts many small firms is a long-term lease of expensive office space.[7] Overly optimistic guaranteed payments to laterals or senior partners also can cause personal liability. These contract liabilities cannot be insured, and therefore smaller firms have a strong incentive to select forms of business that may shield their members from personal liability.

3. THE ECONOMICS OF LAW FIRMS IN THE TWENTY–FIRST CENTURY

The economics of legal practice improved steadily during the late 1990s. Developments in the high technology and telecommunications areas provided a fertile source for new and innovative legal work. Merger activity increased, and the number of negotiated acquisitions of businesses grew steadily. The "bottom line" of most large law firms improved and the number of associates hired increased to reflect the growth in business. While the future appeared rosy, what actually happened at the beginning of 2000 was apparently completely unexpected.

On January 1, 2000, the law firm of Gunderson Dettmer Stough Villeneuve Franklin & Hachigian ("Gunderson Dettmer"), a highly-profitable but little known firm headquartered in Menlo Park, California, announced that it planned to raise salaries for first-year associates in the year 2000 from $100,500 per year ($96,000 in salary plus a guaranteed $4,500 annual bonus) to $145,000 per year ($125,000 in salary plus a guaranteed $20,000 annual bonus). This was base pay for a first year associate: Raises in subsequent years and bonuses for meritorious service in any year were not excluded.

In 2000, Gunderson Dettmer was a firm of about 90 lawyers concentrating on three principal segments of the rapidly emerging "growth company" market: (1) information and communication technology, (2) medical/life science/health care, and (3) consumer/retail products and services. Its four areas of specialization were corporate securities, technology and intellectual property, executive compensation and employment, and taxation. In the furor following its announcement, Gunderson Dettmer felt it necessary to post an elaborate explanation on the internet (http://www.gddsvffh.com/rec_comp.htm) denying that the increase was designed to encourage associates to increase their number of billable hours. Rather, it stated that the increase was designed to encourage associates to remain at the firm and to discourage them from taking jobs with clients. Apparently nine Gunderson Dettmer associates had done precisely that shortly before the announcement.

7. See, e.g., 8182 Maryland Associates v. Sheehan, 14 S.W.3d 576 (Mo. 2000), infra.

The consequences of the Gunderson Dettmer announcement were far reaching.

NATIONAL ASSOCIATION FOR LAW PLACEMENT
THE SALARY WARS AND THEIR AFTERMATH[8]
March 2000.

The "Gunderson Effect" is an epithet characterizing the Year 2000 reverberations that followed one firm's 45% hike in entry-level associate wages last January. Ironically, the Gunderson legacy has evolved into either an "advantage" or an a "albatross" for scores of law firms nationwide as they have been compelled to respond to a compensation strategy that was at best market-specific and at worst unproven as an effective recruitment and retention tool.

When Gunderson Dettmer Stough Villeneuve Franklin & Hachigian boosted first year associates wages * * * they did so in a market where the allure of Silicon Valley dot-coms has precipitated significant brain-drain on law firms. Since January, law firms everywhere have wrestled with the pressure to offer more money to associates. Notwithstanding the groundswell of firms responding with increased salaries, there is agreement that very few firms needed to raise salaries to preclude loss of entry-level associates to sexy Internet start-ups. Those few firms/offices (located in or near the Silicon Valley, San Francisco, Los Angeles and other premier high-tech enterprise sites) quickly followed Gunderson's lead, but, in doing so, firms with a national presence started a coast-to-coast response as they extended the increases to all of their offices, not just those in dot-com country.

As January, February, and March headlines nationwide reveal, firms of all genres in every market have followed suit, some immediately and willingly and others slowly, cautiously, and reluctantly, but without exception, they have done so because law firm managers interpret associate pay raises as a necessary means to sustain their recruitment prowess and preclude inadvertent defections of talent up and down the line.

It is virtually impossible to accurately track and assess the real-time salary fluctuations in individual metropolitan markets, but it is clear that the ripple-effect of the salary raises is spreading from larger markets to smaller markets with expediency. * * *

IMPLICATIONS AND AFTERMATH
the Impact on Law Firms

For some, it's no sweat: Elite law firms with sizeable margins and high profits were able to absorb the latest round of salary hikes without breaking a sweat. Some boast that they could "pay even more, if we had to." As a result, a new hierarchy is evolving in which elite general practice or corporate law firms with national offices as well as boutiques with specialized niches will have prestige status.

---

8. Published by the National Association   and reprinted with permission.
for Law Placement (NALP), Washington, D.C.,

The albatross nests on their necks: Mid-size law firms and law firms of all sizes absent top partner profits and cash reserves are already feeling the weight of the pay increases. Belt-tightening is underway in every realm as many mid-size firms examine the viability of using more contract lawyers, establishing two-tiered compensation tracks, and reducing internal spending. The funds to underwrite associate pay raises come from any of several sources: increased billable hours (by partners and/or associates), increased billable rates (partners and/or associates), partner profits, a firm's cash reserves, and even cuts in personnel costs (hiring fewer associates and augmenting with contract attorneys). Partners as well as associates from firms that are not as profitable as others will be drawn to the wealthiest firms, which will force those less profitable firms to recruit laterally and, in doing so, pose significant new recruitment costs and result in changes in firm culture. Another alternate downside is that with senior associates earning high salaries, some talented lawyers may not care to make partner especially since junior partners may earn about the same as senior associates in less profitable firms.

Partner and associate relationships are being waylaid: It is not hard to imagine that partners whose compensation and/or anticipated profit will be cut by as much as 20% would be a little dismayed over the recent turn of events. Assuming a 2 to 1 partner ratio in a large 500 attorney firm, equity partners will be impacted to the tune of $50,000 or more. Moreover, given the new structures and efforts to relieve salary compression in senior associate ranks, some senior associates will earn more than salaried partners. Why then, will partners remain altruistic toward associates and provide abundant mentoring and coaching for them? Won't partners be ever-the-more demanding, expecting first-year associates who are paid handsomely to be able to perform to near perfection? And it should come as no surprise that evaluations will come earlier and have more teeth than ever before. The Partnership of the future won't carry what they consider "deadwood" further than the door.

Clients wary and decry liability: Firms attempting to incorporate a portion of the pay hikes into billable rates have met with mixed responses, some clients responding with understanding and a willingness to shoulder a fair share of the cost of top talent, and others resisting the trend. In fact, some General Counsels have noted that first-year associates in some firms are earning more than they are, not to mention more than some judges, states attorneys general, and other high-profile attorneys.

Morale of staff, partners, some astute associates declines: Hard-working staffers have watched the bidding wars in awe, noting that "the associates are running the place" and wondering if and when they will ever again benefit from pay raises. Partners, disenchanted with firm profits and the short or long-term prospects for improvement of earnings, may be on the most-wanted list when it comes to retention. And some associates, those who seriously value life balance and who were "content" as opposed to "greedy," are expressing concern about the future of their firms and of their jobs.

Firm culture, pro bono take hits: Meanwhile, the atmosphere in some firms is turning sour. As the battle for billable hours escalates, competition is keen and social interaction lessens. Fewer pro bono hours are volunteered, as are fewer hours for firm recruitment, governance, and community involvement. Leaders from non-profit organizations benefiting from pro bono time fear loss of essential legal services for their clients and non-profit businesses.

Notes

(1) "Sweat bonuses" are widely used arrangements within law firms by which associates receive extra bonuses in a year if they record more than a specified number of billable hours. For example, Morgan, Lewis & Bockius announced in early 2000 that it would pay a bonus of $10,000 to an associate if he or she records 2,000 billable hours or more in a year. This bonus was in addition to assured first year compensation of $115,000. The same firm promised second year associates a base salary of $125,000 with specified bonuses if the associate bills more than 2,000, 2,200 or 2,400 hours during the year. Associate Salaries Explode, 35 Bankruptcy Court Decisions, Volume 35, Issue 25 (May 9, 2000).

(2) Increases in first year associate compensation at large law firms widened the gap between law jobs in the public and private sectors. In 1999, a Department of Justice GS–12 attorney earned between $51,204 and $66,564; an attorney in the Senate Office of Legal Counsel, $47,500. A federal bankruptcy judge with many years' experience earned $129,966 per year. Even federal district court and appellate judges must have felt uncomfortable as law firms offered entry-level associates levels of compensation that approach or exceed the levels they receive. This discomfort was increased by legal restrictions on the power of judges to earn outside income, and led to calls to relax those restrictions.

(3) Revenues received by most large law firms increased significantly in the 1990s. New York's Davis Polk & Wardwell, for example, had revenues of $217 million in fiscal 1989; in fiscal 1999, its revenues had increased to $460 million. Nat'l L.J., N.Y. Pay Edge Drops in 2000, A1, A23, Oct. 2, 2000. However, in many firms personnel costs rose more rapidly than revenues, largely fueled by high salaries for junior associates. See Higher Pay Found to Erode Law Firms' Profit Growth, N.Y. Times, Dec. 12, 2000, at C3.

(4) Many law firms increased their billing rates during the year 2000 in an effort to maintain their revenue base for partners. A study published in the National Law Journal, Some Rates Soar, Others Barely Budge, B13 (Dec. 18, 2000), indicated that a minority of firms increased the billing rates for partners (up to $600 per hour for a few true "rain-making" partners), but more commonly revenue improvement was sought through modest increases in billing rates for associates.

THE YEAR OF THE BUST: 2001

The first indications that the high tech bubble was slowing down appeared in the latter part of 2000. These indications were not taken seriously by many firm managers of highly successful law firms. They remembered the brief slowdown that occurred in the late 1980s and early 1990s, and believed that any decline would be brief and would not affect long term growth. Firms therefore saw no reason to change their plans for 2001, including the number of new associates and summer interns that had been promised jobs, and the compensation levels that were based on the Brobeck Phleger salary scale that had previously been announced to become effective beginning 2001.

The full magnitude of the decline in law business gradually became apparent in the spring and summer of 2001. The decline was first evident in the telecom area but rapidly spread to the high technology area, the "dot-coms." Start-ups that had not developed viable businesses quickly found that the cash window had closed almost overnight. In one telecom area alone, the competitive local exchange carriers, $140 billion had been invested but companies quickly ran out of cash, found themselves unable to raise additional money, and simply defaulted on all planned projects. It has been estimated that 95 percent of the $140 billion invested in this one part of the telecommunication industry was irretrievably lost.

The November 18, 2001 *New York Times* stated that between 1997 and 2000, telecom companies had raised close to one-half trillion dollars but the decline in the value of these companies was "one of the most spectacular investment debacles ever. Bigger than the South Sea Bubble. Bigger than tulip mania. Bigger than dot.bomb. The flameout of the telecommunications sector when it is over will wind up costing investors hundreds of billions of dollars."

The collapse of the dot-com high technology area was not as severe as in the telecom area but followed the same path. Many start-up firms found that there was no way to continue in business without additional capital and there simply was no way to raise that capital. When they closed their doors, lessors and creditors repossessed hardware, office equipment, computers and the like, leaving the dot-coms with liabilities and a business plan, but no assets.

A limited number of new companies survived; many of those that did were taken over by the venture capital firms that had originally financed them while outside investors typically lost their entire investment.

As summer associates and interns began to arrive at large law firms in 2001, it was apparent that there was not enough work to support them. Firms generally honored their basic commitments to these employees and delayed the inevitable reduction. After the September 11, 2001 terrorist attack, many firms announced layoffs. Sherman & Sterling, another major New York firm, announced that it was laying off about 10 percent of its associates, explaining that the firm could not longer maintain a "boom economy work force in a weak economy that has further deteriorated since September 11." An estimated 400 individuals across the country lost their jobs during this period.

The decline in legal business was particularly acute for west coast firms that had grown rapidly during the telecommunications and dot-com bubbles. In November, 2001, Brobeck, Phleger & Harrison announced that it was offering severance pay to associates that would agree to leave the firm voluntarily. Eighty-two associates accepted this offer and left the firm. On February 1, 2002, Brobeck Phleger announced that it was laying off an additional 54 associates and 85 staff members. At the same time, the firm quietly demoted many partners to fixed income status, describing them as having "senior" or "permanent" attorney status. Brobeck later announced that in 2001, it had suffered a 43.6 percent decrease in profits per partner on a 6.1 percent drop in gross revenue and a 14.4 percent decline in revenue per partner. In July of 2002, 18 additional Brobeck partners left the firm and joined California's Clifford Chance.

A number of other west coast firms suffered similar—though significantly smaller—attorney defections or declines in profitability in the 2001–2002 period.

While the decline in legal business was national in scope, many east coast firms posted increases in revenue and a few also recorded increases in overall profitability. In 2001, Sherman & Sterling of New York City posted a five percent increase in gross revenue but a 19 percent drop in revenue per lawyer and a 29.6 percent decrease in profits per partner. Holland & Knight of Tampa, Florida, added more than 100 lateral partners during 2001, resulting in a 28.3 percent increase in gross revenue, but profits per partner fell by 10.1 percent. Some east coast firms also tightened their staffs, laying off associates and transferring weaker partners to fixed income status.

New York firms did considerably better than firms in most cities largely because many of their clients were well-established national firms not directly affected by the dot-com collapse. In 2001, Paul, Weiss, Rifkind, Wharton & Garrison of New York City recorded a 38.8 percent increase in profits per partner, the largest increase of any of the one hundred largest law firms. The majority of the 20 largest New York firms all showed increases in their profits per partner in 2001, which some showing a double-digit gain.

One consequence of the tightening of the market for lawyers in 2001 and 2002 was the quiet disappearance of the high salaries for beginning associates promulgated by Gunderson Dettmer in 2000. School placement counselors therefore increasingly suggested that graduates should apply to smaller and mid-sized firms, or look for staff positions in government or businesses. More recently, the market for corporate lawyers has improved, perhaps as a result of the scandals and resultant legislation in the early years of the new century.

4. RETIREMENT POLICIES IN LAW FIRMS

Many large law firms have programs by which senior partners reaching the age of 60, 62, or 65 are permitted, encouraged, or required to retire, thereby leaving the profit sharing group. Until relatively recently, most law firms did not provide pension benefits for partners. The assumption was that each partner would set aside funds for savings and retirement during his or her productive years at the firm. In specific cases, retirement payments might be informally negotiated when a senior partner agreed to leave the firm. But unfunded pension plans in partnerships face fundamental problems.

BANE v. FERGUSON

United States Court of Appeals, Seventh Circuit, 1989.
890 F.2d 11.

Before POSNER, COFFEY, and KANNE, CIRCUIT JUDGES.

POSNER, CIRCUIT JUDGE.

The question presented by this appeal from the dismissal of the complaint is whether a retired partner in a law firm has either a common law or a statutory claim against the firm's managing council for acts of negligence that, by causing the firm to dissolve, terminate his retirement benefits. It is a diversity case governed by the law of Illinois, rather than a federal-question case governed by the Employee Retirement Income Security Act, 29 U.S.C. §§ 1001 et seq., because ERISA excludes partners from its protections.

Charles Bane practiced corporate and public utility law as a partner in the venerable Chicago law firm of Isham, Lincoln & Beale, founded more than a century ago by Abraham Lincoln's son Robert Todd Lincoln. In August 1985 the firm adopted a noncontributory retirement plan that entitled every retiring partner to a pension, the amount depending on his earnings from the firm on the eve of retirement. The plan instrument provided that the plan, and the payments under it, would end when and if the firm dissolved without a successor entity, and also that the amount paid out in pension benefits each year could not exceed five percent of the firm's net income in the preceding year. Four months after the plan was adopted, the plaintiff retired, moved to Florida with his wife, and began drawing his pension (to continue until his wife's death if he died first) of $27,483 a year. Bane was 72 years old when he retired. So far as appears, he had, apart from social security, no significant source of income other than the pension.

Several months after Bane's retirement, Isham, Lincoln & Beale merged with Reuben & Proctor, another large and successful Chicago firm. The merger proved to be a disaster, and the merged firm was dissolved in April 1988 without a successor whereupon the payment of pension benefits to Bane ceased and he brought this suit. The suit alleges that the defendants were the members of the firm's managing council in the period leading up to the dissolution and that they acted unreasonably in deciding to merge the firm with Reuben & Proctor, in purchasing computers and other office equipment, and in leaving the firm for greener pastures shortly before its dissolution. The suit does not allege that the defendants committed fraud, engaged in self-dealing, or deliberately sought to destroy or damage the law firm or harm the plaintiff; the charge is negligent mismanagement, not deliberate wrongdoing. The suit seeks damages, presumably the present value of the pension benefits to which the Banes would be entitled had the firm not dissolved. * * *

Bane has four theories of liability. The first is that the defendants, by committing acts of mismanagement that resulted in the dissolution of the firm, violated the Uniform Partnership Act * * * [§ 9(3)(c)], which provides that "unless authorized by the other partners * * * one or more but less than all the partners have no authority to: Do any * * * act which would make it impossible to carry on the ordinary business of the partnership." This provision is inapplicable. Its purpose is not to make negligent partners liable to persons with whom the partnership transacts (such as Bane), but to limit the liability of the other partners for the unauthorized act of one partner. See Hackney v. Johnson, 601 S.W.2d 523, 525 (Tex.Civ.App.1980). The purpose in other words is to protect partners. Bane ceased to be a partner when he retired in 1985.

Nor can Bane obtain legal relief on the theory that the defendants violated a fiduciary duty to him; they had none. A partner is a fiduciary of his partners, but not of his former partners, for the withdrawal of a partner terminates the partnership as to him. Adams v. Jarvis, 23 Wis.2d 453, 458, 127 N.W.2d 400, 403 (1964). * * * Even if the defendants were fiduciaries of the plaintiff, moreover, the business-judgment rule would shield them from liability for mere negligence in the operation of the firm, just as it would shield a corporation's directors and officers, who are fiduciaries of the share-holders. * * *

That leaves for discussion Bane's claims of breach of contract and of tort. The plan instrument expressly decrees the death of the plan upon the dissolution of the firm, and nowhere is there expressed a commitment or even an undertaking to maintain the firm in existence, whether for the sake of the plan's beneficiaries or anyone else. Contracts have implicit as well as explicit terms, see, e.g., Wood v. Duff–Gordon, 222 N.Y. 88, 118 N.E. 214 (1917) (Cardozo, J.), and one can imagine an argument that the plaintiff was induced to retire by an implied promise that the managing council would do everything possible to keep the firm going—that without such an implied promise he would not have retired, given his dependence on the firm's retirement plan for his income after he retired. But Bane does not make this argument and anyway it is hopeless. * * *

The last question, which is the most interesting because the most fundamental, is whether the defendants violated a duty of care to the plaintiff founded on general principles of tort law. What is the liability of the managers of a failed enterprise to persons harmed by the failure? When a large firm—whether a law firm, or a manufacturing enterprise, or a bank, or a railroad—fails, and shuts its doors, many persons besides the owners of the firm may be hurt in their pocketbooks—workers, suppliers, suppliers' workers, creditors (like Mr. Bane), and members of these persons' families. * * * We can find no precedent in Illinois law or elsewhere for imposing tort liability on careless managers for the financial consequences of the collapse of the firm to all who are hurt by that collapse. "The act of dissolution of a corporation is not in itself sufficient foundation for [a] tort action even if it results in the breach of contracts. If the dissolution is motivated by good faith judgment for the benefit of the corporation rather than personal gain of the officers, directors or shareholders, no liability attaches to the dissolution." Swager v. Couri, 60 Ill.App.3d 192, 196, 17 Ill.Dec. 457, 460, 376 N.E.2d 456, 459 (1978) (citations omitted). The competence, not the good faith, of the defendants is drawn in question by the complaint. And the principle of *Swager* is as applicable to a partnership as to a corporation. * * *

We are sorry about the financial blow to the Banes but we agree with the district judge that there is no remedy under the law of Illinois.

Notes

(1) The pension plan involved in this case contemplated that retirement payments to former partners were to be made out of future earnings of the firm. In addition to the impermanence of such a plan (as demonstrated by Judge Posner's opinion), these plans almost invariably lead to inter-generational conflict, as younger partners in their most productive years resent losing a portion of their earnings to benefit retired partners. In many instances, productive junior partners left firms in order to be free of unfunded retirement obligations to senior partners. Would the result in Bane v. Ferguson have been any different if the plaintiff could have shown that the partnership was only dissolved to permit the existing partners to avoid their pension obligations under the pension plan? How else might this pension have been funded?

(2) Law firms that provide retirement plans for their retired partners today generally require the beneficiaries themselves to fund the plans during their productive years. In many firms, partners are expected to provide for their own retirement entirely on their own by creation of tax-deferred Keogh or other plans that permit the accumulation of substantial retirement benefits over a career.

D.   LIMITED LIABILITY PARTNERSHIPS (LLPS)

ROBERT W. HAMILTON, REGISTERED LIMITED LIABILITY PARTNERSHIPS: PRESENT AT THE BIRTH (NEARLY)

66 Colo.L.Rev. 1065, 1069–71 (1995).

The LLP is a direct outgrowth of the collapse of real estate and energy prices in the late 1980s, and the concomitant disaster that befell Texas's banks and savings and loan associations. Texas led the nation in bank and savings and loan failures during the 1980s. More than one-third of all the bank failures in the United States occurred in Texas.

Ever since the collapse of these financial institutions across the state, the Federal Deposit Insurance Corporation ("FDIC") and the Resolution Trust Corporation ("RTC") (and its predecessor, the Federal Savings and Loan Insurance Corporation ("FSLIC")) have devoted a significant part of their total resources to the recovery of funds lost in the collapse of Texas institutions. Suit was brought against hundreds of shareholders, directors and officers of failed financial institutions. However, the amounts recovered from the principal wrongdoers were only a tiny fraction of total losses and attention quickly turned to the roles of the lawyers and accountants who had represented the failed financial institutions before their collapse. "Where were the lawyers?" and "Where were the public accountants?" were cries figuratively heard across the state. Claims against lawyers and accountants for malpractice and breach of duty were attractive because the individual professionals sometimes had been deeply involved in the affairs of their clients. Also, these lawyers and accountants were usually associated with partnerships that had substantial malpractice insurance and numerous wealthy partners. As a result, several highly reputable law firms in Texas found themselves in deep trouble because of their bank and thrift work during the "salad days" of the 1980s.

The most vivid example is provided by a major Dallas law firm (hereafter referred to as the "Dallas Law Firm").[9] Long recognized as one of the leading corporate law firms in the state, the Dallas Law Firm in the early 1980s was a traditional general partnership.[10] One Dallas Law Firm partner, Laurence Vineyard, along with four associates, did legal work for three savings and loan associations. * * * In addition to providing legal services, it turned out that Vineyard sat on the board of directors of at least one of the S & Ls and had profitable financial arrangements with the others. These three S & Ls were among the more flagrant "high fliers" which paid little attention to principles of sound financial management and provided lavish benefits and large unsecured loans for their owners. Losses from the collapse of these three S & Ls ran over one billion dollars. Vineyard was deeply involved. He was criminally prosecuted, convicted, sentenced to two five year prison terms, and dis-

---

9. [By the Author] The firm continues in business today under its original name and has requested that it not be specifically identified in this paper.

10. [By the Author] The present Dallas Law Firm is a professional corporation.

barred.[11] His personal assets were insubstantial in light of the losses incurred by the S & Ls, and the FSLIC and FDIC turned their attention to the malpractice insurer for the Dallas Law Firm and to all persons who were partners during the period the firm represented the S & Ls. Caught within the FSLIC/FDIC net were retired partners, partners who had since left the Dallas Law Firm to join other firms,[12] partners who had been promoted from associate to partner, persons who had become "of counsel" to the Dallas Law Firm, and the forty-some partners who had nothing at all to do with representation of the various thrift institutions. The total claims asserted by the FSLIC greatly exceeded the liability insurance available to the firm and the assets of the firm itself. To emphasize this point, in one particularly chilling meeting, FSLIC personnel used an overhead projector to show a slide listing the names of each Dallas Law Firm defendant with estimates of total net worth and the amount likely to be available from each of them to satisfy the government's claims.

Needless to say, the Dallas Law Firm litigation caught the attention of the hundreds of law firms that had represented banks or thrifts during the 1980s. Thousands of lawyers in hundreds of Texas law firms watched this litigation closely as it unfolded in the late 1980s with a "there but for the grace of God go I" reaction. The lawsuit against the Dallas Law Firm was ultimately settled for approximately the amount of malpractice insurance carried by the firm.

Notes

(1) The LLP statute enacted by Texas in 1991 was designed to meet this perceived liability crisis. As originally enacted, it differs in several significant respects from UPA (1997) § 306(c): (a) The Texas statute was limited only to acts of negligence or malpractice and did not cover contract or other liabilities. (b) It required each electing LLP to maintain either a fidelity bond or liquid assets of at least $100,000 for the protection of malpractice creditors. (c) It did not expressly cover obligations of a partner to indemnify other partners [UPA (1914) § 18(b)] or to contribute to the assets of the partnership on winding up [UPA (1914) § 40(d)]. (d) It expressly imposed liability on partners who had a responsibility of oversight of partners or associates that committed acts of negligence or malpractice. Similar statutes were promptly enacted in Delaware and other states.

(2) Almost from the outset, other states developing LLP statutes broadened the limited protection provided by the Texas statute. The first "fixes" to the

---

11. [By the Author] Vineyard was actually convicted in connection with transactions involving a Colorado S & L that occurred after he left the Dallas Law Firm. He was also convicted for diverting loan proceeds from an approved S & L project to the purchase of his personal residence, a transaction that also occurred after he had left the Dallas Law Firm. However, the government cited and relied upon these criminal convictions when raising questions about the validity of transactions he performed for the S & Ls while a partner with the Dallas Law Firm. See United States v. Vineyard, 699 F. Supp. 103 (N.D.Tex.1988) (ordering Vineyard to pay millions of dollars restitution for the damage caused by these loans).

12. [By the Author] FSLIC made a major effort to recover a portion of the losses from the malpractice insurers of the firms to which former Dallas Law Firm partners had moved. Malpractice insurance is written on a "claims made" basis, and notice was given after these lawyers had joined their new firms. Some of these firms had independent potential exposure to S & L liability because of their own representation of S & Ls as well as derivative exposure arising from the claims being asserted against former partners of the Dallas Law Firm. Global settlements were negotiated with some of these firms, involving substantial payments to the federal agencies.

statute related to the problems of indemnification and contribution and the issue whether the shield of limited liability could be "evaded" by artful pleading of a malpractice claim as breach of contract rather than as a tort. As states continued to enact these statutes, the shield of limited liability was broadened significantly to cover claims arising from contract as well as malpractice or tort. Section 306(c) of UPA (1997) (added in 1996) is an example. Such statutes are called "broad shield" statutes (as contrasted with "narrow shield" statutes, that, like the original Texas statute, provide protection only against malpractice or tort claims). About 17 states have adopted broad shield statutes; the Texas statute itself was broadened to a full shield statute in 1997.

(3) The narrow shield statutes (like the original Texas statute) do not affect basic partnership rules except when firms actually face substantial malpractice claims in excess of their malpractice insurance plus the undistributed assets in the partnership. In all other situations, the traditional partnership rules apply. Thus, of all the millions or billions of partnership transactions that occur each year in the United States, very few are affected by the narrow shield statutes.

(4) The same cannot be said of the modern broad shield LLP statutes, which make all electing partnerships into limited liability entities, and which potentially affect basic partnership rules whenever the partnership is unable to satisfy all of its obligations from partnership assets. Is there any policy justification for broadening the shield to cover liability arising from transactions voluntarily entered into? Law and economics scholars, exemplified by Professor Larry Ribstein, have put forth a normative argument that limited liability is the preferred policy for contractual obligations of business entities and therefore the broad shield statutes "get it right." See Larry E. Ribstein, The Deregulation of Limited Liability and the Death of Partnership, 70 Wash.U.L.Q. 417 (1992). Limited liability is preferable, he argues, because it encourages passive investments in firms as well as protecting inadvertent or unwary partners from unexpected and crushing liabilities. Furthermore, he suggests that the shield may easily be "contracted around," so that sophisticated persons dealing with an LLP always may obtain personal liability by express agreement.

(5) These arguments assume that persons dealing with a partnership are or should be aware that the letters "LLP" in the name of the firm reverse the traditional view that partners are jointly and severally liable for partnership obligations. That assumption may not be justified. See Susan Saab Fortney, Professional Responsibility and Liability Issues Related to Limited Liability Partnerships, 39 S.Tex.L.Rev. 399, 414–15 (1998):

> Eighty-five percent of the [questionnaire] respondents (79 persons) reported that they did not "know how a law firm organizing itself as a limited liability partnership or limited liability company affects the malpractice liability of the firm's attorneys." Similarly, 85% (79 persons) indicated that they did not know how incorporation affects attorney malpractice liability. Presumably, the survey respondents as members of a metropolitan Chamber of Commerce possess more business acumen than members of the general population. Nevertheless, the vast majority of respondents did not appreciate the significance of law firms operating as PCs [professional corporations], LLCs or LLPs.

(6) Other concerns about the effect of the LLP election have also been expressed. See Jennifer J. Johnson, Limited Liability for Lawyers: General Partners Need Not Apply, 51 Bus.Law. 85, 139–40 (1995); Robert R. Keating, et al.,

Limited Liability Partnerships: The Next Step in the Evolution of the Unincorporated Business Organization, 51 Bus.Law 147, 184 (1995).

(7) It is true that even under broad shield LLP statutes individual partners may become personally liable because of their own conduct. Indeed, there is no shortage in the literature of possible theories by which the LLP's shield of limited liability may be pierced in litigation: theories of misrepresentation, fraud, fraudulent transfers, and breach of a duty of full and fair disclosure required by general ethical principles.

(8) Many lawyers believe that the LLP shield is more "porous" than the shield provided by corporations or limited liability companies. For example, does the principle that any change in membership in a partnership constitutes a termination of the old partnership and the creation of a new partnership affect the LLP election? Many law firms that have elected LLP status practice in more than one state. Does an LLP registered in State A have a shield of limited liability with respect to its office in State B?[13] There are at least four plausible answers: (a) Yes, State B should as a matter of comity or full faith and credit accord the LLP its statutory protection provided by the laws of State A; (b) no, in State B the LLP is a general partnership because it has never registered as an LLP in State B; (c) maybe, since State B should apply its own LLP statute to foreign LLPs as a matter of public policy; and (d) yes, State B should treat the LLP as if it were a foreign corporation, not a partnership.

(9) Many states now permit law, accounting, and professional firms to conduct business as professional corporations (PCs) or limited liability companies (LLCs) as well as LLPs. However, professional firms do not widely use these alternatives perhaps in part because in some states franchise taxes and filing fees are higher for PCs and LLCs than for LLPs.

E.   MANAGEMENT

NATIONAL BISCUIT CO. v. STROUD
Supreme Court of North Carolina, 1959.
249 N.C. 467, 106 S.E.2d 692.

PARKER, JUSTICE.

C.N. Stroud and Earl Freeman entered into a general partnership to sell groceries under the firm name of Stroud's Food Center. There is nothing in the agreed statement of facts to indicate or suggest that Freeman's power and authority as a general partner were in any way restricted or limited by the articles of partnership in respect to the ordinary and legitimate business of the partnership. Certainly, the purchase and sale of bread were ordinary and legitimate business of Stroud's Food Center during its continuance as a going concern.

---

13. [By the Editors] Some states have enacted registration or filing procedures for foreign LLPs. Rhode Island Gen.Laws, 1956, § 7–12–59, for example, requires foreign LLPs to file a notice with the Rhode Island Secretary of State giving basic information about the LLP. The fee for filing this notice is $1,000 and is valid for two years. By filing this notice, "[t]he internal affairs of foreign registered limited liability partnerships, including the liability of partners for debts, obligations and liabilities of or chargeable to the partnership or another partner or partners, are subject to and governed by the laws of the jurisdiction in which the foreign limited partnership is registered." Assume that a Boston law firm that is a registered LLP in Massachusetts opens a two-person office in Providence, Rhode Island, but because of an oversight fails to file the required notice. What is the potential liability of the two partners stationed in Providence?

Several months prior to February 1956, Stroud advised plaintiff that he personally would not be responsible for any additional bread sold by plaintiff to Stroud's Food Center. After such notice to plaintiff, it from 6 February 1956 to 25 February 1956, at the request of Freeman, sold and delivered bread in the amount of $171.04 to Stroud's Food Center.

In Johnson v. Bernheim, 76 N.C. 139, this Court said: "A and B are general partners to do some given business; the partnership is, by operation of law, a power to each to bind the partnership in any manner legitimate to the business. If one partner go to a third person to buy an article on time for the partnership, the other partner cannot prevent it by writing to the third person not to sell to him on time; or, if one party attempt to buy for cash, the other has no right to require that it shall be on time. And what is true in regard to buying is true in regard to selling. What either partner does with a third person is binding on the partnership. It is otherwise where the partnership is not general, but is upon special terms, as that purchases and sales must be with and for cash. There the power to each is special, in regard to all dealings with third persons at least who have notice of the terms." There is contrary authority. 68 C.J.S. Partnership § 143, pp. 578–579. However, this text of C.J.S. does not mention the effect of the provisions of the Uniform Partnership Act.

The General Assembly of North Carolina in 1941 enacted a Uniform Partnership Act, which became effective 15 March 1941. G.S. Ch. 59, Partnership, Art. 2. * * *

[The Court quotes UPA (1914) §§ 9(1), 9(4), 18(e), 18(h) and the North Carolina version of UPA (1914) § 15, which reads, "All partners are jointly and severally liable for the acts and obligations of the partnership."]

Freeman as a general partner with Stroud, with no restrictions on his authority to act within the scope of the partnership business, so far as the agreed statement of facts shows, had under the Uniform Partnership Act "equal rights in the management and conduct of the partnership business." Under [UPA (1914) § 18(h)] Stroud, his co-partner, could not restrict the power and authority of Freeman to buy bread for the partnership as a going concern, for such a purchase was an "ordinary matter connected with the partnership business," for the purpose of its business and within its scope, because in the very nature of things Stroud was not, and could not be, a majority of the partners. Therefore, Freeman's purchases of bread from plaintiff for Stroud's Food Center as a going concern bound the partnership and his co-partner Stroud. * * *

In Crane on Partnership, 2d Ed., p. 277, it is said: "In cases of an even division of the partners as to whether or not an act within the scope of the business should be done, of which disagreement a third person has knowledge, it seems that logically no restriction can be placed upon the power to act. The partnership being a going concern, activities within the scope of the business should not be limited, save by the expressed will of the majority deciding a disputed question; half of the members are not a majority." * * *

At the close of business on 25 February 1956, Stroud and Freeman by agreement dissolved the partnership. By their dissolution agreement all of the partnership assets, including cash on hand, bank deposits and all accounts receivable, with a few exceptions, were assigned to Stroud, who bound himself by such written dissolution agreement to liquidate the firm's assets and discharge its liabilities. It would seem a fair inference from the agreed statement of facts that the partnership got the benefit of the bread sold and delivered by plaintiff to Stroud's Food Center, at Freeman's request, from 6 February 1956 to 25 February 1956. But whether it did or not, Freeman's acts, as stated above, bound the partnership and Stroud.

The judgment of the court below is affirmed.

RODMAN, J., dissents.

SMITH v. DIXON

Supreme Court of Arkansas, 1965.
238 Ark. 1018, 386 S.W.2d 244.

HOLT, JUSTICE.

The appellee, as purchaser, brought this action against appellants, as sellers, for the specific performance of a contract for the sale of realty and in the alternative sought damages for nonperformance of the contract.

The appellants are E.F. Smith, his wife, and their children and spouses. This entire family constitutes a business firm known as E.F. Smith & Sons, A Partnership. The "Contract For Sale of Realty With Lease" was signed by one of the appellants, W.R. Smith, on behalf of the family partnership.

By the terms of the contract, executed in March 1962, the partnership agreed to sell the 750 acre "Cracraft" plantation for $200,000.00 and convey title to the appellee on January 3, 1963. In the interim, by the lease provisions, the appellee took possession, farmed, and improved a portion of the property. Upon refusal of the appellants to convey the land as recited in the contract, the appellee instituted this action. The chancellor denied specific performance and awarded appellee special damages in the amount of $11,512.73. * * *

The partnership was created a short time after the lands in controversy were acquired by the family in 1951. The court found that:

"Soon after the purchase of 'Cracraft' [the lands in question] and the 'Sterling Place,' the Smiths, at the suggestion and on the recommendation of the financial institutions, who were to finance the farming operations for them on the farms, organized and formed a partnership known as E.F. Smith & Sons. They term the partnership an 'operating partnership'. The general purpose of the firm was to engage in farming operations on the farms, including direct cultivation and renting to others. The operation was later expanded to engage in the general farming business in the area. The partnership agreement was oral and has never been reduced to writing. Mr. W.R. Smith is the predominant member of both the partnership and the Smiths. He serves as the managing partner with general powers, with Mr. Charles Smith in charge of production. The other members of the partnership did not, nor at the present time, appear to have any direct participation or responsibility in the operation. * * *

"The firm, by and through its managing partner, Mr. W.R. Smith, has acted as agent for or under contract with, the Smiths, in the sale of the

'Sterling Place' to Mr. Rankin, in a similar capacity in another land conveyance and as trustee for another purchase."

It appears undisputed that appellant W.R. Smith was authorized by the members of the partnership to negotiate for the sale of the lands in question to the appellee. However, it is claimed that his authorization was based upon different terms of sale, mainly, a price of $225,000.00 instead of $200,000.00. Therefore, it is urged that the contract is unenforceable since it was not signed nor ratified by other members of the family.

In the case of May v. Ewan, 169 Ark. 512, 275 S.W. 754, we held that a partnership is bound by the acts of a partner when he acts within the scope or *apparent* scope of his authority. There we quoted with approval:

> * * * In order to determine the apparent scope of the authority of a partner, recourse may frequently be had to past transactions indicating a custom or course of dealing peculiar to the firm in question.

See, also [UPA (1914) §§ 8–10]. In the case at bar it was customary in past transactions, as in the present one, for the partnership to rely upon the co-partner, W.R. Smith, to transact the business affairs of the firm. We agree with the chancellor that appellant W.R. Smith was acting within the apparent scope of his authority as a partner when he signed the contract and that it is binding and enforceable upon the partnership. * * *

Notes

(1) Is National Biscuit Co. v. Stroud a case of actual authority or apparent authority? What about Smith v. Dixon?

(2) Partnerships and many other agency relationships may involve simultaneous actual and apparent authority. For example, if Freeman had been an employee or agent of Stroud rather than a partner, it is clear that Stroud could revoke any actual authority that Freeman might have to bind him to a purchase of bread simply by notifying Freeman. However, despite such notice, Freeman might still have the power under concepts of apparent authority to bind Stroud to a purchase of bread unless Nabisco is advised of the revocation of authority. In the actual case, of course, Stroud actually advised Nabisco that he did not intend to be bound by further purchases by Freeman yet he was held liable as a result of the court's decision. How can this be?

(3) Would the result in Smith v. Dixon be changed if W.R. Smith had been an agent or employee of E.F. Smith & Sons rather than the "predominant member" or "managing partner with general powers?" In light of the fact that W. R. Smith was the "managing partner" and "predominant member" of the partnership why didn't the court hold that he had actual authority? What do you think is the key fact in this case?

(4) To what extent do the basic concepts of actual authority and apparent authority appear in UPA (1914) §§ 9(1), 9(2), and 9(4)? In UPA (1997) § 301?

(5) What should a person in Stroud's position do if he or she no longer trusts the co-partner and wishes to avoid liability for future bread purchases by the partnership?

(6) How does one ascertain the scope of the phrase "for apparently carrying on in the usual way the business of the partnership" in UPA (1914) § 9(1) or UPA (1997) § 301?

(a) Many partnership agreements contain a recitation of the business to be carried on. For example, "The purpose of the Partnership is to engage in the sale, service, and repair of all types of outboard and inboard motor boats, outboard and inboard motors, and all character of marine equipment and accessories." Alan R. Bromberg, Crane and Bromberg on Partnership 599 (1968). Are such recitations relevant?

(b) Consider Burns v. Gonzalez, 439 S.W.2d 128 (Tex.Civ.App.—San Antonio 1969, writ ref'd n.r.e.), in which the Court concluded that there was no reason to depart from the normal rule that the party who asserts that the particular act of an agent is within the scope of the agent's authority has the burden of proving the extent of that authority.

(7) To what extent may the management rights of partners be varied by agreement? It is important to note that UPA (1914) § 18 is qualified by the phrase "subject to any agreement between them." Does that mean that anything goes? Can management of a partnership be vested solely in one partner or in a person who is not a partner? What is the legal effect of a partnership agreement between A and B that states "X shall have the sole power to manage the business and affairs of the partnership and A and B shall have no power to participate in partnership decisions or to bind the partnership to third persons?" Given the potential responsibility of A and B for partnership liabilities, why would they ever agree to such a provision? Is this not an attempt to eliminate the authority granted partners in UPA (1914) § 9 by agreement? Yet § 9 does not contain the phrase "subject to any agreement among them." If despite such a provision, B obtains a loan from a bank in the partnership name, is the partnership liable to the bank even though B subsequently misappropriates the money? Compare UPA (1914) §§ 9(1), 13, 14, 15; UPA (1997) §§ 103(a), 301.

(8) The partnership agreement is often referred to as "the law of the partnership" for that particular partnership. A partnership is a consensual arrangement and that the substantive rules governing the internal affairs of a partnership may generally be altered by agreement. But see UPA (1997) § 103(b). Third parties are not bound by provisions in the agreement and may enforce rights and liabilities created by UPA (1914) or UPA (1997) without regard to the agreement. See UPA (1997) § 103(b)(10). May the authority granted partners in UPA (1914) § 9 or UPA (1997) § 301 itself be eliminated by agreement if potential creditors are given notice?

(9) UPA (1997) authorizes partnerships and partners to make a public filing of a "statement of partnership authority." See, UPA (1997) § 303; UPA (1997) § 105. UPA (1914) contains no similar provisions. This innovation is patterned upon provisions in the Georgia statute. See Ga. Code Ann. § 14–8–10.1. Does § 303 mean that Nabisco would have to check the public filings before it can safely sell bread on credit to a business such as Stroud's Food Center? With respect to real estate transfers, does not § 303 simply create one more piece of paper that a title examiner must examine in connection with transfers of real estate by partnerships?

ROUSE v. POLLARD
Court of Chancery of New Jersey, 1941.
129 N.J.Eq. 47, 18 A.2d 5, affirmed 130 N.J.Eq. 204, 21 A.2d 801 (1941).

Bigelow, Vice Chancellor.

The seven defendants were partners engaged in the general practice of law, their firm is well-known and enjoying a high reputation for skill and integrity. Complainant was their client. The member of the firm who took care of her legal business was Thomas E. Fitzsimmons. At almost her first interview with him, she disclosed that she owned valuable securities, whereupon he immediately suggested that she sell them and turn the money over to the firm, saying that they would invest for her in good mortgages, and send her the interest every six months. Accordingly, on June 21, 1927, complainant endorsed to Fitzsimmons a check for the proceeds of her securities, $28,253, which he deposited in his personal bank account. Out of this sum, he gave the firm's bookkeeper $350 on account of complainant, for legal services unconnected with this transaction. He paid to her or on her order $403, retaining the balance. For several years he sent her a check every January and July for an amount equal to three percent of the principal sum. In 1931, at her request, he paid complainant $7,000 and thereafter through 1937 continued to pay her interest on $20,500. Meanwhile, the law firm, of which defendants were members, was dissolved at the end of 1932.

In January, 1938, Fitzsimmons was arrested for embezzlement, was found to have defrauded a large number of persons and was sentenced to the State Prison. No mortgages or other securities representing complainant's $20,500 have been discovered and from the vagueness of Fitzsimmons' testimony, I am satisfied that immediately upon receipt of her money in 1927, he converted it to his own use. She may, of course, have a decree against Fitzsimmons but he is insolvent. The question is whether the other defendants are liable to her.

Until after Fitzsimmons' exposure, his co-defendants were entirely ignorant that complainant had entrusted him with any money, or had any dealings with him except for ordinary law work. Neither the payment to the firm of $350 by Fitzsimmons on complainant's account, nor any other circumstance which has been proved, was sufficient to put the partners on notice that he held other funds of complainant. They did not suspect or have reason to suspect him of improper conduct in this or other matters until long after the partnership was dissolved. Complainant can recover only if the partners are answerable for Fitzsimmons' malfeasance. They are responsible only if he was acting as their agent in accepting complainant's money. Certainly he had no express authority to act for his co-defendants in this regard. If there were authority, it existed only by implication from the fact that he and they were partners.

As a general rule, each partner is, by virtue of the partnership relation, authorized to act as the general agent for his co-partners in all matters coming within the scope of the business of the firm, in the same manner and to the same extent as if he had full power of attorney from his co-partners. All the partners are responsible for the act of one of their number as agent, even though he acts for some secret purpose of his own, and not really for the benefit of the firm. Restatement–Agency [2d], sec. 165.[14] Where one partner, by fraudulent promises made in a transaction within the scope of the partnership business, obtains money from a third person and misappropriates

14. [By the Editors] Section 165 provides: "A disclosed or partially disclosed principal is subject to liability upon a contract purported to be made on his account by an agent authorized to make it for the principal's benefit, although the agent acts for his own or other improper purposes, unless the other party has notice that the agent is not acting for the principal's benefit."

it, the other partners are liable. While the agency of a partner extends to all matters connected with the business in which the partnership is engaged, his authority extends no further. If the transaction is outside the partnership business, the other partners are not liable and they are not bound by a statement of the partner who conducts such transaction that he is acting on behalf of the firm.

So we come to the question whether the receipt of complainant's money by Fitzsimmons was a transaction within the scope of defendant's business. The scope of any line of business may be gauged by the usual and ordinary course in which such business is carried on by those engaged in it in the locality where the partnership has its seat. But the scope may be broadened by the actual though exceptional course and conduct of the business of the partnership itself, as carried on with the knowledge, actual or presumed, of the partner sought to be charged.

In their practice, defendants frequently had in their hands moneys belonging to clients, held for a particular purpose such as investment in a certain mortgage. But they were not in the habit of receiving, and indeed never received, money from a client to place on mortgage at their discretion. Fitzsimmons, doubtless in other cases besides the present one, received money for general investment and represented when doing so that he was acting for the firm. But the other members of the firm had no knowledge of such actions or representations on his part.

In England, although the receipt of money to be invested on a particular security may be considered an incident of an attorney's or solicitor's business, the receipt of money for the purpose of investment generally, or to invest it in mortgage as soon as a good mortgage can be found, is not so considered. No proof has been presented to show how the practice of law is usually carried on in New Jersey, and none is necessary, for that is a subject with which the court is familiar. The receipt of money for the purpose of investing it as soon as a good mortgage can be found, as was done by Fitzsimmons in the case at bar, is not part of the practice of law according to the usual and ordinary course pursued in New Jersey.

It follows that Fitzsimmons' partners are not answerable to complainant and as to them the bill will be dismissed.

Notes

(1) If Rouse v. Pollard arose under UPA (1914), which sections would be decisive? § 9? § 13? § 14? § 15?

(2) The opinion of the Court of Errors and Appeals of New Jersey affirming the principal case contains a somewhat fuller description of what happened (130 N.J.Eq. at 205–06, 21 A.2d at 802–03):

> In the course of the incidental conferences Fitzsimmons asked Mrs. Rouse what money she possessed and was informed by her of the amount thereof and the manner in which it was invested. According to Mrs. Rouse:
>
> > He said that securities was a bad thing for a woman in my position to have and he suggested that I turn over my securities and sell them and turn the money over to the firm, that they dealt in gilt edge mortgage bonds, as he said. He said that they did that for their clients and it was

perfectly secure. I asked if it was all right for me and he said that is the only way they would take care of it and I would get my check every six months. He said if I handed it at once they would place it the first of July and I did place it the 15th and the 15th of January was the first check.

Mrs. Rouse wrote to her brokers directing them to sell her securities and to "forward a check for the same payable to me to my attorney, Mr. Thomas E. Fitzsimmons, c/o Riker & Riker, 24 Commerce Street, Newark, N.J." A check for $28,252.67 was sent as directed, was endorsed by Mrs. Rouse "Pay to the order of Thos. E. Fitzsimmons" and was deposited by Fitzsimmons in his personal bank account. No part ever came to the firm except $350, or thereabouts, which was paid by Fitzsimmons to the firm for the legal services rendered, and no member of the firm, other than Fitzsimmons, knew of the transaction. The bill of complaint specifically exonerates the remaining members from any fraud, deceit or misappropriation. On January 16, 1928, Fitzsimmons wrote Mrs. Rouse: "Enclosed herewith find my check for $825, being six months' interest at 6% on the $27,500, which I have invested for you." On July 19, 1932, Fitzsimmons wrote: "I enclose herewith check for $615, representing six months' interest on the money which I have invested for you." For more than ten years interest payments went to Mrs. Rouse by Fitzsimmons' personal check. $7,000 of the principal was returned to her, likewise by Fitzsimmons' check, and the receipt was by Mrs. Rouse to Fitzsimmons, personally. The letter from Fitzsimmons to Mrs. Rouse accompanying the check reads:

> As requested, I enclose herewith check for $7,000, which sum is to be deducted from the amount which I have invested for you on bond and mortgage. I am also enclosing a receipt for such amount which I would request you to sign and return to me.

So, too, the receipt to Mrs. Rouse showing a balance retained to invest is by Fitzsimmons, personally. That was in October of 1931. On December 31, 1932, Fitzsimmons retired from the firm of Riker and Riker, and complainant had actual notice of this fact at that time or shortly thereafter. From then on Fitzsimmons' letters to Mrs. Rouse were written on his own stationery from his new office address, and Mrs. Rouse never thereafter went to, or communicated with, the Riker firm until after she had learned, in the early spring of 1938, of Fitzsimmons' defalcations and arrest.

Do these facts suggest an alternative ground for the decision in Rouse v. Pollard?

(3) The opinion of the Court of Errors and Appeals also gives additional information and detail about the nature of the firm practice of Riker and Riker (130 N.J.Eq. at 208–09, 21 A.2d at 803–04):

> The firm did engage extensively in what is known as a "real estate practice"; it represented banks, building and loan associations and estates; it examined titles, closed mortgages and drew necessary documents relating to mortgage investments by clients; it had clients' funds and trust funds on deposit awaiting the closing or other requirements of transactions for which such funds were held; it did not do a general investment business and it did not accept funds for future, unspecified investment, at the firm's discretion, in mortgages or otherwise.
>
> We do not understand that it is a characteristic function of the practice of law to accept clients' money for deposit and future investment in unspeci-

fied securities at the discretion of the attorney, and we find to the contrary. It is possible that attorneys in isolated instances have done this; just as it is possible that a person of any profession or occupation has done so. It has not, however, been done by lawyers, in this jurisdiction at least, with such frequency or appropriateness as to become a phase of the practice.

Assuming that a person knowledgeable about law firms would understand this, should Mrs. Rouse be held to this standard? If she goes to a well-known law firm for assistance in a divorce settlement, is introduced to a partner, Mr. Fitzsimmons, and is told by him what the scope of the business of the firm is, can't she rely on the accuracy of this information?

(4) What would you suggest an attorney do if she learns that a partner has accepted money under the circumstances Fitzsimmons accepted Mrs. Rouse's funds in the principal case?

ROACH v. MEAD

Supreme Court of Oregon, 1986.
301 Or. 383, 722 P.2d 1229.

Before PETERSON, C.J., and LENT, LINDE, CAMPBELL, CARSON and JONES, JJ.

JONES, JUSTICE.

* * * At trial, defendant, David J. Berentson, moved for a directed verdict, contending that he was not vicariously liable for the negligent acts of his partner, Kenneth E. Mead, because the negligent acts were outside the scope of the partnership's business. The trial court denied the motion, and the jury found defendant liable for $20,000 damages * * *. The Court of Appeals held that defendant attorney was vicariously liable for his former partner's negligence. We affirm the Court of Appeals. * * *

Mead, defendant's former law partner, first represented plaintiff in December 1974 on a traffic charge and later represented plaintiff on several occasions. On November 1, 1979, Mead and defendant formed a law partnership. Mead continued to advise plaintiff on other traffic charges and on business dealings. Defendant prepared plaintiff's income tax returns.

In June 1980, plaintiff sold his meter repair business for $50,000. On November 25, 1980, plaintiff asked for Mead's advice on investing $20,000 in proceeds from the sale. Plaintiff testified that Mead told plaintiff that "he would take [the money] at 15 percent. So, I let him have it. * * * I trusted him and felt he would look out for me." Plaintiff considered Mead's advice to be legal advice; he testified that otherwise he would not have consulted an attorney.

After plaintiff agreed to the loan, Mead executed a promissory note for $20,000 payable on or before November 25, 1982, at 15 percent interest. Mead said that he would be receiving a large sum of money with which he would repay plaintiff. Mead offered to secure the loan with a second mortgage on his house, and plaintiff replied that he should do "whatever you think is best." Mead did not secure the loan.

On May 1, 1981, Mead went to plaintiff's home and requested a $1,500 loan, telling plaintiff he was in financial trouble but "had big money coming in." Plaintiff agreed to the loan and Mead added the $1,500 to the amount due on the promissory note.[15] Mead did not repay any money to plaintiff and later was declared bankrupt.[16]

Plaintiff sued defendant's partnership for negligence, alleging that the partnership failed to disclose the conflicting interests of plaintiff and Mead, to advise plaintiff to seek independent legal advice, to inform plaintiff of the risks involved in an unsecured loan, and to advise plaintiff that the loan would not be legally enforceable because the rate of interest was usurious. * * *

I. VICARIOUS LIABILITY

Plaintiff contends that Mead negligently advised him about the loan and that defendant should be vicariously liable for Mead's negligent legal advice. Defendant, while conceding that Mead was negligent, argues that the transaction between plaintiff and Mead was a personal loan outside the scope of the partnership, and that the evidence did not prove that soliciting personal loans was within Mead's express, implied or apparent authority as defendant's law partner. * * *

[The Court quotes UPA (1914) §§ 9(1), 9(2), 9(4), 13, and 15(a).]

Liability of partners for the acts of co-partners is based on a principal-agent relationship between the partners and the partnership. "Partners are jointly and severally liable for the tortious acts of other partners if they have authorized those acts or if the wrongful acts are committed 'in the ordinary course of the business of the partnership.' [UPA (1914) §§ 13, 15]" *Wheeler v. Green,* 286 Or. 99, 126, 593 P.2d 777 (1979). The issue in this case is whether Mead's failure to advise plaintiff on the legal consequences of the loan was "in the ordinary course of the business of the partnership."

In *Croisant v. Watrud,* 248 Or. 234, 432 P.2d 799 (1967), this court confronted a similar issue of the vicarious liability of a partnership for the wrongful acts of a partner. In *Croisant,* the client of an accountant sued the accounting partnership, claiming damages for the accountant's breach of trust. The accountant collected income from the client's property and then made unauthorized payments to the client's husband from the money. The defendant partnership contended that the collection services were personal dealings of the accountant with the client and not part of the partnership's business. This court held:

> If a third person reasonably believes that the services he has request-
> ed of a member of an accounting partnership is undertaken as a part
> of the partnership business, the partnership should be bound for a
> breach of trust incident to that employment even though those
> engaged in the practice of accountancy would regard as unusual the

---

15. [By the Court] The jury found defendant not liable for [this] additional $1,500 loan, presumably because it determined that the loan was personal and that giving legal advice concerning the loan was not within the scope of the partnership's business.

16. [By the Court] On January 18, 1983, this court accepted Mead's resignation from the bar. He stated that he had chosen not to

contest disciplinary charges alleging that he had "borrowed $45,000 from a client, that he misrepresented the priority of the security given for the loan and that he subsequently forged a satisfaction of the mortgage given as security." 43 Or.St.B.Bull., June 1983, at 42. Mead was convicted of theft by deception because of the loan referred to in the disciplinary charges.

performance of such services [collecting and disbursing funds] by an accounting firm. 248 Or. at 242, 432 P.2d 799.

The court stated that the reasonableness of the third person's belief that "the service he seeks is within the domain of the profession is a question which must be answered upon the basis of the facts in the particular case." *Id.* at 243, 432 P.2d 799.

Defendant contends that *Croisant* may be distinguished from the case at bar because in *Croisant* "the misconduct occurred in the course of * * * activities which the court held could reasonably be viewed as within the scope of the accounting firm's business," while in this case"[t]here was no evidence that the act of an attorney in taking a personal loan from a client could reasonably be viewed as part of the business of a law firm." However, defendant admits that "the evidence most favorable to Plaintiff was simply that Plaintiff thought Mead was giving him investment advice and that the giving of advice regarding legal aspects of loans and investments in general is a normal part of law practice." Defendant thus concedes the validity of plaintiff's argument that plaintiff reasonably believed that investment advice was within the scope of the partnership's business; plaintiff does not contend that soliciting loans from clients was partnership business.

In the case at bar, the jury determined that plaintiff reasonably believed that the partnership's legal services included investment advice. We agree with the Court of Appeals that:

> * * * There is expert and other testimony from which the jury could have found that plaintiff relied on Mead for legal advice concerning the loan, that a lawyer seeking a loan from a client would be negligent if the lawyer did not tell the client to get independent legal advice and that a lawyer advising a client about this particular loan would seek to secure it and would warn the client of the risks involved in providing a usurious interest rate. 76 Or.App. at 85, 709 P.2d 246.

The Court of Appeals' rationale is buttressed by our decisions in bar disciplinary proceedings concerning loans from clients to lawyers. * * *

When a lawyer borrows money from a client, this court requires that the lawyer advise the client about the legal aspects of the loan. Mead's failure to advise plaintiff to seek independent legal advice, that loans usually should be secured and the debtor's financial status checked, and that the rate of interest was usurious were all failures of Mead as a lawyer advising his client. Because these failures occurred within the scope of the legal partnership, responsibility for Mead's negligence was properly charged to defendant as Mead's law partner. The trial court did not err in submitting the negligence issue to the jury. * * *

The Court of Appeals is affirmed.

Notes

(1) Can this case be distinguished from *Rouse v. Pollard?* There were several cases during the 1980s in which liability was imposed on the partnership or copartners in situations similar to *Roach v. Mead.* See Stephen E. Kalish, When a

Law Firm Member Borrows From a Client—The Law Firm's Responsibility: A Professional Model Replaces a Club Model, 37 Kan.L.Rev. 107 (1988). Professor Kalish views *Rouse v. Pollard* as illustrative of the "club model" of law partnerships and *Roach v. Mead* as illustrative of a "professional model."

(2) In the principal case, what differences are there, if any, between the $20,000 loan on which liability was found and the $1500 loan, on which it was not?

(3) Model Rules of Professional Conduct, Rule 1.8:

(a) A lawyer shall not enter into a business transaction with a client or knowingly acquire an ownership, possessory, security or other pecuniary interest adverse to a client unless:

(1) the transaction and terms on which the lawyer acquires the interest are fair and reasonable to the client and are fully disclosed and transmitted in writing to the client in a manner which can be reasonably understood by the client;

(2) the client is given a reasonable opportunity to seek the advice of independent counsel in the transaction; and

(3) the client consents in writing thereto.

Is a law firm liable for malpractice if a partner fails to obtain the written consent required by Rule 1.8(a)(3) for a personal loan from a client?

(4) What principles determine the liability of a partner for the negligence or incompetence of an employee, e.g., a secretary or staff attorney employed by a law firm?

(5) In Fanaras Enterprises, Inc. v. Doane, 423 Mass. 121, 666 N.E.2d 1003 (1996), Fanaras had entered into a retainer arrangement with Doane, an attorney. Under the retainer, Fanaras alleged, Doane was paid fees of $25,000 per quarter "in return for full, total and immediate access to Mr. Doane's legal advice, and so that [Fanaras] would always receive devoted priority service from Attorney Doane." While this arrangement continued, Fanaras also loaned Doane over $400,000, an amount that was to be repaid, with interest of 11 per cent "as soon as Doane obtained sufficient funds by way of selling [two properties he owned] or by way of obtaining a mortgage loan against either or both of those properties." However, Doane secretly placed mortgages against the two properties of over $1,800,000, diverted the funds, defaulted on the mortgages, and declared personal bankruptcy. Fanaras recovered nothing from the properties or from Doane. In an effort to collect from Doane's malpractice insurer, Fanaras sued Doane alleging that Doane was negligent in failing to advise Fanaras "to seek independent legal advice and/or to secure the loans with a mortgage" and that it "relied on Attorney Doane, at all times, to protect my interests in connection with these loans, and he failed to do that." (423 Mass., at 122–24, 666 N.E.2d, at 1004–05) Doane's liability insurer intervened and successfully moved for summary judgment. Held, affirmed:

The fact that the plaintiff paid Doane a substantial retainer "in return for full, total, and immediate access to Mr. Doane's legal advice, and so that Fanaras Enterprises, Inc., would always receive devoted priority service from Attorney Doane," * * * is of no consequence. That arrangement clearly contemplated the plaintiff's right to Doane's prompt legal advice on request. Nowhere * * * is there the slightest suggestion that the plaintiff, through Fanaras or otherwise, requested Doane's advice or assistance with respect to the loans to Doane and obtaining security for their repayment, or with respect to managing the plaintiff's money. To the contrary, the clear implication of the affidavit is that Fanaras did not seek such advice or assistance but merely "relied" on Doane to protect him. That reliance may or may not have been reasonable, but it did not establish an attorney-client relationship or legal malpractice with respect to the loans. It is not enough that, with respect to other matters, the parties were in an attorney-client relationship.

Three Justices dissented:

I believe that in light of the materials the plaintiff has presented, it may well be able to prove at trial that Doane owed it a duty as an attorney in respect to the loans Doane obtained from it. * * * If Doane had been advising Fanaras about Fanaras's dealings with a building owner for whom Fanaras was doing construction work, and that building owner, in Doane's earshot, had solicited a business loan from Fanaras, a jury would surely have been warranted in finding that the "devoted priority" service, for which Fanaras was paying such a high price, extended even without an explicit request to Doane's advising Fanaras about any legal aspects of the loan. Similarly here, the jury might have concluded that Fanaras had put itself in Doane's hands, as far as legal advice went, and that it was a violation of the relationship (if not an attorney-client relationship, then what?) for Doane neither to have advised Fanaras of the need to obtain some security nor, because Doane was now in a conflict of interest situation, to seek outside counsel. Nor would a finding of a conflict somehow preclude a finding of an attorney-client relationship. Much more likely, the conflict was itself a potential breach of Doane's duty, and it would be brazen for Doane to urge that, because of the conflict, there was no relationship on which Fanaras might rely. (423 Mass., at 126–27, 666 N.E.2d, at 1006–07).

Is the result reached in *Doane* consistent with Roach v. Mead?

(6) A lawyer representing an unsophisticated client may assume the role of both legal and business adviser. For a discussion of this, see Robert W. Hamilton, Fundamentals of Modern Business: A Lawyer's Guide, 803–04 (1989).

It is perhaps unnecessary to point out that there is a difference between a lawyer warning a client that a proposed business transaction with third persons is risky or inappropriate, and the lawyer engaging in a direct business transaction with a client. However, what happens if the direct business advice is poor? For example, the value of a proposed options contract increases dramatically but the client declined to invest on the advice of the lawyer. Can the client then sue the attorney for bad advice or for advice that is beyond the competence of a lawyer to give? If the lawyer fails to warn the client about the risk of options and significant losses are incurred, might the lawyer be liable on the theory that attorneys of ordinary competence would have warned the client under such circumstances?

F. DUTIES OF PARTNERS TO EACH OTHER

MEINHARD v. SALMON

Court of Appeals of New York, 1928.
249 N.Y. 458, 164 N.E. 545.

CARDOZO, C.J.

On April 10, 1902, Louisa M. Gerry leased to the defendant Walter J. Salmon the premises known as the Hotel Bristol at the northwest corner of

Forty–Second street and Fifth avenue in the city of New York. The lease was for a term of 20 years, commencing May 1, 1902, and ending April 30, 1922. The lessee undertook to change the hotel building for use as shops and offices at a cost of $200,000. Alterations and additions were to be accretions to the land.

Salmon, while in course of treaty with the lessor as to the execution of the lease, was in course of treaty with Meinhard, the plaintiff, for the necessary funds. The result was a joint venture with terms embodied in a writing. Meinhard was to pay to Salmon half of the moneys requisite to reconstruct, alter, manage, and operate the property. Salmon was to pay to Meinhard 40 percent of the net profits for the first five years of the lease and 50 percent for the years thereafter. If there were losses, each party was to bear them equally. Salmon, however, was to have sole power to "manage, lease, underlet and operate" the building. There were to be certain pre-emptive rights for each in the contingency of death.

The two were coadventurers, subject to fiduciary duties akin to those of partners. King v. Barnes, 109 N.Y. 267, 16 N.E. 332. As to this we are all agreed. The heavier weight of duty rested, however, upon Salmon. He was a coadventurer with Meinhard, but he was manager as well. During the early years of the enterprise, the building, reconstructed, was operated at a loss. If the relation had then ended, Meinhard as well as Salmon would have carried a heavy burden. Later the profits became large with the result that for each of the investors there came a rich return. For each the venture had its phases of fair weather and of foul. The two were in it jointly, for better or for worse.

When the lease was near its end, Elbridge T. Gerry had become the owner of the reversion. He owned much other property in the neighborhood, one lot adjoining the Bristol building on Fifth avenue and four lots on Forty–Second street. He had a plan to lease the entire tract for a long term to some one who would destroy the buildings then existing and put up another in their place. In the latter part of 1921, he submitted such a project to several capitalists and dealers. He was unable to carry it through with any of them. Then, in January, 1922, with less than four months of the lease to run, he approached the defendant Salmon. The result was a new lease to the Midpoint Realty Company, which is owned and controlled by Salmon, a lease covering the whole tract, and involving a huge outlay. The term is to be 20 years, but successive covenants for renewal will extend it to a maximum of 80 years at the will of either party. The existing buildings may remain unchanged for seven years. They are then to be torn down, and a new building to cost $3,000,000 is to be placed upon the site. The rental, which under the Bristol lease was only $55,000, is to be from $350,000 to $475,000 for the properties so combined. Salmon personally guaranteed the performance by the lessee of the covenants of the new lease until such time as the new building had been completed and fully paid for.

The lease between Gerry and the Midpoint Realty Company was signed and delivered on January 25, 1922. Salmon had not told Meinhard anything about it. Whatever his motive may have been he had kept the negotiations to himself. Meinhard was not informed even of the bare existence of a project. The first that he knew of it was in February, when the lease was an accomplished fact. He then made demand on the defendants that the lease be held in trust as an asset of the venture, making offer upon the trial to share the personal obligations incidental to the guaranty. The demand was followed by refusal, and later by this suit. A referee gave judgment for the plaintiff, limiting the plaintiff's interest in the lease, however, to 25 percent. The limitation was on the theory that the plaintiff's equity was to be restricted to one-half of so much of the value of the lease as was contributed or represented by the occupation of the Bristol site. Upon cross-appeals to the Appellate Division, the judgment was modified so as to enlarge the equitable interest to one-half of the whole lease. With this enlargement of plaintiff's interest, there went, of course, a corresponding enlargement of his attendant obligations. The case is now here on an appeal by the defendants.

Joint adventurers, like copartners, owe to one another, while the enterprise continues, the duty of the finest loyalty. Many forms of conduct permissible in a workaday world for those acting at arm's length are forbidden to those bound by fiduciary ties. A trustee is held to something stricter than the morals of the market place. Not honesty alone, but the punctilio of an honor the most sensitive, is then the standard of behavior. As to this there has developed a tradition that is unbending and inveterate. Uncompromising rigidity has been the attitude of courts of equity when petitioned to undermine the rule of undivided loyalty by the "disintegrating erosion" of particular exceptions. Wendt v. Fischer, 243 N.Y. 439, 444, 154 N.E. 303. Only thus has the level of conduct for fiduciaries been kept at a level higher than that trodden by the crowd. It will not consciously be lowered by any judgment of this court.

To the eye of an observer, Salmon held the lease as owner in his own right, for himself and no one else. In fact he held it as a fiduciary, for himself and another, sharers in a common venture. If this fact had been proclaimed, if the lease by its terms had run in favor of a partnership, Mr. Gerry, we may fairly assume, would have laid before the partners, and not merely before one of them, his plan of reconstruction. The pre-emptive privilege, or, better, the pre-emptive opportunity, that was thus an incident of the enterprise, Salmon appropriated to himself in secrecy and silence. He might have warned Meinhard that the plan had been submitted, and that either would be free to compete for the award. If he had done this, we do not need to say whether he would have been under a duty, if successful in the competition, to hold the lease so acquired for the benefit of a venture then about to end, and thus prolong by indirection its responsibilities and duties. The trouble about his conduct is that he excluded his coadventurer from any chance to compete, from any chance to enjoy the opportunity for benefit that had come to him alone by virtue of his agency. This chance, if nothing more, he was under a duty to concede. The price of its denial is an extension of the trust at the option and for the benefit of the one whom he excluded.

No answer is it to say that the chance would have been of little value even if seasonably offered. Such a calculus of probabilities is beyond the science of the chancery. * * *

We have no thought to hold that Salmon was guilty of a conscious purpose to defraud. Very likely he assumed in all good faith that with the approaching end of the venture he might ignore his coadventurer and take the extension for himself. He had given to the enterprise time and labor as well as money. He had made it a success. Meinhard, who had given money but neither time nor labor, had already been richly paid. There might seem to be something grasping in his insistence upon more. Such recriminations are not unusual when coadventurers fall out. They are not without their force if conduct is to be judged by the common standards of competitors. That is not to say that they have pertinency here. Salmon had put himself in a position in which thought of self was to be renounced, however hard the abnegation. He was much more than a coadventurer. He was a managing coadventurer. For him and for those like him the rule of undivided loyalty is relentless and supreme. Wendt v. Fischer, supra, Munson v. Syracuse, etc., R.R. Co., 103 N.Y. 58, 74, 8 N.E. 355. A different question would be here if there were lacking any nexus of relation between the business conducted by the manager and the opportunity brought to him as an incident of management. For this problem, as for most, there are distinctions of degree. If Salmon had received from Gerry a proposition to lease a building at a location far removed, he might have held for himself the privilege thus acquired, or so we shall assume. Here the subject-matter of the new lease was an extension and enlargement of the subject-matter of the old one. A managing coadventurer appropriating the benefit of such a lease without warning to his partner might fairly expect to be reproached with conduct that was underhanded, or lacking, to say the least, in reasonable candor, if the partner were to surprise him in the act of signing the new instrument. Conduct subject to that reproach does not receive from equity a healing benediction.

A question remains as to the form and extent of the equitable interest to be allotted to the plaintiff. The trust as declared has been held to attach to the lease which was in the name of the defendant corporation. We think it ought to attach at the option of the defendant Salmon to the shares of stock which were owned by him or were under his control. The difference may be important if the lessee shall wish to execute an assignment of the lease, as it ought to be free to do with the consent of the lessor. On the other hand, an equal division of the shares might lead to other hardships. It might take away from Salmon the power of control and management, which under the plan of the joint venture, he was to have from first to last. The number of shares to be allotted to the plaintiff should, therefore, be reduced to such an extent as may be necessary to preserve to the defendant Salmon the expected measure of dominion. To that end an extra share should be added to his half.

Subject to this adjustment, we agree with the Appellate Division that the plaintiff's equitable interest is to be measured by the value of half of the entire lease, and not merely by half of some undivided part. A single building covers the whole area. Physical division is impracticable along the lines of the Bristol site, the keystone of the whole. Division of interests and burdens is equally impracticable. Salmon, as tenant under the new lease, or as guarantor of the performance of the tenant's obligations, might well protest if Meinhard, claiming an equitable interest, had offered to assume a liability not equal to Salmon's, but only half as great. He might justly insist that the lease must be accepted by his coadventurer in such form as it had been given, and not constructively divided into imaginary fragments. What must be yielded to the one may be demanded by the other. The lease as it has been executed is single and entire. If confusion has resulted from the union of adjoining parcels, the trustee who consented to the union must bear the inconvenience. Hart v. Ten Eyck, 2 Johns. Ch. 62. * * *

The judgment should be modified by providing that at the option of the defendant Salmon there may be substituted for a trust attaching to the lease a trust attaching to the shares of stock, with the result that one-half of such shares together with one additional share will in that event be allotted to the defendant Salmon and the other shares to the plaintiff, and as so modified the judgment should be affirmed with costs.

ANDREWS, J. (dissenting). * * *

Were this a general partnership between Mr. Salmon and Mr. Meinhard, I should have little doubt as to the correctness of this result, assuming the new lease to be an offshoot of the old. Such a situation involves questions of trust and confidence to a high degree; it involves questions of good will; many other considerations. As has been said, rarely if ever may one partner without the knowledge of the other acquire for himself the renewal of a lease held by the firm, even if the new lease is to begin after the firm is dissolved. Warning of such an intent, if he is managing partner, may not be sufficient to prevent the application of this rule.

We have here a different situation governed by less drastic principles. I assume that where parties engage in a joint enterprise each owes to the other the duty of the utmost good faith in all that relates to their common venture. Within its scope they stand in a fiduciary relationship. I assume prima facie that even as between joint adventurers one may not secretly obtain a renewal of the lease of property actually used in the joint adventure where the possibility of renewal is expressly or impliedly involved in the enterprise. I assume also that Mr. Meinhard had an equitable interest in the Bristol Hotel lease. Further, that an expectancy of renewal inhered in that lease. Two questions then arise. Under his contract did he share in that expectancy? And if so, did that expectancy mature into a graft of the original lease? To both questions my answer is "No." * * *

What then was the scope of the adventure into which the two men entered? It is to be remembered that before their contract was signed Mr. Salmon had obtained the lease of the Bristol property. Very likely the matter had been earlier discussed between them. The $5,000 advance by Mr. Meinhard indicates that fact. But it has been held that the written contract defines their rights and duties. Having the lease, Mr. Salmon assigns no interest in it to Mr. Meinhard. He is to manage the property. It is for him to decide what alterations shall be made and to fix the rents. But for 20 years from May 1, 1902, Salmon is to make all advances from his own funds and Meinhard is to pay him personally on demand one-half of all expenses incurred and all losses sustained "during the full term of said lease," and during the same period Salmon is to pay him a part of the net profits. There was no joint capital provided.

It seems to me that the venture so inaugurated had in view a limited object and was to end at a limited time. There was no intent to expand it into a far greater undertaking lasting for many years. The design was to exploit a particular lease. Doubtless in it Mr. Meinhard had an equitable interest, but in it alone. This interest terminated when the joint adventure terminated. There was no intent that for the benefit of both any advantage should be taken of the chance of renewal—that the adventure should be continued beyond that date. Mr. Salmon has done all he promised to do in return for Mr. Meinhard's undertaking when he distributed profits up to May 1, 1922. Suppose this lease, nonassignable without the consent of the lessor, had contained a renewal option. Could Mr. Meinhard have exercised it? Could he have insisted that Mr. Salmon do so? Had Mr. Salmon done so could he insist that the agreement to share losses still existed, or could Mr. Meinhard have claimed that the joint adventure was still to continue for 20 or 80 years? I do not think so. The adventure by its express terms ended on May 1, 1922. The contract by its language and by its whole import excluded the idea that the tenant's expectancy was to subsist for the benefit of the plaintiff. On that date whatever there was left of value in the lease reverted to Mr. Salmon, as it would had the lease been for thirty years instead of twenty. Any equity which Mr. Meinhard possessed was in the particular lease itself, not in any possibility of renewal. There was nothing unfair in Mr. Salmon's conduct. * * *

The judgment of the courts below should be reversed and a new trial ordered, with costs in all courts to abide the event.

POUND, CRANE, and LEHMAN, JJ., concur with CARDOZO, C.J., * * *

ANDREWS, J., dissents in opinion in which KELLOGG and O'BRIEN, JJ., concur.

Notes

(1) Consider UPA (1914) §§ 20–22. Does § 21 incorporate the broad fiduciary duty of *Meinhard*? An ABA Committee, commenting on this section, states that while it "is often cited as establishing a broad fiduciary duty, in fact, as presently worded, [it] is basically merely an anti-theft provision." UPA Revision Subcommittee of the Committee on Partnerships and Unincorporated Business Organizations, Should the Uniform Partnership Act Be Revised? 43 Bus. Law. 121, 151 (1987). However, many partnership cases cite *Meinhard* and § 21 as establishing a broad fiduciary duty among partners. Indeed, some cases state that this is "one of the highest fiduciary duties recognized in the law." E.g. Huffington v. Upchurch, 532 S.W.2d 576, 579 (Tex.1976). On the other hand, some recent cases do not reflect approval of the broad language in *Meinhard*. See, for example, Bane v. Ferguson, at p. 46, supra.

(2) Is this duty affected by whether or not the partners are dealing with each other at arms length? In Johnson v. Peckham, 132 Tex. 148, 120 S.W.2d 786 (1938), strained relations had developed between two partners and a suit for an accounting and dissolution was pending in a court. Peckham agreed to purchase Johnson's interest in two oil leases that constituted the partnership property for $1,500. Shortly after this transaction was completed, Peckham resold the leases for $10,500. Upon a showing that negotiations for this resale had begun prior to the time Peckham purchased Johnson's interest, Peckham was required to share the profitable resale with Johnson. A judgment for $3,750 (one-half of $10,500 minus $1,500) was entered, the Court quoting the ringing language of Mr. Justice Cardozo in Meinhard v. Salmon. Same result under UPA (1914)?

(3) A partner secretly takes $1,000 from the partnership and invests it in another venture. What rights do his copartners have if the other venture fails? If it is profitable?

(4) An important issue under UPA (1914) is whether the broad fiduciary duties contemplated by that statute may be modified by an express agreement among the parties. Singer v. Singer, 634 P.2d 766 (Okla.App.1981) involved a written partnership agreement for a family oil and gas partnership which stated in paragraph 8:

> Each partner shall be free to enter into business and other transactions for his or her own separate individual account, even though such business or other transaction may be in conflict with and/or competition with the business of this partnership. Neither the partnership nor any individual member of this partnership shall be entitled to claim or receive any part of or interest in such transactions, it being the intention and agreement that any partner will be free to deal on his or her own account to the same extent and with the same force and effect as if he or she were not and never had been members of this partnership. (634 P.2d, at 768)

Members of the partnership discussed the purchase of a tract of land, but before the partnership could act, two members of the family formed their own separate partnership and purchased the land in question. They refused to share the purchase with the original partnership, citing paragraph 8. The court held this conduct permissible:

> We find the defendants had a contract right to do precisely what they did * * *. [P]aragraph 8 is designed to allow and is uniquely drafted to promote spirited, if not outright predatory competition between the partners. Its strong wording leaves no doubt in our minds that its drafters intended to effect such a result. * * * We construe it to legitimize and extend free competition between the partners to partnership prospects and opportunities * * *. (634 P.2d at 772–73)

> From a fiduciary aspect, the permissible boundaries of intra-partnership competition, under paragraph 8, are limited only after the threshold of actual partnership acquisition has been crossed. Had Stanley and Andrea pirated an existing partnership asset or used partnership funds or encumbered [the family partnership] financially, our decision would be different.

Does this case stand for a general proposition that under UPA (1914) basic partnership duties can be waived? For arguments that it does, see J. Dennis Hynes, Fiduciary Duties and RUPA: An Inquiry Into Freedom of Contract, 58–SPG Law & Contemp. Probs. 29 (Spring 1995); Larry E. Ribstein, Fiduciary Contracts in Unincorporated Firms, 54 Wash. & Lee L.Rev. 537 (1997).

(5) UPA (1997) approaches the fiduciary duty issue very differently from UPA (1914). Consider carefully UPA (1997) § 404, particularly the word "only" in § 404(a) and the phrase "is limited to" in § 404(b). This language was inserted because of "a sense that vague, broad statements of a powerful duty of loyalty cause too much uncertainty. * * * [E]ven if there are no bad holdings, overly broad judicial language has left practitioners uncertain about whether their negotiated agreement will be voided. * * * [P]racticing attorneys want to be able to reach a deal, put it down on paper and know that it will not be undone by the application of fiduciary duties." Donald J. Weidner, The Revised Uniform Partnership Act Midstream: Major Policy Decisions, 21 U. Tol. L. Rev. 825, 856 (1990). A description of the last-minute changes made in the language of § 404 is described in J. Dennis Hynes, Fiduciary Duties and RUPA: An Inquiry Into Freedom of Contract, 58–SPG Law & Contemp. Probs. 29 (1995).

(a) Does not UPA (1997) § 404(b)(1) incorporate most of the essence of UPA (1914) § 21? However, UPA (1914) § 21 refers to the "formation, conduct, or liquidation" of the partnership while UPA (1997) § 404(b)(1) refers only to the "conduct or winding up" of the partnership. Under UPA (1997) there is no duty of loyalty in connection with the formation of the partnership. Does that make sense? Should the negotiation of a partnership contract be subject to a broader fiduciary duty than the negotiation of a contract, say, for employment or to purchase a new automobile? Might not a relationship of trust and confidence exist while a partnership agreement is being drafted? See also UPA (1997) § 404(d). There is no similar provision in UPA (1914). Does the combination of UPA (1997) §§ 404(b), (c), and (d), taken together, equal the broadly phrased duty established by *Meinhard* and UPA (1914) § 21 (except with respect to partnership formation)?

(b) Might there be aspects of a duty of loyalty that are not encompassed within the three subsections of UPA (1997) § 404(b)? If so, what?

(c) Does not UPA (1997) § 404(e) significantly undercut § 404(b)? Cannot most breaches of fiduciary duty be justified on the theory that the conduct "furthers the partner's own interest?" What function, if any, does the word "merely" in § 404(e) serve?

(d) The duty of care defined in UPA § 404(c) essentially adopts the duty of care applicable in the corporate context for partnerships. UPA (1914) did not attempt to define a duty of care for partners. For an argument that the relaxed corporate concepts of duty of care are "inappropriate" for partnerships, see Claire Moore Dickerson, Is It Appropriate to Appropriate Corporate Concepts: Fiduciary Duties and the Revised Uniform Partnership Act, 64 U. Colo. L.Rev. 111, 151–56 (1993).

(6) An amended version of "DRULPA," the Delaware Revised Uniform Limited Partnership Act, 6 Del. Code Ann. §§ 17–1101, *et seq.*, became effective on August 1, 2004. One significant change added the word "eliminate" to a list of ways partners can alter fiduciary duties by contract. Section 17–1101(d) provides that in limited partnerships, "[t]o the extent that, at law or in equity, a partner or other person has duties (including fiduciary duties) to a limited partnership or to another partner or to another person that is a party to or is otherwise bound by a partnership agreement, the partner's or other person's duties may be expanded or restricted *or eliminated* by provisions in the partnership agreement; provided that the partnership agreement may not eliminate the implied contractual covenant of good faith and fair dealing" (emphasis added).

What are possible policy goals behind this addition, and what is the probable result of this contracting power? What's at stake if parties can replace partners' fiduciary duties with contractual standards such as the duty of good faith and fair dealing? And how is the duty of good faith and fair dealing different from the duty of loyalty?

In practice, the addition of "eliminate" merely codified the broad manner in which Delaware courts had interpreted the power to restrict fiduciary duties up until 2004. Prior to the amendment, several courts had suggested that parties could eliminate fiduciary duties by contract under certain circumstances. See, e.g., Sonet v. Timber Co., 722 A.2d 319 (Del. Ch. 1998); Gotham Partners, L.P. v. Hallwood Realty Partners, L.P., 840 A.2d 641 (Del. 2003).

G.   PARTNERSHIP PROPERTY

OFFICIAL COMMENT TO SUBDIVISIONS (1) AND (2–B) OF SECTION 25 OF THE UNIFORM PARTNERSHIP ACT[18]

6 Uniform Laws Annotated: Uniform Partnership Act 327 (1969).

Subdivision (1). One of the present principal difficulties in the administration of the law of partnerships arises out of the difficulty of determining the exact nature of the rights of a partner in specific partnership property. That the partners are co-owners of partnership property is clear; but the legal incidents attached to the right of each partner as co-owner are not clear. When the English courts in the seventeenth century first began to discuss the legal incidents of this co-ownership, they were already familiar with two other kinds of co-ownership, joint tenancy and tenancy in common. In joint tenancy on the death of one owner his right in the property passes to the other co-owners. This is known as the right of survivorship. The incident of survivorship fits in with the necessities of partnership. On the death of a partner, the other partners and not the executors of the deceased partner should have a right to wind up partnership affairs. (See [UPA (1914) § 25(d)].) The early courts, therefore, declared that partners were joint tenants of partnership property, the consequence being that all the other legal incidents of joint tenancy were applied to partnership co-ownership. Many of these incidents, however, do not apply to the necessities of the partnership relation and produce most inequitable results. This is not to be wondered at because the legal incidents of joint tenancy grew out of a co-ownership of land not held for the purposes of business. The attempt of our courts to escape the inequitable results of applying the legal incidents of joint tenancy to partnership has produced very great confusion. Practically this confusion has had a more unfortunate effect on substantive rights when the separate creditors of a partner attempt to attach and sell specific partnership property than when a partner attempts to assign specific partnership property not for a partnership purpose but for his own purposes.

The Commissioners, however, believe that the proper way to end the confusion which has arisen out of the attempt to treat partners as joint tenants is to recognize the fact that the rights of a partner as co-owner with his partners of specific partnership property should depend on the necessities of the partnership relation. In short, that the legal incidents of the tenancy in partnership are not necessarily those of any other co-ownership.

In the clauses of this section these incidents of tenancy in partnership are stated with several practical results of value. In the first place the law is greatly simplified in expression. In the second place the danger of the courts reaching an inequitable conclusion by refusing to modify the results of applying the legal incidents of joint tenancy to the partnership relation is done away with. Finally, ground is laid for the simplification of a procedure in those cases where the separate creditor desires to secure satisfaction out of his debtor's interest in the partnership. (Compare [UPA (1914) § 25(2)(c)] with [UPA (1914) § 28(1)].)

18. Reprinted with permission from West Publishing Corporation.

Subdivision (2–b). Clause (b) asserts that the right of a partner as co-owner in specific partnership property is not separately assignable. This peculiarity of tenancy in partnership is a necessary consequence of the partnership relation. If A and B are partners and A attempts to assign all his right in partnership property, say a particular chattel, to C, and the law recognizes the possibility of such a transfer, C would pro tanto become a partner with B; for the rights of A in the chattel are to possess the chattel for a partnership purpose. But partnership is a voluntary relation. B cannot have a partner thrust upon him by A without his, B's, consent.

A cannot confer on C his, A's, right to possess and deal with the chattel for a partnership purpose. Neither can he confer any other rights which he has in the property. A partner has a beneficial interest in partnership property considered as a whole. As profits accrue, he has a right to be paid his proportion, and on the winding up of the business, after the obligations due third persons have been met, he has a right to be paid in cash his share of what remains of the partnership property. These rights considered as a whole are his interest in the partnership; and this beneficial interest he may assign in whole or fractional part, as is indicated in [UPA (1914) § 27]. In a sense, each partner, having thus a beneficial interest in the partnership property considered as a whole, has a beneficial interest in each part, and such beneficial interest might be regarded as assignable if it were not impossible, except by purely arbitrary and artificial rules, to measure a partner's beneficial interest in a specific chattel belonging to the partnership, or any other specific portion of partnership property.

Notes

(1) As indicated in this official comment, the problem of ownership of property, the rights of partners, and the rights of creditors of the partnership and of individual partners are covered in some detail in UPA (1914) §§ 24–28. These sections should be read carefully since they provide firm (and sometimes startling) answers to questions. For example, a person dies leaving a will that provides that son A inherits all his personal property and daughter B inherits all his real estate. His only asset on his death is a one-half interest in a partnership whose sole asset is a valuable piece of real estate. Who is entitled to his interest in that real estate? See UPA (1914) § 26.

(2) Are not the complexities of property ownership in UPA (1914) a consequence of the unwillingness of the draftsmen of that statute to accept the notion that a partnership was an entity separate from the partners? Consider the much simpler property ownership rules adopted by UPA (1997) §§ 203, 204, 501, 502, 503. Section 502 defines the partner's "transferable interest" in a partnership. What is the analogous property interest defined in UPA (1914) § 24? How does UPA (1997) treat the "property interest" that is defined in UPA (1914) § 24 as "the right to participate in management"?

(3) The ability of a *partnership* creditor to proceed against the *individual* property of a partner is dependent only on naming and serving the partner as a defendant in the suit (and possibly obtaining a judgment against both the partner and the partnership and exhausting the assets of the partnership). If these steps are taken, the partner's individual property may be subject to execution, attachment or other process. However, the ability of an *individual* creditor to proceed against *partnership* property is sharply circumscribed. See UPA (1914)

§§ 25(2)(c), 28; UPA (1997) §§ 501, 504. Why are individual creditors seeking to recover from partnership assets treated differently from partnership creditors seeking to recover from individual assets?

(4) What is a "charging order"? See UPA (1914) § 28; UPA (1997) § 504. Precisely what must an individual creditor do in order to obtain such an order? What rights or powers does such a creditor get when she obtains such an order? Is it a "lien" on the partnership interest? Consult Kerry v. Schneider, 239 F.2d 896 (9th Cir.1956); UPA (1997) § 504(b). What other rights does the creditor have or what can he thereafter obtain? J. Gordan Gose, The Charging Order Under the Uniform Partnership Act, 28 Wash.L.Rev. 1, 15–18 (1953), describes the relationship between creditor, debtor, and partnership as follows:

> First, the charging order may enjoin the members of the partnership from making further disbursements of any kind to the debtor partner, except such payments as may be permissible under a legal exemption right properly asserted by the debtor.

> Second, the charging order may formally require the members of the partnership to pay to the creditor any amounts which it would otherwise pay to the debtor partner, exclusive of any amounts payable to the latter under a properly asserted legal exemption right.

> Third, the appointment of a receiver is not indispensable to the collection of the claim out of the debtor partner's share. A receiver should be appointed only where he has some useful function to serve such as the maintenance of a lawsuit, the conduct of a sale or the representation of competing creditors of the debtor partner. It may be that even in such a case, no receiver is necessary since there is no insuperable reason why these services cannot be obtained by some other method. * * *

> * * * Fourth, the debtor's interest should be sold if, and only if, the court is convinced that the creditor's claim will not be satisfied with reasonable expedition by the less drastic process of diverting the debtor's income from the partnership to the payment of the debt.[19] Even in the case of a wholly solvent partnership, the creditor's claim may be so large in relation to the current income of the debtor from the firm as to require sale as the only alternative to long delay in payment.

(5) Where the partnership or a partner is insolvent UPA (1914) §§ 40(h) and (i) establish the "jingle rule" for priority of payment: individual creditors have priority with regard to individual property and partnership creditors have priority with regard to partnership property. For many years, the federal Bankruptcy Act followed the same pattern, but in 1978 it was changed to provide, essentially, that partnership creditors have priority as to partnership property and equivalence with individual creditors as to individual property. 11 U.S.C.A. § 723(c). The most serious criticism of the old "jingle rule" was that partnership creditors consider the net worth of both the partnership and the individual partners in deciding to extend credit to the partnership and should not therefore be subordinated to individual creditors with respect to individual assets. UPA (1997) does not seek to

---

19. [By the Author] There is actually no authority whatsoever as to when a sale should be ordered. Necessarily the order must fall in the area of those "which the circumstances of the case require." The apparent situations in which sale would be necessary are those in which, owing to the size of the claim or the absence of current liquid income, an order to pay over the debtor partner's share of current income and other moneys would not be effective.

define the priorities between partnership and individual creditors, presumably leaving the matter to the federal Bankruptcy Act.

(6) What is the status of an assignee or transferee of a partnership interest? Is she a partner? Is she liable for partnership obligations? Can she compel dissolution and winding up of the partnership? What rights does she have? See UPA (1914) §§ 18(g), 27, 32(2); UPA (1997) § 503.

H.　PARTNERSHIP ACCOUNTING

From an accounting standpoint, the business of the partnership is distinct from the financial affairs of the individual partners. The interests of the partners are usually reflected in capital accounts which are adjusted periodically for income, drawings, and contributions or withdrawals of capital. A capital account essentially sets forth the partner's ownership interest in the partnership. UPA (1997) § 401 describes how each partner's capital account is constructed and maintained: that account equals the capital contributed by the partner less the amount of any distributions to the partner plus the partner's share of the profits less the partner's share of the losses. A partner's capital account may be negative from time to time; upon the final settlement of accounts when the partnership is terminated, a partner with a negative capital account must pay the partnership that amount. UPA (1997) § 807(b). It is not essential that the partnership actually maintain a formal capital account for each partner but all except the most informal partnerships do so.

Financial accounting for partnerships in most respects closely resembles corporate accounting for profits and losses, assets and liabilities. A simple illustration based on the first year's successful operation of the AB Software Store might be helpful.

(1) Income Statement

AB SOFTWARE STORE
Statement of Profit and Loss for Year Ending December 31, 2004

Sales	$417,000	
Cost of Sales	270,000	
GROSS PROFIT		$147,000
Other Expenses:		
Advertising	8,000	
Rentals	24,000	
Depreciation	5,000	
Salaries	32,000	
Miscellaneous	18,000	87,000
NET PROFIT		$60,000

(2) Balance Sheet

AB SOFTWARE STORE
Balance Sheet, December 31, 2004

Assets		Liabilities	
Cash	$19,000	Accounts Payable	$73,000
Accounts Receivable	93,000	Note Payable to A	25,000
Inventory	95,000		
Fixtures (Net of depreciation)	42,000		

Truck (Net of deprecia-tion)	9,000	**Equity** Partner's Capital	160,000
	$258,000		$258,000

(3) Capital Accounts for 2004

	Opening	Income for Year	Drawing for Year	Closing
A	$100,000	$30,000	–0–	$130,000
B	–0–	30,000	–0–	30,000
				$160,000

ROBERT W. HAMILTON AND RICHARD A. BOOTH, BUSINESS BASICS FOR LAW STUDENTS: ESSENTIAL CONCEPTS AND APPLICATIONS (3RD ED.)
Pages 116–21 (2002).[20]

The starting point of the whole subject of accountancy is a very simple equation:

$$Equity = Assets - Liabilities$$

Equity in this equation has nothing to do with the historical courts of equity or with notions of fairness or simple justice: It means ownership or net worth. This equation simply states that the net worth of a business is equal to its assets minus its liabilities.

A balance sheet is in many ways the most fundamental financial statement: It is simply a restatement of this fundamental equation in the form:

Assets = Liabilities + Equity

A balance sheet simply is a presentation of this equation in a chart form:

Assets:	Liabilities + Equity
_____	_____

Every balance sheet, whether it is for General Motors or the smallest retail grocery store, is based on this format. * * *

The asset side of a balance sheet is sometimes referred to as the *left hand side* [and] the liability/equity side is sometimes called the *right hand side* * * *.

There are four fundamental premises underlying financial accounting that can readily be grasped from this simple introduction. First, financial accounting assumes that the business that is the subject of the financial statements is an entity. A person may own several different businesses; if each business maintains its own records, it will be on the assumption that each is independent from the person's other businesses. The equity referred to in that business's balance sheet will be limited to the person's investment in that single business. If a person owns two businesses that keep separate

20. Reprinted with the permission of Aspen Law & Business/Panel Publishers, a division of   Aspen Publishers, Inc. The text set forth above is subject to revision.

financial records, a debt that one business owes the other will be reflected as an asset on one balance sheet and a liability on the other.

Second, all entries have to be in terms of dollars, at least in the United States. All property, tangible or intangible, and obligations shown on a balance sheet, must be expressed in dollars, either historical cost or fair market value or some other method of valuation. Many "assets" or "liabilities" of a business, however, are not reflected at all. A person's friendly smile may be an asset in a sense, but will not appear on a balance sheet because a dollar value is not normally given to a smile. Assets, such as a debt owed to the company or rights to a patent, on the other hand, do appear in balance sheets. * * * Similarly, a company may have a reputation for sharp practices or questionable dealing. While that reputation is doubtless a liability in a sense, it is not the type of liability that appears on a balance sheet. A liability in the balance sheet sense is a recognized debt or obligation to someone else, payable either in money or in something reducible to money. Not all liabilities that in the legal or lay sense meet this test are recognized as liabilities in the accounting sense. * * *

Third, a balance sheet must balance. The fundamental accounting equation itself states an equality: The two sides of the balance sheet restate that equality in somewhat reorganized form. A balance sheet therefore is itself an equality and the sum of the left hand side of the balance sheet must precisely equal the sum of the right hand side. Indeed, when accountants are involved in auditing a complex business, they take advantage of this characteristic by running trial balances on their work to make sure that they have not inadvertently transposed or omitted figures: The mathematical equality of the two sides of the balance sheet provides a check on the accuracy of the accountant's labors. In short, if a balance sheet doesn't balance, somewhere there is a mistake.

Fourth, every transaction that a business enters must be recorded in at least two ways if the balance sheet is to continue to balance. This last point underlies the concept of that mysterious subject, double entry bookkeeping, and is the cornerstone on which modern accounting is built.

Assume that we have a new business that is just starting out, in which the owner has invested $10,000 in cash (for this purpose it makes no difference whether the business is going to be conducted in the form of a proprietorship, partnership, or corporation; all that is important is that it will be accounted for as an entity separate from the owner). The opening balance sheet will look like this:

Assets:		Liabilities:	–0–
Cash	10,000	Owner's Equity	10,000

Now let us assume that the owner buys a used truck for $3,000 cash. The effect of this transaction is to reduce cash by $3,000 and create a new asset on the balance sheet:

Assets:		Liabilities:	–0–
Cash	7,000	Owner's Equity	10,000
Used Truck	3,000		
	10,000		10,000

Voila! The balance sheet still balances. Let us assume next that the owner goes down to the bank and borrows an additional $1,000. This also has a dual effect: it increases cash by $1,000 (because the business is receiving the proceeds of the loan) and increases liabilities by $1,000 (because the business thereafter has to repay the loan). Yet another balance sheet can be created showing the additional effect of this second transaction:

Assets:			Liabilities:	
Cash	8,000		Debt to Bank	1,000
Used Truck	3,000		Owner's Equity	10,000
	11,000			11,000

Further insights should be evident from these two examples: First, a balance sheet records a situation at one instant in time. It is a static concept, an equilibrium that exists at one point in time rather than a record of change from an earlier period. Put another way, every transaction potentially creates a different or new balance sheet when the transaction is recorded. Second, the bottom line of a balance sheet—$11,000 in this example—is not itself a meaningful figure, because transactions such as the bank loan that do not affect the real worth of the business to the owners may increase or decrease the bottom line.

The two transactions described above—the purchase of a used truck and a short-term bank loan—involve a reshuffling of assets and liabilities. From an accounting standpoint, the owner of the business is neither richer nor poorer as a result of them. However, most transactions that a business enters into are of a different type: They involve ordinary business operations leading to a profit or loss in the current accounting period. Consider a simple example. Suppose the business described above involves hauling things in the truck for customers. Thus the company hires a truck driver at a cost of $200 per day to drive the truck and pick up and deliver for it. During that first day the truck driver works very hard and for long hours making deliveries for which the business is paid $500. It is simple to create a *profit and loss statement* or *income statement* for the business for the one day of operation. "Profit and loss" and "income" are synonyms for this purpose. The basic formula is:

$$income = revenues - expenses$$

Obviously, the business had income of $300 ($500 of revenue minus $200 of expense for the truck driver) for its first day of operation. There may have been other expenses as well that arguably should be charged to that first day of operation, but for simplicity, we are ignoring that possibility.

At first glance the income statement appears to have nothing to do with the balance sheet described in the previous section. It is possible, however, to create a new balance sheet to reflect each of these transactions.

First, the payment of the $200 to the truck driver involves a cash payment of $200 by the business; it is easy to record that. But where should the offsetting entry be? The balance sheet cannot look like this:

Assets:			Liabilities:		
	Cash	7,800		Debt to Bank	1,000
	Used Truck	3,000		Equity	10,000
		10,800			11,000

Something is obviously wrong because this balance sheet does not balance. There must be an offsetting entry. It certainly should not be a reduction of liabilities (since the amount of the bank loan is unchanged) or an increase in value of the truck. Perhaps one could view the services as an asset something like the truck, but that does not make much sense because the services are simply gone. One could perhaps argue that no balance sheet should be created until the payment to the truck driver is offset by whatever the device earns during the rest of the day, but that cannot be correct either, because the balance sheet should balance after every transaction, not just at the end of a sequence of transactions. The only possible solution is to reduce "owner's equity" by the payment:

Assets:			Liabilities:		
	Cash	7,800		Debt to Bank	1,000
	Used Truck	3,000		Equity	9,800
		10,800			10,800

Second, the $500 payment for the services rendered:

Assets:			Liabilities:		
	Cash	8,300		Debt to Bank	1,000
	Used Truck	3,000		Equity	10,300
		11,300			11,300

Admittedly, these two balance sheets are not very helpful in showing the relationship between the balance sheet and the income statement. What is needed is a segregation of income items within the equity account so that the permanent investment and the transient changes are shown separately. Thus, the following balance sheet at the end of the period is much more illuminating:

Assets:			Liabilities:		
	Cash	8,300		Debt to Bank	1,000
	Used Truck	3,000		Equity	10,000
				Earnings	300
		11,300			11,300

The important point at present is that the statement of income or profit and loss is itself a right-hand entry on the balance sheet.

The balance sheet is a static concept showing the status of a business at a particular instant in time while the income statement describes the results of operations over some period of time: daily, monthly, quarterly, or annually. In a sense, the balance sheet is a snapshot, the income statement a motion picture. The income statement also serves as the bridge between the balance sheet at the beginning of the period and the balance sheet at the end of the period, because positive income items (revenues) increase owner's equity while negative income items (expenses) reduce it. Most investors and creditors look first at the bottom line of the income statement when evaluating financial statements, because the income statement reflects the operations of the business. The balance sheet usually plays a lesser role in financial analysis.

The concept of profit and loss and accounting periods rests on additional fundamental postulates. First, accounting assumes the continuing existence and activity of the business enterprise as a going concern. In other words, it is assumed that the business will be around for an indefinite number of future accounting periods. If a business is in such dire straits that its continued existence is unlikely, a totally different set of accounting principles must be adopted. Second, each business must adopt a fiscal or accounting period and must report the results of operations for that period as a separate accounting unit. The unit usually chosen is a year—either a **calendar year** or a **fiscal year.** (A fiscal year is a reporting period that the business chooses that ends on a date other than December 31 and may vary somewhat in length from a period of precisely 12 months.) Third, in determining the results of operations during an accounting period, some kind of logical relationship must be created between the revenues and expenses that are taken into account in determining profit or loss for that period. The principle usually followed is that costs allocable to the creation of revenue should be matched with that revenue. Other costs arising from the passage of time are allocated to the accounting period on the basis of that time and not the time of receipt. Fourth, some principles must be established as to when revenue is realized. Usually, the rule that is adopted is that revenues are realized when the business becomes unconditionally entitled to their receipt, not when payment is received. In the case of a contract for the sale of goods, for example, revenue may be realized when the goods are shipped, not when the contract was entered into or when payment is made. As a corollary, property of the business that may have appreciated in market value does not give rise to revenue until the gain is realized by sale or disposition of the property.

This concept is known as **accrual accounting**, and most businesses follow it. Indeed, most businesses of any size are required to use accrual accounting even though **cash basis accounting** might seem simpler. Most individuals use cash basis accounting for tax purposes (even if they do not know it). Accrual accounting, however, tends to give investors and creditors a better sense of the financial health of a business. * * *

Notes

(1) Turning to AB Software Store partnership financial statements, how would the partners' capital accounts look if the store had spent $10,000 rather than $8,000 on advertising in the year in question without any increase in sales? How would they look if both A and B had drawn $5,000 each out of the business at the end of the year in question? If the partnership had lost $6,000 rather than shown a profit of $60,000?

(2) A, despite his desire to limit his financial investment to $100,000, agreed to lend the partnership an additional $25,000, presumably because the store was successful. He therefore has the status both of creditor and of partner. What are his rights as against other general creditors with respect to his loan if the partnership goes under? See UPA (1914) § 40.

(3) In actual operation, a small business such as the AB Software Store would likely use its "cash flow" as a measure of its success or failure. Accounting for cash flow differs from traditional accounting in that it considers only transactions that involve dollars in and dollars out. Traditional accounting, as set forth above, includes some expenses that do not reduce the amount of available cash of the business. An example is the item "depreciation" in AB Software's financial statements. When assets are purchased by a business they are usually recorded in a business's accounting records at their purchase price ("historical cost") with no subsequent adjustment for variations in market value but with an annual charge for "depreciation" to reflect the gradual "wearing out" or "using up" of the asset. See Robert W. Hamilton and Richard A. Booth, Business Basics for Law Students: Essential Concepts and Applications § 6.11 (2002), for a fuller discussion. The AB Software Store has adopted this practice and has deducted from its earnings $5,000 for depreciation of its fixtures and its equipment. Obviously, there was no payment of $5,000 to anyone involved in this transaction. Hence, if everything else were equal, cash flow of the AB Software Store for the first year will be $5,000 higher than its reported earnings. However, there are many items that do not affect earnings but have the opposite effect of reducing cash flow. An obvious example is the repayment of a debt. Most businesses prepare "cash flow" financial statements for internal purposes and to make sure that there will be cash available when foreseeable payments become due. In modern financial analysis, there is usually more emphasis on analysis of cash flow than on accounting earnings. Assume that AB Software Store decides to liquidate and wind up after one year—all the assets are sold, the proceeds used to discharge debts, and the balance distributed to the partners. Given the conventions described in this note, can one determine from the balance sheet how much will be available for distribution to A and B?

I. PARTNERSHIP DISSOLUTION

The dissolution provisions of the two versions of the Uniform Partnership Act differ significantly from each other and were an area of significant controversy in the drafting of UPA (1997). Dissolution provisions are the most complicated sections in both of these statutes. The cases and materials in the balance of this Section primarily deal with UPA (1914). The changes made by UPA (1997) are described in a note at the end of this Section.

In § 29 of UPA (1914), "dissolution" is defined as a change in legal relationship "caused by any partner ceasing to be associated in the carrying on * * * of the business." This definition of the word "dissolution" differs considerably from the lay understanding of that word. It refers to a change in personal relationships among partners within the partnership and has nothing to do with the disposition of assets or closing down or selling the business. As a result of this peculiar definition, for the last eighty years there has been a considerable risk of misunderstanding whenever the word "dissolution" is used in the partnership context. UPA (1914) § 30 defines two additional concepts: Following "dissolution" there is a period of "winding up," which leads to the "termination" of the partnership. Early drafts of UPA (1997) attempted to avoid the basic confusion over the word "dissolution" by not using the "d word" at all; however, it crept back into § 603 and article 8 of UPA (1997). UPA (1997) consistently uses the word "dissociation" to refer to an event that causes a partner to cease being a participant in the partnership;

it is therefore very close to the technical concept of "dissolution" that was used in UPA (1914) § 29. In UPA (1997), "dissolution" is used only when referring to an event that leads to the termination of the partnership.

Notes

(1) Whatever the provisions of UPA (1914), partnership agreements prepared by attorneys usually make careful provisions for the continuation of the business following dissolution. The most common provision is that upon any withdrawal of a partner ("dissolution" in the language of UPA (1914) § 29), the business of the partnership is not to be wound up and terminated but is to be continued by the remaining partners with the interest of the withdrawing partner being paid off in cash on some basis. Where the partnership is continued by agreement, is it not clear under UPA (1914) that "dissolution" has occurred and that a "new" partnership has instantaneously been formed to continue the business? For a court that refused to apply the language of UPA § 29 literally in this very common situation, see Adams v. Jarvis, page 90, infra.

(2) Even in the absence of express agreement, the withdrawal of one or more partners usually does not lead to the closing of the doors of the business. For example, in a partnership of three doctors, A, B, and C, that do not have a partnership agreement providing for the continuation of the business, assume that C withdraws but A and B decide to continue the same practice at the same location under the same name. C may well acquiesce in this decision by A and B since continuation is usually more sensible as a matter of business economics than a piecemeal liquidation and sale of the business. UPA (1914) contains elaborate provisions defining the rights and responsibilities of C if the business is continued after his withdrawal. See Cauble v. Handler, page 86, infra. However, in the absence of a specific agreement to continue, C may compel the winding up of the business. UPA (1914) § 38(1).

(3) Under UPA (1914), does a technical dissolution occur when one or more new partners are admitted but no existing partner withdraws? See UPA (1914) §§ 17, 29.

COLLINS v. LEWIS

Texas Court of Civil Appeals, 1955.
283 S.W.2d 258, writ ref'd n.r.e.

HAMBLEN, CHIEF JUSTICE.

This suit was instituted in the District Court of Harris County by the appellants, who, as the owners of a fifty percent (50%) interest in a partnership known as the LBC Cafeteria, sought a receivership of the partnership business, a judicial dissolution of the partnership, and foreclosure of a mortgage upon appellees' interest in the partnership assets. Appellees denied appellants' right to the relief sought, and filed a cross-action for damages for breach of contract in the event dissolution should be decreed. Appellants' petition for receivership having been denied after a hearing before the court, trial of the issues of dissolution and foreclosure, and of appellees' cross-action, proceeded before the court and a jury. At the conclusion of such trial, the jury, in response to special issues submitted, returned a verdict upon which the trial court entered judgment denying all relief sought by appellants.

The facts are substantially as follows:

In the latter part of 1948 appellee John L. Lewis obtained a commitment conditioned upon adequate financial backing from the Brown–Bellows–Smith Corporation for a lease on the basement space under the then projected San Jacinto Building for the purpose of constructing and operating a large cafeteria therein. Lewis contacted appellant Carr P. Collins, a resident of Dallas, proposing that he (Lewis) would furnish the lease, the experience and management ability for the operation of the cafeteria, and Collins would furnish the money; that all revenue of the business, except for an agreed salary to Lewis, would be applied to the repayment of such money, and that thereafter all profits would be divided equally between Lewis and Collins. These negotiations * * * culminated in the execution between the building owners, as lessors, and Lewis and Collins, as lessees, of a lease upon such basement space for a term of 30 years. Thereafter Lewis and Collins entered into a partnership agreement to endure throughout the term of the lease contract. This agreement is in part evidenced by a formal contract between the parties, but both litigants concede that the complete agreement is ascertainable only from the verbal understandings and exchanges of letters between the principals. It appears to be undisputed that originally a corporation had been contemplated, and that the change to a partnership was made to gain the advantages which such a relationship enjoys under the internal revenue laws. The substance of the agreement was that Collins was to furnish all of the funds necessary to build, equip, and open the cafeteria for business. Lewis was to plan and supervise such construction, and, after opening for business, to manage the operation of the cafeteria. As a part of this undertaking, he guaranteed that moneys advanced by Collins would be repaid at the rate of at least $30,000, plus interest, in the first year of operation, and $60,000 per year, plus interest, thereafter, upon default of which Lewis would surrender his interest to Collins. In addition Lewis guaranteed Collins against loss to the extent of $100,000. * * *

Immediately after the lease agreement had been executed Lewis began the preparation of detailed plans and specifications for the cafeteria. Initially Lewis had estimated, and had represented to Collins, that the cost of completing the cafeteria ready for operation would be approximately $300,000. Due to delays on the part of the building owners in completing the building, and delays in procuring the equipment deemed necessary to opening the cafeteria for business, the actual opening did not occur until September 18, 1952, some 2½ years after the lease had been executed. It likewise appears that the actual costs incurred during that period greatly exceeded the amount previously estimated by Lewis to be necessary. The cause of such increase is disputed by the litigants. Appellants contend that it was brought about largely by the extravagance and mismanagement of appellee Lewis. Appellees contend that it resulted from inflation, increased labor and material costs, caused by the Korean War, and unanticipated but necessary expenses. Whatever may have been the reason it clearly appears that Collins, while expressing concern over the increasing cost, and urging the employment of every possible economy, continued to advance funds and pay expenses, which, by the date of opening for business, had exceeded $600,000.

Collins' concern over the mounting costs of the cafeteria appears to have been considerably augmented by the fact that after opening for business the cafeteria showed expenses considerably in excess of receipts. Upon being informed, shortly after the cafeteria had opened for business, that there existed incurred but unpaid items of cost over and above those theretofore paid, Collins made demand upon Lewis that the cafeteria be placed immediately upon a profitable basis, failing which he (Collins) would advance no more funds for any purpose. There followed an exchange of recriminatory correspondence between the parties, Collins on the one hand charging Lewis with extravagant mismanagement, and Lewis on the other hand charging Collins with unauthorized interference with the management of the business. Futile attempts were made by Lewis to obtain financial backing to buy Collins' interest in the business. Numerous threats were made by Collins to cause Lewis to lose his interest in the business entirely. This suit was filed by Collins in January of 1953.

The involved factual background of this litigation was presented to the jury in a trial which extended over five weeks * * *. At the conclusion of the evidence 23 special issues of fact were submitted to the jury. The controlling issues of fact, as to which a dispute existed, were resolved by the jury in their answers to Issues 1 to 5, inclusive, in which they found that Lewis was competent to manage the business of the LBC Cafeteria; that there is not a reasonable expectation of profit under the continued management of Lewis; that but for the conduct of Collins there would be a reasonable expectation of profit under the continued management of Lewis; that such conduct on the part of Collins was not that of a reasonably prudent person acting under the same or similar circumstances; and that such conduct on the part of Collins materially decreased the earnings of the cafeteria during the first year of its operation. * * * [W]e conclude not only that there is ample support for the findings of the jury which we consider to be controlling, but further that upon the entire record, including such findings, the trial court entered the only proper judgment under the law, and that judgment must be in all things affirmed. * * *

As we understand appellants' position * * * they contend that there is no such thing as an indissoluble partnership; that it is not controlling or even important, in so far as the right to a dissolution is concerned, as to which of the partners is right or wrong in their disputes; and finally, that whenever it is made to appear that the partners are in hopeless disagreement concerning a partnership which has no reasonable expectation of profit, the legal right to dissolution exists. In support of these contentions appellants cite numerous authorities, all of which have been carefully examined. We do not undertake to individually distinguish the authorities cited for the reason that in no case cited by appellants does a situation analogous to that here present exist, namely, that the very facts upon which appellants predicate their right to a dissolution have been found by the jury to have been brought about by appellant Collins' own conduct, in violation of his own contractual obligations.

We agree with appellants' premise that there is no such thing as an indissoluble partnership only in the sense that there always exists the power, as opposed to the right, of dissolution. But legal right to dissolution rests in equity, as does the right to relief from the provisions of any legal contract. The jury finding that there is not a reasonable expectation of profit from the LBC Cafeteria under the continued management of Lewis, must be read in connection with their findings that Lewis is competent to manage the business of LBC Cafeteria, and that but for the conduct of Collins there would be a reasonable expectation of profit therefrom. In our view those are the controlling findings upon the issue of dissolution. It was Collins' obligation to furnish the money; Lewis' to furnish the management, guaranteeing a stated minimum repayment of the money. The jury has found that he was competent, and could reasonably have performed his obligation but for the conduct of Collins. We know of no rule which grants Collins, under such circumstances, the right to dissolution of the partnership. The rule is stated in Karrick v. Hannaman, 168 U.S. 328, 18 S.Ct. 135, 138, 42 L.Ed. 484, as follows: "A court of equity, doubtless, will not assist the partner breaking his contract to procure a dissolution of the partnership, because, upon familiar principles, a partner who has not fully and fairly performed the partnership agreement on his part has no standing in a court of equity to enforce any rights under the agreement." It seems to this Court that the proposition rests upon maxims of equity, too fundamental in our jurisprudence to require quotation.

The basic agreement between Lewis and Collins provided that Collins would furnish money in an amount sufficient to defray the cost of building, equipping and opening the L–C Cafeteria for operation. As a part of the agreement between Lewis and Collins, Lewis executed, and delivered to Collins, a mortgage upon Lewis' interest in the partnership "until the indebtedness incurred by the said Carr P. Collins * * * has been paid in full out of income derived from the said LBC Cafeteria, Houston, Texas." * * *

Collins' right to foreclose [the mortgage on Lewis' interest] depends upon whether or not Lewis has met his basic obligation of repayment at the rate agreed upon. Appellees contend, we think correctly, that he has, in the following manner: the evidence shows that Collins advanced a total of $636,720 for the purpose of building, equipping and opening the cafeteria for business. The proof also shows that Lewis contended that the actual cost exceeded that amount by over $30,000. The litigants differed in regard to such excess, it being Collins' contention that it represented operating expense rather than cost of building, equipping and opening the cafeteria. The jury heard the conflicting proof relative to these contentions, and resolved the question by their answer to Special Issue 20, whereby they found that the minimum cost of building, equipping and opening the cafeteria for operation amounted to $697,603.36. Under the basic agreement of the partners, therefore, this excess was properly Collins' obligation. Upon the refusal of Collins to pay it, Lewis paid it out of earnings of the business during the first year of its operation. Thus it clearly appears that Lewis met his obligation, and the trial court properly denied foreclosure of the mortgage.

In their brief, appellants repeatedly complain that they should not be forced to endure a continuing partnership wherein there is no reasonable expectation of profit, which they say is the effect of the trial court's judgment. The proper and equitable solution of the differences which arise between partners is never an easy problem, especially where the relationship is as involved as this present one. We do not think it can properly be said, however, that the judgment of the trial court denying appellants the dissolution which they seek forces them to endure a partnership wherein there is no reasonable expectation of profit. We have already pointed out the ever present inherent power, as opposed to the legal right, of any partner to terminate the relationship. Pursuit of that course presents the problem of possible liability for such damages as flow from the breach of contract. The alternative course available to appellants seems clearly legible in the verdict of the jury, whose services in that connection were invoked by appellants.

Judgment affirmed.

Notes

(1) The principal case arose before Texas enacted its version of UPA (1914). Would the result have been the same under that Act? See UPA (1914) §§ 31(1)(b), 31(2), 38(2).

(2) Assuming the case had arisen under that Act, would Collins' rights have been different if he could have dissolved the partnership under § 31(1)(b) rather than under § 32? In what way?

(3) Was there a written agreement here? When Collins and Lewis started this venture it appears that they initially planned to form a corporation. Does this fact help explain how Collins got into the mess that he found himself?

(4) Apparently Collins and Lewis are locked into a partnership that is, as a practical matter, not dissolvable. What happens next?

CAUBLE v. HANDLER

Texas Court of Civil Appeals, 1973.
503 S.W.2d 362, writ ref'd n.r.e.

BREWSTER, JUSTICE.

This is a suit brought by the administratrix of the estate of a deceased partner against the surviving partner for an accounting of the partnership assets. No jury was involved and the trial court did not file findings of fact and conclusions of law. Tom Handler, the defendant, was the surviving partner and Thomas Cauble was the deceased partner. The partnership was engaged in selling at retail furniture and appliances and each partner owned a 50% interest.

The trial court awarded the plaintiff, the administratrix of the estate of the deceased partner, a judgment against the surviving partner for $20.95 plus six percent interest thereon from February 2, 1973, the date of the judgment. The judgment also awarded the court appointed auditor a fee in the sum of $1,800.00 for his services in auditing the partnership accounts, taxed the item as court costs, and then taxed the entire court costs against plaintiff. It is from this judgment that plaintiff is appealing. We will refer herein to the parties as they appeared in the court below.

We reverse and remand the case for a new trial.

The plaintiff's first point is that the trial court erred in basing its judgment upon the book value of the partnership assets that were arbitrarily established by defendant. Her eighth point of error is that the court erred in refusing to consider the cash market value of the partnership assets in arriving at its judgment.

We sustain both of these points of error.

It is apparent from the record that the trial court determined the value of the partnership inventory by using the cost or book value thereof. Thomas Cauble died on May 18, 1971. * * * Handler kept the partnership books and took a physical inventory that was used by the partnership tax man in preparing [the] final partnership income tax return. In preparing the inventory Handler testified that he priced each item in the inventory "According to the invoices, according to cost." Again he stated: "Take the count first and then you * * * go back to the invoice and pick up the amount."

The value of the partnership inventory, arrived at as above indicated, was used by the accountant in preparing the final income tax return and was used by the court in determining the value of the plaintiff's interest in the partnership at the date of Cauble's death.

The court erred when he used the cost price or book value of the partnership assets in determining the value of the inventory. The following is from the opinion in the case of Johnson v. Braden, 286 S.W.2d 671 (San Antonio, Tex.Civ.App., 1956, no writ hist.), at page 672: "The judgment must be reversed. Market values of the company assets are wholly absent from the record, and Johnson, on cross-examination, demonstrated that the plaintiff's audit was based on book values. *It should have been based on market value.*" (Emphasis ours.)

See also * * * Hurst v. Hurst, 1 Ariz.App. 227, 401 P.2d 232 (1965). This Hurst case holds that book values are simply arbitrary values and cannot be used. The case also holds that the amount for which the partnership assets were sold four years after the date of dissolution is also not proper evidence to be considered on the issue of market value of the partnership property at date of dissolution. * * *

Much of plaintiff's argument under her first three points of error is devoted to her contention that the trial court erred in failing and refusing to allow her a share of the profit made by Handler by continuing the partnership business between date of dissolution and date of judgment.

We sustain this contention.

The undisputed evidence shows that Handler continued to operate and to control the partnership business after the death of Cauble and down to the trial date, and that he used and sold the assets of the partnership during all that period. The record does not show that this was done with the consent of the administratrix of the deceased's estate.

Exhibit E of the court appointed auditor's report was offered into evidence and it showed that during the period from May 19, 1971, to May 21, 1972, Handler made a net profit of $40,163.42 out of operating the partnership business after dissolution. The fact that this net profit was made is undisputed. As demonstrated above, this auditor's report was legitimate evidence of the amount of those profits.

The defendant * * * admits that plaintiff tried this case on the theory that she was entitled to recover, after the accounting, one-half of the value of the partnership assets, plus a share of the profits from the date of Cauble's death to date of judgment.

The trial court, in its judgment, refused to allow the plaintiff to recover one-half of the profits that were made by Handler after the dissolution of the partnership by his continued operation of the business. Instead the trial court awarded plaintiff a recovery of some interest in the amount of $3,764.89.

It is section 38(1) of [UPA (1914)] that gave the representative of the estate of the deceased partner the right to elect, if she so desired, to have the partnership assets liquidated, the debts paid, and the share of each partner in the surplus paid to him in cash.

The plaintiff in this case did not elect to have this done.

If that election is made it many times results in the sacrifice of going concern values. See "Law of Partnership" by Crane and Bromberg, page 474, note 43.

The following quotation explains the several elections that were open to the plaintiff under the fact situation that we have here. It is from "Law of Partnership" by Crane and Bromberg, Section 86(c), pages 495–496, and is as follows:

> If a partnership is seasonably wound up after dissolution, profits and losses during the liquidation are shared by the partners in proportion to their pre-dissolution ratios, unless they have agreed otherwise. * * *
>
> *The situation changes if the business is not wound up, but continued, whether with or without agreement.* In either case, the noncontinuing partner (or his representative) has a first election between two basic alternatives, either of which can be enforced in an action for an accounting. He can force a liquidation, taking his part of the proceeds and thus sharing in profits and losses after dissolution. Alternatively, he can permit the business to continue (or accept the fact that it has continued) and claim as a creditor (though subordinate to outside creditors) the value of his interest at dissolution. This * * * means he is unaffected by later changes in those values. *If he takes the latter route, he has a second election to receive in addition* either interest * * * *or profits from date of dissolution.* This second election shields him from losses * * *
>
> The second election may seem one-sided. It serves as 'a species of compulsion * * * to those continuing the business * * * to hasten its orderly winding up.' In part it is compensation to the outgoing partner for his liability on partnership obligations existing at dissolution; this liability continues until satisfaction, which would normally occur in the process of winding up. * * *
>
> The second election rests partly on the use of the outgoing partner's assets in the conduct of the business * * * his right to profits ends when the value of his interest is properly paid to him. (Emphasis ours.)

[UPA (1914)] Section 42 * * * gives the representative of the estate of a deceased partner a right to share in the profits, if he elects to do so, if the other partner continues to operate the business after dissolution.

The great weight of authority is to the effect that Sec. 42, giving the option to take profits to the non-continuing partner is applicable regardless of whether the business is continued with or without the consent of the non-continuing partner or the representative of his estate. For a full discussion of this see the law review article in 63 Yale Law Journal 709, entitled "Profit Rights and Creditors' Priorities After a Partner's Death or Retirement:

Section 42 of the UPA" and the additional article on this subject in 67 Harvard Law Review 1271.

It is manifestly clear that the plaintiff in this case elected, as she had a right to do under Sec. 42 to have the value of Cauble's partnership interest at the date of dissolution ascertained and to receive from the surviving partner, Handler, as an ordinary creditor, an amount equal to the value of Cauble's interest in the dissolved partnership at date of dissolution, plus the profits attributable to his right in the property of the dissolved partnership.

The following proceedings that occurred during the trial show that this election was made by plaintiff:

"THE COURT: You think they're making an election for the profits, is that correct, sir?

"MR. OWENS: The way they've been introducing their evidence and talking here I presume they have.

"MR. SCHATTMAN: That's correct.

"THE COURT: If you have not done so that is your election?

"MR. SCHATTMAN: Right.

"THE COURT: All right, then that disposes of that point."

Although the undisputed evidence showed that Handler made over $40,163.42 by operating the partnership business after dissolution the Court refused to allow plaintiff to recover from Handler the Cauble estate's share of those profits, which plaintiff had a right to do. In lieu of profits, which plaintiff elected to recover, the Court awarded her six percent interest on what he found to be the cost or book value of the Cauble interest in the partnership at date of dissolution. This interest amounted to $3,764.89, which sum was considerably less than a one-half interest in the $40,163.42 in profits that Handler made out of his operation of the partnership business after dissolution.

This error was obviously prejudicial to plaintiff.

In plaintiff's fifth point of error she contends that the trial court erred in taxing all the costs incurred in connection with the accounting case, including the court appointed auditor's fee of $1,800.00, against the plaintiff. * * *

The record does not reveal the court's reason for taxing all the court costs, including the $1,800.00 court appointed auditor's fee, against just one of the two partners involved in this accounting suit. * * *

We recognize that the trial court does have a broad discretion in taxing the costs in a case like this and there are occasions where the costs have been taxed against just one partner. But, as a general rule, the costs that are incurred in an accounting case are ordered paid out of the partnership estate. This results in the costs being paid by the partners in proportion to their interest in the business.

It would seem that in the ordinary case both partners would benefit by having the state of the account between them legally adjudicated so that the partnership can be terminated. One partner is not obligated to accept the adverse party's word for the state of the partnership account. * * *

Reversed and remanded for a new trial.

Notes

(1) In addition to the basic elections provided by UPA (1914) described in the principal case, the Act also provides answers for a number of other questions that may arise when a partnership business is simply continued after dissolution. For example:

(a) What are the rights of creditors of the old partnership with respect to the assets of the continuing business? See UPA (1914) § 41.

(b) In view of the agency that exists between partners, what must a retiring partner do to avoid liability for subsequent partnership obligations? See UPA (1914) § 35(1)(b).

(c) If a creditor knows that a partner has retired and deals with the successor partnership, does that release the retired partner from preretirement partnership obligations? See UPA (1914) § 36(2).

ADAMS v. JARVIS

Supreme Court of Wisconsin, 1964.
23 Wis.2d 453, 127 N.W.2d 400.

Action for declaratory judgment construing a medical partnership agreement between three doctors. Plaintiff-respondent withdrew from the partnership seven years after it was formed. * * *

The dispute concerns the extent of the plaintiff's right to share in partnership assets, specifically accounts receivable. The relevant portions of the agreement provide:

* * *

13. Fiscal Year—Share of Profits and Losses. The partnership fiscal year shall coincide with the calendar year. Net profits and losses of the partnership shall be divided among the individuals in the same proportion as their capital interests in the partnership, except as hereinafter provided for partners who become incapacitated or have withdrawn from the partnership, or the estates of the deceased partners. * * *

15. Conditions of Termination. Partnership shall not terminate under certain conditions. The incapacity, withdrawal or death of a partner shall not terminate this partnership. Such partner, or the estate or heirs of a deceased partner shall continue to participate in partnership profits and losses, as provided in this agreement, but shall not participate in management, the making of partnership decisions, or any professional matters. On the happening of any of the above events, the books of the partnership shall not be closed until the end of the partnership fiscal year.

16. Withdrawal. No withdrawal from the firm shall be effective until at least thirty (30) days have elapsed from the date on which written notice of such intention is given the other partners by registered mail to their last known address.

As used herein 'withdrawal' shall refer to any situation in which a partner leaves the partnership, at a time when said partnership is not dissolving, pursuant to a written agreement of the parties to do so. The withdrawing partner shall be entitled to receive from the continuing partners the following:

(1) Any balance standing to his credit on the books of the partnership;

(2) That proportion of the partnership profits to which he was entitled by this agreement in the fiscal year of his withdrawal, which the period from the beginning of such year to the effective date of withdrawal shall bear to the whole of the then current fiscal year. Such figure shall be ascertained as soon as practicable after the close of the current fiscal year and shall be payable as soon as the amount thereof is ascertained. All drawings previously made during the then fiscal year shall be first charged against the share in net partnership profits as above computed. If there shall have been losses for such fiscal year, or overdrawings, or losses and the whole of any overdrawings or loans, shall be determined and charged against his capital account, and if in excess thereof, shall be paid by him or his estate promptly after the close of the fiscal year, plus

(3) The amount of his capital account on the effective date of his withdrawal (after deduction of any losses required to be paid in subdivision (2) above).

In the event such withdrawing partner dies prior to receiving any or all of the above payments, his personal representative, heirs or assigns shall receive the same payments at the same time as those to which he would have been entitled by the terms had he lived. Payment of the items set forth in subdivisions (1) and (3) above shall be made according to and evidenced by a promissory note, executed by the remaining partners, payable in twelve (12) equal quarterly installments, the first of which shall be payable at the end of the six (6) months following the effective date of such withdrawal. Acceleration of said note shall be permitted at the sole discretion of the two remaining partners. Such note shall bear interest at Two (2) Percent, payable with each installment.

It is further agreed that in the event of the withdrawal of any partner or partners, any and all accounts receivable for any current year and any and all years past shall remain the sole possession and property of the remaining member or members of THE TOMAHAWK CLINIC.
* * *

18. Dissolution. Should this partnership be dissolved by agreement of the parties, all accounts and notes shall be liquidated and all firm assets sold or divided between the partners at agreed valuations. The books of the partnership shall then be closed and distribution made in proportion to the capital interests of the partners as shown by the partnership books. No drawings should be paid once the partnership has begun to wind up its affairs, although liquidating dividends based on estimates may be paid from time to time. No dissolution shall be effective until the end of the then fiscal year, and until ninety (90) days have elapsed from the date on which written agreement to such dissolution shall have been executed by the parties hereto.

This agreement shall be binding not only upon the parties hereto, but also upon their heirs, executors, administrators, successors, and assigns, and the wives of said partners have signed this agreement as witnesses, after being advised of the terms of this agreement."

The trial court decided that the withdrawal of the plaintiff worked a dissolution of the partnership under [UPA (1914) §§ 29, 30]; that the partnership assets should be liquidated and applied to the payment of partnership interests according to the scheme set forth in [UPA (1914) § 38] for the reason that paragraphs 15 and 16 of the partnership agreement did not apply in the case of a statutory dissolution; that plaintiff's interest was one-third of the net worth, including therein accounts receivable of the partnership as of May 31, 1961; that plaintiff should recover from defendants the value of his partnership interest; and gave judgment accordingly, but retained jurisdiction for supplementary proceedings. Defendants appeal.

BEILFUSS, JUSTICE.

1. Does a withdrawal of a partner constitute a dissolution of the partnership under [UPA (1914) §§ 29, 30], notwithstanding a partnership agreement to the contrary?

2. Is plaintiff, as withdrawing partner, entitled to a share of the accounts receivable?

WITHDRAWAL

* * * [The court quotes UPA (1914) §§ 29, 30.]

The partnership agreement as set forth above (paragraph 15) specifically provides that the partnership shall not terminate by the withdrawal of a partner. We conclude the parties clearly intended that even though a partner withdrew, the partnership and the partnership business would continue for the purposes for which it was organized. Paragraph 18 of the agreement provides for a dissolution upon agreement of the parties in the sense that the partnership would cease to function as such subject to winding up of its affairs.

While the withdrawal of a partner works a dissolution of the partnership under the statute as to the withdrawing partner, it does not follow that the rights and duties of remaining partners are similarly affected. The agreement contemplates a partnership would continue to exist between the remaining partners even though the personnel constituting the partnership was changed.

Persons with professional qualifications commonly associate in business partnerships. The practice of continuing the operation of the partnership business, even though there are some changes in partnership personnel, is also common. The reasons for an agreement that a medical partnership should continue without disruption of the services rendered is self evident. If the partnership agreement provides for continuation, sets forth a method of paying the withdrawing partner his agreed share, does not jeopardize the rights of creditors, the agreement is enforceable. The statute does not specifically regulate this type of withdrawal with a continuation of the business. The statute should not be construed to invalidate an otherwise enforceable contract entered into for a legitimate purpose.

The provision for withdrawal is in effect a type of winding up of the partnership without the necessity of discontinuing the day-to-day business.

[UPA (1914) § 38] contemplates a discontinuance of the day-to-day business but does not forbid other methods of winding up a partnership.

The agreement does provide that Dr. Adams shall no longer actively participate and further provides for winding up the affairs insofar as his interests are concerned. In this sense his withdrawal does constitute a dissolution. We conclude, however, that when the plaintiff, Dr. Adams, withdrew, the partnership was not wholly dissolved so as to require complete winding up of its affairs, but continued to exist under the terms of the agreement. The agreement does not offend the statute and is valid.

ACCOUNTS RECEIVABLE

* * * [The Court quotes UPA (1914) § 38(1).]

The trial court concluded that the withdrawal constituted a statutory dissolution; that partnership assets shall be liquidated pursuant to the statute and that the plaintiff was entitled to a one-third interest in the accounts receivable.

[UPA (1914) § 38(1)], applies only "unless otherwise agreed." The distribution should therefore be made pursuant to the agreement.

Paragraphs 15 and 16 of the contract as set forth above provide for the withdrawal of a partner and the share to which he is entitled. Subject to limitations not material here, paragraph 16 provides that a withdrawing partner shall receive (1) any balance to his credit on partnership books, (2) his proportionate share of profits calculated on a fiscal year basis, and (3) his capital account as of the date of his withdrawal. Paragraph 16 further provides that in event of withdrawal "any and all accounts receivable for any current year and any and all years past shall remain the sole possession and property of the remaining member or members of THE TOMAHAWK CLINIC."

* * *

We conclude the parties to the agreement intended accounts receivable to be restricted to customer or patient accounts receivable.

The provision of the agreement is clear and unambiguous. There is nothing in the record to suggest the plaintiff's bargaining position was so unequal in the negotiations leading up to the agreement that the provision should be declared unenforceable upon the grounds of public policy. Legitimate business and good will considerations are consistent with a provision retaining control and ownership of customer accounts receivable in an active functioning professional medical partnership. We hold the provision on accounts receivable enforceable.

Because of our determination that the partnership agreement is valid and enforceable the judgment of the trial court insofar as it decrees a dissolution of the partnership and a one-third division of the accounts receivable to the plaintiff must be reversed and remanded to the trial court with directions to enter judgment in conformity with this opinion.

* * * The trial court may conduct such proceedings as are necessary to effectuate a distribution pursuant to the agreement.

The parties have stipulated that the plaintiff ceased to be an active partner as of June 1, 1961. The agreement provides that the partnership fiscal year shall coincide with the calendar year. It further provides that his share of the partnership profits upon withdrawal shall be calculated upon the whole year and in proportion to his participation of the whole fiscal year. He is, therefore, entitled to 5/12 or 1/3, or 5/36 of the profits for the fiscal year ending December 31, 1961.

Such of the accounts receivable as were collected during the year 1961 do constitute a part of the profits for 1961. The plaintiff had no part of the management of the partnership after June 1, 1961; however, his eventual distributive share of profits is dependent, in some degree, upon the management of the business affairs and performance of the continuing partners for the remainder of the fiscal year. Under these circumstances the continuing partners stand in a fiduciary relationship to the withdrawing partner and are obligated to conduct the business in a good faith manner including a good faith effort to liquidate the accounts receivable consistent with good business practices.

Judgment reversed with directions to conduct supplementary proceedings to determine distributive share of plaintiff and then enter judgment in conformity with this opinion.

Notes

(1) If the business is to continue after dissolution, the critical problem of how the interest of the departed partners is to be liquidated must be addressed in the partnership agreement. As the principal case holds, such an agreement will be enforced in lieu of rights otherwise given by statute in the absence of agreement.

(2) What was the potential problem with year-end accounts receivable that caused the court in the next-to-last paragraph of its opinion to refer to the partners' fiduciary duties to each other?

(3) The manner of liquidating a former partner's interest in The Tomahawk Clinic set forth in the partnership agreement probably worked reasonably fairly, given the economics of most medical practices. Would you recommend that similar provisions be used in, say, a law partnership specializing in plaintiff personal injury litigation?

(4) A drafter of a continuation agreement must resolve several basic questions that are not unlike the problems faced by a drafter of share transfer restrictions in closely held corporations. See, pp. 487–488, infra. Generally, fair treatment of the retiring interest is the ultimate aim; there is often an element of Russian roulette in drafting these provisions since clauses are usually reciprocal and it cannot be determined in advance which partner will be the first to withdraw. How were the following matters handled by the agreement in Adams v. Jarvis?

(a) First, a determination must be made as to the types of dissolution which trigger the clause. The most common provision covers death or retirement, but it may also cover other types of dissolution, such as expulsion or bankruptcy.

(b) Second, what is to happen to the outgoing interest? There are several alternatives that have widely varying income tax consequences. The other partners may simply purchase the interest. They may arrange to have the interest purchased by an acceptable third person. Or the partnership may purchase the interest. Or the assets of the partnership may be sold as a unit to the remaining partners who are to continue the business. Or the outgoing interest may continue to share in future earnings on a more or less permanent basis.

(c) Third, is the disposition to be optional or mandatory from the standpoint of the remaining partners? In other words, may the remaining partners elect to terminate, ignoring the provision in the agreement?

(d) Fourth, how much is the withdrawing interest to receive? Valuation is usually a complex task, and the best method depends on the nature of the business. Appraisal of each asset by an independent appraiser may be most appropriate in the case of a real estate partnership, but hopelessly inadequate in a law firm where most of the assets are represented by contingent work in progress. What would be a fair basis for valuing an interest in a large law firm?

The following suggestions cover the most popular techniques of valuation:

> A fixed sum; book value, perhaps with supplemental appraisals; appraisal; capitalization of earnings in the past; a fraction of future earnings over a specified period of time; negotiation after the fact; a right of first refusal to meet the best offer obtainable elsewhere by the withdrawing interest; a sum based on a fraction of the partner's income from the partnership during the previous year or an average of several years.

(e) Fifth, is the payment to be made in a lump sum, or over time?

(f) Sixth, how is the cash to be raised to meet the required payments (life insurance, borrowing, funds generated by the business's regular operations)?

(g) Seventh, may the retiring interest compete with the partnership interest? If not, how much of the consideration is to be allocated to the covenant not to compete?

(h) Eighth, should the retiring interest have power to inspect books and records or demand an audit?

8182 MARYLAND ASSOCIATES, LIMITED PARTNERSHIP v. SHEEHAN

Supreme Court of Missouri, En Banc, 2000.
14 S.W.3d 576.

WILLIAM RAY PRICE, JR. CHIEF JUSTICE. * * *

On April 5, 1984, the Missouri general partnership of Popkin, Stern, Heifitz, Lurie, Sheehan, Reby & Chervitz, a law firm, entered into a lease agreement with 8182 Maryland. Defendant Richard J. Sheehan, a general partner of Popkin, Stern, Heifitz, Lurie, Sheehan, Reby & Chervitz, signed the lease along with the other thirteen general partners. This lease was for the use of two floors and space in the parking garage of an office building that had yet to be constructed. The term of the lease was 120 months and commenced on the date the space was made "ready for occupancy" by 8182 Maryland. Rent was to be paid on the first day of each month. The lease was silent as to liability for incoming or withdrawing partners from Popkin, Stern, Heifitz, Lurie, Sheehan, Reby & Chervitz. The lease did, however, contain a clause requiring the written consent of the landlord for assignment of the lease.

In October of 1985, Sheehan withdrew from the partnership.[21] On December 31, 1985, Sheehan assigned his interest in the partnership to the remaining partners. * * * In January of 1986, Sheehan's resignation became effective and the partnership formally adopted the shorter name of "Popkin & Stern." Apparently, the lease with 8182 Maryland was not expressly assigned in writing by the old partnership of Popkin, Stern, Heifitz, Lurie, Sheehan, Reby & Chervitz to the new partnership of Popkin & Stern, nor did Popkin & Stern assume the obligations of the lease in writing. On or before April 26, 1986, Popkin & Stern began occupancy of the leased premises.

At varying points between January 1, 1985, and January 1, 1986, Defendants Timothy Noelker, Douglas Burdette, Barbara Lageson, and Jeffrey Klar became partners of Popkin & Stern. There is no evidence in the record that any partnership agreement signed by these partners contained language concerning personal liability on the lease for incoming partners. None were asked to sign the lease agreement or any assumption agreement. It does not appear that the lease agreement was ever expressly assigned in writing to any of the new partnerships that resulted from the changing composition of the firm, or that any of these new partnerships assumed the obligation of the lease in writing. Noelker, Burdette, Lageson, and Klar all withdrew from the firm on or before December 1, 1989. None entered into a withdrawal agreement with any Popkin & Stern partnership or 8182 Maryland.

In September of 1991, Popkin & Stern defaulted on its lease obligation to 8182 Maryland and subsequently filed for bankruptcy in 1992. The third amended petition in this case, filed on January 13, 1993, alleged that 8182 Maryland suffered damages in the amount of $865,488.53 for past-due rent and the partnership's pro rata share of the building's operating expenses and parking garage expenses and $4,891,975.91 for the "present value of the Premises for the remainder of the stated term over the reasonable value of the Premises for the remainder of the stated term," a remedy the lease expressly allowed to the landlord upon the partnership's default. 8182 Maryland named as defendants all past and present general partners of the firm since April 4, 1984, but has dismissed thirty-six of those defendants.

Noelker and Klar filed partial motions for summary judgment seeking to limit any recovery of damages to partnership assets, not their individual assets. The trial court entered an order of partial summary judgment in favor of Noelker on January 22, 1993, and in favor of Klar on February 10, 1993. Later, Sheehan, Noelker, Klar, Burdette, and Harris filed separate motions for summary judgment requesting the circuit court dismiss, in all respects, the third amended petition against each of them. * * * The trial court granted these motions * * * [and] it is from the granting of these motions that 8182 Maryland appeals. * * *

III.   MISSOURI PARTNERSHIP LAW

Partnership law in Missouri is governed by the Uniform Partnership Law (UPL). The UPL is nearly identical to the [1914] Uniform Partnership Act (UPA), adopted in most states. * * *

---

21. [By the Court] Sheehan resigned from the firm to become the Assistant Chief Litigation Counsel, Division of Enforcement, Securities and Exchange Commission in Washington, D.C. He subsequently joined the New York Stock Exchange as vice president for enforcement and became first vice president and assistant general counsel for Dean Witter.

Central to the determination of personal liability for Defendant Sheehan and Defendants Noelker, Burdette, Lageson, and Klar is the legal effect the withdrawal of existing partners and the addition of incoming partners has on a partnership. The withdrawal of an existing partner dissolves the partnership. * * * [The Court quotes UPA (1914) § 29]. Dissolution, however, is not a termination of the partnership business. * * * [The Court quotes UPA (1914) § 30]. A partner's personal liability is not discharged merely by the dissolution of the partnership. [UPA (1914) § 36(1)]. However, a partner may be "discharged from any existing liability upon dissolution of the partnership by an agreement to that effect between himself, the partnership creditor and the person or partnership continuing the business." UPL § 358.360.2 [similar to UPA (1914) § 36(2)]. Under certain circumstances, such an agreement may even be inferred.

* * * The result is that the old firm continues until its affairs are wound up and a new partnership is formed, consisting of the remaining members of the old partnership. Ohlendorf v. Feinstein, 636 S.W.2d 687, 689 (Mo.App.1982). Any creditors of the old partnership also become creditors of the new partnership continuing the business. Section 358.410.

The UPL does not expressly make the admission of a new partner a ground for dissolution. However, "[i]t is universally admitted that any change in membership dissolves a partnership, and creates a new partnership." Comment, UPA § 41; see also Ellingson v. Walsh, O'Connor & Barneson, 15 Cal.2d 673, 104 P.2d 507, 509 (1940).

* * * Under Missouri common law, a partnership is dissolved by the admission of a new partner. Mudd v. Bast, 34 Mo. 465, 468 (1864).

IV. THE CLAIM AGAINST SHEEHAN

Defendant Sheehan was a partner who personally signed the lease, but withdrew from the partnership of Popkin, Stern, Heifitz, Lurie, Sheehan, Reby & Chervitz before the lease agreement commenced or was breached by Popkin & Stern. There is no doubt Sheehan was personally liable for the lease while still a partner at Popkin, Stern, Heifitz, Lurie, Sheehan, Reby & Chervitz. [The court quotes UPA (1914) §§ 9(1) and 15]. When Sheehan and the other general partners of Popkin, Stern, Heifitz, Lurie, Sheehan, Reby & Chervitz signed the lease agreement with 8182 Maryland, each partner of the partnership became personally liable on the agreement.

A.

Sheehan first claims his withdrawal from the partnership terminated his personal liability because his withdrawal became effective before the lease agreement "commenced." We do not agree. A party becomes liable on a contractual agreement, even a lease agreement with a future date of commencement, at the moment it is executed. * * * Commencement, under the terms of this lease, was merely the starting point for the collection of rent and the possibility of occupancy, not the beginning of contractual liability. Once Sheehan signed the lease agreement, he became jointly and severally liable for all existing and future obligations under that lease.

B.

Sheehan also claims his liability terminated at withdrawal because he withdrew before any breach of the lease occurred. We again disagree. When Sheehan withdrew from Popkin, Stern, Heifitz, Lurie, Sheehan, Reby & Chervitz, the partnership was dissolved, and the new partnership of Popkin & Stern resulted among the remaining partners. Dissolution, however, "of the partnership does not of itself discharge the existing liability of any partner." [UPA (1914) § 36(1)]; see also Thompson by Thompson v. Gilmore, 888 S.W.2d 715, 716 (Mo.App.1994) ["Under Missouri law, including the adoption of the Uniform Partnership Act, 'dissolution does not relieve the partners from their liability for performance of contracts theretofore made.' "]. Liability for partnership obligations does not die simply by disassociating oneself from the partnership business.

Moreover, withdrawing partners retain personal liability after withdrawal, even for contingent obligations. In *Thompson*, two partners of a law partnership that contracted with Thompson for representation in a wrongful death action, subsequently withdrew. The remaining partners failed to file Thompson's claim before the statute of limitations ran. The court expressly held the two partners who had withdrawn liable for the contingent obligation assumed by the law firm before they left. Thompson by Thompson v. Gilmore, at 716. * * *

V.

Defendants Noelker, Burdette, Lageson, and Klar became partners of Popkin & Stern at various times subsequent to the lease agreement, but all left the partnership before the breach occurred. Defendants rely exclusively on [UPA (1914) § 17] for the proposition that their liability can only be satisfied out of partnership assets. [The court quotes § 17.]

Defendants argue that because the lease was a pre-existing obligation of the previous partnership, which they never signed, they cannot be held individually liable for the lease obligations.

A.

We have not had occasion to interpret [§ 17]. Several other states, however, have adopted identical language in their partnership laws and have analyzed the implications of that section in the context of lease agreements.* * * Generally, these states have approached the issue of liability by focusing upon when the obligation of a lease "arises." * * *

Ellingson v. Walsh, O'Connor & Barneson, 15 Cal.2d 673, 104 P.2d 507 (1940), however, approached the question by interpreting California's version of UPA section 17 in the dual context of property and contract law theories, traditionally referred to as privity of contract and privity of estate. In *Ellingson*, a partner who joined a partnership after the execution of a lease agreement contested his personal liability for a breach of the lease. The court, however, found that * * *

* * * although the original partnership expressly assumed the lease and was, therefore, liable both under the lease contract and as a tenant, the addition of a new partner caused the first partnership to be dissolved and a new partnership came into being composed of the old members and the new

partner. "This second partnership did not expressly assume the obligations of the lease, but it occupied the premises. Whether it was liable contractually on the lease is immaterial; it became liable for rent as a tenant." Thus, the members of the new partnership were liable for rent not because of when the obligation of a lease arose, but because they were in occupation of the premises. This liability "arises and binds * * * continually throughout the period of * * * occupation." Id. at 510.

B.

The analysis set out in *Ellingson* provides the clearest framework for determining the personal liability of partners relative to a partnership lease consistent with the UPA and Missouri landlord/tenant law. In Missouri, a lease agreement has a dual nature; it is both a conveyance and a contract. "As between the lessor and lessee, a lease creates a contractual relationship, privity of contract, as well as being a conveyance of an estate in land which creates privity of estate." Incentive Realty, Inc. v. Hawatmeh, 983 S.W.2d [156 at 160 (Mo. App. 1998)]. Privity of contract carries with it the obligations in the written lease agreement, while privity of estate carries with it liability for rent and any other covenants running with the land.

Thus, the original partnership of Popkin, Stern, Heifitz, Lurie, Sheehan, Reby & Chervitz had privity of contract upon signing the lease agreement. When Sheehan withdrew, however, the original partnership was dissolved and a new one, Popkin & Stern, comprised of the remaining members of the original partnership, was formed. This new partnership continued the partnership business, acquiring the creditors of the old partnership. Although not a party to the lease between Popkin, Stern, Heifitz, Lurie, Sheehan, Reby & Chervitz and 8182 Maryland, Popkin & Stern occupied the leased premises and paid the rent. Unfortunately, there was no assignment and/or assumption agreement specifically defining the relationship of the old partnership and its partners, the new partnership and its partners, and 8182 Maryland.

"When a party other than a tenant is shown to be in possession of the premises, and paying rent therefor, there is a presumption that the lease has been assigned to him." Milton R. Friedman, Friedman on Leases section 7.501c1 (4th ed.1997). The lease was, therefore, presumably assigned to the resulting partnership. Over the years, each time an old partner left or a new partner joined the partnership, a similar dissolution occurred, and when the remaining partners joined by any incoming partners continued to occupy the leased premises and pay rent, another assignment of the lease to the resulting partnership was presumed. * * *

Due to its occupation of the premises and presumed assignment, Popkin & Stern, and each partnership thereafter was in privity of estate with 8182 Maryland. * * * Privity of estate creates liability only for payment of rent and other covenants running with the land [only] while the tenant is in possession. Thus, each succeeding Popkin & Stern partnership, and each of the partnerships' varying partners, became jointly and severally liable for rent payments only during the period their partnerships were in privity of estate with 8182 Maryland. When each Defendant withdrew from the partnership they were a member of, that partnership ceased to exist and ceased to occupy the land. Its privity of estate ended, and thus the withdrawing partner's personal liability for rent ended as well.

* * * Defendants Noelker, Burdette, Lageson, and Klar are not personally liable for rent arising subsequent to the time they were members of a partnership in occupation of the premises when the lease breach occurred subsequent to their withdrawal. We affirm the judgments entered in their favor.

All concur.

Notes

(1) If this opinion is correct, individual partners of law firms should be cautious about simply signing long-term leases for expensive office space. Would the LLP election eliminate this risk? Might not sophisticated landlords insist that all partners sign personal guarantees of future rental payments? Are members of the law firm who sign the original lease protected from liability if they thereafter elect LLP status?

(2) The risk of liability on leases can be reduced by using a short-term lease with successive renewal options or by having the law firm create a corporation or LLC to enter into the lease and subsequently sublet the space to the firm. However, a sophisticated landlord in that situation would probably insist on receiving some protection against a premature departure as well as a financial benefit for agreeing to such arrangements.

LAMPERT, HAUSLER & RODMAN, PC
v. JOHN F. GALLANT, ET AL.

Superior Court of Massachusetts at Suffolk, 2004.
18 Mass.L.Rptr. 614, 2004 WL 3120801.

VAN GESTEL, J.

This matter comes before the Court on a motion by the plaintiff, Lampert, Hausler & Rodman, P.C. ("LH & R"), seeking partial summary judgment on the issue of liability alone against the defendant John F. Gallant ("Gallant") on Count II of the complaint and on Count I of the third-party counterclaim. Count II claims a breach of fiduciary duty by Gallant to LH & R and Count I claims a breach of fiduciary duty by LH & R to Gallant.

BACKGROUND

Former partners/shareholders in a law firm, are locked in a professionally ugly battle over which lawyers get how much in fees from matters incomplete at the time of a split-up. Of greatest concern to LH & R are certain unfinished contingent fee cases that followed Gallant and the other defendant as departing lawyers.

[The parties] never expended the effort to create a written agreement addressing the division of unfinished business or the dissolution of the firm. Thus, when Gallant, a shareholder in Gallant, Hausler & Lampert, P.C., "resigned" and certain clients followed him to his new firm, the question of allocation of fees and disbursements gave birth to this lawsuit.

Now, LH & R, seizing upon the close corporation status of the professional corporation, presses Gallant, who is still a shareholder, to abide by his fiduciary duties. For Gallant, who established his new firm, and is practicing law in the same town as LH & R, this is difficult because his mere competition is being held out as a breach.

The fiduciary duties of lawyers in a partnership to their former law firm with regard to alleged improper solicitation of clients are well established in Massachusetts. See, e.g., *Meehan v. Shaughnessy; Cohen, 404 Mass. 419, 433–38, 535 N.E.2d 1255 (1989)*. That Gallant, Hausler & Lampert, P.C. is a closely held professional corporation in the practice of law does not diminish those fiduciary duties. However, other factors may have an effect thereon.

Also earlier, when LH & R lamented that following Massachusetts law will result in placing clients in the awkward and uncomfortable position of having to take a stand in the midst of an unseemly clash among their present and former lawyers over fees that the clients have paid or will have to pay, this Court stated that sheltering the clients from this burden must come from the lawyers acting professionally, not by a trial judge overlooking law recently expressed by the Supreme Judicial Court.

DISCUSSION

Given that LH & R is a law firm, *Rule 5.6 of the Massachusetts Rules of Professional Conduct*, found in SJC Rule 3:07, must be given recognition. In significant part, this Rule provides that:

* * *

A lawyer shall not participate in offering or making:

(b) an agreement in which a restriction on the lawyer's right to practice is part of the settlement of a controversy.

Pettingell v. Morrison, Mahoney & Miller, 426 Mass. 253, 687 N.E.2d 1237 (1997), provides guidance here. In *Pettingell*, the Supreme Judicial Court clarified the law in Massachusetts under its former Rule DR 2–108(A) and, in footnote 4 at page 255, noted that substantively DR 2–108(A) is the same as *Rule 5.6 of the Massachusetts Rules of Professional Conduct* that became effective on January 1, 1998. Then, at page 257, the SJC said:

The objective of DR 2–108(A) is to permit a lawyer who leaves a law firm to act for clients of the law firm without being discouraged from doing so by a provision for the forfeiture of funds. A forfeiture provision tends to discourage client free choice by encouraging a lawyer who leaves a firm not to compete. The broad prophylactic object of DR 2–108(A) is to forbid the inclusion of such a provision in all partnership agreements.

The SJC went on to say, at page 258:

Without adopting a per se rule, we join with the vast majority of jurisdictions that have generally declined to give effect to forfeiture provisions There may be situations in which, although a forfeiture provision is inappropriate, some reasonable recognition of a law firm's loss due to the departure of a partner should be recognized. A law firm's legitimate interest in its survival and well-being might justify a limitation on payments to a withdrawing partner in particular circumstances ... but that limitation would be more difficult to justify if it applied to a withdrawing partner who competes but not to all departing partners ... A situation warranting an offsetting claim by a firm might arise when a departing partner leaves the surviving partners with onerous partnership debts, threatening the financial integrity of the firm.

There are no special interests in LH & R's survival brought to the attention of this Court.

"The concern [in *Rule 5.6*] is to protect the clients and potential clients of the withdrawing lawyer and the law firm." *Id*. at 257.

The *Pettingell* court made absolutely clear that the "basic concerns of [*Rule 5.6*] are the interests of clients, not the interrelationship of the partners and former partners as such." *Id*. at 255. "The strong public interest in allowing clients to retain counsel of their choice outweighs any professional benefits derived from a restrictive covenant." *Meehan, supra, 404 Mass. at 431*.

Rule 5.6 does not permit the enforcement of a "fiduciary duty" that restricts the right of a lawyer to practice after termination of the relationship. But here, of course, it is argued that the relationship has not terminated because of Gallant's continuing position as a shareholder in LH & R. Indeed, Gallant himself enforces that argument by pressing with vigor his own alleged right to have the other shareholders of LH & R extend ongoing fiduciary duties to him.

This Court was told not to carve out, just for lawyers, a special exclusion to the fiduciary duties of shareholders in a closely held corporation. Indeed, the argument went, lawyers, more than all other kinds of shareholders, are fully equipped to understand the obligations that they have assumed when they choose to conduct their practice in the form of a professional corporation.

But, this Court is not free, nor should it be, to overlook the Rules of Professional Conduct or the teachings in *Pettingell* and *Meehan*.[22] To do otherwise abandons the very persons that the SJC says must be protected—clients and potential clients.

Again *Pettingell* provides some guidance. There the SJC was addressing a forfeiture clause in a written partnership agreement that would restrict the rights of lawyers to practice after withdrawal from a law firm. Among other things, the law firm argued that the forfeiture clause was not severable from the balance of the agreement. The SJC saw "no merit" in this claim. *Pettingell, supra, 426 Mass. at 258*. The firm further contended that "if the forfeiture clause is not enforced, its financial obligations to the [departing lawyers] should similarly not be recognized." *Id*. Noting that that argument had been unsuccessful elsewhere, see e.g., *Jacob v. Norris, McLaughlin & Marcus*, 128 N.J. 10, 33, 607 A.2d 142 (1992), the SJC said:

> We see no reason not to enforce the agreement generally but deny enforcement of the offending provision. To do otherwise would result in the enforcement of the forfeiture and would conflict with the public policy that compels denial of the enforcement of that provision.

Id. at 258–59. In short, the constraint of the disciplinary rules trumps what otherwise would be a valid provision in a contract.

---

22. [By the court] Additionally, a professional corporation organized to practice law is among the kinds of limited liability entities specifically regulated by SJC Rule 3:06.

This Court sees no compelling reason why it should not apply a similar approach to the present situation. Thus, it sees no basis not to enforce the fiduciary duties between and among the shareholders of LH & R generally but to deny enforcement of so much thereof as would prohibit Gallant—or Lampert or Hausler—from practicing law. To do otherwise would result in the enforcement of a condition contrary to *Rule 5.6 of the Rules of Professional Conduct* as interpreted in *Pettingell* and *Meehan* and would conflict with the public policy that compels denial of the enforcement of that kind of condition for the good of clients and potential clients.* * *

Order

For the foregoing reasons, the plaintiff's motion for partial summary judgment on issues of liability only with respect to Count II of the complaint and Count I of the third-party counterclaim is *ALLOWED* with respect to all breaches of those fiduciary duties owed by John F. Gallant to the plaintiff and with respect to all breaches of those fiduciary duties owed by Alan G. Lampert and Douglas E. Hausler to John F. Gallant, except insofar as any such fiduciary duties may otherwise prohibit John F. Gallant, Alan G. Lampert or Douglas E. Hausler from practicing law in, or not within, the law firm formerly known as Gallant, Lampert & Hausler, P.C.

Notes

(1) What if a lawyer announces that he is retiring from law practice and therefore is entitled to a pension or "continuation payments" under the law firm's contract; shortly thereafter he decides to join another firm or open his own office in the same community? May the firm discontinue making the pension or "continuation payments?" For an affirmative answer, cf. Donnelly v. Brown, Winick, Graves, Gross, Baskerville, Schoenebaum and Walker, 599 N.W.2d 677 (Iowa 1999).

(2) May a partner be expelled if there is no express expulsion power in the partnership agreement? In a partnership at will, a majority of the partners can reach much the same result by dissolving the partnership voluntarily and immediately reconstituting a new partnership under the same name but without the partner whose presence is no longer desired. For an example see Dawson v. White & Case, 88 N.Y.2d 666, 649 N.Y.S.2d 364, 672 N.E.2d 589 (1996). Might the "expelled partner" have a right to participate in the subsequent business under UPA (1914) § 38(2)(b)? To compel a winding up under id. § 37? What if the partnership is for a term?

(3) UPA (1914) §§ 32(1)(c) or (d), 38(2) contemplate a "wrongful dissolution," in which a partner "who engaged in wrongful conduct" may be removed by judicial order, and whose financial rights thereafter are reduced by the loss suffered by his wrongful conduct. What is the relationship between "wrongful dissolution" and "expulsion"? Does the partnership have a choice as to which theory to adopt? Assume in a partnership at will a partner engages in wrongful conduct. Is it meaningful to say that he was "expelled"? Should his recovery against the firm be limited to that provided by § 38(2)? Consult Robert W. Hillman, Misconduct as a Basis for Excluding or Expelling a Partner: Effecting Commercial Divorce and Securing Custody of the Business, 78 Nw.U.L.Rev. 527 (1983).

(4) Sections 31(1)(d) and 38, second sentence, of UPA (1914) both contemplate that an expulsion must be "bona fide." What does "bona fide" mean in this context? That the other partners have "cause" to expel the partner? That they have a good reason to do so that may not rise to the level of cause? That they have a plausible reason to do so that is not merely pretextual? That these words should simply be ignored in the reality of the modern partnership? Is it significant that UPA (1997) § 601(3) omits this phrase? For a thoughtful analysis, see Paula J. Dailey, The Law of Partnership Expulsions: Fiduciary Duty and Good Faith, 21 Cardozo L.Rev. 181, 185–86 (1999).

GIBBS v. BREED, ABBOTT & MORGAN

New York Supreme Court, 2000.
271 A.D.2d 180, 710 N.Y.S.2d 578.

MAZZARELLI, J.

Plaintiffs Charles Gibbs and Robert Sheehan are former partners of Breed Abbott & Morgan ("BAM") who specialize in trust and estate law. They withdrew from BAM in July 1991 to join Chadbourne & Parke ("Chadbourne"), and brought this action for monies due to them under their BAM partnership. Defendants asserted various counterclaims alleging that plaintiffs breached their fiduciary duty to BAM. * * * Plaintiffs appeal from the trial court's determination that, in the course of both partners' planning and eventually implementing their withdrawal from BAM, they breached their fiduciary duty to the partnership.

From January 1991 until July 1991, plaintiffs were the only partners in the Trusts and Estates department ("T/E") at BAM; plaintiff Gibbs was the head of the department. * * * The BAM trusts and estates department also employed three associate attorneys, Warren Whitaker (fifteenth year), Austin Wilkie (fourth year), and Joseph Scorese (first year); two accountants, Lois Wetzel and Ellen Furst; and two paralegals, Lee Ann Riley and Ruth Kramer. * * *

On June 19, 1991, both plaintiffs informed Stephen Lang, BAM's presiding partner, that they had accepted offers to join Chadbourne. Lang asked Gibbs not to discuss his departure with any of the T/E associates, and Gibbs agreed not to do so. * * *

On June 24, 1991, Gibbs and Sheehan sent Chadbourne a memo listing the names of the personnel in the T/E department at BAM, their respective salaries, their annual billable hours, and the rate at which BAM billed out these employees to clients. The memo included other information about the attorneys, including the colleges and law schools they attended, and their bar admissions. This list had been prepared by Sheehan on April 26, 1991, months before the partners announced they were leaving. Sheehan specifically testified that the memo was prepared in anticipation of discussions with prospective firms, and both Gibbs and Sheehan testified at trial that the recruitment of certain associates and support personnel was discussed with different firms between March and May, as the partners were considering various affiliations. While Gibbs and Sheehan were still partners at BAM, Chadbourne interviewed four BAM employees that Gibbs had indicated he was interested in bringing to Chadbourne with him. On June 27, 1991, plaintiffs submitted their written resignations. Before Gibbs and Sheehan left BAM, they wrote letters to clients served by them, advising that they were leaving BAM and that other attorneys at BAM could serve them. These letters did not mention the fact that the two partners were moving to Chadbourne. Although the partnership agreement required 45 days notice of an intention to withdraw, BAM waived this provision upon plaintiffs' production of their final billings for work previously performed. Gibbs left BAM on July 9, 1991, and Sheehan left on July 11, 1991, both taking various documents, including their respective "chronology" or desk files.[23] With the assistance of his chronology file, Gibbs began to contact his former clients on July 11, 1991. On July 11th, Chadbourne made employment offers to Whitaker, Wilkie, Wetzel, and Riley. Wilkie, Wetzel, and Riley accepted that same day; Whitaker accepted on July 15, 1991. In the following weeks, 92 of the 201 BAM T/E clients moved their business to Chadbourne.

After hearing all the testimony and the parties' arguments, the trial court determined that Gibbs' actions in persuading his partner Sheehan to leave BAM, "and the way in which the leave was orchestrated, were done, at least partially, with the intention of crippling BAM's Trusts and Estates ("T/E") department", and constituted a breach of loyalty to BAM. The court also found that Gibbs and Sheehan had breached their fiduciary duties to BAM by sending Chadbourne the April 26, 1991 memo detailing personal information about the individuals in the T/E Department at BAM, because this gave Chadbourne a competitive advantage in offering employment to other members of the department. Finally, the court found that Gibbs and Sheehan breached their fiduciary duties to BAM by taking their chronology files with them to Chadbourne. Specifically, the court concluded that by taking their respective chronology files, the partners "to a large degree hobbled their former partners in their effort to rebuild the Trusts and Estates department, in order to maintain a viable department, and in their ability to serve clients without undue disruption."

With respect to damages, the court concluded that both Gibbs and Sheehan were entitled to recover their share of BAM profits accruing until the end of July 1991, and that Sheehan was entitled to the remainder of his capital account with the firm. Although there was no evidence that the partners had improperly solicited former BAM clients, the court found that despite BAM's efforts to mitigate damages by hiring a new partner and two associates into the T/E Department, that department suffered financial losses as a result of plaintiffs' conduct, and concluded that it was entitled to recover lost profits for a reasonable period following plaintiffs' departure. * * * Gibbs and Sheehan were held jointly and severally liable for $1,861,045. The court also awarded defendants prejudgment interest and attorneys' fees. The court's liability finding should be modified, the damage award vacated, and the matter remanded for a determination of the financial loss, if any, occasioned by plaintiffs' disloyal act of supplying competitors with BAM's confidential employee data.

23. The "chronology" or desk files contained copies of every letter written by the respective attorneys during the previous years. The letters included those written to adversaries about pending legal matters, letters written to clients, and letters written to others about ongoing BAM matters. These letters were du- plicates of those kept in BAM's regular client files, but defendants allege that due to the fact that the files are arranged chronologically, active matters are more easily referenced. The original correspondences, left with the firm, have been filed by client and are dispersed throughout the department.

The members of a partnership owe each other a duty of loyalty and good faith, and "[a]s a fiduciary, a partner must consider his or her partners' welfare, and refrain from acting for purely private gain" (*Meehan v. Shaughnessy,* 404 Mass. 419, 434, 535 N.E.2d 1255) (Mass.1989). Partners are constrained by such duties throughout the life of the partnership and "[t]he manner in which partners plan for and implement withdrawals ... is [still] subject to the constraints imposed on them by virtue of their status as fiduciaries" (Robert Hillman, *Loyalty in the Firm: A Statement of General Principles on the Duties of Partners Withdrawing From Law Firms,* 55 Wash & Lee L.Rev. 997 (1998)). According the trial court's findings on issues of fact and credibility appropriate deference, we uphold that portion of the court's liability determination which found that plaintiffs breached their fiduciary duty as partners of the firm they were about to leave by supplying confidential employee information to Chadbourne while still partners at BAM. * * * However, we find no breach with respect to Gibbs' interactions with Sheehan, or with respect to either partner's removal of his desk files from BAM.

Defendants did not establish that Gibbs breached any duty to BAM by discussing with Sheehan a joint move to another firm, or that Sheehan's decision was based upon anything other than his own personal interests. * * *

However, the record supports the court's finding that both partners committed a breach of their fiduciary duty to the BAM partners by supplying Chadbourne, and presumably the other partnerships they considered joining, with the April 26, 1991 memorandum describing the members of BAM's T/E department, their salaries, and other confidential information such as billing rates and average billable hours, taken from personnel files. Moreover, a closer examination of the record does not support the dissent's conclusion that these partners did not engage in surreptitious recruiting. The partners may not have discussed with firm employees the possibility of moving with them prior to June 20, 1991, but they indicated to Chadbourne the employees they were interested in prior to this date, and Gibbs specifically testified that he refrained from telling one of his partners, to whom he had a duty of loyalty, about his future plans to recruit specific associates and support staff from the partnership.

There is no evidence of improper client solicitation in this case, nor is it an issue on this appeal. * * * [T]he fiduciary restraints upon a partner with respect to client solicitation are not analogous to those applicable to employee recruitment. By contrast to the lawyer-client relationship, a partner does not have a fiduciary duty to the employees of a firm which would limit its duty of loyalty to the partnership. Thus, recruitment of firm employees has been viewed as distinct and "permissible on a more limited basis than * * * solicitation of clients" (Hillman, *supra* at 1031). Pre-withdrawal recruitment is generally allowed "only after the firm has been given notice of the lawyer's intention to withdraw" (*id.*).

However, here, * * * [t]here is ample support in the record for the trial court's finding that the preparation and sending of the April 26, 1991 memo, combined with the subsequent hiring of certain trusts and estates personnel, constituted an egregious breach of plaintiff's fiduciary duty to BAM. * * * Because the memo gave Chadbourne confidential BAM employment data as well as other information reflecting BAM's valuation of each employee, Chadbourne was made privy to information calculated to give it an unfair advantage in recruiting certain employees (*see, Bancroft–Whitney Co. v. Glen,* 64 Cal.2d 327, 49 Cal.Rptr. 825, 411 P.2d 921 (1966). [breach of fiduciary duty for corporate officer to surreptitiously provide competitor with selective list of qualified employees and their salaries]).

While partners may not be restrained from inviting qualified personnel to change firms with them (*see, Denburg v. Parker Chapin Flattau & Klimpl,* 82 N.Y.2d 375, 382, 604 N.Y.S.2d 900, 624 N.E.2d 995 (1993). [striking down provision which would restrain partner from competing with his former firm] *citing, Jacob v. Norris, McLaughlin & Marcus,* 128 N.J. 10, 607 A.2d 142 (1992). [striking down provision which would prohibit partner form soliciting firm employees for a year after leaving the firm]), here Gibbs and Sheehan began their recruiting while still members of the firm and prior to serving notice of their intent to withdraw. They did so without informing their partners that they were disseminating confidential firm data to competitors. * * * The dissent's analysis, that once the firm was notified of the partners' departure, there was no breach of fiduciary duty, is flawed. The breach occurred in April of 1991 and could not be cured by any after-the-fact notification by the fiduciary who committed the breach that he was withdrawing from the firm. Chadbourne still had the unfair advantage of the confidential information from the April 1991 memo, and still had the upper hand, which was manifested by its ability to tailor its offers and incentives to the BAM recruits.

Contrary to the dissent, I would characterize the memo distributed to prospective competitors as confidential. The data was obtained from BAM personnel files which Sheehan had unique access to as a BAM partner. The dissent's statement that such financial information is generally known to ''headhunters'' is without foundation.

With respect to the specific associates and support staff whose compensation was disseminated in the April 1991 memo, the information disclosed to Chadbourne incorporated these individuals' bonuses. Bonus payments are confidential, often voted by the partnership, based upon the unique quality of an individual's work, the number of hours billed, and many other intangible factors. These lump sum payments often constitute a substantial portion of an associate's salary, and the payments are certainly not available to the public. Finally, support staff also receive bonuses paid to them at the discretion of the individual partners, from their personal accounts. This information is highly individualized and also privileged. Sheehan abused his fiduciary duty to the partnership by accessing personnel files to obtain the actual gross compensation of the associates and support staff he and Gibbs wished to bring with them, including bonuses, and disclosing this information to Chadbourne.

Moreover, the memo contained more than a list of salaries. It itemized each of the employees' annual billable hours, and the rates at which BAM billed these employees out to their clients, information which was not otherwise publicly available. These facts go directly to a potential employee's value and were accessible only to members of the BAM partnership. Selected partners providing BAM's confidential information, which they were able to obtain by virtue of their position as fiduciaries, to Chadbourne was an act of disloyalty to their partnership. The confidential information placed Chadbourne, as a competing prospective employer, in the advantageous position of conducting interviews of the associates and support staff with more knowledge than any firm could obtain through independent research, as well as providing it with information BAM partners did not know it had, thereby prejudicing their own efforts to retain their associates and support staff.

* * *

All concur except WALLACH and SAXE, JJ. who concur in part and dissent in part in an Opinion by SAXE, J.

SAXE, J. (concurring in part and dissenting in part)

What is prohibited is *actual* competition with the firm while still a member of it. An overall guiding principle limiting the conduct of departing partners is that the process must be handled properly and fairly, so that the withdrawing partner, while in possession of information that the firm lacks (namely, his impending departure), may not take unfair advantage of that information. * * *

An equally important principle in these circumstances, providing something of a counterweight to the duty of loyalty partners owe one another, is "the important value of client freedom of choice in legal representation" (*see, Graubard Mollen Dannett & Horowitz v. Moskovitz,* 86 N.Y.2d 112, 120, 629 N.Y.S.2d 1009, 653 N.E.2d 1179, *supra*). Imposition of a limitation which restricts the ability of a departing partner to offer the client the ability to continue to serve as counsel may violate the ethical prohibition against restricting an attorney's practice of law (Code of Professional Responsibility DR 2–108[A]). * * *

Under the circumstances, plaintiffs' preliminary compilation of information regarding the salaries, billable hours and standard billing rates of the employees they sought to bring with them, and their providing it to Chadbourne after giving notice to Breed, Abbott, provides no support for a liability determination against them.

First of all, there is no showing, nor did the trial court find, that the purportedly confidential information was provided to Chadbourne—or any other firm—during the period that plaintiffs were interviewing, or at any time before they gave notice to Breed, Abbott. * * *

Furthermore, although the salaries and bonuses paid to associates may be termed "confidential", in fact this information is often the greatest unkept secret in the legal profession. Unlike the earnings of law firm partners, which vary widely even within most firms, depending upon such factors as billable hours and "rainmaking" ability, the earnings of associates and support staff at large firms are relatively circumscribed, with each firm setting standard rates for both salaries and bonuses. Such information is widely known outside the firms themselves: the salary levels and bonuses paid to associates at large New York firms are regularly published in professional publications such as the New York Law Journal. Salary levels, bonuses and other financial information regarding employees' billing rates are well known to professional "headhunters", the agencies that specialize in recruiting and placing lawyers and law firm support staff, and associates' background information is available from sources such as the Martindale–Hubbell directory.

Therefore, while plaintiffs obtained the salary information regarding the associates and staff in question through their position as partners at Breed, Abbott, it was information that could as easily been obtained elsewhere. The concept that this information is some sort of trade secret does not comport with the realities of the practice of law. * * *

I perceive nothing in plaintiffs' conduct constituting any violation of fiduciary duty, and accordingly, I would reverse and dismiss the counterclaims in their entirety.

Note

The majority and dissent both express the view that the legal standards that control departing lawyers' solicitation of clients are different from the legal standards that regulate departing lawyers' recruitment of lawyers. Why is this so? One reason may be to protect the important value of client freedom of choice in legal representation. This value may conflict with the duty of loyalty that partners owe to each other as partners. It may be that lawyers must be allowed to notify their clients of their departure in order to allow the clients to have freedom of choice.

BOHATCH v. BUTLER & BINION

Supreme Court of Texas, 1998.
977 S.W.2d 543.

ENOCH, JUSTICE, delivered the opinion of the Court, in which GONZALEZ, OWEN, BAKER, and HANKINSON, JUSTICES, join.

Partnerships exist by the agreement of the partners; partners have no duty to remain partners. The issue in this case is whether we should create an exception to this rule by holding that a partnership has a duty not to expel a partner for reporting suspected overbilling by another partner. The trial court rendered judgment for Colette Bohatch on her breach of fiduciary duty claim against Butler & Binion and several of its partners (collectively, "the firm"). The court of appeals held that there was no evidence that the firm breached a fiduciary duty and reversed the trial court's tort judgment; however, the court of appeals found evidence of a breach of the partnership agreement and rendered judgment for Bohatch on this ground. 905 S.W.2d 597. We affirm the court of appeals' judgment.

I. FACTS

Bohatch became an associate in the Washington, D.C., office of Butler & Binion in 1986 after working for several years as Deputy Assistant General Counsel at the Federal Energy Regulatory Commission. John McDonald, the managing partner of the office, and Richard Powers, a partner, were the only other attorneys in the Washington office. The office did work for Pennzoil almost exclusively. Bohatch was made partner in February 1990. She then began receiving internal firm reports showing the number of hours each attorney worked, billed, and collected. From her review of these reports, Bohatch became concerned that McDonald was overbilling Pennzoil and discussed the matter with Powers. Together they reviewed and copied portions of McDonald's time diary. Bohatch's review of McDonald's time entries increased her concern.

On July 15, 1990, Bohatch met with Louis Paine, the firm's managing partner, to report her concern that McDonald was overbilling Pennzoil. Paine said he would investigate. Later that day, Bohatch told Powers about her conversation with Paine. The following day, McDonald met with Bohatch and informed her that Pennzoil was not satisfied with her work and wanted her work to be supervised. Bohatch testified that this was the first time she had ever heard criticism of her work for Pennzoil.

The next day, Bohatch repeated her concerns to Paine and to R. Hayden Burns and Marion E. McDaniel, two other members of the firm's management committee, in a telephone conversation. Over the next month, Paine and Burns investigated Bohatch's complaint. They reviewed the Pennzoil bills and supporting computer print-outs for those bills. They then discussed the allegations with Pennzoil in-house counsel John Chapman, the firm's primary contact with Pennzoil. Chapman, who had a long-standing relationship with McDonald, responded that Pennzoil was satisfied that the bills were reasonable.

In August, Paine met with Bohatch and told her that the firm's investigation revealed no basis for her contentions. He added that she should begin looking for other employment, but that the firm would continue to provide her a monthly draw, insurance coverage, office space, and a secretary. After this meeting, Bohatch received no further work assignments from the firm.

In January 1991, the firm denied Bohatch a year-end partnership distribution for 1990 and reduced her tentative distribution share for 1991 to zero. In June, the firm paid Bohatch her monthly draw and told her that this draw would be her last. Finally, in August, the firm gave Bohatch until November to vacate her office.

By September, Bohatch had found new employment. She filed this suit on October 18, 1991, and the firm voted formally to expel her from the partnership three days later, October 21, 1991.

The trial court granted partial summary judgment for the firm on Bohatch's wrongful discharge claim, and also on her breach of fiduciary duty and breach of the duty of good faith and fair dealing claims for any conduct occurring after October 21, 1991 (the date Bohatch was formally expelled from the firm). The trial court denied the firm's summary judgment motion on Bohatch's breach of fiduciary duty and breach of the duty of good faith and fair dealing claims for conduct occurring before October 21, 1991. The breach of fiduciary duty claim and a breach of contract claim were tried to a jury. The jury found that the firm breached the partnership agreement and its fiduciary duty. It awarded Bohatch $57,000 for past lost wages, $250,000 for past mental anguish, $4,000,000 total in punitive damages (this amount was apportioned against several defendants), and attorney's fees. The trial court rendered judgment for Bohatch in the amounts found by the jury, except it disallowed attorney's fees because the judgment was based in tort. After suggesting remittitur, which Bohatch accepted, the trial court reduced the punitive damages to around $237,000.

All parties appealed. The court of appeals held that the firm's only duty to Bohatch was not to expel her in bad faith. 905 S.W.2d at 602. The court of appeals stated that " '[b]ad faith' in this context means only that partners cannot expel another partner for self-gain." Finding no evidence that the firm expelled Bohatch for self-gain, the court concluded that Bohatch could not recover for breach of fiduciary duty. Id. at 604. However, the court concluded that the firm breached the partnership agreement when it reduced Bohatch's tentative partnership distribution for 1991 to zero without notice, and when it terminated her draw three months before she left. The court concluded that Bohatch was entitled to recover $35,000 in lost earnings for 1991 but none for 1990, and no mental anguish damages. Accordingly, the court rendered judgment for Bohatch for $35,000 plus $225,000 in attorney's fees.

II. Breach of Fiduciary Duty

We have long recognized as a matter of common law that "[t]he relationship between * * * partners * * * is fiduciary in character, and imposes upon all the participants the obligation of loyalty to the joint concern and of the utmost good faith, fairness, and honesty in their dealings with each other with respect to matters pertaining to the enterprise." Fitz–Gerald v. Hull, 150 Tex. 39, 237 S.W.2d 256, 264 (1951) (quotation omitted). Yet, partners have no obligation to remain partners; "at the heart of the partnership concept is the principle that partners may choose with whom they wish to be associated." Gelder Med. Group v. Webber, 41 N.Y.2d 680, 394 N.Y.S.2d 867, 870–71, 363 N.E.2d 573, 577 (1977). The issue presented, one of first impression, is whether the fiduciary relationship between and among partners creates an exception to the at-will nature of partnerships; that is, in this case, whether it gives rise to a duty not to expel a partner who reports suspected overbilling by another partner. * * * Courts in other states have held that a partnership may expel a partner for purely business reasons. See St. Joseph's Reg'l Health Ctr. v. Munos, 326 Ark. 605, 934 S.W.2d 192, 197 (1996).

The fiduciary duty that partners owe one another does not encompass a duty to remain partners or else answer in tort damages. Nonetheless, Bohatch and several distinguished legal scholars urge this Court to recognize that public policy requires a limited duty to remain partners—i.e., a partnership must retain a whistleblower partner. They argue that such an extension of a partner's fiduciary duty is necessary because permitting a law firm to retaliate against a partner who in good faith reports suspected overbilling would discourage compliance with rules of professional conduct and thereby hurt clients.

While this argument is not without some force, we must reject it. A partnership exists solely because the partners choose to place personal confidence and trust in one another. See Holman, 522 P.2d at 524 ("The foundation of a professional relationship is personal confidence and trust."). Just as a partner can be expelled, without a breach of any common law duty, over disagreements about firm policy or to resolve some other "fundamental schism," a partner can be expelled for accusing another partner of overbilling without subjecting the partnership to tort damages. Such charges, whether true or not, may have a profound effect on the personal confidence and trust essential to the partner relationship. Once such charges are made, partners may find it impossible to continue to work together to their mutual benefit and the benefit of their clients. The threat of tort liability for expulsion would tend to force partners to remain in untenable circumstance—suspicious of and angry with each other—to their own detriment and that of their clients whose matters are neglected by lawyers distracted with intra-firm frictions.

We emphasize that our refusal to create an exception to the at-will nature of partnerships in no way obviates the ethical duties of lawyers. Such duties sometimes necessitate difficult decisions, as when a lawyer suspects overbilling by a colleague. The fact that the ethical duty to report may create an irreparable schism between partners neither excuses failure to report nor transforms expulsion as a means of resolving that schism into a tort. We hold that the firm did not owe Bohatch a duty not to expel her for reporting suspected overbilling by another partner.

III. BREACH OF THE PARTNERSHIP AGREEMENT

The court of appeals concluded that the firm breached the partnership agreement by reducing Bohatch's tentative distribution for 1991 to zero without the requisite notice. 905 S.W.2d at 606. The firm contests this finding on the ground that the management committee had the right to set tentative and year-end bonuses. However, the partnership agreement guarantees a monthly draw of $7,500 per month regardless of the tentative distribution. Moreover, the firm's right to reduce the bonus was contingent upon providing proper notice to Bohatch. The firm does not dispute that it did not give Bohatch notice that the firm was reducing her tentative distribution. Accordingly, the court of appeals did not err in finding the firm liable for breach of the partnership agreement. Moreover, because Bohatch's damages sound in contract, and because she sought attorney's fees at trial under section 38.001(8) of the Texas Civil Practice and Remedies Code, we affirm the court of appeals' award of Bohatch's attorney's fees. * * *

We affirm the court of appeals' judgment. * * *

HECHT, JUSTICE, concurring in the judgment.[24]

The Court holds that partners in a law firm have no common-law liability for expelling one of their number for accusing another of unethical conduct. The dissent argues that partners in a law firm are liable for such conduct. Both views are unqualified; neither concedes or even considers whether "always" and "never" are separated by any distance. I think they must be. I have trouble justifying a 500–partner firm's expulsion of a partner for reporting overbilling of a client that saves the firm not only from ethical complaints but from liability to the client. But I cannot see how a five-partner firm can legitimately survive one partner's accusations that another is unethical. Between two such extreme examples I see a lot of ground. This case does not force a choice between diametrically opposite views. Here, the report of unethical conduct, though made in good faith, was incorrect. That fact is significant to me because I think a law firm can always expel a partner for bad judgment, whether it relates to the representation of clients or the relationships with other partners, and whether it is in good faith. I would hold that Butler & Binion did not breach its fiduciary duty by expelling Colette

24. [By the Editors] Justice Hecht's full opinion is considerably longer than the com- bined majority and dissenting opinions.

Bohatch because she made a good-faith but nevertheless extremely serious charge against a senior partner that threatened the firm's relationship with an important client, her charge proved groundless, and her relationship with her partners was destroyed in the process. I cannot, however, extrapolate from this case, as the Court does, that no law firm can ever be liable for expelling a partner for reporting unethical conduct. Accordingly, I concur only in the Court's judgment. * * *

No court has considered whether expulsion of a partner from a law firm for reporting unethical conduct is a breach of fiduciary duty. Several courts have concluded that expulsion to remedy a fundamental schism in a professional firm is not a breach of fiduciary duty. There is hardly a schism more fundamental than that caused by one partner's accusing another of unethical conduct. If a partner can be expelled because of disagreements over nothing more significant than firm policy and abrasive personal conduct, as cases have held, surely a partner can be expelled for accusing another partner of something as serious as unethical conduct. Once such charges are raised, I find it hard to imagine how partners could continue to work together to their mutual benefit and the benefit of their clients. The trust essential to the relationship would have been destroyed. Indeed, I should think that a lawyer who was unable to convince his or her partners to rectify the unethical conduct of another would choose to withdraw from the firm rather than continue in association with lawyers who did not adhere to high ethical standards.

But I am troubled by the arguments of the distinguished amici curiae that permitting a law firm to retaliate against a partner for reporting unethical behavior would discourage compliance with rules of conduct, hurt clients, and contravene public policy. Their arguments have force, but they do not explain how a relationship of trust necessary for both the existence of the firm and the representation of its clients can survive such serious accusations by one partner against another. The threat of liability for expulsion would tend to force partners to remain in untenable circumstances—suspicious of and angry with each other—to their own detriment and that of their clients whose matters are neglected by lawyers distracted with intra-firm frictions. If "at the heart of the partnership concept is the principle that partners may choose with whom they wish to be associated", Gelder, 394 N.Y.S.2d at 870–871, 363 N.E.2d at 577, surely partners are not obliged to continue to associate with someone who has accused one of them of unethical conduct.

Pennzoil's conclusion that Butler & Binion's fees were reasonable, reached after being made aware of Bohatch's concerns that McDonald's time was overstated, establishes that Butler & Binion did not collect excessive fees from Pennzoil. A fee that a client as sophisticated as Pennzoil considers reasonable is not clearly excessive simply because a lawyer believes it could have been less. Bohatch's argument that Pennzoil had other reasons not to complain of Butler & Binion's bills is simply beside the point. Whatever its motivations, Pennzoil found the bills reasonable, thereby establishing that McDonald had not overbilled in violation of ethical rules.

Bohatch's real concern was not that fees to Pennzoil were excessive—she had never even seen the bills and had no idea what the fees, or fee arrangements, were—but that McDonald was misrepresenting the number of hours he worked. The District of Columbia Code of Professional Responsibility at the time also prohibited lawyers from engaging in "conduct involving dishonesty, fraud, deceit or misrepresentation." Id. DR 1–102(A)(4). But there is no evidence that McDonald actually engaged in such conduct. At most, Bohatch showed only that McDonald kept sloppy time records, not that he deceived his partners or clients. Neither his partners nor his major client accused McDonald of dishonesty, even after reviewing his bills and time records.

Butler & Binion's expulsion of Bohatch did not discourage ethical conduct; it discouraged errors of judgment, which ought to be discouraged. Butler & Binion did not violate its fiduciary duty to Bohatch. * * *

I would not hold that being correct is enough, only that being incorrect precludes recovery, at least in these circumstances. My criticism of the Court is not that another bright-line rule—one based on whether a report was correct—would be better, but that no bright-line rule should be adopted when the full ramifications of so broad a rule have not been adequately considered. It should come as no surprise to anyone that a lawyer can be fired for being incorrect, albeit in good faith. A lawyer can always be terminated for being incorrect about legal matters. It is, after all, a lawyer's judgment that is important, not her sincerity. Bohatch's charges were not merely an innocent mistake. They caused the expenditure of a significant amount of time in investigation, the report of possible overbilling to one of the firm's major clients, potentially jeopardizing that relationship, and an impossible strain on three lawyers working together on the same business for the same client in a small but important office of the firm. Without offering a solution to the problems the amici raise, the Court adopts an absolute rule: a law firm that expels a partner for reporting ethics violations has no liability to the partner under any circumstances. The rule is ill-advised, particularly when it is far broader than necessary to address Bohatch's claims. * * *

SPECTOR, J., joined by PHILLIPS, CHIEF JUSTICE, dissenting.

[W]hat's the use you learning to do right when it's troublesome to do right and ain't no trouble to do wrong, and the wages is just the same?—The Adventures of Huckleberry Finn.

The issue in this appeal is whether law partners violate a fiduciary duty by retaliating against one partner for questioning the billing practices of another partner. I would hold that partners violate their fiduciary duty to one another by punishing compliance with the Disciplinary Rules of Professional Conduct. Accordingly, I dissent.

* * * I would hold that in this case the law partners violated their fiduciary duty by retaliating against a fellow partner who made a good-faith effort to alert her partners to the possible overbilling of a client. * * *

The duty to prevent overbilling and other misconduct exists for the protection of the client. Even if a report turns out to be mistaken or a client ultimately consents to the behavior in question, as in this case, retaliation against a partner who tries in good faith to correct or report perceived misconduct virtually assures that others will not take these appropriate steps in the future. * * *

The Court's writing in this case sends an inappropriate signal to lawyers and to the public that the rules of professional responsibility are subordinate to a law firm's other interests. Under the majority opinion's vision for the legal profession, the wages would not even be the same for "doing right"; they diminish considerably and leave an attorney who acts ethically and in good faith without recourse. Accordingly, I respectfully dissent.

Notes

(1) Assume that you are a junior partner in a large law firm. You discover that the senior partner with whom you work may be doing legal work "on the side" in his own name and not turning the fees over to the firm. Should you take the matter to the managing partner or a member of the management committee? Might you not then suffer the same fate as Colette Bohatch? On the other hand, if you do nothing and the misconduct later comes to light, might you not be blamed for failing to report the misconduct and be expelled for that reason?

(2) Assume a law firm's partnership agreement does not contain an express provision authorizing expulsion but provides that the agreement may be amended by a majority vote. May a law firm amend its partnership agreement to include an expulsion clause and then immediately apply it to expel a specific partner? If so, do fiduciary duties or the duty of good faith require that there be disclosure as to the identity of the target before the amendment is adopted?

(3) As the principal case suggests, whistleblowers (those who report questionable corporate governance or accounting incidents both house and to other authorities) are not afforded much protection under the common law or partnership statutes. Although Bohatch received compensation arising from the firm's breach of the partnership agreement, the court found that the partnership owed her no fiduciary duties in the situation, and thus they could freely expel her from the partnership. While this is still true for law firms and other non-publicly traded partnerships and companies, Congress has given protection to whistleblowers in publicly-traded firms in a provision of the Sarbanes–Oxley Act of 2003. The statute requires the audit committee of the board of directors to set up procedures for handling complaints by whistleblowers within the company.[26] Sections 806 and 1107 of the Act, reproduced below, provide further protection for whistleblowers by making it illegal to retaliate against or to harass people who assist in an investigation of the company's violations of securities laws:

> No (publicly–traded) company or any officer, employee... or agent of such company, may discharge, demote, suspend, threaten, harass, or in any other manner discriminate against an employee because of any lawful act done by the employee to provide information ... or otherwise assist in an investigation regarding any conduct which the employee reasonably believes constitutes a violation of ... any rule or regulation of the Securities and Exchange Commission, or any provision of Federal law relating to fraud against shareholders...

26. Public Law 107–204, Section 301(4), amending Section 10A of the Securities Exchange Act of 1934, (15 U.S.C. Section 78f), provides that public company audit committees must establish procedures for: (A) the receipt, retention, and treatment of complaints received by the issuer regarding accounting, internal accounting controls, or auditing matters; and (B) the confidential, anonymous submission by employees of the issuer of concerns regarding questionable accounting matters.

Whoever knowingly, with intent to retaliate, takes any action harmful to any person, including interference with the lawful employment or livelihood of any person, for providing to a law enforcement officer any truthful information relating to the commission or possible commission of any Federal offense, shall be fined or imprisoned for not more than 10 year, or both.

Would these provisions of Sarbanes–Oxley have been a problem for the defendant law firm, Butler & Binion, had they been in place in 1998? Would they have been of any use to Colette Bohatch?

* * *

Dissolution Under UPA (1997). The technical definition of "dissolution" set forth in UPA (1914) may be traced to the partial acceptance in that Act of the view that a partnership was an aggregate of the partners. By the time of the development of UPA (1997), it had become clear that the entity theory of partnership was accepted and that a new approach toward dissolution was called for. An influential article by Professor Larry E. Ribstein (A Statutory Approach to Partner Dissociation, 65 Wash. U. L.Q. 357 (1987)) not only added the word "dissociation" to the partnership lexicon but also pointed out that "cessation of partner status" was an event that was independent of the question whether the business should be "dissolved" and wound up. In other words, it should be possible for a partner to leave or be "dissociated" and yet have the partnership continue if the value of the withdrawing partner's interest is paid to him. UPA (1997) adopts this approach.

UPA (1997) recognizes that partners need not be individuals; they may be corporations, limited liability companies, and other types of entities.

The major features of the dissolution provisions of UPA (1997) are as follows:

(1) The death, withdrawal, cessation of existence, or expulsion of a partner is a "dissociation." UPA (1997) § 601. Events causing dissociation of a partner who is an individual were broadened from similar provisions relating to "dissolution" under UPA (1914) in various ways, most notably by broadening the power to expel partners without express authorization in the partnership agreement (§ 601(4)) or by judicial order (§ 601(5)). Events causing dissociation of a partner which is not an individual are identified (§§ 601(4), (8)–(10)).

(2) The basic distinction between "rightful" and "wrongful" dissociation is retained in the new statute, but the definition of "wrongful" dissociation in a partnership for a term or particular undertaking is broadened (§ 602(b)).

(3) A partnership continues in existence despite dissociation of a partner. It may continue in existence indefinitely with the dissociated partner becoming entitled to the value of her partnership interest in cash under article 7, or it may be dissolved and wound up under article 8.

(4) Dissolution and winding up are required in only the limited circumstances set forth in § 801. Two provisions are of particular importance: a) in a partnership at will, any partner who dissociates by his express will may compel dissolution and winding up; and, b) in a partnership for a definite term or particular undertaking, if one partner dissociates wrongfully (or a dissociation occurs because of death or dissolution of a partner), dissolution and winding up of the partnership occurs only if one-half of the remaining members agree to dissolve the partnership within 90 days after the dissociation. Once an event requiring dissolution and winding up occurs, the partnership is to be wound up unless all the partners (including any dissociated partner other than a wrongfully dissociating partner) agree.

(5) If a partner dissociates, but the business is not dissolved and wound up, the partner is entitled to receive the "buyout price." § 701(a). This price is defined in § 701(b). If the dissociation was wrongful, damages may offset the buyout price, § 701(c), and the payment may be deferred until the expiration of the term or completion of the undertaking, "unless the partner establishes to the satisfaction of the court that earlier payment will not cause undue hardship to the business of the partnership." § 701(h). "A deferred payment must be adequately secured and bear interest." Id.

(6) UPA (1997) does not have the election [in § 42 of UPA (1914)] that permits a former partner in a partnership that does not wind up to take either a share of post-dissolution profits or interest on his capital account as compensation for the use of his capital. Under UPA (1997) § 701(b), last sentence, a dissociated partner is entitled only to interest on the amount to be paid the dissociated partner from the date of dissociation to the date of payment.

(7) A dissociated partner has apparent authority to bind the partnership, § 702, and may be liable for post-dissociation partnership liabilities incurred within two years after the dissociation. § 703. Either a dissociated partner or the partnership may file a public statement of dissociation to limit this apparent authority. § 704.

(8) A partnership "*is dissolved*" when one of the events requiring winding up listed in UPA (1997) § 801 occurs, but this list is exclusive. After dissolution, the partnership continues in existence for the purpose of winding up. § 802(a). The apparent authority of partners to bind the partnership continues after dissolution, but any partner who has not wrongfully dissociated may file a public statement of dissolution to give notice that the partnership is in the winding up process. § 806. Section 807 describes the final settlement of partnership accounts upon winding up. Partnership assets must be applied to the discharge of partnership liabilities, and if the assets are insufficient, individual partners are required to contribute in accordance with their respective loss sharing ratios. Partners with negative balances in their accounts are required to restore those balances to zero to ensure that all partners receive the amounts in their accounts. Any excess assets remaining are distributable to the partners in accordance with their profit sharing ratios. In general, section 807 is considerably more precise about the winding up process than the corresponding provisions of UPA (1914).

J. INADVERTENT PARTNERSHIPS

A recurring issue in partnership law is whether an arrangement between persons may unintentionally constitute a partnership so that a creditor who dealt with A may force B to pay its claim. At common law, a sharing of profits was often deemed conclusive of the existence of a partnership. Consider UPA (1914) §§ 6, 7. Section 7(4) states that such sharing is "prima facie evidence" of a partnership except that in certain cases "no such inference shall be drawn." May "prima facie evidence" be rebutted? If no "inference" of partnership is to be drawn in certain situations, does that mean no partnership exists, or does it mean that a partnership might be found to exist on the basis of other information? Finally, what is the significance of the co-ownership requirement in § 6 in this context? Does this definition help in determining when an arrangement is a partnership as compared to something else? Is §7 more helpful than §6?

UPA (1997) § 202(c)(3) states that a person who receives a share of the profits of a business "is presumed to be a partner" unless the payments are received in some other capacity. Is a "presumption" of partnership any different than "prima facie evidence" of a partnership? Is this simply an instance where the drafters of UPA (1997) cleaned up some rather archaic language in UPA (1914)?

MARTIN v. PEYTON

Court of Appeals of New York, 1927.
246 N.Y. 213, 158 N.E. 77.

Andrews, J.

* * * Today only those who are partners between themselves may be charged for partnership debts by others. [UPA (1914) § 7] There is one exception. Now and then a recovery is allowed where in truth such relationship is absent. This is because the debtor may not deny the claim. [UPA (1914) § 16]

Partnership results from contract, express or implied. If denied, it may be proved by the production of some written instrument, by testimony as to some conversation, by circumstantial evidence. If nothing else appears, the receipt by the defendant of a share of the profits of the business is enough. [UPA (1914) § 7]

Assuming some written contract between the parties, the question may arise whether it creates a partnership. If it be complete, if it expresses in good faith the full understanding and obligation of the parties, then it is for the court to say whether a partnership exists. It may, however, be a mere sham intended to hide the real relationship. Then other results follow. In passing upon it, effect is to be given to each provision. Mere words will not blind us to realities. Statements that no partnership is intended are not conclusive. If as a whole a contract contemplates an association of two or more persons to carry on as co-owners a business for profit, a partnership there is. [UPA (1914) § 6] On the other hand, if it be less than this, no partnership exists. Passing on the contract as a whole, an arrangement for sharing profits is to be considered. It is to be given its due weight. But it is to be weighed in connection with all the rest. It is not decisive. It may be merely the method adopted to pay a debt or wages, as interest on a loan or for other reasons.

An existing contract may be modified later by subsequent agreement, oral or written. A partnership may be so created where there was none before. And again, that the original agreement has been so modified may be proved by circumstantial evidence—by showing the conduct of the parties.

In the case before us, the claim that the defendants became partners in the firm of Knauth, Nachod & Kuhne, doing business as bankers and brokers, depends upon the interpretation of certain instruments. There is nothing in their subsequent acts determinative of or indeed material upon this question. And we are relieved of questions that sometimes arise. "The plaintiff's position is not," we are told, "that the agreements of June 4, 1921, were a false expression or incomplete expression of the intention of the parties. We say that they express defendants' intention and that that intention was to create a relationship which as a matter of law constitutes a partnership." Nor may the claim of the plaintiff be rested on any question of estoppel. "The plaintiff's claim," he stipulates, "is a claim of actual partnership, not of partnership by estoppel, and liability is not sought to be predicated upon [§ 16] of the [1914 Uniform] Partnership [Act]."

Remitted then, as we are, to the documents themselves, we refer to circumstances surrounding their execution only so far as is necessary to make them intelligible. And we are to remember that although the intention of the parties to avoid liability as partners is clear, although in language precise and definite they deny any design to then join the firm of K.N. & K.; although they say their interests in profits should be construed merely as a measure of compensation for loans, not an interest in profits as such; although they provide that they shall not be liable for any losses or treated as partners, the question still remains whether in fact they agree to so associate themselves with the firm as to "carry on as co-owners a business for profit."

In the spring of 1921 the firm of K.N. & K. found itself in financial difficulties. John R. Hall was one of the partners. He was a friend of Mr. Peyton. From him he obtained the loan of almost $500,000 of Liberty bonds, which K.N. & K. might use as collateral to secure bank advances. This, however, was not sufficient. The firm and its members had engaged in unwise speculations, and it was deeply involved. Mr. Hall was also intimately acquainted with George W. Perkins, Jr., and with Edward W. Freeman. He also knew Mrs. Peyton and Mrs. Perkins and Mrs. Freeman. All were anxious to help him. He therefore, representing K.N. & K., entered into negotiations with them. While they were pending a proposition was made that Mr. Peyton, Mr. Perkins, and Mr. Freeman, or some of them, should become partners. It met a decided refusal. Finally an agreement was reached. It is expressed in three documents, executed on the same day, all a part of the one transaction. They were drawn with care and are unambiguous. We shall refer to them as "the agreement," "the indenture," and "the option."

We have no doubt as to their general purpose. The respondents were to loan K.N. & K. $2,500,000 worth of liquid securities, which were to be returned to them on or before April 15, 1923. The firm might hypothecate them to secure loans totaling $2,000,000, using the proceeds as its business necessities required. To insure respondents against loss K.N. & K. were to turn over to them a large number of their own securities which may have been valuable, but which were of so speculative a nature that they could not be used as collateral for bank loans. In compensation for the loan, the respondents were to receive 40 percent of the profits of the firm until the return was made, not exceeding, however, $500,000, and not less than $100,000. Merely because the transaction involved the transfer of securities and not of cash does not prevent its being a loan, within the meaning of section 11. The respondents also were given an option to join the firm if they, or any of them, expressed a desire to do so before June 4, 1923.

Many other detailed agreements are contained in the papers. Are they such as may be properly inserted to protect the lenders? Or do they go further? Whatever their purpose, did they in truth associate the respondents with the firm so that they and it together thereafter carried on as co-owners a business for profit? The answer depends upon an analysis of these various provisions.

As representing the lenders, Mr. Peyton and Mr. Freeman are called "trustees." The loaned securities when used as collateral are not to be mingled with other securities of K.N. & K., and the trustees at all times are to be kept informed of all transactions affecting them. To them shall be paid all dividends and income accruing therefrom. They may also substitute for any of the securities loaned securities of equal value. With their consent the firm may sell any of its securities held by the respondents, the proceeds to go, however, to the trustees. In other similar ways the trustees may deal with these same securities, but the securities loaned shall always be sufficient in value to permit of their hypothecation for $2,000,000. If they rise in price, the excess may be withdrawn by the defendants. If they fall, they shall make good the deficiency.

So far, there is no hint that the transaction is not a loan of securities with a provision for compensation. Later a somewhat closer connection with the firm appears. Until the securities are returned, the directing management of the firm is to be in the hands of John R. Hall, and his life is to be insured for $1,000,000, and the policies are to be assigned as further collateral security to the trustees. These requirements are not unnatural. Hall was the one known and trusted by the defendants. Their acquaintance with the other members of the firm was of the slightest. These others had brought an old and established business to the verge of bankruptcy. As the respondents knew, they also had engaged in unsafe speculation. The respondents were about to loan $2,500,000 of good securities. As collateral they were to receive others of problematical value. What they required seems but ordinary caution. Nor does it imply an association in the business.

The trustees are to be kept advised as to the conduct of the business and consulted as to important matters. They may inspect the firm books and are entitled to any information they think important. Finally, they may veto any business they think highly speculative or injurious. Again we hold this but a proper precaution to safeguard the loan. The trustees may not initiate any transaction as a partner may do. They may not bind the firm by any action of their own. Under the circumstances the safety of the loan depended upon the business success of K.N. & K. This success was likely to be compromised by the inclination of its members to engage in speculation. No longer, if the respondents were to be protected should it be allowed. The trustees therefore might prohibit it, and that their prohibition might be effective, information was to be furnished them. Not dissimilar agreements have been held proper to guard the interests of the lender.

As further security each member of K.N. & K. is to assign to the trustees their interest in the firm. No loan by the firm to any member is permitted and the amount each may draw is fixed. No other distribution of profits is to be made. So that realized profits may be calculated, the existing capital is stated to be $700,000, and profits are to be realized as promptly as good business practice will permit. In case the trustees think this is not done, the question is left to them and to Mr. Hall, and if they differ then to an arbitrator. There is no obligation that the firm shall continue the business. It may dissolve at any time. Again we conclude there is nothing here not properly adapted to secure the interest of the respondents as lenders. If their compensation is dependent on a percentage of the profits, still provision must be made to define what these profits shall be.

The "indenture" is substantially a mortgage of the collateral delivered by K.N. & K. to the trustees to secure the performance of the "agreement." It certainly does not strengthen the claim that the respondents were partners.

Finally we have the "option." It permits the respondents, or any of them, or their assignees or nominees to enter the firm at a later date if they desire to do so by buying 50 percent or less of the interests therein of all or any of the members at a stated price. Or a corporation may, if the respondents and the members agree, be formed in place of the firm. Meanwhile, apparently with the design of protecting the firm business against improper or ill-judged action which might render the option valueless, each member of the firm is to place his resignation in the hands of Mr. Hall. If at any time he and the trustees agree that such resignation should be accepted, that member shall then retire, receiving the value of his interest calculated as of the date of such retirement.

This last provision is somewhat unusual, yet it is not enough in itself to show that on June 4, 1921, a present partnership was created, nor taking these various papers as a whole do we reach such a result. It is quite true that even if one or two or three like provisions contained in such a contract do not require this conclusion, yet it is also true that when taken together a point may come where stipulations immaterial separately cover so wide a field that we should hold a partnership exists. As in other branches of the law, a question of degree is often the determining factor. Here that point has not been reached.

The judgment appealed from should be affirmed, with costs.

CARDOZO, C.J., and POUND, LEHMAN, KELLOGG, and O'BRIEN, JJ., concur.

SMITH v. KELLEY

Court of Appeals of Kentucky, 1971.
465 S.W.2d 39.

CLAY, COMMISSIONER.

Appellant brought this suit for a partnership accounting. The Chancellor adjudged no partnership existed and dismissed appellant's claim. Appellant contends on appeal that the judgment is "erroneous".

With one exception, there is little dispute about the facts. In 1964 appellees Kelley and Galloway were partners in an accounting business. Appellant left another firm and came to work for them. For three and one-half years appellant drew $1,000 a month, plus $100 a month for travel expenses. At the end of each year he was paid a relatively small additional sum as a bonus out of the profits of the business. Not until appellant left the Kelley–Galloway firm in 1968 did he make any claim that he was entitled to a fixed percentage of the profits. In this lawsuit he asserts he had a twenty-percent interest therein.

There was no writing evidencing a partnership agreement. However, during the years appellant worked for the firm he was held out to the public as a partner. In a contract entered into between Kelley, Galloway, appellant and a third party, appellant was designated a partner. Partnership tax returns listed him as such; so did a statement filed with the Kentucky Board of

Accountancy. In a suit filed in the circuit court against a third party, he was designated a partner.

On the other hand, Kelley, Galloway and another employee of the firm testified there was no agreement that Smith would be a partner or have a right to share in the profits; he made no contribution to the assets of the partnership; he took no part in the management; he had no authority to hire or fire employees or to make purchases for the firm; he did not sign any notes when the firm was borrowing money; and he was not obligated to stand any losses of the firm.

A partnership is a contractual relationship and the intention to create it is necessary. As to third parties, a partnership may arise by estoppel, but our question is whether the parties intended to and did create such a relationship as would entitle appellant to share in the profits.

The Chancellor found that the original partners had at no time agreed that appellant would be entitled to share in a percentage of the profits. This was a matter of credibility and the Chancellor, who heard the evidence, chose to believe appellees. His finding on this point was not clearly erroneous and would seem to be dispositive of the case. In addition however, the conduct of the parties over a three-and-one-half-year period confirms the conclusion that, though appellant was held out to the public as a partner, between themselves a partnership relationship was not intended to be and was not created. We find no error in the court's findings of fact or conclusions of law.

Appellant relies on Guthrie v. Foster, 256 Ky. 753, 76 S.W.2d 927 (1934), wherein the Chancellor's finding that a partnership existed was based on certain facts similar to those we have in this case. However, there were other considerations in the cited case that do not appear here and it is not controlling.

We have examined the [1914] Uniform Partnership Act, and particularly [§§ 6, 7(1), 7(4), 18(a), 18(e), 18(g)], and find the trial court's decision took cognizance of the essential elements of a partnership therein prescribed.

The judgment is affirmed.

Notes

(1) In Smith v. Kelley, assume that a customer of the accounting firm of Kelley & Galloway sues the partnership for malpractice and adds Smith as a defendant. Is Smith liable?

(2) Would Smith be liable if a customer of Kelley & Galloway was injured in a slip-and-fall accident in the waiting room of the partnership?

(3) UPA (1997) § 308 uses the phrase "purported partner" rather than "partner by estoppel." Is that phrase an improvement?

Chapter Three

THE LIMITED PARTNERSHIP: WITH SPECIAL REFERENCE TO FEDERAL INCOME TAXATION

A. INTRODUCTION

An attorney forming a new business venture today may select from a complex menu of business forms. One of the most significant factors—and not infrequently the controlling one—in making this selection is the manner in which income or loss from the firm is taxed under the Internal Revenue Code.

Income taxation of corporations is mechanical and often costly as contrasted with the taxation of partnerships. Furthermore, mandatory internal management rules for corporations, in many states, are often not well-suited for small firms owned by one or a few persons.

Historically, the limited partnership has been the form of business most responsive to concerns of limited liability and favorable income tax treatment. Its widespread use is declining with the development of modern unincorporated business forms and "significant" changes in federal income tax rules. However, it continues to be the business form of choice in certain important contexts.

B. FEDERAL INCOME TAXATION: BASIC PRINCIPLES[1]

When considering taxes in the business context, one must take into account not only the taxation of the business itself but also the interrelationship with the taxation of the individual owners.

Initially, all businesses compute income for tax purposes in the same manner, deducting business expenses from receipts in order to compute taxable income. After determination of the business's taxable income, however, the tax treatment to some extent depends on the business form.

---

1. [By the Editors] The discussion below is based on tax rates and the tax structure in effect at the end of the year 2002. During the presidential campaign of 2002, both of the principal candidates promised changes in federal income tax rules. However, the changes proposed modifications of tax rates rather than changes in the general tax structure described below. An exception involved proposals to drastically reduce, and eventually eliminate entirely, the federal estate tax discussed below in connection with family limited partnerships.

In broad terms, the Internal Revenue Code recognizes two distinct methods of taxing business income, which are generally described as "corporate" and "partnership" taxation. Corporate income taxation is described in Subchapters C and S of the Internal Revenue Code, while partnership income taxation is described in Subchapter K. The differences between these two basic methods of taxing business income drive the selection of business form for specific enterprises.

(a) Corporate Tax Rates

Corporations historically have been treated as separate taxable entities under the Internal Revenue Code with their own sets of rules and their own tax schedules. The rates applicable to traditional corporations are set forth in Subchapter C. In 2005, corporations are subject to tax on income at the following rates:[2]

Table 1

Corporate Tax Rates

If Taxable Income Is Over	But Not Over	The Tax Is	Of the Amount Over
–0–	$50,000	15%	–0–
$50,000	75,000	$7,500 + 25%	$50,000
75,000	100,000	13,750 + 34%	75,000
100,000	335,000	22,250 + 39%	100,000
335,000	10,000,000	113,900 + 34%	335,000
10,000,000	15,000,000	3,400,000 + 35%	10,000,000
15,000,000	18,333,333	5,150,000 + 38%	15,000,000
18,333,333	———	6,416,667 + 35%	18,333,333

Notes

(1) It is important to distinguish between *marginal* tax rates and *average* tax rates. The *marginal* tax rate applicable to a corporation with exactly $75,000 of income is 34 percent because that is the rate applicable to each additional dollar of taxable income the corporation earns above $75,000 (up to $100,000). However, the *average* tax rate on such income is 18 percent since a corporation's tax bill on exactly $75,000 of taxable income is $13,750 (15 percent of $50,000 plus 25 percent of $25,000). A corporation with precisely $100,000 of taxable income owes $22,250; that is an average rate of 22.25 percent, but the marginal tax rate on each additional dollar of income is 39 percent up to $335,000.

(2) Where do the mysterious numbers $7,500, $13,750 in Table 1 come from? Hint: calculate the precise tax due on $50,000 of income taxed at 15%; then calculate the precise tax due on an additional $25,000 of income taxed at 25%.

(3) The tax structure for corporations in general is mildly progressive; it is "progressive" because additional income is taxed at increasingly higher effective rates. A tax structure is "regressive" if lower amounts of income are taxed at higher rates than higher amounts of income. When a corporation's income is in

2. [By the Editors] This table is a composite table building in special surtaxes at the $100,000 and $15,000,000 levels.

the $100,000–$335,000 range, it is subject to a marginal rate of 39 percent; above $335,000 the tax rate reverts to 34 percent. These declines in marginal rates may be viewed as regressive even though the effective rate of taxation on corporate income can never exceed 34 percent at any level of income up to $10,000,000 or 35 percent at any level of income. These special surtaxes on corporations are designed to gradually eliminate the benefit of the lower brackets for corporations that have incomes over $100,000 and $15,000,000 respectively.

(4) Corporations subject to the tax rates set forth in Table 1 are called C corporations, named after Subchapter C of the Internal Revenue Code. The taxation of S corporations is discussed at page 131, infra.

(b) Individual Tax Rates

There are four different individual income tax rate schedules based primarily on marital status, plus elaborate sets of tax tables based on the rate schedules and used mostly by persons with relatively small incomes. In addition, there is a special tax schedule for the income of trusts and estates. For purposes of considering the interaction of personal and corporate tax rates upon business income, however, a detailed consideration of this complex structure is unnecessary. It is simplest to use the tax schedule for married taxpayers filing joint tax returns for the year 2006:

Table 2

2004 Income Tax Rates
(Married Taxpayers Filing Joint Return)

If taxable income is:	The tax is:
Not over $36,900	15% of taxable income
Over $36,900 but under $89,150	$5,535 + 25% of excess over $36,900
Over $89,150 but under $140,000	$20,165 + 28% of excess over $89,150
Over $140,000 but under $250,000	$35,928.50 + 33% of excess over $140,000
Over $250,000	$75,528.50 + 35% of excess over $250,000.[3]

Tax rate schedules for individuals involve a higher tax rate than the schedule for married taxpayers filing joint returns.

Note

In the years during and after World War II, marginal rates on individual taxpayers were extremely high by modern standards, the top bracket rising above 90 percent. As late as 1980, the highest marginal rate for joint returns was 70

---

3. [By the Editors] Other provisions of the Internal Revenue Code "phase out" taxpayers' personal exemptions and a portion of taxpayers' personal deductions for high income taxpayers, beginning at specified threshold amounts (approximately $150,000 of taxable income for taxpayers filing a joint return). These phase out provisions may be viewed as a type of surtax (similar to that applicable to corporations at the $100,000 and $15,000,000 levels of income) that create interim rates higher than those set forth in the above table at certain levels of income. However, for technical reasons these phase out provisions cannot be simply reflected in this Table in the same way that the effect of the corporate surtaxes is reflected.

percent for taxable income in excess of $215,400. A major policy implemented by the Reagan administration in the 1980s was to reduce high marginal rates. This policy resulted in a maximum marginal rate of 28 percent in 1986, a date which is a watershed in much of the discussion that follows. Between 1986 and 2000, however, the general trend has been toward higher marginal rates. The Bush Administration has again sought to cap marginal rates. The Economic Growth and Tax Relief of Reconciliation Act of 2001 and the Jobs and Growth Tax Relief Reconciliation Act of 2003 provide various revisions to the tax code, including capping marginal tax rates on individuals at 35 percent. However, most of these provisions are subject to "sunset clauses" that will cause these amendments to rates to expire after 2008 if not readopted by Congress, so that rates would return to pre-2001 higher rates.

(c) The Taxation of Capital Gains or Losses

Before 1986, at the same time that the maximum individual tax rates of 70 percent or more were in effect, the maximum tax rate on a different form of income—long-term capital gains arising from the sale or exchange of capital assets held for more than 6 months—was only 25 percent. Capital assets are assets held for profit making or investment purposes. This dramatic difference in rates created strong incentives to structure transactions or establish long-term strategies that transmute ordinary income into long-term capital gain in order to make the 25 percent rather than the 70 percent rate applicable. To a somewhat lesser extent, this same incentive exists today.

The technical rules with respect to the treatment of capital gains were relatively complex before 1986 and are even more complex today. Long term capital gains or losses are defined to be gains or losses on assets held for more than one year. In general, the current maximum tax rate on long term capital gains is 15 percent. Short term capital gains are taxed at ordinary income tax rates. Capital losses are available to offset capital gains plus up to $3,000 of ordinary income in any year; excess capital losses may be carried over to offset capital gains in future years. In making these various calculations and determining the net amount of gain or loss, and its character as short term or long term, short term gains and losses are separately netted to determine the net short term capital gain or loss. Long term capital gains and losses are netted in the same manner to establish the net long term gain or loss. The two are then combined to determine the net capital gain or loss for the year.

(d) Estate Taxes

An issue of major importance to people who own small businesses is the effect of the federal estate taxes on their succession plans. When the owner of a small business dies, estate taxes must be paid on the appraised value of that business before it can be passed to the owner's heirs.

As a result, it is generally more economical to sell a business before death than to pass it to one's heirs under existing tax law. Many Republican politicians objected to this situation, and further oppose the estate tax on the grounds that it retards economic growth, decreases investment, and stifles the creation of new jobs by slowing the growth of business. In 2001, President George W. Bush obtained passage of the Tax Relief Act of 2001 which contained a reduction in the estate tax from 2001 until 2009, and phased out the tax entirely by 2010. Currently, the statute provides that after 2010 the estate tax automatically goes back to 2001 levels. However, there is a real possibility that the elimination of the estate tax will be made permanent after 2010. Many people, however, oppose total repeal of the estate tax since it would primarily benefit the most affluent taxpayers.

The following are the applicable estate tax rates and unified credit exemption amount under the 2005 tax laws:

Year [of Death]	Estate Exemption	Estate Tax Rate
2004	$1.5 million	48%
2005	$1.5 million	47%
2006	$2 million	46%
2007	$2 million	45%
2008	$2 million	45%
2009	$3.5 million	45%
2010	Taxes Repealed	0

ROBERT W. HAMILTON AND RICHARD A. BOOTH, BUSINESS BASICS FOR LAW STUDENTS: ESSENTIAL CONCEPTS AND APPLICATIONS

Third Ed. (2002).[4]
Page 215

The calculation of the amount of the gain from sales or exchanges [of property] involves the use of technical language that is fundamental to any understanding of the tax laws:

a.   **Basis** is the investment the seller of the property has in the property. It is the cost or purchase price of the property that the seller pays or incurs in acquiring the property. In the case of property acquired by gift, the basis in the hands of the donee is usually the same as the basis in the hands of the donor (**a substituted basis**); in the case of property acquired by inheritance, it is generally the fair market value of the assets on the death of the decedent (**a stepped–up basis**).

b.   **Adjusted basis** is the basis of the property, (1) plus capital improvements made by the seller, commissions originally paid by the seller, legal costs for defending or perfecting title, and so forth, and (2) minus returns of capital, particularly **depreciation** claimed as tax deductions, **depletion**, deducted **casualty losses**, insurance reimbursements, and the like.

c.   The **amount realized** includes the cash received for the property on a sale or the fair market value of the property received in exchange for the property. Selling expenses, including brokerage commissions the seller pays, reduce the amount realized. In the case of property subject to a mortgage, the amount realized also includes the amount of mortgage debt that the seller is relieved from paying as a result of the sale. For example, if an owner of real estate encumbered by a $50,000 mortgage sells the property for $10,000 cash over and above the mortgage, which the buyer agrees to assume and pay, the amount realized from the sale is $60,000, not $10,000. If the property is sold

4. Reprinted with the permission of Aspen   ers, Inc.
Law & Business, a Division of Aspen Publish-

with the seller giving the buyer $5,000 for assuming the mortgage of $50,000, the amount realized is $45,000.

d. **Gain** on a transaction equals the amount realized minus the adjusted basis. If the adjusted basis is greater than the amount realized, the difference is the loss.

* * *

On the death of a taxpayer, the potential tax on unrealized gain is in effect forgiven (by giving the estate or heirs a "stepped up" basis equal to current market value at date of death). This is a significant benefit that may well dictate business strategy. For example, for an elderly taxpayer, borrowing funds on the security of the appreciated shares for living expenses may be sensible.

(e) The Taxation of Partnerships and Corporations

When personal and corporate income tax rates are compared, the differences at first blush seem modest or insignificant. Both individual and corporate rates begin at 15 percent of taxable income and then progress to a maximum of 35 percent for corporations and 35.6 percent for individuals in 2004. There does not seem to be any difference between them. However, that turns out not to be the case.

(1) **Proprietorships**. Consider first the tax treatment of a proprietorship, a business wholly owned by a single individual, and conducted in her own name.

ROBERT W. HAMILTON, BUSINESS ORGANIZATIONS: UNINCORPORATED BUSINESSES AND CLOSELY HELD CORPORATIONS[5]

A proprietorship is not a separate taxable entity. Its income or loss is reported on the proprietor's personal income tax return. For example, if a proprietor files a joint return with his or her spouse, the business income or loss of each proprietorship owned by either or both of them must be included in that joint return.

The manner of reporting the income and expenses of a proprietorship is interesting because it reflects a pragmatic compromise between the legal view that a proprietorship is not a separate entity from its owner and the economic view that the proprietorship's financial affairs should not be intermixed with the proprietor's personal affairs. The Internal Revenue Code requires an individual taxpayer who is also an entrepreneur to file the long-form personal income tax return—the form 1040. The Internal Revenue Code also requires a separate tax form, Schedule C, to be prepared to record the gain or loss from each business owned by the taxpayer. Schedule C must be attached to the taxpayer's form 1040 and the income or loss of the proprietorship is added to or subtracted from the proprietor's other income in order to determine her

5. Reprinted with the permission of Aspen Law & Business, a Division of Aspen Publish-   ers, Inc.

final liability to Uncle Sam. A separate Schedule C must be filed for each business. State income taxation works much the same way (though many states base their tax on the taxpayer's federal tax return and do not require a completely separate accounting of income or loss). * * *

Every entrepreneur operating a sole proprietorship must also take into account the requirements of the Self Employment Contributions Act of 1954 ("SECA"), imposing a tax on Schedule C income equal (in 2001) to 12.4 percent of proprietorship income up to $80,400 for old age survivors and disability insurance (OASI) and an additional uncapped 2.9 percent for Medicare. If the entrepreneur is also an employee of another firm, the OASI tax is applied first against the salary of the employee and the proprietorship income is taxed only to the extent the salary is less than $80,400.

* * *

(2) **Unincorporated Business Forms.** Under regulations adopted by the Treasury Department in 1997, an unincorporated business entity (including a business entity formed under state law as a general partnership, limited partnership, limited liability partnership, or limited liability company) that has at least two owners generally will be classified for federal income tax purposes as a partnership, and therefore will be subject to taxation under subchapter K of the Internal Revenue Code. Alternatively the entity may elect to be classified for federal income tax purposes as a corporation. An unincorporated business entity that has a single owner generally will be disregarded as an entity separate from its owner for federal income tax purposes (i.e., its activities will be treated in the same manner as a sole proprietorship or branch or division of the owner), unless the entity elects to be classified for federal income tax purposes as a corporation. Because it is largely elective, this tax classification regime is commonly referred to as "check the box." There is a statutory exception to this elective regime in the case of publicly–traded partnerships, which generally will be classified for federal income tax purposes as corporations.

Under the partnership tax regime of subchapter K, the partnership itself does not pay any tax. It does, however, compute its taxable income and file an informational return (Form 1065) with the IRS. For federal income tax purposes, the income or loss reported by the partnership is "passed through" to the partners, in accordance with the partnership agreement. The partnership must provide each partner with a statement (Form K–1) informing the partner of his, her, or its respective shares of the partnership's income and deductions. Each partner must then include these amounts directly on his, her, or its income tax return. Taxation is therefore imposed solely at the level of owners, not at the entity level.

It is important to appreciate that while both proprietorships and unincorporated business forms are taxed as extensions of the individual taxpayers who are the owners of the enterprise, the amounts allocated are based on the income calculations of the proprietorship or unincorporated business form and not on the amounts actually distributed in cash or property to the proprietor, partner or member.

The apparent simplicity of the pass-through tax treatment provided by subchapter K is quite deceptive. The allocation of losses among general partners, in particular, opened the door to tax avoidance on a major scale. With the development of limited liability for some partners in LLCs and LLPs, partnership taxation easily became the most complex area of tax law. See, e.g., Christine R. Strong and Susan P. Hamill, Allocations Attributable to Partner Nonrecourse Liabilities: Issues Revealed by LLCs and LLPs, 51 Alabama L.Rev. 603 (2000).

In general terms the SECA tax is imposed on general partners, I.R.C.§ 1402(a), but not on limited partners unless the payments constitute "guaranteed payments" (I.R.C.§ 1402(a)(13)). The SECA tax is applicable to earnings of individual members of limited liability companies to the extent attributable to a trade or business.

(3) **C Corporations.** C corporations have their own special tax schedule (see Table 1, page 124, supra). However, when comparing the tax consequences of conducting a business in corporate or unincorporated form, it is essential to recognize that the corporate rate is not in lieu of, but is in addition to, the tax on the ultimate shareholders. There is, in short, double taxation of business earnings if a C corporation makes distributions to shareholders. An example should make this clear. If the corporation has taxable income of precisely $75,000, the corporation must pay a corporate income tax of $13,750, leaving $61,250 available for distribution to the shareholders; if the corporation then distributes the $61,250 to its shareholders, all of whom are in the 35 percent bracket, the shareholders will owe another $21,437.50, for a total tax bill at both levels of $35,187.50. The effective combined tax rate on $75,000 of corporate income is 48 percent. In contrast, if the business were conducted in an unincorporated form, there is no tax at all at the entity level, and the maximum additional tax (calculated at the rate of 35 percent) would be $26,250. In other words, on the assumption that all income is to be distributed to shareholders, the failure to obtain conduit or pass-through tax treatment results in nearly $9000 of additional federal income taxes in a single year!

Indeed, if the corporate and individual taxpayers are both at the highest marginal rates, which are both currently at 35 percent, the combined tax rate on a distribution by a C corporation that is subject to the 35 percent rate to its shareholders who are all in the 35 percent bracket is about 60 percent. There is thus a 20 percent differential or bias against C corporation tax status at the highest levels of income.

(4) **S Corporations.** The double tax treatment of closely held C corporations was widely viewed by shareholders in those corporations as unfair and discriminatory. In the 1950s, Subchapter S was added to the Internal Revenue Code to give some relief from the double tax treatment. Subchapter S requires an affirmative election by the corporation and is not available to all closely–held corporations. A corporation that makes this election is called an "S corporation" or a "sub S corporation."

The S corporation election is a tax election and not a corporate law election: an S corporation possesses all of the normal attributes of a corporation under state law, but is taxed in a different way than C corporations. To be eligible for S corporation treatment, corporations must not have more than 75 individual shareholders; the maximum number of shareholders in an S corporation was originally set at ten and gradually increased over the years.

An S corporation, in addition to meeting the maximum 75 shareholder requirement, may not have shareholders who are nonresident aliens or certain artificial entities, and may not have issued more than one class of stock (except for classes of common stock that differ only in voting rights). Before 1996, S corporations also were not permitted to have corporate shareholders or own stock in another corporation; these restrictions have been eliminated. There is no maximum size limitation for S corporations, though doubtless most of them are small. Most S corporations have only one shareholder.

S corporations are taxed on a modified conduit basis that is similar in many respects to that applicable to unincorporated business forms: the corporation files a return showing the earnings allocable to each shareholder, who must include that amount in his or her personal income tax return. That amount is includible whether or not any distributions are made by the corporation. However, the tax treatment of S corporations is not identical to that of unincorporated business forms in all respects, and in several respects is less advantageous to the taxpayer than the conduit tax provided by Subchapter K. However, an S corporation does have the basic feature of conduit or pass-through taxation that is typical of the partnership and proprietorship forms of business, and as a result is a plausible alternative to a partnership from a tax standpoint.

Notes

(1) The tax treatment of C corporations has been the subject of considerable theoretical discussion, both historically and at present. One basic problem is that it is unclear where the ultimate incidence of the corporate income tax falls, whether on consumers, employees, shareholders, or other businesses. At the beginning of President Reagan's second term in 1985 there was a brief flirtation with the idea that the corporate income tax should be abolished. However, as the compromises that eventually became the Tax Reform Act of 1986 were hammered out, this idea was abandoned. Instead, there was increased reliance on the corporate income tax as a source of revenue.

(2) There have been numerous proposals over the years to "integrate" the corporate and individual income tax structures and thereby eliminate the "double tax" on corporate shareholders. Other industrialized countries generally do not have a double tax structure. President Reagan's proposal to repeal the corporate income tax was one example of such a proposal. Alternatively, one could eliminate dividends from the taxable income of shareholders. Yet another approach would treat the payment of tax by a corporation as a kind of withholding tax with respect to income ultimately distributed to shareholders. Yet another approach would in effect extend S corporation tax treatment to all corporations. These proposals, however, all have formidable problems because of the different types of taxpayers, tax-exempt entities, foreign shareholders, and the like. For interesting analyses of the double tax structure and the problems of integration proposals, see American Law Institute, Federal Income Tax Project; Alvin C. Warren, Jr., Reporter's Study of Corporate Tax Integration (1993); U.S. Dep't of the Treasury, Integration of the Individual and Corporate Tax System: Taxing Business Income Once (1992).

(f) Business Tax–Planning Strategies

Tax planning for businesses involves several considerations:

First, everyone has to pay taxes on their income, or at least account to the federal government for it by filing a tax return. In this respect, taxation is more immediate and certain than the risk of unlimited liability for owners. The danger that a business may incur a liability in excess of business assets may or may not materialize depending on what happens in the future; but liability for taxes is a certainty, not a possibility. Hence tax planning is a routine and often dominant aspect of every significant business venture.

Second, taxpayers quite legitimately expect to minimize their tax liability to the extent they may legally do so. There is a basic distinction between legitimate tax avoidance [usually called "tax planning"] on the one hand and tax evasion that may lead to fraud penalties or worse, on the other.[6] The selection of business forms in order to take advantage of differences in tax schedules or the S corporation election is clearly permissible tax planning.

Third, in tax planning one must usually concentrate on the marginal rate of taxation, not the average rate. As a practical matter, most individuals considering an investment in a business venture will already have income from other sources that exceeds $36,900, so every dollar of income obtained from the business venture will be taxed at 25 percent or more; the 15 percent individual tax rate is simply irrelevant in most situations.[7] Where there are several different investors or owners, they are likely to be in different tax brackets. Generally, the strategy that minimizes the tax obligations of the owner or investor who is in the highest tax bracket will be followed, though that is not always true.[8]

Fourth, in selecting the form of business, the total tax liabilities of both business and owners must be taken into account. Under current tax rates, it is usually advantageous to conduct a small business in a form that permits conduit tax treatment. But that is not true in all situations. In some tax regimes, the widespread use of the C corporation minimizes effective taxes.[9]

---

6. [By the Editors] The claiming of personal exemptions for household pets is an example of criminal tax evasion while electing S corporation status is an example of acceptable tax avoidance. While this may seem obvious, the line between legitimate avoidance and improper evasion is often shadowy. In addition to criminal sanctions, the Internal Revenue Service possesses authority to impose civil sanctions in situations where criminal prosecution is thought to be inappropriate. The IRS possesses power to review and reject specific tax avoidance transactions. For example, the IRS has statutory power to compel accounting changes so as "to clearly reflect income" (I.R.C.§ 446) that may result in significant tax liability arising from apparently proper tax avoidance transactions. The IRS may also take advantage of a court-created doctrine relating to "step transactions" that permits it to treat a series of transactions as a single transaction so as to clearly reflect income. Many courts have also accepted an argument often made by the IRS that form should not be elevated over substance, and that the substance should determine how a transaction is taxed. Review of tax avoidance transactions under these various doctrines typically arise in audits of tax returns and do not normally lead to the imposition of penalties (other than the payment of interest on tax deficiencies) on the taxpayer.

7. [By the Editors] The same is not true of a newly formed corporation. That entity will be taxed at the 15 percent rate for its income up to $75,000, though the 5 percent surtax will wipe out the benefit of that lower tax rate after the corporation's taxable income grows. Since new businesses may be placed in several different corporations, multiple use of the 15 percent bracket may be available in many situations.

8. [By the Editors] A revised version of the "Golden Rule" for business is "He who has the gold, rules." Typically, the person in the highest tax bracket will be contributing capital that is essential for the success of the enterprise, and hence his tax minimization becomes the goal of tax planning.

9. [By the Editors] Consider John W. Lee, A Populist Political Perspective of the Business Tax Entities Universe: "Hey The Stars May Lie But The Numbers Never Do," 78 Tex. L.Rev. 885, 887–88 (2000):

Before 1986, corporate tax rates were lower than individual tax rates at most levels of income; corporate tax rates were capped at 46 percent of income while individual marginal tax rates were 50 percent or higher. As a result, total taxes were minimized if a C corporation was employed and a policy was adopted of never paying dividends that were taxable as such to shareholders. To minimize tax bills before 1986, therefore, profitable corporations often accumulated large amounts of undistributed earnings.[10] Of course, at some point the owners will wish to enjoy the fruits of their successful enterprise. One widely followed strategy was to accumulate the maximum amount possible within the corporation at the favorable corporate rates and then sell all the stock in the business at a price that presumably reflected the accumulated income within the corporation. Alternatively, the corporation might redeem all the stock of a shareholder. Properly structured, the gain on either the sale or the redemption of the stock would be taxed to the shareholder at favorable capital gains tax rates. This basic strategy was so common in pre–1986 tax strategy that it had its own name: the "accumulation/bail out" strategy.

The S corporation election was less attractive than the accumulation/bail out strategy in the era of very high marginal individual tax rates. For a profitable corporation, the S corporation election was disastrous, since it moved taxable income away from the corporation with its lower rates and into the returns of the individual shareholders to be taxed at the much higher individual marginal rates. However, with the lower marginal individual rates now in effect, the S corporation election may be more advantageous than the accumulation/bail out strategy if the owners wish to withdraw income from the business for their own use.

The conventional wisdom * * * holds that the choice of tax entity for a new, closely held, or private, small income venture is a passthrough entity. * * * [T]he reality in taxland is that either the regular or Subchapter C Corporation * * * or the Subchapter S corporation * * * tends in most market segments to be the tax entity of choice for small businesses conducted in an entity form rather than as a sole partnership. * * *

Notwithstanding the concern of conventional wisdom over double taxation of C Corporations and shareholders, * * * profitable small income, private C Corporations and their mostly high income, active owners apparently pay less federal income tax at the owner and entity levels combined than they would under direct pass through taxation with tax-free withdrawal of profits, as in a single level of taxation * * * [in a Subchapter S corporation or unincorporated entity]. * * * [T]hirty-seven percent of C Corporations report, on the average, about $40,000, which is taxable at fifteen percent (with sixty-one percent reporting no income or a loss). In sharp contrast, eighty percent of their owners are taxable at the higher individual income brackets. Furthermore, a second level of outside shareholder-level taxation on the retained earnings is avoided at least half the time, when the shareholder holds the small C Corporation private stock * * * until her death without receiving dividends. When the taxation is not avoided, it is greatly reduced on a present value basis by a long-deferred and often installment-reported capital gains sale.

The tax saving described by Mr. Lee is based on the accumulation/bail-out strategy discussed in the following text. Income earned by the C corporation is taxed at the low 15% and 25% brackets and accumulated. No distributions are made and the stock is subsequently sold (with the gain taxed at the long term capital rates of 15%) or held until the death of the stockholder, when the step-up in basis permits the capital gains tax to be avoided entirely.

10. [By the Editors] The Internal Revenue Code contains a penalty tax aimed at unreasonable accumulations of income in a corporation for the purpose of avoiding the taxation of dividends to shareholders. While this tax did limit the strategy described in the text, it was only applicable to large accumulations unrelated to the reasonable needs of the enterprise, and could often be avoided as a practical matter. This penalty tax has become much less important as a result of the current marginal rates applicable to corporations and individuals.

More recently, it seems that owners of small businesses organized as S corporations have been concentrating distributions into dividends instead of salaries, while paying what the IRS considers salaries that are too low. The purpose of this allocation is to permit the owner-employees of the small businesses to reduce payments for FICA (social security) and Medicare taxes, because these taxes are applicable to distributions characterized as "salary" but not to payments dubbed "dividends." A study by the Department of the Treasury's Inspector General for Tax Administration found that a number of S corporations paid salaries as low as $5000 per year, while reporting significant income, and paying dividends of as much as $500,000. The Treasury views this sort of pattern as blatant abuse of the tax system.

A second pre–1986 tax strategy that enabled a corporation to minimize the impact of double taxation of corporate income involved "zeroing out" a C corporation's taxable income. This strategy relied on the fact that, while distributions in the form of dividends are not deductible by corporations, payments to shareholders in the form of salaries, rent, and interest are deductible by the corporation (so long as the payments are reasonable in amount).[11] The distribution of income in the form of salaries, rent, and interest to shareholders thus eliminated the corporate tax on that income and in effect shifted it to the shareholders, since such payments are taxable as ordinary income to the shareholders who receive them. One could minimize the total tax bill of a corporation by a judicious determination of how much salary and related benefits could be paid to the shareholders. The goal was to reduce the taxable income of the corporation and increase the taxable income of the shareholder by the amount of the deductible payments so that the total tax bill was minimized. However, the process of "zeroing out" was often not precise and if the corporation was extremely successful, it might not be possible to shift the optimal amount of taxable income to shareholders and justify those deductions as reasonable.[12] As a result, under pre–1986 tax rates, the "zeroing out" process was often not carried to its ultimate conclusion. Partial "zeroing out" might be combined with the accumulation/bail out strategy.

A final strategy popular in the pre–1986 period involved start-up businesses that expected losses temporarily. In this situation, it was attractive to have the business be taxed on a conduit or pass-through basis, since that enabled the shareholders to take advantage of the losses to shield other individual income from taxation. In effect, the losses of the business served as a kind of tax shelter for its shareholders. A common pattern then was initially

---

11. [By the Editors] The suggestion was sometimes made that the corporation should not pay dividends but provide living benefits indirectly or secretly; the corporation might pay shareholders' grocery bills or provide automobiles at no expense to shareholders. Such suggestions may move across the shadowy line between permissible tax planning and improper tax evasion. Certainly if the Internal Revenue Service learned that excessive benefits were being provided (as it might, for example, from an audit of the corporate books), it would, at the least, insist that deductions by the corporation be disallowed. If the recipient did not include the value of the benefits as income subject to taxation, benefits would also be taxed to the individual shareholders as informal dividends. In addition, tax fraud penalties might be assessed and criminal prosecution pursued in egregious cases.

12. [By the Editors] A more serious problem was that distributions in these forms sometimes led to friction within the corporate family since payments could not be made in proportion to shareholdings without running serious risk that the IRS might subsequently claim that they were in fact non-deductible dividends.

to conduct a business as a partnership or proprietorship until it became profitable and then to incorporate. The accumulation/bail out strategy would be followed thereafter.

The 1986 Tax Reform Act changed these various strategies in fundamental ways. First of all, it imposed significant restrictions on the deductibility of passive losses in an effort to stamp out "abusive" tax shelters. These restrictions continue to prevent the widespread use of loss businesses as tax shelters. Secondly, and much more fundamentally, it reduced the marginal rates on individuals to a maximum of 28 percent (now again at 35 percent), a rate that was lower than the corporate tax rate. Overnight, tax strategies changed dramatically. For a profitable enterprise, an unincorporated business form provided dramatic tax savings over a traditional corporation. Subchapter S suddenly became an attractive tax strategy for profitable as well as loss corporations. And, as a further important consequence, modifications to the limited partnership form developed and briefly threatened to lead to the "disincorporation" of much of large American business.

C. LIMITED PARTNERSHIPS WITH CORPORATE GENERAL PARTNERS

The original concept of a limited partnership is described in Chapter 1. The typical limited partnership in the late 1970s and early 1980s bore little resemblance to the hypothetical small-town hardware store described in that Chapter. The typical limited partnership of that era was a federal income tax driven business in which there were hundreds of limited partners and one general partner that was a corporation or another limited partnership.

The three basic principles were critical to this major change in the limited partnership: (1) the potential liability of limited partners and their agents for taking part in control of the business had to be significantly restricted; (2) it had to be clear that limited partners did not have the power to withdraw from a limited partnership during the term of the partnership agreement; and (3) corporations and other limited liability entities had to be eligible to serve as the sole general partner of a limited partnership.[13] Each of these principles was duly established.

1. *Narrowing the Potential Liability of Limited Partners.* Section 7 of ULPA (1916), in its entirety, stated, "A limited partner shall not become liable as a general partner unless, in addition to the exercise of his rights and powers as a limited partner, he takes part in the control of the business." There was considerable doubt under this sparse language as to how much activity by the limited partner would constitute "taking part" in control of the business, and thus incurring the liabilities of a general partner. This uncertainty of itself made the limited partnership form of business somewhat unattractive, since there are always possible crisis situations in which inactive investors would expect to intervene or participate in management in an effort to save their investment. Also, § 7 gave little guidance in the following

---

13. [By the Editors] As a corollary it was also necessary to establish the principle that shareholders, directors and officers of the corporate general partner did not become general partners in the limited partnership simply because of their participation in the management of the corporate general partner.

recurring situations. May limited partners retain the power to remove the general partner and substitute another person in that position? May a limited partner also act as an employee or agent of the limited partnership? May he or she act as a surety for the limited partnership or have the power to approve or disapprove amendments to the limited partnership agreement? Under ULPA (1916) one could not be sure. Under the case law arising under that statute, the test appeared to depend on whether the limited partner had actually exercised the powers he had reserved. Nevertheless, there was some judicial sympathy for the marginally-active limited partner. For example:

(a) In Silvola v. Rowlett, 129 Colo. 522, 272 P.2d 287 (1954), a limited partner was held not generally liable for partnership obligations even though he "express[ed] opinions as to the advisability of transactions when his suggestions or opinion[s] [were] sought by the general partner."

(b) In Rathke v. Griffith, 36 Wash.2d 394, 218 P.2d 757 (1950), a limited partner was named to the "board of directors" of the limited partnership but did not actually participate in the day-to-day decisions of the business. Even though the limited partner had also signed a few documents on behalf of the limited partnership, the court refused to hold the limited partner liable to creditors who were unaware of such documents.

* * *

This uncertainty was an important factor that led to the decision to "modernize" the 1916 statute. The result was the development of an entirely new Revised Uniform Limited Partnership Act in 1976; significant amendments were made in 1985. This amended statute, often referred to as "RULPA" is referred to here simply as "ULPA (1976)." ULPA (1976) has been adopted by 48 states. The extent to which limited partners may participate in the affairs of the limited partnership is set forth in §§ 303 and 304.

ULPA (1976)

§ 303. Liability to Third Parties

(a) Except as provided in subsection (d), a limited partner is not liable for the obligations of a limited partnership unless he [or she] is also a general partner or, in addition to the exercise of his [or her] rights and powers as a limited partner, he [or she] participates in the control of the business. However, if the limited partner participates in the control of the business, he [or she] is liable only to persons who transact business with the limited partnership reasonably believing, based upon the limited partner's conduct, that the limited partner is a general partner.

(b) A limited partner does not participate in the control of the business within the meaning of subsection (a) solely by doing one or more of the following:

(1) being a contractor for or an agent or employee of the limited partnership or of a general partner or being an officer, director, or shareholder of a general partner that is a corporation;

(2) consulting with and advising a general partner with respect to the business of the limited partnership;

(3) acting as surety for the limited partnership or guaranteeing or assuming one or more specific obligations of the limited partnership;

(4) taking any action required or permitted by law to bring or pursue a derivative action in the right of the limited partnership;

(5) requesting or attending a meeting of partners;

(6) proposing, approving, or disapproving, by voting or otherwise, one or more of the following matters:

(i) the dissolution and winding up of the limited partnership;

(ii) the sale, exchange, lease, mortgage, pledge, or other transfer of all or substantially all of the assets of the limited partnership;

(iii) the incurrence of indebtedness by the limited partnership other than in the ordinary course of its business;

(iv) a change in the nature of the business;

(v) the admission or removal of a general partner;

(vi) the admission or removal of a limited partner;

(vii) a transaction involving an actual or potential conflict of interest between a general partner and the limited partnership or the limited partners;

(viii) an amendment to the partnership agreement or certificate of limited partnership; or

(ix) matters related to the business of the limited partnership not otherwise enumerated in this subsection (b), which the partnership agreement states in writing may be subject to the approval or disapproval of limited partners;

(7) winding up the limited partnership * * *; or

(8) exercising any right or power permitted to limited partners under this Act and not specifically enumerated in this subsection (b).

(c) The enumeration in subsection (b) does not mean that the possession or exercise of any other powers by a limited partner constitutes participation by him [or her] in the business of the limited partnership.

(d) A limited partner who knowingly permits his [or her] name to be used in the name of the limited partnership * * * is liable to creditors who extend credit to the limited partnership without actual knowledge that the limited partner is not a general partner.

§ 304. Person Erroneously Believing Himself [or Herself] Limited Partner

(a) Except as provided in subsection (b), a person who makes a contribution to a business enterprise and erroneously but in good faith believes that he [or she] has become a limited partner in the enterprise is not a general partner in the enterprise and is not bound by its obligations by reason of making the contribution, receiving distributions from the enterprise, or exercising any rights of a limited partner, if, on ascertaining the mistake, he [or she]:

(1) causes an appropriate certificate of limited partnership or a certificate of amendment to be executed and filed; or

(2) withdraws from future equity participation in the enterprise by executing and filing in the office of the Secretary of State a certificate declaring withdrawal under this section.

(b) A person who makes a contribution of the kind described in subsection (a) is liable as a general partner to any third party who transacts business with the enterprise (i) before the person withdraws and an appropriate certificate is filed to show withdrawal, or (ii) before an appropriate certificate is filed to show that he [or she] is not a general partner, but in either case only if the third party actually believed in good faith that the person was a general partner at the time of the transaction.

———

It is important to recognize that most of this careful articulation of the scope of limited partners' potential liability became moot with the development and widespread acceptance of a simpler concept: that a corporation with nominal assets could be the sole general partner of a limited partnership. The essential point is that under sections 303(b)(1) and (c) officers, directors, or shareholders of a general partner did not themselves become general partners of the limited partnership merely by taking part in the management of the general partner.

2. *Limited Partners have no right to withdraw before the expiration of the term of a limited partnership.* Sections 602 and 603 of ULPA (1976) provide (in an inconspicuous way) that in limited partnerships for a term, limited partners, unlike general partners, have no power to withdraw prematurely from the limited partnership:

§ **602**. A general partner may withdraw from a limited partnership at any time by giving written notice to the other partners but if the withdrawal violates the partnership agreement, * * * [the withdrawing general partner may be liable for damages.]

§ **603.** A limited partner may withdraw from a limited partnership at the time or upon the happening of events specified in writing in the partnership agreement. If the agreement does not specify in writing the time or the events upon the happening of which a limited partner may withdraw * * * [the limited partner may withdraw on six months notice to the limited partnership].

* * *

The import of § 603 can best be appreciated by considering a limited partnership agreement that provides that there shall be no withdrawals during a term of, say, fifty years. Under ULPA (1976) limited partners cannot withdraw from or cause the dissolution of the limited partnership during that 50–year period. Limited partners may be able to sell or dispose of their limited partnership interests to some third person, but the capital invested by the limited partner remains in the limited partnership until the 50–year term expires.

3. *Limited Liability Entities as Sole General Partners.*

ROBERT W. HAMILTON, CORPORATE GENERAL PARTNERS OF LIMITED PARTNERSHIPS
1 J. Small & Emerging Bus. L. 73, 78–87 No. 1 (1997).

A limited partnership with a corporation as the sole general partner creates a totally different kind of entity than the traditional limited partnership. If the general partner is only marginally capitalized, the limited partnership becomes a limited liability entity not unlike a corporation. No individual is personally liable for the firm's debts. Most of the capital is provided by passive investors who, as limited partners, have no right to participate in management. Furthermore, control of the limited partnership is vested solely in the hands of the corporate general partner; in turn, control of that entity may be vested exclusively in the persons who organize the venture but provide only a small fraction of the capital needed by the enterprise. Since there is no legal prohibition against limited partners serving as shareholders, directors, or officers of the corporate general partner, organizers of the venture may also participate in the sharing of profits and losses as limited partners as well as through the corporate general partner.[14]

What was the incentive that gave rise to the rather sudden development of corporate general partners beginning in about 1970? The answer, in a word, was taxes; federal income taxes, to be precise. The 1970s were the era of tax shelters. A business form was needed that assured that losses could be passed through to investors, that investors had no personal responsibility for losses, and that the promoters of the tax shelter could run things without personal responsibility for debts and losses arising when the business ultimately collapsed. The limited partnership with a corporate general partner filled this need perfectly.[15] During the 1970s many thousands of real estate and oil and gas ventures were created in the limited partnership form primarily to provide tax deductions for affluent professionals and investors based on tax deductions for depreciation in real estate ventures, and for tangible and intangible drilling expenses and depletion in oil and gas ventures.

14. [By the Author] The conceptual problem of whether a limited partner could retain his shield of limited liability while participating in the management of the corporate general partner created problems in Texas in the 1970s. In Delaney v. Fidelity Lease Ltd., 526 S.W.2d 543, 545–46 (Tex.1975) the Texas Supreme Court imposed personal liability on those limited partners basically on a "too many hats" approach. Shortly thereafter, the Texas Attorney General, relying primarily on Delaney, opined that a corporation could not be the sole general partner of a limited partnership. Op. Tex. Att'y Gen. H–1229 (1978). This opinion flew so squarely in the face of the partnership statutes and widespread current practice that six law professors teaching corporation law objected in a letter to the Attorney General. 16 Bull. of Sec. on Corp., Bank. & Bus. L. 24 (No. 1 Sept. 1978). The Attorney General then backed down. Op. Tex. Att'y Gen. No. H–1229A (1978). By this time the tax shelter business discussed below was in full swing, and

the Texas Legislature in 1979 adopted amendments that made it perfectly clear (1) that corporations could be general partners and (2) that limited partners had a safe harbor from liability if they participated in the management of the general partner. 1979 Tex. Gen. Laws 1781, now codified in Tex. Rev. Civ. Stat. Ann. art. 6132b §§ 6–A, 15 (West Supp. 1997). When the same issue arose in other states, decisions usually rejected the Delaney approach. See Frigidaire Sales Corp. v. Union Properties, Inc., 562 P.2d 244, 246 (Wash.1977); Western Camps, Inc. v. Riverway Ranch Enters., 138 Cal. Rptr. 918, 927 (Cal.Ct.App.1977). The issue was ultimately laid to rest by ULPA (1976)§ 303(b)(1) which created a "safe harbor" for limited partners who were "an officer, director or shareholder of a general partner that is a corporation."

15. [By the Author] Various other business forms were sometimes used as tax shelters. * * *

The era of tax shelters ended with the enactment of the Tax Reform Act of 1986.[16] However, the changes in marginal tax rates for individuals and corporations made in that statute opened up entirely new tax saving devices which utilized limited partnerships with corporate general partners. * * * As a result, the creation of limited partnerships with corporate general partners continued at a faster rate after 1986 than before, despite the closing of tax shelters.

* * * [W]here limited partnerships are used today, it is the norm to use a corporation as the sole general partner. Probably the most common allocation of financial benefits is 99% to the limited partners and 1% to the general partner. In these situations, the general partner is usually under the direct control of some but not all of the limited partners. The 99/1 division minimizes the tax disadvantages * * *.

A corporate general partner differs from an individual general partner in several basic respects. * * *

First, a corporate general partner is subject to the control of somebody else. With an individual as a general partner, there is no doubt as to whose decisions will be evaluated under applicable principles of fiduciary duty. Where a corporate general partner is involved, the decision-maker may be a panel of individuals or a single person whose identity may or may not be known to limited partners and whose financial interest in the limited partnership may be great or may be small.[17]

Second, it is relatively easy to control transfers of managerial authority to third persons when individual general partners are involved. Restrictions on transfers of general partnership interests without the consent of the limited partners appear in both statutes and limited partnership agreements, and, while it may be possible to evade these limitations through a delegation of duties rather than an assignment of interest itself, such a delegation does not eliminate the continuing responsibility of the general partner. However, a corporate general partner is inherently an economic entity which itself may be the subject of purchase or sale. The individuals involved in the ownership and management of the business of the corporate general partner may change without a change in the identity of the general partner itself. The simplest example is the sale of shares by the shareholders of the general partner to an unrelated third person. Further, the same result can be achieved through mergers or other transactions that arguably may not involve a sale or transfer at all. Thus, a corporate general partner is unlike an individual general partner in the basic respect that control may be shifted from one group to another without apparently affecting the continuous existence of the corporate general partner. From the standpoint of inactive investors who are limited partners, of course, the identity of those in control of the general partner is usually more important than the formal identity of the general partner itself.

---

16. [By the Author] Tax Reform Act of 1986, Pub. L. No. 99–514, 100 Stat. 2085 (1986) (codified as amended in scattered sections of 26 U.S.C.).

17. [By the Author] The financial interest of the general partner in the limited partnership may be known, but the economic interest of the decision maker in the corporate general partner may be small or unknown.

Third, a corporate general partner may be entirely acceptable and responsible as a general partner even though its assets are nominal or relatively insignificant in comparison to the size of the business it is managing. This is likely where the shareholders or managers of the corporate general partner also own substantial limited partnership interests. A claim of breach of fiduciary duty against a general partner is not worth very much if the general partner itself is a corporation with nominal assets. Recovery, if there is to be recovery, depends on finding some theory to hold the parties that manage the general partner liable for the general partner's breach of duty.

Fourth, even if a corporate general partner is reasonably capitalized at the outset, subsequent transactions may largely bleed off these assets to the corporate owners without the consent of the limited partnership and without involving a fraudulent conveyance, but with significantly increased potential risks to limited partners.

Finally, there are potential conflicts of fiduciary duty whenever a corporation (as contrasted with an individual) is the general partner of a limited partnership. The general partner obviously owes fiduciary duties to the limited partnership and to the limited partners. Corporate officers and directors also owe fiduciary duties to the shareholders of a corporate partner. These fiduciary duties may conflict. This conflict is likely to be particularly intense when there are shareholders of the corporate general partner who have no direct financial interest in the limited partnership. If the shareholders of the corporate general partner gain more from a breach of fiduciary duty than the limited partners lose, it makes economic sense for the managers of the corporate general partner to breach duties to the limited partners and maximize the gain to the corporate general partner. However, the rhetoric of fiduciary duties in this situation appears to indicate the contrary: That the duties owed by the corporate general partner to the limited partners trump the duties owed by the officers and directors of the corporate general partner to the shareholders. Cases state that a corporation that is the sole general partner owes "the duty * * * to exercise the utmost good faith, fairness, and loyalty" for the benefit of the limited partnership.[18] This statement seems to require that officers and directors of the corporate general partner favor the duties to the limited partnership and the limited partners above any duty to the shareholders.

IN RE USACAFES, L.P. LITIGATION

Court of Chancery of Delaware, 1991.
600 A.2d 43.

ALLEN, CHANCELLOR.

These consolidated actions arise out of the October 1989 purchase by Metsa Acquisition Corp. of substantially all of the assets of USACafes, L.P., a Delaware limited partnership (the "Partnership") at a cash price of $72.6 million or $10.25 per unit. Plaintiffs are holders of limited partnership units. They bring these cases as class actions on behalf of all limited partnership

---

18. Boxer v. Husky Oil Co., 429 A.2d 995, 1984).
997 (Del.Ch.1981), *aff'd,* 483 A.2d 633 (Del.

unit holders except defendants. The relief sought includes, inter alia, the imposition of constructive trusts on certain funds received by defendants in connection with the Metsa sale and an award of damages to the class resulting from the sale.

The Partnership was formed in the 1986 reorganization of the business of USACafes, Inc., a Nevada corporation. Also formed as part of that reorganization was USACafes General Partner, Inc. (the "General Partner"), a Delaware corporation that acts as the general partner of the Partnership. Both the Partnership and the General Partner are named as defendants in this action. A second category of defendants is composed of Sam and Charles Wyly, brothers who together own all of the stock of the General Partner, sit on its board, and who also personally, directly or indirectly, own 47% of the limited partnership units of the Partnership. Sam Wyly chairs the Board of the General Partner. * * *

The * * * most central theory [of the amended complaint] involves an alleged breach of the duty of loyalty. In essence, it claims that the sale of the Partnership's assets was at a low price, favorable to Metsa, because the directors of the General Partner all received substantial side payments that induced them to authorize the sale of the Partnership assets for less than the price that a fair process would have yielded. Specifically, it is alleged that, in connection with the sale, (1) the Wylys received from Metsa more than $11 million in payments (or promises to pay in the future) which were disguised as consideration for personal covenants not to compete; (2) the General Partner (which the Wylys wholly own) received a $1.5 million payment right in consideration of the release of a claim that plaintiffs assert was nonexistent * * *. In sum, it is alleged that between $15 and $17 million was or will be paid to the directors and officers of the General Partner by or with the approval of Metsa; those payments are alleged to constitute financial inducements to the directors of the General Partner to refrain from searching for a higher offer to the Partnership. Plaintiffs add that, even assuming that Metsa was the buyer willing to pay the best price, some part at least of these "side payments" should have gone to the Partnership. * * *

* * * [T]he Wyly defendants and the other director defendants move under Rule 12(b)(6) to dismiss the breach of fiduciary duty claims in the amended complaint asserting that, while the General Partner admittedly did owe fiduciary duties to the limited partners, they as directors of the General Partner owe no such duties to those persons. The whole remedy of the limited partners for breach of the duties of loyalty and care, it is said, is against the General Partner only and not its directors. * * *

I turn first to the director defendants' motion to dismiss for failure to state a claim with respect to the sale of the Partnership's assets. The gist of this motion is the assertion that the directors of the General Partner owed the limited partners no duty of loyalty or care. In their view their only duty of loyalty was to the General Partner itself and to its shareholders (i.e., the Wyly brothers). Thus, in alleging that the director defendants breached duties of loyalty and care running to them, the directors say the limited partners have asserted a legal nullity.

In my opinion the assertion by the directors that the independent existence of the corporate General Partner is inconsistent with their owing fiduciary duties directly to limited partners is incorrect. Moreover, even were it correct, their position on this motion would have to be rejected in any event because the amended complaint expressly alleges that they personally participated in the alleged breach by the General Partner itself, which admittedly did owe loyalty to the limited partners.

The first basis of this holding is the more significant. While I find no corporation law precedents directly addressing the question whether directors of a corporate general partner owe fiduciary duties to the partnership and its limited partners, the answer to it seems to be clearly indicated by general principles and by analogy to trust law. I understand the principle of fiduciary duty, stated most generally, to be that one who controls property of another may not, without implied or express agreement, intentionally use that property in a way that benefits the holder of the control to the detriment of the property or its beneficial owner. There are, of course, other aspects—a fiduciary may not waste property even if no self interest is involved and must exercise care even when his heart is pure—but the central aspect of the relationship is, undoubtedly, fidelity in the control of property for the benefit of another.[19] See generally Robert Flannigan, The Fiduciary Obligation, 9 Oxford J. Legal St. 285 (1989).

While the parties cite no case treating the specific question whether directors of a corporate general partner are fiduciaries for the limited partnership, a large number of trust cases do stand for a principle that would extend a fiduciary duty to such persons in certain circumstances. The problem comes up in trust law because modernly corporations may serve as trustees of express trusts. Thus, the question has arisen whether directors of a corporate trustee may personally owe duties of loyalty to *cestui que trusts* of the corporation. A leading authority states the accepted answer:

> The directors and officers of [a corporate trustee] are certainly under a duty to the beneficiaries not to convert to their own use property of the trust administered by the corporation * * *. Furthermore, the directors and officers are under a duty to the beneficiaries of trusts administered by the corporation not to cause the corporation to misappropriate the property * * *. The breach of trust need not, however, be a misappropriation * * *. Any officer [director cases are cited in support here] who knowingly causes the corporation to commit a breach of trust causing loss * * * is personally liable to the beneficiary of the trust.
>
> Moreover, a director or officer of a trust institution who improperly acquires an interest in the property of a trust administered by the institution is subject to personal liability. He is accountable for any profit * * *. Even where the trustee [itself] is not liable, however, because it had no knowledge that the director was making the purchase, the director * * * is liable to the beneficiaries * * *. The directors and officers are in a fiduciary relation not merely to the [corporation] * * * but to the beneficiaries of the trust administered by the [corporation].

A. Scott & W. Fratcher, The Law of Trusts § 326.3, at 304–306 (4th ed. 1989) (citing cases).

---

19. [By the Court] Thus, for example, a borrower of money is not considered a fiduciary for the lender simply because she is bound to return the principle [*sic*] sum plus interest. The "property" is held by the borrower for her own benefit.

The theory underlying fiduciary duties is consistent with recognition that a director of a corporate general partner bears such a duty towards the limited partnership. That duty, of course, extends only to dealings with the partnership's property or affecting its business, but, so limited, its existence seems apparent in any number of circumstances. Consider, for example, a classic self-dealing transaction: assume that a majority of the board of the corporate general partner formed a new entity and then caused the general partner to sell partnership assets to the new entity at an unfairly small price, injuring the partnership and its limited partners. Can it be imagined that such persons have not breached a duty to the partnership itself? And does it not make perfect sense to say that the gist of the offense is a breach of the equitable duty of loyalty that is placed upon a fiduciary? It appears true that the same result might be rationalized as aider and abettor liability, but I am unsure what such indirection would add that is useful where a self-dealing transaction or other diversion of partnership property is alleged. Indeed in some instances, for example the use by a director of confidential information concerning the partnership's business not yet known by the board of the general partner, there may be no breach of loyalty or care by the general partner itself to abet, yet there may be director liability to the partnership by the director. * * * It is not necessary here to attempt to delineate the full scope of that duty. It may well not be as broad as the duty of the director of a corporate trustee.[20] But it surely entails the duty not to use control over the partnership's property to advantage the corporate director at the expense of the partnership. That is what is alleged here. * * *

The motions of the individual defendants, the General Partner, and the Partnership to dismiss the claims arising out of the sale of the Partnership's assets are denied. * * *

Notes

(1) The basic issue addressed by Chancellor Allen in *USACafes* has arisen in a number of cases. Most cases impose a fiduciary duty on the controllers of the corporate general partner, see e.g. Wilson v. Friedberg, 323 S.C. 248, 473 S.E.2d 854 (App.1996) ("corporate veil" of corporate general partner pierced because sole shareholder intermingled partnership assets and failed to keep adequate records). Some cases impose liability without discussion of the theory but simply state that X was in complete control of the corporate general partner and therefore was responsible for breaches of duty by the general partner.

(2) A basic principle of partnership law is that no partner can be compelled to accept another person as a partner against his or her will. For example, an attempt by a general partner to assign his interest in a partnership to a person who is not a partner is effective to transfer only his financial interest unless the other partners are willing to accept the assignee as a partner. See UPA (1914) § 27; UPA (1994) § 502. Should the same rule be applicable to direct transfers of partnership interests by *general*[21] partners of limited partnerships? ULPA (1976)

---

20. [By the Court] For example, I imply nothing on such questions as whether a director of a corporate general partner might be held liable directly to the partnership on a "corporate" opportunity theory or for waste of partnership assets (two possible consequences of characterizing such persons as fiduciaries for the partnership).

21. [By the Editors] Transfers by limited partners to third persons involve only transfers of financial interests and therefore do not raise

§ 702 provides that such an assignee may be become a limited partner if authorized by the partnership agreement.

(3) The transfer of *shares* in a corporate general partner is not of itself a transfer of a *partnership* interest. The corporation remains the same entity even if all the shares are sold to a third person. Arguably, therefore, the limited partners have no basis for objecting when the shareholders of the corporate general partner sell all or a controlling block of their shares in the corporation to someone else. However, the limited case law contradicts this notion. See *In re* Integrated Resources, Inc., 1990 WL 325414 (Bankr.S.D.N.Y.1990). For more on this case, see Robert W. Hamilton, Corporate General Partners of Limited Partnerships, 1 J. Small & Emerging Bus. L. 73, 92–3 (1997).

(4) The identity of corporate general partners also may change through mergers or similar transactions without any formal transfer of the general partnership interest. Such a transaction (unlike a sale of controlling shares) does involve a change in the corporate form of the general partner and arguably may therefore constitute either a "transfer" or "assignment" in violation of prohibitions against assignment in limited partnership agreements or in breach of the general prohibition against assigning management powers by general partners. The leading case is Star Cellular Tel. Co., Inc. v. Baton Rouge CGSA, Inc., 1993 WL 294847 (Del.Ch.1993) (per Jacobs, Ch.), aff'd, 647 A.2d 382 (Del.1994). The agreement provided that:

> The General Partner may transfer or assign its General Partner's interest only after written notice to all the other Partners and the unanimous vote of all the other Partners to permit such transfer and to continue the business of the Partnership with the assignee of the General Partner as General Partner. * * * Withdrawal of the General Partner (which will also be deemed its withdrawal as a Limited Partner) will cause the dissolution and termination of the Partnership * * * unless it is continued by the unanimous consent of the remaining Partners * * *.

The importance of the court's decision lies in its analysis, not in its conclusion: it did not focus on the meaning of the words "transfer" or "assign" or on the question whether a merger under the applicable corporation statutes was or was not defined to be a transfer. Rather, the court based its decision on whether the transaction was of a type that could adversely affect the interests of the non-assigning parties. In other words, the test was not a mechanical or linguistic one but rather one based on results and impact. The court concluded that the merger of subsidiaries into a new subsidiary involved in that case did not adversely affect the interests of the limited partners.

(5) As a result of the 1987 Tax Act, there is now one invariable rule about conduit-type taxation. If a business has ownership interests that are publicly–traded, that business will be taxed as a C corporation no matter what business form is adopted.

(6) Under the tax rates in effect in 2005, the name of the game for most closely-held businesses is to continue to take advantage of conduit or pass-through taxation. This means (i) the use of unincorporated business forms that provide conduit tax treatment, (ii) the election of subchapter S if the corporation is eligible, or (iii) the "zeroing out" of income by a C corporation as much as possible—to 100 percent if that can be defended in a tax audit. Taxation as a C

the same issue. Such transfers are generally permitted.

corporation is generally to be avoided though, as indicated earlier, there are some situations in which this is not the case.

D.   CHECK THE BOX

The *Kintner* regulations were originally developed by the Internal Revenue Service in response to the development of limited partnerships with corporate general partners. The IRS considered taking the position that unlimited personal liability was the touchstone for partnership taxation, but eventually moved to the tax classification based on the presence of "corporate" characteristics defined in the *Kintner* regulations. Efforts by the IRS to maintain economic meaning and substance in the *Kintner* regulations led to extremely detailed substantive rules for limited partnerships and LLCs, numerous private rulings by the IRS as new twists developed, and the creation of a cottage industry in large law firms as individual attorneys specialized in the nuances of the application of the *Kintner* regulations to LLCs and limited partnerships. This approach toward classification was widely criticized by commentators. See e.g. Larry E. Ribstein, The Deregulation of Limited Liability and the Death of Partnership, 70 Wash. U. L.Q. 417, 451 (1992) ("there is no normative basis for the tax distinction between 'corporations' and 'partnerships,'" and "the classification is unsuitable as an arbitrary line because it entails significant costs"); see also Rebecca S. Rudnick, Who Should Pay the Corporate Tax in a Flat Tax World?, 39 Case W. Res. L. Rev. 965, 1047–61 (1988–89).

Effective January 1, 1997, the Internal Revenue Service adopted new regulations for the classification of business forms. 26 C.F.R. Parts 1, 301, 602, TD 8697, 61 Fed.Reg. 66,584 (1996). These new regulations, popularly known as "check the box," state that the *Kintner* rules had become "increasingly formalistic," and that the new regulations replace those rules "with a much simpler approach that generally is elective."

While the detailed "check the box" regulations are relatively complex, the basic principles can be stated simply:

(1) An entity will be classified as a corporation for tax purposes if it is created under a statute that "describes or refers to the entity as incorporated as a corporation, body corporate, or body politic" or as "a joint-stock company or joint stock association." Such an entity must be taxed as a C corporation or as an S corporation (if it qualifies).

(2) An entity that is not classified as a corporation and has at least two members can elect to be classified for tax purposes either as a corporation or as a partnership by making an election at the time it files its first tax return. If the entity does not formally elect to be taxed as a corporation it will be taxed as a partnership. Existing entities with two or more members retain the tax status they had immediately before the new regulations go into effect.

(3) An entity that has only one member may elect to be taxed as a corporation or it will be taxed as a "nothing," i.e. as though it has no separate existence from its owner. This principle is of primary importance to limited liability companies described in the following chapter.

(4) If an entity elects to change its classification, it may not change its classification back within five years without permission of the Commissioner.

The conversion of an entity that is currently taxable as a corporation to a partnership is itself a taxable event, treated as though the corporation dissolved and reconstituted itself as a partnership. The conversion in the opposite direction, i.e. from a partnership to a corporation, will usually (though not always) be tax-free.

Notes

(1) This regulation was generally received with shouts of joy by practitioners because it truly simplified what was formerly a complex and arcane area of business law. One comment captures the general euphoria: "Surfs up. An unincorporated entity can look, walk and quack like a corporation in every respect—have officers and a board of managers, uninterruptible life, certificates that are freely transferable as well as limited liability—without risking classification as a corporation. However, don't organize the entity under any statute that refers to the entity as a joint stock company or association." Comment of John Debruyn by electronic mail, August 31, 1996.

(2) Under check-the-box, closely held corporations (and a variety of similar corporate-type business forms) must be taxed as corporations. Of course, most such corporations may elect S corporation treatment, but they will never be eligible for the more flexible subchapter K treatment unless they go through the tax-costly process of dissolving the corporation and reforming as an LLC or limited partnership.

(3) The great advantage of check-the-box from the standpoint of business planners is that with respect to unincorporated business forms—proprietorships, general partnerships, limited partnerships, and limited liability companies—the tax treatment is not related either to the business form that is selected or the exposure of owners to personal liability. As a result, unincorporated business forms may elect to be taxed under Subchapter K, Subchapter S, or Subchapter C without regard to the type of unincorporated business form selected.

E. TWENTY–FIRST CENTURY LIMITED PARTNERSHIPS: LEVERAGE BUYOUT COMPANIES, VENTURE CAPITAL FIRMS AND FAMILY LIMITED PARTNERSHIPS

The development of the limited liability company has sharply reduced the popularity of limited partnerships in many contexts. LLCs are so much simpler and more flexible than LPs that it is sometimes difficult for closely–held businesses to justify the use of LPs.[22] We continue to study LPs in part because many pre–1997 limited partnerships are large economic entities that remain in existence and will likely persist in the LP form in part because the LP is still the clear choice in two important but narrow types of enterprises: sophisticated arrangements called venture capital funds and family limited partnerships.

---

22. [By the Editors] Popularity of the limited partnership form is to some extent dependent on tax and other costs of competing business forms. For example, Texas and some other states impose a franchise tax on limited liability companies and corporations but not on general or limited partnerships. In these states, firms may be formed as limited partnerships or limited liability partnerships and then elect alternative income tax treatment under Check the Box.

The decline in the general use of the LP led to a revision of ULPA (1976) in 2001. The new statute, named "ReRulpa" (or "Re–RULPA") provides as a default rule that general partners are not liable for debts of the limited partnership unless they expressly agree to assume liability. In effect, ReRulpa makes the LLLP the default rule. This tentative decision has been somewhat controversial. Since the majority of the states have adopted the earlier version of the ULPA (1976) with the 1985 amendments, that version continues to govern this business form for all practical purposes in corporate law.

The Prefatory Note to the final version of Re—Rulpa describes the goal of this new statute as follows:

> Re–RULPA is being drafted for a business world in which limited liability partnerships and limited liability companies can meet many of the needs formerly met by limited partnerships. Re–RULPA therefore targets two types of enterprises that seem largely beyond the scope of LLPs and LLCs: (i) sophisticated manager-entrenched commercial deals whose participants commit for the long term, and (ii) estate planning arrangements (family limited partnerships). Re–RULPA accordingly assumes that, more often than not, people utilizing the act will want:
>
> • strong, centralized management, strongly entrenched, and
>
> • passive investors with little right to exit the entity.

The first type of entity that continues to use the traditional LP structure involves sophisticated commercial arrangements that feature highly centralized management (the venture capitalists) in which large investors commit funds for relatively long periods of time and have very limited rights to compel liquidation or the repurchase of their interests. There are two groups of modern economic entities that typically are organized as limited partnerships: venture capital firms and leveraged buyout companies. Both involve management and investment of huge amounts of capital—typically individual contributions in the millions of dollars—provided by wealthy individuals and institutional investors. The investors are limited partners who receive periodic distributions of income from the LP. The venture capital firm or leveraged buyout company serves as the general partner in these limited partnerships. Withdrawals of capital by the LPs are regulated by contract. The limited partnership structure assures continuous centralized management, centralized investment decisions made by managers of the general partner free of involvement by the limited partners, who contribute capital and share in the economic returns.

A leveraged buyout company collects money from investors and combines those funds with money borrowed from financial institutions to buy controlling interests in operating companies. The assets of the company being acquired are typically used as collateral to secure the repayment of the borrowed funds. The term "leverage" means debt, and refers to the fact that the companies acquired in leveraged buyouts have a lot of debt in relation to the amount of equity on their balance sheets, and thus are highly "leveraged." These companies have a high risk of bankruptcy because they do not have very stable, predictable earnings. Unexpected fluctuations in earnings will cause such companies to fail to make the scheduled payment of principal and interest on their outstanding debt obligations.

Venture capital limited partnerships are professionally-managed pools of capital that invest their money in equity securities of closely-held companies at early and medium stages of their development. Venture capitalists usually sit on the boards of the companies in which they have invested and take a very active role in the corporate governance of these firms.[23]

Venture capital funds typically are organized as limited partnerships run by general partners with experience in all aspects of managing young companies. The limited partners provide virtually all of the capital that the venture fund uses to make investments. The general partner that manages the venture fund and provides expertise to the companies in which the fund invests contributes only a small portion of the capital. Venture capital general partners are able to help with brand development, financial controls, accounting, marketing, and choosing lawyers, accountants and investment bankers. Venture capitalists also help companies choose managers to help run the non-creative aspects of the companies in their portfolios. In other words, venture capital general partners help with the development of the companies in which they invest up to the point at which they sell shares to the public.

Usually, the partnership agreements between U.S. venture capital funds and their investors limit the term of the investment to 7–10 years, at which time the fund is liquidated and the money returned to investors. Successful venture capital limited partnerships easily attract money from investors when they begin a new funding cycle.

Venture capital firms are highly specialized. Some firms invest only in certain industry sectors such as biotechnology, computer peripherals, or fashion retailing. Other firms invest only in companies in certain geographical regions or only in companies that are in the very early (or very late) stages of their development businesses.

While venture capital investing is a modest fraction of overall capital investment in corporations (venture capital funds are limited partnerships, while the businesses in which they invest are corporations), the U.S. venture capital industry is, by far, the largest in the world. Moreover, the venture capital industry is important in certain industry sectors, particularly biotechnology and high technology companies. A number of very successful companies including Apple Computer, Cisco Systems, Compaq, Lotus Development Corp., Seagate Technologies, and Sun Microsystems began life as portfolio companies of venture capital firms.

The limited partnership structure is well-tailored to the venture capitalist business. Although venture capitalists generally do not receive a majority of the equity in the companies in which they invest, they typically control a majority of the seats on the boards of portfolio companies. Venture capital firms receive preferred stock (or sometimes, debt instruments) in portfolio companies, which has significant voting rights and which can be converted into common stock and liquidated if and when the portfolio company makes a public offering. These arrangements work well, as evidenced by the fact that,

23. Shannon W. Stevenson, The Venture Capital Solution to the Problem of Close Corporation Shareholder Fiduciary Duties, 41 Duke L.J. 1139 (2001); Bernard S. Black and Ronald J. Gilson, Venture Capital and the Structure of Capital Markets: Banks Versus Stock Markets, 47 Journal of Financial Economics 47 Journal of Financial Economics 243 (1998); William A. Sahlman, The Structure and Governance of Venture Capital Organizations, 27 Journal of Financial Economics 473 (1990).

while there is a tremendous amount of litigation among investors in closely–held corporations, there has been very little litigation between venture capital firms and the portfolio companies they create or between venture capital firms and their investors. This is particularly surprising in light of the high rate of failure of portfolio companies. A rough rule of thumb in the industry is that a failure rate of 80% is considered quite good for venture capitalists that specialize in investing in early stages of new ventures. Of course, very little litigation is not the same thing as no litigation. Problems do arise, as the following case demonstrates.

IN RE SPREE.COM CORP.

United States Bankruptcy Court, Eastern District of Pennsylvania, 2001.
2001 WL 1518242.

The plaintiff Cashback Liquidation Company commenced suit against [a venture capital fund called Technology Crossover Ventures, LP, (TCV), along with Technology Crossover Ventures, Inc., which was the corporate general partner of the TCV limited partnership, and some of the investors in TCV, including one Mark Tesler]. Mark Tesler served as a member of Plaintiff's board of directors [and] as the representative, agent and/or employee of the TCV Investor Defendants. The gravamen of the Complaint is that the TCV Defendants and Tesler (collectively referred to as the "Defendants") made certain damaging statements to a reporter from the Wall Street Journal about Plaintiff's business without authorization or consent and in violation of the parties' agreement and the duties of confidentiality, loyalty and due care imposed on Tesler as a board member and on the TCV Investor Defendants [who were his] principals. It is alleged that these statements which then formed the basis of an article in the Wall Street Journal on August 24, 2000 (the "Article") had a chilling effect on Plaintiff's existing and prospective ability to raise necessary capital, resulting ultimately in the need to file for bankruptcy protection. * * *

The offending portion of the article is quoted in paragraph 44 of the Complaint [ ]:

"What do we want to do with this puppy? The cash runs out soon" says venture capitalist Mark Tesler. Mr. Tesler is sitting around a giant conference table littered with coffee cups, plates of ham sandwiches and lots of paper. He and 18 other partners and associates of Technology Crossover Ventures have gathered behind closed doors at a Palo Alto, California hotel one hot Monday morning in late July. This mission: to figure out ways for the 100–plus companies in their portfolio to survive the tricky financing environment that has been in place since April's stock market slump.

Mr. Tesler is talking about Spree.com Corp., a business-to-business Internet company in which TCV has invested $5 million. Spree (unrelated to the Spree telephone calling card) is in the early stages of building a sales pipeline for its new business model, and will need more cash to complete its plans. "They're going to be looking at us for more capital, aren't they?" says Jay Hoag, a partner and, with Rick Kimball, co-founder of TCV. "I don't want to be supporting them until who knows when." The partners agree to keep funding Spree, awaiting some key sales milestones.

But, muses Mr. Hoag, "There's nothing easy about this story." Spree executives didn't return calls seeking comment for this article. * * *

The Confidentiality Clause is contained in paragraph 7 of the Agreement and provides in pertinent part:

> *Confidentiality*. The Investors agree to keep the information heretofore or hereafter furnished to the Investors by the company or on the Company's behalf (the "Confidential Material") confidential. Notwithstanding the foregoing, the term "Confidential Material" does not include information that (a) is or becomes publicly available other than through breach of this provision by the Investors; (b) is already known to the Investors at the time of the disclosure; [or] (c) is without reference to the Confidential Material. The Investors agree to take reasonable precautions to safeguard the Confidential Material from disclosure to anyone other than appropriate employees, officers, directors, partners and representatives, including auditors and attorneys, of the Investors, which persons shall be advised of the confidential nature of the material. * * *

The question then is whether statements made to the reporter and thereafter published contained "Confidential Material" as defined by the Agreement. Plaintiff contends that "the public statement that Spree's cash 'runs out soon' constituted a wrongful disclosure of information unavailable to the public." In response, Defendants point out Plaintiff's admissions that "[i]n or about July and August of 2000, Spree geared up for and embarked on a 'road show' to solicit additional third party investors for capital contributions and/or financing," and "[p]rior to and during August of 2000, a number of prospective investors expressed an interest in providing additional capital and/or financing in Spree." As Tesler's allegedly wrongful statement was made after the acknowledged road show, Defendants question how disclosure to the reporter concerning Spree.com's need for money could have breached a confidence. I agree. Plaintiff's admission that it had previously embarked on its fund solicitation program leads to the inescapable conclusion that it would have already disclosed its financial condition to those prospective investors. * * * Any solicitation of funds would require a complete disclosure of Plaintiff's financial condition. It is inconceivable that Plaintiff would not disclose its cash position in connection with securing new funding. Since any information that is or becomes publicly available other than through breach of the Confidentiality Agreement is not "Confidential Material," the statement that Spree is "running out of cash" does not provide the basis for a claim for breach of contract.

Plaintiff also highlights several other references in the article that it contends are actionable breaches of contract. Specifically, it mentions Tesler's characterization of the Plaintiff as a "puppy." The parties have both presented me with articles using that term, the Defendants affectionately; the Plaintiff derogatively.[24] Indeed the "puppy" reference is proffered, among other things, as support for the Plaintiff's contention that the article was "as

---

24. [By the Court:] I refuse to take judicial notice of the meaning of that term from these materials and quite frankly, I am surprised by the request that I do so. Its use is susceptible of shades of meaning, none of which implicate "Confidential Material." Defendants also request that I take judicial notice of the "well known and indisputable crash of the dot.com market" in evaluating the Complaint.

a whole" derogatory. Whether the article was derogatory misses the point. The issue is whether any "Confidential Material" was disclosed. * * *

The Plaintiff's Fifth Claim deals with prospective contracts with third parties. Plaintiff has correctly identified the elements of this tortious interference claim as (1) the existence of one or more contracts between plaintiff and a third party; (2) a purpose or intent by defendant to harm the plaintiff by preventing completion of a contractual relationship; (3) improper conduct by defendant which is neither privileged nor justified; and (4) actual legal harm resulting from defendant's actions. Defendants first argue that the Complaint fails to plead the existence of any prospective contracts. This position appears born of an illogical reading of paragraph 21 of the Complaint which avers "[e]xisting venture capital investors * * * previously made verbal commitments to contribute a portion of additional funds needed to meet Spree.com's future business plan (including the TCV Investor Defendants)." * * * The complaint pleads that these other existing Investors (*i.e.,* signatories to the Agreement) did not honor their verbal commitments to provide additional funds as a direct and proximate result of the Defendants' conduct. * * *

[With regard to the Fifth Claim], Plaintiff has pled facts that, if proven, would establish lack of privilege or justification as to Tesler. It alleges the existence of a fiduciary duty of care by Tesler, which he breached by statements made to the press which he knew would and did indeed injure the corporation by foreclosing prospective financing agreements being negotiated. It contends that Tesler put Plaintiff's economic well-being at risk to enhance its image in the marketplace. It is the beyond the "rules of the game" for a director to make such public statements with knowledge of the injurious consequences.

* * *

3. The Fifth Claim is DISMISSED to the extent it alleges tortious interference with existing contracts as to all remaining Defendants.

4. All remaining Defendants shall file an answer to this Complaint. * * *

Notes

(1) For more about venture capital funds, visit the following websites, http://www.newspring ventures.com/ aboutvc.asp, and http://www.newspring ventures.com/ dictionary.asp.

(2) In re Spree.com Corp. v. Tesler illustrates an important aspect of the business relationship between venture capitalists and portfolio companies. In their initial investments, venture capitalists generally do not put enough money in the companies in which they invest to allow those companies to fulfill their business plans. This so-called "staged investment" approach gives the venture capitalists considerable power over the entrepreneur. If the entrepreneur is uncooperative, or if the business does not appear to have good prospects after the initial investment, the venture capitalist can refuse to make investments in the future (unless, of course, it has made a contractual commitment of some kind to keep investing). By contrast, if the investments were not staged, the entrepreneur usually will want to keep pursuing the project until the venture capitalist's money runs out.

(3) Clearly, the general partner of a venture capital limited partnership, like other general partners of limited partnerships, owes fiduciary duties to the limited partners. Did the confidentiality agreement in this case affect the fiduciary duties owed by the general partner?

(4) The plaintiffs are alleging that the remarks by the venture capitalist that appeared in the Wall Street Journal constituted a breach of fiduciary duty and tortious interference with the plaintiffs' prospective contractual relations with the investors in the venture capital limited partnership. How did these "prospective contractual relations" arise? Should not investors have power to "pull the plug" and refuse to make further investments in enterprises if they conclude they are not viable? Might an investor in some circumstances agree unconditionally to provide additional funds? Such an unqualified provision, however, is not common: In most venture capital arrangements, the supplier of capital reserves the power to "pull the plug" at its sole discretion.

(5) Another form of entity, that avails itself of the limited partnership form are family limited partnerships ("FLPs"). These family arrangements are created by affluent individuals primarily to minimize gift and estate taxes. An FLP also facilitates management of personal assets, simplifies the annual gifting of assets to the younger generation, and assures that unrestricted funds are not transferred to younger adults before they are capable of handling them. FLPs are widely popular:

> There are no federal or state laws that preclude the funding of family limited partnerships with marketable securities and/or municipal bonds. And although the Internal Revenue Service (IRS) has no affinity for family limited partnerships under these circumstances, its challenges to such partnerships have not been successful.

> Proper establishment of a family limited partnership requires a number of steps. First, the family limited partnership agreement must contain certain provisions that restrict the ability of a limited partner to withdraw from the partnership. Such restrictions on transferability permit gifts of limited partnership interests to be discounted because valuation computation [for gift and estate taxes] are made on a "going concern" basis rather than upon a "liquidation" basis.*

The FLP permits saving on gift and estate taxes because these taxes are calculated on the basis of the value of the interest received by the donee, not the cost of the interest to the donor. The FLP also simplifies the making of gifts, since a parent can simply give each child one additional limited partnership unit every year, a transaction that does not involve a transfer of cash, property, or securities.

Needless to say, the Internal Revenue Service is not overjoyed by the increasing use of FLPs as gift or estate tax avoidance devices. The area has become increasingly complex as the IRS has taken positions that limit the discounts available, only to be met with additional ingenious variations on the FLP device to avoid those limitations. Congress has also enacted statutes designed to limit the FLP device.

---

* Herbert L. Zuckerman and Jay A. Soled, Family Limited Partnerships with a Twist, Experience, Spring 1997, at 34.

Chapter Four

LIMITED LIABILITY COMPANIES

A. INTRODUCTION

The limited liability company ("LLC") was the product of innovative professionals creating solutions when the current legal system failed to meet client needs. As described by Professor Hamill: "Since the late 1960s, Hamilton Brothers Oil Company had been involved in international oil and gas exploration using foreign LLCs, primarily the Panamanian limitada. Unlike the U.S. entities available at that time, limitadas provided direct limited liability [for all owners] and the ability to secure partnership classification for * * * tax purposes." Susan Pace Hamill, The Origins Behind the Limited Liability Company, 59 Ohio St.L.J. 1459, 1463–64 (1998).

Because no similar domestic entity existed in the United States, representatives of Hamilton Brothers Oil Company developed legislation that authorized an unincorporated domestic entity to be created that resembled the limitada. An initial effort to obtain enactment in Alaska failed, but the same legislation was introduced in Wyoming, where it was enacted on March 4, 1977, apparently without controversy.[1] The critical question then became whether the Internal Revenue Service would issue a favorable ruling that an unincorporated entity that provided limited liability for all its members would be eligible for partnership taxation. A favorable tax ruling was obtained in 1988. Revenue Ruling 88–76, 1988–2 Cum.Bull. 360. Once the tax issue was resolved, states quickly adopted LLC statutes to take advantage of the flexibility of this new business form. By 1995, all 50 states had adopted LLC statutes.

Because of concern that diversity in state laws might create serious problems for interstate LLCs, attempts to develop prototype or uniform state LLC statutes began almost immediately after the LLC's tax status was recognized. However, the rush by states to enact LLC statutes was underway, and most states enacted LLC statutes before efforts to develop standardized statutes came to fruition. The first standardized product was a "Prototype Limited Liability Company Act," proposed in 1992 by a committee of the American Bar Association. Concepts developed in this prototype statute were incorporated into many state statutes.

---

1. [By the Editors] Five years later a similar statute was enacted in Florida.

The Uniform Limited Liability Company Act was promulgated by the National Conference of Commissioners on Uniform State Laws in 1996. As of 2007, only eight states and the U.S. Virgin Islands have adopted this statute.

SUSAN PACE HAMILL, THE LIMITED LIABILITY COMPANY: A CATALYST EXPOSING THE CORPORATE INTEGRATION QUESTION

95 Mich.L.Rev. 393, 446 (1996).[2]

The rise of the domestic limited liability company (LLC)[3] from obscurity to its present position as a viable, mainstream alternative to the corporation or partnership was met with enormous enthusiasm by the business community and the practicing bar. * * * [T]he LLC offers for the first time a domestic entity that combines the tax advantages of a partnership with limited liability protection for all members, an advantage commonly associated with corporations. * * *

By combining the best of both worlds, partnership taxation and limited liability, the LLC revolution can be characterized as tax driven. Nevertheless, some commentators believe that it is the LLC's superior business provisions that will cause LLCs to continue to rise in popularity. Although the LLC's business provisions may be characteristic of either partnerships or corporations, in toto they produce a truly unique and new business entity that cannot be aligned categorically with either of the more traditional forms. For example, the statutory provisions addressing the management and control of the LLC generally vest agency authority and governance rights in all members, as if they were partners in a general partnership. However, LLC members, unlike general partners, can adopt a management structure resembling those of corporations or limited partnerships by appointing managers. The LLC's managers, holding the power to make important policy decisions and to bind the LLC in day-to-day business transactions, take on the roles held both by general partners of limited partnerships and by corporate directors and officers.

Regardless of whether the motivation is tax or business related, the use and acceptance of LLCs as a serious alternative to the partnership and the corporation exponentially increased between 1988 and 1995 * * *. Indeed, some commentators believe the LLC will largely replace the partnership and the closely held corporation and emerge as the dominant form of business for nonpublicly traded entities.

The rise of the LLC, however, has not been greeted with uniform zeal. Said one critic: "The federal government has opened up a candy store."[4] This

2. Reprinted with permission from The Michigan Law Review Association.

3. [By the Author] The LLC is an unincorporated business organization that contains dissolution, management and transferability provisions similar to those of a general partnership but that can easily be altered to resemble the limited partnership or to approach the corporate model. A related unincorporated business entity that appeared in 1991, the limited liability partnership (LLP), essentially operates as a general partnership for business purposes, while offering the partners either partial or total limited liability protection. The articles written on LLCs and LLPs are too numerous to cite completely.

4. [By the Author] New York Contemplates Cost of Partnership Treatment for Limited Li-

pithy comment metaphorically sums up the underlying and often unarticulated concern hidden in the shadows of the LLC euphoria. * * *

Notes

(1) "The LLC is not simply an entity that provides its members with limited liability, but one that is non-corporate in nature. * * * [An important aspect of this structure is that] LLCs generally are not subject to restrictions as to finance and management that historically have bound corporations. In particular, there is no need to create special 'surplus' accounts for dividends and no special requirement for management by a board of directors or equivalent body." Robert R. Keatinge, et al., The Limited Liability Company: A Study of an Emerging Entity, 47 Bus.Law. 378, 385 (1992).

As noted above, the purpose of forming a limited liability company is to create an entity that offers investors the protections of limited liability and the flow-through tax status of partnerships. Unlike partnerships, where entity profits flow through to individual partners for income tax purposes, corporations are treated as separate taxable entities under the Internal Revenue Code. Hence, from the investors' perspective, the income of a corporation is subject to double taxation.

The Treasury regulations that were in effect when the original LLC statutes were enacted provided that in order for a business organization such as a limited liability company to qualify for pass-through tax treatment and thereby avoid the double taxation on distributions, it must possess more "noncorporate characteristics" than "corporate characteristics." The regulations provided that a firm would be considered a corporation rather than a partnership if it had three of the following "corporate" characteristics: (1) continuity of life; (2) free transferability of interests; (3) centralization of management; and (4) limited liability. Because limited liability companies offer limited liability as a matter of course, to ensure partnership tax status limited liability companies must lack two of the three remaining characteristics. Moreover, the Internal Revenue Service made it clear that it would grant partnership (i.e., pass-through) tax status to limited liability companies only if they did not possess the corporate characteristics of continuity of life and free transferability of interests.

In 1997, the IRS replaced the old tax rules with "check the box." See page 146. Under these rules, business entities such as LLCs can choose for themselves whether to be taxed as a partnership (pass-through taxation) or as a corporation (entity taxation). However certain entities are not eligible for this election, and must be taxed as corporations. These include: (1) entities organized under a Federal or state statute that refers to the entity as a "corporation" or as "incorporated"; (2) certain foreign entities that are specifically listed in the regulations as per se corporations; and (3) business entities that are taxable as corporations under other provisions of the Internal Revenue Code, such as publicly–traded firms, real estate mortgage investments conduits, and regulated investment companies.

Now taxpayers can decide for themselves whether their LLCs (and other unincorporated business associations) should be taxed as partnerships or corporations. Moreover, the IRS now permits LLCs to achieve pass-through tax treatment even if they have only one owner.

ability Companies, 1992 Tax Notes Today, 243–10 (quoting from James W. Wetzler, New York State Commissioner of Taxation and Finance).

Some early state statutes, such as those in Colorado, Virginia and Nevada, required that LLCs expire after a certain fixed period. Without continuity of life for LLCs organized in these states, these statutes ensured that non-corporate characteristics dominated over the corporate characteristics. Other early statutes required LLCs to have more than one owner in order to resemble traditional partnerships. The "Check the Box" rules also removed virtually any incentive that investors might have for organizing as a Subchapter S corporation rather than as an LLC. Thus, the "Check the Box" rules have been described as causing "the true birth of the single-member LLC."[5]

As you will recall from Chapter 3, Subchapter S was added to the Internal Revenue Code in the middle of the last century to allow certain corporations to be taxed as partnerships at the election of their shareholders. In the wake of the "Check the Box" rules, it is not obvious why shareholders would ever elect Subchapter S status. LLCs, for example, can have an unlimited number of investors, while Subchapter S corporations are limited to 75. Subchapter S corporations cannot have non-US residents among their investors, while LLCs can; also shares in S corporations cannot be owned by C or S corporations or by LLCs, while LLCs can be owned by other LLCs, or by C or S corporations. However, for some firms, the Subchapter S form still makes sense. In particular, Subchapter S corporations can engage in mergers, stock-for-stock swaps, and other corporate reorganizations on a tax-free basis, while LLCs cannot. This difference is very important for businesses that hope to merge with or to be acquired by other corporations. Such businesses, if they want pass-through tax treatment, normally elect Subchapter S status rather than LLC status.

(2) Larry E. Ribstein, The Emergence of the Limited Liability Company, 51 Bus.Law. 1, 2–3, 6–10 (1995):[6]

> The LLC is * * * best understood in terms of four general characteristics: (i) limited liability; (ii) partnership tax features; (iii) chameleon management— that is, the ability to choose between centralized and direct member-management; and (iv) creditor-protection provisions. These characteristics, in turn, are best understood in light of the development of the LLC as an alternative to existing business forms.

(3) One important question about LLCs is the extent to which liability for LLC obligations may be imposed on LLC members based on analogous principles applicable to "piercing the corporate veil" of closely–held corporations, discussed in Chapter 7 of this casebook. In very general terms, veil-piercing in corporate law is based on equitable and common-sense principles that logically should apply to LLCs to the same extent as they apply to corporations.[7] However, the piercing issue has not been definitively resolved though every indication is that the corporate principle will be applied to LLCs. In Ditty v. CheckRite, Ltd., 973 F.Supp. 1320, 1335–36 (D.Utah 1997), the court, citing nine law review articles, concluded that "[w]hile there is little case law discussing veil piercing theories

---

5. J. William Callison & Maureen A. Sullivan, Limited Liability Companies: A State-by-State Guide to Law and Practice 30 (Supp. 1999).

6. Reprinted with permission from the American Bar Association.

7. [By the Editors] In C & J Builders & Remodelers, LLC v. Geisenheimer, 1998 WL 203400 (Conn.Super.Ct.1998) the court stated "the plaintiff C & J Builders and Remodelers,

LLC, and the signer of the contract Charles Pagano d/b/a C & J Builders and Remodelers, [are] 'practically identical' in relation to the defendant owners * * *. The defendant is prejudiced in no way by resolving this dispute through arbitration as anticipated in the construction contract, as opposed to litigation in court." Is that in effect a decision to pierce the veil of an LLC?

outside the corporate context, most commentators assume that the doctrine applies to limited liability companies." The court concluded however, that "[p]laintiffs have not produced evidence sufficient to permit a finding, as a matter of law, that the protective veil of DeLoney & Associates should be pierced to hold Richard DeLoney personally liable * * *."

An unpublished study dated April 17, 1999, by J. William Callison entitled "Limits of Limited Liability: Veil Piercing in the Limited Liability Company," prepared for the Spring Meeting of the Business Law Section of the American Bar Association lists ten cases, and concludes, "[I]t is likely that courts will apply corporate veil piercing principles to LLCs."[8] Id, at 6. He notes that in at least six states, LLC statutes specifically direct that corporate principles of piercing should be applied to LLCs, and that decisions in various other states indicate that the piercing doctrine will be applied to LLCs for essentially the same policy reasons as are applicable to corporations.[9]

(4) While the LLC provides limited liability for all investors, it does not involve "incorporation" in the traditional sense of that term as used in corporation statutes. Perhaps a closer analogy is to the limited liability of partners achieved by a public filing under the limited partnership statutes. Indeed, from a liability standpoint, an LLC may be conceptualized as a limited partnership in which there are no general partners and no liability for participation in management of the enterprise.

(5) "[I]n all but one state new corporation formations (without differentiation between C and S Corporations) outnumber[ed] new LLC formations—usually by a margin of 2:1 to 3:1 or greater for 1995–1998." John W. Lee, A Populist Perspective of the Business Entities Universe: "Hey The Stars May Lie But the Numbers Never Do," 78 Tex.L.Rev. 885, 887 (2000). Apparently, the tables turned after 1998 and by 2003, LLCs "comprised a majority of new business filings in 19 states and made up 41.84% of business filings nationwide." Howard M. Friedman, "The Silent LLC Revolution—The Social Cost of Academic Neglect," 3 Creighton L. Rev. 35, 36 (2004).

Assume that you are asked to form a manager-managed LLC that will have ten or more participants, some of whom are inactive investors and several of whom are active managers who will contribute to the enterprise. There is an obvious analogy to a closely-held corporation. To what extent should the LLC you form adopt corporate procedures? This type of question simply is not addressed by LLC statutes.

For example, as described in subsequent chapters, corporations have traditional mandatory internal procedures: decisions made by boards of directors and shareholders must be voted upon at meetings; notice of meetings must be given unless expressly waived; action is taken by resolution duly proposed at a meeting and adopted by a vote; minutes of meetings are prepared by the corporate secretary and placed in a minute book and retained

8. [By the Editors] For a more recent case that purports to apply corporate veil piercing principles to an LLC, see New England National LLC v. Kabro of East Lyme, 2000 WL 254590 (Conn.Super.Ct.2000).

9. *See also* Hollowell v. Orleans Regional Hospital LLC, 217 F.3d 379, 385, n. 7 (5th Cir.2000); Warren Johnson, Limited Liability Companies (LLC): Is the LLC Liability Shield Holding Up Under Judicial Scrutiny?, 35 New Eng. L. Rev., 177, 213 (2000).

permanently; and so forth. LLC statutes contain virtually none of these requirements. The corporate requirements, while often a nuisance, may have real benefits in some situations. For example, when a bank officer demands to see proof that a specific individual is authorized to sign a promissory note on behalf of a corporation, it is essential to have a record that establishes that authority. Presumably that would be a certified resolution or excerpt from minutes of a meeting at which that authority was granted by the board of directors. If these formalities are a good idea for corporations, should they also be adopted by multi-member LLCs? Attorneys are split on this issue, and many do not recommend formal corporate procedures for LLCs. After all, a major reason to use an LLC was to avoid such requirements. A significant minority, however, adopt corporate procedures for use in multiple-member LLCs on the theory that at some point specific proof of prior actions will be necessary, and that documented transactions and relationships reduce the likelihood that veil-piercing arguments may arise.

Corporations reflect equity ownership through the issuance of stock typically represented by certificates. Should LLCs do likewise? The Texas Limited Liability Company Act (Art. 1528n, § 4.05 B) states that an LLC "may provide that a member's membership interest may be evidenced by a certificate of membership interest issued by the limited liability company, may provide for the assignment or transfer of membership interests represented by a certificate, and may make other provisions with respect to the certificate." Some other states have a similar provision, and the use of certificates presumably is elective in other states. Would you recommend that ownership certificates be used in an LLC? Assume that a member wishes to make a gift of a portion of his membership interest to a child. Would a statement in some obscure record that "Mr. X assigned a ten percent interest in his membership interest to his daughter" stand up at some later date? If certificates of membership are used in an LLC, is there a risk that they may be considered "securities" subject to the antifraud provisions of Rule 10b–5 of the Securities Exchange Act of 1934? Rule 10b–5 is discussed in detail beginning at p. 813, infra; it broadly requires full disclosure in connection with purchases or sales of closely held or publicly traded securities and creates a federal cause of action for transactions that violate the Rule.

For that matter, might LLC membership interests be analogized to shares of corporate stock and Rule 10b–5 applied on that basis? For a negative (but preliminary) answer, see Great Lakes Chemical Corp. v. Monsanto Co., 96 F.Supp. 2d 376 (D.Del.2000). If Rule 10b–5 is not applicable to LLCs, might it encourage the use of this new business form rather than corporations for many ventures?

B. THE UNIFORM LIMITED LIABILITY COMPANY ACT

Provisions in LLC statutes are obviously drawn from both corporate and partnership statutes. ULLCA has had limited acceptance since its promulgation in part because it embodies more partnership concepts than most existing state LLC statutes. Examples include the following: An operating agreement may be oral. ULLCA § 103. Partnership concepts of "dissociation" and "dissolution" are applicable to LLCs. ULLCA §§ 601, 701, 801. Membership interests are patterned after interests in a partnership. For example, transferees are admitted as members only with the unanimous consent of the remaining members (though the operating agreement may make such interests more freely transferable). ULLCA § 503. The rights of a creditor of an LLC against a member involve a charging order. ULLCA § 504(a). LLCs may be manager-managed rather than member-managed, but an affirmative election to be manager-managed must be made in the articles of organization. ULLCA § 203(a)(6). In most states, the default rule is exactly the opposite: corporate-type management is the default rule. Voting in a member-managed LLC is on a per capita basis as in a general partnership. ULLCA § 404(a).

In some respects ULLCA follows the corporate model. An LLC is formed by filing "articles of organization" in a governmental office. ULLCA §§ 202, 203. The name of the LLC must contain words or abbreviations indicating that the entity is an LLC. ULLCA § 105(a). Provisions are made for reserved (ULLCA § 106) and registered (ULLCA § 107) names. The LLC must maintain a registered office and registered agent for service of process. ULLCA § 108. Restrictions on distributions are based on the corporate model. ULLCA § 406. A foreign LLC must obtain a certificate of authority to transact business in another state. ULLCA §§ 1002, 1004.

In other respects ULLCA departs significantly from the corporate model. ULLCA provides extreme flexibility with respect to internal organization and financing; there are relatively few mandatory statutory requirements, and internal relationships are largely governed by an "operating agreement"—a contract—rather than by statutory provisions. ULLCA § 103. Another difference is that in a corporation the articles of incorporation control over bylaws in case of a conflict; ULLCA provides that the operating agreement controls over the articles of organization in case of conflict. ULLCA § 203(c).

These comparisons and contrasts with corporations should not be over-emphasized. Many state corporation statutes permit small, closely-held corporations to elect partnership-type management within a corporate structure. See Chapter 9, section D. Some state LLC statutes also specifically provide corporate type remedies in areas in which ULLCA is silent. See for example, Md. Corp. & Assoc. Code § 4A–705. Also see Froelich v. Erickson, 96 F.Supp.2d 507, 527 (D.Md. 2000).

C. CONTRACTUAL ASPECTS OF LIMITED LIABILITY COMPANIES

THE SCOPE OF FIDUCIARY DUTIES IN AN LLC

Fiduciary duties require that the person who owes such duties, such as a majority or controlling investor, act in the best interest of the party to whom such duties are owed, such as a minority investor. The two most basic fiduciary duties are the duty of care and the duty of loyalty. The duty of care provides that parties must act in a non-negligent manner, which means that they must act on an informed basis. The duty of loyalty encompasses self-dealing, as well as any actions that place the fiduciary in a role that competes with the LLC. The duty of loyalty requires that transactions that pose conflicts of interest be structured and consummated so as to mitigate such conflicts and to protect the party to whom the fiduciary duties are owed.

In addition, it generally is acknowledged that the duties of care and loyalty also subsume other duties that are articulated in a variety of ways. These different articulations always include the duty to act in good faith and the duty of complete candor and disclosure, which require fiduciaries to disclose all information material to their relationship to the beneficiary, as well as all information that the minority investor would find relevant in making decisions about its investment, and all information necessary to make any other information disclosed not misleading.

Long-standing public policy forbids companies and individuals who owe fiduciary duties from taking any action that is in any way adverse or contrary to the interests of those to whom the fiduciary duties are owed. In their most elemental form, fiduciary duties require fiduciaries such as majority or controlling investors to refrain from engaging in transactions that would, if effectuated, make themselves better off at the expense of the minority investors or others to whom they owe fiduciary duties. It is even more clearly a breach of fiduciary duty to engage in a transaction that makes the majority investor better off while leaving the minority investor worse off.

As the history of LLCs shows, the LLC organizational form borrows attributes from both corporations and partnerships. Both partnerships and corporations feature fiduciary duties as part of their default rule structure. LLCs are no different. Indeed, it would be illogical to presume that combining two forms of business organization in which fiduciary duties play a large role could possibly result in the creation of a new form of business organization in which fiduciary duties are lacking or diminished.

Should fiduciary duties in an LLC be analogous to those of a general partnership, a limited partnership, or a corporation? Should an LLC have the power to define the scope of fiduciary duty in its operating agreement? Specific states have adopted various positions. California and Illinois provide that an LLC member or manager has fiduciary duties to the LLC similar to those of a partner in a partnership. Cal. Corp. Code § 17153 (Supp. 1998); Ill. Stat. Ch. 805 § 180/15–3. ULLCA adopts an approach that is similar to the duties owed by directors to a corporation, ULLCA § 409(a)-(d) (though a controversial exception may exist for members who are not managers of the LLC).

Delaware adopts the most liberal position, in effect allowing each LLC to elect the fiduciary regime it desires.[1] An amended version of the Delaware Limited Liability Company Act, 6 Del. Code Ann. §§ 18–1101, *et seq.*, became effective on August 1, 2004.[2] One significant change added the word "eliminate" to a list of ways LLC members and managers can alter fiduciary duties by contract. Section 18–1101(c) provides that in LLCs, "[t]o the extent that, at law or in equity, a member or manager or other person has duties (including fiduciary duties) to a limited liability company or to another member or manager or to another person that is a party to or is otherwise bound by a limited liability company agreement, the member's or manager's or other person's duties may be expanded or restricted or *eliminated* by

---

1. [By the Editors] For specific examples, see Sonet v. Timber Co., 722 A.2d 319, 320, 322 (Del. Ch. 1998); Elf Atochem North America, Inc. v. Jaffari and Malek L.L.C., infra.

2. This change occurred concurrently with the DRUPA amendment for Delaware limited partnerships. See Chapter 2 and 6 Del. Stat. Ann. § 17–1101(d).

provisions in the limited liability company agreement; provided, that the limited liability company agreement may not eliminate the implied contractual covenant of good faith and fair dealing." (emphasis added).

What's at stake if parties can replace fiduciary duties with contractual standards such as the duty of good faith and fair dealing? And how is the duty of good faith and fair dealing different from the duty of loyalty? Consider the following case.

BLACKMORE PARTNERS, L.P. v. LINK ENERGY LLC

Court of Chancery of Delaware, 2004.
864 A.2d 80.

LAMB, Vice Chancellor.

A former equity unit holder of a solvent limited liability company brings this purported class action suit against the company and directors for breach of fiduciary duty in connection with a transaction that rendered the equity units worthless. The complaint alleges that the directors breached their fiduciary duties by approving (as they were authorized to do without a vote of the unit holders) a sale of substantially all the company's assets in a transaction that resulted in the distribution to the company's creditors of 100% of available funds in an amount that exceeded the total amount of their claims. The plaintiff also alleges that the defendants violated their fiduciary duties by failing to consider alternative transactions that would have provided a better result for the company's equity holders.

The defendants have moved to dismiss the complaint for failure to state a claim upon which relief can be granted, in accordance with Rule 12(b)(6) of the Court of Chancery Rules. The question presented is whether a complaint that does not contain specific allegations that a majority of the directors were either interested in the transaction or lacked independence may nevertheless survive a motion to dismiss on the basis of a permissible inference that the actions of the directors amounted to a breach of the duty of loyalty. The court holds that the well-pleaded allegations of fact found in the complaint, if true, could support a reasonable inference of disloyal conduct. This is all that is required to survive a motion to dismiss.

I.

A. THE PARTIES

Link Energy LLC is a Delaware limited liability company formed in November of 2002, in anticipation of assuming and continuing the business of EOTT Energy Partners, L.P. upon its emergence from bankruptcy. Link, and EOTT Energy Partners before it, engaged in the purchasing, gathering, transporting, trading, storage and resale of crude oil and related activities.

In October of 2002, EOTT Energy Partners filed for Chapter 11 restructuring in the United States Bankruptcy Court for the Southern District of Texas. As part of the restructuring plan approved by the bankruptcy court, EOTT Energy Partners' publicly traded common units were cancelled and its former common unit holders received equity units in Link representing 3% of Link's newly issued equity units. Moreover, as part of the restructuring, EOTT Energy Partners cancelled $235 million of its outstanding 11% senior unsecured notes in exchange for which the holders received a pro rata share of $104 million in 9% senior unsecured notes issued by Link and a pro rata share of the Link equity units. The remaining equity units were distributed to other allowed unsecured creditors.

* * *

Plaintiff Blackmore Partners, L.P. is a Delaware investment partnership. Blackmore beneficially owned 16,239 Link equity units through March 16, 2004 and remains a unit holder.

B. THE SALE OF LINK'S ASSETS

At the time the company emerged from bankruptcy, its capital structure was highly leveraged. According to periodic statements made by Link, business forecasts were not being met and the company's high cost of capital was putting it at a competitive disadvantage. Therefore, Link's management and board announced that they were considering alternatives to continuing operation and engaged Lehman Brothers Inc. as an advisor. In March 2004, Link agreed to sell its assets and business to Plains All American Pipeline, L.P. for $290 million. Under the terms of the Link LLC operating agreement the board of directors had the power to effectuate that transaction without a vote of unit holders. Link has now sold substantially all of its assets, ceased all of its principal business, and is in the process of winding up.

On March 16, 2004, Link issued a press release regarding the late filing of its 10–K report, due on March 31, 2004. In its press release, Link disclosed that it was in negotiations to sell all of its operating assets, and that any proceeds would be used to pay its creditors. The press release reported that the proposed transaction required of Link's board of directors and the board of directors of the buyer and continued:

Based on current projections, the company's management believes that its unit holders would receive a minimal amount, if any, after payment of, or otherwise making provision for, all of its liabilities, obligations and contingencies, which are substantial. There can be no assurance, however, that there will be any funds to distribute to unit holders.

The day following the press release, Links units traded at $1 per unit, down from over $5 per unit. Before they were eventually stopped regular trading, the units traded at, or below, $0.20.

According to the amended complaint, after Link's March 16 announcement, certain unit holders who were not also 9% note holders, including a representative of the plaintiff, contacted Link to discuss an alternative transaction to avoid the asset sale. This so-called "Alternative Proposal," which is described only in the most conclusory terms, allegedly would have involved an infusion of equity into the company that would have allowed Link to remain independent, obviating the need to redeem the 9% notes. The amended complaint also alleges in a conclusory fashion that ChevronTexaco was "willing and eager" to take over some of Link's marketing activities, which were limited by Link's inability to obtain substantial letters of credit for such activities. This relationship with ChevronTexaco would allegedly have been extremely beneficial to Link, allowing it to increase its revenue while improving its balance sheet. After receiving the Alternative Proposal, Link's management communicated that Link would not do anything without first discussing a transaction with the plaintiff and other unit holders.

On March 31, 2004, without any further contact with the plaintiff or the other unit holders, Link made public in a press release its sale of assets to Plains. According to the press release, Link was to receive $290 million in consideration: $273 million in cash from Plains and the assumption of certain obligations, and $17 million in cash from Texas New Mexico Pipe Line Company, a wholly owned subsidiary of Shell Pipeline Company, in consideration for settling outstanding litigation with that company. From these proceeds, $265 million of the $290 million was to be used to repay debt, including the 9% notes. However, in addition to the value of the principal and the accrued interest, the 9% note holders also received their pro rata share of the $25 million remaining from the sale of Link's assets. This $25 million kicker was in return for the note holders waiving covenants in the notes that required any purchaser of the Link's assets to assume the notes. The March 31 press release stated: "The potential premium is in exchange for the senior note holders' waiver and modification of certain provisions of the notes, including the right to have Plains assume the notes, and approximates the premium on the notes reflected by the estimated market value if Plains had assumed the notes." The press release also restated the belief of Link's board, later confirmed, that the unit holders would receive no distributions under the sale.

The press release does not say that Link was on the verge of returning to insolvency, nor does it say that maintenance of the status quo was untenable. Instead, it states that "[t]his sale is in Link Energy's long-term best interest in order to protect the value of the assets, the needs of our customers, and the jobs of our employees." The press release does not address any concern for the interests of the common unit holders, the value of whose interest in Link was wiped out by the transaction.

* * *

In the amended complaint, Blackmore alleges that the board members violated their fiduciary duties owed to Link's equity holders by approving the sale of substantially all of Link's assets to Plains. The amended complaint raises two distinct, but related, claims. First, it alleges that Link's board favored the 9% note holders, to whom they did not owe a fiduciary duty, at the expense of the unit holders, to whom they did owe a fiduciary duty. Specifically, the amended complaint alleges that the board violated its fiduciary duty by approving the distribution of the $25 million excess consideration to the 9% note holders. As alleged in the amended complaint: "In approving the distribution, the [Director Defendants] deployed the LLC's power against its unit holders, failed to act with a rational basis and failed to act in good faith with regard to the unit holders. This distribution plan constitutes a breach of duty owed to plaintiff and the Class by defendants."[3] Second, the plaintiff alleges that the board failed to maximize unit holder value in a sale of control transaction and, therefore, violated its duty of loyalty under *Revlon*.

On August 18, 2004, the defendants renewed their 12(b)(6) motion to dismiss. They allege that the plaintiff has failed to state a claim upon which

---

3. [By the Court] Compl. ¶ 36.

relief can be granted. They argue that, since Link's LLC Operating Agreement contains an exculpatory clause based on 8 *Del. C.* 102(b)(7), claims for breach of the duty of care are barred.[4] Furthermore, the defendants argue that, to sustain a claim for breach of the duty of loyalty, the plaintiff bears the burden of pleading facts sufficient for this court to infer that the board's decision was motivated by self-interest, lack of independence or bad faith, and that the plaintiff has failed to meet that burden. Therefore, they argue, the plaintiff's action should be dismissed.

* * *

Once a board of directors determines to sell the corporation in a change of control transaction, its responsibility is to endeavor to secure the highest value reasonably attainable for the stockholders.[5] This obligation is a contextually-specific application of the directors' duty to act in accordance with their fiduciary obligations, and there is no single blueprint that a board must follow to fulfill its duties. Rather, the board's actions must be evaluated in light of the relevant circumstances to determine whether they were undertaken with due diligence and in good faith. If no breach of duty is found, the board's actions are entitled to the protections of the business judgment rule.

As Vice Chancellor Strine pointed out in *McMillan v. Intercargo Corp.,* the presence of the exculpatory clause in the LLC Agreement:

... has an important, but confined, influence on the court's analysis of this motion. Because the plaintiff[ ] may not recover damages for a breach of the duty of care by the defendant directors, the court's focus is necessarily upon whether the complaint alleges facts that, if true, would buttress a conclusion that the defendant directors breached their duty of loyalty or otherwise engaged in conduct not immunized by the exculpatory charter provision.

Thus, to survive the motion to dismiss, the complaint must allege particularized facts that support an inference of disloyalty or a lack of good faith.

* * *

The complaint alleges, and for purposes of this motion the court assumes as true, that the Director Defendants approved a transaction that disadvantaged the holders of Link's equity units. Until the announcement of the transaction, the units had significant, if not substantial, trading value. Indeed, there is a basis in the complaint to infer that the value of Link's assets exceeded its liabilities by least $25 million. Moreover, the facts alleged support an inference that Link was neither insolvent nor on the verge of re-entering bankruptcy. Yet, as a result of the transaction at issue, those units were rendered valueless.

In the circumstances, the allegation that the Defendant Directors approved a sale of substantially all of Link's assets and a resultant distribution of proceeds that went exclusively to the company's creditors raises a reason-

4. [By the Court] This provision is authorized by 6 *Del. C.* § 18–1101(c)(2), which provides that a manager's "duties and liabilities may be expanded or restricted by provisions in the limited liability company agreement."

5. [By the Court] *McMillan,* 768 A.2d at 502 (citing *Revlon, Inc. v. MacAndrews & Forbes Holdings, Inc.,* 506 A.2d 173, 182 (Del. 1986)).

able inference of disloyalty or intentional misconduct. Of course, it is also possible to infer (and the record at a later stage may well show) that the Director Defendants made a good faith judgment, after reasonable investigation, that there was no future for the business and no better alternative for the unit holders. Nevertheless, based only the facts alleged and the reasonable inferences that the court must draw from them, it would appear that no transaction could have been worse for the unit holders and reasonable to infer, as the plaintiff argues, that a properly motivated board of directors would not have agreed to a proposal that wiped out the value of the common equity and surrendered all of that value to the company's creditors.

In an analogous case, Chancellor Allen recognized "[t]he broad principle that if directors take action directed against a class of securities they should be required to justify" their action.[6] Thus, while on a more complete record, it may appear that the Director Defendants took no such action or were justified in acting as they did, this court cannot now conclude that the complaint does not state a claim for breach of the duty of loyalty or other misconduct not protected by the exculpatory provision in Link's operating agreement. For this reason, the Rule 12(b)(6) motion to dismiss must be denied.

For the foregoing reasons, the defendants' motion to dismiss pursuant to Rule 12(b)(6) is DENIED. IT IS SO ORDERED.

Notes

1. In this case, the Link board chose to benefit the noteholders (to whom they did not owe a fiduciary duty) at the expense of the unitholder (to whom they did owe a fiduciary duty). Should the court find that this is a violation of the duty of loyalty? Can you think of a reasonable business decision to favor the noteholders?

2. Why might a board essentially transfer all of the value of the LLC's units to the LLC's creditors? The later decision provides a possible answer. In Blackmore Partners, L.P. v. Link Energy, L.L.C., 2005 WL 2709639 (Del. Ch. 2005), the court declared that once the LLC slipped into the "zone of insolvency," the main duty of the directors shifted from the owners to the creditors. Therefore, the court held that the board members were not liable to the unitholders and that they did not breach any of their duties. Does this make sense? Even if Link was insolvent, do the directors have a duty to the owners over the creditors? Should they?

ELF ATOCHEM NORTH AMERICA, INC. v. JAFFARI AND MALEK LLC

Supreme Court of Delaware, 1999.
727 A.2d 286.

Before VEASEY, CHIEF JUSTICE, WALSH and BERGER, JUSTICES.

VEASEY, CHIEF JUSTICE: This is a case of first impression before this Court involving the Delaware Limited Liability Company Act (the "Act"). The limited liability company ("LLC") is a relatively new entity that has emerged in recent years as an attractive vehicle to facilitate business relationships and transactions. The wording and architecture of the Act is somewhat complicat-

---

6. [By the Court] *Orban v. Field,* 1993 WL 547187, at *9 (Del.Ch. Dec. 30, 1993).

ed, but it is designed to achieve what is seemingly a simple concept—to permit persons or entities ("members") to join together in an environment of private ordering to form and operate the enterprise under an LLC agreement with tax benefits akin to a partnership and limited liability akin to the corporate form.

This is a purported derivative suit brought on behalf of a Delaware LLC calling into question whether: (1) the LLC, which did not itself execute the LLC agreement in this case ("the Agreement") defining its governance and operation, is nevertheless bound by the Agreement; and (2) contractual provisions directing that all disputes be resolved exclusively by arbitration or court proceedings in California are valid under the Act. Resolution of these issues requires us to examine the applicability and scope of certain provisions of the Act in light of the Agreement. We hold that: (1) the Agreement is binding on the LLC as well as the members; and (2) since the Act does not prohibit the members of an LLC from vesting exclusive subject matter jurisdiction in arbitration proceedings (or court enforcement of arbitration) in California to resolve disputes, the contractual forum selection provisions must govern. Accordingly, we affirm the judgment of the Court of Chancery. * * *

FACTS

Plaintiff below-appellant Elf Atochem North America, Inc., a Pennsylvania Corporation ("Elf"), manufactures and distributes solvent-based maskants to the aerospace and aviation industries throughout the world. Defendant below—appellee Cyrus A. Jaffari is the president of Malek, Inc., a California Corporation. Jaffari had developed an innovative, environmentally-friendly alternative to the solvent-based maskants that presently dominate the market. For decades, the aerospace and aviation industries have used solvent-based maskants in the chemical milling process.[11] Recently, however, the Environmental Protection Agency ("EPA") classified solvent-based maskants as hazardous chemicals and air contaminants. To avoid conflict with EPA regulations, Elf considered developing or distributing a maskant less harmful to the environment. In the mid-nineties, Elf approached Jaffari and proposed investing in his product and assisting in its marketing. Jaffari found the proposal attractive since his company, Malek, Inc., possessed limited resources and little international sales expertise. Elf and Jaffari agreed to undertake a joint venture that was to be carried out using a limited liability company as the vehicle.

On October 29, 1996, Malek, Inc. caused to be filed a Certificate of Formation with the Delaware Secretary of State, thus forming Malek LLC, a Delaware limited liability company under the Act. The certificate of formation is a relatively brief and formal document that is the first statutory step in creating the LLC as a separate legal entity. The certificate does not contain a comprehensive agreement among the parties, and the statute contemplates that the certificate of formation is to be complemented by the terms of the Agreement.[12] Next, Elf, Jaffari and Malek, Inc. entered into a series of

---

11. [By the Court] Manufactures of airplanes and missiles use maskants in the process of chemical milling in order to reduce the weight of their products. Chemical milling is a process where a caustic substance is placed on metal parts in order to dissolve the metal with which it comes into contact. Maskants are used to protect those areas of metal intended to be preserved.

12. [By the Court] See 6 Del.C. § 18–201(d), which provides: "A limited liability company agreement may be entered into either

agreements providing for the governance and operation of the joint venture. Of particular importance to this litigation, Elf, Malek, Inc., and Jaffari entered into the Agreement, a comprehensive and integrated document of 38 single-spaced pages setting forth detailed provisions for the governance of Malek LLC, which is not itself a signatory to the Agreement.

The Agreement is the operative document for purposes of this Opinion * * *. Under the Agreement, Elf contributed $1 million in exchange for a 30 percent interest in Malek LLC. Malek, Inc. contributed its rights to the water-based maskant in exchange for a 70 percent interest in Malek LLC.

The Agreement contains an arbitration clause covering all disputes. The clause, Section 13.8, provides that "any controversy or dispute arising out of this Agreement, the interpretation of any of the provisions hereof, or the action or inaction of any Member or Manager hereunder shall be submitted to arbitration in San Francisco, California * * *." Section 13.8 further provides: "No action * * * based upon any claim arising out of or related to this Agreement shall be instituted in any court by any Member except (a) an action to compel arbitration * * * or (b) an action to enforce an award obtained in an arbitration proceeding. * * * " The Agreement also contains a forum selection clause, Section 13.7, providing that all members consent to: "exclusive jurisdiction of the state and federal courts sitting in California in any action on a claim arising out of, under or in connection with this Agreement or the transactions contemplated by this Agreement, provided such claim is not required to be arbitrated pursuant to Section 13.8"; and personal jurisdiction in California. The Distribution Agreement contains no forum selection or arbitration clause.

ELF'S SUIT IN THE COURT OF CHANCERY

On April 27, 1998, Elf sued Jaffari and Malek LLC, individually and derivatively on behalf of Malek LLC, in the Delaware Court of Chancery, seeking equitable remedies. Among other claims, Elf alleged that Jaffari breached his fiduciary duty to Malek LLC, pushed Malek LLC to the brink of insolvency by withdrawing funds for personal use, interfered with business opportunities, failed to make disclosures to Elf, and threatened to make poor quality maskant and to violate environmental regulations. Elf also alleged breach of contract, tortious interference with prospective business relations, and (solely as to Jaffari) fraud. The Court of Chancery granted defendants' motion to dismiss based on lack of subject matter jurisdiction. The court held that Elf's claims arose under the Agreement or the transactions contemplated by the agreement, and were directly related to Jaffari's actions as manager of Malek LLC. Therefore, the court found that the Agreement governed the question of jurisdiction and that only a court of law or arbitrator in California is empowered to decide these claims. Elf now appeals the order of the Court of Chancery dismissing the complaint.

CONTENTIONS OF THE PARTIES

Elf claims that the Court of Chancery erred in holding that the arbitration and forum selection clauses in the Agreement governed, and thus

before, after or at the time of the filing of a certificate of formation and, whether entered into before, after or at the time of such filing, may be made effective as of the formation of the limited liability company or at such other time or date as provided in the limited liability company agreement."

deprived that court of jurisdiction to adjudicate all of Elf's claims, including its derivative claims made on behalf of Malek LLC. Elf contends that, since Malek LLC is not a party to the Agreement, it is not bound by the forum selection provisions. Elf also argues that the court erred in failing to classify its claim as derivative on behalf of Malek LLC against Jaffari as manager. Therefore, Elf claims that the Court of Chancery should have adjudicated the dispute. Finally, Elf argues that the dispute resolution clauses of the Agreement are invalid under Section 109(d) of the Act, which, it alleges, prohibits the parties from vesting exclusive jurisdiction in a forum outside of Delaware.[13] * * *

GENERAL SUMMARY OF BACKGROUND OF THE ACT

The phenomenon of business arrangements using "alternative entities" has been developing rapidly over the past several years. Long gone are the days when business planners were confined to corporate or partnership structures.* * *

The Delaware [Limited Liability Company] Act was adopted in October 1992. * * * To date, the Act has been amended six times with a view to modernization. The LLC is an attractive form of business entity because it combines corporate-type limited liability with partnership-type flexibility and tax advantages. The Act can be characterized as a "flexible statute" because it generally permits members to engage in private ordering with substantial freedom of contract to govern their relationship, provided they do not contravene any mandatory provisions of the Act. Indeed, the LLC has been characterized as the "best of both worlds."

The Delaware Act has been modeled on the popular Delaware LP Act. In fact, its architecture and much of its wording is almost identical to that of the Delaware LP Act. Under the Act, a member of an LLC is treated much like a limited partner under the LP Act. The policy of freedom of contract underlies both the Act and the LP Act.[14]

In August 1994, nearly two years after the enactment of the Delaware LLC Act, the Uniform Law Commissioners promulgated the Uniform Limited Liability Company Act (ULLCA).[15] To coordinate with later developments in federal tax guidelines regarding manager-managed LLCs, the Commissioners adopted minor changes in 1995. The Commissioners further amended the ULLCA in 1996. Despite its purpose to promote uniformity and consistency,

13. [By the Court] See 6 Del.C. § 18–109(d), which provides: "In a written limited liability company agreement or other writing, a manager or member may consent to be subject to the nonexclusive jurisdiction of the courts of, or arbitration in, a specified jurisdiction, or the exclusive jurisdiction of the courts of the State of Delaware, or the exclusivity of arbitration in a specified jurisdiction or the State of Delaware * * *."

14. [By the Court] * * * [C]ompare 6 Del.C. § 18–1101(b) ("It is the policy of * * * [the LLC Act] to give the maximum effect to the principle of freedom of contract and to the enforceability of limited liability company agreements") with 6 Del.C. § 17–1101(c) ("It

is the policy of * * * [the LP Act] to give maximum effect to the principle of freedom of contract and to the enforceability of partnership agreements.")

15. [By the Court] Jennifer J. Johnson, Limited Liability for Lawyers: General Partners Need Not Apply, 51 Bus.Law. 85, n. 69 (1995). In addition to the ULLCA, a Prototype Limited Liability Company Act ("Prototype Act") was drafted by the Subcommittee on Limited Liability Companies of the ABA Section of Business Law. The Prototype Act was released in the Fall of 1993 and has formed the basis for several LLC statutes enacted since that time. * * *

the ULLCA has not been widely popular. In fact, only seven jurisdictions have adopted the ULLCA since its creation in 1994. A notable commentator on LLCs has argued that legislatures should look to either the Delaware Act or the Prototype Act created by the ABA when drafting state statutes.[16]

POLICY OF THE DELAWARE ACT

The basic approach of the Delaware Act is to provide members with broad discretion in drafting the Agreement and to furnish default provisions when the members' agreement is silent.[17] The Act is replete with fundamental provisions made subject to modification in the Agreement (e.g. "unless otherwise provided in a limited liability company agreement* * *.").[18]

Although business planners may find comfort in working with the Act in structuring transactions and relationships, it is a somewhat awkward document for this Court to construe and apply in this case. To understand the overall structure and thrust of the Act, one must wade through provisions that are prolix, sometimes oddly organized, and do not always flow evenly. Be that as it may as a problem in mastering the Act as a whole, one returns to the narrow and discrete issues presented in this case.

FREEDOM OF CONTRACT

Section 18–1101(b) of the Act, like the essentially identical Section 17–1101(c) of the LP Act, provides that "[i]t is the policy of [the Act] to give the maximum effect to the principle of freedom of contract and to the enforceability of limited liability company agreements." Accordingly, the following observation relating to limited partnerships applies as well to limited liability companies:

> The Act's basic approach is to permit partners to have the broadest possible discretion in drafting their partnership agreements and to furnish answers only in situations where the partners have not expressly made provisions in their partnership agreement. Truly, the partnership agreement is the cornerstone of a Delaware limited partnership, and effectively constitutes the entire agreement among the partners with respect to the admission of partners to, and the creation, operation and termination of, the limited partnership. Once partners exercise their contractual freedom in their partnership agreement, the partners have a great deal of certainty that their partnership agreement will be enforced in accordance with its terms.[19]

16. [By the Court] See Larry E. Ribstein, A Critique of the Uniform Limited Liability Company Act, 25 Stetson L.Rev. 311, 329 (1995).

17. [By the Court] According to Lubaroff & Altman [Delaware Limited Liability Companies, in Delaware Law of Corporations & Business Organizations, § 20.1 (R. Franklin Balli & Jess A. Finkelstein ed., 1998)], "the Act gives members virtually unfettered discretion to define contractually their business understanding, and then provides assurance that their understanding will be enforced in accordance with the terms of their limited liability company agreement."

18. [By the Court] * * * For example, members are free to contract among themselves concerning management of the LLC, including who is to manage the LLC, the establishment of classes of members, voting procedures for holding meetings of members, or considering matters without a meeting. See Lubaroff & Altman, supra * * * at § 20.4.

19. [By the Court] Martin I. Lubaroff & Paul Altman, Delaware Limited Partnerships § 1.2 (1999) (footnote omitted). In their article on Delaware limited liability companies, Lubaroff and Altman use virtually identical language in describing the basic approach of the LLC Act. Clearly, both the LP Act and the LLC

In general, the commentators observe that only where the agreement is inconsistent with mandatory statutory provisions will the members' agreement be invalidated. Such statutory provisions are likely to be those intended to protect third parties, not necessarily the contracting members. As a framework for decision, we apply that principle to the issues before us, without expressing any views more broadly. * * *

MALEK LLC's FAILURE TO SIGN THE AGREEMENT DOES NOT AFFECT THE MEMBERS' AGREEMENT GOVERNING DISPUTE RESOLUTION

Elf argues that because Malek LLC, on whose behalf Elf allegedly brings these claims, is not a party to the Agreement, the derivative claims it brought on behalf of Malek LLC are not governed by the arbitration and forum selection clauses of the Agreement. Elf argues that Malek LLC came into existence on October 29, 1996, when the parties filed its Certificate of Formation with the Delaware Secretary of State. The parties did not sign the Agreement until November 4, 1996. Elf contends that Malek LLC existed as an LLC as of October 29, 1996, but never agreed to the Agreement because it did not sign it. Because Malek LLC never expressly assented to the arbitration and forum selection clauses within the Agreement, Elf argues it can sue derivatively on behalf of Malek LLC * * *. We are not persuaded by this argument. Section 18–101(7) defines the limited liability company agreement as "any agreement, written or oral, of the member or members as to the affairs of a limited liability company and the conduct of its business." Here, Malek, Inc. and Elf, the members of Malek LLC, executed the Agreement to carry out the affairs and business of Malek LLC and to provide for arbitration and forum selection. Notwithstanding Malek LLC's failure to sign the Agreement, Elf's claims are subject to the arbitration and forum selection clauses of the Agreement. The Act is a statute designed to permit members maximum flexibility in entering into an agreement to govern their relationship. It is the members who are the real parties in interest. The LLC is simply their joint business vehicle. This is the contemplation of the statute in prescribing the outlines of a limited liability company agreement. * * *

[We] find no reason why the members cannot alter the default jurisdictional provisions of the statute and contract away their right to file suit in Delaware. For example, Elf argues that Section 18–110(a), which grants the Court of Chancery jurisdiction to hear claims involving the election or removal of a manager of an LLC, applies to the case at bar because Elf is seeking removal of Jaffari. While Elf is correct on the substance of Section 18–110(a), Elf is unable to convince this Court that the parties may not contract to avoid the applicability of Section 18–110(a). We hold that, because the policy of the Act is to give the maximum effect to the principle of freedom of contract and to the enforceability of LLC agreements, the parties may contract to avoid the applicability of [6 Del. C.]. * * * Here, the parties contracted as clearly as practicable when they relegated to California in Section 13.7 [of the Agreement] "any" dispute "arising out of, under or in connection with [the] Agreement or the transactions contemplated by [the] Agreement * * *." Likewise, in Section 13.8: "[n]o action at law or in equity

Act are uniform in their commitment to "max-   * * * at § 20.4.
imum flexibility." See Lubaroff & Altman,

based upon any claim arising out of or related to" the Agreement may be brought, except in California, and then only to enforce arbitration in California. * * *

We affirm the judgment of the Court of Chancery dismissing Elf Atochem's amended complaint for lack of subject matter jurisdiction.

Notes

(1) Consider ULLCA § 103. Would the freedom of contract approach taken by the Delaware Court permit an operating agreement to change the "nonwaivable provisions" of this section? This section appears to contemplate an either/or election between these two alternative management structures. In the real world, LLC members may prefer a form of management that contains elements of both alternatives. The "freedom of contract" approach taken by the Delaware court clearly would permit such mixed-control devices. It is perhaps less clear under ULLCA. Might the last sentence of ULLCA § 103(a) authorize such an arrangement?

(2) At least one other court has taken a different view of the enforceability of Operating Agreements against the LLC itself. In Bubbles & Bleach, LLC v. Becker, 1997 WL 285938 (N.D.Ill.1997), the court held that the failure of Bubbles & Bleach, LLC (B & B), a Wisconsin LLC, to sign a contract containing an arbitration clause and a choice-of-forum clause rendered those clauses unenforceable, because the LLC was not a party to them.

(3) In addition to differences of opinion about the nature of LLC Operating Agreements, the courts in B & B and Elf Atochem also differed in their views about the fundamental nature of the LLC, with the Delaware court viewing it as an aggregate-type of entity like a partnership, and the District Court for the Northern District of Illinois viewing the LLC as an entity, like a corporation. See, Note, "Freedom of" or "Freedom From"? The Enforceability of Contracts and the Integrity of the LLC, 50 Duke L.J. 1087, 1090 (2001).

D.　CHARACTERISTICS OF AN LLC

ABRY PARTNERS V, L.P. v. F & W ACQUISITION LLC

Court of Chancery of Delaware, 2006.
891 A.2d 1032.

STRINE, Vice Chancellor.

This case involves a request by the buy-side of a corporate acquisition contract (the Stock Purchase Agreement) to rescind that contract. The plaintiffs, a group of entities affiliated with a sophisticated private equity firm named ABRY Partners ("Buyer"), bought a portfolio company from an entity owned by another sophisticated private equity firm, Providence Equity Partners ("Seller"). The portfolio company that was purchased by the Buyer, F & W Publications ("Company"), was in the business of publishing magazines and selling books.

As in many acquisition agreements involving private equity firms, the Stock Purchase Agreement carefully delineated the representations and warranties that were being made by the portfolio Company that was being sold and by the owner of that Company. By its plain and unambiguous terms, the Stock Purchase Agreement stated the Buyer's promise that it was not relying upon representations and warranties not contained within the Agreement's four corners and that no such extra-contractual representations had been made.

More critically for purposes of this case, the Stock Purchase Agreement went further. By its terms, it purports to limit the liability of the Seller for any misrepresentation of fact contained within the Agreement to exposure for a claim for damages in arbitration (an "Indemnity Claim") not to exceed the amount of a contractually-established Indemnity Fund. That fund is set at $20 million, or 4% of the $500 million purchase price paid by the Buyer for the portfolio company. By its terms, the Stock Purchase Agreement makes an Indemnity Claim the exclusive remedy of the Buyer for misrepresentation and bars a rescission claim of the nature the Buyer has pled in this court.

The Seller has moved to dismiss this case for failure to state a claim. It asserts that the contractual limitation on liability should be enforced and that the Buyer should be limited to the remedy of an Indemnity Claim for no more than $20 million. Given the sophisticated nature of the parties, and the express stipulation that the exclusive remedy provision of the Agreement was specifically bargained for and was reflected in setting the deal price, the Seller argues that there is no principled basis for the Buyer to escape its voluntarily-accepted limitation on its remedial options.

Although the Buyer makes many counter-arguments that I reject, its most forceful and convincing response is that the contractual limitation on liability is unenforceable as a matter of public policy. Recognizing that the case law of this court gives effect to non-reliance provisions that disclaim reliance on extra-contractual representations, the Buyer has premised its rescission claim solely on the falsity of representations and warranties contained within the Stock Purchase Agreement itself. In other words, the Buyer has accepted that it had promised that the only representations of fact it was relying upon and the only representations of fact made to it were contained within the Agreement itself, and that this court's jurisprudence will hold it to that promise.

But the Buyer claims that this State's public policy will not go further and tolerate an attempt by a contracting party to immunize itself from a rescission claim premised on false representations of fact contained within a written contract and recognized by the parties to be the factual predicate for their decision to contract. To do so would be to sanction unethical business practices of an abhorrent kind and to create an unwise incentive system for contracting parties that would undermine the overall reliability of promises made in contracts.

For reasons I explain, I conclude that Delaware law permits sophisticated commercial parties to craft contracts that insulate a seller from a rescission claim for a contractual false statement of fact that was not intentionally made. In other words, parties may allocate the risk of factual error freely as to any error where the speaking party did not consciously convey an untruth. In that context, there is no moral imperative to impinge on the ability of rational parties dealing at arms-length to shape their own arrangements, and courts are ill-suited to set a uniform rule that is more efficient than the specific outcomes negotiated by particular contracting parties to deal with the myriad situations they face.

But the contractual freedom to immunize a seller from liability for a false contractual statement of fact ends there. The public policy against fraud is a strong and venerable one that is largely founded on the societal consensus that lying is wrong. Not only that, it is difficult to identify an economically-sound rationale for permitting a seller to deny the remedy of rescission to a buyer when the seller is proven to have induced the contract's formation or closing by lying about a contractually-represented fact.

For these reasons, when a seller intentionally misrepresents a fact embodied in a contract—that is, when a seller lies—public policy will not permit a contractual provision to limit the remedy of the buyer to a capped damage claim. Rather, the buyer is free to press a claim for rescission or for full compensatory damages. By this balance, I attempt to give fair and efficient recognition to the competing public policies served by contractual freedom and by the law of fraud.

* * *

According to the complaint, the Buyer expressed to the Seller and CSFB [Credit Suisse First Boston] that its offer would be based largely on the Company's free cash flow, as measured by its earnings before interest, taxes, depreciation, and amortization ("EBITDA"). Specifically, the Buyer alleged that it would be willing to pay ten times EBITDA for the twelve months ending June 30, 2005, which would result in a price of approximately $480 million. According to the Buyer, the Seller, through Dominguez, suggested to Company management a desire to show the Buyer that the Company would generate EBITDA of approximately $51 million in that period, which would justify a purchase price of $510 million. The negotiations resulted in the Buyer agreeing to purchase all the stock of the Company for $500 million through the Stock Purchase Agreement. That Agreement was inked on June 11, 2005. The contemplated sale of stock closed on August 5, 2005.

C. AFTER CLOSING THE SALE, THE BUYER DISCOVERS THAT THE COMPANY'S FINANCIAL STATEMENTS WERE INACCURATE

Once the Buyer assumed ownership of the Company, it began to uncover a host of serious financial and operational problems. So serious were these problems that the Buyer came to the conclusion that it had been defrauded by the Seller and the Company in connection with the Stock Purchase Agreement.

Specifically, the Buyer alleges that it has become apparent that the Seller and Company management, working in concert, schemed together to manipulate the Company's financial statements in order to fraudulently induce the Buyer into purchasing the Company at an excessive price. Thus, the Buyer claims that the Company's December 2004, March 2005, and June 2005 financial statements contained material misrepresentations and did not accurately portray the Company's financial condition.

With respect to the December 2004 financial statements, the Buyer alleges that the Company manipulated its earnings by overstating magazine revenues through a scheme known as "backstarting," which involves inflating revenues by providing new magazine subscribers with back issues of a magazine when they receive their first issue under the subscription. This allows a publisher to report income earlier by using up more of a subscription in the first month. The Buyer also argues that the Company misstated its performance by using outdated estimates rather than actual numbers to reflect newsstand revenue, failing to account for book returns correctly, and establishing inadequate reserves for obsolete inventory and uncollectible accounts receivable. The Buyer contends that this resulted in overstated net revenues, which in turn inflated the Company's EBITDA.

The Buyer argues that the March 2005 financial statements continued the same transgressions that occurred in the December 2004 statements and then exacerbated them with other shenanigans. To wit, the Buyer claims that the Company did not merely inaccurately account for book returns, but that it fraudulently and intentionally reduced the Company's book return reserves by $500,000 in order to increase reported earnings.[1] Similarly, the Buyer also accuses the Company of "channel stuffing" in order to inflate the quarterly revenues reflected in the March 2005 statements. Channel stuffing, in this context, involved the Company offering higher-than-normal discounts to book retailers and discounts to more customers than normal, which artificially inflated revenues. Allegedly, this practice leads to more returns than normal because book retailers cannot sell the entire inventory and therefore return the unsold books to the Company, and the Buyer contends that the Company failed adequately to account for the expected increase in returns.

The Buyer avers that the manipulation of the Company's financial statements became even more blatant and pervasive in the June 2005 financial statements. The Buyer argues that the June 2005 financial statements are particularly important because they were received from the Company less than a week before the August 5 closing. Therefore, the Buyer alleges, the Company and the Seller had an incentive to make them look good to ensure that the Buyer would close the deal.

The June 2005 financial statements are allegedly tainted with the same improprieties as the December 2004 and March 2005 financial statements. But the Company is alleged to have engaged in additional chicanery in order to show good end-of-quarter results. To that end, the Company: (1) extended, by a week, the quarterly reporting period of a subsidiary in the United Kingdom in order to increase the revenues and earnings depicted in the June 2005 financial statements; (2) shipped magazines in June that were scheduled to arrive in July in order to recognize revenues from those magazines in June rather than July; (3) manipulated its book club by moving a book club cycle from the second half of 2005 into June to inflate revenues; and (4) reported revenues related to a conference held in June 2005 but delayed reporting expenses from that same conference. That is, the Company allegedly made the quarter ending in June 2005 look artificially better by shorting later financial periods.

* * *

1. [By the Court] In April, the Company partially corrected this by reversing $200,000 of the entry.

The Buyer contends that the various misrepresentations and non-disclosures resulted in it purchasing the Company for a grossly overstated value. Specifically, the Buyer alleges that the true value of the Company was more like $400 million than $500 million and that it would never have closed had it known that the Company was propping up its performance with unethical business and accounting practices.

When it learned of these improprieties, the Buyer asked the Seller to rescind the transaction and to take back ownership of the Company. The Seller refused and this suit ensued.

* * *

The first specific provision of the Stock Purchase Agreement requiring recitation is § 7.8, which states:

Acquiror acknowledges and agrees that neither the Company nor the Selling Stockholder has made any representation or warranty, expressed or implied, as to the Company or any Company Subsidiary or as to the accuracy or completeness of any information regarding the Company or any Company Subsidiary furnished or made available to Acquiror and its representatives, except as expressly set forth in this Agreement . . . and neither the Company nor the Selling Stockholder shall have or be subject to any liability to Acquiror or any other Person resulting from the distribution to Acquiror, or Acquiror's use of or reliance on, any such information or any information, documents or material made available to Acquiror in any "data rooms," "virtual data rooms," management presentations or in any other form in expectation of, or in connection with, the transactions contemplated hereby.

This is a critical provision. It operates to define what information the Buyer relied upon in deciding to execute the Agreement. By its plain terms, the Buyer promised that neither the Company nor the Seller had made any representation or warranty as to the accuracy of any information about the Company except as set forth in the Agreement itself. The Buyer further promised that neither the Seller nor the Company would have any liability to the Buyer or any other person for any extra-contractual information made available to the Buyer in connection with the contemplated sale of the Company. Because of this provision, the Buyer was careful to amend its complaint and to premise its claims solely upon alleged misrepresentations of facts that are represented and warranted in the Stock Purchase Agreement itself.

* * *

Likewise, § 7.10 of the Agreement contained a provision requiring the Company to provide unaudited, month-end financial statements for the period between signing and closing, and requiring the Company to represent that those financial statements were "true and correct in all material respects, were prepared in accordance with GAAP . . . and present fairly in all material respects the financial position of the Company and the Company Subsidiaries on a consolidated basis." Likewise, in § 6.2(j) of the Agreement, the Company covenanted that it would not change its accounting methods in effect as of

December 31, 2004 unless mandated by law or a change in GAAP. Those covenants bound only the Company, not the Seller.

* * *

But the plain terms and structure of the Agreement make it clear that the Seller was not making the much more extensive representations made by the Company in the much longer part of the Agreement setting forth the Company's representations and warranties, which is Article III. Article III contains twenty-two general representations and warranties, many of which had extensive subparts. These representations and warranties were made only by the Company. Article III, in § 3.23, also reinforces the promise of the Buyer that it was not relying on extra-contractual representations by stating:

EXCEPT AS EXPRESSLY SET FORTH IN THIS *ARTICLE III,* THE COMPANY MAKES NO REPRESENTATION OR WARRANTY, EXPRESSED OR IMPLIED, AT LAW OR IN EQUITY IN RESPECT OF THE COMPANY OR THE COMPANY SUBSIDIARIES, OR ANY OF THEIR RESPECTIVE ASSETS, LIABILITIES OR OPERATIONS, INCLUDING WITH RESPECT TO MERCHANTABILITY OR FITNESS FOR ANY PARTICULAR PURPOSE, AND ANY SUCH OTHER REPRESENTATIONS OR WARRANTIES ARE HEREBY EXPRESSLY DISCLAIMED. ACQUIROR HEREBY ACKNOWLEDGES AND AGREES THAT, EXCEPT TO THE EXTENT SPECIFICALLY SET FORTH IN THIS *ARTICLE III,* THE ACQUIROR IS ACQUIRING THE COMPANY ON AN "AS IS, WHERE IS" BASIS. THE DISCLOSURE OF ANY MATTER OR ITEM IN ANY SCHEDULE HERETO SHALL NOT BE DEEMED TO CONSTITUTE AN ACKNOWLEDGEMENT THAT ANY SUCH MATTER IS REQUIRED TO BE DISCLOSED.

If this was all the Stock Purchase Agreement said, the contract's plain terms would most logically be read to preclude any suit by the Buyer against the Seller for all representations and warranties made by the Company. Why? Because (i) the Buyer promised that it was only relying on representations and warranties expressly set forth in the Agreement and expressly disclaimed reliance on any other extra-contractual information; and (ii) the Agreement plainly indicates that the representations and warranties of the Company are those of the Company alone, and not those of the Seller.

For the obvious reason that it would own the Company after closing, the Buyer naturally wanted the Seller to back up the Company's representations and warranties. The Buyer accomplished that objective to a precisely negotiated extent. For starters, as a closing condition, the Seller was required by § 8.2(h)(i) of the Stock Purchase Agreement to provide an Officer's Certificate stating that the closing conditions relating to the accuracy of not only the Seller's, but the Company's, representations and warranties were satisfied, that the Company and Seller had complied with the covenants applicable to them, and also that the Company had not suffered events that had or would reasonably be expected to constitute an MAE [Material Adverse Effect]. In compliance with that requirement, the Seller, through Dominguez, provided the Officer's Certificate, which stated:

Pursuant to Section 8.2(h)(i) of the Agreement, the undersigned duly elected and authorized officer of the Selling Stockholder, hereby certifies that

... (1) Each representation and warranty of the Company set forth in Article III and the Selling Stockholder set forth in Article IV of the Agreement or in each case deemed made pursuant to Section 7.10(a) is true and correct as of the Closing Date ... (2) Each of the Selling Stockholder and the Company have performed and complied in all material respects with the agreements and covenants required to be performed or complied with by it on or prior to the Closing Date ... (3) Since the date of the Agreement, there has been no change, event or condition of any character (whether or not covered by insurance) which, in the aggregate, has had or would reasonably be expected to have a Company Material Adverse Effect.

* * *

Section 9.1(c), however, goes on to limit the aggregate liability of the Seller for conduct covered by § 9.1(a) to the amount of the escrowed Indemnity Fund, which was established to be $20 million in § 2.4(b). This limitation is part of a very textured subsection that also permits the Buyer to seek damages for breaches of representations and warranties, without reference to materiality qualifications placed on them in the bring-down clause—that is, the clause of the Agreement that brings the representations and warranties down from the time of signing to the time of closing in the form of closing conditions. In other words, through the Indemnity Claim process, the Buyer clawed back the materiality qualifiers the Company and Seller extracted on the representations and warranties for purposes of closing.

The Stock Purchase Agreement also addresses the exclusivity of the Indemnity Claim provisions of the Agreement. To that end, § 9.9(a) (the "Exclusive Remedy Provision") provides:

Except as may be required to enforce post-closing covenants hereunder ... after the Closing Date the indemnification rights in this *Article IX* are and shall be the sole and exclusive remedies of the Acquiror, the Acquiror Indemnified Persons, the Selling Stockholder, and the Company with respect to this Agreement and the Sale contemplated hereby; *provided* that this sentence shall not be deemed a waiver by any party of its right to seek specific performance or injunctive relief in the case of another party's failure to comply with the covenants made by such other party.

* * *

Further, the Agreement requires that Indemnity Claims be arbitrated in Massachusetts if they cannot be resolved consensually. Despite the selection of Massachusetts as an arbitration forum, the Agreement, in § 9.5 and § 11.9, also makes clear that Delaware law governs any claim submitted to arbitration. First, § 9.5(e) provides that "[e]xcept as may be otherwise expressly provided herein, for any Contested Claim submitted to arbitration, the burden of proof shall be as it would be if the claim were litigated in a judicial proceeding governed exclusively by the internal Laws of the State of Delaware applicable to contracts executed and entered into within the State of Delaware." Second, in a general choice of law provision in § 11.9(a), the parties also agreed that the Stock Purchase Agreement would be "governed by, and construed in accordance with, the Laws of the State of Delaware, regardless of the Laws that might otherwise govern under applicable principles of conflicts of law." Finally, § 11.9(c)(i) of the Agreement invests the courts of Delaware with exclusive jurisdiction over any dispute regarding the Agreement, including cases seeking review of an arbitrator's ruling or award, and embodies the parties' consent to the jurisdiction of this State's courts.

In this case, the Buyer does not argue that it is suing the Seller to cause it to specifically perform, or to enjoin the Seller from failing to comply with, a covenant of the Seller itself. Rather, the Buyer seeks an order requiring the Seller to take back the Company and return to the Buyer $500 million largely on the basis that the Company made false representations and warranties and the Seller provided a false Officer's Certificate, thereby fraudulently inducing the Buyer to sign the Agreement and later close the deal.

* * *

The Seller's primary argument is that the Stock Purchase Agreement precludes the Buyer from obtaining the relief it seeks in this court. That argument is premised on several elements of the Agreement, which I have described in detail. In summary, though, the argument proceeds as follows. The Stock Purchase Agreement is a carefully negotiated document that allocates economic risk. It was entered into by sophisticated players in the private equity markets. In that Agreement, the parties carefully set forth which representations and warranties were made by the Company and which were made by the Seller. The Buyer also explicitly promised that the only information it relied upon in entering into the Agreement was that represented and warranted in the Agreement itself, thus contractually pledging that it had not relied on extra-contractual representations. In addition, the Buyer agreed to the Exclusive Remedy Provision stating that the only remedy that it had against the Seller for contractual misrepresentations was limited to a claim in arbitration for damages, i.e., an Indemnity Claim. And, in that event, the Seller's liability is capped at the extent of the Indemnity Fund for $20 million. Furthermore, the Agreement explicitly indicated that the Exclusive Remedy Provision and limitation on liability contained in the contract were bargained for and reflected in the sale price.

Instead of seeking the relief permitted to it by the Agreement-an Indemnity Claim-the Buyer is bringing a claim for rescission in court. Not only that, the Buyer is seeking to hold the Seller responsible for representations and warranties made by the Company, when the Seller only agreed to back Company representations to the extent of the Indemnity Fund.

The Seller believes that the Buyer's attempt to avoid the terms of the Stock Purchase Agreement is improper and mandates dismissal. Having signed a contract explicitly disclaiming access to the very remedy it now seeks, the Buyer has contractually forsaken its current preferred remedy and must be held to its bargain. The Seller contends that a deal between sophisticated parties with the free right to walk away is a deal, and the law of this State should honor it.

* * *

1. *Do The Terms Of The Stock Purchase Agreement Purport To Limit The Liability Of The Seller For Intentional, Fraudulent Misrepresentations?*

The Buyer argues that this court need not reach its argument that public policy precludes the Agreement from barring its fraud-based rescission claim.

According to the Buyer, the Agreement cannot be reasonably read to subject fraud claims, rather than merely breach of contract claims, to the Exclusive Remedy Provision. I find that argument unpersuasive and inconsistent with the plain language of the Stock Purchase Agreement.

Section 9.1 clearly requires the Seller to indemnify the Buyer, but only to the extent of funds on deposit in the Indemnity Fund for damages determined "to have arisen out of or to have resulted from, in connection with, or by virtue of facts or circumstances (i) which constitute an *inaccuracy, misrepresentation, breach of,* default in, or failure to perform, *any of the representations, warranties or covenants.*" The Exclusive Remedy Provision establishes an Indemnity Action as the sole remedy both "with respect to" the Stock Purchase Agreement and "the Sale contemplated hereby."

Recognizing the difficulties that this language presents for it, the Buyer advances two arguments to support its position. First, the Buyer asks me to interpret the word "misrepresentation" in § 9.1 of the Agreement as encompassing negligent and innocent misrepresentations only, not fraudulent misrepresentations. But that argument is not a convincing one, given the common understanding of the term misrepresentation in our legal lexicon. Misrepresentation is defined by Black's Law Dictionary as "the act of making a false or misleading statement about something, [usually] with the intent to deceive." Further, modern legal usage appears to place an even stronger emphasis on the breadth of the term. Specifically, "this word is broad enough to describe a fraudulent as well as a negligent or innocent statement."[2]

* * *

2. *Is The Buyer Permitted To Seek Rescission In This Court Despite The Exclusive Remedy Terms Of The Stock Purchase Agreement?*

Having determined that the Stock Purchase Agreement's plain terms would, if given legal effect, preclude the Buyer from seeking rescission, I must now consider the Buyer's argument that public policy intervenes to trump contractual freedom and to prevent that preclusion. That public policy argument continues a longstanding debate within American jurisprudence about society's relative interest in contractual freedom versus establishing universal minimum standards of truthful conduct for contracting parties.

* * *

As the Buyer notes, there is a strong tradition in American law that holds that contracts may not insulate a party from damages or rescission resulting from the party's fraudulent conduct.

* * *

On the other hand, there is also a strong American tradition of freedom of contract, and * * * [t]he Seller stresses this strain in our law to buttress its argument that contracts between sophisticated parties with equal bargaining strength should be honored without intrusion by the policy concerns of unelected judges.

* * *

---

2.   [By the Court] Bryan A. Garner, A Dictionary of Modern Legal Usage 567 (2d ed. 1995).

Delaware is also sensitive to the need for commerce to proceed in a rational and certain way. We also respect the ability of sophisticated businesses, such as the Buyer and Seller, to make their own judgments about the risk they should bear and the due diligence they undertake, recognizing that such parties are able to price factors such as limits on liability. Contributing to that respect is our knowledge that judicial decisions are not the only way that commercial norms of fair play are instilled. This case is a good example. If the Seller, a private equity firm, gets a rap as a fraudster who tries to sell portfolio companies based on false representations, that Seller will pay a price. Although there are a lot more private equity firms today than there were a decade ago, the nature of that market is still such that reputational factors are likely to be important. Having a bad reputation is likely to be costly, as buyers will tend to discount the value of the tainted seller's portfolio companies as a form of self-protection as well as to demand greater remedial flexibility in the sales contract.

* * *

I resolve this case in the following manner. To the extent that the Stock Purchase Agreement purports to limit the Seller's exposure for its own conscious participation in the communication of lies to the Buyer, it is invalid under the public policy of this State. That is, I find that the public policy of this State will not permit the Seller to insulate itself from the possibility that the sale would be rescinded if the Buyer can show either: 1) that the Seller knew that the Company's contractual representations and warranties were false; or 2) that the Seller itself lied to the Buyer about a contractual representation and warranty. This will require the Buyer to prove that the Seller acted with an illicit state of mind, in the sense that the Seller knew that the representation was false and either communicated it to the Buyer directly itself or knew that the Company had. In this case, that distinction is largely of little importance because of the Officer's Certificate provided by the Seller. In that certificate, the Seller certified that (1) each representation and warranty of the Company and Seller was true and correct as of the closing date; (2) the Seller and Company performed and complied in all material respects with the agreements and covenants required to be performed or complied with; and (3) between the date of signing the Stock Purchase Agreement and closing, there had been no change, event or condition of any character which had or would reasonably be expected to constitute a material adverse effect for the Company.

By contrast, the Buyer may not obtain rescission or greater monetary damages upon any lesser showing. If the Company's managers intentionally misrepresented facts to the Buyer without knowledge of falsity by the Seller, then the Buyer cannot obtain rescission or damages, but must proceed with an Indemnity Claim subject to the Indemnity Fund's liability cap. Likewise, the Buyer may not escape the contractual limitations on liability by attempting to show that the Seller acted in a reckless, grossly negligent, or negligent manner. The Buyer knowingly accepted the risk that the Seller would act with inadequate deliberation. It is an experienced private equity firm that could have walked away without buying. It has no moral justification for escaping its own voluntarily-accepted limits on its remedies against the Seller absent proof that the Seller itself acted in a consciously improper manner.

In sum, I conclude that the Seller's motion to dismiss the complaint in its entirety must be denied. But the Buyer may only obtain its desired relief—rescission or in the alternative, full compensatory damages—if it meets the burden of proof described.

IV. Conclusion

For the foregoing reasons, the Seller's motion to dismiss is granted as ... the negligent misrepresentation count, and granted as to the remaining counts to the extent described. The motion is otherwise denied.

IT IS SO ORDERED.

Notes

1. What is the balance that the court strikes between contractual freedom and fraud? How does Vice Chancellor Strine draw the line? Is his distinction a compelling one? In your opinion, were the Seller's business practices fair?

2. Strine carefully chooses to describe misrepresentation as lying rather than fraud, and has an interesting rationale. Is this distinction helpful or distracting? Remember 6 Del. Stat. Ann. § 18–1101(c) states "... the limited liability company agreement may not eliminate the implied contractual covenant of good faith and fair dealing." There is a similar statute for limited partnerships at 6 Del. Stat. Ann. § 17–1101(d). Does the exculpatory clause violate these statutes? In other words, would intentional misrepresentation violate the covenant of good faith and fair dealing? If so, how is it possible for the parties in this case to contract around the covenant? Does the court address this issue?

3. The exculpatory clause in this case is unique, since it limited the Seller's liability not only for information provided about the Company, but also for intentional misrepresentations within the contract itself. The clause therefore created a precarious balance, with the freedom to contract on the one hand and the public policy interest against lying on the other hand. Does the court get it right? How much should it matter that the parties are sophisticated and that the contract was the result of careful drafting extensive negotiation between them?

4. Strine also points out an additional constraint: since the two funds belonged to a rather small private equity community, he reasoned that concerns about professional reputation would additionally safeguard against fraud. How strong is this argument?

POORE v. FOX HOLLOW ENTERPRISES

Superior Court of Delaware, 1994.
1994 WL 150872.

Steele, Judge.

Pursuant to Superior Court Civil Rule 12(f), Tammy Poore filed a Motion to Strike Appellee's Answering Brief for failure to properly file an answer in Superior Court through Delaware counsel. * * * During the oral arguments concerning this Motion, Douglas E. Campbell admitted he drafted the answering brief himself. Although Mr. Campbell stated he did not have a license to practice law in Delaware, he believed because Fox Hollow Enterprises is a Limited Liability Company and not a corporation, he could represent this company in Superior Court without a Delaware licensed attorney. * * *

The Delaware Supreme Court has held a corporation cannot appear or conduct business in court without representation by Delaware counsel. Transpolymer Industries, Inc. v. Chapel Main Corp., Del.Supr., No. 284, 1990, Horsey, J. (Sept. 18, 1990) (ORDER). The Supreme Court reasoned "[a] corporation, though a legally recognized entity, is regarded as an artificial or fictional entity, and not a natural person. While a natural person may represent himself or herself in court even though he or she may not be an attorney licensed to practice, a corporation being an artificial entity, can only act through its agents and, before a court only through an agent duly licensed to practice law." Id. (citations omitted).

The threshold question presented to this Court concerns whether or not it should apply this theory of corporate representation to Delaware Limited Liability Companies. As an alternative business entity under Delaware law, the Court must decide if a Limited Liability Company more closely resembles a partnership, which may represent itself in Court, or a corporation, which requires representation by legal counsel. * * *

The Court recognizes the Delaware General Assembly enacted the DLLCA to serve as an alternative business entity which allows the combination of the best features of both partnerships and corporations. The Delaware statute treats a properly structured LLC as a partnership for federal income tax purposes while affording limited liability for members and managers, similar to the limited liability afforded to shareholders and directors of a Delaware corporation. 6 Del.C. § 18–303, 18–1106(a).

Although the statute treats an LLC as a partnership for federal income tax purposes, an LLC is largely a creature of contract—with management, economic, voting and other rights and obligations being primarily specified in the LLC agreement. Walter C. Tuthill & Denison H. Hatch, Jr., Delaware Limited Liability Companies, March 5, 1993, at 3. An LLC formed under the DLLCA constitutes a separate legal entity. 6 Del.C. § 18–201(b). Additionally, the interest of a member in the LLC is analogous to shareholders of a corporation. A member usually contributes personal property and has no interest in specific assets owned by the LLC. 6 Del.C. § 18–701. Moreover, a member or manager of an LLC cannot be held liable for the company's debts or obligations above his or her contribution to the company. 6 Del.C. § 18–303.

The Court finds these aspects of the LLC constitute a distinct, but artificial entity under Delaware law. Because of the limited liability inherent in the LLC and the contractual nature of this entity, the Court finds the Delaware Legislature did not intend [to say that] a member or manager of an LLC could appear in Court to represent the entity without representation by Delaware legal counsel. Ultimately, regulation of the practice of law rests in the Delaware Supreme Court, not the legislature. The underlying purpose of the rule prohibiting the appearance of a corporation by anyone other than a member of the Delaware Bar also applies to the representation of Limited Liability Companies.

Because Fox Hollow Enterprises did not obtain Delaware legal counsel to represent its interests in this appeal, the Court grants Appellant's Motion to Strike Appellee's Answering Brief pursuant to Superior Court Civil Rule 12(f).

Note

The Oklahoma Constitution, art. 28, §§ 4, 10, contains the following provisions with respect to the holders of liquor store licenses:

No retail package store or wholesale distributor's license shall be issued to:

(a) A corporation, business trust or secret partnership.

(b) A person or partnership unless such person or all of the copartners including limited partners shall have been residents of the State of Oklahoma for at least ten (10) years immediately preceding the date of application for such license.

(c) A person or a general or limited partnership containing a partner who has been convicted of a violation of a prohibitory law relating to the sale, manufacture, or the transportation of alcoholic beverages which constituted a felony or misdemeanor.

(d) A person or a general or limited partnership containing a partner who has been convicted of a felony.

In Meyer v. Oklahoma Alcoholic Beverage Laws Enforcement Commission, 890 P.2d 1361 (1995), the Oklahoma Court of Appeals held that an LLC was not eligible to receive a package store license. Is that right? The court reasoned as follows:

Meyer argues that an LLC is essentially a partnership. However, the act creating the business form is in Title 18, which is entitled "Corporations." Furthermore, a provision in our Uniform Partnership Act states that "any association formed under any other statute of this state * * * is not a partnership under this act, unless such association would have been a partnership in this state prior to adoption of this act." 54 O.S.1991 § 206(2).

Meyer claims that its expert witness, the only witness in all the proceedings, testified that an LLC was a partnership. However, contrary to Meyer's contention, the witness's testimony was not so unequivocal. The totality of the testimony was that an LLC is a hybrid that has attributes of both corporations and partnerships. The witness indicated an LLC is more like a partnership, but noted the primary difference is that all owners/members have limited liability in an LLC—something not found in partnerships. We conclude that the limitation of liability of all LLC members is a substantial difference especially relevant to the provisions of our liquor laws.

Our examination of the pertinent constitutional provisions leads us to conclude that their evident purpose was the assignment of personal responsibility for compliance with the liquor laws. Thus, business forms that did not insure such personal responsibility were excluded from eligibility for licensing.

The [Oklahoma Limited Liability Company Act] does exactly what its name indicates. It creates a form of business that has as its most important feature the limitation of liability of its members. This liability limitation is also a shield from the very responsibility and accountability that the constitutional provisions regarding alcoholic beverage laws and enforcement sought to impose. * * *

The Oklahoma constitutional provision and statutes involved in *Meyer* were drafted at a time when the only business forms available were partnerships or corporations. The issue was therefore one of classification, could an LLC be classified as a "partnership" or as a "corporation"? There must be hundreds (or thousands) of existing federal and state statutory and regulatory provisions that are based on the premise that all businesses may be classified either as corporations or partnerships. Might it be possible to develop a statutory "fix" for the classification problem by a provision that states, e.g., that for administrative purposes an LLC should always be treated as a partnership? Might there be problems if such a statute were enacted without first examining each provision of the Internal Revenue Code?

E.   INSPECTION RIGHTS FOR LLC RECORDS

MARIE L. KASTEN v. DORAL DENTAL USA, LLC

Court of Appeals of Wisconsin, 2006.
2006 WL 861382.

Before SNYDER, P.J., BROWN and ANDERSON, JJ.

ISSUES

1.   Whether WIS. STAT. § 183.0405 (2003–04),[1] part of the Wisconsin Limited Liability Company Law (WLLCL), grants a broad right of member access to limited liability company records that, absent contrary language in the LLC operating agreement, embraces informal and nonfinancial records.

2.   If the court determines that the statute grants members a broad inspection right, whether e-mails can be classified as "records" under WIS. STAT. § 183.0405(2) such that they are subject to a member's inspection.

FACTS

Doral Dental USA, LLC, is a Wisconsin LLC that was organized in August 1996. As part of a divorce settlement in 2001, Marie L. Kasten received a 23.1% membership interest in Doral Dental.

In late 2002 and 2003, Doral Dental began negotiating with potential buyers. In February 2003, Kasten started requesting certain documents from Doral Dental. She requested, inter alia, "various business records, financial and tax records and ledgers, invoices, agreements, contracts, employment records, letters of intent" and the "most current status of negotiations with suitors for Doral." Kasten apparently requested these documents because she was concerned that the transactions that were in negotiations would adversely impact her interest in the company. Kasten has requested numerous other documents since that time.

Doral Dental complied with some, but not all, of Kasten's requests. In November 2003, Kasten filed a lawsuit to enforce her rights, pursuant to WIS. STAT. § 183.0405 and Doral Dental's operating agreement, to inspect and copy the remaining Doral Dental records and documents. In July 2004, Kasten filed a motion to compel, claiming that Doral Dental had not provided several of the documents she had requested. Her requests included "drafts of the sales documents and exhibits" and e-mail correspondence "by/to/from" various

---

1.   [By the Court] All references to the Wisconsin Statutes are to the 2003–04 version   unless otherwise noted.

LLC members and their counsel and "between officers or directors" of Doral Dental.

The court held that Kasten was not entitled to inspect the e-mails or drafts of documents she requested. The court concluded that e-mails are not "documents or records," but "communications." The court, however, ruled that Kasten had the right to inspect other written correspondence.

DISCUSSION

This case presents a classic books-and-records dispute, but in an emerging context. Kasten maintains that the WLLCL and the operating agreement for Doral Dental grant her, in her capacity as a member of the LLC, the right to inspect and copy LLC e-mails and document drafts.[2] A careful and considered canvas of LLC jurisprudence reveals that the scope of a member's right to inspect an LLC's records and the question of whether an e-mail is a company record subject to a member's inspection have not been touched upon in Wisconsin.

Parties' arguments. Kasten maintains that the WLLCL and the operating agreement grant her the right to inspect and copy e-mails and "drafts of documents." She urges a broad interpretation of a member's inspection rights based upon the language in Wis. Stat. § 183.0405(2) granting members the right to inspect "any other limited liability company record" and the language in the operating agreement granting members the right to inspect "all other Company records" and "Company documents."

Doral Dental, on the other hand, reads Wis. Stat. § 183.0405(2) and the operating agreement as granting only a narrow right to inspect the documents and records specifically enumerated in § 183.0405(1). Doral Dental further asserts that, at most, the statutory term "record" and the agreement's term "documents" refer to finalized records maintained to "reflect significant company transactions or events or its financial condition." Doral Dental posits that the e-mails and drafts do not qualify as such.

The WLLCL and the operating agreement. The WLLCL's provisions concerning a member's inspection rights are found in Wis. Stat. § 183.0405. Section 183.0405(1) sets forth a list of records that an LLC is required to keep at its principal place of business.[3] Section 183.0405(2) provides that any member may, upon reasonable request, inspect and copy any required LLC record under subsec. (1) at that member's own expense during ordinary business hours and "unless otherwise provided in an operating agreement, any other limited liability company record, wherever the record is located."

The operating agreement references member rights to inspection in two places and seems to grant similar inspection rights as the WLLCL. The agreement states in pertinent part:

> *Books of Account.* The Manager shall maintain full and accurate books of account for the Company at the principal Company office. Each Member

---

2. [By the Court] Because her appeal requires the court to engage in statutory and contract construction, it presents questions of law subject to the court's independent review.

See Gottsacker v. Monnier, 2005 WI 69, ¶ 13, 281 Wis.2d 361, 697 N.W.2d 436.

3. The Court includes the text of Wisconsin Stat. § 183.0405.

shall have access to and the right to inspect and copy such books and all other Company records at all reasonable times.

* * *

Company Books. Upon reasonable request, each Member shall have the right, during ordinary business hours, to inspect and copy Company documents at the requesting Member's expense.

Scope of inspection rights. Doral Dental's argument that WIS. STAT. § 183.0405(2) limits member inspection to the records enumerated in § 183.0405(1) does not seem consistent with the language of the statute itself. As Doral Dental points out, the WLLCL clearly provides that any member may, upon reasonable request, inspect and copy any LLC record required under subsec. (1). Sec. 183.0405(2). However, the statute seems to go one step further. It also provides that, unless otherwise stated in an operating agreement, the member's right to inspect and copy records extends to "any other" records of the LLC, regardless of whether they are required to be kept by the statute. *See*§ 183.0405(2); J. WILLIAM CALLISON AND MAUREEN A. SULLIVAN, LIMITED LIABILITY COMPANIES: A STATE-BY-STATE GUIDE TO LAW AND PRACTICE § 15.59 (2005).

* * *

On the one hand, Doral Dental cites to other corporate inspection statutes that it claims confirm its narrow understanding of the term "records." The Wisconsin Uniform Limited Partnership Act, WIS. STAT. ch. 179, permits limited partner inspection of only the records required to be maintained by the statute. WIS. STAT. § 179.05(2). These records include the partnership's tax returns and records, financial statements of the partnership and other formal documents pertaining to the finances of the partnership. Sec. 179.05(1). In a similar vein, the Wisconsin Business Corporation Law, WIS. STAT. ch. 180, limits shareholder inspection to formal company documents such as minutes of meetings, bylaws and accounting records. *See* WIS. STAT. §§ 180.1602 and 180.1601. The WLLCL does borrow liberally from these two statutes and a member of an LLC, depending on the structure of the LLC as set forth in the operating agreement, does share certain characteristics with partners and shareholders. *See* JOSEPH W. BOUCHER ET AL., LLCS AND LLPS: A WISCONSIN HANDBOOK § 1.10 (rev. ed. 1999). Doral Dental further rejects a broad reading of the statute on the basis that it would impose a hefty burden on LLCs in that it would require them to make nearly all company files and documents available to its members.

On the other hand, as Kasten points out, the WLLCL, unlike the other statutes, explicitly refers to "any other limited liability company record." WIS. STAT. § 183.0405(2). It is difficult to infer an implicit limitation on the availability of company documents in the face of this broad language. Furthermore, as Kasten observes, the statute also states that the member may inspect the other records "unless otherwise provided in an operating agreement." *See*§ 183.0405(2). The statute therefore can be read as granting a broad right of inspection and leaving it up to the LLCs to narrowly tailor their inspection rights to suit their own purposes and management structure.[4] This under-

---

4. Doral Dental maintains that its operating agreement is more restrictive than the statute because a member's inspection rights fall under the headings "Books of Account"

standing is consistent with the WLLCL drafter's intention to create a business entity characterized by flexibility and freedom of contract. *Gottsacker v. Monnier,* 2005 WI 69, ¶ 19, 281 Wis.2d 361, 697 N.W.2d 436.

* * *

E-mails as records. If the court determines that the WLLCL contemplates a broad grant of access to company records, the more interesting question of whether an e-mail is a company "record" comes into play. The trial court drew a distinction between e-mails and written correspondence and concluded that Kasten was only entitled to inspect written correspondence.

* * *

On the one hand, e-mail correspondence may be of a different character than most company files and documents and, as a result, may not be properly characterized as a company record. E-mail, unlike like other written correspondence, most often takes on a frank, conversational tone and involves messages that, like work product to attorneys, reflect unguarded thoughts in progress or comments. E-mail messages frequently contain statements that never would have been made in a formal memorandum or company record or that are not related to company finances.

[The court declined to rule and, pursuant to Wis. Stat. Rule 809.61, certified the appeal in this case to the Wisconsin Supreme Court for its review and determination.]

Notes

(1)   This case asks to what degree to the members of a Wisconsin LLC have inspection rights for the LLC's records. The Wisconsin Supreme Court will determine whether this right extends to informal records, which do not necessarily contain financial information, and whether an email is a "record." What is the rationale behind the right of inspection granted in Wisc. Stat. Ann. § 183.0405?

(2)   Section 183.0405 (2) and (3) provide:

(2) Upon reasonable request, a member may, at the member's own expense, inspect and copy during ordinary business hours any limited liability company record * * * unless otherwise provided in an operating agreement, any other limited liability company record, wherever the record is located.

(3) Members or, if the management of the limited liability company is vested in one or more managers, managers shall provide, to the extent that the circumstances render it just and reasonable, true and full information of all things affecting the members to any member or to the legal representative of any member upon reasonable request of the member or the legal representative.

Imagine you sit on the Wisconsin Supreme Court. Does Mrs. Kasten's request qualify under these guidelines? Was the information she demanded "just" and

and "Company Books." However, the operating agreement does not simply speak to "Company Books" or "Books of Account"; like the statute, it also provides member inspection of *"all other Company records."* (Emphasis add-

ed.) It further contains a reference to company "documents," a term that potentially could be construed even more broadly than the term "records."

"reasonable"? What sort of legal principles should be used to determine how much access LLC members should have and when? Should the requesting member's stake in the LLC make any difference in your answer?

(3) On its website, the Wisconsin Supreme Court frames the issue this way:

In her appeal, Kasten argues that the circuit court erred in holding that Doral's managers were not required to produce Doral's e-mails and drafts of documents. Kasten writes: "The circuit court's ruling shrouds critical management communications and motivations under an unjustified cloak of secrecy . . ."

Doral, on the other hand, argues that the statute and the operating agreement grant only a narrow right of inspection. Doral says that, at most, the word "record" in the statute and the word "document" in the LLC agreements refer to finalized records that "reflect significant company transactions or events or its financial conduct."

The Supreme Court will determine the scope of an LLC member's right to inspect records, and whether e-mails and draft documents count as records.[5]

In your opinion, whose argument is more compelling? Should LLC managers have the right to keep certain records from members? Which ones? Should emails be protected or open to inspection?

(4) Of the business forms discussed thus far, which have inspection rights similar to these? Are there any key differences?

(5) Suppose a member of an LLC signed an LLC agreement that purported to remove all rights to inspect internal LLC documents. What would be the result? Del. G. C. L. § 18–305 gives members of LLCs the right, "subject to such reasonable standards (including standards governing what information and documents are to be furnished at what time and location and at whose expense) as may be set forth" in the LLC agreement or by the manager or members. The statute, however, goes on to provide that "[t]he rights of a member or manager to obtain information . . . may be restricted in an original limited liability company or in any subsequent amendment approved or adopted by *all* of the members and in compliance with any applicable provisions of the limited liability company agreement." How does this language mesh with Del. G.C.L. § 1101(c), discussed earlier in this chapter, which allows LLC's and LLC members to eliminate their fiduciary duties to one another?

(6) Chapter 16 of this casebook deals with the issue of investor access to books and records in the corporate context. Does the court appear to treat the LLC in the context of access to books and records more like a partnership or more like a corporation?

F. A FINAL LOOK

Assume that you are advising A and B as to the form of business enterprise they should select for the software store discussed in chapter 1. Would you recommend that they select a general partnership? A limited partnership? A limited liability partnership? A limited liability company? A corporation? If you recommend that they use an LLC (and presumably that is

5. See http://wicourts. gov/sc/orasyn/ Dis-   seqNo=27011.
playDocument.   html?content   =html   &

an attractive choice), should the enterprise be member-managed or manager-managed? If it is member-managed, how do you ensure that A's veto power will be effective? How would you structure a manager-managed LLC (in which B is the manager) to protect A's veto power?

Also in connection with the AB Software Store, assume that you have represented A on legal matters for several years but you have never represented B. B does not have a lawyer. When A asks you to give advice on the best form of business for the software store, B indicates that he relies on your judgment and will accept your recommendation. Do you have to take B's interest into account as well as A's? In some circumstances, a choice may be more favorable to A than to B. See Chapter 8, Part E, infra. Does B become your client if he relies on you but you fail to warn him about possible problems? Are you "counsel for the venture"? Consider Model Rules of Professional Conduct 1.7 (1983):

(a) A lawyer shall not represent a client if the representation of that client will be directly adverse to another client, unless:

(1) the lawyer reasonably believes the representation will not adversely affect the relationship with the other client; and

(2) each client consents after consultation.

(b) A lawyer shall not represent a client if the representation of that client may be materially limited by the lawyer's responsibilities to another client or to a third person, or by the lawyer's own interests, unless:

(1) the lawyer reasonably believes the representation will not be adversely affected; and

(2) the client consents after consultation. When representation of multiple clients in a single matter is undertaken, the consultation shall include explanation of the implications of the common representation and the advantages and risks involved.

Does that rule apply to your situation? If so, how do you explain "the implications of the common representation and the advantages and risks involved" to B in making the decision of the business form to select?

Finally, consider a situation that many traditional law firms have faced. Assume that you are the senior partner in an "old line" law firm that has conducted business in the general partnership form for more than fifty years. It has more than 20 regular clients, including six that provide a major portion of your firm's business.

(a) You decide that the time has come to convert your law firm to a limited liability entity. Should your firm elect to be an LLP? An LLC? A professional corporation?

(b) Once you announced your decision to adopt a limited liability business form, a junior partner raises a question: Does the firm have any obligation to advise its clients that the form of the firm has changed? Do you believe that the letters "LLC," "LLP," or "LP" in the future letterhead will be adequate warning to clients that the liability rules with respect to the firm have changed? Or should we send a letter to every client stating that the change in legal form has the effect of limiting the personal liability of partners? Not surprisingly, most firms converting to a limited liability business form have not sent out such letters.

CHARACTERISTICS OF ALTERNATIVE TYPES OF BUSINESS ORGANIZATION[20]

Characteristics	Sole Proprietorship	General Partnership	Limited liability Partnership	Limited Liability Company	S–Corporation	Corporation
Formation	No filing required	No filing required Agreement of parties involved. No permission required	Filing with state official required	Filing with state official required	Filing with state official required	Filing with state official required
Duration	Sole Proprietor determines.	Dissolved by Partner's death or bankruptcy	Dissolved when partners dissociate and wind up the business of the partnership	Sometimes limited by state law	Perpetual	Perpetual
Liability	Sole Proprietor has unlimited liability	Partners have unlimited liability	Partners liable for their own actions and actions of those under their control and supervision; partners not typically liable for the debts of the LLP	Members not typically liable for the debts of the LLC	Shareholders are typically not personally liable for the debts of the corporation	Shareholders are typically not personally liable for the debts of the corporation
Simplicity of Operation	Yes	Yes	Yes	More formal than sole proprietorship, less formal than corporation	Formality of board of directors, officers, annual meetings and annual reporting	Formality of board of directors, officers, annual meetings and annual reporting
Management	Sole Proprietor has full control of management and operations	Typically each partner has an equal voice unless otherwise arranged	Typically each partner has a voice unless otherwise arranged	Members of LLC manage and control the entity unless Articles of Organization provide otherwise	The corporation is managed by or under the direction of the board of directors who are elected by the shareholders.	The corporation is managed by or under the direction of the board of directors who are elected by the shareholders.
Taxation	Not a taxable entity. Sole proprietor pays all taxes	Not a taxable entity. Income/loss is passed through to members of the partnership	Not a taxable entity. Income/loss is passed through to members of the partnership	Not a taxable entity. Income/loss is passed through to members of the LLC	Not a taxable entity. Income/loss is passed through to the shareholders	Corporation is a taxable entity.
Double Taxation	No	No	No	No	No	Yes
Cost of Formation	None	None	Filing fee with the State	Filing fee with the state	Filing fee with the state	Filing fee with the state
Raising Equity Capital	Not unless individual puts in money	Contributions from partners or an addition of more partners	Contribution from partners or addition of more partners	Possible to sell interests. Subject to operating agreement restrictions	Sell shares of stock to raise capital	Sell shares of stock to raise capital
Transferability of Interest	No	No	Free transferability of interest—can transfer right to economic interest without consent of others, but cannot transfer rights to participate in management and control	Possibly	Yes, subject to consent	Shares of stock are easily transferable

20.   Chart developed by the Editors.

Chapter Five

THE DEVELOPMENT OF CORPORATION LAW IN THE UNITED STATES: JURISDICTIONAL COMPETITION

In England the power to award corporate charters was first assumed by the Crown and later by Parliament. In the American colonies, in the pre-revolutionary period, colonial legislatures granted some corporate charters under the presumed authority of the British Parliament. For many years, this power was exercised sparingly, usually limited to ventures of a public or quasi-public nature. Charters often contained numerous restrictions. Perhaps as a result of the English heritage (which often combined corporate charters with grants of monopoly power), corporations were viewed with suspicion and mistrust.

Following independence and the adoption of the Federal Constitution, state legislatures continued to grant corporate charters, many of them for banks. After the War of 1812, the number of corporate charters increased rapidly; in addition to banks, corporations were formed to construct canals and turnpikes. Many of these early charters granted special privileges in the form of monopolies or exclusive franchises. Intensive industrial development began in about 1825. The corporation proved to be an ideal instrument for this development since it could raise large amounts of capital from numerous investors and provide centralized direction of large industrial concerns.

The Federal Government incorporated the Bank of the United States by statute in 1791. However, doubt continued to exist as to the general power of the Federal Government to create corporations for general economic purposes, and as a result states continued to form business corporations. Even today, with the power of the Federal Government to create corporations firmly established, that power is rarely exercised and then only for predominantly public purposes. The formation of business corporations in the United States is firmly in the hands of the states, as is control over the relationships between the investors and the managers of business organizations. As the Supreme Court has noted, "[c]orporations are creatures of state law, and investors commit their funds to corporate directors on the understanding that, except where federal law *expressly* requires certain responsibilities of directors with respect to stockholders, state law will govern the internal affairs of the corporation." Santa Fe Industries v. Green, 430 U.S. 462, 479, 97 S.Ct. 1292, 51 L.Ed.2d 480 (1977); Business Roundtable v. S.E.C. 905 F.2d 406 (D.C.Cir.1990).

Originally, state legislatures approved each individual corporate charter. Approval of a charter was a political act, involving lobbying, political influence, campaign contributions, and sometimes worse. The first general incorporation statutes permitting businesses to incorporate by action of an administrative agency without specific legislative approval were adopted in Pennsylvania in 1836 and in Connecticut in 1840. This innovation quickly became popular so that by 1859 twenty-five out of the then existing thirty-eight states and territories had enacted general incorporation statutes. By 1890, all states had adopted general incorporation statutes.

The enactment of general and unlimited corporation statutes by New Jersey and other states, followed by Delaware's enactment of its General Corporation Law in 1899, touched off a vigorous jurisdictional competition for corporate charters among the states. This race is vividly described in the following excerpt.

LOUIS K. LIGGETT CO. v. LEE

Supreme Court of the United States, 1933.
288 U.S. 517, 548–65, 53 S.Ct. 481, 490–96, 77 L.Ed. 929, 944–54.

MR. JUSTICE BRANDEIS, dissenting. * * *

* * * The prevalence of the corporation in America has led men of this generation to act, at times, as if the privilege of doing business in corporate form were inherent in the citizen; and has led them to accept the evils attendant upon the free and unrestricted use of the corporate mechanism as if these evils were the inescapable price of civilized life, and, hence, to be borne with resignation. Throughout the greater part of our history a different view prevailed. Although the value of this instrumentality in commerce and industry was fully recognized, incorporation for business was commonly denied long after it had been freely granted for religious, educational, and charitable purposes. It was denied because of fear. Fear of encroachment upon the liberties and opportunities of the individual. Fear of the subjection of labor to capital. Fear of monopoly. Fear that the absorption of capital by corporations, and their perpetual life, might bring evils similar to those which attended mortmain. There was a sense of some insidious menace inherent in large aggregations of capital, particularly when held by corporations. So at first the corporate privilege was granted sparingly; and only when the grant seemed necessary in order to procure for the community some specific benefit otherwise unattainable. The later enactment of general incorporation laws does not signify that the apprehension of corporate domination had been overcome. The desire for business expansion created an irresistible demand for more charters; and it was believed that under general laws embodying safeguards of universal application the scandals and favoritism incident to special incorporation could be avoided. The general laws, which long embodied severe restrictions upon size and upon the scope of corporate activity, were, in part, an expression of the desire for equality of opportunity.

(a) Limitation upon the amount of the authorized capital of business corporations was long universal. The maximum limit frequently varied with the kinds of business to be carried on, being dependent apparently upon the supposed requirements of the efficient unit. Although the statutory limits were changed from time to time, this principle of limitation was long retained. Thus in New York the limit was at first $100,000 for some businesses and as little as $50,000 for others. Until 1881 the maximum for business corporations in New York was $2,000,000; and until 1890, $5,000,000. In Massachusetts the limit was at first $200,000 for some businesses and as little as $5,000 for others. Until 1871 the maximum for mechanical and manufacturing corporations was $500,000; and until 1899, $1,000,000. The limit of $1,000,000 was retained for some businesses until 1903.

In many other states, including the leading ones in some industries, the removal of the limitations upon size was more recent. Pennsylvania did not remove the limits until 1905. * * * Michigan did not remove the maximum limit until 1921. * * * Missouri did not remove its maximum limit until 1927. Texas still has such a limit for certain corporations.

(b) Limitations upon the scope of a business corporation's powers and activity were also long universal. At first, corporations could be formed under the general laws only for a limited number of purposes—usually those which required a relatively large fixed capital, like transportation, banking and insurance, and mechanical, mining, and manufacturing enterprises. Permission to incorporate for "any lawful purpose" was not common until 1875; and until that time the duration of corporate franchises was generally limited to a period of 20, 30, or 50 years. All, or a majority, of the incorporators or directors, or both, were required to be residents of the incorporating state. The powers which the corporation might exercise in carrying out its purposes were sparingly conferred and strictly construed. Severe limitations were imposed on the amount of indebtedness, bonded or otherwise. The power to hold stock in other corporations was not conferred or implied. The holding company was impossible.

(c) The removal by the leading industrial states of the limitations upon the size and powers of business corporations appears to have been due, not to their conviction that maintenance of the restrictions was undesirable in itself, but to the conviction that it was futile to insist upon them; because local restriction would be circumvented by foreign incorporation. Indeed, local restriction seemed worse than futile. Lesser states, eager for the revenue derived from the traffic in charters, had removed safeguards from their own incorporation laws.[1] Companies were early formed to provide charters for

1. [By the Justice] The traffic in charters quickly became widespread. In 1894 Cook on Stock and Stockholders (3d Ed.) Vol. II, pp. 1604, 1605, thus described the situation: "New Jersey is a favorite state for incorporations. Her laws seem to be framed with a special view to attracting incorporation fees and business fees from her sister states and especially from New York, across the river. She has largely succeeded in doing so, and now runs the state government very largely on revenues derived from New York enterprises." * * *

In 1906 John S. Parker thus described the practice, in his volume Where and How—A Corporation Handbook (2d Ed.) p. 4:

Many years ago the corporation laws of New Jersey were so framed as to invite the incorporation of companies by persons residing in other states and countries. The liberality and facility with which corporations could there be formed were extensively advertised, and a great volume of incorporation swept into that state. * * *

The policy of New Jersey proved profitable to the state, and soon legislatures of other states began active competition. * * *

Delaware and Maine also revised their laws, taking the New Jersey act as a model, but with lower organization fees and annual tax-corporations in states where the cost was lowest and the laws least restrictive.[2] The states joined in advertising their wares.[3] The race was one not of diligence but of laxity. Incorporation under such laws was possible: and the great industrial States yielded in order not to lose wholly the prospect of the revenue and the control incident to domestic incorporation.

The history of the changes made by New York is illustrative. The New York revision of 1890, which eliminated the maximum limitation on authorized capital, and permitted intercorporate stockholding in a limited class of cases, was passed after a migration of incorporation from New York, attracted by the more liberal incorporation laws of New Jersey. But the changes made by New York in 1890 were not sufficient to stem the tide. In 1892, the Governor of New York approved a special charter for the General Electric Company, modeled upon the New Jersey act, on the ground that otherwise the enterprise would secure a New Jersey charter. Later in the same year the New York corporation law was again revised, allowing the holding of stock in other corporations. But the New Jersey law still continued to be more attractive to incorporators. By specifically providing that corporations might be formed in New Jersey to do all their business elsewhere, the state made its policy unmistakably clear. Of the seven largest trusts existing in 1904, with an aggregate capitalization of over two and a half billion dollars, all were organized under New Jersey law; and three of these were formed in 1899. During the first seven months of that year, 1336 corporations were organized under the laws of New Jersey, with an aggregate authorized capital of over two billion dollars. The Comptroller of New York, in his annual report for 1899, complained that "our tax list reflects little of the great wave of organization that has swept over the country during the past year and to

es. Arizona and South Dakota also adopted liberal corporation laws, and contenting themselves with the incorporation fees, require no annual state taxes whatever.

West Virginia for many years has been popular with incorporators, but in 1901, in the face of the growing competition of other states, the legislature increased the rate of annual taxes. And West Virginia thus lost her popularity. See Conyngton and Bennett, Corporation Procedure (Rev.Ed.1927), p. 712. On the other hand, too drastic price cutting was also unprofitable. The bargain prices in Arizona and South Dakota attracted wild cat corporations. Investors became wary of corporations organized under the laws of Arizona or South Dakota and both states fell in disrepute among them and consequently among incorporators. See Conyngton on Corporate Organizations (1913) c. 5.

2. [By the Justice] Thus, in its pamphlet "Business Corporations Under the Laws of Maine" (1903), the Corporation Trust Company enumerated among the advantages of the Maine laws: The comparatively low organization fees and annual taxes; the absence of restrictions upon capital stock or corporate indebtedness; the authority to issue stock for services as well as property, with the judgment of the directors as to their value conclusive;

and, significantly enough, "the method of taxation, which bases the annual tax upon the stock issued, does not necessitate inquiry into or report upon the intimate affairs of the corporation." * * * See, also, the Red Book on Arizona Corporation Laws (1908), published by the Incorporating Company of Arizona, especially page 5:

The remoteness of Arizona from the Eastern and Southern States has in a measure delayed the promulgation of the generousness of its laws. New Jersey, Delaware and West Virginia have become widely known as incorporating states. More recently Arizona, [South] Dakota, New Mexico and Nevada have come into more or less prominence by the passage of laws with liberal features.

3. [By the Justice] Thus, in an official pamphlet containing the corporation laws of Delaware (1901), the secretary of state wrote in the preface: "It is believed that no state has on its statute books more complete and liberal laws than these"; and the outstanding advantages were then enumerated. * * * See, also, "The General Corporation Act of New Jersey" (1898), edited by J.B. Dill, issued by the secretary of state: "Since 1875 it has been the announced and settled policy of New Jersey to attract incorporated capital to the State. * * * " P. xvii.

which this state contributed more capital than any other state in the Union." "It is time," he declared, "that great corporations having their actual head-quarters in this State and a nominal office elsewhere, doing nearly all of their business within our borders, should be brought within the jurisdiction of this State not only as to matters of taxation but in respect to other and equally important affairs." In 1901 the New York corporation law was again revised. * * *

Able, discerning scholars have pictured for us the economic and social results of thus removing all limitations upon the size and activities of business corporations and of vesting in their managers vast powers once exercised by stockholders—results not designed by the states and long unsuspected. They show that size alone gives to giant corporations a social significance not attached ordinarily to smaller units of private enterprise. Through size, corporations, once merely an efficient tool employed by individuals in the conduct of private business have become an institution—an institution which has brought such concentration of economic power that so-called private corporations are sometimes able to dominate the state. The typical business corporation of the last century, owned by a small group of individuals, managed by their owners, and limited in size by their personal wealth, is being supplanted by huge concerns in which the lives of tens or hundreds of thousands of employees and the property of tens or hundreds of thousands of investors are subjected, through the corporate mechanism, to the control of a few men. Ownership has been separated from control; and this separation has removed many of the checks which formerly operated to curb the misuse of wealth and power. And, as ownership of the shares is becoming continually more dispersed, the power which formerly accompanied ownership is becoming increasingly concentrated in the hands of a few. The changes thereby wrought in the lives of the workers, of the owners and of the general public are so fundamental and far-reaching as to lead these scholars to compare the evolving "corporate system" with the feudal system; and to lead other men of insight and experience to assert that this "master institution of civilised life" is committing it to the rule of a plutocracy. * * *

In the twentieth and twenty-first centuries, Delaware in particular has maintained a hospitable climate for corporations. The success of this small state in attracting and retaining corporation business has been the subject of considerable scholarly interest and debate.

Notes

(1) The importance of the law of the state of incorporation (in addition to such mundane matters as differences in franchise taxes) is greatly enhanced by the so-called "internal affairs rule," that provides that foreign courts should apply the law of the state of incorporation to issues relating to the internal affairs of a foreign corporation. Consult MBCA § 15.05(c); Restatement of Conflict of Laws (2d) § 302. See generally Phaedon J. Kozyris, Corporate Wars and Choice of Law, 1985 Duke L.J. 1; Deborah DeMott, Perspectives on Choice of Law for Corporate Internal Affairs, 48 Law & Contemp. Probs. 161 (Summer 1985).

(2) California is the principal state that has sought to apply specific provisions of its corporation statutes to corporations formed in other states but whose principal business activities are in California. West's Ann.Cal.Corp.Code § 2115 requires corporations with "specified minimum contacts" in California to comply with designated provisions of the California statute: among others, sections dealing with cumulative voting, limitations on distributions, inspection rights of shareholders, and dissenters' rights. The section is not applicable to corporations with shares listed on national securities exchanges or NASDAQ. The constitutionality of this approach has not been definitively resolved. Wilson v. Louisiana–Pacific Resources, Inc., 138 Cal.App.3d 216, 187 Cal.Rptr. 852 (1982) upheld the imposition of the California cumulative voting provisions upon a Utah corporation that was subject to § 2115; the California shareholders' inspection statute was applied to a foreign corporation in Valtz v. Penta Inv. Corp., 139 Cal.App.3d 803, 188 Cal.Rptr. 922 (1983). But see Arden–Mayfair, Inc. v. Louart Corp., 385 A.2d 3 (Del.Ch.1978), holding the California statute inapplicable under "generally recognized choice of law principles" and discussing an unreported California lower court decision holding § 2115 unconstitutional. For a further discussion of litigation with respect to § 2115 and similar statutes see Norwood P. Beveridge Jr., The Internal Affairs Doctrine: The Proper Law of a Corporation, 44 Bus. Law 693, 702–09 (1989).

On January 1, 2003, a new law, called the "California Corporate Disclosure Act" went into effect in California. The Act requires companies incorporated in California, as well as companies qualified to do business in California, to make an annual filing of certain corporate information with the California Secretary of State. Among the information that must be filed is information beyond that contained in the quarterly and annual filings on Forms 10Q and 10K that public corporations must make with the Securities and Exchange Commission under the Securities Exchange Act of 1934. The California Corporate Disclosure Act requires companies making reports under the Act to describe any "other services" that the independent auditor used by the reporting company has performed during the previous 24 months. The Act also requires corporations to file information about the compensation of directors and executive officers, and about loans to directors.

(3) While it is clear that Delaware competes vigorously to maintain its dominant position in the jurisdictional competition for corporate charters, it is less clear how effective other states have been at competing with Delaware. For the view that "Delaware's dominant position in the incorporations market is far stronger and more secure than has been previously recognized" and that "structural features of the market for corporate law * * * make it unprofitable for other small states to challenge Delaware's position," see Bebchuk and Hamdani, Vigorous Race or Leisurely Walk: Reconsidering the Debate on State Competition Over Corporate Charters, 112 Yale L.J. 553 (2002). Professors Bebchuk and Hamdani point out that small states like South Dakota could cut taxes by half if they could capture the sort of revenues that Delaware garners from its incorporation business. Nonetheless, Bebchuk and Hamdani argue that "network and learning externalities" make it difficult for other states to compete with Delaware. By this the authors mean that corporations find Delaware incorporation valuable precisely because other corporations locate there. As more and more corporations choose to incorporate in Delaware, Delaware incorporations become increasingly valuable and other states find it increasingly difficult to compete.

See Guhan Subramanian, The Influence of Antitakeover Statutes on Incorporation Choice: Evidence on the "Race" Debate and Antitakeover Overreaching, 150 U. Pa. L. Rev. 1795 (2002). The article finds that managers generally migrate to (and fail to migrate from) typical antitakeover statutes. However, the states with arguably the most severe antitakeover statutes (Massachusetts, Ohio, and Pennsylvania) do not attract incorporation business. Professor Subramanian finds that managers of public companies are somewhat (26%) more likely to remain in their headquarters state instead of reincorporating to Delaware or some third state if the headquarters state allows the typical array of antitakeover devices (these devices are discussed in Chapter 12). Working on the assumption that these devices are bad for shareholders, Professor Subramanian takes the view that his results are generally consistent with the "race-to-the-bottom" view.

For more discussion on the subject, see Robert M. Lawless, Nevada's Position in the Market for Corporate Charters, Nevada Lawyer, Aug. 2002; Lucian Bebchuk, Alma Cohen, and Allen Farrell, Does the Evidence Favor State Competition in Corporate Law?, 90 Cal. L. Rev. 1775 (2002).

(4) In 1999, the Chief Justice of the Delaware Supreme Court, E. Norman Veasey, stated that a major reason for the success of Delaware General Corporation Law was the "transformation of the archaic Judicial Branch structure and judicial selection method that existed at the end of the Nineteenth Century to a modern judicial selection system which, together with a modern corporation law, propelled the Delaware bench and bar to international prominence." E. Norman Veasey, The Drama of Judicial Branch Change in this Century, 17 Delaware Lawyer (Winter 1999–2000), at 4, 4–5. He described the current role of the State of Delaware in the corporation world as follows:

> * * * [D]epoliticizing the Judiciary attract[ed] to the Bench quality people whose focus is likely to be on service and scholarship. This may well be the central reason why Delaware has attracted over 300,000 corporations, including more than half of the Fortune 500 and half of the New York Stock Exchange corporations. It has also attracted some of the finest lawyers in America to our Bar. The role of the Judiciary complements the outstanding work of the Bar, the General Assembly and the Secretary of State's office.

(5) Professor Roberta Romano examined the diffusion of corporate law innovations such as limits on director liability and takeover regulation and concluded that changes in corporate law are produced via a dynamic process in which states initially experiment with various approaches to solving a perceived problem. After this experimentation period, a majority settles on one formula. The result is "substantial uniformity across the states." Roberta Romano, The States as a Laboratory: Legal Innovation and State Competition For Corporate Charters, 23 Yale J. on Reg. 209, 246 (2006). She described the relationship between federalism and corporate law innovation as follows:

> The development of corporate law has been left to the states with sporadic federal intervention: the New Deal laws regulating the issuance of securities, the terms of cash takeover bids, and most recently, audit committees and executive loans. Federalism has succeeded in this domain because the states have sorted out amongst themselves who has exclusive jurisdiction over corporate law to minimize conflict by adopting an "internal affairs" jurisdictional rule in which the governing choice of law rule is the corporation's statutory domicile. This contrasts with other potential conflict rules, such as physical domicile (the corporate law conflicts rule in most of continental Europe) or the domicile of the buyer or seller of a firm's securities (U.S. states' securities law conflicts rule). The latter conflicts rule would subject

firms operating across state lines to multiple legal regimes in the absence of federal regulation.

* * *

The states' agreement on the internal affairs jurisdictional rule has had important consequences for the development of corporate law. The ease of selecting a domicile whose exclusive jurisdiction is legally recognized has resulted in considerable experimentation and innovation in corporate law, as states have sought to retain locally-domiciled firms by offering up-to-date codes to meet changing business conditions. The output of this competition has been, for the most part, welfare-enhancing. This contention may be best illustrated by the fact that consumers of corporate law—investors, managers, and their lobbying organizations—have not advocated replacing the states' authority with either the federal government, or purely private contracts and self-regulating organizations, despite some academic support for both of those alternatives. In this regard, the production of corporate law stands as an exemplar of the advantage of a federal system: State competition for incorporations has spurred an innovative legal process that is responsive to a rapidly changing business environment to the benefit of firms and their investors.

Id. at 210–11.

(6) In their 1932 seminal work on the corporation, Adolph Berle and Gardiner Means discussed what the authors perceived to be the social and economic problems generated by the separation of ownership and control in the modern publicly held corporation. At the heart of Berle and Means' account of the role of the corporation in society was their statistical work in which they made two famous claims. First they claimed that the top 200 corporations in America were vastly larger and controlled far more wealth than all other companies. This top 200, according to Berle and Means' data, controlled almost 50% of U.S. corporate wealth and 38% of the nation's business assets. Compounding this concentration of economic power was the fact that the top managers of these firms owned only a very small fraction of the shares in these firms, but controlled all of their assets. From this observation sprang the famous notion of the "problem" of "the separation of ownership and control" of the modern public corporation.

Berle and Mean's ultimate empirical observations were that:

The rise of the modern corporation has brought a concentration of economic power which can compete on equal terms with the modern state.... Where its own interests are concerned, it even attempts to dominate the state. The future may see the economic organism, now typified by the corporation, not only on an equal plane with the state, but possibly even superseding it as the dominant form of social organization.[1]

The corporation never approached being the political and economic monolith that Berle and Means feared for the simple reason that competition, in product markets, labor markets, and, above all, capital markets, imposed serious constraints on the freedom of managers and other corporate actors to pursue their own, selfish ends at the expense of investors. Competition imposes rigorous discipline, including the ultimate sanction of bankruptcy, on firms that pursue their own interests at the expense of their investors.

Berle and Means' concern about the concentration of economic and political power in the hands of managers can be found in current discussions of corporate

---

1. Berle and Means, The Modern Corporation and Private Property, at 313.

regulation, with some commentators worrying that management wields undue influence over the kind of legislation that is passed and uses this influence to entrench its own power. The regulation of the market for corporate control has been cited as one area in which managers have been able to use their power to protect their authority. Treatment of the conflicts of interest between managers and firms in the context of contests for corporate control has emerged as a major theme in the law and economics of corporate law. Lucian Bebchuk, John Coates and Guhan Subramanian generally take the view that incumbent managers are not sufficiently constrained in their self-serving efforts to entrench themselves in their jobs. A seemingly benign anti-takeover tactic, staggering the terms of corporate directors, impedes takeovers by extending the amount of time required for outside acquirers to gain control of boards of directors, even after they have acquired ownership of a controlling block of voting shares. Earlier work by John Pound had shown that the pro-management tilt of the regulation of the market for corporate control can be attributed to the fact that incumbent management is in a far better structural position to galvanize into an effective political coalition to lobby for protectionist legislation than shareholders are to oppose it.[2]

Thus, modern corporate law scholarship has confronted the myriad ways in which government regulation reflects firm operation and performance. On the one hand, regulations in the form of Sarbanes–Oxley, the Foreign Corrupt Practices Act, and rigid scrutiny of technical accounting conventions have greatly increased the personal risks associated with serving as a manager or director of a business regulated by the Securities and Exchange Commission and the federal securities laws. On the other hand, managers have been able to entrench themselves in office by persuading both state and federal regulators and judges to acquiesce in their efforts to legalize a dizzying array of anti-takeover devices that constantly threaten to undermine the vitality of the market for corporate control. Specifically, the modern American public corporation is, according to Mark Roe, due to political adaptation, rather than to the efficiency characteristics of this organizational form.[3] In particular, according to Roe, the "massive dissociation of wealth from active management"[4] is due to regulation that constrains banks and other sophisticated financial institutions from involving themselves in corporate governance. These same rules are convenient to managers because they generate an organizational structure that leaves managers with a great deal of freedom to pursue their own ends.

(7) Several event studies were conducted in the 1980s to try to determine the effect of management discretion to choose the state of incorporation and thus the law that governs the corporation. The studies concluded that the choice benefited shareholders, but some criticized the studies for placing too much import on the change in stock price after reincorporation and failing to account for other possible explanations for a shift in stock price. Responding to such criticism, Professor Robert Daines used a different methodology to test the economic effects on corporations of reincorporating in Delaware. Professor Daines compared the "Tobin's Q" of companies incorporated in Delaware with the Tobin's Q of companies not incorporated in Delaware. Tobin's Q measures the relationship between the market value of a company's stock and the book value of the

2. John Pound, The Rise of the Political Model of Corporate Governance and Corporate Control, 68 N.Y.U. L. Rev. 1003–71 (1993).

3. Mark J. Roe, A Political Theory of American Corporate Finance, 91 Colum. L. Rev. 10 (1991).

4. Id. at 13 (quoting Adolf Berle and Gardiner Means).

company's assets. Tobin's Q is a widely used measure of the value of a company's assets as they are presently deployed. The greater the difference between the market value of the firm's stock and the book value of the assets, the more efficiently management is deploying those assets. Professor Daines found that Delaware companies had a higher Tobin's Q than other companies, even after controlling for a wide range of other factors. This implies that incorporating in Delaware allows for a more efficient deployment of a firm's assets. Robert Daines, Does Delaware Improve Firm Value?, 62 J. Fin. Econ. 525 (2001).

(8) The high quality of the Delaware judiciary in corporate matters does not entirely explain Delaware's spectacular success in the incorporation business. Writing in 1976, Professor Seligman suggested that the advantage of Delaware lies "not [in] her statute alone, but rather [in] the manner in which her judiciary interprets it." Joel Seligman, A Brief History of Delaware's General Corporation Law of 1899, 1 Del.J.Corp.Law 249, 284 (1976). In reaching this conclusion, Professor Seligman relied primarily on an earlier article by Professor William L. Cary, a former chairman of the SEC, who, after reviewing a number of Delaware decisions, concluded that "there is no public policy left in Delaware corporate law except the objective of raising revenue. * * * Consciously or unconsciously, fiduciary standards and standards of fairness generally have been relaxed. In general, the judicial decisions can best be reconciled on the basis of a desire to foster incorporation in Delaware." William L. Cary, Federalism and Corporate Law: Reflections Upon Delaware, 83 Yale L.J. 663, 670, 684 (1974). Professor Cary attributed this attitude to the relationship between the Delaware bench, bar, and state government:[10]

> What is striking about the membership of the court in the last 23 years is that almost all the justices were drawn from the group responsible for the 1967 revision of the corporation law. In fact, two of them were members of the Commission. A majority of the justices practiced law in the firms which represent the important corporations registered in Delaware. * * * Three left the bench, two of them to return to leading firms in Delaware, and one to become Governor. With the exception of Justice Carey, who served from 1945 on the bench in various roles, all but two of the justices have been directly involved in major political positions in the state. The three chief justices have been chronologically (1) Attorney General, (2) Secretary of State and Governor, and (3) the Democratic candidate for Attorney General. Two other justices were Chairman of the State Planning Commission and attorney for the Delaware Senate. The whole process is reminiscent of musical chairs. In such a small state as Delaware, with a population of 548,000 and a bar of 733, of whom 423 are in private practice, we have in microcosm the ultimate example of the relationship between politics, the bar, and the judiciary. There is certainly nothing "wrong" or surprising about these relationships. Yet it is clear that Delaware may be characterized as a tight little club in which the corporate bar cites unreported decisions before the courts in which they practice. Thus major participation in state politics and in the leading firms inevitably would align the Delaware judiciary solidly with Delaware legislative policy. Indeed, as outstanding members of the bar, they may have contributed to its formulation before they became judges, and at any rate, might be disloyal to their state to pursue any other course.

10. Reprinted by permission of The Yale Law Journal Company and Fred B. Rothman & Company from *The Yale Law Journal,* Vol. 83, pp. 690–92.

This was harsh criticism and it is not surprising that defenders of the Delaware Corporation Act reacted sharply and with outrage. E.g. S. Samuel Arsht, Reply to Professor Cary, 31 Bus.Law. 1113 (1976):

> Professor Cary premises his advocacy of a Federal Corporate Minimum Standards Act upon the alleged deficiencies of state law, particularly focusing upon Delaware, its statutes, bench and bar. I submit that Professor Cary's analysis of the Delaware experience is biased, unscholarly and wholly unfair. If his articles had to measure up to the required standards of an SEC disclosure document, they would be found woefully deficient.

(9) Whatever the merits of Professor Cary's complaints about the "cozy" relationship between the Delaware judiciary, the Bar, and the legislature in the 1970s, it is clear that the Delaware judiciary is highly regarded today. The Delaware Chancery Court, the trial court in which most corporation issues are litigated, is a specialized business and corporation court that is the envy of other states.[11] This court sits without a jury and handles local equity matters as well as major commercial disputes. Corporations often prefer to litigate issues in Delaware rather than elsewhere because of the knowledge, expertise, sophistication and experience of the Chancellor and the four Vice Chancellors on corporate matters.

(10) Ralph Winter, Government and the Corporation 9 (1978):

> Rejecting full federal chartering as "politically unrealistic," Cary calls for federal minimum-standards legislation. He claims this legislation, designed to "raise" the standards of management conduct, would increase public confidence—and investment—in American corporations. This last claim, it is absolutely critical to note, is not that an overriding social goal is sacrificed by state law but that Delaware is preventing *private* parties from optimizing their *private* arrangements.
>
> With all due respect to Cary and to the almost universal academic support for his position, it is implausible on its face. The plausible argument runs in exactly the opposite direction. (1) If Delaware permits corporate management to profit at the expense of shareholders and other states do not, then earnings of Delaware corporations must be less than earnings of comparable corporations chartered in other states; therefore, shares in the Delaware corporations must trade at lower prices. (2) Corporations with lower earnings will be at a disadvantage in raising debt or equity capital. (3) Corporations at a disadvantage in the capital market will be at a disadvantage in the product market, and their share price will decline, thereby increasing chances of a takeover that would replace management. To avoid this result, corporations must seek legal systems more attractive to capital. (4) States desiring corporate charters will thus try to provide legal systems that optimize the shareholder-corporation relation. * * *

(11) Efforts to explain the success of Delaware have become virtually a cottage industry for corporate theorists. For example, it has been suggested that Delaware is successful because it reduces regulatory costs through limiting net-

11. [By the Editors] Several states have created specialized business courts modeled roughly after the Delaware Chancery Court. The trend towards such courts "is in its inception but is gaining strength." Report of Ad Hoc Committee on Business Courts, Business Courts: Toward a More Efficient Judiciary, 52 Bus. Law. 947, 960 (1997). This report indicates that three states (New York, Illinois, and North Carolina) have established business courts since 1992, and that studies are underway in at least six additional states.

work externalities,[13] because of its "regulatory responsiveness,"[14] or because of the superiority of its Court of Chancery.[15] Another explanation is the advantage provided by the large developed body of case law in Delaware.[16] A less generous explanation is the apparent dependence of Delaware legislators on corporate and corporate-related campaign contributions which assures they will quickly address corporate needs. Finally, it has been suggested that the willingness of Delaware judges to engage in corporate lawmaking explains Delaware's success.[17] Certainly, a partial explanation lies in the efficiency of the Delaware courts in considering and resolving significant corporate litigation.[18]

(12) As of late 2002, Delaware was the state of incorporation for 51 percent of all U.S. public companies, over 50 percent of companies listed on the New York Stock Exchange and 63 percent of the companies on Fortune Magazine's list of the 500 largest companies in the United States. The number of new incorporations in Delaware is in the range of 45,000 per year.

(13) To some extent, corporate law rules are likely to reflect societal attitudes about the larger role of corporations within society. See Marco Pagano & Paolo Volpin, The Political Economy of Finance, Oxford Rev. Econ. Pol'y, Vol. 17, no. 4 (2001). (Chart shows the different perspectives on corporate governance that distinguish Anglo–American corporate governance systems from corporate governance systems in continental Europe and Asia.):

Differences in Perspectives on Corporate Governance:

Preferences of Senior Managers about Corporate Objectives

Survey question	Possible Answers	Japan	Germany	France	USA	UK
(1) Whose Company is it?	All stakeholders	97.1	82.7	78	24.4	29.5
	The shareholders	2.9	17.3	22	75.6	70.5
(1) No. of respondents:		68	110	50	82	78
(2) Which is more important?	Job Security Dividends	97.1 2.9	59.1 40.9	60.4 39.6	10.8 89.2	10.7 89.3
(2) No. of respondents:		68	105	68	83	75

13. [By the Editors] Marcel Kahan and Michael Klausner, Standardization and Innovation in Corporate Contracting (or "The Economics of Boilerplate"), 83 Va.L.Rev. 713, 763–74 (1997).

14. [By the Editors] Roberta Romano, The Genius of American Corporate Law 38 (1993).

15. [By the Editors] Curtis Alva, Delaware and the Market for Corporate Charters: History and Agency, 15 Del.J.Corp.Law 885, 918 (1990).

16. [By the Editors] Stephen J. Massey, Chancellor Allen's Jurisprudence and the Theory of Corporate Law, 17 Del.J.Corp.L. 683, 702 n. 79 (1992); Henry G. Manne, The Judiciary and Free Markets, 21 Harv. J.L. & Pub. Pol'y 11, 18 (1997).

17. [By the Editors] Jill E. Fisch, The Peculiar Role of the Delaware Courts in the Competition for Corporate Charters, 68 Cincinnati L.Rev. 1061 (2000). The author states: "The article concludes that Delaware lawmaking offers Delaware corporations a variety of benefits, including flexibility, responsiveness, insulation from undue political influence, and transparency. These benefits increase Delaware's ability to adjust its corporate law to changes in the business world."

18. [By the Editors] See Mark J. Lowenstein, Delaware As Demon: Twenty Years After Professor Cary's Polemic, 71 U.Colo.L.Rev. 497, 505 (2000):

Regardless of the provisions of the corporate code, Delaware's superior judiciary would persist and provide a good reason to incorporate in Delaware. The Delaware Chancery Court * * * hears 500 business-related cases a year. The Chancery Court resolves those cases promptly, and its decisions are rarely appealed. Only five percent of its decisions are appealed to the state Supreme Court— Delaware has no intermediate appellate court—and in those appeals the Supreme Court upholds the Chancery Court in seventy-five percent of the cases. If a case is appealed to the Supreme Court, that court generally renders a decision in about thirty days from submission. Thus, litigants know that Delaware will provide a prompt resolution of their dispute, and corporate managers might well value this in deciding where to incorporate.

DOLE FOOD COMPANY, INC., PROXY STATEMENT

June 8, 2001.

PROPOSAL NO. 3

REINCORPORATION IN DELAWARE

INTRODUCTION

For the reasons set forth below, the Board believes that it is in the best interests of Dole and its stockholders to change the state of incorporation of Dole from Hawaii to Delaware (the "Proposed Reincorporation"). * * *

The Proposed Reincorporation will be effected by merging Dole–Hawaii into a new Delaware corporation that is a wholly-owned subsidiary of Dole–Hawaii (the "Merger"). Upon completion of the Merger, Dole–Hawaii, as a corporate entity, will cease to exist and Dole–Delaware will succeed to the assets and liabilities of Dole–Hawaii and will continue to operate the business of Dole under its current name, Dole Food Company, Inc.

NO CHANGE IN THE CORPORATE NAME, BOARD MEMBERS, BUSINESS, MANAGEMENT, CAPITALIZATION, BOARD OF DIRECTORS STRUCTURE, EMPLOYEE BENEFIT PLANS OR LOCATION OF PRINCIPAL FACILITIES OF DOLE WILL OCCUR AS A RESULT OF THE PROPOSED REINCORPORATION.

Dole–Hawaii Common Stock is listed for trading on the New York Stock Exchange and the Pacific Exchange and, after the Merger, Dole–Delaware Common Stock will be traded on the New York Stock Exchange and the Pacific Exchange under the same symbol ("DOL") as the shares of Dole–Hawaii Common Stock are currently traded. There will be no interruption in the trading of Dole's Common Stock as a result of the Merger. * * * The Proposed Reincorporation includes the implementation of a new certificate of incorporation and by-laws for Dole–Delaware (the "Delaware Charter" and "Delaware By–Laws") to replace the current articles of association and by-laws of Dole–Hawaii (the "Hawaii Charter" and "Hawaii By–Laws"). As a Delaware corporation, Dole–Delaware will be subject to the Delaware General Corporation Law (the "Delaware Law"). Dole–Hawaii is subject to the corporation laws of Hawaii. Differences between the Delaware Charter and By–Laws, on the one hand, and the Hawaii Charter and By–Laws, on the other hand, must be viewed in the context of the differences between the Delaware Law and the corporation law of Hawaii. * * *

PRINCIPAL REASONS FOR THE REINCORPORATION PROPOSAL

For many years, Delaware has followed a policy of encouraging incorporation in that state and, in furtherance of that policy, has been a leader in adopting, construing, and implementing comprehensive, flexible corporate laws responsive to the legal and business needs of corporations organized under its laws. Many corporations have initially chosen Delaware, or chosen to reincorporate in Delaware, in a manner similar to that proposed by Dole.

The Board of Directors believes that the principal reasons for considering such a reincorporation are:

- the development in Delaware over the last century of a well-established body of case law construing the Delaware General Corporation Law, which provides businesses with a greater measure of predictability than exist in any other jurisdiction; the certainty afforded by the well-established principles of corporate governance under the Delaware Law are of benefit to Dole and its stockholders and should increase Dole's ability to attract and retain outstanding directors and officers;

- the Delaware Law itself, which is generally acknowledged to be the most advanced and flexible corporate statute in the country;

- the Delaware Court of Chancery, which brings to its handling of complex corporate issues a level of experience, a speed of decision and a degree of sophistication and understanding unmatched by any other court in the country, and the Delaware Supreme Court, the only appeals court, which is highly regarded and currently consists primarily of former Vice Chancellors and corporate practitioners; and

- the Delaware General Assembly, which each year considers and adopts statutory amendments that have been proposed by the Corporation Law Section of the Delaware bar to meet changing business needs.

The Proposed Reincorporation will effect only a change in the legal domicile of Dole and other changes of a legal nature. The material changes are described in this Proxy Statement. The Proposed Reincorporation will NOT result in any change in the name, business, management, capitalization, board of directors structure, fiscal year, assets, liabilities or location of the principal facilities of Dole. The directors elected at the Annual Meeting to serve on the Board of Dole–Hawaii will become the directors of Dole–Delaware. * * *

COMPARISON OF THE CHARTERS AND BY-LAWS OF DOLE–HAWAII AND
DOLE–DELAWARE AND SIGNIFICANT DIFFERENCES BETWEEN
THE CORPORATION LAWS OF HAWAII AND DELAWARE

GENERAL. The Delaware Law and the corporation law of Hawaii differ in several respects. It is not practical to summarize all of the differences in this Proxy Statement, but the differences that could materially affect the rights of stockholders are discussed below.

Some of the provisions in the Delaware Charter and Delaware By–Laws, in conjunction with the Delaware Law, alter the rights of stockholders and the power of management, as compared with provisions in the Hawaii Charter and Hawaii By–Laws, in conjunction with the Hawaii Act. Some of these alterations could reduce stockholder participation in important corporate decisions and may have "anti-takeover" implications, some of which may make takeovers harder to accomplish and some of which may make takeovers easier to accomplish. The alterations are discussed in greater detail in the following pages of this Proxy Statement. The Proposed Reincorporation is not being proposed in response to any present attempt, known to the Board, to acquire control of Dole, to obtain representation on the Board, or to take significant corporate action that would materially affect the governance of Dole.

Dole does not now have in place, and has no present plans to put in place, the panoply of anti-takeover provisions frequently employed by Delaware (and other) public companies, including so-called shareholder rights ("poison pill") plans, a classified board of directors, "continuing director" charter provisions, or similar measures.

STOCKHOLDER VOTING. The Hawaii Act generally provides that the majority of the votes entitled to be cast on a matter constitutes a quorum for action on that matter, and that action on the matter by a voting group is approved if the votes cast within the group in favor of the matter exceed the votes cast opposing the matter, unless the articles of incorporation or the Hawaii Act require a greater number of affirmative votes. The Delaware Law generally provides that the certificate of incorporation or by-laws of a corporation may specify the size of a quorum and the vote necessary for the transaction of any business, but the quorum cannot be set at less than one-third of the shares entitled to vote at the meetings or of the shares of a class or series of shares entitled to a separate vote. Absent a specification in the certificate of incorporation or by-laws, a majority of the shares entitled to vote constitutes a quorum * * *

DIRECTOR LIABILITY AND INDEMNIFICATION. Under the Hawaii Act, a corporation's articles of incorporation (or by-laws adopted prior to July 1, 1996) may contain a provision eliminating or limiting the liability of directors to the corporation or its stockholders for monetary damages for any action taken, or any failure to take action, as a director, but such provision may not eliminate or limit the personal liability of a director for the amount of a financial benefit received by the director to which the director is not entitled, an intentional infliction of harm on the corporation or the stockholders, a violation of the provisions of the Hawaii Act relating to unlawful distributions, or an intentional violation of criminal law. A Hawaii By–Law adopted prior to July 1, 1996 contains such a provision.

Under the Delaware Law, a corporation's certificate of incorporation may contain a similar provision, eliminating or limiting the personal liability of directors to the corporation or its stockholders for monetary damages for breach of fiduciary duty as a director, but such provision may not eliminate or limit the liability of a director for any breach of the director's duty of loyalty to the corporation or its stockholders, acts or omissions not in good faith or which involve intentional misconduct or a knowing violation of law, wilful or negligent payment of unlawful dividends or stock purchases or redemptions, or any transaction from which the director derived an improper personal benefit. The Delaware Charter contains such a provision.

The provisions of the Hawaii Act and the Delaware Law are substantially similar with respect to indemnification of officers and directors. * * * The Delaware Law requires indemnification when there has been a successful defense on the merits or otherwise. If the individual loses or settles, the Delaware Law provides for permissive indemnification (i.e., it is not required, but the corporation may indemnify). The Delaware Law generally permits indemnification of expenses, including attorneys' fees, actually and reasonably incurred in the defense or settlement of a derivative or third-party action, provided there is a determination (a) by a majority vote of the directors who are not parties to such action, suit or proceeding, even though less than a quorum, (b) by a committee of such directors designated by majority vote of such directors, even though less than a quorum, (c) by independent legal counsel or (d) by a majority vote of a quorum of the stockholders, that the person seeking indemnification acted in good faith and in a manner reasonably believed to be in or not opposed to the best interests of the corporation. Without court approval, however, no indemnification may be made in respect of any derivative action in which such person is adjudged liable for negligence or misconduct in the performance of his or her duty to the corporation. Under Delaware law, indemnification and expense advancement may be made obligatory, and broader indemnification than set forth in the Delaware Law may be made permissive or obligatory, subject to certain limitations. The Delaware By–Laws provide for indemnification of officers and directors to the fullest extent permitted by the Delaware Law.

Expenses incurred by an officer or director in defending an action may be paid in advance, under the Hawaii Act and the Delaware Law, if the director or officer undertakes to repay such amounts if it is ultimately determined that he or she is not entitled to indemnification. In addition, both states authorize a corporation's purchase of indemnity insurance for the benefit of its officers, directors, employees and agents whether or not the corporation would have the power to indemnify against the liability covered by the policy.

The Delaware By–Laws provide for the advancement of expenses incurred by a director or officer in defending a proceeding, subject to an undertaking by such director or officer to repay such amount should it be determined that he is not entitled to be indemnified by Dole–Delaware. These provisions are similar to provisions of the Hawaii By–Laws.

Insofar as indemnification for liabilities arising under the Securities Act of 1933 may be permitted to directors, officers, or persons controlling Dole pursuant to the foregoing provisions, Dole is informed that, in the opinion of the Securities and Exchange Commission, such indemnification is against public policy and therefore unenforceable.

DIVIDENDS AND DISTRIBUTIONS. A Hawaii corporation, unless otherwise restricted by its articles of incorporation, may authorize and make distributions unless, after giving effect thereto, the corporation would be unable to pay its debts as they become due in the usual course of business or the total assets of the corporation would be less than the sum of its total liabilities plus (unless otherwise provided in its articles of incorporation) the amount that would be needed, if the corporation were to be dissolved at the time as of which the distribution is measured, to satisfy the preferential rights upon dissolution of stockholders whose preferential rights are superior to those receiving the distribution. The Hawaii Charter does not contain any such provisions with respect to payment of distributions. Generally, a director who votes for or assents to an illegal distribution is liable to the corporation, jointly and severally with all other directors so voting or assenting, for the amount of the distribution in excess of the amount that could have legally been paid.

The Delaware Law generally allows dividends to be paid out of surplus of the corporation or, if there is no surplus, out of the net profits of the corporation for the current fiscal year or the prior fiscal year. The directors of a Delaware corporation are prohibited from making distributions to stockholders except in the manner provided by the Delaware Law. In case of any wilful or negligent violation of the provisions of the Delaware Law governing distributions, the directors under whose administration the violation occurred (except for those directors who dissented) are, for a period of six years, jointly and severally liable to the corporation and, in the event of the corporation's insolvency or dissolution, to its creditors for the full amount of the distribution unlawfully made.

Notes

(1) Beginning in the 1960s and early 1970s there has been a trend toward the gradual expansion of federal law at the expense of state law. These earlier expansions were largely based on broad construction of antifraud concepts in the 1934 Act and Rule 10b–5 promulgated thereunder, but this trend had stabilized by the mid–1970s. In the early 1980s another movement toward federalization of state corporation law developed from the conservative "law and economics" movement's theory that a national market for "corporate control" of publicly–held corporations existed with which states were powerless to interfere. The United States Supreme Court abruptly dismantled this theory in CTS Corp. v. Dynamics Corp. of America, 481 U.S. 69, 107 S.Ct. 1637, 95 L.Ed.2d 67 (1987). Justice Powell's majority opinion strongly restated the traditional role of states in the regulation of state-created publicly–held corporations:

> We think the Court of Appeals failed to appreciate the significance, for Commerce Clause analysis, of the fact that state regulation of corporate governance is regulation of entities whose very existence and attributes are a product of state law. * * *

> * * * Every State in this country has enacted laws regulating corporate governance. By prohibiting certain transactions, and regulating others, such laws necessarily affect certain aspects of interstate commerce. This necessarily is true with respect to corporations with shareholders in States other than the State of incorporation. Large corporations that are listed on national exchanges, or even regional exchanges, will have shareholders in many States and shares that are traded frequently. The markets that facilitate this national and international participation in ownership of corporations are essential for providing capital not only for new enterprises but also for established companies that need to expand their businesses. This beneficial free market system depends at its core upon the fact that a corporation— except in the rarest situations—is organized under, and governed by, the law of a single jurisdiction, traditionally the corporate law of the State of its incorporation.

> These regulatory laws may affect directly a variety of corporate transactions. Mergers are a typical example. In view of the substantial effect that a merger may have on the shareholders' interests in a corporation, many States require supermajority votes to approve mergers. See * * * MBCA § 11.03. By requiring a greater vote for mergers than is required for other transactions, these laws make it more difficult for corporations to merge. State laws also may provide for "dissenters' rights" under which minority shareholders who disagree with corporate decisions to take particular actions are entitled to sell their shares to the corporation at fair market value. See * * * MBCA § 13.02. By requiring the corporation to purchase the shares of dissenting sharehold-

ers, these laws may inhibit a corporation from engaging in the specified transactions.[30]

It thus is an accepted part of the business landscape in this country for States to create corporations, to prescribe their powers, and to define the rights that are acquired by purchasing their shares. A State has an interest in promoting stable relationships among parties involved in the corporations it charters, as well as in ensuring that investors in such corporations have an effective voice in corporate affairs.

481 U.S. at 89–91, 107 S.Ct. at 1649–51, 95 L.Ed.2d at 85–86.

(2) More recently, some of the provisions of the Sarbanes–Oxley Act of 2002 override traditional state law. For example, executive compensation, which typically is the province of state law, is affected by Sarbanes–Oxley in a couple of ways. First, Section 1103 gives the Securities and Exchange Commission the power to seek a freeze of "extraordinary payments" made to corporate officers and directors during the course of an SEC investigation into possible securities law violations. If the officer or director is charged with violating a securities law, the funds can be frozen until the conclusion of legal proceedings. Second, Section 304 requires CEOs and CFOs to reimburse the company for any bonus or equity-based compensation or profits received from the sale of securities during the 12–month period after the first publication of a financial statement that later turned out to be erroneous and had to be restated. This provision was inserted in the statute as a response to the widespread public perception that corporate officers manipulated their companies' financial statements in order to trigger incentive-based executive compensation agreements or to make insider trading profits. Also, Sarbanes–Oxley increases the SEC's power to bar people from serving as officers or directors of public companies. Prior to the passage of the Act, in order to bar somebody from serving as an officer or director, the SEC had to make a showing that the person demonstrated "substantial unfitness" to serve as an officer or director. Over time, this provision had been interpreted to mean that the SEC had to show "egregious misconduct" or that a person had engaged in "repeated violations of securities laws." Now, the SEC need only show that a person is "unfit" (rather than substantially unfit), and the SEC can bar people from serving as officers and directors for misconduct that falls far short of being egregious or recidivist.

The nature and scope of fiduciary duties has long been the province of state law, and Sarbanes–Oxley does not change this. However, Section 307 of the Act, which contains significant new provisions regulating the conduct of corporate lawyers (another area that traditionally has been the province of state law), requires the SEC to develop rules of professional conduct for lawyers of public companies. The rules that the SEC develops require that lawyers report "evidence

---

30. [By the Court] Numerous other common regulations may affect both nonresident and resident shareholders of a corporation. Specified votes may be required for the sale of all of the corporation's assets. See * * * MBCA § 12.02. The election of directors may be staggered over a period of years to prevent abrupt changes in management. See * * * MBCA § 8.06. Various classes of stock may be created with differences in voting rights as to dividends and on liquidation. See * * * MBCA § 6.01(c). Provisions may be made for cumulative voting. See * * * MBCA § 7.28. Corpora- tions may adopt restrictions on payment of dividends to ensure that specified ratios of assets to liabilities are maintained for the benefit of the holders of corporate bonds or notes. See MBCA [§ 6.40] (noting that a corporation's articles of incorporation can restrict payment of dividends); * * *. Where the shares of a corporation are held in States other than that of incorporation, actions taken pursuant to these and similar provisions of state law will affect all shareholders alike wherever they reside or are domiciled. * * *

of a material violation of the securities laws, or breach of fiduciary duty or similar violation'' by a public company or any of its agents, to the general counsel or the CEO of the company. If this person does not respond ''appropriately'' the lawyer is required to report the evidence to the audit committee of the board of directors, or to some other committee of the board that is comprised solely of independent directors.

Chapter Six

THE FORMATION OF A CLOSELY HELD CORPORATION

This chapter assumes that a decision has been made to form a corporation, and the issues are how, where, and, most importantly, what happens if things are not done correctly.

A. WHERE TO INCORPORATE

Selection of the state of incorporation involves an appraisal of two factors: (a) a dollars-and-cents analysis of the relative cost of incorporating, or qualifying as a foreign corporation, under the statutes of the states under consideration, and (b) a consideration of the advantages and disadvantages of the substantive corporation laws of these states. As a practical matter the choice usually comes down to the jurisdiction where the business is to be conducted or Delaware, the most popular outside jurisdiction.

If the corporation is closely–held and its business is to be conducted largely or entirely within a single state, local incorporation is almost always to be preferred. The cost of forming a Delaware corporation and qualifying it to transact business in another state will be greater than forming a local corporation in that state to begin with. In addition, the cost of operating a local business through a Delaware corporation qualified to transact business in the state will almost certainly be greater than the cost of operating a local corporation. Income and franchise taxes are usually the same for both domestic and qualified foreign corporations, but again the Delaware taxes must be added. In 1991, the Delaware franchise taxes were increased significantly, thereby reducing the attractiveness of that state for small out-of-state corporations. Another disadvantage of Delaware incorporation is the possibility of being forced to defend a suit in that distant state rather than where the corporation has its principal place of business. The Delaware statute may offer some flexibility not available in other states, in that § 831 of the GCL permits a corporation with less than 30 shareholders to be managed directly by the shareholders. Many states, however, have adopted § 7.32 of the MBCA, which also permits non-traditional management arrangements.

B. HOW TO INCORPORATE

How should one go about forming a corporation? At one time, this probably involved the employment of an attorney familiar with the incorporation process of the selected state. Today, many states accept corporate filings electronically, and a number of internet companies offer to provide, for a fee, incorporation services for any state.

Many internet companies promise to file the corporate documents with the Secretary of State on-line, and serve as a registered agent for the corporation. Others offer assured filing within 24 hours. All accept credit cards for payment. The official website of the state of Delaware's Division of Corporations[1] offers a variety of services, including "Same Day" and even "2–Hour" processing of corporate filings, provided that the filings are received no later than 6:00PM, and a fee of $500 is paid.[2] Whether or not all this is a bargain, or even if it results in the formation of a corporation that meets the needs of the founders, obviously depends on a variety of factors. If the corporation involves issues of any complexity, or there is any possibility whatsoever of disagreements arising among the founders of the corporation (or their heirs), it will almost certainly be necessary to utilize the services of an attorney to assure that the documents accord with the needs of the investors.

Assume that you are an attorney "just starting out," and are asked to draft specialized provisions for a corporation to be formed. There are significant issues that must be addressed. The first is what substantive provisions should be reduced to writing, and whether these provisions should be placed in the articles of incorporation, the bylaws, or a shareholders' agreement. The modern trend is to limit the articles of incorporation to provisions required by law to appear in that public document. The other substantive provisions are placed in documents such as the bylaws or shareholders' agreement that are not filed of public record.

In forming a corporation, there is always a danger of overlooking some obvious matter or using "boiler plate" language that may have been suitable for the last corporation but is egregiously inappropriate for this corporation. Many corporations may be stamped from a single mold and be perfectly satisfactory, but some cannot. Depending on such matters as the nature of the business, the agreements among the shareholders and their mutual degree of trust and confidence, a considerable amount of individualized drafting may be necessary. Read MBCA §§ 2.01–2.03, 2.05–2.06, 7.32.

The formal requirements for filing of documents are set forth in MBCA, Chapter 1, particularly §§ 1.20–1.26. These minimal requirements are similar to those adopted by most states, and the trend is towards limiting the procedures for forming a corporation to those specified in the MBCA. Generally, the trend in most states is towards the simplification of the process of incorporation wherever possible, and incorporation by postcard or electronic filing is feasible in many states. However, about a dozen states still require

---

1. http://www.state.de.us/corp/special.htm.

2. A complete list of current fees is available at http://www.state.de.us/corp/corpfee3.htm#Domestic.

the filing or recording of the articles of incorporation in one or more counties as well as with a state official. About a half-dozen states still require publication of the articles of incorporation as well as filing with a state official.

Consider again MBCA §§ 2.02, 1.20. Would the following document, submitted to the Secretary of State with the appropriate fee (a) be accepted for filing under the MBCA, and (b) result in the formation of a corporation?

ARTICLES OF INCORPORATION

1.   The name of the corporation is AB Software Store, Inc.

2.   The corporation is authorized to issue 1,000 shares of stock.

3.   The street address of the corporation's registered office is 125 Main Street, City of _____, State of _____ and the name of the corporation's registered agent at that address is Robert B_____.

4.   The name and address of the incorporator is Robert B_____, 125 Main Street, City of _____, State of _____.

/s/ Robert B_____

Robert B_____, Incorporator.

———

Whatever minor technical defects may exist in this form, incorporation under the MBCA appears to be a very simple process that hardly requires the services of an attorney (if a "plain vanilla" corporation such as that described above is desired).[3] This apparent simplicity is somewhat deceptive since articles of incorporation usually will have to contain express provisions on additional topics if the desires of the interested parties are to be fully carried out. Consider, for example, MBCA § 6.01 in the situation where it is contemplated that the corporation will issue shares of stock of more than one class. If it is contemplated that the corporation may have a significant number of shareholders, careful consideration should also be given to limiting the liability of directors [MBCA § 2.02(b)(4), discussed in Chapter 11] and adjusting the scope of the right of directors and officers to indemnification [MBCA §§ 2.02(b)(5), 8.50–8.59, discussed in Chapter 14]. The Official Comment to MBCA § 2.02 contains a two-page list of provisions "that may be elected only in the articles of incorporation" and a shorter list of provisions "that may be elected either in the articles of incorporation or in the bylaws."

Notes

(1) So far as formal requirements for filing are concerned, the Committee on Corporate Laws in 1997 amended Chapter 1 of the MBCA to authorize electronic filing of documents as a guide for the adoption of such procedures by states.

---

3.   [By the Editors] Also, it should be obvious that modern articles of incorporation provide relatively little useful information to third persons about the owners of the corporation, its assets, or the nature of its business. For example, the incorporator, "Robert B_____," might be an attorney, an employee of a law firm, or an employee of a corporation service company. Somewhat more meaningful information may sometimes be obtained from other filed documents. See for example, MBCA § 16.21.

Among the numerous technical changes made by these amendments are definitions of the concepts of "delivery," of "electronic transmissions," and of "signatures." MBCA §§ 1.40(5), (7A), 22A. At the same time, the Committee recognized that the development of reliable and inexpensive copying machines made unnecessary the filing requirement that a copy of a document accompany the document itself. These are innovative provisions that probably will be widely followed in the future. Older requirements, such as that documents be acknowledged or verified before a notary public and his or her acknowledgement and notarial seal be attached, also serve little real purpose as a practical matter, and may gradually disappear.

(2) The processing of filed documents by the Secretary of State under the MBCA is described in § 1.25, a section that was also significantly amended in 1997. The date the existence of the corporation begins is described in § 2.03, as is the legal effect of the decision by the Secretary of State to file the document. Chapter 1 of the MBCA does not reflect a very expansive approach to the powers of the office of Secretary of State. For example, the Secretary of State may not prescribe a mandatory form for articles of incorporation (§ 1.21(b)), his filing duty is expressly defined as "ministerial" (§ 1.25(d)), and he is expressly commanded to file a document if it "satisfies the requirements of section 1.20" (MBCA § 1.25(a)).

This restrictive view of the powers of the Secretary of State rests on the experience of attorneys in a number of states where the office of Secretary of State viewed its powers broadly, purported to adopt rules or regulations in addition to the requirements of the corporation statute,[4] and often conducted wide-ranging review of the propriety of specific provisions of documents filed with it. One can envision the frustration of an attorney who, after negotiating a complex provision for inclusion in a proposed articles of incorporation (or other document), is faced with the task of persuading a relatively low-level employee in the office of the Secretary of State that the provision is consistent with the Secretary of State's view of the meaning of the corporation statute.

Of course, the office of Secretary of State has considerable political "clout" in the legislatures of most states, and therefore, these provisions may not be accepted in some states. As of 2000, fourteen states that generally followed the MBCA in revising their corporation statutes had granted the Secretary of State greater review power than provided by § 1.25.

(3) *Names.* Consider, for example, the requirement that the corporation have a name, and the requirements relating to that name in MBCA § 4.01. Consider also MBCA §§ 4.02, 4.03.

(a) The critical language in § 4.01(b) is that a corporate name "must be distinguishable upon the records of the secretary of state" from other corporate names. Earlier versions of the MBCA required that a corporate name "not be the same as, or deceptively similar to, the name" of an existing corporation. MBCA (1969) § 8. Many secretaries of state construed this or other similar language to require a determination whether the proposed name constituted unfair competition with existing corporations. The Official Comment to § 4.01 states that "confusion in an absolute or linguistic sense is the appropriate test under the Model Act, not the competitive relationship between the corporations, which is the

---

4. [By the Editors] In this connection, consider also MBCA § 1.30. Contrast this narrow grant of authority with § 139 of the 1969 Model Act, which granted the secretary of state the power and authority "reasonably necessary to enable him to administer this Act efficiently and to perform the duties therein imposed upon him."

test for fraud or unfair competition." In enforcing whatever statutory standard is applicable, the secretary of state "simply maintains an alphabetical list of 'official' corporate names as they appear from corporate records and makes his decision * * * by comparing the proposed name with those on the list." Official Comment to § 4.01. Today, this list is usually maintained electronically, and in some states, may be accessible to the public.

(b) Is the current test a desirable one for determining name availability? The "distinguishable upon the records of the secretary of state" language was taken from § 102(1) of the Delaware General Corporation Law. In Trans–Americas Airlines, Inc. v. Kenton, 491 A.2d 1139 (Del.1985), Transamerica Corporation, the nationally-known conglomerate, had long associated the name "Transamerica" with the activities of a wholly owned subsidiary named "Trans International Airlines, Inc.," which operated a worldwide air charter service. This association took the form of national advertising by Transamerica and using the word "Transamerica" on many of the airplanes operated by the subsidiary. Trans International Airlines, Inc. was permitted by the Delaware Secretary of State to change its name to "Transamerica Airlines, Inc." An entirely unrelated corporation named "Trans–Americas Airlines, Inc." complained to the Secretary of State and filed suit after the Secretary of State refused to revoke the registration of the name "Transamerica Airlines, Inc." The Delaware Supreme Court accepted the lower court's conclusion that " 'Transamerica Airlines, Inc.' is distinguishable from the name 'Trans–Americas Airlines, Inc.,' on the records of the [Secretary of State]," and held that the statute did not authorize the Secretary of State to reject a name on the ground that it was "confusingly similar" to a name or names already in use.

(c) Because of the widespread adoption of earlier versions of the Model Act, the statutes of many states today contain a "deceptively similar" standard (though sometimes phrased in different words) that makes it clear that prevention of unfair competition is at least partially the objective of corporate name regulation. The extent to which secretaries of state actually attempt to police against unfair competition apparently varies widely from state to state. Many secretaries of state have also evolved "house rules" about name availability that may lead to rather peculiar results.

(d) As noted in MBCA § 4.01(e), corporations may generally conduct business under an assumed or fictitious name to the same extent that an individual may. (The general test for the lawfulness of doing business under an assumed or fictitious name is that it is proper to do so if the purpose is not to defraud. See e.g. United States v. Dunn, 564 F.2d 348, 354 n. 12 (9th Cir.1977)).

(e) What purposes are served by "reserved names" (MBCA § 4.02) and "registered names" (MBCA § 4.03)?

(4) *Duration.* MBCA § 3.02 automatically grants every corporation "perpetual duration and succession in its corporate name," unless its articles of incorporation provide otherwise. Earlier versions of the Model Act required that the articles of incorporation affirmatively set forth "[t]he period of duration, which may be perpetual." MBCA (1969) § 54(b); see also id. § 4(a). Some state corporation acts today contain provisions similar to the 1969 Act. Since almost all corporations elected perpetual status under these provisions, MBCA § 3.02 does not reflect a significant change. Why might a corporation with less than a perpetual duration ever be created?

(5) *Purposes.* Historically, a great deal of importance was attached to the statement of purposes in the articles of incorporation. It "is undoubtedly the most

important part of the corporate charter, for this clause, together with the general act under which it is drawn, is the true measure of the powers of the corporation." Louis S. Berkoff, The Object Clause in Corporate Articles, 4 Wis.L.Rev. 424 (1928). During the nineteenth and early twentieth centuries, corporations were formed for a specific "purpose" that had to be "fully stated;" general purpose and multiple purpose clauses were not accepted in many states. As a result, a great deal of litigation involved the question of whether a corporation had exceeded its purposes in some transaction. See the discussion of *ultra vires* in part C in this Chapter. This problem has just about disappeared under modern statutes. See MBCA § 3.01(a). Indeed, the disappearance of litigation over the scope of purpose clauses is one of the more visible and sensible changes in corporation law in the last half-century.

(a) The first step in this development was recognition that a corporation may list multiple purposes without any limitation on the number of purposes specified and without any obligation that the corporation actually pursue all the purposes contained in its articles. The result was that form books were developed that contained hundreds of possible purpose clauses.

Such clauses were generally drafted on the theory that they should be as broad as possible when describing some line or kind of business. Since the number of purposes was unlimited, furthermore, it was possible to string together a large number of such clauses to produce articles of incorporation that were impressively long, and unreadable. Purpose clauses in this era often ran pages in length but usually gave little or no information as to what precise business the corporation actually planned to engage in.

(b) The next step, quite logically, was to eliminate the excessive verbiage of purposes clauses by permitting incorporation "for the transaction of any lawful business," or similar language that did not require specification of particular lines or kinds of business. These clauses, however, were not quickly accepted; their use did not become widespread until the second half of the twentieth century. The 1969 Model Act permitted this streamlined language (which, after all, did little more than what a long statement of specific purposes did), but it continued to require an affirmative statement of the purposes of the corporation in the articles of incorporation "which may be stated to be, or to include, the transaction of any or all lawful business for which corporations may be incorporated under this Act." MBCA (1969) § 54(c).

(c) Why might articles of incorporation today ever include a narrow purposes clause? There are several possible explanations: (1) some types of corporations may be engaged in businesses subject to state regulation that permit incorporation under general business statutes (see MBCA § 3.01(b)) but require limitations on certain types of corporate activities; (2) some persons may be uncomfortable with the complete lack of useful information about the purpose of the corporation permitted by the MBCA, preferring that some description of the principal business of the corporation appear in the articles of incorporation (without restricting the corporation to that business); and (3) in closely–held corporations, a limited purposes clause may be used where one or more persons interested in the corporation (but not controlling its affairs) wish to restrict the lines of business the corporation may enter. Other justifications may exist as well.

(6) *Powers.* Historically, one often encountered provisions in articles of incorporation that dealt with corporate "powers" as well as corporate "purposes." The distinction between "powers" and "purposes" is not self-evident; it can best be appreciated by comparing the list of "general powers" in MBCA § 3.02 with a

"purpose" such as operating a software store. The distinction between "purposes" and "powers" certainly was not understood by many practitioners, since articles of incorporation clauses dealing with "powers" were often indiscriminately mixed in with "purposes." A useful psychological device that aids in distinguishing "powers" from "purposes" is mentally to precede each statement with the phrase "to engage in the business of * * * " and then to use the present participle form of the applicable verb. Thus, instead of saying, "The purpose for which the corporation is organized is to operate a software store," say "The purpose for which the corporation is organized is *to engage in the business of* operating a software store." By transposing the verb form from the infinitive to the present participle form, the distinction between powers such as "to sue and be sued" and purposes such as "to operate a software store" becomes accentuated.

(a) Is it necessary or desirable to make any references to corporate powers in modern articles of incorporation? Consider MBCA § 2.02(c). Most attorneys agree that it is preferable to take this subsection at face value, at least in states where the statutory powers are sufficiently broad to encompass various acts that raised *ultra vires* problems in an earlier era, such as the power of a corporation to enter into a general partnership or to guarantee the debts of customers or third persons.

(b) Today, all statutes contain a list of general powers analogous to those found in MBCA § 3.02. In addition, provisions relating to specific powers may be "tucked away" in substantive provisions themselves. See, e.g. MBCA § 8.51. Section 3.02 contains several changes from earlier versions of similar sections in earlier Model Acts. Perhaps most important is the addition of the introductory phrase, "has *the same powers as an individual* to do all things necessary or convenient to carry out its business and affairs" (emphasis added). As of 2005, over twenty-five states include this phrase in their corporation statutes.

MBCA § 3.02 begins with the phrase "[u]nless its articles of incorporation provide otherwise." Why might it be desirable to preclude a corporation from exercising specific powers? Consider, for example, § 3.02(15), which according to the Official Comment was included in addition to § 3.02(13) to permit "contributions for purposes that may not be charitable, such as for political purposes or to influence elections." Might an investor wish to preclude such contributions? What other kinds of restrictions on powers might a cautious investor wish to impose on a corporation in which he or she is making a significant investment as a minority shareholder?

(7) *Registered office and registered agent.* The designation of a registered office and registered agent, and the statutory provisions relating thereto (see MBCA §§ 5.01–5.04) are designed to ensure that every corporation has publicly stated a current place where it may be found for purposes of service of process, tax notices, and the like. Often a corporation designates its registered office to be its principal business office. In such a case, the registered agent usually is a corporate officer or employee. The principal disadvantage of this is the possibility that legal documents or communications may be mixed in with routine business mail or advertisements and not receive the attention they deserve. For this reason, many attorneys suggest that they be designated as a registered agent and their office be designated as the registered office. Corporation service companies also routinely provide registered offices and registered agents for a fee.

The MBCA deals with several mundane questions that may arise in connection with registered offices and registered agents. For example: (a) What happens when a process server goes to the designated street address and finds no office and/or no registered agent on which process may be served? (b) How can a corporation service company effectively discontinue acting as a registered agent when its annual fee is not paid? (c) What is to prevent a person from being named a registered agent without his knowledge or consent?

(8) *"Initial directors" and "incorporators."* Under earlier versions of the Model Act the organization of the corporation was accomplished by "initial directors" named in the articles of incorporation; the "incorporators" executed the articles of incorporation but did not meet. MBCA (1969) § 57. A number of states, however, provided that the incorporators were to complete the organization of the corporation, and therefore did not require that initial directors be named in the articles of incorporation. MBCA § 2.05 in effect gives the drafter of articles of incorporation an option as to how the organization of the corporation is to be completed. Factors that might be considered in this regard include, (a) will it be necessary for shareholders to meet shortly after the formation of the corporation to elect permanent directors and conduct other business, and (b) do the real parties in interest desire anonymity?

Should an attorney serve as incorporator or initial director? In most states it is clear that no liability attaches to the role of incorporator; the same may not necessarily be true of the position of director, which, as discussed in a later chapter, may carry with it certain fiduciary duties and potential liabilities. Some cautious attorneys refuse as a matter of principle to serve as directors of corporations though there is no ethical objection to doing so.

(9) *The number of incorporators, directors or shareholders.* Blackstone noted that "Three make a corporation." Until mid-century, statutes required that there be at least three incorporators and three directors. Further, there were often residency requirements, shareholding requirements, and the like. So far as incorporators are concerned, the trend is clearly to reduce the minimum number to one and to allow corporations or other artificial entities to serve as incorporators; all but a handful of states now follow the Model Act in this regard. Of course, in view of the limited role of incorporators, this result is probably reasonable.

What about a minimum number of shareholders and directors? There apparently has never been in recent history a requirement that a corporation have at least three shareholders. A North Carolina case that appears to have so held, Park Terrace v. Phoenix Indem. Co., 243 N.C. 595, 91 S.E.2d 584 (1956), was promptly overruled by statute. Assuming this is so, what then about directors? See MBCA § 8.03(a). As of 2005, approximately nine states still required a board of at least three directors, though a number of these states permit a corporation with one or two shareholders to reduce the size of the board to the number of shareholders.

(10) *Initial Capital.* One interesting aspect of the articles of incorporation set forth above is that there is no reference to dollars: no dollar figure is associated with the shares of stock (i.e. no minimum issuance price is established) and no minimum capitalization of the corporation is set forth.

(a) The matter of the issuance price for shares is discussed in Chapter 8 and discussion of that issue is deferred until then.

(b) Shouldn't a new corporation be required to have at least some minimum amount of capital before it is launched into the business world? Until relatively recently there was such a requirement in most states. Prior to 1969, the Model Act prohibited a corporation from transacting any business or incurring any indebtedness "until there has been paid in for the issuance of shares consideration of the value of at least one thousand dollars." MBCA (1966) § 51. The articles of incorporation also had to contain a recitation to the same effect. Id. § 48(g). These provisions have largely disappeared in the United States:

It is probably true that in most states there was never a serious attempt to enforce these minimum capitalization requirements by holding up the certificate of incorporation, though some states did require the submission of an affidavit or certificate that the required amount had been contributed. Much more important was the question whether initial or subsequent directors who acquiesced to the conduct of business before the minimum capital was in fact paid in might be personally liable either for the minimum capital, or more dangerously, or for all debts of the corporation incurred before the required capital was paid in. The Model Act (MBCA (1966 Ed.) § 43(e)) minimized the potential impact of the minimum capitalization requirement by providing that directors who assent to the commencement of business are "jointly and severally liable to the corporation for such part of one thousand dollars as shall not have been received before commencing business, but such liability shall be terminated when the corporation has actually received one thousand dollars as consideration for the issuance of shares." Not all states followed this provision. Tri–State Developers, Inc. v. Moore, 343 S.W.2d 812 (Ky.1961), for example, a corporation began business with $500 rather than the required minimum of $1,000. The court upheld a judgment for $10,180.34 under such a statute. Kentucky eliminated entirely the minimum capital requirement in 1972. See Ky.B.C.A. § 271B.2–020 (1989).

The lack of minimum capitalization requirements in the U.S. is in sharp contrast to legal regimes in the European Union, which require that countries that belong to the EU must have minimum capital of at least € 25,000 before they can commence business. This capital must be in the form of "assets capable of economic assessment, and may not consist of such things as a promise to perform work or to supply services."[5] Do you think that it was sensible to eliminate all minimum capital requirements? Considering today's prices and today's conditions, shouldn't the move be in the opposite direction? Or is this simply an illustration of the race of laxity?

What happens after the articles of incorporation are filed? See MBCA §§ 2.05, 2.06. In addition to preparing and filing the articles of incorporation, attorneys usually handle other details in connection with the formation of a corporation. They may:

(1) Prepare the corporate bylaws;

(2) Prepare the notice calling the meeting of the initial board of directors, minutes of this meeting, and waivers of notice if necessary;

(3) Obtain a corporate seal and minute book for the corporation;

(4) Obtain blank certificates for the shares of stock, arrange for their printing or typing, and ensure that they are properly issued;

(5) Arrange for the opening of the corporate bank account;

5. Second Council Directive 77/91 of 13 December 1976 on Coordination of Safeguards Which, for the Protection of the Interests of Members and Others, are Required by Member States of Companies Within the Meaning of the Second paragraph of Article 58 of the Treaty, in Respect of the Formation of Public Limited Liability Companies and the Maintenance and Alteration of Their Capital, with a View to Making Such Safeguards Equivalent, 1977 O.J. (L. 26) 1.

(6) Prepare employment contracts, voting trusts, shareholder agreements, share transfer restrictions, and other special arrangements which are to be entered into with respect to the corporation and its shares;

(7) Obtain taxpayer identification numbers, occupancy certificates, and other governmental permits or consents to the operation of the business; and

(8) Evaluate whether the corporation should file an S corporation election, assuming that election is available.

Where there are to be several shareholders, consideration should be given to the manner of governance of the corporation after it is formed. There are numerous "boiler plate" forms for articles of incorporation and bylaws. But these forms create a corporation that may not be well suited for a closely–held corporation with multiple shareholders. A carefully-crafted shareholders' agreement may be necessary to provide appropriate protections for shareholders both in terms of participation in management and the power to "exit" in case of controversy. In some cases, these appropriate provisions may be effective if they are placed in the bylaws or articles of incorporation, but it is a mistake to assume that participants in a corporation automatically have the same freedom as partners in a partnership or members in an LLC to structure the form of governance in any manner they wish. The traditional rule was that the governance structure set forth in the corporation statute was mandatory—even a corporation with a single shareholder was required to have a board of directors, officers, meetings, and so forth. The gradual erosion of this rule is described in Chapter 9, Section A.

MBCA § 7.32 was added to the MBCA in 1991 (see Changes in the Revised Model Business Corporation Act—Amendments Pertaining to Closely Held Corporations, 46 Bus. Law. 297 (1990)). This section represents a new approach toward the problem of governance in corporations with a few shareholders. As of 2005, over eighteen states had adopted § 7.32, some with minor variations or limitations. In addition to § 7.32, most states have adopted some provisions designed to ameliorate to some extent the traditional rules of corporate management when applied to small corporations. In deciding what form of governance should be adopted for such a corporation, care must be taken to work within the confines of provisions authorized in the specific state, since failing to do so runs the risk that the manner of governance selected may later be held invalid.

Different considerations apply if the corporation contemplates that it will make a public offering of its shares after its formation. During the 1990s, many internet and "high-tech" companies were formed with the specific contemplation of receiving funds from venture capital firms and later "going public" through a public offering. These corporations included in their articles of incorporation provisions authorizing the issue of senior classes of securities and other provisions appropriate for a publicly–held corporation, e.g., proxy voting, registration of securities ownership, and similar matters.

In more traditional businesses, it is relatively uncommon for a newly formed business to contemplate an initial public offering shortly after its formation. More likely, a corporation will operate as a closely–held entity for several years before reaching a position that it might decide to "go public." When that decision is made, specialized securities counsel must be retained to assure that the offering is in compliance with the requirements of the federal

Securities Act of 1933. This may involve amendments to articles of incorporation and bylaws as well as a full review of pre-offering transactions and arrangements between the corporation and its shareholders to determine whether disclosure of, or offers to rescind, specific prior transactions may be necessary.

MINUTES OF ORGANIZATIONAL MEETING OF DIRECTORS OF ABC CORPORATION

The organizational meeting of the Board of Directors of ABC Corporation was duly convened in _____, _____ on _____, __, 20__, at _____ __.M.

All directors were present at the meeting and each director waived notice of the time, place of the meeting and of the purposes for which it was held, as evidenced by execution of a waiver of notice, which is attached hereto.

By unanimous consent, Ms. Barbara Brown served as chairperson of the meeting and Mr. Walter White served as secretary of the meeting.

The secretary presented and read to the meeting a copy of the articles of incorporation of the corporation. He reported that an original and a copy of the articles of incorporation had been duly filed with the office of the Secretary of State, together with the required filing fee, and that the Secretary of State had issued a fee receipt dated _____.

The secretary presented to the meeting a minute book for the corporation. Thereupon motion duly made, seconded and unanimously adopted, it was:

RESOLVED, That the minute book presented to this meeting be adopted as the minute book for this corporation, and that the secretary of this meeting be instructed to place therein the articles of incorporation and certificate of incorporation of the corporation.

The chairperson then read to the meeting a draft of the bylaws which had been prepared for the regulation and management of the affairs of the corporation. On motion duly made, seconded and unanimously adopted, it was:

RESOLVED, That the bylaws submitted at and read to this meeting are hereby approved as the bylaws of this corporation, and the secretary of this meeting is hereby instructed to copy such bylaws, at length, in the minute book of the corporation.

The chairperson then presented a form of stock certificate to be used to represent shares issued by the corporation. On motion duly made, seconded and unanimously adopted, it was:

RESOLVED, That the form of stock certificate presented to this meeting is hereby approved and adopted, and the secretary of this meeting is hereby instructed to insert a specimen of such stock certificate in the minute book of the corporation.

The chairperson then presented to the meeting a form of corporate seal for use by the corporation. On motion duly made, seconded and unanimously adopted, it was:

RESOLVED, That the corporate seal, an impression of which is affixed in the margin of the bylaws, is hereby approved and adopted as the official corporate seal of this corporation.

The chairperson then called for the election of officers of the corporation. On motion duly made, seconded and unanimously adopted, the following persons were elected to the offices set opposite their respective names:

Barbara Brown	President
George Green	Vice President and Treasurer
Walter White	Vice President and Secretary

each such officer to serve in accordance with the provisions of the bylaws and until his or her successor shall have been elected and shall have qualified.

Thereupon, on motion duly made, seconded and unanimously adopted, Ms. Brown not voting, it was resolved that Ms. Brown be paid a salary of $_____ per month, payable monthly, but that the other officers of the corporation not be paid any regular salary.

Barbara Brown, George Green and Walter White each submitted written offers to purchase one thousand (1,000) shares of the corporation at a price of ten dollars ($10) per share. On motion duly made, seconded and unanimously adopted, it was:

RESOLVED, That this corporation accept the following offers to purchase shares of the corporation:

Name	Number of Shares	Total Price
Barbara Brown	1,000	$10,000.00
George Green	1,000	$10,000.00
Walter White	1,000	$10,000.00

FURTHER RESOLVED, That upon payment to this corporation of the respective sums payable to this corporation, the officers of this corporation are hereby authorized and directed to issue to the respective purchasers certificates representing fully paid and nonassessable shares of this corporation for the shares so purchased.

Ms. Brown reported to the meeting that she had incurred and paid the following sums to the following persons for the following purposes in connection with the formation of the corporation:

$100.00   to the secretary of state of _____ as the statutory fee for filing the articles of incorporation.

$277.20   to Mr. Jones for legal services in connection with drafting the articles of incorporation, bylaws and other matters directly related to the formation of the corporation.

It was thereupon resolved that Ms. Brown should be reimbursed for such expenses in the total sum of $377.20 and the treasurer was instructed to pay Ms. Brown such sum as soon as possible out of corporate funds.

On motion duly made, seconded and unanimously adopted, it was

RESOLVED that the _____ Bank be chosen as the depository of the funds of the corporation, and the _____ and the _____ were each authorized to draw checks on the corporation's bank account in such bank. A form of resolution furnished by such bank was then presented to the meeting and, after being read and fully understood, such form of resolution was adopted and is attached to these minutes as an exhibit.

There being no further business, on motion duly made, seconded and unanimously adopted, the meeting was adjourned.

_____

Secretary

We consent to the foregoing actions

_____

_____

_____

Alternate form:

WAIVER

We, the undersigned, being all the original directors of ABC Corporation named in the articles of incorporation, do hereby waive notice and the call by the incorporators of said corporation of the organization meeting of the directors of said corporation, and agree that the organization meeting shall be held at _____, in the city of _____, _____ _____ o'clock ___.M. on the _____ day of _____, 20__.

_____

_____

_____

Notes

(1) Under the MBCA, there may be only one initial director or one incorporator who organizes the corporation. Where only a single person is acting, much of the "playacting" flavor of these minutes should disappear and a simpler formulation followed, e.g. "The director of the corporation determines that * * *."

(2) Most of the miscellaneous matters relating to the launching of a new corporation are accomplished at a meeting of the incorporators or initial directors. The attorney will normally draft the minutes of this meeting. In some circumstances, it may be necessary to have a meeting of the shareholders to elect permanent directors; the attorney normally drafts the minutes of this meeting also.

(3) If the corporation is small and closely–held, it is not necessary to actually hold meetings of incorporators, directors, or shareholders. See MBCA §§ 2.05, 7.04, 8.21. Similar provisions appear in all corporation statutes. Thus, a consent signed by all the incorporators, directors, or shareholders is effective as a legal matter. If the consent procedure is not utilized (as may be the case, for example, where one individual is absent, or where the number of persons involved is large), it is generally desirable to actually hold a meeting, using the minutes as a form of script.

(4) At the very early stages of corporate formation, there is unlikely to be significant disagreement, dissent, or controversy. See, however, Walsh v. Search Exploration, Inc., 16 Del.J.Corp.L. 1640 (Del.Ch.1990). Del.Gen.Corp.L. § 211, provides in part that "[i]f there be a failure to hold the annual meeting * * * for a period of 13 months after the organization of the corporation * * * the Court of Chancery may summarily order a meeting to be held * * *." Compare MBCA § 7.03(a)(1).

————

The bylaws of a corporation constitute the internal set of operating rules for the corporation. See MBCA § 2.06. They are usually prepared by the attorney who oversees the formation of the corporation. Numerous sample bylaws are available in form books; corporation service and internet companies also provide sample sets of bylaws as part of their services in connection with the formation of a corporation. Bylaws may vary from a brief one or two page document to elaborate provisions covering all aspects of corporate management and operation. Since officers and directors of a corporation are usually not familiar with the provisions of the applicable corporation statute and may not be familiar with special requirements set forth in the articles of incorporation, a sensible practice is to restate such provisions in the bylaws for the benefit of the corporate officers and shareholders. The following excerpt from a form set of bylaws[6] gives their flavor:

ARTICLE III. BOARD OF DIRECTORS

Section 1. *General Powers.* The business and affairs of the corporation shall be managed by its board of directors.

Section 2. *Number, Tenure, and Qualifications.* The number of directors of the corporation shall be _____. Directors shall be elected at the annual meeting of stockholders, and the term of office of each director shall be until the next annual meeting of stockholders and the election and qualification of his or her successor. Directors need not be residents of the State of _____, _____ *[but shall be stockholders of the corporation] [and need not be stockholders of the corporation].*

Section 3. *Regular Meetings.* A regular meeting of the board of directors shall be held without notice other than this bylaw immediately after and at the same place as the annual meeting of stockholders. The board of directors may provide, by resolution, the time and place for holding additional regular meetings without other notice than such resolution. Additional regular meetings shall be held at the principal office of the corporation in the absence of any designation in the resolution.

Section 4. *Special Meetings.* Special meetings of the board of directors may be called by or at the request of the president or any _____ *[two]* directors, and shall be held at the principal office of the corporation or at such other place as the directors may determine.

6. American Jurisprudence, Legal Forms, Second Edition, September 2002, Chapter 74. Corporations, Sample Bylaws, Copyright, 2002, West Publishing Company, reprinted with permission.

Section 5. *Notice.* Notice of any special meeting shall be given at least _____ *[48 hours or as the case may be]* before the time fixed for the meeting, by written notice delivered personally or mailed to each director at his or her business address, or by telegram. If mailed, such notice shall be deemed to be delivered when deposited in the United States mail so addressed, with postage thereon prepaid, not less than _____ days prior to the commencement of the above-stated notice period. If notice is given by telegram, such notice shall be deemed to be delivered when the telegram is delivered to the telegraph company. Any director may waive notice of any meeting. The attendance of a director at a meeting shall constitute a waiver of notice of such meeting, except where a director attends a meeting for the express purpose of objecting to the transaction of any business because the meeting is not lawfully called or convened. Neither the business to be transacted at, nor the purpose of, any regular or special meeting of the board of directors need be specified in the notice or waiver of notice of such meeting.

Section 6. *Quorum.* A majority of the number of directors fixed by these bylaws shall constitute a quorum for the transaction of business at any meeting of the board of directors, but if less than such majority is present at a meeting, a majority of the directors present may adjourn the meeting from time to time without further notice.

Section 7. *Board Decisions.* The act of the majority of the directors present at a meeting at which a quorum is present shall be the act of the board of directors _____ *[except that vote of not less than _____ (fraction) of all the members of the board shall be required for the amendment of or addition to these bylaws or as the case may be].*

Section 8. *Vacancies.* Any vacancy occurring in the board of directors may be filled by the affirmative vote of a majority of the remaining directors though less than a quorum of the board of directors. A director elected to fill a vacancy shall be elected for the unexpired term of his or her predecessor in office. Any directorship to be filled by reason of an increase in the number of directors shall be filled by election at an annual meeting or at a special meeting of stockholders called for that purpose.

Section 9. *Compensation.* By resolution of the board of directors, the directors may be paid their expenses, if any, of attendance at each meeting of the board of directors, and may be paid a fixed sum for attendance at each meeting of the board of directors or a stated salary as director. No such payment shall preclude any director from serving the corporation in any other capacity and receiving compensation therefor.

Section 10. *Presumption of Assent.* A director of the corporation who is present at a meeting of the board of directors at which action on any corporate matter is taken shall be presumed to have assented to the action taken unless his or her dissent shall be entered in the minutes of the meeting or unless he or she shall file his or her written dissent to such action with the person acting as the secretary of the meeting before the adjournment thereof or shall forward such dissent by registered mail to the secretary of the corporation immediately after the adjournment of the meeting. Such right to dissent shall not apply to a director who voted in favor of such action.

Note

Lawyers typically use checklists when preparing documents such as bylaws or articles of incorporation in order to make sure that they do not omit any important provision. A checklist for the bylaw provisions pertaining to directors would normally include the following: (1) number and qualifications; (2) increase or decrease in number: (3) resignation and removal; (4) filling vacancies; (5) powers and duties; (6) meetings of directors; (7) committees; (8) compensation and indemnification. What other sorts of information might such a checklist contain?

C. THE DECLINE OF THE DOCTRINE OF *ULTRA VIRES*

[handwritten: — Beyond the scope of legal authority]

A classic English case presents the doctrine of *ultra vires* in its full rigor and glory. In Ashbury Ry. Carriage & Iron Co. v. Riche, 33 L.T.R. 450, 1875 WL 13580 (1875), the charter of a corporation authorized it to "sell or lend all kinds of railway plant, to carry on the business of mechanical engineers and general contractors, & c." The corporation entered into contracts with one Riche to purchase a concession to construct and operate a railway line in Belgium. Riche was apparently to construct the railroad line, and the corporation was to raise the necessary capital. After partial performance, the corporation repudiated the contract. The House of Lords concluded that the corporation was not liable to Riche because owning and operating a railway line was *ultra vires*. Lord Chancellor Cairns declared:

[handwritten: Purpose is to sell/lend railway plants not own railways.]

> * * * In a case such as your Lordships have now to deal with, it is not a question whether the contract sued upon involves that which is *malum prohibitum* or *malum in se,* or is a contract contrary to public policy, and illegal in that sense. I assume the contract in itself to be perfectly legal; to have nothing in it obnoxious to any of the powers involved in the expressions which I have used. The question is not the illegality of the contract, but the competency and power of the company to make the contract. I am of the opinion that this contract was, as I have said, entirely beyond the objects of the memorandum of association. If so it was thereby placed beyond the powers of the company to make the contract. If so it is not a question whether the contract ever was ratified or not ratified. If it was a contract void at its beginning, it was void for this reason—because the company could not make the contract. If every shareholder of the company had been in this room, and every shareholder of the company had said, "That is a contract which we desire to make, which we authorize [sic] the directors to make, to which we sanction the placing the seal of the company," the case would not have stood in any different position to that in which it stands now. The company would thereby, by unanimous assent, have been attempting to do the very thing which by the Act they were prohibited from doing.

[handwritten left margin: Conduct that is just evil.]
[handwritten right margin: Conduct prohibited by statute]

Several things may be noted about this case. First, while it involves a purposes clause that is narrower than the activities actually engaged in by the corporation, the activities themselves were not inherently unlawful or beyond the powers of corporations generally. At the time, British law apparently did not permit corporations to amend their memoranda of association so that a new corporation would have to have been formed to operate the Belgian railroad. Presumably, however, nothing prevented that from being done with the same membership and management. Modern practice in drafting articles of incorporation greatly reduces but does not eliminate the possibility that similar problems will arise in the future. Second, the result of the case hardly seems reasonable or fair. After entering into what appears to be an entirely reasonable business contract, and presumably receiving benefits thereunder, the corporation is permitted to avoid the contract on the basis of a defense that was entirely within its power to correct. Third, the argument that corporations simply are unable to commit *ultra vires* acts threatens to be very unsettling. It might be used, for example, to set aside completed transactions, including sales of goods and land, which the corporation now regrets. It also would appear to be a handy defense for the corporation to avoid liability to injured plaintiffs in tort cases. Thus, almost from the first, the law of *ultra vires* became, in effect, a judicial attempt to avoid the harsh and undesirable but apparently logically compelled consequences of a judicially-created doctrine.

Some courts avoided the *ultra vires* doctrine by construing purposes clauses broadly and finding implied purposes from the language used. A famous example is the conclusion by the United States Supreme Court that a railway company might engage in the business of leasing and running a seaside resort hotel. Jacksonville M.P. Ry. & Nav. Co. v. Hooper, 160 U.S. 514, 16 S.Ct. 379, 40 L.Ed. 515 (1896). Other doctrines that have found acceptance include estoppel, unjust enrichment, quasi-contract, and waiver. In particular, these doctrines were applied to ensure that completed transactions would not be disturbed, and to permit tort claimants to recover for injuries suffered as a consequence of the corporation's conduct of an *ultra vires* business. *Ultra vires* continued to be applied, however, in connection with executory agreements and, when all is said and done, the doctrine was an undesirable one, involving harsh and erratic consequences.

One superficially-plausible justification for the doctrine arises from the fact that articles of incorporation are on public file; it seems reasonable to argue that one is charged with notice of whatever unexpected provision might appear in public documents. From a business standpoint, that argument is unrealistic: it assumes people will check articles of incorporation when in fact they do not, and that when they do check the articles, they will make business judgments based on a reading of what often is essentially boilerplate legalese.

711 KINGS HIGHWAY CORP. v. F.I.M.'S MARINE REPAIR SERV., INC.

Supreme Court of New York, 1966.
51 Misc.2d 373, 273 N.Y.S.2d 299.

Victor L. Anfuso, Justice.

Defendant corporation moves pursuant to CPLR 3211, subdiv. [a], par. 7 for judgment dismissing the complaint for legal insufficiency or in the alternative for summary judgment pursuant to CPLR 3212.

The verified complaint alleges that on or about April 20, 1965, the plaintiff, owner of premises known as 711–715 Kings Highway in the County of Kings, City of New York, entered into a written lease agreement with defendant whereby plaintiff leased the aforesaid premises to defendant for a period of 15 years commencing July 1, 1966; that with the exception of a security deposit of $5,000 paid by defendant to plaintiff pursuant to the lease agreement, which sum plaintiff now tenders or offers to return to defendant, the lease remains wholly executory; that under the terms of the lease the demised premises were to be used as a motion picture theatre; that the purposes for which the defendant corporation was formed were restricted generally to marine activities including marine repairs and the building and equipment of boats and vessels, as set forth in the certificate of incorporation; that the execution of the subject lease calling for defendant's use of the demised premises as a motion picture theatre, and the conduct and operation of a motion picture theatre business for profit by the defendant are acts which fall completely outside the scope of the powers and authority conferred by the defendant's corporate charter, thereby rendering invalid the lease agreement entered into by the parties. The complaint then prays for a declaratory judgment declaring the lease to be invalid or in the alternative for rescission, and further, that the defendant be enjoined from performing, or exercising any rights, under the lease.

In the opinion of the court, Section 203 of the New York Business Corporation Law embraces the situation presented by the factual allegations of the complaint and requires a dismissal of the complaint for failure to state a cause of action. This section provides as follows:

> That no act of a corporation and no transfer of property to or by a corporation, otherwise lawful, shall be invalid by reason of the fact that the corporation was without capacity or power to do such act or engage in such transfer except that such lack of capacity or power may be asserted (1) in an action brought by a shareholder to enjoin a corporate act or (2) in an action by or in the right of a corporation against an incumbent or former officer or director of the corporation or (3) in an action or special proceeding brought by the Attorney General.

[handwritten margin note: Statute greatly narrows doctrine of ultra vires.]

It is undisputed that the present case does not fall within the stated exceptions contained in Section 203. It is accordingly clear from the language of the statutory provision hereinabove referred to that there is no substance to plaintiff's argument, in opposition to the instant motion, which is predicated on a want of corporate power to do an act or enter into an agreement beyond the express or implied powers of the corporation conferred by the corporate charter.

Neither is there merit to the plaintiff's contention that Section 203 applies only where ultra vires is raised as a defense. Notwithstanding the fact that this section is entitled "Defense of ultra vires" it seems that except in the three stated situations set forth in the section, which are not applicable to the instant case, ultra vires may not be invoked as a sword in support of a cause of action any more than it can be utilized as a defense. To hold otherwise would render meaningless those provisions in Section 203 which permit ultra vires to be invoked in support of the actions or proceedings set forth as exceptions to the general language of this section.

Finally plaintiff's contention that the ultra vires doctrine still applies fully to executory contracts must be rejected. By virtue of Section 203 the doctrine may not be invoked even though the contract which is claimed to be ultra vires is executory, as in the instant case. See Revisers' Notes and Comments on Section 203 of the Business Corporation Law.

Accordingly the defendant's motion for judgment dismissing the complaint for insufficiency is granted. * * *

Notes

(1) Consider MBCA § 3.04. Does this give the court the needed flexibility to protect legitimate and reasonable business relationships on the one hand while protecting shareholders who may have relied on a narrow purposes clause as protection against undesired business expansion on the other?

(2) Do not MBCA § 3.04(b)(1) and (c) give shareholders greater rights to set aside executory transactions than the corporation itself? Might not a corporation, having entered into a disadvantageous *ultra vires* transaction, enlist a shareholder to intervene and seek the cancellation of the contract? Of course, if it is advantageous for the corporation to avoid a transaction, it probably will also be advantageous from the standpoint of the shareholder since it will increase the value of his shares.

(3) In Tallahatchie Valley Elec. Power Ass'n v. Miss. Propane Gas Ass'n, 812 So.2d 912, Util. L. Rep. P 26,803 (Miss.2002), Miss. Propane, a trade association representing manufacturers of propane gas, sued Tallahatchie Power (TVEPA) when TVEPA began selling propane gas. TVEPA was organized pursuant to state and federal statutory provisions designed to encourage the dissemination of electric energy, particularly in rural areas. The Mississippi Supreme Court held that TVEPA had exceeded its statutory authority when it acquired a subsidiary that sold propane gas. TVEPA then argued that the lawsuit brought against it by the Gas Association was essentially an ultra vires action, and that the plaintiffs therefore lacked standing to bring the suit because only the company's shareholders, or the state itself has standing to bring a law suit claiming that a corporate action is ultra vires. The Mississippi Supreme Court agreed that the lawsuit involved an ultra vires claim because it challenged TVEPA's power to act pursuant to statutory authority and its corporate charter. However, it held that the association nevertheless had standing because it was a trade group that represented companies that were shareholders in TVEPA. On the merits, the Court refused to enjoin TVEPA's subsidiary's sales of non-electric energy products such as propane gas, even though this line of business was ultra vires for TVEPA. The Court reasoned that the members of the association had "no legal right to be free of the lawful competition posed by" TVEPA's subsidiary, and concluded that the association did not assert any "legally cognizable injury upon which the relief sought may be granted." The Court, in other words, held that TVEPA's ownership of the subsidiary violated state statutes, but that the competition that its subsidiary was engaging in was lawful. The court noted that the subsidiary was a separate legal entity, legally distinct from its parent. Thus, it appears that while TVEPA broke the law by acquiring a subsidiary that was engaged in a business that the parent could not lawfully engage in, the subsidiary did not violate the law because it was engaged in what was, for it (though not for its corporate parent), a legal competitive enterprise. In light of this holding, what would an appropriate remedy be in this case?

(4) Cucchi v. New York City Off–Track Betting Corp., 818 F.Supp. 647, 657–58 (S.D.N.Y.1993), plaintiff contended that she had been fired as an employee of

defendant in violation of the statutory provisions regulating the defendant, and that therefore her firing was *ultra vires*. This argument was rejected by the court on the ground that the doctrine of *ultra vires* as embodied in § 203 could be invoked only by a shareholder or by the state through its attorney-general and not by an employee.

SULLIVAN v. HAMMER

Court of Chancery of Delaware, 1990.
1990 WL 114223.

HARTNETT, VICE CHANCELLOR:

I

On April 25, 1989, defendant Occidental Petroleum Corporation ("Occidental") mailed to its stockholders a Proxy Statement for the Company's 1989 annual meeting, which reported that a Special Committee of Occidental had approved a proposal to provide financial support for The Armand Hammer Museum of Art and Cultural Center ("the Museum"). The Museum is to be located adjacent to and be physically integrated with Occidental's Los Angeles headquarters building, the Occidental Petroleum Center. Dr. Armand Hammer, who is over 90 years old, is the founder and Chairman of the Board of Occidental.

The Proxy Statement referred to the financial support that Occidental would provide to the Museum, including: (a) funding construction costs estimated at approximately $50 million and granting the Museum a 30–year rent-free lease in the Occidental Petroleum Center; (b) funding an annuity for the Museum, at an estimated after-tax cost of $24 million; and (c) granting the Museum an option to purchase the Museum complex and the Occidental Petroleum Center at the end of the 30–year lease term for $55 million, their estimated fair market value at that time.

[handwritten margin note: Terms of Proxy Statement]

The Proxy Statement also set forth a description of Dr. Hammer's employment agreements, including a provision for Occidental to contribute to the Armand Hammer Foundation a lump sum approximating seven times Dr. Hammer's aggregate compensation during the year prior to his death. These disclosures had appeared in Occidental's public filings for several years.

Plaintiffs filed this action asserting class and derivative claims on May 9, 1989. The complaint alleges, * * * that Occidental's expenditures and commitments with respect to the Museum and its obligations to the Armand Hammer Foundation pursuant to Dr. Hammer's employment contract constitute a gift and waste of corporate assets * * *[and] that Dr. Hammer had breached his duty of loyalty by causing Occidental to make these expenditures for his personal benefit. The complaint sought injunctive, declaratory, rescissory and other equitable relief.

On May 9, 1989, plaintiff's counsel accepted defendants' invitation to enter into settlement discussions and between May 24, 1989 and June 3, 1989, met to discuss a possible settlement. As a condition of entering into and continuing these discussions, plaintiffs' counsel demanded and were provided with documents relating to the Museum and Occidental's charitable contributions, among other matters. Plaintiffs' counsel made an effort to include Mr. Kahn's New York counsel in the settlement negotiations but were rebuffed.

On May 12, 1989, Occidental issued a supplement to its Proxy Statement. Plaintiffs concede that the supplemental disclosures provided the corrective disclosures the Sullivan * * * complaint sought.

On June 3, 1989, subject to plaintiffs' right to pursue additional discovery to confirm the fairness and adequacy of the settlement, the parties entered into a written Memorandum of Understanding setting forth the general terms of a proposed settlement of the litigation and providing for the negotiations of a formal Stipulation of Settlement to be executed within thirty days for submission to this Court for approval. * * *

On August 4, 1989, a Special Committee of Occidental's Board of Directors retained former Chancellor Grover C. Brown of the law firm of Morris, James, Hitchens & Williams as its independent counsel to review the merits of the actions taken by the Board of Occidental and to advise the members of the Special Committee with respect to any financial support to be given by Occidental to the Museum. On October 6, 1989, Occidental's Board of Directors delegated to the Special Committee the additional authority to approve or disapprove the proposed settlement agreement in this action after consulting with and considering the advice of its independent counsel.

The Special Committee reexamined the proposal for the financial support by Occidental to the Museum. Also, through its independent counsel, the Special Committee met with and discussed possible settlement of the litigation * * *. The Special Committee subsequently, and for the first time, formally approved the challenged charitable contributions. Furthermore, the Special Committee was advised by its special counsel regarding the litigations and determined that, in its opinion, it was in the best interests of Occidental to agree to the proposed settlement presented in this action.

* * * Counsel for plaintiffs also engaged in further negotiations with the defendants, the Special Committee and its counsel on the aspects of the settlement. Plaintiffs' counsel asserted that he evaluated or reevaluated the challenged transactions, the relative strength of plaintiffs' complaint, the activities of the Special Committee and the claims made by Kahn and various others opposing settlement of this litigation.

On January 24, 1990, counsel for all the parties in this action presented to the Court a fully executed Stipulation and Agreement of Compromise, Settlement and Release ("the Stipulation of Settlement"). The Court then directed that, solely for settlement purposes, this action would be maintained as a stockholder derivative action and as a class action by plaintiffs, as representatives of the Class * * *.

II

* * * The proposed Settlement, inter alia, provides:

(1) the Museum building shall be named the "Occidental Petroleum Cultural Center Building" with the name displayed appropriately on the building.

(2) Occidental shall be treated as a corporate sponsor by the Museum for as long as the Museum occupies the building.

(3) Occidental's contribution of the building shall be recognized by the Museum in public references to the facility.

(4) Three of Occidental's directors shall serve on the Museum's Board (or no less than one-third of the total Museum Board) with Occidental having the option to designate a fourth director.

(5) there shall be an immediate loan of substantially all of the art collections of Dr. Hammer to the Museum and there shall be an actual transfer of ownership of the collections upon Dr. Hammer's death or the commencement of operation of the Museum whichever later occurs.

(6) All future charitable contributions by Occidental to any Hammer-affiliated charities shall be limited by the size of the dividends paid to Occidental's common stockholders. At current dividend levels, Occidental's annual contributions to Hammer-affiliated charities pursuant to this limitation could not exceed approximately 3 cents per share.

(7) Any amounts Occidental pays for construction of the Museum in excess of $50 million and any amounts paid to the Foundation upon Dr. Hammer's death must be charged against the agreed ceiling on limitations to Hammer-affiliated charities.

(8) Occidental's expenditures for the Museum construction shall not exceed $50 million, except that an additional $10 million may be expended through December 31, 1990 but only if such additional expenditures do not enlarge the scope of construction and if such expenditures are approved by the Special Committee. Amounts in excess of $50 million must be charged against the limitation on donations to Hammer-affiliated charities.

(9) Occidental shall be entitled to receive 50% of any consideration received in excess of a $55 million option price for the Museum property or 50% of any consideration the Museum receives from the assignment or transfer of its option or lease to a third party. * * *

Terms of Settlement

* * * The settlement in the Court's opinion leaves much to be desired.

The Court's role in reviewing the proposed Settlement, however, is quite restricted. If the Court was a stockholder of Occidental it might vote for new directors, if it was on the Board it might vote for new management and if it was a member of the Special Committee it might vote against the Museum project. But its options are limited in reviewing a proposed settlement to applying Delaware law to the facts adduced in the record and then determining in its business judgment whether, on balance, the settlement is reasonable.

Delaware law clearly favors the voluntary settlement of litigation. *Polk v. Good, Del. Supr., 507 A.2d 531 (1986); Neponsit Investment Co. v. Abramson, Del. Supr., 405 A.2d 97 (1979); Rome v. Archer, Del. Supr., 197 A.2d 49 (1964).* It is neither necessary nor desirable for the Court to try the case or to decide any of the issues on the merits prior to determining whether a settlement should be approved. *Polk v. Good, 507 A.2d at 536; Gladstone v. Bennett, Del. Supr., 153 A.2d 577, 583 (1959).* Rather, the Court must look to the facts and circumstances upon which the claim is based, and the possible defenses thereto, and must then exercise its own business judgment and determine the overall reasonableness of the settlement. *Polk v. Good, 507 A.2d at 536; Neponsit Investment Co. v. Abramson, 405 A.2d at 100; Rome v. Archer, 197 A.2d at 53.* In short, it is the function of the Court to decide whether the proposed settlement is fair and reasonable in light of the factual and legal circumstances of the case. In re: Resorts International Shareholders Litigation, Del. Ch., C.A. No. 9470–NC, Hartnett, V.C. (Sept. 7, 1988), aff'd sub. nom., In re Resorts International Shareholders Litigation *Appeals, Del. Supr., 570 A.2d 259 (1990)*.

The factors to be considered in the Court's review are:

(1) the probable validity of the claims, (2) the apparent difficulties in enforcing the claims through the courts, (3) the collectibility of any judgment recovered, (4) the delay, expense and trouble of litigation, (5) the amount of the compromise as compared with the amount and collectibility of the judgment, and (6) the views of the parties involved, pro and con.

Polk v. Good, 507 A.2d at 536 (citations omitted). * * *

The Court must therefore consider the benefit to the class and whether the benefit is reasonable when compared to the range of potential recovery. See In re Beatrice Companies, Inc. Litigation, Del. Ch., C.A. No. 8240–NC, Allen, C. (Apr. 16, (1986), aff'd, *Del. Supr., 522 A.2d 865 (1987)*.

IV

The potential for ultimate success on the merits here is, realistically, very poor. The business judgment rule, as consistently reiterated by the Delaware Supreme Court, stands as an almost impenetrable barrier to the plaintiffs.

The business judgment rule "is a presumption that in making a business decision the directors of a corporation acted on an informed basis, in good faith and in the honest belief that the action taken was in the best interests of the company." *Aronson v. Lewis, Del. Supr., 473 A.2d 805, 812 (1984)*. The presumption, which protects a board-approved transaction, can be overturned only if a plaintiff can show that a majority of the directors expected to derive personal financial benefit from the transaction, that they lacked independence, that they were grossly negligent in failing to inform themselves, or that the decision of the Board was so irrational that it could not have been the reasonable exercise of the business judgment of the Board. Cf. Tomczak v. Morton Thiokol, Inc., Del. Ch., C.A. No. 7861–NC, Hartnett, V.C. (Nov. 30, 1989).

The plaintiffs have not shown any facts which would show that the directors have any self-interest in the transaction either from a personal financial interest or from a motive for entrenchment in office. *Grobow v. Perot, Del. Supr., 539 A.2d 180 (1988)*. Nor is there any evidence in the record showing that the members of the Special Committee are in fact dominated by Dr. Hammer or anyone else.

The record also shows that the directors and the Special Committee gave due consideration to the transaction. Cf. *Smith v. Van Gorkom, Del. Supr., 488 A.2d 858 (1985)*.

It is therefore highly probable that, in deciding a motion to dismiss or for summary judgment or after trial, this Court would find that the decisions of the directors are entitled to the presumption of propriety afforded by the business judgment rule. In Re: Resorts International Shareholders Litigation, Del. Ch., C.A. No. 9470–NC, Hartnett, V.C. (Sept. 7, 1988), aff'd sub. nom., *In* *re Resorts International Shareholders Litigation Appeals, Del. Supr., 570 A.2d 259 (1990).* * * *

This Court, therefore, must review the claims of plaintiffs against a presumption that the acts of the directors are valid.

VI

This court's role in reviewing the gift by Occidental Petroleum Corporation to the Museum is also severely limited.

The test of whether a corporation may make a charitable gift is its reasonableness. *Theodora Holding Corp. v. Henderson, Del. Ch., 257 A.2d 398 (1969).*

It is clear that the Museum qualifies as a charity. From the present record it is also clear that the present gift (as now limited) is within the range of reasonableness.

It is therefore reasonably probable that plaintiffs would also fail to prevail on this claim.

VII

Against this background of weakness of plaintiffs' claims, the Court must weigh the consideration being received by the class.

While the consideration to be received by the class is speculative, I find, on balance, in the exercise of my business judgment, that it is adequate to support the settlement.

Plaintiffs' claim that "the proposed settlement: (1) reinforces and assures Occidental's identification with and meaningful participation in the affairs of the Museum; (2) reinforces and protects the charitable nature and consequences of Occidental's gifts by securing prompt delivery and irrevocable transfer of the art collections to the Museum; (3) imposes meaningful controls upon the total construction costs that Occidental will pay, which have already forced the reduction of the construction budget by $19.4 million; (4) places meaningful restrictions upon Occidental's future charitable donations to Hammer-affiliated entities and avoids increases in posthumous payments to the Foundation or any other designated recipient after Dr. Hammer's death; (5) restores to Occidental an equitable portion of any appreciation of the properties in the event the Museum exercises its option and disposes of the properties or transfers its option for value; and (6) guarantees that the art collections will continue to be located in the Los Angeles area and remain available for the enjoyment of the American public rather than dissipated into private collections or sold abroad." Obviously the value of these benefits is speculative.

Benefits of compromise

Plaintiffs * * * submitted an affidavit of Kenneth A. Budenstein of Duff & Phelps Financial Consulting Co. in which it is claimed that the monetary value of having the Museum Building called the "Occidental Petroleum Cultural Center Building" is approximately $10 million.

Although the Court views this estimate with a good deal of skepticism, * * * it seems clear that Occidental will receive good will from the gift and will be able to utilize the adjacent Museum in the promotion of its business purposes.

I therefore find that the benefit to the stockholders of Occidental is sufficient to support the settlement and is adequate, if only barely so, when compared to the weakness of plaintiffs' claims.

In summary, the settlement is approved.

Notes

(1) In First Nat'l Bank v. Bellotti, 435 U.S. 765, 98 S.Ct. 1407, 55 L.Ed.2d 707 (1978) and Consolidated Edison Co. v. Public Serv. Comm'n, 447 U.S. 530, 100 S.Ct. 2326, 65 L.Ed.2d 319 (1980), the Supreme Court recognized that corporate political speech had constitutional protection. A more recent decision in this line of cases, Austin v. Michigan Chamber of Commerce, 494 U.S. 652, 110 S.Ct. 1391, 108 L.Ed.2d 652 (1990), held that because of the essential nature of a corporation, "narrowly drawn" limitations on corporate political speech were constitutionally permissible. See Charles D. Watts, Jr., Corporate Legal Theory Under the First Amendment: *Bellotti* and *Austin,* 46 U.Miami L.Rev. 317 (1991). In this line of cases, commercial speech—speech directly affecting the property, business, or assets of the corporation—is not involved. At the time of these decisions, applicable state law generally did not expressly authorize corporate political contributions or payments to influence public elections; indeed, the statutes of some states specifically prohibited them. The "black letter" rule has long been that corporations are state creations with limited powers granted by the states. Head & Amory v. Providence Ins. Co., 6 U.S. (2 Cranch) 127, 169, 2 L.Ed. 229 (1804). If the power to make political contributions or payments to influence public elections on matters unrelated to the business of the corporation was not expressly granted by the statutes of the state of incorporation, where did corporations obtain the basic power to exercise these constitutional rights established by the Supreme Court? Does MBCA § 3.02(15) authorize these expenditures?

(2) Is there risk in broadly authorizing corporate powers in statutes such as MBCA § 3.02 without any kind of restriction or limitation? Or does the holding in *Sullivan v. Hammer* itself provide a suitable restriction?

(3) Charitable contributions by corporations, particularly publicly held corporations, have been the subject of some criticism. Are you impressed by the argument that the function of business corporations is profit, and that charitable contributions are inconsistent with that function since they involve gifts of corporate assets? What about the argument that shareholders, rather than corporate management, should be permitted to decide which charities to support since that choice is essentially a personal rather than a business–related one? Should a distinction be drawn between charitable contributions that may benefit the corporation directly (e.g., General Motors making contributions to support hospitals in areas close to General Motors plants), and more general contributions (e.g., to Harvard University)? For a thoughtful discussion of these issues, see Melvin Aron Eisenberg, Corporate Conduct that Does Not Maximize Shareholder Gain: Legal Conduct, Ethical Conduct, the Penumbra Effect, Reciprocity, the Prisoner's Dilemma, Sheep's Clothing, Social Conduct, and Disclosure, 28 Stetson L.Rev. 1 (1998).

D. PREMATURE COMMENCEMENT OF BUSINESS

1. PROMOTERS

The term "promoter" includes a "person who, acting alone or in conjunction with one or more other persons, directly or indirectly takes initiative in founding and organizing the business or enterprise of an issuer."[7] A promoter is often referred to as the "founder" or "organizer" of an enterprise. S.E.C. Rule 405, 17 C.F.R. § 230.405 (2000). The formation of a business enterprise largely involves business rather than legal problems. If the new business needs a plant, the promoter must locate one and rent or buy it. If a key person is essential for the success of the venture, the promoter must negotiate a contract of employment with him. If a distributive network for the business product or a source of raw materials is necessary, the promoter must make the arrangements. In any event, capital must be raised, either through the sale of equity interests in the business, or through loans, or commonly, a combination of both.

One important aspect of the promoter relationship is that the promoter owes significant fiduciary duties to other participants in the venture. The scope of these duties is described in Post v. United States, 407 F.2d 319, 328 (D.C.Cir.1968), cert. denied, 393 U.S. 1092, 89 S.Ct. 863, 21 L.Ed.2d 784 (1969), as follows:

> By elementary legal principles, promoters stand in a fiduciary relationship exacting good faith in their intracompany activities and demanding adherence to a high standard of honesty and frankness. Not the lesser of the promoter's manifold responsibilities outlaw secret profit-making and command the dedication of corporate funds to corporate purposes. And it cannot be doubted that promoters of stock corporations who employ the mails in deceitful violation of their fiduciary obligations may incur the full condemnation of the law.

In *Post*, defendants were convicted of conspiracy and mail fraud stemming from their activities in promotion of a country club in the Washington metropolitan area. The court upheld the following jury instruction as an accurate statement of both what a promoter does and what his fiduciary duty entails:

> The jury are instructed that a promoter is a person who sets in motion machinery that brings about the incorporation and organization of a corporation, brings together the persons interested in the enterprise to be conducted by the corporation, aids in inducing persons to become members of the corporation, and in procuring from them membership fees to carry out purposes set forth in the corporation's articles of incorporation. If from the evidence in this case the jury should find beyond a reasonable doubt that the defendants were promoters of Lakewood Country Club, Inc., then you are instructed that the defendants stood in a fiduciary relation to both the corporation as a separate legal entity and the members, including those persons who it was to be anticipated would make application to and would become members in Lakewood Country Club, Inc. Such a fiduciary relationship on the part of the defendants, should you find them to be the promoters of the Lakewood Country Club, Inc., required that they exercise the utmost good faith in their relations

7. [By the Editors] According to S.E.C. Rule 405, 17 C.F.R. § 230.405 (2000), the term "promoter" also includes a person "who, in connection with the founding and organizing of the business or enterprise of an issuer, directly or indirectly receives in consideration of services or property, or both services and property, 10 percent or more of any class of securities of the issuer or 10 percent or more of the proceeds from the sale of any class of such securities."

with the corporation and the members, including fully advising the corporation and members and persons who it was to be anticipated would become members, of any interest which the defendants had that would in any way affect the corporation, the members and anticipated members. Such a full disclosure requirement, if you should find the defendants to be promoters, would obligate them to faithfully make known all facts which might have influenced prospective members in deciding whether or not to purchase memberships. And this full disclosure would include the duty to refrain from misrepresenting any material facts, as well as the duty to make known any personal interest the defendants had in any transaction relating to the country club enterprise.

Also you are instructed that if you should find beyond a reasonable doubt that the defendants were promoters of the Lakewood Country Club, Inc., and that the funds obtained by them from members of the club corporation to accomplish the purposes of the corporation were used by them for the club's benefit, they were properly used. On the other hand, if you should find beyond a reasonable doubt that the defendants were the promoters of the club corporation, and that they had intentionally converted those funds to their own personal use, such would be a fraud on the members of the club corporation, since such funds were in the nature of trust funds as to which the defendants had a fiduciary obligation. And in that connection you are further instructed that for promoters to knowingly use their fiduciary position to obtain secret profits at the expense of the corporation of its members would not only be a breach of that fiduciary duty but an act of fraud.

407 F.2d 319, 328, n. 51.

Notes

(1) *Post v. United States* is unusual in that it involved a criminal prosecution of a promoter; most reported promoter cases involve civil suits brought against the promoter by injured parties. In *Post*, however, civil suits against the promoters were foreclosed because the promoters voluntarily agreed to relinquish control of the Lakewood Country Club project in exchange for a general release from civil liability. Presumably, representatives of the Club agreed to this settlement because prospects of recovering the converted funds from the promoters were not good.

(2) If a subsequent investor has dealt directly with the promoter in connection with the investment, there is little doubt that the promoter is liable for common law fraud in the event of misrepresentation. An additional federal remedy for fraud, or for mere nondisclosure of a material fact, may be available under Rule 10b–5. See Chapter 13, section B. A Rule 10b–5 case must be brought in the federal courts. Rule 10b–5 is applicable only if the fraud or nondisclosure is "in connection with the purchase or sale of a security" and the transaction involves use of a "telephone or other interstate means of communication or any other interstate facility."

(3) In addition to subsequent investors in the enterprise, who else may attack transactions between a promoter and the corporation on the ground the transaction violates the promoter's fiduciary duty? At least the following possibilities exist:

(a) *General creditors of the corporation or their representatives, usually trustees in bankruptcy or receivers.* These suits are based on a theory that the promoters converted corporate assets to their own use in fraud of creditors. See, e.g., Frick v. Howard, 23 Wis.2d 86, 126 N.W.2d 619 (1964).

(b) *Co-promoters.* It is clear that a promoter is in a fiduciary relationship with his or her co-promoters, Geving v. Fitzpatrick, 56 Ill.App.3d 206, 14 Ill.Dec. 175, 371 N.E.2d 1228 (1978). Co-promoters may be viewed as partners in a venture to create the business. However, if the venture is incorporated, complications may arise from the injection of the corporation into the picture, and the substitution of corporate relationships for joint venture relationships.

(c) *The corporation.* The corporation itself may bring suit against its promoters after it has come under the control of subsequent investors or other persons. Two classic cases involving this issue arise out of the same promotional scheme at the beginning of this century. In this scheme, the promoters had sold property to the corporation formed by them for shares with a par value equal to about three times what they had paid for the property, and about twice what the property was worth at the time of the transfer. The United States Supreme Court in Old Dominion Copper Mining & Smelting Co. v. Lewisohn, 210 U.S. 206, 28 S.Ct. 634, 52 L.Ed. 1025 (1908), an action by the corporation against one of the principal promoters, concluded that since the promoters and the shareholders were identical at the time of the transaction, there were no members of the corporation who were not informed of the facts at the time of the fraud, and corporate assent was therefore given with full knowledge. As a result, there was no breach of duty or wrong committed against the corporation. It was immaterial, the court said, that thereafter, outsiders subscribed for shares in ignorance of the true facts because "of course, legally speaking, a corporation does not change its identity by adding a cubit to its stature." In Old Dominion Copper Mining & Smelting Co. v. Bigelow, 203 Mass. 159, 89 N.E. 193 (1909), an action by the corporation against the other principal promoter, on the other hand, the Massachusetts court argued that promoters stand in the same fiduciary position to the corporation when uninformed shareholders are expected to be brought in after the wrong has been perpetrated as they do when there are current shareholders to whom no disclosure is made. While a wrong is committed immediately against the corporation, there is no one to enforce the remedy until the new shareholders come in. The views of the Massachusetts court appear to have gained ascendancy in cases in which the promoters plan to invite the public to become subscribers for shares. See Northridge Co-op. Section No. 1, Inc. v. 32nd Avenue Constr. Corp., 2 N.Y.2d 514, 161 N.Y.S.2d 404, 141 N.E.2d 802 (1957).

(4) In recent years, litigation involving promoters' fraud has declined. This is partly due to Rule 10b–5 and partly due to enhanced enforcement of a different federal statute, the Federal Securities Act of 1933, which makes it unlawful to use means of interstate commerce or the mails to sell publicly a security unless a registration statement has been filed with the S.E.C. setting forth required information.

STANLEY J. HOW & ASSOC., INC. v. BOSS

United States District Court, Southern District of Iowa, 1963.
222 F.Supp. 936.

[Editor: This was an action to recover on a contract for the performance of architectural services. The plaintiff alleged that it had performed the required services and was entitled to a fee of $38,250, of which it had received only $14,500. It seeks to collect the difference from Boss, a promoter of a corporation. The pertinent parts of the contract (with italics added) are as follows:

> This agreement made as of the twentieth (20th) day of April in the year Nineteen Hundred and Sixty–One by and between *Boss Hotels Company, Inc. hereinafter called the Owner,* and Stanley J. How and Associates, Inc. hereinafter called the Architect * * *.

> The Owner agrees to pay the Architect for such services a fee of six (6) percent of the construction cost of the Project, with other payments and reimbursements as hereinafter provided.

> The Owner and the Architect each binds himself, his partners, successors, legal representatives and assigns to the other party to this Agreement and to the partners, successors, legal representatives and assigns of such other party in respect to all covenants of this Agreement.

> Except as above, neither the Owner nor the Architect shall assign, sublet or transfer his interest in this Agreement without written consent of the other.

> IN WITNESS WHEREOF the parties hereto have made and executed this Agreement the day and year first above written.

> *Owner:* /s/ Edw. A. Boss   Architect:
>
> *By: Edwin A. Boss, agent for a*   Stanley J. How and Associates,
> *Minnesota corporation to be formed* Inc.
> *who will be the obligor.*
>   /s/ Stanley J. How

This contract was the Standard Form of Agreement between Owner and Architect printed by the American Institute of Architects. The blanks were originally filled in by a representative of the plaintiff; as originally prepared, the signature clause as well as the caption referred to "Boss Hotels Co., Inc." as the "owner." However, when the contract was presented to Boss, he erased the words "Boss Hotel Co., Inc." and inserted the language "By: Edwin A. Boss, agent for a Minnesota corporation to be formed who will be the obligor." He then asked Mr. How, "Is this all right?" or "Is this acceptable, this manner of signing?" or words to that effect. How said "Yes," and the contracts were then signed by defendant and Stanley J. How. Defendant caused an Iowa corporation named Minneapolis–Hunter Hotel Co. to be formed to construct the project. The checks sent to plaintiff for partial payments under the contract bore the name of this corporation. The project was ultimately abandoned after a substantial amount of architectural work had been performed under the contract.

HANSON, DISTRICT JUDGE.

* * * To what extent [the Minneapolis–Hunter Hotel Co.] actually came into being is not clear in the record. No corporate charter, by-laws, or resolutions were offered into evidence. At any rate, if this new corporation exists, there are no assets in it to pay the amount due on the contract.

There really is not much debate as to what the law is on the questions raised. Both parties site [*sic*] King Features Syndicate, Dept. of Hearst Corp.

International News Service Division v. Courrier, 241 Iowa 870, 43 N.W.2d 718, 41 A.L.R.2d 467, for the proposition that a promoter, though he may assume to act on behalf of the projected corporation and not for himself, will be personally liable on his contract unless the other party agreed to look to some other person or fund for payment. * * *

[The court then summarizes Comment b to Section 326 of the Restatement of Agency. This comment, as revised in the Restatement of Agency, Second, reads:

b. *Promoters.* The classic illustration of the rule stated in this Section is the promoter. When a promoter makes an agreement with another on behalf of a corporation to be formed, the following alternatives may represent the intent of the parties:

(1) They may understand that the other party is making a revocable offer to the nonexistent corporation which will result in a contract if the corporation is formed and accepts the offer prior to withdrawal. This is the normal understanding.

(2) They may understand that the other party is making an irrevocable offer for a limited time. Consideration to support the promise to keep the offer open can be found in an express or limited promise by the promoter to organize the corporation and use his best efforts to cause it to accept the offer.

(3) They may agree to a present contract by which the promoter is bound, but with an agreement that his liability terminates if the corporation is formed and manifests its willingness to become a party. There can be no ratification by the newly formed corporation, since it was not in existence when the agreement was made.

(4) They may agree to a present contract on which, even though the corporation becomes a party, the promoter remains liable either primarily or as surety for the performance of the corporation's obligation.

Which one of these possible alternatives, or variants thereof, is intended is a matter of interpretation on the facts of the individual case.

[The third] possible interpretation is not very important in this case because a novation was not pleaded or argued. * * *

In the present case, the contract was signed: "Edwin A. Boss, agent for a Minnesota corporation to be formed who will be the obligor." The defendant argues that this is an agreement that the new corporation is solely liable. The problem here is what is the import of the words "who will be the obligor." It says nothing about the present obligor. The words "will be" connote something which will take place in the future. * * *

About the closest case to the present in terms of signature is O'Rorke v. Geary, 207 Pa. 240, 56 A. 541, where the contract was signed "D.J. Geary for a bridge company to be organized and incorporated as party of the second part." The payments were to be made monthly and work was to be done before it was possible for the corporation to make the payments. The court held the promoter personally liable. * * *

* * * [T]his is a situation where the parties used ambiguous words to describe their intentions. To resolve this ambiguity, it is helpful to resort to the usual rules of interpretation of ambiguous contracts. * * *

Mr. How's testimony and his business record * * * show that he did not intend that the new corporation was the sole obligor on the contract. He stated that he believed Boss Hotel Co., Inc. or Boss Hotels was liable on the contract. This is not inconsistent with thinking Mr. Boss was liable on the contract, but it is inconsistent with intending that the new corporation was to be solely liable on the contract. Promoters other than the one signing the contract may be liable on the contract also. In this case, Boss Hotel Co., Inc. was not made a party but this does show a reason why Mr. How might state that he felt Boss Hotel Co., Inc. was liable on the contract. The oral testimony on this point was only generally to the effect that the parties agreed that the contract was all right as written, but did tend to support the conclusion that Mr. Boss was intended to be the present obligor on the contract. * * *

It might well be that the parties were thinking about an understanding such as the [third] type wherein there would be a future novation. However, the defendant didn't feel this was the situation. He did not plead or argue novation or agreement to that effect. Therefore, the only issue was whether the contract was a continuing offer to the then nonexistent corporation or was an agreement that Mr. Boss was a present obligor. While the agreement was not completely clear, the words "who will be the obligor," are not enough to offset the rule that the person signing for the nonexistent corporation is normally to be personally liable. This is especially true when considered in light of other circumstances of this case and would be true even without the inference that the law puts on this situation. * * *

The defendant argues that a practical construction has been put on the contract to the effect the plaintiff agreed to look solely to the credit of the new corporation. For this construction, the defendant relies upon the fact that the two checks which were given to Mr. Boss carried the letterhead of the new corporation and were signed by Edwin Hunter. * * * This would be an attempt to penalize the plaintiff for being patient and not demanding strict compliance. The court feels there was no waiver of rights and none was pleaded. * * *

In this case, the defendant was the principal promoter, acting for himself personally and as President of Boss Hotels, Inc. The promoters abandoned their purpose of forming the corporation. This would make the promoter liable to the plaintiff unless the contract be construed to mean: (1) that the plaintiff agreed to look solely to the new corporation for payment, and (2) that the promoter did not have any duty toward the plaintiff to form the corporation and give the corporation the opportunity to assume and pay the liability. * * *

At the time the specifications and drawings were completed, the amount owed the plaintiff was 75% of 6% of $850,000.00 (the reasonable cost estimate). This would amount to $38,250.00. $14,500.00 of this amount has been paid leaving an amount of $23,750.00 due to the plaintiff.

Accordingly the court concludes that the plaintiff, Stanley J. How & Associates, Inc., should have and recover judgment against the defendant,

Edwin A. Boss, in the sum of $23,750.00, with interest and costs and, accordingly, a judgment will be entered. * * *

Notes

(1) Is it not a fair inference from the circumstances surrounding the execution of the contract in this case that both parties probably contemplated that the architect was to look solely to some corporation for payment, that neither party thought that Boss was to be *personally* liable and that, therefore, the holding of the court in effect gives the plaintiff an unjustified windfall? In light of this argument, how persuasive is the Court's reliance on O'Rorke v. Geary, holding that where performance is called for before the corporation is formed, there is an inference that the promoter intended to be personally liable?

(2) Consider the following sections of the Restatement (Second) of Agency. Do they suggest alternative grounds by which a promoter might be held liable if he executes a contract in the name of a not-yet-formed corporation but without including the phrase "a corporation to be formed"?

§ 329 Agent Who Warrants Authority

A person who purports to make a contract, conveyance or representation on behalf of another who has full capacity but whom he has no power to bind, thereby becomes subject to liability to the other party thereto upon an implied warranty of authority, unless he has manifested that he does not make such warranty or the other party knows that the agent is not so authorized.

§ 330 Liability for Misrepresentation of Authority

A person who tortiously misrepresents to another that he has authority to make a contract, conveyance, or representation on behalf of a principal whom he has no power to bind, is subject to liability to the other in an action of tort for loss caused by reliance upon such misrepresentation.

§ 331 Agent Making No Warranty or Representation of Authority

A person who purports to make a contract, conveyance or representation on behalf of a principal whom he has no power to bind thereby is not subject to liability to the other party thereto if he sufficiently manifests that he does not warrant his authority and makes no tortious misrepresentation.

(3) Presumably, it would have been entirely feasible for Boss to have formed a new corporation or LLC to construct the project under the laws of either Minnesota or Iowa. If he had done so, and thereafter the contract had been entered into in the name of the new corporation or LLC, the possibility of a successful suit by the architect against Boss personally would have been very slight. The fact that cases involving promoter liability on contracts continue to arise with some regularity probably indicates that many promoters do not have legal advice in the early stages of the promotion, since presumably an attorney would insist that basic rights and obligations be expressed reasonably clearly, and that some provision should be made for obvious contingencies such as a total failure of the promotion. An attorney representing the promoter would normally recommend that a corporation or LLC be formed and that all contracts be taken in the name of that entity exclusively. The attorney should also recommend that

the agreement expressly provide that the other party should look only to the entity for payment. Of course, counsel for the other party would doubtless recommend that the promoter expressly assume personal responsibility for performance of the contract.

(4) In Yari v. Giles, 2002 WL 534642 (Tex.App. Amarillo 2002), Liglia Giles, a commercial tenant in a strip shopping center signed a lease with Bob Yari, the promoter who was developing the shopping center, and planned to incorporate it as Perisco, Inc. The lease recited that it was an agreement between Perisco, Inc., as landlord and Giles and Giles' company, LRG Enterprises, Inc., as tenant. The lease was signed on August 25, but Perisco was not formed until over two months later, on November 3. Giles sued Yari personally for unreasonably refusing his requests to place a sign outside of his store. In concluding that Yari was personally liable for breaching the terms of the lease, the court held that "[t]he rule is well-established * * * that a contract made by the promoter of a corporation before the corporate existence does not become a contract of the corporation when it is formed. The promoter is not liable where the other party knows the corporation does not exist. (Yari) presented no evidence that (Giles) knew Perisco was not a corporation at the time the lease was executed. Therefore the rule making promoters personally liable is applicable." In Coopers & Lybrand v. Fox, 758 P.2d 683 (Colo.App.1988), Garry Fox was in the process of forming a new business to be called "Fox and Partners, Inc." On November 3, 1981 he met with a representative of Coopers & Lybrand and arranged for a tax opinion and other accounting services. Articles of incorporation were filed on December 4, 1981. After rendering the services, Coopers & Lybrand sent a bill for $10,827 to "Mr. Garry R. Fox, Fox and Partners, Inc." When the bill was not paid, suit was brought against Garry Fox individually. The Court held that Fox was personally liable for the debt. Contrast this result with that in Quaker Hill, Inc. v. Parr, 148 Colo. 45, 364 P.2d 1056 (1961). Consider also Goodman v. Darden, Doman & Stafford Assoc., 100 Wash.2d 476, 670 P.2d 648, 652–53 (1983).

(5) A "head count" of the numerous cases involving the personal liability of promoters would doubtless show that a majority of the cases hold the defendant-promoter personally liable on one theory or another.

(6) McArthur v. Times Printing Co., 48 Minn. 319, 51 N.W. 216 (1892) deals with the issue of when corporations will be liable for the contracts entered into by promoters. In *McArthur,* a promoter contracted with the plaintiff on behalf of the defendant company for services as an advertising solicitor before the company had been incorporated. Plaintiff began his services and continued them after incorporation until he was discharged. According to the court, while "no formal arrangements were made relating to the contract * * * all the shareholders and directors knew of the contract. Nobody repudiated or complained of the contract after incorporation." The court took the position that a corporation is not liable on a promoter's contract unless it expressly or impliedly adopts (or "ratifies") it.

(7) The court's position in *McArthur* appears to be generally accepted, though the issue has arisen in only a few litigated cases. For an example of implied adoption, see Stolmeier v. Beck, 232 Neb. 705, 441 N.W.2d 888 (1989). In Framingham Sav. Bank v. Szabo, 617 F.2d 897 (1st Cir.1980) the Court applied the "extreme minority" rule of Massachusetts that a newly–formed corporation "could not become bound to the contract by ratification or adoption of the putative agent's bargain. Rather, to bind itself the corporation must introduce 'into the transaction such elements as would be sufficient foundation for a new contract.' The corporation can become liable on the terms of the original contract,

but only if its post-incorporation acts are sufficient independently to bind it to a new contract." 617 F.2d at 898. Considering that corporations act only through agents, do you think results will often differ if a court applies the general rule or the "extreme minority" rule applied in Massachusetts?

(8) 2 Williston on Contracts § 306, at 431 (3d ed. 1959) states that "it seems more nearly to correspond with the intentions of the parties to suggest that when the corporation assents to the contract, it assents to take the place of the promoter—a change of parties to which the other side of the contract assented in advance." Is that true? If this inference were adopted, might promoters facing an unwanted pre-formation contractual liability form a corporation with nominal assets and arrange to have that corporation adopt the contract?

2. DEFECTIVE INCORPORATION

ROBERTSON v. LEVY

Court of Appeals, District of Columbia, 1964.
197 A.2d 443.

HOOD, CHIEF JUDGE.

On December 22, 1961, Martin G. Robertson and Eugene M. Levy entered into an agreement whereby Levy was to form a corporation, Penn Ave. Record Shack, Inc., which was to purchase Robertson's business. Levy submitted articles of incorporation to the Superintendent of Corporations on December 27, 1961, but no certificate of incorporation was issued at this time. Pursuant to the contract an assignment of lease was entered into on December 31, 1961, between Robertson and Levy, the latter acting as president of Penn Ave. Record Shack, Inc. On January 2, 1962, the articles of incorporation were rejected by the Superintendent of Corporations but on the same day Levy began to operate the business under the name Penn Ave. Record Shack, Inc. Robertson executed a bill of sale to Penn Ave. Record Shack, Inc. on January 8, 1962, disposing of the assets of his business to that "corporation" and receiving in return a note providing for installment payments signed "Penn Ave. Record Shack, Inc. by Eugene M. Levy, President." The certificate of incorporation was issued on January 17, 1962. One payment was made on the note. The exact date when the payment was made cannot be clearly determined from the record, but presumably it was made after the certificate of incorporation was issued. Penn Ave. Record Shack, Inc. ceased doing business in June 1962 and is presently without assets. Robertson sued Levy for the balance due on the note as well as for additional expenses incurred in settling the lease arrangement with the original lessor. In holding for the defendant the trial court found that [§ 139 of the 1950 Model Act],[8] relied upon by Robertson, did not apply and further that Robertson was estopped to deny the existence of the corporation.

The case presents the following issues on appeal: Whether the president of an "association" which filed its articles of incorporation, which were first rejected but later accepted, can be held personally liable on an obligation

---

8. [By the Editors] This section reads as follows:

§ 139. Unauthorized Assumption of Corporate Powers

All persons who assume to act as a corporation without authority so to do shall be jointly and severally liable for all debts and liabilities incurred or arising as a result thereof.

entered into by the "association" before the certificate of incorporation has been issued, or whether the creditor is "estopped" from denying the existence of the "corporation" because, after the certificate of incorporation was issued, he accepted the first installment payment on the note.

The Business Corporation Act of the District of Columbia, Code 1961, is patterned after the Model Business Corporation Act which is largely based on the Illinois Business Corporation Act of 1933. On this appeal, we are concerned with an interpretation of [§§ 50 and 139 of the 1950 Model Act]. Several states have substantially enacted the Model Act, but only a few have enacted both sections similar to those under consideration. A search of the case law in each of these jurisdictions, as well as in our own jurisdiction, convinces us that these particular sections of the corporation acts have never been the subject of a reported decision.

For a full understanding of the problems raised, some historical grounding is not only illuminative but necessary. In early common law times private corporations were looked upon with distrust and disfavor. This distrust of the corporate form for private enterprise was eventually overcome by the enactment of statutes which set forth certain prerequisites before the status was achieved, and by court decisions which eliminated other stumbling blocks. Problems soon arose, however, where there was substantial compliance with the prerequisites of the statute, but not complete formal compliance. Thus the concepts of de jure corporations, de facto corporations, and of "corporations by estoppel" came into being.

Taking each of these in turn, a de jure corporation results when there has been conformity with the mandatory conditions precedent (as opposed to merely directive conditions) established by the statute. A de jure corporation is not subject to direct or collateral attack either by the state in a *quo warranto* proceeding or by any other person.

A *de facto* corporation is one which has been defectively incorporated and thus is not de jure. The Supreme Court has stated that the requisites for a corporation de facto are: (1) A valid law under which such a corporation can be lawfully organized; (2) An attempt to organize thereunder; (3) Actual user of the corporate franchise. Good faith in claiming to be and in doing business as a corporation is often added as a further condition. A de facto corporation is recognized for all purposes except where there is a direct attack by the state in a *quo warranto* proceeding. The concept of de facto corporation has been roundly criticized.[9]

Cases continued to arise, however, where the corporation was not de jure, where it was not de facto because of failure to comply with one of the four requirements above, but where the courts, lacking some clear standard or guideline, were willing to decide on the equities of the case. Thus another concept arose, the so-called "corporation by estoppel." This term was a complete misnomer. There was no corporation, the acts of the associates having failed even to colorably fulfill the statutory requirements; there was no estoppel in the pure sense of the word because generally there was no holding out followed by reliance on the part of the other party. Apparently estoppel

9. [By the Court] Ballantine § 20 ("a baffling and discouraging maze,"); Stevens, Corporations, pp. 135–6 (1949) ("inaccurate and confusing,"); Frey, Legal Analysis and the De Facto Doctrine, 100 U.Pa.L.Rev. 1153, 1180 (1952) ("legal conceptualism at its worst,").

can arise whether or not a de facto corporation has come into existence. Estoppel problems arose where the certificate of incorporation had been issued as well as where it had not been issued, and under the following general conditions: where the "association" sues a third party and the third party is estopped from denying that the plaintiff is a corporation; where a third party sues the "association" as a corporation and the "association" is precluded from denying that it was a corporation; where a third party sues the "association" and the members of that association cannot deny its existence as a corporation where they participated in holding it out as a corporation; where a third party sues the individuals behind the "association" but is estopped from denying the existence of the "corporation"; where either a third party, or the "association" is estopped from denying the corporate existence because of prior pleadings.

One of the reasons for enacting modern corporation statutes was to eliminate problems inherent in the de jure, de facto and, estoppel concepts. * * *

The first portion of [§ 50] sets forth a *sine qua non* regarding compliance. No longer must the courts inquire into the equities of a case to determine whether there has been "colorable compliance" with the statute. The corporation comes into existence only when the certificate has been issued. Before the certificate issues, there is no corporation de jure, de facto or by estoppel. After the certificate is issued under [§ 50], the de jure corporate existence commences. Only after such existence has begun can the corporation commence business through compliance with section [§ 48(g) of MBCA (1950)] by paying into the corporation the minimum capital, and with [§ 51 of that Act], which requires that the capitalization be no less than $1,000. These latter two sections are given further force and effect by [a non-Model Act section] which declares that directors of a corporation are jointly and severally liable for any assets distributed or any dividends paid to shareholders which renders the corporation insolvent or reduces its net assets below its stated capital.

The authorities which have considered the problem are unanimous in their belief that [MBCA (1950) §§ 50 and 139] have put to rest de facto corporations and corporations by estoppel. Thus the Comment to [§ 50], * * * after noting that de jure incorporation is complete when the certificate is issued, states that:

> Since it is unlikely that any steps short of securing a certificate of incorporation would be held to constitute apparent compliance, the possibility that a de facto corporation could exist under such a provision is remote.[10]

Similarly, Professor Hornstein in his work on Corporate Law and Practice (1959) observes at § 29 that: "Statutes in almost half the jurisdictions

---

10. [By the Editors] The comment to § 56 of MBCA (1969) was even more unambiguous:

Under the unequivocal provisions of the Model Act, any steps short of securing a certificate of incorporation would not constitute apparent compliance. Therefore a de facto corporation cannot exist under the Model Act.

The comment to § 146 (identical to § 139 of the 1950 Act) added "Abolition of the concept of de facto incorporation, which at best was fuzzy, is a sound result. No reason exists for its continuance under general corporate laws, where the process of acquiring de jure incorporation is both simple and clear. The vestigial appendage should be removed."

have virtually eliminated the distinction between de jure and de facto corporations [citing § 139 of the Model Act]." * * *

The portion of [§ 50] which states that the certificate of incorporation will be "conclusive evidence" that all conditions precedent have been performed eliminates the problems of estoppel and de facto corporations once the certificate has been issued. The existence of the corporation is conclusive evidence against all who deal with it. Under [§ 139], if an individual or group of individuals assumes to act as a corporation before the certificate of incorporation has been issued, joint and several liability attaches. We hold, therefore, that the impact of these sections, when considered together, is to eliminate the concepts of estoppel and *de facto* corporateness under the Business Corporation Act of the District of Columbia. It is immaterial whether the third person believed he was dealing with a corporation or whether he intended to deal with a corporation.[11] The certificate of incorporation provides the cut off point; before it is issued, the individuals, and not the corporation, are liable.

Turning to the facts of this case, Penn Ave. Record Shack, Inc. was not a corporation when the original agreement was entered into, when the lease was assigned, when Levy took over Robertson's business, when operations began under the Penn Ave. Record Shack, Inc. name, or when the bill of sale was executed. Only on January 17 did Penn Ave. Record Shack, Inc. become a corporation. Levy is subject to personal liability because, before this date, he assumed to act as a corporation without any authority so to do. Nor is Robertson estopped from denying the existence of the corporation because after the certificate was issued he accepted one payment on the note. An individual who incurs statutory liability on an obligation under [§ 139] because he has acted without authority, is not relieved of that liability where, at a later time, the corporation does come into existence by complying with section [§ 50]. Subsequent partial payment by the corporation does not remove this liability.

The judgment appealed from is reversed with instructions to enter judgment against the appellee on the note and for damages proved to have been incurred by appellant for breach of the lease.

Reversed with instructions.

Notes

(1) Several decisions in states that adopted both §§ 50 and 139 of the MBCA accept the result reached in Robertson v. Levy, holding that there can be no limited liability before the certificate of incorporation is filed. See, Booker Custom Packing Co., Inc. v. Sallomi, 149 Ariz. 124, 716 P.2d 1061 (App.1986); Thompson & Green Mach. Co., Inc. v. Music City Lumber Co., Inc., 683 S.W.2d 340 (Tenn.App.1984).

(2) In Sherwood & Roberts–Oregon, Inc. v. Alexander, 269 Or. 389, 525 P.2d 135 (1974), the Court refused to apply §§ 50 and 139 when no attempt was made at all to incorporate. The Court further held that the promoters were not liable on

---

11. [By the Court] In the present case, Robertson admitted intending to deal with a corporation.

the ground that the third person had agreed not to look to the promoter for payment of the note that had been executed in the name of the nonexistent corporation. Can that be right?

(3) When applying §§ 50 and 139 should a distinction be drawn between active participants and inactive investors? Can such a distinction be justified under the common law of de facto corporations? Under the language of § 139? What does "assume to act" mean in that section? Does it refer to all participants in an active promotion? Only the active promoter?

(4) MBCA (1984) makes significant changes in the provisions of MBCA (1950).

(5) In Cantor v. Sunshine Greenery, Inc., 165 N.J.Super. 411, 398 A.2d 571 (1979), the plaintiff sued William J. Brunetti on a lease he had signed in the name of Sunshine Greenery, Inc. on December 16, 1974. It turned out that the name "Sunshine Greenery, Inc." had been reserved for Brunetti by the New Jersey Secretary of State on November 21. Brunetti and Sharyn N. Sansoni signed a certificate of incorporation (equivalent to articles of incorporation) on December 3, and mailed it to the Secretary of State on the same date with a check for the filing fee. For some unexplained reason, the document was not officially filed by the Secretary of State until December 18, 1974, two days after the execution of the lease. The court held that Sunshine Greenery, Inc. was a *de facto* corporation and Brunetti was not personally liable.

(6) Can you see factual differences between *Sunshine Greenery* and *Robertson* that might justify the difference in result? Another possible basis for reconciling the two cases is the difference in statutory provisions in the District of Columbia and New Jersey. As indicated in *Robertson,* the critical provisions in the District of Columbia were drawn directly from §§ 50 and 139 of the 1950 Model Act. New Jersey was not a Model Act state. See N.J.Stat.Ann. § 14A:2–7(2).

(7) Before the development of the 1950 Model Act provisions set forth in *Robertson* there was a tendency to hold all participants in a corporation that was neither *de facto* nor *de jure* personally liable. See Harry G. Henn and John R. Alexander, Laws of Corporations and Other Business Associations 343 (3d. 1983).

(8) In Cranson v. International Business Machines Corp., 234 Md. 477, 200 A.2d 33, Cranson, was not held personally liable for the debts of his defectively incorporated association, the Real Estate Service Bureau. Cranson had agreed to invest in the Real Estate Service Bureau and to become an officer and a director of the new company. Cranson and his fellow investors hired a lawyer who assured them that the corporation had been formed under the laws of Maryland. Cranson paid for and received stock certificates, and the company set up bank accounts and maintained corporate books and records, despite the fact that, unknown to Cranson, due to an oversight on the part of the attorney, the certificate of incorporation was not filed with the Secretary of State until after the business had purchased eight typewriters from IBM on credit. The court held that because I.B.M. dealt with the Bureau as if it were a corporation and relied on its credit rather than that of Cranson, it was "estopped to deny the corporate existence of the Bureau."

The court in Cranson distinguished between the doctrine of *de facto* corporation and the doctrine of corporation by estoppel. The court observed that both doctrines are applied to protect officers of defectively incorporated associations. The doctrine of *de facto* corporations is applied to cases where elements show: (1) the existence of law authorizing incorporation; (2) an effort in good faith to incorporate under the existing law; and (3) actual use or exercise of corporate powers. The doctrine of *estoppel* to deny the corporate existence is applied where the person seeking to hold the officer personally liable has contracted with the association in a manner that recognizes and admits its existence as a corporation.

> The court observed that, while some cases assimilate these two doctrines, they are not dependent upon one another. Where the three elements of a *de facto* corporation are found, there exists an entity which is a corporation *de jure* against all persons but the state. However, the estoppel theory is only applied to facts of each case and may be invoked even where there is no corporation *de facto*. In Cranson, even though some of the requirements for a *de facto* corporation are missing, this does not preclude the application of the estoppel doctrine. * * *

Cranson v. International Business Machines Corp., 234 Md. 477, 200 A.2d 33 (1964).

(9) In Harry Rich Corp. v. Feinberg, 518 So.2d 377 (Fla.App.1987), Feinberg found himself in essentially the same position that Cranson did. He had been shown articles of incorporation that he believed had been properly filed. Florida had adopted MBCA § 139; the Court, however, held that Feinberg was not liable under that section since "assume to act" should be construed to permit recovery "only where the individual acts with actual or constructive knowledge that no corporation exists." 518 So.2d at 381. The Court also relied on a non-Model Act statute enacted in Florida that prohibits a defectively-formed corporation from using its lack of legal organization as a defense against claims brought by third persons.

(10) Consider MBCA § 2.04, a deceptively simple statute. The Official Comment explains:

> A review of recent case law indicates * * * that even in states with * * * [statutes that provide expressly that those who prematurely act as or on behalf of a corporation are personally liable on all transactions entered into or liability incurred before incorporation], courts have continued to rely on common law concepts of de facto corporations, de jure corporations, and corporations by estoppel that provide uncertain protection against liability for preincorporation transactions. These cases caused a review of the underlying policies represented in earlier versions of the Model Act and the adoption of a slightly more flexible or relaxed standard.

> Incorporation under modern statutes is so simple and inexpensive that a strong argument may be made that nothing short of filing articles of incorporation should create the privilege of limited liability. A number of situations have arisen, however, in which the protection of limited liability arguably should be recognized even though the simple incorporation process established by modern statutes has not been completed. * * *

Other "arguable" exceptions referred to in the Official Comment include situations:

(a) Where a corporate organizer enters into a transaction in the name of the corporation when he reasonably and honestly believes that articles have been filed but they have not been due to attorney neglect or other cause.

(b) Where a transaction is entered into after the articles have been mailed or delivered to the filing office but have not been received in the filing office through no fault of the filer.

(c) Where a person knows that no corporation has been formed, but insists that his contract be immediately entered into in the name of the corporation.

(11) Several states have enacted statutes that are similar to MBCA § 2.04, but use different language. Colo. Rev. Stat. 7–102–104 (1997), for example, uses the phrase "good faith belief" that authority exists. Fla. Stat. Ann. § 607.0204 substitutes "actual knowledge" for "knowing." And, Va. Code Ann. § 13.1–622 uses the phrase "knew or reasonably should have known that there was no incorporation."

(12) There are literally hundreds of reported cases that involve defects in the incorporation process. The number has declined significantly in recent years by reason of changes in the incorporation process in many states, particularly the adoption of the MBCA and the elimination of multiple procedural requirements, multiple filings, and mandatory minimum capitalization. However, a handful of states continue to have one or more of these requirements. And cases involving *de facto* corporations continue to arise. See, for example, Grabarek v. J's Const. & Masonry, Inc., 2002 WL 1837845 (Conn.Super.2002), in which the court held that the defendant, J's Construction, was a de facto corporation despite plaintiffs' arguments that there was no evidence that the defendants "ever took steps in good faith towards incorporation."

(13) As noted in the Court's opinion in *Robertson*, the consequences of defective incorporation have long troubled courts and commentators. The common law *de facto* doctrine, as applied by courts, in particular, has been the subject of much academic analysis and criticism. Despite the efforts of the draftsmen of the MBCA, courts still refer to common law principles in resolving cases arising in MBCA states. Rather surprisingly, this academic controversy appears to have been rekindled in the late 1990s. It began in 1952, when Professor Alexander Frey of the University of Pennsylvania Law School published an article attempting to classify all *de facto* corporation cases arising prior to 1952. Alexander Hamilton Frey, Legal Analysis and the "De Facto" Doctrine, 100 U.Pa.L.Rev. 1153, 1174 (1952). He considered 212 cases.[12] His classification was based on the nature of the defect, whether there had been dealings on a corporate basis (roughly, whether the plaintiffs had contracted with the firm without knowing whether it was incorporated), and whether the suit sought to hold active or inactive investors personally liable. This study, it should be noted, involves only cases that predate the earliest version of the Model Act.

(14) Professor Frey's analysis concluded that the defective incorporation doctrines were misused by courts and that rather than aiding analysis, they tended to be misleading. He stated that the *de facto* doctrine was "just so much jargon and ought to be abandoned," 100 U.Pa.L.Rev., at 1178, since it involved "legal conceptualism at its worst." Id., at 1180. He found 72 cases in which good faith attempts at compliance with legal requirements had been made but the *de facto* doctrine protected investors in only 42 of the 72 cases. He also found 38

---

12. [By the Editors] Professor Frey's research has been replicated by later scholars who conclude that it suffers from serious defects. See, for example, Norwood P. Beveridge, Corporate Puzzles: Being A True And Complete Explanation of De Facto Corporations and Corporations by Estoppel, their Historical Development, Attempted Abolition, and Eventual Rehabilitation, 22 Okla. City U.L.Rev. 935, 940, n. 15 (1997): "Many of Professor Frey's Cases are mischaracterized. * * * One case is counted twice * * *. Two others had at the time of his article been overruled either expressly * * *, or overruled by implication. * * * Some did not even deal with corporations at all, but with business trusts * * *, Pennsylvania partnership associations * * *, or other forms of business organizations. Frey's claim * * * to have catalogued all reported cases on the question [also] cannot be credited. * * *"

cases in which there were clearly dealings on a corporate basis and no attempt to incorporate, but defendants escaped personal liability in only 13 of these 38 cases.

(15) In 1990, another article updated Professor Frey's analysis. Wayne N. Bradley, An Empirical Study of Defective Incorporation, 39 Emory L.J. 523 (1990). It considered 131 additional cases that were decided between January 1, 1970 and November 1, 1989. Bradley concluded that there was an increase in the tendency of courts to hold individual shareholders of defective corporations personally liable when sued by third parties. He also concluded that personal liability is almost always imposed where there are business activities, but no attempt at all to incorporate.

(16) The database created by the Frey/Bradley articles has led to continued scholarly analysis. Fred S. McChesney, Doctrinal Analysis and Statistical Modeling in Law: The Case of Defective Incorporation, 71 Wash. U.L.Q. 493, 500–03 (1993) points out that cases cannot be unambiguously classified as involving "de facto corporations" or "corporations by estoppel:"

> In jurisdictions recognizing the doctrines of de facto corporation and corporation by estoppel, there is virtual unanimity as to the elements of each. As a practical matter, though, case reviews by legal commentators have repeatedly found that courts do not generally follow the supposed requirements—indeed, it is not clear that courts understand the difference between the two. * * *

> In Frey's *de facto* corporation cases, the importance of attempted compliance was reduced * * * by the fact that courts awarded limited liability only when the plaintiff was already dealing with the firm as a corporation. In no cases where dealings were not on a corporate basis did defendants' good faith attempts at statutory compliance result in limited liability. In other words, in all of the cases where courts invoked the de facto corporation doctrine to uphold limited liability, defendants had satisfied the test for corporation by estoppel anyway. Courts seemed frequently to confuse the two doctrines, making the relevance of the distinction even less clear. * * * Conversely, Frey's results also indicated that outcomes in the estoppel cases were apparently influenced by steps defendants had taken to achieve corporation status. Frey reported two groups of estoppel cases. In neither was an attempt at statutory compliance made, obviating doctrinally the possibility of de facto corporate status. But in one group the defendants had taken some steps toward incorporation (e.g., drawing up and signing articles of incorporation) and apparently believed in good faith that they were acting as a corporation. In the second group, the firm's principals had no reason to think they were acting as a corporation, yet held the firm out as such. As long as corporation by estoppel was the defense, the distinction should make no difference in those cases where plaintiffs had dealt with the firm as a corporation. Yet, limited liability was granted in 44 percent of the first group of cases (11 of 25), but almost never (8 percent) in the second group (2 of 13 cases). Thus, just as estoppel elements appear important in the de facto corporation cases, the elements of de facto corporate status (attempted compliance) apparently influence judges to decree corporations by estoppel. * * *

He then applies a multiple regression analysis on cases from Frey's analysis to reach the following conclusion:

> * * * Frey's sample had already indicated that it is not unusual for defendants to seek to comply with the statute and at the same time for plaintiffs to deal with defendant(s) as a corporation. The empirical results here indicate

that both factors affect judges' decisions in common-law defective incorporation situations. * * *

Thus, one should not view the cases as falling into the two traditional boxes, de facto corporation and corporation by estoppel. The results here make it easier to understand (if not excuse) judges' frequent inability to enunciate a clear distinction in the two subsets of cases. Evaluated by what they do, not by what they say, judges apply one unitary doctrine—that of defective incorporation. That doctrine should be viewed as consisting of several factors, including defendants' attempt to comply with the statute and plaintiffs' treatment of the firm as a corporation. However, neither is sufficient; each merely adds to the likelihood that limited liability will be recognized. The apparent confusion shown by many judges in distinguishing the two doctrines reflects the fact that they are really not two doctrines at all.

(17) Wayne N. Bradley also points out that issues relating to *de facto* corporations arise in a variety of different contexts. For example, he cites thirty-one cases in which the *defendant* attempted to escape liability by claiming that the *plaintiff* was not a valid corporation at the time of the transaction; this argument failed in twenty-four cases. In nine cases the defendant attempted to escape liability by asserting that it was not itself a properly formed corporation; not surprisingly, this defense failed in all nine cases. 39 Emory L.J., at 560–66.

FRONTIER REFINING COMPANY V. KUNKEL'S, INC.

Supreme Court of Wyoming, 1965.
407 P.2d 880.

JUSTICE GRAY delivered the opinion of the Court.

Plaintiff Frontier Refining Company commenced an action against Kunkel's, Inc., as a partnership, and George Fairfield, Clifford D. Kunkel and Harlan Beach, as members thereof, to recover a balance claimed due on an open account. By its amended complaint, Frontier alleged that the individual defendants by oral agreement were associated in the business of operating a service station and truck terminal in Cheyenne, Wyoming, as a partnership under the name of Kunkel's, Inc., and were indebted to plaintiff in the sum of $6,732.32 for gasoline sold by plaintiff to said partnership. The defendant Kunkel was never served and the action proceeded against the defendants Fairfield and Beach. Both denied that any partnership was ever created between the individual defendants; denied that they were ever associated in the operation of any business with the defendant Kunkel under the name of Kunkel's, Inc.; and affirmatively alleged that the defendant Kunkel operated the business as an individual. Upon trial, the court found that the business known as Kunkel's, Inc., was not a partnership composed of the individual defendants; found generally for the defendants; and judgment was entered dismissing the action. Frontier appeals from the judgment. Hereafter we shall refer to the individual defendants by their last names.

* * * [I]t is Frontier's position that when this occurs the parties are individually liable as partners for the debts incurred in the business venture. To support its position Frontier cites, among other authorities, the general rule set forth in 68 C.J.S. Partnership § 40, p. 462, which states:

* * * In most jurisdictions the rule is * * * to the effect that, where two or more persons hold themselves out as a corporation, or permit an

association of which they are incorporators, stockholders, or members to be so held out, when there is no corporation either de jure or de facto, they will all be liable individually as partners for its debts and on contracts entered into either by themselves or by others as agents of the pretended corporation and in its name * * *.

* * * Nevertheless, as an initial approach to the problem here, we have been somewhat bothered as to whether or not such rule, which was laid down independently of statute, affords the remedy which Frontier seeks to pursue. A statutory remedy relating to the matter was in effect at the time the business transactions here took place. Section 17–36.122, W.S.1957, provides as follows:

All persons who assume to act as a corporation without authority so to do shall be jointly and severally liable for all debts and liabilities incurred or arising as a result thereof.

* * * In order that the basis for the conclusion reached be understood, it is necessary to relate the evidence in some detail. In this connection, however, we might point out that much of the testimony upon which appellant relies was in conflict with the evidence favorable to the defendants. * * *

With respect to the facts, the record discloses that Frontier was a refiner and distributor of petroleum products. About the middle of May 1962 Kunkel became interested in taking over a filling station and truck stop in Cheyenne, Wyoming, owned by Frontier and which was then under lease to one "Woody" Griffitt. Such lease, however, was about to be terminated. Kunkel talked with B. L. Warren, zone manager of Frontier, and advised Warren that he had no money to finance the venture but was acquainted with Fairfield and would talk with Fairfield to see "if he could raise the money." Kunkel then went to the Gas Hills area in Wyoming where Fairfield in association with Beach was engaged in a mining venture, and according to the testimony of Fairfield the approach of Kunkel was to obtain a loan. Fairfield declined and there was then some conversation with respect to the formation of a corporation. Fairfield advised Kunkel that if he and Beach went in on the venture it would have to be on that basis. Apparently very little was said concerning the details of the formation of the corporation except that it would be Kunkel's responsibility to see that the business was incorporated—which was not even attempted—and Kunkel was not to "open the door" unless that had been done. It was understood also that Kunkel would manage the business of the corporation and in order to get it started Fairfield and Beach would purchase the equipment from Griffitt and would then take stock for their investment. Each defendant was to receive one-third of the stock of the corporation.

A short time later Fairfield came to Cheyenne and looked over the station. Warren, Frontier's employee, testified that this was about June 1, 1962; that he talked with Fairfield at that time; that he was told by Fairfield that the business would be a corporation; and that he was also told "Cliff [Kunkel] would be able to go on it." However, Fairfield testified that he did not see Warren at that time and had never said anything to Warren about a proposed corporation. Neither is there evidence that Beach ever discussed such matters with anyone. In this connection, however, Warren on May 28, 1962, by written memorandum advised Frontier that the business was to be incorporated under the name of "Kunkel's Incorporated" and would be financed by Fairfield and Beach and that both would be officers of the corporation. Warren also submitted with the memorandum a financial statement of Kunkel, which he said was not to be considered that of the corporation. No financial statement of Fairfield or Beach was ever obtained or submitted to Frontier.

Also, on June 1, 1962, Frontier entered into a sublease agreement for the station with "CLIFFORD D. KUNKEL DBA KUNKEL'S INC.," as sublessee, which was to become effective on June 12, 1962. Other agreements were entered into in the same manner and with one exception the agreements were signed "C. D. Kunkel" without reference to the purported corporate name or any corporate capacity. The exception was the "Distributor's Contract" which set forth the conditions relating to the purchase and sale of petroleum products. Here the name "Kunkel's, Inc." preceded the signature. Right here we might also point out Fairfield's testimony to the effect that he never saw these agreements until sometime in November 1962, and that he had not previously discussed with Kunkel the negotiation of such agreements.

Soon after the agreements were made, Kunkel, unknown to Fairfield or Beach, took over the station and commenced doing business. The first sale of gasoline by Frontier to the station was made on June 13, 1962, and was billed "Clifford D. Kunkel dba Kunkel Inc." Subsequent sales were billed in the same manner. Some thirty days after the initial sale Frontier discovered that through error the products purchased by the station were not paid for at the time of delivery as had been provided in the "Distributor's Contract," and an indebtedness in excess of $5,000 accrued during that period.

It is also in evidence that Fairfield and Beach put some $11,000 into the venture, but the exact dates that these payments were made cannot be ascertained from the record. However, the testimony of Fairfield tends to show that two of the checks aggregating the sum of $10,000 to be used for the purchase of the inventory and equipment from Griffitt were made subsequent to the time that Kunkel opened the station. With respect to all of these payments Fairfield testified that he was not aware of Kunkel's failure at that time to incorporate the business and there is no evidence that he was aware of the indebtedness that had accrued during the thirty-day period. Fairfield also denied the testimony of Warren that Fairfield, when the delinquency was called to his attention, gave assurances that the account would be paid.

* * * However, the foregoing, when carefully analyzed, lends sufficient support to the trial court's conclusion that the facts here were such that individual liability could not be imposed upon Fairfield and Beach on the theory that they were partners in the venture under general rules of law relating to a purported corporation.

In the first instance the trial court was entitled to infer that Kunkel was the sole source of the information given to Frontier concerning a proposed corporation under the name of Kunkel's, Inc., and that neither Fairfield nor Beach, expressly or impliedly, authorized Kunkel to make such representations or to enter into contracts with Frontier in the name of "Kunkel's, Inc." Such fact would lend substantial support to a conclusion that neither Fairfield nor Beach held themselves out as a corporation, an essential element under the general rule advanced by Frontier.

Another inference that could readily be drawn was that the indebtedness was not incurred in the name of a pretended corporation. At the outset of the business relations between Frontier and the venture in question, Frontier with full knowledge that a corporation had not yet been formed chose to transact its business with Kunkel as an individual. * * * Now, after extending credit by mistake, it attempts to explain that the reason its business transactions were entered into with Kunkel as an individual was the lack of a corporate entity with which to contract. Such explanation would hardly prevent the trial court from concluding that Frontier did not extend credit or intend to extend credit to "Kunkel's, Inc.," and that Frontier was content to look only to Kunkel for performance of its agreements. It has been determined that a creditor, under such circumstances, will be held to his bargain. *Guilford Builders Supply Company v. Reynolds, 249 N.C. 612, 107 S.E.2d 80, 83.* * * *

It appears to us also that Frontier's position is inconsistent. When it became obvious that the business operated by Kunkel was insolvent, Frontier obtained from him a chattel mortgage naming "Clifford D. Kunkel, individually and doing business as Kunkel's, Inc." as mortgagor and signed simply as "C. D. Kunkel." The mortgage disclosed on its face that it was not executed in the name of or on behalf of a corporation, pretended or otherwise. It covered the equipment used in the station and was given to secure the indebtedness owing Frontier. Subsequently Fairfield, claiming to own such equipment, took possession of it. Thereupon Frontier, in a companion case, brought an action in replevin to recover possession of the property in order that its mortgage might be foreclosed. With respect to this proceeding the trial court found that the mortgage was valid and entered judgment for Frontier. That judgment has now become final, no appeal having been taken by either of the parties. As a consequence, Frontier is in this position. In this appeal it is protesting the finding of the trial court that there was no partnership composed of the individual defendants. Yet, in the companion case—consolidated for trial with this case—it accepts the fruits of a judgment which carries with it an inherent finding by the trial court that Kunkel, as an individual, was Frontier's debtor and the owner of the property pledged to secure such debt. To permit Frontier to disavow such judgment to the extent of imposing liability upon Fairfield and Beach under the general rule advanced by Frontier, would be unconscionable. Imposition by the courts of the general rules relating to a defective corporation are subject to equitable principles, *Loverin v. McLaughlin, 161 Ill. 417, 44 N.E. 99, 105;* and we think the statement in the opinion of the Supreme Court of Iowa, *Schumacher v. Sumner Telephone Co., 161 Iowa 326, 142 N.W. 1034, 1038, Ann.Cas.1916A, 201*—a case presenting a much closer question than does the case here—is quite pertinent. There the court said:

> * * * To recover, appellant must bring himself clearly within the benefit of some established rule or principle of the law, and in this we think he has failed. There is very little shown to commend his demand against the appellees to equitable consideration, and the court ought not to go out of its way to discover grounds for compelling payment of his claim by parties who did not contract the debt, who had no knowledge of its existence until suit was begun thereon, who gave no authority to Robish to borrow money on their account, and where the lender did not part with his money relying upon their conduct or credit. * * *

Finding no error in the proceedings, we affirm the judgment.

Affirmed.

Notes

(1) The defendants in this case avoided personal liability on the ground that they were creditors, not partners. But did not the defendants specifically decline to loan money to this venture? What then was the legal basis for the decision? The court says, "In order to prevail, the plaintiff must bring himself clearly within the benefit of some established rule or principle of the law, and in this we think he has failed." But what about the argument that the business was a partnership because a partnership will be said to exist "where the evidence as a whole reasonably shows that the parties have entered into a contractual relation whereby they have combined their property, labor, and skill in an enterprise or business as co-owners for the purpose of joint profit"? See Brcka v. Falcon Electric Corp., 2001 WL 641524 (Minn.App.2001).

(2) The principal case illustrates the risk of entering a business relationship without double-checking to make sure that a proper filing has been made with the relevant authorities. Here the risk was that the investors would be treated as partners, rather than as creditors.

(3) In light of the fact that the business suffered losses and somebody had to bear these losses, which party was in the best position to shoulder them as between the creditors and the outside investors? Is this issue best decided on a case-by-case basis or as a matter of general policy?

Chapter Seven

DISREGARD OF THE CORPORATE ENTITY

A. THE COMMON LAW DOCTRINE OF PIERCING THE CORPORATE VEIL

BARTLE v. HOME OWNERS CO-OP.

Court of Appeals of New York, 1955.
309 N.Y. 103, 127 N.E.2d 832.

FROESSEL, JUDGE.

Plaintiff, as trustee in bankruptcy of Westerlea Builders, Inc., has by means of this litigation attempted to hold defendant liable for the contract debts of Westerlea, defendant's wholly owned subsidiary. Defendant, as a cooperative corporation composed mostly of veterans, was organized in July, 1947, for the purpose of providing low-cost housing for its members. Unable to secure a contractor to undertake construction of the housing planned, Westerlea was organized for that purpose on June 5, 1948. With building costs running considerably higher than anticipated, Westerlea, as it proceeded with construction on some 26 houses, found itself in a difficult financial situation. On January 24, 1949, the creditors, pursuant to an extension agreement, took over the construction responsibilities. Nearly four years later, in October, 1952, Westerlea was adjudicated as bankrupt. Meanwhile, defendant had contributed to Westerlea not only its original capital of $25,000 but additional sums amounting to $25,639.38.

Plaintiff's principal contention on this appeal is that the courts below erred in refusing to "pierce the corporate veil" of Westerlea's corporate existence; as subordinate grounds for recovery he urged that the defendant equitably pledged its assets toward the satisfaction of the debts of the bankrupt's creditors, and that the doctrine of unjust enrichment should apply.

The trial court made detailed findings of fact which have been unanimously affirmed by the Appellate Division, 285 App.Div. 1113, 140 N.Y.S.2d 512, which are clearly supported by the evidence, and by which we are bound. It found that while the defendant, as owner of the stock of Westerlea, controlled its affairs, the outward indicia of these two separate corporations was at all times maintained during the period in which the creditors extended credit; that the creditors were in no wise misled; that there was no fraud; and

258

that the defendant performed no act causing injury to the creditors of Westerlea by depletion of assets or otherwise. The trial court also held that the creditors were estopped by the extension agreement from disputing the separate corporate identities.

We agree with the courts below. The law permits the incorporation of a business for the very purpose of escaping personal liability. Generally speaking, the doctrine of "piercing the corporate veil" is invoked "to prevent fraud or to achieve equity", International Aircraft Trading Co. v. Manufacturers Trust Co., 297 N.Y. 285, 292, 79 N.E.2d 249, 252. But in the instant case there has been neither fraud, misrepresentation nor illegality. Defendant's purpose in placing its construction operation into a separate corporation was clearly within the limits of our public policy.

The judgment appealed from should be affirmed, without costs.

VAN VOORHIS, JUDGE (dissenting).

The judgment of the Appellate Division should be reversed on the law, as it seems to me, and plaintiff should have judgment declaring defendant to be liable for the debts of the bankrupt, Westerlea Builders, Inc., and that defendant holds its real property subject to the claims of creditors of Westerlea. Not only is Westerlea a wholly owned subsidiary of defendant, Home Owners, having the same directors and management, but also and of primary importance, business was done on such a basis that Westerlea could not make a profit. Home Owners owned a residential subdivision; Westerlea was organized as a building corporation to erect homes for stockholders of Home Owners upon lots in this tract. Home Owners arranged with Westerlea for the construction of houses and then would sell the lots on which such houses had been erected to Home Owners' stockholders—at prices fixed by Home Owners' price policy committee in such amounts as to make no allowance for profit by Westerlea. The object was to benefit Home Owners' stockholders by enabling them to obtain their houses at cost, with no builder's profit.

The consequence is that described by Latty, Subsidiaries and Affiliated Corporations at pages 138–139: "The subsidiaries had, to begin with, nothing, made nothing, and could only end up with nothing. It is not surprising that the parent was held liable in each case." And again: "This set-up is often, though not necessarily, found in combination with a scheme whereby the corporation cannot possibly make profits (or can at the most make only nominal profits), and whereby all the net income in the course of the corporation's business is drained off as operating charges of one sort or another. The presence of this additional factor should remove any doubt that may remain as to the right of the creditor of the corporation not to be limited to the corporate assets for the satisfaction of his debt."

In the present instance, Westerlea was organized with a small capital supplied by Home Owners, which soon became exhausted. Thereafter, it had no funds and could acquire none over and beyond the actual cost of the houses which it was building for stockholders of Home Owners. Those stockholders obtained the entire benefit of Westerlea's operations by obtaining these houses at cost. Not only was Westerlea allowed no opportunity to make money, but it was placed in a position such that if its business were successful and times remained good, it would break even, otherwise it would inevitably become insolvent. The stockholders of Home Owners became the beneficiaries of its insolvency. This benefit to the stockholders of Home Owners was analogous to dividends, at least it was something of value which was obtained by them from Home Owners by virtue of their stock ownership. Under the circumstances, this benefit to its stockholders was a benefit to Home Owners as a corporation.

It follows that Westerlea was merely an agent of Home Owners to construct houses at cost for Home Owners stockholders, and therefore Home Owners is rendered liable for Westerlea's indebtedness.

CONWAY, C.J., and DESMOND, DYE, FULD and BURKE, JJ., concur with FROESSEL, J.

VAN VOORHIS, J., dissents in an opinion.

DEWITT TRUCK BROKERS v.
W. RAY FLEMMING FRUIT CO.

United States Court of Appeals, Fourth Circuit, 1976.
540 F.2d 681.

Before RUSSELL and WIDENER, CIRCUIT JUDGES, and THOMSEN, SENIOR DISTRICT JUDGE.[1]

DONALD RUSSELL, CIRCUIT JUDGE:

In this action on debt, the plaintiff seeks, by piercing the corporate veil under the law of South Carolina, to impose individual liability on the president of the indebted corporation individually.[2] The District Court, making findings of fact which may be overturned only if clearly erroneous, pierced the corporate veil and imposed individual liability. The individual defendant appeals. We affirm.

At the outset, it is recognized that a corporation is an entity, separate and distinct from its officers and stockholders, and that its debts are not the individual indebtedness of its stockholders. This is expressed in the presumption that the corporation and its stockholders are separate and distinct. And this oft-stated principle is equally applicable, whether the corporation has many or only one stockholder. But this concept of separate entity is merely a legal theory, "introduced for purposes of convenience and to subserve the ends of justice," and the courts "decline to recognize [it] whenever recognition of the corporate form would extend the principle of incorporation 'beyond its legitimate purposes and [would] produce injustices or inequitable consequences.'" Krivo Industrial Supp. Co. v. National Distill. & Chem. Corp. (5th Cir.1973), 483 F.2d 1098, 1106. Accordingly, "in an appropriate case and in furtherance of the ends of justice," the corporate veil will be pierced and the corporation and its stockholders "will be treated as identical." 18 Am.Juris.2d at 559.

This power to pierce the corporate veil, though, is to be exercised "reluctantly" and "cautiously" and the burden of establishing a basis for the disregard of the corporate fiction rests on the party asserting such claim. Coryell v. Phipps (5th Cir.1942), 128 F.2d 702, 704, aff., 317 U.S. 406, 63 S.Ct. 291, 87 L.Ed. 363 (1943).

---

1. [By the Court] Sitting by designation.

2. [By the Court] The corporate defendant, it is conceded, is not responsive to judgment.

The circumstances which have been considered significant by the courts in actions to disregard the corporate fiction have been "rarely articulated with any clarity." Swanson v. Levy (9th Cir.1975), 509 F.2d 859, 861–2. Perhaps this is true because the circumstances "necessarily vary according to the circumstances of each case," and every case where the issue is raised is to be regarded as "*sui generis,* [to] * * * be decided in accordance with its own underlying facts." Since the issue is thus one of fact, its resolution "is particularly within the province of the trial court" and such resolution will be regarded as "presumptively correct and [will] be left undisturbed on appeal unless it is clearly erroneous."

Contrary to the basic contention of the defendant, however, proof of plain fraud is not a necessary element in a finding to disregard the corporate entity. * * * [E]qually as well settled * * * is the rule that the mere fact that all or almost all of the corporate stock is owned by one individual or a few individuals, will not afford sufficient grounds for disregarding corporateness. But when substantial ownership of all the stock of a corporation in a single individual is combined with other factors clearly supporting disregard of the corporate fiction on grounds of fundamental equity and fairness, courts have experienced "little difficulty" and have shown no hesitancy in applying what is described as the "alter ego" or "instrumentality" theory in order to cast aside the corporate shield and to fasten liability on the individual stockholder. Iron City S. & G. Div. of McDonough Co. v. West Fork Tow. Corp., [N.D.W.Va. 1969] 298 F.Supp. at 1098.

But, in applying the "instrumentality" or "alter ego" doctrine, the courts are concerned with reality and not form, with how the corporation operated and the individual defendant's relationship to that operation. * * * [T]he authorities have indicated certain facts which are to be given substantial weight in this connection. One fact which all the authorities consider significant in the inquiry, and particularly so in the case of the one-man or closely-held corporation, is whether the corporation was grossly undercapitalized for the purposes of the corporate undertaking. Mull v. Colt Co. (S.D.N.Y.1962), 31 F.R.D. 154, 163; Automotriz Del Golfo De Cal. v. Resnick (1957), 47 Cal.2d 792, 306 P.2d 1, 63 A.L.R.2d 1042, 1048, with annotation.[3] And, "[t]he obligation to provide adequate capital begins with incorporation and is a continuing obligation thereafter * * * during the corporation's operations." Other factors that are emphasized in the application of the doctrine are

---

3. [By the Court] * * * In *Mull, supra,* 31 F.R.D. at 163, the Court quoted from Ballentine, Corporations, 303 (rev. ed. 1946):

  * * * It is coming to be recognized as the policy of the law that shareholders should in good faith put at the risk of the business unencumbered capital reasonably adequate for its prospective liabilities. If the capital is illusory or trifling compared with the business to be done and the risks of loss, this is a ground for denying the separate entity privilege.

In Note, Disregard of the Corporate Entity: Contract Claims, 28 Ohio S.L.J. 441 (1967), the author argues that undercapitalization as a factor in determining whether to pierce the corporate veil should be inapplicable in contract cases; cf., however, Note, Limited Liability: A Definite Judicial Standard for the Inadequate Capitalization Problem, 47 Temple L.Q. 32 (1974). The reasoning is that when one extends credit or makes any other contractual arrangement with a corporation, it is to be assumed he acquaints himself with the corporation's capitalization and contracts on such basis, and not on the individual credit of the dominant stockholder. In this case, however, that reasoning would be inapplicable, since the plaintiff did not rely on the corporation's capitalization but received an assurance from Flemming of personal liability.

failure to observe corporate formalities,[4] non-payment of dividends, the insolvency of the debtor corporation at the time, siphoning of funds of the corporation by the dominant stockholder,[5] non-functioning of other officers or directors, absence of corporate records, and the fact that the corporation is merely a facade for the operations of the dominant stockholder or stockholders. The conclusion to disregard the corporate entity may not, however, rest on a single factor, whether undercapitalization, disregard of corporation's formalities, or what-not, but must involve a number of such factors; in addition, it must present an element of injustice or fundamental unfairness. * * *

If these factors, which were deemed significant in other cases concerned with this same issue, are given consideration here, the finding of the District Court that the corporate entity should be disregarded was not clearly erroneous. Certainly the [W. Ray Flemming Fruit Company] was, in practice at least, a close, one-man corporation from the very beginning. Its incorporators were the defendant Flemming, his wife and his attorney. It began in 1962 with a capitalization of 5,000 shares, issued for a consideration of one dollar each. In some manner which Flemming never made entirely clear, approximately 2,000 shares were retired. At the times involved here Flemming owned approximately 90% of the corporation's outstanding stock, according to his own testimony, though this was not verified by any stock records. Flemming was obscure on who the other stockholders were and how much stock these other stockholders owned, giving at different times conflicting statements as to who owned stock and how much. His testimony on who were the officers and directors was hardly more direct. He testified that the corporation did have one other director, Ed Bernstein, a resident of New York. It is significant, however, that, whether Bernstein was nominally a director or not, there were no corporate records of a real directors' meeting in all the years of the corporation's existence and Flemming conceded this to be true. Flemming countered this by testifying that Bernstein traveled a great deal and that his contacts with Bernstein were generally by telephone. The evidence indicates rather clearly that Bernstein was * * * "nothing more than [a] figure-head[s]," who had "attended no directors' meeting," and even more crucial, never received any fee or reimbursement of expenses or salary of any kind from the corporation.

The District Court found, also, that the corporation never had a stockholders' meeting. * * * It is thus clear that corporate formalities, even rudimentary formalities, were not observed by the defendant.

---

4. [By the Court] House of Koscot Dev. Corp. v. American Line Cosmetics, Inc. (5th Cir.1972), 468 F.2d 64, 66–7 (" * * * Turner ignored normal corporate formalities * * * "); Lakota Girl Scout C., Inc. v. Havey Fund–Rais. Man., Inc. (8th Cir.1975), 519 F.2d 634, 638 (" * * * corporate formalities [were] not followed * * * "). While disregard of corporate formalities is a circumstance to be considered, it is generally held to be insufficient in itself, without some other facts, to support a piercing of the corporate veil.

Cf., Zubik v. Zubik (3d Cir.1967), 384 F.2d 267, 271, cert. denied, 390 U.S. 988, 88 S.Ct. 1183, 19 L.Ed.2d 1291 (1968), n. 4, where the Court stated that "[i]n the context of an attempt by an outside party to pierce the corporate veil of such a closely-held corporation, the informalities are considered of little consequence." * * *

See, however, Harrison v. Puga (1971), 4 Wash.App. 52, 480 P.2d 247, 254, where the Court said that if the defendants disregarded the corporate formalities, they could hardly complain if the court did likewise.

5. [By the Court] Chatterley v. Omnico, 26 Utah 2d 88, 485 P.2d 667, 670.

Beyond the absence of any observance of corporate formalities is the purely personal matter in which the corporation was operated. No stockholder or officer of the corporation other than Flemming ever received any salary, dividend, or fee from the corporation, or, for that matter, apparently exercised any voice in its operation or decisions. In all the years of the corporation's existence, Flemming was the sole beneficiary of its operations and its continued existence was for his exclusive benefit. During these years, he was receiving from $15,000 to $25,000 each year from a corporation, which, during most of the time, was showing no profit and apparently had no working capital. Moreover, the payments to Flemming were authorized under no resolution of the board of directors of the corporation, as recorded in any minutes of a board meeting. Actually, it would seem that Flemming's withdrawals varied with what could be taken out of the corporation at the moment: If this amount were $15,000, that was Flemming's withdrawal; if it were $25,000 that was his withdrawal. * * *

That the corporation was undercapitalized, if indeed it were not without any real capital, seems obvious. Its original stated "risk capital" had long since been reduced to approximately $3,000 by a reduction in the outstanding capital, or at least this would seem to be inferable from the record, and even this, it seems fair to conclude, had been seemingly exhausted by a long succession of years when the corporation operated at no profit. The inability of the corporation to pay a dividend is persuasive proof of this want of capital. In fact, the defendant Flemming makes no effort to refute the evidence of want of any capital reserves on the part of the corporation. It appears patent that the corporation was actually operating at all times involved here on someone else's capital. This conclusion follows from a consideration of the manner in which Flemming operated in the name of the corporation during the year when plaintiff's indebtedness was incurred.

The corporation was engaged in the business of a commission agent, selling fruit produce for the account of growers of farm products such as peaches and watermelons in the Edgefield, South Carolina, area. It never purported to own such products; * * * it (always acting through Flemming) sold the products as agent for the growers. Under the arrangement with the growers, it was to remit to the growers the full sale price, less any transportation costs incurred in transporting the products from the growers' farm or warehouse to the purchaser and its sales commission. An integral part of these collections was * * * represented by the plaintiff's transportation charges. Accordingly, during the period involved here, the corporation had as operating funds seemingly only its commissions and the amount of the plaintiff's transportation charges, for which the corporation had claimed credit in its settlement with its growers. At the time, however, Flemming was withdrawing funds from the corporation at the rate of at least $15,000 per year; and doing this, even though he must have known that the corporation could only do this by withholding payment of the transportation charges due the plaintiff, which in the accounting with the growers Flemming represented had been paid the plaintiff. And, it is of some interest that the amount due the plaintiff for transportation costs was approximately the same as the $15,000 minimum annual salary the defendant testified he was paid by the corporation. Were the opinion of the District Court herein to be reversed, Flemming would be permitted to retain substantial sums from the operations of the corporation without having any real capital in the undertaking, risking nothing of his own and using as operating capital what he had collected as due the plaintiff. Certainly, equity and fundamental justice support individual liability of Flemming for plaintiff's charges, payment for which he asserted in his accounting with the growers that he had paid and for which he took credit on such accounting. This case patently presents a blending of the very factors which courts have regarded as justifying a disregard of the corporate entity in furtherance of basic and fundamental fairness.

Finally, it should not be overlooked that at some point during the period when this indebtedness was being incurred—whether at the beginning or at a short time later is not clear in the record the plaintiff became concerned about former delays in receipt of payment for its charges and, to allay that concern, Flemming stated to the plaintiff, according to the latter's testimony as credited by the District Court, that "he (i.e., Flemming) would take care of [the charges] personally, if the corporation failed to do so * * *." On this assurance, the plaintiff contended that it continued to haul for the defendant. The existence of this promise by Flemming is not disputed. * * * This assurance was given for the obvious purpose of promoting the *individual* advantage of Flemming. This follows because the only person who could profit from the continued operation of the corporation was Flemming. When one, who is the sole beneficiary of a corporation's operations and who dominates it, as did Flemming in this case, induces a creditor to extend credit to the corporation on such an assurance as given here, that fact has been considered by many authorities sufficient basis for piercing the corporate veil. Weisser v. Mursam Shoe Corporation (2d Cir.1942), 127 F.2d 344, 145 A.L.R. 467. The only argument against this view is bottomed on the statute of frauds. But reliance on such statute is often regarded as without merit in a case where the promise or assurance is given "at the time or before the debt is created," for in that case the promise is original and without the statute. Goldsmith v. Erwin (4th Cir.1950), 183 F.2d 432, 435–6, 20 A.L.R.2d 240, with annotation. A number of courts, including South Carolina, however, have gone further and have held that, where the promisor owns substantially all the stock of the corporation and seeks by his promise to serve his personal pecuniary advantage, the question whether such promise is "within the statute of frauds" is a fact question to be resolved by the trial court and this is true whether the promise was made before the debt was incurred or during the time it was being incurred. Amer. Wholesale Corp. v. Mauldin (1924), 128 S.C. 241, 244–5, 122 S.E. 576. This is that type of case and may well have been resolved on this issue.

For the reasons stated, we conclude that the findings of the District Court herein are not clearly erroneous and the judgment of the District Court is
    Affirmed.

Notes

(1) One should not let the talismanic phrase, "piercing the corporate veil," obscure reality. The issue in piercing the corporate veil cases is whether a shareholder should be held personally liable for a corporate obligation. The decision to "pierce" in *DeWitt* does not mean that the Fruit Company was no longer a corporation. It remains in business; its name remains in the records of

the Secretary of State; it has the privilege of filing federal and state income tax returns, and so forth. Further, it does not necessarily mean that *all* the shareholders are personally liable for *all* the obligations of the corporation. While DeWitt may be able to "pierce," other creditors may not; Fleming may be held personally liable on a "piercing" theory but the other shareholder (if there in fact was one) may continue to be protected by the shield of limited liability. Basically, the piercing issue only involves the question whether a specific shareholder is personally liable for a specific corporate obligation, and the court's conclusion uses "piercing the corporate veil" as a justification to impose or refuse to impose liability.

(2) The rhetoric and reasoning in *DeWitt* is typical of many "piercing the corporate veil" cases: long on rhetoric and contradictory general principles but short on reasoning. Indeed, perhaps in no other area are courts more prone to decide real life disputes by characterization, epithet, and metaphor: "alter ego," "instrumentality," "sham," "subterfuge," or "tool," to select a few. Various terms are often combined in artful phraseology. Philip L. Blumberg, The Law of Corporate Groups: Procedural Law 8 (1983)[6] states, "This is jurisprudence by metaphor or epithet. It does not contribute to legal understanding because it is an intellectual construct, divorced from business realities. * * * Courts state that the corporate entity is to be disregarded because the corporation is, for example, a mere 'alter ego.' But they do not inform us why this is so, except in very broad terms that provide little general guidance. As a result, we are faced with hundreds of decisions that are irreconcilable and not entirely comprehensible. Few areas of the law have been so sharply criticized by commentators." Courts, on the other hand, often appear unconcerned by the vagueness of the doctrines they are formulating. One court observed that a "guiding concept behind veil piercing cases is the need for the court to 'avoid an over-rigid preoccupation with questions of structure and apply the preexisting and overarching principle that liability is imposed to reach an equitable result.'" Litchfield Asset Management Corp. v. Howell, 70 Conn.App. 133, 799 A.2d 298 (2002).

The vagueness of the articulated legal standards for piercing the corporate veil presents significant challenges for corporate lawyers required to advise clients in an area of understandably great personal concern to them since personal liability may well be involved. The rules are not getting any clearer. In Great Neck Plaza v. Le Peep Restaurants, 37 P.3d 485 (Colo.App.2001), the court articulated a ten factor test for determining whether to pierce the corporate veil, but made it clear that the court may consider only "certain factors" and it may consider factors other than the ten listed factors. The court did not specify which, if any, of the factors was essential, or whether any factors were more or less important than others. Id. at 490.

On the other hand, it is important to bear in mind that it is one thing to say that the rationales in the various piercing the corporate veil cases are not articulated so as to give iron-clad guidance to future potential litigants but quite another thing to say that courts often (or even sometimes) pierce the corporate veil in situations when it is inappropriate to do so. Despite the vagueness of the language in many veil piercing opinions, there are very few cases in which the corporate veil is actually pierced. Courts appear to be rather reluctant to disregard the corporate form. However, that reluctance appears to be diminished in cases brought in the parent-subsidiary context.

6. Reprinted with permission of Aspen Publishing Co.

However, even in the parent-subsidiary context, courts generally take the view that a parent corporation possesses a separate existence and is treated separately from a subsidiary unless there are circumstances clearly involving fraud, manifest unfairness, or misconduct. Courts are aware that over-utilization of their equitable power to pierce the corporate veil would make the corporate form useless: "any court must start from the general rule that the corporate entity should be recognized and upheld, unless specific, unusual circumstances call for an exception. * * * Care should be taken on all occasions to avoid making 'the entire theory of the corporate entity useless.' " Koch v. First Union Corporation, 2002 WL 372939 (Pa.Com.Pl.2002).

(3) Statistically speaking, piercing the corporate veil is entirely a phenomenon of closely held corporations, and predominantly one-person corporations. The corporate form is simply never pierced so as to impose liability against shareholders in a publicly traded corporation. Robert B. Thompson, The Limits of Liability in the New Limited Liability Entities, 32 Wake Forest L.Rev. 1, 9–10 (1997):

> * * * In an earlier empirical study, I reported that among the 1600 reported cases of piercing the veil, there was no case in which shareholders of a publicly held corporation were held liable. After additional analysis of that data base, I can make a broader statement. Piercing occurs only within corporate groups or in close corporations with fewer than ten shareholders. None of the close corporations in which piercing occurred had more than nine shareholders.

> * * * Those who are only passive investors, as the shareholders of a large corporation, will be insulated from the liability of the enterprise, while those who take a more active role in the business are subject to liability.

(4) Several cases involving contractual liability accept the argument that a third party who knowingly and voluntarily agrees to deal with a marginally financed corporation without requesting assurances from the shareholders personally cannot hold the shareholders personally liable. In O'Hazza v. Executive Credit Corp., 246 Va. 111, 431 S.E.2d 318, 323 (1993), for example, the court stated:

> [T]he record does not show that ECC was the victim of fraud, of any type, perpetrated by the O'Hazzas or by anyone else. Hughes had been involved with the corporation on at least 10 previous deals. * * * Hughes knew the financial situation of the corporation prior to advancing Guy O'Hazza the money for the hotel project. Hughes was a voluntary creditor who had the knowledge and opportunity to investigate the corporation before he agreed to loan the funds. We agree with the O'Hazzas' position that ECC "knowingly made a risky loan to a corporation on shaky financial footing with the hope of making a profit."

See also Consumer's Co-op. of Walworth County v. Olsen, 142 Wis.2d 465, 419 N.W.2d 211 (1988) (sophisticated creditor continued to extend credit despite delinquencies in payment in violation of its own internal policies with respect to extension of credit).

(5) Is it sound to argue that public policy requires attention to be paid to corporate formalities and that ignoring the corporate entity where formalities have been ignored furthers this policy? Or may one argue that a shareholder should be liable because he is not permitted first to ignore the rules of corporate behavior and then to claim the advantage of the corporate shield?

BAATZ v. ARROW BAR

Supreme Court of South Dakota, 1990.
452 N.W.2d 138.

SABERS, JUSTICE.

Kenny and Peggy Baatz (Baatz), appeal from summary judgment dismissing Edmond, LaVella, and Jacquette Neuroth, as individual defendants in this action. * * * Kenny and Peggy were seriously injured in 1982 when Roland McBride crossed the center line of a Sioux Falls street with his automobile and struck them while they were riding on a motorcycle. McBride was uninsured at the time of the accident and apparently is judgment proof.

Baatz alleges that Arrow Bar served alcoholic beverages to McBride prior to the accident while he was already intoxicated. Baatz commenced this action in 1984, claiming that Arrow Bar's negligence in serving alcoholic beverages to McBride contributed to the injuries they sustained in the accident. Baatz supports his claim against Arrow Bar with the affidavit of Jimmy Larson. Larson says he knew McBride and observed him being served alcoholic beverages in the Arrow Bar during the afternoon prior to the accident, while McBride was intoxicated. * * *

Edmond and LaVella Neuroth formed the Arrow Bar, Inc. in May 1980. During the next two years they contributed $50,000 [$5,000 (?)] to the corporation pursuant to a stock subscription agreement. The corporation purchased the Arrow Bar business in June 1980 for $155,000 with a $5,000 down payment. Edmond and LaVella executed a promissory note personally guaranteeing payment of the $150,000 balance. In 1983 the corporation obtained bank financing in the amount of $145,000 to pay off the purchase agreement. Edmond and LaVella again personally guaranteed payment of the corporate debt. Edmond is the president of the corporation, and Jacquette Neuroth serves as the manager of the business. Based on the enactment of SDCL 35–4–78 and 35–11–1 and advice of counsel, the corporation did not maintain dram shop liability insurance at the time of the injuries to Kenny and Peggy.[7]

In 1987 the trial court entered summary judgment in favor of Arrow Bar and the individual defendants. Baatz appealed that judgment and we reversed

---

7. [By the Editors] Section 35–4–78(2) makes it a misdemeanor for any licensed bar to sell an alcoholic beverage to "any person who is obviously intoxicated at the time." In Walz v. City of Hudson, 327 N.W.2d 120 (S.D.1982) the Court held that this section created a private cause of action for persons injured by patrons who were sold alcoholic beverages in violation of this section. In 1985, the South Dakota Legislature attempted to overrule Walz by (1) adding a sentence to 35–4–78(2) stating that "no licensee is civilly liable to any injured person * * * for any injury suffered * * * because of the intoxication of any person due to the sale of any alcoholic beverage in violation of the provisions of this section," and (2) adding 35–11–1 which made a formal legislative finding that "the consumption of alcoholic bev-

erages, rather than the serving of alcoholic beverages, is the proximate cause of any injury inflicted upon another by an intoxicated person" and therefore "abrogated" the Walz holding. Apparently, while this legislation was pending, the attorney recommended that the Arrow Bar not obtain dram shop insurance even though the Baatz law suit had been filed in 1984. However, in Baatz v. Arrow Bar, 426 N.W.2d 298 (1988) the South Dakota Supreme Court held that the attempted abrogation was invalid both retrospectively and prospectively. The court's opinion does not make clear how the attorney's recommendation not to purchase dram shop insurance presumably in 1985 affected the Baatz litigation filed in 1984 for injuries that occurred in 1982.

and remanded to the trial court for trial. * * * Shortly before the trial date, Edmond, LaVella, and Jacquette moved for and obtained summary judgment dismissing them as individual defendants. Baatz appeals. We affirm.

A trial court may grant summary judgment only when there are no genuine issues of material fact. * * * When determining whether a genuine issue of material fact exists, the evidence must be viewed most favorably to the non-moving party and reasonable doubts are to be resolved against the moving party. Groseth Int'l, Inc. v. Tenneco, Inc., 410 N.W.2d 159 (S.D.1987). * * *

Baatz claims that even if Arrow Bar, Inc. is the licensee, the corporate veil should be pierced, leaving the Neuroths, as the shareholders of the corporation, individually liable. A corporation shall be considered a separate legal entity until there is sufficient reason to the contrary. Mobridge Community Indus., Inc. v. Toure, Ltd., 273 N.W.2d 128 (S.D.1978). When continued recognition of a corporation as a separate legal entity would "produce injustices and inequitable consequences," then a court has sufficient reason to pierce the corporate veil. Farmers Feed & Seed, Inc. v. Magnum Enter., Inc., 344 N.W.2d 699, 701 (S.D.1984). Factors that indicate injustices and inequitable consequences and allow a court to pierce the corporate veil are:

1) fraudulent representation by corporation directors;

2) undercapitalization;

3) failure to observe corporate formalities;

4) absence of corporate records;

5) payment by the corporation of individual obligations; or

6) use of the corporation to promote fraud, injustice, or illegalities.

When the court deems it appropriate to pierce the corporate veil, the corporation and its stockholders will be treated identically. Mobridge, supra.

Baatz advances several arguments to support his claim that the corporate veil of Arrow Bar, Inc. should be pierced, but fails to support them with facts, or misconstrues the facts.

First, Baatz claims that since Edmond and LaVella personally guaranteed corporate obligations, they should also be personally liable to Baatz. However, the personal guarantee of a loan is a contractual agreement and cannot be enlarged to impose tort liability. Moreover, the personal guarantee creates individual liability for a corporate obligation, the opposite of (factor 5), above. As such, it supports, rather than detracts from, recognition of the corporate entity.

Baatz also argues that the corporation is simply the alter ego of the Neuroths, and, in accord with Loving Saviour Church v. United States, 556 F.Supp. 688 (D.S.D.1983), aff'd, 728 F.2d 1085 (8th Cir.1984), the corporate veil should be pierced. Baatz' discussion of the law is adequate, but he fails to present evidence that would support a decision in his favor in accordance with that law. When an individual treats a corporation "as an instrumentality through which he [is] conducting his personal business," a court may disregard the corporate entity. Larson v. Western Underwriters, Inc., 77 S.D. 157, 163, 87 N.W.2d 883, 886 (1958). Baatz fails to demonstrate how the Neuroths were transacting personal business through the corporation. In fact, the evidence indicates the Neuroths treated the corporation separately from their individual affairs.

Baatz next argues that the corporation is undercapitalized. Shareholders must equip a corporation with a reasonable amount of capital for the nature of the business involved. See Curtis v. Feurhelm, 335 N.W.2d 575 (S.D.1983). Baatz claims the corporation was started with only $5,000 in borrowed capital, but does not explain how that amount failed to equip the corporation with a reasonable amount of capital. In addition, Baatz fails to consider the personal guarantees to pay off the purchase contract in the amount of $150,000, and the $50,000 stock subscription agreement. There simply is no evidence that the corporation's capital in whatever amount was inadequate for the operation of the business. Normally questions relating to individual shareholder liability resulting from corporate undercapitalization should not be reached until the primary question of corporate liability is determined. Questions depending in part upon other determinations are not normally ready for summary judgment. See Van Knight Steel Erection, Inc. v. Housing and Redev. Auth. of the City of St. Paul, 430 N.W.2d 1 (Minn.Ct.App.1988); see also Candee Constr. Co., Inc. v. South Dakota Dep't of Transp., 447 N.W.2d 339, 346 (S.D.1989) (Sabers, J., dissenting). However, simply asserting that the corporation is undercapitalized does not make it so. Without some evidence of the inadequacy of the capital, Baatz fails to present specific facts demonstrating a genuine issue of material fact.

Finally, Baatz argues that Arrow Bar, Inc. failed to observe corporate formalities because none of the business' signs or advertising indicated that the business was a corporation. Baatz cites SDCL 47–2–36 as requiring the name of any corporation to contain the word corporation, company, incorporated, or limited, or an abbreviation for such a word. In spite of Baatz' contentions, the corporation is in compliance with the statute because its corporate name—Arrow Bar, Inc.—includes the abbreviation of the word incorporated. Furthermore, the "mere failure upon occasion to follow all the forms prescribed by law for the conduct of corporate activities will not justify" disregarding the corporate entity. Larson, supra, 77 S.D. at 164, 87 N.W.2d at 887 (quoting P.S. & A. Realties, Inc. v. Lodge Gate Forest, Inc., 205 Misc. 245, 254, 127 N.Y.S.2d 315, 324 (1954)). Even if the corporation is improperly using its name, that alone is not a sufficient reason to pierce the corporate veil. This is especially so where, as here, there is no relationship between the claimed defect and the resulting harm.

In addition, the record is void of any evidence which would support imposition of individual liability by piercing the corporate veil under any of the other factors listed above in 1), 4) or 6).

In summary, Baatz fails to present specific facts that would allow the trial court to find the existence of a genuine issue of material fact. There is no indication that any of the Neuroths personally served an alcoholic beverage to McBride on the day of the accident. Nor is there any evidence indicating that the Neuroths treated the corporation in any way that would produce the injustices and inequitable consequences necessary to justify piercing the corporate veil. In fact, the only evidence offered is otherwise. Therefore, we affirm summary judgment dismissing the Neuroths as individual defendants.

WUEST, C.J., AND Morgan and MILLER, JJ., CONCUR.

HENDERSON, JUSTICE (dissenting).

This corporation has no separate existence. It is the instrumentality of three shareholders, officers, and employees. * * *

A corporate shield was here created to escape the holding of this Court relating to an individual's liability in a dram shop action. * * * As a result of this holding, the message is now clear: Incorporate, mortgage the assets of a liquor corporation to your friendly banker, and proceed with carefree entrepreneuring.

In both of these briefs, the parties argue, all in all, about the facts. One may reasonably conclude that there exists questions of fact. * * * [The] Baatzes had their case thrown out of court when many facts were in dispute. I am reminded of the old lawyer, before a jury, who expressed his woe of corporations. He cried out to the jury: "A corporation haveth no soul and its hind end you can kicketh not." * * *

Peggy Baatz, a young mother, lost her left leg; she wears an artificial limb; Kenny Baatz, a young father, has had most of his left foot amputated; he has been unable to work since this tragic accident. Peggy uses a cane. Kenny uses crutches. Years have gone by since they were injured and their lives have been torn asunder.

Uninsured motorist was drunk, and had a reputation of being a habitual drunkard; Arrow Bar had a reputation of serving intoxicated persons. (Supported by depositions on file). An eyewitness saw uninsured motorist in an extremely intoxicated condition, shortly before the accident, being served by Arrow Bar. * * * This evidence must be viewed most favorably to the nonmoving party. American Indian Agr. Credit Consortium, Inc. v. Ft. Pierre Livestock, Inc., 379 N.W.2d 318 (S.D.1985). A police officer testified, by deposition, that uninsured motorist was in a drunken stupor while at the Arrow Bar.

* * * Arrow Bar, Inc. is being used to justify any wrongs perpetrated by the incorporators in their individual capacity. Conclusion: Fraud is perpetrated upon the public. At a deposition of Edmond Neuroth (filed in this record), this "President" of "the corporation" was asked why the Neuroth family incorporated. His answer: "Upon advice of counsel, as a shield against individual liability." The corporation was undercapitalized (Neuroths borrowed $5,000 in capital). * * * In Loving Saviour Church, it was held that a chiropractor could not use a church to escape income taxes; here, a corporation conceived in undercapitalization as "a shield," in the words of "the President," should not be used as an artifice to avoid the intent of SDCL 35–4–78(2). * * *

Therefore, I respectfully dissent.

Notes

(1) Tort cases involving the "piercing" doctrine have a different flavor than contract cases. Consider Robert W. Hamilton, The Corporate Entity, 49 Tex. L.Rev. 979, 983–85 (1971).[8]

8. Published originally in 49 Texas Law Review 979, 979–1009 (1971). Copyright 1971 by the Texas Law Review Association. Reprinted by permission.

Secondly, a major consideration in determining whether the shareholders or the third party should bear the loss is whether the third party dealt voluntarily with the corporation or whether he is an involuntary creditor, typically a tort claimant. In a contract case, the plaintiff has usually dealt in some way with the corporation and should be aware that the corporation lacks substance. In the absence of some sort of deception, the creditor more or less assumed the risk of loss when he dealt with a "shell"; if he was concerned, he should have insisted that some solvent third person guarantee the performance by the corporation. In tort cases, on the other hand, there is usually no element of voluntary dealing, and the question is whether it is reasonable for businessmen to transfer a risk of loss or injury to members of the general public through the device of conducting business in the name of a corporation that may be marginally financed. The issues of public policy raised by tort claims bear little relationship to the issues raised by a contract claim. It is astonishing to find that this fundamental distinction is only dimly perceived by many courts, which indiscriminately cite and purport to apply, tort precedents in contract cases and vice versa.

(2) Robert B. Thompson, Piercing the Corporate Veil: An Empirical Study, 76 Cornell L.Rev. 1036 (1991),[9] examined 1,583 cases involving the piercing the corporate veil doctrine decided before 1985. The conclusions reached from this massive survey include the following: * * *

b) The corporate veil was pierced in about 40 percent of the reported cases. This percentage remained stable over more than four decades, was about the same in state and federal courts, and variations from state to state did not appear to be statistically significant.

d) 779 cases in the survey involved contract claims and 226 involved tort claims.[10] The corporate veil was pierced in 327 of the contracts cases (42 percent) and 70 of the torts cases (31 percent).

e) Undercapitalization was a factor in 19 percent of the contracts cases in which the corporate veil was pierced (61 of 327), but was a factor in only 13 percent of the tort cases in which piercing occurred (9 of 70). A failure to follow corporate formalities was cited in 20 percent of the contracts cases and 11 percent of the torts cases.

(3) As discussed in Chapter 6, most state corporation statutes today do not require any minimum amount of capital. It is literally possible today to form a corporation with one cent or one dollar of capital. Of course, to actually form a corporation with essentially zero capital to engage in a risky business would appear to be extremely dangerous in light of the rhetoric in many piercing cases about "inadequate capital." In *Baatz*, for example, the corporation began with $5,000 in cash and some personal guarantees, which the majority held was sufficient to avoid the inadequate capitalization argument. However, should that really be the test? The cash plus the personal guarantees was sufficient to permit the Neuroths to purchase the Arrow Bar, but certainly not sufficient to cover possible unexpected liabilities, let alone the serious injuries to the members of the Baatz family. If the test should be some amount of "free" capital sufficient to cover unexpected liabilities, the question becomes, how much? Is the problem in *Baatz* the conscious decision not to purchase dram shop insurance? Might there be

---

9. Copyright 1991 by Cornell University. All rights reserved.

10. [By the Editors] The remaining cases were classified as "criminal" or "statute" cases.

malpractice on the part of the attorney who recommended that the purchase of such insurance was unnecessary?

(4) In 1999, Professor Thompson announced that he had extended his survey of piercing cases to include cases through 1996. Robert B. Thompson, Piercing the Veil Within Corporate Groups: Corporate Shareholders as Mere Investors, 13 Conn. J. Int'l Law 379 (1999). This expansion generated an additional 2,200 cases, making his sample a total of 3,800 cases. He concludes that "courts are less likely to pierce the veil in cases involving tort claims as opposed to those involving contractual claims; this finding is surprising given even stronger statements of commentators that a tort setting makes for a much stronger case for [piercing the veil] since the plaintiff had no opportunity to bargain for the lack of liability." Id, at 384–385.

RADASZEWSKI v. TELECOM CORP.

United States Court of Appeals, Eighth Circuit, 1992.
981 F.2d 305.

Before RICHARD S. ARNOLD, CHIEF JUDGE, HEANEY, SENIOR CIRCUIT JUDGE, and MAGILL, CIRCUIT JUDGE.

RICHARD S. ARNOLD, CHIEF JUDGE.

This is an action for personal injuries filed on behalf of Konrad Radaszewski, who was seriously injured in an automobile accident on August 21, 1984. Radaszewski, who was on a motorcycle, was struck by a truck driven by an employee of Contrux, Inc. The question presented on this appeal is whether the District Court had jurisdiction over the person of Telecom Corporation, which is the corporate parent of Contrux. This question depends, in turn, on whether, under Missouri law, Radaszewski can "pierce the corporate veil," and hold Telecom liable for the conduct of its subsidiary, Contrux, and Contrux's driver. The District Court held that it lacked jurisdiction. We agree, though for different reasons.

In general, someone injured by the conduct of a corporation or one of its employees can look only to the assets of the employee or of the employer corporation for recovery. The shareholders of the corporation, including, if there is one, its parent corporation, are not responsible. This is a conscious decision made by the law of every state to encourage business in the corporate form. Obviously the decision has its costs. Some injuries are going to go unredressed because of the insolvency of the corporate defendant immediately involved, even when its shareholders have plenty of money. To the general rule, though, there are exceptions. There are instances in which an injured person may "pierce the corporate veil," that is, reach the assets of one or more of the shareholders of the corporation whose conduct has created liability. In the present case, the plaintiff seeks to hold Telecom Corporation liable for the conduct of an employee of its wholly owned subsidiary, Contrux, Inc.

Under Missouri law, a plaintiff in this position needs to show three things. The leading case is *Collet v. American National Stores, Inc.*, 708 S.W.2d 273 (Mo.App.1986). The Missouri Court of Appeals had this to say:

A tripartite test has been developed for analysis of the question. To "pierce the corporate veil," one must show:

(1) Control, not mere majority or complete stock control, but complete domination, not only of finances, but of policy and business practice in respect to the transaction attacked so that the corporate entity as to this transaction had at the time no separate mind, will or existence of its own; and

(2) Such control must have been used by the defendant to commit fraud or wrong, to perpetrate the violation of a statutory or other positive legal duty, or dishonest and unjust act in contravention of plaintiff's legal rights; and

(3) The aforesaid control and breach of duty must proximately cause the injury or unjust loss complained of.

Id. at 284.

It is common ground among all parties that Telecom, as such, has had no contact with Missouri. If it is subject to jurisdiction over its person in Missouri courts, it is only because of the conduct of Contrux, its subsidiary. So the issue of jurisdiction over the person depends on whether the corporate veil of Contrux can be pierced to bring Telecom into the case. As it happens, this is also the question upon which Telecom's substantive liability depends. (We assume for present purposes that Contrux is liable—this has not yet been proved.) * * *

Undercapitalizing a subsidiary, which we take to mean creating it and putting it in business without a reasonably sufficient supply of money, has become a sort of proxy under Missouri law for the second *Collet* element. On the prior appeal, for example, we said that "Missouri courts will disregard the existence of a corporate entity that is operated while undercapitalized." 891 F.2d at 674. *Collet, supra*, 708 S.W.2d at 286–87. The reason, we think, is not because undercapitalization, in and of itself, is unlawful (though it may be for some purposes), but rather because the creation of an undercapitalized subsidiary justifies an inference that the parent is either deliberately or recklessly creating a business that will not be able to pay its bills or satisfy judgments against it. This point has been made clear by the Supreme Court of Missouri. In *May Department Stores Co. v. Union Electric Light & Power Co.*, 341 Mo. 299, 327, 107 S.W.2d 41, 55 (1937), the Court found an improper purpose in a case where a corporation was "operating it without sufficient funds to meet obligations to those who must deal with it." Similarly, in *Consolidated Sun Ray, Inc. v. Oppenstein*, 335 F.2d 801 (8th Cir.1964), we said: "Making a corporation a supplemental part of an economic unit and operating it without sufficient funds to meet obligations to those who must deal with it would be circumstantial evidence tending to show either an improper purpose or reckless disregard of the rights of others." *Id.* at 806–07.

Here, the District Court held, and we assume, that Contrux was undercapitalized in the accounting sense. Most of the money contributed to its operation by Telecom was in the form of loans, not equity, and when Contrux first went into business, Telecom did not pay for all of the stock that was issued to it. This is a classic instance of watered stock, of putting a corporation into business without sufficient equity investment. Telecom in effect concedes that Contrux's balance sheet was anemic, and that, from the point of view of generally accepted accounting principles, Contrux was inadequately capitalized. Telecom says, however, that this doesn't matter, because Contrux had $11,000,000 worth of liability insurance available to pay judgments like the one that Radaszewski hopes to obtain. No one can say, therefore, the argument runs, that Telecom was improperly motivated in setting up Contrux, in the sense of either knowingly or recklessly establishing it without the ability of pay tort judgments.

In fact, Contrux did have $1,000,000 in basic liability coverage, plus $10,000,000 in excess coverage. This coverage was bound on March 1, 1984, about five and one-half months before the accident involving Radaszewski. Unhappily, Contrux's [excess liability] insurance carrier became insolvent two years after the accident and is now in receivership. (This record does not show the financial status of the receivership. We thus do not know whether any money would ever be available from the insurance company to pay a judgment in favor of Radaszewski, if he obtains one.) But this insurance, Telecom points out, was sufficient to satisfy federal financial-responsibility requirements. Under 49 C.F.R. § 387, motor carriers must maintain "financial reserves (e.g., insurance policies or surety bonds) sufficient to satisfy liability amounts set forth in this subpart covering public liability." 49 C.F.R. § 387.5. It is undisputed that the amount of insurance maintained by Contrux exceeded federal requirements, and that Contrux, at all times during its operations, was considered financially responsible by the relevant federal agency, the Interstate Commerce Commission.

The District Court rejected this argument. Undercapitalization is undercapitalization, it reasoned, regardless of insurance. The Court said: "The federal regulation does not speak to what constitutes a properly capitalized motor carrier company. Rather, the regulation speaks to what constitutes an appropriate level of *financial responsibility*." *Konrad Radaszewski v. Contrux, Inc.*, No. 88–0445–CV–W–1 (W.D.Mo. Oct. 26, 1990), slip op. 7 n. 6 (emphasis in original). This distinction escapes us. The whole purpose of asking whether a subsidiary is "properly capitalized," is precisely to determine its "financial responsibility." If the subsidiary is financially responsible, whether by means of insurance or otherwise, the policy behind the second part of the *Collet* test is met. Insurance meets this policy just as well, perhaps even better, than a healthy balance sheet. * * *

The doctrine of limited liability is intended precisely to protect a parent corporation whose subsidiary goes broke. That is the whole purpose of the doctrine, and those who have the right to decide such questions, that is, legislatures, believe that the doctrine, on the whole, is socially reasonable and useful. We think that the doctrine would largely be destroyed if a parent corporation could be held liable simply on the basis of errors in business judgment. Something more than that should be shown, and *Collet* requires something more than that. In our view, this record is devoid of facts to show that "something more." * * *

We * * * affirm the judgment of the District Court dismissing the complaint for want of jurisdiction, but modify that judgment to provide that it is with prejudice as to Radaszewski's complaint against Telecom.

HEANEY, SENIOR CIRCUIT JUDGE, dissenting.

I respectfully dissent. * * * In my view, Contrux's liability insurance is a relevant factor to be considered, but a fact finder after a trial might well find that this factor alone does not require a verdict for the defendant. * * *

Notes

(1) Do you agree that the piercing doctrine should not apply in a tort case if the corporation has acquired liability insurance against that risk even if, under the circumstances, the plaintiff is unable to recover under that insurance?

(2) What is meant by "undercapitalization"? If a corporation is adequately capitalized when it is formed, but thereafter suffers operating losses, is it then undercapitalized? If so, does that mean the shareholders must infuse additional capital in that corporation or suffer the possible application of the piercing the corporate veil doctrine? For negative answers, see Consumer's Co-op. of Walworth County v. Olsen, 142 Wis.2d 465, 419 N.W.2d 211, 218–19 (1988); CNC Service Center, Inc. v. CNC Service Center, 753 F.Supp. 1427 (N.D.Ill.1991). What about a corporation that was formed some time ago, and is reactivated by shareholders to go into a new business? Should undercapitalization be measured at the time it goes into the new business or when it was originally incorporated? What about a corporation that is adequately capitalized for its continuing business A, but then goes into a new business B? If the capital is inadequate for businesses A and B combined, is it thereafter undercapitalized with respect to a claim arising from business A?

(3) What should count as capital? Liability insurance? Should such insurance be relevant in contracts cases? Capital invested by the shareholders in the form of loans to an otherwise undercapitalized business? Should it make any difference if the shareholders plan to have the corporation repay those loans or whether they plan to leave the funds in the corporation indefinitely? In O'Hazza v. Executive Credit Corp., 246 Va. 111, 431 S.E.2d 318 (1993), the Court concluded that a corporation was adequately capitalized when the shareholders contributed $10,000 in initial capital and then loaned the corporation approximately $140,000 "without expectation of repayment." Should such subjective intentions play any role in the piercing the corporate veil doctrine? See also Arnold v. Phillips, 117 F.2d 497, 501–02 (5th Cir.1941) (distinction made between loans before the enterprise was launched and loans thereafter to keep the business afloat).

(4) Frank H. Easterbrook and Daniel R. Fischel, The Economic Structure of Corporate Law 57 (1991):[11]

> [Parent corporations should not always] be liable for the debts of those in which they hold stock. Far from it. Such general liability would give unaffiliated firms a competitive advantage. Think of the taxicab business. Taxi firms may incorporate each cab or put just a few cabs in a firm. If courts routinely pierced this arrangement and put the assets of the full venture at risk for the accidents of each cab, then "true" single-cab firms would have lower costs of operation because they alone could cut off liability. That would create a perverse incentive because, as we have emphasized, larger firms are apt to carry more insurance. Potential victims of torts would not gain from a legal rule that promoted corporate disintegration. As a result, courts properly disregard the corporate form only when the corporate arrangement has increased risks over what they would be if firms generally were organized as separate ventures.

Do you agree? Do Easterbrook and Fischel correctly state "the law"?

(5) In Minton v. Cavaney, 56 Cal.2d 576, 15 Cal.Rptr. 641, 364 P.2d 473 (1961), Cavaney, an attorney, duly incorporated the Seminole Hot Springs Corporation, a corporation that thereafter leased and operated a public swimming pool. No stock was ever issued by the corporation and no capital was ever invested. Cavaney served as a director and as secretary and treasurer of Seminole; the corporate records were stored in his office. Cavaney testified on deposition that he was only a "temporary" or "accommodation" director and officer, but there was also testimony that he expected to receive a portion of the corporation's stock. During the first year of the pool's operation, the plaintiffs' daughter drowned in the pool. Cavaney died sometime thereafter. The plaintiffs obtained a $10,000 default judgment against Seminole and, since that corporation had no assets, sought to hold Cavaney's estate personally liable on the judgment. Held: Cavaney's estate could be held personally liable on the plaintiffs' claim on a theory of alter ego, but his estate can relitigate the issues of Seminole's negligence and the amount of damages, since Cavaney was not a party to the original proceeding. The Court rejected Cavaney's claim that he should not be liable because he was merely a temporary or accommodation director with the understanding that he would not exercise any of the duties of a director: "A person may not in this manner divorce the responsibilities of a director from the statutory duties and powers of that office." 15 Cal.Rptr. at 644, 364 P.2d at 476. This and similar cases illustrate the dangers of an attorney agreeing to serve even briefly as a director or officer of a corporation created by the attorney.

(6) Minton v. Cavaney is cited in California for the proposition that inadequate initial capitalization alone is sufficient to pierce the corporate veil. In Slottow v. American Cas. Co., 10 F.3d 1355, 1360 (9th Cir.1993), for example, the court stated "FNT's initial capitalization of $500,000 was woefully inadequate for a corporation that handled trust agreements of the magnitude involved here. The investors claimed damages in the range of $10,000,000; * * * Under California law, inadequate capitalization of a subsidiary may alone be a basis for holding the parent corporation liable * * *." But see Paul Steelman, Ltd. v. Omni Realty Partners, 110 Nev. 1223, 885 P.2d 549, 550 (1994).

FLETCHER v. ATEX, INC.

United States Court of Appeals, Second Circuit, 1995.
68 F.3d 1451.

Before: KEARSE, CALABRESI, AND Cabranes, Circuit Judges.

JOSE A. CABRANES, CIRCUIT JUDGE:

Facts:

Pros. History

* * * The plaintiffs-appellants filed suit against Atex, Inc. ("Atex") and its parent, Eastman Kodak Company ("Kodak"), to recover for repetitive stress injuries that they claim were caused by their use of computer keyboards manufactured by Atex. * * * [A summary judgment was entered dismissing Kodak as a defendant and plaintiff's appeal.]

* * * From 1981 until December 1992, Atex was a wholly-owned subsidiary of Kodak. In 1987, Atex's name was changed to Electronic Pre–Press Systems, Inc., ("EPPS"), but its name was changed back to Atex in 1990. In December 1992, Atex sold substantially all of its assets to an independent third party and again changed its name to 805 Middlesex Corp., which holds the proceeds from the sale. Kodak continues to be the sole shareholder of 805 Middlesex Corp. * * *

The district court correctly noted that "[u]nder New York choice of law principles, '[t]he law of the state of incorporation determines when the corporate form will be disregarded and liability will be imposed on shareholders.'" * * * Because Atex was a Delaware corporation, Delaware law determines whether the corporate veil can be pierced in this instance.

Delaware law permits a court to pierce the corporate veil of a company "where there is fraud or where [it] is in fact a mere instrumentality or alter ego of its owner." Geyer v. Ingersoll Publications Co., 621 A.2d 784, 793 (Del.Ch.1992). Although the Delaware Supreme Court has never explicitly adopted an alter ego theory of parent liability for its subsidiaries, lower Delaware courts have applied the doctrine on several occasions, as has the United States District Court for the District of Delaware. * * * [U]nder an alter ego theory, there is no requirement of a showing of fraud. To prevail on an alter ego claim under Delaware law, a plaintiff must show (1) that the parent and the subsidiary "operated as a single economic entity" and (2) that an "overall element of injustice or unfairness * * * [is] present." Harper v. Delaware Valley Broadcasters, Inc., 743 F.Supp. 1076, 1085 (D.Del.1990), aff'd, 932 F.2d 959 (3d Cir.1991) (internal quotation marks omitted).

To prevail on an alter ego theory of liability, a plaintiff must show that the two corporations "'operated as a single economic entity such that it would be inequitable * * * to uphold a legal distinction between them.'" * * * Among the factors to be considered in determining whether a subsidiary and parent operate as a "single economic entity" are:

> [W]hether the corporation was adequately capitalized for the corporate undertaking; whether the corporation was solvent; whether dividends were paid, corporate records kept, officers and directors functioned properly, and other corporate formalities were observed; whether the dominant shareholder siphoned corporate funds; and whether, in general, the corporation simply functioned as a facade for the dominant shareholder.

Harco Nat'l Ins. Co. v. Green Farms, Inc., No. CIV.A. 1331, 1989 WL 110537, at *4, (Del.Ch. Sept.19, 1989) (quoting United States v. Golden Acres, Inc., 702 F.Supp. 1097, 1104 (D.Del.1988)). As noted above, a showing of fraud or wrongdoing is not necessary under an alter ego theory, but the plaintiff must demonstrate an overall element of injustice or unfairness. Harco, 1989 WL 110537, at *5.

A plaintiff seeking to persuade a Delaware court to disregard the corporate structure faces "a difficult task." Harco, 1989 WL 110537, at *4. Courts have made it clear that "[t]he legal entity of a corporation will not be disturbed until sufficient reason appears." Id. Although the question of domination is generally one of fact, courts have granted motions to dismiss as well as motions for summary judgment in favor of defendant parent companies where there has been a lack of sufficient evidence to place the alter ego issue in dispute. See, e.g., Akzona, Inc. v. Du Pont, 607 F.Supp. 227, 237 (D.Del.1984) (rejecting plaintiffs' alter ego theory of liability on a motion to dismiss). * * *

Kodak has shown that Atex followed corporate formalities, and the plaintiffs have offered no evidence to the contrary. Significantly, the plaintiffs have not challenged Kodak's assertions that Atex's board of directors held regular meetings, that minutes from those meetings were routinely prepared and maintained in corporate minute books, that appropriate financial records and other files were maintained by Atex, that Atex filed its own tax returns and paid its own taxes, and that Atex had its own employees and management executives who were responsible for the corporation's day-to-day business. The plaintiffs' primary arguments regarding domination concern (1) the defendant's use of a cash management system; (2) Kodak's exertion of control over Atex's major expenditures, stock sales, and the sale of Atex's assets to a third party; (3) Kodak's "dominating presence" on Atex's board of directors; (4) descriptions of the relationship between Atex and Kodak in the corporations' advertising, promotional literature, and annual reports; and (5) Atex's assignment of one of its former officer's mortgage to Kodak in order to close Atex's asset-purchase agreement with a third party. The plaintiffs argue that each of these raises a genuine issue of material fact about Kodak's domination of Atex, and that the district court therefore erred in granting summary judgment to Kodak on the plaintiffs' alter ego theory. We find that the district court correctly held that, in light of the undisputed factors of independence cited by Kodak, "the elements identified by the plaintiffs * * * [were] insufficient as a matter of law to establish the degree of domination necessary to disregard Atex's corporate identity."

First, the district court correctly held that "Atex's participation in Kodak's cash management system is consistent with sound business practice and does not show undue domination or control." The parties do not dispute the mechanics of Kodak's cash management system. Essentially, all of Kodak's domestic subsidiaries participate in the system and maintain zero-balance bank accounts. All funds transferred from the subsidiary accounts are recorded as credits to the subsidiary, and when a subsidiary is in need of funds, a transfer is made. At all times, a strict accounting is kept of each subsidiary's funds.

Courts have generally declined to find alter ego liability based on a parent corporation's use of a cash management system. See, e.g., In re Acushnet River & New Bedford Harbor Proceedings, 675 F.Supp. 22, 34 (D.Mass.1987) (Without "considerably more," "a centralized cash management system * * * where the accounting records always reflect the indebtedness of one entity to another, is not the equivalent of intermingling funds" and is insufficient to justify disregarding the corporate form.); United States v. Bliss, 108 F.R.D. 127, 132 (E.D.Mo.1985) (cash management system indicative of the "usual parent-subsidiary relationship"); Japan Petroleum Co. (Nigeria) v. Ashland Oil Inc., 456 F.Supp. 831, 838, 846 (D.Del.1978) (finding segregation of subsidiary's accounts within parent's cash management system to be "a function of administrative convenience and economy, rather than a manifestation of control"). The plaintiffs offer no facts to support their speculation that Kodak's centralized cash management system was actually a "complete commingling" of funds or a means by which Kodak sought to "siphon[ ] all of Atex's revenues into its own account."

Second, the district court correctly concluded that it could find no domination based on the plaintiffs' evidence that Kodak's approval was required for Atex's real estate leases, major capital expenditures, negotiations for a sale of minority stock ownership to IBM, or the fact that Kodak played a significant role in the ultimate sale of Atex's assets to a third party. Again, the parties do not dispute that Kodak required Atex to seek its approval and/or participation for the above transactions. However, this evidence, viewed in the light most favorable to the plaintiffs, does not raise an issue of material fact about whether the two corporations constituted "a single economic entity." Indeed, this type of conduct is typical of a majority shareholder or parent corporation. See Phoenix Canada Oil Co. v. Texaco, 842 F.2d 1466, 1476 (3d Cir.1988) (declining to pierce the corporate veil where subsidiary required to secure approval from parent for "large investments and acquisitions or disposals of major assets"), cert. denied, 488 U.S. 908, 109 S.Ct. 259, 102 L.Ed.2d 247 (1988); Akzona v. Du Pont, 607 F.Supp. 227, at 237 (D.Del.1984), (same, where parent approval required for expenditures exceeding $850,000); Japan Petrol., 456 F.Supp. at 843 (finding no parent liability where parent approval required for expenditures exceeding $250,000). In Akzona, the Delaware district court noted that a parent's "general executive responsibilities" for its subsidiary's operations included approval over major policy decisions and guaranteeing bank loans, and that that type of oversight was insufficient to demonstrate domination and control. Akzona, 607 F.Supp. at 238 (internal quotation marks omitted). Similarly, the district court in the instant case properly found that the presence of Kodak employees at periodic meetings with Atex's chief financial officer and comptroller to be "entirely appropriate." 861 F.Supp. at 245 (citing Akzona, 607 F.Supp. at 238); see Acushnet, 675 F.Supp. at 34 ("The quarterly and annual reports made [to the parent] do not represent an untoward intrusion by the owner into the corporate enterprise. The right of shareholders to remain informed is similarly recognized in many public and closely held corporations").

The plaintiffs' third argument, that Kodak dominated the Atex board of directors, also fails. Although a number of Kodak employees have sat on the Atex board, it is undisputed that between 1981 and 1988, only one director of Atex was also a director of Kodak. Between 1989 and 1992, Atex and Kodak had no directors in common. Parents and subsidiaries frequently have overlapping boards of directors while maintaining separate business operations. In Japan Petroleum, the Delaware district court held that the fact that a parent and a subsidiary have common officers and directors does not necessarily demonstrate that the parent corporation dominates the activities of the subsidiary. 456 F.Supp. at 841; see Scott–Douglas Corp. v. Greyhound Corp., 304 A.2d 309, 314 (Del.Super.Ct.1973) (same). Since the overlap is negligible here, we find this evidence to be entirely insufficient to raise a question of fact on the issue of domination.

[handwritten margin note: Kodak's presence on Atex's board of directors was not overwhelming and it is also typical]

Fourth, the district court properly rejected the plaintiffs' argument that the descriptions of the relationship between Atex and Kodak and the presence of the Kodak logo in Atex's promotional literature justify piercing the corporate veil. The plaintiffs point to several statements in both Kodak's and Atex's literature to evidence Kodak's domination of its subsidiary. For example, plaintiffs refer to (1) a promotional pamphlet produced by EPPS (a/k/a Atex) describing Atex as a business unit of EPPS and noting that EPPS was an "agent" of Kodak; (2) a document produced by Atex entitled "An Introduction to Atex Systems," which describes a "merger" between Kodak and Atex; (3) a statement in Kodak's 1985 and 1986 annual reports describing Atex as a "recent acquisition[ ]" and a "subsidiar[y] * * * combined in a new division"; and (4) a statement in an Atex/EPPS document, "Setting Up TPE 6000 on the Sun 3 Workstation," describing Atex as "an unincorporated division of

Electronic Pre–Press Systems, Inc., a Kodak company." They also refer generally to the fact that Atex's paperwork and packaging materials frequently displayed the Kodak logo.

It is clear from the record that Atex never merged with Kodak or operated as a Kodak division. The plaintiffs offer no evidence to the contrary, apart from these statements in Atex and Kodak documents that they claim are indicative of the true relationship between the two companies. Viewed in the light most favorable to the plaintiffs, these statements and the use of the Kodak logo are not evidence that the two companies operated as a "single economic entity." See Coleman v. Corning Glass Works, 619 F.Supp. 950, 956 (W.D.N.Y.1985) (upholding corporate form despite "loose language" in annual report about "merger" and parent's reference to subsidiary as a "division"), aff'd, 818 F.2d 874 (1987); Japan Petrol., 456 F.Supp. at 846 (noting that representations made by parent in its annual reports that subsidiary serves as an agent "may result from public relations motives or an attempt at simplification"); American Trading & Prod. Corp. v. Fischbach & Moore, Inc., 311 F.Supp. 412, 416 (N.D.Ill.1970) ("boastful" advertising and consideration of subsidiaries as "family" do not prove that corporate identities were ignored). * * *

Finally, even if the plaintiffs did raise a factual question about Kodak's domination of Atex, summary judgment would still be appropriate because the plaintiffs offer no evidence * * * of an "overall element of injustice or unfairness" that would result from respecting the two companies' corporate separateness. * * *

Notes

(1) Philip I. Blumberg, The Multinational Challenge to Corporation Law: The Search for a New Corporate Personality viii (1993):

> Under traditional law, the fragmentation of an integrated business among a number of affiliated companies as a matter of legal form * * * achieves legal consequences of great importance. In sanctioning this result, the traditional law ignores the fact that despite the legal restructuring, only one business is involved—a business being conducted collectively by interlinked companies under common ownership and control.

Blumberg's basic thesis—extended over seven volumes entitled "The Law of Corporate Groups"—is that a parent corporation with numerous subsidiaries should be viewed as a single economic enterprise for liability and other purposes. Do you agree? Despite Professor Blumberg's efforts to develop a "law" applicable to all corporate groups, judicial decisions lend scant support to his thesis in the liability area.

(2) Large publicly held corporations usually have numerous wholly owned subsidiaries. The number of subsidiaries of a single major company such as Exxon Corporation may easily run into the hundreds. Subsidiaries are created to operate in separate geographic areas, to operate businesses acquired by the parent corporation that are not closely related to the principal business, to provide services to other subsidiaries, and, generally, to operate in business areas in which the corporate management believes the business may be run most efficiently by a separately-organized corporation. In many instances, a corporation acquires one or more subsidiaries almost by accident in a transaction to acquire some desired

business. The opinion in *Atex* does not indicate how Kodak happened to acquire a wholly owned subsidiary that was involved in the manufacture of computer keyboards, but it might easily have occurred as part of Kodak's interest in the computer business or as the result of an acquisition of an unrelated business that happened to own Atex.

(3) A parent corporation may operate a business either as a separate subsidiary or as a division or department of the parent corporation itself. If the business is operated as a division or department, there is no legal separation between the parent and the business, and the parent is personally liable for the obligations of that business. If it is operated as a subsidiary, on the other hand, there is legal separation and the parent probably will not be liable on the subsidiary's obligations. The managerial differences between a subsidiary and a division are not as clear as might be thought, since a "division" can be set up with a board of directors and other "corporate" characteristics. Usually, the limitation of parental liability is not the dominant factor in a decision to conduct a specific business in the form of a subsidiary rather than a division. More important is the perceived benefit by the parent in terms of operational efficiency, e.g., to give the managers of a subsidiary in an unrelated business a greater degree of independence or to have outsiders on the subsidiary's board of directors. However, where the subsidiary's business seems unduly risky (or is of a type for which it is difficult to assess the risk), the element of limited liability may become a factor. And no matter why the subsidiary was originally incorporated, when unexpected potential or actual liabilities arise, it is quite likely that the parent corporation may seek to avoid direct responsibility by relying on the separate existence of the subsidiary. The plaintiffs in turn usually argue that the subsidiary's corporate veil should be pierced in order to impose liability directly on the parent.[12]

(4) Many subsidiaries of large publicly held corporations are themselves immense businesses, with sales and assets in the billions of dollars, and profits in the millions of dollars. They have their own work force, their own managers, and their own board of directors (usually comprised of executives of the subsidiary and the parent corporation and, sometimes, individuals not affiliated with either). Large subsidiaries are almost certain to have almost complete operational freedom in their day-to-day activities. However, they are subject to control by the parent corporation in non-operational areas similar to areas in which Atex was subject to direct control by Kodak; these areas of control may be justified by economic or legal considerations:

(a) A parent corporation must file a consolidated income tax return including its subsidiaries, and accounting rules require that published financial statements consolidate the operations of all wholly and majority-owned subsidiaries. Uniform accounting principles and practices for all subsidiaries are

---

12. [By the Editors] Piercing arguments may be made for other reasons as well. A plaintiff may seek to add the parent corporation as a defendant even though the subsidiary is clearly able to respond in damages if exemplary damages are being sought on the theory that such damages may be larger if the assets of the parent are considered along with those of the subsidiary. Piercing arguments also arose in the wake of the stranding of the Exxon Valdez in Alaska where the issue was the proper interpretation of excess liability insurance policies issued by Lloyds of London. It turned out that the Exxon Valdez was owned and operated by a wholly-owned Exxon subsidiary, Exxon Shipping Company. While Exxon did not attempt to limit its own responsibility for the costs of the Exxon Valdez disaster to Alaska residents, it did argue strenuously that Exxon Shipping Company was a separate insured for purposes of the Lloyds' policies; the insurers, in turn, attempted to pierce the corporate veil and claim there was only a single insured. This single issue, which involved hundreds of millions of dollars of insurance coverage, was ultimately settled, following a jury verdict favorable to Exxon in litigation in Houston, Texas.

therefore highly desirable. Accounting personnel may be provided by the parent to do all the bookkeeping for each subsidiary, for which a charge usually is imposed by the parent.

(b) Routine legal services are likely to be provided by the parent for all subsidiaries, though subsidiaries may be authorized to hire local counsel in areas in which the parent has no other operations.

(c) Subsidiaries usually are not permitted to borrow money from banks or third parties. The parent corporation is able to borrow larger amounts of money on more favorable terms than any subsidiary so that central financing of major capital improvements is sensible from an economic standpoint. Such a policy also permits the parent corporation to allocate capital funds among its various subsidiaries so as to maximize the overall return of the enterprise.

(d) Employees may from time transfer or be transferred from one subsidiary to another or to or from the parent. In order to facilitate these transfers, the parent corporation typically creates common pension, profit sharing, and retirement plans for all employees of both parents and subsidiaries; it also may establish salary scales so that transfers are simplified and inter-corporate competition for salaries and "perks" eliminated. Employees may be regularly "lent," "borrowed", or "assigned" on a temporary basis to or by the various corporations that make up the corporate family. The advantage of having easy transferability of employees within the corporate family is particularly apparent with respect to specialists since it avoids each subsidiary having to employ its own.

(e) Cash concentration systems similar to that described in the principal case permit the corporation to receive a higher return on excess funds than would be possible if each subsidiary maintained its own separate banking accounts. It also makes sure that idle funds are not left in non-interest bearing accounts even for a brief period. Cash concentration systems function in a manner very similar to a bank, with the parent and its various subsidiaries being its customers.

(f) Because large corporations usually have internal legal staffs, the documentation with respect to separate subsidiaries is usually maintained with a care and fastidiousness to detail that is unusual in a corporation with human shareholders. Minutes, consents, waivers, and so forth are routinely generated in great detail. Rules exist in some corporate families about careful identification of which "hat" each employee is wearing when he or she takes specific actions. Companies also may have policies limiting the use of corporate stationery. Despite these efforts, however, there usually can be found extemporaneous comments or statements that blur the legal existence between parent and subsidiary. The incidents described in the principal case are fairly typical in this regard.

———

The cases set forth above give a flavor of the common law of piercing the corporate veil jurisprudence. As of about 1980, there appeared to exist a national jurisprudence on piercing the corporate veil. Courts usually cited cases from various jurisdictions without discrimination in their attempts to apply whatever standards and doctrines that existed in this area to the specific facts before them, and there appeared to be general agreement on what the underlying standards were. However, doctrines in this area have shown a considerable capacity to mutate, and there are many indications today that states are "going their own way" and developing individualized tests for piercing the corporate veil. See generally Stephen B. Presser, Piercing the Corporate Veil (1991) (state-by-state analysis of precedents relating to piercing the corporate veil, updated by annual supplements). Examples of these mutations follow.

Texas. The Texas law of piercing the corporate veil took a bizarre turn in Castleberry v. Branscum, 721 S.W.2d 270 (Tex.1986), a case decided by a five-four vote. The court rewrote the traditional piercing rhetoric so broadly that it appeared likely that thereafter shareholders' protection from liability on both contract and tort corporate obligations had become entirely dependent on a jury's determination that the transaction met some undefined and abstract standard of fairness. The Court held, first, that the corporate veil may be pierced if the corporate fiction is used "as a means of perpetrating fraud" or as "a sham to perpetrate a fraud," and either "actual fraud" or "constructive fraud" was sufficient: The difference between "actual" and "constructive" fraud is that "[a]ctual fraud usually involves dishonesty of purpose or intent to deceive, whereas constructive fraud is the breach of some legal or equitable duty which, irrespective of moral guilt, the law declares fraudulent because of its tendency to deceive others, to violate confidence, or to injure public interest." Archer v. Griffith, 390 S.W.2d 735, 740 (Tex.1964). Furthermore, the distinction between tort and contract claimants (a distinction that several earlier Texas opinions had accepted) was expressly rejected; in either type of case, plaintiffs may hold shareholders personally liable if they can establish "a sham to perpetrate a fraud" which involves "a flexible fact-specific approach focusing on equity." Castleberry v. Branscum, 721 S.W.2d at 273.

Probably equally as troubling, the issue whether the corporate veil should be pierced was held to be a question of fact for the jury rather than a question of law for the judge. If the plaintiff presented evidence sufficient to permit the issue to be submitted to the jury, the jury decision controlled. Finally, the doctrine of piercing the corporate veil was subdivided into a multi-tiered classification comprised of seven or eight independent categories. However, the classification created by the Court was highly confusing, with overlapping requirements and vague definitional provisions. For example, "alter ego" was found to be "separate from" the other listed categories and "only one of the bases for disregarding the corporate fiction." Alter ego involves "such unity between corporation and individual that the separateness of the corporation has ceased and holding only the corporation liable would result in injustice." Id. at 272.

The *Castleberry* opinion caused grave concern within the Texas business community since it appeared that it might no longer be safe to conduct business in corporate form in Texas. These concerns, in turn, almost immediately gave rise to calls for legislative correction. The Texas Legislature responded by enacting a statute in 1989 that was apparently the first legislative attempt to codify, or partially codify, the piercing the corporate veil doctrine. Vernon's Ann. Texas Bus. Corp. Act art. 2.21 now reads[13] as follows:

---

13. [By the Editors] This statute was amended in 1993 and 1997.

A.　A holder of shares, an owner of any beneficial interest in shares, or a subscriber for shares * * *, or any affiliate thereof or of the corporation shall be under no obligation to the corporation or to its obligees with respect to: * * *

　　(2) any contractual obligation of the corporation or any matter relating to or arising from the obligation on the basis that the holder, owner, subscriber, or affiliate is or was the alter ego of the corporation, or on the basis of actual fraud or constructive fraud, a sham to perpetrate a fraud, or other similar theory, unless the obligee demonstrates that the holder, owner, subscriber, or affiliate caused the corporation to be used for the purpose of perpetrating and did perpetrate an actual fraud on the obligee primarily for the direct personal benefit of the holder, owner, subscriber, or affiliate; or

　　(3) any obligation of the corporation on the basis of the failure of the corporation to observe any corporate formality, including without limitation: (a) the failure to comply with any requirement of this Act or of the articles of incorporation or bylaws of the corporation; or (b) the failure to observe any requirement prescribed by this Act or by the articles of incorporation or bylaws for acts to the taken by the corporation, its board of directors, or its shareholders.

B.　The liability of a holder, owner, or subscriber of shares of a corporation or any affiliate thereof or the corporation for an obligation that is limited by Section A of this article is exclusive and preempts any other liability imposed on a holder, owner, or subscriber of shares of a corporation or any affiliate thereof or of the corporation for that obligation under common law or otherwise, except that nothing contained in this article shall limit the obligation of a holder, owner, subscriber, or affiliate to an obligee of the corporation when:

　　(1) the holder, owner, subscriber, or affiliate has expressly assumed, guaranteed, or agreed to be personally liable to the obligee for the obligation; or

　　(2) the holder, owner, subscriber, or affiliate is otherwise liable to the obligee for the obligation under this Act or another applicable statute.

Do you believe this statute limits too narrowly the scope of the piercing the corporate veil doctrine? One of the peculiarities of art. 2.21A is that it applies only with respect to "contractual obligations." What law in Texas should apply to piercing issues in tort cases under this legislation? *Castleberry*? Or, the former "general" law of piercing the corporate veil?

Subsequent developments in Texas reveal that judges and lawyers apparently read cases more often than they read statutes. In several cases courts continued to cite and rely on the broad language of *Castleberry* as authority in contracts cases without referring to Art. 2.21. See, e.g. Gonzales County Water Supply Corp. v. Jarzombek, 918 S.W.2d 57 (Tex.App.1996). It is possible, of course, that this is the fault of the lawyers or the judge's law clerks rather than the judges themselves. In Western Horizontal Drilling, Inc. v. Jonnet Energy Corp., 11 F.3d 65, 69, n. 5 (5th Cir.1994), the Court noted, "We recognize that the Texas Supreme Court seems to be ignoring the amendments to article 2.21 and continues to permit a failure to observe corporate formalities as a means of proving alter ego. * * *."[14] And, in one unreported case, a court held that "denuding of assets" remained a ground for piercing the corporate veil under *Castleberry* not covered by article 2.21. Gradually, however, the existence of this novel statute is coming to the attention of lawyers and judges. See Mike Tanskersley, What If They Made a Law and No One Noticed? Texas Lawyer, December 16, 1996, p.3; Thomas Oldham, Piercing the corporate Veil Under Texas Law, 58 Tex.B.J. 1013 (1995).

Notes

Was the *Castleberry* court correct in holding that the issue whether a corporate veil is to be pierced is a question of fact for the jury to decide rather than a question of law for the court? Some courts state that "piercing" is an "equitable" doctrine and therefore is to be tried to the Court, e.g., Consumer's Co-op. of Walworth County v. Olsen, 142 Wis.2d 465, 419 N.W.2d 211, 213 (1988) but other courts follow the Texas position, e.g., Wm. Passalacqua Builders, Inc. v. Resnick Developers South, Inc., 933 F.2d 131, 134–36 (2d Cir.1991).

The Second Circuit. This federal court developed a theory about New York law in the 1990s (that appeared to have slim basis in New York state court precedents) that in parent/subsidiary cases the corporate veil may be pierced "in two broad situations: to prevent fraud or other wrong, *or* where a parent dominates and controls a subsidiary." Carte Blanche (Singapore) Pte., Ltd. v. Diners Club Int'l, Inc., 2 F.3d 24, 26 (2d Cir.1993) (emphasis added). The disjunctive ("or") means, according to the Second Circuit, that domination and control alone is sufficient to justify piercing the corporate veil in some circumstances even in the absence of a showing of inequity or unfairness. See Wm. Passalacqua Builders, Inc. v. Resnick Developers South, Inc., 933 F.2d 131 (2d Cir.1991); Itel Containers Int'l Corp. v. Atlanttrafik Express Serv. Ltd., 909 F.2d 698, 703 (2d Cir.1990); Thomson–CSF, S.A. v. American Arbitration Ass'n, 64 F.3d 773, 777 (2d Cir.1995).[15] If one corporation owns all the stock of another, how can it avoid "dominating" and "controlling" the subsidiary? According to the Second Circuit, factors that might be considered include:

> [T]he triers of fact are entitled to consider factors that would tend to show that defendant was a dominated corporation, such as: (1) the absence of the formalities and paraphernalia that are part and parcel of the corporate existence, *i.e.,* issuance of stock, election of directors,

14. [By the Editors] The court then completely misreads the intent of article 2.21 by stating, "The amendments overruled Castleberry to the extent that a failure to observe the corporate formalities is no longer a factor in proving the alter ego theory in contract claims. Thus, to pierce the corporate veil using the alter ego theory in a contract claim, the claimant must look to the remaining factors outlined in *Castleberry*." 11 F.3d at 68.

15. [By the Editors] See, however, Campo v. 1st Nationwide Bank, 857 F.Supp. 264, 271 (E.D.N.Y.1994), where the Court without comment substitutes an "and" for the critical "or" when citing *Carte Blanche* and *Passalacqua*, and then concludes that the complaint alleges sufficient facts under both branches to state a cause of action.

keeping of corporate records and the like, (2) inadequate capitalization, (3) whether funds are put in and taken out of the corporation for personal rather than corporate purposes, (4) overlap in ownership, officers, directors, and personnel, (5) common office space, address and telephone numbers of corporate entities, (6) the amount of business discretion displayed by the allegedly dominated corporation, (7) whether the related corporations deal with the dominated corporation at arms length, (8) whether the corporations are treated as independent profit centers, (9) the payment or guarantee of debts of the dominated corporation by other corporations in the group, and (10) whether the corporation in question had property that was used by other of the corporations as if it were its own.

Wm. Passalacqua Builders, Inc. v. Resnick Developers South, Inc., 933 F.2d at 139. Except for number (3), are these appropriate standards for holding a parent corporation liable for the debts of a subsidiary if there is no other evidence of fraud or injustice? More recent Second Circuit decisions indicate a retreat from these earlier holdings by the simple substitution of "and" for "or" at the critical point in the test for piercing the corporate veil. American Fuel Corp. v. Utah Energy Development Co., 122 F.3d 130 134 (2d Cir.1997); Thrift Drug, Inc. v. Universal Prescription Adm'rs, 131 F.3d 95, 97 (2d Cir.1997); Golub v. Kidder Peabody & Co., 2000 WL 1024688 (S.D.N.Y. 2000); Goya Foods, Inc. v. Unanue, 233 F.3d 38, 43 (1st Cir.2000), applying New York law. However, Mercury Time, Inc. v. Gruen Marketing Corp., 1999 WL 342299 (S.D.N.Y.1999), cites both the "and" construction of *American Fuel* and the "or" construction of *Passalacqua* in the course of its opinion.

Alaska. Alaska state courts have developed a different piercing standard for parent/subsidiary cases. In McKibben v. Mohawk Oil Co., 667 P.2d 1223 (Alaska 1983) the court described the test as follows:

Two theories may be used to justify disregarding the corporate status of a subsidiary. First, a parent corporation may be held liable for the wrongful conduct of its subsidiary when the parent uses a separate corporate form "to defeat public convenience, justify wrong, commit fraud, or defend crime." Jackson v. General Electric Co., 514 P.2d 1170, 1172–73 (Alaska 1973); Elliott v. Brown, 569 P.2d 1323, 1326 (Alaska 1977). Second, a parent corporation may be held liable on the alternative theory that the subsidiary is the mere instrumentality of the parent. Uchitel Co. v. Telephone Co., 646 P.2d 229, 234 (Alaska 1982); Jackson, 514 P.2d at 1173. In the latter instance, liability is imposed "simply because the two corporations are so closely intertwined that they do not merit treatment as separate entities." Id.

The criteria for determining when two corporations are "closely intertwined" depends on eleven factors, including, for example, (1) the parent corporation owns all or most of the capital stock of the subsidiary, (2) the parent and subsidiary corporations have common directors or officers, (3) the parent corporation finances the subsidiary, (4) the parent corporation subscribes to all the capital stock of the subsidiary or otherwise causes its incorporation, (5) the parent corporation pays the salaries and other expenses of the subsidiary, and (6) the subsidiary has grossly inadequate capital. However, it is not necessary that all eleven factors be found in order to pierce the corporate veil.

In City of Fairbanks v. Amoco Chemical Co., 46 F.3d 1139 (9th Cir.1995), the Ninth Circuit construed Alaska law as permitting piercing under either the "mere instrumentality" or "defeat the public convenience" tests, but held that a mere finding of under-capitalization is not sufficient to establish that the corporation is a "mere instrumentality."

The problems with the list of factors approach are that (1) it puts weight on some factors that appear relatively unimportant or at least less important than others, (2) it encourages a mechanical counting of factors, and (3) as a practical matter it probably does not improve the predictability of result. However, Alaska is not alone. The court in Perry v. Household Retail Services, Inc., 953 F.Supp. 1370 (M.D.Ala.1996) (involving the question whether Household International, Inc. was subject to personal service in Alabama and was responsible for an obligation of its wholly owned subsidiary, Household Retail Services, Inc.) used factors very similar to the above list, stating that these factors "are certain circumstances which are important, and which, if present in the proper combination are controlling." However, "[n]o one of these factors is dispositive; nor does the list exhaust the relevant factors."

Notes

(1) A choice of law issue often arises in piercing cases since states may develop different rules with respect to the piercing doctrine. Consider, for example, a Delaware corporation that transacts all of its business in Illinois; its shares are owned by Illinois residents and the decision to incorporate in Delaware was based on the perceived benefits of Delaware law. Assume further that this corporation either breaches a contract or commits a tortious act in Illinois that injures citizens of Illinois who bring suit in an Illinois court, naming both the corporation and its shareholders as co-defendants. Should the court apply Illinois or Delaware "veil piercing" principles in determining the liability of the shareholders? As suggested by *Fletcher*, there is a plausible argument that Delaware law should apply, since the relationship of shareholders to their corporation may be viewed as a matter of "internal affairs" of the corporation to be governed by the law of the state of incorporation under section 307 of the Restatement of Conflicts of Law (Second).[16] A number of cases support this approach.[17] Also proceeding on this theory, Texas in 1989 amended Art. 8.02A of its Business Corporation Act to make clear that *Castleberry* should never apply to a qualified foreign corporation:

> A foreign corporation which shall have received a certificate of authority under this Act shall * * * enjoy the same, but no greater, rights and

16. [By the Editors] "The local law of the state of incorporation will be applied to determine the existence and extent of a shareholder's liability to the corporation for assessments or contributions *and to its creditors for corporate debts.*" [emphasis added]

17. [By the Editors] In many of the cases that discuss the choice of law issue, however, the Court indicates it can find no substantive difference between the laws of the two relevant states, and applies "general" veil piercing concepts without deciding which state law is applicable.

privileges as a domestic corporation * * *; provided, however, that only the laws of the jurisdiction of incorporation of a foreign corporation shall govern (1) the internal affairs of the foreign corporation, including but not limited to the rights, powers, and duties of its board of directors and shareholders and matters relating to its shares, and (2) the liability, if any of shareholders of the foreign corporation for the debts, liabilities, and obligations of the foreign corporation for which they are not otherwise liable by statute or agreement.

If an *unregistered* corporation is sued in Texas, article 8.02(a) has no application and presumably suit can be maintained against it in Texas courts. Does that make sense? If the internal affairs rule is to apply to a foreign corporation registered in Texas, is it not *a fortiori* that it should also apply to a foreign corporation that has even lesser contacts with the state of Texas? See generally, P. Blumberg, The Law of Corporate Groups: Substantive Law, ch. 27.

(2) Choice of law issues in torts cases apparently involve different considerations than those involved in contracts cases. In § 145 of the Restatement (Second) of Conflict of Laws (1969), it is suggested that the local law of the state that has the "most significant relationship to the occurrence and the parties" should apply in a torts case. Is not § 145 fundamentally inconsistent with § 307 in this area? If, in the hypothetical referred to in note (1), suit is brought in Illinois against the Delaware corporation on an automobile accident that occurred in Illinois, should not § 145 of the Second Restatement "trump" § 307 and the "internal affairs" rule, and require the application of Illinois piercing principles? Would it make any difference if Illinois veil-piercing law gives no indication that it views torts cases differently from contracts cases? If an accident involving a Delaware corporation occurred in Texas injuring Texas residents, would article 8.02 of the Texas Business Corporation Act compel the application of Delaware law despite the fact that Delaware has virtually no relationship with the case? What might be covered by the last clause of article 8.02, "the debts, liabilities, and obligations of the foreign corporation for which they [the shareholders] *are not otherwise liable by statute or agreement*?"

(3) The Delaware law of piercing is pro-defendant. In Harco National Insurance Co. v. Green Farms, Inc., 1989 WL 110537, at *6 (Del.Ch.1989), the court stated that "[p]ersuading a Delaware court to disregard the corporate entity is a difficult task." In LaSalle National Bank v. Perelman, 82 F.Supp.2d 279, 295 (D.Del.2000), the court added that "[i]n order to prevail on a claim to pierce the corporate veil and hold the corporation's shareholders liable, a plaintiff must prove that the corporate form causes fraud or similar injustice. * * * Absent a showing of fraud or that a subsidiary is in fact the mere alter ego of the parent, a common central management alone is not a proper basis for disregarding the separate corporate existence."

B. SHOULD THE PIERCING DOCTRINE BE ABOLISHED?

In an often quoted passage, Frank H. Easterbrook and Daniel R. Fischel, Limited Liability and the Corporation, 52 U.Chi.L.Rev. 89 (1985) stated,

> Limited liability is a fundamental principle of corporate law. Yet liability has never been absolutely limited. Courts occasionally allow creditors to "pierce the corporate veil," which means that shareholders must satisfy creditors' claims. "Piercing" seems to happen freakishly. Like lightning,

it is rare, severe, and unprincipled. There is a consensus that the whole area of limited liability, and conversely of piercing the corporate veil, is among the most confusing in corporate law.

We argue to the contrary that economic analysis—in particular, the theory of the firm and the economics of insurance—explains the legal treatment of limited liability. Both the rules and the exceptions serve valuable functions.

In their book, The Economic Structure of Corporate Law, ch. 2 (1991) the authors develop this thesis at greater length.

In a somewhat similar analysis, Professor Stephen Bainbridge, in his article, Abolishing Veil Piercing, 26 J.Corp.Law 479 (2001), comments that veil-piercing is "rare, unprincipled, and arbitrary." He adds, "Judicial opinions in this area tend to open with vague generalities and close with conclusory statements, with little or no concrete analysis in between. There simply are no bright-line rules for deciding when courts will pierce the corporate veil." However, he also states that "there are only two classes of cases in which personal liability ought to be in play: (1) where the creditor was misled by the shareholder and, as a result of that misrepresentation, forewent the protections of a personal guarantee; (2) where the shareholder has siphoned funds out of the firm, so that it is *ex post* undercapitalized." 26 J.Corp.Law, at 517.

Some lawyers in a chat group have argued that the piercing doctrine is unnecessary because the transactions in which it is applied involve fraudulent transfers that may be attacked either under well-established statutory or common law principles. The Uniform Fraudulent Transfers Act ("UFTA"), approved in 1984, has been adopted in about 40 states.

Among the remedies provided to an injured creditor by UFTA are "avoidance of the transfer or obligation to the extent necessary to satisfy the creditor's claim" and "any other relief the circumstances may require." (Section 7). Would these remedies permit a plaintiff to recover in a tort case such as *Baatz,* where the corporation is nominally financed and the owners do not purchase liability insurance? Are the other transactions involved in the foregoing cases all subject to attack as fraudulent transfers? Even if there is substantial overlap between "piercing" situations and fraudulent transfers, should piercing be retained as a kind of supplemental remedy independent of UFTA? One response made to the argument that piercing only involves fraudulent transfers in disguise was that the very vagueness and uncertainty of the piercing doctrine encourages adequate capitalization (and the purchase of liability insurance) by corporations to begin with. Do you agree?

C. THE PIERCING DOCTRINE IN FEDERAL/STATE RELATIONS

UNITED STATES v. BESTFOODS

Supreme Court of the United States, 1998.
524 U.S. 51, 118 S.Ct. 1876, 141 L.Ed.2d 43.

JUSTICE SOUTER delivered the opinion of the Court.

The United States brought this action for the costs of cleaning up industrial waste generated by a chemical plant. The issue before us, under the

Comprehensive Environmental Response, Compensation, and Liability Act of 1980 (CERCLA), 94 Stat. 2767, as amended, 42 U.S.C. § 9601 et seq., is whether a parent corporation that actively participated in, and exercised control over, the operations of a subsidiary may, without more, be held liable as an operator of a polluting facility owned or operated by the subsidiary. We answer no, unless the corporate veil may be pierced. But a corporate parent that actively participated in, and exercised control over the operations of the facility itself, may be held directly liable in its own right as an operator of the facility.

I

In 1980, CERCLA was enacted in response to the serious environmental and health risks posed by industrial pollution. * * * "As its name implies, CERCLA is a comprehensive statute that grants the President broad power to command government agencies and private parties to clean up hazardous waste sites." * * * If it satisfies certain statutory conditions, the United States may, for instance, use the "Hazardous Substance Superfund" to finance cleanup efforts, see 42 U.S.C. §§ 9601(11), 9604, which it may then replenish by suits brought under § 107 of the Act against, among others, "any person who at the time of disposal of any hazardous substance owned or operated any facility." 42 U.S.C. § 9607(a)(2). So, those actually "responsible for any damage, environmental harm, or injury from chemical poisons may be tagged with the cost of their actions," S.Rep. No. 96–848, pp. 6119 (1980).[18] The term "person" is defined in CERCLA to include corporations and other business organizations, see 42 U.S.C. § 9601(21), and the term "facility" enjoys a broad and detailed definition as well, see § 9601(9).[19] The phrase "owner or operator" is defined only by tautology, however, as "any person owning or operating" a facility, § 9601(20)(A)(ii), and it is this bit of circularity that prompts our review. Cf. Exxon Corp. v. Hunt, supra, at 363, 106 S.Ct., at 1109 (CERCLA, "unfortunately, is not a model of legislative draftsmanship").

II

In 1957, Ott Chemical Co. (Ott I) began manufacturing chemicals at a plant near Muskegon, Michigan, and its intentional and unintentional dumping of hazardous substances significantly polluted the soil and ground water at the site. In 1965, respondent CPC International Inc.[20] incorporated a wholly owned subsidiary to buy Ott I's assets in exchange for CPC stock. The new company, also dubbed Ott Chemical Co. (Ott II), continued chemical manufacturing at the site, and continued to pollute its surroundings. CPC kept the

---

18. [By the Court] "CERCLA * * * imposes the costs of the cleanup on those responsible for the contamination." Pennsylvania v. Union Gas Co., 491 U.S. 1, 7 (1989). "The remedy that Congress felt it needed in CERCLA is sweeping: everyone who is potentially responsible for hazardous-waste contamination may be forced to contribute to the costs of cleanup." Id., at 21 (plurality opinion of Brennan, J.).

19. [By the Court] "The term 'facility' means (A) any building, structure, installation, equipment, pipe or pipeline (including any pipe into a sewer or publicly owned treatment works), well, pit, pond, lagoon, impoundment, ditch, landfill, storage container, motor vehicle, rolling stock, or aircraft, or (B) any site or area where a hazardous substance has been deposited, stored, disposed of, or placed, or otherwise come to be located; but does not include any consumer product in consumer use or any vessel."

20. [By the Court] CPC has recently changed its name to Bestfoods. Consistently with the briefs and the opinions below, we use the name CPC herein.

managers of Ott I, including its founder, president, and principal shareholder, Arnold Ott, on board as officers of Ott II. Arnold Ott and several other Ott II officers and directors were also given positions at CPC, and they performed duties for both corporations.

In 1972, CPC sold Ott II to Story Chemical Company, which operated the Muskegon plant until its bankruptcy in 1977. Shortly thereafter, when respondent Michigan Department of Natural Resources (MDNR) examined the site for environmental damage, it found the land littered with thousands of leaking and even exploding drums of waste, and the soil and water saturated with noxious chemicals. MDNR sought a buyer for the property who would be willing to contribute toward its cleanup, and after extensive negotiations, respondent Aerojet–General Corp. arranged for transfer of the site from the Story bankruptcy trustee in 1977. Aerojet created a wholly owned California subsidiary, Cordova Chemical Company (Cordova/California), to purchase the property, and Cordova/California in turn created a wholly owned Michigan subsidiary, Cordova Chemical Company of Michigan (Cordova/Michigan), which manufactured chemicals at the site until 1986.[21]

By 1981, the federal Environmental Protection Agency had undertaken to see the site cleaned up, and its long-term remedial plan called for expenditures well into the tens of millions of dollars. To recover some of that money, the United States filed this action under § 107 in 1989, naming five defendants as responsible parties: CPC, Aerojet, Cordova/California, Cordova/Michigan, and Arnold Ott.[22] (By that time, Ott I and Ott II were defunct.) After the parties (and MDNR) had launched a flurry of contribution claims, counterclaims, and cross-claims, the District Court consolidated the cases for trial in three phases: liability, remedy, and insurance coverage.

So far, only the first phase has been completed; in 1991, the District Court held a 15–day bench trial on the issue of liability. Because the parties stipulated that the Muskegon plant was a "facility" within the meaning of 42 U.S.C. § 9601(9), that hazardous substances had been released at the facility, and that the United States had incurred reimbursable response costs to clean up the site, the trial focused on the issues of whether CPC and Aerojet, as the parent corporations of Ott II and the Cordova companies, had "owned or operated" the facility within the meaning of § 107(a) (2).

The District Court said that operator liability may attach to a parent corporation both directly, when the parent itself operates the facility, and indirectly, when the corporate veil can be pierced under state law. See CPC Int'l, Inc. v. Aerojet–General Corp., 777 F.Supp. 549, 572 (W.D.Mich.1991).

The court explained that, while CERCLA imposes direct liability in situations in which the corporate veil cannot be pierced under traditional concepts of corporate law, "the statute and its legislative history do not suggest that CERCLA rejects entirely the crucial limits to liability that are inherent to corporate law." Id., at 573. As the District Court put it, "a parent

---

21. [By the Court] Cordova/California and MDNR entered into a contract under which Cordova/California agreed to undertake certain cleanup actions, and MDNR agreed to share in the funding of those actions and to indemnify Cordova/California for various expenses. The Michigan Court of Appeals has held that this agreement requires MDNR to indemnify Aerojet and its Cordova subsidiaries for any CERCLA liability that they may incur in connection with their activities at the Muskegon facility.

22. [By the Court] Arnold Ott settled out of court with the Government on the eve of trial.

corporation is directly liable under section 107(a)(2) as an operator only when it has exerted power or influence over its subsidiary by actively participating in and exercising control over the subsidiary's business during a period of disposal of hazardous waste. A parent's actual participation in and control over a subsidiary's functions and decision-making creates 'operator' liability under CERCLA; a parent's mere oversight of a subsidiary's business in a manner appropriate and consistent with the investment relationship between a parent and its wholly owned subsidiary does not.''

Applying that test to the facts of this case, the District Court held both CPC and Aerojet liable under § 107(a)(2) as operators. As to CPC, the court found it particularly telling that CPC selected Ott II's board of directors and populated its executive ranks with CPC officials, and that a CPC official, G.R.D. Williams, played a significant role in shaping Ott II's environmental compliance policy.

After a divided panel of the Court of Appeals for the Sixth Circuit reversed in part, United States v. Cordova/Michigan, 59 F.3d 584, that court granted rehearing en banc and vacated the panel decision, 67 F.3d 586 (1995).

This time, 7 judges to 6, the court again reversed the District Court in part. 113 F.3d 572 (1997). The majority remarked on the possibility that a parent company might be held directly liable as an operator of a facility owned by its subsidiary: "At least conceivably, a parent might independently operate the facility in the stead of its subsidiary; or, as a sort of joint venturer, actually operate the facility alongside its subsidiary." Id., at 579. But the court refused to go any further and rejected the District Court's analysis with the explanation "that where a parent corporation is sought to be held liable as an operator pursuant to 42 U.S.C. § 9607(a)(2) based upon the extent of its control of its subsidiary which owns the facility, the parent will be liable only when the requirements necessary to pierce the corporate veil [under state law] are met. In other words, * * * whether the parent will be liable as an operator depends upon whether the degree to which it controls its subsidiary and the extent and manner of its involvement with the facility, amount to the abuse of the corporate form that will warrant piercing the corporate veil and disregarding the separate corporate entities of the parent and subsidiary." Id., at 580.

Applying Michigan veil-piercing law, the Court of Appeals decided that * * * CPC was [not] liable for controlling the actions of its subsidiaries, since the parent and subsidiary corporations maintained separate personalities and the [parent] did not utilize the subsidiary corporate form to perpetrate fraud or subvert justice.

We granted certiorari, 522 U.S. 1024 (1997), to resolve a conflict among the Circuits over the extent to which parent corporations may be held liable under CERCLA for operating facilities ostensibly under the control of their subsidiaries.[23] We now vacate and remand.

---

23. [By the Court] Compare United States v. Cordova/Michigan, 113 F.3d 572, 580 (C.A.6 1997) (case below) (parent may be held liable for controlling affairs of subsidiary only when the corporate veil can be pierced), and Joslyn Mfg. Co. v. T.L. James & Co., 893 F.2d 80, 82– 83 (C.A.5 1990) (same), cert. denied, 498 U.S. 1108 (1991) (but cf. Riverside Market Dev. Corp. v. International Bldg. Prods., Inc., 931 F.2d 327, 330 (C.A.5) (parent companies that actually participate in the wrongful conduct cannot hide behind the corporate veil, and can

III

It is a general principle of corporate law deeply "ingrained in our economic and legal systems" that a parent corporation (so-called because of control through ownership of another corporation's stock) is not liable for the acts of its subsidiaries. Douglas & Shanks, Insulation from Liability Through Subsidiary Corporations, 39 Yale L.J. 193 (1929) (hereinafter Douglas); see also Berkey v. Third Ave. R. Co., 244 N.Y. 84, 85, 155 N.E. 58 (1926) (Cardozo, J.); 1 W. Fletcher, Cyclopedia of Law of Private Corporations § 33, p. 568 (rev. ed. 1990) ("Neither does the mere fact that there exists a parent-subsidiary relationship between two corporations make the one liable for the torts of its affiliate"); Horton, Liability of Corporation for Torts of Subsidiary, 7 A.L.R.3d 1343, 1349 (1966) ("Ordinarily, a corporation which chooses to facilitate the operation of its business by employment of another corporation as a subsidiary will not be penalized by a judicial determination of liability for the legal obligations of the subsidiary") * * *. Thus it is hornbook law that "the exercise of the 'control' which stock ownership gives to the stockholders * * * will not create liability beyond the assets of the subsidiary. That 'control' includes the election of directors, the making of by-laws * * * and the doing of all other acts incident to the legal status of stockholders. Nor will a duplication of some or all of the directors or executive officers be fatal." Douglas 196 (footnotes omitted). Although this respect for corporate distinctions when the subsidiary is a polluter has been severely criticized in the literature, see, e.g., Note, Liability of Parent Corporations for Hazardous Waste Cleanup and Damages, 99 Harv.L.Rev. 986 (1986), nothing in CERCLA purports to reject this bedrock principle, and against this venerable common-law backdrop, the congressional silence is audible. Cf. Edmonds v. Compagnie Generale Transatlantique, 443 U.S. 256, 266–267 (1979) ("silence is most eloquent, for such reticence while contemplating an important and controversial change in existing law is unlikely"). The Government has indeed made no claim that a corporate parent is liable as an owner or an operator under § 107 simply because its subsidiary is subject to liability for owning or operating a polluting facility.

But there is an equally fundamental principle of corporate law, applicable to the parent-subsidiary relationship as well as generally, that the corporate veil may be pierced and the shareholder held liable for the corporation's conduct when, inter alia, the corporate form would otherwise be misused to accomplish certain wrongful purposes, most notably fraud, on the shareholder's behalf. See, e.g., Anderson v. Abbott, supra, at 362 ("there are occasions when the limited liability sought to be obtained through the corporation will be qualified or denied"); P. Blumberg, Law of Corporate Groups: Tort, Contract, and Other Common Law Problems in the Substantive Law of Parent and Subsidiary Corporations §§ 6.01–6.06 (1987 and 1996 Supp.)

be held directly liable without veil-piercing), cert. denied, 502 U.S. 1004 (1991)), with United States v. Kayser–Roth Corp., 910 F.2d 24, 27 (C.A.1 1990) (parent actively involved in the affairs of its subsidiary may be held directly liable as an operator of the facility, regardless of whether the corporate veil can be pierced), cert. denied, 498 U.S. 1084 (1991), Schiavone v. Pearce, 79 F.3d 248, 254–255 (C.A.2 1996) (same), Lansford–Coaldale Joint Water Auth. v. Tonolli Corp., 4 F.3d 1209, 1220–1225 (C.A.3 1993) (same), Jacksonville Elec. Auth. v. Bernuth Corp., 996 F.2d 1107, 1110 (C.A.11 1993) (same), and Nurad, Inc. v. William E. Hooper & Sons Co., 966 F.2d 837, 842 (C.A.4) (parent having authority to control subsidiary is liable as an operator, even if it did not exercise that authority), cert. denied, 506 U.S. 940 (1992).

(discussing the law of veil piercing in the parent-subsidiary context). Nothing in CERCLA purports to rewrite this well-settled rule, either. CERCLA is thus like many another congressional enactment in giving no indication "that the entire corpus of state corporation law is to be replaced simply because a plaintiff's cause of action is based upon a federal statute," Burks v. Lasker, 441 U.S. 471, 478 (1979), and the failure of the statute to speak to a matter as fundamental as the liability implications of corporate ownership demands application of the rule that "[i]n order to abrogate a common-law principle, the statute must speak directly to the question addressed by the common law," United States v. Texas, 507 U.S. 529, 534 (1993) (internal quotation marks omitted). The Court of Appeals was accordingly correct in holding that when (but only when) the corporate veil may be pierced,[24] may a parent corporation be charged with derivative CERCLA liability for its subsidiary's actions.[25]

IV

A

If the act rested liability entirely on ownership of a polluting facility, this opinion might end here; but CERCLA liability may turn on operation as well as ownership, and nothing in the statute's terms bars a parent corporation from direct liability for its own actions in operating a facility owned by its subsidiary. As Justice (then-Professor) Douglas noted almost 70 years ago, derivative liability cases are to be distinguished from those in which "the alleged wrong can seemingly be traced to the parent through the conduit of its own personnel and management" and "the parent is directly a participant in the wrong complained of." Douglas 207, 208. In such instances, the parent is

---

24. [By the Court] There is significant disagreement among courts and commentators over whether, in enforcing CERCLA's indirect liability, courts should borrow state law, or instead apply a federal common law of veil piercing. Compare, e.g., U.S. v. Cordova Chemical Co. of Michigan, 113 F.3d 572, at 584–585 (6th Cir.1997) (Merritt, J., concurring in part and dissenting in part)(arguing that federal common law should apply); Brotherhood of Locomotive Engineers v. Springfield Terminal Ry. Co., 210 F.3d 18 (1st Cir.2000) (federal common law of piercing should apply to claimed violation of the Railway Labor Act); Lansford–Coaldale Joint Water Auth. v. Tonolli Corp., 4 F.3d, at 1225 ("given the federal interest in uniformity in the application of CERCLA, it is federal common law, and not state law, which governs when corporate veil-piercing is justified under CERCLA"), and Aronovsky & Fuller, Liability of Parent Corporations for Hazardous Substance Releases under CERCLA, 24 U.S.F.L.Rev. 421, 455 (1990) ("CERCLA enforcement should not be hampered by subordination of its goals to varying state law rules of alter ego theory"), with, e.g., 113 F.3d, at 580 ("Whether the circumstances in this case warrant a piercing of the corporate veil will be determined by state law"), and Dennis, Liability of Officers, Directors and Stockholders under CERCLA: The Case for Adopting State Law, 36 Vill.L.Rev. 1367 (1991) (arguing that state law should apply). Cf. * * * Note, Piercing the Corporate Law Veil: The Alter Ego Doctrine Under Federal Common Law, 95 Harv.L.Rev. 853 (1982) (arguing that federal common law need not mirror state law, because "federal common law should look to federal statutory policy rather than to state corporate law when deciding whether to pierce the corporate veil"). Since none of the parties challenges the Sixth Circuit's holding that CPC and Aerojet incurred no derivative liability, the question is not presented in this case, and we do not address it further.

25. [By the Court] Some courts and commentators have suggested that this indirect, veil-piercing approach can subject a parent corporation to liability only as an owner, and not as an operator. See, e.g., Lansford–Coaldale Joint Water Auth. v. Tonolli Corp., supra, at 1220; Oswald, Bifurcation of the Owner and Operator Analysis under CERCLA, 72 Wash. U.L.Q. 223, 281–282 (1994) (hereinafter Oswald). We think it is otherwise, however. If a subsidiary that operates, but does not own, a facility is so pervasively controlled by its parent for a sufficiently improper purpose to warrant veil piercing, the parent may be held derivatively liable for the subsidiary's acts as an operator.

directly liable for its own actions. See H. Henn & J. Alexander, Laws of Corporations 347 (3d ed. 1983) (hereinafter Henn & Alexander) ("Apart from corporation law principles, a shareholder, whether a natural person or a corporation, may be liable on the ground that such shareholder's activity resulted in the liability"). The fact that a corporate subsidiary happens to own a polluting facility operated by its parent does nothing, then, to displace the rule that the parent "corporation is [itself] responsible for the wrongs committed by its agents in the course of its business," Mine Workers v. Coronado Coal Co., 259 U.S. 344, 395 (1922), and whereas the rules of veil-piercing limit derivative liability for the actions of another corporation, CERCLA's "operator" provision is concerned primarily with direct liability for one's own actions. See, e.g., Sidney S. Arst Co. v. Pipefitters Welfare Ed. Fund, 25 F.3d 417, 420 (C.A.7 1994) ("the direct, personal liability provided by CERCLA is distinct from the derivative liability that results from piercing the corporate veil") (internal quotation marks omitted). It is this direct liability that is properly seen as being at issue here.

Under the plain language of the statute, any person who operates a polluting facility is directly liable for the costs of cleaning up the pollution. This is so regardless of whether that person is the facility's owner, the owner's parent corporation or business partner, or even a saboteur who sneaks into the facility at night to discharge its poisons out of malice. If any such act of operating a corporate subsidiary's facility is done on behalf of a parent corporation, the existence of the parent-subsidiary relationship under state corporate law is simply irrelevant to the issue of direct liability. See Riverside Market Dev. Corp. v. International Bldg. Prods., Inc., 931 F.2d 327, 330 (C.A.5) ("CERCLA prevents individuals from hiding behind the corporate shield when, as 'operators,' they themselves actually participate in the wrongful conduct prohibited by the Act"); United States v. Kayser–Roth Corp., 910 F.2d 24, 26 (C.A.1 1990) ("a person who is an operator of a facility is not protected from liability by the legal structure of ownership").[26]

This much is easy to say; the difficulty comes in defining actions sufficient to constitute direct parental "operation." Here of course we may again rue the uselessness of CERCLA's definition of a facility's "operator" as "any person * * * operating" the facility, which leaves us to do the best we can to give the term its "ordinary or natural meaning." Bailey v. United States, 516 U.S. 137, 145 (1995) (internal quotation marks omitted). In a mechanical sense, to "operate" ordinarily means "[t]o control the functioning of; run: operate a sewing machine." American Heritage Dictionary 1268 (3d ed. 1992); see also Webster's New International Dictionary 1707 (2d ed. 1958) ("to work; as, to operate a machine"). And in the organizational sense more obviously intended by CERCLA, the word ordinarily means "[t]o conduct the affairs of; manage: operate a business." American Heritage Dictionary, supra, at 1268; see also Webster's New International Dictionary, supra, at 1707 ("to man-

---

26. [By the Court] See Oswald 257 ("There are * * * instances * * * in which the parent has not sufficiently overstepped the bounds of corporate separateness to warrant piercing, yet is involved enough in the facility's activities that it should be held liable as an operator. Imagine, for example, a parent who strictly observed corporate formalities, avoided intert-wining officers and directors, and adequately capitalized its subsidiary, yet provided active, daily supervision and control over hazardous waste disposal activities of the subsidiary. Such a parent should not escape liability just because its activities do not justify a piercing of the subsidiary's veil").

age"). So, under CERCLA, an operator is simply someone who directs the workings of, manages, or conducts the affairs of a facility. To sharpen the definition for purposes of CERCLA's concern with environmental contamination, an operator must manage, direct, or conduct operations specifically related to pollution, that is, operations having to do with the leakage or disposal of hazardous waste, or decisions about compliance with environmental regulations.

B

With this understanding, we are satisfied that the Court of Appeals correctly rejected the District Court's analysis of direct liability. But we also think that the appeals court erred in limiting direct liability under the statute to a parent's sole or joint venture operation, so as to eliminate any possible finding that CPC is liable as an operator on the facts of this case.

1

By emphasizing that "CPC is directly liable under section 107(a)(2) as an operator because CPC actively participated in and exerted significant control over Ott II's business and decision-making," 777 F.Supp., at 574, the District Court applied the "actual control" test of whether the parent "actually operated the business of its subsidiary," as several Circuits have employed it, see, e.g., United States v. Kayser–Roth Corp., supra, at 27 (operator liability "requires active involvement in the affairs of the subsidiary"); Jacksonville Elec. Auth. v. Bernuth Corp., 996 F.2d 1107, 1110 (C.A.11 1993) (parent is liable if it "actually exercised control over, or was otherwise intimately involved in the operations of, the [subsidiary] corporation immediately responsible for the operation of the facility". The well-taken objection to the actual control test, however, is its fusion of direct and indirect liability; the test is administered by asking a question about the relationship between the two corporations (an issue going to indirect liability) instead of a question about the parent's interaction with the subsidiary's facility (the source of any direct liability)). If, however, direct liability for the parent's operation of the facility is to be kept distinct from derivative liability for the subsidiary's own operation, the focus of the enquiry must necessarily be different under the two tests. "The question is not whether the parent operates the subsidiary, but rather whether it operates the facility, and that operation is evidenced by participation in the activities of the facility, not the subsidiary. Control of the subsidiary, if extensive enough, gives rise to indirect liability under piercing doctrine, not direct liability under the statutory language." Oswald 269; see also Schiavone v. Pearce, 79 F.3d 248, 254 (C.A.2 1996) ("Any liabilities [the parent] may have as an operator, then, stem directly from its control over the plant"). The District Court was therefore mistaken to rest its analysis on CPC's relationship with Ott II, premising liability on little more than "CPC's 100–percent ownership of Ott II" and "CPC's active participation in, and at times majority control over, Ott II's board of directors." 777 F.Supp., at 575. The analysis should instead have rested on the relationship between CPC and the Muskegon facility itself.

In addition to (and perhaps as a reflection of) the erroneous focus on the relationship between CPC and Ott II, even those findings of the District Court that might be taken to speak to the extent of CPC's activity at the facility itself are flawed, for the District Court wrongly assumed that the actions of the joint officers and directors are necessarily attributable to CPC. The District Court emphasized the facts that CPC placed its own high-level officials on Ott II's board of directors and in key management positions at Ott II, and that those individuals made major policy decisions and conducted day-to-day operations at the facility: "Although Ott II corporate officers set the day-to-day operating policies for the company without any need to obtain formal approval from CPC, CPC actively participated in this decision-making because high-ranking CPC officers served in Ott II management positions." Id., at 559; see also id., at 575 (relying on "CPC's involvement in major decision-making and day-to-day operations through CPC officials who served within Ott II management, including the positions of president and chief executive officer," and on "the conduct of CPC officials with respect to Ott II affairs, particularly Arnold Ott"); id., at 558 ("CPC actively participated in, and at times controlled, the policy-making decisions of its subsidiary thorough its representation on the Ott II board of directors") * * * [and] "through representation in the highest levels of the subsidiary's management"). In imposing direct liability on these grounds, the District Court failed to recognize that "it is entirely appropriate for directors of a parent corporation to serve as directors of its subsidiary, and that fact alone may not serve to expose the parent corporation to liability for its subsidiary's acts." American Protein Corp. v. AB Volvo, 844 F.2d 56, 57(C.A.2), cert. denied, 488 U.S. 852 (1988).

This recognition that the corporate personalities remain distinct has its corollary in the "well established principle [of corporate law] that directors and officers holding positions with a parent and its subsidiary can and do 'change hats' to represent the two corporations separately, despite their common ownership." Lusk v. Foxmeyer Health Corp., 129 F.3d 773, 779 (C.A.5 1997). Since courts generally presume "that the directors are wearing their 'subsidiary hats' and not their 'parent hats' when acting for the subsidiary," P. Blumberg, Law of Corporate Groups: Procedural Problems in the Law of Parent and Subsidiary Corporations § 1.02.1, at 12 (1983); it cannot be enough to establish liability here that dual officers and directors made policy decisions and supervised activities at the facility. The Government would have to show that, despite the general presumption to the contrary, the officers and directors were acting in their capacities as CPC officers and directors, and not as Ott II officers and directors, when they committed those acts.[27] The District Court made no such enquiry here, however, disregarding entirely this time-honored common law rule.

In sum, the District Court's focus on the relationship between parent and subsidiary (rather than parent and facility), combined with its automatic attribution of the actions of dual officers and directors to the corporate parent, erroneously, even if unintentionally, treated CERCLA as though it displaced or fundamentally altered common law standards of limited liability.

---

27. [By the Court] We do not attempt to recite the ways in which the Government could show that dual officers or directors were in fact acting on behalf of the parent. Here, it is prudent to say only that the presumption that an act is taken on behalf of the corporation for whom the officer claims to act is strongest when the act is perfectly consistent with the norms of corporate behavior, but wanes as the distance from those accepted norms approaches the point of action by a dual officer plainly contrary to the interests of the subsidiary yet nonetheless advantageous to the parent.

Indeed, if the evidence of common corporate personnel acting at management and directorial levels were enough to support a finding of a parent corporation's direct operator liability under CERCLA, then the possibility of resorting to veil piercing to establish indirect, derivative liability for the subsidiary's violations would be academic. There would in essence be a relaxed, CERCLA-specific rule of derivative liability that would banish traditional standards and expectations from the law of CERCLA liability. But, as we have said, such a rule does not arise from congressional silence, and CERCLA's silence is dispositive.

2

We accordingly agree with the Court of Appeals that a participation-and-control test looking to the parent's supervision over the subsidiary, especially one that assumes that dual officers always act on behalf of the parent, cannot be used to identify operation of a facility resulting in direct parental liability. Nonetheless, a return to the ordinary meaning of the word "operate" in the organizational sense will indicate why we think that the Sixth Circuit stopped short when it confined its examples of direct parental operation to exclusive or joint ventures, and declined to find at least the possibility of direct operation by CPC in this case.

In our inquiry into the meaning Congress presumably had in mind when it used the verb "to operate," we recognized that the statute obviously meant something more than mere mechanical activation of pumps and valves, and must be read to contemplate "operation" as including the exercise of direction over the facility's activities. The Court of Appeals recognized this by indicating that a parent can be held directly liable when the parent operates the facility in the stead of its subsidiary or alongside the subsidiary in some sort of a joint venture. We anticipated a further possibility above, however, when we observed that a dual officer or director might depart so far from the norms of parental influence exercised through dual office holding as to serve the parent, even when ostensibly acting on behalf of the subsidiary in operating the facility. Yet another possibility, suggested by the facts of this case, is that an agent of the parent with no hat to wear but the parent's hat might manage or direct activities at the facility.

Identifying such an occurrence calls for line-drawing yet again, since the acts of direct operation that give rise to parental liability must necessarily be distinguished from the interference that stems from the normal relationship between parent and subsidiary. Again, norms of corporate behavior (undisturbed by any CERCLA provision) are crucial reference points. Just as we may look to such norms in identifying the limits of the presumption that a dual officeholder acts in his ostensible capacity, so here we may refer to them in distinguishing a parental officer's oversight of a subsidiary from such an officer's control over the operation of the subsidiary's facility. "[A]ctivities that involve the facility but which are consistent with the parent's investor status, such as monitoring of the subsidiary's performance, supervision of the subsidiary's finance and capital budget decisions, and articulation of general policies and procedures, should not give rise to direct liability." Oswald 282. The critical question is whether, in degree and detail, actions directed to the facility by an agent of the parent alone are eccentric under accepted norms of parental oversight of a subsidiary's facility.

There is, in fact, some evidence that CPC engaged in just this type and degree of activity at the Muskegon plant. The District Court's opinion speaks of an agent of CPC alone, who played a conspicuous part in dealing with the toxic risks emanating from the operation of the plant. G.R.D. Williams worked only for CPC; he was not an employee, officer, or director of Ott II, and thus, his actions were of necessity taken only on behalf of CPC. The District Court found that "CPC became directly involved in environmental and regulatory matters through the work of * * * Williams, CPC's governmental and environmental affairs director. Williams * * * became heavily involved in environmental issues at Ott II." 777 F.Supp., at 561. He "actively participated in and exerted control over a variety of Ott II environmental matters," and he "issued directives regarding Ott II's responses to regulatory inquiries," id., at 575.

We think that these findings are enough to raise an issue of CPC's operation of the facility through Williams's actions, though we would draw no ultimate conclusion from these findings at this point. Not only would we be deciding in the first instance an issue on which the trial and appellate courts did not focus, but the very fact that the District Court did not see the case as we do suggests that there may be still more to be known about Williams's activities. Indeed, even as the factual findings stand, the trial court offered little in the way of concrete detail for its conclusions about Williams's role in Ott II's environmental affairs, and the parties vigorously dispute the extent of Williams's involvement. Prudence thus counsels us to remand, on the theory of direct operation set out here, for reevaluation of Williams's role, and of the role of any other CPC agent who might be said to have had a part in operating the Muskegon facility.[28]

V

The judgment of the Court of Appeals for the Sixth Circuit is vacated, and the case is remanded with instructions to return it to the District Court for further proceedings consistent with this opinion.

Notes

(1) This significant opinion resolved complex and long-standing disputes among the circuits as to the proper interpretation of CERCLA. See n. 23, supra. Might the Court's analysis of "operator" have relevance in establishing piercing liability in a "run of the mill" case involving individual rather than corporate shareholders? What might a shareholder who is an individual do that would involve "operating" a business that is beyond the normal activities of a shareholder? Can an individual who is also the president and chief executive officer of a corporation ever be an "operator" of the business? Or are these questions moot because such activity would be grounds for piercing the corporate veil in any event? For a case holding that a corporate officer can be personally liable under provisions of state environmental law assigning liability to "any person creating a condition or maintaining a facility or condition that reasonably could be expected to create a source of pollution to waters of state," see BEC Corporation v. Department of Environmental Protection, 256 Conn. 602, 775 A.2d 928 (2001).

---

28. [By the Court] There are some passages in the District Court's opinion that might suggest that, without reference to Williams, some of Ott II's actions in operating the facility were in fact dictated by, and thus taken on behalf of, CPC. * * *

(2) The question of whether piercing in CERCLA cases should be governed by federal or state law was not resolved. This has not been definitively resolved as of the time this casebook went to press. The conflicting views are described in footnote 24. The issue of whether the parent company "owned" or "operated" the site where environmental damage occurred should clearly be decided under federal law construing those terms because these terms are contained in CERCLA. Only in analyzing the question of whether a parent should be held liable under a veil-piercing theory does the issue of state law versus federal law arise. Since CERCLA does not specifically mention piercing the corporate veil, and instead creates a separate liability regime for parent corporations, is there any reason not to apply state piercing law in CERCLA cases? What federal statutory policy, if any, might be involved in these cases?

(3) Piercing issues also pertain to employment discrimination arising under title VII of the Civil Rights Act of 1964. The supervisor whose action is the cause for complaint may be on the payroll of the parent while the employee is on the payroll of the subsidiary. In Garcia v. Elf Atochem North America, 28 F.3d 446 (5th Cir.1994) (abrogated on other grounds by Oncale v. Sundowner Offshore Services, 523 U.S. 75, 118 S.Ct. 998, 140 L.Ed.2d 201 (1998)), the court stated that the test was whether the parent and subsidiary were part of a "single, integrated enterprise," and there was a four-fold test for this determination: "(1) interrelation of operations, (2) centralized control of labor relations, (3) common management, and (4) common ownership or financial control." See also Gabriele v. Cole Nat'l Corp., 78 F.Supp.2d 61, 65 (N.D.N.Y.1999). Is this simply another way of describing traditional tests for piercing the corporate veil? If not, is it more stringent or less stringent than those tests?

STARK v. FLEMMING

United States Court of Appeals, Ninth Circuit, 1960.
283 F.2d 410.

[Editor: The Secretary of Health, Education and Welfare ruled that Mrs. Stark was not entitled to old-age benefits. The District Court affirmed, 181 F.Supp. 539 (N.D.Cal.1959).]

Proc. History

PER CURIAM.

* * * Appellant placed her assets—a farm and a duplex house—in a newly organized corporation. Then she began to draw $400 per month as salary. The Secretary has found the corporation was a sham. There is no doubt that the corporation was set up to qualify appellant in a short time for social security payments.

But here there seems to have been proper adherence to the normal corporate routines. And it is difficult to understand how the corporate arrangement would not have to be respected by others than the Secretary. And we think he must respect it, too.

Congress could have provided that the motivation to obtain social security by organizing a corporation would defeat the end. It did not.

The Secretary is justified in taking exception to the amount paid Mrs. Stark for her services by which she sought to qualify herself for the maximum amount of social security payments. The salary left little or nothing for a return on capital, and the capital was substantial.

So, we think the Secretary is entitled to make an objective reappraisal of the salary to determine what would have been a reasonable salary for Mrs. Stark for the services she performed. One legitimate approach would be: What would a commercial farm agency in the vicinity of the farm have charged? And what would a rental agency in the vicinity of the duplex have charged for the same service? And perhaps, she might be allowed slightly more than such agencies. It is not for us to review such determinations within reasonable limits. When the Secretary determines a reasonable salary, then the amount of social security payments can be readily computed.

We, therefore, hold that the district court's judgment should be vacated and that the case should go back through the district court for direction to the Secretary to reevaluate the case on an approach consistent with what we have indicated herein.

Reversed.

ROCCOGRANDI v. UNEMPLOYMENT COMP. BD. OF REVIEW

Superior Court of Pennsylvania, 1962.
197 Pa.Super. 372, 178 A.2d 786.

MONTGOMERY, JUDGE.

The appellants are all members of a family who are involved in the wrecking business together. Each owns 40 shares of stock in the company which has 205 outstanding shares, and all three are officers of the company. The officers of the company, during periods of insufficient work to employ all the members of the family, hold a meeting and by majority vote decide which members shall be "laid off." It was decided by majority vote of all the stockholders that the appellants would be "laid off" because it was their respective turns. Immediately thereafter claims for unemployment compensation benefits were filed by the three appellants. The Bureau of Employment Security denied the claims on the grounds that the appellants were self-employed. Upon appeal the referee reversed the bureau and held the appellants to be entitled to benefits. The Board of Review reversed the referee's decision, holding that the appellants had sufficient control to lay themselves off and that they did just that. Therefore the appellants were self-employed and must be denied eligibility for benefits under section 402(h) and section 402(b)(1) of the law, 43 P.S. § 802(b)(1), (h).

This case is ruled by De Priest Unemployment Compensation Case, 196 Pa.Super. 612, 177 A.2d 20, in which this Court held that the corporate entity may be ignored in determining whether the claimants, in fact, were "unemployed" under the act, or were self-employed persons whose business merely proved to be unremunerative during the period for which the claim for benefits was made.

Decisions affirmed.

Notes

(1) Do the questions raised by these two cases relate to the nature of corporateness, or do they merely involve an interpretation of the Federal Social

Security Act or Pennsylvania Unemployment Compensation Act? If the former, is the question the same as in the traditional piercing cases? In other words, are the courts trying to accomplish something in these two cases that is different from what the courts were trying to accomplish in other piercing cases?

(2) In connection with Stark v. Flemming, compare the basically inconsistent decision in Vogel v. Sullivan, 735 F.Supp. 1353 (N.D.Ill.1990) (plaintiff may not transmute self-employment income into salary simply by incorporating his apartment house).

(3) State unemployment compensation statutes provide an exemption from contributions for employers who employ less than a minimum number of employees, often eight. May an employer avoid liability under these statutes by splitting his business among several different corporations so that each corporation has less than the minimum number of employees? See State v. Dallas Liquor Warehouse No. 4, 147 Tex. 495, 217 S.W.2d 654 (1949).

D. "REVERSE" PIERCING

CARGILL, INC. v. HEDGE
Supreme Court of Minnesota, 1985.
375 N.W.2d 477.

SIMONNET, JUSTICE.

Do the owner-occupants of a farm, by placing their land in a family farm corporation, lose their homestead exemption from judgment creditors? The trial court and the court of appeals said no. We agree and affirm.

On October 24, 1973, defendant-respondent Sam Hedge and his wife Annette entered into a contract for deed for the purchase of a 160-acre farm. On March 1, 1974, the Hedges assigned their vendees' interest to Hedge Farm, Inc., a Minnesota corporation qualified as a family farm corporation under Minn. Stat. § 500.24, subd. 1(c)(1973), and took possession. Between 1976 and 1979, Sam Hedge purchased farm supplies and services on account from plaintiff-appellant Cargill, Inc., totaling about $17,000. Apparently not until 1980, however, after Cargill had started suit on the account, did it become aware of the Hedges' corporation. Eventually, pursuant to a confession of judgment, judgment was entered in favor of Cargill and against Sam Hedge and Hedge Farms, Inc., for $12,707.08.

An execution sale was held on July 15, 1982, with Cargill as the successful bidder. Shortly before the 1-year redemption period expired, the district court, on motion of the judgment debtor, enjoined further proceedings on the execution, tolled the redemption period, and allowed Annette to join the proceedings as an intervenor. Subsequently, the trial court ruled that the Hedges had a right to exempt from the execution 80 acres constituting their homestead. The court of appeals affirmed, ruling that Annette Hedge, as sole shareholder of Hedge Farm, Inc., had an "equitable interest" in the corporate property, and that this interest, coupled with the Hedges' occupancy, satisfied the homestead statute. The court implied that it was willing to reach the same result by "piercing the corporate veil." *Cargill, Inc. v. Hedge*, 358 N.W.2d 490 (Minn. Ct. App. 1984). We granted Cargills' petition for further review.

The right to a homestead exemption from execution is a constitutional right. Minn. Const. art. 1, § 12. This right exempts from seizure or sale "the house owned and occupied by the debtor as his dwelling place, together with the land upon which it is situated," Minn. Stat. § 510.01 (1984); in rural areas, 80 acres may be exempted, Minn. Stat. § 510.02 (1984). Clearly, a corporation, an artificial entity needing no dwelling, is not entitled to a homestead exemption. *E.g., Sugg v. Pollard*, 184 N.C. 494, 115 S.E. 153 (1922). If there is to be a homestead exemption here, it must be one personal to the Hedges, notwithstanding the existence of their corporation.

Annette hedge is the sole stockholder of Hedge Farm, Inc. The court of appeals felt that this gave Annette an "equitable interest" in the property which, together with occupancy, constituted the kind of ownership which would allow the Hedges to assert a homestead exemption in the corporate property. But if Annette is the sole "owner" of the farm, there is no need to assert any homestead exemption because Annette is not a debtor. In any event, the "equitable interest" rationale seems to us conceptually ill-adapted to resolving the issue of creditors' rights we have here, especially since the relationship of a shareholder to a corporation is also implicated. We decline to adopt any equitable interest theory.

We do think, however, that the approach of a reverse pierce of the corporate veil may be used. In *Roepke v. Western National Mutual Insurance Co.*, 302 N.W.2d 350 (Minn. 1981), we disregarded the corporate entity to further the purposes of the No-Fault Act. Although title to six motor vehicles was in a corporation, in *Roepke* we nevertheless treated the vehicles as if they had been owned by the deceased, sole shareholder of the corporation, so that the decedent could be deemed an "insured" under the no-fault policy for the purpose of survivors' benefits. It seemed unfair to deprive the business owner of no-fault coverage he would have had if he had operated as a sole proprietorship. We stressed that the decedent had been president and sole stockholder of the corporation, that all six vehicles were used as family vehicles, and that no one in the family owned any other vehicles. Later, in *Kuennen v. Citizens Security Mutual Insurance Co.*, 330 N.W.2d 886 (Minn. 1983), we made clear that policy reasons for a pierce do not alone justify disregarding the corporate entity. We refused a reverse pierce in *Kuennen*, where the decedent held only 51% of the stock and used only two of the four corporate vehicles for family use. Thus the degree of identity between the individual and his or her corporation, the extent to which the corporation is an alter ego, is important. Also important is whether others, such as a creditor or other shareholders, would be harmed by a pierce.

Here there is a close identity between the Hedges and their corporation. While the Hedges maintained some of the corporate formalities, such as keeping corporate minutes, filing corporate tax returns, and dealing with the Production Credit Association as a corporation, realistically, as the trial court found, they operated the farm as their own. They had no lease with the corporation and paid no rent. The farmhouse was their family home. Annette Hedge owned all the stock. Mr. and Mrs. Hedge and their daughters were the corporate directors with Sam Hedge as president, Patricia as vice-president, and Annette as secretary-treasurer. None of the officers received any salary. The corporation was as much an alter ego for the Hedges as Mr. Roepke's corporation was for him.

In this case, too, we have strong policy reasons for a reverse pierce, much stronger than in *Roepke*, namely, furtherance of the purpose of the homestead exemption. * * *

One of the features of a corporation is limiting creditor liability to the corporate assets. We are aware of the danger of a debtor being able to raise or lower his corporate shield, depending on which position best protects his property. Consequently, a reverse pierce should be permitted in only the most carefully limited circumstances. This is such a case, and we so hold. Disregarding the entity Hedge Farm, Inc., we treat the Hedge farm as if owned by Sam and Annette Hedge as vendees under their contract for deed. As a co-vendee, Sam Hedge, the debtor, is entitled to claim a homestead exemption in 80 acres of his farm, and the creditors' execution sale of the exempted 80 acres is void.

Affirmed.

KELLEY, J., took no part in the consideration or decision of this case.

Notes

(1) Gregory S. Crespi, The Reverse Pierce Doctrine: Applying Appropriate Standards, 16 J. Corp. L. 33, 36–7 (1990):

> [The traditional piercing the corporate veil jurisprudence] is almost wholly irrelevant to the interesting and diverse set of situations that are collectively referred to by the cases and commentary as involving a "reverse pierce" of the corporate veil. In a reverse pierce claim, either a corporate insider or a person with a claim against a corporate insider is attempting to have the insider and the corporate entity treated as a single person for some purpose. * * * [R]everse pierce claims implicate different policies and require a different analytical framework from the more routine corporate creditor veil-piercing attempts.

Crespi's analysis indicates, however, that reverse piercing claims have been met with skepticism and outright rejection by many courts. If the plaintiffs can rely on the corporate form to escape personal liability from creditors, and also rely on reverse piercing to keep the corporation's assets out of the grasp of creditors, is there any way for creditors to protect themselves?

(2) Workers' Compensation statutes provide an administrative remedy for injured employees and prohibit suits brought against the "employer" of the injured employee. However, suits against third parties whose negligence contributed to the injury are not barred. In Sims v. Western Waste Industries ("WWI"), 918 S.W.2d 682 (Tex.App.1996), writ denied, an injured employee of a subsidiary corporation sued the parent corporation of his employer, alleging that the parent was involved in the design, manufacture and marketing of the truck involved in the employee's accident. The parent filed a motion for summary judgment arguing that it was the alter ego of the employer and therefore protected by the statutory bar against suits brought against the employer. A summary judgment in favor of the parent corporation was reversed:

> We are not persuaded that the legislature ever intended parent corporations, who deliberately chose to establish a subsidiary corporation, to be allowed to assert immunity under the Texas Workers' Compensation Act by reverse piercing of the corporate veil they themselves established. WWI has accepted the benefits of establishing a subsidiary corporation in Texas and will not be

allowed to disregard that entity now that it is to their gain to do so. We hold that Texas law does not permit a parent corporation to assert the alter ego theory of piercing the corporate veil of their subsidiary and thereby assert Workers' Compensation immunity as a defense to a suit by the subsidiary's employee. Point of error one is sustained. We reverse the judgment of the trial court and remand for trial.

918 S.W.2d, at 686. Accord: Reboy v. Cozzi Iron & Metal, Inc., 9 F.3d 1303, 1308, n. 9 (7th Cir.1993), where the court stated: "Moreover we agree with the district court and the Reboys that Cozzi's defensive use of the 'piercing the corporate veil' doctrine may simply be inappropriate under Indiana law. There are no cases in Indiana allowing the doctrine to be used to gain immunity under the Worker's Compensation Act. Moreover, the defensive use of the 'piercing the corporate veil' doctrine in the employment context has been addressed and soundly rejected in at least one other circuit. See Boggs v. Blue Diamond Coal Co., 590 F.2d 655, 662 (6th Cir.1979)."

(3) Some courts have rejected the doctrine of reverse piercing. One concern is that reverse piercing elevates the claims of one set of creditors (the individual creditors of the shareholder) above the claims of another set of creditors (the creditors of the corporation). Another concern is that reverse piercing circumvents normal debt collection practices and procedures, such as obtaining a charging order against a shareholder's interest in the company.

PEPPER v. LITTON

Supreme Court of the United States, 1939.
308 U.S. 295, 60 S.Ct. 238, 84 L.Ed. 281.

[Editor: Pepper sued the Dixie Splint Coal Company for an accounting of royalties due Pepper under a lease. While this case was pending, Litton, the sole shareholder of Dixie Splint, caused Dixie Splint to confess a judgment in favor of Litton based on alleged claims for back salary. After Pepper obtained a judgment, Litton caused execution to be issued on his judgment; Litton purchased the corporate assets at the resulting sale, and then caused Dixie Splint to file a voluntary petition in bankruptcy. The trustee in bankruptcy brought suit in state court to have the judgment obtained by Litton set aside and the execution sale quashed; the trustee lost. Smith v. Litton, 167 Va. 263, 188 S.E. 214 (1936). Litton then filed a claim in the bankruptcy court based on the portion of the judgment not satisfied by the proceeds of the execution sale. The District Court disallowed Litton's claim in its entirety and directed that the trustee should recover for the benefit of the bankrupt's estate the property purchased by Litton at the execution sale. The Court of Appeals reversed on the ground that the state court decision was res judicata.]

MR. JUSTICE DOUGLAS, delivered the opinion of the Court.

This case presents the question of the power of the bankruptcy court to disallow either as a secured or as a general or unsecured claim a judgment obtained by the dominant and controlling stockholder of the bankrupt corporation on alleged salary claims. * * *

The findings of the District Court, amply supported by the evidence, reveal a scheme to defraud creditors reminiscent of some of the evils with which 13 Eliz. c. 5 was designed to cope. But for the use of a so-called "one-man" or family corporation, Dixie Splint Coal Company, of which respondent was the dominant and controlling stockholder, that scheme followed an ancient pattern. * * *

In the first place, res judicata did not prevent the District Court from examining into the Litton judgment and disallowing or subordinating it as a claim. * * *

In the second place, even though we assume that the alleged salary claim on which the Litton judgment was based was not fictitious but actually existed, we are of the opinion that the District Court properly disallowed or subordinated it.

Courts of bankruptcy are constituted by §§ 1 and 2 of the bankruptcy act, 30 Stat. 544, 11 U.S.C.A. §§ 1(8), 11, and by the latter section are invested "with such jurisdiction at law and in equity as will enable them to exercise original jurisdiction in bankruptcy proceedings." Consequently this Court has held that for many purposes "courts of bankruptcy are essentially courts of equity, and their proceedings inherently proceedings in equity". Local Loan Co. v. Hunt, 292 U.S. 234, 240, 54 S.Ct. 695, 697, 78 L.Ed. 1230, 93 A.L.R. 195. * * *

That equitable power also exists in passing on claims presented by an officer, director, or stockholder in the bankruptcy proceedings of his corporation. The mere fact that an officer, director, or stockholder has a claim against his bankrupt corporation or that he has reduced that claim to judgment does not mean that the bankruptcy court must accord it *pari passu* treatment with the claims of other creditors. Its disallowance or subordination may be necessitated by certain cardinal principles of equity jurisprudence. A director is a fiduciary. Twin–Lick Oil Company v. Marbury, 91 U.S. 587, 588, 23 L.Ed. 328. So is a dominant or controlling stockholder or group of stockholders. Southern Pacific Company v. Bogert, 250 U.S. 483, 492, 39 S.Ct. 533, 537, 63 L.Ed. 1099. Their powers are powers in trust. See Jackson v. Ludeling, 21 Wall. 616, 624, 22 L.Ed. 492. Their dealings with the corporation are subjected to rigorous scrutiny and where any of their contracts or engagements with the corporation is challenged the burden is on the director or stockholder not only to prove the good faith of the transaction but also to show its inherent fairness from the viewpoint of the corporation and those interested therein. Geddes v. Anaconda Copper Mining Company, 254 U.S. 590, 599, 41 S.Ct. 209, 212, 65 L.Ed. 425. The essence of the test is whether or not under all the circumstances the transaction carries the earmarks of an arm's length bargain. If it does not, equity will set it aside. While normally that fiduciary obligation is enforceable directly by the corporation, or through a stockholder's derivative action, it is, in the event of bankruptcy of the corporation, enforceable by the trustee. For that standard of fiduciary obligation is designed for the protection of the entire community of interests in the corporation—creditors as well as stockholders. * * *

Though disallowance of such claims will be ordered where they are fictitious or a sham, these cases do not turn on the existence or nonexistence of the debt. Rather they involve simply the question of order of payment. At times equity has ordered disallowance or subordination by disregarding the corporate entity. That is to say, it has treated the debtor-corporation simply as a part of the stockholder's own enterprise, consistently with the course of conduct of the stockholder. But in that situation as well as in the others to which we have referred, a sufficient consideration may be simply the violation of rules of fair play and good conscience by the claimant; a breach of the fiduciary standards of conduct which he owes the corporation, its stockholders and creditors. * * *

On such a test the action of the District Court in disallowing or subordinating Litton's claim was clearly correct. Litton allowed his salary claims to lie dormant for years and sought to enforce them only when his debtor corporation was in financial difficulty. Then he used them so that the rights of another creditor were impaired. * * * Litton, though a fiduciary, was enabled by astute legal maneuvering to acquire most of the assets of the bankrupt not for cash or other consideration of value to creditors but for bookkeeping entries representing at best merely Litton's appraisal of the worth of Litton's services over the years.

This alone would be a sufficient basis for the exercise by the District Court of its equitable powers in disallowing the Litton claim. But when there is added the existence of a "planned and fraudulent scheme," as found by the District Court, the necessity of equitable relief against that fraud becomes insistent. No matter how technically legal each step in that scheme may have been, once its basic nature was uncovered it was the duty of the bankruptcy court in the exercise of its equity jurisdiction to undo it. Otherwise, the fiduciary duties of dominant or management stockholders would go for naught; exploitation would become a substitute for justice; and equity would be perverted as an instrument for approving what it was designed to thwart. * * *

In view of these considerations we do not have occasion to determine the legitimacy of the "one-man" corporation as a bulwark against the claims of creditors.[29]

Accordingly the judgment of the Circuit Court of Appeals is reversed and that of the District Court is affirmed.

Reversed.

Notes

(1) The doctrine applied in Pepper v. Litton is usually referred to as the "Deep Rock" doctrine, after the name of a corporation involved in an earlier case. Could the court have "pierced the corporate veil" of Dixie Splint Coal Co. and avoided Litton's claim on the theory that one cannot owe a debt to oneself? If the latter approach had been followed, Litton might have become personally liable for Dixie Splint's debts. What tests should the court use in determining whether to pierce or to subordinate? Is it simply a matter of relative degrees of bad faith or improper conduct? The absence of reasonably objective tests in this area has led to considerable confusion and some inconsistency in results.

---

29. [By the Court] On this point the District Court said: "An examination of the facts disclosed here shows the history of a deliberate and carefully planned attempt on the part of Scott Litton and Dixie Splint Coal Company to avoid the payment of a just debt. I speak of Litton and Dixie Splint Coal Company because they are in reality the same. In all the experience of the law, there has never been a more prolific breeder of fraud than the one-man corporation. It is a favorite device for the escape of personal liability. This case illustrates another frequent use of this fiction of corporate entity, whereby the owner of the corporation, through his complete control over it, undertakes to gather to himself all of its assets to the exclusion of its creditors."

(2) Section 510(c) of the Bankruptcy Act of 1978, 11 U.S.C.A. § 510(c), provides that " * * * after notice and a hearing, the Court may * * * under principles of equitable subordination, subordinate for purposes of distribution all or part of an allowed claim to all or part of another allowed claim or all or part of an allowed interest to all or part of another allowed interest * * *." H.R.Rep. No. 595, 95th Cong., 1st Sess., at 359 (1977) states that "[t]his section [was] intended to codify case law, such as *Pepper v. Litton* * * *."

(3) Do the tests for subordination under the Deep Rock doctrine differ in degree or kind from the tests applicable to piercing the corporate veil?

E. SUCCESSOR LIABILITY

What happens to a corporate liability when the company is acquired by another company? What happens to a corporate liability when a company simply ceases doing business? Courts are split on the issue of whether it is fair to impose liability on a successor company. Courts sometimes impose such liability on successor corporations in order to impose liability on the party who is better able to bear it (possibly through insurance), or who is the only plausible defendant to compensate an injured plaintiff, or to protect the good name and reputation of the preceding company, or to prevent fraud.

Courts that decline to impose successor liability argue that the doctrine is inappropriate because it fails to respect the corporate forms of the companies involved, and that it is unfair because it holds a corporation liable for an obligation that was not its fault. Courts also argue that imposing liability will not deter misbehavior because the compensation paid is not from the wrongdoer, but from an innocent party. The courts argue that when mergers and other financial arrangement are made, finality is necessary in order to permit the free transferability of assets. Obviously, corporations will be reluctant to make acquisitions if there is significant uncertainty about their contingent liability for the debts and other obligations of the companies they acquire.

From a policy perspective, the imposition of successor liability is difficult because it has both significant potential costs and significant potential benefits. The imposition of successor liability makes it more difficult to transfer assets. The free transferability of assets is important to the creditors of the company being acquired, because they want to transform the assets of the business into cash so that their claims can be paid. On the other hand, there is always the risk that corporate assets will be sold for less than fair consideration, or that, once the assets are sold, the cash will disappear into the hands of the corporation's shareholders.

NISSEN CORP. v. MILLER

Court of Appeals of Maryland, 1991.
323 Md. 613, 594 A.2d 564.

CHASANOW, J.

On January 31, 1981, Frederick B. Brandt (Brandt) purchased from Atlantic Fitness Products (Atlantic) a treadmill that was designed, manufactured, and marketed by American Tredex Corporation (American Tredex). Later the same year, on July 31, Nissen Corporation (Nissen) entered into an asset purchase agreement with American Tredex. Pursuant to that agreement, Nissen purchased the trade name, patents, inventory and other assets of American Tredex. Nissen also assumed some of American Tredex's obligations and liabilities, but the contract expressly excluded assumption of liability for injuries arising from any product previously sold by American Tredex. The contract contemplated the continuation of the selling corporation, American Tredex, for five years and that during that period American Tredex would be known by a new name, AT Corporation.

* * *

Over five years after his purchase of the treadmill, on October 18, 1986, Brandt was injured while trying to adjust the running treadmill. More than a year later, on December 31, 1987, American Tredex (then known as AT Corporation) was administratively dissolved. Brandt and his wife filed suit on September 1, 1988, against American Tredex, AT Corporation, Nissen, and Atlantic, seeking damages for negligence, strict liability, breach of express and implied warranties, and loss of consortium. Atlantic cross-claimed against Nissen for indemnity and contribution. Nissen filed a motion for summary judgment, which was granted. * * * Brandt and Atlantic appealed to the Court of Special Appeals. In Miller v. Nissen Corp., 83 Md.App. 448, 575 A.2d 758 (1990), the Court of Special Appeals reversed the trial court. We granted Nissen's petition for writ of certiorari on the issue of whether it, as a successor to American Tredex, is liable to Brandt for his injuries.

The issue in the instant case is whether this Court should adopt the general rule of nonliability of successor corporations, with its four well-recognized traditional exceptions, or whether we should add a fifth exception for "continuity of enterprise."

The general or traditional rule of corporate successor liability has been stated by many cases and treatises:

> [A] corporation which acquires all or part of the assets of another corporation does not acquire the liabilities and debts of the predecessor, unless: (1) there is an express or implied agreement to assume the liabilities; (2) the transaction amounts to a consolidation or merger; (3) the successor entity is a mere continuation or reincarnation of the predecessor entity; or (4) the transaction was fraudulent, not made in good faith, or made without sufficient consideration. Thus, the general rule is one of successor nonliability, subject to four 'traditional' exceptions * * *

1 American Law of Products Liability 3d § 7.1, at 10–12 (Travers, rev. ed. 1990).* * *

* * * All parties agree that this Court should adopt the general rule of nonliability of a successor corporation, with its four traditional exceptions. Brandt and Atlantic (Respondents) contend we should also adopt the more liberal "continuity of enterprise" theory as a fifth exception in products liability cases. * * *

Respondents would only be entitled to recover if we expand the traditional "mere continuation" or continuity of entity exception and add the "continuity of enterprise" exception to the general rule of nonliability of corporate successors. The mere continuation or continuity of entity exception applies where "there is a continuation of directors and management, shareholder interest and, in some cases, inadequate consideration. The gravamen of the traditional 'mere continuation' exception is the continuation of the corporate entity rather than continuation of the business operation." 1 Frumer & Friedman, supra, at 2.06[2][c], at 2–182 to 2–183 (emphasis in original, footnote omitted); * * * This exception focuses on the continuation of management and ownership. In contrast, the continuity of enterprise theory focuses on continuation of the business operation or enterprise where there is no continuation in ownership. * * *

Respondents do not contend that Nissen is a "mere continuation" of American Tredex or that the sale of assets in the instant case falls within any of the traditional exceptions to the rule of nonliability of corporate successors, nor would the record support such an argument. Only if we expand the traditional exceptions to include a "continuity of enterprise" exception would Brandt be entitled to proceed against Nissen.

Brandt urges that we adopt the continuity of enterprise theory because it "is limited, proper and pertinent to the rights of a consumer who has suffered a personal injury for which some entity must be held responsible." He argues that "courts have logically prevented the evasion of liability by any part of the manufacturing and selling chain" and that, in recognition of this public policy, we should "not allow a major corporation to purchase only the benefits in an asset purchase transaction while denying its attendant liabilities to the consuming public, particularly where the successor corporation has held itself out to the public as the sponsor of the injury-causing entity." Atlantic further argues that the traditional rule evolved to protect the rights of creditors and shareholders in the corporate context and is inapplicable in the case of products liability plaintiffs and that "[a] corporation contemplating not only the acquisition of the assets of another corporation, but also the continuation of the basic enterprise of that corporation must accept the burdens as well as the benefits of such a transaction." Atlantic contends that, because Nissen enjoyed American Tredex's goodwill and held itself out as the effective continuation of American Tredex, selling replacement parts, performing some contracts, retaining some employees, honoring existing 90–day warranties, and servicing customer accounts, it should bear the burden of American Tredex's liability for defective products.

Nissen counters that it was not part of the "manufacturing and selling chain"; it merely purchased American Tredex's assets. That transaction was fully negotiated, including the requirement that the predecessor corporation continue in existence after the sale, presumably so that it would be subject to suit in cases such as this. The price Nissen paid for the business was based on the total contract, including the provision that the predecessor retain all liability for injuries caused by defective products sold by it before the asset purchase. Nissen argues that we should adhere to "[t]he longstanding general rule and its well-defined limited exceptions" because they "have functioned well to balance the rights of creditors and successor corporations by preserving traditional principles of corporate law and promoting the free alienability of business assets while maintaining adequate protection for the interests of consumers and creditors from fraudulent and unjust corporate transactions."

Nissen urges that the expansion of the traditional rule that Respondents propose would impose liability not only upon "a major corporation * * * where the successor corporation has held itself out to the public as the sponsor of the injury causing entity," but also upon the small corporation that purchases assets and carries on a business but abandons its predecessor's defective, injury-causing designs or practices.

* * * Respondents argue that public policy demands that we accept the continuity of enterprise doctrine because, as stated by Brandt in his brief, "some entity must be held responsible" where "a consumer * * * has suffered a personal injury." In *Phipps*, however, we clarified the basis for our adoption of strict products liability:

> [T]he theory of strict liability is not a radical departure from traditional tort concepts. Despite the use of the term "strict liability" the seller is not an insurer, as absolute liability is not imposed on the seller for any injury resulting from the use of his product. Proof of a defect in the product at the time it leaves the control of the seller implies fault on the part of the seller sufficient to justify imposing liability for injuries caused by the product. * * *

* * * It is clear from our decisions that inherent in our recognition of strict products liability is the concept that sellers who place defective and unreasonably dangerous products on the market are at fault when a user is injured by that activity and should bear responsibility. A corporate successor is not a seller and bears no blame in bringing the product and the user together. It seems patently unfair to require such a party to bear the cost of unassumed and uncontemplated products liability claims primarily because it is still in business and is perceived as a "deep pocket."

Respondent Atlantic argues that, because Nissen reaped the benefits of the goodwill of American Tredex, it would be unfair to permit it to escape the burden of paying American Tredex's tort liabilities. This argument lacks merit. It overlooks the fact that, if American Tredex products do cause injuries, Nissen will suffer a resultant loss in the value of the goodwill it purchased.

Although Brandt contends that we should "not allow a major corporation to purchase only the benefits in an asset purchase transaction while denying its attendant liabilities to the consuming public," he overlooks the fact that the remedy he seeks for this "injustice" may be unfairly broad. Were we to adopt continuity of enterprise, not only would liability be imposed upon "a major corporation," but it would also be imposed upon the small business operation which may not be in a position to spread the risk or insure against it. * * *

Brandt also complains that he was not "alerted to internal corporate changes which would prevent the protection properly due to a consumer of a product." We cannot accept the proposition implied by this argument that consumers retain products in reliance upon their ability to sue a certain entity if a problem develops with the product. Brandt was notified of the sale of American Tredex. Had he realized that he would not be able to sue the successor if he was injured, we doubt that he would have scrapped his treadmill and purchased a new one. Nissen did more than was required of it by providing the needed replacement parts at Brandt's request. The fact that

Nissen maintained a network to service American Tredex customers and, in fact, furnished parts to Brandt for his treadmill does not give rise to successor liability. Furthermore, we should not penalize Nissen for retaining a few of American Tredex's employees or for assuming some of American Tredex's commitments. All of these actions on Nissen's part have important societal value. While we recognize the societal value of permitting consumers to recover from those responsible when they are injured by a product, Nissen is not one of those responsible for Brandt's injuries.

The Restatement (Second) of Torts § 402A, upon which Maryland strict liability in tort law is based, Phipps, 278 Md. at 353, 363 A.2d at 963, does not contemplate imposition of liability upon successor corporations. * * * As was noted by the Third Circuit in Polius:

> [T]he Restatement reaffirms the notion of a causal relationship between the defendant's acts and the plaintiff's injury—a concept that is fundamental to tort law. The corporate successor theories espoused by Michigan and California brush aside this bedrock requirement and impose liability on entities which in fact had no connection with the acts causing injury.

> Even the wholesaler or retailer who sells a defective product has some causal connection with the plaintiff's injury. The same cannot be said of the owner of a new business who manufactures an improved, defect-free, version of a product in a facility purchased from his predecessor * * *. Under the continuity of enterprise theory, a new owner who continues his predecessor's operations may be liable if he manufactures some but not all of a number of items. If the new owner continues to manufacture ten items but decides not to produce one because it is too dangerous, he might nevertheless be liable for claims which his predecessor set in motion through the dangerous product.

802 F.2d at 81–82. The Polius court concluded that "the continuity of enterprise theory * * * proposes an ill-considered extension of liability to an entity having no causal relationship with the harm." Id. at 82.

* * *

For the reasons set forth in this opinion, we reject the continuity of enterprise theory of successor corporate liability. Like the majority of our sister states, we adhere to the general rule of nonliability of successor corporations, with its four traditional exceptions, in products liability cases.

ELDRIDGE, J. and HINKEL, J., dissenting:

We concur with the majority in the adoption of the general rule of nonliability of successor corporations, together with its four traditional exceptions. We would, however, adopt a fifth exception for "continuity of enterprise" with regard to defective products. Therefore, we dissent.

Notes

(1) What is the justification for the general rule that a corporation that acquires all of the assets of another corporation generally does not assume the liabilities of the first corporation absent an agreement to assume such liabilities, some other special facts, or fraud?

(2) An interesting question: What happens if a company offers viable products and services, and has a stable and productive workforce, but also has past or prospective tort liabilities in an amount greater than the total value of the firm. Commentators have observed that this situation poses extremely difficult problems. Any merger or other transfer of assets should not make the corporation's creditors *worse off* than they would have been if the transaction had not occurred. On the other hand, the creditors should not be placed in a *better* position as a result of an acquisition or other change in control, because this would reduce the incentives of an acquirer to take over the company. See Mark J. Roe, Mergers, Acquisitions, and Tort: A Comment on the Problem of Successor Corporation Liability, 70 Va. L.Rev. 1559, 1562 (1984).

(3) When corporations decide to dissolve and distribute their assets to shareholders, issues closely related to those involved in piercing the corporate veil cases arise. When a corporation decides to wind up its business, there is always a risk that the proceeds of any asset sale will be distributed to the corporation's shareholders before the claims of all of the creditors have been satisfied. On the other hand, people running businesses want to be able to stop doing business and take their money out of the company without worrying that creditors will appear years later, and declare that their claims were not paid. Similarly, when all of the assets of the corporation are sold, the lawyers for the selling corporation will normally be consulted about how (and when) the proceeds from the sale are to be distributed to shareholders. The members of the board of directors of the selling corporation should be particularly concerned that proper procedures are followed, because corporate directors will be personally liable if a corporation makes an improper distribution of its assets.

(4) The purpose of Chapter 14 of the MBCA is to provide a clear set of instructions for dissolving a corporation in such as way as to extinguish corporate liabilities. MBCA Section 14.02 requires a shareholder vote for dissolution. A simple majority will suffice for dissolution, unless the corporation's articles of incorporation specify that a super-majority is required. MBCA Section 14.03 provides that a corporation must file articles of dissolution after receiving shareholder authorization in order to dissolve the corporation. The corporation is dissolved "upon the effective date of its articles of dissolution." MBCA Section 14.03(b). What is the effect of dissolution? MBCA Section 14.05 states that after dissolution, the corporation may only carry on business associated with the process of winding up and the rights and duties of shareholders and directors are not affected. In addition, suits by or against the corporation are not altered. Section 14.06 sets forth the rules for dissolving corporations to follow in order to extinguish known claims against the dissolved corporation. Section 14.06(a) provides that the dissolved corporation may dispose of the known claims against it by notifying its known creditors, and permit them to file a claim against the corporation. If no claim is filed by the creditor by the deadline set by the corporation (which must be at least 120-days from the date of the written notice), the claim is barred. A corporation that receives a claim from a creditor during that 120 day period can reject the claim. If the corporation rejects the claim, it is barred unless the creditor commences a proceeding within 90 days from the date of the rejection notice. Section 14.06(c).

Chapter Eight

FINANCIAL MATTERS AND
THE CORPORATION

A. DEBT AND EQUITY CAPITAL

Every firm needs financing in order to conduct its operations. The financing that firms use to fund their business activities is called "capital."[1] Capital may be obtained from a variety of different sources, e.g., (1) by borrowing funds from friends, or commercial sources such as banks or on credit cards, (2) by capital contributions from the owners of the firm, (3) by capital contributions from outside investors who thereafter either remain inactive or become active co-owners of the firm, or (4) by retaining earnings of the business rather than distributing them to owners.

The critical distinction in finance is the distinction between "equity capital" and "debt." Debt is associated with the idea of borrowing. The main characteristics of debt are that it must, at some point, be repaid, that interest on the amount borrowed must be paid periodically, and that the repayment of principal and interest is not contingent on the success of the business.

"Equity," by contrast, is synonymous with "ownership" and has nothing to do with the word "equity" in its traditional historical or legal meaning. Rather, the principal characteristic of equity is that, conceptually, the value of an owner's equity in a piece of property equals the market value of that property minus the market value of the debts that are liens against that property. Equity capital is composed of contributions by the original entrepreneurs in the firm; capital contributed by subsequent investors usually in exchange for ownership interests in the business, and retained earnings of the enterprise.

Based on these fundamental characteristics of debt and equity, debt claims sometimes are referred to as "fixed claims," while equity claims are

---

1. [By the Editors] The word "capital" is a broad term that may be used in a wide variety of different contexts and has several meanings. For example, the term is used: (a) to describe the money or other consideration that a firm receives from issuing stock; (b) the amount of a firm's legally required capital (discussed in this chapter); (c) a firm's "net worth," i.e., the amount by which a firm's assets exceed its total liabilities; (d) a firm's "capital plant," that is, the plant equipment and other long-lived physical assets that a firm uses in its operations; and (e) all of the money and property that a firm owns or uses. In this chapter we use the term "capital" to refer to the amount of equity and debt used by the firm to fund its business activities.

referred to as "residual claims" to connote the idea that fixed claimants (creditors) are entitled to be repaid the principal and interest owed to them on the loans they have made, while residual claimants (equity owners) have a claim on everything that is left over after the fixed claimants have been paid.

This Chapter considers primarily the raising of equity capital by corporations through the sale of its securities. It considers debt financing only to a limited extent. A word of caution at the outset is appropriate. An important federal statute, the Securities Act of 1933, 15 U.S.C.A. § 77a et seq., imposes substantial disclosure requirements on the public sale of securities using the mails or the facilities of interstate commerce. Public offerings of securities must be registered with the U.S. Securities and Exchange Commission, and failure to do so can result in criminal and civil penalties. In addition, states have statutes called "blue sky laws" that regulate the sale of securities within the specific state. These federal and state statutes are potentially applicable whenever a business seeks funds; they are not limited to large transactions or to transactions in which capital is raised with the assistance of professional underwriters. These statutes are discussed briefly in Section F of this Chapter. In real life, potential applicability of these statutes must be considered whenever a firm is raising capital from third parties.

B. TYPES OF EQUITY SECURITIES

There is a recognized nomenclature for equity securities issued by corporations. The following brief discussion is essential background for those unfamiliar with this nomenclature; it also illustrates that while the language is sometimes arcane, the underlying ideas are not complicated.

1. SHARES GENERALLY

It is helpful to begin with fundamental concepts. "Shares" are defined in MBCA § 1.40(22) as the "units into which the proprietary interests in a corporation are divided." Further, a corporation may create and issue different "classes" of shares with different preferences, limitations, and relative rights. MBCA §§ 1.40(2), 6.01(a). Each class must have a "distinguishing designation," and all shares within a single class must have identical rights. If a corporation issues only one class of shares, they may be referred to as "common shares," "capital shares," or simply "shares" or "stock." The various designations and rights of shares of different classes must be set forth in the articles of incorporation. MBCA § 6.01.

MBCA § 6.01(b) sets forth two fundamental rights of holders of common shares: (1) They are entitled to vote for the election of directors and on other matters coming before the shareholders, and (2) They are entitled to the net assets of the corporation (after making allowance for debts), when distributions are made in the form of dividends or liquidating distributions.

MBCA § 6.01(b) permits these essential attributes of common shares to be placed in different classes of shares in whole or in part, but requires that one or more classes with these attributes must always be authorized. Section 6.03(c) adds that at least one share of each class with these basic attributes must always be outstanding—that is, issued to some person or persons.[2]

---

2. [By the Editors] When a new corporation is in the process of being formed, there may be a brief period between the filing of the articles of incorporation and the organizational meet-

2. COMMON AND PREFERRED SHARES

If a corporation has more than one class of shares, a customary distinction is between "common" shares and "preferred" shares. These terms are not defined in the MBCA but have commonly accepted meanings and are used almost ubiquitously.

"Common shares" are a class or classes of shares that have the fundamental rights of voting for directors and receiving the net assets of the corporation as described above. MBCA §§ 6.01(b), 6.03(c). Often these two fundamental rights are combined in a single class of "common shares," but they may also be divided among different classes of shares. Holders of common shares have non-financial rights as well: a right to inspect books and records (see MBCA § 16.02), a right to sue on behalf of the corporation to right a wrong committed against it (see MBCA §§ 7.40–7.47), a right to financial information (see MBCA § 16.20), and so forth.

Common shares may be defined in various ways. The United States Supreme Court identified the characteristics usually associated with common stock as: (i) the right to receive dividends contingent upon an apportionment of profits, (ii) negotiability (capable of being transferred by delivery or endorsement when the transferee takes the instrument for value, in good faith, and without notice of conflicting title claims or defenses), (iii) the ability to be pledged or hypothecated (ability to be pledged as security or collateral for a debt, without delivery of title or possession), (iv) the conferring of voting rights in proportion to the number of shares owned, and (v) the capacity to increase in value. United Housing Foundation, Inc. v. Forman, 421 U.S. 837, 95 S.Ct. 2051, 44 L.Ed.2d 621 (1975).[3]

Whatever the niceties of definition, because common shares represent the residual ownership interest in the corporation, their financial interest is open-ended in the sense that they benefit as the business prospers and the corporate assets increase.

"Preferred shares" are typically classes of shares with rights that are preferential to those assigned to the common shares, but limited in some way. For example, a class of preferred stock might have the right to receive a distribution of five dollars per share before the common shares become entitled to any distribution. Preferred shares are usually (but not always) non-voting. However, voting power often is assigned to preferred shares if the company misses scheduled dividend payments on its preferred stock, or if it

---

ing where the issuance of shares is authorized. Thus there may be a brief period during which the corporation is in existence but no shares are issued or outstanding. The assumption is that the corporation will not enter into business transactions until after the organizational meeting is held, since prior to the organizational meeting, the corporation will not have officers to act on its behalf, will not have a bank account, and will not have any assets because no stock will have been issued. It is possible, however, for a corporation to commence business before articles of incorporation are filed or before a formal organizational meeting is held. Typically, in those cases there will be no doubt as to the persons who are to own the common shares of the corporation and who therefore are in fact the shareholders. Premature commencement of business creates a risk of personal liability being imposed on shareholders for transaction entered into in the name of the corporation.

3. [By the Editors] This definition was set forth in a case involving the issue whether a "share of stock" that entitled the owner to lease an apartment in a housing cooperative was a "security"; housing cooperative shares possess virtually none of the enumerated characteristics.

fails to meet some other financial test. MBCA § 13.01(6) contains a partial definition of "preferred shares."

Preferred shares entitle the holders to a "priority" or "preference" in payment as against the holders of common shares. This priority or preference may be either in the payment of dividends or in the making of distributions out of the capital of a corporation, or very commonly in both. A "priority" or "preference" simply means that the holders of preferred shares are entitled to a specified distribution before anything can be paid on the common shares. For example, the dividend preference of $5 per year mentioned above means only that nothing can be paid to the holders of common shares until the preferred shareholders are first paid their $5 per share. Preferred shares are often described by reference to the amount of their dividend preference or by a percentage of the stock's par or stated value. Thus, a "$5.00 preferred" has a dividend preference of $5.00 per year, while a "5% preferred" has a dividend preference equal to five percent of the share's par value. Preferred shareholders typically have limited or "capped" rights to earnings, but that is not always the case.

The precise scope of the rights of a preferred shareholder is traditionally established by detailed provisions in the articles of incorporation creating that class of shares. These provisions are called the "preferred shareholder's contract" and may not be amended without the consent of holders of some statutorily designated fraction of the preferred shares themselves.

Funds may be distributed to common or preferred shareholders in the form of "dividends" or "distributions." A "dividend" is a distribution from current or retained earnings; payments to shareholders out of capital are called "distributions." If earnings of the corporation are retained by the corporation and not distributed, the value of common shares will increase but the value of preferred shares may not (since their rights are usually limited or capped).

The MBCA sets forth rules for distributions generally, but does not set forth special rules for dividends. MBCA §§ 1.40(6), 6.40. Decisions whether or not to make a distribution to common shareholders, and if so, how much, are matters within the business judgment of directors. Typically, common shareholders have no legal basis for complaint if distributions or dividends on common shares are omitted over extended periods of time.

Where a corporation has only one class of shares outstanding, that class obviously consists of common shares, even though they may be described in the articles of incorporation as "capital stock" or simply "stock" or "shares." The MBCA consistently uses the word "shares" rather than "stock" in describing equity security interests, but the Official Comment to § 6.01 points out that "no specific designation is required by the Model Act."

Many corporations begin their life with only a modest amount of capital raised by the sale of shares. As noted earlier, the statutes in a few states prescribe a minimum initial capitalization—often $1,000. The Model Act contained such a requirement until 1969 when it was eliminated on the grounds "that the protection sought to be achieved was illusory and that the provision served no useful purpose." Comment to MBCA (1969) § 56. The MBCA currently does not contain a minimum capital requirement.

3. SPECIAL RIGHTS OF PUBLICLY TRADED PREFERRED SHARES

Rights and privileges usually given to publicly traded preferred shares include the following:

Cumulative Dividend Rights. The dividend preference of preferred shares may be cumulative, noncumulative, or partially cumulative. A cumulative dividend simply means that if a preferred dividend is not paid in any year, it accumulates and must be paid (along with the following years' unpaid cumulative dividends) before any dividend may be paid on the common shares in a later year. For example, if a preferred share has a $5.00 cumulative dividend preference, and that dividend is omitted in one year, not only may no dividend be paid on the common shares in that year, but also in the following year, no dividend may be paid on the common shares unless the holder of the preferred share receives $10.00 in dividends, making up for the omission in the prior year. A noncumulative dividend is not carried over from one year to the next; if no dividend is declared during the year, the preferred shareholder loses the right to receive the dividend for that year. A noncumulative dividend that is not paid during the year simply disappears, and the following year is a new ball game. A partially cumulative dividend typically is cumulative to the extent there are earnings in the year, and noncumulative with respect to any excess dividend preference. Unpaid cumulative dividends are not debts of the corporation, but a right of priority in future distributions. Unlike interest on a debt, dividends on preferred shares may be paid only from funds that are legally available for making distributions. Many state statutes, however, liberally permit the payment of cumulative preferred dividends from various capital accounts. Typically, publicly-traded preferred shares have cumulative dividend rights.

Voting. Preferred shares are usually nonvoting shares (though many exceptions exist, particularly in closely held corporations). In order to provide some protection for preferred shareholders, it is customary to provide that nonvoting preferred shares obtain a right to vote for the election of a specified number of directors if preferred dividends have been omitted for a specified period.

Liquidation Preferences. Preferred shares usually have a liquidation preference as well as a dividend preference. The liquidation preference is often fixed at a specified price per share, payable upon the dissolution of the corporation before anything may be paid to the common shares. Like preferred dividends, a liquidation preference is not a debt but a claim to priority if and when funds are available. The amount of the liquidation preference is usually a fixed amount, so that the holders of the preferred do not share in any general appreciation in value of the corporation's assets.

Redemption Rights. Preferred shares may be made redeemable at the option of the *corporation,* usually at a price fixed by the articles of incorporation at the time the class of preferred shares was created. A right to "redeem" shares simply means that the corporation has the power to buy back the redeemable shares at any time at the fixed price, and the shareholder has no choice but to accept that price. (If the shareholder refuses to turn in his certificates, the corporation simply deposits the redemption price in a bank and refuses to recognize that the shares are outstanding or that they have rights with respect to the corporation other than the right to the redemption price.) When a corporation elects to exercise the redemption privilege, it "calls" the stock for redemption. Typically, the power to call redeemable shares may be exercised only after a specified period of time has elapsed; also the redemption price is usually set somewhat in excess of the amount of the share's liquidation preference. For example, preferred shares that are entitled to receive $100.00 per share on liquidation may be made redeemable at any time for $105.00 plus any unpaid cumulative dividends.

Conversion Rights. Preferred shares may be made convertible at the option of the *holder* into common shares at a fixed ratio specified in the articles of incorporation; convertible preferred shares are attractive when the common shares are publicly traded, so that an active market exists for the conversion securities. A conversion privilege allows the holders of the preferred shares to obtain a part of the long term appreciation of the corporation's assets if the holders are willing to give up their preferred rights by converting their shares into common shares. Typically, the conversion ratio is established so that the common shares must appreciate substantially in price before it is profitable to convert the preferred shares. When the price of the common shares rises above this level, the preferred shares fluctuate in price with the common shares. Convertible shares are also usually redeemable, but typically the privilege to convert continues for a limited period of time after the call for redemption. A conversion is described as "forced" when shares are called for redemption at a time when the market value of the shares obtainable on conversion exceeds the redemption price.

Protective Provisions. Preferred shares may also have certain financial protections, such as sinking fund provisions, which require the corporation to set aside a certain amount each year to redeem a specified portion of the preferred stock issue. In addition, convertible preferred shares usually contain elaborate provisions protecting the conversion privilege from dilution in case of share dividends, share splits, or the issuance of additional common shares. The importance of these protections cannot be minimized since preferred shareholders have not fared well on arguments based on fiduciary duty and the like. See Lawrence E. Mitchell, The Puzzling Paradox of Preferred Stock (And Why We should Care About It), 51 Bus.Law. 443. 443–44 (1996) (arguing that preferred stockholders' rights are often not recognized in judicial proceedings and that they should instead rely exclusively on their contract as a source of rights).[4]

Of course, it is well-settled that corporations and their directors owe fiduciary duties to common shareholders. Perhaps the reason that preferred shareholders have fared so poorly when making fiduciary duty claims is that courts have no principled basis for dealing with such claims by preferred shareholders when those claims compete directly with the fiduciary claims of common shareholders. After all, both classes of claimants are competing for the same cash flows.

Participating Preferred. The preferred shares described above are nonparticipating. Nonparticipating shares are entitled to the specified dividend payment and the specified liquidation preference, and nothing more no matter how profitable the corporation. "Participating preferred" shares are entitled

---

4. Cited with permission from the American Bar Association.

to the specified dividend and, after the common shares receive a specified amount, they share with the common in additional distributions on some predetermined basis. Such shares combine some of the features of common and preferred. They are sometimes referred to as "Class A common" or by a similar designation that shows that their right to participate is open-ended and therefore they have one of the major attributes of common shares. Preferred shares that are participating in dividend distributions usually have liquidation preferences that are tied in some way to the amounts receivable by the common shares on liquidation.

Classes of Preferred. A corporation may issue different classes of preferred shares. A corporation, for example, may issue "Class A preferred" and "Class B preferred" with different dividend rates, different rights on dissolution, and different priorities. The Class A preferred may be junior to the Class B in terms of priorities or it may be superior to or on par with the Class B. Both are "senior" securities, however, because both have preferential rights over common shares.

Series of Preferred. MBCA § 6.02(a)(2) refers to "one or more series within a class." The concept of a "series within a class" arose because of problems of raising substantial amounts of capital through the issuance of preferred shares. In preferred share financing, it is often advantageous to tailor the price, dividend, and other terms of the shares to the market conditions current at the time of issue. It was inconvenient and expensive to amend the articles of incorporation of a corporation with many shareholders to create a new class of preferred shares whenever a new issue was to be sold; as a result, a number of states authorized the creation of a "class" of preferred shares that contained no financial terms at all but authorized the board of directors to carve out different "series" of shares from within the class, and designate the financial terms of each series when it was issued. Preferred shares for which the board of directors is authorized to establish terms are often called "blank shares." MBCA § 6.02 is a somewhat broader "blank shares" provision since it authorizes the board to establish "classes" as well as "series." In practice, however, there is usually no economic difference between a "class" of preferred shares and a "series within a class" of preferred shares: both have unique financial terms, but all shares within the "class" or "series" have identical preferences, limitations and relative rights (see MBCA § 6.02(c)). The Official Comment to MBCA § 6.02 states that the labels "class" and "series" are "often a matter of convenience"; it does not seem sensible to limit the power of directors merely because of historical nomenclature.

The terms of one or more "series" may also be specified in the articles of incorporation if that is desired. However, the term "series" is most widely used in connection with preferred shares the financial terms of which may be established by the board of directors following procedures similar to those set forth in MBCA § 6.02.

4. CLASSES OF COMMON SHARES

Section 6.01 of the MBCA, like all state statutes, authorizes the creation of classes of common shares by appropriate provision in the articles of incorporation; such classes may vary in terms of management, financial or voting rights. For example, classes of nonvoting common shares, classes with multiple or fractional votes per share, classes entitled to twice the dividend of another class, classes entitled to a preference or priority in distributions to another class, and classes entitled to elect a specified number of directors are all permissible. Different classes of common shares are often designated by alphabetical reference, e.g., "Class A common shares," or sometimes by description, e.g., "nonvoting common stock." Classes of common shares are widely used as planning devices in closely held corporations (as are classes of preferred shares).

———

From the foregoing description, it should be clear that the precise line between "preferred" and "common" shares, at the margin at least, was always a shadowy one. There might be little or no difference, for example, between a "participating preferred" and a "Class A common" except the title. Developments during the 1970s and early 1980s also tended to blur this distinction (as well as the distinction between "debt securities" and preferred shares). Extremely high interest rates during this period led to the development of novel financing devices. This period, for example, saw the development of "flexible rate" preferred, where the amount of the dividend was tied to interest rates or some other objective criteria, or left discretionary with the board of directors.

Because of these developments, § 6.01 of the MBCA makes a significant philosophical break with the past by studiously avoiding the words "preferred shares" and "common shares," and by establishing a scheme of consummate generality designed to accommodate the most innovative and ingenious creator of new classes or types of shares.

When considering classes of debt or equity securities, not too much weight should be given to the name. A class may be described as a "senior preferred" and yet be subordinate to virtually all other classes of preferred shares with much more modest titles. Modern equity and debt issues often have unique or fanciful names, e.g., "senior reset preferred stock," debt exchangeable for common stock ("DECS"), or "preferred equity redemption cumulative stock" ("PERCS") that give little or no clue as to either the nature of the securities involved or their investment quality.[5]

Notes

(1) A corporation may create a class of *preferred* shares that is redeemable (callable) at the option of the holder. Such shares have some of the characteristics of a demand note, and are widely used as a financing device. They are not (or arguably may not be) permitted by the statutes of some states.

(2) What about creating *common* shares that are redeemable at the option of the holder? Is there any possible evil that might arise from such shares? Some states prohibit this kind of security except in specified limited circumstances. One well-known and universally accepted example of such shares are shares of "mutual funds" the issuer of which stands ready at any time to redeem shares at net

---

5. For a succinct description of equity-linked securities, see http://www.math.ust.hk/ faculty/maykwok/courses/FINA690G/convert_ secur_ 690G.pdf (*accessed February 19, 2005*).

asset value. Is there any reason to permit redeemable preferred stock, but to prohibit redeemable common stock?

(3) What about creating *common* shares that are callable at the option of the corporation? The great majority of states impose limitations on this type of security or prohibit them entirely. In older versions of the Model Act, a right of redemption at the corporation's option could be created only in connection with shares with preferential rights; several states authorize callable or redeemable common shares only if there is another class of common shares that is not callable or redeemable. E.g. West's, Ann.Cal.Corp.Code § 402; N.Y. McKinney's Bus.Corp. Law § 512(c). What possible evils might be created if the corporation had the power generally to "call" common shares at a predetermined price?

(4) Although it is very common (and universally legal) for preferred stock to be convertible into common stock, most state statutes prohibit shares with an "upstream conversion" right, that is, the right to convert common shares into preferred shares, or to convert either common or preferred shares into debt securities or interests. What possible evils might arise if shareholders generally had the power to convert their equity interests into more senior common stock or into debt?

(5) The MBCA permits the creation of all types of shares referred to in the previous paragraphs without restriction or limitation. Indeed, the MBCA goes even further in some respects, permitting, for example, the creation of shares that are redeemable at the option of a third person, e.g. the holders of other classes of shares, or the creation of shares that are redeemable at a price "determined in accordance with a designated formula or by reference to extrinsic data or events." MBCA § 6.01(c)(2).

Is this total freedom a good idea? It may be justified on several grounds: (1) there is no evidence of demonstrated harm caused by these types of securities in states that permit their use. (2) The rights of classes of shares are determined in part by contractual negotiation, and elimination of restrictions may be justified on the ground of "freedom of contract." (3) Essentially the same results may usually be attained by contractual commitments between investors and the corporation independent of the articles of incorporation, and there seems to be no reason why persons cannot place their commitments in the articles of incorporation if they wish. And, finally, (4) upstream conversions and similar transactions are potentially less damaging to creditors and other senior security holders than the reacquisition of shares by the corporation for cash.

C. ISSUANCE OF SHARES: HEREIN OF SUBSCRIPTIONS, PAR VALUE AND WATERED STOCK

1. SHARE SUBSCRIPTIONS AND AGREEMENTS TO PURCHASE SECURITIES

Historically, the traditional method of raising capital for a new corporation was by public subscriptions pursuant to which persons agreed to purchase a specified number of shares contingent upon a specified amount of capital being raised. Usually these subscriptions were "preincorporation subscriptions" solicited before the corporation was formed; the actual formation of the corporation would occur only if a sufficient number of preincorporation subscriptions had been obtained to assure the success of the venture. After being formed, the corporation would make "calls" on the subscribers for them to actually pay to the corporation the amounts they promised to pay in their subscriptions. The common law of subscription agreements grappled with a number of problems arising from raising capital in this fashion, including the revocability of subscriptions before acceptance, the basis on which calls are to be made, and the remedies available to the new corporation if a subscription was not paid. These issues are now usually resolved in an unambiguous way by statute. See MBCA § 6.20. The use of preincorporation subscription agreements declined in importance with the development of the modern investment banking industry, which permitted large amounts of capital to be raised for a single venture on a nationwide basis.

Subscription agreements may be used to a limited extent in connection with the capitalization of a closely held business with a small number of investors. Modern practice, however, is to use simple contractual agreements to purchase securities rather than a formal subscription agreement. In the words of the annotation to MBCA (1969), "today financing by subscription is the exception." Comment to MBCA (1969) § 17.

2. AUTHORIZATION AND ISSUANCE OF COMMON SHARES UNDER THE MBCA

Assume that a corporation has been formed under the MBCA, and that it is desired to create only a single class of common shares. These shares, or some of them, are to be issued equally to two persons, A and B, for an aggregate consideration of $10,000 in cash or for specified property, the value of which is uncertain but probably about $10,000. How many shares should be authorized, how many shares should be issued, and what price should be established as the issue price for such shares?

Under the MBCA, the answers to these questions simple and straightforward. Any number of shares may be issued at any price so long as the combination (number of shares x price) totals $10,000. It may be 5,000 shares each at $1 per share, 500 shares each at $10 per share, 50 shares each at $100 per share, 5 shares each at $1,000 per share, one share each at $5,000, or any combination in between. The only constraint is that the price be the same for both A and B, since they are buying the same class of shares. Also, the number of shares authorized in the corporation's articles of incorporation must, of course, be at least equal to the number of shares that the corporation plans to issue. Since it is always possible that the corporation will need more capital at a later date, the authorization of some excess shares may be sensible: and it is perfectly legal for a corporation to authorize more shares than it plans to issue. On the other hand, it may not be desirable to authorize vastly more shares than the corporation plans to issue for a couple of reasons. First, limiting the number of shares may protect minority shareholders since a majority shareholder may be able to issue authorized but unissued shares more easily than he can secure an amendment to the articles of incorporation increasing the authorized shares. Since, as will subsequently appear, the issuance of shares in some situations may harm the minority's interest, greater protection is generally given the minority if only the number of shares actually to be issued is authorized. Second, some states impose taxes based on authorized shares: authorizing unnecessary shares may simply increase one's taxes. On balance, most attorneys recommend that some shares be authorized

Hypothetical amt. It doesn't need to be $10k

in excess of what is proposed to be issued, even if there is some additional tax cost.

3. PAR VALUE AND STATED CAPITAL

"Par value" is an arbitrary dollar value assigned to shares of stock which, after being assigned, represents the minimum amount for which each share may be sold. Generally, there is no minimum or maximum value that must be assigned. In most states, shares may also have "no par value," which means that the Board of Directors will assign a value to the stock below which the shares cannot be issued.

In over twenty states, the articles of incorporation must state the "par value" of the shares of each class (or state that the shares are issued "with no par value" or "without par value"). The remaining states, like the MBCA, either have eliminated entirely or made optional the concept of par value.[6] The current trend is toward the elimination of this concept as an historical anomaly. Par value provisions involve archaic and confusing common law concepts of legal capital and watered stock, and, in most jurisdictions that retain the par value concept, they form the basis for restrictions on dividends, corporate share repurchases, and other transactions involving a direct or indirect distribution of corporate assets to shareholders

Consider MBCA (1969), §§ 54(d), 15 (second sentence), 18, 21. As these statutory provisions make clear, par value is established in the articles of incorporation as a fundamental part of the description of the shares. It is whatever amount that is designated as par value by the drafter; it may be one mill, one cent, one dollar, ten dollars, or some other amount. Originally, par value had considerable importance because it was widely viewed as the amount for which shares would be issued: shares with a par value of one hundred dollars per share could be subscribed for at one hundred dollars per share with confidence that all other identical shares would also be issued for $100. In effect, par value originally ensured proportionality of treatment of widely dispersed shareholders, increased confidence in the resale market that the shares had real value (and were not "mere pieces of paper"), and assured the population in general that corporations had in fact been capitalized as advertised by the par values of the shares they issued.

It did not take long, however, for unscrupulous promoters to turn this practice to their own advantage. In the leading case of Hospes v. Northwestern Mfg. & Car Co., 48 Minn. 174, 50 N.W. 1117, 1118 (1892), for example, the Court summarized the allegations of the complaint as follows:

> Briefly stated, the allegations of the complaint are that on May 10, 1882, Seymour, Sabin & Co. owned property of the value of several million dollars, and a business then supposed to be profitable. That, in order to continue and enlarge this business, the parties interested in Seymour, Sabin & Co., with others, organized the car company, to which was sold the greater part of the assets of Seymour, Sabin & Co. at a valuation of $2,267,000, in payment of which there were issued to Seymour, Sabin &

---

6. [By the Editors] The Statutory Supplement contains the provisions of MBCA (1969) relating to par value. The discussion below is tied to these individual provisions, the text of which should be carefully examined. While not all states adopted the 1969 Model Act par value provisions, they are typical of these statutes, and raise the basic issues that must be addressed under all state statutes that retain these concepts.

Co. shares of the preferred stock of the car company of the par value of $2,267,000, it being then and there agreed by both parties that this stock was in full payment of the property thus purchased. It is further alleged that the stockholders of Seymour, Sabin & Co., and the other persons who had agreed to become stockholders in the car company, were then desirous of issuing to themselves, and obtaining for their own benefit, a large amount of common stock of the car company, "without paying therefor, and without incurring any liability thereon or to pay therefor;" and for that purpose, and "in order to evade and set at naught the laws of this state," they caused Seymour, Sabin & Co. to subscribe for and agree to take common stock of the car company of the par value of $1,500,000. That Seymour, Sabin & Co. thereupon subscribed for that amount of the common stock, but never paid therefor any consideration whatever, either in money or property. That thereafter these persons caused this stock to be issued to D.M. Sabin as trustee, to be by him distributed among them. That it was so distributed without receipt by him or the car company from any one of any consideration whatever, but was given by the car company and received by these parties entirely "gratuitously." * * *

The common stock issued by the car company is a species of "watered stock," since the corporation did not receive the par value for the stock when it was issued. What should be done about this? Is there a danger that innocent creditors might rely on the fact that shares with a specified par value are outstanding and assume that the corporation had at least the specified amount of capital? The Court believed that this was a potential problem, and concluded that under some circumstances the recipients of watered shares should be required to pay in the par value even though they had never agreed to do so. The Court, however, had some difficulty with the rationale:

[The plaintiff] plants itself upon the so-called "trust-fund" doctrine that the capital stock of a corporation is a trust fund for the payment of its debts; its contention being that such a "bonus" issue of stock creates, in case of the subsequent insolvency of the corporation, a liability on part of the stockholder in favor of creditors to pay for it, notwithstanding his contract with the corporation to the contrary.

This "trust fund" doctrine, commonly called the "American doctrine," has given rise to much confusion of ideas as to its real meaning, and much conflict of decision in its application. * * * The phrase that "the capital of a corporation constitutes a trust fund for the benefit of creditors" is misleading. Corporate property is not held in trust, in any proper sense of the term. A trust implies two estates or interests—one equitable and one legal; one person, as trustee, holding the legal title, while another, as the *cestui que trust,* has the beneficial interest. Absolute control and power of disposition are inconsistent with the idea of a trust. The capital of a corporation is its property. It has the whole beneficial interest in it, as well as the legal title. It may use the income and profits of it, and sell and dispose of it, the same as a natural person. It is a trustee for its creditors in the same sense and to the same extent as a natural person, but no further. * * *

Another proposition which we think must be sound is that creditors cannot recover on the ground of contract when the corporation could not.

Their right to recover in such cases must rest on the ground that the acts of the stockholders with reference to the corporate capital constitute a fraud on their rights. We have here a case where the contract between the corporation and the takers of the shares was specific that the shares should not be paid for. * * * In such a case the creditors undoubtedly may have rights superior to the corporation, but these rights cannot rest on the implication that the shareholder agreed to do something directly contrary to his real agreement, but must be based on tort or fraud, actual or presumed. In England, since the act of 1867, there is an implied contract created by statute that "every share in any company shall be deemed and be taken to have been issued and to be held subject to the payment of the whole amount thereof in cash." This statutory contract makes every contrary contract void. Such a statute would be entirely just to all, for every one would be advised of its provisions, and could conduct himself accordingly. And in view of the fact that "watered" and "bonus" stock is one of the greatest abuses connected with the management of modern corporations, such a law might, on grounds of public policy, be very desirable. But this is a matter for the legislature, and not for the courts. We have no such statute * * *.

It is well settled that an equity in favor of a creditor does not arise absolutely and in every case to have the holder of "bonus" stock pay for it contrary to his actual contract with the corporation. Thus, no such equity exists in favor of one whose debt was contracted prior to the issue, since he could not have trusted the company upon the faith of such stock. Handley v. Stutz, 139 U.S. 417, 11 Sup.Ct.Rep. 530. It does not exist in favor of a subsequent creditor who has dealt with the corporation with full knowledge of the arrangement by which the "bonus" stock was issued, for a man cannot be defrauded by that which he knows when he acts. It has also been held not to exist where stock has been issued and turned out at its full market value to pay corporate debts. The same has been held to be the case where an active corporation, whose original capital has been impaired, for the purpose of recuperating itself issues new stock, and sells it on the market for the best price obtainable, but for less than par, (Handley v. Stutz, supra) although it is difficult to perceive, in the absence of a statute authorizing such a thing, (of which every one dealing with the corporations is bound to take notice) any difference between the original stock of a new corporation and additional stock issued by a "going concern." It is difficult, if not impossible, to explain or reconcile these cases upon the "trust-fund" doctrine, or, in the light of them, to predicate the liability of the stockholder upon that doctrine. But by putting it upon the ground of fraud, and applying the old and familiar rules of law on that subject to the peculiar nature of a corporation and the relation which its stockholders bear to it and to the public, we have at once rational and logical ground on which to stand. The capital of a corporation is the basis of its credit. It is a substitute for the individual liability of those who own its stock. People deal with it and give it credit on the faith of it. They have a right to assume that it has paid in capital to the amount which it represents itself as having; and if they give it credit on the faith of that representation, and if the representation is false, it is a fraud upon them; and, in case the corporation becomes insolvent, the law, upon the plainest principles of common justice, says to the delinquent stockholder, make that representation good by paying for your stock. It certainly cannot require the invention of any new doctrine in order to enforce so familiar a rule of equity. It is the misrepresentation of fact in stating the amount of capital to be greater than it really is that is the true basis of the liability of the stockholder in such cases; and it follows that it is only those creditors who have relied, or who can fairly be presumed to have relied, upon the professed amount of capital, in whose favor the law will recognize and enforce an equity against the holders of "bonus" stock. This furnishes a rational and uniform rule, to which familiar principles are easily applied, and which frees the subject from many of the difficulties and apparent inconsistencies into which the "trust-fund" doctrine has involved it; and we think that, even when the trust-fund doctrine has been invoked, the decision in almost every well-considered case is readily referable to such a rule.

50 N.W., at 1119–21. The Court then concluded that subsequent creditors should not be required to allege and prove affirmatively that they relied on the capital represented by the bonus shares, but that lack of reliance might be a defense. In other words, the capitalization of a corporation as established by the par values of its issued shares was a public representation on which subsequent creditors might rely and compel the shareholders to make good their representation, unless the corporation could establish that the creditors extended credit knowing the represented capital was not there. Finally, the Court concluded that the particular plaintiff involved in the Hospes case (a newly formed corporation that had bought up claims against the original car company at significant discounts) had not sufficiently alleged its own bona fides to be allowed to maintain suit.

Notes

(1) The shares issued by the car company in the Hospes case are usually described as "bonus shares," because nothing was paid for them. "Watered shares" are technically shares issued for property worth less than their par value, while "discount shares" are shares issued for cash but less than par. All three types are usually lumped under the single phrase "watered stock." As indicated in *Hospes,* recipients of such shares are potentially liable to subsequent creditors of the corporation.

(2) The notion that funds paid in for stock constitute a "trust fund" for creditors has a strange fascination for many courts. See e.g. Wood v. Dummer, 30 Fed.Cas. 435, No. 17,944 (C.C.Me.1824). While most of these cases are old, the language appears in some fairly recent decisions, and it is possible that it may influence decisions in some cases. The idea that corporate capital constitutes a "trust fund" is a fiction for the reasons recognized in the quoted excerpts from *Hospes.* For a short and convincing explanation of why the "trust fund" argument is circular and indeterminate, see C. Robert Morris, Some Notes on "Reliance," 75 Minn. L.Rev. 815, 815–20 (1991).

HANEWALD v. BRYAN'S INC.

Supreme Court of North Dakota, 1988.
429 N.W.2d 414.

MESCHKE, JUSTICE.

Harold E. Hanewald appealed from that part of his judgment for $38,600 plus interest against Bryan's, Inc. which refused to impose personal liability upon Keith, Joan, and George Bryan for that insolvent corporation's debt. We reverse the ruling that Keith and Joan Bryan were not personally liable.

On July 19, 1984, Keith and Joan Bryan incorporated Bryan's, Inc. to "engage in and operate a general retail clothing, and related items, store * * *." The Certificate of Incorporation was issued by the Secretary of State on July 25, 1984. The first meeting of the board of directors elected Keith Bryan as president and Joan Bryan as secretary-treasurer of Bryan's, Inc. George Bryan was elected vice-president, appointed registered agent, and designated manager of the prospective business. The Articles of Incorporation authorized the corporation to issue "100 shares of common stock with a par value of $1,000 per share" with "total authorized capitalization [of] $100,000.00." Bryan's, Inc. issued 50 shares of stock to Keith Bryan and 50 shares of stock to Joan Bryan. The trial court found that "Bryan's, Inc. did not receive any payment, either in labor, services, money, or property, for the stock which was issued."

On August 30, 1984, Hanewald sold his dry goods store in Hazen to Bryan's, Inc. Bryan's, Inc. bought the inventory, furniture, and fixtures of the business for $60,000, and leased the building for $600 per month for a period of five years. Bryan's, Inc. paid Hanewald $55,000 in cash and gave him a promissory note for $5,000, due August 30, 1985, for the remainder of the purchase price. The $55,000 payment to Hanewald was made from a loan by the Union State Bank of Hazen to the corporation, personally guaranteed by Keith and Joan Bryan.

Bryan's, Inc. began operating the retail clothing store on September 1, 1984. The business, however, lasted only four months with an operating loss of $4,840. In late December 1984, Keith and Joan Bryan decided to close the Hazen store. Thereafter, George Bryan, with the assistance of a brother and local employees, packed and removed the remaining inventory and delivered it for resale to other stores in Montana operated by the Bryan family. Bryan's, Inc. sent a "Notice of Rescission" to Hanewald on January 3, 1985, in an attempt to avoid the lease. The corporation was involuntarily dissolved by operation of law on August 1, 1986, for failure to file its annual report with the Secretary of State.

Bryan's, Inc. did not pay the $5,000 promissory note to Hanewald, but paid off the rest of its creditors. Debts paid included the $55,000 loan from Union State Bank and a $10,000 loan from Keith and Joan Bryan. The Bryan loan had been, according to the trial court, "intended to be used for operating costs and expenses."

Hanewald sued the corporation and the Bryans for breach of the lease agreement and the promissory note, seeking to hold the Bryans personally liable. The defendants counterclaimed, alleging that Hanewald had fraudulently misrepresented the business' profitability in negotiating its sale. After a trial without a jury, the trial court entered judgment against Bryan's, Inc. for $38,600 plus interest on Hanewald's claims and ruled against the defendants on their counterclaim. The defendants have not cross appealed these rulings.

The trial court, however, refused to hold the individual defendants personally liable for the judgment against Bryan's, Inc., stating:

Trial Crt. Says only Corp. is liable

> Bryan's, Inc. was formed in a classic manner, the $10,000.00 loan by Keith Bryan being more than sufficient operating capital. Bryan's, Inc. paid all obligations except the obligation to Hanewald in a timely fashion, and since there was no evidence of bad faith by the Bryans, the corporate shield of Bryan's, Inc. should not be pierced.

Reason: Corp. was on up and up so no viel piercing

Hanewald appealed from the refusal to hold the individual defendants personally liable.

Insofar as the judgment fails to impose personal liability upon Keith and Joan Bryan, the corporation's sole shareholders, we agree with Hanewald that the trial court erred. We base our decision on the Bryans' statutory duty to pay for shares that were issued to them by Bryan's, Inc.

Organizing a corporation to avoid personal liability is legitimate. Indeed, it is one of the primary advantages of doing business in the corporate form. However, the limited personal liability of shareholders does not come free. As this court said in *Bryan v. Northwest Beverages*, 69 N.D. 274, 285 N.W. 689, 694 (1939), "[t]he mere formation of a corporation, fixing the amount of its capital stock, and receiving a certificate of incorporation, do not create anything of value upon which the company can do business." It is the shareholders' initial capital investments which protects their personal assets from further liability in the corporate enterprise. Thus, generally, shareholders are not liable for corporate debts beyond the capital they have contributed to the corporation.

capital investment is what creates corp. shield in this state, not certificate of incorporation.

This protection for corporate shareholders was codified in the statute in effect when Bryan's, Inc. was incorporated and when this action was commenced * * *. [The Court quotes MBCA (1969) § 25, first paragraph.] This statute obligated shareholders to pay for their shares as a prerequisite for their limited personal liability.

The kinds of consideration paid for corporate shares may vary. Article XII, § 9 of the state constitution says that "[n]o corporation shall issue stock or bonds except for money, labor done, or money or property actually received; and all fictitious increase of stock or indebtedness shall be void." [The Court summarizes and quotes from MBCA (1969) § 19.] The purpose of these constitutional and statutory provisions is "to protect the public and those dealing with the corporation * * *." *Bryan v. Northwest Beverages, supra*, 285 N.W. at 694.

In this case, Bryan's, Inc. was authorized to issue 100 shares of stock each having a par value of $1,000. Keith Bryan and Joan Bryan, two of the original incorporators and members of the board of directors, were each issued 50 shares. The trial court determined that "Bryan's, Inc. did not receive any payment, either in labor, services, money, or property, for the stock which was issued." Bryans have not challenged this finding of fact on this appeal. We hold that Bryans' failure to pay for their shares in the corporation makes them personally liable under [MBCA (1969) § 25], for the corporation's debt to Hanewald.

Drafters' comments to § 25 of the Model Business Corporation Act, * * * sketched the principles:

> The liability of a subscriber for the unpaid portion of his subscription and the liability of a shareholder for the unpaid balance of the full consideration for which his shares were issued are based upon contract principles. The liability of a shareholder to whom shares are issued for overvalued property or services is a breach of contract. These liabilities have not been considered to be exceptions to the absolute limited liability concept.

> Where statutes have been silent, courts have differed as to whether the cause of action on the liabilities of shareholders for unpaid consideration for shares issued or to be issued may be asserted by a creditor directly, by the corporation itself or its receiver, or by a creditor on behalf of the corporation. The Model Act is also silent on the subject for the reason that it can be better treated elsewhere." 1 Model Business Corporation Act Annotated 2d, Comment to § 25, at pp. 509–510 (1971).

This court, in *Marshall–Wells Hardware Co. v. New Era Coal Co.*, 13 N.D. 396, 100 N.W. 1084 (1904), held that creditors could directly enforce shareholders' liabilities to pay for shares held by them under statutes analogous to [MBCA (1969) § 25]. We believe that the shareholder liability created by [MBCA (1969) § 25] may likewise be enforced in a direct action by a creditor of the corporation.

Our conclusion comports with the generally recognized rule, derived from common law, that "a shareholder is liable to corporate creditors to the extent his stock has not been paid for." 18A Am.Jur.2d *Corporations* § 863 (1985). *See also, id.* at §§ 906 and 907. One commentator has observed:

> For a corporation to issue its stock as a gratuity violates the rights of existing stockholders who do not consent, and is a fraud upon subsequent subscribers, and upon subsequent creditors who deal with it on the faith of its capital stock. The former may sue to enjoin the issue of the stock, or to cancel it if it has been issued, and has not reached the hands of a bona fide purchaser; and the latter, according to the weight of authority, may compel payment by the person to whom it was issued, to such extent as may be necessary for the payment of their claims. 11 W. Fletcher, *Cyclopedia of the Law of Private Corporations* § 5202, at p. 450 (1986).

The shareholder "is liable to the extent of the difference between the par value and the amount actually paid," and "to such an extent only as may be necessary for the satisfaction of" the creditor's claim. 11 W. Fletcher, *supra*, § 5241, at pp. 550, 551.

The defendants asserted, and the trial court ruled, that the $10,000 loan from Keith and Joan Bryan to the corporation was nevertheless "more than sufficient operating capital" to run the business. However, a shareholder's loan is a debt, not an asset, of the corporation. Where, as here, a loan was repaid by the corporation to the shareholders before its operations were abandoned, the loan cannot be considered a capital contribution.[7]

We conclude that the trial court, having found that Keith and Joan Bryan had not paid for their stock, erred as a matter of law in refusing to hold them personally liable for the corporation's debt to Hanewald. The debt to Hanewald does not exceed the difference between the par value of their stock and the amount they actually paid. Therefore, we reverse in part to remand for entry of judgment holding Keith and Joan Bryan jointly and severally liable for the entire corporate debt to Hanewald. The judgment is otherwise affirmed.

Notes

(1) Is the liability imposed on the Bryans based on the theories developed in the Hospes case, or does it arise from the force of the statutes themselves? Under MBCA (1969), is there watered stock liability if:

(a) The directors fraudulently recite that property is worth $2,000 when it is really worth only $1,000, and then issue shares with a par value of $2,000 for it?

(b) The directors reasonably and nonfraudulently recite that property is worth $1,000, but then issue shares with a par value of $2,000 for it? As a practical matter, the last paragraph of MBCA (1969) § 19 eliminates many potential problems in this area.

(2) In most states watered stock liability arises only in connection with the original issuance of shares. If a corporation reacquires some of its shares after they have been lawfully issued, it may resell those shares at any price it desires without giving rise to watered stock liability. The theory is that these shares remain "issued" even though they are held in the corporation's treasury and their resale at less than par does not water the corporation's stock account. These shares (called "treasury shares") have an intermediate status under most statutes: they are not viewed as "outstanding" for purposes of dividends, quorum, and voting purposes, but are viewed as "issued" so that their "reissuance" does not violate the restrictions imposed by the par value statutes. See Brumfield v. Horn, 547 So.2d 415 (Ala.1989). There is some contrary authority. MBCA § 6.31 eliminates the concept of treasury shares (for reasons to be discussed later) and treats reacquired shares as authorized but unissued shares. However, most states still retain the concept of treasury shares.

4. ELIGIBLE AND INELIGIBLE CONSIDERATION FOR SHARES

Consider MBCA (1969) § 19. The idea that only the actual receipt of certain types of property or services by a corporation will support the issuance of shares is not technically a part of the par value structure, but it is closely

---

7. [By the Court] There are some circumstances in which a shareholder's loan to the corporation may be treated as a capital contribution. *See* 12B W. Fletcher, *Cyclopedia of the Law of Private Corporations* § 5739 (1984). In bankruptcy proceedings, for example, a shareholder's loans to his corporation can be treated as capital contributions when a corporation is deemed undercapitalized. *See Pepper v. Litton*, 308 U.S. 295, 60 S.Ct. 238, 84 L.Ed. 281 (1939). However, the result in this class of cases is an equitable subordination of the shareholder's claim to the claims of other creditors, which is consistent in principle with the result we reach today.

aligned with it and must be taken into account whenever shares are being issued under a traditional statute.

What purpose is served by § 19? There are at least two possibilities: first, it was designed to protect creditors of the corporation who may rely on its capital in extending credit, since it attempts to assure that there is something "real" which can be levied against and sold; second, it may protect other investors (who invest "real" assets such as money or property) from dilution of their interests.

What happens when shares are issued for a combination of past and future services in a jurisdiction in which it is legal to issue shares for services already provided, but not for future services? In a jurisdiction like Delaware that is favorably-disposed to the idea that there is nothing wrong with issuing shares for future services, a court held that all stock issued in consideration for a combination of past and future services is presumed valid unless the party challenging the validity of the consideration paid can allocate the part of the stock that was issued for past services and the part issued for future services. See Coates v. Parnassus Systems, Inc., 2002 WL 534595 (Tex.App.—Austin, 2002).

Obviously, in some circumstances a contract to perform services may have considerable value. If Jane Fonda enters into a contract to perform in a film, the producer could presumably borrow large sums solely on the strength of the Fonda contract. If Ms. Fonda is to receive a twenty-five percent interest in the corporation producing the film, can the corporation issue shares to her reflecting that interest when she signs the contract? If not, how can she be given the interest that her contract entitles her to at the outset of the filming?

Consider, on the other hand, John Q. Promoter, who sells 75 percent of his newly formed corporation's shares to outsiders for cash, and issues the remaining 25 percent to himself in exchange for his contract to perform services of an indefinite nature in the future. The investors determine that Promoter's future services are of no benefit to the corporation. Section 19 of MBCA (1969) may permit the corporation to cancel the shares issued to Promoter, thus allowing the investors to avoid dilution of their interests in the corporation. Is there any basis for attacking such a transaction on grounds other than § 19?

Shares issued for a promissory note are also prohibited by MBCA (1969) § 19. Again it is possible to divine an intention either to protect creditors of the corporation or to protect other investors who contribute cash while the promoter puts in an uncollectible promissory note. Courts have held that if a corporation does issue shares for a promissory note in violation of this section, the corporation may nevertheless enforce the note; the corporation, however, also may be able to cancel the offending shares for failing to comply with § 19. Presumably, a note executed by John D. Rockefeller is "as good as gold," and yet shares cannot be issued to John D. in exchange for that note. On the other hand, if John D.'s note is owned by a third person, Pam Smith, may Smith be issued shares in consideration of John D.'s note?

Another problem may be raised by the language in MBCA (1969) § 19, "other property, tangible or intangible." What about claimed secret processes, formulas, conditional or contingent contract rights, "good will," capitalized research costs that have not yet led to a marketable product, and other intangible "property"? Intangibles are often not only difficult to value; their very existence may be so ephemeral as not to constitute "property" at all in the eyes of some courts, at least for purposes of § 19. There are several decisions in which this question has been raised, usually in the context of seeking to cancel shares issued in exchange for such "property."

Notes

(1) What about issuing shares for a promise to pay money in the future that is not evidenced by a promissory note? Is not that literally permitted by MBCA (1969) § 19? The New York analogue to this section uses the phrase "obligations of the subscriber for future payments" rather than "promissory notes." N.Y.— McKinney's Bus.Corp.Law § 504(b). What about a *secured* promissory note? General Bonding & Casualty Ins. Co. v. Moseley, 110 Tex. 529, 222 S.W. 961 (1920), held that a note secured by a valid first trust lien on real estate was permissible consideration; cf. American Radiator & Standard Sanitary Corp. v. United States, 155 Ct.Cl. 515, 295 F.2d 939 (1961). For a case upholding the issue of shares for services of uncertain value previously rendered, see Haft v. Dart Group, 841 F.Supp. 549, 573 (D.Del.1993).

(2) As indicated in the text, these restrictions on eligible consideration for shares are not technically part of the par value structure. A state may abolish par value and yet decide to retain these traditional restrictions on eligible consideration (as California, for example, has done). North Dakota and several other states have placed language similar to MBCA (1969) § 19 in their state constitutions. In these states, it may not be possible to abolish par value and other aspects of the legal capital regime without constitutional amendments.

(3) Consider MBCA §§ 6.21(b), 6.21(d), 6.21(e). Do these sections provide adequate protection against a transaction like that of John Q. Promoter referred to in the text? In many cases, of course, the corporation will elect to follow the escrow procedure suggested in § 6.21(e), thereby avoiding possible dilution. MBCA § 6.21(d) may initially appear to be a completely pro-corporation provision; in fact, it was primarily intended as a pro-lawyer provision, to provide the basis for subsequent legal opinions that outstanding shares were validly issued and non-assessable without requiring a historical review of a transaction that may have occurred many years earlier. Courts have not applied this statute broadly and literally. For example, Haft v. Dart Group Corporation, 1994 WL 643185 (Del.Ch. Nov. 14, 1994), held that a similar provision does not preclude a shareholder from attacking grants of options to purchase shares at favorable prices because they constituted gift or waste.

(4) The Official Comment to MBCA § 6.21 states that the term "benefit" should be "broadly construed to include, for example, a reduction of a liability, a release of a claim, or benefits obtained by a corporation by contribution of its shares to a charitable organization or as a prize in a promotion." For a thoughtful analysis of appropriate non-profit maximizing corporate conduct, see Melvin Aron Eisenberg, Corporate Conduct that Does Not Maximize Shareholder Gain: Legal Conduct, Ethical Conduct, the Penumbra Effect, Reciprocity, the Prisoner's Dilemma, Sheep's Clothing, Social Conduct, and Disclosure, 28 Stetson L.Rev. 1 (1998).

(5) The Official Comment to § 6.21 also states that "[i]n the realities of commercial life, there is sometimes a need for the issuance of shares for contract rights or * * * intangible property or benefits." Do you agree? If you were

drafting a new corporation statute, would you follow § 6.21 in this regard, or would you retain some or all of old § 19?

5. PAR VALUE IN MODERN PRACTICE

The early practice of creating shares with a par value equal to the proposed issuance price long ago fell into disuse. Today, the practice most often followed is to use "nominal" par value that is one cent, ten cents, or one dollar per share when the shares are issued for several dollars or more per share. The use of no par shares—for reasons discussed below—is a distant second.[8] Under current practice, par value serves only a minor function and is in no way an indication of the price at which the shares are issued. There is, however, one significant carryover from the earlier practice: to avoid watered stock liability the issuance price for shares of stock with par value must always be equal to or greater than par value.

Several factors caused the movement away from par value as a representation of the purchase price of shares and the development of nominal par value shares. Doubtless, concern about watered stock liability, particularly where property of uncertain value is being contributed, was a factor. If high par value shares are given in exchange for such property, arguments may later arise that the property was not worth the par value of the shares received and the recipients might be sued for the difference. Another factor was the possible loss of flexibility of pricing shares. When a secondary market for previously issued shares develops, a corporation raising capital by selling shares in effect competes with that market. A corporation issuing shares with a par value of $100 may not be able to reduce the price below that figure and may have to stop selling shares if the market price of the previously-issued shares dropped below $100 per share. (At that point interested investors can get a better price by buying previously issued shares in the secondary market than they can from the corporation which is locked into the $100 price by the par value.)

Still another factor was that nominal par shares increase corporate flexibility in making distributions in the future. Consider MBCA (1969) § 21, and its possible application to "high par," "nominal par," and "no par" alternatives when forming a corporation. Consider the following alternatives:

(i) The corporation issues 10 shares of $100 par value stock for $1,000 in cash.

(ii) The corporation issues 10 shares of $1 par value stock for $1,000 in cash.

(iii) The corporation issues 10 shares of no par value stock for $1,000 in cash.

The appropriate accounting for alternatives (i) and (ii) are as follows:

Alternative (i)		
Assets	Liabilities	0
Cash 1000	Capital accounts	
	Stated Capital	1000

8. [By the Editors] The fact that a case such as Hanewald v. Bryan's Inc. arose in the 1980s can be explained only on the basis that the person forming the corporation was unaware of modern practice and the dangers of placing a high par value on shares.

		Capital Surplus	0
	1000		1000

Alternative (ii)

Assets		Liabilities	0
Cash	1000	Capital accounts	
		Stated Capital	10
		Capital Surplus	990
	1000		1000

In connection with alternative (iii), MBCA (1969) § 21 provides that the entire $1,000 should be treated as stated capital unless the directors determine to allocate to capital surplus "any portion of the consideration received for the issuance of such shares." (Does "any portion" include "all"?) Not all states give the directors total freedom to allocate the proceeds from no par shares to capital surplus. Some states do not permit such allocation at all (in which case, alternative (iii) becomes identical to alternative (i)), while others permit only a partial allocation. Before 1985, Texas, for example, permitted allocation of only 25 percent of the consideration to capital surplus. Vernon's Ann.Tex.Stat.Bus.Corp.Act, art. 2.17B (1980). Assuming that such a restriction is applicable, and the directors elect to classify the maximum amount possible to capital surplus, alternative (iii) becomes:

Alternative (iii)

Assets		Liabilities	0
Cash	1000	Capital accounts	
		Stated Capital	750
		Capital Surplus	250
	1000		1000

Now, a logical question is: What difference does it make if the capital contribution is recorded as stated capital or capital surplus? Rather surprisingly, it does make a difference, which can best be appreciated if a balance sheet is drawn up after the corporation (financed as suggested in alternative (ii)) has (1) borrowed $1,000 from a bank, and (2) had two years of operations during which it has earned and accumulated an aggregate of $2,000 from its earnings. Further, for simplicity, it will be assumed that all of the assets are held by the corporation in the form of cash. The balance sheet looks like this:

Assets		Liabilities	$1,000
Cash	$4,000	Capital accounts	
		Earned Surplus	$2,000
		Stated Capital	10
		Capital Surplus	990
	$4,000		$4,000

At this point the shareholders decide they want to distribute to themselves some or all of the $4,000. If the balance sheet is to continue to balance, every dollar taken from the left-hand column must obviously be reflected by the reduction of a right-hand column entry. The significance of the right-hand entries is that they in effect limit or monitor the distribution of assets from the left-hand column. The distributions permitted by a corporation are evaluated in accordance with MBCA (1969) §§ 45, 46, and 6.

Under these statutes, capitalizing a corporation with large amounts of capital surplus gave that corporation greater freedom and flexibility to make distributions or reacquire its own shares than it would have had if it were capitalized with large amounts of stated capital. In the above examples, the corporation, no matter how capitalized, could use the $2,000 of earned surplus to reacquire shares or make a distribution to shareholders. However, the corporation capitalized solely with stated capital (alternative (i)) would be limited to that amount; the corporation created with no par shares (alternative (iii)) would have available for distribution an additional $250 of capital surplus, for total potential distributions of $2250; the corporation capitalized most flexibly (alternative (ii)) could legally distribute $2990 out of its assets (subject, however, to the general insolvency tests in the 1969 Model Act). Admittedly, this increase in flexibility does not seem to be of earthshaking significance, and indeed may raise policy questions about whether corporations should have the freedom to distribute virtually all their capital as permitted in alternative (ii).

Where the consideration for no par shares may be allocated to capital surplus without limitation (as permitted by § 18 of MBCA (1969)), either no par or nominal par shares give the same amount of freedom. No par shares, however, ever gained the popularity and widespread use of nominal par shares. One factor that, in the past, undoubtedly encouraged the use of nominal par shares, and discouraged the use of both high par and no par, was the federal excise tax statute, repealed in 1965, that imposed a documentary stamp tax on issues and transfers of securities. This tax was based on "the par or face value of each certificate" of par value stock and "the actual value of each certificate" of no-par stock. I.R.C. § 4301 (1954), repealed by Pub.L. No. 89–44, Tit. IV, § 401(a), 79 Stat. 148 (1965). Several states may continue to measure their taxes on a similar basis.

TED J. FIFLIS, HOMER KRIPKE, & PAUL M. FOSTER, ACCOUNTING FOR BUSINESS LAWYERS
(4th ed. 1991), p. 433.[9]

* * * [A] prospective creditor who inspects the balance sheet of a corporation and finds a low par or stated capital and most of the net worth embodied in capital surplus should know * * * that corporation laws to some extent permit the distribution of capital surplus as well as earned surplus to stockholders, giving creditors no protection beyond the legal capital consisting of par or stated capital.

Not equally well-known is the fact that just as lawyers minimized the effect of the rule that the legal capital must be paid-in to the corporation, by use of low par or low stated value no-par stock, so too they minimized the effect of the rule limiting distributions out of legal capital by various techniques permitting reduction of legal capital without creditors' approval. The conclusion is that corporation law provides creditors with very little actual protection * * *.

As a result creditors today do not rely upon statutory protection against shareholder distributions. Trade creditors rely instead on security interests or

9. Reprinted with permission from West Publishing Corporation.

careful monitoring of their receivables while commercial lenders require disclosure of financial data, security interests, and contractual limitations on distributions. It is in the areas of disclosure and statutory and contractual limitations that the practitioner must understand the accounting in order to serve his clients properly. * * *

Notes

(1) Is there any public relations value in the use of high par value stock? Is such stock desirable in order to ensure protection to creditors? Does a high par value tend to keep share prices high? What problems can high par value stock create for a corporation? Of course, from the creditors' standpoint, assets reflected as stated capital are somewhat preferable to assets reflected as capital surplus since they are more "locked in" and unavailable for distribution to shareholders. Consider, however, MBCA (1969) § 58(d), (e), (h), and (i).

(2) It is important to distinguish conceptually between "no par shares" in states that retain the par value structure, and shares issued in states that, like the MBCA, have eliminated par value. The issuance of "no par shares" in par value states affects the stated capital and capital surplus accounts, may create watered stock liability in certain circumstances, and may affect the distributions a corporation may lawfully make. States that have eliminated the par value structure have eliminated the watered stock concept and have also generally eliminated mandatory capital accounts. They have also established different rules relating to when distributions lawfully may be made.

(3) Of course, it is not strictly true that the MBCA has "eliminated" the concept of par value. See MBCA § 2.02(b)(2)(iv). The Official Comment explains that optional par value provisions may be of use "to corporations which are to be qualified in foreign jurisdictions in that franchise or other taxes are computed upon the basis of par value." In addition, optional par value may also be given effect "essentially as a matter of contract between the parties." Where a corporation formed in a state that has abolished par value contemplates multistate operations, lawyers usually recommend that an optional par value be adopted to minimize tax consequences if the corporation becomes subject to taxation in a state that uses par value as a measure of tax liability.

TORRES v. SPEISER

Supreme Court, Appellate Division, New York, 2000.
268 A.D.2d 253, 701 N.Y.S.2d 360.

MEMORANDUM DECISION.

Order, Supreme Court, Bronx County (Kenneth Thompson, Jr., J.), entered December 24, 1998, which denied plaintiff's motion for partial summary judgment with respect to his claim that the sale of his minority interest in defendant corporation to the individual defendant is invalid, unanimously affirmed, without costs.

There is no merit to plaintiff's argument that the sale of his stock is invalid under Business Corporation Law § 504 because the price of the stock was less than its par value and such defect could not be cured by the individual defendant's promises of future consideration. While section 504 prohibits an initial issuance of stock in a new corporation for less than par value or before the full purchase price is paid, it has no bearing on a re-sale of issued shares among shareholders, as occurred here (see, Vohra v. Prasad Realty Corp., 174 A.D.2d 735, 571 N.Y.S.2d 768). Nor can summary judgment be granted to plaintiff on the ground that the individual defendant's promises to assist him in establishing a check cashing business in Puerto Rico that he was to manage, and to establish a corporation to own that business the stock of which was to be divided between himself and defendant in a "mutually acceptable manner", were material terms of his agreement to retransfer his stock that are so indefinite as not to be susceptible to enforcement, and that the entire transaction therefore was nothing more than an unenforceable agreement to agree. There are issues of fact in this regard as to partial performance of the purported agreement. We have considered defendant's other arguments and find them unpersuasive.

Note

This case illustrates the narrow role played by the concept of par value in modern corporation law. Par value relates only to the original issuance of shares, and has no application whatever to subsequent transactions in the shares themselves, which may be bought or sold at any mutually acceptable price. The role of par value is declining in other contexts as well. For example, before 1992 in Texas, certain corporate taxes were computed on the basis of the corporation's "taxable capital." Taxable capital included both the corporation's "stated capital" and its "surplus." Stated capital was defined as the sum of the par value of all shares of the corporation having a par value that have been issued plus the consideration fixed by the corporation for all shares without par value that have been issued. Surplus was defined as the corporation's net assets less its "stated capital." Under this tax regime, capital-intensive industries bore the brunt of the tax, even in unprofitable years. In 1991, the legislature amended the franchise-tax act to establish "earned surplus" as the tax base from which to calculate the major portion of a corporation's franchise tax. "Earned surplus" is the corporation's reportable federal net income, less certain foreign-source income, plus officer and director compensation. As applicable here, "[t]he rates of the franchise tax are * * * 0.25 percent per year of privilege period of net taxable capital; and * * * 4.5 percent of net taxable earned surplus." See Rylander v. Palais Royal, Inc., 81 S.W.3d 909, 912–13 (Tex.App.—Austin, 2002).

D.   DEBT FINANCING

"Bonds" and "debentures" are evidences of long term indebtedness that are usually referred to as "debt securities." Both involve unconditional promises to pay a stated sum in the future, and to make payments of interest periodically until then. Technically, a "debenture" is an unsecured corporate obligation while a "bond" is secured by a lien or mortgage on corporate property. However, the word "bond" is often used indiscriminately to cover both bonds and debentures. Bonds and debentures historically were payable to bearer; anyone in possession of the piece of paper could obtain payment of the debt; the owner kept debt securities in a lock box to protect against theft. Interest coupons reflecting the periodic obligation to pay interest were attached to each debt security. Each coupon was a promise to make a specified payment of interest on a specific date. As the date an interest payment became due approached, the owner would cut off ("clip" was the verb universally used) the interest coupon and submit it to the corporation for payment.

A registered bond is one that has been registered in the name of a specific individual and from which the coupons have been removed; interest is paid directly to the registered owner by check. All new bonds are issued today in registered form in order to minimize income tax evasion. Of course, registered bonds are freely transferable.[10]

In recent years, novel types of debt instruments have been created, and new words have entered the common vocabulary. Zero coupon bonds, often called "zeroes," pay no interest at all; they sell at a substantial discount from face value and upon maturity the holder receives the face value. The entire difference between original issue price and face value represents interest payable upon the maturity of the "zero."[11] Junk bonds, widely used in takeovers, are simply below investment-grade debt instruments. Many other novel variations exist. See generally Robert W. Hamilton and Richard A. Booth, Business Basics for Law Students: Essential Terms and Concepts and Applications (Third Ed.), §§ 14.20–14.25.

While primary attention is paid to equity securities in this casebook, it should be pointed out that from an economic standpoint, debt financing is considerably more important than equity financing. Most large publicly held corporations regularly engage in debt financing but rarely raise capital through issuance of equity securities. Indeed, in recent years many publicly held corporations have reduced the amount of equity securities outstanding through repurchases of shares while at the same time increasing their outstanding indebtedness.

Even greater reliance on debt is common in European capital markets because the introduction of the euro eliminated currency risk between EU member nations. Government bonds in Europe are trading at near all-time lows, and many companies are refinancing debt at a lower cost. The high-yield issuance market has grown as well, but is still young compared to the U.S. market. In Europe, the bond market has been enhanced by the slowdown of the equities markets. When, as at present, interest rates are low and equity markets are weak, borrowers in need of financing find it cheaper to issue bonds.[12]

---

10. [By the Editors] Other typical characteristics of debt securities are: (1) Interest payments are usually fixed obligations, due in any event, and expressed as a percentage of the face amount of the security. However, income bonds, which condition the obligation to pay interest on adequate corporate earnings, are also used. Somewhat rarer are so-called participating bonds, where the interest obligation increases with corporate earnings. (2) Debt securities are usually subject to redemption, permitting the corporation to pay off the obligation before it is due, often at a premium over the face value. (3) Debt securities may be subordinated to the payment of other obligations. (4) Debt securities may be convertible into other classes of stock, usually common stock. Convertible debentures are treated as equity securities for many purposes. See, e.g.,

15 U.S.C.A. § 78c(a)(11). (5) Some states authorize holders of bonds or debentures to participate in the selection of the board of directors upon specified contingencies. Many of these characteristics are also present in preferred shares.

11. [By the Editors] For income tax purposes, however, a holder of a "zero" must include in taxable income an allocable portion of the discount even though it is not to be received until some time in the distant future; as a result, "zeroes" are attractive investments primarily for tax-exempt or tax-deferred entities.

12. Standard & Poor's, EU Bond Market Resilient Despite Economic Slowdown, at http://www.gtnews.com/articles6/4194.pdf.

As has previously been indicated, the distinction between debt and equity may not be at all clear at the margin. It is usually advantageous to engage to some extent in debt financing. The notion that the best business is a debt-free business, while sounding attractive, is not consistent either with the minimization of income taxes or with the maximization of profits. A sharp distinction must be drawn, however, between debt owed to third persons, and debt owed to shareholders.

1. THE CONCEPT OF LEVERAGE

Debt owed to third persons creates leverage. Leverage is favorable to the borrower when the borrower is able to earn more on the borrowed capital than the cost of the borrowing. The entire excess is allocable to the equity accounts of the corporation, thereby increasing the rate of return on the equity invested in the corporation. An example should help to make this clear. Assume that a corporation has a total invested capital of $500,000. Let us consider the earnings per share on two alternative assumptions: (a) all this capital is invested as equity capital, e.g., 50,000 shares sold at $10.00 per share, and (b) half is borrowed on a long-term basis, and the other half is contributed capital, e.g., 25,000 shares sold at $10.00 per share.

ALTERNATIVE A

Assumed net earnings	$25,000	$100,000	$150,000	$200,000
Number of shares	50,000	50,000	50,000	50,000
Earnings per share	$ 0.50	$ 2.00	$ 3.00	$ 4.00

ALTERNATIVE B

Assumed net earnings	$25,000	$100,000	$150,000	$200,000
Interest on bonds (8% on $250,000)	$20,000	$ 20,000	$ 20,000	$ 20,000
Earnings allocable to common[13]	$ 5,000	$ 80,000	$130,000	$180,000
Number of shares	25,000	25,000	25,000	25,000
Earnings per share	$ 0.20	$ 3.20	$ 5.20	$ 7.20

In alternative B, the interest represents a fixed claim, i.e. the charge for obtaining the use of $250,000 of capital. When earnings are low, debt service takes up most of the earnings: in the hypothetical above, if earnings drop below $20,000, alternative B will show losses while alternative A continues to show modest profits until earnings drop to zero. When earnings increase above $20,000, however, the per share earnings under alternative B rise much more rapidly than alternative A even though the shares are otherwise identical. In effect, in alternative B, the common shareholders are getting $500,000 to work for them even though they contributed only $250,000, at the cost of the fixed interest charge which they must meet out of their own capital if necessary. Even this fixed charge is partially offset by the tax saving resulting from the deductibility of the interest.[14] This is leverage, a device well

---

13. [By the Editors] Computed simply by subtraction and without regard to reduction in income taxes as a result of the increased interest deduction.

14. [By the Editors] Nonparticipating preferred stock owned by third persons also creates leverage, which technically is a phenomenon of a senior, limited position rather than of

understood by real estate syndicates and promoters who seek to obtain the largest possible mortgage and the smallest possible equity investment of their own. The risk, of course, is that the income from the project may not be sufficient to cover the fixed charges, and the investors may quickly be wiped out.[15]

Debt financing is attractive during periods of high inflation because the loans will ultimately be repaid with inflated dollars. Of course, the competition for loans in such circumstances may cause high interest charges which will offset, either wholly or partially, this advantage of debt financing.

Leverage can generally be obtained only by the use of other people's money.[16] Conflicts inevitably arise between the interests of fixed-claimants (creditors) and the interests of residual claimants (shareholders). Suppose for example that a firm that has been capitalized pursuant to Alternative B in the above example, has a choice between two investments. Investment #1 has a 100% chance of resulting in net earnings of $25,000. Investment #2 has an 80% chance of resulting in net earnings of $200,000 and a 20% chance of resulting in net earnings of zero. Which of these investments will the shareholders prefer? Which of these investments will the bondholders prefer? Much of what corporate lawyers do is to draft loan agreements, bond covenants, articles of incorporation and other documents that, in whole or in part, attempt to reconcile the conflicts that inevitably exist between the interests of creditors and the interests of equity holders

2. TAX TREATMENT OF DEBT

In a C corporation, there are usually tax advantages for shareholders who are individuals to lend to the corporation a portion of their investment in the corporation rather than making a contribution to capital. Interest payments on debt are deductible by the borrower whereas dividend payments on equity securities are not.[17] A loan by a shareholder to his corporation therefore reduces the double tax problem of a C corporation. On the other hand, if the shareholder is a corporation, the shareholder may prefer to receive payments in the form of dividends rather than interest because of the dividend-received

debt. However, the tax advantage of debt—the deductibility of the interest—is lost if preferred stock is used, with the result that most leverage situations created today involve the issuance of debt. On the other hand, a corporation is entitled to a credit for dividends received, including dividends paid upon preferred stock.

15. [By the Editors] An economist might show impatience with an example such as that set forth in the text. Assuming that both the common shares and the bonds are publicly traded (and with certain further simplifying assumptions), the economist would argue that the total value of the securities issued by the enterprise (the aggregate market value of all issued common shares plus all issued bonds) would be independent of the amount of debt in the capital structure of the enterprise. In other words, any increase in value of the common stock by reason of the corporation's capital

structure would be offset by a decrease in the market price for the bonds. Even if this principle, first set forth by Miller and Modigliani, is abstractly accepted, a leveraged capital structure such as set forth in the example may benefit the common shareholders at the expense of the debtholders. Also, this relationship may not be visible to the holders of the bonds in situations where the debt is not publicly or widely held.

16. [By the Editors] Some leverage may also be obtained if loans by shareholders are made on a basis other than in proportion to their shareholdings.

17. [By the Editors] There are additional differences between interest payments and dividends. For example, dividends are taxable to the provider of capital only if the corporation has earnings and profits, while interest is taxable in any event.

deduction, even though this causes the "borrower" to lose the benefit of an interest deduction.

Because of the tax advantages of loans by individual shareholders to C corporations, there is an extensive jurisprudence as to whether debt should be reclassified as equity for tax purposes. A classic case is Slappey Drive Indus. Park v. United States, 561 F.2d 572 (5th Cir.1977), where the court stated:

> Articulating the essential difference between * * * [debt and equity] is no easy task. Generally, shareholders place their money "at the risk of the business" while lenders seek a more reliable return. That statement of course glosses over a good many considerations with which even the most inexperienced investor is abundantly familiar. A purchaser of General Motors stock may bear much less risk than a bona fide lender to a small corporation.

> Nevertheless, the "risk of the business" formulation has provided a shorthand description that courts have repeatedly invoked. Contributors of capital undertake the risk because of the potential return; in the form of profits and enhanced value, on their underlying investment. Lenders, on the other hand, undertake a degree of risk because of the expectancy of timely repayment with interest. Because a lender, unrelated to the corporation, stands to earn only a fixed amount of interest, he usually is unwilling to bear a substantial risk of corporate failure or to commit his funds for a prolonged period. A person ordinarily would not advance funds likely to be repaid only if the venture is successful without demanding the potential enhanced return associated with an equity investment.

> These considerations provide only imperfect guidance when the issue relates to a shareholder's purported loan to his own corporation, the usual situation encountered in debt-equity cases. It is well established that shareholders may loan money to their corporations and achieve corresponding tax treatment. When making such loans they could hardly be expected to ignore their shareholder status; their motivations will not match those of potential lenders who have no underlying equity interest. The "risk of the business" standard, though, continues to provide a backdrop for our analysis. While we should not expect a creditor-shareholder to evidence motivations and behavior conforming perfectly to those of a mere creditor, neither should we abandon the effort to determine whether the challenged transaction is in substance a contribution to capital masquerading as debt.

The Court then identified 13 factors that may be relevant in making the classification, and concluded that "[i]n the case at bar the most telling * * * factor is the corporate debtors' consistent failure to repay the debts on the due dates or to seek postponements. More generally, that failure and the corresponding absence of timely interest payments combine with * * * [the defendants'] testimony regarding the parties' view of their relationships to make clear that these transactions were in substance not at all the type arrangements for which debt treatment is appropriate."

The issue whether debt should be reclassified as equity for tax purposes arises in the S corporation context as well. A corporation eligible to be taxed as an S corporation may have only one class of stock. If an S corporation issues debt to shareholders that might be reclassified as equity under the C corporation precedents, is that corporation's S corporation status at risk? The IRS first took a rather literalistic approach in its regulations, arguing that "administrative complexities" compelled disallowance of S corporation status in all reclassification cases. Some courts accepted this view, but others did not, holding the regulations invalid. The leading case invalidating the regulations was Portage Plastics Co., Inc. v. United States, 486 F.2d 632 (7th Cir.1973). In 1982, Congress largely solved this problem by creating a "safe harbor" for "straight debt," the existence of which does not disqualify a corporation from the S corporation election. I.R.C. § 1361(c)(5) defines "straight debt" as debt that involves a written unconditional promise to pay a sum certain in money if (a) interest rates and interest payment dates are not contingent on profits, the borrower's discretion, or similar factors, (b) there is no direct or indirect convertibility into stock, and (c) the creditor is an eligible shareholder under Chapter S.[18]

Notes

(1) A "debt/equity ratio" is the mathematical ratio between a corporation's liabilities and the shareholders' equity. For example, a corporation with $10,000 of equity that borrows $100,000 has a debt/equity ratio of 10:1. This ratio may be calculated on an aggregate or overall liabilities basis (taking into account debts and obligations owed to persons other than shareholders) or on an "inside" basis (taking into account only debts owed to shareholders). At one time the Internal Revenue Service proposed regulations to the effect that debt would not be viewed as "excessive" if the corporation's "outside" ratio was less than 10:1 and its "inside" ratio was less than or equal to 3:1. Is this a sensible way to create a "safe harbor" for shareholder-created debt? Would such a "safe harbor" be desirable?

(2) At one time, it was thought that under case law an inside debt/equity ratio of 4:1 or higher would be decisive in reclassifying the debt as equity. This ratio test, originally based on a statement in John Kelley Co. v. Comm'r, 326 U.S. 521, 66 S.Ct. 299, 90 L.Ed. 278 (1946), was generally rejected by courts in favor of the more flexible approach set forth in *Slappey Drive*.

(3) A corporation with a high debt/equity ratio is sometimes referred to as a "thin corporation."

3. DEBT AS A PLANNING DEVICE

The advantages of debt as a planning device in closely held corporations are well illustrated by Obre v. Alban Tractor Co., 228 Md. 291, 179 A.2d 861 (1962). Obre and Nelson formed a new corporation, Annel Corporation, to engage in the dirt moving and road building business. Obre agreed to contribute to the corporation equipment and cash worth $65,548.10 while Nelson agreed to contribute $10,000 in cash and equipment. The equipment values were based on an independent appraisal. The parties agreed that control was to be shared equally from the outset. Acting upon the advice of "a

---

18. [By the Editors] There was an irony in the attempts by the IRS to disqualify corporations from S corporation treatment on the basis of the existence of reclassifiable debt interests, since this special tax election was originally created to eliminate the double tax treatment that gives rise to the incentive for shareholders to create thin corporations to begin with.

well-known and reputable firm of certified public accountants," the parties capitalized the corporation as follows:

Obre: $10,000 par value voting common stock
           $20,000 par value non voting preferred stock
           $35,548.10 unsecured promissory note

Nelson: $10,000 par value voting common stock

The venture was an economic failure, shortly ending up in a state insolvency proceeding. In this proceeding, Obre successfully claimed the right to participate as an unsecured creditor to the extent of his $35,548.10 unsecured note. The unpaid trade creditors argued that a "subordinating equity" principle required that this note be treated as equity—a capital contribution—rather than as a valid debt. The Court rejected this argument, stating that there was no showing of undercapitalization, fraud, misrepresentation, or estoppel. In deciding that Annel Corporation was not undercapitalized, the Court treated Obre's preferred stock as an equity investment so that the corporation had begun business with $40,000 of equity and only $35,548.10 of debt. The Court held that there was no showing that $40,000 of equity capital was inadequate for a business such as that of Annel Corporation. The Court also relied on the fact that Obre's "loan" to the corporation was either known to the creditors or could easily have been discovered by examining public state tax filings, by requesting a financial statement, or by obtaining a credit report.

Notes

(1) The "subordinating equity" concept is essentially the Deep Rock doctrine in a state law context. Do you think the trade creditors might have been more successful if they had placed Annel Corporation in federal bankruptcy proceedings?

(2) Was the Annel Corporation adequately capitalized? Isn't it reasonably clear that even $75,548.10 was not enough capital and that $40,000 was inadequate? Should this be a matter of proof or of presumption?

(3) Why did those certified public accountants recommend that a significant portion of Obre's contribution be in the form of debt rather than simply having a preferred stock investment of $55,548.10?

E.   PLANNING THE CAPITAL STRUCTURE FOR THE CLOSELY HELD CORPORATION

Attorneys are often requested to review and make recommendations about the proposed capital structure of newly-formed closely held ventures. Usually, the capital structure will be an integral part of broader control considerations in which individual participants attempt to ensure their continued right to participate in the venture and the attorney reviews the entire "package" as a single unit. Tax considerations may also be of critical importance. In reviewing proposed capital structures, an attorney will generally have several basic concerns, including:

(1) Will the structure "work"; i.e., will it stand up in the event of later disagreement and possible legal attack?

(2) Will the structure actually provide the desired result? For example, a person desiring a guaranteed, unconditional periodic payment who is asked to accept preferred stock should be made aware that the directors may usually forego declaring dividends on the preferred if they so desire.

(3) Will the desired tax treatment be available, or more likely; is the structure created one that makes the desired tax treatment probable if not certain? In this regard, the availability of the S corporation election may be of major importance to the participants.

(4) Might the structure give rise to unexpected liabilities? The most likely sources of unexpected liabilities are the possible application of the concepts of par value and watered stock (in states that still recognize such concepts) and, possibly, the ubiquitous doctrine of piercing the corporate veil.

(5) Are the clients' financial contributions reasonably protected and reasonably fairly treated in the event of unexpected or calamitous occurrences causing the sudden and premature termination of the venture?

This is only a partial list. Depending on the circumstances, participants will usually have additional concerns about the capital structure. For example, a person planning on contemplated periodic payments for living expenses may wish to have assurance that corporate matters are handled conservatively and not in a way that may jeopardize future distributions. Other persons may wish to have a major voice in fiscal management and future plans to raise additional capital which may affect their roles in the venture. Considerations about capital structure obviously shade over into questions relating to control over the venture in general, and indeed should be addressed as part of the broader considerations of control.

Notes

(1) These various factors may be illustrated by an extensive analysis of the incorporation of the AB Software Store, where A is to contribute $100,000 in cash and B is to render services in exchange for a "salary" and a 50 percent interest in the business. Further, assume that B is to have "earned out" his 50 percent interest at the end of two years. Assuming that the corporation is formed under the 1969 Model Act, consider the following alternatives:

(a) At the outset of the venture, A and B are each issued 1,000 shares of stock, par value of $100 per share. Does B have watered stock liability? What about MBCA (1969) § 19, second paragraph?

(b) At the outset of the venture, 100 shares of stock, $1.00 par value, are issued to A for $100,000; 100 shares are issued to B only after he has performed services for two years in consideration of such services. Does this avoid the § 19 and watered stock problems? What happens if A decides to close out the business after eighteen months? Where does B stand? (B, however, may have a breach of contract action against A if A wrongfully excludes B from the venture in violation of the agreement.)

(c) At the outset of the venture, 100 shares of stock, par value of $1, are issued to A for $100,000; B executes a promissory note for $100,000, payable in two years out of future services, and B is issued 100 shares in exchange for that note. Again consider MBCA (1969) § 19. As indicated earlier, some states permit shares to be issued in exchange for a promissory note; in those states, B presumably would be simultaneously a shareholder and a debtor.

(d) At the outset of the venture, shares of common stock are issued to A and B at different prices. For example, using $1.00 par value shares, 100 shares are issued to A for $100,000 and 100 shares are issued to B for $100. B actually pays the $100. So long as there is full disclosure, is there anything improper in issuing otherwise identical shares for different prices? Even if this is proper, what happens if there is a fire shortly after the venture is begun, covered by insurance, and the parties decide to liquidate and distribute the insurance proceeds? Would not B be entitled to $50,000, even though he invested only $100? There is also an income tax problem from B's standpoint, since the bargain purchase of shares will probably be treated as compensation to B which is fully taxable in the year in which he receives the shares. This income tax problem is involved in some of the other alternatives as well, including alternatives (b) and (c).

(e) At the outset of the venture, two classes of common shares are created with identical rights per share on dissolution, but with different voting rights:

(i) Class A common, par value $1.00 per share, one vote per share, 10,000 shares issued to A for $10.00 per share, or a total of $100,000.

(ii) Class B common, par value $1.00 per share, one thousand votes per share, 10 shares issued to B for $10.00 per share, or a total of $100.

If this technique were followed, how should the relative dividend rights of the two shares be established? (If dividend rights differ, which will probably be the case, the S corporation election is unavailable.) Generally, the MBCA permits multiple or fractional votes per share; some state statutes, however, permit only single votes per share. Obviously, essentially the same structure could be created with fractional votes per share.

(f) At the outset of the venture, a single class of shares is created with a par value of $1.00 per share, and 10 shares are issued to A for $100 and 10 shares are issued to B for $100. A then lends the corporation $99,800 to complete the capitalization. Would that loan qualify for the "straight debt" safe harbor for the S corporation election? What should be the terms of repayment? Of interest? Is it fair to B to require that a commercial rate of interest be paid to A?

(g) At the outset of the venture, two classes of shares, preferred and common, are created each with a par value of $1.00 per share; 10 shares of common stock are issued to A for $100, 10 shares of common stock are issued to B for $100, and 9,980 shares of preferred stock are issued to A at $10 per share for $99,800, completing the capitalization. How should the dividend right of the preferred stock be established? Why is this alternative less attractive than others?

(h) Combine alternatives (f) and (g) as follows: at the outset of the venture, two classes of shares, preferred and common, are created each with a par value of $1.00 per share; ten shares of common are issued to A and B for $100 each; A is also issued 5,000 shares of preferred for $50,000 and lends the corporation the remaining $49,800, completing the capitalization. Is this an improvement over both alternatives (f) and (g)? Does it resemble the structure proposed by that "well-known and reputable firm of certified public accountants" in *Obre*?

(i) Combine alternatives (d) and (f) as follows: at the outset of the venture, one class of common stock with a par value of $1.00 per share is created, and ten shares are issued to A for $50,000 and ten shares to B for $100. A then lends the corporation the remaining $49,900. Is this the best solution?

(2) In the AB Software Store, A is a passive investor, putting in capital but not participating in the day-to-day affairs of the store. As indicated above, such investors often demand, and are entitled to receive, some sort of return on their investment. The choice of "how much" and "when" are obviously sensitive business decisions that must be negotiated. From the standpoint of the venture, if the S corporation election is unavailable, it is usually advantageous for such payments to be in deductible form rather than as nondeductible dividends on, say, a special class of preferred shares. On the other hand, it is also usually desirable to give the corporation the option to defer or omit such payments if business demands dictate. That, of course, means that the debt is no longer within the "straight debt" safe harbor for the S corporation election. On such issues it is not uncommon for different participants to have different and inconsistent goals which must be accommodated, adjusted, or compromised before the venture can begin.

(3) In many of the above alternatives, the interests of A and B are potentially, if not actually, adverse. If B is without a lawyer, an attorney representing A faces ethical problems that must be addressed. B is very likely to resist retaining a lawyer for reasons of cost, and may wish to rely on A's lawyer to represent his interests as well as A's. If you were A's lawyer in this situation, would you feel comfortable in giving B advice as well as A? Are the problems associated with par value, classes of stock, watered stock, S corporation election, Deep Rock, and other issues arising in the capitalization area of such complexity that you should insist B retain his own lawyer? In an electronic symposium dealing with a situation similar to this, most practicing attorneys stated they would not agree to represent both parties because of concerns about mandatory disclosure, conflict of interest, and about being sued if the venture turns out badly. Several law professors argued that there should be some basis on which an attorney can give limited assistance to a party with full disclosure of the limits to the person involved without incurring liability for malpractice.

(4) Assume that A and B decide to form an LLC. Must the same problems be faced? Because an LLC may elect to be taxed under subchapter K, the answer is basically "no." This is yet another reason to prefer the LLC form of business, at least where no later public offering is contemplated.

F. PUBLIC OFFERINGS

The goal for many closely-held corporations is to "go public," that is, to raise often substantial amounts of capital by making a public offering of their securities through the services of an underwriter. These transactions are known as initial public offerings ("IPOs").

Going public has both significant costs and significant benefits to the owners of the company. Of course, the principal benefit of going public is to raise additional capital for expansion. Many successful closely held corporations, however, can finance their growth from retained earnings, or from loans from a small number of investors. However, going public often has the advantage of reducing a corporation's need to rely on bank debt. Money raised in public offerings often is used to pay down pre-existing indebtedness. Public offerings of equity enable a company to use the money for projects with a long-term time horizon.

Selling securities through a public offering also gives the existing shareholders liquidity. Shareholders who owned illiquid shares in closely held corporations often sell their shares after a public offering in order to diversify their investment portfolios. Funds acquired by a corporation in a public offering sometimes are used to make acquisitions of other companies. Also, public offerings have the benefit of enabling a company to better compete for employees, since options in publicly traded shares, and other stock-based compensation, can be offered to prospective employees. Companies whose shares are publicly traded also are preferred by prospective employees, and by customers and suppliers, since they tend to be better known.

Many closely-held companies feel uncomfortable with the amount of disclosure that must be made during the process of making an IPO. Companies that have engaged in conflict of interest transactions, for example, may decided not to go public because they are unwilling to disclose the details of those transactions. Similarly, prior to an IPO, management will have to "clean up its balance sheet." Some argue that this process sometimes requires companies to sacrifice long-term investments in order to meet short-term objectives.

In addition, the process of going public involves substantial legal risks. The company is strictly liable under Section 11 of the Securities Act of 1933 for material misstatements and omissions in the Registration Statement (which contains the prospectus and other documents that must be filed with the SEC before the company may make an IPO). Even after a company goes public it must file quarterly and annual financial reports under the Securities Exchange Act and comply with strict internal accounting control measures and record-keeping requirements. Also, a publicly held company must constantly deal with analysts and outside shareholders. The following excerpt from Professor Hazen's treatise provides a compelling explanation for the intensive regulation of public securities offerings in this country.

THOMAS LEE HAZEN, TREATISE ON THE LAW OF SECURITIES REGULATION
Vol. 1, pp. 6–8 (2d ed. 1990).[19]

Beginning in the late nineteenth century the eastern industrialists found fertile ground for securities in the developing American frontier. There were many questionable practices, and as a result, pressures arose to regulate the marketing of fraudulently valued securities. Accordingly in 1911 Kansas passed the first state security statutory regulation which is also known as a "blue sky law" because of its purpose to protect the Kansas farmers against the industrialists selling them a piece of the blue sky. A number of states followed suit and blue sky laws began to spring up throughout the country; today all states have blue sky legislation.[20] The state blue sky laws not only focused on disclosure but also required that all securities registered thereunder "qualify" on a merit basis; that is, the state securities commissioner had the power to pass on the merits of the investment. Notwithstanding the broad regulatory potential of the merit approach, the blue sky laws proved to be relatively ineffective in stamping out securities frauds, especially on a national

---

19. Reprinted with the permission of West Publishing Corporation.

20. [By the Editors] *See* Paul G. Mahoney, The Origins of the Blue–Sky Laws: A Test of

Competing Hypotheses, 46 J.L. & Econ. 229 (2003).

level. For a while federal legislation was successfully resisted. The stock market crash of 1929 can be viewed as the straw that broke the camel's back.

Although the general economic condition went a long way toward causing the Wall Street crash of 1929, the number of fraudulently floated securities that contributed to the great crash cannot be underestimated. In fact, the congressional hearings are replete with examples of outrageous conduct that most certainly had a great impact on our nation's disastrous economy. As a result, Congress entered into the regulatory arena with the Securities Act of 1933 which is also known as the "Truth in Securities" Act.[21] At the time of enactment, the 1933 Act was administered by the Federal Trade Commission. * * * The 1933 Act * * * is directed primarily at the distribution of securities. Subject to certain enumerated exemptions, the Securities Act of 1933 generally, requires the registration of all securities being placed in the hands of the public for the first time.[22] After considerable debate, Congress decided not to follow the pattern of the state acts and eschewed the idea of a merit approach, opting instead for a system of full disclosure. The theory behind the federal regulatory framework is that investors are adequately protected if all * * * aspects of the securities being marketed are fully and fairly disclosed and thus there is no need for the more time-consuming merit analysis of the securities being offered. The Securities Act of 1933 contains a number of private remedies for investors who are injured due to violations of the Act.[23] There are also general anti-fraud provisions which bar material omissions and misrepresentations in connection with the sale of securities. The scope of the Securities Act of 1933 is limited; first, insofar as it covers only distributions of securities and second, as its investor protection reach extends only to purchasers of securities.

21. [By the Author] 15 U.S.C.A. §§ 77a–77aa.

22. [By the Author] * * * This includes not only primary distributions (sold by the issuer), but also secondary distributions wherein the securities are sold by individuals or institutions who did not acquire the securities in a public offering.

23. [By the Editors] The most important of these private remedies are the following: 1) Section 11 permits purchasers of securities in a registered offering to bring suits for losses incurred if the prospectus contains misleading statements of material facts. Reliance by the purchaser on the false statement is not required, but a purchaser cannot recover if he or she knew of the misstatement when making the purchase. The issuer is strictly liable under Section 11; officers, directors, underwriters, and other persons named in the registration statement as having prepared or certified any part of the registration statement, may also be liable unless they can establish that they made a reasonable investigation or relied on experts. 2) Section 12(1) permits any purchaser of securities that should have been registered, but were not, to rescind the purchase without regard to fault or misstatement. If the securities are no longer owned by the purchaser, the defendant is liable for damages based on the loss calculated as the difference between the plaintiff's purchase price and sales price. 3) Section 12(2) imposes liability on any seller for material misstatements or omissions in connection with the sale of securities subject only to the defense that the seller did not know and with reasonable care would not have known that the statement was false or omitted. Purchasers have the right to bring suit to recover their losses if there are incomplete or inaccurate disclosures of material facts in the prospectus, without regard to intent or negligence. Persons who may be liable include the issuer itself, its responsible directors and officers, the underwriters, holders of controlling interests, and the sellers of the securities in a secondary offering. In 1995, the Supreme Court in Gustafson v. Alloyd Co., 513 U.S. 561, 115 S.Ct. 1061, 131 L.Ed.2d 1 (1995), sharply narrowed § 12(2) by limiting it to misstatements in the public documents filed in connection with the offering.

The draconian nature of these civil remedies is softened by reason of a relatively short statute of limitations: one year from the date of discovery but in no event more than three years after the public distribution.

In 1934 Congress enacted the Securities Exchange Act of 1934[24] which is a more omnibus regulation. The extent of the regulation was so vast that Congress felt it was not possible to continue overburdening the Federal Trade Commission with this new administrative responsibility and thus established the Securities and Exchange Commission ["SEC"] which is now one of the largest federal agencies. The Exchange Act of 1934 is directed at regulating all aspects of public trading of securities. * * *

Whenever a corporation makes an offering of shares, consideration must be given to the possible application of the state and federal securities laws. If the offering is made to only a few persons, one or more exemptions will often be available, though that cannot be absolutely guaranteed simply by the size of the offering; if the offering is made in a public manner or to numerous persons, there is a presumption that compliance with * * * federal law will be necessary unless an exemption is clearly available.

———

Full compliance with the Securities Act of 1933, 15 U.S.C.A. §§ 77a–77aa, involves the filing of a registration statement with the Securities and Exchange Commission pursuant to Section 5 of the Act. A registration statement consists of two parts: 1) a "prospectus," a document that is to be distributed to potential and actual investors, and 2) additional information that must be submitted to the SEC and is publicly available but need not be included in the prospectus. Registration of an issue by an "unseasoned company," i.e. one whose shares are not widely traded in the public markets and which has never previously filed a registration statement under the 1933 Act, is an expensive, complex and often messy process. Schneider, Manko & Kant, Going Public: Practice, Procedure, and Consequences (Bowne, 1997):[25]

> Once the decision has been made to go public, the parties immediately face perhaps the most important decision to be made—selecting the managing underwriter. Investment banking firms vary widely in prestige, financial strength, and ability to provide the various services the company can expect. Some underwriters are not ordinarily interested in first offerings, while others specialize in them. * * * In selecting the managing underwriter, advice should be obtained from experienced advisers who have a background in the area of public offerings. * * *
>
> For the average first offering, a very substantial amount of preliminary work is required that does not relate directly to preparing the registration statement as such. To have a vehicle for the offering, the business going public normally must be conducted as a single corporation or a parent corporation with subsidiaries. In most cases, the business is not already in such a neat package when the offering project commences. It often is conducted by a number of corporations under common ownership, by partnerships, or by combinations of business entities. Considerable work must be done in order to reorganize the various entities by mergers,

---

24. [By the Editors] 15 U.S.C.A. § 78(a) et seq. The most important antifraud provision under this Act is Rule 10b–5, discussed at length in Chapter 13.

25. As quoted in Robert W. Hamilton and Richard Booth, Corporation Finance, Cases and Materials 185–90 (2000).

liquidations, and capital contributions. Even when there is a single corporation, a recapitalization almost always is required so that the company will have an appropriate capital structure for the public offering. * * *

Among other common projects in preparing to go public, it often is necessary to enter into, revise, or terminate employment agreements, adopt stock option plans and grant options thereunder, transfer real estate, revise leases, rewrite the corporate charter and bylaws, engage a transfer agent and registrar, rearrange stockholdings of insiders, draw, revise or cancel agreements among shareholders, revamp financing arrangements, prepare and order stock certifications, obtain a CUSIP number (a separate identification number for each publicly traded security recognized on an industry-wide basis), and secure a tentative trading symbol. * * *

Legal fees for a first offering can vary over a wide range depending on the size and complexity of the offering, the ease with which information can be assembled and verified, the extent of risk factors or other difficult disclosures, and other factors. Fees in the range of $150,000 to $450,000 would be typical.[26] * * *

Notes

(1) The registration statement of a company making an IPO must contain information about 27 items described in Schedule A of the 1933 Act; additional disclosure requirements appear in SEC Regulation S–K and on the registration statement form (form S–1) itself. The company must also arrange to have certified financial statements prepared in accordance with Regulation S–X for the previous three years. Preparation of these financial statements by an independent auditor is often complicated by incomplete or misleading financial records. Virtually all closely held companies find that their existing financial statements must be significantly revised to meet the requirements of Regulation S–X even if they were originally prepared by an outside auditor and were believed to be entirely suitable for their own needs while privately held.

(2) Securities registration from the standpoint of the attorney is a highly specialized and complex matter. The "corporate check" required for an IPO usually involves the cooperation of two sets of attorneys: Those representing the issuer and those representing the underwriter. Because the 1933 Act imposes substantial civil liabilities, the attorneys must examine carefully the background of prior transactions, determine whether disclosure may be required of transactions between the issuer and the managers, determine whether prior issues of securities were lawfully made pursuant to an available exemption, and so forth. The process by which attorneys verify the accuracy and completeness of registration statements is usually referred to as a "due diligence" investigation. A sloppily-prepared or incomplete registration statement may subject the attorneys to personal liability to investors as well as causing damage to their reputations if they are named as parties in a securities fraud or disciplinary proceeding. The number of suits filed against attorneys under the 1933 Act is surprisingly large,

---

26. [By the Editors] In addition, accounting fees ranging from $100,000, to 250,000, printing expenses ranging from $75,000 to $175,000, and the SEC's filing fee at the rate of 1/33 of one percent of the maximum aggregate offering price of the securities, will be incurred.

and this type of practice is viewed as a high-risk practice. Insurers may be reluctant to write malpractice insurance for securities attorneys in solo practice or with small firms. See Stephen J. Choi & A.C. Pritchard, Behavioral Economics and the SEC, 56 Stan. L. Rev. 1 (2003) (applying behavioral insights to securities regulation).

(3) Robert W. Hamilton and Richard Booth, Corporation Finance: Cases and Materials 184–85 (3d Ed. 2000):

> Once complete, the registration statement is then filed with the SEC. The SEC's Division of Corporate Finance reviews the registration statement and typically issues a lengthy comment letter specifying areas in which more disclosure or specificity is required. During the review process, a preliminary prospectus (sometimes called a "red herring") is circulated to potential investors. (A prospectus is in essence the same document as the registration statement but without the exhibits.) Securities may not be sold, however, until the registration statement becomes effective. In theory, a registration statement becomes effective automatically 20 calendar days after it is filed, but each change in the registration statement, whether in response to SEC comments or for any other reason, starts a new 20–day waiting period. When the registration statement is about to become effective, the price of the offering is sent in a final pricing amendment, and the SEC waives the new 20–day waiting period that would otherwise be required. The securities may then be sold to investors. A final prospectus must, however, be delivered to everyone who purchases the securities over the following 40 to 90 days depending on the circumstances of the offering.

(4) Section 12(g) of the Securities Exchange Act of 1934, 15 U.S.C.A. § 78(l)(g) requires every corporation that has (i) shares registered on a national securities exchange or (ii) 500 or more shareholders of record and more than $10,000,000 of assets to register that class with the Securities and Exchange Commission. This requirement is technically independent of and separate from the registration requirement set forth in the Securities Act of 1933. However, almost all corporations that go through a full-scale 1933 Act registration will almost immediately become subject to this 1934 Act registration requirement. The 1934 Act registration requirement triggers a variety of continuous disclosure obligations and application of proxy rules, "short swing" profit recapture under § 16(b) of the 1934 Act, annual reports to shareholders, and the like. Indeed, most of the continuous disclosure requirements for publicly held corporations are imposed by the regulations under § 12(g) of the 1934 Act.

(5) In addition to the registration requirements of the securities acts, public offerings traditionally had to comply with state blue sky laws in the states in which securities are to be offered for sale. In 1996 Congress enacted a major statute, the National Securities Markets Improvement Act ("NSMIA"), Pub.L. 104–290, 110 Stat. 3416 (1996), that rationalized and simplified the registration process for registered public corporations by preempting significant portions of the state blue sky laws. For negative evaluations of this statute, see Rutherford B. Campbell, Jr., Blue Sky Laws and Recent Congressional Preemption Failure, 22 J.Corp.L. 175 (1997); F. Hodge O'Neal, Corporate and Securities Law Symposium, 78 Wash. U.L.Q. 397 (2000). However, NSMIA arguably does not preempt or affect the blue sky registration process for securities that are sold publicly pursuant to an *exemption* from the federal registration process, and, today, as described below, most capital raising by closely held corporations is pursuant to one or more of these exemptions.

(6) New technological developments have had a dramatic effect on the dissemination of information about publicly traded securities. Many registered (and some unregistered) securities are now offered for sale on the internet or electronic communications networks and often touted through "chat rooms" or anonymous postings of questionable information. The traditional registration process was designed for a simpler era, and the Securities & Exchange Commission has struggled to respond to these new developments. For example, the SEC has found it necessary to increase dramatically its fraud section in order to respond to complaints of egregious misrepresentations in connection with the sale of securities. For a recent example of touting a small publicly traded stock, see "Teenager in Stock–Fraud Case Kept $500,000 in Profits—The Line Between Proper and Improper Activity on Web Grows Increasing Fuzzy," Wall Street Journal, October 20, 2000, at C1 (describing a case of a fraudulent stock offering on the internet initially unnoticed by regulators). Additionally, several companies have offered unregistered "free stock" over the internet to investors if they will simply visit the company's web site. The purpose is to create a public market for the shares, clearly a valuable adjunct to any marginal corporation's activities. The SEC has taken a dim view of these offerings and, in April 1999, required full-scale registration of "free" stock issues. The cost of registration may deter many marginal issuers, though at least two companies have actually registered issues of free stock.

SECURITIES AND EXCHANGE COMM'N
v. RALSTON PURINA CO.

Supreme Court of the United States, 1953.
346 U.S. 119, 73 S.Ct. 981, 97 L.Ed. 1494.

Mr. Justice Clark delivered the opinion of the Court.

Section [4(2)] of the Securities Act of 1933 exempts "transactions by an issuer not involving any public offering" from the registration requirements of § 5. We must decide whether Ralston Purina's offerings of treasury stock to its "key employees" are within this exemption. On a complaint brought by the Commission under § 20(b) of the Act seeking to enjoin respondent's unregistered offerings, the District Court held the exemption applicable and dismissed the suit. The Court of Appeals affirmed. The question has arisen many times since the Act was passed; an apparent need to define the scope of the private offering exemption prompted certiorari. 345 U.S. 903, 73 S.Ct. 643.

Ralston Purina manufactures and distributes various feed and cereal products. Its processing and distribution facilities are scattered throughout the United States and Canada, staffed by some 7,000 employees. At least since 1911 the company has had a policy of encouraging stock ownership among its employees; more particularly, since 1942 it has made authorized but unissued common shares available to some of them. Between 1947 and 1951, the period covered by the record in this case, Ralston Purina sold nearly $2,000,000 of stock to employees without registration and in so doing made use of the mails.

In each of these years, a corporate resolution authorized the sale of common stock "to employees * * * who shall, without any solicitation by the Company or its officers or employees, inquire of any of them as to how to purchase common stock of Ralston Purina Company." A memorandum sent to branch and store managers after the resolution was adopted advised that "[t]he only employees to whom this stock will be available will be those who take the initiative and are interested in buying stock at present market prices." Among those responding to these offers were employees with the duties of artist, bakeshop foreman, chow loading foreman, clerical assistant, copywriter, electrician, stock clerk, mill office clerk, order credit trainee, production trainee, stenographer, and veterinarian. The buyers lived in over fifty widely separated communities scattered from Garland, Texas, to Nashua, New Hampshire and Visalia, California. The lowest salary bracket of those purchasing was $2,700 in 1949, $2,435 in 1950 and $3,107 in 1951. The record shows that in 1947, 234 employees bought stock, 20 in 1948, 414 in 1949, 411 in 1950, and the 1951 offer, interrupted by this litigation, produced 165 applications to purchase. No records were kept of those to whom the offers were made; the estimated number in 1951 was 500.

The company bottoms its exemption claim on the classification of all offerees as "key employees" in its organization. Its position on trial was that "A key employee * * * is not confined to an organization chart. It would include an individual who is eligible for promotion, an individual who especially influences others or who advises others, a person whom the employees look to in some special way, an individual, of course, who carries some special responsibility, who is sympathetic to management and who is ambitious and who the management feels is likely to be promoted to a greater responsibility." That an offering to all of its employees would be public is conceded.

The Securities Act nowhere defines the scope of [§ 4(2)'s] private offering exemption. Nor is the legislative history of much help in staking out its boundaries. * * *

Decisions under comparable exemptions in the English Companies Acts and state "blue sky" laws, the statutory antecedents of federal securities legislation have made one thing clear—to be public, an offer need not be open to the whole world. In Securities and Exchange Comm. v. Sunbeam Gold Mines Co., 9 Cir., 1938, 95 F.2d 699, 701, this point was made in dealing with an offering to the stockholders of two corporations about to be merged. Judge Denman observed that:

> In its broadest meaning the term 'public' distinguishes the populace at large from groups of individual members of the public segregated because of some common interest or characteristic. Yet such a distinction is inadequate for practical purposes; manifestly an offering of securities to all redheaded men, to all residents of Chicago or San Francisco, to all existing stockholders of the General Motors Corporation or the American Telephone & Telegraph Company, is no less 'public', in every realistic sense of the word, than an unrestricted offering to the world at large. Such an offering, though not open to everyone who may choose to apply, is none the less 'public' in character, for the means used to select the particular individuals to whom the offering is to be made bear no sensible relation to the purposes for which the selection is made. * * * To determine the distinction between 'public' and 'private' in any particular context, it is essential to examine the circumstances under which the distinction is sought to be established and to consider the purposes sought to be achieved by such distinction.

The courts below purported to apply this test. The District Court held, in the language of the Sunbeam decision, that "The purpose of the selection bears a 'sensible relation' to the class chosen," finding that "The sole purpose of the 'selection' is to keep part stock ownership of the business within the operating personnel of the business and to spread ownership throughout all departments and activities of the business." The Court of Appeals treated the case as involving "an offering, without solicitation, of common stock to a selected group of key employees of the issuer, most of whom are already stockholders when the offering is made, with the sole purpose of enabling them to secure a proprietary interest in the company or to increase the interest already held by them."

Exemption from the registration requirements of the Securities Act is the question. The design of the statute is to protect investors by promoting full disclosure of information thought necessary to informed investment decisions. * * * Since exempt transactions are those as to which "there is no practical need for * * * [the bill's] application," the applicability of [§ 4(2)] should turn on whether the particular class of persons affected need the protection of the Act. An offering to those who are shown to be able to fend for themselves is a transaction "not involving any public offering."

The Commission would have us go one step further and hold that "an offering to a substantial number of the public" is not exempt under [§ 4(2)]. We are advised that "whatever the special circumstances, the Commission has consistently interpreted the exemption as being inapplicable when a large number of offerees is involved." But the statute would seem to apply to a "public offering" whether to few or many. It may well be that offerings to a substantial number of persons would rarely be exempt. * * * [T]here is no warrant for superimposing a quantity limit on private offerings as a matter of statutory interpretation.

The exemption, as we construe it, does not deprive corporate employees, as a class, of the safeguards of the Act. We agree that some employee offerings may come within [§ 4(2)], e.g., one made to executive personnel who because of their position have access to the same kind of information that the act would make available in the form of a registration statement. Absent such a showing of special circumstances, employees are just as much members of the investing "public" as any of their neighbors in the community. * * *

Keeping in mind the broadly remedial purposes of federal securities legislation, imposition of the burden of proof on an issuer who would plead the exemption seems to us fair and reasonable. Agreeing, the court below thought the burden met primarily because of the respondent's purpose in singling out its key employees for stock offerings. But once it is seen that the exemption question turns on the knowledge of the offerees, the issuer's motives, laudable though they may be, fade into irrelevance. The focus of inquiry should be on the need of the offerees for the protections afforded by registration. The employees here were not shown to have access to the kind of information which registration would disclose. The obvious opportunities for pressure and imposition make it advisable that they be entitled to compliance with § 5.

Reversed.

THE CHIEF JUSTICE and MR. JUSTICE BURTON dissent.

Notes

(1) Could Ralston Purina have avoided the impact of the holding in this case by structuring its stock sale plan in the form of a sale to a corporate officer (such as the president or a vice president) who clearly did not need the protection of the Act, and then having that officer sell shares to employees who asked about the possibility of stock purchases? In a word, the answer is "no." Section 2(11) of the 1933 Act, 15 U.S.C.A. § 77(b), defines an "underwriter" to mean "any person who has purchased from an issuer with a view to, or offers or sells for an issuer in connection with, the distribution of any security * * *." Thus, the officer becomes an "underwriter" and the suggested transaction violates § 5 of the Act.

(2) Section 2(11) of the 1933 Act also states that the term "issuer" in the provision quoted in note (2) includes "any person directly or indirectly controlling or controlled by the issuer, or any person under direct or indirect common control with the issuer." The effect of this language is to impose on controlling or controlled persons the same obligation as is imposed on issuers under the Securities Act. Thus, the sole shareholder of a successful company cannot avoid the registration requirements of the 1933 Act simply by selling shares from his personal portfolio to the public rather than arranging for the corporation to sell shares directly. However, if a major shareholder of a corporation that is going public wishes to obtain personally a portion of the capital to be raised in the offering, he may include a portion of his own holdings in the registration statement prepared on behalf of the corporation. The shares so registered would then be sold as part of the public offering. This type of transaction, known as a "secondary offering," is quite common.

(3) It is also quite common for a corporation that has made a registered public offering to have outstanding previously-issued shares that have not been registered. How can a person who acquires shares in a legitimate § 4(2) transaction, ever safely resell those shares in light of this definition? The SEC has adopted Rule 144, 17 C.F.R. § 230.144, to establish guidelines for the resale of unregistered shares (often called "restricted stock") by investors without concern that the seller may be deemed to be an "underwriter" under § 2(11). Rule 144 basically establishes a one-year holding requirement; this Rule is complex, however, and cannot be simply summarized. Rule 144 is not exclusive, so resales in some circumstances within the one year period may be consistent with the original nonpublic offering exemption even though they do not comply with Rule 144.

SECURITIES ACT RELEASE NO. 33–5450

39 Fed.Reg. 2353 (1974).

Background and Purpose

Section 3(a)(11) of the Securities Act of 1933 exempts "any security which is a part of an issue offered and sold only to persons resident within a single State * * * where the issuer of such security is a person resident and doing business within or, if a corporation, incorporated by and doing business within, such State." [This section] * * * was intended to allow issuers with localized operations to sell securities as part of a plan of local financing. Congress apparently believed that a company whose operations are restricted to one area should be able to raise money from investors in the immediate vicinity without having to register the securities with a federal agency. In theory, the investors would be protected both by their proximity to the issuer and by state regulation. Rule 147 reflects this Congressional intent and is limited in its application to transactions where state regulation will be most effective. The Commission has consistently taken the position that the exemption applies only to local financing provided by local investors for local companies. To satisfy the exemption, the entire issue must be offered and sold exclusively to residents of the state in which the issuer is resident and doing business. An offer or sale of part of the issue to a single non-resident will destroy the exemption for the entire issue.

Certain basic questions have arisen in connection with interpreting section 3(a)(11). They are:

1. What transactions does the section cover;

2. What is "part of an issue" for purposes of the Section;

3. When is a person "resident within" a state or territory for purposes of the section; and

4. What does "doing business within" mean in the context of the Section?

The courts and the Commission have addressed themselves to these questions in the context of different fact situations, and some general guidelines have been developed. Certain guidelines were set forth by the Commission in Securities Act Release No. 4434 and, in part, are reflected in Rule 147. However, in certain aspects, as pointed out below, the rule differs from past interpretations.

THE TRANSACTION CONCEPT

Although the intrastate offering exemption is contained in section 3 of the Act, which section is phrased in terms of exempt "securities" rather than "transactions", the legislative history and Commission and judicial interpretations indicate that the exemption covers only specific transactions and not the securities themselves. Rule 147 reflects this interpretation.

THE "PART OF AN ISSUE" CONCEPT

The determination of what constitutes "part of an issue" for purposes of the exemption, i.e. what should be "integrated", has traditionally been dependent on the facts involved in each case. * * * [The Commission refers to the same factors that are discussed in Rule 230.502, page 361, infra.]

THE "PERSON RESIDENT WITHIN" CONCEPT

The object of the section 3(a)(11) exemption—i.e., to restrict the offering to persons within the same locality as the issuer who are, by reason of their proximity, likely to be familiar with the issuer and protected by the state law governing the issuer—is best-served by interpreting the residence requirement narrowly. In addition, the determination of whether all parts of the issue have been sold only to residents can be made only after the securities have "come to rest" within the state or territory. Rule 147 retains these concepts, but provides more objective standards for determining when a person is considered a resident within a state for purposes of the rule and when securities have come to rest within a state.

Because the primary purpose of the intrastate exemption was to allow an essentially local business to raise money within the state where the investors would be likely to be familiar with the business and with the management, the doing business requirement has traditionally been viewed strictly. First, not only should the business be located within the state, but the principal or predominant business must be carried on there. Second, substantially all of the proceeds of the offering must be put to use within the local area.

Rule 147 reinforces these requirements by providing specific percentage amounts of business that must be conducted within the state, and of proceeds from the offering that must be spent in connection with such business. In addition, the rule requires that the principal office of the issuer be within the state. * * *

[The text of Rule 147 itself is omitted.]

Note

The combination of *Ralston Purina* and the narrow Rule 147 construction of the § 3(a)(11) exemption obviously complicates the raising of capital by small businesses that can ill-afford the cost of a full-scale Form S–1 registration. As a result, it was widely believed that the registration process had a negative impact on capital-raising by small businesses. In 1980, Congress enacted legislation (described below) designed to minimize this impact. In 1982, the SEC adopted Regulation D, a series of limited offering exemptions predominantly for small businesses. In 1992, it adopted a series of additional amendments to its regulations pursuant to its so-called "Small Business Initiative."

SECURITIES ACT RELEASE NO. 33–6389
47 Fed.Reg. 11251 (1982).

SUMMARY

The Commission announces the adoption of a new regulation governing certain offers and sales of securities without registration under the Securities Act of 1933 and a uniform notice of sales form to be used for all offerings under the regulation. The regulation replaces three exemptions and four forms, all of which are being rescinded. The new regulation is designed to simplify and clarify existing exemptions, to expand their availability, and to achieve uniformity between federal and state exemptions in order to facilitate capital formation consistent with the protection of investors. * * *

I. Background

Regulation D is the product of the Commission's evaluation of the impact of its rules and regulations on the ability of small businesses to raise capital. This study has revealed a particular concern that the registration requirements and the exemptive scheme of the Securities Act impose disproportionate restraints on small issuers. * * *

Coincident with the Commission's small business program, Congress enacted the Small Business Investment Incentive Act of 1980 (the "Incentive Act") [94 Stat. 2275 (codified in scattered sections of 15 U.S.C.A.)]. The

Incentive Act included three changes to the Securities Act: the addition of an exemption in Section 4(6) for offers and sales solely to accredited investors,[27] the increase in the ceiling of Section 3(b) from $2,000,000 to $5,000,000,[28] and the addition of Section 19(c) which, among other things, authorized "the development of a uniform exemption from registration for small issuers which can be agreed upon among several States or between the States and the Federal Government." * * *

Commentary to the Commission criticized the complexity of the exemptive scheme as it relates to all issuers. * * *

SECURITIES WITHOUT REGISTRATION UNDER THE SECURITIES ACT OF 1933
17 C.F.R. § 230.501 et seq. (2000).

PRELIMINARY NOTES

1. The following rules relate to transactions exempted from the registration requirements of section 5 of the Securities Act of 1933 (the *Act*). * * *

2. Nothing in these rules obviates the need to comply with any applicable state law relating to the offer and sale of securities. Regulation D is intended to be a basic element in a uniform system of Federal–State limited offering exemptions consistent with the provisions of sections 18 and 19(c) of the Act. * * *

6. In view of the objectives of these rules and the policies underlying the Act, regulation D is not available to any issuer for any transaction or chain of transactions that, although in technical compliance with these rules, is part of a plan or scheme to evade the registration provisions of the Act. In such cases, registration under the Act is required. * * *

§ 230.501 Definitions and terms used in Regulation D.

As used in Regulation D, the following terms shall have the meaning indicated:

(a) *Accredited investor.* *Accredited investor* shall mean any person who comes within any of the following categories, or who the issuer reasonably believes comes within any of the following categories, at the time of the sale of the securities to that person:

(1) Any bank * * * or any savings and loan association or other institution * * * whether acting in its individual or fiduciary capacity;

---

27. [By the Editors] Section 4(6) provides an exemption for "transactions involving offers or sales by an issuer solely to one or more accredited investors, if the aggregate offering price of an issue of securities offered in reliance on this paragraph does not exceed * * * [$5,000,000], if there is no advertising or public solicitation in connection with the transaction by the issuer or anyone acting on the issuer's behalf, and if the issuer files such notice with the Commission as the Commission shall prescribe."

28. [By the Editors] Section 3(b) provides:

The Commission may from time to time by its rules and regulations, and subject to such terms and conditions as may be prescribed therein, add any class of securities to the securities exempted as provided in this section, if it finds that the enforcement of this subchapter with respect to such securities is not necessary in the public interest and for the protection of investors by reason of the small amount involved or the limited character of the public offering; but no issue of securities shall be exempted under this subsection where the aggregate amount at which such issue is offered to the public exceeds [$5,000,000].

any [registered] broker or dealer * * * any insurance company * * * any investment company * * * or a business development company * * * any Small Business Investment Company [or certain employee benefit plans]. * * *

(3) Any organization described in section 501(c)(3) of the Internal Revenue Code, corporation, Massachusetts or similar business trust, or partnership, not formed for the specific purpose of acquiring the securities offered, with total assets in excess of $5,000,000;

(4) Any director, executive officer, or general partner of the issuer of the securities being offered or sold, or any director, executive officer, or general partner of a general partner of that issuer;

(5) Any natural person whose individual net worth or joint net worth with that person's spouse, at the time of his purchase, exceeds $1,000,000;

(6) Any natural person who had an individual income in excess of $200,000 in each of the two most recent years or joint income with that person's spouse in excess of $300,000 in each of those years and has a reasonable expectation of reaching the same income level in the current year;

(7) Any trust, with total assets in excess of $5,000,000, not formed for the specific purpose of acquiring the securities offered, whose purchase is directed by a sophisticated person as described in § 230.506(b)(2)(ii); and

(8) Any entity in which all of the equity owners are accredited investors. * * *

(e) *Calculation of number of purchasers.* For purposes of calculating the number of purchasers under §§ 230.505(b) and 230.506(b) only, the following shall apply:

(1) The following purchasers shall be excluded:

(i) Any relative, spouse or relative of the spouse of a purchaser who has the same principal residence as the purchaser;

(ii) Any trust or estate in which a purchaser and any of the persons related to him as specified in paragraph (e)(1)(i) or (e)(1)(iii) of this section collectively have more than 50 percent of the beneficial interest (excluding contingent interests);

(iii) Any corporation or other organization of which a purchaser and any of the persons related to him as specified in paragraph (e)(1)(i) or (e)(1)(ii) of this section collectively are beneficial owners of more than 50 percent of the equity securities (excluding directors' qualifying shares) or equity interests; and

(iv) Any accredited investor. * * *

§ 230.502 General conditions to be met.

The following conditions shall be applicable to offers and sales made under Regulation D (§§ 230.501–230.508):

(a) *Integration.* All sales that are part of the same Regulation D offering must meet all of the terms and conditions of Regulation D. Offers and sales that are made more than six months before the start of a Regulation D offering or are made more than six months after completion of a Regulation D offering will not be considered part of that Regulation D offering, so long as during those six month periods there are no offers or sales of securities by or for the issuer that are of the same or a similar class as those offered or sold under Regulation D * * *.

NOTE: The term *offering* is not defined in the Act or in Regulation D. If the issuer offers or sells securities for which the safe harbor rule in paragraph (a) of this § 230.502 is unavailable, the determination as to whether separate sales of securities are part of the same offering (i.e. are considered *integrated*) depends on the particular facts and circumstances. Generally, transactions otherwise meeting the requirements of an exemption will not be integrated with simultaneous offerings being made outside the United States in compliance with Regulation S. See Release No. 33–6863.

The following factors should be considered in determining whether offers and sales should be integrated for purposes of the exemptions under Regulation D:

(a) Whether the sales are part of a single plan of financing;

(b) Whether the sales involve issuance of the same class of securities;

(c) Whether the sales have been made at or about the same time;

(d) Whether the same type of consideration is received; and

(e) Whether the sales are made for the same general purpose.

(b) *Information requirements.* (1) *When information must be furnished.* If the issuer sells securities under § 230.505 or § 230.506 to any purchaser that is not an accredited investor, the issuer shall furnish the information specified in § 230.502(b)(2) of this section to such purchaser a reasonable time prior to sale. * * *

(c) *Limitation on manner of offering.* Except as provided in § 230.504(b)(1), neither the issuer nor any person acting on its behalf shall offer or sell the securities by any form of general solicitation or general advertising, including, but not limited to, the following:

(1) Any advertisement, article, notice or other communication published in any newspaper, magazine, or similar media or broadcast over television or radio; and

(2) Any seminar or meeting whose attendees have been invited by any general solicitation or general advertising, * * *.

(d) *Limitations on resale.* Except as provided in § 230.504(b)(1), securities acquired in a transaction under Regulation D shall have the status of securities acquired in a transaction under section 4(2) of the Act and cannot be resold without registration under the Act or an exemption therefrom. The issuer shall exercise reasonable care to assure that the purchasers of the securities are not underwriters within the meaning of section 2(11) of the Act, which reasonable care may be demonstrated by the following:

(1) Reasonable inquiry to determine if the purchaser is acquiring the securities for himself or for other persons;

(2) Written disclosure to each purchaser prior to sale that the securities have not been registered under the Act and, therefore, cannot be resold unless they are registered under the Act or unless an exemption from registration is available; and

(3) Placement of a legend on the certificate or other document that evidences the securities stating that the securities have not been registered under the Act and setting forth or referring to the restrictions on transferability and sale of the securities.

While taking these actions will establish the requisite reasonable care, it is not the exclusive method to demonstrate such care. Other actions by the issuer may satisfy this provision. * * *

§ 230.504   Exemption for limited offerings and sales of securities not exceeding $1,000,000.

(a) *Exemption*. Offers and sales of securities that satisfy the conditions in paragraph (b) of this § 230.504 * * * shall be exempt from the provisions of section 5 of the Act under section 3(b) of the Act.

(b) *Conditions to be met*. (1) To qualify for exemption under this § 230.504, offers and sales must satisfy the terms and conditions of §§ 230.501 and 230.502(a), (c) and (d), except that the provisions of § 230.502(c) and (d) will not apply to offers and sales of securities under this § 230.504 that are made:

(i) Exclusively in one or more states that provide for the registration of the securities, and require the public filing and delivery to investors of a substantive disclosure document before sale, and are made in accordance with those state provisions;

(ii) In one or more states that have no provision for the registration of the securities or the public filing or delivery of a disclosure document before sale, if the securities have been registered in at least one state that provides for such registration, public filing and delivery before sale, offers and sales are made in that state in accordance with such provisions, and the disclosure document is delivered before sale to all purchasers (including those in the states that have no such procedure); or

(iii) Exclusively according to state law exemptions from registration that permit general solicitation and general advertising so long as sales are made only to "accredited investors" as defined in § 230.501(a). * * *

(2) The aggregate offering price for an offering of securities under this § 230.504, as defined in § 230.501(c), shall not exceed $1,000,000, less the aggregate offering price for all securities sold within the twelve months before the start of and during the offering of securities under this § 230.504, in reliance on any exemption under section 3(b), or in violation of section 5(a) of the Securities Act.

Note 1: The calculation of the aggregate offering price is illustrated as follows:

If an issuer sold $900,000 on June 1, 1987 under this § 230.504 and an additional $4,100,000 on December 1, 1987 under § 230.505, the issuer could not sell any of its securities under this § 230.504 until December 1, 1988. Until then the issuer must count the December 1, 1987 sale towards the $1,000,000 limit within the preceding twelve months.

Note 2: If a transaction under § 230.504 fails to meet the limitation on the aggregate offering price, it does not affect the availability of this § 230.504 for the other transactions considered in applying such limitation. For example, if an issuer sold $1,000,000 worth of its securities on January 1, 1988 under this § 230.504 and an additional $500,000 worth on July 1, 1988, this § 230.504 would not be available for the later sale, but would still be applicable to the January 1, 1988 sale.

§ 230.505 Exemption for limited offers and sales of securities not exceeding $5,000,000.

(a) *Exemption.* Offers and sales of securities that satisfy the conditions in paragraph (b) of this section by an issuer that is not an investment company shall be exempt from the provisions of section 5 of the Act under section 3(b) of the Act.

(b) *Conditions to be met*—(1) *General conditions.* To qualify for exemption under this section, offers and sales must satisfy the terms and conditions of §§ 230.501 and 230.502.

(2) *Specific conditions*—(i) *Limitation on aggregate offering price.* The aggregate offering price for an offering of securities under this § 230.505, as defined in § 203.501(c), shall not exceed $5,000,000, less the aggregate offering price for all securities sold within the twelve months before the start of and during the offering of securities under this section in reliance on any exemption under section 3(b) of the Act or in violation of section 5(a) of the Act. * * *

(ii) *Limitation on number of purchasers.* There are no more than or the issuer reasonably believes that there are no more than 35 purchasers of securities from the issuer in any offering under this section. * * *

§ 230.506 Exemption for limited offers and sales without regard to dollar amount of offering.

(a) *Exemption.* Offers and sales of securities by an issuer that satisfy the conditions in paragraph (b) of this section shall be deemed to be transactions not involving any public offering within the meaning of section 4(2) of the Act.

(b) *Conditions to be met*—(1) *General conditions.* To qualify for an exemption under this section, offers and sales must satisfy all the terms and conditions of §§ 230.501 and 230.502.

(2) *Specific Conditions*—(i) *Limitation on number of purchasers.* There are no more than or the issuer reasonably believes that there are no more than 35 purchasers of securities from the issuer in any offering under this section. * * *

(ii) *Nature of purchasers.* Each purchaser who is not an accredited investor either alone or with his purchaser representative(s) has such knowledge and experience in financial and business matters that he is capable of evaluating the merits and risks of the prospective investment, or the issuer reasonably believes immediately prior to making any sale that such purchaser comes within this description.

§ 230.508 Insignificant deviations from a term, condition or requirement of Regulation D.

(a) A failure to comply with a term, condition or requirement of § 230.504, § 230.505 or § 230.506 will not result in the loss of the exemption from the requirements of section 5 of the Act for any offer or sale to a particular individual or entity, if the person relying on the exemption shows:

(1) The failure to comply did not pertain to a term, condition or requirement directly intended to protect that particular individual or entity; and

(2) The failure to comply was insignificant with respect to the offering as a whole, provided that any failure to comply with paragraph (c) of § 230.502, paragraph (b)(2) of § 230.504, paragraphs (b)(2)(i) and (ii) of § 230.505 and paragraph (b)(2)(i) of § 230.506 shall be deemed to be significant to the offering as a whole; and

(3) A good faith and reasonable attempt was made to comply with all applicable terms, conditions and requirements of § 230.504, § 230.505 or § 230.506. * * *

Notes

(1) Rule 508 was added in 1989, SEC Rel. No. 33–6825, 54 Fed.Reg. 11369 (1989), to "alleviate the draconian consequences of an innocent and insignificant defect in perfecting an exemption from registration." Stanley Keller, Securities Exemptions: The Saga of a Substantial Compliance Defense, Insights, Vol. 3, No. 8, p. 11 (Aug. 1989) (noting that the substantial compliance test in Rule 508 will not create a significant change in practice).[29] See also Carl W. Schneider, A Substantial Compliance ("I & I") Defense and Other Changes are Added to SEC Regulation D, 44 Bus.Law. 1207 (1989).

(2) The SEC's (1992) "Small Business Initiative" involved a series of new regulations and rule amendments designed to ease the regulatory burdens imposed on small businesses. SEC Rel. Nos. 33–6949, 34–30968, 39–30968, 57 Fed. Reg. 36,442 (1992). The principal changes made by this initiative are:

(a) *Regulation A.* The oldest and at one time the most widely used "small business" regulation adopted by the SEC under § 3(b) is Regulation A (affectionately known as "Reg. A" by securities lawyers). 17 C.F.R. § 230.251, et seq. While technically an exemption under § 3(b), it actually involves a somewhat streamlined registration process at the regional offices of the SEC. See generally Harvey Frank, The Processing of Small Issues of Securities

---

29. Insights: The Corporate & Securities Law Advisor. Copyright by Prentice Hall Law & Business.

Under Regulation A, 1962 Duke L.J. 507. The late 1980s saw a significant reduction in Reg. A filings: from $408 million in 1981 to $34 million in 1991. The principal reasons for this decline were the $1.5 million ceiling on Reg. A issues and the cost of the Reg. A qualification process itself. The 1992 Small Business Initiative made several changes to make Reg. A more attractive: the ceiling was increased to $5 million, the information required to be disclosed was simplified and integrated to some extent with the uniform filings proposed by the North American Securities Administrators Association (NASAA) under state blue sky laws, and the information was permitted to be presented in a question-and-answer format. The SEC also simplified reporting requirements under the Securities Exchange Act of 1934 for small businesses with revenue of less than $25 million for each of two consecutive years.

(b) *Testing the Waters.* Rule 254, 17 C.F.R. § 230.254(a), permits a potential Reg. A user to publish or deliver to prospective purchasers a written document to determine whether there is investor interest in the contemplated offering. This document may be distributed without any review by the central offices of the SEC; basically the only requirement is that a copy be filed with an appropriate regional office, and include the name and telephone number of a person able to answer possible questions about the document. Testing the waters obviously permits a potential issuer to defer investing funds in the Reg. A process until after it has a pretty good idea that the offer will be successful.

(c) *Rule 504.* Perhaps the most important change was the amendment of Rule 504 of Regulation D so as to permit offerings by non-reporting issuers of up to $1 million essentially with no registration requirement at all (except for continued application of broad antifraud provisions). This change required similar action to be taken at the state level if it was to be implemented in fact.

See Rutherford B. Campbell, Jr., Blue Sky Laws and Recent Congressional Preemption Failure, 22 J.Corp.L. 175, 181–85 (1997) (evaluating the small offering exemptions offered by the SEC and noting that they meet both the needs of small issuers to raise capital effectively and the needs of the investors by providing fraud protections).

(3) While the issue is not free from doubt, NSMIA does not apparently preempt state requirements with respect to any of these small business related exemptions. As stated by Professor Campbell, "Glaringly absent from * * * [the list of transactions preempted by NSMIA] are securities issued in transactions under Section 3(a)(11), which includes Rule 147, under Section 3(b), which includes Rule 504, 505 and Regulation A, and under the common law of Section 4(2)." 22 J.Corp.L., at 198–99. Professor Campbell argues strongly that the relief granted from overlapping blue sky regulation benefits only companies that raise large amounts of capital and leaves the smaller enterprise fully subject to the complex and sometimes costly blue sky process.

SMITH v. GROSS

United States Court of Appeals, Ninth Circuit, 1979.
604 F.2d 639.

Before CARTER and GOODWIN, CIRCUIT JUDGES, and WATERS, DISTRICT JUDGE.

PER CURIAM:

Gerald and Mary Smith appeal from the district court's judgment dismissing their action against the defendants. The Smiths brought suit against

Gross, Gaddie, and the two corporate defendants for violation of the federal securities laws. The district court dismissed the suit without prejudice for lack of subject matter jurisdiction on the ground that there was no security involved in the transactions between the parties. * * *

We reverse. The transaction between the parties involved an investment contract.[30]

FACTS

The following statement of facts is taken from the Smiths' amended complaint and Gerald Smith's affidavit. Seller Gross, in a promotional newsletter, solicited buyer-investors to raise earthworms in order to help Gross reach his quotas of selling earthworms to fishermen. In the newsletter, buyers were promised that the seller's growing instructions would enable buyers to have a profitable farm, that the time involved would be similar to raising a garden, that the earthworms double in quantity every sixty days, and that the seller would buy back all bait size worms produced by buyers at $2.25 per pound. After responding to the newsletter, the Smiths were told by Gross that very little work was required, that success was guaranteed by the agreement to repurchase the Smiths' production, and that Gross needed the Smiths' help in the common enterprise of supplying worms for the bait industry. The Smiths alleged that they would not have purchased the worms without Gross' promise to repurchase the Smiths' production at $2.25 per pound. The Smiths were assured that they need not be worried about the market for worms because Gross would handle the marketing.

The Smiths alleged that, contrary to Gross' representations, worms multiply at a maximum of eight rather than 64 times per year, and that they could achieve the promised profits only if the multiplication rate was as fast as represented and Gross purchased the Smiths' production at $2.25 per pound. They also alleged that $2.25 is greater than the true market price and that Gross could pay that price only by selling the worms to new worm farmers at inflated prices. The price at which Gross sold the worms to worm farmers was ten times in excess of the true market value. There is little market for worms in the Phoenix area. * * *

INVESTMENT CONTRACT

The Smiths contend that the transactions between the parties involved an investment contract type of security. In SEC v. W.J. Howey Co., 328 U.S. 293, 301, 66 S.Ct. 1100, 1104, 90 L.Ed. 1244 (1946), the Supreme Court set out the conditions for an investment contract: "[t]he test is whether the scheme involves [1] an investment of money [2] in a common enterprise [3] with profits to come solely from the efforts of others." This court in SEC v. Glenn W. Turner Enterprises, Inc., 474 F.2d 476, 482 (9th Cir.), cert. denied, 414 U.S. 821, 94 S.Ct. 117, 38 L.Ed.2d 53 (1973), held that despite the Supreme Court's use of the word "solely", the third element of the *Howey* test is "whether the efforts made by those other than the investor are the undeniably significant ones, those essential managerial efforts which affect

---

30. [By the Editors] Section 2(1) of the Securities Act of 1933 defines "security." (See Statutory Supplement.) If the interest sold to the plaintiffs is an "investment contract", the defendants have sold a security, and since that security was not registered under the Securities Act of 1933, the plaintiffs have the statutory right to rescind the transaction under § 12.

the failure or success of the enterprise." The *Turner* court defined a common enterprise as "one in which the fortunes of the investor are interwoven with and dependent upon the efforts and success of those seeking the investment or of third parties." Id. at 482 n. 7.

We find this case virtually identical with Miller v. Central Chinchilla Group, Inc., 494 F.2d 414 (8th Cir.1974). In *Miller,* the defendants entered into contracts under which they sold chinchillas to the plaintiffs with the promise to repurchase the offspring. The plaintiffs were told that it was simple to breed chinchillas according to the defendants' instructions and that the venture would be highly profitable. The plaintiffs alleged that the chinchillas were difficult to raise and had a high mortality rate, and that the defendants could return the promised profits only if they repurchased the offspring and sold them to other prospective chinchilla raisers at an inflated price.

The *Miller* court focused on two features in holding that there was an investment contract: (1) the defendants persuaded the plaintiffs to invest by representing that the efforts required of them would be very minimal; and (2) that if the plaintiffs diligently exerted themselves, they still would not gain the promised profits because those profits could be achieved only if the defendants secured additional investors at the inflated prices. 494 F.2d at 417. Both of these features are present in the instant case. We find *Miller* to be persuasive and consistent with *Turner.*

The defendants argue that *Miller* is distinguishable on the ground that there the contract prohibited buyers from reselling to anyone other than the sellers; whereas here the buyers were free to resell to anyone they wanted to. The defendants contend that this distinguishing feature shows that the agreement was not a common enterprise.

The defendants' argument is without merit. There was a common enterprise as required by *Turner.* The Smiths alleged that, although they were free under the terms of the contract to sell their production anywhere they wished, they could have received the promised profits only if the defendants repurchased above the market price, and that the defendants could have repurchased above the market price only if the defendants secured additional investors at inflated prices. Thus, the fortune of the Smiths was interwoven with and dependent upon the efforts and success of the defendants.

We also find that here, as in *Miller,* the third element of an investment contract set forth in *Turner*—that the efforts of those other than the investor are the undeniably significant ones—was present here. The *Miller* court noted that the plaintiffs there had been assured by the sellers that the effort needed to raise chinchillas was minimal. The significant effort necessary for success in the endeavor was that of the seller in procuring new investors who would purchase the chinchillas at inflated prices. Here, the Smiths alleged that they were promised that the effort necessary to raise worms was minimal and they alleged that they could not receive the promised income unless the defendants purchased their harvest.

We find the analysis in *Miller* persuasive and hold that the Smiths alleged facts that, if true, were sufficient to establish an investment contract.

The defendants contend that the agreement between the parties was analogous to a franchise agreement. Franchise agreements are not securities. See, e.g., Bitter v. Hoby's International, Inc., 498 F.2d 183 (9th Cir.1974). This argument is not persuasive. The franchise cases are distinguishable. In *Bitter* this court focused on the fact that a franchisee independently determines his own success. Here, according to the Smiths' allegations, the only market in the Phoenix area for their production was the guaranteed right to resell to the sellers, and, thus, the Smiths were not solely responsible for their own success. We also note that the ultimate buyers in *Bitter* were the consuming public and not as here the offering party.

The facts as alleged in the Smiths' amended complaint and affidavit establish that an investment contract existed. * * * The judgment of the district court is reversed.

Notes

(1) The legal approach taken in this case permits a large number of ingenious investment schemes to be attacked successfully under the securities laws. Many of these investments are at best marginal and at worst fraudulent, though some entirely legitimate ones become ensnared in the broad definition of "security." The leading case is unquestionably SEC v. W.J. Howey Co., cited in the Court's opinion. Basically, this case involved the sale of plots of land planted in citrus; purchases were made in narrow strips of land arranged so that each contained a single row of 48 trees. The cultivation, harvesting, and marketing of the crop were largely centrally provided through service contracts with the seller of the land; the seller was also heavily involved in citrus production on adjoining land. The Supreme Court held that this arrangement constituted a "security" and thereby established the legal principle applied in the principal case.

(2) The broad definition of "security" set forth in this line of cases may seem necessary in order to protect investors in marginal, nontraditional schemes. The SEC, in particular, has long argued for a broad and expansive definition, but courts have not always accepted this position. As stated by Professor John C. Coffee, "The SEC has generally looked at any kind of unorthodox instrument or syndicate and tried to see whether or not investors need protection. Courts have been more doctrinal and formal." Quoted in Karen Donovan, SEC Defines "Securities" Expansively, National Law Journal, March 31, 1997, B1, at B2. Recent litigation involves several interesting issues:

(a) Is the solicitation of a settlement proposal, which "caps" the liability of "names" previously involved in insurance syndicates promulgated by Lloyd's of London in the United States, an offering of a "security"? For a negative answer, see Allen v. Lloyd's of London, 94 F.3d 923 (4th Cir.1996).

(b) Is a "Ponzi scheme"[31] in which the Foundation for New Era Philanthropy Inc. solicited donations from wealthy individuals, churches, foundations, and educational institutions on the basis of a promise to double their money in six months, a sale of securities? For an affirmative answer, see SEC v. Bennett, 904 F.Supp. 435 (E.D.Pa.1995); same case, 889 F.Supp. 804 (E.D.Pa.1995).

---

31. [By the Editors] A ponzi scheme is "a fraudulent investment scheme in which money contributed by later investors generates artificially high dividends for the original investors, whose example attracts even larger investments." Black's Law Dictionary [Second Pocket Edition] 536, col. 1 (2001).

(c) Is the sale of existing life insurance policies on the lives of HIV positive individuals to investors in order to permit the insureds to receive a portion of the face value of their policies during their lifetimes, a sale of securities? For a negative answer, see SEC v. Life Partners, Inc., 102 F.3d 587 (D.C.Cir.1996) [one judge dissenting].

(d) Is a "pyramid scheme"[32] in which much of the sales efforts to resell interests are made by investors in the enterprise a sale of securities to those investors? For a negative answer in a criminal prosecution see United States v. Holtzclaw, 950 F.Supp. 1306 (S.D.W.Va.1997) [investors did not rely solely or primarily on the efforts of others].

(3) In Landreth Timber Co. v. Landreth, 471 U.S. 681, 105 S.Ct. 2297, 85 L.Ed.2d 692 (1985), the Supreme Court rejected the so-called "sale of business doctrine" and held that the sale of all or a majority of the shares of a closely held corporation constituted the sale of a "security" subject to the federal securities acts. The principal argument of the court was a literal one based on the language of § 2(1). This holding makes available the protections of the antifraud provisions of the securities acts to all sales of closely held shares (assuming that the facilities of interstate commerce are used).

G. ISSUANCE OF SHARES BY A GOING CONCERN: PREEMPTIVE RIGHTS, DILUTION & RECAPITALIZATIONS

STOKES v. CONTINENTAL TRUST CO. OF CITY OF NEW YORK

Court of Appeals of New York, 1906.
186 N.Y. 285, 78 N.E. 1090.

This action was brought by a stockholder to compel his corporation to issue to him at par such a proportion of an increase made in its capital stock as the number of shares held by him before such increase bore to the number of all the shares originally issued, and in case such additional shares could not be delivered to him for his damages in the premises. The defendant is a domestic banking corporation in the city of New York, organized in 1890, with a capital stock of $500,000, consisting of 5,000 shares of the par value of $100 each. The plaintiff was one of the original stockholders, and still owns all the stock issued to him at the date of organization, together with enough more acquired since to make 221 shares in all. On the 29th of January, 1902, the defendant had a surplus of $1,048,450.94, which made the book value of the stock at that time $309.69 per share. On the 2d of January, 1902, Blair & Co., a strong and influential firm of private bankers in the city of New York, made the following proposition to the defendant: "If your stockholders at the special meeting to be called for January 29th, 1902, vote to increase your capital stock from $500,000 to $1,000,000 you may deliver the additional stock to us as soon as issued at $450 per share ($100 par value) for ourselves and our associates, it being understood that we may nominate ten of the 21 trustees to

32. [By the Editors] A familiar pyramid scheme is the chain letter. A pyramid scheme is "a property-distribution scheme in which a participant pays for the chance to receive compensation for introducing new persons to the scheme, as well as for when those new persons themselves introduce participants." Black's Law Dictionary, ibid., at 574, col. 2.

be elected at the adjourned annual meeting of stockholders." The directors of the defendant promptly met and duly authorized a special meeting of the stockholders to be called to meet on January 29, 1902, for the purpose of voting upon the proposed increase of stock and the acceptance of the offer to purchase the same. Upon due notice a meeting of the stockholders was held accordingly, more than a majority attending either in person or by proxy. A resolution to increase the stock was adopted by the vote of 4,197 shares, all that were cast. Thereupon the plaintiff demanded from the defendant the right to subscribe for 221 shares of the new stock at par, and offered to pay immediately for the same, which demand was refused. A resolution directing a sale to Blair & Co. at $450 a share was then adopted by a vote of 3,596 shares to 241. The plaintiff voted for the first resolution, but against the last, and before the adoption of the latter he protested against the proposed sale of his proportionate share of the stock, and again demanded the right to subscribe and pay for the same, but the demand was refused. On the 30th day of January, 1902, the stock was increased, and on the same day was sold to Blair & Co. at the price named, although the plaintiff formerly renewed his demand for 221 shares of the new stock at par, and tendered payment therefor, but it was refused upon the ground that the stock had already been issued to Blair & Co. Owing in part to the offer of Blair & Co. which had become known to the public, the market price of the stock had increased from $450 a share in September, 1901, to $550 in January, 1902, and at the time of the trial, in April, 1904, it was worth $700 per share. Prior to the special meeting of the stockholders, by authority of the board of directors, a circular letter was sent to each stockholder, including the plaintiff, giving notice of the proposition made by Blair & Co. and recommending that it be accepted. Thereupon the plaintiff notified the defendant that he wished to subscribe for his proportionate share of the new stock, if issued, and at no time did he waive his right to subscribe for the same. Before the special meeting, he had not been definitely notified by the defendant that he could not receive his proportionate part of the increase, but was informed that his proposition would "be taken under consideration." After finding these facts in substance, the trial court found, as conclusions of law, that the plaintiff had the right to subscribe for such proportion of the increase, as his holdings bore to all the stock before the increase was made; that the stockholders, directors, and officers of the defendant had no power to deprive him of that right, and that he was entitled to recover the difference between the market value of 221 shares on the 30th of January, 1902, and the par value thereof, or the sum of $99,450, together with interest from said date. The judgment entered accordingly was reversed by the Appellate Division, and the plaintiff appealed to this court, giving the usual stipulation for judgment absolute in case the order of reversal should be affirmed.

VANN, J. (after stating the facts). * * * Thus the question presented for decision is whether according to the facts found the plaintiff had the legal right to subscribe for and take the same number of shares of the new stock that he held of the old? The subject is not regulated by statute, and the question presented has never been directly passed upon by this court, and only to a limited extent has it been considered by courts in this state. * * *

If the right claimed by the plaintiff was a right of property belonging to him as a stockholder, he could not be deprived of it by the joint action of the other stockholders, and of all the directors and officers of the corporation. What is the nature of the right acquired by a stockholder through the ownership of shares of stock? What rights can he assert against the will of a majority of the stockholders, and all the officers and directors? While he does not own and cannot dispose of any specific property of the corporation, yet he and his associates own the corporation itself, its charter, franchises, and all rights conferred thereby, including the right to increase the stock. He has an inherent right to his proportionate share of any dividend declared, or of any surplus arising upon dissolution, and he can prevent waste or misappropriation of the property of the corporation by those in control. Finally, he has the right to vote for directors and upon all propositions subject by law to the control of the stockholders, and this is his supreme right and main protection. Stockholders have no direct voice in transacting the corporate business, but through their right to vote they can select those to whom the law intrusts the power of management and control. * * * This right to vote for directors, and upon propositions to increase the stock or mortgage the assets, is about all the power the stockholder has. So long as the management is honest, within the corporate powers, and involves no waste, the stockholders cannot interfere, even if the administration is feeble and unsatisfactory, but must correct such evils through their power to elect other directors. Hence, the power of the individual stockholder to vote in proportion to the number of his shares is vital, and cannot be cut off or curtailed by the action of all the other stockholders, even with the co-operation of the directors and officers.

In the case before us the new stock came into existence through the exercise of a right belonging wholly to the stockholders. As the right to increase the stock belonged to them, the stock when increased belonged to them also, as it was issued for money and not for property or for some purpose other than the sale thereof for money. By the increase of stock the voting power of the plaintiff was reduced one-half, and while he consented to the increase he did not consent to the disposition of the new stock by a sale thereof to Blair & Co. at less than its market value, nor by sale to any person in any way except by an allotment to the stockholders. * * * The plaintiff had power, before the increase of stock, to vote on 221 shares of stock, out of a total of 5,000, at any meeting held by the stockholders for any purpose. By the action of the majority, taken against his will and protest, he now has only one-half the voting power that he had before, because the number of shares has been doubled while he still owns but 221. This touches him as a stockholder in such a way as to deprive him of a right of property. Blair & Co. acquired virtual control, while he and the other stockholders lost it. We are not discussing equities, but legal rights, for this is an action at law, and the plaintiff was deprived of a strictly legal right. If the result gives him an advantage over other stockholders, it is because he stood upon his legal rights, while they did not. The question is what were his legal rights, not what his profit may be under the sale to Blair & Co., but what it might have been if the new stock had been issued to him in proportion to his holding of the old. The other stockholders could give their property to Blair & Co., but they could not give his. * * *

We are thus led to lay down the rule that a stockholder has an inherent right to a proportionate share of new stock issued for money only and not to purchase property for the purposes of the corporation or to effect a consolidation, and while he can waive that right, he cannot be deprived of it without his consent except when the stock is issued at a fixed price not less than par, and he is given the right to take at that price in proportion to his holding, or in some other equitable way that will enable him to protect his interest by acting on his own judgment and using his own resources. This rule is just to all and tends to prevent the tyranny of majorities which needs restraint, as well as virtual attempts to blackmail by small minorities which should be prevented. * * *

[The court concluded that the plaintiff's damages should have been measured by the difference between the $450 sale price and the $550 market value of the shares rather than the difference between par value and market value of the shares.]

The order appealed from should be reversed and the judgment of the trial court modified by reducing the damages from the sum of $99,450, with interest from January 30, 1902, to the sum of $22,100, with interest from that date, and by striking out the extra allowance of costs, and as thus modified the judgment of the trial court is affirmed, without costs in this court or in the Appellate Division to either party.

HAIGHT, J. (dissenting). [Opinion omitted].

CULLEN, C.J., and WERNER and HISCOCK, JJ., concur with VANN, J.; WILLARD BARLETT, J., concurs with HAIGHT, J.; O'BRIEN, J., absent.

Notes

(1) The common law preemptive right discussed in *Stokes* is now embodied in state statutes, of which there is considerable diversity. See MBCA § 6.30, which provides standard terms on an elective basis to codify many aspects of the preemptive right.

(2) It is now generally accepted that the preemptive right is not an inherent aspect of the ownership of shares but a right that may be granted or withheld by the articles of incorporation. The MBCA adopts an "opt in" clause: Under § 6.30(a), no preemptive right exists unless provision for it is expressly made. As a result, a "plain vanilla" corporation whose articles of incorporation contain the statutory minima will not have preemptive rights. Would not the converse (i.e. that a corporation has preemptive rights unless expressly denied in the articles of incorporation) be preferable? At least nineteen states have adopted an "opt out" rather than an "opt in" provision.

(3) If a corporation elects preemptive rights, should that right extend to shares issued as compensation to directors or officers? See MBCA § 6.30(b)(3)(i) and (ii). Does that not tend to frustrate the purpose of preemptive rights whenever one shareholder is an officer of the corporation and others are not? Why should shares "sold otherwise than for money" [MBCA § 6.30(b)(3)(iv)] not be subject to preemptive rights? What is the justification for excluding shares issued within six months of the formation of the corporation? See MBCA § 6.30(b)(3)(iii). What about shares that are offered preemptively, but not purchased? May they be sold entirely free of such rights in the future? See MBCA § 6.30(b)(6).

KATZOWITZ v. SIDLER

Court of Appeals of New York, 1969.
24 N.Y.2d 512, 301 N.Y.S.2d 470, 249 N.E.2d 359.

KEATING, JUDGE.

Isador Katzowitz is a director and stockholder of a close corporation. Two other persons, Jacob Sidler and Max Lasker, own the remaining securities and, with Katzowitz, comprise Sulburn Holding Corp.'s board of directors. Sulburn was organized in 1955 to supply propane gas to three other corporations controlled by these men. Sulburn's certificate of incorporation authorized it to issue 1,000 shares of no par value stock for which the incorporators established a $100 selling price. Katzowitz, Sidler and Lasker each invested $500 and received five shares of the corporation's stock.

The three men had been jointly engaged in several corporate ventures for more than 25 years. In this period they had always been equal partners and received identical compensation from the corporations they controlled. Though all the corporations controlled by these three men prospered, disenchantment with their inter-personal relationship flared into the open in 1956. At this time, Sidler and Lasker joined forces to oust Katzowitz from any role in managing the corporations. * * *

Before the issue could be tried, the three men entered into a stipulation in 1959 whereby Katzowitz withdrew from active participation in the day-to-day operations of the business. The agreement provided that he would remain on the boards of all the corporations, and each board would be limited to three members composed of the three stockholders or their designees. Katzowitz was to receive the same compensation and other fringe benefits which the controlled corporations paid Lasker and Sidler. The stipulation also provided that Katzowitz, Sidler and Lasker were "equal stockholders and each of said parties now owns the same number of shares of stock in each of the defendant corporations and that such shares of stock shall continue to be in full force and effect and unaffected by this stipulation, except as hereby otherwise expressly provided." The stipulation contained no other provision affecting equal stock interests.

The business relationship established by the stipulation was fully complied with. Sidler and Lasker, however, were still interested in disassociating themselves from Katzowitz. * * *

In December of 1961 Sulburn was indebted to each stockholder to the extent of $2,500 for fees and commissions earned up until September, 1961. Instead of paying this debt, Sidler and Lasker wanted Sulburn to loan the money to another corporation which all three men controlled. Sidler and Lasker called a meeting of the board of directors to propose that additional securities be offered at $100 per share to substitute for the money owed to the directors. The notice of meeting for October 30, 1961 had on its agenda "a proposition that the corporation issue common stock of its unissued common capital stock, *the total par value [of] which shall equal the total sum of the fees and commissions now owing by the corporation to its * * * directors*". (Emphasis added.) Katzowitz made it quite clear at the meeting that he would not invest any additional funds in Sulburn in order for it to make a loan to this other corporation. The only resolution passed at the meeting was that the corporation would pay the sum of $2,500 to each director.

With full knowledge that Katzowitz expected to be paid his fees and commissions and that he did not want to participate in any new stock issuance, the other two directors called a special meeting of the board on December 1, 1961. The only item on the agenda for this special meeting was the issuance of 75 shares of the corporation's common stock at $100 per share. The offer was to be made to stockholders in "accordance with their respective preemptive rights for the purpose of acquiring additional working capital". The amount to be raised was the exact amount owed by the corporation to its shareholders. The offering price for the securities was 1/18th the book value of the stock. Only Sidler and Lasker attended the special board meeting. They approved the issuance of the 75 shares.

Notice was mailed to each stockholder that they had the right to purchase 25 shares of the corporation's stock at $100 a share. The offer was to expire on December 27, 1961. Failure to act by that date was stated to constitute a waiver. At about the same time Katzowitz received the notice, he received a check for $2,500 from the corporation for his fees and commissions. Katzowitz did not exercise his option to buy the additional shares. Sidler and Lasker purchased their full complement, 25 shares each. This purchase by Sidler and Lasker caused an immediate dilution of the book value of the outstanding securities.

On August 25, 1962 the principal asset of Sulburn, a tractor trailer truck, was destroyed. On August 31, 1962 the directors unanimously voted to dissolve the corporation. Upon dissolution, Sidler and Lasker each received $18,885.52 but Katzowitz only received $3,147.59.

The plaintiff instituted a declaratory judgment action to establish his right to the proportional interest in the assets of Sulburn in liquidation less the $5,000 which Sidler and Lasker used to purchase their shares in December, 1961.

Special Term (Westchester County) found the book value of the corporation's securities on the day the stock was offered at $100 to be worth $1,800. The court also found that "the individual defendants * * * decided that in lieu of taking that sum in cash [the commissions and fees due the stockholders], they preferred to add to their investment by having the corporate defendant make available and offer each stockholder an additional twenty-five shares of unissued stock." The court reasoned that Katzowitz waived his right to purchase the stock or object to its sale to Lasker and Sidler by failing to exercise his preemptive right and found his protest at the time of dissolution untimely.

On the substantive legal issues and findings of fact, the Appellate Division [two Justices dissenting, 29 App.Div.2d 955, 289 N.Y.S.2d 324] was in agreement with Special Term. The majority agreed that the book value of the corporation's stock at the time of the stock offering was $1,800. The Appellate Division reasoned, however, that showing a disparity between book value and offering price was insufficient without also showing fraud or overreaching. Disparity in price by itself was not enough to prove fraud. The Appellate Division also found that the plaintiff had waived his right to object to his recovery in dissolution by failing to either exercise his pre-emptive rights or take steps to prevent the sale of the stock.

The concept of pre-emptive rights was fashioned by the judiciary to safeguard two distinct interests of stockholders—the right to protection against dilution of their equity in the corporation and protection against dilution of their proportionate voting control. (Ballantine, Corporations [rev. ed., 1946], § 209.) After early decisions (Gray v. Portland Bank, 3 Mass. 364; Stokes v. Continental Trust Co., 186 N.Y. 285, 78 N.E. 1090, 12 L.R.A., N.S., 969), legislation fixed the right enunciated with respect to proportionate voting but left to the judiciary the role of protecting existing shareholders from the dilution of their equity (e.g., Stock Corporation Law, § 39, now Business Corporation Law, Consol.Laws, c. 4, § 622; see Drinker, The Preemptive Right of Shareholders to Subscribe to New Shares, 43 Harv.L.Rev. 586; Alexander Hamilton Frey, Shareholders' Pre-emptive Rights, 38 Yale L.J. 563).

It is clear that directors of a corporation have no discretion in the choice of those to whom the earnings and assets of the corporation should be distributed. Directors, being fiduciaries of the corporation, must, in issuing new stock, treat existing shareholders fairly. Though there is very little statutory control over the price which a corporation must receive for new shares the power to determine price must be exercised for the benefit of the corporation and in the interest of all the stockholders.

Issuing stock for less than fair value can injure existing shareholders by diluting their interest in the corporation's surplus, in current and future earnings and in the assets upon liquidation. Normally, a stockholder is protected from the loss of his equity from dilution, even though the stock is being offered at less than fair value, because the shareholder receives rights which he may either exercise or sell. If he exercises, he has protected his interest and, if not, he can sell the rights, thereby compensating himself for the dilution of his remaining shares in the equity of the corporation.[33]

When new shares are issued, however, at prices far below fair value in a close corporation or a corporation with only a limited market for its shares, existing stockholders, who do not want to invest or do not have the capacity to invest additional funds, can have their equity interest in the corporation diluted to the vanishing point.

The protection afforded by stock rights is illusory in close corporations. Even if a buyer could be found for the rights, they would have to be sold at an inadequate price because of the nature of a close corporation. Outsiders are normally discouraged from acquiring minority interests after a close corporation has been organized. Certainly a stockholder in a close corporation is at a total loss to safeguard his equity from dilution if no rights are offered and he does not want to invest additional funds.

Though it is difficult to determine fair value for a corporation's securities and courts are therefore reluctant to get into the thicket, when the issuing

---

33. [By the Court] There is little justification for issuing stock far below its fair value. The only reason for issuing stock below fair value exists in publicly held corporations where the problem of floating new issues through subscription is concerned. The reason advanced in this situation is that it insures the success of the issue or that it has the same psychological effect as a dividend.

price is shown to be markedly below book value in a close corporation and when the remaining shareholder-directors benefit from the issuance, a case for judicial relief has been established. In that instance, the corporation's directors must show that the issuing price falls within some range which can be justified on the basis of valid business reasons. If no such showing is made by the directors, there is no reason for the judiciary to abdicate its function to a majority of the board or stockholders who have not seen fit to come forward and justify the propriety of diverting property from the corporation and allow the issuance of securities to become an oppressive device permitting the dilution of the equity of dissident stockholders.

The defendant directors here make no claim that the price set was a fair one. No business justification is offered to sustain it. Admittedly, the stock was sold at less than book value. The defendants simply contend that, as long as all stockholders were given an equal opportunity to purchase additional shares, no stockholder can complain simply because the offering dilutes his interest in the corporation.

The defendants' argument is fallacious.

The corollary of a stockholder's right to maintain his proportionate equity in a corporation by purchasing additional shares is the right not to purchase additional shares without being confronted with dilution of his existing equity if no valid business justification exists for the dilution.

A stockholder's right not to purchase is seriously undermined if the stock offered is worth substantially more than the offering price. Any purchase at this price dilutes his interest and impairs the value of his original holding. "A corporation is not permitted to sell its stock for a legally inadequate price at least where there is objection. Plaintiff has a right to insist upon compliance with the law whether or not he cares to exercise his option. He cannot block a sale for a fair price merely because he disagrees with the wisdom of the plan but he can insist that the sale price be fixed in accordance with legal requirements." (Bennett v. Breuil Petroleum Corp., [34 Del.Ch. 6, 14–15, 99 A.2d 236, 241 (1953).]) Judicial review in this area is limited to whether under all the circumstances, including the disparity between issuing price of the stock and its true value, the nature of the corporation, the business necessity for establishing an offering price at a certain amount to facilitate raising new capital, and the ability of stockholders to sell rights, the additional offering of securities should be condemned because the directors in establishing the sale price did not fix it with reference to financial considerations with respect to the ready disposition of securities.

Here the obvious disparity in selling price and book value was calculated to force the dissident stockholder into investing additional sums. No valid business justification was advanced for the disparity in price, and the only beneficiaries of the disparity were the two director-stockholders who were eager to have additional capital in the business.

It is no answer to Katzowitz' action that he was also given a chance to purchase additional shares at this bargain rate. The price was not so much a bargain as it was a tactic, conscious or unconscious on the part of the directors, to place Katzowitz in a compromising situation. The price was so fixed to make the failure to invest costly. However, Katzowitz at the time might not have been aware of the dilution because no notice of the effect of the issuance of the new shares on the already outstanding shares was disclosed. In addition, since the stipulation entitled Katzowitz to the same compensation as Sidler and Lasker, the disparity in equity interest caused by their purchase of additional securities in 1961 did not affect stockholder income from Sulburn and, therefore, Katzowitz possibly was not aware of the effect of the stock issuance on his interest in the corporation until dissolution.

No reason exists at this time to permit Sidler and Lasker to benefit from their course of conduct. Katzowitz' delay in commencing the action did not prejudice the defendants. By permitting the defendants to recover their additional investment in Sulburn before the remaining assets of Sulburn are distributed to the stockholders upon dissolution, all the stockholders will be treated equitably. Katzowitz, therefore, should receive his aliquot share of the assets of Sulburn less the amount invested by Sidler and Lasker for their purchase of stock on December 27, 1961.

Accordingly, the order of the Appellate Division should be reversed, with costs, and judgment granted in favor of the plaintiff against the individual defendants.

BURKE, SCILEPPI, BERGAN, BREITEL and JASEN, JJ., concur with KEATING, J.

FULD, C.J., dissents and votes to affirm on the opinion at the Appellate Division.

Notes

(1) The transaction involved in *Katzowitz* is a type of "freeze-out." A similar type of freeze-out occurs when inside shareholders pay for their additional shares by canceling debts owed to them by the corporation (representing, in effect, capital that they have already invested in the business) while outside shareholders are put to the painful choice of investing fresh capital over which they lose effective control or see their proportionate interest decline drastically. A classic example is Hyman v. Velsicol Corp., 342 Ill.App. 489, 97 N.E.2d 122 (1951), where an outside shareholder was given the choice of investing an additional $136,000 in order to stay even or watching his proportional interest decline from 20 percent to a fraction of one percent. What did the shareholder do? He sued, of course, but lost when the Court concluded that the plan "was not an abuse of discretion" and was not "fraudulently oppressive." As in *Katzowitz*, the shareholder's preemptive right was fully protected and shares were issued at par value, arguably below "true value." However, there was some business justification for the transaction since the majority shareholders were canceling outstanding indebtedness owed to them and the plaintiff was a former employee who was interested in a competing business.

(2) Some freeze-out cases have been brought under the theory that the plan constitutes a violation of fiduciary duties, discussed in a later chapter. See generally, Mark K. Kessler, Elimination of Minority Interests by Cash Merger: Two Recent Cases, 30 Bus.Law. 699 (1975). Cases have also adopted the view that transactions literally complying with statutory requirements may be set aside if they do not meet a standard of "entire fairness" when they involve conflict of interest transactions. See Weinberger v. UOP, Inc., p. 785 infra; see also Alpert v. 28 Williams St. Corp., 63 N.Y.2d 557, 483 N.Y.S.2d 667, 473 N.E.2d 19 (1984). The modern trend seems clearly to be running in the direction of imposing a fiduciary duty on dilutive transactions such as those involved in *Katzowitz*. In the words of

the Mississippi Supreme Court, "[t]he traditional view that shareholders have no fiduciary duty to each other, and transactions constituting 'freeze-outs' or 'squeezeouts' generally cannot be attacked as a breach of duty of loyalty or good faith to each other, is outmoded." Fought v. Morris, 543 So.2d 167, 169 (Miss. 1989). See also Johnston v. Wilbourn, 760 F.Supp. 578, 582 (S.D.Miss.1991). In the light of this trend, it is doubtful that older cases such as Hyman v. Velsicol (note (2) above) would be decided the same way if they arose today. See generally F. Hodge O'Neal, Oppression of Minority Shareholders: Protecting Minority Rights, 35 Clev.St.L.Rev. 121 (1987).

LACOS LAND COMPANY v. ARDEN GROUP, INC.

Court of Chancery of Delaware, New Castle County, 1986.
517 A.2d 271.

ALLEN, CHANCELLOR. This action constitutes a multi-pronged attack upon a proposed recapitalization of defendant Arden Group, Inc., authorized by a vote of Arden's shareholders at their June 10, 1986 annual meeting. The recapitalization, if effectuated, will create a new Class B Common Stock possessing ten votes per share and entitled, as a class, to elect seventy-five percent of the members of Arden's board of directors. This new stock is, pursuant to the terms of a presently pending exchange offer, available on a share-for-share basis to all holders of Arden's Class A Common Stock. It is, however, acknowledged by defendants that the new Class B Common Stock has been deliberately fashioned to be attractive mainly to defendant Briskin— Arden's principal shareholder and chief executive officer. Thus, the recapitalization is not itself a device to raise capital but rather is a technique to transfer stockholder control of the enterprise to Mr. Briskin.

Plaintiff is an Arden stockholder owning approximately 4.5% of Arden's Class A Common Stock * * *. Defendants are the members of Arden's board of directors. Pending is an application to preliminarily enjoin the issuance of Class B Common Stock * * *.

I.

The new supervoting common stock whose issuance is sought to be enjoined will differ from Arden's other authorized class of common stock, Class A Common Stock, most importantly, in its enhanced voting power, its diminished dividend rights and in restrictions upon its transfer.

Specifically, with respect to voting rights, the recent charter amendment provides that "on every matter submitted to a vote or consent of the stockholder, every holder of Class A Common Stock shall be entitled to one vote * * * for each share * * * and every holder of Class B Common Stock shall be entitled to 10 votes * * * for each share * * *."

As to the election of directors, the restated certificate provides that Class A shares, together with the Company's preferred stock, voting as a class shall "be entitled to elect 25% of the total number of directors to be elected" rounded up to the nearest whole number. The Class B shares are entitled to vote as a separate class and to elect the remaining 75% of directors to be elected.[34]

---

34. If, on the record date for the meeting to elect directors, the Class B shares equal less than 12 1/2% of the total of Class A and Class B shares together, then Class A will continue

With respect to dividend rights, Class A Common Stock will, following the initial issuance of Class B shares, have the right to receive a one-time dividend of $.30 per share; Class B shares are to have no right to participate to any extent in that cash dividend. Excepting this one-time $.30 dividend, each share of Class B stock is to be entitled to participate in all dividends declared and paid with respect to a share of Class A stock but only to the extent of 90% of such dividend.

Class B shares may be transferred only to a Permitted Transferee,[35] but under certain circumstances may be converted on a share-for-share basis into Class A stock. A transfer of Class B to a person other than a Permitted Transferee at a time when conversion to Class A would be permitted would convert the transferred stock into Class A stock. Generally, Class B stock may, at the option of the holder, be converted to Class A stock on a share-for-share basis at the earlier of (i) the third anniversary of its issuance or (ii) the death of the holder.

II.

The creation of a dual common stock structure with one class exercising effective control of the company is, of course, not a novel idea, although it is one that, thanks to its potential as an anti-takeover device, has recently emerged from the reaches of the corporation law chorus to strut its moment upon center stage where corporate drama is acted out. In this instance, the notion of employing this dual common stock structure apparently originated with defendant Briskin.

Mr. Briskin became Arden chief executive officer in 1976 at a time when the Company was apparently in a desperate condition. Its stock was then trading between $1 and $2 per share. Briskin's stewardship has apparently been active and effective. While Arden has paid no dividends since 1970, during Briskin's tenure Arden's stock price has risen steadily; currently Arden common stock is publicly trading at around $25 per share, a price somewhat higher than the range of prices at which its stock traded in the weeks prior to the announcement of the plan that is the subject matter of this litigation.

In instigating the dual common stock voting structure, Mr. Briskin was apparently not responding to any specific threat to existing policies or practices of Arden posed by a specific takeover threat. Rather, he apparently was motivated to protect his power to control Arden's business future. Such a motivation, while it may be suspect—since it may reflect not a desire to protect business policies and capabilities for the benefit of the corporation and its shareholders but rather a wish simply to retain the benefits of office—does not itself constitute a wrong. See, e.g., Unocal Corp. v. Mesa Petroleum Co., Del. Supr., 493 A.2d 946, 955 (1985).

to vote as a class in the filling of 25% of the positions to be filled but will have the right to vote in the Class B election as well, with Class B shares continuing to be entitled to ten votes per share.

35. For a natural person Permitted Transferees include (1) the holder's spouse or any lineal descendant of a grandparent of the holder or the holder's spouse, (2) the trustee of any trust for the benefit of the holder or a Permitted Transferee, (3) charitable organizations, (4) a corporation or partnership under majority control of the holder or a Permitted Transferee and (5) the holder's estate.

In this instance, Briskin initially took his idea to the board of directors at its November 22, 1985 meeting. The Board established a three member committee of non-officer directors to consider the matter. Prior to the committee's first meeting, its chairman sent the other two committee members the proxy statement of another company that had adopted a dual class common stock structure, together with materials on other companies that had adopted supervoting plans and some materials relating to a report written by Professor Fischel on "Organized Exchanges and the Regulation of Dual Class Common Stock." The special committee retained neither independent counsel nor an independent financial advisor. At its first meeting, held on April 7, 1986, the chairman of this group distributed to the committee a draft report that he had previously prepared which gave approval to a supervoting stock plan. The committee reviewed this draft and suggested changes. The chairman noted the suggested changes and prepared a final three page report which was signed four days later at the committee's second, and final, meeting.

The committee's report was presented to the board at its April 22 meeting at which time the board approved the supervoting stock plan.

At that meeting the board fixed the date of the Company's annual meeting for June 10, 1986. Management of the Company prepared a proxy statement describing the proposed charter amendments authorizing the new supervoting Class B Common Stock, describing the Exchange Offer by which it was proposed that such new stock be distributed and setting out the background of, and the reasons for, this proposal.

At the June 10 annual meeting, the Arden stockholders approved the proposed certificate amendments. Of 2,303,170 shares outstanding, 1,463,155 voted in favor (64%) and 325,004 (14%) voted to reject the proposal. Of the affirmative votes, 427,347 were voted by Briskin or his family and 388,493 were voted by a trustee as directed by Arden's management. As to the preferred stock, 74.4% of the 136,359 shares outstanding voted in favor of the proposal, more than half of which were voted by a trustee as directed by Arden's management.

As a consequence of the stockholders' approval of the proposal, the Company, on June 18, 1986, distributed to all holders of its Class A Common Stock an Offering Circular offering to exchange for each share of such common stock one share of Class B Common Stock with the rights, preferences, etc. described above.

III.

Our corporation law provides great flexibility to shareholders in creating the capital structure of their firm. [Citation omitted.] Differing classes of stock with differing voting rights are permissible under our law, 8 Del.C. sec. 151(a); [Citation omitted.]; restriction on transfers are possible, 8 Del.C. sec. 202, and charter provisions requiring the filling of certain directorates by a class of stock are, if otherwise properly adopted, valid. [Citation omitted.] Thus, each of the significant characteristics of the Class B Common Stock is in principle a valid power or limitation of common stock. The primary inquiry therefore is whether the Arden shareholders have effectively exercised their will to amend the Company's restated certificate of incorporation so as to authorize the implementation of the dual class common stock structure. * * *

For the reasons that follow I conclude that plaintiff has demonstrated a reasonable probability that on final hearing it will be demonstrated that the June 10, 1986 vote of the Arden shareholders has been fundamentally and fatally flawed and that, therefore, the amendments to Arden's restated certificate of incorporation purportedly authorized by that vote are voidable. * * * I conclude provisionally on the basis of the record now available, that the June 10 vote was inappropriately affected by an explicit threat of Mr. Briskin that unless the proposed amendments were approved, he would use his power (and not simply his power qua shareholder) to block transactions that may be in the best interests of the company, if those transactions would dilute his ownership interest in Arden. I use the word threat because such a position entails, in my opinion, the potential for a breach of Mr. Briskin's duty, as the principal officer of Arden and as a member of its board of directors, to exercise corporate power unselfishly, with a view to fostering the interests of the corporation and all of its shareholders. * * *

IV.

Judging from what is stated in the proxy materials, Arden's board in recommending the charter amendments and Arden's shareholders in approving them were both placed, inappropriately, in a position that made it significantly less likely than it might otherwise have been that approval of the plan to effectively transfer all shareholder power to Mr. Briskin would have been given.

To a shareholder who wondered why his board of directors was recommending a plan expected to place all effective shareholder power in a single shareholder, the proxy statement gives a clear answer: Mr. Briskin is demanding it; it's not such a big deal anyway since, as a practical matter, he has great power already; and if he doesn't get these amendments, he may exercise his power to thwart corporate transactions that may be in the Company's best interests. Thus, in order for the board to be "permitted to consider" certain transactions that might threaten to reduce Mr. Briskin's control, the board approved the proposal. This story is disclosed more or less straight forwardly in the proxy solicitation materials.

As to Mr. Briskin's position, the proxy statement states:

Purpose and Effects of the Proposal

1. Purpose. Mr. Briskin, the Company's largest single stockholder * * * has informed the Company of his concern that certain transactions which could be determined by the Board of Directors to be in the best interests of all of the stockholders, such as the issuance of additional voting securities in connection with financings or mergers or acquisitions by the Company, might make the Company vulnerable to an unsolicited or hostile takeover attempt or to an attempt at "greenmail," and that he would not give his support to any such transactions for which his approval might be required unless steps were taken to secure his voting position in the Company.

As to the asserted fact that Mr. Briskin already really has, as a practical matter, the power to control the Company, the proxy statement says (immediately following the foregoing quoted matter):

As a practical matter, given the present stock ownership of Mr. Briskin and certain supermajority vote requirements and other provisions of the existing Certificate (see "Possible Adverse Consequences"), explicit or implicit approval of Mr. Briskin would be required for every such major transaction the Company might choose to engage in (whether or not a vote of stockholders is actually required). Similarly, it is unlikely that the Company would engage in transactions to which Mr. Briskin is opposed. Such transactions, including the issuance of additional capital stock, although dilutive of Mr. Briskin's stock ownership, could be in the best interests of stockholders other than Mr. Briskin. * * *

Thus, Arden shareholders were unmistakably told that should they fail to approve the proposed amendments, Mr. Briskin "would not give his support to any transaction [that might make the Company vulnerable to an unsolicited or hostile takeover attempt] for which his approval might be required." Using the term in the vague way which we ordinarily do, a vote in such circumstances as these could be said to be "coerced." But that label itself supplies no basis to conclude that the legal effect of the vote is impaired in any way. * * *

The determination of whether it was inappropriate for Mr. Briskin to structure the choice of Arden's shareholders (and its directors), as was done here, requires, first, a determination of which of his hats—shareholder, officer or director—Mr. Briskin was wearing when he stated his position concerning the possible withholding of his "support" for future transactions unless steps were taken "to secure his voting position." If he spoke only as a shareholder, and should have been so understood, an evaluation of the propriety of his position might be markedly different than if the "support" referred to could be or should be interpreted as involving the exercise of his power as either an officer or director of Arden.

On this point defendants' position at oral argument confirms that which the proxy language itself indicates—that, in taking this position, Mr. Briskin did not limit, and could not be understood to have limited, himself to exercising only stockholder power. Defendants have emphasized that Briskin's "practical" power derives in part from his notable success as a chief executive officer; his history of success, I was reminded, creates influence and his position confers power to initiate board consideration of important matters. Moreover, the proxy statement made clear that the approval that Briskin threatened to withhold included approval of transactions that did not require a vote of stockholders. * * * Accordingly, the conclusion seems inescapable that, in announcing an intent to withhold support for corporate action that might entail, for instance, the issuance of stock, even if that act might be in the best interests of the corporation, unless "steps were taken to preserve his voting position," Mr. Briskin could not be understood to have been acting only as a shareholder.

As a director and as an officer, of course, Mr. Briskin has a duty to act with complete loyalty to the interests of the corporation and its shareholders. Weinberger v. UOP, Inc., Del. Supr., 457 A.2d 701 (1983); Guth v. Loft, Del.

Supr., 23 Del. Ch. 255, 5 A.2d 503 (1939). His position as stated to the shareholders in the Company proxy statement seems inconsistent with that obligation. In form at least, the statement by a director and officer that he will not give his support to a corporate transaction unless steps are taken to confer a personal power or benefit, suggests an evident disregard of duty. However, the nature of the quid pro quo sought by Mr. Briskin in this case is at least consistent with a benign or selfless motive. The Class B stock he sought to have the board recommend and the stockholders approve would transfer complete control of the enterprise to him for an indefinite period, but it is a control that may not be transferred generally and so it is unlikely that Mr. Briskin was motivated to gain access to a control premium for his stock by insisting on a device of this kind as a price of his supporting certain types of future action.

Mr. Briskin's motivation in fact, however, need not be determined in order to conclude that the stockholder vote of June 10, 1986 was fatally flawed by the implied (indeed, the expressed) threats that unless the proposed amendments were authorized, he would oppose transactions "which could be determined by the Board of Directors to be in the best interests of all of the stockholders." As a corporate fiduciary, Mr. Briskin has no right to take such a position, even if benevolently motivated in doing so. Shareholders who respect Mr. Briskin's ability and performance—and who are legally entitled to his undivided loyalty—were inappropriately placed in a position in which they were told that if they refused to vote affirmatively, Mr. Briskin would not support future possible transactions that might be beneficial to the corporation. A vote of shareholders under such circumstances cannot, in the face of a timely challenge by one of the corporation's shareholders, be said, in my opinion, to satisfy the mandate of Section 242(b) of our corporation law requiring shareholder consent to charter amendments. * * *

For the Foregoing reasons, plaintiff's motion shall be granted. Plaintiff shall submit a form of implementing order on notice.

Notes

(1) Since it appears clear that Mr. Briskin was firmly in control of this corporation anyway, why did he want to effectuate this recapitalization?

(2) Can you think of any reasons for doing the proposed recapitalization challenged in Lacos Land v. Arden Group, Inc., that would have passed judicial scrutiny? If so, was Briskin being punished in the principal case for his honesty?

H. DISTRIBUTIONS BY A CLOSELY HELD CORPORATION

GOTTFRIED v. GOTTFRIED

Supreme Court of New York, 1947.
73 N.Y.S.2d 692.

CORCORAN, JUSTICE.

This action was brought in the early part of 1945 by minority stockholders of Gottfried Baking Corporation (hereinafter called "Gottfried"), to compel the Board of Directors of that corporation to declare dividends on its common stock. The defendants are Gottfried itself, its directors, and Hanscom Baking Corporation (hereinafter called "Hanscom"), a wholly owned subsidiary of Gottfried. Gottfried is a closely held family corporation. All of its stockholders, with minor exceptions, are children of the founder of the business, Elias Gottfried, and their respective spouses.

Both corporations are engaged in the manufacture and sale of bakery products; Gottfried for distribution at wholesale, and Hanscom for distribution at retail in its own stores. Each corporation functions separately, in the manufacture and sale of its respective products.

At the end of 1946 the outstanding capitalization of Gottfried consisted of 4500 shares of "A" stock, without nominal or par value, and 20,862 shares of common stock without par value. The "A" stock is entitled to dividends of $8 per share before any dividends may be paid upon the common stock, as well as a further participation in earnings. At the end of 1944, immediately before this action was commenced, Gottfried also had outstanding preferred stock in the face amount of $79,000, and Hanscom had outstanding $86,000 face amount of preferred stock. The plaintiffs in the aggregate owned approximately 38% of each of these classes of securities. The individual defendants owned approximately 62 percent.

From 1931 until 1945 no dividends had been paid upon the common stock, although dividends had been paid regularly upon the outstanding preferred stock and intermittently upon the "A" stock. There seems to be no question with respect to the policy of the Board of Directors in not declaring dividends prior to 1944. An analysis of the financial statements of the corporation shows a net working capital deficit at the end of 1941, in which year a consolidated loss of $109,816 had been incurred. Moreover, until the end of 1943 the earned surplus was relatively small in relation to the volume of business done and the growing requirements of the business.

Although the action was brought in the early part of 1945 to compel the declaration of dividends upon the common stock, dividends actually were declared and paid upon said stock in 1945, and subsequently. The purpose of the action now, therefore, is to compel the payment of dividends upon the common stock in such amount as under all the circumstances is fair and adequate.

The action is predicated upon the claim that the policy of the Board of Directors with respect to the declaration of dividends is animated by considerations other than the best welfare of the corporations or their stockholders. The plaintiffs claim that bitter animosity on the part of the directors, who own the controlling stock, against the plaintiff minority stockholders, as well as a desire to coerce the latter into selling their stock to the majority interests at a grossly inadequate price, and the avoidance of heavy personal income taxes upon any dividends that might be declared, have been the motivating factors that have dominated the defendants. Plaintiffs, contend, moreover, that the defendants by excessive salaries, bonuses and corporate loans to themselves or some of them, have eliminated the immediate need of dividends in so far as they were concerned, while at the same time a starvation dividend policy with respect to the minority stockholders—not on the payroll—operates designedly to compel the plaintiffs to sacrifice their stock by sale to the defendants.

There is no essential dispute as to the principles of law involved. If an adequate corporate surplus is available for the purpose, directors may not withhold the declaration of dividends in bad faith. But the mere existence of an adequate corporate surplus is not sufficient to invoke court action to compel such a dividend. There must also be bad faith on the part of the directors.

There are no infallible distinguishing ear-marks of bad faith. The following facts are relevant to the issue of bad faith and are admissible in evidence: Intense hostility of the controlling faction against the minority; exclusion of the minority from employment by the corporation; high salaries, or bonuses or corporate loans made to the officers in control; the fact that the majority group may be subject to high personal income taxes if substantial dividends are paid; the existence of a desire by the controlling directors to acquire the minority stock interests as cheaply as possible. But if they are not motivating causes they do not constitute "bad faith" as a matter of law.

The essential test of bad faith is to determine whether the policy of the directors is dictated by their personal interests rather than the corporate welfare. Directors are fiduciaries. Their *cestui que trust* are the corporation and the stockholders as a body. Circumstances such as those above mentioned and any other significant factors, appraised in the light of the financial condition and requirements of the corporation, will determine the conclusion as to whether the directors have or have not been animated by personal, as distinct from corporate, considerations.

The court is not concerned with the direction which the exercise of the judgment of the Board of Directors may take, provided only that such exercise of judgment be made in good faith. It is axiomatic that the court will not substitute its judgment for that of the Board of Directors.

It must be conceded that closely held corporations are easily subject to abuse on the part of dominant stockholders, particularly in the direction of action designed to compel minority stockholders to sell their stock at a sacrifice. But close corporation or not, the court will not tolerate directorate action designed to achieve that or any other wrongful purpose. Even in the absence of bad faith, however, the impact of dissension and hostility among stockholders falls usually with heavier force in a closely held corporation. In many such cases, a large part of a stockholder's assets may be tied up in the corporation. It is frequently contemplated by the parties, moreover, that the respective stockholders receive their major livelihood in the form of salaries resulting from employment by the corporation. If such employment be terminated, the hardship suffered by the minority stockholder or stockholders may be very heavy. Nevertheless, such situations do not in themselves form a ground for the interposition of a court of equity.

There is no doubt that in the present case bitter dissension and personal hostility have existed for a long time between the individual plaintiffs and defendants. The plaintiffs Charles Gottfried and Harold Gottfried have both been discontinued from the corporate payrolls.

It is true too that several of the defendants have in recent years received as compensation substantial sums. * * *

The evidence also discloses that substantial advances or loans have been made from time to time to several of the defendants, part of which still remain outstanding. Advances and loans of this character in varying amounts likewise had been made for many years to stockholders and directors. Without passing upon the propriety or legality of these transactions, the evidence does not sustain an inference that they were made with a view to the dividend policy of the corporation. They were incurred, in large part, long before any controversy arose with respect to dividends, nor is the aggregate amount thereof of sufficient magnitude to affect in a material way the capacity of Gottfried to pay dividends.

Plaintiff Charles Gottfried testified that Benjamin Gottfried, one of the defendants, told him that he and the other minority stockholders would never get any dividends because the majority could freeze them out and that the majority had other ways than declaring dividends of getting money out of the companies. Benjamin Gottfried denied that he had ever made such statements. There is no evidence, moreover, that such statements were made by any of the other defendants. The court does not believe that this disputed testimony carries much weight upon the question of a concerted policy on the part of the directors to refrain from declaring dividends for the purpose of "freezing out" the plaintiffs.

Nor does the evidence with respect to the financial condition of the corporation and its business requirements sustain the plaintiffs' claims. * * * The evidence discloses that * * * expenditures [actually made in 1945] * * * included the retirement of the then outstanding preferred stocks of Gottfried and Hanscom in the sum of $165,000. Since all the parties held these preferred stocks in the same ratio as they held Gottfried "A" stock and common stock, each of the stockholders, including the plaintiffs, participated proportionately in the benefits of such retirement. After said retirement their respective pro rata interests in Gottfried were precisely the same as before these distributions were made. From this point of view the plaintiffs were in at least as good a position as a result of this preferred stock retirement as though dividends had been paid upon the common stock in the sum of $165,000, which is almost equivalent to the entire net earnings for the year 1944. It is noteworthy in this connection, moreover, that the retirement of the preferred stock was urged by both Charles and Harold Gottfried, two of the plaintiffs, at the annual meeting of the stockholders of Gottfried held on December 5, 1944. Harold went so far as to request that funds be borrowed from a bank in order to effect such retirement. These stockholders certainly cannot complain because a sum almost equivalent to the prior year's entire net income was defrayed, in accordance with their own request, in the form of retirement of preferred stock rather than by payment of dividends on the common stock.

Other major items of expenditure in 1945, * * * were payments of dividends on Gottfried preferred stock in the sum of $5,031, dividends on Hanscom preferred stock in the sum of $5,597, and dividends on the "A" stock of $36,000. In all of these payments of dividends on stock prior to the common stock the plaintiffs were pro rata beneficiaries. In 1945 there were also payments upon outstanding mortgages in the sum of $133,626. Reduction of mortgage indebtedness seems to have been a standard policy of Gottfried when its financial condition permitted it. Payments for sites for new plants and properties deemed necessary for the corporations' operations aggregated more than $214,000.

In addition to the above-mentioned expenditures * * * Gottfried in 1945 paid $31,532 in dividends on the common stock. It may be, of course, that the payment of these dividends was stimulated by the commencement of this suit. The fact remains that they were paid. * * *

The ratio of dividends paid in 1945 to the earnings of the immediately preceding year was 44.87%.

Under these circumstances, it may not be said that the directorate policy regarding common stock dividends at the time the suit was brought was unduly conservative. It certainly does not appear to have been inspired by bad faith. * * *

The complaint is dismissed and judgment directed for the defendants. Settle judgment.

DODGE v. FORD MOTOR CO.

Supreme Court of Michigan, 1919.
204 Mich. 459, 170 N.W. 668.

OSTRANDER, C.J.

[Editor: Plaintiffs are minority shareholders in the Ford Motor Company. At the time, Henry Ford, president of the company, owned 58 percent of the outstanding capital stock.] * * *

When plaintiffs made their complaint and demand for further dividends, the Ford Motor Company had concluded its most prosperous year of business. The demand for its cars at the price of the preceding year continued. It could make and could market in the year beginning August 1, 1916, more than 500,000 cars. Sales of parts and repairs would necessarily increase. The cost of materials was likely to advance, and perhaps the price of labor; but it reasonably might have expected a profit for the year of upwards of $60,000,000. It had assets of more than $132,000,000, a surplus of almost $112,000,000, and its cash on hand and municipal bonds were nearly $54,000,000. Its total liabilities, including capital stock, was a little over $20,000,000. It had declared no special dividend during the business year except the October, 1915, dividend. It had been the practice, under similar circumstances, to declare larger dividends. Considering only these facts, a refusal to declare and pay further dividends appears to be not an exercise of discretion on the part of the directors, but an arbitrary refusal to do what the circumstances required to be done. These facts and others call upon the directors to justify their action, or failure or refusal to act. In justification, the defendants have offered testimony tending to prove, and which does prove, the following facts: It had been the policy of the corporation for a considerable time to annually reduce the selling price of cars, while keeping up, or improving, their quality. As early as in June, 1915, a general plan for the expansion of the productive capacity of the concern by a practical duplication of its plant had been talked over by the executive officers and directors and agreed upon; not all of the details having been settled, and no formal action of directors having been taken. The erection of a smelter was considered, and engineering and other data in connection therewith secured. In consequence, it was determined not to reduce the selling price of cars for the year beginning August 1, 1915, but to maintain the price and to accumulate a large surplus to pay for the proposed expansion of plant and equipment, and perhaps to build a plant for smelting ore. It is hoped, by Mr. Ford, that eventually, 1,000,000 cars will be annually produced. The contemplated changes will permit the increased output.

The plan, as affecting the profits of the business for the year beginning August 1, 1916, and thereafter, calls for a reduction in the selling price of the cars. It is true that this price might be at any time increased, but the plan called for the reduction in price of $80 a car. The capacity of the plant, without the additions thereto voted to be made (without a part of them at least), would produce more than 600,000 cars annually. This number, and more, could have been sold for $440 instead of $360, a difference in the return for capital, labor, and materials employed of at least $48,000,000. In short, the plan does not call for and is not intended to produce immediately a more profitable business, but a less profitable one; not only less profitable than formerly, but less profitable than it is admitted it might be made. The apparent immediate effect will be to diminish the value of shares and the returns to shareholders.

It is the contention of plaintiffs that the apparent effect of the plan is intended to be the continued and continuing effect of it, and that it is deliberately proposed, not of record and not by official corporate declaration, but nevertheless proposed, to continue the corporation henceforth as a semi-eleemosynary institution and not as a business institution. In support of this contention, they point to the attitude and to the expressions of Mr. Henry Ford.

Mr. Henry Ford is the dominant force in the business of the Ford Motor Company. No plan of operations could be adopted unless he consented, and no board of directors can be elected whom he does not favor. One of the directors of the company has no stock. One share was assigned to him to qualify him for the position, but it is not claimed that he owns it. A business, one of the largest in the world, and one of the most profitable, has been built up. It employs many men, at good pay.

"My ambition," said Mr. Ford, "is to employ still more men, to spread the benefits of this industrial system to the greatest possible number, to help them build up their lives and their homes. To do this we are putting the greatest share of our profits back in the business."

"With regard to dividends, the company paid sixty percent on its capitalization of two million dollars, or $1,200,000, leaving $58,000,000 to reinvest for the growth of the company. This is Mr. Ford's policy at present, and it is understood that the other stockholders cheerfully accede to this plan."

He had made up his mind in the summer of 1916 that no dividends other than the regular dividends should be paid, "for the present."

"Q. For how long? Had you fixed in your mind anytime in the future, when you were going to pay? A. No.

"Q. That was indefinite in the future? A. That was indefinite; yes, sir."

The record, and especially the testimony of Mr. Ford, convinces that he has to some extent the attitude towards shareholders of one who has dispensed and distributed to them large gains and that they should be content to take what he chooses to give. His testimony creates the impression, also, that he thinks the Ford Motor Company has made too much money, has had too large profits, and that, although large profits might be still earned, a sharing of them with the public, by reducing the price of the output of the company, ought to be undertaken. We have no doubt that certain sentiments, philanthropic and altruistic, creditable to Mr. Ford, had large influence in determining the policy to be pursued by the Ford Motor Company—the policy which has been herein referred to.

* * * There should be no confusion (of which there is evidence) of the duties which Mr. Ford conceives that he and the stockholders owe to the general public and the duties which in law he and his codirectors owe to protesting, minority stockholders. A business corporation is organized and carried on primarily for the profit of the stockholders. The powers of the directors are to be employed for that end. The discretion of directors is to be exercised in the choice of means to attain that end, and does not extend to a change in the end itself, to the reduction of profits, or to the nondistribution of profits among stockholders in order to devote them to other purposes.

There is committed to the discretion of directors, a discretion to be exercised in good faith, the infinite details of business, including the wages which shall be paid to employees, the number of hours they shall work, the conditions under which labor shall be carried on, and the price for which products shall be offered to the public.

It is said by appellants that the motives of the board members are not material and will not be inquired into by the court so long as their acts are within their lawful powers. As we have pointed out, and the proposition does not require argument to sustain it, it is not within the lawful powers of a board of directors to shape and conduct the affairs of a corporation for the merely incidental benefit of shareholders and for the primary purpose of benefiting others, and no one will contend that, if the avowed purpose of the defendant directors was to sacrifice the interests of shareholders, it would not be the duty of the courts to interfere.

We are not, however, persuaded that we should interfere with the proposed expansion of the business of the Ford Motor Company. In view of the fact that the selling price of products may be increased at any time, the ultimate results of the larger business cannot be certainly estimated. The judges are not business experts. It is recognized that plans must often be made for a long future, for expected competition, for a continuing as well as an immediately profitable venture. The experience of the Ford Motor Company is evidence of capable management of its affairs. It may be noticed incidentally, that it took from the public the money required for the execution of its plan, and that the very considerable salaries paid to Mr. Ford and to certain executive officers and employees were not diminished. We are not satisfied that the alleged motives of the directors, in so far as they are reflected in the conduct of the business, menace the interests of shareholders.

It is enough to say, perhaps, that the court of equity is at all times open to complaining shareholders having a just grievance.

Assuming the general plan and policy of expansion and the details of it to have been sufficiently, formally, approved at the October and November, 1917, meetings of directors, and assuming further that the plan and policy and the details agreed upon were for the best ultimate interest of the company and therefore of its shareholders, what does it amount to in justification of a refusal to declare and pay a special dividend or dividends? The Ford Motor Company was able to estimate with nicety its income and profit. It could sell more cars than it could make. Having ascertained what it would cost to produce a car and to sell it, the profit upon each car depended upon the selling price. That being fixed, the yearly income and profit was determinable, and, within slight variations, was certain. * * *

Defendants say, and it is true, that a considerable cash balance must be at all times carried by such a concern. But, as has been stated, there was a large daily, weekly, monthly, receipt of cash. The output was practically continuous and was continuously, and within a few days, turned into cash. Moreover, the contemplated expenditures were not to be immediately made. The large sum appropriated for the smelter plant was payable over a considerable period of time. So that, without going further, it would appear that, accepting and approving the plan of the directors, it was their duty to distribute on or near the 1st of August, 1916, a very large sum of money to stockholders.

In reaching this conclusion, we do not ignore, but recognize, the validity of the proposition that plaintiffs have from the beginning profited by, if they have not lately, officially, participated in, the general policy of expansion pursued by this corporation. We do not lose sight of the fact that it had been, upon an occasion, agreeable to the plaintiffs to increase the capital stock to $100,000,000 by a stock dividend of $98,000,000. These things go only to answer other contentions now made by plaintiffs, and do not and cannot operate to estop them to demand proper dividends upon the stock they own. It is obvious that an annual dividend of 60 percent, upon $2,000,000 or $1,200,000, is the equivalent of a very small dividend upon $100,000,000, or more.

The decree of the court below fixing and determining the specific amount to be distributed to stockholders is affirmed. * * *

STEERE, FELLOWS, STONE, and BROOKE, JJ., concurred with OSTRANDER, J.

MOORE, J. * * * I do not agree with all that is said by [JUSTICE OSTRANDER] in his discussion of the question of dividends. I do agree with him in his conclusion that the accumulation of so large a surplus establishes the fact that there has been an arbitrary refusal to distribute funds that ought to have been distributed to the stockholders as dividends. I therefore agree with the conclusion reached by him upon that phase of the case.

BIRD, C.J., and KUHN, J., concurred with MOORE, J.

WILDERMAN v. WILDERMAN

Court of Chancery of Delaware, 1974.
315 A.2d 610.

Marvel, Vice Chancellor:

Eleanor M. Wilderman, the plaintiff in this action, sues in her own right and in her capacity as a stockholder with an interest in one-half of the issued and outstanding stock of the defendant Marble Craft Company, Inc. She primarily seeks a ruling to the effect that the defendant Joseph M. Wilderman (the president of the corporate defendant and her former husband) for the fiscal years ending March 31, from 1971 through 1973, caused excessive and unauthorized payments to be made to himself out of earnings of the corporate defendant and that such payments, made in the form of unearned and unauthorized salary and bonuses, must accordingly be returned to the treasury of Marble Craft Company.

Plaintiff asks that upon the Court-ordered return of such excessive payments to the corporate treasury that they be treated as corporate profits and required to be distributed as dividends, thereby opening the way to plaintiff to share in the net corporate profits as a stockholder with a 50% equity in her corporation. Plaintiff also asks that appropriate adjustments be made in the corporate defendant's pension plan so as to reflect the return to the corporate treasury of amounts found to be excessive compensation received by the defendant for the fiscal years in question. Also sought is an injunction against disbursement by the individual defendant of moneys from corporate funds or the transfer by such defendant of corporate assets without the approval of the board of directors of the corporation. Finally, plaintiff seeks an order directing the continuance of the business of the corporate defendant under a custodian as provided for under the provisions of 8 Del.C. s 226.

Marble Craft is engaged in the business of installing ceramic tile and marble facings in residences and commercial buildings, such business having been organized by the individual parties to this action some fifteen years ago, being originally operated from the family home. Defendant's initial knowledge of the tile business was gained while working briefly for his father-in-law prior to going into business with his former wife, and there is no doubt but that defendant has been the major force in the business of the corporate defendant inasmuch as he has done most of the estimating, supervising and business getting for the corporation, working up to sixty hours or more per week on corporate business. Plaintiff, on the other hand, has been primarily a bookkeeper for the business, although there is no doubt but that plaintiff is fully versed in the tile business, her father having started such a business in 1929. Significantly, in the beginning of the enterprise the parties' respective compensation was not entirely disparate, as it is now, defendant having initially drawn $125 a week compared to plaintiff's $75.

The business proved successful as a family venture, and in 1961 it was incorporated under the name of Marble Craft Company, Inc., its authorized capital shares consisting of one hundred shares of stock being issued to plaintiff and defendant as joint tenants in exchange for the assets of the business. By-laws providing for the election of two directors were adopted, and the parties, as the duly elected directors, thereupon chose themselves to fill the designated corporate offices, defendant being elected president and the plaintiff vice president, secretary, and treasurer.

The controversy here involved primarily centers around the amount of compensation which defendant has caused to be paid to himself for the fiscal years 1971, 1972 and 1973, compensation which had its origin in a policy[36] designed to avoid corporate taxation by paying out the net corporate profits of Marble Craft Company in the form of executive compensation before the end of each taxable year, thus avoiding double taxation. Accordingly, dividends attributable to corporate profits have never been formally paid until ordered by the Court in the course of this litigation. Such policy of avoiding dividend payments initially worked to the advantage of both parties and their two children, the financial advantage to plaintiff in the plan having been virtually destroyed by the parties' separation and divorce. Thus, following the breakup of the home, plaintiff was largely excluded from the benefits enuring to defendant as a result of the large amounts he proceeded to pay himself. Asserting his authority as the chief executive officer of the corporate defendant, defendant caused the amount of compensation to be paid to him to be increased from $25,000 in 1963 to $60,000 in 1970, the last year for which salary payments to defendant are not questioned, such salary having concededly been authorized by corporate resolution. Next, despite the pendency of this action defendant paid himself a bonus of $71,738.71 in addition to a flat salary of $20,800 for the fiscal year 1971, the salary being based on an authorized draw of $400 per week, this being the first year after marital differences arose in which defendant could not point to at least tacit corporate authorization as to the full amount of his compensation. For the fiscal year 1972 defendant paid himself total compensation of $35,000, a year in which corporate profits were substantially lower than those of the previous year due to a building trades strike, and for the fiscal year ending March 31, 1973, defendant caused payment to himself of total compensation in the amount of $86,893.40. During this same period plaintiff received the annual sum of $7,800 for her services to the corporation.

On June 26, 1972, in an effort to work out some accommodation between the parties, a custodian was appointed by order of this Court as provided for by 8 Del.C. § 226(a)(2). However, the deadlock between the parties persisted, and on March 29, 1973, the defendant having caused the sum of $86,893.40[37] to be paid to himself as compensation for such fiscal year, an order was entered, on the recommendation of the custodian, which stipulated that such payment was without prejudice to the right to contest defendant's compensation in excess of his authorized salary of $20,800. Also authorized and paid on the custodian's recommendation was a dividend of $20,000 to be divided equally between plaintiff and defendant.

36. [By the Court] This policy, however, encountered the opposition of the Internal Revenue Service which reduced the deduction allowable to Marble Craft for salary paid to defendant from $30,000 to $20,000 for 1965, from $30,000 to $25,000 for 1966, and from $60,000 to $40,000 for 1970. Presumably the effect of this action was twofold (1) the amount of disallowance was taxed as income to the corporation, and (2) the amount of disallowance less the tax due thereon became a de facto dividend.

37. [By the Court] Based on an authorized salary of $35,000 per annum plus 15% of gross receipts in excess of $300,000, a formula which was operative through the fiscal year 1970.

The authority to compensate corporate officers is normally vested in the board of directors, 8 Del.C. § 122(5), and the compensating of corporate officers is usually a matter of contract. * * * By early April 1971 the management of Marble Craft was clearly deadlocked with its owner-managers in complete disagreement as to the amount of compensation to be paid the defendant, the payment of anything above a $400 weekly salary being opposed by plaintiff. Therefore, the only amount agreed upon by the board and hence the only authorized payment to Mr. Wilderman for the fiscal years 1971, 1972 and 1973 would appear to have been at the rate of $20,800 per year, or $400 per week, and that additional compensation received by him for the years in question must find its authorization in the theory of quantum meruit.

Turning from the issue of corporate authorization of defendant's salary to the issue of the reasonableness of the compensation paid Mr. Wilderman, plaintiff contends that the compensation paid to defendant for the years in question was unreasonable, plaintiff arguing that although courts are hesitant to inquire into the reasonableness of executive compensation when it is fixed by a disinterested board, the standard for fixing executive compensation is obviously more strict when it is fixed by the recipient himself. And where, as in the case at bar, the recipient's vote as a director was necessary to the fixing of the amount of his compensation, then the burden of showing the reasonableness of such compensation clearly falls upon its recipient. This is so, of course, because of the fiduciary position which directors hold towards their corporation and its stockholders.

As to the facts to be considered in reaching a determination of the question as to whether or not defendant has met the burden he must carry there is little authority in Delaware. In Hall v. Isaacs, [37 Del.Ch. 530, 146 A.2d 602 (1958), affirmed in part 39 Del.Ch. 244, 163 A.2d 288 (1960)] the Court was of the view that evidence of what other executives similarly situated received was relevant, and in Meiselman v. Eberstadt, [39 Del.Ch. 563, 170 A.2d 720 (1961)] the ability of the executive was considered. Other factors which have been judicially recognized elsewhere are whether or not the Internal Revenue Service has allowed the corporation to deduct the amount of salary alleged to be unreasonable. Other relevant factors are whether the salary bears a reasonable relation to the success of the corporation, the amount previously received as salary, whether increases in salary are geared to increases in the value of services rendered, and the amount of the challenged salary compared to other salaries paid by the employer. See 2 Washington and Rothschild, Compensating the Corporate Executive, 848–873 (3rd Ed.1962). Dr. Seligman, an expert, testified that on the basis of a financial analysis of Marble Craft and its present earnings that reasonable compensation for defendant would range between $25,000 and $35,000. It also appears that the Internal Revenue Service proposes to permit Marble Craft a deduction of $52,000 for defendant's 1971 compensation of $92,538.

On the present record I am not convinced that defendant has discharged his burden as to the reasonableness of amounts he has drawn for all of the years in question. * * * Thus, while for the fiscal years 1971, 1972 and 1973 Mr. Wilderman was technically entitled to be compensated for his services in the amount of only $20,800, I am of the opinion that in light of the nature of defendant's services to the corporation, which appear to have been important to its success, that he is entitled to compensation in the amount of $45,000 for the fiscal year 1971 and the same amount for fiscal 1973. Defendant's compensation of $35,000 for the fiscal year ending 1972 will be left undisturbed. Accordingly, he will be ordered to return $47,538 in excess compensation to the corporate treasury for fiscal 1971 and $41,893.40 for fiscal 1973, both amounts with interest.

Additionally, because payments to the Marble Craft pension fund have been tied to defendant's compensation for the years in question, defendant will be directed to repay to the defendant Marble Craft excessive payments to such fund in the same ratio as the refunds of his excessive compensation. * * *

An appropriate order may be submitted on notice.

Notes

(1) In Mann–Paller Found., Inc. v. Econometric Research, Inc., 644 F.Supp. 92 (D.D.C.1986), the majority shareholder of the defendant corporation received compensation in the amount of $347,745 in 1985; the minority shareholder received nothing since no dividend was declared. The minority shareholder sued to recover $191,369.10 on the theory that the compensation to the majority shareholder constituted a *"de facto* dividend" that had not been paid in proportion to shareholdings. The Court granted summary judgment for the defendants: The suit failed as a claim to compel the payment of a dividend since it did not allege "that the withholding of [a dividend] is explicable only on the theory of an oppressive or fraudulent abuse of discretion" (644 F.Supp. at 98); the suit also failed as a claim alleging improper compensation to a shareholder-employee since such a suit must be brought in the name of and for the benefit of the corporation (a derivative suit) rather than directly on behalf of a minority shareholder. Compare Murphy v. Country House, Inc., 349 N.W.2d 289 (Minn.App.1984).

(2) Other courts have agreed with the basic principles of *Wilderman* that where one party in effect sets his own compensation, he then has the burden of establishing its fundamental fairness. Lynch v. Patterson, 701 P.2d 1126 (Wyo. 1985); Giannotti v. Hamway, 239 Va. 14, 387 S.E.2d 725 (1990). Cases of this type shade off into discussions of the responsibilities of directors in self-dealing cases discussed in Chapter 12, section A.

ROBERT W. HAMILTON, BUSINESS ORGANIZATIONS: UNINCORPORATED BUSINESSES AND CLOSELY HELD CORPORATIONS[38]
Pages 304–05 (1997).

Superficially, a purchase by a corporation of its own shares may not be thought of as involving a distribution at all. It may appear to be the purchase of an asset rather than the making of a distribution. That analysis, however, confuses transactions in which the corporation repurchases *its own stock* and transactions in which it purchases stock *issued by another corporation.* The former is a distribution, the latter is an investment.

When a corporation buys back its own stock, it does not receive anything of value in the hands of the corporation. The remaining shareholders continue

---

38. Reprinted with permission of Aspen   Aspen Publishers, Inc.
Law & Business/Panel Publishers, a division of

to own 100 percent of the corporate assets (now reduced by the amount of the payment used to reacquire the shares). A corporation cannot treat stock in itself that it has purchased as an asset any more than it can treat its authorized but unissued stock as an asset. One cannot own 10 percent of oneself and have one's total worth be 110 percent of the value of one's assets. This point is so fundamental that it may be well to re-read the last few sentences.

Stock issued by another corporation is entirely different. That does not create the same circularity problem. Shares of corporation B have value based on the assets owned by corporation *B*; if shares of corporation B are purchased by corporation *A* they are an asset in the hands of corporation *A*.

The fact that a repurchase of shares constitutes a distribution can be most easily appreciated by considering a proportionate repurchase of stock by the corporation from each shareholder. Assume that three persons each own 100 shares of stock in a corporation, its entire outstanding stock. The shareholders decide that each of them will sell 10 shares back to the corporation for $100 per share, or a total of $1,000 each. When the transaction is completed, each shareholder continues to own one-third of the corporation (now represented by 90 shares rather than 100 shares), the corporation is $3,000 poorer and the shareholders are each $1,000 richer. Clearly, there has been a distribution even though the transaction was cast in the form of a repurchase of stock rather than a direct distribution of assets by the corporation. * * *

Under most state statutes, the 30 shares reacquired by the corporation in the previous example are called *treasury shares*. Treasury shares are viewed as being held by the corporation in a sort of twilight zone until they are either retired permanently or resold to someone else in the future. Treasury shares are not an asset of the corporation even though they are salable and may be sold at some later time. Exactly the same thing can be said of every share of authorized but unissued stock.

Assume that the corporation in the example described above decides to resell the treasury shares to X (a nonshareholder) for $3,000. The interests of each of the three original shareholders have been diluted: There are now four shareholders owning shares in the ratio 90:90:90:30. The corporation could have paid the original shareholders a cash dividend of $1,000 each and then sold 33 shares of authorized but unissued stock to X for $3,000 with * * * the same economic result. * * *

A repurchase of shares by the corporation is a distribution even if the corporation purchases only shares owned by one shareholder rather than proportionately from each shareholder. Such a transaction is a disproportionate distribution (i.e., one not shared proportionately by all shareholders). The corporation has made a distribution to a single shareholder equal to the purchase price it paid for the shares. This transaction is not all bad from the standpoint of the other shareholders, however, since it simultaneously increases their percentage interest in the corporation. For example, if the corporation with three shareholders in the above example repurchased all 100 shares owned by shareholder *A* for $10,000, the interests of shareholders *B* and C in the corporation are both increased from 33.3 percent to 50 percent. The assets of the corporation are reduced by the $10,000 purchase price paid to shareholder *A* to eliminate his or her interest in the corporation. Whether or not this is a "winner" for *A* or for *B* and *C* depends on the value of the assets in the corporation before the share repurchase.

Notes

(1) Consider the situation where one shareholder in a closely held corporation wishes to leave the enterprise, and the other shareholders are willing to purchase her shares. The price may be established either by negotiation or by prior agreement. How should the transaction be structured? Should the remaining shareholders each purchase their proportional number of shares? Should the corporation purchase the departing shares? Does it make any economic difference which way the transaction is structured?

A redemption of shares by the corporation also provides tax benefits. From the standpoint of the departing shareholder, there is no difference: a redemption of shares is treated as a sale or exchange of the shares giving rise to short or long-term capital gain or loss equal to the difference between the redemption price of the shares and the shareholder's basis.[39] But what about the tax position of the other shareholders if the corporation is a C corporation with earnings and profits? If the corporation distributed the redemption price to the other shareholders in order for them to purchase the shares, there would clearly have been a taxable dividend. In Holsey v. Commissioner, 258 F.2d 865 (3d Cir.1958), the court held in this kind of situation that the remaining shareholders could not be taxed on the increase in wealth until the gain was realized by a sale of the shares.[40] One situation in which a tax will be imposed on the non-redeeming shareholders is where they are obligated by contract to purchase the stock of the retiring shareholder. If the corporation redeems the stock, its payment discharges a personal obligation of the nonredeemed shareholder and is a constructive dividend to him.[41]

Thus, a disproportionate redemption of stock permits the distribution of earnings of a C corporation to shareholders at a minimum tax cost.

(2) Redemptions of shares are treated by corporation statutes as a distribution subject to the legal restraints on dividends and distributions described in the following section. A redemption in violation of these restrictions probably may be enjoined. See e.g. Neimark v. Mel Kramer Sales, Inc., 102 Wis.2d 282, 306 N.W.2d 278 (App.1981). What should be done if the shareholders wish to have the corporation redeem the shares but the corporation fails to meet fully these tests for the legality of the redemption?

(3) A very common feature of disproportionate redemption transactions is that the corporation may pay only a portion of the purchase price in cash when the transaction is closed, the balance being represented by promissory notes

---

39. [By the Editors] Exceptions to the statement in the text exist. For example, if the sale is "essentially equivalent to a dividend," the redemption is treated as a dividend giving rise to ordinary income rather than as a sale or exchange giving rise to a capital gain or loss.

40. The Internal Revenue Service acquiesced in this result. Rev.Rul. 58–614, 1958–2 C.B. 920. See generally William J. Rands, Closely Held Corporations: Federal Tax Consequences of Stock Transfer Restrictions, 7 J.Corp.Law 449, 456–57 (1982).

41. [By the Editors] An example is Sullivan v. United States, 363 F.2d 724, 729 (8th Cir. 1966) cert. denied 387 U.S. 905, 87 S.Ct. 1683, 18 L.Ed.2d 622 (1967). Such a transaction is a constructive dividend to the remaining shareholders for exactly the same reason that use of corporate funds to pay a valid debt of a shareholder is a constructive dividend to that shareholder.

payable over an extended period of time. The deferred purchase price may simply reflect the reality that the corporation lacks liquid assets sufficient to acquire the redeemed shares entirely for cash at the closing. The future payments may be made out of subsequent earnings or cash flow, thereby in effect making payment of the purchase price in part contingent on the future success of the business. A deferred sale may also reflect further tax planning within a C corporation, since future earnings may in effect be diverted for the benefit of shareholders without incurring the double taxation on dividends.

DONAHUE v. RODD ELECTROTYPE CO.

Supreme Judicial Court of Massachusetts, 1975.
367 Mass. 578, 328 N.E.2d 505.

Before TAURO, C.J., and REARDON, QUIRICO, BRAUCHER, KAPLAN and WILKINS, JJ.

TAURO, CHIEF JUSTICE.

The plaintiff, Euphemia Donahue, a minority stockholder in the Rodd Electrotype Company of New England, Inc. (Rodd Electrotype), a Massachusetts corporation, brings this suit against the directors of Rodd Electrotype, Charles H. Rodd, Frederick I. Rodd and Mr. Harold E. Magnuson, against Harry C. Rodd, a former director, officer, and controlling stockholder of Rodd Electrotype and against Rodd Electrotype (hereinafter called defendants). The plaintiff seeks to rescind Rodd Electrotype's purchase of Harry Rodd's shares in Rodd Electrotype and to compel Harry Rodd "to repay to the corporation the purchase price of said shares, $36,000, together with interest from the date of purchase." The plaintiff alleges that the defendants caused the corporation to purchase the shares in violation of their fiduciary duty to her, a minority stockholder of Rodd Electrotype.

The trial judge, after hearing oral testimony, dismissed the plaintiff's bill on the merits. He found that the purchase was without prejudice to the plaintiff and implicitly found that the transaction had been carried out in good faith and with inherent fairness. The Appeals Court affirmed with costs. Donahue v. Rodd Electrotype Co. of New England, Inc., 307 N.E.2d 8 (1974). * * *

The evidence may be summarized as follows: In 1935, the defendant, Harry C. Rodd, began his employment with Rodd Electrotype, then styled the Royal Electrotype Company of New England, Inc. (Royal of New England). At that time, the company was a wholly-owned subsidiary of a Pennsylvania corporation, the Royal Electrotype Company (Royal Electrotype). Mr. Rodd's advancement within the company was rapid. The following year he was elected a director, and, in 1946, he succeeded to the position of general manager and treasurer.

In 1936, the plaintiff's husband, Joseph Donahue (now deceased), was hired by Royal of New England as a "finisher" of electrotype plates. His duties were confined to operational matters within the plant. Although he ultimately achieved the positions of plant superintendent (1946) and corporate vice president (1955), Donahue never participated in the "management" aspect of the business.

In the years preceding 1955, the parent company, Royal Electrotype, made available to Harry Rodd and Joseph Donahue shares of the common stock in its subsidiary, Royal of New England. Harry Rodd took advantage of the opportunities offered to him and acquired 200 shares for $20 a share. Joseph Donahue, at the suggestion of Harry Rodd, who hoped to interest Donahue in the business, eventually obtained fifty shares in two twenty-five share lots priced at $20 a share. The parent company at all times retained 725 of the 1,000 outstanding shares. One Lawrence W. Kelley owned the remaining twenty-five shares.

In June of 1955, Royal of New England purchased all 725 of its shares owned by its parent company. The total price amounted to $135,000. Royal of New England remitted $75,000 of this total in cash and executed five promissory notes of $12,000 each, due in each of the succeeding five years. Lawrence W. Kelley's twenty-five shares were also purchased at this time for $1,000. A substantial portion of Royal of New England's cash expenditures was loaned to the company by Harry Rodd, who mortgaged his house to obtain some of the necessary funds.

The stock purchases left Harry Rodd in control of Royal of New England. Early in 1955, before the purchases, he had assumed the presidency of the company. His 200 shares gave him a dominant eighty percent interest. Joseph Donahue, at this time, was the only minority stockholder.

Subsequent events reflected Harry Rodd's dominant influence. In June, 1960, more than a year after the last obligation to Royal Electrotype had been discharged, the company was renamed the Rodd Electrotype Company of New England, Inc. In 1962, Charles H. Rodd, Harry Rodd's son (a defendant here), who had long been a company employee working in the plant, became corporate vice president. In 1963, he joined his father on the board of directors. In 1964, another son, Frederick I. Rodd (also a defendant), replaced Joseph Donahue as plant superintendent. By 1965, Harry Rodd had evidently decided to reduce his participation in corporate management. That year Charles Rodd succeeded him as president and general manager of Rodd Electrotype.

From 1959 to 1967, Harry Rodd pursued what may fairly be termed a gift program by which he distributed the majority of his shares equally among his two sons and his daughter, Phyllis E. Mason. Each child received thirty-nine shares. Two shares were returned to the corporate treasury in 1966.

We come now to the events of 1970 which form the grounds for the plaintiff's complaint. In May of 1970, Harry Rodd was seventy-seven years old. The record indicates that for some time he had not enjoyed the best of health and that he had undergone a number of operations. His sons wished him to retire. Mr. Rodd was not averse to this suggestion. However, he insisted that some financial arrangements be made with respect to his remaining eighty-one shares of stock. A number of conferences ensued. Harry Rodd and Charles Rodd (representing the company) negotiated terms of purchase for forty-five shares which, Charles Rodd testified, would reflect the book value and liquidating value of the shares.

A special board meeting convened on July 13, 1970. As the first order of business, Harry Rodd resigned his directorship of Rodd Electrotype. The remaining incumbent directors, Charles Rodd and Mr. Harold E. Magnuson (clerk of the company and a defendant and defense attorney in the instant suit), elected Frederick Rodd to replace his father. The three directors then authorized Rodd Electrotype's president (Charles Rodd) to execute an agreement between Harry Rodd and the company in which the company would purchase forty-five shares for $800 a share ($36,000).

The stock purchase agreement was formalized between the parties on July 13, 1970. Two days later, a sale pursuant to the July 13 agreement was consummated. At approximately the same time, Harry Rodd resigned his last corporate office, that of treasurer.

Harry Rodd completed divestiture of his Rodd Electrotype stock in the following year. * * * Thus, in March, 1971, the shareholdings in Rodd Electrotype were apportioned as follows: Charles Rodd, Frederick Rodd and Phyllis Mason each held fifty-one shares; the Donahues[42] held fifty shares.

A special meeting of the stockholders of the company was held on March 30, 1971. At the meeting, Charles Rodd, company president and general manager, reported the tentative results of an audit conducted by the company auditors and reported generally on the company events of the year. For the first time, the Donahues learned that the corporation had purchased Harry Rodd's shares. According to the minutes of the meeting, following Charles Rodd's report, the Donahues raised questions about the purchase. They then voted against a resolution, ultimately adopted by the remaining stockholders, to approve Charles Rodd's report. * * *

A few weeks after the meeting, the Donahues, acting through their attorney, offered their shares to the corporation on the same terms given to Harry Rodd. Mr. Harold E. Magnuson replied by letter that the corporation would not purchase the shares and was not in a financial position to do so.[43] This suit followed.

In her argument before this court, the plaintiff has characterized the corporate purchase of Harry Rodd's shares as an unlawful distribution of corporate assets to controlling stockholders. She urges that the distribution constitutes a breach of the fiduciary duty owed by the Rodds, as controlling stockholders, to her, a minority stockholder in the enterprise, because the Rodds failed to accord her an equal opportunity to sell her shares to the corporation. The defendants reply that the stock purchase was within the powers of the corporation and met the requirements of good faith and inherent fairness imposed on a fiduciary in his dealings with the corporation. They assert that there is no right to equal opportunity in corporate stock purchases for the corporate treasury. For the reasons hereinafter noted, we agree with the plaintiff and reverse the decree of the Superior Court. However, we limit the applicability of our holding to "close corporations" * * *. Whether the holding should apply to other corporations is left for decision in another case, on a proper record. * * *

42. [By the Court] Joseph Donahue gave his wife, the plaintiff, joint ownership of his fifty shares in 1962. In 1968, they transferred five shares to their son, Dr. Robert Donahue. On Joseph Donahue's death, the plaintiff became outright owner of the forty-five share block. This was the ownership pattern which obtained in March, 1971.

43. [By the Court] Between 1965 and 1969, the company offered to purchase the Donahue shares for amounts between $2,000 and $10,000 ($40 to $200 a share). The Donahues rejected these offers.

A. *Close Corporations.* In previous opinions, we have alluded to the distinctive nature of the close corporation, but have never defined precisely what is meant by a close corporation. There is no single, generally accepted definition. Some commentators emphasize an "integration of ownership and management" (Note, Statutory Assistance for Closely Held Corporations, 71 Harv.L.Rev. 1498 [1958]), in which the stockholders occupy most management positions. Others focus on the number of stockholders and the nature of the market for the stock. In this view, close corporations have few stockholders; there is little market for corporate stock. * * * We accept aspects of both definitions. We deem a close corporation to be typified by: (1) a small number of stockholders; (2) no ready market for the corporate stock; and (3) substantial majority stockholder participation in the management, direction and operations of the corporation.

As thus defined, the close corporation bears striking resemblance to a partnership. Commentators and courts have noted that the close corporation is often little more than an "incorporated" or "chartered" partnership. Ripin v. United States Woven Label Co., 205 N.Y. 442, 447, 98 N.E. 855, 856 (1912) ("little more (though not quite the same as) than chartered partnerships"). The stockholders "clothe" their partnership "with the benefits peculiar to a corporation, limited liability, perpetuity and the like." In the Matter of Surchin v. Approved Bus. Mach. Co., Inc., 55 Misc.2d 888, 889, 286 N.Y.S.2d 580, 581 (Sup.Ct.1967). In essence, though, the enterprise remains one in which ownership is limited to the original parties or transferees of their stock to whom the other stockholders have agreed,[44] in which ownership and management are in the same hands, and in which the owners are quite dependent on one another for the success of the enterprise. Many close corporations are "really partnerships, between two or three people who contribute their capital, skills, experience and labor." Kruger v. Gerth, 16 N.Y.2d 802, 805, 263 N.Y.S.2d 1, 3, 210 N.E.2d 355, 356 (1965) (Desmond, C.J., dissenting). Just as in a partnership, the relationship among the stockholders must be one of trust, confidence and absolute loyalty if the enterprise is to succeed. Close corporations with substantial assets and with more numerous stockholders are no different from smaller close corporations in this regard. All participants rely on the fidelity and abilities of those stockholders who hold office. Disloyalty and self-seeking conduct on the part of any stockholder will engender bickering, corporate stalemates, and, perhaps, efforts to achieve dissolution.

In Helms v. Duckworth, 101 U.S.App.D.C. 390, 249 F.2d 482 (1957), the United States Court of Appeals for the District of Columbia Circuit had before it a stockholders' agreement providing for the purchase of the shares of a deceased stockholder by the surviving stockholder in a small "two-man" close corporation. The court held the surviving stockholder to a duty "to deal fairly,

---

44. [By the Court] The original owners commonly impose restrictions on transfers of stock designed to prevent outsiders who are unacceptable to the other stockholders from acquiring an interest in the close corporation. These restrictions often take the form of agreements among the stockholders and the corporation or by-laws which give the corporation or the other stockholders a right of "first refusal" when any stockholder desires to sell his shares. In a partnership, of course, a partner cannot transfer his interest in the partnership so as to give his assignee a right to participate in the management or business affairs of the continuing partnership without the agreement of the other partners. [UPA (1914)] § 27. See Hazen v. Warwick, 256 Mass. 302, 308, 152 N.E. 342 (1926).

honestly, and openly with * * * [his] fellow stockholders." Id. at 487. Judge Burger, now Chief Justice Burger, writing for the court, emphasized the resemblance of the two-man close corporation to a partnership: "In an intimate business venture such as this, stockholders of a close corporation occupy a position similar to that of joint adventurers and partners. While courts have sometimes declared stockholders 'do not bear toward each other that same relation of trust and confidence which prevails in partnerships,' this view ignores the practical realities of the organization and functioning of a small 'two-man' corporation organized to carry on a small business enterprise in which the stockholders, directors, and managers are the same persons" (footnotes omitted). Id. at 486.

Although the corporate form provides * * * advantages for the stockholders (limited liability, perpetuity, and so forth), it also supplies an opportunity for the majority stockholders to oppress or disadvantage minority stockholders. The minority is vulnerable to a variety of oppressive devices, termed "freeze-outs," which the majority may employ. See, generally, Note, Freezing Out Minority Shareholders, 74 Harv.L.Rev. 1630 (1961). An authoritative study of such "freeze-outs" enumerates some of the possibilities: "The squeezers [those who employ the freeze-out techniques] may refuse to declare dividends; they may drain off the corporation's earnings in the form of exorbitant salaries and bonuses to the majority shareholder-officers and perhaps to their relatives, or in the form of high rent by the corporation for property leased from majority shareholders * * *; they may deprive minority shareholders of corporate offices and of employment by the company; they may cause the corporation to sell its assets at an inadequate price to the majority shareholders * * *." F.H. O'Neal and J. Derwin, Expulsion or Oppression of Business Associates, 42 (1961). In particular, the power of the board of directors, controlled by the majority, to declare or withhold dividends and to deny the minority employment is easily converted to a device to disadvantage minority stockholders.

The minority can, of course, initiate suit against the majority and their directors. Self-serving conduct by directors is proscribed by the director's fiduciary obligation to the corporation. However, in practice, the plaintiff will find difficulty in challenging dividend or employment policies. Such policies are considered to be within the judgment of the directors. This court has said: "The courts prefer not to interfere * * * with the sound financial management of the corporation by its directors, but declare as a general rule that the declaration of dividends rests within the sound discretion of the directors, refusing to interfere with their determination unless a plain abuse of discretion is made to appear." Crocker v. Waltham Watch Co., 315 Mass. 397, 402, 53 N.E.2d 230, 233 (1944). Judicial reluctance to interfere combines with the difficulty of proof when the standard is "plain abuse of discretion" or bad faith, to limit the possibilities for relief. Although contractual provisions in an "agreement of association and articles of organization" or in by-laws have justified decrees in this jurisdiction ordering dividend declarations, generally, plaintiffs who seek judicial assistance against corporate dividend or employment policies[45] do not prevail.

---

45. [By the Court] Attacks on allegedly excessive salaries voted for officers and directors fare better in the courts. See Stratis v. Andreson, 254 Mass. 536, 150 N.E. 832 (1926); Saga-

Thus, when these types of "freeze-outs" are attempted by the majority stockholders, the minority stockholders, cut off from all corporation-related revenues, must either suffer their losses or seek a buyer for their shares. Many minority stockholders will be unwilling or unable to wait for an alteration in majority policy. Typically, the minority stockholder in a close corporation has a substantial percentage of his personal assets invested in the corporation. Galler v. Galler, 32 Ill.2d 16, 27, 203 N.E.2d 577 (1964). The stockholder may have anticipated that his salary from his position with the corporation would be his livelihood. Thus, he cannot afford to wait passively. He must liquidate his investment in the close corporation in order to reinvest the funds in income-producing enterprises.

At this point, the true plight of the minority stockholder in a close corporation becomes manifest. He cannot easily reclaim his capital. In a large public corporation, the oppressed or dissident minority stockholder could sell his stock in order to extricate some of his invested capital. By definition, this market is not available for shares in the close corporation. In a partnership, a partner who feels abused by his fellow partners may cause dissolution by his "express will * * * at any time" ([UPA (1914)] § 31[1][b] and [2]) and recover his share of partnership assets and accumulated profits.[46] [UPA (1914)] § 38. If dissolution results in a breach of the partnership articles, the culpable partner will be liable in damages. [UPA (1914)] § 38(2)(a)II. By contrast, the stockholder in the close corporation or "incorporated partnership" may achieve dissolution and recovery of his share of the enterprise assets only by compliance with the rigorous terms of the applicable chapter of the General Laws. Rizzuto v. Onset Cafe, Inc., 330 Mass. 595, 597–598, 116 N.E.2d 249 (1953). "The dissolution of a corporation which is a creature of the Legislature is primarily a legislative function, and the only authority courts have to deal with this subject is the power conferred upon them by the Legislature." Leventhal v. Atlantic Fin. Corp., 316 Mass. 194, 205, 55 N.E.2d 20, 26 (1944). To secure dissolution of the ordinary close corporation subject to G.L. c. 156B, the stockholder, in the absence of corporate deadlock, must own at least fifty percent of the shares or have the advantage of a favorable provision in the articles of organization. The minority stockholder, by definition lacking fifty percent of the corporate shares, can never "authorize" the corporation to file a petition for dissolution under G.L. c. 156B, § 99(a), by his own vote. He will seldom have at his disposal the requisite favorable provision in the articles of organization.

Thus, in a close corporation, the minority stockholders may be trapped in a disadvantageous situation. No outsider would knowingly assume the position of the disadvantaged minority. The outsider would have the same difficulties. To cut losses, the minority stockholder may be compelled to deal with the majority. This is the capstone of the majority plan. Majority "freeze-out" schemes which withhold dividends are designed to compel the minority

---

lyn v. Meekins, Packard & Wheat, Inc., 290 Mass. 434, 195 N.E. 769 (1935). What is "reasonable compensation" is a question of fact. Black v. Parker Mfg. Co., 329 Mass. 105, 116, 106 N.E.2d 544 (1952). The proof which establishes an excess over such "reasonable compensation" appears easier than the proof which would establish bad faith or plain abuse of discretion.

46. [By the Court] The partnership agreement may control the amount and timing of distribution in a way which is disadvantageous to the retiring partner.

to relinquish stock at inadequate prices. When the minority stockholder agrees to sell out at less than fair value, the majority has won.

Because of the fundamental resemblance of the close corporation to the partnership, the trust and confidence which are essential to this scale and manner of enterprise, and the inherent danger to minority interests in the close corporation, we hold that stockholders[47] in the close corporation owe one another substantially the same fiduciary duty in the operation of the enterprise[48] that partners owe to one another. In our previous decisions, we have defined the standard of duty owed by partners to one another as the "utmost good faith and loyalty." Cardullo v. Landau, 329 Mass. 5, 8, 105 N.E.2d 843 (1952). Stockholders in close corporations must discharge their management and stockholder responsibilities in conformity with this strict good faith standard. They may not act out of avarice, expediency or self-interest in derogation of their duty of loyalty to the other stockholders and to the corporation.

We contrast this strict good faith standard with the somewhat less stringent standard of fiduciary duty to which directors and stockholders[49] of all corporations must adhere in the discharge of their corporate responsibilities. Corporate directors are held to a good faith and inherent fairness standard of conduct (Winchell v. Plywood Corp., 324 Mass. 171, 177, 85 N.E.2d 313 [1949]) and are not "permitted to serve two masters whose interests are antagonistic." Spiegel v. Beacon Participations, Inc., 297 Mass. 398, 411, 8 N.E.2d 895, 904 (1937). "Their paramount duty is to the corporation, and their personal pecuniary interests are subordinate to that duty." Durfee v. Durfee & Canning, Inc., 323 Mass. 187, 196, 80 N.E.2d 522, 527 (1948).

The more rigorous duty of partners and participants in a joint adventure, here extended to stockholders in a close corporation, was described by then Chief Judge Cardozo of the New York Court of Appeals in Meinhard v. Salmon, 249 N.Y. 458, 164 N.E. 545 (1928): "Joint adventurers, like copartners, owe to one another, while the enterprise continues, the duty of the finest loyalty. Many forms of conduct permissible in a workaday world for those acting at arm's length, are forbidden to those bound by fiduciary ties. * * * Not honesty alone, but the punctilio of an honor the most sensitive, is then the standard of behavior." Id. at 463–464, 164 N.E. at 546.

Application of this strict standard of duty to stockholders in close corporations is a natural outgrowth of the prior case law. In a number of cases

---

47. [By the Court] We do not limit our holding to majority stockholders. In the close corporation, the minority may do equal damage through unscrupulous and improper "sharp dealings" with an unsuspecting majority. See Helms v. Duckworth, 101 U.S.App.D.C. 390, 249 F.2d 482 (1957).

48. [By the Court] We stress that the strict fiduciary duty which we apply to stockholders in a close corporation in this opinion governs *only* their actions relative to the operations of the enterprise and the effects of that operation on the rights and investments of other stockholders. We express no opinion as to the standard of duty applicable to transactions in the shares of the close corporation when the corporation is not a party to the transaction. Cf. Andrews, The Stockholder's Right to Equal Opportunity in the Sale of Shares, 78 Harv. L.Rev. 505 (1965).

49. [By the Court] The rule set out in many jurisdictions is: "The majority has the right to control; but when it does so, it occupies a fiduciary relation toward the minority, as much so as the corporation itself or its officers and directors." Southern Pac. Co. v. Bogert, 250 U.S. 483, 487–488, 39 S.Ct. 533, 535, 63 L.Ed. 1099 (1919).

involving close corporations, we have held stockholders participating in management to a standard of fiduciary duty more exacting than the traditional good faith and inherent fairness standard because of the trust and confidence reposed in them by the other stockholders. * * *

[W]e have imposed a duty of loyalty more exacting than that duty owed by a director to his corporation (Spiegel v. Beacon Participations, Inc., 297 Mass. 398, 410–411, 8 N.E.2d 895 [1937]) or by a majority stockholder to the minority in a public corporation because of facts particular to the close corporation in the cases. In the instant case, we extend this strict duty of loyalty to all stockholders in close corporations. The circumstances which justified findings of relationships of trust and confidence in these particular cases exist universally in modified form in all close corporations. See Kruger v. Gerth, 16 N.Y.2d 802, 806, 263 N.Y.S.2d 1, 210 N.E.2d 355 (1965) (Fuld, J., dissenting). Statements in other cases which suggest that stockholders of a corporation do not stand in a relationship of trust and confidence to one another will not be followed in the close corporation context.

B. *Equal Opportunity in a Close Corporation.* Under settled Massachusetts law, a domestic corporation, unless forbidden by statute, has the power to purchase its own shares. Dupee v. Boston Water Power Co., 114 Mass. 37, 43 (1873). * * * When the corporation reacquiring its own stock is a close corporation, the purchase is subject to the additional requirement, in the light of our holding in this opinion, that the stockholders, who, as directors or controlling stockholders, caused the corporation to enter into the stock purchase agreement, must have acted with the utmost good faith and loyalty to the other stockholders.

To meet this test, if the stockholder whose shares were purchased was a member of the controlling group, the controlling stockholders must cause the corporation to offer each stockholder an equal opportunity to sell a ratable number of his shares to the corporation at an identical price.[50] Purchase by the corporation confers substantial benefits on the members of the controlling group whose shares were purchased. These benefits are not available to the minority stockholders if the corporation does not also offer them an opportunity to sell their shares. The controlling group may not, consistent with its strict duty to the minority, utilize its control of the corporation to obtain special advantages and disproportionate benefit from its share ownership. Cf. Victor Brudney and Marvin A. Chirelstein, Fair Shares in Corporate Mergers and Takeovers, 88 Harv.L.Rev. 297, 334 (1974).

The benefits conferred by the purchase are twofold: (1) provision of a market for shares; (2) access to corporate assets for personal use. By definition, there is no ready market for shares of a close corporation. The purchase creates a market for shares which previously had been unmarketable. It transforms a previously illiquid investment into a liquid one. If the close corporation purchases shares only from a member of the controlling group, the controlling stockholder can convert his shares into cash at a time when none of the other stockholders can. Consistent with its strict fiduciary duty,

---

50. [By the Court] Of course, a close corporation may purchase shares from one stockholder without offering the others an equal opportunity if all other stockholders give advance consent to the stock purchase arrangements through acceptance of an appropriate provision in the articles of organization, the corporate by-laws or a stockholder's agreement. Similarly, all other stockholders may ratify the purchase.

the controlling group may not utilize its control of the corporation to establish an exclusive market in previously unmarketable shares from which the minority stockholders are excluded. See Jones v. H.F. Ahmanson & Co., 1 Cal.3d 93, 115, 81 Cal.Rptr. 592, 460 P.2d 464 (1969).

The purchase also distributes corporate assets to the stockholder whose shares were purchased. Unless an equal opportunity is given to all stockholders, the purchase of shares from a member of the controlling group operates as a *preferential* distribution of assets. In exchange for his shares, he receives a percentage of the contributed capital and accumulated profits of the enterprise. The funds he so receives are available for his personal use. The other stockholders benefit from no such access to corporate property and cannot withdraw their shares of the corporate profits and capital in this manner unless the controlling group acquiesces. Although the purchase price for the controlling stockholder's shares may seem fair to the corporation and other stockholders under the tests established in the prior case law, the controlling stockholder whose stock has been purchased has still received a relative advantage over his fellow stockholders, inconsistent with his strict fiduciary duty—an opportunity to turn corporate funds to personal use.

The rule of equal opportunity in stock purchases by close corporations provides equal access to these benefits for all stockholders. We hold that, in any case in which the controlling stockholders have exercised their power over the corporation to deny the minority such equal opportunity, the minority shall be entitled to appropriate relief.[51] To the extent that language in Spiegel v. Beacon Participations, Inc., 297 Mass. 398, 431, 8 N.E.2d 895 (1937), and other cases suggests that there is no requirement of equal opportunity for minority stockholders when a close corporation purchases shares from a controlling stockholder, it is not to be followed.

C. *Application of the Law to this Case.* We turn now to the application of the learning set forth above to the facts of the instant case.

The strict standard of duty is plainly applicable to the stockholders in Rodd Electrotype. Rodd Electrotype is a close corporation. Members of the Rodd and Donahue families are the sole owners of the corporation's stock. * * * Through their control of these management positions and of the majority of the Rodd Electrotype stock, the Rodds effectively controlled the corporation. In testing the stock purchase from Harry Rodd against the applicable strict fiduciary standard, we treat the Rodd family as a single controlling group. We reject the defendants' contention that the Rodd family cannot be treated as a unit for this purpose. From the evidence, it is clear that the Rodd family was a close-knit one with strong community of interest.

---

51. [By the Court] Under the Massachusetts law, "[n]o stockholder shall have any preemptive right to acquire stock of the corporation except to the extent provided in the articles of organization or in a by-law adopted by and subject to amendment only by the stockholders." G.L. c. 156B, § 20. We do not here suggest that such preemptive rights are required by the strict fiduciary duty applicable to the stockholders of close corporations. However, to the extent that a controlling stockholder or other stockholder, in violation of his fiduciary duty, causes the corporation to issue stock in order to expand his holdings or to dilute holdings of other stockholders, the other stockholders will have a right to relief in court. Even under the traditional standard of duty applicable to corporate directors and stockholders generally, this court has looked favorably upon stockholder challenges to stock issues which, in violation of a fiduciary duty, served personal interests of other stockholder/directors and did not serve the corporate interest. See, e.g., Elliott v. Baker, 194 Mass. 518, 80 N.E. 450 (1907).

* * *. Moreover, a strong motive of interest requires that the Rodds be considered a controlling group. When Charles Rodd and Frederick Rodd were called on to represent the corporation in its dealings with their father, they must have known that further advancement within the corporation and benefits would follow their father's retirement and the purchase of his stock. * * *

On its face, then, the purchase of Harry Rodd's shares by the corporation is a breach of the duty which the controlling stockholders, the Rodds, owed to the minority stockholders, the plaintiff and her son. The purchase distributed a portion of the corporate assets to Harry Rodd, a member of the controlling group, in exchange for his shares. The plaintiff and her son were not offered an equal opportunity to sell their shares to the corporation. In fact, their efforts to obtain an equal opportunity were rebuffed by the corporate representative. As the trial judge found, they did not, in any manner, ratify the transaction with Harry Rodd.

Because of the foregoing, we hold that the plaintiff is entitled to relief. Two forms of suitable relief are set out hereinafter. The judge below is to enter an appropriate judgment. The judgment may require Harry Rodd to remit $36,000 with interest at the legal rate from July 15, 1970, to Rodd Electrotype in exchange for forty-five shares of Rodd Electrotype treasury stock. * * * In the alternative, the judgment may require Rodd Electrotype to purchase all of the plaintiff's shares for $36,000 without interest. In the circumstances of this case, we view this as the equal opportunity which the plaintiff should have received. Harry Rodd's retention of thirty-six shares, which were to be sold and given to his children within a year of the Rodd Electrotype purchase, cannot disguise the fact that the corporation acquired one hundred percent of that portion of his holdings (forty-five shares) which he did not intend his children to own. The plaintiff is entitled to have one hundred percent of her forty-five shares similarly purchased.[52] * * * The case is remanded to the Superior Court for entry of judgment in conformity with this opinion.

So ordered.

WILKINS, JUSTICE (concurring).

I agree with much of what the Chief Justice says in support of granting relief to the plaintiff. However, I do not join in any implication * * * that the rule concerning a close corporation's purchase of a controlling stockholder's shares applies to all operations of the corporation as they affect minority stockholders. That broader issue, which is apt to arise in connection with salaries and dividend policy, is not involved in this case. The analogy to partnerships may not be a complete one.

Notes

(1) The basic holding of *Donahue* that fiduciary relationships exist within closely held corporations has been widely cited and accepted. Courts in more than

---

52. [By the Court] If there has been a significant change in corporate circumstances since this case was argued, this is a matter which can be brought to the attention of the court below and may be considered by the judge in granting appropriate relief in the form of a judgment.

25 states have either cited *Donahue* approvingly or have cited cases that relied upon *Donahue* for this proposition. This is a major change in approach from earlier cases.

(2) Even though *Donahue* talks about freeze-outs, the actual transaction in that case involves an arguably unfair redemption of shares. Courts have generally followed *Donahue* in this respect, and set aside a partial redemption of the majority's shares to the exclusion of the minority, e.g., Estate of Schroer v. Stamco Supply, Inc., 19 Ohio App.3d 34, 482 N.E.2d 975 (1984); Tillis v. United Parts, Inc., 395 So.2d 618 (Fla.App.1981), or the redemption of a third person's shares in order to assure the retention of control by one faction, e.g., Comolli v. Comolli, 241 Ga. 471, 246 S.E.2d 278 (1978). In Toner v. Baltimore Envelope Co., 304 Md. 256, 498 A.2d 642 (1985), the Court, while accepting the idea that fiduciary duties exist within a closely held corporation, declined to adopt "a per se equal opportunity rule" in the case of a selective redemption of shares by a closely held corporation. The Court commented that while controlling shareholders may violate fiduciary duties in such repurchases, that conclusion "should be based on all of the relevant facts." 498 A.2d at 650. The Court viewed cases such as *Donahue* and *Comolli* as establishing a "per se test." Essentially consistent with *Toner* is Delahoussaye v. Newhard, 785 S.W.2d 609 (Mo.App.1990).

(3) The broad language in *Donahue* has been invoked by plaintiffs in several Massachusetts cases where employee-shareholders were fired for reasons that did not constitute good cause. The leading case is Wilkes v. Springside Nursing Home, Inc., 370 Mass. 842, 353 N.E.2d 657 (1976), where the Court ordered the reinstatement of a minority shareholder to the corporate payroll after he had been fired in connection with an attempted freeze-out. However, the Massachusetts Supreme Court in its opinion in *Wilkes* retreated to some extent from the broad "equal opportunity" language of *Donahue*. The Court stated:

> We are concerned that untempered application of the strict good faith standard enunciated in *Donahue* to cases such as the one before us will result in the imposition of limitations on legitimate action by the controlling group in a close corporation which will unduly hamper its effectiveness in managing the corporation in the best interests of all concerned. The majority, concededly, have certain rights to what has been termed "selfish ownership" in the corporation which should be balanced against the concept of their fiduciary obligation to the minority.

> Therefore, when minority stockholders in a close corporation bring suit against the majority alleging a breach of the strict good faith duty owed to them by the majority, we must carefully analyze the action taken by the controlling stockholders in the individual case. It must be asked whether the controlling group can demonstrate a legitimate business purpose for its action. In asking this question, we acknowledge the fact that the controlling group in a close corporation must have some room to maneuver in establishing the business policy of the corporation. It must have a large measure of discretion, for example, in declaring or withholding dividends, deciding whether to merge or consolidate, establishing the salaries of corporate officers, dismissing directors with or without cause, and hiring and firing corporate employees.

> When an asserted business purpose for their action is advanced by the majority, however, we think it is open to minority stockholders to demonstrate that the same legitimate objective could have been achieved through an alternative course of action less harmful to the minority's interest. If called on

to settle a dispute, our courts must weigh the legitimate business purpose, if any, against the practicability of a less harmful alternative.

Applying this approach to the instant case, it is apparent that the majority stockholders in Springside have not shown a legitimate business purpose for severing Wilkes from the payroll of the corporation or for refusing to reelect him as a salaried officer and director. * * * There was no showing of misconduct on Wilkes' part as a director, officer or employee of the corporation which would lead us to approve the majority action as a legitimate response to the disruptive nature of an undesirable individual bent on injuring or destroying the corporation. On the contrary, it appears that Wilkes had always accomplished his assigned share of the duties competently, and that he had never indicated an unwillingness to continue to do so. 353 N.E.2d at 663–64.

The Court returned to the same theme in Zimmerman v. Bogoff, 402 Mass. 650, 524 N.E.2d 849 (1988), where it said, "the *Donahue* remedy is not intended to place a strait jacket on legitimate corporate activity. Where the alleged wrongdoer can demonstrate a legitimate business purpose for his action, no liability will result unless the wronged shareholder succeeds in showing that the proffered legitimate objective could have been achieved through a less harmful, reasonably practicable, alternative mode of action." 524 N.E.2d at 853.

These cases create a potential conflict with the well-accepted employment at will doctrine, which states "that an employer may terminate an at-will employee at any time with or without cause * * * [unless] the termination violates a clearly established public policy." King v. Driscoll, 418 Mass. 576, 580, 638 N.E.2d 488, 491 (1994). The public policy exception, furthermore, is interpreted "narrowly." Ibid. In three subsequent cases, the Massachusetts court refused to allow *Donahue* to intrude upon the employment at will doctrine. In *King,* no breach of duty was found where an employee had been fired for agreeing to serve as a plaintiff in a derivative suit, but his shares were repurchased on terms set forth in the original contract of employment. In Blank v. Chelmsford Ob/Gyn, P.C., 420 Mass. 404, 649 N.E.2d 1102 (1995), no breach of a *Donahue* duty was found where the plaintiff's employment agreement provided that the employment could be terminated by written notice, "such notice shall be effective to terminate this contract on the last day of the sixth month following," and the plaintiff's employment was terminated in accordance with that contract. In Merola v. Exergen Corp., 423 Mass. 461, 668 N.E.2d 351 (1996), an employee/shareholder was terminated for personal non-economic reasons, but the Court held *Donahue* was not violated because the plaintiff's investment in the stock was not tied to employment in any formal way and the termination did not lead to the financial gain of the controlling shareholder.

(4) Does an attorney who represents a closely held corporation have an obligation with respect to minority shareholders if, for example, negotiations occur regarding the redemption of some of the controlling shares? See Schaeffer v. Cohen, Rosenthal, et al., 405 Mass. 506, 541 N.E.2d 997 (1989), where the Court stated, "Just as an attorney for a partnership owes a fiduciary duty to each partner, it is fairly arguable that an attorney for a close corporation owes a fiduciary duty to the individual shareholders." 541 N.E.2d at 1002. However, the resolution of this issue was not necessary for the decision in the case and a subsequent case declined to extend a duty to attorneys who represent individual shareholders rather than the corporation. Kurker v. Hill, 44 Mass.App.Ct. 184, 689 N.E.2d 833 (1998). A lawyer may be liable when his or her client breaches a

fiduciary duty if the lawyer is found to have aided-and-abetted that breach and the transaction takes place in a jurisdiction that imposes liability for aiding and abetting. In Chem–Age Industries, Inc. v. Glover, 652 N.W.2d 756 (S.D.2002), the court was confronted with the question of whether a lawyer who incorporates a business on behalf of an individual client owes a duty of care to the corporation and its investors. The client in this case obtained substantial funds from two investors, then had the lawyer incorporate the business. Once the business was incorporated, the client misappropriated the investors' funds, giving some of the ill-gotten gains to the lawyer. The court dismissed the plaintiff's direct claims against the lawyer for malpractice on the grounds that the lawyer had not contracted to give legal advice to the plaintiffs and in fact had little contact with them. The court, however, refused to dismiss that portion of the lawsuit claiming that the corporation was damaged by the lawyer's negligent representation. The court also held that there were material questions of fact as to whether the lawyer had knowingly provided substantial assistance to the client in connection with the client's breaches of his fiduciary duty.

(5) There are costs as well as benefits to the approach taken by the court in *Donahue*. Just as majority shareholders in closely held corporations can abuse and take advantage of the minority, so too can the minority abuse the majority if the minority has too much power. Concerns have been raised that proposals to protect minority shareholders in closely held corporations by giving them the power to compel the corporation to repurchase their shares have been criticized. See Frank Easterbrook and Daniel R. Fischel, Close Corporations and Agency Costs, 38 Stanford L. Rev. 271, 285–89 (1986)(arguing that the automatic buy-out right gives minority shareholders the ability to impose costs on other investors that is absent under a fault standard for involuntary dissolution).

More generally, in The Economic Structure of Corporate Law,[53] Easterbrook and Fischel argue that corporation law is a matter of contract and the "[t]he role of corporate law * * * is to adopt a background term that prevails unless varied by contract. And the background term should be the one that is either picked by contract expressly or is the operational assumption of successful firms." Id. at 36. In the case of closely held corporations where "a court is unavoidably entwined in a dispute, it must decide what the parties would have agreed to had they written a contract resolving all contingencies." Id. at 245. Do you agree that this is the appropriate standard (a standard that is generally accepted by law and economics scholars) for determining what duties courts should imply? Easterbrook and Fischel also argue that the costs of the imposition of strict fiduciary duties are so great that "it is conceivable, indeed certain, that there will be situations where all parties decide that they are better off without" these duties. 38 Stanford L. Rev. 271 at 285. As a result, they contend the decision in *Donahue* is totally wrong.

(6) Following an approach consistent with the contractual perspective described above, Delaware appears to have flatly rejected the approach of *Donahue*. In Nixon v. Blackwell, 626 A.2d 1366, 1380 (Del.1993) the Delaware Supreme Court stated, "[I]t would do violence to normal corporate practice and our corporation law to fashion an *ad hoc* ruling which would result in a court-imposed stockholder buy-out for which the parties had not contracted." The court added, for good measure, that to do so "would be inappropriate judicial legislation." The proper standard to review the decision in question according to the Delaware court was the "entire fairness" test discussed in chapter 12, Section A, infra.

---

53. Reprinted by permission of the publishers from *The Economic Structure of Corporate Law* by Frank H. Easterbrook and Daniel R. Fischel, Cambridge, Mass.: Harvard University Press, Copyright © 1991 by the President and Fellows of Harvard College.

However, the facts of Nixon v. Blackwell are quite different from those of *Donahue*. See Robert A. Ragazzo, Toward A Delaware Common Law of Closely Held Corporations, 77 Wash.U.L.Q. 1099, 1125–27 (1999). Professor Ragazzo suggests that principles which the Delaware Supreme Court has developed for publicly held corporations may provide protection for shareholders in closely held corporations in *Donahue*-type situations.

I. LEGAL RESTRICTIONS ON DISTRIBUTIONS

About 37 states today have adopted section 6.40 of the Model Business Corporation Act, some with minor variations or changes, as the standard test for the legality of distributions of capital, of dividends and of reacquisitions of shares. The remaining states retain older tests that build on traditional concepts of corporate capital. Included among the states retaining older concepts are the commercially important states of Delaware, New Jersey, New York, and Ohio. It is fair to state that the problems involved in determining the legality of distributions of capital, dividends and reacquisitions under older statutes were among the most complex and confusing in the entire field of corporate law. The provisions of the current MBCA go a long way toward rationalizing these restrictions and it is likely that the remaining states will eventually revise their statutes in this area.

1. THE MODEL BUSINESS CORPORATION ACT

Section 6.40 of the MBCA sweeps away most of the complex issues and problems under earlier statutes. One of the important issues faced by the revisers of the Model Act was whether the validity of distributions should be measured exclusively by an insolvency test, or whether both an insolvency test and a balance sheet test should be retained. A balance sheet test requires consideration of underlying accounting principles if the test is to have any substance. The decision to retain a balance sheet test by the Committee was based on several considerations: The historical reliance on balance sheet tests in state statutes, protection for senior securities interests provided by § 6.40(c)(2), and the desire for specific tests, so far as practical, in evaluating the lawfulness of distributions. There was some sentiment for the incorporation of "generally accepted accounting principles" (GAAP) into the section, at least as a "safe harbor" for directors approving a distribution, but the final compromise on this issue now appears in the general language of § 6.40(d). The decision not to include a specific reference to GAAP was based partially on concern that the content of GAAP principles have varied over time. Is there anything wrong with a state statute incorporating by reference a changing body of principles controlled by other persons? Is that an invalid delegation of lawmaking authority to a private body?

OFFICIAL COMMENT TO § 6.40

* * *

2. *Equity Insolvency Test*

* * * [O]lder statutes prohibited payments of dividends if the corporation was, or as a result of the payment would be, insolvent in the equity sense. This test is retained, appearing in section 6.40(c)(1).

In most cases involving a corporation operating as a going concern in the normal course, information generally available will make it quite apparent that no particular inquiry concerning the equity insolvency test is needed. While neither a balance sheet nor an income statement can be conclusive as to this test, the existence of significant shareholders' equity and normal operating conditions are of themselves a strong indication that no issue should arise under that test. Indeed, in the case of a corporation having regularly audited financial statements, the absence of any qualification in the most recent auditor's opinion as to the corporation's status as a "going concern," coupled with a lack of subsequent adverse events, would normally be decisive.

It is only when circumstances indicate that the corporation is encountering difficulties or is in an uncertain position concerning its liquidity and operations that the board of directors or, more commonly, the officers or others upon whom they may place reliance under section 8.30(b), may need to address the issue. Because of the overall judgment required in evaluating the equity insolvency test, no one or more "bright line" tests can be employed. However, in determining whether the equity insolvency test has been met, certain judgments or assumptions as to the future course of the corporation's business are customarily justified, absent clear evidence to the contrary. These include the likelihood that (a) based on existing and contemplated demand for the corporation's products or services, it will be able to generate funds over a period of time sufficient to satisfy its existing and reasonably anticipated obligations as they mature, and (b) indebtedness which matures in the near-term will be refinanced where, on the basis of the corporation's financial condition and future prospects and the general availability of credit to businesses similarly situated, it is reasonable to assume that such refinancing may be accomplished. To the extent that the corporation may be subject to asserted or unasserted contingent liabilities, reasonable judgments as to the likelihood, amount, and time of any recovery against the corporation, after giving consideration to the extent to which the corporation is insured or otherwise protected against loss, may be utilized. There may be occasions when it would be useful to consider a cash flow analysis, based on a business forecast and budget, covering a sufficient period of time to permit a conclusion that known obligations of the corporation can reasonably be expected to be satisfied over the period of time that they will mature.

In exercising their judgment, the directors are entitled to rely, under section 8.30(b) as noted above, on information, opinions, reports, and statements prepared by others. Ordinarily, they should not be expected to become involved in the details of the various analyses or market or economic projections that may be relevant. Judgments must of necessity be made on the basis of information in the hands of the directors when a distribution is authorized. They should not, of course, be held responsible as a matter of hindsight for unforeseen developments. This is particularly true with respect to assumptions as to the ability of the corporation's business to repay long-term obligations which do not mature for several years, since the primary focus of the directors' decision to make a distribution should normally be on the corporation's prospects and obligations in the shorter term, unless special factors concerning the corporation's prospects require the taking of a longer term perspective. * * *

4. *Balance Sheet Test*

Section 6.40(c)(2) requires that, after giving effect to any distribution, the corporation's assets equal or exceed its liabilities plus (with some exceptions) the dissolution preferences of senior equity securities. Section 6.40(d) authorizes asset and liability determinations to be made for this purpose on the basis of either (1) financial statements prepared on the basis of accounting practices and principles that are reasonable in the circumstances or (2) a fair valuation or other method that is reasonable in the circumstances. The determination of a corporation's assets and liabilities and the choice of the permissible basis on which to do so are left to the judgment of its board of directors. In making a judgment under section 6.40(d), the board may rely under section 8.30(b) upon opinions, reports, or statements, including financial statements and other financial data prepared or presented by public accountants or others.

Section 6.40 does not utilize particular accounting terminology of a technical nature or specify particular accounting concepts. In making determinations under this section, the board of directors may make judgments about accounting matters, giving full effect to its right to rely upon professional or expert opinion. * * *

a. Generally accepted accounting principles

The board of directors should in all circumstances be entitled to rely upon reasonably current financial statements prepared on the basis of generally accepted accounting principles in determining whether or not the balance sheet test of section 6.40(c)(2) has been met, unless the board is aware that it would be unreasonable to rely on the financial statements because of newly-discovered or subsequently arising facts or circumstances. But section 6.40 does not mandate the use of generally accepted accounting principles; it only requires the use of accounting practices and principles that are reasonable in the circumstances. While publicly-owned corporations subject to registration under the Securities Exchange Act of 1934 must, and many other corporations in fact do, utilize financial statements prepared on the basis of generally accepted accounting principles, a great number of smaller or closely-held corporations do not. Some of these corporations maintain records solely on a tax accounting basis and their financial statements are of necessity prepared on that basis. Others prepare financial statements that substantially reflect generally accepted accounting principles but may depart from them in some respects (e.g., footnote disclosure). These facts of corporate life indicate that a statutory standard of reasonableness, rather than stipulating generally accepted accounting principles as the normative standard, is appropriate in order to achieve a reasonable degree of flexibility and to accommodate the needs of the many different types of business corporations which might be subject to these provisions, including in particular closely-held corporations. Accordingly, the revised Model Act contemplates that generally acceptable accounting principles are always "reasonable in the circumstances" and that other accounting principles may be perfectly acceptable, under a general standard of reasonableness, even if they do not involve the "fair value" or "current value" concepts that are also contemplated by section 6.40(d).

b. Other principles

Section 6.40(d) specifically permits determinations to be made under section 6.40(c)(2) on the basis of a fair valuation or other method that is reasonable in the circumstances. Thus the statute authorizes departures from historical cost accounting and sanctions the use of appraisal and current value methods to determine the amount available for distribution. No particular method of valuation is prescribed in the statute, since different methods may have validity depending upon the circumstances, including the type of enterprise and the purpose for which the determination is made. For example, it is inappropriate in most cases to apply a "quick-sale liquidation" method to value an enterprise, particularly with respect to the payment of normal dividends. On the other hand, a "quick-sale liquidation" valuation method might be appropriate in certain circumstances for an enterprise in the course of reducing its asset or business base by a material degree. In most cases, a fair valuation method or a going-concern basis would be appropriate if it is believed that the enterprise will continue as a going concern.

Ordinarily a corporation should not selectively revalue assets. It should consider the value of all of its material assets, whether or not reflected in the financial statements (e.g., a valuable executory contract). Likewise, all of a corporation's material obligations should be considered and revalued to the extent appropriate and possible. In any event, section 6.40(d) calls for the application under section 6.40(c)(2) of a method of determining the aggregate amount of assets and liabilities that is reasonable in the circumstances.

Section 6.40(d) also refers to some "other method that is reasonable in the circumstances." This phrase is intended to comprehend within section 6.40(c)(2) the wide variety of possibilities that might not be considered to fall under a "fair valuation" or "current value" method but might be reasonable in the circumstances of a particular case.

5. *Preferential Dissolution Rights and the Balance Sheet Test*

Section 6.40(c)(2) provides that a distribution may not be made unless the total assets of the corporation exceed its liabilities plus the amount that would be needed to satisfy any shareholder's superior preferential rights upon dissolution if the corporation were to be dissolved at the time of the distribution. This requirement in effect treats preferential dissolution rights of shares for distribution purposes as if they were liabilities for the sole purpose of determining the amount available for distributions, and carries forward analogous treatment of shares having preferential dissolution rights from earlier versions of the Model Act. * * *

8. *Application to Reacquisition of Shares*

The application of the equity insolvency and balance sheet tests to distributions that involve the purchase, redemption, or other acquisition of the corporation's shares creates unique problems; section 6.40 provides a specific rule for the resolution of these problems as described below.

a. Time of measurement

Section 6.40(e)(1) provides that the time for measuring the effect of a distribution under section 6.40(c), if shares of the corporation are reacquired, is the earlier of (i) the payment date, or (ii) the date the shareholder ceased to be a shareholder with respect to the shares, except as provided in section 6.40(g).

b. When tests are applied to redemption-related debt

In an acquisition of its shares, a corporation may transfer property or incur debt to the former holder of the shares. The case law on the status of this debt is conflicting. However, share repurchase agreements involving payment for shares over a period of time are of special importance in closely held corporate enterprises. Section 6.40(e) provides a clear rule for this situation: the legality of the distribution must be measured at the time of the issuance or incurrence of the debt, not at a later date when the debt is actually paid, except as provided in section 6.40(g). Of course, this does not preclude a later challenge of a payment on account of redemption-related debt by a bankruptcy trustee on the ground that it constitutes a preferential payment to a creditor.

c. Priority of debt distributed directly or incurred in connection with a reacquisition of shares

Section 6.40(f) provides that indebtedness created to acquire the corporation's shares or issued as a distribution is on a parity with the indebtedness of the corporation to its general, unsecured creditors, except to the extent subordinated by agreement. General creditors are better off in these situations than they would have been if cash or other property had been paid out for the shares or distributed (which is proper under the statute), and no worse off than if cash had been paid or distributed and then lent back to the corporation, making the shareholders (or former shareholders) creditors. The parity created by section 6.40(f) is logically consistent with the rule established by section 6.40(e) that these transactions should be judged at the time of the issuance of the debt.

9. *Treatment of Certain Indebtedness*

Section 6.40(g) provides that indebtedness need not be taken into account as a liability in determining whether the tests of section 6.40(c) have been met if the terms of the indebtedness provide that payments of principal or interest can be made only if and to the extent that payment of a distribution could then be made under section 6.40. This has the effect of making the holder of the indebtedness junior to all other creditors but senior to the holders of all classes of shares, not only during the time the corporation is operating but also upon dissolution and liquidation. It should be noted that the creation of such indebtedness, and the related limitations on payments of principal and interest, may create tax problems or raise other legal questions.

Although section 6.40(g) is applicable to all indebtedness meeting its tests, regardless of the circumstances of its issuance, it is anticipated that it will be applicable most frequently to permit the reacquisition of shares of the corporation at a time when the deferred purchase price exceeds the net worth of the corporation. This type of reacquisition will often be necessary in the case of businesses in early stages of development or service businesses whose value derives principally from existing or prospective net income or cash flow rather than from net asset value. In such situations, it is anticipated that net worth will grow over time from operations so that when payments in respect of the indebtedness are to be made the two insolvency tests will be satisfied. In the meantime, the fact that the indebtedness is outstanding will not prevent distributions that could be made under subsection (c) if the indebtedness were not counted in making the determination.

Notes

(1) One feature of dividend statutes is that there is little litigation involving their application. They are primarily a problem for the corporate attorney striving to ensure that a directorial decision does not inadvertently give rise to personal liability. From time to time, however, they arise in unexpected fashion in litigation that has nothing to do with a simple distribution of assets to shareholders. In re C–T of Virginia, Inc., 958 F.2d 606 (4th Cir.1992), for example, the court held that a leveraged buyout (see Chapter 14) does not constitute a "distribution" of assets subject to § 6.40. *Contra* is Matter of Munford, Inc., 97 F.3d 456 (11th Cir.1996) arising under the Georgia statute.

(2) In Minnelusa Co. v. Andrikopoulos, 929 P.2d 1321 (Colo.1996), the court held that a corporation executing a promissory note to repurchase stock could not later use the Colorado stock repurchase statute to invalidate the promissory note on the theory that its execution rendered the corporation insolvent. The court stated that the invalidity of a corporate stock repurchase agreement could be raised only by persons who are injured or prejudiced thereby and not by the corporation itself. Such a defense also was held not to be available to a shareholder who personally guaranteed the corporate performance of such a promissory note.

(3) In 2000, § 6.40(h) was added to the Model Act to make clear that upon dissolution the distribution rules of § 14.09 are applicable rather than the provisions of § 6.40.

The following are brief descriptions of the older tests that continue to have relevancy in some states.

J. NON–MODEL ACT STATUTES

State statutes not based on the current MBCA establish a variety of tests for the legality of distributions.

1. PURE INSOLVENCY TEST

Massachusetts applies a pure insolvency test to all transactions: liability is imposed on directors if the distribution renders the corporation insolvent or left with insufficient property to pay its debts.

Other states apply a variety of different tests.

2. "EARNED SURPLUS" DIVIDEND STATUTES

MBCA (1969) established the general tests for the legality of a dividend as (1) the availability of "earned surplus" out of which the dividend may be paid, and (2) a solvency test to be applied immediately after giving effect to the dividend. See MBCA (1969) § 45. Eight states continue to follow this pattern. The definition of "earned surplus" in MBCA (1969) § 2(1), apparently contemplated the aggregation of income from all profit-and-loss statements going back to the time the corporation was organized. This approach creates practical and theoretical problems that are described in William P. Hackney, The Financial Provisions of the Model Business Corporation Act, 70 Harv. L.Rev. 1357, 1368–69 (1957):[54]

> Even for a new corporation, the air of simplicity about a statutory rule allowing dividends only out of the undistributed balance of all corporate income is misleading. Actually, the correct computation of income for any one year is not only incredibly difficult but is so far from an exact science—which of course it does not purport to be—that it is meaningless to attempt to say precisely in dollars what any corporation's income actually is. The determination of income requires allocations of receipts, expenses, and losses to fiscal periods, such allocations being sometimes based on fact but sometimes estimated, or conventional, or based on assumptions as to future events which may prove invalid. Accounting principles are not fundamental truths, capable of scientific proof, but are derived from experience and reason; proved utility is the criterion. Rapidly changing accounting principles show that accounting income is not a fixed concept but one subject to both differences of opinion and variations from year to year. One "sophisticated accountant" has been quoted as defining income as "anything which good accounting practice accepts as income."

> Nor is it clear what is meant by the Model Act definition's repetitive terms, "net profits," "income," and "gains and losses." Paragraphs 28–34 of Accounting Terminology Bulletin No. 1 indicate that while these terms have had varying meanings in the past there is an increasing tendency to regard the terms "income" and "profit and loss" as coextensive. There is no indication of how the term "gains" might differ in meaning from "profits" or from "income," nor why the word "earnings" is left out of the definition, nor why the word "net" must precede "profits" but not "income," "gains," or "losses." * * *

The earned surplus statutes raise two additional questions that are answered in various ways in specific state statutes: (1) May a corporation eliminate deficits in earned surplus by transferring amounts from capital surplus or some other surplus account to earned surplus? See MBCA (1969) § 2(1), which inferentially permits such transfers. Such a transaction is called a "quasi-reorganization," and is not permitted under the statutes of some states. (2) May a corporation with a negative earned surplus from earlier years pay a dividend out of current earnings, or must it first apply current earnings to eliminate past deficits? MBCA (1969) contained an alternative § 45(a), which allowed dividends from current earnings; such dividends, usually known as "nimble dividends," are not permitted in some states. Only three states apparently continue to permit such dividends at the present time.

3. "IMPAIRMENT OF CAPITAL" DIVIDEND STATUTES

A few non-Model Act statutes establish a test for determining the legality of dividends that appears to be based on a balance sheet rather than income statement analysis. The Delaware statute, for example, permits a corporation to pay dividends basically "out of its surplus," Del.Gen.Corp.Law § 170, and

54. Copyright 8 1957 by the Harvard Law Review Association.

defines "surplus" to include everything in excess of the aggregate par values of the issued shares plus whatever else the corporation has elected to add to its capital account. New York also applies a "surplus" test but adds the requirement that "the net assets of the corporation remaining after such declaration, payment or distribution shall at least equal the amount of its stated capital * * *." N.Y.—McKinney's Bus.Corp.Law § 510(b). Other statutes talk in terms of not "impairing capital" or of prohibiting dividends "except from surplus, or from the net profits arising from the business." This last clause in particular seems to clearly contemplate the payment of dividends out of sources other than earnings (because of the use of the disjunctive "or"). All of these impairment of capital statutes were construed to permit such distributions. For example, Randall v. Bailey, 288 N.Y. 280, 43 N.E.2d 43 (1942), arising under an earlier version of the New York statute, involved, among other issues, an attempt by a corporation to create surplus by writing up the value of appreciated assets on its books. The Court permitted the corporation to increase its dividend-paying capacity by such a bookkeeping entry. Presumably, such a "reevaluation surplus" is "surplus" under such statutes and payments out of it would not "impair capital." Could an argument be made that reevaluation surplus might be "earned surplus" as a "gain" under the definition of "earned surplus" in MBCA (1969) § 2(1)? Randall v. Bailey also involved an asset of "good will" that apparently was added to the balance sheet as a balancing entry in an earlier corporate acquisition. This entry, of course, did not represent any specific property. In applying the balance sheet tests of "surplus" for determining when a dividend can be paid, shouldn't only "real" assets be counted? The Court permitted recognition of the asset of good will under the circumstances, but the lower court commented that "[d]irectors obviously cannot create assets by fiat." 23 N.Y.S.2d 173, 177 (1940).

Cases such as Randall v. Bailey raise a basic question: to what extent should the legality of dividends be determined on the basis of accounting conventions or principles? For example, from an accounting standpoint, write-ups of assets to reflect market appreciation are generally frowned on if not flatly prohibited. Should "generally accepted accounting principles" (which are subject to change from time to time and do not command universal respect in any event) be relevant in deciding whether a corporation may legally pay a dividend out of "reevaluation surplus"? These statutes rely on accounting concepts in establishing limitations on distributions; on the other hand, it seems odd to make the legality of dividends depend on the shifting sands of accounting rules or conventions. Further, since much of the litigation relating to the legality of dividends arose in the context of creditors seeking to surcharge directors for declaring unlawful dividends, transactions such as those involved in Randall v. Bailey also raise the question whether directors can rely on the books of the corporation as presented to them by corporate officers or on the advice of attorneys or accountants for the corporation as to the availability of funds for the payment of dividends. Compare MBCA §§ 6.40(d), 8.33.

4. DISTRIBUTIONS OF CAPITAL SURPLUS

MBCA (1969) § 46 permits distributions to be made out of "capital surplus" with the proper authorization. Currently seven states follow this pattern while 12 other states authorize such distributions by provisions that vary substantially from the 1969 Act. Statutes in several states require the approval of a majority or two-thirds of the shareholders to authorize such a distribution. A few states adopt the phrase "partial liquidation" for such distributions to emphasize that they are not distributions of earnings but distributions of part of the capital of the corporation. Some statutes also impose special limitations on capital surplus created by the reduction of stated capital (e.g., by amending the articles to reduce the par value of outstanding shares or by canceling previously outstanding shares). Surplus so created is defined as "reduction surplus" in a few states.

Notes

(1) As a practical matter, it is quite possible for a corporation to have adequate earned surplus at the time of the original closing, but that earned surplus may be dissipated through operating losses before the payments are to be made. Similarly, it is possible that a corporation may meet the solvency test at the time of the original repurchase but not at the time later payments come due. The limited case law on this issue appears to apply both standards to each payment, though that makes little sense, at least in the case of earned surplus limitations. Consult David R. Herwitz, Installment Repurchase of Stock: Surplus Limitations, 79 Harv.L.Rev. 303 (1965). For a case rejecting this conclusion, but based on the precise language of a state corporation statute, see Williams v. Nevelow, 513 S.W.2d 535 (Tex.1974). The MBCA § 6.40(e)(2) essentially accepts the conclusion in *Williams*.

(2) Reacquisitions of shares on a deferred payment basis also raise a question: should a former shareholder who holds promissory notes of the corporation for part of the purchase price of shares be treated on a parity with general trade creditors, or should his or her claim be subordinated? A leading case subordinating this debt is Robinson v. Wangemann, 75 F.2d 756 (5th Cir.1935). The MBCA squarely addresses this question in MBCA § 6.40(e)(1) and (f) and places such a creditor on a parity with general trade creditors.

Chapter Nine

MANAGEMENT AND CONTROL
OF CORPORATION

A. THE TRADITIONAL ROLES
OF SHAREHOLDERS AND
DIRECTORS

McQUADE v. STONEHAM

Court of Appeals of New York, 1934.
263 N.Y. 323, 189 N.E. 234.

Pound, Chief Judge.

The action is brought to compel specific performance of an agreement between the parties, entered into to secure the control of National Exhibition Company, also called the Baseball Club (New York Nationals or "Giants"). This was one of Stoneham's enterprises which used the New York polo grounds for its home games. McGraw was manager of the Giants. McQuade was at the time the contract was entered into a city magistrate. He resigned December 8, 1930.

Defendant Stoneham became the owner of 1,306 shares, or a majority of the stock of National Exhibition Company. Plaintiff and defendant McGraw each purchased 70 shares of his stock. Plaintiff paid Stoneham $50,338.10 for the stock he purchased. As a part of the transaction, the agreement in question was entered into. It was dated May 21, 1919. Some of its pertinent provisions are:

VIII. The parties hereto will use their best endeavors for the purpose of continuing as directors of said Company and as officers thereof the following:

Directors:

Charles A. Stoneham,

John J. McGraw,

Francis X. McQuade

—with the right to the party of the first part [Stoneham] to name all additional directors as he sees fit:

Officers:

419

Charles A. Stoneham, President,

John J. McGraw, Vice President,

Francis X. McQuade, Treasurer.

IX. No salaries are to be paid to any of the above officers or directors, except as follows:

President	$45,000
Vice–President	7,500
Treasurer	7,500

X. There shall be no change in said salaries, no change in the amount of capital, or the number of shares, no change or amendment of the by-laws of the corporation or any matters regarding the policy of the business of the corporation or any matters which may in anywise affect, endanger or interfere with the rights of minority stockholders, excepting upon the mutual and unanimous consent of all of the parties hereto. * * *

XIV. This agreement shall continue and remain in force so long as the parties or any of them or the representative of any, own the stock referred to in this agreement, to wit, the party of the first part, 1,166 shares, the party of the second part 70 shares and the party of the third part 70 shares, except as may otherwise appear by this agreement. * * *

In pursuance of this contract Stoneham became president and McGraw vice president of the corporation. McQuade became treasurer. In June, 1925, his salary was increased to $10,000 a year. He continued to act until May 2, 1928, when Leo J. Bondy was elected to succeed him. The board of directors consisted of seven men. The four outside of the parties hereto were selected by Stoneham and he had complete control over them. At the meeting of May 2, 1928, Stoneham and McGraw refrained from voting, McQuade voted for himself, and the other four voted for Bondy. Defendants did not keep their agreement with McQuade to use their best efforts to continue him as treasurer. On the contrary, he was dropped with their entire acquiescence. At the next stockholders' meeting he was dropped as a director although they might have elected him.

The courts below have refused to order the reinstatement of McQuade, but have given him damages for wrongful discharge, with a right to sue for future damages.

The cause for dropping McQuade was due to the falling out of friends. McQuade and Stoneham had disagreed. The trial court has found in substance that their numerous quarrels and disputes did not affect the orderly and efficient administration of the business of the corporation; that plaintiff was removed because he had antagonized the dominant Stoneham by persisting in challenging his power over the corporate treasury and for no misconduct on his part. The court also finds that plaintiff was removed by Stoneham for protecting the corporation and its minority stockholders. We will assume that Stoneham put him out when he might have retained him, merely in order to get rid of him.

Defendants say that the contract in suit was void because the directors held their office charged with the duty to act for the corporation according to their best judgment and that any contract which compels a director to vote to keep any particular person in office and at a stated salary is illegal. Directors are the exclusive executive representatives of the corporation, charged with administration of its internal affairs and the management and use of its assets. They manage the business of the corporation. (General Corporation Law, Consol.Laws, c. 23, § 27.) "An agreement to continue a man as president is dependent upon his continued loyalty to the interests of the corporation." Fells v. Katz, 256 N.Y. 67, 72, 175 N.E. 516, 517. So much is undisputed.

Plaintiff contends that the converse of this proposition is true and that an agreement among directors to continue a man as an officer of a corporation is not to be broken so long as such officer is loyal to the interests of the corporation and that, as plaintiff has been found loyal to the corporation, the agreement of defendants is enforceable.

Although it has been held that an agreement among stockholders whereby it is attempted to divest the directors of their power to discharge an unfaithful employee of the corporation is illegal as against public policy (Fells v. Katz, supra), it must be equally true that the stockholders may not, by agreement among themselves, control the directors in the exercise of the judgment vested in them by virtue of their office to elect officers and fix salaries. Their motives may not be questioned so long as their acts are legal. The bad faith or the improper motives of the parties does not change the rule. Manson v. Curtis, 223 N.Y. 313, 324, 119 N.E. 559, Ann.Cas.1918E, 247. Directors may not by agreements entered into as stockholders abrogate their independent judgment. Creed v. Copps, 103 Vt. 164, 152 A. 369, 71 A.L.R. 1287, annotated.

Stockholders may, of course, combine to elect directors. That rule is well settled. As Holmes, C.J., pointedly said (Brightman v. Bates, 175 Mass. 105, 111, 55 N.E. 809, 811): "If stockholders want to make their power felt, they must unite. There is no reason why a majority should not agree to keep together." The power to unite is, however, limited to the election of directors and is not extended to contracts whereby limitations are placed on the power of directors to manage the business of the corporation by the selection of agents at defined salaries.

The minority shareholders whose interest McQuade says he has been punished for protecting, are not, aside from himself, complaining about his discharge. He is not acting for the corporation or for them in this action. It is impossible to see how the corporation has been injured by the substitution of Bondy as treasurer in place of McQuade. As McQuade represents himself in this action and seeks redress for his own wrongs, "we prefer to listen to [the corporation and the minority stockholders] before any decision as to their wrongs." Faulds v. Yates, 57 Ill. 416, 417, 11 Am.Rep. 24.

It is urged that we should pay heed to the morals and manners of the market place to sustain this agreement and that we should hold that its violation gives rise to a cause of action for damages rather than base our decision on any outworn notions of public policy. Public policy is a dangerous guide in determining the validity of a contract and courts should not interfere lightly with the freedom of competent parties to make their own contracts. We do not close our eyes to the fact that such agreements, tacitly or openly arrived at, are not uncommon, especially in close corporations where the stockholders are doing business for convenience under a corporate organization. We know that majority stockholders, united in voting trusts, effectively manage the business of a corporation by choosing trustworthy directors to reflect their policies in the corporate management. Nor are we unmindful that McQuade has, so the court has found, been shabbily treated as a purchaser of stock from Stoneham. We have said: "A trustee is held to something stricter than the morals of the market place" (Meinhard v. Salmon, 249 N.Y. 458, 464, 164 N.E. 545, 546, 62 A.L.R. 1), but Stoneham and McGraw were not trustees for McQuade as an individual. Their duty was to the corporation and its stockholders, to be exercised according to their unrestricted lawful judgment. They were under no legal obligation to deal righteously with McQuade if it was against public policy to do so.

The courts do not enforce mere moral obligations, nor legal ones either, unless someone seeks to establish rights which may be waived by custom and for convenience. We are constrained by authority to hold that a contract is illegal and void so far as it precludes the board of directors, at the risk of incurring legal liability, from changing officers, salaries, or policies, or retaining individuals in office, except by consent of the contracting parties. On the whole, such a holding is probably preferable to one which would open the courts to pass on the motives of directors in the lawful exercise of their trust. * * *

The judgment of the Appellate Division and that of the Trial Term should be reversed and the complaint dismissed, with costs in all courts.

CRANE, KELLOGG, O'BRIEN, and HUBBS, JJ., concur with POUND, C.J.

LEHMAN, J., concurs in result in opinion in which CROUCH, J., concurs. [This concurring opinion is omitted.]

Notes

(1) 2 Model Bus.Corp.Act Ann. (3d ed.), Historical Background to Section 8.01, at 8–7:[1]

Business corporations in common law jurisdictions have long followed the tradition of a representative form of governance by the election of a board of directors by the shareholders, voting by interest and not per capita. The board has traditionally been charged with the duty and responsibility of managing the business and affairs of the corporation, determining corporate policies, and selecting the officers and agents who carry on the detailed administration of the business. In large, publicly held corporations, the role of directors has been increasingly seen as involving oversight and review rather than actual management.

Legal writers have developed various theories as to the status of directors and the source of their powers: (1) the agency theory (all powers reside in the shareholders who have delegated certain powers to the directors as their agents); (2) the concession theory (the powers of directors are derived from the state, which authorizes them to perform certain functions, so that this power does not flow from the shareholders); (3) the Platonic guardian theory

---

1. Reprinted from *Model Business Corporation Act Annotated* with the permission of the   American Bar Association.

(the board is an aristocracy or group of overseers created by statutory enactment); and (4) the sui generis theory (directors are not agents; they are fiduciaries whose duties run to the corporation but their relationship with the corporation is sui generis since they are not trustees). Of these various theories, the first has been generally rejected, and probably most commentators today would agree that the fourth most accurately describes the modern role of directors.

Of course, most agreements among shareholders are valid. Arguments about invalidity arise in connection with agreements that encroach on the domain of the board of directors, which may be problematic, or which are related to matters like the election of directors that are in the domain of the shareholders. However, shareholder agreements must be carefully drafted if shareholders are to elect directors when resignations create board vacancies, since state law generally provides that the board of directors can fill such vacancies. See McIlquham v. Feste, 2001 WL 1497179 (Del.Ch. Nov. 16, 2001).

(2) Two subsequent cases have largely defined the scope of the principle originally set forth in Manson v. Curtis and articulated in the principal case:

(a) In Clark v. Dodge, 269 N.Y. 410, 199 N.E. 641 (1936), Clark owned 25 percent and Dodge owned 75 percent of the stock of each of two corporations. Clark and Dodge entered into a written agreement under seal in which it was agreed that Clark would continue to manage the business, and in that connection, would disclose a secret formula to Dodge's son that was necessary for the successful operation of the business. In return, Dodge agreed that he would vote his shares and also vote as director to ensure (i) Clark would be retained as general manager (so long as he should be "faithful, efficient and competent"), (ii) Clark would receive one-fourth of the net income either by way of salary or dividends, and (iii) no unreasonable salary would be paid to reduce the net income so as to materially affect Clark's profits. The agreement also provided that Clark would be retained as a director, and that Clark agreed to bequeath his stock— assuming no issue survived him—to Dodge's wife and children. After a falling out, Clark sought specific performance of the agreement, which was granted despite the provisions restricting Dodge's discretion as a director. The Court found that the contract was not illegal as against public policy as discussed within McQuade v. Stoneham, 263 N.Y. 323, 189 N.E. 234, upon the authority of which the complaint was dismissed by the Appellate Division. The Court reasoned that objections on grounds of public policy are largely meaningless in the context of this case:

> Where the directors are the sole stockholders, there seems to be no objection to enforcing an agreement among them to vote for certain people as officers.
>
> * * *
>
> If there was any invasion of the powers of the directorate under that agreement, it is so slight as to be negligible; and certainly there is no damage suffered by or threatened to anybody. The broad statements in the McQuade opinion, applicable to the facts there, should be confined to those facts. Id. at 415, 417.

(b) In Long Park v. Trenton–New Brunswick Theatres Co., 297 N.Y. 174, 77 N.E.2d 633 (1948), all the shareholders of the theatre company entered into an agreement giving one shareholder "full authority and power to supervise and direct the operation and management" of certain theatres. Such shareholder could be removed as manager only by arbitration among the shareholders. The Court stated:

> By virtue of these provisions the management of all theatres leased or operated by Trenton or any subsidiary is vested in Keith, without approval of the directors, and this management may not be changed by the directors but only [by arbitration]. The directors may neither select nor discharge the manager, to whom the supervision and direction of the management and operation of the theatres is delegated with full authority and power. Thus, the powers of the directors over the management of its theatres, the principal business of the corporation, were completely sterilized. Such restrictions and limitations upon the powers of the directors are clearly in violation of section 27 of the General Corporation Law of this State and the New Jersey statute. * * *
>
> We think these restrictions and limitations went far beyond the agreement in Clark v. Dodge, 269 N.Y. 410, 199 N.E. 641. We are not confronted with a slight impingement or innocuous variance from the statutory norm, but rather with the deprivation of all the powers of the board insofar as the selection and supervision of the management of the corporation's theatres, including the manner and policy of their operation, are concerned. * * *

77 N.E.2d at 634–35.

(3) Precisely what is the status of the rule of the McQuade case following these two decisions?

GALLER v. GALLER

Supreme Court of Illinois, 1964.
32 Ill.2d 16, 203 N.E.2d 577.

UNDERWOOD, JUSTICE.

Plaintiff, Emma Galler, sued in equity for an accounting and for specific performance of an agreement made in July, 1955, between plaintiff and her husband, of one part, and defendants, Isadore A. Galler and his wife, Rose, of the other. Defendants appealed from a decree of the superior court of Cook County granting the relief prayed. The First District Appellate Court reversed the decree and denied specific performance, affirming in part the order for an accounting, and modifying the order awarding master's fees. (45 Ill.App.2d 452, 196 N.E.2d 5.) That decision is appealed here on a certificate of importance.

There is no substantial dispute as to the facts in this case. From 1919 to 1924, Benjamin and Isadore Galler, brothers, were equal partners in the Galler Drug Company, a wholesale drug concern. In 1924 the business was incorporated under the Illinois Business Corporation Act, each owning one half of the outstanding 220 shares of stock. In 1945 each contracted to sell 6 shares to an employee, Rosenberg, at a price of $10,500 for each block of 6 shares, payable within 10 years. They guaranteed to repurchase the shares if Rosenberg's employment were terminated, and further agreed that if they sold their shares, Rosenberg would receive the same price per share as that paid for the brothers' shares. Rosenberg was still indebted for the 12 shares in July, 1955, and continued to make payments on account even after Benjamin Galler died in 1957 and after the institution of this action by Emma Galler in 1959. Rosenberg was not involved in this litigation either as a party or as a witness, and in July of 1961, prior to the time that the master in chancery hearings were concluded, defendants Isadore and Rose Galler purchased the 12 shares from Rosenberg. A supplemental complaint was filed by the plaintiff, Emma Galler, asserting an equitable right to have 6 of the 12 shares transferred to her and offering to pay the defendants one half of the amount that the defendants paid Rosenberg. The parties have stipulated that pending disposition of the instant case, these shares will not be voted or transferred. For approximately one year prior to the entry of the decree by the chancellor in July of 1962, there were no outstanding minority shareholder interests.

In March, 1954, Benjamin and Isadore, on the advice of their accountant, decided to enter into an agreement for the financial protection of their immediate families and to assure their families, after the death of either brother, equal control of the corporation. In June, 1954, while the agreement was in the process of preparation by an attorney-associate of the accountant, Benjamin suffered a heart attack. Although he resumed his business duties some months later, he was again stricken in February, 1955, and thereafter was unable to return to work. During his brother's illness, Isadore asked the accountant to have the shareholders' agreement put in final form in order to protect Benjamin's wife, and this was done by another attorney employed in the accountant's office. On a Saturday night in July, 1955, the accountant brought the agreement to Benjamin's home, and 6 copies of it were executed there by the two brothers and their wives. The accountant then collected all signed copies of the agreement and informed the parties that he was taking them for safe keeping. Between the execution of the agreement in July, 1955, and Benjamin's death in December, 1957, the agreement was not modified. Benjamin suffered a stroke late in July, 1955, and on August 2, 1955, Isadore and the accountant and a notary public brought to Benjamin for signature two powers of attorney which were retained by the accountant after Benjamin executed them with Isadore as a witness. The plaintiff did not read the powers and she never had them. One of the powers authorized the transfer of Benjamin's bank account to Emma and the other power enabled Emma to vote Benjamin's 104 shares. Because of the state of Benjamin's health, nothing further was said to him by any of the parties concerning the agreement. It appears from the evidence that some months after the agreement was signed, the defendants Isadore and Rose Galler and their son, the defendant, Aaron Galler sought to have the agreements destroyed. The evidence is undisputed that defendants had decided prior to Benjamin's death they would not honor the agreement, but never disclosed their intention to plaintiff or her husband.

On July 21, 1956, Benjamin executed an instrument creating a trust naming his wife as trustee. The trust covered, among other things, the 104 shares of Galler Drug Company stock and the stock certificates were endorsed by Benjamin and delivered to Emma. When Emma presented the certificates to defendants for transfer into her name as trustee, they sought to have Emma abandon the 1955 agreement or enter into some kind of a noninterference agreement as a price for the transfer of the shares. Finally, in September, 1956, after Emma had refused to abandon the shareholders' agreement, she did agree to permit defendant Aaron to become president for one year and agreed that she would not interfere with the business during that year. The stock was then reissued in her name as trustee. During the year 1957 while

Benjamin was still alive, Emma tried many times to arrange a meeting with Isadore to discuss business matters but he refused to see her.

Shortly after Benjamin's death, Emma went to the office and demanded the terms of the 1955 agreement be carried out. Isadore told her that anything she had to say could be said to Aaron, who then told her that his father would not abide by the agreement. He offered a modification of the agreement by proposing the salary continuation payment but without her becoming a director. When Emma refused to modify the agreement and sought enforcement of its terms, defendants refused and this suit followed.

During the last few years of Benjamin's life both brothers drew an annual salary of $42,000. Aaron, whose salary was $15,000 as manager of the warehouse prior to September, 1956, has since the time that Emma agreed to his acting as president, drawn an annual salary of $20,000. In 1957, 1958, and 1959, a $40,000 annual dividend was paid. Plaintiff has received her proportionate share of the dividend.

The July, 1955, agreement in question here, entered into between Benjamin, Emma, Isadore and Rose, recites that Benjamin and Isadore each own 47 1/2% of the issued and outstanding shares of the Galler Drug Company, an Illinois corporation, and that Benjamin and Isadore desired to provide income for the support and maintenance of their immediate families. No reference is made to the shares then being purchased by Rosenberg. The essential features of the contested portions of the agreement are substantially as set forth in the opinion of the Appellate Court: (2) that the bylaws of the corporation will be amended to provide for a board of four directors; that the necessary quorum shall be three directors; and that no directors' meeting shall be held without giving ten days notice to all directors. (3) The shareholders will cast their votes for the above named persons (Isadore, Rose, Benjamin and Emma) as directors at said special meeting and at any other meeting held for the purpose of electing directors. (4, 5) In the event of the death of either brother his wife shall have the right to nominate a director in place of the decedent. (6) Certain annual dividends will be declared by the corporation. The dividend shall be $50,000 payable out of the accumulated earned surplus in excess of $500,000. If 50% of the annual net profits after taxes exceeds the minimum $50,000, then the directors shall have discretion to declare a dividend up to 50% of the annual net profits. If the net profits are less than $50,000, nevertheless the minimum $50,000 annual dividend shall be declared, providing the $500,000 surplus is maintained. Earned surplus is defined. (9) The certificates evidencing the said shares of Benjamin Galler and Isadore Galler shall bear a legend that the shares are subject to the terms of this agreement. (10) A salary continuation agreement shall be entered into by the corporation which shall authorize the corporation upon the death of Benjamin Galler or Isadore Galler, or both, to pay a sum equal to twice the salary of such officer, payable monthly over a five-year period. Said sum shall be paid to the widow during her widowhood, but should be paid to such widow's children if the widow remarries within the five-year period. (11, 12) The parties to this agreement further agree and hereby grant to the corporation the authority to purchase, in the event of the death of either Benjamin or Isadore, so much of the stock of Galler Drug Company held by the estate as is necessary to provide sufficient funds to pay the federal estate tax, the Illinois inheritance tax and other administrative expenses of the estate. If as a result of such purchase from the estate of the decedent the amount of dividends to be received by the heirs is reduced, the parties shall nevertheless vote for directors so as to give the estate and heirs the same representation as before (2 directors out of 4, even though they own less stock), and also that the corporation pay an additional benefit payment equal to the diminution of the dividends. In the event either Benjamin or Isadore decides to sell his shares he is required to offer them first to the remaining shareholders and then to the corporation at book value, according each six months to accept the offer.

The Appellate Court found the 1955 agreement void because "the undue duration, stated purpose and substantial disregard of the provisions of the Corporation Act outweigh any considerations which might call for divisibility" and held that "the public policy of this state demands voiding this entire agreement".

While the conduct of defendants towards plaintiff was clearly inequitable, the basically controlling factor is the absence of an objecting minority interest, together with the absence of public detriment. * * * [Discussion of Illinois cases omitted.]

The power to invalidate the agreements on the grounds of public policy is so far reaching and so easily abused that it should be called into action to set aside or annul the solemn engagement of parties dealing on equal terms only in cases where the corrupt or dangerous tendency clearly and unequivocally appears upon the face of the agreement itself or is the necessary inference from the matters which are expressed, and the only apparent exception to this general rule is to be found in those cases where the agreement, though fair and unobjectionable on its face, is a part of a corrupt scheme and is made to disguise the real nature of the transaction. * * *

At this juncture it should be emphasized that we deal here with a so-called close corporation. Various attempts at definition of the close corporation have been made. For a collection of those most frequently proffered, see O'Neal, Close Corporations, § 1.02 (1958). * * * Moreover, it should be recognized that shareholder agreements similar to that in question here are often, as a practical consideration, quite necessary for the protection of those financially interested in the close corporation. While the shareholder of a public-issue corporation may readily sell his shares on the open market should management fail to use, in his opinion, sound business judgment, his counterpart of the close corporation often has a large total of his entire capital invested in the business and has no ready market for his shares should he desire to sell. He feels, understandably, that he is more than a mere investor and that his voice should be heard concerning all corporate activity. Without a shareholder agreement, specifically enforceable by the courts, insuring him a modicum of control, a large minority shareholder might find himself at the mercy of an oppressive or unknowledgeable majority. Moreover, as in the case at bar, the shareholders of a close corporation are often also the directors and officers thereof. With substantial shareholding interests abiding in each member of the board of directors, it is often quite impossible to secure, as in the large public-issue corporation, independent board judgment free from personal motivations concerning corporate policy. For these and other reasons too voluminous to enumerate here, often the only sound basis for protection is afforded by a lengthy, detailed shareholder agreement securing the rights and obligations of all concerned. For a discussion of these and other considerations, see Note, "A Plea for Separate Statutory Treatment of the Close Corporation", 33 N.Y.U.L.Rev. 700 (1958).

* * * [T]here has been a definite, albeit inarticulate, trend toward eventual judicial treatment of the close corporation as *sui generis*. Several shareholder-director agreements that have technically "violated" the letter of the Business Corporation Act have nevertheless been upheld in the light of the existing practical circumstances, i.e., no apparent public injury, the absence of a complaining minority interest, and no apparent prejudice to creditors. However, we have thus far not attempted to limit these decisions as applicable only to close corporations and have seemingly implied that general considerations regarding judicial supervision of all corporate behavior apply.

The practical result of this series of cases, while liberally giving legal efficacy to particular agreements in special circumstances notwithstanding literal "violations" of statutory corporate law, has been to inject much doubt and uncertainty into the thinking of the bench and corporate bar of Illinois concerning shareholder agreements. See e.g., Cary, "How Illinois Corporations May Enjoy Partnership Advantages: Planning for the Closely Held Firm," 48 N.W.U.L.Rev. 427; Note, "The Validity of Stockholders' Voting Agreements in Illinois," 3 U.Chi.L.Rev. 640.

It is therefore necessary, we feel, to discuss the instant case with the problems peculiar to the close corporation particularly in mind.

It would admittedly facilitate judicial supervision of corporate behavior if a strict adherence to the provisions of the Business Corporation Act were required in all cases without regard to the practical exigencies peculiar to the close corporation. West v. Camden, 135 U.S. 507, 10 S.Ct. 838, 34 L.Ed. 254. However, courts have long ago quite realistically, we feel, relaxed their attitudes concerning statutory compliance when dealing with close corporate behavior, permitting "slight deviations" from corporate "norms" in order to give legal efficacy to common business practice. See e.g., Clark v. Dodge, 269 N.Y. 410, 199 N.E. 641; Benintendi v. Kenton Hotel, 294 N.Y. 112, 60 N.E.2d 829, 159 A.L.R. 280 (dissenting opinion subsequently legislatively approved). This attitude is illustrated by the following language in Clark v. Dodge: "Public policy, the intention of the Legislature, detriment to the corporation, are phrases which in this connection [the court was discussing a shareholder-director agreement whereby the directors pledged themselves to vote for certain people as officers of the corporation] mean little. Possible harm to bona fide purchasers of stock or to creditors or to stockholding minorities have more substance; but such harms are absent in many instances. If the enforcement of a particular contract damages nobody—not even, in any perceptible degree, the public—one sees no reason for holding it illegal, even though it impinges slightly upon the broad provisions of [the relevant statute providing that the business of a corporation shall be managed by its board of directors]. Damage suffered or threatened is a logical and practical test, and has come to be the one generally adopted by the courts. See 28 Columbia Law Review 366, 372." Clark v. Dodge, 199 N.E. 641, 642.

Again, "As the parties to the action are the complete owners of the corporation, there is no reason why the exercise of the power and discretion of the directors cannot be controlled by valid agreement between themselves, provided that the interests of creditors are not affected." Clark v. Dodge, 199 N.E. 641, 643, quoting from Kassel v. Empire Tinware Co., 178 App.Div. 176, 180, 164 N.Y.S. 1033, 1035. * * *

Perhaps, as has been vociferously advanced, a separate comprehensive statutory scheme governing the close corporation would best serve here. See Note "A Plea for Separate Statutory Treatment of the Close Corporation", 33 N.Y.U.L.Rev. 700. Some states have enacted legislation dealing specifically with the close corporation.

At any rate, however, the courts can no longer fail to expressly distinguish between the close and public-issue corporation when confronted with problems relating to either. What we do here is to illuminate this problem—before the bench, corporate bar, and the legislature, in the context of a particular fact situation. To do less would be to shirk our responsibility, to do more would, perhaps be to invade the province of the legislative branch.

We now, in the light of the foregoing, turn to specific provisions of the 1955 agreement.

The Appellate Court correctly found many of the contractual provisions free from serious objection, and we need not prolong this opinion with a discussion of them here. That court did, however, find difficulties in the stated purpose of the agreement as it relates to its duration, the election of certain persons to specific offices for a number of years, the requirement for the mandatory declaration of stated dividends (which the Appellate Court held invalid), and the salary continuation agreement.

Since the question as to the duration of the agreement is a principal source of controversy, we shall consider it first. The parties provided no specific termination date, and while the agreement concludes with a paragraph that its terms "shall be binding upon and shall inure to the benefits of" the legal representatives, heirs and assigns of the parties, this clause is, we believe, intended to be operative only as long as one of the parties is living. It further provides that it shall be so construed as to carry out its purposes, and we believe these must be determined from a consideration of the agreement as a whole. Thus viewed, a fair construction is that its purposes were accomplished at the death of the survivor of the parties. While these life spans are not precisely ascertainable, and the Appellate Court noted Emma Galler's life expectancy at her husband's death was 26.9 years, we are aware of no statutory or public policy provision against stockholder's agreements which would invalidate this agreement on that ground. * * *

The clause that provides for the election of certain persons to specified offices for a period of years likewise does not require invalidation. In Kantzler v. Benzinger, 214 Ill. 589, 73 N.E. 874, this court upheld an agreement entered into by all the stockholders providing that certain parties would be elected to the offices of the corporation for a fixed period. In Faulds v. Yates, 57 Ill. 416, we upheld a similar agreement among the majority stockholders of a corporation, notwithstanding the existence of a minority which was not before the court complaining thereof.

We turn next to a consideration of the effect of the stated purpose of the agreement upon its validity. The pertinent provision is: "The said Benjamin A. Galler and Isadore A. Galler desire to provide income for the support and maintenance of their immediate families." Obviously, there is no evil inherent in a contract entered into for the reason that the persons originating the terms desired to so arrange their property as to provide post-death support for those dependent upon them. Nor does the fact that the subject property is corporate stock alter the situation so long as there exists no detriment to minority stock interests, creditors or other public injury. It is, however, contended by defendants that the methods provided by the agreement for implementation of the stated purpose are, as a whole, violative of the Business Corporation Act to such an extent as to render it void *in toto*.

The terms of the dividend agreement require a minimum annual dividend of $50,000, but this duty is limited by the subsequent provision that it shall be operative only so long as an earned surplus of $500,000 is maintained. It may be noted that in 1958, the year prior to commencement of this litigation, the corporation's net earnings after taxes amounted to $202,759 while its earned surplus was $1,543,270, and this was increased in 1958 to $1,680,079 while earnings were $172,964. The minimum earned surplus requirement is designed for the protection of the corporation and its creditors, and we take no exception to the contractual dividend requirements as thus restricted.

The salary continuation agreement is a common feature, in one form or another, of corporate executive employment. It requires that the widow should receive a total benefit, payable monthly over a five-year period, aggregating twice the amount paid her deceased husband in one year. This requirement was likewise limited for the protection of the corporation by being contingent upon the payments being income tax-deductible by the corporation. The charge made in those cases which have considered the validity of payments to the widow of an officer and shareholder in a corporation is that a gift of its property by a noncharitable corporation is in violation of the rights of its shareholders and *ultra vires*. Since there are no shareholders here other than the parties to the contract, this objection is not here applicable, and its effect, as limited, upon the corporation is not so prejudicial as to require its invalidation.

Having concluded that the agreement, under the circumstances here present, is not vulnerable to the attack made on it, we must consider the accounting feature of this action. The trial court allowed the relief prayed, an action we deem proper except as to the master's fees which were modified by the Appellate Court. Since no question is here raised regarding them, we affirm the action of that court in this respect. The questions as to salary which the Appellate Court correctly held were improperly increased became ones of fact to be determined by the trial court.

We hold defendants must account for all monies received by them from the corporation since September 25, 1956, in excess of that theretofore authorized.

Accordingly, the judgment of the Appellate Court is reversed except insofar as it relates to fees, and is, as to them affirmed. The cause is remanded to the circuit court of Cook County with directions to proceed in accordance herewith.

Affirmed in part and reversed in part, and remanded with directions.

Notes

(1) Like *Donahue* (see page 397, supra), this decision and opinion has had a significant impact on the development of close corporation law. Its call for special legislative treatment of closely held corporations has led to statutory developments in most states. These statutes permit closely held corporations to depart dramatically from the traditional statutory scheme of shareholders/directors/officers in specified circumstances. As a result, it is possible—by appropriate planning—to create corporations that vary widely from the traditional statutory scheme envisioned in *McQuade*. It is important, however, to follow whatever statutory scheme has been adopted in the specific state, since a deviation may risk invalidation of the entire arrangement. Many states have adopted more than one of the following alternative approaches.

(2) *Modification of the Statutory Scheme by Provisions in the Articles of Incorporation.* The statutes of about 30 states permit the authority normally placed in the board of directors to be vested in other persons or organizations by an appropriate provision in the articles of incorporation (or in some instances for some types of provisions, in the bylaws). Many of these statutes also provide that if managerial authority is vested in persons or organizations other than the board of directors, those persons or organizations then have the duties, responsibilities, and liabilities of directors. Two states expressly permit shareholders to do anything that the board of directors may do so long as they act with the consent of all the shareholders.

(3) *Integrated Close Corporation Statutes.* About 17 states have followed the suggestion made by Justice Underwood in *Galler* and enacted special close corporation statutes. While these statutes vary from state to state, they share one common characteristic: they are all integrated "opt in" statutes that may be elected by a corporation that meets the statutory definition of a close corporation.

(a) The definition usually involves a numerical limit on the number of shareholders (Delaware's maximum is 30); this type of definition obviously creates problems when a corporation grows so that the number of shareholders exceed the limit, though that apparently rarely occurs as a practical matter. Some state statutes provide that the election may continue even if the number of shareholders exceed the numerical limit, apparently on the theory that a corporation with a large number of shareholders will find the close corporation election to be unwieldy. The election to take advantage of the integrated close corporation statute is usually evidenced by a provision in the corporation's articles of incorporation which simply states that "[t]his Corporation is a statutory close corporation."

(b) Delaware Gen.Corp.Law §§ 341–356, enacted in 1967, is a fairly typical Close Corporation statute, though a number of states have subsequently added novel features. With respect to the role of the board of directors, Del.Gen.Corp.Law § 350 broadly validates agreements that restrict discretion of directors which might be invalid under *McQuade*; § 351 authorizes a corporation to dispense entirely with a board of directors and provide for direct management by shareholders; § 354 validates written agreements among shareholders that "treat the corporation as if it were a partnership or to arrange relations among the stockholders or between the stockholders and the corporation in a manner that would be appropriate only among partners." Section 352 provides for the judicial appointment of a "custodian" if the corporation is threatened with irreparable injury or deadlock while § 353 provides for the judicial appointment of a provisional director "if the directors are so divided respecting the management of the corporation's business cannot be obtained with the consequence that the business and affairs of the corporation can no longer be conducted to the advantage of the stockholders generally"; these two provisions, it should be noted, are not "opt in" provisions but rather are automatically applicable to all electing close corporations. Section 355 authorizes close corporations to adopt a provision that mandates dissolution at the request of "any stockholder, or * * * the holders of any specified number or percentage of shares of any class of stock, an option to have the corporation the corporation dissolved at will or upon the occurrence of any specified event or contingency."

(c) Some close corporation statutes permit a corporation to dispense with bylaws, annual meetings, and other formal requirements imposed on corporations generally. Some statutes add for good measure that the exercise of any of the powers granted to statutory close corporations "is not a ground for imposing personal liability on the shareholders for liabilities of the corporation," or provisions to the same effect.

(d) Most of the legal commentary discussing the growth of these integrated close corporation statutes has been either purely reportorial or uncritically enthusiastic. For a critical examination (and perhaps an unnecessarily negative analysis) see Dennis S. Karjala, A Second Look at Special Close Corporation Legislation, 58 Tex.L.Rev. 1207 (1980); Dennis S. Karjala, An Analysis of Close Corporation Legislation in the United States, 21 Ariz.St.L.J. 663 (1989). Several observations may be made about these statutes:

(i) They are based on little or no empirical examination of the need for such legislation. Provisions appear to be based on intuitive views as to what a close corporation probably needs; of course, as close corporation statutes have proliferated, the major source for provisions becomes statutes already enacted in other states.

(ii) The statutes, where available, do not appear to be widely used. A study of a sample of 1,033 Texas filings showed that close corporation statutes were elected in only 37 instances (3.71%). Richard A. Blunk, Analyzing Texas Articles of Incorporation: Is the Statutory Close Corporation Format Viable? 34 Sw.L.J. 941 (1980). Since this study, however, the Texas statute was considerably simplified and it is possible that its use has increased somewhat since then. In Maryland, over 50 percent of the corporations are statutory close corporations but that is apparently a result of a provision that in electing corporations, workers' compensation insurance does not have to be provided for officers and directors who are also employees. To the extent this data is reliable and indicative of practices in other states, two conclusions might be drawn: (a) close corporation statutes may not be really needed, or (b) attorneys are very cautious about trying new and untested devices. There also may be uncertainty about whether potential liability for breach of fiduciary duties might be increased by election of this new device.

(4) *Authorization of Shareholder Agreements.* MBCA § 7.32, which was added to the Model Act in 1992, was designed to be the ultimate solution to the close corporation management problem. The Official Comment states that it "rejects the older line of cases [epitomized by Long Park, Inc. v. Trenton–New Brunswick Theatres Co. and] adds an important element of predictability currently absent

from the Model Act and affords participants in closely-held corporations greater contractual freedom to tailor the rules of their enterprise." See particularly §§ 7.32(a)(1), 7.32(b). When § 7.32 was approved, the Committee on Corporate Laws also withdrew a "Model Close Corporation Supplement" that was based on the Delaware model with refinements; this model close corporation supplement generally had not been enacted in states that used the MBCA as the basis for revisions of their corporation statutes. The decision to withdraw this integrated close corporation statute was also partially based on the belief of members of the Committee, that relatively few corporations actually elected close corporation status in states where that election was available.

(5) *Galler* arose because an accountant preparing an estate plan for a client whose principal assets were shares in a closely held corporation was apparently unaware of corporate legal norms. An estate planner who has some degree of sophistication about corporation law can usually develop and effectuate an estate plan for a client within the confines of traditional corporate principles and, if not, through the use of the flexibility provided by the various statutes discussed in these notes. In the Matter of the Estate of Hirshon, 13 N.Y.2d 787, 242 N.Y.S.2d 218, 192 N.E.2d 174 (1963), the testator, who owned 68 percent of the stock of a closely held corporation, created a testamentary trust and directed the trustees to vote for themselves as directors of the corporation. His will contained detailed rules for the subsequent governance of the corporation. For example, it directed that one Arthur V. Graseck "be elected and retained in office as president of the corporation to be in charge of the general management thereof," and that the testator's widow (and, upon her death, his daughter) be named as chairman of the board of directors with a minimum compensation of $12,000 per annum plus a bonus. The Court invalidated these detailed rules under the *McQuade* principle.

ZION v. KURTZ

Court of Appeals of New York, 1980.
50 N.Y.2d 92, 428 N.Y.S.2d 199, 405 N.E.2d 681.

MEYER, JUDGE.

On these appeals we conclude that when all of the stockholders of a Delaware corporation agree that, except as specified in their agreement, no "business or activities" of the corporation shall be conducted without the consent of a minority stockholder, the agreement is, as between the original parties to it, enforceable even though all formal steps required by the statute have not been taken. We hold further that the agreement made by the parties to this action was violated when the corporation entered into two agreements without the minority stockholder's consent. * * *

[Editor: Harold Kurtz formed a Delaware corporation, Lombard–Wall Group, Inc. ("Group"). Group acquired all the stock of Lombard–Wall Incorporated ("LBW"), in a complex transaction in which Abraham Zion made available assets that were used as security for a loan to finance the acquisition. As part of the transaction, Zion acquired all the Class A stock of Group while Kurtz continued to own all of the Class B stock. Zion and Kurtz also executed a shareholders' agreement, which provided in § 3.01(a) that without the consent of the holders of the Class A stock, Group would not "engage in any business or activities of any kind, directly or indirectly, whether through any Subsidiary or by way of a loan, guarantee or otherwise, other than the acquisition and ownership of the stock of LBW as contemplated by this

Agreement * * *." The articles of incorporation of Group did not refer to this veto power. Group's board of directors approved two agreements over the objection of Zion. Zion brought suit to cancel the two agreements as violating the shareholders' consent agreement.]

The stockholders' agreement expressly provided that it should be "governed by and construed and enforced in accordance with the laws of the State of Delaware as to matters governed by the General Corporation Law of that State," and that is the generally accepted choice-of-law rule with respect to such "internal affairs" as the relationship between shareholders and directors (cf. Greenspun v. Lindley, 36 N.Y.2d 473, 478, 369 N.Y.S.2d 123, 330 N.E.2d 79; see Restatement, Conflict of Laws 2d, § 302, Comment g). Subdivision (a) of section 141 of the General Corporation Law of Delaware provides that the business and affairs of a corporation organized under that law "shall be managed by a board of directors, except as may be otherwise provided in this chapter or in its certificate of incorporation." Included in the chapter referred to are provisions relating to close corporations, which explicitly state that a written agreement between the holders of a majority of such a corporation's stock "is not invalid, as between the parties to the agreement, on the ground that it so relates to the conduct of the business and affairs of the corporation as to restrict or interfere with the discretion or powers of the board of directors" (§ 350) * * *.

Clear from those provisions is the fact that the public policy of Delaware does not proscribe a provision such as that contained in the shareholders' agreement here in issue even though it takes all management functions away from the directors. Folk, in his work on the Delaware Corporation Law, states concerning section 350 that "Although some decisions outside Delaware have sustained 'reasonable' restrictions upon director discretion contained in stockholder agreements, the theory of § 350 is to declare unequivocally, as a matter of public policy, that stockholder agreements of this character are not invalid," that section 351 "recognizes a special subclass of close corporations which operate by direct stockholder management," and with respect to section 354 that it "should be liberally construed to authorize all sorts of internal agreements and arrangements which are not affirmatively improper or, more particularly, injurious to third parties."

Defendants argue, however, that Group was not incorporated as a close corporation and the stockholders' agreement provision was never incorporated in its certificate. The answer is that any Delaware corporation can elect to become a close corporation by filing an appropriate certificate of amendment (Del.General Corporation Law, § 344) and by such amendment approved by the holders of all of its outstanding stock may include in its certificate provisions restricting directors' authority (ibid., § 351). Here, not only did defendant Kurtz agree in paragraph 8.05(b) of the stockholders' agreement to "without further consideration, do, execute and deliver, or cause to be done, executed and delivered, all such further acts, things and instruments as may be reasonably required more effectively to evidence and give effect to the provisions and the intent and purposes of this Agreement," but also as part of the transaction by which the * * * guarantee was made and Zion became a Group stockholder, defendant Kurtz, while he was still the sole stockholder and sole director of Group, executed a consent to the various parts of the transaction under which he was "authorized and empowered to execute and deliver, or cause to be executed and delivered, all such other and further instruments and documents and take, or cause to be taken, all such other and further action as he may deem necessary, appropriate or desirable to implement and give effect to the Stockholders Agreement and the transactions provided for therein." Since there are no intervening rights of third persons, the agreement requires nothing that is not permitted by statute, and all of the stockholders of the corporation assented to it, the certificate of incorporation may be ordered reformed, by requiring Kurtz to file the appropriate amendments, or more directly he may be held estopped to rely upon the absence of those amendments from the corporate charter (see Delaney, The Corporate Director: Can His Hands Be Tied In Advance, 50 Col.L.Rev. 52, 66).[2]

The result thus reached accords with the weight of authority which textwriter F. Hodge O'Neal tells us sustains agreements made by all shareholders dealing with matters normally within the province of the directors (1 Close Corporations § 5.24, p. 83), even though the shareholders could have, but had not, provided similarly by charter or by-law provision sanctioned by statute (ibid., § 5.19, pp. 73–74). Moreover, though we have not yet had occasion to construe subdivision (b) of section 620 of the Business Corporation Law,[3] which did not become effective until September 1, 1963, it is worthy of note that in adopting that provision the Legislature had before it the Revisers' Comment that: "Paragraph (b) expands the ruling in Clark v. Dodge, 269 N.Y. 410, 199 N.E. 637 [641] (1936), and, to the extent therein provided, overrules Long Park, Inc. v. Trenton–New Brunswick Theatres Co., 297 N.Y. 174, 77 N.E.2d 633 (1948); Manson v. Curtis, 223 N.Y. 313, 119 N.E. 559 (1919) and McQuade v. Stoneham, 263 N.Y. 323, 189 N.E. 234 (1934)." Thus it is clear that no New York public policy stands in the way of our application of the Delaware statute and decisional law above referred to * * *.

For the foregoing reasons the order of the Appellate Division should be modified, as above indicated.

GABRIELLI, JUDGE (dissenting in part).

* * * I conclude that the agreement requiring plaintiff's consent was invalid under well-established public policies. * * * [It was] an illegal attempt by shareholders to deprive the board of directors of its inherent authority to exercise its discretion in managing the affairs of the corporation. * * * I would, [therefore,] reverse the determination of the Appellate Division with

---

2. [By the Court] The fallacy of the dissent is that it converts a shield into a sword. The notice devices on which the concept of the dissent turns are wholly unnecessary to protect the original parties, who may be presumed to have known what they agreed to. To protect an original party who has not been hurt (indeed, has expressly agreed to the limitation he is being protected against and affirmatively covenanted to see to it that all necessary steps to validate the agreement were taken) because a third party without notice could have been hurt had he been involved can only be characterized as a perversion of the liberal legislative purpose demonstrated by the Delaware statutes quoted in the text above.

3. [By the Court] That provision reads: "(b) A provision in the certificate of incorporation otherwise prohibited by law because it improperly restricts the board in its management of the business of the corporation, or improperly transfers to one or more shareholders or to one or more persons or corporations to be selected by him or them, all or any part of such management otherwise within the authority of the board under this chapter, shall nevertheless be valid: (1) If all the incorporators or holders of record of all outstanding shares, whether or not having voting power, have authorized such provision in the certificate of incorporation or an amendment thereof; and (2) If, subsequent to the adoption of such provision, shares are transferred or issued only to persons who had knowledge or notice thereof or consented in writing to such provision."

respect to plaintiff's * * * cause of action and hold that plaintiff cannot maintain a suit based upon defendants' failure to obtain his consent prior to executing the disputed * * * agreements.

It is beyond dispute that shareholder agreements such as the one relied upon by plaintiff in this case are, as a general rule, void as against public policy. Section 3.01 of the agreement, as interpreted both by plaintiff and by a majority of this court, would have precluded the board of directors of Group from taking any action on behalf of the corporation without first obtaining plaintiff's consent. This contractual provision, if enforced, would effectively shift the authority to manage every aspect of corporate affairs from the board to plaintiff, a minority shareholder who has no fiduciary obligations with respect to either the corporation or its other shareholders. * * *

Under the statutes of Delaware, the State in which Group was incorporated, the authority to manage the affairs of a corporation is vested solely in its board of directors (Del.General Corporation Law, § 141, subd. [a]). The same is true under the applicable New York statutes (Business Corporation Law, § 701). Significantly, in both States, the courts have declined to give effect to agreements which purport to vary the statutory rule by transferring effective control of the corporation to a third party other than the board of directors (see Abercrombie v. Davies, 35 Del.Ch. 599, 604–611, 123 A.2d 893, rev'd on other grounds 36 Del.Ch. 371, 130 A.2d 338 * * *). The common-law rule in Delaware was aptly stated in Abercrombie v. Davies, 35 Del.Ch. at p. 611, 123 A.2d at p. 899, supra: "So long as the corporate form is used as presently provided by our statutes this Court cannot give legal sanction to agreements which have the effect of removing from directors in a very substantial way their duty to use their own best judgment on management matters."

True, the common-law rule has been modified somewhat in recent years to account for the business needs of the so-called "close corporation." The courts of our State, for example, have been willing to enforce shareholder agreements where the incursion on the board's authority was insubstantial (Clark v. Dodge, 269 N.Y. 410, 199 N.E. 641) or where the illegal provisions were severable from the otherwise legal provisions which the shareholder sought to enforce (Triggs v. Triggs, 46 N.Y.2d 305, 413 N.Y.S.2d 325, 385 N.E.2d 1254). Neither the courts of our State nor the courts of Delaware, however, have gone so far as to hold that an agreement among shareholders such as the agreement in this case, which purported to "sterilize" the board of directors by completely depriving it of its discretionary authority, can be regarded as legal and enforceable. To the contrary, the common-law rule applicable to both closely and publicly held corporations continues to treat agreements to deprive the board of directors of substantial authority as contrary to public policy.

Indeed, there heretofore has been little need for the courts to modify the general common-law rule against "sterilizing" boards of directors to accommodate the needs of closely held corporations. This is because the Legislatures of many States, including New York and Delaware, have enacted laws which enable the shareholders of closely held corporations to restrict the powers of the board of directors if they comply with certain statutory prerequisites (Del.General Corporation Law, §§ 350, 351; Business Corporation Law, § 620, subd. [b]). The majority apparently construes these statutes as indications that the public policies of the enacting States no longer proscribe the type of agreement at issue here in cases involving closely held corporations. Hence, the majority concludes that there is no bar to the enforcement of the shareholder agreement in this case, even though the statutory requirements for close corporations were not fulfilled. I cannot agree.

Under Delaware law, as the majority notes, the shareholders of a close corporation are free to enter into private, binding agreements among themselves to restrict the powers of their board of directors (Del.General Corporation Law, § 350). The same appears to be true under the present New York statutes (Business Corporation Law, § 620, subd. [b]). Both the Delaware and the New York statutory schemes, however, contemplate that such variations from the corporate norm will be recorded on the face of the certificate of incorporation (Del.General Corporation Law, § 351; Business Corporation Law, § 620, subd. [b]). New York additionally requires that the existence of a substantial restriction on the powers of the board "shall be noted conspicuously on the face or back of every certificate for shares issued by [the] corporation" (Business Corporation Law, § 620, subd. [g]). Significantly, in both Delaware and New York, a provision in the certificate of incorporation restricting the discretion of the board has the effect of shifting liability for any mismanagement from the directors to the managing shareholders (Del.General Corporation Law, § 351, subds. [2]–[3]; Business Corporation Law, § 620, subd. [f]).

In my view, these statutory provisions are not merely directory, but rather are evidence of a clear legislative intention to permit deviations from the statutory norms for corporations only under controlled conditions. In enacting these statutes, which are tailored for "close corporations," the Legislatures of Delaware and New York were apparently attempting to accommodate the needs of those who wished to take advantage of the limited liability inherent in the corporate format, but who also wished to retain the internal management structure of a partnership (see, generally, 1 O'Neal, Close Corporations, § 5.02). At the same time, however, the Legislatures were obviously mindful of the danger to the public that exists whenever shareholders privately agree among themselves to shift control of corporate management from independent directors to the shareholders, who are not necessarily bound by the fiduciary obligations imposed upon the board. In order to protect potential purchasers of shares and perhaps even potential creditors of the corporation, the Legislatures of Delaware and New York imposed specific strictures upon incorporated businesses managed by shareholders, the most significant of which is the requirement that restrictions on the statutory powers of the board of directors be evidenced in the certificate of incorporation. This requirement is an essential component of the statutory scheme because it ensures that potential purchasers of an interest in the corporation will have at least record notice that the corporation is being managed in an unorthodox fashion. Absent an appropriate notice provision in the certificate, there can be no assurance that an unsuspecting purchaser, not privy to the private shareholder agreement, will not be drawn into an investment that he might otherwise choose to avoid.

Since I regard the statutory requirements discussed above as essentially prophylactic in nature, I cannot subscribe to the notion that the agreement in this case should be enforced merely because there has been no showing that the interests of innocent third parties have actually been impaired. As is apparent from the design of the relevant statutes, the public policies of our own State as well as those of the State of Delaware remain opposed to shareholder agreements to "sterilize" the board of directors unless notice of the agreement is provided in the certificate of incorporation. Where such notice is provided, the public policy objections to the agreement are effectively eliminated and there is no further reason to preclude enforcement (see Lehrman v. Cohen, 43 Del.Ch. 222, 235, 222 A.2d 800). On the other hand, where, as here, the shareholders have entered into a private agreement to "sterilize" the board of directors and have failed to comply with the simple statutory prerequisites for "close corporations," the agreement must be deemed void and unenforceable in light of the inherent potential for fraud against the public. Indeed, since it is this very potential for public harm which renders these agreements unlawful, the mere fortuity that no one was actually harmed, if that be the case, cannot be the controlling factor in determining whether the agreement is legally enforceable. For the same reason, the illegality in the instant agreement cannot be cured retroactively, as the majority suggests, by requiring defendants to file the appropriate amendments to the certificate of incorporation. And, of course, it is elementary that a party to an agreement cannot be estopped from asserting its invalidity when the agreement is prohibited by law or is contrary to public policy (e.g., Brick v. Campbell, 122 N.Y. 337, 25 N.E. 493).

By its holding today, the majority has, in effect, rendered inoperative both the language and the underlying purpose of the relevant Delaware and New York statutes governing "close corporations." According to the majority's reasoning, the only requirements for upholding an otherwise unlawful shareholder agreement which concededly deprives the directors of all discretionary authority are that all of the shareholders concur in the agreement and that no "intervening rights of third persons" exist at the time enforcement of the agreement is sought. The statutes in question also recognize these factors as conditions precedent to the enforcement of shareholder agreements to "sterilize" a corporate board of directors. But the laws of both jurisdictions go further, requiring in each case that the "close corporation" give notice of its unorthodox management structure through its filed certificate of incorporation. The obvious purpose of such a requirement is to prevent harm to the public before it occurs. If, as the majority's holding suggests, this requirement of notice to the public through the certificate of incorporation is without legal effect unless and until a third party's interests have actually been impaired, then the prophylactic purposes of the statutes governing "close corporations" would effectively be defeated. It is this aspect of the majority's ruling that I find most difficult to accept.

For all of the foregoing reasons, I must respectfully dissent and cast my vote to modify the order of the Appellate Division by directing dismissal of plaintiff's first cause of action.

JASEN, JONES and FUCHSBERG, JJ., concur with MEYER, J,

GABRIELLI, J, dissents in part and votes to modify in a separate opinion in which COOKE, C.J., and WACHTLER, J., concur.

Notes

(1) Why should a court reach out like this and apply a Delaware statute when it is clear on the face of the statute that it is not applicable? Obviously, the majority was swayed by its belief that the application of close corporation statutes and the enforcement of shareholder agreements was desirable from a policy standpoint. If the result in *Zion* is accepted, what is left of the *McQuade* principle in states with close corporation statutes? Dubin v. Muchnick, 108 Misc.2d 1042, 438 N.Y.S.2d 920, 922 (1981) states that *Zion* has "apparently swept all of the earlier authorities into the realm of legal history."

(2) In Nixon v. Blackwell, 626 A.2d 1366 (Del.1993), the Delaware Supreme Court refused to apply the Delaware close corporation statute to a nonelecting close corporation, stating that the statute "is a narrowly constructed statute which applies only to a corporation which is designated as a 'close corporation' in its certificate of incorporation, and which fulfills other requirements [set forth by the statute]." Further, it is improper to apply special provisions to a nonelecting Delaware close corporation "because the provisions of [the Delaware statute] relating to close corporations and other statutory schemes preempt the field in their respective areas." 626 A.2d at 1380. Is it not clear from these statements that the Delaware courts would reject entirely the rationale of *Zion*? Since that case is at least nominally an application of Delaware law, what is left of the holding of the principal case?

MATTER OF AUER v. DRESSEL

Court of Appeals of New York, 1954.
306 N.Y. 427, 118 N.E.2d 590.

DESMOND, JUDGE.

This article 78 of the Civil Practice Act proceeding was brought by class A stockholders of appellant R. Hoe & Co., Inc., for an order in the nature of mandamus to compel the president of Hoe to comply with a positive duty imposed on him by the corporation's by-laws. Section 2 of article I of those by-laws says that "It shall be the duty of the President to call a special meeting whenever requested in writing so to do, by stockholders owning a majority of the capital stock entitled to vote at such meeting." On October 16, 1953, petitioners submitted to the president written requests for a special meeting of class A stockholders, which writings were signed in the names of the holders of record of slightly more than 55% of the class A stock. The president failed to call the meeting and, after waiting a week, the petitioners brought the present proceeding. The answer of the corporation and its president was not forthcoming until October 28, 1953, and it contained, in response to the petition's allegation that the demand was by more than a majority of class A stockholders, only a denial that the corporation and the president had any knowledge or information sufficient to form a belief as to the stockholding of those who had signed the requests. Since the president, when he filed that answer, had had before him for at least ten days the signed requests themselves, his denial that he had any information sufficient for a belief as to the adequacy of the number of signatures was obviously perfunctory and raised no issue whatever. There was no discretion in this corporate officer as to whether or not to call a meeting when a demand therefor was put before him by owners of the required number of shares. The important right of stockholders to have such meetings called will be of little practical value if corporate management can ignore the requests, force the stockholders to commence legal proceedings, and then, by purely formal denials, put the stockholders to lengthy and expensive litigation, to establish facts as to stockholdings which are peculiarly within the knowledge of the corporate officers. In such a situation, Special Term did the correct thing in disposing of the matter summarily, as commanded by section 1295 of the Civil Practice Act.

The petition was opposed on the further alleged ground that none of the four purposes for which petitioners wished the meeting called was a proper one for such a class A stockholders' meeting. Those four stated purposes were these: (A) to vote, upon a resolution indorsing the administration of petitioner Joseph L. Auer, who had been removed as president by the directors, and demanding that he be reinstated as such president; (B) voting upon a proposal to amend the charter and by-laws to provide that vacancies on the board of directors, arising from the removal of a director by stockholders or by resignation of a director against whom charges have been preferred, may be filled, for the unexpired term, by the stockholders only of the class theretofore represented by the director so removed or so resigned; (C) voting upon a proposal that the stockholders hear certain charges preferred, in the requests, against four of the directors, determine whether the conduct of such directors or any of them was inimical to the corporation and, if so, to vote upon their removal and vote for the election of their successors; and (D) voting upon a proposal to amend the by-laws so as to provide that half of the total number of directors in office and, in any event, not less than one-third of the whole authorized number of directors constitute a quorum of the directors.

The Hoe certificate of incorporation provides for eleven directors, of whom the class A stockholders, more than a majority of whom join in this petition, elect nine and the common stockholders elect two. The obvious purpose of the meeting here sought to be called (aside from the endorsement and reinstatement of former president Auer) is to hear charges against four of the class A directors, to remove them if the charges be proven, to amend the by-laws so that the successor directors be elected by the class A stockholders, and further to amend the by-laws so that an effective quorum of directors will be made up of no fewer than half of the directors in office and no fewer than one third of the whole authorized number of directors. No reason appears why the class A stockholders should not be allowed to vote on any or all of those proposals.

The stockholders, by expressing their approval of Mr. Auer's conduct as president and their demand that he be put back in that office, will not be able, directly, to effect that change in officers, but there is nothing invalid in their so expressing themselves and thus putting on notice the directors who will stand for election at the annual meeting. As to purpose (B), that is, amending the charter and by-laws to authorize the stockholders to fill vacancies as to class A directors who have been removed on charges or who have resigned, it seems to be settled law that the stockholders who are empowered to elect directors have the inherent power to remove them for cause, In re Koch, 257 N.Y. 318, 321, 322, 178 N.E. 545, 546. Of course, as the Koch case points out, there must be the service of specific charges, adequate notice and full opportunity of meeting the accusations, but there is no present showing of any lack of any of those in this instance. Since these particular stockholders have the right to elect nine directors and to remove them on proven charges, it is not inappropriate that they should use their further power to amend the by-laws to elect the successors of such directors as shall be removed after hearing, or who shall resign pending hearing. Quite pertinent at this point is Rogers v. Hill, 289 U.S. 582, 589, 53 S.Ct. 731, 734, 77 L.Ed. 1385, which made light of an argument that stockholders, by giving power to the directors to make by-laws, had lost their own power to make them; quoting a New Jersey case, In re Griffing Iron Co., 63 N.J.L. 168, 41 A. 931, the United States Supreme Court said: " 'It would be preposterous to leave the real owners of the corporate property at the mercy of their agents, and the law has not done so.' " Such a change in the bylaws, dealing with class A directors only, has no effect on the voting rights of the common stockholders, which rights have to do with the selection of the remaining two directors only. True, the certificate of incorporation authorizes the board of directors to remove any director on charges, but we do not consider that provision as an abdication by the stockholders of their own traditional, inherent power to remove their own directors. Rather, it provides an additional method. Were that not so, the stockholders might find themselves without effective remedy in a case where a majority of the directors were accused of wrongdoing and, obviously, would be unwilling to remove themselves from office.

We fail to see, in the proposal to allow class A stockholders to fill vacancies as to class A directors, any impairment or any violation of paragraph (h) of article Third of the certificate of incorporation, which says that class A stock has exclusive voting rights with respect to all matters "other than the election of directors." That negative language should not be taken to mean that class A stockholders, who have an absolute right to elect nine of these eleven directors, cannot amend their by-laws to guarantee a similar right, in the class A stockholders and to the exclusion of common stockholders, to fill vacancies in the class A group of directors.

There is urged upon us the impracticability and unfairness of constituting the numerous stockholders a tribunal to hear charges made by themselves, and the incongruity of letting the stockholders hear and pass on those charges by proxy. Such questions are really not before us at all on this appeal. The charges here are not, on their face, frivolous or inconsequential, and all that we are holding as to the charges is that a meeting may be held to deal with them. Any director illegally removed can have his remedy in the courts.

The order should be affirmed, with costs, and the Special Term directed forthwith to make an order in the same form as the Appellate Division order with appropriate changes of dates.

Van Voorhis, Judge (dissenting).

* * * An examination of the request for a special meeting by these stockholders indicates that none of the proposals could be voted upon legally at the projected meeting. The purposes of the meeting are listed as A, B, C and D. Purpose A is described as "Voting upon a resolution endorsing the administration of Joseph L. Auer, as President of the corporation, and demanding his immediate reinstatement as President." For the stockholders to vote on this proposition would be an idle gesture, since it is provided by

section 27 of the General Corporation Law, Consol.Laws, c. 23, that "The business of a corporation shall be managed by its board of directors." The directors of Hoe have been elected by the stockholders for stated terms which have not expired, and it is their function and not that of the stockholders to appoint the officers of the corporation, Stock Corporation Law, Consol.Laws, c. 59, § 60.

Purpose B of the special meeting is to vote upon a proposal to amend the certificate and the by-laws so as to provide "that vacancies on the Board of Directors arising from the removal of a director by stockholders or by resignation of a director against whom charges have been preferred may be filled, for the unexpired term, only by the stockholders of the class theretofore represented by the director so removed." This proposal is interwoven with the next one (C), which is about to be discussed, which is to remove four directors from office before the expiration of their terms in order to alter the control of the corporation. Proposal B must be read in the context that the certificate of incorporation provides for eleven directors, of whom the class A stockholders elect nine and the common stockholders two. So long as any class A shares are outstanding, the voting rights with respect to all matters "other than the election of directors" are vested exclusively in the holders of class A stock, with one exception now irrelevant. This means that the common stockholders are entitled to participate directly in the election of two directors, who, in turn, are authorized by the certificate to vote to fill vacancies occurring among the directors elected by the class A shareholders. This proposed amendment would deprive the directors elected by the common stockholders of the power to participate in filling the vacancies which petitioners hope to create among the class A directors, four of whom they seek to remove by proposal C which is about to be discussed. Such an alteration would impair the existing right of the common stockholders to participate in filling vacancies upon the board of directors and could not be legally adopted at this meeting demanded by petitioners from which the common stockholders are excluded. * * *

Purpose C of the special meeting is to vote "upon a proposal that the Stockholders (1) hear the charges preferred against Harry K. Barr, William L. Canady, Neil P. Cullom and Edwin L. Munzert, and their answers thereto; (2) determine whether such conduct on their part or on the part of any of them was inimical to the best interest of R. Hoe & Co., Inc., and if so (3) vote upon the removal of said persons or any of them as directors of R. Hoe & Co., Inc., for such conduct, and (4) vote for the election of directors to fill any vacancies on the Board of Directors which the Stockholders may be authorized to fill." By means of this proposal, it is sought to change the control of the corporation and to accomplish what A could not achieve, viz., remove the existing president and reappoint Mr. Joseph L. Auer as president of the corporation. Neither the language nor the policy of the corporation law subjects directors to recall by the stockholders before their terms of office have expired, merely for the reason that the stockholders wish to change the policy of the corporation. In People ex rel. Manice v. Powell, 201 N.Y. 194, 201, 94 N.E. 634, 637, this court said that "It would be somewhat startling to the business world if we definitely announced that the directors of a corporation were mere employés and that the stockholders of the corporation have the power to convene from time to time and remove at will any or all of the directors, although their respective terms of office have not expired." Fraud or breach of fiduciary duty must be shown, Matter of Koch, 257 N.Y. 318, 178 N.E. 545. In that event, directors may be removed from office before expiration of term by an action brought under subdivision 4 of section 60 of the General Corporation Law. In addition to such procedure, paragraph Fourteenth of the certificate of incorporation states: "Any director of the corporation may at any time be removed for cause as such director by resolution adopted by a majority of the whole number of directors then in office, provided that such director, prior to his removal, shall have received a copy of the charges against him and shall have had an opportunity to be heard thereon by the board. The By–Laws may provide the manner of presentation of the charges and of the hearing thereon."

Petitioners have instituted this proceeding on the theory that although no power is conferred upon the stockholders by the certificate or the by-laws to remove directors before the expiration of their terms, with or without cause, power to do so for cause is inherent in them as the body authorized to elect the directors, citing Matter of Koch, 257 N.Y. 318, 178 N.E. 545, supra. Petitioners have argued that the grant of this power to the board of directors to remove some of their number for cause after trial, does not eliminate what is asserted to be the inherent right of the stockholders to do likewise. No cases are cited in support of the latter proposition. * * * Such cases as have been cited in support of a power in the stockholders to remove directors for cause are clear in holding that such action can be taken only subject to the rule that "specific charges must be served, adequate notice must be given, and full opportunity of meeting the accusations must be afforded." Matter of Koch, 257 N.Y. 318, 322, 178 N.E. 545, 546, supra.

Although the demand by these petitioners for a special meeting contains no specification of charges against these four directors, the proxy statement, circulated by their protective committee, does describe certain charges. No point appears to be made of the circumstance that they are not contained in the demand for the meeting. Nevertheless, although this proxy statement enumerates these charges and announces that a resolution will be introduced at the special meeting to hear them, to determine whether sufficient cause exists for the removal of said persons as directors, and, if so, to remove them and to fill the resulting vacancies, the stockholders thus solicited are requested to sign proxies running to persons nominated by petitioners' protective committee. Inasmuch as this committee, with which petitioners are affiliated, has already charged in the most forceful terms that at least one of these directors has been guilty of misconduct and that "his *clique* of directors have removed Joseph L. Auer as President," it is reasonable to assume that the case of the accused directors has already been prejudged by those who will vote the proxies alleged to represent 255,658 shares of class A stock, and that the 1,200 shareholders who are claimed to have signed proxies have (whether they know it or not) voted, in effect, to remove these directors before they have been tried. The consequence is that these directors are to be adjudged guilty of fraud or breach of faith in absentia by shareholders who have neither heard nor ever will hear the evidence against them or in their behalf. Such a procedure does not conform to the requirements of Matter of Koch, supra, nor the other authorities which have been cited, and is far removed from "a law which hears before it condemns, which proceeds upon inquiry, and renders judgment only after trial." Brief by Daniel Webster in Trustees of Dartmouth Coll. v. Woodward, 4 Wheat. [U.S.] 518, 581, 4 L.Ed. 629. The charges against these directors enumerated in the proxy statement are described as having been preferred by one John Kadel and are to the effect that these four accused directors supported a resolution on July 2, 1953, that severance pay of $50,000 be granted to Mr. Auer "upon condition that he resign and that he sign an agreement not to participate, with any stockholders group or otherwise, in any action against any of the directors or officers of the Company." This money was not in fact paid to Auer. The charge based thereon against these directors is that there was a breach of trust in offering to pay $50,000 of the corporation's money in consideration of a covenant by Auer not to participate (as the minutes of the directors' meeting of July 2, 1953, actually read) in "any hostile action against the company, its officers and directors." It is not clear how this constituted actionable misconduct in view of the circumstance that none of this money actually was paid, and that there was no showing in this record any misconduct on the part of these four directors which might have furnished a basis for a stockholders' derivative action by Auer against these directors. It is not so plain that these directors should be subjected to trial by stockholders, acting through proxies who are evidently prepared to oust them with or without cause that a mandamus order should, in any event, be issued to compel the calling of a special meeting for that purpose. The other charges, viz., that Mr. Cullom was paid $300 a month as rental for office space in his suite at 63 Wall Street, and that he engaged one of his personal friends and clients in connection with appraisal proceedings involving the common stock of the company for which the friend was paid $5,000 are not supplemented by further facts indicating that such conduct was hostile to the interest of the corporation.

It is not for the courts to determine which of these warring factions is pursuing the wiser policy for the corporation. If these petitioners consider that the stockholders made a mistake in the election of the present directors, they should not be permitted to correct it by recalling them before the expiration of their terms on charges of fraud or breach of fiduciary duty without a full and fair trial, which, if not conducted in court under section 60 of the General Corporation Law, is required to be held before the remaining directors under paragraph Fourteenth of the certificate of incorporation. The difficulty inherent in conducting such a trial by proxy may well have been the reason on account of which the incorporators delegated that function to the board of directors under paragraph Fourteenth of the certificate of incorporation. If it were to develop (the papers before the court do not contain evidence of such a fact) that enough of the other directors would be disqualified so that it would be impossible to obtain a quorum for the purpose, it may well be doubted that these directors could be tried before so large a number of stockholders sitting in person (if it were possible to assemble them in one place) or that they could sit in judgment by proxy. In ancient Athens evidence is said to have been heard and judgment pronounced in court by as many as 500 jurors known as ducats, but in this instance, if petitioners be correct in their figures, there are 1,200 class A stockholders who have signed requests or proxies, and these are alleged to hold only somewhat more than half of the outstanding shares. Since it would be impossible for so large a number to conduct a trial in person, they could only do so by proxy. Voting by proxy is the accepted procedure to express the will of large numbers of stockholders on questions of corporate policy within their province to determine, and it would be suitable in this instance if the certificate of incorporation had reserved to stockholders the power to recall directors without cause before expiration of term, as in Abberger v. Kulp, 156 Misc. 210, 281 N.Y.S. 373, but it is altogether unsuited to the performance of duties which partake of the nature of the judicial function, involving, as this would need to do if the accused directors are to be removed before the expiration of their terms, a decision after trial that they have been guilty of faithlessness or fraud. Section 60 of the General Corporation Law is always available for that purpose if the occasion requires.

The final proposal to be voted on at this special meeting (D) relates simply to an amendment to the by-laws so as to provide that a quorum shall consist of not less than one half of the number of directors holding office and in no event less than one third of the authorized number of directors. Section 8 of article II of the by-laws already provides that one half of the total number of directors shall constitute a quorum; the modification that a quorum shall in no event be less than one third of the authorized number of directors whom petitioners seek to eliminate.

Inasmuch as we consider that for the foregoing reasons none of the business for which the special meeting is proposed to be called could legally be transacted, this proceeding should be dismissed. * * *

The petition should be dismissed, with costs in all courts.

Lewis, C.J., and Dye, Fuld and Froessel, JJ., concur with Desmond, J.

Van Voorhis, J., dissents in opinion in which Conway, J., concurs.

Notes

(1) Unlike the earlier principal cases in this Section, this case involves a publicly held corporation: at the time of this litigation, R. Hoe & Co., Inc. had 6,000 shareholders and some 460,000 Class A shares outstanding. The principal difference between a publicly held corporation and a closely held corporation from the management standpoint is that in a publicly held corporation, ownership and management are usually vested in quite different persons or groups. In a closely held corporation, the majority shareholder is likely to be the chief executive officer and possess the ability to name or remove directors virtually at will. See MBCA § 8.08. In contrast, most publicly held corporations have professional managers who in the aggregate own an insignificant fraction of the corporation's outstanding shares. Because shareholders are numerous and diffuse, the "owners" of a publicly held corporation are not a cohesive group. Indeed, the simple process of calling a shareholders meeting involves, at the least, communicating with thousands of widely scattered shareholders. Subsequent chapters of this book discuss at length the nature of control and management in the publicly held corporation. The purpose of this note is to call attention to examples of provisions in state corporation statutes that are designed primarily or exclusively for the large publicly held corporation. Many other examples can be cited.

(a) Traditional corporation statutes provide that the business and affairs of a corporation shall be managed "by" the board of directors. MBCA § 8.01(b) and the statutes of many states add "or under the direction of" following the word "by" to reflect the reality that boards of directors of publicly held corporations do not actually manage the business and affairs of a corporation.

(b) MBCA § 8.09 provides that directors may be removed by judicial proceeding in the case of "fraudulent or dishonest conduct, or gross abuse of authority or discretion, with respect to the corporation." If a director accused of serious misconduct stubbornly refuses to resign, removal by judicial proceeding is often simpler and less expensive than calling a shareholders meeting to remove the director. It is possible that this provision may also be utilized by a closely held corporation which has evenly divided voting power at the shareholder level or action is subject to a veto by a minority shareholder.

(c) MBCA §§ 7.23 and 7.24 contain special rules for shareholder voting by proxy that, as a practical matter, are almost exclusively a phenomenon of publicly held corporations.

(2) Consider again the practical difficulties discussed in the dissenting opinion of holding a shareholders' meeting of R. Hoe & Co., Inc. to pass on the removal of the directors for cause. If such a meeting is to be held, how should it be structured to give even minimal "due process" to the directors threatened with removal? Do you think the conduct described in the dissenting opinion constitutes "cause" for removal?

B. SHAREHOLDER VOTING AND AGREEMENTS

SALGO v. MATTHEWS

Court of Civil Appeals of Texas, 1973.
497 S.W.2d 620, writ ref'd n.r.e.

GUITTARD, JUSTICE.

This equitable proceeding involves a proxy contest for control of General Electrodynamics Corporation, a Texas corporation. Stockholders Joe W. Matthews and Paul Thorp, representing the faction opposed to current management, sought the aid of the district court in requiring the president, as chairman of the stockholders' meeting, and the election inspector appointed by him, to accept certain disputed proxies, count the votes of the stockholders cast under these proxies, and declare that the candidates supported by plaintiffs had been elected directors of the corporation. We hold that the court erred in granting injunctive relief, both temporary and final, in absence of any showing that plaintiffs could not have obtained adequate relief by the statutory remedy of quo warranto after the completion of the election. * * *

[The incumbent management faction was headed by Francis Salgo, the president of Electrodynamics. At the meeting, Salgo appointed Julian Meer, a well-known attorney, as election inspector. During the course of examining and tabulating proxy appointments,] plaintiffs presented to defendant Meer four proxy documents purporting to have been executed in plaintiffs' favor on behalf of Pioneer Casualty Company, the registered owner of 29,934 shares of stock. Beneficial title to these shares had been transferred to Don Shepherd, who was in bankruptcy, and two of the proxy documents were signed, "Pioneer Casualty Company By Don Shepherd." Plaintiffs also presented to the inspector an order of the 126th District Court of Travis County, Texas, directing Tom I. McFarling as receiver of Pioneer Casualty Company to give Shepherd a proxy to vote these shares by giving his proxy to plaintiffs

Matthews and Thorp, and plaintiffs also presented a proxy document signed by the receiver in accordance with this order. Defendant Meer refused to accept any of these proxies, and their validity is the principal matter in controversy. Defendant Meer also refused to accept two telegraphic proxies aggregating 5,000 shares from stockholders Candis and Wrobliske when plaintiff Thorp presented them to him on the afternoon of November 9. * * *

* * * [W]e hold that the inspector was not subject to judicial control in the performance of his duties because he had discretionary authority to make a preliminary determination of the validity of the proxies for the purpose of tabulating them, counting the votes, and certifying the result, although the correctness of his decision was subject to review after the election by proceeding in quo warranto. * * *

Our holding that an election inspector has discretionary authority to determine the validity of disputed proxies for the purpose of declaring the result of the election should not be interpreted as meaning that he may go beyond the corporate records in determining the identity of stockholders entitled to vote. Defendants argue that the trial court's findings establish that beneficial ownership of the 29,934 shares registered in the name of Pioneer Casualty Company was not in Pioneer's receiver or in Don Shepherd, to whom these shares had been transferred, but was vested in Shepherd's bankruptcy trustee, and, consequently, that neither the receiver nor Shepherd had the right to vote. We assume that Shepherd's trustee was the beneficial owner, but, as against the corporation and its officers, beneficial ownership does not carry with it the right to vote without having the shares transferred on the books. A bylaw of General Electrodynamics Corporation provides that stock is transferable only on its books. This bylaw indicates the strong interest of the corporation and its stockholders in determining stock ownership quickly by reference to the corporate records. If beneficial title is in dispute, that dispute cannot properly be decided by the election inspector, and neither should the losing faction be able to go into court to invalidate the election on the ground that the ownership of certain shares was not correctly shown by the corporate records. For even greater reason the election should not be interrupted or suspended while complicated questions of title to stock are litigated to final judgment.

The rule that under such a bylaw, eligibility to vote at corporate elections is determined by the corporate records rather than by the ultimate judicial decision of beneficial title of disputed shares is well sustained by authority. In re Giant Portland Cement Co., 26 Del.Ch. 32, 21 A.2d 697 (Ch.1941). This rule is in accordance with Tex.Bus.Corp.Act Ann. art. 2.27(A) (1956), V.A.T.S., which provides, "The original stock transfer books shall be prima-facie evidence as to who are the shareholders entitled * * * to vote at any meeting of shareholders." According to E. Aranow & H. Einhorn, [Proxy Contests for Corporate Control (1957) at 386], although such a statute uses the term "prima-facie," it has the effect of making stock records conclusive on the inspector. The term "prima-facie" avoids any implication that the stock record is conclusive in a suit concerning title to the stock.

The binding effect of the stock record on corporate officers does not leave a beneficial owner without remedy. He may be presumed to know that the record owner can vote the stock. The beneficial owner can protect his interest by requiring a transfer on the books or by demanding a proxy from the record owner, and if voluntary compliance is not forthcoming, relief is available by injunction or mandamus. In the present case Shepherd's trustee, the beneficial owner, made no effort to vote the shares. He sought no proxy from the receiver or the receivership court. In these circumstances neither the corporate officers nor any of the other stockholders were in a position to assert that only the trustee had the right to vote.

The question presented to the inspector was, who was entitled to act for the record owner? The shares were registered in the name of Pioneer Casualty Company, which was in receivership and had no officers to act for it. The only person entitled to act for Pioneer was its receiver under orders of the 126th district court of Travis County. The receiver, acting under such an order, gave a proxy to Shepherd to act for Pioneer, with instructions to give a further proxy to plaintiffs Matthews and Thorp, and Shepherd, acting for Pioneer in accordance with the proxy to him, gave a proxy to plaintiffs. This transaction was essentially the same as if the receiver, acting under the court's order, had given the proxy directly to plaintiffs. The recitation in the order that Shepherd was the beneficial owner is of no consequence, since the beneficial owner, whether Shepherd or his trustee, had no right under the bylaws to vote the shares as against General Electrodynamics Corporation and its officers. * * * Since the stockholder of record was Pioneer Casualty Company, and the receiver was authorized by court order to act for Pioneer, the inspector's proper course was to accept the stock record as determining that the right to vote was in Pioneer Casualty Company, and to accept the proxies given by the receiver to Shepherd and by him to plaintiffs as valid.

Defendants argue that if the inspector was authorized to go behind the stock book and recognize the voting rights of the receiver for Pioneer Casualty Company, he was authorized to go further and determine the beneficial ownership of the stock for the purpose of the election. We do not agree. The inspector was bound by the stock book to consider Pioneer Casualty Company the legal owner for the purpose of the election, but he was required to determine who could act for the record owner, just as if someone had challenged the authority of a person purporting to act as an officer of a corporate stockholder. Since Pioneer was in receivership, the inspector could consider that fact and should have treated the receiver as the authorized representative of the record owner. It is quite another matter to say that the inspector should have inquired into beneficial ownership of the stock and recognized the right of Shepherd or his trustee in bankruptcy to vote the shares. * * *

Reversed and rendered.

Notes

(1) Underlying the holding in the principal case is the basic concept that shares are always registered in the name of a specific person on the records of the corporation. See MBCA §§ 6.25(b)(2), 7.07(a). The person in whose name shares are registered is called the "record holder" and may or may not be the person who is the actual owner of the shares, usually referred to as the "beneficial owner." Generally speaking, the corporation may treat the record owner as the owner of the shares for purposes such as voting, the payment of dividends or distributions,

and determining to whom shares have been transferred. In *Salgo*, the record owner was a person different from the beneficial owner and the Court held that the corporation must determine who has been authorized to vote the shares by the record owner. Where the record owner and the beneficial owner are different persons it is clear, as dicta in the principal case states, that the beneficial owner can compel the record owner (by court process, if necessary) to execute a proxy appointment in the name of the beneficial owner so that the owner may vote the shares as he or she desires. The beneficial owner also has the power to compel the record owner to turn over any distributions made by the corporation and, ultimately, to reregister the shares in the name of the beneficial owner when requested to do so. Why do some beneficial owners allow shares to be held of record by someone else, sometimes for extended periods? As discussed subsequently, shares of publicly held corporations are usually held of record by nominees or by brokerage firms ("in street name") in order to facilitate transfer.

(2) The traditional practice is to issue certificates representing shares in the name of the record owner. For an example of a share certificate, see page 486, infra. See also MBCA § 6.25. Share certificates usually come attached to a "stub" that may be filled in when the certificate is actually issued by the corporation to a shareholder. In closely held corporations, the record of shareholders may simply consist of these stubs; in publicly held corporations, much more elaborate records may be kept by a "transfer agent," typically a commercial bank. These records, of course, reveal only the record owner, not the beneficial owner. MBCA § 6.26, and the statutes of many states, also authorize a corporation to issue uncertificated shares, i.e., shares that are not represented by certificates. This is a relatively recent innovation for closely held corporations, and it appears today that most corporations continue to prefer to issue certificated shares, though there is a slight saving in cost in using uncertificated shares.

(3) Shareholder voting and entitlement to distributions are determined from the records of the corporation. It is not necessary for a record shareholder to exhibit the share certificate (in the case of certificated shares) in order to vote or receive a distribution. When a corporation conducts a vote it must determine which shareholders are entitled to notice and to vote at the meeting. State statutes provide that the board of directors may fix a record date, or cut-off date for determining who the shareholders of record are. Sometimes these cut-off dates can present problems, even for large publicly traded companies, that, presumably, are assisted by expert counsel. In McKesson Corporation v. Derdiger 793 A.2d 385 (Del.Ch.2002), McKesson, a large Delaware Corporation whose shares trade on the New York Stock Exchange, after distributing its proxy materials to shareholders, sued for a declaratory judgment that its annual meeting, if held as scheduled, would not be void for noncompliance with Delaware law regarding the fixing of record dates for shareholders for voting at that meeting. McKesson had set May 25, 2001 as the record date for stockholders to be eligible to vote at the annual meeting, and announced that the annual meeting would be held on July 25, 2001, exactly 60 days later. However, Section 213(a) of the Delaware General Corporation Law, provides that the record date cannot be set "more than 60 * * * days *before* the date of the annual meeting." McKesson's May 25, 2001 record date was 61 days before the Annual Meeting. The Delaware Chancery Court reasoned that since one day before July 25, is July 24, 60 days before July 25 must by May 26, and thus, May 25 must be more than 60 days before the date of the annual meeting. The court further opined that "the Legislature includes immutable time limits in statutes to serve particular purposes and such time limits are usually strictly enforced." However, despite the noncompliance, the court ultimately

decided that the actions taken on the July 25 Annual Meeting were valid, but suggested that it might not be willing to do so again in future cases. The mechanics of establishing the date on which shareholders entitled to vote will be determined is set forth in MBCA § 7.07. See also § 7.20.

(4) Action by shareholders at a meeting requires the existence of a quorum and the approval by the requisite number of votes at a meeting at which a quorum is present. See MBCA §§ 7.25(a), 7.25(c), 7.26, 7.27, 7.28(a). These are often viewed as mundane, technical matters, but there are a number of substantive issues that may arise.

Cumulative vs. Straight Voting. The workings of these two methods of voting to elect directors can be most simply described by an illustration. Let us assume a corporation with two shareholders, A with 18 shares, and B with 82 shares. Further, let us assume that there are five directors and each shareholder nominates five candidates. Directors run "at large" rather than for specific places; hence the five persons receiving the most votes are elected. If only straight voting is permitted, A may cast 18 votes for each of five candidates and B may cast 82 votes for each of five candidates. The result, of course, is that all five of B's candidates are elected. If cumulative voting is permitted the number of total votes that each shareholder may cast is first computed and each shareholder is permitted to distribute these votes as he sees fit over one or more candidates. In the example above, A is entitled to cast a total of 90 votes (18x5) and B is entitled to cast 410 votes (82x5). If A casts all 90 votes for A_1, A_1 is ensured of election because B cannot divide 410 votes among five candidates in such a way as to give each candidate more than 90 votes and preclude A_1's election. Obviously, the effect of cumulative voting is that it increases minority participation on the board of directors. In straight voting, the shareholder with 51 percent of the vote elects the entire board; in cumulative voting, a relatively small faction (18 percent in the above example) may obtain representation on the board. Whether this is good or bad depends on one's point of view.[4]

One undesirable aspect of cumulative voting is that it tends to be a little tricky. If a shareholder casts votes in an irrational or inefficient way, he may not get the directorships his position entitles him to; when voting cumulatively it is relatively easy to make a mistake in spreading votes around. The most graphic illustrations of this are the cases where a majority shareholder votes in such a way that he elects only a minority of the directors. This is most

---

4. [By the Editors] Numerous arguments for and against cumulative voting have been made. Arguments in favor of such voting include: (1) it is democratic in that persons with large (but minority) holdings should have a voice in the conduct of the corporation; (2) it is desirable to have as many viewpoints as possible represented on the board of directors; and (3) the presence of a minority director may discourage conflicts of interest by management since discovery is considerably more likely. Arguments in opposition include: (1) the introduction of a partisan on the board is inconsistent with the notion that the board should represent all interests in the corporation; (2) a partisan director may cause disharmony which reduces the efficiency of the board; (3) a partisan director may criticize management unreasonably so as to make it less willing to take risky (but desirable) action; (4) a partisan director may leak confidential information; and (5) in practice cumulative voting is usually used to further narrow partisan goals, particularly to give an insurgent group a toehold in the corporation in an effort to obtain control. *See* Jeffrey N. Gordon, Institutions as Relational Investors: A New Look at Cumulative Voting, 94 Colum.L.Rev. 124 (1994).

likely to occur when one shareholder votes "straight" and another cumulates. For example, if A has 60 shares and B only 40, with five directors to be elected, B may nevertheless elect a majority of the board if A votes "straight" and B knows that A is doing so. The result might look like this:

A_1–60, A_2–60, A_3–60, A_4–60, A_5–60; B_1–67, B_2–66, B_3–65, B_4–1, B_5–1.

This is daring of B because he is spreading his vote over three persons when he can be sure only of electing two. If B decides to do this, and A knows that B will try to elect three persons, then A, by properly cumulating his votes, can elect four directors, in effect "stealing" one of B's.[5]

The following formula is useful in determining the number of shares needed to elect one director:

$$\frac{S}{D + 1} + 1.$$

where S equals the total number of shares voting, and D equals the number of directors to be elected.[6] The analogous formula to elect n directors is:

$$\frac{nS}{D + 1} + 1.$$

Note

In Stancil v. Bruce Stancil Refrigeration, Inc., 81 N.C.App. 567, 344 S.E.2d 789 (1986), all the shares of stock of a North Carolina corporation were owned by two brothers: Bruce Stancil (12,500 shares) and Howard Stancil (12,500 shares). North Carolina requires cumulative voting by statute for corporations with less than 2,000 shareholders and provides that directors are elected by a "plurality of the votes cast." N.C.Gen.Stat. § 55–67(c). Before the election in question, the board of directors consisted of Bruce Stancil, Eva Stancil (Bruce's wife), and Howard Stancil. At the shareholders' meeting, each brother was represented by counsel. Bruce, "without a majority vote or consent, asserted his 'right' to act as chairman of the meeting and in fact conducted the proceedings at the meeting, acting with and upon the advice and consultation of his attorney, Wiley L. Lane, Jr." 344 S.E.2d at 790. Howard announced that he planned to vote cumulatively in conformity with the North Carolina statutes but Bruce did not acknowledge this statement (or grant the recess the North Carolina statute provides for after such an announcement is made). Bruce nominated himself, his wife, Eva, and one Sarah Barnes. Howard nominated himself, his wife, Clara, and one Henry Babb. The trial court's findings and conclusions describe what happened then:

15.   The Respondent, Bruce Stancil, cast his votes for his nominees for director as follows:

5. [By the Editors] The results of such an election might be as follows: A_1–73, A_2–74, A_3–75, A_4–76, A_5–2, B_1–67, B_2–66, B_3–65, B_4–1, B_5–1.

6. [By the Editors] A minor modification may sometimes be necessary. The first portion of the formula, $S/(D+1)$ establishes the maximum number of shares voted for a single person which are *insufficient* to elect that person as a director. Any share, or fraction thereof, in excess of that amount will be sufficient to elect a director. The formula in the text ignores fractional shares which sometimes may lead to a one-share error. For example, where there are 100 shares voting and five directors to be elected, the first portion of the formula is 100/(5 + 1) or 100/6. In this example, 16 shares will not elect a director, but 17 shares will, since the first part of the formula yields 16 2/3. The formula in the text yields an answer of 17 2/3.

Bruce Stancil	12,500 Votes
Sarah Barnes	12,500 Votes
Eva Stancil	12,500 Votes

The Petitioner, Howard K. Stancil, cast his votes for his nominees for director as follows:

Howard K. Stancil	18,750	Votes
Clara Stancil	18,750	Votes
Henry Babb	0	Votes

16.   The Respondent, Bruce Stancil, after casting 12,500 votes for each of his three nominees (totaling 37,500 votes as allowed by law), purported to cast an additional 18,750 votes against Howard Stancil and 18,750 votes against Clara Stancil.

17.   There is no provision in the North Carolina Business Corporation Act providing for the casting of shareholder votes against a nominee for director, and the purported "votes" cast by the Respondent, Bruce Stancil, subsequent to the casting of his affirmative votes totaling 37,500 for his three nominees, were void and of no lawful effect.

18.   Bruce Stancil, Sarah Barnes and Eva Stancil, all being Respondents herein and recipients of 12,500 votes each, failed, as to each of them, to receive a plurality of the votes cast, as required by G.S. 55–67(c), and were not lawfully elected as directors of the Respondent corporation.

344 S.E.2d at 791. The appellate court affirmed the trial court's conclusion as to the result of the election. Does the board of directors now consist of Howard and Clara with one vacancy? What about the possible application of a statute similar to MBCA § 8.05(e)? If you had been Wiley L. Lane, Jr., what should you have done to preserve your client's apparently dominant position on the board of directors?

HUMPHRYS v. WINOUS CO.

Supreme Court of Ohio, 1956.
165 Ohio St. 45, 133 N.E.2d 780.

BELL, JUSTICE.

It can not be disclaimed that by reason of the stock distribution of this particular corporation a classification of the three directors into three classes containing one director each effectively divests the minority shareholders of a measure of control they formerly exercised over the corporation by electing one member of the board through the expedient of cumulative voting.

The issue herein, however, is not whether a particular result was accomplished but whether, under the statutes, such a result can legally be accomplished.

Section 1701.64, Revised Code, provides, in part, as follows:

The articles or the code of regulations may provide for the term of office of all of the directors or, if classified upon the basis of the expiration of the terms of office of the directors, of each class thereof, provided that no term shall be fixed for a period of more than three years from the date of their election and until the election of their successors.

Section 1701.58, Revised Code, after providing that any shareholder may, upon giving 24 hours notice of his desire to do so, cumulate such voting power as he possesses and give one candidate as many votes as the number of directors multiplied by the number of his votes equals, then provides that "such right to vote cumulatively shall not be restricted or qualified by the articles or the code of regulations."

The Court of Appeals sustained the contention of appellees and held that, since Section 1701.58, Revised Code, was specific in character, it constituted a limitation upon the applicability of Section 1701.64, Revised Code, and that, since the classification by appellants, attempted under the authority of Section 1701.64, Revised Code, did restrict the right to vote cumulatively as specifically guaranteed by Section 1701.58, Revised Code, such classification was invalid.

[The Court notes the historical development of an interest in cumulative voting to protect the rights of minority shareholders dating back to John H. Doyle's 1893 address to the Ohio State Bar Association and the subsequent recommendation submitted to the Ohio State Bar Association by the Committee on Judicial Administration and Legal Reform.]

* * *

If we may assume that the General Assembly was motivated by the recommendation of the bar association, it is obvious that it intended to assure minority representation on a corporate board of directors by permitting cumulative voting.

The provision for classification of directors appears for the first time in Ohio as * * * part of the General Corporation Act, effective June 9, 1927, 112 Ohio Laws, p. 32. * * *

Strangely enough, however, prior to 1955, there were only two cases which discussed the effect of classification of directors on cumulative voting. In Pittsburgh Steel Co. v. Walker (Court of Common Pleas, Allegheny County, Pennsylvania, 1944), three judges said there was doubt as to the constitutionality of the staggered system, but did not pass directly on the question. In Heeps v. Byers Co. (Court of Common Pleas, Allegheny County, Pennsylvania, 1950), one judge denied a preliminary injunction against the holding of a staggered-voting election on constitutional and other grounds. The Supreme Court of Pennsylvania, in affirming the judgment of the lower court, merely denied any right to question the granting of preliminary injunctions. Cohen v. A.M. Byers Co., 363 Pa. 618, 70 A.2d 837.

But on February 1, 1955, the Circuit Court of Cook County, Illinois, decided the case of Wolfson v. Avery. The action grew out of the much-publicized battle between Sewell Avery and Louis E. Wolfson for control of the board of directors of Montgomery Ward & Company. The Wolfson group sought a declaratory judgment that a bylaw of Montgomery Ward providing for the annual election of only one-third of the nine members of the board of directors is in violation of Section 3, Article XI of the Illinois Constitution, S.H.A., which among other things, provides for cumulative voting. Since the bylaw is specifically authorized by Section 35 of the Illinois Business Corporation Act, Illinois Revised Statutes 1953, Chapter 32, paragraph 157.35, the complaint also sought to have that portion of the statute declared unconstitutional. The Circuit Court granted the plaintiff's motion for judgment on the pleadings, declaring Section 35 of the Business Corporation Act unconstitutional.

The trial judge in the Wolfson case adopted the theory that the Constitution requires that a minority shareholder be given the right—by cumulative voting—to exercise his "maximum voting strength proportionate to his share holding." He rejected the argument that the constitutional provision merely gives minority shareholders an opportunity to have some representation on the board of directors, whether proportionate or not. 23 Law Week, 2393.

The Supreme Court of Illinois, 6 Ill.2d 78, 126 N.E.2d 701, 711, after reviewing at some length the proceedings of the constitutional convention and the publications which interpreted the constitutional provision which was ratified on July 2, 1870, concluded that "Section 35 of the Business Corporation Act, in authorizing the classification of directors, is inconsistent with the constitutional right of a stockholder to cumulate his shares through multiplying them by the 'number of directors,' and cannot be sustained."

The Illinois court, in disposing of the defendant's reliance upon the fact that a law authorizing classification was passed by the first Illinois Legislature, and that this Legislature included 13 members who had served on the Constitutional Convention, said that "that is a fact to be given some weight, but it is by no means controlling (cf. Marbury v. Madison, 1 Cranch. 137, 2 L.Ed. 60) and in this case it must yield to the evidence supplied by the constitutional debates and the contemporary accounts in the press."

* * * As distinguished from a conflict between a constitutional provision and a statutory provision as in the Wolfson case, we have here a conflict between two statutory provisions. * * *

That cumulative voting is generally accepted is evidenced by the facts that mandatory cumulative voting provisions are found in the Constitutions of 13 states and in the statutes of eight others, and that permissive cumulative voting is authorized in 18 states. Cumulative voting is provided for in [MBCA (1950) § 31], drawn by the American Bar Association, and in Section 28 of the Model Business Corporation Act, proposed by the Commissioners on Uniform State Laws. Despite the seemingly obvious conflict between classification of directors and cumulative voting, provisions for staggered elections are made in approximately 33 states. See Williams, Cumulative Voting for Directors (1951), 7; Cumulative Voting and Classification of Directors, St. John's Law Review, 83, 86.

The problem will never arise in three jurisdictions because annual election of all directors is required by statute. See Section 22, Title 10, Alabama Code; Sections 805, 2201, California Corporation Code; Section 44–109, Wyoming Compiled Statutes.

Obviously, a provision in the articles or code of regulations to the effect that a shareholder may not vote cumulatively would restrict the right given by statute and would therefore be invalid in Ohio. Similarly a provision that a shareholder could vote cumulatively only if he held a certain percentage of the corporate stock would be invalid. But the same result might easily be accomplished without running afoul of the prohibition of Section 1701.58, Revised Code.

And majority shareholders have in many instances succeeded in curtailing or eliminating cumulative voting through a number of devices. In states where the right to vote cumulatively is permissive rather than mandatory, the charters of certain corporations have been amended to replace cumulative voting with straight voting. Cumulative voting may also be circumvented by removing minority-elected directors without cause. A third method employed to prevent effective use of cumulative voting is that of reducing the number of directors.

For example, suppose in a corporation having a board of nine members a minority shareholder, by cumulating his voting power, is able to elect one member of the board. But suppose, also, at the next meeting, the code of regulations is amended to reduce the directorate from nine to seven, as permitted under Section 1701.68, Revised Code. The minority shareholder, although not deprived of his *right* to vote cumulatively, has been deprived of representation on the board just as effectively as if he had not had the right. Similar examples could be given, depending on the number of shares held by the minority and the number of directors to be elected. Can it be said that the legislative intent in enacting Section 1701.58, Revised Code, was to limit Section 1701.64, Revised Code, and not limit Section 1701.68, Revised Code, and other sections of the corporation act? We do not think so.

If effect is to be given to both enactments of the General Assembly, the guaranty provided in Section 1701.58, Revised Code, must be construed as one granting a *right* that may not be restricted or qualified rather than one *ensuring* minority representation on the board of directors.

To hold otherwise would require a complete annihilation of the provision for classification because any classification would necessarily be a restriction or qualification on the effectiveness of cumulative voting, and no corporation could ever avail itself of the privilege of classification. We do not believe the General Assembly intended any such result.

Both the Ohio State Bar Association and the General Assembly recognized that, under the law of Ohio as it existed in January 1954, the action taken here by the corporation could have been accomplished. Consequently, the bar association recommended a change in the corporation law of Ohio to the effect that any class of directors could contain not less than two directors. In commenting on the proposed change, the Corporation Law Committee of the association said: "A new provision is that the number of directors in a given class shall be not less than two. This is for the purpose of meeting the objection that has been raised to the effect that under the present law the majority shareholders may fix the number of directors at three, each director to be in a separate class so that at each annual meeting only one director is to be elected. This device would prevent the minority, even though holding 49 per cent of the shares, from electing a single director."

Subsequently, Section 1701.57, Revised Code, was enacted, supplanting former Section 1701.64, Revised Code, to require that each class of directors must consist of not less than three directors each. 126 Ohio Laws, H70, effective October 11, 1955. Thus did the General Assembly obviate the possibility of a recurrence of the action taken by The Winous Company.

It can not be gainsaid that the action taken here effectively eliminated the minority shareholders from exercising any control over the corporation.

But we are of the opinion that the throwing of an aura of uncertainty and confusion around the statutory provision for classification of directors is not required by the construction of the statutory provision for cumulative voting. We hold, therefore, that Section 1701.58, Revised Code, guarantees to minority shareholders only the right of cumulative voting and does not necessarily guarantee the effectiveness of the exercise of that right to elect minority representation on the board of directors. * * *

The judgment of the Court of Appeals is reversed and the judgment of the Court of Common Pleas is modified and, as modified, is affirmed.

Judgment reversed.

MATTHIAS, STEWART and TAFT, JJ., concur.

WEYGANDT, C.J., and HART, J., dissent.

WEYGANDT, CHIEF JUSTICE, dissents on the ground of the cogent reasoning of the Court of Appeals that "the right of a shareholder in an Ohio corporation to cumulate his vote has been provided by statute in this state for more than fifty years. The legislature in adopting the revision of the statute dealing with corporate organization in 1927, showed clearly that it intended to strengthen the cumulative voting provision by adding to existing law the provision that a corporation cannot restrict cumulative voting by its articles or code of regulations. And when in the same act the legislature, for the first time provides that there may be classification of directors when provided for by its code of regulations, it could not have been intended that the exercise of such right could be so used as to nullify the right of cumulative voting. When the minimum number of three directors is provided for, and their terms of office are for three years, one to be elected each year, the right to cumulative voting is, in such case, *completely nullified*"—an utterly futile result hardly contemplated by the emphatic language of the General Assembly in its attempt to *strengthen* the right. (Italics supplied.)

Notes

(1) Consider MBCA §§ 7.28(b), (c), (d), 8.04. Under the MBCA, cumulative voting, like preemptive rights, is an "opt in" election to be chosen by an appropriate provision in the articles of incorporation. As of 2002, 30 states had adopted an "opt in" provision while thirteen states had an "opt out" election. Seven states make cumulative voting mandatory for all corporations, five by provision in state constitutions. The number of states with mandatory cumulative voting, however, is declining. In 1990, California, long the bastion of mandatory cumulative voting, made that manner of voting permissive for corporations with shares listed on a public exchange or with more than 800 shareholders of record. Cal.Gen.Corp.Law § 301.5. If a corporation has opted to grant cumulative voting under the Model Act, may it thereafter amend the articles of incorporation by less than unanimous vote to delete that requirement? See MBCA § 10.01. Section 13.02(a)(4)(iv) of MBCA (1984) granted a right of dissent and appraisal to such a shareholder; however, the 1999 amendments eliminated this limited statutory right to an appraisal so that it now exists only if the corporation elects affirmatively to provide that right.

(2) What devices are available to minimize the impact of cumulative voting where that voting is mandatory? What about creating classes of directors consist-

ing of one director each, such as involved in the Winous Co. case? See MBCA § 8.06.[7] A decision to classify the board of directors may be attacked as a breach of fiduciary duty in some circumstances if made without business justification and in the midst of a proxy campaign to elect one director. Coalition to Advocate Pub. Util. Responsibility, Inc. v. Engels, 364 F.Supp. 1202 (D.Minn.1973). What about removal of a director elected by minority votes? See MBCA §§ 8.08, 8.09. What about "freezing out" the minority director by denying that director access to information, refusing to appoint him or her to any committees, and then holding "unofficial meetings" and "ramming through decisions * * * with little discussion"? It is reported that these tactics were used by a public corporation, Bunker–Ramo Corp. against a director elected by a dissident group. Kaufman, Directors of Bunker–Ramo Seek to Expel Unwelcome Suitor's Chief From Board, Wall St. J., March 31, 1980, at 10. See Jeffrey N. Gordon, Institutions as Relational Investors: A New Look at Cumulative Voting, 94 Colum.L.Rev. 124 (1994).

(3) Where a board is composed of three or more directors, several states permit the staggering of elections if the corporation does not have cumulative voting. Staggering a three-person board means that each director serves for three years and only one director stands for election each year. Is there anything wrong with that? When coupled with a provision that permits removal of directors only for cause, this makes outside takeovers by share purchases or proxy fights more difficult, since the successful outsider will only be able to replace one group of directors each year. During the 1980s, a number of publicly held corporations adopted a classified board of directors, coupled with a prohibition against removal of directors except for cause, as a takeover defense.

(4) Professor Lani Guinier, (who had been nominated by President Bill Clinton to head the Civil Rights Division of the Department of Justice), has advocated that cumulative voting be made available to increase the power of minority groups to elect representatives in municipal elections. See Lani Guinier, Groups, Representation, and Race–Conscious Redistricting: A Case of the Emperor's New Clothes, 71 Tex. L. Rev. 1589 (1993).

RINGLING BROS.–BARNUM & BAILEY COMBINED SHOWS v. RINGLING

Supreme Court of Delaware, 1947.
29 Del.Ch. 610, 53 A.2d 441.

PEARSON, JUDGE.

The Court of Chancery was called upon to review an attempted election of directors at the 1946 annual stockholders meeting of the corporate defendant. The pivotal questions concern an agreement between two of the three present stockholders, and particularly the effect of this agreement with relation to the exercise of voting rights by these two stockholders. At the time of the meeting, the corporation had outstanding 1000 shares of capital stock held as follows: 315 by petitioner Edith Conway Ringling; 315 by defendant Aubrey B. Ringling Haley (individually or as executrix and legatee of a deceased husband); and 370 by defendant John Ringling North. The purpose of the meeting was to elect the entire board of seven directors. The shares could be

---

7. [By the Editors] Section 8.06, as approved in 1984, limited the application of this section to boards consisting of nine or more directors. It was amended to eliminate this limitation in 1999. Do you agree that this change was desirable?

voted cumulatively. Mrs. Ringling asserts that by virtue of the operation of an agreement between her and Mrs. Haley, the latter was bound to vote her shares for an adjournment of the meeting, or in the alternative, for a certain slate of directors. Mrs. Haley contends that she was not so bound for reason that the agreement was invalid, or at least revocable.

The two ladies entered into the agreement in 1941. * * * The agreement recites that each party was the owner "subject only to possible claims of creditors of the estates of Charles Ringling and Richard Ringling, respectively" (deceased husbands of the parties), of 300 shares of the capital stock of the defendant corporation; that in 1938 these shares had been deposited under a voting trust agreement which would terminate in 1947, or earlier, upon the elimination of certain liability of the corporation; that each party also owned 15 shares individually; that the parties had "entered into an agreement in April 1934 providing for joint action by them in matters affecting their ownership of stock and interest in" the corporate defendant; that the parties desired "to continue to act jointly in all matters relating to their stock ownership or interest in" the corporate defendant (and the other corporation). The agreement then provides as follows:

"Now, Therefore, in consideration of the mutual covenants and agreements hereinafter contained the parties hereto agree as follows:

1. Neither party will sell any shares of stock or any voting trust certificates in either of said corporations to any other person whosoever, without first making a written offer to the other party hereto of all of the shares or voting trust certificates proposed to be sold, for the same price and upon the same terms and conditions as in such proposed sale, and allowing such other party a time of not less than 180 days from the date of such written offer within which to accept same.

2. In exercising any voting rights to which either party may be entitled by virtue of ownership of stock or voting trust certificates held by them in either of said corporation, each party will consult and confer with the other and the parties will act jointly in exercising such voting rights in accordance with such agreement as they may reach with respect to any matter calling for the exercise of such voting rights.

3. In the event the parties fail to agree with respect to any matter covered by paragraph 2 above, the question in disagreement shall be submitted for arbitration to Karl D. Loos, of Washington, D.C. as arbitrator and his decision thereon shall be binding upon the parties hereto. Such arbitration shall be exercised to the end of assuring for the respective corporations good management and such participation therein by the members of the Ringling family as the experience, capacity and ability of each may warrant. The parties may at any time by written agreement designate any other individual to act as arbitrator in lieu of said Loos.

4. Each of the parties hereto will enter into and execute such voting trust agreement or agreements and such other instruments as, from time to time they may deem advisable and as they may be advised by counsel are appropriate to effectuate the purposes and objects of this agreement.

5. This agreement shall be in effect from the date hereof and shall continue in effect for a period of ten years unless sooner terminated by mutual agreement in writing by the parties hereto.

6. The agreement of April 1934 is hereby terminated.

7. This agreement shall be binding upon and inure to the benefit of the heirs, executors, administrators and assigns of the parties hereto respectively."

The Mr. Loos mentioned in the agreement is an attorney and has represented both parties since 1937, and, before and after the voting trust was terminated in late 1942, advised them with respect to the exercise of their voting rights. At the annual meetings in 1943 and the two following years, the parties voted their shares in accordance with mutual understandings arrived at as a result of discussions. In each of these years, they elected five of the seven directors. Mrs. Ringling and Mrs. Haley each had sufficient votes, independently of the other, to elect two of the seven directors. By both voting for an additional candidate, they could be sure of his election regardless of how Mr. North, the remaining stockholder, might vote.[8]

Some weeks before the 1946 meeting, they discussed with Mr. Loos the matter of voting for directors. They were in accord that Mrs. Ringling should cast sufficient votes to elect herself and her son; and that Mrs. Haley should elect herself and her husband; but they did not agree upon a fifth director. The day before the meeting, the discussions were continued, Mrs. Haley being represented by her husband since she could not be present because of illness. In a conversation with Mr. Loos, Mr. Haley indicated that he would make a motion for an adjournment of the meeting for sixty days, in order to give the ladies additional time to come to an agreement about their voting. On the morning of the meeting, however, he stated that because of something Mrs. Ringling had done, he would not consent to a postponement. Mrs. Ringling then made a demand upon Mr. Loos to act under the third paragraph of the agreement "to arbitrate the disagreement" between her and Mrs. Haley in connection with the manner in which the stock of the two ladies should be voted. At the opening of the meeting, Mr. Loos read the written demand and stated that he determined and directed that the stock of both ladies be voted for an adjournment of sixty days. Mrs. Ringling then made a motion for adjournment and voted for it. Mr. Haley, as proxy for his wife, and Mr. North voted against the motion. Mrs. Ringling (herself or through her attorney, it is immaterial which,) objected to the voting of Mrs. Haley's stock in any manner other than in accordance with Mr. Loos' direction. The chairman ruled that the stock could not be voted contrary to such direction, and declared the motion for adjournment had carried. Nevertheless, the meeting proceeded to the election of directors. Mrs. Ringling stated that she would continue in the meeting "but without prejudice to her position with respect to the voting of

---

8. [By the Court] Each lady was entitled to cast 2205 votes (since each had the cumulative voting rights of 315 shares, and there were 7 vacancies in the directorate). The sum of the votes of both is 4410, which is sufficient to allow 882 votes for each of 5 persons. Mr. North, holding 370 shares, was entitled to cast 2590 votes, which obviously cannot be divided so as to give to more than two candidates as many as 882 votes each. It will be observed that in order for Mrs. Ringling and Mrs. Haley to be sure to elect five directors (regardless of how Mr. North might vote) they must act together in the sense that their combined votes must be divided among five different candidates and at least one of the five must be voted for by both Mrs. Ringling and Mrs. Haley.

the stock and the fact that adjournment had not been taken." Mr. Loos directed Mrs. Ringling to cast her votes.

882 for Mrs. Ringling,

882 for her son, Robert, and

441 for a Mr. Dunn, who had been a member of the board for several years.

She complied. Mr. Loos directed that Mrs. Haley's votes be cast

882 for Mrs. Haley,

882 for Mr. Haley, and

441 for Mr. Dunn.

Instead of complying, Mr. Haley attempted to vote his wife's shares

1103 for Mrs. Haley, and

1102 for Mr. Haley.

Mr. North voted his shares

864 for a Mr. Woods,

863 for a Mr. Griffin, and

863 for Mr. North.

The chairman ruled that the five candidates proposed by Mr. Loos, together with Messrs. Woods and North, were elected. The Haley–North group disputed this ruling insofar as it declared the election of Mr. Dunn; and insisted that Mr. Griffin, instead, had been elected. A directors' meeting followed in which Mrs. Ringling participated after stating that she would do so "without prejudice to her position that the stockholders' meeting had been adjourned and that the directors' meeting was not properly held." Mr. Dunn and Mr. Griffin, although each was challenged by an opposing faction, attempted to join in voting as directors for different slates of officers. Soon after the meeting, Mrs. Ringling instituted this proceeding.

The Vice Chancellor determined that the agreement to vote in accordance with the direction of Mr. Loos was valid as a "stock pooling agreement" with lawful objects and purposes, and that it was not in violation of any public policy of this state. He held that where the arbitrator acts under the agreement and one party refuses to comply with his direction, "the Agreement constitutes the willing party * * * an implied agent possessing the irrevocable proxy of the recalcitrant party for the purpose of casting the particular vote." It was ordered that a new election be held before a master, with the direction that the master should recognize and give effect to the agreement if its terms were properly invoked.

Before taking up defendants' objections to the agreement, let us analyze particularly what it attempts to provide with respect to voting, including what functions and powers it attempts to repose in Mr. Loos, the "arbitrator." The agreement recites that the parties desired "to continue to act jointly in all matters relating to their stock ownership or interest in" the corporation. The parties agreed to consult and confer with each other in exercising their voting rights and to act jointly—that is, concertedly; unitedly; towards unified courses of action—in accordance with such agreement as they might reach.

Thus, so long as the parties agree for whom or for what their shares shall be voted, the agreement provides no function for the arbitrator. His role is limited to situations where the parties fail to agree upon a course of action. In such cases, the agreement directs that "the question in disagreement shall be submitted for arbitration" to Mr. Loos "as arbitrator and his decision thereon shall be binding upon the parties." These provisions are designed to operate in aid of what appears to be a primary purpose of the parties, "to act jointly" in exercising their voting rights, by providing a means for fixing a course of action whenever they themselves might reach a stalemate.

Should the agreement be interpreted as attempting to empower the arbitrator to carry his directions into effect? Certainly there is no express delegation or grant of power to do so, either by authorizing him to vote the shares or to compel either party to vote them in accordance with his directions. The agreement expresses no other function of the arbitrator than that of deciding questions in disagreement which prevent the effectuation of the purpose "to act jointly." The power to enforce a decision does not seem a necessary or usual incident of such a function. Mr. Loos is not a party to the agreement. It does not contemplate the transfer of any shares or interest in shares to him, or that he should undertake any duties which the parties might compel him to perform. They provided that they might designate any other individual to act instead of Mr. Loos. The agreement does not attempt to make the arbitrator a trustee of an express trust. What the arbitrator is to do is for the benefit of the parties, not for his own benefit. Whether the parties accept or reject his decision is no concern of his, so far as the agreement or the surrounding circumstances reveal. We think the parties sought to bind each other, but to be bound only to each other, and not to empower the arbitrator to enforce decisions he might make.

From this conclusion, it follows necessarily that no decision of the arbitrator could ever be enforced if both parties to the agreement were unwilling that it be enforced, for the obvious reason that there would be no one to enforce it. Under the agreement, something more is required after the arbitrator has given his decision in order that it should become compulsory: at least one of the parties must determine that such decision shall be carried into effect. Thus, any "control" of the voting of the shares, which is reposed in the arbitrator, is substantially limited in action under the agreement in that it is subject to the overriding power of the parties themselves.

The agreement does not describe the undertaking of each party with respect to a decision of the arbitrator other than to provide that it "shall be binding upon the parties." It seems to us that this language, considered with relation to its context and the situations to which it is applicable, means that each party promised the other to exercise her own voting rights in accordance with the arbitrator's decision. The agreement is silent about any exercise of the voting rights of one party by the other. The language with reference to situations where the parties arrive at an understanding as to voting plainly suggests "action" by each, and "exercising" voting rights by each, rather than by one for the other. There is no intimation that this method should be different where the arbitrator's decision is to be carried into effect. Assuming that a power in each party to exercise the voting rights of the other might be a relatively more effective or convenient means of enforcing a decision of the arbitrator than would be available without the power, this would not justify implying a delegation of the power in the absence of some indication that the parties bargained for that means. The method of voting actually employed by the parties tends to show that they did not construe the agreement as creating powers to vote each other's shares; for at meetings prior to 1946 each party apparently exercised her own voting rights, and at the 1946 meeting, Mrs. Ringling, who wished to enforce the agreement, did not attempt to cast a ballot in exercise of any voting rights of Mrs. Haley. We do not find enough in the agreement or in the circumstances to justify a construction that either party was empowered to exercise voting rights of the other.

Having examined what the parties sought to provide by the agreement, we come now to defendants' contention that the voting provisions are illegal and revocable. They say that the courts of this state have definitely established the doctrine "that there can be no agreement, or any device whatsoever, by which the voting power of stock of a Delaware corporation may be irrevocably separated from the ownership of the stock, except by an agreement which complies with Section 18" of the Corporation Law, Rev.Code 1935, § 2050, and except by a proxy coupled with an interest. They rely on Perry v. Missouri–Kansas P.L. Co., 22 Del.Ch. 33, 191 A. 823; In re Public Industrial Corporation, 19 Del.Ch. 398, reported as In re Chilson, 168 A. 82; Aldridge v. Franco Wyoming Oil Co., 24 Del.Ch. 126, 7 A.2d 753, affirmed in 24 Del.Ch. 349, 14 A.2d 380; Belle Isle Corporation v. Corcoran, Del.Sup., 49 A.2d 1; and contend that the doctrine is derived from Section 18 itself, Rev.Code of Del.1935, § 2050. The statute reads, in part, as follows:

> Sec. 18. Voting Trusts: * * *—One or more stockholders may by agreement in writing deposit capital stock of an original issue with or transfer capital stock to any person or persons, or corporation or corporations authorized to act as trustee, for the purpose of vesting in said person or persons, corporation or corporations, who may be designated Voting Trustee or Voting Trustees, the right to vote thereon for any period of time determined by such agreement, not exceeding ten years, upon the terms and conditions stated in such agreement. Such agreement may contain any other lawful provisions not inconsistent with said purpose. * * * Said Voting Trustees may vote upon the stock so issued or transferred during the period in such agreement specified; stock standing in the names of such Voting Trustees may be voted either in person or by proxy, and in voting said stock, such Voting Trustees shall incur no responsibility as stockholder, trustee or otherwise, except for their own individual malfeasance.[9]

In our view, neither the cases nor the statute sustain the rule for which the defendants contend. Their sweeping formulation would impugn well-recognized means by which a shareholder may effectively confer his voting rights upon others while retaining various other rights. For example, defendants' rule would apparently not permit holders of voting stock to confer upon stockholders of another class, by the device of an amendment of the certificate

9. [By the Editors] Omitted portions of the section provide requirements for the filing of a copy of the agreement in the principal Delaware office of the corporation for the issuance of certificates of stock to the voting trustees, for the voting of stock where there are more than one voting trustee, and for the extension of the agreement for additional periods, not exceeding ten years each. The current Delaware voting trust statute, Del. G.C.L. § 218, was amended in 1994 to eliminate the ten-year limitation on the life of a voting trust but retained the requirement that a copy be filed with the corporation.

of incorporation, the exclusive right to vote during periods when dividends are not paid on stock of the latter class. The broad prohibitory meaning which defendants find in Section 18 seems inconsistent with their concession that proxies coupled with an interest may be irrevocable, for the statute contains nothing about such proxies. The statute authorizes, among other things, the deposit or transfer of stock in trust for a specified purpose, namely, "vesting" in the transferee "the right to vote thereon" for a limited period; and prescribes numerous requirements in this connection. Accordingly, it seems reasonable to infer that to establish the relationship and accomplish the purpose which the statute authorizes, its requirements must be complied with. But the statute does not purport to deal with agreements whereby shareholders attempt to bind each other as to how they shall vote their shares. Various forms of such pooling agreements, as they are sometimes called, have been held valid and have been distinguished from voting trusts. We think the particular agreement before us does not violate Section 18 or constitute an attempted evasion of its requirements, and is not illegal for any other reason. Generally speaking, a shareholder may exercise wide liberality of judgment in the matter of voting, and it is not objectionable, that his motives may be for personal profit, or determined by whims or caprice, so long as he violates no duty owed his fellow shareholders. Heil v. Standard G. & E. Co., 17 Del.Ch. 214, 151 A. 303. The ownership of voting stock imposes no legal duty to vote at all. A group of shareholders may, without impropriety, vote their respective shares so as to obtain advantages of concerted action. They may lawfully contract with each other to vote in the future in such way as they, or a majority of their group, from time to time determine. Reasonable provisions for cases of failure of the group to reach a determination because of an even division in their ranks seem unobjectionable. The provision here for submission to the arbitrator is plainly designed as a deadlock-breaking measure, and the arbitrator's decision cannot be enforced unless at least one of the parties (entitled to cast one-half of their combined votes) is willing that it be enforced. We find the provision reasonable. It does not appear that the agreement enables the parties to take any unlawful advantage of the outside shareholder, or of any other person. It offends no rule of law or public policy of this state of which we are aware.

Legal consideration for the promises of each party is supplied by the mutual promises of the other party. The undertaking to vote in accordance with the arbitrator's decision is a valid contract. The good faith of the arbitrator's action has not been challenged and, indeed, the record indicates that no such challenge could be supported. Accordingly, the failure of Mrs. Haley to exercise her voting rights in accordance with his decision was a breach of her contract. It is no extenuation of the breach that her votes were cast for two of the three candidates directed by the arbitrator. His directions to her were part of a single plan or course of action for the voting of the shares of both parties to the agreement, calculated to utilize an advantage of joint action by them which would bring about the election of an additional director. The actual voting of Mrs. Haley's shares frustrates that plan to such an extent that it should not be treated as a partial performance of her contract.

Throughout their argument, defendants make much of the fact that all votes cast at the meeting were by the registered shareholders. The Court of

Chancery may, in a review of an election, reject votes of a registered shareholder where his voting of them is found to be in violation of rights of another person. Compare: In re Giant Portland Cement Co., Del.Ch., 21 A.2d 697. It seems to us that upon the application of Mrs. Ringling, the injured party, the votes representing Mrs. Haley's shares should not be counted. Since no infirmity in Mr. North's voting has been demonstrated, his right to recognition of what he did at the meeting should be considered in granting any relief to Mrs. Ringling; for her rights arose under a contract to which Mr. North was not a party. With this in mind, we have concluded that the election should not be declared invalid, but that effect should be given to a rejection of the votes representing Mrs. Haley's shares. No other relief seems appropriate in this proceeding. Mr. North's vote against the motion for adjournment was sufficient to defeat it. With respect to the election of directors, the return of the inspectors should be corrected to show a rejection of Mrs. Haley's votes, and to declare the election of the six persons for whom Mr. North and Mrs. Ringling voted.

This leaves one vacancy in the directorate. The question of what to do about such a vacancy was not considered by the court below and has not been argued here. For this reason, and because an election of directors at the 1947 annual meeting (which presumably will be held in the near future) may make a determination of the question unimportant, we shall not decide it on this appeal. If a decision of the point appears important to the parties, any of them may apply to raise it in the Court of Chancery, after the mandate of this court is received there.

An order should be entered, directing a modification of the order of the Court of Chancery in accordance with this opinion.

Notes

(1) Robert B. Thompson, Teaching Business Associations: Norms, Economics and Cognitive Learning, 34 Ga.L.Rev. 997, 998–99 (2000), describes the background of this famous case:

> John Ringling, the most flamboyant of five Ringling brothers, had sent the circus spiraling toward disaster by borrowing to purchase a competitor who had secured the traditional opening dates of the season at the old Madison Square Garden. The purchase unfortunately occurred on the cusp of what became the Great Depression. The ensuing financial debacle left the banks with significant control over the circus, much to the consternation of the family. It took a wonder-kid from the next generation, John Ringling North, to regain family control. His arrogance as savior, however, offended the two women who had inherited the remaining two-thirds of the stock of the circus following the death of all the members of the founding generation.

> These two controlling shareholders are the parties to [the] agreement at issue, and they worked in harmony for a short time to exclude North. It was the Great Hartford Circus Fire of 1944 that undid their alliance. The husband of one, who happened to be on the scene at the time of the fire, went to jail. The son of the other, who happened to be away at the time of the tragedy did not and apparently showed little sympathy for the plight of his co-venturer. John Ringling North saw his opening and went to join on visiting day. The

result was a defection of one shareholder, which led to the question about the agreement's enforceability.

(2) See also President and Fellows of Harvard Coll. v. Glancy, 2003 WL 21026784 (Del.Ch. Mar. 21, 2003), upholding claim that voting trustees breached their fiduciary duties to plaintiffs by executing a shareholders agreement that bound the trustees to discriminate against plaintiffs by providing other shareholder groups with representation among the trustees and on the board.

(3) Consider MBCA § 7.31. The Official Comment states that section 7.31(b) "avoids the result reached in the Ringling case." Does it?

NEW YORK—MCKINNEY'S BUS.CORP.LAW

§ 609. Proxies.

(a) Every shareholder entitled to vote at a meeting of shareholders or to express consent or dissent without a meeting may authorize another person or persons to act for him by proxy.

(b) No proxy shall be valid after the expiration of eleven months from the date thereof unless otherwise provided in the proxy. Every proxy shall be revocable at the pleasure of the shareholder executing it, except as otherwise provided in this section.

(c) The authority of the holder of a proxy to act shall not be revoked by the incompetence or death of the shareholder who executed the proxy unless, before the authority is exercised, written notice of an adjudication of such incompetence or of such death is received by the corporate officer responsible for maintaining the list of shareholders.

(d) Except when other provision shall have been made by written agreement between the parties, the record holder of shares which he holds as pledgee or otherwise as security or which belong to another, shall issue to the pledgor or to such owner of such shares, upon demand therefor and payment of necessary expenses thereof, a proxy to vote or take other action thereon.

(e) A shareholder shall not sell his vote or issue a proxy to vote to any person for any sum of money or anything of value, except as authorized in this section and section 620 (Agreements as to voting; provision in certificate of incorporation as to control of directors); provided, however, that this paragraph shall not apply to votes, proxies or consents given by holders of preferred shares in connection with a proxy or consent solicitation made available on identical terms to all holders of shares of the same class or series and remaining open for acceptance for at least twenty business days.

(f) A proxy which is entitled "irrevocable proxy" and which states that it is irrevocable, is irrevocable when it is held by any of the following or a nominee of any of the following:

(1) A pledgee;

(2) A person who has purchased or agreed to purchase the shares;

(3) A creditor or creditors of the corporation who extend or continue credit to the corporation in consideration of the proxy if the proxy states that it was given in consideration of such extension or continuation of credit, the amount thereof, and the name of the person extending or continuing credit;

(4) A person who has contracted to perform services as an officer of the corporation, if a proxy is required by the contract of employment, if the proxy states that it was given in consideration of such contract of employment, the name of the employee and the period of employment contracted for;

(5) A person designated by or under an agreement under paragraph (a) of section 620.

(g) Notwithstanding a provision in a proxy, stating that it is irrevocable, the proxy becomes revocable after the pledge is redeemed, or the debt of the corporation is paid, or the period of employment provided for in the contract of employment has terminated, or the agreement under paragraph (a) of section 620 has terminated; and in a case provided for in subparagraphs (f)(3) or (4), becomes revocable three years after the date of the proxy or at the end of the period, if any, specified therein, whichever period is less, unless the period of irrevocability is renewed from time to time by the execution of a new irrevocable proxy as provided in this section. This paragraph does not affect the duration of a proxy under paragraph (b).

(h) A proxy may be revoked, notwithstanding a provision making it irrevocable, by a purchaser of shares without knowledge of the existence of the provision unless the existence of the proxy and its irrevocability is noted conspicuously on the face or back of the certificate representing such shares.

(i) Without limiting the manner in which a shareholder may authorize another person or persons to act for him as proxy pursuant to paragraph (a) of this section, the following shall constitute a valid means by which a shareholder may grant such authority.

(1) A shareholder may execute a writing authorizing another person or persons to act for him as proxy. Execution may be accomplished by the shareholder or the shareholder's authorized officer, director, employee or agent signing such writing or causing his or her signature to be affixed to such writing by any reasonable means including, but not limited to, by facsimile signature.

(2) A shareholder may authorize another person or persons to act for the shareholder as proxy by transmitting or authorizing the transmission of a telegram, cablegram or other means of electronic transmission to the person who will be the holder of the proxy or to a proxy solicitation firm, proxy support service organization or like agent duly authorized by the person who will be the holder of the proxy to receive such transmission, provided that any such telegram, cablegram or other means of electronic transmission must either set forth or be submitted with information from which it can be reasonably determined that the telegram, cablegram or other electronic transmission was authorized by the shareholder. If it is determined that telegrams, cablegrams, or other electronic transmissions are valid, the inspectors or, if there are no inspectors, such other persons making that determination shall specify the nature of the information on which they relied.

(j) Any copy, facsimile telecommunication or other reliable reproduction of the writing or transmission created pursuant to paragraph (i) of this section may be substituted or used in lieu of the original writing or transmission for any and all purposes for which the original writing or transmission could be used, provided that such copy, facsimile telecommunication or other reproduction shall be a complete reproduction of the entire original writing or transmission.

NEW YORK—MCKINNEY'S BUS.CORP.LAW

§ 620. Agreements as to Voting; Provision in Certificate of Incorporation as to Control of Directors

(a) An agreement between two or more shareholders, if in writing and signed by the parties thereto, may provide that in exercising any voting rights, the shares held by them shall be voted as therein provided, or as they may agree, or as determined in accordance with a procedure agreed upon by them. * * *

Notes

(1) A proxy appointment, like other grants of authority to an agent, is usually revocable whether or not it is stated to be irrevocable. Several situations exist, however, where the common law courts felt it necessary to recognize irrevocable proxies. These situations were usually analyzed as those involving a "proxy coupled with an interest," a notion roughly analogous to a "power coupled with an interest" in the law of agency. The leading case is Hunt v. Rousmanier's Adm'rs, 21 U.S. (8 Wheat.) 174, 5 L.Ed. 589 (1823). Of course, the phrase "proxy coupled with an interest" does not help to decide anything, and at common law the whole area was one of confusion. See Proctor L. Thomas, Irrevocable Proxies, 43 Tex.L.Rev. 733 (1965). In New York, the vagueness of this test is eliminated by § 609(f), which covers the most common kinds of "interests" that a proxy may be "coupled" with, thereby becoming irrevocable. Compare the language of MBCA § 7.22(d) with § 609 of the New York statute in this regard.

(2) In Haft v. Haft, 671 A.2d 413, 421–23 (Del.Ch.1995), Chancellor Allen held that an irrevocable proxy granted to the chief executive officer of the corporation was enforceable because of the CEO's interest in the corporation:

> No Delaware court has been required to address this question under the language of amended Section 212. In now doing so, it is appropriate to acknowledge that the corporate law has tended to distrust and discourage the separation of the shareholder claim as equity investor (i.e., the right to enjoy distributions on stock if, as, and when declared) from the right to vote stock. For example, there was for many years a rather clear rule against the sale of a corporate vote unattached to the sale of the underlying stock. A powerful argument can be advanced that generally the congruence of the right to vote and the residual rights of ownership will tend towards efficient wealth production.
>
> A proxy is, of course, a means temporarily to split the power to vote from the residual ownership claim of the stockholder. In the vast number of instances in which proxies to vote stock are used, however, this split occasions no significant divergence between the interests of the proxy holder and the holder of the residual corporate interest because the proxy is of relatively short duration and in all events is revocable unilaterally. Thus, in effect, the grant of the proxy represented a judgment (which may be enforced through revocation) that the holder of the proxy will exercise it in the economic

interest of the residual owner. A potentially inefficient split between the interests of the voter and the interests of the residual owners may, however, develop when the proxy is irrevocable. Such a holder is free from the unilateral control of the grantor and may be expected to be inclined to exercise voting rights in a way that benefits himself. There is of course, as a general matter, nothing legally suspect in contracting parties exercising contracted-for rights in a self-interested manner.[10] Yet the exercise of voting control over corporations by persons whose interest in them is not chiefly or solely as a residual owner will create circumstances in which the corporation will be less than optimally efficient in the selection of risky investment projects. (A simple, if gross, example: the holder of an irrevocable proxy with voting control might simply refuse to elect a board that will accept the best investment projects (those with the highest risk adjusted rate of return) unless some side payment to him is arranged). The special additional costs associated with such a divorce between ownership and voting (the costs being expressed either as an otherwise unnecessary expense or as the selection of non-optimizing investment projects) will of course tend to diminish as the voter's interest becomes aligned with the residual owner's interest.

In this light, the dicta of In re Chilson may be thought to offer a means of limiting the agency costs that irrevocable proxies occasion. By recognizing only an interest in the stock itself as an interest that will support the irrevocability of a proxy, the rule of *Chilson* would eliminate a class of cases in which the incentives of the proxy holder to exploit the corporation would be greatest, that is, those in which she simply has no economic interest at all in the residual equity of the firm. Of course the Chilson rule does not entirely eliminate the inefficient incentive structure that the divorce of voting power and benefit occasions; the proxy voter/secured lender still is a creditor and thus may not be inclined to accept high-risk/high-reward projects, even if they have a positive risk-adjusted net present value. But the Chilson rule would moderate the effect. * * *

In this instance, I confess to the view that a corporation law rule allowing for the specific enforceability of an irrevocable proxy that is coupled only with the holder's interest in maintaining a salaried office seems mischievous in terms of its possible efficiency effects. But in light of the 1967 amendment to the Delaware statutory law * * * and the absence of contrary precedent, I am required to express the opinion that such an interest—the interest that Herbert Haft had and retains as the senior executive officer of Dart—is sufficient under our law to render specifically enforceable the express contract for an irrevocable proxy. * * *

(3) Consider § 609(e) of the New York statute, a provision that has no analogue in the MBCA. In Schreiber v. Carney, 447 A.2d 17 (Del.Ch.1982), the Court was faced with a situation where a major shareholder committed itself to withdraw its opposition to a merger in exchange for a favorable loan from a participant in the merger. There was full disclosure of the arrangement to the

---

10. [By the Chancellor] I note that this statement is subject to qualification in at least three circumstances: (1) a contract between a fiduciary and the person or entity for whom she acts (the "trust" or "corporation" etc.); (2) a contract between a fiduciary and a person who is an express beneficiary of the "trust" etc., if the contract relates to the business of the "trust" and (3) an implied obligation of good faith and fair dealing, which under certain circumstances will be found to impose a limitation on a arm's-length contracting party's ability to exercise legal rights in a way that deprives the other contracting party of the substance of the express bargain that the parties had reached.

independent shareholders, who overwhelmingly approved the proposed transaction. The Court stated:

> It is clear that the loan constituted vote-buying as that term has been defined by the courts. Vote-buying, despite its negative connotation, is simply a voting agreement supported by consideration personal to the stockholder, whereby the stockholder divorces his discretionary voting power and votes as directed by the offeror. The record clearly indicates that Texas International purchased or "removed" the obstacle of Jet Capital's opposition. Indeed, this is tacitly conceded by the defendants. However, defendants contend that the analysis of the transaction should not end here because the legality of vote-buying depends on whether its object or purpose is to defraud or in some manner disenfranchise the other stockholders. Defendants contend that because the loan did not defraud or disfranchise any group of shareholders, but rather enfranchised the other shareholders by giving them a determinative vote in the proposed merger, it is not illegal *per se*. Defendants, in effect, contend that vote-buying is not void *per se* because the end justified the means. * * *

> The present case presents a peculiar factual setting in that the proposed vote-buying consideration was conditional upon the approval of a majority of the disinterested stockholders after a full disclosure to them of all pertinent facts and was purportedly for the best interests of all Texas International stockholders. * * *

> There are essentially two principles which appear in [the traditional vote-buying] cases. The first is that vote-buying is illegal *per se* if its object or purpose is to defraud or disenfranchise the other stockholders. A fraudulent purpose is as defined at common law, as [sic] a deceit which operates prejudicially upon the property rights of another.

> The second principle which appears in these old cases is that vote-buying is illegal *per se* as a matter of public policy; the reason being that each stockholder should be entitled to rely upon the independent judgment of his fellow stockholders. Thus, the underlying basis for this latter principle is again fraud but as viewed from a sense of duty owed by all stockholders to one another. The apparent rationale is that by requiring each stockholder to exercise his individual judgment as to all matters presented, "[t]he security of the small stockholders is found in the natural disposition of each stockholder to promote the best interests of all, in order to promote his individual interests." Cone v. Russell, 48 N.J.Eq. 208, 21 A. 847, 849 (1891). In essence, while self interest motivates a stockholder's vote, theoretically, it is also advancing the interests of the other stockholders. Thus, any agreement entered into for personal gain, whereby a stockholder separates his voting right from his property right was considered a fraud upon this community of interests. * * *

> An automatic application of this rationale to the facts in the present case, however, would be to ignore an essential element of the transaction. The agreement in question was entered into primarily to further the interests of Texas International's other shareholders. Indeed, the shareholders, after reviewing a detailed proxy statement, voted overwhelmingly in favor of the loan agreement. Thus, the underlying rationale for the argument that vote-buying is illegal *per se,* as a matter of public policy, ceases to exist when measured against the undisputed reason for the transaction.

Moreover, the rationale that vote-buying is, as a matter of public policy, illegal *per se* is founded upon considerations of policy which are now outmoded as a necessary result of an evolving corporate environment. * * *

This is not to say, however, that vote-buying accomplished for some laudable purpose is automatically free from challenge. Because vote-buying is so easily susceptible of abuse it must be viewed as a voidable transaction subject to a test for intrinsic fairness.

447 A.2d at 23–26. The Court refused to grant summary judgment invalidating the transaction on the ground that it constituted vote-buying.

(4) For an argument sharply criticizing Delaware's liberal rules regarding corporate vote-buying, and arguing that vote buying problems are likely to increase as more corporations utilize the internet and other advances in electronic communications technology, see Douglas Cole, E–Proxies for Sale? Corporate Vote–Buying in the Internet Age, 76 Wash. L. Rev. 793 (2001). The Delaware courts appear to have significantly liberalized the rules regarding vote-buying even beyond the holding in Schreiber v. Carney where the Court declared that vote-buying was no longer illegal per-se. Hewlett v. Hewlett–Packard Company, 2002 WL 818091 (Del.Ch. Apr. 30, 2002) arose out of the hotly contested shareholder vote on the proposed merger of Hewlett Packard Company and Compaq Computer Corporation, which, before their merger, were the second and third largest computer companies in the United States. Walter B. Hewlett opposed the merger and waged a vigorous proxy contest to defeat it. Nine days after the vote in which Hewlett–Packard's shareholders apparently had approved the merger, Walter Hewlett and a group of other merger opponents filed a lawsuit seeking a declaration that the merger was invalid because it had not been validly approved by the shareholders. One of the plaintiffs' principal claims was that Hewlett–Packard had illegally bought the votes of Deutsche Bank (which voted 17 million shares in favor of the merger) since Hewlett–Packard gave the bank a significant amount of new business when it added Deutsch Bank as a co-manager. Prior to this transaction, the proxy committee of Deutsch Bank's Asset Management Division had decided to vote against the merger. Immediately after the new arrangement was implemented, Deutsch Bank switched its votes in favor of the merger.

In upholding this vote-buying arrangement, the Delaware Court of Chancery stated that the appropriate standard for evaluating vote-buying claims is the one articulated in Schreiber v. Carney: vote-buying is illegal *per se* if "the object or purpose is to defraud or in some way disenfranchise the other shareholders." The court also stated that "because vote-buying is so easily susceptible of abuse it must be viewed as a voidable transaction subject to a test for intrinsic fairness." In *Hewlett* however, the court noted that this proposition "seems difficult to reconcile" with the Delaware legislature's "explicit validation of shareholder agreements." It distinguished *Schreiber* on the ground that it was the management of the defendant corporation that was buying votes in favor of a corporation in Schreiber. The court distinguished situations in which management buys votes and situations in which shareholders buy votes, stating that "[s]hareholders are free to do whatever they want with their votes, including selling them to the highest bidder." Management on the other hand, "may not use corporate assets to buy votes in a hotly contested proxy contest about an extraordinary transaction that would significantly transform the corporation unless it can be demonstrated, as it was in *Schreiber*, that management's vote-buying activity does not have a deleterious effect on the corporate franchise."

The court then denied Hewlett–Packard's motion to dismiss the plaintiffs' vote-buying claims because it found that the plaintiffs successfully alleged that HP bought votes from Deutsche Bank with corporate assets, and because no steps were taken to ensure that the shareholder franchise was protected. However, the court stated that, at trial, the plaintiffs would bear the burden of presenting sufficient evidence to support a finding that Deutsche Bank was coerced by Hewlett–Packard management, and that the decision of Deutsch Bank to switch its votes was not made by Deutsch Bank for other than independent business reasons.

(5) Del.Gen.Corp.Law § 228 permits action by shareholders without a meeting if written consent, setting forth the action taken "shall be signed by the holders of outstanding stock having not less than the minimum number of votes that would be necessary to authorize or take such action at a meeting at which all shares entitled to vote thereon were present and voted." Contrast MBCA § 7.04. Not so for § 228 of the Delaware statute, which allows decisions by majority action to be effected in publicly held corporations without holding a meeting. Through this device, an aggressor who is able to obtain a majority of the outstanding voting shares may act immediately to replace the board of directors, oust incumbent management, amend bylaws, and defuse anti-takeover defenses. As noted by the Delaware Supreme Court, the "broad use [of § 228] in takeover battles, which we now observe, was not contemplated" in 1967 when this section was added to the Delaware General Corporation Law. Allen v. Prime Computer, Inc., 540 A.2d 417, 419 (Del.1988).

(6) Should consents be subject to the same rules of revocability as an ordinary proxy? Or should consents be deemed to be "self executing" so that once a majority has executed consents, the corporation has irrevocably acted? Or should they be analogized to voting agreements which are not revocable because they constitute contracts? In Calumet Indus., Inc. v. MacClure, 464 F.Supp. 19 (N.D.Ill. 1978), the Court accepted the proxy analogy, a view that was also accepted in dictum in Allen v. Prime Computer, Inc., supra. See also Pabst Brewing Co. v. Jacobs, 549 F.Supp. 1068 (D.Del.1982). Accepting that result, how long should a consent remain effective? In 1987, the Delaware legislature amended § 228 by adding a new subsection (c) that requires all consents to be dated and provides that consents are effective only if they are received within 60 days after the first dated consent is delivered to the corporation.

(7) Effective July 1, 2000, Delaware amended its General Corporation Law to permit "electronic-only" meetings at a web site and there was no physical place of meeting at all. Del. G.C.L. § 211(a)(2). At such a "meeting," shareholders may use remote communication to participate and "be deemed present in person and vote at a meeting of stockholders whether such meeting is to be held at a designated place or solely by means of remote communication." Voting by electronic transmission is authorized if information is submitted "from which it can be determined that the electronic transmission was authorized by stockholder or proxy holder." Id, § 211(e). Delaware also amended its GCL in several other significant respects in 2000 to recognize modern technology. It authorized written shareholder consents to be delivered electronically so long as the e-mail or telecopy was printed out before it is delivered. Electronic notice to stockholders is permitted if the stockholder has consented to delivery of notice in that form. Notices delivered to stockholders by telecopy or e-mail are deemed given when "directed" to the proper phone number or e-mail address. Director action by unanimous consent and directors' resignations also may be made by electronic transmission. Consideration was also given to permitting meetings of directors by remote communica-

tion, but it was felt that current practice of holding meetings by telephone conference call provided sufficient flexibility.

BROWN v. McLANAHAN

United States Court of Appeals, Fourth Circuit, 1945.
148 F.2d 703.

Before Parker, Soper, and Dobie, Circuit Judges.

Dobie, Circuit Judge.

This appeal from an order granting a motion to dismiss, involves the equitable rights attaching to certain voting trust certificates representing shares of preferred stock of the Baltimore Transit Company (hereinafter called the Company).

The appellant, Dorothy K. Brown (hereinafter referred to as plaintiff), as the holder of voting trust certificates representing 500 shares of the preferred stock of the Company, brought a class action against the voting trustees, the directors of the Company, the Company itself, the indenture trustee for the holders of the Company's debentures, and the debenture holders as a class (herein collectively referred to as defendants), seeking to set aside as unlawful an amendment of the Company's charter which purports to vest voting rights in the debenture holders. On oral argument before this Court, it was stated that the holders of 45,000 shares of preferred stock have indicated their approval of this suit.

The securities involved in this litigation were issued under a plan of reorganization of the United Railways and Electric Company of Baltimore, and The Maryland Electric Railways Company and Subsidiary Companies, under Section 77B of the Bankruptcy Act, 11 U.S.C.A. § 207. The plan was approved by the United States District Court for the District of Maryland. In re United Railways & Electric Co. of Baltimore's Reorganization, 11 F.Supp. 717.

That part of the reorganization plan relevant to the question before us may be briefly summarized.

The plan provided for the issuance of three types of securities. Debentures in the amount of $22,083,381 and 233,427 shares of preferred stock were issued to the holders of all first lien bonds on the basis of $500 principal amount of debentures, and five shares of preferred stock, par value $100 per share for each $1,000 principal amount of the bonds; 169,112 shares of new common stock, without par value, were issued to the old common stockholders and to unsecured creditors.

Under the plan of reorganization, voting rights were vested exclusively in the preferred and common stock. Each share of preferred entitled the holder to one vote on all corporate matters (except that the power to elect one director was exclusively vested in the common stock) and further, so long as any six months' installment of dividends on the preferred remained in arrears, the holders of the preferred stock held the *exclusive right* to vote for the election of all but one director. Three shares of common stock entitled the holder to one vote.

The plan also provided for the establishment of a voting trust of all the preferred and common stock of the reorganized company for a period of ten years, the maximum period permitted by Maryland law. In accordance with this provision, all the stock was issued to eight voting trustees under a voting trust agreement which was to terminate on July 1, 1945. The trustees in turn issued voting trust certificates to those entitled to distribution under the plan. Under the plan, the voting rights were to revert, on termination of the trust, to the certificate holders in proportion to the number of shares represented.

No dividends have ever been paid on the preferred stock, and pursuant to the charter provision, at all times since dividends have been in arrears, the exclusive right to elect all but one director has been vested in the preferred stock.

The eight voting trustees are also a majority of the directors of the Company, elected as such by their own vote as trustees. On June 21, 1944, *without notice of any kind to the certificate holders,* the directors passed a resolution recommending, and the voting trustees as stockholders voted to adopt, an amendment to the Company's charter.

Article VII of the Voting Trust Agreement, by authority of which the trustees purportedly acted, provides in part as follows:

(1) Until the termination of the trusts of this instrument the entire right to vote upon or with respect to all shares of Preferred and/or Common Stock deposited, or at any time held hereunder, and the right to otherwise authorize, approve or oppose on behalf of said shares of stock any corporate action of The Baltimore Transit Company shall be vested exclusively in said Trustees; without limiting the generality or scope of the foregoing provisions such rights shall include the right to vote or act with respect to any amendment of the certificate of incorporation of the Company, the increase, reduction, classification, reclassification of its capital stock, change in the par value, preference and restrictions and qualifications of all shares, the creation of any debts or liens, any amendment to the By–Laws, the election or removal of directors, the acceptance of stock in payment of dividends as well as every other right of an absolute owner of said shares * * *

Briefly, the amendment effected several changes in voting rights. It eliminated the arrearage clause which had provided for exclusive voting rights in the preferred stock. It also granted voting rights to the holders of debentures, one vote for each $100 principal amount of the debentures, thus creating approximately 221,000 new votes eligible to be cast in all corporate matters. And, further, as of the date of termination of the voting trust agreement on July 1, 1945, the common stockholders would be deprived of their exclusive right to elect one director.

These facts are all substantially set forth in plaintiff's complaint. The complaint alleges, and for purposes of the motion to dismiss these allegations must be accepted as true, that the creation of 221,000 new votes in the debentures will dilute the voting power of the stock; that the amendment will deprive the voting trust certificate holders of their right to control the management of the Company, and the election of its directors after the expiration of the voting trust; that these voting trustees are holders of substantial amounts of debentures, either in their own right, or as officers of various banks.

Plaintiff contends that the action of the voting trustees in adopting the amendment was a breach of the fiduciary duty owed to the certificate holders and seeks fourfold relief that: (1) The amendment of June 21, 1944, be declared null and void; (2) the voting trustees be removed; (3) the voting trust be terminated; and (4) damages be allowed in the alternative.

The crux of the complaint is that the voting trustees, faced with the fact that the voting trust would shortly expire and that they would no longer be able to control the corporation, proceeded to amend its charter so that they would be able to hold on to the control by giving voting rights to the debentures (thereby enhancing the value of these debentures) which were largely owned or controlled by them or by corporations in which they were interested and to take away from the preferred stock the power of control which resided in it when dividends were in arrears. * * *

Plaintiff contends that such action on the part of the trustees was invalid for three reasons: (1) Because it was beyond the powers vested in the trustees to diminish the voting power, which they held in trust for the holders of preferred stock as well as for other stockholders and debenture holders, so that upon the termination of the trust they would not be able to return it to those from whom they had received it in the same condition in which it was received; (2) because it was an abuse of trust to use the voting power which the trustees held in trust for the benefit of preferred stockholders as well as of the debenture holders to the advantage of the latter and the detriment of the former; and (3) that it was an abuse of trust to use the voting power for their own benefit and the benefit of corporations in which they were interested and to the detriment of preferred stockholders who were beneficiaries of the trust. We think the action of the trustees was invalid for all three reasons. As to the third reason, it could well be that the evidence at the trial may show the facts to be different from the facts as alleged. There seems to be no dispute as to the facts to which the first and second reasons apply.

As to the first and second reasons, we think it perfectly clear that it was not intended by the voting trust agreement to vest the trustees with power either to impair the voting power of the preferred stock which they held in trust or to use the power for the benefit of the debenture holders and to the detriment of the holders of preferred stock. It is true that the power to amend the charter for proper purposes was conferred upon them; but at the time of the creation of the voting trust it was not permissible under the law to vest voting power in the debenture holders. An amendment of the law made it legal to do this; but it could not have been intended at the time of the creation of the voting trust that the trustees should exercise the voting power in a way which the law did not then recognize and which would result in taking from the holders of stock a part of the very power which they had conferred upon the trustees to be held in trust for their benefit. It is elementary that a trustee may not exercise powers granted in a way that is detrimental to the *cestuis que trustent*; nor may one who is trustee for different classes favor one class at the expense of another. Such an exercise of power is in derogation of the trust and may not be upheld, even though the thing done be within the scope of powers granted to the trustees in general terms. It is well settled that the depositaries of the power to vote stock are trustees in the equitable sense, Henry L. Doherty & Co. v. Rice, C.C., 186 F. 204, 214, and a voting trust is a trust in the accepted equitable view. * * *

Defendants strongly urge that the real beneficiaries here and now are the debenture holders and not the certificate holders. Such cases as Mackin v. Nicollet Hotel, 8 Cir., 25 F.2d 783, and Clark v. Foster, 98 Wash. 241, 167 P. 908, are cited for the proposition that it is the existence of a voting trust, in many cases restricting the powers of the stockholder, that attracts lending by bondholders. Assuming the correctness of this contention, we still find no such situation here. This plan of reorganization was an attempt to salvage utility companies sinking in the quagmire of bankruptcy. These debenture holders accepted, in lieu of their old obligations, two kinds of property, ownership of the company and a creditor's lien. Ownership control, for purposes of judicious management, was placed in the hands of trustees. When the debenture holders sold their ultimate rights to stock ownership with its attendant control of the Company's affairs, they retained only their creditor's lien. We are not at liberty here to distort the established rules of property and to find that by some process of corporate alchemy the legal ownership of the Company has been transmuted into evidence of debt.

The sale of the voting trust certificates by the original holders vested all equitable rights in their transferees and we cannot say that one might sell the equitable rights in preferred stock to a bona fide purchaser, and subsequently by indirection, impair or destroy the inherent equitable property in those certificates, to the benefit of the original seller. Meinhard v. Salmon, 249 N.Y. 458, 464, 164 N.E. 545, 62 A.L.R. 1. * * *

We are of the opinion, and so hold, that the action taken by these trustees was beyond the limit of their authority. The motion to dismiss should therefore have been denied.

The judgment of the District Court will be reversed and the cause remanded for further proceedings in accordance with the views herein expressed. The amendment to the charter of June 21, 1944 should be declared void, but what further relief should be granted upon the complaint is a matter resting in the sound discretion of the District Court.

Reversed and remanded.

Notes

(1) Consider MBCA § 7.30. An earlier version of the Delaware voting trust statute, Del.Gen.Corp.Law § 218 is set forth in *Ringling Bros.*, page 457, supra. It is important to recognize that the procedural requirements with respect to the creation of a voting trust—particularly the filing of a copy of the voting trust agreement with the corporation—is essential for its validity. This rule is a reflection of the fact that the early attitude of courts to voting trusts was unfavorable, and mistrust may still continue to some extent in some states. The comment of Mr. Justice Douglas (in a nonjudicial context) that a voting trust is "little more than a vehicle for corporate kidnapping," William O. Douglas, Democracy and Finance 43 (1940), is a clear reflection of this early attitude. The Securities and Exchange Commission has historically opposed the use of voting trusts, and the New York Stock Exchange refuses to list voting stock where there

exists "a voting trust, irrevocable proxy, or any similar arrangement to which the company or any of its officers or directors is a party, either directly or indirectly."

(2) There has been some recognition that a voting trust should be viewed as simply another control mechanism that may in certain situations be the subject of abuse but generally is no more subject to criticism than other control devices. This perspective is most clearly set forth in Oceanic Exploration Co. v. Grynberg, 428 A.2d 1, 7–8 (Del.1981). Most voting trust statutes, like § 7.30 of the MBCA, mandate a ten year life span for voting trusts. Compare this section with § 7.31, which has no maximum period for the existence of a voting agreement. In 1994, Delaware amended its voting trust statute to eliminate the 10–year provision, perhaps a further recognition that the early attitude towards voting trusts was misplaced.

(3) If creditors do not trust a dominant shareholder, they may insist that controlling shares be placed in a voting trust as a condition to the extension of credit. The most spectacular illustration of this was the voting trust in which creditors of Trans World Airlines, Inc. required Howard Hughes to place his 75 percent of TWA stock in 1966 as a condition to making loans of over $80 million to finance the purchase of jumbo jets by TWA. After the trust was created, Hughes had no voice in TWA management, and that corporation brought suit against Hughes Tool Company and Hughes individually for damages under the antitrust laws for conduct occurring prior to the creation of the voting trust. Who was the *cestui* of that voting trust under Brown v. McLanahan? Hughes later agreed to sell the shares of TWA in the voting trust, and this sale took place when TWA was near its historic high in price. Mr. Hughes received a check for over $550,000,000 from this sale. See John McDonald, Howard Hughes's Biggest Surprise, Fortune, July 1, 1966, at 119–20. Despite the sale, the antitrust suit continued. Major stopping points include Trans World Airlines, Inc. v. Hughes, 332 F.2d 602 (2d Cir.1964), cert. dismissed as improvidently granted 380 U.S. 248, 85 S.Ct. 934, 13 L.Ed.2d 817 (1965), upholding the entry of a default judgment for the refusal of Hughes Tool Company to submit to discovery and, particularly, the refusal of Howard Hughes to submit to a deposition, and Trans World Airlines, Inc. v. Hughes, 449 F.2d 51 (2d Cir.1971) affirming a judgment against Hughes for $137,611,435.95 and the ultimate reversal of the case by the United States Supreme Court on a ground that had been repeatedly argued but never accepted during approximately 10 years of litigation. Hughes Tool Co. v. Trans World Airlines, Inc., 409 U.S. 363, 93 S.Ct. 647, 34 L.Ed.2d 577 (1973), rehearing denied 410 U.S. 975, 93 S.Ct. 1435, 35 L.Ed.2d 707 (1973).

(4) Regulatory agencies may insist that voting control of a regulated corporation be placed in a voting trust as a condition for permitting private parties to acquire the regulated corporation or, more commonly, the parent corporation of a regulated corporation when the corporation is a relatively small portion of the parent's business. For example, § 102(a) of the Interstate Transportation Act, 49 U.S.C.A. § 11323(a), provides that certain acquisitions of rail carriers may only be carried out with the approval and authorization of the Surface Transportation Board. For an example of the use of the voting trust under a predecessor section, see Chicago West Pullman Corporation and Chicago West Pullman Transportation Corporation, Finance Docket No. 31390, 1989 WL 237934 (I.C.C. Feb. 21, 1989). The Federal Communications Commission follows a somewhat similar practice with respect to transfers of holders of radio or television licenses. Some state insurance commissions permit transfers of control of regulated insurance companies if the shares are placed in an irrevocable voting trust with acceptable trustees.

(5) In Hall v. Staha, 303 Ark. 673, 800 S.W.2d 396 (1990), Hatfield and Staha formed a Delaware limited partnership, MED–MAX Associates Limited Partnership, and transferred their stock in Dunhall Pharmaceuticals, Inc., a profitable seller of pharmaceuticals, to the limited partnership. The limited partnership also obtained Dunhall shares from a number of other shareholders in exchange for limited partnership interests; Hatfield and Staha also exchanged some shares owned by other persons for limited partnership interests. MED–MAX ultimately acquired 50.5 percent of the Dunhall stock. While Hatfield and Staha were the general partners, there was no disclosure of the identity of the limited partners. The Court held that MED–MAX was an illegal voting trust since it was a "secret, uncontrolled, combination of stockholders formed to acquire voting control of a corporation to the possible detriment of the nonparticipating stockholders." 800 S.W.2d at 402. The votes cast by MED–MAX at a shareholders' meeting were invalidated. Is there any reason why a limited partnership cannot be a voting trust?

LEHRMAN v. COHEN

Supreme Court of Delaware, 1966.
43 Del.Ch. 222, 222 A.2d 800.

HERRMANN, JUSTICE.

The primary problem presented on this appeal involves the applicability of the Delaware Voting Trust Statute. Other questions involve the legality of stock having voting power but no dividend or liquidation rights except repayment of par value, and an alleged unlawful delegation of directorial duties and powers.

These are the material facts:

Giant Food Inc. (hereinafter the "Company") was incorporated in Delaware in 1935 by the defendant N.M. Cohen and Samuel Lehrman, deceased father of the plaintiff Jacob Lehrman. From its inception, the Company was controlled by the Cohen and Lehrman families, each of which owned equal quantities of the voting stock, designated Class AC (held by the Cohen family) and Class AL (held by the Lehrman family) common stock. The two classes of stock have cumulative voting rights and each is entitled to elect two members of the Company's four-member board of directors.

Over the years, as may have been expected, there were differences of opinion between the Cohen and Lehrman families as to operating policies of the Company. Samuel Lehrman died in 1949; each of his children inherited part of his stock in the Company; but a dispute arose among the children regarding an *inter vivos* gift of certain shares made to the plaintiff by his father shortly before his death. To eliminate the Lehrman family dispute and its possible disruption of the affairs of the Company, an arrangement was made which settled the dispute and permitted the plaintiff to acquire all of the outstanding Class AL stock, thereby vesting in him voting power equal to that held by the Cohen family. The arrangement involved repurchase by the Company of the stock held by the plaintiff's brothers and sister, their relinquishment of any claim to the stock gift, and an equalizing surrender of certain stock by the Cohens to the Company for retirement. An essential part of the arrangement, upon the insistence of the Cohens, was the establishment of a fifth directorship to obviate the risk of deadlock which would have continued if the equal division of voting power between AL and AC stock were continued.

To implement the arrangement, on December 31, 1949, the Company's certificate of incorporation was amended, *inter alia,* to create a third class of voting stock, designated Class AD common stock, entitled to elect the fifth director. Article Fourth of the amendment to the certificate of incorporation provided for the issuance of one share of Class AD stock, having a par value of $10 and the following rights and powers:

> The holder of Class AD common stock shall be entitled to all of the rights and privileges pertaining to common stock without any limitations, prohibitions, restrictions or qualifications except that the holder of said Class AD stock shall not be entitled to receive any dividends declared and paid by the corporation, shall not be entitled to share in the distribution of assets of the corporation upon liquidation or dissolution either partial or final, except to the extent of the par value of said Class AD common stock, and in the election of Directors shall have the right to vote for and elect one of the five Directors hereinafter provided for.

> The corporation shall have the right, at any time, to redeem and call in the Class AD stock by paying to the holder thereof the par value of said stock, provided however, that such redemption or call shall be authorized and directed by the affirmative vote of four of the five Directors hereinafter provided for.[11]

By resolution of the board of directors, the share of Class AD stock was issued forthwith to the defendant Joseph B. Danzansky, who had served as counsel to the Company since 1944. All corporate action regarding the creation and the issuance of the Class AD stock was accomplished by the unanimous vote of the AC and AL stockholders and of the board of directors. In April 1950, pursuant to the arrangement, Danzansky voted his share of AD stock to elect himself as the Company's fifth director; and he served as such until the institution of this action in 1964. During that entire period, the AC and AL stock have been voted to elect two directors each. From 1950 through 1964, Danzansky regularly attended board meetings, raised and discussed general items of business, and voted on all issues as they came before the board. He was not obliged to break any deadlock among the directors prior to October 1, 1964 because no such deadlock arose before that date.

Beginning in December 1959, 200,000 shares of non-voting common stock of the Company were sold in a public issue for over $3,000,000. Each prospectus published in connection with the public issue contained the following statement:

> Common Stock AD is not a participating stock, and the only purpose for the provision and issuance of such stock is to prevent a deadlock in case the Directors elected by the Common Stock AC and the Directors elected by the Common Stock AL cannot reach an agreement.

11. [By the Court] Article Fourth of the amendment also co-related the Class AL and the Class AC common stock as follows:

"The holders of Class AL common stock shall be entitled to all of the rights and privileges pertaining to common stock without any limitations, prohibitions, restrictions, or qualifications except that the holder or holders of said Class AL common stock, in the election of Directors, shall have the right to vote for and elect two of the five Directors hereinafter provided for."

Similarly, a letter on behalf of the Company to the Commissioner of Internal Revenue, dated July 15, 1959, contained the following statement:

As can be seen from the enclosed certified copy of the stock provisions of the certificate of Incorporation, as amended, the Class AD common stock is not a participating stock, the only purpose for the provision and issuance of such a stock being to prevent a deadlock in case the AC and AL Directors cannot reach an agreement.

From the outset and until October 1, 1964, the defendant N.M. Cohen was president of the Company. On that date, a resolution was adopted at the Company's annual stockholders' meeting to give Danzansky a fifteen year executive employment contract at an annual salary of $67,600, and options for 25,000 shares of the non-voting common stock of the Company. The AC and AD stock were voted in favor and the AL stock was voted against the resolution. At a directors meeting held the same day, Danzansky was elected president of the Company by a 3–2 vote, the two AL directors voting in opposition. On December 11, 1964, Danzansky resigned as director and voted his share of AD stock to elect as the fifth director Millard F. West, Jr., a former AL director and investment banker whose firm was one of the underwriters of the public issue of the Company's stock. The newly constituted board ratified the election of Danzansky as president; and, on January 27, 1965, after the commencement of this action and after a review and report by a committee consisting of the new AD director and one AL director, Danzansky's employment contract was approved and adopted with certain modifications.

The plaintiff brought this action on December 11, 1964, basing it upon two claims: The First Claim charges that the creation, issuance, and voting of the one share of Class AD stock resulted in an arrangement illegal under the law of this State for the reasons hereinafter set forth. The Second Claim, addressed to the events of October 1, 1964, charges that the election of Danzansky as president of the Company and his employment contract violated the terms of the 1959 deadlock-breaking arrangement, as made between the holders of the AC and AL stock, and constituted breaches of contract and fiduciary duty. The plaintiff and the defendants filed cross-motions for summary judgment as to the First Claim. The Court of Chancery, after considering the contentions now before us and discussed infra, granted summary judgment in favor of the defendants and denied the plaintiff's motion for summary judgment. The plaintiff appeals.

I.

The plaintiff's primary contention is that the Class AD stock arrangement is, in substance and effect, a voting trust; that, as such, it is illegal because not limited to a ten year period as required by the Voting Trust Statute. The defendants deny that the AD stock arrangement constitutes a disguised voting trust; but they concede that if it is, the arrangement is illegal for violation of the Statute. Thus, issue is clearly joined on the point.

The criteria of a voting trust under our decisions have been summarized by this Court in Abercrombie v. Davies, 36 Del.Ch. 371, 130 A.2d 338 (1957). The tests there set forth, accepted by both sides of this cause as being applicable, are as follows: (1) the voting rights of the stock are separated from the other attributes of ownership; (2) the voting rights granted are intended to be irrevocable for a definite period of time; and (3) the principal purpose[12] of the grant of voting rights is to acquire voting control of the corporation.

Adopting and applying these tests, the plaintiff says, as to the first element, that the AD arrangement provides for a divorcement of voting rights from beneficial ownership of the AC and AL stock; that the creation and issuance of the share of AD stock is tantamount to a pooling by the AC and AL stockholders of a portion of their voting stock and giving it to a trustee, in the person of the AD stockholder, to vote for the election of the fifth director; that after the creation of the AD stock, the AC and AL stockholders each hold but 40% of the voting power, and the AD stockholder holds the controlling balance of 20%; that the AD stock has no property rights except the right to a return of the $10 paid as the par value; and that, therefore, there has been a transfer of the voting rights devoid of any participating property rights. So runs the argument of the plaintiff in support of his contention that the first of the *Abercrombie* criteria for a voting trust is met.

The contention is unacceptable. The AD arrangement did not separate the voting rights of the AC or the AL stock from the other attributes of ownership of those classes of stock. Each AC and AL stockholder retains complete control over the voting of his stock; each can vote his stock directly; no AL or AC stockholder is divested of his right to vote his stock as he sees fit; no AL or AC stock can be voted against the shareholder's wishes; and the AL and AC stock continue to elect two directors each.

The AD stock arrangement, as we view it, became a part of the capitalization of the Company. The fact that there is but a single share, or that the par value is nominal, is of no legal significance; the one share and the $10 par value might have been multiplied many times over, with the same consequence. It is true that the creation of the separate class of AD stock may have diluted the voting *power* which had previously existed in the AC and AL stock—the usual consequence when additional voting stock is created—but the creation of the new class did not divest and separate the voting *rights* which remain vested in each AC and AL shareholder, together with the other attributes of the ownership of that stock. The fallacy of the plaintiff's position lies in his premise that since the voting power of the AC and AL stock was reduced by the creation of the AD stock, the percentage of reduction became the *res* of a voting trust. In any recapitalization involving the creation of additional voting stock, the voting power of the previously existing stock is diminished; but a voting trust is not necessarily the result.

Since the holders of the Class AC and Class AL stock of the Company did not separate the voting rights from the other attributes of ownership of those classes when they created the Class AD stock, the first *Abercrombie* test of a voting trust is not met.

This conclusion disposes of the second and third *Abercrombie* tests * * *.

In the final analysis, the essence of the question raised by the plaintiff in this connection is this: Is the substance and purpose of the AD stock

---

12. [By the Court] It is noteworthy, in this connection, that in Abercrombie, this Court distinguished between purpose and motive, stating that it considered only purpose to be material (130 A.2d 338, 341).

arrangement sufficiently close to the substance and purpose of § 218 to warrant its being subjected to the restrictions and conditions imposed by that Statute? The answer is negative not only for the reasons above stated, but also because § 218 regulates trusts and pooling agreements amounting to trusts, not other and different types of arrangements and undertakings possible among stockholders. Compare Ringling Bros.–Barnum & Bailey Combined Shows Inc. v. Ringling, 29 Del.Ch. 610, 53 A.2d 441 (1947); Abercrombie v. Davies, supra. The AD stock arrangement is neither a trust nor a pooling agreement.

We hold, therefore, that the Class AD stock arrangement is not controlled by the Voting Trust Statute.

II.

The plaintiff's second point is that even if the Class AD stock arrangement is not a voting trust in substance and effect, the AD stock is illegal, nevertheless, because the creation of a class of stock having voting rights only, and lacking any substantial participating proprietary interest in the corporation, violates the public policy of this State as declared in § 218.

The fallacy of this argument is twofold: First, it is more accurate to say that what the law has disfavored, and what the public policy underlying the Voting Trust Statute means to control, is the separation of the vote from the stock—not from the stock ownership. Clearly, the AD stock arrangement is not violative of that public policy. Secondly, there is nothing in § 218, either expressed or implied, which requires that all stock of a Delaware corporation must have both voting rights and proprietary interests. Indeed, public policy to the contrary seems clearly expressed by 8 Del.C. § 151(a) which authorizes, in very broad terms, such voting powers and participating rights as may be stated in the certificate of incorporation. Non-voting stock is specifically authorized by § 151(a); and in the light thereof, consistency does not permit the conclusion, urged by the plaintiff, that the present public policy of this State condemns the separation of voting rights from beneficial stock ownership.

We conclude that the plaintiff's contention in this regard cannot withstand the force and effect of § 151(a). In our view, that Statute permits the creation of stock having voting rights only, as well as stock having property rights only. The voting powers and the participating rights of the Class AD stock being specified in the Company's certificate of incorporation, we are of the opinion that the Class AD stock is legal by virtue of § 151(a). * * *

We are told that if the AD stock arrangement is allowed thus to stand, our Voting Trust Statute will become a "dead letter" because it will be possible to evade and circumvent its purpose simply by issuing a class of non-participating voting stock, as was done here. We have three negative reactions to this argument:

First, it presupposes a divestiture of the voting rights of the AC and AL stock—an untenable supposition as has been stated. Secondly, it fails to take into account the main purpose of a Voting Trust Statute: to avoid secret, uncontrolled combinations of stockholders formed to acquire voting control of the corporation to the possible detriment of non-participating shareholders. It may not be said that the AD stock arrangement contravenes that purpose.

Finally on this point, if we misconceive the legislative intent, and if the AD stock arrangement in this case reveals a loophole in § 218 which should be plugged, it is for the General Assembly to accomplish—not for us to attempt by interstitial judicial legislation.

III.

The plaintiff advances yet another reason for invalidating the AD stock. The essence of this argument is that the only function of that class of stock is to break directorial deadlocks; that the issuance of the AD stock is merely a technical device to permit that result; that, as such, it is illegal because it permits the AC and AL directors of the Company to delegate their statutory duties to the AD director as an arbitrator.

We see nothing inherently wrong or contrary to the public policy of this State, as plaintiff seems to suggest, about a device, otherwise lawful, designed by the stockholders of a corporation to break deadlocks of directors. The plaintiff says in this connection, that if public policy sanctioned such device, our General Corporation Law would provide for it. The fallacy of this argument lies in the assumption that legislative silence is a dependable indicator of public policy. We know of no reason, either under our statutes or our decisions, which would prevent the stockholders of a Delaware corporation from protecting themselves and their corporation, by a plan otherwise lawful, against the paralyzing and often fatal consequences of a stalemate in the directorate of the corporation. We hold, therefore, that the AD stock arrangement had a proper purpose.

As to the means adopted for the accomplishment of that purpose, we find the AD stock arrangement valid by virtue of § 141(a) of the Delaware Corporation Law which provides:

> The business of every corporation organized under the provisions of this chapter shall be managed by a board of directors, except as hereinafter or in its certificate of incorporation otherwise provided.

The AD stock arrangement was created by the unanimous action of the stockholders of the Company by amendment to the certificate of incorporation. The stockholders thereby provided how the business of the corporation is to be managed, as is their privilege and right under § 141(a). It was this stockholder action which delegated to the AD director whatever powers and duties he possesses; they were not delegated to him by his fellow directors, either out of their own powers and duties, or otherwise.

It is settled, of course, as a general principle, that directors may not delegate their duty to manage the corporate enterprise. But there is no conflict with that principle where, as here, the delegation of duty, if any, is made not by the directors but by stockholder action under § 141(a), via the certificate of incorporation.

In our judgment, therefore, the AD stock arrangement is not invalid on the ground that it permits the AC and AL directors of the Company to delegate their statutory duties to the AD director.

On this point, the plaintiff relies mainly upon the Chancery Court decision in Abercrombie v. Davies, 35 Del.Ch. 599, 611, 123 A.2d 893 (1956). There, in considering an agreement requiring all eight directors to submit a disputed question to an arbitrator if seven were unable to agree, the Chancery Court stated that legal sanction may not be accorded to an agreement, at least when made by less than all the stockholders, which takes from the board of directors the power of determining substantial management policy. The plaintiff's reliance is misplaced, because, *inter alia,* the *Abercrombie* arrangement was not created by the certificate of incorporation, within the authority of § 141(a). * * *

Our conclusions upon these questions make it unnecessary to discuss the defendants' contentions that the plaintiff's action is barred by the principles of estoppel, laches, acquiescence and ratification.

Finding no error in the judgment below, it is affirmed.

Notes

(1) What happens (a) if a director misses both a board meeting and a shareholders' meeting, (b) at the missed meetings the corporation's bylaws are amended to permit the issuance of a new class of voting stock with the power to elect a director, and (c) the new stock is issued to an ally of the shareholder who was present at the meetings? Suppose further that these transactions result in a change in control of the corporation? See Schaefer v. Ulinski, 253 Wis.2d 845, 644 N.W.2d 293 (App.2002). In refusing to void the issuance of the new stock, the court stated that the notices of both the board meeting and the shareholders' meeting made specific reference to the proposed actions. The court appears to have been influenced by the fact that the maneuver prevented a deadlock from occurring in the company's board of directors.

(2) Cases support the ability of Delaware corporations to create unusual share voting patterns. For example:

(a) Providence and Worcester Co. v. Baker, 378 A.2d 121 (Del.1977). The corporation's certificate of incorporation provided that a shareholder was entitled to (i) one vote per share for each share he owned up to fifty shares and (ii) one vote for every twenty shares he owned in excess of fifty, but (iii) no shareholder might vote more than one fourth of all the outstanding shares. The Court upheld this voting arrangement under the Delaware statute. These voting restrictions, it should be noted, did not limit the power of persons to cast large numbers of votes by proxy but rather limited the voting power of individual owners of shares. Would this voting arrangement be upheld under the last sentence of MBCA § 6.01(a)?

(b) Williams v. Geier, 671 A.2d 1368 (Del.1996). This case upheld a "tenure voting" plan by a 3–2 vote. Under this plan each share of common stock of Cincinnati Milacron, Inc. on the date the plan was implemented became entitled to 10 votes. However, if a share was sold or transferred thereafter, its voting power was immediately reduced to one vote per share; if the new holder retained the share for three years, it resumed being entitled to 10 votes per share. A family group owned more than 50 percent of Milacron, a publicly held corporation, but only three of the ten directors were associated with the family group. The stated reasons for recommending this plan was to (a) provide current and longer-term shareholders with a greater voice in the company, (b) permit the issuance of additional shares of common stock with minimal dilution of voting rights, and (c) discourage takeovers. Tenure voting clearly benefits a controlling family group in this situation, since it not only discourages takeovers but also deters transfers of shares by individual members of that group.

LING AND CO. v. TRINITY SAV. AND LOAN ASS'N

Supreme Court of Texas, 1972.
482 S.W.2d 841.

REAVLEY, JUSTICE.

Trinity Savings and Loan Association sued Bruce W. Bowman for the balance owed on a promissory note and also to foreclose on a certificate for 1500 shares of Class A Common Stock in Ling & Company, Inc. pledged by Bowman to secure payment of the note. Ling & Company was made a party to the suit by Trinity Savings and Loan because of Ling & Company's insistence that the transfer of its stock was subject to restrictions that were unfulfilled. Bowman did not appear and has not appealed from the judgment against him. The trial court entered summary judgment in favor of Trinity Savings and Loan, against the contentions of Ling & Company, foreclosing the security interest in the stock and ordering it sold. The court of civil appeals affirmed. 470 S.W.2d 441. We reverse the judgments and remand the case to the trial court.

The objection to the foreclosure and public sale of this stock is based upon restrictions imposed upon the transfer of the stock by the articles of incorporation of Ling & Company. It is conceded that no offer of sale has been made to the other holders of this class of stock and that the approval of the pledge of the stock has not been obtained from the New York Stock Exchange. It is the position of Trinity Savings and Loan that all of the restrictions upon the transfer of any interest in this stock are invalid and of no effect. This has been the holding of the courts below.

The face and back of the stock certificate are reproduced and attached to this opinion.

The restrictions appear in Article Four of the Ling & Company articles of incorporation, as amended and filed with the Secretary of State in 1968. Section D requires the holder to obtain written approval of the New York Stock Exchange prior to the sale or encumbrance of the stock if, at the time, Ling & Company is a member corporation of the Exchange. Then Section E(4) prevents the sale of the stock without first affording the corporation the opportunity to buy and, if it fails to purchase, giving that opportunity to all holders of the same class of stock. The method of computation of the price, based upon the corporate books, is provided in this section of the articles.

The court of civil appeals struck down the restrictions for [two] reasons: the lack of conspicuous notice thereof on the stock certificate, [and] the unreasonableness of the restrictions * * *.

CONSPICUOUSNESS

The Texas Business Corporation Act as amended in 1957, V.A.T.S.Bus. Corp.Act, art. 2.22, subd. A, provides that a corporation may impose restrictions on the transfer of its stock if they are "expressly set forth in the articles of incorporation * * * and * * * copied at length or in summary form on the face or so copied on the back and referred to on the face of each certificate

* * * ." Article 2.19, subd. F, enacted by the Legislature at the same time, permits the incorporation by reference on the face or back of the certificate of the provision of the articles of incorporation which restricts the transfer of the stock. The court of civil appeals objected to the general reference to the articles of incorporation and the failure to print the full conditions imposed upon the transfer of the shares. However, reference is made on the face of the certificate to the restrictions described on the reverse side; the notice on the reverse side refers to the particular article of the articles of incorporation as restricting the transfer or encumbrance and requiring "the holder hereof to grant options to purchase the shares represented hereby first to the Corporation and then pro rata to the other holders of the Class A Common Stock * * * ." We hold that the content of the certificate complies with the requirements of the Texas Business Corporation Act.

There remains the requirement of the Texas [Uniform Commercial] Code that the restriction or reference thereto on the certificate must be conspicuous. Sec. [8–204] requires that a restriction on transferability be "noted conspicuously on the security." Sec. [1–201(10)] defines "conspicuous" and makes the determination a question of law for the court to decide. It is provided that a conspicuous term is so written as to be noticed by a reasonable person. Examples of conspicuous matter are given there as a "printed heading in capitals * * * [or] larger or other contrasting type or color." This means that something must appear on the face of the certificate to attract the attention of a reasonable person when he looks at it. 1 Anderson, Uniform Commercial Code 87 (2nd ed. 1970). The line of print on the face of the Ling & Company certificate does not stand out and cannot be considered conspicuous.

Our holding that the restriction is not noted conspicuously on the certificate does not entitle Trinity Savings and Loan to a summary judgment under this record. Sec. [8–204] provides that the restriction is effective against a person with actual knowledge of it. The record does not establish conclusively that Trinity Savings and Loan lacked knowledge of the restriction on January 28, 1969, the date the record indicates when Bowman executed an assignment of this stock to Trinity Savings and Loan.

REASONABLENESS

Art. 2.22, subd. A of the Texas Business Corporation Act provides that a corporation may impose restrictions on disposition of its stock if the restrictions "do not unreasonably restrain or prohibit transferability." The court of civil appeals has held that the restrictions on the transferability of this stock are unreasonable for two reasons: because of the required approval of the New York Stock Exchange and because of successive options to purchase given the corporation and the other holders of the same class of stock.

Ling & Company in its brief states that it was a brokerage house member of the New York Stock Exchange at an earlier time and that Rule 315 of the Exchange required approval of any sale or pledge of the stock. Under these circumstances, we must disagree with the court of civil appeals holding that this provision of article 4D of the articles of incorporation is "arbitrary, capricious, and unreasonable." Nothing appears in the summary judgment proof on this matter, and the mere provision in the article is no cause for vitiating the restrictions as a matter of law.

It was also held by the intermediate court that it is unreasonable to require a shareholder to notify all other record holders of Class A Common Stock of his intent to sell and to give the other holders a ten day option to buy. The record does not reveal the number of holders of this class of stock; we only know that there are more than twenty. We find nothing unusual or oppressive in these first option provisions. See 2 O'Neal, Close Corporations, § 7.13 (1971). Conceivably the number of stockholders might be so great as to make the burden too heavy upon the stockholder who wishes to sell and, at the same time, dispel any justification for contending that there exists a reasonable corporate purpose in restricting the ownership. But there is no showing of that nature in this summary judgment record. * * *

The summary judgment proof does not justify the holding that restrictions on the transfer of this stock were ineffective as to Trinity Savings and Loan Association. The judgment below is reversed and the cause is remanded to the trial court.

DANIEL, J., concurs in result.

For Value Received.____ hereby sell, assign, and transfer
unto_____
_____Shares
of the Capital Stock represented by the within
Certificate; and do hereby irrevocably constitute and appoint
_____Attorney
to transfer the said Stock on the books of the within named
Corporation with full power of substitution in the premises
Dated_____ 19
In presence of

NOTICE: The shares represented by this certificate are subject to all the terms, conditions and provisions of the Articles of Incorporation of the Corporation, as the same may be amended from time to time, which Articles are incorporated herein by reference as though fully set forth herein. Copies of the Articles of Incorporation may be obtained from the Secretary of State of the State of Texas or upon written request therefor from the Secretary of the Corporation. Reference is specifically made to the provisions of Article Four of the Articles of Incorporation which set forth the designations, preferences, limitations and relative rights of the shares of each class of capital stock authorized to be issued, which deny pre-emptive rights, prohibit cumulative voting, restrict the transfer, sale, assignment, pledge, hypothecation or encumbrance of any of the shares represented hereby under certain conditions, and which under certain conditions require the holder hereof to grant options to purchase the shares represented hereby first to the Corporation and then pro rata to the other holders of the Class A Common Stock, all as set forth in said Article Four. Reference is also specifically made to the provisions of Article Nine which vests the power to adopt, alter, amend or repeal the by-laws in the Board of Directors except to the extent such power may be modified or divested by action of shareholders representing a majority of the holders of the Class A Common Stock.

(A5775)

Notes

(1) Consider MBCA §§ 6.27, 1.40(3). Share transfer restrictions essentially constitute contractual obligations that limit the power of owners to freely transfer their shares. There are several different justifications for imposing share transfer restrictions, and the type of restriction imposed may depend on the objective. Consider MBCA § 6.27(c). What kinds of "status" are referred to in subsection (c)(1)? The Official Comment refers to election of close corporation status under an integrated close corporation statute, subchapter S, and "entitlement to a program or eligibility for a privilege administered by governmental agencies or national securities exchanges." Presumably, the share transfer restriction involved in *Ling* was of the latter type, designed to allow the New York Stock Exchange to police ownership interests in member firms. MBCA § 6.27(c)(3) also refers to "other reasonable purpose[s]" which presumably includes provisions designed to enable owners in closely held corporations to remain close, i.e., to select the persons with whom they will be associated in business, and to permit withdrawing participants to liquidate their investments on some reasonable basis.

(2) A variety of possible share transfer restrictions are described in MBCA § 6.27(d). In closely held corporations, the two most common types of restrictions are buy-sell agreements (see subsection (d)(1)) and option agreements (see subsection (d)(2)). An option does not guarantee the shareholder a specified price, whereas a buy-sell agreement does. The restrictions described in subsections (d)(3) and (d)(4) are potentially more onerous since they may prohibit all transfers to anyone at any price; it will be noted that they are valid only if the prohibition "is not manifestly unreasonable." Does it follow that (d)(1) and (d)(2) restrictions are valid even if they are "manifestly unreasonable?"

Couldn't most, if not all, of the problems faced by minority shareholders in closely-held corporations be solved if minority shareholders demanded a "buy-sell agreement?" Such agreements, if properly drafted, enable shareholders to require either the corporation or their fellow shareholders to buy out their equity interest in the corporation at some mutually-agreed-upon price, upon the occurrence of some mutually-agreed-upon triggering event. Certainly such agreements appear to solve the "freeze-out" and lack of liquidity problems that minority shareholders in closely held corporations often face. At a minimum, lawyers counseling investors who are about to become minority shareholders in a corporation, should insist that their clients at least consider seeking the protections afforded by buy-sell agreements.

Some share transfer restrictions in closely held corporations are phrased as rights of first refusal, giving the corporation or the shareholders an opportunity to meet the best price the shareholder has been able to obtain from outsiders.

(3) There are two basic types of buy-sell agreements. See Rodney J. Waldbaum, Buy–Sell Agreements, The Practical Accountant, May/June 1972, at pp. 17–25:

> * * * The first type is a cross-purchase agreement between the shareholders. Each shareholder agrees to personally purchase his proportionate share of the stock of the other shareholders in the event of their death, and binds his estate to sell the shares he owns to the surviving shareholders in proportion to their respective holdings. The capitalization of the corporation remains unchanged.

> The second type is a stock-redemption agreement. The corporation becomes a party to the agreement as well as the shareholders. The corporation would agree to redeem or purchase the shares of the first shareholder to die, and each of the two shareholders would bind his estate to sell or tender for redemption the shares he owns. Upon the death of the first shareholder, the corporation buys his shares using corporate funds.

> Both types of buy-sell agreements fix the price to be paid for the shares and specify the terms for payment. * * *

(4) The traditional view is that share transfer restrictions constitute a restraint on alienation, and therefore are strictly construed. This attitude is changing. One case, for example, has described this attitude as "anachronistic." Bruns v. Rennebohm Drug Stores, Inc., 151 Wis.2d 88, 442 N.W.2d 591, 596 (App.1989). Nevertheless, because of this historic approach, it is important to specify clearly and unambiguously the essential attributes of the restrictions. This should include such matters as whether the purchase is optional or mandatory, the persons who may or must purchase the shares and the sequence in which they may purchase, the manner in which the price is to be determined, the time periods during which persons may decide whether or not to purchase (if an option), and the events (e.g., proposed sale, death, bankruptcy, family gift, etc.) which triggered the restriction.

Buy-sell agreements can provide a means for minority shareholders to protect their interests in a closely held corporation. Yet many fail to do so. One commentator has observed that "people enter closely-held businesses in the same manner as they enter marriage: optimistically and ill-prepared." Charles W. Murdock, The Evolution of Effective Remedies for Minority Shareholders and Its Impact Upon Valuation of Minority Shares, 65 Notre Dame L. Rev. 425, 426 (1990). Courts have moved to protect minority shareholders from "oppression," discussed in Section D, infra. The following excerpt discusses some possible reasons why shareholders do not bargain for buy-sell agreements when investing in close corporations.

DOUGLAS K. MOLL, MINORITY OPPRESSION & THE LIMITED LIABILITY COMPANY: LEARNING (OR NOT) FROM CLOSE CORPORATION HISTORY

40 Wake Forest L. Rev. 883, 911–16 (2005).

Employment contracts, buy/sell agreements, and supermajority provisions * * * are all useful in safeguarding the minority shareholder from oppression. If the majority shareholder refused to consent to some or all of these protective arrangements, the minority shareholder could refuse to invest in the venture.

Despite this apparent opportunity for ex ante bargaining, it is widely recognized that close corporation investors typically fail to engage in such contracting. A number of reasons have been advanced for this failure. Because close corporation owners are frequently linked by family or other personal relationships, there is often an initial atmosphere of mutual trust that diminishes the sense that contractual protection is needed. Commentators have also argued that close corporation owners are often unsophisticated in business and legal matters such that the need for contractual protection is rarely recognized.

Even if an investor did recognize that planning for dissension was useful, barriers to effective contracting would still exist. In light of the countless ways in which oppressive conduct can occur, it is quite difficult to foresee all (if not most) of the situations that may require contractual protection. This inability to appreciate the universe of potential problems may result in incomplete contracting or, possibly, in no contracting at all. Further, the typical decision to invest in a close corporation venture is, for all intents and purposes, a decision to engage in a long-term association with other shareholders that will involve significant personal interaction in the future. Effective contracting for protection is particularly challenging in such a setting, as the parties usually seek to avoid harming their relationship during the contracting process. Indeed, a minority shareholder may be hesitant to even raise the topic of dissension because of a fear that it will damage the trust between the shareholders—trust that is critical to the operation of any small business. This hesitation may result in no planning for dissension at all.

Even if the topic of dissension is broached, a similar concern exists that any "hard feelings" created by the bargaining process will hinder the parties' abilities to work together in the future. Given this concern and the related desire to preserve as much goodwill between the shareholders as possible, a minority investor at the outset of a close corporation venture is likely to feel constrained in its ability to freely exercise any bargaining advantage that it has—i.e., constrained in its ability to fully "flex" its bargaining "muscle" against the majority shareholder. When the typical familiarity between close corporation participants is factored into the analysis, the minority shareholder is likely to feel even more constrained, as the shareholder will be concerned that fair (but hard) bargaining may harm both a business and a family/friendship relationship. Unlike discrete, single-interaction transactions, therefore, effective contracting in the close corporation setting is frequently hindered by relationship-oriented concerns. As a result, contractual protection for the minority shareholder is often incomplete or nonexistent.

For all of these reasons, it is rare for effective ex ante contracting to occur between close corporation investors. This systemic failure to "self-protect" exacerbates the oppression problem and underscores the need for a judicial response.

Notes

(1) When drafting a buy-sell agreement, determining the method of valuation is extremely important. There are several alternative approaches the parties can choose. The shareholders can retain an outside expert to appraise the value of the company's stock. This has the advantage of involving a neutral third party. The parties may want to determine ex ante how the appraiser will be selected to prevent charges of bias. One drawback is the high cost associated with retaining professional appraisers. The shareholders may choose to refer to the corporation's book value. This method has the advantage of being relatively straightforward, although the book value of the company may not accurately reflect its value as a going concern. Another option is for the parties to set a value for the shares, subject to periodic reevaluation.

(2) Consider the restrictions on corporate repurchases. MBCA § 6.40 governs distributions by corporations. Such distributions may take the form of dividend payments, as well as repurchases or other acquisitions by the corporation of its own shares of stock set forth in MBCA § 6.40, discussed in Chapter 8, Section I, supra. Might these provisions require a corporation to refuse to repurchase shares pursuant to a buy-sell agreement? If so, a carefully prepared estate plan may go awry.

(3) Buy-sell agreements that are triggered by the death of a shareholder may raise serious estate tax problems for the decedent's estate. The stock is likely to be the principal asset in the estate and have considerable (but uncertain) value. The critical question is whether the amount received pursuant to the buy-sell agreement determines the value of the stock for estate tax purposes. Prior to 1990 this issue was largely governed by case law, but today is addressed by § 2703 of the Internal Revenue Code:

(a) General rule.—For purposes of this subtitle, the value of any property shall be determined without regard to:

(1) any option, agreement, or other right to acquire or use the property at a price less than the fair market value of the property (without regard to such option, agreement, or right), or

(2) any restriction on the right to sell or use such property.

(b) Exceptions.—Subsection (a) shall not apply to any option, agreement, right, or restriction which meets each of the following requirements:

(1) It is a bona fide business arrangement.

(2) It is not a device to transfer such property to members of the decedent's family for less than full and adequate consideration in money or money's worth.

(3) Its terms are comparable to similar arrangements entered into by persons in an arms' length transaction."

If these requirements are not met it is quite possible that the Internal Revenue Service may seek a valuation for estate tax purposes considerably higher than the amount actually received by the estate as payment for the shares.

(4) Share transfer restrictions obviously may provide considerable protection to minority shareholders who may otherwise lose control over corporate affairs, to shareholders who retire, and to the heirs or devisees of deceased shareholders. Share transfer restrictions may also be designed, however, for the benefit of the corporation and its controlling shareholders who may be able to eliminate undesired shareholders at attractive prices. Some restrictions appear to be designed to ensure that shares of highly profitable corporations owned by a relatively few family members remain in the hands of the family over one or more generations. A share transfer restriction with this goal in mind is drafted so as to cover gifts and bequests of shares as well as sales to third persons. The option to trigger the buy-sell obligation is vested in the corporation rather than in one or more shareholders. And the price is likely to be set at a low and fixed level with no provision for adjustment based on the success of the corporation. Grandon v. Amcore Trust Co., 225 Ill.App.3d 630, 167 Ill.Dec. 670, 588 N.E.2d 311 (1992), cert. denied 146 Ill.2d 627, 176 Ill.Dec. 797, 602 N.E.2d 451 (1992), for example, involved the Sterling Gazette Company, a corporation owned by the Grandon family that had published the "Sterling Daily Gazette," a daily newspaper, since 1903. Thirty-three shares of the Sterling Gazette Company had left the Grandon family in the 1960s, when Preston Grandon, the majority shareholder at the time, gave them to his third wife, Marie, who in turn placed them in two trusts for the benefit of her children from an earlier marriage. The share certificates received by Marie, those issued in her name, and the shares issued in the names of the trusts, all contained a restrictive legend that provided that the purchaser of the stock agreed to resell the stock to Sterling Gazette Company for $250 per share upon the shareholder's death or severance of his connection with the company. This legend setting a $250 price had been in effect since before 1964 (when Marie acquired the shares). In 1986, the company sought to acquire the shares from the trusts for $250 per share since manifestly the trusts and their beneficiaries had no connection with the company. The Court concluded that the restriction was unenforceable since there was no reference to a buy-sell agreement in the articles of incorporation or the bylaws, and the gift of the shares to Marie did not constitute acceptance by her of a buy-sell agreement. Presumably, $250 represented only a tiny fraction of the value of the shares in the Sterling Gazette Company in 1986.

Many cases hold that a share transfer restriction is valid even though it compels a shareholder to sell shares at an arbitrary price that may not reflect the real value of the shares. See, e.g., Unigroup, Inc. v. O'Rourke Storage & Transfer Co., 980 F.2d 1217 (8th Cir.1992)(book value); In re Estate of Mather, 410 Pa. 361, 189 A.2d 586 (1963)(price of $1 per share upheld despite contention that shares were worth $1,060 per share); Allen v. Biltmore Tissue Corp., 2 N.Y.2d 534, 161 N.Y.S.2d 418, 141 N.E.2d 812 (1957)(repurchase at original price issued).

C. DEADLOCKS

GEARING v. KELLY

Court of Appeals of New York, 1962.
11 N.Y.2d 201, 227 N.Y.S.2d 897, 182 N.E.2d 391.

PER CURIAM.

Appellants, who own 50% of the stock of the Radium Chemical Company, Inc., seek, within the provisions of section 25 of the General Corporation Law, Consol.Laws, c. 23, to set aside the election of a director.

In NY setting aside corp. elections is equitable

In a proceeding under that section, the court sits as a court of equity which may order a new election "as justice may require." We have concluded, as did the majority of the Appellate Division, that appellants have failed to show that justice requires a new election, in that they may not now complain of an irregularity which they themselves have caused.

P had notice of meeting but intentionally skipped to prevent quorum.

No clean hands."

No remedy!!

Mrs. Meacham stayed away from the meeting of March 6, 1961 for the sole purpose of preventing a quorum from assembling, and intended, in that manner, to paralyze the board. There can be no doubt, and indeed it is not even suggested, that she lacked notice or any manner found it temporarily inconvenient to present herself at that particular time and place. It is certain, then, that Mrs. Meacham's absence from the noticed meeting of the board was intentional and deliberate. Much is said by appellants about a desire to protect their equal ownership of stock through equal representation on the board. It is, however, clear that such balance was voluntarily surrendered in 1955. Whether this was done in reliance on representations of Kelly, Sr., as alleged in the plenary suit, is properly a matter for that litigation, rather than the summary type of action here.

The relief sought by appellants, the ordering of a new election, would, furthermore, be of no avail to them, for Mrs. Meacham would then be required, as evidence of her good faith, to attend. Such a futile act will not be ordered.

The identity of interests of the appellants is readily apparent. Mrs. Gearing has fully indorsed and supported all of the demands and actions of her daughter, and has associated herself with the refusal to attend the directors' meeting. A court of equity need not permit Mrs. Gearing to attack actions of the board of directors which were marred through conduct of the director whom she has actively encouraged. To do so would allow a director to refuse to attend meetings, knowing that thereafter an associated stockholder could frustrate corporate action until all of their joint demands were met.

The failure of Mrs. Meacham to attend the directors' meeting, under the present circumstances, bars appellants from invoking an exercise of the equitable powers lodged in the courts under the statute.

The order appealed from should be affirmed, with costs.

FROESSEL, JUDGE (dissenting).

The bylaws of Radium Chemical Company, Inc., provided for a board of four directors, a majority of whom "shall constitute a quorum for the transaction of business." Prior to 1955 the board consisted of appellant Meacham, who had succeeded her father (appellant Gearing's late husband), respondent Kelly, Sr., and Margaret E. Lee. In 1955 Kelly, Jr., was elected to the then vacant directorship. The board continued thus until Margaret Lee offered her resignation in 1961 and, on March 6 of that year, at a meeting of the board of directors at which she and the two Kellys were present, her resignation was accepted. Thereupon the two Kellys elected Julian Hemphill, a son-in-law of Kelly, Sr., to replace Margaret Lee.

I agree with Justice Eager, who dissented in the Appellate Division, that two members of the board were insufficient to constitute a quorum in this case for the purpose of electing the new director. It necessarily follows that the election of Julian Hemphill is not merely irregular, as the majority hold, but is wholly void and must be set aside.

Section 25 of the General Corporation Law grants to the court two alternatives in a case such as this: (1) to confirm the election, or (2) to order a new election as justice may require (Matter of Faehndrich, 2 N.Y.2d 468, 474, 161 N.Y.S.2d 99, 104, 141 N.E.2d 597, 600). As we held in the case just cited, the clause "as justice may require" does not enlarge the court's power nor authorize it to grant different relief from that specified in the statute. There is no basis whatever here for the application of the doctrine of estoppel, and in no event could it reasonably be applied to the nondirector, appellant Gearing, a substantial stockholder in this corporation. The purported election is, therefore, a nullity.

This is a mere contest for control, and the court should not assist either side, each of which holds an equal interest in the corporation, particularly where, as here, petitioners were willing that director Meacham attend meetings for the purpose of transacting all the necessary business of the board, but were unwilling that she attend a meeting, the purpose of which was to strip them of every vestige of control. Appellant Meacham had surrendered nothing in 1955 when she permitted Kelly, Jr., to become a director as well as his father, for Margaret Lee was then a third director.

The statute mandates a new election and that should be ordered. It is no answer to say that the results will probably be the same. If the parties are deadlocked, whether as directors or stockholders, and choose to remain that way, they have other remedies, and I see no reason why we should help one side or the other by disregarding a bylaw that follows the statute (General Corporation Law, § 27), particularly when it results in giving the Kellys complete control of the corporation.

I would, therefore, reverse the order appealed from, and modify the order of Special Term by ordering a special election and affirming it in all other respects.

DESMOND, C.J., and FULD, VAN VOORHIS, BURKE and FOSTER, JJ., concur in Per Curiam opinion.

FROESSEL, J., dissents in an opinion in which DYE, J., concurs.

Note

Many state statutes relating to the filling of vacancies on the board of directors are based on the first sentence of MBCA (1969) § 38: "[a]ny vacancy occurring in the board of directors may be filled by the affirmative vote of a majority of the remaining directors though less than a quorum of the board of directors." If this statute had been in effect in New York at the time Gearing v. Kelly arose, would the Kellys need the presence of Mrs. Meacham in order to elect Hemphill? What does the clause "though less than a quorum" in § 38 modify? Compare MBCA § 8.10(a)(3). Does the language of that section resolve all possible ambiguity? Consider also the possible application of MBCA § 8.05(e) to the facts of this case.

IN RE RADOM & NEIDORFF, INC.

Court of Appeals of New York, 1954.
307 N.Y. 1, 119 N.E.2d 563.

DESMOND, JUDGE.

Radom & Neidorff, Inc., the proposed dissolution of which is before us here, is a domestic corporation which has for many years, conducted, with great success, the business of lithographing or printing musical compositions. For some thirty years prior to February 18, 1950, Henry Neidorff, now deceased, husband of respondent Anna Neidorff, and David Radom, brother-in-law of Neidorff and brother of Mrs. Neidorff, were the sole stockholders, each holding eighty shares. Henry Neidorff's will made his wife his executrix and bequeathed her the stock, so that, ever since his death, petitioner-appellant David Radom and Anna Neidorff, brother and sister, have been the sole and equal stockholders. Although brother and sister, they were unfriendly before Neidorff's death and their estrangement continues. On July 17, 1950, five months after Neidorff's death, Radom brought this proceeding, praying that the corporation be dissolved under section 103 of the General Corporation Law, Consol.Laws, c. 23, the applicable part of which is as follows:

> § 103. *Petition in Case of Deadlock*
>
> Unless otherwise provided in the certificate of incorporation, if a corporation has an even number of directors who are equally divided respecting the management of its affairs, or if the votes of its stockholders are so divided that they cannot elect a board of directors, the holders of one-half of the stock entitled to vote at an election of directors may present a verified petition for dissolution of the corporation as prescribed in this article.

NY law allows petition to dissolve when there is a deadlock.

That statute, like others in article 9 of the General Corporation Law, describes the situations in which dissolution may be petitioned for, but, as we shall show later, it does not mandate the granting of the relief in every such case.

The petition here stated to the court that the corporation is solvent and its operations successful, but that, since Henry Neidorff's death, his widow (respondent here) has refused to co-operate with petitioner as president, and that she refuses to sign his salary checks, leaving him without salary, although he has the sole burden of running the business. It was alleged, too, that, because of "unresolved disagreements" between petitioner and respondent, election of any directors, at a stockholders' meeting held for that purpose in June, 1950, had proved impossible. A schedule attached to the petition showed corporate assets consisting of machinery and supplies worth about $9,500, cash about $82,000, and no indebtedness except about $17,000 owed to petitioner (plus his salary claim). Mrs. Neidorff's answering papers alleged that, while her husband was alive, the two owners had each drawn about $25,000 per year from the corporation, that, shortly after her husband's death, petitioner had asked her to allow him alone to sign all checks, which request she refused, that he had then offered her $75,000 for her stock, and, on her rejection thereof, had threatened to have the corporation dissolved and to buy it in at a low price or, if she should be the purchaser, that he would start a competing business. She further alleged that she has not, since her husband's death, interfered with Radom's conduct of the business and has signed all corporate checks sent her by him except checks for his own salary which, she says, she declined to sign because of a stockholder's derivative suit brought by her against Radom, and still pending, charging him with enriching himself at this corporation's expense.

Because of other litigation now concluded, see Matter of Radom's Estate, 305 N.Y. 679, 112 N.E.2d 768, to which Mrs. Neidorff was not a party, but which had to do with a contest as to the ownership of the Radom stock, respondent's answering papers in this dissolution proceeding were not filed until three years after the petition was entered. From the answering papers it appears, without dispute, that for those three years, the corporation's profits before taxes had totaled about $242,000, or an annual average of about $71,000, on a gross annual business of about $250,000, and that the corporation had, in 1953, about $300,000 on deposit in banks. There are many other accusations and counteraccusations in these wordy papers, but the only material facts are undisputed: first, that these two equal stockholders dislike and distrust each other; second, that, despite the feuding and backbiting, there is no stalemate or impasse as to corporate policies; third, that the corporation is not sick but flourishing; fourth, that dissolution is not necessary for the corporation or for either stockholders; and, fifth, that petitioner, though he is in an uncomfortable and disagreeable situation for which he may or may not be at fault, has no grievance cognizable by a court except as to the nonpayment of his salary, hardly a ground for dissolving the corporation.

Five most important facts
1. Stock-holder animosity
2. Corporate policies are in order
3. Corp. is makin money
4. Dissolution not necessary
5. P's only complaint is that he isn't gettin paid

Special Term held that these papers showed a basic and irreconcilable conflict between the two stockholders requiring dissolution, for the protection of both of them, if the petition's allegations should be proven. An order for a reference was, accordingly, made, but respondent appealed therefrom, and no hearings were held by the Referee. The Appellate Division reversed the order and dismissed the petition, pointing out, among other things, that not only have the corporation's activities not been paralyzed but that its profits have increased and its assets trebled during the pendency of this proceeding, that the failure of petitioner to receive his salary did not frustrate the corporate business and was remediable by means other than dissolution. The dismissal of the proceeding was "without prejudice, however, to the bringing of another proceeding should deadlock in fact arise in the selection of a board of directors, at a meeting of stockholders to be duly called, or if other deadlock should occur threatening impairment or in fact impairing the economic operations of the corporation." 282 App.Div. 854, 124 N.Y.S.2d 424, 425. Petitioner then appealed to this court.

It is worthy of passing mention, at least, that respondent has, in her papers, formally offered, and repeated the offer on the argument of the appeal before us, "to have the third director named by the American Arbitration Association, any Bar Association or any recognized and respected public body."

Clearly, the dismissal of this petition was within the discretion of the Appellate Division. General Corporation Law, § 106. There is no absolute right to dissolution under such circumstances. Even when majority stockhold-

standard
for
dissolution

1. interest
of stockholders
so discordant
as to prevent
efficient
management, or

2. object of
corporate
existence
is frustrated

ers file a petition because of internal corporate conflicts, the order is granted only when the competing interests "are so discordant as to prevent efficient management" and the "object of its corporate existence cannot be attained." Hitch v. Hawley, 132 N.Y. 212, 221, 30 N.E. 401, 404. The prime inquiry is, always, as to necessity for dissolution, that is, whether judicially-imposed death "will be beneficial to the stockholders or members and not injurious to the public," General Corporation Law, § 117; Hitch v. Hawley, supra. * * * Taking everything in the petition as true, this was not such a case, and so there was no need for a reference, or for the taking of proof, under sections 106 and 113 of the General Corporation Law.

The order should be affirmed, with costs.

FULD, JUDGE (dissenting).

Section 103 of the General Corporation Law, insofar as here relevant, permits a petition for dissolution of a corporation by the holders of one half of the shares of stock entitled to vote for directors "if the votes of its stockholders are so divided that they cannot elect a board of directors." That is the precise situation in the case before us, for the petition explicitly recites that petitioner Radom and respondent Neidorff "are hopelessly deadlocked with respect to the management and operation of the corporation" and that serious disputes have developed between them with the result that "the votes of the two stockholders are so divided that they cannot elect a Board of Directors." * * *

For upwards of thirty years, petitioner Radom and Henry Neidorff, respondent's husband, shared equally in the ownership and management of Radom & Neidorff, Inc. Through all that time, their relationship was harmonious as well as profitable. Neidorff died in 1950, at which time respondent, through inheritance, acquired her present 50% stock interest in the business. Since then, all has been discord and conflict. The parties, brother and sister, are at complete loggerheads; they have been unable to elect a board of directors; dividends have neither been declared nor distributed, although the corporation has earned profits; debts of the corporation have gone unpaid, although the corporation is solvent; petitioner, who since Neidorff's death has been the sole manager of the business, has not received a penny of his salary—amounting to $25,000 a year—because respondent has refused to sign any corporate check to his order. More, petitioner's business judgment and integrity, never before questioned, have been directly attacked in the stockholder's derivative suit, instituted by respondent, charging that he has falsified the corporation's records, converted its assets and otherwise enriched himself at its expense. Negotiations looking to the purchase by one stockholder of the other's interest were begun—in an effort to end the impasse—but they, too, have failed.

In very truth, as petitioner states in his papers, "a corporation of this type, with only two stockholders in it cannot continue to operate with incessant litigation and feuding between the two stockholders, and with differences as fundamental and wholly irreconcilable as are those of Mrs. Neidorff and myself. * * * [S]ettlement of these differences cannot be effected, while continuance on the present basis is impossible, so that there is no alternative to judicial dissolution." Indeed, petitioner avers, in view of the unceasing discord and the fact that he has had to work without salary and advance his own money to the corporation, he does not, whether or not dissolution be granted, "propose to continue to labor in and operate this business."

It is, then, undisputed and indisputable that the stockholders are not able to elect a board of directors. In addition, it is manifest, on the facts alleged, that the Supreme Court could find that the stockholders are hopelessly deadlocked vis-à-vis the management of the corporation; that the corporation cannot long continue to function effectively or profitably under such condition; that petitioner's resignation as president and manager—which he contemplates—will be highly detrimental to the interests of both corporation and stockholders and cannot help but result in substantial loss; and that petitioner is not responsible for the deadlock that exists. In such circumstances, the requisite statutory hearing may well establish that dissolution is indispensable, the only remedy available. As the high court of New Jersey recently declared in applying to somewhat comparable facts a statute similar to section 103 of our General Corporation Law, Matter of Collins–Doan Co., 3 N.J. 382, 396, 70 A.2d 159, 166, 13 A.L.R.2d 1250, "In the case at hand, *there is a want of that community of interest essential to corporate operation.* Dissolution will serve the interests of the shareholders as well as public policy. * * * And, if the statutory authority be deemed discretionary in essence, there is no ground for withholding its affirmative exercise here, *for there is no alternative corrective remedy.* * * * " (Emphasis supplied.)

Here, too, the asserted dissension, the court could find, permits of no real or effective remedy but a section 103 dissolution. And that is confirmed by a consideration of the alternatives seemingly open to petitioner. He could remain as president and manager of the corporation, without compensation, completely at odds with his embittered sister—certainly neither a natural nor a satisfying way in which to conduct a business. Or he could carry out his present plan to quit the enterprise—and thereby risk a loss, to corporation and stockholders, far greater than that involved in terminating the business. Or he could, without quitting, set up a competing enterprise and thereby expose himself to suit for breach of fiduciary duty to the corporation. Cf. Duane Jones Co. v. Burke, 306 N.Y. 172, 117 N.E.2d 237. It is difficult to believe that the legislature could have intended to put one in petitioner's position to such a choice. Reason plainly indicates, and the law allows, the reasonable course of orderly dissolution pursuant to section 103.

Respondent, however, suggests that, in view of the fact that petitioner is managing the business profitably, he should continue to do so, defend against the stockholder's suit which she brought attacking his honor and integrity and himself start an action for the compensation denied him for more than three years. But, it seems self-evident, more and further litigation would only aggravate, not cure, the underlying deadlock of which petitioner complains. And, if he were to bring the suggested suit for salary due him, the question arises, whom should he sue, and who is to defend? The mere proposal that petitioner embark on a series of actions against the corporation, of which he is president and half owner, indicates the extent of the present impasse, as well as the futility of perpetuating it. The same is true of the other alternative suggested by respondent, namely, that the third of the three directors, required by section 5 of the Stock Corporation Law, Consol.Laws, c. 59, be appointed by an impartial party. The deadlock of which petitioner complains is between the stockholders, not the directors, and when stockholders are deadlocked, section 103 calls for dissolution, not arbitration. Beyond that, and even if the offer to elect an impartial director were relevant, it would still be necessary to inquire when it was made and under what circumstances. It does not justify, alone or in conjunction with the other facts, a summary dismissal of the proceeding without a hearing.

Although respondent relies on the fact that the corporation is now solvent and operating at a profit, it is manifest that, if petitioner carries out his plan to resign as president and quits the business, there may be irreparable loss, not alone to him and respondent, as the owners of the corporation, but also to the corporation's creditors. Quite apart from that, however, the sole issue under section 103 is whether there is a deadlock as to the management of the corporation, not whether business is being conducted at a profit or loss. Whether the petition should or should not be entertained surely cannot be made to turn on proof that the corporation is on the verge of ruin or insolvency.

* * * By virtue of other provisions of Article 9 of the General Corporation Law—sections 101 and 102—directors and stockholders may seek dissolution, when the corporation is insolvent, in order to prevent further loss to the owners and creditors. Section 103, however—which bears the title, *"Petition in case of deadlock"*—was designed to serve a far different purpose. As amended in 1944, upon the recommendation of the Law Revision Commission, that section provides for dissolution "if the votes of its stockholders are so divided that they cannot elect a board of directors." Nothing in the statute itself or in its legislative history suggests that a "Petition in case of deadlock" must wait until the corporation's profits have dried up and financial reverses set in. Had the commission or the legislature intended to incorporate such a qualification into section 103, it could readily have done so. The only test envisaged by the commission, however, was that which the legislature enacted, and a court may not import any other. * * *

The order of the Appellate Division should be reversed and that at Special Term affirmed.

CONWAY, DYE and VAN VOORHIS, JJ., concur with DESMOND, J.

FULD, J., dissents in opinion in which LEWIS, C.J., and FROESSEL, J., concur.

Notes

(1) See MBCA § 14.30(2), a statute that is typical of many state involuntary dissolution statutes. The Official Comment to this section makes it clear that the use of the word "may" in the preambular material preserves the Court's discretion (applied in *Radom*) "as to whether dissolution is appropriate even though grounds exist under the specific circumstances." Why should not the remedy of involuntary dissolution be generally available to minority shareholders in closely held corporations to the same extent that remedy is available to partners in a general partnership?

(2) Courts are often reluctant to order dissolution, despite the fact that they clearly have the power to do so. Courts also have a wide range of other equitable remedies available to them. For example, in Haseotes v. Bentas, 2002 WL 31058540 (Del.Ch. Sept. 3, 2002), the four member board of Cumberland Farms,

Inc. was deadlocked. Shareholders petitioned for the appointment of a custodian. The court denied this motion, and instead ordered the parties to conduct a shareholders' meeting for the purpose of electing a board of directors. The "court-ordered shareholders' meeting did not eliminate the deadlock, as each party continued to refuse to vote for any candidate acceptable to the other side. Ultimately the court agreed to appoint a tie-breaking custodian who was vested with the power to vote on matters of corporate governance when the board deadlocked." However, the custodian was not explicitly directed to vote on every issue, and there is some evidence that the custodian "expressly disclaimed any authority to vote and has taken the position that even if he did have the authority he would not exercise it." There was no demand on the Custodian to take action because any such demand would appear to be futile since there has been an express refusal to act. Presumably, the Plaintiffs will continue to litigate. 2002 WL 31058540, at *6.

(3) Compare MBCA §§ 14.01, 14.02, 14.20. Might a dissatisfied shareholder in a closely held corporation be able to use these alternative dissolution provisions to avoid the limitations of § 14.30(2)?

D. MODERN REMEDIES FOR OPPRESSION, DISSENSION OR DEADLOCK

Involuntary dissolution was the original statutory remedy developed for deadlock situations where the corporation was on dead center and the participants had no way to resolve the situation. As early as 1933, a few states broadened their involuntary dissolution statutes to include oppression, significant misconduct by the directors (or by those in control of the corporation), and the misapplication or wasting of assets. Earlier versions of the Model Act adopted this pattern, which gradually found its way into most corporation statutes. MBCA § 14.30(2) is thus typical of most state statutes dealing with involuntary dissolution.

Recent developments have broadened available remedies in the closely held corporation in two directions. First, the kinds of conduct within a closely held corporation that are viewed as oppressive have been broadened both by statute and by judicial decisions analogizing the closely held corporation to a partnership. Second, remedies available to minority shareholders in closely held corporations have been broadened both by specific statutory provisions (including, but by no means limited to, the integrated close corporation statutes discussed in Zion v. Kurtz and the following notes) and by judicial decisions in states whose statutes still state that dissolution is the remedy for such conduct. See Robert B. Thompson, The Shareholder's Cause of Action for Oppression, 48 Bus. Law. 699 (1993).

DAVIS v. SHEERIN

Court of Appeals of Texas, 1988.
754 S.W.2d 375, error denied.

Before EVANS, C.J., and SAM BASS and DUNN, JJ.

DUNN, JUSTICE.

This is an appeal from portions of a trial court's judgment, in which James L. Sheerin ("appellee") was declared to own a 45% share in a corporation * * *. The major challenges are against an ordered buy-out of appellee's stock in the corporation * * *. William H. Davis ("appellant") is the owner of the remaining 55% interest in * * * [the corporation].

In May of 1985, appellee brought suit individually in his own right, and as a shareholder on behalf of W.H. Davis Co., Inc., a Texas corporation ("the corporation"), against William H. Davis and Catherine L. Davis ("appellants") based on allegations of appellants' oppressive conduct toward appellee as a minority shareholder, and their breaches of fiduciary duties owed to appellee and the corporation. * * *

In 1955, William Davis and appellee incorporated a business, initially started by William Davis, in which appellant Davis owned 55% and appellee owned 45% of the corporation's stock. Appellants and appellee all served as directors and officers, with William Davis serving as president and running the day-to-day operations of the business. Appellee, unlike appellants, was not employed by the corporation. In 1960, appellee and appellant William Davis formed a partnership for the purpose of acquiring real estate.

The precipitating cause of appellee's lawsuit in 1985 was appellants' denial of appellee's right to inspect the corporate books, unless appellee produced his stock certificate. Appellants claimed that appellee had made a gift to them, in the late 1960's, of his 45% interest. * * *

Following a six-week trial to a jury, the trial court, in addition to declaring that appellee owned a 45% interest in the corporation, * * * ordered [a] "buy-out" by appellants of appellee's 45% of the stock in the corporation for $550,000, the fair value determined by the jury * * *.

In points of error one through seven, appellants challenge the court's order that they buy-out appellee's 45% interest in the corporation. Appellants' basic argument is two fold: (1) the remedy of a "buy-out" is not available to a minority shareholder under Texas law, and (2) if such a remedy were available, the facts of this case are not appropriate for, nor do the jury's findings support, the application of this remedy based on the court's determination of oppressive conduct.

The Texas Business Corporation Act does not expressly provide for the remedy of a "buy-out" for an aggrieved minority shareholder. Tex.Bus.Corp. Act. art. 7.05 (Vernon 1980) does provide for the appointment of a receiver, with the eventual possibility of liquidation, for aggrieved shareholders who can establish the existence of one of five situations, including illegal, oppressive, or fraudulent conduct by those in control.

Nor do we find any Texas cases where the particular remedy of a "buy-out" has been ordered, unless provided for in a contract between the parties. But courts of other jurisdictions have recognized a "buy-out" as an appropriate remedy, even in the absence of express statutory or contractual authority. See *Alaska Plastics, Inc. v. Coppock,* 621 P.2d 270 (Alaska 1980); *Sauer v. Moffitt,* 363 N.W.2d 269 (Iowa Ct.App.1984); *McCauley v. Tom McCauley & Son, Inc.,* 104 N.M. 523, 724 P.2d 232 (Ct.App.1986) (granting the option of liquidation or "buy-out"); *In re Wiedy's Furniture Clearance Center Co.,* 108 A.D.2d 81, 487 N.Y.S.2d 901 (1985); *Delaney v. Georgia–Pacific Corp.,* 278 Or. 305, 564 P.2d 277 (1977). Alaska, Iowa, New Mexico, New York, and Oregon all have statutes that provide for liquidation as the remedy for oppressive acts, and, in the above cited cases, the courts allowed a "buy-out" as a less harsh remedy. Other states' statutes specifically provide for a "buy-out," either as a remedy for an aggrieved minority shareholder, * * * [citing the statutes of five states], or as an option available to a majority shareholder to avoid a liquidation order * * * [citing the statutes of two states].

Both parties rely on *Patton v. Nicholas,* 154 Tex. 385, 279 S.W.2d 848 (1955), to support their respective arguments in favor of or against a court's authority in Texas to order a "buy-out." In that case, the court reversed an order of liquidation in a suit brought by an aggrieved minority shareholder, although it found that liquidation might be an appropriate remedy in some instances. * * * [A discussion of earlier Texas law is omitted.]

We conclude that Texas courts, under their general equity power, may decree a "buy-out" in an appropriate case where less harsh remedies are inadequate to protect the rights of the parties.

Court creates remedy of "buy-out" through its equitable powers.

Having decided that a "buy-out" is an available remedy under the court's general equity powers, we must decide whether it was appropriate in this case. The trial court's judgment reflects that its "buy-out" order was based on the jury's finding of conspiracy to deprive appellee of his stock, on the evidence and arguments, and on its conclusion that appellants acted oppressively against appellee and would continue to do so. * * *

Oppressive conduct is the most common violation for which a "buy-out" was found to be an appropriate remedy in other jurisdictions. *See, e.g. Alaska Plastics,* 621 P.2d 270, *Wiedy's,* 487 N.Y.S.2d 901; *McCauley,* 724 P.2d 232; *Baker v. Commercial Body Builders, Inc.,* 264 Or. 614, 507 P.2d 387 (1973). Courts take an especially broad view of the application of oppressive conduct to a closely-held corporation, where oppression may more easily be found. *Skierka v. Skierka Bros. Inc.,* 629 P.2d 214 (Mont.1981). An ordered "buy-out" of stock at its fair value is an especially appropriate remedy in a closely-held corporation, where the oppressive acts of the majority are an attempt to "squeeze out" the minority, who do not have a ready market for the corporation's shares, but are at the mercy of the majority.

The Texas Business Corporation Act, which provides a cause of action based on oppressive conduct, does not define oppressive conduct. Nor do we find any Texas decision providing a definition. We therefore turn again to decisions of other jurisdictions to consider what constitutes oppressive conduct.

Oppressive conduct has been described as an expansive term that is used to cover a multitude of situations dealing with improper conduct, and a narrow definition would be inappropriate. *McCauley,* 724 P.2d at 236. Courts may determine, according to the facts of the particular case, whether the acts complained of serve to frustrate the legitimate expectations of minority shareholders, or whether the acts are of such severity as to warrant the requested relief.

The New York court in *Wiedy's* held that oppression should be deemed to arise only when the majority's conduct substantially defeats the expectations that objectively viewed were both reasonable under the circumstances and were central to the minority shareholder's decision to join the venture. *Wiedy's,* 487 N.Y.2d at 903.

Courts in states with statutes containing situations establishing causes of action for minority shareholders, similar to those allowed in the Texas statute, have held that oppressive conduct is an independent ground for relief not requiring a showing of fraud, illegality, mismanagement, wasting of assets, nor deadlock, the other grounds available for shareholders, though these factors are frequently present. *Fix v. Fix Material Co., Inc.*, 538 S.W.2d 351, 358 (Mo.Ct.App.1976) (citing *Gidwitz v. Lanzit Corrugated Box Co.*, 20 Ill.2d 208, 170 N.E.2d 131, 135[1] (1960)).

While noting that general definitions are of little value for application in a specific case, the Oregon Supreme Court in *Baker* cited the most quoted definitions of oppressive conduct as:

> burdensome, harsh and wrongful conduct," "a lack of probity and fair dealing in the affairs of a company to the prejudice of some of its members," or "a visible departure from the standards of fair dealing, and a violation of fair play on which every shareholder who entrusts his money to a company is entitled to rely.

Baker, 507 P.2d at 393. * * *

Our review of the record shows that the jury made the following findings in regards to appellants' conduct:

(1) appellants conspired to deprive appellee of his stock ownership in the corporation;

(2) appellants received informal dividends by making profit sharing contributions for their benefit and to the exclusion of appellee, and that this was a willful breach of fiduciary duty;

(3) appellants wasted corporate funds by using them for their legal fees, and that this was a willful breach of fiduciary duty;

(4) appellants did not convert appellee's stock;

(5) appellants were not paid excessive compensation;

(6) there was no malicious suppression of dividends;

(7) various purchases or investments did not constitute a breach of fiduciary duty; and

(8) appellants did not conspire to breach their fiduciary duty.

The jury also found that appellee did not make a gift of his stock to appellants, represent that he would, nor agree to do so in the future. * * *

Even though there were findings of the absence of some of the typical "squeeze out" techniques used in closely held corporations, e.g., no malicious suppression of dividends or excessive salaries, we find that conspiring to deprive one of his ownership of stock in a corporation, especially when the corporate records clearly indicate such ownership, is more oppressive than either of those techniques. Appellant's conduct not only would substantially defeat any reasonable expectations appellee may have had, as required by the New York Court in *Wiedy's,* but would totally extinguish any such expectations. * * * We therefore hold that the jury's finding of conspiracy to deprive appellee of his interest in the corporation, together with the acts of willful breach of a fiduciary duty as found by the jury, and the undisputed evidence indicating that appellee would be denied any future voice in the corporation, are sufficient to support the trial court's conclusion of oppressive conduct and the likelihood that it would continue in the future. * * *

Appellants' oppressive conduct, along with their attempts to purchase appellee's stock, are indications of their desire to gain total control of the corporation. That is exactly what a "buy-out" will achieve. We disagree with appellants' suggestion that a "buy-out" is a more drastic remedy than liquidation. *See Stefano v. Coppock*, 705 P.2d 443, 446 (Alaska 1985). This is especially true in light of the fact that appellants do not challenge the jury's finding of $550,000 as the fair value of appellee's stock, which is the amount set by the trial court for the "buy-out." * * *

Based on the facts of this case, we find that a "buy-out" was an appropriate remedy, and that the trial court did not abuse its discretion.

Notes

(1) Cases that hold that a court may order a buyout even where the statute, like MBCA § 14.30(2), only refers to dissolution as the appropriate remedy may not be as radical as they first appear. Consider Harry J. Haynsworth, The Effectiveness of Involuntary Dissolution Suits as a Remedy for Close Corporation Dissension, 35 Clev.St.L.Rev. 25, 50–55 (1987):

> The 1984 and 1985 involuntary dissolution cases present an interesting statistical profile. There were a total of forty-seven cases that qualified for the sample. Forty-five of the cases came from twenty different states * * *.

> Ten of the cases in the sample involved technical legal issues in which no decision on the type of relief, if any, had been made at the time the opinion was issued. * * *

> Of the remaining thirty-seven cases, a buy-out was the most frequent relief ordered by the court or elected by the defendants. This result occurred in twenty of the decisions (fifty-four percent). Dissolution was ordered in ten of the cases (twenty-seven percent). In four of the cases (eleven percent), no substantial relief was granted to the plaintiff on the merits. Finally, in the three other cases (eight percent) relief other than either dissolution or a buy-out was the exclusive remedy ordered; and in eleven of the dissolution and buy-out cases (thirty percent of the total and thirty-seven percent of the dissolution and buy-out cases), additional relief was also granted. This additional relief included compensatory damages, punitive damages, an accounting, cancellation of issued stock, partial liquidation and other innovative orders * * *.

> That a court-supervised buy-out was the predominant form of ultimate relief and that a buy-out occurred twice as frequently as a court-ordered liquidation is not surprising. A buy-out, assuming fair value is received for the shares, gives the plaintiff a cash-out right that he or she would not otherwise have, and in many cases, this is undoubtedly the principal motivation behind the lawsuit. Getting rid of a dissatisfied shareholder permanently is also advantageous to the corporation and remaining shareholders. Moreover, * * * judges have consistently stated that dissolution should be ordered only as a last resort when no alternative remedy is feasible; and the dissolution cases in the sample used in this article illustrate that in this instance, judges are practicing what they preach.

What is somewhat surprising is the number of cases in which a court-supervised buy-out is the result of the involuntary dissolution suit. In a previous study of the fifty-four involuntary dissolution opinions decided between 1960–1976 conducted by Professors J.A.C. Hetherington and Michael P. Dooley of the University of Virginia,[13] a court-ordered or court supervised buy-out was involved in only three of the cases, whereas dissolution was ordered in sixteen of the twenty-seven cases in which some affirmative relief was granted.

Professors Hetherington and Dooley not only analyzed the judicial opinions issued between 1960 and the end of 1976, but they also followed up on each case to determine the ultimate outcome. Interestingly, out of all the cases, including those for which relief had been denied, fifty-four percent actually ended up with one side buying out the other. This is exactly the same percentage as the buy-out cases in the 1984–1985 decisions. This parallelism suggests that recent decisions more accurately mirror the results ultimately negotiated by the parties than the decisions rendered a decade or more ago.

(2) In 1991, the Committee on Corporate Laws added MBCA § 14.34. Closely held shares by definition have no market value. How is "fair value" to be determined under § 14.34? A somewhat analogous determination of "fair value" is required in the appraisal procedure under MBCA § 13.30, but the Official Comment to § 14.34 points out that the "two proceedings are not wholly analogous, * * * and the court should consider all relevant facts and circumstances of the particular case in determining fair value." In 2002, 21 states had enacted § 14.34. However, several states authorize a buyout remedy only in connection with corporations that have elected special close corporation treatment, though decisions such as Zion v. Kurtz (p. 433, supra) and the principal case may make that distinction less important than might first appear.

(3) The word "oppressive" does not carry "an essential inference of imminent disaster; it can contemplate a continued course of conduct." Gidwitz v. Lanzit Corrugated Box Co., 20 Ill.2d 208, 214, 170 N.E.2d 131, 135 (1960). See also Giannotti v. Hamway, 239 Va. 14, 387 S.E.2d 725 (1990). The *Gidwitz* and *Giannotti* courts stated that "oppressive" is not synonymous with "illegal" or "fraudulent" and its application does not necessarily involve a finding of mismanagement or misapplication of assets. Other courts have referred to general concepts of "a lack of probity and fair dealing" or departure from standards of "fair play." White v. Perkins, 213 Va. 129, 134, 189 S.E.2d 315, 319–20 (1972); Giannotti v. Hamway, 239 Va. 14, 387 S.E.2d 725 (1990). Still, other courts have associated "oppressive" with violations of the fiduciary duty of good faith and fair dealing imposed by Donahue v. Rodd Electrotype, page 397, supra, and similar cases. See also Robert B. Thompson, The Shareholder's Cause of Action for Oppression, 48 Bus.Law. 699 (1993).

(4) Most oppression cases involve actions by majority shareholders that injure minority shareholders. However, minority shareholders also owe duties to the majority and breach of these duties may be viewed as oppressive in some instances. In Rexford Rand Corp. v. Ancel, 58 F.3d 1215 (7th Cir.1995), Gregory, a minority shareholder, was fired as an employee of the corporation for reasons that were in dispute. The corporation subsequently failed to file its annual report with the state of Illinois, and was administratively dissolved, thereby making its name generally available. Gregory, learning of this, reserved the name "Rexford Rand

---

13. [By the Author] Hetherington & Dooley, Illiquidity And Exploitation: A Proposed Statutory Solution to the Remaining Close Corporation Problem, 63 Va.L.Rev. 1 (1976).

Corporation" for his own use and began conducting business under that name in competition with the corporation. The court, relying on concepts developed in *Donahue*, held this conduct violated a duty owed to the corporation and required the name to be transferred back to the original corporation:

> * * * In addition, minority shareholders owe a duty of loyalty to a close corporation in certain circumstances. Minority shareholders have an obligation as de facto partners in the joint venture not to do damage to the corporate interests. * * * Rexford Rand contends that Gregory acted unscrupulously and thus breached his duty of loyalty by reserving the Rexford Rand name for himself rather than informing Selwyn and Albert that Illinois was preparing to administratively dissolve the corporation.
>
> Gregory acknowledges that, under normal circumstances, he would have owed a duty of loyalty to Rexford Rand. He argues, however, that his duty terminated after the alleged freeze-out, which deprived him of his position in the corporation as well as the benefits of his stock ownership. The Illinois courts have never decided whether a freeze-out terminates a minority shareholder's duty of loyalty to a close corporation. * * * Our research indicates that only one court has addressed the question of whether a freeze-out terminates a shareholder's fiduciary duty to a close corporation. In J Bar H, Inc. v. Johnson, 822 P.2d 849 (Wyo.1991), the Supreme Court of Wyoming stated that "where a shareholder/director/employee of a close corporation has been wrongfully terminated from employment with the corporation and has been unjustly prevented from fulfilling her function as a director or officer, she can no longer be considered to act in a fiduciary capacity for the corporation." Id. at 861. The court reasoned that "the fiduciary duty not to compete depends on the ability to exercise the status which creates it." A minority shareholder who has been frozen out no longer exercises the influence over corporate affairs that gives rise to a fiduciary duty. Consequently, no fiduciary duty should remain after a freeze-out. * * *
>
> While we understand the reluctance of the J Bar H court to place a fiduciary duty on a shareholder who has been frozen out, we do not believe that *J Bar H* achieves the optimal result. Gregory may have been the victim of oppressive activity, and he may have believed that reserving the Rexford Rand name for his own use would induce Albert and Selwyn to buy out his stock at a fair price. Gregory's desire to obtain a fair buyout is not itself objectionable * * *. The method by which he sought to induce a settlement, however, is troubling. By appropriating the corporate name, Gregory threatened to cause serious damage to the well-being of the corporation and to imperil Selwyn and Albert's investment as well as his own. The freeze-out did not deprive Gregory of his status as a shareholder, and as a shareholder in a close corporation, Gregory should have placed the interests of the corporation above his personal interests. * * *. If shareholders take it upon themselves to retaliate any time they believe they have been frozen out, disputes in close corporations will only increase. Rather, if unable to resolve matters amicably, aggrieved parties should take their claims to court and seek judicial resolution. Thus, the decision of the district court returning the name to the corporation * * * is affirmed.

(5) In Muellenberg v. Bikon Corp., 143 N.J. 168, 669 A.2d 1382, 1388–89 (1996), majority and minority shareholders sharply disputed who was primarily at fault in oppressing the other; the court, after carefully weighing the equities, concluded that it was appropriate to require the majority shareholders to sell their

shares to the minority shareholder. The court stated "while a minority buy-out of the majority is an uncommon remedy, it was the appropriate one here."

ABREU v. UNICA INDUS. SALES, INC.

Appellate Court of Illinois, 1991.
224 Ill.App.3d 439, 166 Ill.Dec. 703, 586 N.E.2d 661.

JUSTICE GREIMAN delivered the opinion of the court:

Defendants appeal from an adverse decision in a shareholder's derivative action where the trial court found defendants had breached fiduciary obligations by usurping corporate opportunities and repeatedly attempting to acquire secret product formulas. The trial court awarded plaintiff monetary and injunctive relief, attorney fees, and appointed a provisional director to oversee the new board of directors and to break any deadlock between directors.

Defendants raise five issues on appeal: (1) whether the appointment of plaintiff's son-in-law, the General Manager of Operations of the company, as provisional director violates the statute authorizing such appointment; (2) even if such appointment was appropriate under the statute, whether the trial court erred in refusing to remove the provisional director for allegedly failing to carry out the trial court's instructions and follow statutory guidelines; (3) whether the trial court properly awarded attorney fees to plaintiff separate from the damages award; (4) whether the trial court's injunction protecting the company's product formulas is overly broad; and (5) whether damages were properly awarded.

Plaintiff Zenaida Abreau's husband, Manuel ("Manny") Abreau was co-founder and 50% owner of Ebro Foods, Inc. ("Ebro"), a company that develops and manufactures food products. Manny ran the company as its president until his death in November 1987. Plaintiff succeeded to her husband's stock interests and is currently president of Ebro. Defendants Ralph and William Steinbarth ("Ralph" and "William") are co-owners and the only directors of defendant La Preferida, Inc., the other 50% shareholder in Ebro and a company that distributed Ebro's products.

In a thoughtful 42–page opinion, the trial judge carefully and explicitly set out his findings. The trial court found that Ralph created Ebro Industrial Sales, Inc., as a minority-owned business (later renamed Unica Industrial Sales, Inc.) to directly compete with Ebro Foods, Inc. in securing the business of Kraft Foods and awarded damages of $211,269 to Ebro for the lost Kraft business. The trial court also found that defendants repeatedly tried to obtain the master formulas for Ebro's products so that they might have the product made elsewhere and sell it themselves without going through Ebro. The court determined that ownership of the formulas is exclusive to Ebro and that all shareholders are enjoined from disclosing the formulas or data from which the formulas may be ascertained. The court also removed Ralph as director and five other people from employment at Ebro, finding that there had been oppressive and fraudulent self-dealing conduct that threatened the viability of Ebro as a solvent corporation.

Since Ebro was left with only two directors, plaintiff and La Preferida's candidate, Emil Smider, the trial court appointed a provisional director to stabilize the two hostile factions in the best interest of Ebro, pursuant to section 12.55(b) of the Illinois Business Corporation Act ("IBCA").

[Editor: IBCA § 12.55 read in part as follows:

ALTERNATIVE REMEDIES TO JUDICIAL DISSOLUTION.—(a) In either an action for dissolution pursuant to Section 12.50 or in an action which alleges the grounds for dissolution set fourth in Section 12.50 but which does not seek dissolution, the Circuit Court, in lieu of dismissing the action or ordering dissolution, may retain jurisdiction and:

✓ (1) Appoint a provisional director;   — *Illinois crts csn appoint provisional*

(2) Appoint a custodian; or   *directors,*

(3) In an action by a shareholder, order a purchase of the complaining shareholder's shares * * *.

(b) A provisional director may be appointed in the discretion of the court if it appears that such action by the court will remedy the grounds alleged by the complaining shareholder to support the jurisdiction of the court under Section 12.50. A provisional director may be appointed notwithstanding the fact that there is no vacancy on the board of directors and shall have all the rights and powers of a duly elected director, including the right to notice of and to vote at meetings of directors, until such time as the provisional director is removed by order of court or, unless otherwise ordered by court, removed by a vote of the shareholders sufficient either to elect a majority of the board of directors or if greater than majority voting is required by the articles of incorporation or the by-laws, to elect the requisite number of directors needed to take action. * * *]

Defendants first contend the trial court erred in appointing Silvio Vega ("Vega"), General Manager of Operations at Ebro and plaintiff's son-in-law, to serve as provisional director because the IBCA implicitly requires the provisional director to be an impartial third party. While the statute does not explicitly require the provisional director be impartial, defendants argue that because 11 of 16 state statutes enacting the remedy of provisional directors expressly require impartiality, the rest of the statutes assume impartiality. * * *

D's first argument — Provisional Director must be impartial and Silvio Vega is P's son-in-law: not impartial

We disagree that there is a strict requirement of impartiality in appointing a provisional director. Defendant's presumptive reading of legislative intent overlooks the fact that when the legislature enacted the IBCA in 1983, it was well aware of other states' statutes expressly requiring some degree of impartiality and chose to bypass that language and place reliance on the trial court's discretion. * * *

A provisional director is appointed as an alternative remedy to judicial dissolution in times of corporate strife to help guide the company through crisis toward the goal of stabilization and prosperity. When appointing a provisional director, the trial court considers only the best interests of the corporation, and not those of any warring factions. If the trial court, based upon the particular situation, finds that there is no traditionally independent third party with the skills and abilities necessary to fulfill the position within an urgent time frame, it may use its discretion to appoint a provisional director in the best interest of the corporation, whether or not that person has

Court's answer to D's argument provisional director need not be totally impartial, just best under circumstances

been aligned or appears to have been aligned with a particular group of shareholders.

To impose a strict requirement that the court find and appoint a traditionally impartial independent third party, and allow that person time to familiarize himself with the history and goals of the company and its current crisis situation, regardless of the urgency of the situation or the availability of highly competent people who may not be traditionally impartial, is to ignore the mission of section 12.55.

In this case, we find the appointment of Vega was made in the best interest of the corporation and that even though he could not be described as traditionally impartial, the trial court properly exercised discretion, given the circumstances of the case and Vega's background.

We reject the trial judge's reasoning that his right to appoint Vega is founded in the misdeeds of the defendants. The statute imposes upon the court a more goal-oriented approach.

Best interest under circumstance test is a balancing test.

Factors that a trial court may balance in evaluating candidates for provisional director include: degree and quality of past involvement in the corporation; an understanding of the corporation's history and current situation; experience and abilities in providing a cooperative and unifying element; need for immediate appointment; degree of impartiality; and above all, a true interest in the viability and advancement of the corporation as an entity and not allegiance to one of the deadlocked factions.

Defendants argue that Vega is merely a parrot or handmaiden of plaintiff, voting with plaintiff on matters simply because he is her son-in-law. We uphold the trial court's finding that this is an inaccurate and unfair description of Vega, given his experience, knowledge and involvement in the corporation.

Vega has worked for Ebro for over 17 years and is familiar with every aspect of the corporation; he holds a CPA degree that enables him to understand the financial complexities of the business; he has complete knowledge of the history of Ebro's relationship with La Preferida and the Steinbarths, and the symbiosis between the two companies.

While defendants recognize that the remedy is for the benefit of the corporation whose viability is threatened by the intershareholder dispute, they state that the intent of the statute is not to create an imbalance on the board in favor of the complaining shareholder. Defendants are correct in this interpretation, but overlook the fact that they have retained all of the shareholder rights that they had prior to the appointment of the provisional director.

Defendants cite *Gidwitz v. Lanzit Corrugated Box Co.* (1960), 20 Ill.2d 208, 170 N.E.2d 131, to support its argument that Vega should be removed because defendants are effectively prohibited from participating in major corporate decisions because Vega creates a *de facto* majority in favor of plaintiff. In *Gidwitz*, dissident factions arose among shareholders of a corporation and the court dissolved the corporation because it found that the president, with the support of other family members owning one-half of the shares, ran the company oppressively. The court stated that the business was run by the president almost as a sole proprietorship with no regard for the views of the other one-half of the shareholders and directors.

We find this case differs from *Gidwitz* in that the trial court made no findings that any of Vega's actions were "oppressive," nor did it find that La Preferida was excluded from participating in the management of Ebro.

We agree with the trial court's findings in this case that a simple split in votes, however consistent, does not create a *de facto* majority, nor does it disenfranchise a shareholder. Corporation law does not guarantee shareholders the outcome of a vote, merely a right to vote. Given the trial court's findings in the underlying derivative suit, it is to be expected that a provisional director, bound by duty to act in the best interests of the corporation, might be wary of votes cast by the offending shareholder in the suit. Simply because the provisional director does not agree with a voting shareholder does not automatically evidence improper impartiality.

[handwritten margin note: Rationale on why this Provisional director did not give control to one of the family factions.]

We find Vega's appointment was properly within the discretion of the trial court and posed no infringement on defendants' shareholder rights.

Defendants next contend that even if the appointment of Vega is valid, he should be removed from office because he performed certain acts that are inconsistent with his statutory and court-imposed duties and responsibilities. Defendants argue that Vega failed his responsibilities as provisional director when he:

[handwritten margin note: D's argument 2 Vega should be removed for failing to comply with the law.]

(1) submitted a proposal to Kraft for the sale of jalapeno peppers which entailed additional expenses for Ebro of approximately $300,000 without prior review by or approval of the Board of Directors;

(2) terminated La Preferida's 25–year role as the exclusive distributor of the "El Ebro" line of food products without presenting a cost-benefit analysis to or seeking the approval of the Board of Directors;

(3) hired a new auditor to prepare a certified audit for 1990 without the approval of the Board of Directors;

(4) voted against a proposal limiting management's ability to make financial and operational commitments on behalf of the corporation;

(5) voted in favor of reimbursing plaintiff for attorneys' fees and costs and to pay directly the attorneys' fees and costs on appeal even though there was no deadlock on the issue and even though defendant's director asked that the vote be postponed so he could further consider the issue;

(6) failed to attempt to reach any compromise prior to voting on disputed proposals;

(7) failed to ensure the preparation of complete and accurate minutes of board meetings; and

(8) failed to provide defendant's director an agenda for a meeting until the start of the meeting.

Because a provisional director is an officer of the court, it is the trial court's duty to oversee the provisional director's actions. Upon reviewing the evidence and the parties' arguments, the trial court found that even though technical inaccuracies may have occurred regarding board procedure, none of

[handwritten margin note: Court does oversee provisional director.]

the oversights, either separate or cumulative, were enough to justify removal of Vega. The court found that the provisional director breached no duty to the corporation and remains committed to the best interests of Ebro.

We find the record upholds the trial court's determinations, and we affirm, with the exception of the charges involving the unilateral management decision to hire a new certified auditor and the mode of approval of attorney fees for Zenaida, which we reverse as inconsistent with the duties of a provisional director. * * *

It is generally accepted, unless corporate bylaws provide otherwise, that it is improper for management of a corporation to directly hire the auditors whose mission it is to evaluate management's performance. Auditors are often selected by a committee of independent non-management directors or by a full board of directors. (R. Knepper, *Liability of Corporate Officers and Directors*, sec. 1.03, at 5–6 (4th Ed.1988); Brodsky & Adamski, Corporate Officers & Directors, sec. 8.05, at 8 (1984); Farrell, *The Audit Committee–A Lawyer's View*, 28 Bus.Law. 1089, 1091 (1973).) While there is no Illinois law directly addressing this issue, we find that in the instant case, any decision regarding the selection of a new auditor should have been reserved for the full Board of Directors and not made unilaterally by management, absent any contrary corporate bylaws. We find invalid Vega's unilateral appointment of an auditor and order the full Board of Directors to vote on selection of an auditor.

We also hold invalid the Board of Directors' vote to reimburse plaintiff and order that the proposal be put to a vote that incorporates proper procedure. In that decision, plaintiff and Vega voted in favor of reimbursing plaintiff for attorney fees while Smider abstained, stating he needed more time to study the proposal. The trial court determined that all relief for plaintiff's attorney fees be considered by the corporation directly and that the board must find a way to "filter" it down to plaintiff. From the record it appears that the process used to reach the outcome of the vote was deficient in that Vega and plaintiff improperly voted.

Provisional directors appointed under section 12.55 are officers of the court and serve at the discretion and direction of the court. The trial court specifically instructed Vega to vote only upon deadlocked matters. We do not find Smider's abstention on the vote created a deadlock. Smider stated that he abstained from the vote because he had received the proposal only a short while before the meeting. Smider requested that the decision be postponed so he could vote on the matter cognizant of all relevant information. The trial court had instructed Vega, as provisional director, to ensure that the board of Directors operated in a "very formal fashion—the board of directors meetings would be set meetings; people would know when they would be; agendas would be kept; that a record of the board of directors meeting would be kept * * * that there be some record so that people can validate what was said."

We do not find it unreasonable under the circumstances for Smider to ask that the vote be postponed until he could thoroughly review the proposal for reimbursement; to vote without doing so would be an abdication of his duty as director to vote only when fully informed. Because there was no deadlock, we find Vega improperly voted on this issue. * * *

[W]e reiterate the trial court's admonition that in a uniquely structured corporate situation such as this, it is highly prudent to retain outside counsel to avoid further complications in the decision-making process. Complex issues regarding legality of votes and the division of corporate responsibility between management and the board need to be examined carefully in order to adhere to corporate bylaws and corporation law. * * *

For all of the foregoing reasons, we affirm in part and reverse and remand in part in accordance with this opinion.

Note

It will be noted that Preferida, a corporation, owned 50 per cent of the stock of Ebro. Could Preferida itself be a director? The general assumption in the United States is that only natural individuals can serve as directors. See MBCA § 8.03(a): A board of directors must consist of one or more *"individuals * * *."* In many European and other countries, artificial entities routinely serve as directors, acting through individuals as agents of the director.

E.   ACTION BY DIRECTORS AND OFFICERS

IN THE MATTER OF DRIVE–IN DEVELOPMENT CORP.

United States Court of Appeals, Seventh Circuit, 1966.
371 F.2d 215.

SWYGERT, CIRCUIT JUDGE.

The principal question in this appeal relates to the circumstances which may bind a corporation to a guaranty of the obligations of a related corporation when it is contended that the corporate officer who executed the guaranty had no authority to do so. The facts giving rise to the question underlie a claim filed by the National Boulevard Bank of Chicago in an arrangement proceeding under chapter XI of the Bankruptcy Act, 11 U.S.C.A. §§ 701–799, in which the Drive In Development Corporation ["Drive In"] was the debtor. National Boulevard's claim was disallowed by the referee, whose decision was confirmed by the district court.

Drive In was one of four subsidiary companies controlled by Tastee Freez Industries, Inc., a holding company that conducted no business of its own. * * *

[Editor: The officers of Drive In executed a guarantee of payment to induce National Boulevard Bank to make a loan to Drive In's parent corporation. The guarantee was executed by one Maranz on behalf of Drive In as "Chairman" and one Dick attested to its execution as secretary. National Boulevard requested a copy of the authorizing resolution of the board of directors of Drive In. A copy, certified by Dick with the corporate seal affixed, was duly delivered. No such resolution, however, was contained in Drive In's corporate minute book, and the directors' testimony left it uncertain as to whether any such resolution had ever been considered or approved at a directors meeting. National Boulevard advanced substantial sums under the guaranty.]

Turning to the merits of the objections to National Boulevard's claim, the referee found that Drive In's minute book did not show that a resolution authorizing Maranz to sign the guaranty was adopted by the directors and that Dick could not recall a specific directors' meeting at which such a resolution was approved. From these findings, the referee concluded that Maranz, who signed the guaranty on behalf of Drive In, had no authority, "either actual or implied or apparent," to bind Drive In. This conclusion was erroneous. Drive In was estopped to deny Maranz' express authority to sign the guaranty because of the certified copy of a resolution of Drive In's board of directors purporting to grant such authority furnished to the bank by Dick, whether or not such a resolution was in fact formally adopted. Dick was the secretary of the corporation. Generally, it is the duty of the secretary to keep the corporate records and to make proper entries of the actions and resolutions of the directors. Therefore it was within the authority of Dick to certify that a resolution such as challenged here was adopted. Statements made by an officer or agent in the course of a transaction in which the corporation is engaged and which are within the scope of his authority are binding upon the corporation. Consequently Drive In was estopped to deny the representation made by Dick in the certificate forwarded to National Boulevard, in the absence of actual or constructive knowledge on the part of the bank that the representation was untrue. * * *

The objectors argue that since William Schneider, a vice president of National Boulevard, requested Dick to furnish the certified copy of a resolution granting authority to execute the guaranty, and since Hugh Driscoll, another vice president of National Boulevard, was also a director of Tastee Freez and was familiar with the organization of the subsidiaries, the bank was somehow in a position to know that no resolution had in fact been adopted by Drive In's board of directors. These facts, however, fall far short of proving such knowledge on the part of National Boulevard.

* * * Although intercorporate contracts of guaranty do not usually occur in the regular course of commercial business, here the interrelationship of Tastee Freez and its subsidiaries presented a situation in which the guaranty was not so unusual as would ordinarily obtain. Furthermore, the realities of modern corporate business practices do not contemplate that those who deal with officers or agents acting for a corporation should be required to go behind the representations of those who have authority to speak for the corporation and who verify the authority of those who presume to act for the corporation. * * *

The order of the district court confirming the referee's order is reversed in part and affirmed in part.

Notes

(1) What if the third person really should know that the directors could not have adopted the resolution being certified by the secretary on the date specified? In Keystone Leasing Corp. v. Peoples Protective Life Ins. Co., 514 F.Supp. 841 (E.D.N.Y.1981), the Court refused to grant the third person the benefit of the estoppel principle set forth in *Drive In* where the third person "must have been aware" that the transaction had not been authorized by the board of directors.

(2) The estoppel recognized in this case is based on the authority of the secretary of the corporation to execute documents and affix the corporate seal. If a document is appropriately executed and sealed by the corporate secretary, third

parties without specific knowledge about the actions taken may rely with confidence on the document. It is obviously sensible for such parties to accept documents at their face value and not inquire into the details of their approval and execution.

LEE v. JENKINS BROS.

United States Court of Appeals, Second Circuit, 1959.
268 F.2d 357.

MEDINA, CIRCUIT JUDGE. * * *

[Editor: In 1919, the Crane Company agreed to sell its Bridgeport, Connecticut, plant to a New Jersey Corporation, Jenkins Brothers. Jenkins Brothers felt it needed to employ competent personnel, and sought to employ Lee, the business manager of Crane Company. Yardley, the President of Jenkins Brothers and a substantial stockholder, met with Lee at a hotel on June 1, 1920, and sought to entice him to join Jenkins Brothers. Also present was a vice president and his wife, though at the time of the trial in October 1957 only Lee was alive to describe the conversation.]

First, Lee testified:

> As far as the pension that I had earned with Crane Company he said the company [Jenkins Brothers] would pay that pension (and) if they didn't or, if anything came up, he would assume the liability himself, he would guarantee payment of the pension; and in consideration of that promise I agreed to go to work for Jenkins Bros. on June 1, 1920.

> The amount of the pension referred to by Mr. Yardley was a maximum of $1500 a year and that would be paid me when I reached the age of 60 years; regardless of what happened in the meantime, if I were with the company or not, I would be given a credit for those 13 years of service with the maximum pension of $1500.

Later Lee put it this way:

> Mr. Farnham Yardley said that Jenkins would assume the obligation for my credit pension record with Crane Company and, if anything happened and they did not pay it, he would guarantee it himself.

> Mr. Yardley's words were 'regardless of what happens, you will get that pension if you join our company.'

Finally, Lee summarized his position:

> My claim is that the company through the chairman of the board of directors and the president, promised me credit for my 13 years of service with Crane Company, regardless of what happened I would receive a pension at the age of 60, not to exceed $1,500 a year. If I was discharged in 1921 or 1922 or left I would still get that pension. That is what I am asking for.

> This agreement was never reduced to writing.

Lee's prospects with Jenkins turned out to be just about as bright as he had hoped. He subsequently became vice president and general manager in charge of manufacturing and a director of the company. At that time he was receiving a salary of $25,000 from Jenkins, $8,000 more from an affiliate, plus an annual 10 percent bonus. In 1945, however, after 25 years with Jenkins, Lee was discharged at the age of 55 * * *.

In the discussion which follows we assume *arguendo,* that there was evidence sufficient to support a finding that Yardley orally agreed on behalf of the corporation that Lee would be paid at the age of 60 a pension not to exceed $1500, and that Yardley's words "regardless of what happens" were, as Lee contends, to be interpreted as meaning that Lee would receive this pension even if he were not working for Jenkins at the time the pension became payable. Jenkins asserts that Yardley had no authority to bind it to such an "extraordinary" contract, express, implied, or apparent and the trial court so found. There is nothing in the proofs submitted by Lee to warrant any finding of actual authority in Yardley. The Certificate of Incorporation and By–Laws of Jenkins are not in evidence nor was any course of conduct shown as between the corporation and Yardley. Accordingly, on the phase of the case now under discussion, we are dealing only with apparent authority. See 2 Fletcher, Cyclopedia Corporations, Section 449 (Perm.Ed.1954). * * *

The ascertainment of the Connecticut law on this critical question of Yardley's apparent authority is a far from simple task. The Connecticut cases have not yet quite come to grips with the question. Hence, it is necessary to consult the "general" law on the subject, on the assumption that, if a general rule can be found, Connecticut would follow it. * * *

Our question on this phase of the case then boils itself down to the following: can it be said as a matter of law that Yardley as president, chairman of the board, substantial stockholder and trustee and son-in-law of the estate of the major stockholder, had no power in the presence of the company's most interested vice president to secure for a "reasonable" length of time badly needed key personnel by promising an experienced local executive a life pension to commence in 30 years at the age of 60, even if Lee were not then working for the corporation, when the maximum liability to Jenkins under such a pension was $1500 per year.

A survey of the law on the authority of corporate officers does not reveal a completely consistent pattern. For the most part the courts perhaps have taken a rather restrictive view on the extent of powers of corporate officials, but the dissatisfaction with such an approach has been manifested in a variety of exceptions such as ratification, estoppel, and promissory estoppel. * * *

The rule most widely cited is that the president only has authority to bind his company by acts arising in the usual and regular course of business but not for contracts of an "extraordinary" nature. The substance of such a rule lies in the content of the term "extraordinary" which is subject to a broad range of interpretation.

The growth and development of this rule occurred during the late nineteenth and early twentieth centuries when the potentialities of the corporate form of enterprise were just being realized. As the corporation became a more common vehicle for the conduct of business it became increasingly evident that many corporations, particularly small closely held ones, did not normally function in the formal ritualistic manner hitherto envisaged. While the boards of directors still nominally controlled corporate affairs, in reality officers and managers frequently ran the business with little, if any, board supervision. The natural consequence of such a development was that third parties commonly relied on the authority of such officials in almost all the multifarious transactions in which corporations engaged. The pace of modern business life was too swift to insist on the approval by the board of directors of every transaction that was in any way "unusual."

The judicial recognition given to these developments has varied considerably. Whether termed "apparent authority" or an "estoppel" to deny authority, many courts have noted the injustice caused by the practice of permitting corporations to act commonly through their executives and then allowing them to disclaim an agreement as beyond the authority of the contracting officer, when the contract no longer suited its convenience. Other courts, however, continued to cling to the past with little attempt to discuss the unconscionable results obtained or the doctrine of apparent authority. Such restrictive views have been generally condemned by the commentators.

The summary of holdings pro and con in general on the subject of what are and what are not "extraordinary" agreements is inconclusive at best * * *. But the pattern becomes more distinct when we turn to the more limited area of employment contracts.

It is generally settled that the president as part of the regular course of business has authority to hire and discharge employees and fix their compensation. In so doing he may agree to hire them for a specific number of years if the term selected is deemed reasonable. But employment contracts for life or on a "permanent" basis are generally regarded as "extraordinary" and beyond the authority of any corporate executive if the only consideration for the promise is the employee's promise to work for that period. Jenkins would have us analogize the pension agreement involved herein to these generally condemned lifetime employment contracts because it extends over a long period of time, is of indefinite duration, and involves an indefinite liability on the part of the corporation.

It is not surprising that lifetime employment contracts have met with substantial hostility in the courts, for these contracts are often oral, uncorroborated, vague in important details and highly improbable. Accordingly, the courts have erected a veritable array of obstacles to their enforcement. They have been construed as terminable at will, too indefinite to enforce, *ultra vires,* lacking in mutuality or consideration, abandoned or breached by subsequent acts, and the supporting evidence deemed insufficient to go to the jury, as well as made without proper authority.

Where reasons have been given to support the conclusion that lifetime employments are "extraordinary," and hence made without authority, a scrutiny of these reasons may be helpful for their bearing on the analogous field of pension agreements. It is said that: they unduly restrict the power of the shareholders and future boards of directors on questions of managerial policy; they subject the corporation to an inordinately substantial amount of liability; they run for long and indefinite periods of time. Of these reasons the only one applicable to pension agreements is that they run for long and indefinite periods of time. There the likeness stops. Future director or shareholder control is in no way impeded; the amount of liability is not disproportionate; the agreement was not only not unreasonable but beneficial and necessary to the corporation; and pension contracts are commonly used fringe benefits in employment contracts. Moreover, unlike the case with life employment contracts, courts have often gone out of their way to find pension promises binding and definite even when labeled gratuitous by the employer. The consideration given to the employee involved is not at all dependent on profits or sales, nor does it involve some other variable suggesting director discretion.

In this case Lee was hired at a starting salary of $4,000 per year plus a contemplated pension of $1500 per year in thirty years. Had Lee been hired at a starting salary of $10,000 per year the cost to the corporation over the long run would have been substantially greater, yet no one could plausibly contend that such an employment contract was beyond Yardley's authority.

The cases on executive authority to make pension agreements are few. In West v. Hunt Foods, Inc., 1951, 101 Cal.App.2d 597, 225 P.2d 978, the most recent case on the subject, a nonsuit was reversed on the theory that the jury might have decided in plaintiff's favor either upon the basis of authority in the president and vice-president to make the promise of a pension or on the basis of a promissory estoppel. In Langer v. Superior Steel Corp., 1935, 318 Pa. 490, 178 A. 490, authority was found lacking in the president, who acted in direct violation of a directors' resolution, to promise a pension for life in return for past services. His apparent authority was not discussed. In Plowman v. Indian Refining Co., D.C.E.D.Ill.1937, 20 F.Supp. 1, the vice president was found to lack authority gratuitously to promise 18 employees life pensions at half wages. * * *

Apparent authority is essentially a question of fact. It depends not only on the nature of the contract involved, but the officer negotiating it, the corporation's usual manner of conducting business, the size of the corporation and the number of its stockholders, the circumstances that give rise to the contract, the reasonableness of the contract, the amounts involved, and who the contracting third party is, to list a few but not all of the relevant factors. In certain instances a given contract may be so important to the welfare of the corporation that outsiders would naturally suppose that only the board of directors (or even the shareholders) could properly handle it. It is in this light that the "ordinary course of business" rule should be given its content. Beyond such "extraordinary" acts, whether or not apparent authority exists is simply a matter of fact.

Accordingly, we hold that, assuming there was sufficient proof of the making of the pension agreement, Connecticut, in the particular circumstances of this case, would probably take the view that reasonable men could differ on the subject of whether or not Yardley had apparent authority to make the contract, and that the trial court erred in deciding the question as a matter of law. We do not think Connecticut would adopt any hard and fast rule against apparent authority to make pension agreements generally, on the theory that they were in the same category as lifetime employment contracts. * * *

Notes

(1) The comments in the principal case about the relative roles of the board of directors and the president of a corporation are not only representative of judicial thinking but also seem firmly grounded in the language of corporation

statutes. See MBCA §§ 8.01, 8.41, last paragraph. In the absence of a § 7.32–type agreement, decisions by even the smallest corporations are to be made by the board of directors, not the officers or shareholders.

(2) Corporation statutes generally specify that every corporation will have designated officers, usually a president, a secretary, and a treasurer. Earlier versions of the MBCA also specified these officers, but the Model Act generally does not. Compare MBCA §§ 8.40(a), 8.40(c), 1.40(20). The Official Comment to § 8.40 suggests that "[e]xperience has shown * * * that little purpose is served by a statutory requirement that there be certain officers, and statutory requirements may sometimes create problems of implied or apparent authority or confusion with nonstatutory offices the corporation desires to create."

(3) Presumably, the chief executive officer of a small corporation, no matter what her formal title, will be required to take a number of actions on her own authority. For example, who is to hire secretaries, order needed equipment and supplies and the like? Where does one go to find the basis of authority? One possible source is the bylaws of the corporation, which usually describe the roles and responsibilities of the principal officers. James R. Burkhard, Proposed Model Bylaws To Be Used With The Revised Model Business Corporation Act (1984), 46 Bus.Law. 189, 225–26 (1990),[14] suggests the following descriptions of the roles of the president, secretary, and treasurer:

§ 4.4 President.

The president shall be the principal executive officer of the corporation and, subject to the control of the board of directors, shall in general supervise and control all of the business and affairs of the corporation. He shall, when present, preside at all meetings of the shareholders and of the board of directors. He may sign, with the secretary or any other proper officer of the corporation thereunto authorized by the board of directors, certificates for shares of the corporation and deeds, mortgages, bonds, contracts, or other instruments which the board of directors has authorized to be executed, except in cases where the signing and execution thereof shall be expressly delegated by the board of directors or by these bylaws to some other officer or agent of the corporation, or shall be required by law to be otherwise signed or executed; and in general shall perform all duties incident to the office of president and such other duties as may be prescribed by the board of directors from time to time. * * *

§ 4.6 The Secretary.

The secretary shall: (a) keep the minutes of the proceedings of the shareholders and of the board of directors in one or more books provided for that purpose; (b) see that all notices are duly given in accordance with the provisions of these bylaws or as required by law; (c) be custodian of the corporate records and of any seal of the corporation and if there is a seal of the corporation, see that it is affixed to all documents the execution of which on behalf of the corporation under its seal is duly authorized; (d) when requested or required, authenticate any records of the corporation; (e) keep a register of the post office address of each shareholder which shall be furnished to the secretary by such shareholder; (f) sign with the president, or a vice-president, certificates for shares of the corporation, the issuance of which

14. Copyright (1990) by the American Bar Association. All rights reserved. Reprinted with permission of the American Bar Association and its Section of Business Law.

shall have been authorized by resolution of the board of directors; (g) have general charge of the stock transfer books of the corporation; and (h) in general perform all duties incident to the office of secretary and such other duties as from time to time may be assigned to him by the president or by the board of directors. * * *

§ 4.7 The Treasurer.

The treasurer shall: (a) have charge and custody of and be responsible for all funds and securities of the corporation; (b) receive and give receipts for moneys due and payable to the corporation from any source whatsoever, and deposit all such moneys in the name of the corporation in such banks, trust companies, or other depositories as shall be selected by the board of directors; and (c) in general perform all of the duties incident to the office of treasurer and such other duties as from time to time may be assigned to him by the president or by the board of directors. If required by the board of directors, the treasurer shall give a bond for the faithful discharge of his duties in such sum and with such surety or sureties as the board of directors shall determine. * * *

(4) Again consider MBCA § 8.01(b). Does this grant of authority to directors have a negative implication with respect to the actual or apparent authority of corporate officers? Assume that all corporate powers are being exercised "under the direction of" (rather than "by") the board of directors, as is almost always the case in large, publicly held corporations and often the case in closely held corporations as well. Should that give the senior officers of the corporation greater authority than a senior executive with the same title might have in a corporation where corporate powers are being exercised "by" the board? The line between the authority of operating officers entering into binding corporate commitments on their own and the area reserved to the board of directors is often unclear. In cases of doubt, should not the operating officer refer the question to the board? What if the board is large and meets infrequently? Consider also American Law Institute, Principles of Corporate Governance: Analysis and Recommendations 84–86 (1994) (noting that questions concerning the authority of senior executives are normally special issues of agency law, the relevant concepts being those of actual and apparent authority, and that the accepted modern rule is that the president has apparent authority by virtue of that position to take actions in the ordinary course of business, but not extraordinary actions).

(5) Another issue that has given rise to litigation is whether a corporate president has power to commence a lawsuit without the prior authorization of the board of directors. For examples of such litigation, see Keogh Corp. v. Howard, Weil, Labouisse, Friedrichs Inc., 827 F.Supp. 269 (S.D.N.Y.1993)(suit instituted by corporate president alleged that Howard, Weil obtained control of Keogh's board of directors through extortion, bribery, and fraud in violation of the Racketeer Influenced and Corrupt Organizations Act; suit dismissed because only the board of directors had authority to "initiate litigation out of the ordinary course of business"); Anmaco, Inc. v. Bohlken, 13 Cal.App.4th 891, 16 Cal.Rptr.2d 675, 679 (1993)(there is no "presumptive or implied authority in the president to institute litigation in the name of the corporation against a co-director and equal shareholder. Pressing the corporation into litigation as a plaintiff is inappropriate where the other shareholder-director could claim equal authority to bring suit in the corporate name. This is particularly obvious in the instant case where Bohlken is not only an equal director and shareholder, but is also Chief Executive Officer of the

company. The proper vehicle for such a suit, when the gravamen of the complaint is injury to the corporation, is a shareholder's derivative action.'').

F. TRANSACTIONS IN CONTROLLING SHARES

DeBAUN v. FIRST WESTERN BANK AND TRUST CO.

Court of Appeals of California, 1975.
46 Cal.App.3d 686, 120 Cal.Rptr. 354.

Thompson, Associate Justice.

This appeal primarily concerns the duty of a majority shareholder to the corporation whose shares he holds in selling the shares when possessed of facts establishing a reasonable likelihood that the purchaser intends to exercise the control to be acquired by him to loot the corporation of its assets. We conclude that in those circumstances the majority shareholder owes a duty of reasonable investigation and due care to the corporation.

Facts

Alfred S. Johnson Incorporated (Corporation) was incorporated by Alfred S. Johnson in 1955 to process color photographs to be reproduced in printed form. All of the 100 outstanding shares of Corporation were originally owned by Johnson. Subsequently, Johnson sold 20 of his shares to James DeBaun, Corporation's primary salesman, and 10 shares to Walter Stephens, its production manager. In November of 1964, Johnson was seriously ill so that managerial control of Corporation was assumed by DeBaun, Stephens, and Jack Hawkins, Corporation's estimator.

Johnson died testate on January 15, 1965. His will named appellant First Western Bank and Trust Company (Bank) as executor and trustee of a trust created by the will. The 70 shares of Corporation owned by Johnson at the time of his death passed to the testamentary trust. George Furman, an employee of Bank, was charged with the direct administration of the trust. While Bank took no hand in the management of Corporation leaving it to the existing management team, Furman attended virtually all directors' meetings. Bank, through its nominee, voted the 70 shares at stockholders' meetings.

Under the guidance of DeBaun and Stephens, the net after tax profit of Corporation increased dramatically as illustrated by the following table:

Fiscal year ending August 31	Net Profit
1964	$15,903
1965	$42,316
1966	$58,969
1967	$37,583
1968 (10 mos.)	$56,710

On October 27, 1966, Bank's trust department determined that the investment in Corporation was not appropriate for the trust and decided to sell the 70 shares. Bank also decided that no one connected with Corporation should be made aware of its decision to sell until a sale was firm. It caused an appraisal of Corporation to be made by General Appraisal Company which estimated the value of Corporation as a going concern at $326,000. Bank retained W.H. Daum Investment Company (Daum) to find a buyer and to assist it in the sale.

DeBaun and Stephens were not told of the Bank's plans. In March of 1968, a competitor of Corporation showed DeBaun a letter from Daum indicating that Corporation was for sale. Subsequently, both DeBaun and Stephens were contacted by two potential buyers who sought to purchase their shares. They refused to sell, agreeing to hold their shares because they had " * * * a good job * * * and percentage of the company * * *. " At the request of Daum's representative, DeBaun submitted an offer for the 70 shares held by Bank. The offer was rejected as inadequate.

On May 15 and 20, 1968, Bank received successive offers for the 70 shares from Raymond J. Mattison, acting in the name of S.O.F. Fund, an inter vivos revocable trust of which he was both settlor and trustee. A sketchy balance sheet of S.O.F. Fund was submitted with the second offer. The offers were rejected. Anticipating a further offer from Mattison and his trust, Furman, acting for Bank, ordered a Dun & Bradstreet report on Mattison and the fund. The report was received on May 24, 1968. It noted pending litigation, bankruptcies, and tax liens against corporate entities in which Mattison had been a principal, and suggested that S.O.F. Fund no longer existed.

As of May 24, I. Earl Funk, a vice-president of Bank, had personal knowledge that: (1) on October 24, 1957, the Los Angeles Superior Court had entered a judgment against Mattison in favor of Bank's predecessor in interest for compensatory and punitive damages as the result of Mattison's fraudulent misrepresentations and a fraudulent financial statement to obtain a loan; and (2) the judgment remained unsatisfied in 1968 and was an asset of Bank acquired from its predecessor in an acquisition of 65 branch banks.

On May 27, 1968, Mattison submitted a third offer to purchase the 70 shares of Corporation held by Bank. The offer proposed that S.O.F. Fund would pay $250,000 for the shares, $50,000 in marketable securities as a down payment with the balance payable over a five-year period. Bank made a counter offer, generally accepting the terms of the Mattison proposal but providing that: (1) the $200,000 balance of the purchase price was to be secured by a pledge of marketable securities valued at a like amount; and (2) Corporation would pay no dividends out of "pre-sale" retained earnings. On June 4, 1968, representatives of Bank met with Oroville McCarrol, who had been a trust officer of Bank's predecessor in interest and was counsel for Mattison. McCarrol proposed that Corporation use its assets to secure the unpaid balance of the purchase price rather than Mattison supplying the security in the form of marketable securities. He proposed also the elimination of the restriction against dividends from pre-sale retained earnings. Despite reservations by Bank personnel on the legality of the use of corporate assets to secure an obligation of a major shareholder, Bank determined to pursue the McCarrol modification further. Troubled by the Dun & Bradstreet report, personnel of Bank met with Mattison and McCarrol on June 27. Mattison explained that it had been his practice to take over failing companies so that the existence of the litigation and tax liens noted in the Dun & Bradstreet report was not due to his fault. Not entirely satisfied, Furman wrote to McCarrol requesting a written report on the status of all pending litigation in which Mattison was involved. McCarrol telephoned his response, declining to represent the status of the litigation but noting that the information was publicly available. Partly because Ralph Whitsett, Furman's immediate superior at Bank, knew McCarrol as a former trust officer of Bank's predecessor in interest, and partly because during a luncheon with Mattison at the Jonathan Club Robert Q. Parsons, the officer at Daum in charge of the transaction, had noted that Mattison was warmly received by his fellow members and reported that fact to Furman, Bank did not pursue its investigation into the public records of Los Angeles County where a mass of derogatory information lay.

As of July 1, 1968, the public records of Los Angeles County revealed 38 unsatisfied judgments against Mattison or his entities totalling $330,886.27, and 54 pending actions claiming a total of $373,588.67 from them. The record also contained 22 recorded abstracts of judgments against Mattison or his entities totalling $285,704.11, and 18 tax liens aggregating $20,327.97. Bank did not investigate the public record and hence was unaware of Mattison's financial track record.

While failing to pursue the investigation of the known information adverse to Mattison, Bank's employees knew or should have known that if his proposal through McCarrol were accepted the payment of the $200,000 balance of the purchase price would necessarily come from Corporation. They assumed that the payments would be made by Mattison from distributions of the Corporation which he would cause it to make after assuming control. They were aware that Corporation would not generate a sufficient aftertax cash flow to pay dividends in a sufficient amount to permit the payments of interest and principal on the $200,000 balance as scheduled in the McCarrol proposal, and knew that Mattison could make those payments only by resorting to distribution of "pre-sale" retained earnings and assets of Corporation.

On July 11, 1968, Bank accepted the McCarrol modification by entering into an exchange agreement with S.O.F. Fund. The agreement obligated S.O.F. to retain a working capital of not less than $70,000, to refrain from intercompany transactions except in the ordinary course of business for adequate consideration, and to furnish monthly financial statements and a certified annual audit report to Bank. It provides that Bank is to transfer its 70 shares of Corporation to Mattison as trustee of S.O.F. Fund, and that the stock will be held by Bank in pledge to secure the fund's obligation. There is provision for acceleration of the unpaid balance of the purchase price if Mattison defaults in any provision of the agreement. The contract obligated Mattison to cause Corporation to execute a security agreement to secure Mattison's obligation to Bank covering all "furniture, fixtures and equipment of [Corporation]." Mattison agreed also to cause Corporation's principal banking business to be maintained with Bank.

The exchange agreement having been executed, Bank gave Mattison a proxy to vote the 70 shares of Corporation at a special meeting of shareholders of Corporation to be held on July 11 at 3 p.m. Furman attended that meeting and an ensuing directors' meeting, as did Mattison. At the shareholders' meeting, DeBaun and Stephens were told that the shares of Corporation owned by Bank had been sold by it on an installment basis to Mattison and that Bank intended to take a pledge of those shares. A new board of directors was elected of which Mattison had control although DeBaun and Stephens remained as directors. DeBaun and Stephens were informed by Furman that a security agreement had been signed to protect Corporation in the event of death or default of Mattison and that in such an event Bank would "foreclose on the stock." Furman did not supply DeBaun or Stephens with a copy of the security agreement or inform them that in fact [it] hypothecated corporate assets as security for Mattison's debt to Bank. Relying upon Furman's statement of the effect of the agreement and misled by his failure to disclose its material terms, and by the further representation that the document was simply a formal requirement of Mattison's purchase of the majority shares, DeBaun and Stephens participated in a unanimous vote approving the execution by Corporation of the security agreement. A directors' meeting was then convened at which Mattison was elected president of Corporation.

At the moment of Bank's sale of the controlling shares to Mattison, Corporation was an eminently successful going business with a bright future. It had cash of $76,126.15 and other liquid assets of over $122,000. Its remaining assets were worth $60,000. Its excess of current assets over current liabilities and reserve for bad debts was $233,391.94, and its net worth about $220,000. Corporation's earnings indicated a pattern of growth. Mattison immediately proceeded to change that situation. Beginning with the date that he acquired control, Mattison implemented a systematic scheme to loot Corporation of its assets. His first step was to divert $73,144 in corporate cash to himself and to MICO, a shell company owned by Mattison. The transfer was made in exchange for unsecured noninterest bearing notes but for no other consideration. On August 2, 1968, Mattison caused Corporation to assign to MICO all of Corporation's assets, including its receivables in exchange for a fictitious agreement for management services. He diverted all corporate mail to a post office box from which he took the mail, opened it, and extracted all incoming checks to the corporation before forwarding the mail on. He ceased paying trade creditors promptly, as had been Corporation's practice, delaying payment of trade creditors to the last possible moment and, to the extent he could, not paying some at all. He delayed shipments on new orders. To cover his activities, Mattison removed the corporate books and records.

In September 1968, DeBaun left Corporation's employ as a salesman because of Mattison's policy of not filling orders and because Mattison had drastically reduced DeBaun's compensation. * * * Mattison continued to loot the corporation, although at a reduced pace by reason of its depleted assets. He collected payments from employees to pay premiums on a voluntary health insurance plan although the policy covering the plan was terminated in September for failure to pay premiums. He issued payroll checks without sufficient funds and continued not to pay trade creditors. Mattison did not supply Bank with the financial reports required by the exchange agreement.

While Bank was not aware of the initial transfer of cash to MICO, it did learn of the other misconduct of Mattison as it occurred. Although the conduct was a breach of the exchange agreement, Bank took no action beyond seeking an oral explanation from Mattison. In December 1968, Stephens also left Corporation's employ.

Bank took no action in the matter until April 25, 1969. On that date, it filed an action in the superior court seeking the appointment of a receiver. On April 30, Bank called a special shareholders' meeting of Corporation at which it voted its shares with those of DeBaun and Stephens to elect a new board of directors replacing the Mattison group. Faced with resistance from Mattison, Bank pursued neither its receivership nor its ouster of the board until June 20, 1969, when it shut down the operations of Corporation. By that time, Corporation was hopelessly insolvent. Its debts exceeded its assets by over $200,000, excluding its contingent liability to Bank, as a result of the fraudulently obtained hypothecation of corporate assets to secure Mattison's debt. Both the federal Internal Revenue Service and California State Board of Equalization had filed liens upon corporate assets and notices to withhold funds. A trade creditor had placed a keeper on the corporate premises.

On July 10, 1969, Bank, pursuant to the security agreement, sold all of Corporation's then remaining assets for $60,000. $25,000 of the proceeds of sale was paid to release the federal tax lien while the remaining $35,000 was retained by Bank. After the sale, Corporation had no assets and owed $218,426 to creditors.

Respondents filed two related actions against Bank. One asserted their right to recover, as shareholders, for damage caused by Bank. The other was a stockholders' derivate [sic] action brought on behalf of Corporation * * *. The two cases were consolidated. Bank demurred to both complaints. In the demurrer to the first action, it contended that respondents DeBaun and Stephens, as shareholders, lacked capacity to pursue their claim. In the demurrer to the second complaint, Bank took the opposite tack, contending that its liability did not run to Corporation. The demurrer to the first complaint was sustained without leave to amend, and the demurrer to the second complaint was overruled. The case at bench proceeded to trial before a judge as a derivate [sic] action. The trial court held for respondents, finding that Bank had breached duties it owed as a majority controlling shareholder to the corporation it controlled. It assessed monetary damages in the amount of $473,836, computed by adding to $220,000, the net asset value of the corporation at the date of transfer of the shares to Mattison, an amount equal to anticipated after-tax earnings of the corporation for the ensuing 10–year period, taking into account an 8 percent growth factor. The court additionally awarded Corporation an amount equal to the sum it would be required to pay and the cost of defending valid claims existing against it when it became defunct. Pursuant to Fletcher v. A.J. Industries, Inc., 266 Cal.App.2d 313, 320–321, 72 Cal.Rptr. 146, the trial court awarded counsel for respondents attorneys' fees payable from the fund recovered for Corporation's benefit. It denied respondents' claim for punitive damages. This appeal from the resulting judgment followed. * * *

Breach of Duty

Early case law held that a controlling shareholder owed no duty to minority shareholders or to the controlled corporation in the sale of his stock. (See e.g., Ryder v. Bamberger, 172 Cal. 791, 158 P. 753 (1916).) Decisional law, however, has since recognized the fact of financial life that corporate control by ownership of a majority of shares may be misused. Thus the applicable proposition now is that "[i]n any transaction where the control of the corporation is material," the controlling majority shareholder must exercise good faith and fairness "from the viewpoint of the corporation and those interested therein." (Remillard Brick Co. v. Remillard–Dandini, 109 Cal. App.2d 405, 420, 241 P.2d 66, 75 quoted in Jones v. H.F. Ahmanson & Co., 1 Cal.3d 93, 110, 81 Cal.Rptr. 592, 600, 460 P.2d 464, 472.) That duty of good faith and fairness encompasses an obligation of the controlling shareholder in possession of facts "[s]uch as to awaken suspicion and put a prudent man on his guard [that a potential buyer of his shares may loot the corporation of its assets to pay for the shares purchased] * * * to conduct a reasonable adequate investigation [of the buyer]." (Insuranshares Corporation v. Northern Fiscal Corp. (E.D.Pa.1940) 35 F.Supp. 22, 25.)

Here Bank was the controlling majority shareholder of Corporation. As it was negotiating with Mattison, it became directly aware of facts that would have alerted a prudent person that Mattison was likely to loot the corporation. Bank knew from the Dun & Bradstreet report that Mattison's financial record was notable by the failure of entities controlled by him. Bank knew that the only source of funds available to Mattison to pay it for the shares he was purchasing lay in the assets of the Corporation. The after-tax net income from the date of the sale would not be sufficient to permit the payment of dividends to him which would permit the making of payments. An officer of Bank possessed personal knowledge that Mattison, on at least one occasion, had been guilty of a fraud perpetrated on Bank's predecessor in interest and had not satisfied a judgment Bank held against him for damages flowing from that conduct.

Armed with knowledge of those facts, Bank owed a duty to Corporation and its minority shareholders to act reasonably with respect to its dealings in the controlling shares with Mattison. It breached that duty. Knowing of McCarrol's refusal to express an opinion on litigation against Mattison and his entities, and that the information could be obtained from the public records, Bank closed its eyes to that obvious source. Rather, it relied upon Mattison's friendly reception by fellow members of the Jonathan Club and the fact that he was represented by a lawyer who had been a trust officer of Bank's predecessor in interest to conclude that indicators that Mattison was a financial bandit should be ignored. Membership in a club, whether it be the Jonathan or the informal group of ex-trust officers of Bank, does not excuse investigation. Nor can Bank be justified in accepting Mattison's uncorroborated statement that the past financial disasters of his entities reported by Dun & Bradstreet were due to his practice of acquiring failing companies. Only one who loots a failed company at the expense of its creditors can profit from its acquisition. Mattison's constantly repeated entry into the transactions without ever pulling a company from the morass was a strong indication that he was milking the companies profitably. Had Bank investigated, as any prudent man would have done, it would have discovered from the public records the additional detail of Mattison's long, long trail of financial failure that would have precluded its dealings with him except under circumstances where his obligation was secured beyond question and his ability to loot Corporation precluded. * * *

Measure of Damages

Appellant contends finally that the trial court improperly multiplied the measure of damages by adding to net asset value on the date of Bank's tortious conduct an estimate for future net profit and an obligation that Bank discharge the valid existing obligations of Corporation. The record refutes the contention.

The trial judge arrived at a value of the corporation as a going concern at the time of appellant's breach by adding to the value of Corporation's tangible assets a goodwill factor computed on the basis of future net income reasonably to be anticipated from the Corporation's past record. This the trial court was authorized to do in determining "the amount which will compensate for all the detriment proximately caused * * *" by appellant's breach of duty. Appellant's breach damaged Corporation not only in the loss of its assets but also in the loss of its earning power. Since the trial court's determination of loss of earning power was based upon a past record of earnings and not speculation, it is supported by substantial evidence. The trial court's order requiring appellant to pay all valid claims of creditors against Corporation is also proper as necessary to restore Corporation to the condition in which it existed prior to the time that Bank contributed to its destruction. Prior to Bank's action, Corporation was a going concern with substantial net assets. As a proximate result of Bank's dereliction of duty, Corporation acquired a negative net worth of about $218,000. Total damage to Corporation is thus the sum necessary to restore the negative net worth, plus the value of its tangible assets, plus its going business value determined with reference to its future profits reasonably estimated. That is the measure which the trial court applied. Since the derivative action is equitable in nature, the court properly framed part of its judgment in terms of an obligation dependent upon future contingencies rather than at a fixed dollar amount.

Disposition

The judgment is affirmed. The matter is, however, remanded to the trial court with directions to hold a hearing to determine the additional amount payable to respondents from the fund recovered by them for benefit of Corporation for counsel fees due for services on this appeal.

Notes

(1) The American Law Institute, Principles of Corporate Governance: Analysis and Recommendations § 5.16,[15] provides:

A controlling shareholder has the same right to dispose of voting equity securities as any other shareholder, including the right to dispose of those securities for a price that is not made proportionally available to other shareholders, but the controlling shareholder does not satisfy the duty of fair dealing to the other shareholders if:

(a) The controlling shareholder does not make disclosure concerning the transaction to other shareholders with whom the controlling shareholder deals in connection with the transaction; or

(b) It is apparent from the circumstances that the purchaser is likely to violate the duty of fair dealing under Part V in such a way as to obtain a significant financial benefit for the purchaser or an associate.

Would "it [be] apparent" to the First Western Bank that Mattison was likely to loot the Alfred S. Johnson Corporation? Is not the ALI test too lax? The Comment to § 5.16 discusses the language of § 5.16(b) further:

> * * * Affirmative investigation by the controlling shareholder is not required in the absence of facts that would alert a reasonable person to the need for further inquiry. What is necessary to trigger that inquiry, however, must be determined in the context of the transaction. The mere fact that the controlling shareholder receives a substantial premium for its shares, or that the purchaser has a general reputation for aggressive acquisitions, is not itself sufficient to trigger such an inquiry. What is required are facts sufficient to put the controlling shareholder on notice that it would be imprudent to proceed with the transaction without making further inquiry as to the purchaser and its motives for acquiring control of the corporation.

Does the commentary set forth a stricter test than § 5.16(b)?

(2) The leading decision in Delaware as to liability for sale to a looter is Harris v. Carter, 582 A.2d 222, 235 (Del.Ch.1990). The test suggested there is:

> Thus, I conclude that while a person who transfers corporate control to another is surely not a surety for his buyer, when the circumstances would alert a reasonably prudent person to a risk that his buyer is dishonest or in some material respect not truthful, a duty devolves upon the seller to make such inquiry as a reasonably prudent person would make, and generally to exercise care so that others who will be affected by his actions should not be injured by wrongful conduct.

(3) Many cases involve a purchase price that seems unreasonably high given the business being purchased. Should the manifest willingness of an unknown purchaser to pay an unreasonably high price be a suspicious circumstance? Some courts have refused to draw an adverse inference even though the premium seems extreme. In Clagett v. Hutchison, 583 F.2d 1259 (4th Cir.1978), for example, the majority shareholder was offered $43.75 per share at a time when the price in a "thinly traded * * * public market" varied between $7.50 and $10.00 per share; the Court held that this price "cannot be said to be so unreasonable as to place [the seller] on notice of the likelihood of fraud on the corporation or the remaining stockholders." 583 F.2d at 1262. One Judge dissented.

(4) Frank H. Easterbrook & Daniel R. Fischel, The Economic Structure of Corporate Law 126, 129–31 (1991):[16]

> Sales of controlling blocs of shares provide a good example of transactions in which the movement of control is beneficial. The sale of control may lead to new offers, new plans, and new working arrangements with other firms that reduce agency costs and create gains from new business relationships. The premium price received by the seller of the control bloc amounts to an unequal distribution of the gains. Sales at a premium are lawful, and the controlling shareholder generally has no duty to spread the bounty. * * *
>
> A specter of "looting" haunts opinions about corporate control transactions. * * * Certainly the sellers of control can detect knavery at a lower cost than the public shareholders who are not parties to the transaction. Yet it is difficult if not impossible to detect looters early on. Looting is by nature a one-time transaction. Once looters have plundered one firm, their reputation

---

16. Reprinted by permission of the publishers from *The Economic Structure of Corporate Law* by Frank H. Easterbrook and Daniel R. Fischel, Cambridge, Mass.: Harvard University Press, Copyright 1991 by the President and Fellows of Harvard College.

(or their residence in jail) prevents them from doing so again. But when they first obtain control, the may appear innocuous. Any rule that blocks sales in advance is equivalent to a program of preventive detention for people who have never robbed banks but have acquisitive personalities.

Although sellers could spend substantial sums investigating buyers and investors and still more in litigating over the quality of investigation, almost all of these efforts would be wasted. If investigations blocked transfers, most of these refusals would be false positives. That is, they would be refusals that reduced the gains available from transferring control. * * *

We do not suggest that the legal system should disregard looting, but the best remedies are based on deterrence rather than prior scrutiny. Looters, when caught, may be fined or imprisoned. Penalties could be made high enough to be effective, making the transaction unprofitable *ex ante*. The costs of deterrence are less than the costs of dealing with looting through a system of prior scrutiny that would scotch many valuable control shifts as a by-product.

(5) Robert W. Hamilton, Private Sale of Control Transactions: Where We Stand Today, 36 Case W.Res.L.Rev. 248, 267–68 (1985):

It is possible that Easterbrook and Fischel are correct when they infer that the costs of an *ex ante* requirement exceed its benefits, but I doubt it. In the first place, in my personal experience, it is not true that looters abscond and only first-time looters ply their trade. Rather, persons on the fringe of the law often quietly merge into the general economy and surface from time to time, hoping that their background is not discovered, and if it is, quietly disappear again. As a result, routine and inexpensive credit checks on persons offering to buy asset-rich companies often turn up substantially negative factors. * * *

Second, while it is possible that the *ex ante* investigation would turn up some "false positives," I do not see why this should be so. What is supposed to be investigated is not whether the purchaser has dismantled companies in the past, but whether he has a reputation for honesty and the apparent wherewithal to finance a transaction of the magnitude under consideration without recourse to the corporation's assets in a way that defrauds creditors and minority shareholders. If a person does not meet this standard, one wonders whether he is really a "false positive."

Finally, the *ex post* deterrence proposed by Easterbrook and Fischel in the form of criminal sanctions is not very attractive. Even if it is assumed that punishment for this type of conduct will be quick and sure—hardly characteristics of current criminal sanctions against white-collar crime—the result is that the innocent shareholders and others "left behind" will usually suffer the entire economic loss, while the majority shareholders who sold to the thieves may keep the entire purchase price, premium and all. The thieves, of course, go to jail. This result seems so obviously unjust from the standpoint of the minority shareholders that it seems unreasonable to embrace it on the basis of entirely theoretical considerations of economic "efficiency."

PERLMAN v. FELDMANN

United States Court of Appeals, Second Circuit, 1955.
219 F.2d 173.

CLARK, CHIEF JUDGE.

This is a derivative action brought by minority stockholders of Newport Steel Corporation to compel accounting for, and restitution of, allegedly illegal gains which accrued to defendants as a result of the sale in August, 1950, of their controlling interest in the corporation. The principal defendant, C. Russell Feldmann, who represented and acted for the others, members of his family,[17] was at that time not only the dominant stockholder, but also the chairman of the board of directors and the president of the corporation. Newport, an Indiana corporation, operated mills for the production of steel sheets for sale to manufacturers of steel products, first at Newport, Kentucky, and later also at other places in Kentucky and Ohio. The buyers, a syndicate organized as Wilport Company, a Delaware corporation, consisted of end-users of steel who were interested in securing a source of supply in a market becoming ever tighter in the Korean War. Plaintiffs contend that the consideration paid for the stock included compensation for the sale of a corporate asset, a power held in trust for the corporation by Feldmann as its fiduciary. This power was the ability to control the allocation of the corporate product in a time of short supply, through control of the board of directors; and it was effectively transferred in this sale by having Feldmann procure the resignation of his own board and the election of Wilport's nominees immediately upon consummation of the sale.

The present action represents the consolidation of three pending stockholders' actions in which yet another stockholder has been permitted to intervene. Jurisdiction below was based upon the diverse citizenship of the parties. Plaintiffs argue here, as they did in the court below, that in the situation here disclosed the vendors must account to the nonparticipating minority stockholders for that share of their profit which is attributable to the sale of the corporate power. Judge Hincks denied the validity of the premise, holding that the rights involved in the sale were only those normally incident to the possession of a controlling block of shares, with which a dominant stockholder, in the absence of fraud or foreseeable looting, was entitled to deal according to his own best interests. Furthermore, he held that plaintiffs had failed to satisfy their burden of proving that the sales price was not a fair price for the stock per se. Plaintiffs appeal from these rulings of law which resulted in the dismissal of their complaint.

The essential facts found by the trial judge are not in dispute. Newport was a relative newcomer in the steel industry with predominantly old installations which were in the process of being supplemented by more modern facilities. Except in times of extreme shortage Newport was not in a position to compete profitably with other steel mills for customers not in its immediate geographical area. Wilport, the purchasing syndicate, consisted of geographically remote end-users of steel who were interested in buying more steel from Newport than they had been able to obtain during recent periods of tight supply. The price of $20 per share was found by Judge Hincks to be a fair one for a control block of stock, although the over-the-counter market price had not exceeded $12 and the book value per share was $17.03. But this finding

---

17. [By the Court] The stock was not held personally by Feldmann in his own name, but was held by the members of his family and by personal corporations. The aggregate of stock thus held amounted to 33% of the outstanding Newport stock and gave working control to the holder. The actual sale included 55,552 additional shares held by friends and associates of Feldmann, so that a total of 37% of the Newport stock was transferred.

was limited by Judge Hincks' statement that "[w]hat value the block would have had if shorn of its appurtenant power to control distribution of the corporate product, the evidence does not show." It was also conditioned by his earlier ruling that the burden was on plaintiffs to prove a lesser value for the stock.

Both as director and as dominant stockholder, Feldmann stood in a fiduciary relationship to the corporation and to the minority stockholders as beneficiaries thereof. Pepper v. Litton, 308 U.S. 295, 60 S.Ct. 238, 84 L.Ed. 281. His fiduciary obligation must in the first instance be measured by the law of Indiana, the state of incorporation of Newport. Although there is no Indiana case directly in point, the most closely analogous one emphasizes the close scrutiny to which Indiana subjects the conduct of fiduciaries when personal benefit may stand in the way of fulfillment of trust obligations. In Schemmel v. Hill, 91 Ind.App. 373, 169 N.E. 678, 682, 683, McMahan, J., said: "Directors of a business corporation act in a strictly fiduciary capacity. Their office is a trust. When a director deals with his corporation, his acts will be closely scrutinized. Directors of a corporation are its agents, and they are governed by the rules of law applicable to other agents, and, as between themselves and their principal, the rules relating to honesty and fair dealing in the management of the affairs of their principal are applicable. They must not, in any degree, allow their official conduct to be swayed by their private interest, which must yield to official duty. In a transaction between a director and his corporation, where he acts for himself and his principal at the same time in a matter connected with the relation between them, it is presumed, where he is thus potential on both sides of the contract, that self-interest will overcome his fidelity to his principal, to his own benefit and to his principal's hurt." And the judge added: "Absolute and most scrupulous good faith is the very essence of a director's obligation to his corporation. The first principal duty arising from his official relation is to act in all things of trust wholly for the benefit of his corporation."

In Indiana, then, as elsewhere, the responsibility of the fiduciary is not limited to a proper regard for the tangible balance sheet assets of the corporation, but includes the dedication of his uncorrupted business judgment for the sole benefit of the corporation, in any dealings which may adversely affect it. Irving Trust Co. v. Deutsch, 2 Cir., 73 F.2d 121, certiorari denied 294 U.S. 708, 55 S.Ct. 405, 79 L.Ed. 1243; Meinhard v. Salmon, 249 N.Y. 458, 164 N.E. 545, 62 A.L.R. 1. Although the Indiana case is particularly relevant to Feldmann as a director, the same rule should apply to his fiduciary duties as majority stockholder, for in that capacity he chooses and controls the directors, and thus is held to have assumed their liability. Pepper v. Litton, supra, 308 U.S. 295, 60 S.Ct. 238. This, therefore, is the standard to which Feldmann was by law required to conform in his activities here under scrutiny.

It is true, as defendants have been at pains to point out, that this is not the ordinary case of breach of fiduciary duty. We have here no fraud, no misuse of confidential information, no outright looting of a helpless corporation. But on the other hand, we do not find compliance with that high standard which we have just stated and which we and other courts have come to expect and demand of corporate fiduciaries. In the often-quoted words of Judge Cardozo: [The Court quotes the classic language from Meinhard v.

Salmon[18]]. The actions of defendants in siphoning off for personal gain corporate advantages to be derived from a favorable market situation do not betoken the necessary undivided loyalty owed by the fiduciary to his principal.

The corporate opportunities of whose misappropriation the minority stockholders complain need not have been an absolute certainty in order to support this action against Feldmann. If there was possibility of corporate gain, they are entitled to recover. * * *

This rationale is equally appropriate to a consideration of the benefits which Newport might have derived from the steel shortage. In the past Newport had used and profited by its market leverage by operation of what the industry had come to call the "Feldmann Plan." This consisted of securing interest-free advances from prospective purchasers of steel in return for firm commitments to them from future production. The funds thus acquired were used to finance improvements in existing plants and to acquire new installations. In the summer of 1950 Newport had been negotiating for cold-rolling facilities which it needed for a more fully integrated operation and a more marketable product, and Feldmann plan funds might well have been used toward this end.

Further, as plaintiffs alternatively suggest, Newport might have used the period of short supply to build up patronage in the geographical area in which it could compete profitably even when steel was more abundant. Either of these opportunities was Newport's, to be used to its advantage only. Only if defendants had been able to negate completely any possibility of gain by Newport could they have prevailed. It is true that a trial court finding states: "Whether or not, in August, 1950, Newport's position was such that it could have entered into 'Feldmann Plan' type transactions to procure funds and financing for the further expansion and integration of its steel facilities and whether such expansion would have been desirable for Newport, the evidence does not show." This, however, cannot avail the defendants, who—contrary to the ruling below—had the burden of proof on this issue, since fiduciaries always have the burden of proof in establishing the fairness of their dealings with trust property. Pepper v. Litton, supra.

Defendants seek to categorize the corporate opportunities which might have accrued to Newport as too unethical to warrant further consideration. It is true that reputable steel producers were not participating in the gray market brought about by the Korean War and were refraining from advancing their prices, although to do so would not have been illegal. But Feldmann plan transactions were not considered within this self-imposed interdiction; the trial court found that around the time of the Feldmann sale Jones & Laughlin Steel Corporation, Republic Steel Company, and Pittsburgh Steel Corporation were all participating in such arrangements. In any event, it ill becomes the defendants to disparage as unethical the market advantages from which they themselves reaped rich benefits.

We do not mean to suggest that a majority stockholder cannot dispose of his controlling block of stock to outsiders without having to account to his corporation for profits or even never do this with impunity when the buyer is an interested customer, actual or potential, for the corporation's product. But

---

18. *See* Meinhard v. Salmon, 249 N.Y. 458 (1928), *supra* chap. 2, page 64.

when the sale necessarily results in a sacrifice of this element of corporate good will and consequent unusual profit to the fiduciary who has caused the sacrifice, he should account for his gains. So in a time of market shortage, where a call on a corporation's product commands an unusually large premium, in one form or another, we think it sound law that a fiduciary may not appropriate to himself the value of this premium. Such personal gain at the expense of his coventurers seems particularly reprehensible when made by the trusted president and director of his company. In this case the violation of duty seems to be all the clearer because of this triple role in which Feldmann appears, though we are unwilling to say, and are not to be understood as saying, that we should accept a lesser obligation for any one of his roles alone.

Hence to the extent that the price received by Feldmann and his codefendants included such a bonus, he is accountable to the minority stockholders who sue here. And plaintiffs, as they contend, are entitled to a recovery in their own right, instead of in right of the corporation (as in the usual derivative actions), since neither Wilport nor their successors in interest should share in any judgment which may be rendered. See Southern Pacific Co. v. Bogert, 250 U.S. 483, 39 S.Ct. 533, 63 L.Ed. 1099. Defendants cannot well object to this form of recovery, since the only alternative, recovery for the corporation as a whole, would subject them to a greater total liability.

The case will therefore be remanded to the district court for a determination of the question expressly left open below, namely, the value of defendants' stock without the appurtenant control over the corporation's output of steel. We reiterate that on this issue, as on all others relating to a breach of fiduciary duty, the burden of proof must rest on the defendants. Judgment should go to these plaintiffs and those whom they represent for any premium value so shown to the extent of their respective stock interests.

The judgment is therefore reversed and the action remanded for further proceedings pursuant to this opinion.

SWAN, CIRCUIT JUDGE (dissenting).

With the general principles enunciated in the majority opinion as to the duties of fiduciaries I am, of course, in thorough accord. But, as Mr. Justice Frankfurter stated in Securities and Exchange Comm. v. Chenery Corp., 318 U.S. 80, 85, 63 S.Ct. 454, 458, 87 L.Ed. 626, "to say that a man is a fiduciary only begins analysis; it gives direction to further inquiry. To whom is he a fiduciary? What obligations does he owe as a fiduciary? In what respect has he failed to discharge these obligations?" My brothers' opinion does not specify precisely what fiduciary duty Feldmann is held to have violated or whether it was a duty imposed upon him as the dominant stockholder or as a director of Newport. Without such specification I think that both the legal profession and the business world will find the decision confusing and will be unable to foretell the extent of its impact upon customary practices in the sale of stock.

The power to control the management of a corporation, that is, to elect directors to manage its affairs, is an inseparable incident to the ownership of a majority of its stock, or sometimes, as in the present instance, to the ownership of enough shares, less than a majority, to control an election. Concededly a majority or dominant shareholder is ordinarily privileged to sell his stock at the best price obtainable from the purchaser. In so doing he acts on his own behalf, not as an agent of the corporation. If he knows or has reason to believe that the purchaser intends to exercise to the detriment of the corporation the power of management acquired by the purchase, such knowledge or reasonable suspicion will terminate the dominant shareholder's privilege to sell and will create a duty not to transfer the power of management to such purchaser. The duty seems to me to resemble the obligation which everyone is under not to assist another to commit a tort rather than the obligation of a fiduciary. But whatever the nature of the duty, a violation of it will subject the violator to liability for damages sustained by the corporation. Judge Hincks found that Feldmann had no reason to think that Wilport would use the power of management it would acquire by the purchase to injure Newport, and that there was no proof that it ever was so used. Feldmann did know, it is true, that the reason Wilport wanted the stock was to put in a board of directors who would be likely to permit Wilport's members to purchase more of Newport's steel than they might otherwise be able to get. But there is nothing illegal in a dominant shareholder purchasing from his own corporation at the same prices it offers to other customers. That is what the members of Wilport did, and there is no proof that Newport suffered any detriment therefrom.

My brothers say that "the consideration paid for the stock included compensation for the sale of a corporate asset," which they describe as "the ability to control the allocation of the corporate product in a time of short supply, through control of the board of directors; and it was effectively transferred in this sale by having Feldmann procure the resignation of his own board and the election of Wilport's nominees immediately upon consummation of the sale." The implications of this are not clear to me. If it means that when market conditions are such as to induce users of a corporation's product to wish to buy a controlling block of stock in order to be able to purchase part of the corporation's output at the same mill list prices as are offered to other customers, the dominant stockholder is under a fiduciary duty not to sell his stock, I cannot agree. For reasons already stated, in my opinion Feldmann was not proved to be under any fiduciary duty as a stockholder not to sell the stock he controlled.

Feldmann was also a director of Newport. Perhaps the quoted statement means that as a director he violated his fiduciary duty in voting to elect Wilport's nominees to fill the vacancies created by the resignations of the former directors of Newport. As a director Feldmann was under a fiduciary duty to use an honest judgment in acting on the corporation's behalf. A director is privileged to resign, but so long as he remains a director he must be faithful to his fiduciary duties and must not make a personal gain from performing them. Consequently, if the price paid for Feldmann's stock included a payment for voting to elect the new directors, he must account to the corporation for such payment, even though he honestly believed that the men he voted to elect were well qualified to serve as directors. He can not take pay for performing his fiduciary duty. There is no suggestion that he did do so, unless the price paid for his stock was more than its value. So it seems to me that decision must turn on whether finding 120 and conclusion 5 of the district judge are supportable on the evidence. They are set out in the margin.[19]

19. [By the Judge] "120. The 398,927 shares of Newport stock sold to Wilport as of   August 31, 1950, had a fair value as a control block of $20 per share. What value the block

Judge Hincks went into the matter of valuation of the stock with his customary care and thoroughness. He made no error of law in applying the principles relating to valuation of stock. Concededly a controlling block of stock has greater sale value than a small lot. While the spread between $10 per share for small lots and $20 per share for the controlling block seems rather extraordinarily wide, the $20 valuation was supported by the expert testimony of Dr. Badger, whom the district judge said he could not find to be wrong. I see no justification for upsetting the valuation as clearly erroneous. Nor can I agree with my brothers that the $20 valuation "was limited" by the last sentence in finding 120. The controlling block could not by any possibility be shorn of its appurtenant power to elect directors and through them to control distribution of the corporate product. It is this "appurtenant power" which gives a controlling block its value as such block. What evidence could be adduced to show the value of the block "if shorn" of such appurtenant power, I cannot conceive, for it cannot be shorn of it. * * *

The final conclusion of my brothers is that the plaintiffs are entitled to recover in their own right instead of in the right of the corporation. This appears to be completely inconsistent with the theory advanced at the outset of the opinion, namely, that the price of the stock "included compensation for the sale of a corporate asset." If a corporate asset was sold, surely the corporation should recover the compensation received for it by the defendants. Moreover, if the plaintiffs were suing in their own right, Newport was not a proper party. The case of Southern Pacific Co. v. Bogert, 250 U.S. 483, 39 S.Ct. 533, 63 L.Ed. 1099, relied upon as authority for the conclusion that the plaintiffs are entitled to recover in their own right, relates to a situation so different that the decision appears to me to be inapposite.

I would affirm the judgment on appeal.

Notes

(1) On remand, Judge Hincks took a deep breath and concluded that the "enterprise value" of a share of Newport stock was $14.67, so that Feldmann had received a premium of $5.33 per share, or a total premium of $2,126,280. The plaintiffs, representing sixty-three percent of the stock, were therefore entitled to a judgment of $1,339,769, plus interest. Perlman v. Feldmann, 154 F.Supp. 436 (D.Conn.1957).

(2) Accepting Judge Hincks' allocation, why should the recovery go to the plaintiffs personally rather than to the corporation, as would normally be the case with derivative suit recoveries? The ALI's Principles of Corporate Governance lists nine similar cases, and generalizes them in § 7.18(e) as follows:

> (e) The court having jurisdiction over a derivative action may direct that all or a portion of the award be paid directly to individual shareholders, on a pro-rata basis, when such a payment is equitable in the circumstances and adequate provision has been made for the creditors of the corporation.

would have had if shorn of its appurtenant power to control distribution of the corporate product, the evidence does not show."

5. "Even if Feldmann's conduct in cooperating to accomplish a transfer of control to Wilport immediately upon the sale constituted a breach of a fiduciary duty to Newport, no part of the moneys received by the defendants in connection with the sale constituted profits for which they were accountable to Newport."

The American Law Institute, Principles of Corporate Governance: Analysis and Recommendations § 7.18(e) at 232. The explanatory text states:

In general, when a substantial portion of the shares are held either by persons who had aided or abetted the defendants to commit the fiduciary breach or by non-contemporaneous holders who had suffered no injury because they had bought their shares at a price reflecting the injury done to the corporation, the case for a pro-rata recovery in favor of the other eligible shareholders will be strongest. However, it should not be assumed that pro-rata recovery should be granted merely because persons who committed or aided the breach remain as shareholders. A corporate recovery in such an instance does not mean that the defendants will receive unjust enrichment. To the contrary, proration of a partial recovery among other shareholders reduces the damages defendants must pay and thereby minimizes both the sanction against them and the amount of compensation that will benefit creditors and others affected by an injury to the corporation. That defendants continue as shareholders is, however, highly relevant if the court determines that there is a possibility that defendants will divert the recovery. This possibility will be greatest when the defendants remain in control of the corporation.

Another instance in which a pro-rata recovery is justified arises when shareholders who were earlier injured by a wrong for which they have not been adequately compensated have been eliminated as the result of a fundamental corporate change. In these circumstances, a derivative action is a more practical means by which to address such a wrong than is the appraisal remedy, because the appraisal remedy grants relief only against the corporation (and thus indirectly against its current shareholders) rather than against the alleged wrongdoer. * * *

(3) Is it desirable for courts to evolve a single, consistent position with respect to premiums paid for controlling shares? (To date they have not done so.) At least the following arguments seem defensible:

(a) In the absence of fraud or foreseeable looting, a person may sell his or her property for what he can get or refuse to sell it at all. That is what economic freedom is all about. (A number of cases have adopted this position which is the dominant position today.)

(b) A purchaser is really seeking control of the corporate assets when he buys the controlling shares. If he wants the assets, he should buy them from the corporation, in which case, all the shareholders would receive the same amount per share. In effect, this translates all sale of control cases into corporate opportunity cases. (Some courts have adopted this position, particularly where the purchasers first approached the corporation seeking to buy its assets, and the controlling shareholder proposes a stock deal. See, e.g., Commonwealth Title Ins. & Trust Co. v. Seltzer, 227 Pa. 410, 76 A. 77 (1910).)

(c) If it is part of the deal for the selling shareholder to resign his position with the corporation (as it almost always is), that is what the premium *really* is for. This approach in effect translates virtually all sale of control cases into sale of corporate office cases. (Some courts have tried this approach, particularly where the premium is set aside and its payment is made contingent on the resignations. E.g., Porter v. Healy, 244 Pa. 427, 91 A. 428 (1914).)

(d) It is simply immoral for a shareholder knowingly to take a greater price for his shares than other shareholders, since each share is actually identical with every other share. The additional amount must be for the control and that should belong to the corporation. See, e.g., David Cowan Bayne, The Noninvestment Value of Control Stock, 45 Ind.L.J. 317 (1970). See also, William D. Andrews, The Stockholder's Right to Equal Opportunity in the Sale of Shares, 78 Harv.L.Rev. 505, 515–17 (1965) (suggesting the "rule" that whenever a controlling stockholder sells his shares, every other holder of shares (of the same class) is entitled to have an equal opportunity to sell his shares, or a pro rata part of them, on substantially the same terms).

(4) Frank H. Easterbrook & Daniel R. Fischel, The Economic Structure of Corporate Law 117–18 (1991):

> A sharing requirement also may make an otherwise profitable transaction unattractive to the prospective seller of control. Suppose the owner of a control bloc of shares finds that his perquisites or the other amenities of his position are worth $10. A prospective acquirer of control concludes that, by eliminating these perquisites and other amenities, it could produce a gain of $15. The shareholders in the company benefit if the acquirer pays a premium of $11 to the owner of the controlling bloc, ousts the current managers, and makes the improvements. The net gains of $4 inure to each investor according to his holdings, and although the acquirer obtains the largest portion because it holds the largest bloc, no one is left out. If the owner of the control bloc must share the $11 premium with all of the existing shareholders, however, the deal collapses. The owner will not part with his bloc for less than a $10 premium. A sharing requirement would make the deal unprofitable to him, and the other investors would lose the prospective gain from the installation of better managers.

Compare Robert W. Hamilton, Private Sale of Control Transactions: Where We Stand Today, 36 Case Western Res.L.Rev. 248, 256–57 (1985):

> There are several problems with this kind of analysis, however. The hypothetical the authors create assumes the correctness of their thesis. The assumption [is] that the purchasers of control will reduce the "perquisites or the other amenities" enjoyed as a result of the seller's position by $10, thereby producing a corporate gain of $15, * * *. One can equally plausibly assume that the buyer feels that he can enjoy the same "perquisites or the other amenities" as the seller enjoyed, and even increase them to, for instance, $14. On this assumption, the minority shareholders are clearly worse off as a result of the sale, and both the purchaser and seller of the control shares are benefiting at the minority shareholders' expense. * * *

> There is another problem with the Easterbrook–Fischel hypothetical. Assume that the control stock sold in the hypothetical consists of 55% of the outstanding shares; if the buyers are content to allow the $15 increase in value to remain in the corporation, they will obtain 55% of the $15 increase in value by reason of their 55% stock ownership, or $8.25. In other words, if they abandon the "perquisites and other amenities," they will pay $11 in order to obtain an increase in investment value of only $8.25. They would obviously be better off if they retain the sellers' "percs" worth $10 and seek to squeeze out another couple of dollars here and there from additional "percs," rather than eliminating the "percs." * * *

> The basic question is: If the new purchasers are rational profit maximizers, why should they share the $15 increase in value with the minority? It is not true that minority shareholders always share ratably in all increases in value with the majority shareholders. It would appear to be rational (and certainly

practical) to place the minority shareholders on "starvation returns" from the corporation while increasing salaries or other "percs" to the new controlling shareholders in order to obtain all the additional $15 in gains. Why should the minority be given any of it? Starvation returns may also persuade the minority to sell their shares at low prices to the majority so that at some time thereafter the purchasers may own all of the outstanding shares and obtain all of the benefits of their skills. In short, I do not view hypothetical examples, such as those put forth by Easterbrook and Fischel, to prove anything more than that there *may be* idealized situations where everyone is better off as a result of the transfer of control; they do not prove that there are such situations, or their frequency.

For an evaluation of all aspects of the sale of control issue, see Einer Elhauge, The Triggering Function of Sale of Control Doctrine, 59 U. Chi. L. Rev. 1465 (1992) (arguing the choice that courts must make when selecting between the two approaches (equal sharing versus the deregulatory school) is based on a classification of cases that effectively avoids underdeterring harmful transfers of control and overdeterring beneficial transfers of control). For yet another analysis and proposal to solve the private sale of control problem, see Yedidia Z. Stern, The Private Sale of Corporate Control: A Myth Dethroned, 25 J.Corp.L. 511 (2000).

(5) In Petition of Caplan, 20 A.D.2d 301, 246 N.Y.S.2d 913 (1964), the Court vacated the election of seven directors who acquired their positions after a minority shareholder, Ray Cohn, had sold his 3% interest in the corporation to Defiance Industries. Defiance, in turn, sold its newly acquired interest to A.M. Sonnabend, a condition of the agreement being that the six Defiance directors (formerly controlled by Cohn) would be replaced by Sonnabend nominees prior to closing the deal. In vacating the election of these directors and holding the elections to be illegal, the Court announced the principle that the management of a corporation is not the subject of trade and cannot be bought apart from actual stock control.

(6) Carter v. Muscat, 21 A.D.2d 543, 251 N.Y.S.2d 378 (1964), involved seriatim resignations of directors in connection with transfer of 9.7 percent of the outstanding shares. Full disclosure of the change in control was made to the shareholders and some of the new directors were thereafter reelected at annual shareholders meetings. After quoting from *Petition of Caplan,* the Court said: "When a situation involving less than 50% of the ownership of stock exists, the question of what percentage of ownership of stock is sufficient to constitute working control is likely to be a matter of fact, at least in most circumstances." 21 A.D.2d at 545, 251 N.Y.S.2d at 381. The change in control was upheld, the Court relying on the disclosure, the absence of objection, and the subsequent election of directors as "endorsements" of the substituted directors.

(7) Section 14(f) of the Securities Exchange Act of 1934, added in 1970, provides that if there is an "arrangement or understanding" with persons acquiring more than five percent of the stock of a registered publicly traded corporation by tender offer or purchase, and "any persons are to be elected or designated as directors of the issuer, otherwise than at a meeting of security holders, and the persons so elected or designated will constitute a majority of the directors," the issuer must disseminate certain information to the SEC and to all holders of record entitled to vote at a meeting. The information must identify the persons to whom control was transferred, describe the transaction by which control was transferred, the source of any consideration paid, the identity of the new directors, transactions with the issuer, the remuneration to be paid to

directors and management, and the amount of securities held by principal shareholders. See Rule 14f–1, 17 C.F.R. § 240.14f–1 (2000).

Chapter Ten

CONTROL AND MANAGEMENT IN THE PUBLICLY HELD CORPORATION

A. "SOCIAL RESPONSIBILITY" OR THE LACK THEREOF

FRANK RENE LOPEZ, CORPORATE SOCIAL RESPONSIBILITY IN A GLOBAL ECONOMY AFTER SEPTEMBER 11: PROFITS, FREEDOM, AND HUMAN RIGHTS

55 Mercer L. Rev. 739, 753–54 (2004).

[C]orporate political clout is not limited to the United States. In fact, given the vulnerability of developing countries, large global corporations exert even more control over foreign countries—especially underdeveloped countries. Underdeveloped countries often lack the power to negotiate or make demands of large global corporations seeking cheap labor. Developing countries are disadvantaged in trade negotiations with global corporations. For example, developing countries often lack resources and negotiating experience, and have very little to offer in complex deal making. Even if a country has labor laws on the books that protect children and workers, government officials often do not enforce them due to corruption, weak bargaining power, or fear that the corporation will relocate to another country.

Some global corporations are so large they can establish their own foreign policy independent of U.S. foreign policy. Years ago, a director of Nestle Corporation commented that Nestle was neither a Swiss Corporation nor a multinational corporation but rather had its own nationality, " 'a Nestle nationality.' " There is much truth to the comment that global corporations have their own nationality. If they can influence both the United States and other countries, in a very real sense, large global corporations do have their own nationality and can create their own foreign policy.

Although countries attempt to establish strong social safety nets to take care of their workers and children, it is difficult to integrate a developing country's economy into the global economy and to simultaneously protect the people. The policies and practices of the World Trade Organization ("WTO") and financial institutions, such as the World Bank and the International

[handwritten margin note: Corporations don't just exercise political influence in U.S. They probably have more influence in developing nations.]

Monetary Fund ("IMF"), facilitate international commerce and marginalize human welfare, equity, and social justice. With the pressure of competition stemming from the race to the bottom, developing countries often lower their regulatory requirements for global corporations, ignoring or eliminating laws that protect children or laws that make it difficult to terminate workers. In the final analysis, developing countries remain at the mercy of large global corporations whose primary objective is maximizing profits at any price.

[margin note: Developing Nations' policies on corporate regulation may be undercut by IMF/WTO policies that encourage global commerce]

THOMAS CRAMPTON, A TREND WITH LEGS AS WELL AS A HEART; DOING GOOD IS BECOMING A PRIORITY FOR COMPANIES

International Herald Tribune, Jan. 28, 2006, at 15.

"In the last few years, companies have begun to move beyond traditional philanthropy and basic compliance into a new kind of corporate and social responsibility," said Jane Nelson, director of the corporate responsibility program at the John F. Kennedy School of Government at Harvard. "It is the new business environment that has prompted concrete steps by corporations."

Critical shifts in the business environment highlighted by Nelson include a lower tolerance for bad behavior on the part of activists, and heightened compliance in the wake of Enron and other corporate scandals, combined with the global reach of even the most local media.

"Enron brought legislation to industry and, believe me, industry really does not like to be legislated," said Alan Hassenfeld, chairman of the toy manufacturer Hasbro. "Myself and other business leaders prefer to move forward with corporate responsibility before the government starts getting any ideas." * * *

[margin note: Interesting comments considering Hasbro's problems with corporate misconduct in China one year after this article (child labor, unsafe conditions, and sexual harassment)]

Needless to say, Nelson of Harvard added, corporate motivations are often selfish. Globalization of the media, for example, means companies can no longer hide their bad practices so easily. "It used to be that a company could hide an oil spill in a distant land," Nelson said. "Now the media and activists are quick to pick up and spread the news." The result, Nelson said, is that "in the last three years you can see a large number of industries that have set up bodies intended to improve corporate responsibility. This is not the end, but it is an important first step." * * *

Beyond business, however, there is now a greater awareness of corporate social responsibility even within the United Nations system. Last July, in recognition of the growing importance of the issue, the world body named John Ruggie as the first special representative of the secretary general on business and human rights. Ruggie's mandate includes finding ways to enhance accountability and responsibility for transnational businesses.

"My phone certainly is ringing much more often these days with companies calling about corporate responsibility," said Juan Somavia, director general of the International Labor Organization, a UN agency. "Companies are very eager for an institution to certify compliance with the standards of corporate responsibility." * * *

Companies and employees may be on board, but shareholders remain difficult to convince, said Amy Butte, chief financial officer of the New York Stock Exchange. "There is definitely increased disclosure and discussion about the topic these days," Butte said. "Once companies are rewarded by the market for socially responsible investments, a virtuous cycle will kick off."

WILLIAM ALLEN,[2] OUR SCHIZOPHRENIC CONCEPTION OF THE BUSINESS CORPORATION

14 Cardozo L.Rev. 261, 264–76 (1992).

Two inconsistent conceptions have dominated our thinking about corporations since the evolution of the large integrated business corporation in the late nineteenth century. Each conception could claim dominance for a particular period, or among one group or another, but neither has so commanded agreement as to exclude the other from the discourses of law or the thinking of business people.

In the first conception, the corporation is seen as the private property of its stockholder-owners. The corporation's purpose is to advance the purposes of these owners (predominantly to increase their wealth), and the function of directors, as agents of the owners, is faithfully to advance the financial interests of the owners. I call this the property conception of the corporation * * *.

The second conception sees the corporation not as the private property of stockholders, but as a social institution. According to this view, the corporation is not strictly private; it is tinged with a public purpose. The corporation comes into being and continues as a legal entity only with governmental concurrence. The legal institutions of government grant a corporation its juridical personality, its characteristic limited liability, and its perpetual life. This conception sees this public facilitation as justified by the state's interest in promoting the general welfare. Thus, corporate purpose can be seen as including the advancement of the general welfare. The board of directors' duties extend beyond assuring investors a fair return, to include a duty of loyalty, in some sense, to all those interested in or affected by the corporation. * * * The corporation itself is, in this view, capable of bearing legal *and* moral obligations. To law and economics scholars, who have been so influential in academic corporate law, this model is barely coherent and dangerously wrong. * * *

Dodge v. Ford Motor Co. reflects as pure an example as exists of the property conception of the corporation. In this conception, the corporation is seen as it is in its nineteenth century roots, as essentially a sort of limited liability partnership. The rights of creditors, employees and others are strictly limited to statutory, contractual, and common law rights. Once the directors have satisfied those legal obligations, they have fully satisfied all claims of these "constituencies." This property view of the nature of corporations, and of the duties owed by directors, equates the duty of directors with the duty to maximize profits of the firm for the benefit of shareholders.

This model of the public corporation is highly coherent and offers several alternative arguments to support the legitimacy of corporate power in our democracy. The first argument in favor of the property concept is political and

2. [By the Editors] William T. Allen was Chancellor of the Delaware Chancery Court until 1997. He currently is a professor of law at New York University.

normative. It is premised on the conclusionary notion that shareholders "own" the corporation, and asserts that to admit the propriety of non-profit maximizing behavior is to approve agents spending other people's money in pursuit of their own, perhaps eccentric, views of the public good. * * *

The second rationale for the property model is that the model, and action consistent with it, maximize wealth creation. This rationale asserts that the purpose of business corporations is the creation of wealth, nothing else. It asserts that business corporations are not formed to assist in self-realization through social interaction; they are not formed to create jobs or to provide tax revenues, they are not formed to endow university departments or to pursue knowledge. All of these other things—job creation, tax payments, research, and social interaction—desirable as they may be, are said to be side effects of the pursuit of profit for the residual owners of the firm.

This argument asserts that the creation of more wealth should always be the corporation's objective, regardless of who benefits. The sovereign's taxing and regulatory power can then address questions of social costs and re-distribution of wealth. * * *

[T]he last quarter of the nineteenth century saw the emergence of social forces that would oppose the conception of business corporations as simply the property of contracting stockholders. The scale and scope of the modern integrated business enterprise that emerged in the late nineteenth century required distinctive professional management skills and huge capital invest-ments that often necessitated risk sharing through dispersed stock ownership. National securities markets emerged and stockholders gradually came to look less like flesh and blood owners and more like investors who could slip in or out of a particular stock almost costlessly. These new giant business corpora-tions came to seem to some people like independent entities, with purposes, duties, and loyalties of their own; purposes that might diverge in some respect from shareholder wealth maximization.

Henry Ford's losing position in *Dodge v. Ford Motor Co.* reflected an idea that was in the air. Others saw these new corporate social actors as different. * * *

This social entity conception sees the purpose of the corporation as not individual but social. Surely contributors of capital (stockholders and bond-holders) must be assured a rate of return sufficient to induce them to contribute their capital to the enterprise. But the corporation has other purposes of perhaps equal dignity: the satisfaction of consumer wants, the provision of meaningful employment opportunities, and the making of a contribution to the public life of its communities. Resolving the often conflict-ing claims of these various corporate constituencies calls for judgment, indeed calls for wisdom, by the board of directors of the corporation. But in this view no single constituency's interest may significantly exclude others from fair consideration by the board. This view appears to have been the dominant view among business leaders for at least the last fifty years. * * *

One would think that whether the corporation law endorses the property conception or the social entity conception would have important conse-quences. * * * [But] for the fifty years preceding that contentious decade [the 1980s], we did not share agreement on the legal nature of the public business corporation and that failure did not seem especially problematic.

Arguments in favor of property conception

1. Maximizing shareholder wealth prevents corporate agents from pursuing eccentric views of public welfare through corporate form.

2. Corporations are only supposed to generate wealth. Gov't regulators handle social welfare problems

Argument for social institution theory

1. shareholders come and go in modern corporations, but concerns independent of shareholder profits remain corporations should be sensitive and responsive to these issues.

The law "papered over" the conflict in our conception of the corporation by invoking a murky distinction between long-term profit maximization and short-term profit maximization. Corporate expenditures which at first blush did not seem to be profit maximizing, could be squared with the property conception of the corporation by recognizing that they might redound to the long-term benefit of the corporation and its shareholders. Thus, without purporting to abandon the idea that directors ultimately owe loyalty only to stockholders and their financial interests, the law was able to approve reasonable corporate expenditures for charitable or social welfare purposes or other actions that did not maximize current profit. * * *

DANIEL R. FISCHEL, THE CORPORATE GOVERNANCE MOVEMENT

35 Vand.L.Rev. 1259, 1268–70 (1982).

It has become fashionable to argue that the pursuit of profit maximization by corporations is at variance with the public interest. Proponents of this argument, however, face the insuperable problem of defining what the public interest is, and when the pursuit of profit maximization should be sacrificed for these ends. As Harold Demsetz has remarked, centuries of philosophers and economists have tried and failed to provide any workable definition of "the fair price," "the just wage," or "fair competition," let alone what constitutes "the good society."[4] * * *

Although potential conflict exists between profit maximization and pursuit of other goals, far more consistency is present between the two than generally assumed. A successful business venture provides jobs to workers and goods and services that consumers want to buy. While these benefits may not appear to be particularly dramatic, they should not be underestimated, as the tens of thousands of workers in distressed industries who have had to give back concessions previously won or have lost their jobs outright will readily attest. Much the same is true in other areas. * * * Frequently this harmony of interests exists, but is difficult to perceive. Firms that close plants to move to different geographical areas commonly are accused, for example, of lacking a sense of responsibility to affected workers and the community as a whole. The difficulty with this argument is that it ignores the presumably greater benefits that will accrue to workers and the community in the new locale where the firm can operate more profitably. A firm that causes dislocations by moving a plant is behaving no more "unethically" than a firm that causes dislocations by, say, inventing a new technology that causes competitors to go out of business.

I do not mean to suggest that profit maximization will always lead to the socially optimal result. In those situations in which externalities are present— pollution is the most common example—a firm may impose costs on others without providing compensation. But even this situation is misunderstood. If a firm dumps pollutants in a stream, the firm imposes costs on the users of the stream that may exceed the benefits to the firm. It does not follow, however, that pollution is immoral behavior which should be halted. Consider

---

4. [By the Author] Demsetz, Social Responsibility in the Enterprise Economy, 10 Sw.   U.L.Rev. 1, 1 (1978).

the reciprocal case in which the firm does not pollute because of concern for users of the stream and instead relies on a more expensive method of disposing wastes. In this situation, the users of the stream impose costs on the firm's investors, employees, and consumers that may exceed the benefits to users of the stream. Neither polluting nor failing to pollute is *a priori* the "ethically" or "morally" correct course of action. * * *

Notes

(1) For more on the corporate social responsibility debate, see Frank H. Easterbrook & Daniel R. Fischel, The Economic Structure of Corporate Law 38 (1991); Einer Elhauge, Sacrificing Corporate Profits in the Public Interest, 80 N.Y.U.L. Rev. 733 (2005); Jay W. Lorsch, Pawns or Potentates: The Reality of America's Corporate Boards 37–38 (1989); Lawrence E. Mitchell, Talking with My Friends: A Response to a Dialogue on Corporate Irresponsibility, 70 Geo. Wash. L. Rev. 988 (2002); Richard A. Rodewald, The Corporate Social Responsibility Debate: Unanswered Questions About the Consequences of Moral Reform, 25 Am. Bus.L.J. 443 (1987); and Larry E. Ribstein, Accountability and Responsibility in Corporate Governance, 81 Notre Dame L. Rev. 1431 (2006).

(2) In 2003 the United Nations took steps toward regulating transnational corporations by developing the Norms on the Responsibilities of Transnational Corporations and Other Business Enterprises with Regard to Human Rights. The Norms made transnational corporations responsible for protecting human rights within their spheres of influence and activities. Among the enumerated rights and obligations were the right to non-discriminatory treatment; certain workers' rights such as the right to collective bargaining and prohibitions on child labor; and obligations to protect the environment. Many Western countries opposed the promulgation of the Norms and in 2005, any further attempts to ratify the Norms were abandoned. For in-depth discussion of the Norms, see Larry Cata Backer, Multinational Corporations, Transnational Law: The United Nations' Norms on the Responsibilities of Transnational Corporations as a Harbinger of Corporate Social Responsibility in International Law, 37 Colum. Hum. Rts. L. Rev 287 (2006).

(3) Chancellor Allen suggests (see 14 Cardozo. L. Rev. at 274–76) that the event that caused the Delaware courts to confront the difficult choice between the property and social entity conceptions of the corporation was the takeover movement of the 1980s described in Chapter 15 of this casebook. In his words:

> * * * Two things made the takeover phenomenon very problematic for the legal theory of the corporation.
>
> The first is that the takeover movement put so much at stake. The issue in the takeover cases was not whether a donation of corporate funds could be made to a museum or college * * *. The issue was frequently whether all of the shareholders would be permitted to sell their shares, whether a change in corporate control would occur; and often whether a radical restructuring of the enterprise would go forward, with dramatic effects on creditors, employees, management, suppliers, and communities. As the junk bond market grew in size, larger and larger enterprises were faced with these prospects. * * *
>
> A second difference between the issues of the takeover era and those of the prior sixty years was that the short-term/long-term distinction was really of little analytical or rhetorical use in resolving the takeover issues. The most pressing of these issues involved the question whether a board of directors

could take action that precluded shareholders from accepting a non-coercive, all cash tender offer.[5] That question obviously raised the further question: Whose interest is the board of directors supposed to foster or protect when substantially all of the shareholders want to sell control of the corporation? The long-term/short-term distinction could not persuasively be used to answer or evade that question when it arose in this context. It is one thing to say that an expenditure of corporate funds that benefits the community—an education grant or the installation of an unmandated pollution control device—is really for the long-term financial benefit of shareholders. * * * It is, however, rather a different thing to justify precluding the shareholders from selling their stock at a large immediate profit on the ground that in the long run that will be good for them. While one might of course say that, many people would find it disturbing to put such a result on the basis that directors know what is better for shareholder than they themselves do. * * *

Courts were not anxious to grapple with this question. To resolve the matter seemed plainly to call for the making of policy in an environment that was warmly contested by powerful interests and in which no widely accepted doctrine offered a clear guide. * * *

Nevertheless, ultimately both our courts and, more importantly, our legislatures have, in effect, endorsed the entity view. In *Paramount Communications, Inc. v. Time, Inc.*[6], the Delaware Supreme Court seems to have expressed the view that corporate directors, if they act in pursuit of some vision of the *corporation's* long-term welfare, may take action that precludes shareholders from accepting an immediate high-premium offer for their shares. This important case might be interpreted as constituting implicit judicial acknowledgment of the social entity conception, as clearly as *Dodge v. Ford Motor Co.* reflects the alternative property conception of the corporation.

THE AMERICAN LAW INSTITUTE, PRINCIPLES OF CORPORATE GOVERNANCE: ANALYSIS & RECOMMENDATIONS[7]

§ 2.01 The Objective and Conduct of the Corporation

(a) Subject to the provisions of Subsection (b) and § 6.02 (Action of Directors That Has the Foreseeable Effect of Blocking Unsolicited Tender Offers), a corporation should have as its objective the conduct of business activities with a view to enhancing corporate profit and shareholder gain.

(b) Even if corporate profit and shareholder gain are not thereby enhanced, the corporation, in the conduct of its business:

(1) Is obliged, to the same extent as a natural person, to act within the boundaries set by law;

(2) May take into account ethical considerations that are reasonably regarded as appropriate to the responsible conduct of business; and

---

5. [By the Author] *See* Lucian A. Bebchuk, *The Pressure to Tender: An Analysis and a Proposed Remedy*, 12 Del.J.Corp.L. 911 (1987); *see also* John C. Coffee, Jr., *The Uncertain Case for Takeover Reforms: An Essay on Stockholders, Stakeholders and Bust–Ups*, 1988 Wis. L.Rev. 435, 439 ("[T]he problem of coercion in takeovers * * * represents the hobgoblin of the law professors.").

6. [By the Author] 571 A.2d 1140 (Del. 1989).

7. Copyright (1994) by The American Law Institute. Reprinted with the permission of the American Law Institute.

(3) May devote a reasonable amount of resources to public welfare, humanitarian, educational, and philanthropic purposes.

Note

Many transactions (such as charitable contributions) that provide no direct benefit to the corporation may be justified on the theory that the directors are maximizing the "long term" profits of the business. While doubtless many such actions do in fact benefit the corporation on a long term basis, the problem is that practically any expenditure can be justified by this argument, and its acceptance virtually means that "anything goes" so far as the use of corporate assets is concerned. Does § 2.01(b) adequately channel the power to enter into non-profit-maximizing transactions? For a careful examination of this section see Melvin Aron Eisenberg, Corporate Conduct that Does Not Maximize Shareholder Gain: Legal Conduct, Ethical Conduct, the Penumbra Effect, Reciprocity, the Prisoner's Dilemma, Sheep's Clothing, Social Conduct, and Disclosure, 28 Stetson L.Rev. 1 (1998). For a criticism of many aspects of the ALI's *Principles of Corporate Governance,* see Douglas M. Branson, Corporate Governance (1993). Consider also Henry Hansmann and Reinier Kraakman, The End of History for Corporate Law, 89 Geo. L.J. 439, 441–42 (2001) (arguing there is convergence on a consensus that the best means to this end of pursuing aggregate social welfare is to make corporate managers strongly accountable to shareholder interests and, at least in direct terms, only to those interests).

ILLINOIS BUSINESS CORPORATION ACT
Illinois–Smith–Hurd Ann. 805 ILCS 5/8.85.

5/8.85 Discharge of Duties—Considerations

In discharging the duties of their respective positions, the board of directors, committees of the board, individual directors and individual officers may, in considering the best long term and short term interests of the corporation, consider the effects of any action (including without limitation, action which may involve or relate to a change or potential change in control of the corporation) upon employees, suppliers and customers of the corporation or its subsidiaries, communities in which offices or other establishments of the corporation or its subsidiaries are located, and all other pertinent factors.

[handwritten margin note: Employs bot concepts. Think about profits, but consider other factors be engaging in transactions.]

PENNSYLVANIA BUSINESS CORPORATION LAW
15 Penn. Stat. § 1715.

§ 1715 Exercise of Powers Generally

(a) General rule.—In discharging the duties of their respective positions, the board of directors, committees of the board and individual directors of a business corporation may, in considering the best interests of the corporation, consider to the extent they deem appropriate:

(1) The effects of any action upon any or all groups affected by such action, including shareholders, employees, suppliers, customers and creditors of the corporation, and upon communities in which offices or other establishments of the corporation are located.

[handwritten margin note: Same idea as Illinois code. Integrates both models.]

(2) The short-term and long-term interests of the corporation, including benefits that may accrue to the corporation from its long-term plans and the possibility that these interests may be best served by the continued independence of the corporation.

(3) The resources, intent and conduct (past, stated and potential) of any person seeking to acquire control of the corporation.

(4) All other pertinent factors.

(b) Consideration of interests and factors.—The board of directors, committees of the board and individual directors shall not be required, in considering the best interests of the corporation or the effects of any action, to regard any corporate interest or the interests of any particular group affected by such action as a dominant or controlling interest or factor. * * *

Notes

(1) These statutes, generally known as "other constituency" or "alternative constituency" statutes, have been extremely popular. Two-thirds of states have adopted similar statutes, which vary considerably in language. This phenomenon is "[o]ne of the most remarkable but least remarked developments in corporation law in many years." James J. Hanks, Jr., Non–Stockholder Constituency Statutes: An Idea Whose Time Should Never Have Come, Insights, Vol. 3, No. 12, at 20 (Dec. 1989). Of the states with constituency statutes, only Connecticut's requires management to consider the interests of non-shareholders. Conn. Gen. Stat. § 33–756 (2006) (directors "shall consider . . . the interests of the corporation's employees, customers, creditors and suppliers, and . . . community and societal considerations"). While considerable law review commentary has been devoted to these statutes, they have been surprisingly non-controversial at the state level; indeed, they have been enacted almost routinely with little or no attention paid to the fact that they may dramatically change the basic ground rules of corporate governance. Their genesis, however, is clear: they were enacted in response to the fear of takeovers during the 1980s. As described by Hanks, "Opponents of hostile takeovers apparently felt that by giving directors a wider range of factors upon which to base a rejection of a takeover offer, they would help protect the directors from liability and thus encourage them to resist takeover offers." Id.

(2) Many comments about constituency statutes are very negative. For example, Lynda J. Oswald: Shareholders v. Stakeholders: Evaluating Corporate Constituency Statutes Under the Takings Clause, 24 J.Corp.L. 1, 2 (1998): "[T]hese constituency statutes blur the lines of corporate control and ownership and create a class of managers whose decisions are utterly discretionary and unfettered by the normal (albeit) weak constraints imposed by traditional corporate law doctrine."

(3) Committee on Corporate Laws, Other Constituencies Statutes: Potential for Confusion, 45 Bus. Law. 2253, 2269 (1990):[8]

> The Committee believes that the better interpretation of these [constituency] statutes, and one that avoids such consequences [i.e., creating conflicts of duty for directors and undermining the effectiveness of the system that has

8. Copyright (1990) by the American Bar Association. All rights reserved. Reprinted with permission of the American Bar Association and its Section of Corporation, Banking and Business Law.

made the corporation an efficient device for the creation of jobs and wealth], is that they confirm what the common law has been: directors may take into account the interests of other constituencies but only as and to the extent that the directors are acting in the best interests, long as well as short term, of the shareholders and the corporation. * * *

(4) In the wake of recent corporate scandals, corporations have begun to espouse non-shareholder stakeholder rhetoric:

> In recent years stakeholder rhetoric has permeated official corporate documents. Thus, the annual reports of many large corporations justify the firm's existence in terms of service to the community, not profit. According to The Economist, annual reports increasingly trumpet corporate programs focusing on non-shareholders like employee outreach, environmental protection, and community development. These reports talk only hesitantly about profit maximization. Hence, 88% of annual reports of Fortune 500 companies discuss activities with, and corporate commitment to, other stakeholders, ranging from employees to suppliers and creditors. Another 74% of these reports highlight the importance of such stakeholders in the first five pages of the report. Moreover, many annual reports discuss other interests throughout the document.

> In a radical shift away from profit speak, a few companies address their annual report to groups other than shareholders. For example, the annual report of General Electric Company begins with a "letter to stakeholders" as opposed to the traditional "letter to shareholders." According to General Electric, their reference to stakeholders is meant to capture the company's commitment to groups beyond shareholders. The rhetoric in these reports underscores corporate focus on stakeholders, as well as the prominence these concerns now receive.

Lisa M. Fairfax, The Impact of Stakeholder Rhetoric on Corporate Norms, 31 Iowa J. Corp. L. 675, 691–92 (2006). Business schools have begun to emphasize social responsibility as part of their curricula, ensuring that future corporate managers become accustomed to thinking about non-shareholder interests. Id. at 695.

[handwritten margin note: Business schools and corp. seem to be following social institution theory.]

(5) An interesting fact is that although over 30 states have enacted constituency statutes, there has been no reported litigation under them in the majority of those states. These statutes have apparently been invoked only by corporate directors after they have been sued for seeking to defeat takeover attempts. See Jonathan Springer, Corporate Law Corporate Constituency Statutes: Hollow Hopes and False Fears, 1999 Ann.Surv.Am.L. 85, 121 (1999) (concluding that concerns about the increased discretion afforded directors by constituency statutes, which are thought to release directors from liability for decisions which take constituency interests into account, have been unfounded). See also Vincent F. Garrity, Jr. & Mark A. Morton, Would the CSX/Conrail Express Have Derailed in Delaware? A Comparative Analysis of Lock–Up Provisions Under Delaware and Pennsylvania Law, 51 U.Miami L.Rev. 677 (1997) and "Epilogue," 51 U. Miami L.Rev., at 711–12, by the same authors. For a generally favorable review of constituency statutes see Edward S. Adams and John H. Matheson, A Statutory Model for Corporate Constituency Concerns, 49 Emory L.J. 1085 (2000).

[handwritten margin note: No one really sues corporations for ignoring non-stakeholder stakeholders. Instead corp. officers rely on constituency statutes to defend themselves when sued by stock-holders for not maximizing profits.]

B. SHAREHOLDERS

1. IN GENERAL

UNITED STATES TEMPORARY NATIONAL ECONOMIC COMMITTEE [BUREAUCRACY AND TRUSTEESHIP IN LARGE CORPORATIONS]
Monograph No. 11, pp. 19–23 (1940).

THE SEPARATION OF OWNERSHIP AND CONTROL

Another result of industrial concentration and the diffusion of ownership is so important that it deserves special consideration. It is the separation of ownership from control. Theoretically, of course, the holders of a majority of the voting stock control a corporation. But "the assumption that the owners of common or voting stock control a company is for the most part a fiction so far as the large corporations listed on exchanges are concerned."

In large public corporations management is more disconnected from ownership. Since there are so many smaller stockholders, there is less opportunity to control the board's decisions.

Three general types or sources of control may be differentiated: control by the holders of a majority of the voting stock, control by an active minority, and control by management. * * * The most common form of control among the large corporations may be termed management control. When stockholding is sufficiently diffuse the position of management becomes almost impregnable.

Management does not need to own stock; the strategic advantages of its location are quite sufficient. A presumption of worth is in its favor and, more concretely, the proxy machinery is at its disposal. Management chooses the proxy committee and by making appointments from among the members of management assures its own continuance. The effectiveness of this machinery is too formidable for small stockholders to overcome. The Financial Editor of the Chicago Daily News, for example, describes the situation thus:

Taking industry as a whole, the methods of using proxies gives the average stockholder [no] * * * chance to express an opinion * * *. He can agree or keep still. The proxy which is sent out lets him vote for the management: if he objects he can come to the meeting and register a kick. When he gets there he will be in the minority.

The management usually enters the meeting with enough votes to carry any measure, regardless of those present.

JOSEPH A. LIVINGSTON, THE AMERICAN STOCKHOLDER[9]
Pp. 60–61, 67 (1958).

Here's a natural question: If a stockholder is not satisfied with a company's management, why should he start a proxy fight, why should he sue, why shouldn't he just sell his stock and be done with it?

Answer: That is what most stockholders do.

9. From The American Stockholder by Joseph A. Livingston. Reprinted by permission of Joseph A. Livingston. Copyright © 1958 by Joseph A. Livingston. Reprinted by permission of J.B. Lippincott Company.

It is the easiest, cheapest, and, from many points of view, the most practical way to express stockholder dissatisfaction with a management, a company, or an industry.

The right to sell is a vote. And the stock market—Wall Street—is the polling booth. If the price of a stock goes up, it registers stockholder-investor-satisfaction. If it goes down, it registers dissatisfaction in the market place. * * *

This right to sell stock—to vote for or against a management—in the market place—is different from a vote at a stockholders' meeting. When a stockholder votes against a slate of directors, he is exercising his right as a stockholder, as an owner. He hopes to change the management and improve the company. But a stockholder who sells says to hell with it. He is not going to reform the company. He is not an owner trying to increase the value of his property. He says, in effect, "Include me out." * * *

Thus, the market-place vote has power. It is a positive warning, a financial warning, to an incumbent management, of stockholder dissatisfaction. It lets the officers know that dissatisfaction has got beyond the discussion stage. The "big boys" are selling. So, the management might bestir itself—make changes—to strengthen the company's position. For that reason, selling stock is not an entirely empty gesture. True, the big investors do not fight for a change; they do not stay with the company that is retrogressing. But their leave-taking has an effect.

DANIEL R. FISCHEL, EFFICIENT CAPITAL MARKET THEORY, THE MARKET FOR CORPORATE CONTROL, AND THE REGULATION OF CASH TENDER OFFERS

57 Tex.L.Rev. 1, 3–5, 8–9 (1978).

An efficient capital market[10] is one in which a trader cannot improve his overall chances of speculative gain by obtaining public information about the

10. [By the Author] Two major implications of efficient capital market theory are that (1) security prices adjust rapidly and in an unbiased manner to any new information, and (2) price changes behave in a random manner. B. Lev, Financial Statement Analysis: A New Approach 212 (1974). If prices of securities did not adjust rapidly and without bias, investors could profit by trading during the time during which securities did not reflect all available information or during periods when the market either overcompensated or undercompensated for new information. Similarly, if security prices did not move randomly, investors could capitalize on systematic price movements to earn above average returns.

The empirical support for efficient capital market theory exists in three forms—weak, semi-strong, and strong. The weak form has focused on the significance of securities' past price movements. Repeated studies have demonstrated that historic patterns of past prices are of no value in predicting future price move-

ments. The semi-strong form asserts that security prices reflect all publicly available information about that security. Empirical tests of the semi-strong form have tested the speed of adjustment of security prices to such events as stock splits, annual earnings announcements and large secondary offerings of common stock. These tests indicate a quick price adjustment process in which the information revealed by specific events is anticipated by the market. The strong form of efficient capital market theory is that even nonpublic information is quickly reflected in security prices. Tests of the strong form have proven inconclusive. Several studies of professionally managed mutual funds have concluded that these funds, despite huge expenditures to identify mispriced securities, were unable to consistently outperform the market. Other studies have found, however, that corporate insiders can profit by trading on inside information not available to other investors.

companies whose securities are in the market and evaluating that information intelligently in determining which stocks to buy and sell. Paradoxically, the efficiency of the market results from the competitive efforts of securities analysts and investors who strive to earn superior returns by identifying mispriced securities—securities that are either overvalued or undervalued. The goal of securities analysis is to discover information that suggests differences between current market prices and what these prices "should" be, the securities' intrinsic values. The securities analyst acts on this information by buying, selling, or recommending securities. The process ensures that market prices reflect all available information. * * * [I]n an efficient capital market in which a large number of buyers and sellers react through a market mechanism such as the New York Stock Exchange to cause market prices to reflect fully and instantly all available information about a company's securities, investors should not be able to "beat the market" systematically by identifying undervalued or overvalued securities. * * *

Efficient capital market theory implies that if a publicly traded company is poorly or less than optimally managed, the price of its securities will reflect this fact accurately and promptly. That a capital market is efficient, however, does not imply that there is a similarly efficient mechanism whereby control shifts from less capable managers to others who can manage corporate assets more profitably. The market for corporate control, so called by Henry Manne in his ground-breaking work on the subject,[11] must perform that function in our economic system.

Poor performance of a company's securities in the capital market is a common indication of poor management. The lower the market price of the securities compared to what it would be with better management, the more attractive the firm is to outsiders with the ability to take the firm over. The most common takeover device is the merger. This takeover device is not available, however, when incumbent management opposes the shift in control because merger statutes uniformly require approval by the directors of the two corporations. The two techniques that can be used to shift control when there is opposition are the direct purchase of shares and the proxy contest. * * *

One of the basic themes of corporation law is the significance for shareholders of the modern corporation's separation of ownership and control. In their famous work on this subject, Professors Berle and Means assumed that managers do not seek to maximize what is most important to shareholders—appreciation of the shareholders' underlying investment.

Berle and Means failed to recognize, however, that unity of ownership and control is not a necessary condition of efficient performance of a firm. If the owner of a wholly owned firm is its manager, he will make operating decisions that maximize his utility. After the owner-manager sells equity in the firm to raise capital, however, his incentive to search out new profitable ventures diminishes because he now bears only a fraction of the losses resulting from less profitable investments. The agency relationship between shareholders and managers inevitably calls into question the identity of the

---

11. [By the Author] E.g., Manne, Cash Tender Offers for Shares—A Reply to Chairman Cohen, 1967 Duke L.J. 231; Manne, Merg- ers and the Market for Corporate Control, 73 J.Pol.Econ. 110 (1965).

agent's decisions with decisions that would maximize the welfare of shareholders.

Various market mechanisms exist, however, to minimize this divergence of interests between managers and shareholders. As Alchian has illustrated, an architect or builder does not share in its profits or losses (as only the owners do) absent contractual arrangement. Yet the architect or builder is vitally interested in the success of the building. The greater the profits generated by his efforts, the greater the demand for his services. Corporate managers are in precisely the same situation. While they do not directly share in the profits of an enterprise, successful performance increases the demand for their services as managers. Managers have a further incentive to maximize profit if their compensation is in some way linked to performance—stock options are a common example of this type of arrangement. Intensity of competition in the firm's product market also provides an incentive for managerial efficiency.

The market for corporate control and the threat of cash tender offers in particular are of great importance in creating incentives for management to maximize the welfare of shareholders. Theoretically, shareholders may oust poor management on their own initiative, but the costs to individual shareholders of monitoring management performance and campaigning for its defeat in shareholder elections when performance is poor are prohibitive. On the other hand, inefficient performance by management is reflected in share price thus making the corporation a likely candidate for a takeover bid. Since a successful takeover bid often results in the displacement of current management, managers have a strong incentive to operate efficiently and keep share prices high.

Notes

(1) See Robert W. Hamilton and Richard A. Booth, Business Basics for Law Students: Essential Terms and Concepts, § 15.2 (1998) (defending the efficient capital market hypothesis theory as a valid and substantiated economic theory and explaining that anomalies in market pricing may be attributable to noise or chaos, which includes several intangibles, inherent in active trading markets). Consider also Richard A. Booth, Stockholders, Stakeholders and Bagholders (Or How Stockholder Diversification Affects Fiduciary Duty), 53 Bus.Law. 429, 433–34, 442 (1998) (explaining that diversified investors are risk-neutral while undiversified investors are risk-adverse and that the former has supplanted the latter as the quintessential "reasonable stockholder" to whom management owes fiduciary duties).

(2) "In typical healthy, publicly held corporations with fairly active trading in securities, managers should try to act in blissful ignorance of all of the reasons that the share price may deviate from intrinsic value. Managers should seek to adopt an investment policy calculated to maximize what the price of each share would be in a fully omniscient and perfectly efficient market, adhering to the naive hope that virtue will be rewarded." Henry T.C. Hu, Risk, Time, and Fiduciary Principles in Corporate Investment, 38 U.C.L.A. L.Rev. 277, 358–59 (1990). In several articles, Professor Hu argues that this approach, which he terms the "blissful shareholder wealth maximization standard," tends to maximize the true or intrinsic value of each share. Is this standard appropriate in corporations with some fully-diversified and some undiversified shareholders?

2. THE GROWTH OF INSTITUTIONAL INVESTORS

RICHARD H. KOPPES, CORPORATE GOVERNANCE: INSTITUTIONAL INVESTORS, NOW IN CONTROL OF MORE THAN HALF THE SHARES OF U.S. CORPORATIONS, DEMAND MORE ACCOUNTABILITY

The National Law Journal, April 14, 1997, p. B5.[12]

Nothing has so defined the revolution of corporate governance over the last 20 years as the rise of institutional investors. This key group has become a powerful force in corporate America. As activists, institutional investors have set the standards and terms for the corporate governance reform movement and are changing the face of American business.

Aging baby boomers have fueled the increase in public and private funds from approximately $2 trillion in 1986 to more than $5 trillion today—accounting for a sizable portion of all institutional investments.

While patterns of share ownership in the United States are almost always changing in one way or another, the 1990s marked a watershed: For the first time on record, institutional investors controlled more than half the shares in American corporations. By contrast, as recently as 40 years ago, these institutions together held less than 10 percent of the outstanding shares. Progressive institutionalization has been the dominant ongoing change in U.S. share ownership.

This change in ownership structure has had a number of important consequences over time. Many institutional investors have such large holdings that they have become permanent, long-term shareowners of major corporations. As buy-and-hold players, institutional investors have become the patient capital of companies. As a result they have an economic interest in using corporate governance to improve performance.

And as the size of their holdings has grown, institutional investors have discovered ownership rights. The practice of simply selling shares in disgust has given way to the realization that taking an active role as an owner makes economic sense.

Notes

(1) The principal kinds of institutional investors are (a) pension funds created by corporate employers, by states and cities for their employees, and by universities, churches, and foundations; (b) mutual funds (and other types of investment companies) that offer opportunities to invest in broad portfolios of securities; (c) insurance companies, both life and casualty; (d) foundations; (e) university and charitable endowments; (f) banks investing trust funds; (g) brokerage firms; and (h) a variety of investment vehicles for sophisticated investors, many in the form of limited partnerships.

(2) The growth of institutional investors described by Mr. Koppes is graphically revealed by statistics. In 1953, individual investors held 90 percent of all

12. Reprinted with permission from April 14, 1997 issue of The National Law Journal.

outstanding shares listed on the New York Stock Exchange, while institutional investors held less than 10 percent. By 1992, more than 50 percent of all NYSE shares were held by institutional investors. Just over one percent of U.S. households own two-thirds of all publicly traded equity securities directly held by individuals. Of course, many additional individuals own stock indirectly through institutional investors such as mutual funds, annuities, and retirement or profit-sharing plans. The Wharton School & The New York Stock Exchange, Inc., The Policy Implications of Stockownership Patterns 3–5 (1993). In terms of dollars, "[I]t took a decade for all institutions to see their assets nearly triple, from $672.6 billion in 1970 to $1.9 trillion in 1980. The next decade brought more than a tripling in assets, to $6.3 trillion in 1990, and then a staggering increase of slightly more than 75 percent in five-and-one-half years, to $11.1 trillion at the end of the second quarter of 1996." The Conference Board, Institutional Investment Report: Patterns of Institutional Investment and Control in the United States, No. 1, vol. 1, January 1997, at 4.

Another indication of institutional investor activity is the growth of larger securities transactions. The New York Stock Exchange collects data on "block transactions" involving single trades of 10,000 shares or more. In 1970, there were 17,217 such transactions, representing 13 percent of the total value of all shares traded on the NYSE. In 1995, the number of such transactions had risen to 1,963,889, representing 53.6 percent of the value of all shares traded on the NYSE. The Conference Board, The Brancato Report on Institutional Investment: Equity Turnover and Investment Strategies, vol. 3, Ed. 2, at 16 (May 1996). In 1999, the number of block trades had increased to 4,195,721, involving 82.7 billion shares, though the percent of the value of all shares traded on NYSE declined to 50.2 percent (because of the growth of exchange trading generally). New York Stock Exchange Fact Book (1999 Data) 4, 16, 93. And these figures understate the trading activities of institutional investors, since there exist several proprietary computerized trading systems open only to institutional investors that do not report transactions in NYSE-listed shares.

(3) Even though the collective holdings of institutional investors may carry with them potential control over individual companies, it is unusual for any single institutional investor to own more than 3 percent of the voting shares of a major company. For example, the 7th largest corporation in mid–1996 was IBM Corporation; 50.4 percent of its shares were owned by institutional investors. Five institutional investors alone owned 11.6 percent of its shares; ten owned 16.8 percent, 20 owned 20.5 percent, and 25 owned 26.1 percent. Ibid., at 33.

(4) Institutional investors almost always have fiduciary duties to persons other than the issuers of the portfolio securities in which they invest. For example, pension funds have a duty to the employees covered by the fund to maximize the funds available for retirement benefits. These duties to third parties are construed by some institutional investors as requiring that they strive to maximize the gain to the institutional investor even though the gain is on a short term basis. This short-horizon investment philosophy, when being applied by a relatively small number of shareholders which collectively may own more than 50 percent of the outstanding securities issued by the largest domestic corporations, is itself a source of concern. However, as suggested by Mr. Koppes, many institutional investors, particularly employee retirement plans, do not adopt a policy of short-term maximization of gains but view themselves as permanent investors in individual companies.

BERNARD BLACK, SHAREHOLDER PASSIVITY REEXAMINED

89 Mich.L.Rev. 520, 521–24 (1990).

The problem of who watches the watchers is as old as government, and not much more tractable for corporate than for government organizations. In theory, the shareholders of public companies elect directors, who watch corporate officers, who manage/watch the company on the shareholders' behalf. But since Berle and Means, we have understood that this theory is a fiction. The managers—the current officers and directors—pick the directors, and the shareholders rubberstamp the manager's choices. Perhaps thrice in a thousand cases, unhappy shareholders mount a proxy fight. About one fourth of the time, they win.

Most modern corporate scholars, especially those with a law-and-economics bent, accept shareholder passivity as inevitable. They rely on market forces, especially takeovers, to limit managerial discretion. The critics' claim, stripped to its essentials, is that shareholders don't care much about voting except in extreme cases and never will. Collective action problems, which arise because each shareholder owns a small fraction of a company's stock, explain why shareholders can't be expected to care. I will call this view the "passivity story." * * *

I argue that the critics' legal analysis is misdirected; their factual assumptions about shareholder size are obsolete; and their collective action explanation for passivity is superficial. Shareholder voting, historically only a minor nuisance to corporate managers, can become an important part of the multist-rand web of imperfect constraints on managers, *if* legal rules permit. My emphasis is on the formal act of voting. Much actual oversight undoubtedly will be informal, but meaningful informal oversight will take place only if the formal power is available should it be needed. * * *

The passivity story also assumes a company with thousands of anonymous shareholders, each owning a tiny fraction of the company's voting stock. That assumption, never wholly true, is increasingly obsolete. Institutional investors have grown large enough so that a limited number of institutions own a sizeable percentage of the shares of most public companies. Moreover, the fastest growing institutions are public pension funds and mutual funds, which face fewer direct conflicts of interest in monitoring corporate managers than the corporate pension funds and bank trust departments who were formerly the principal institutional shareholders. Large institutions can combine forces, form trade groups to represent their collective interest, and one way or another act as monitors of corporate managers, if they see profit in doing so. Legal obstacles notwithstanding, some institutions are trying to do just that.

MICHAEL B. DORFF, SOFTENING PHAROAH'S HEART: HARNESSING ALTRUISTIC THEORY AND BEHAVIORAL LAW AND ECONOMICS TO REIN IN EXECUTIVE SALARIES

51 Buffalo L. Rev. 811, 834–36 (2003).

The free market school has also argued that institutional investors will eventually solve problems—such as those with executive compensation—that stem from the split between ownership and control in public corporations. Unlike most other types of shareholders, institutional investors, such as mutual funds, private and public pension funds, banks, and insurance companies, typically own large amounts of stock. These entities possess the potential to reunify ownership and control. Institutional investors may own large enough blocks of a company's stock to exercise real control, especially if they act in concert. Moreover, concentrated stock ownership may mean that the rewards that come from close monitoring of corporate activities outweigh the associated costs. As a result, institutional investors should possess a strong incentive to oppose any attempt by the CEO to act contrary to the shareholders' interests.

Unfortunately, this theory has often not borne out well in practice, in part because of two popular investment strategies, diversification and indexing. Most institutional investors diversify their holdings to reduce risk exposure. Dividing investments among many different companies limits the consequences of a disaster suffered by any single corporation. But by limiting their investments in any one company, institutional investors also sharply reduce their incentive to monitor any particular corporation's management.

Many institutional investors now also employ indexing for part or all of their equity investments. Indexing involves buying stock in all of the companies in a particular sector index or in the market as a whole, often weighted according to market capitalization. Academic studies have asserted that in the long-term, the vast majority of investors who choose individual stocks will underperform the relevant market index. An additional advantage of indexing is that it eliminates the need for expensive research on individual corporations. In other words, institutional investors who practice indexing need not monitor corporate behavior and, therefore, will not want to bear the expense of an active role in managing the corporation.

Another reason institutional investors may not prove an effective panacea is that institutional investors often have close ties to the corporations in which they invest. Institutional investors include private and public pension funds, mutual funds, insurance companies, and banks. With the exception of public pension funds, all of these entities may seek business from the same companies whose stock they own. * * *

Notes

(1) Despite the potential obstacles to institutional investor activism identified by Professor Dorff, institutional investors have increasingly participated in corporate governance over the past two decades. Less clear is whether activism on the part of institutional investors has improved firm performance. Professor Roberta Romano has argued that institutional investors have focused on reforms that have

not been proven to improve performance, such as limiting executive compensation and altering the structure of the board. Roberta Romano, Less Is More: Making Institutional Investor Activism a Valuable Mechanism of Corporate Governance, 18 Yale J. on Reg. 174 (2001). One kind of institutional investor may have a greater impact on firm performance than others. Recently some have found evidence that activism on the part of hedge funds notably improves firm performance. See Mark Hulbert, A Good Word for Hedge Fund Activism, N.Y. Times, Feb. 18, 2007, at Section 3.

(2) The development of activism by institutional investors has gone through several distinct phases.

(a) Prior to the 1980s, institutional investors tended to view themselves purely as investors who should support rather than confront management. During this period investments by individual institutional investors were much smaller than they are today, and it may have been possible for them to dispose of holdings on the open market if they were dissatisfied with management. In other words, institutional investors could act in much the same way as individual shareholders and exercise the "Wall Street rule" if they were not satisfied with management.

(b) Institutional investor involvement in the oversight or monitoring of portfolio companies began during the takeover movement of the 1980s. With the development of poison pills (often called "shareholder rights plans" by management) and other defensive tactics in the mid–1980s, management of target companies were able to block cash offers for target company shares at premiums that were often 50 percent or more above the prior market price. (For a discussion of poison pills and other defensive tactics, see Chapter 15.) Faced with the significant loss of profitable resale opportunities, a few large institutional investors introduced shareholder proposals in 1985 and 1986 seeking the withdrawal of poison pills. (The rather arcane law of shareholder proposals under the SEC proxy regulations is discussed in Part 4 of Section D of this Chapter.) In the spring of 1987, shareholder proposals on this topic were introduced by institutional investors in more than 60 companies. However, efforts to organize institutional investors were limited because of concern that direct communication among investors might be viewed as solicitation of proxies in violation of the SEC proxy regulations. As described in the subsequent note, these restrictions were significantly relaxed in 1992.

Shareholder proposals to revoke poison pills in the 1980s had only a few instances of spectacular success—for example, in 1988, a 51.9 percent favorable vote of shareholders of USAir Group and a 61.2 percent favorable vote of shareholders of Santa Fe/Southern Pacific. In the aggregate, during the 1989 "proxy season," support for these proposals averaged 27.9 percent of the shares voting, up only slightly from the 26.4 percent during the 1988 season.

In the 1990s, as economic conditions began to improve (accompanied by a revival of the takeover movement and a return of unsolicited takeover bids), the attention of institutional investors again turned to proposals to eliminate poison pills, with much greater success than in the earlier period. Joann S. Lublin, "Poison Pills" Are Giving Shareholders a Big Headache, Union Proposals Assert, Wall St. J., May 23, 1997, p. c1, col. 3, states that in 1997 14 measures to eliminate poison pills had been voted on and had garnered an average of 53.7 percent of the ballots cast, and that between 1988 and 1996, 52 non-binding resolutions to curb poison pills had won a majority of the votes cast; thereafter, half of the companies involved had abandoned their poison pills.

(c) As described in Chapter 15, the takeover movement of the 1980s ended rather unexpectedly in about 1990 following the collapse of the brokerage firm of Drexel Burnham, Lambert, Inc., the criminal conviction of Michael Milkin, and changes in economic and political conditions generally. Attention turned from poison pills and other defensive tactics to the more traditional issues of managerial efficiency, profitability of the enterprise, and executive compensation. The early 1990s were a recessionary period which occurred at the same time many industries were facing unexpected technological and structural change. Many respected and well-known corporations announced massive losses, huge layoffs, and major changes in product lines. At the same time, unfavorable publicity was directed at high levels of executive compensation, which appeared to be little affected by poor performance of the enterprise. During this period, a surprisingly large number of Chief Executive Officers lost their jobs. While the extent of the involvement of institutional investors in these developments is impossible to document, it is generally believed that their influence was substantial. Articles describing these events commonly refer to the influence of "activist shareholders" and "pressure" from shareholders. E.g., John A. Byrne, Requiem for Yesterday's CEO: Old–Style Execs Who Can't Adapt Are Losing Their Hold, Bus. Wk., Feb. 15, 1993, at 32, 33; Judith H. Dobrzynski, Activist Boards, Yes. Panicky Boards, No, Bus. Wk., Dec. 28, 1992, at 40; and Judith H. Dobrzynski, A GM Postmortem: Lessons for Corporate America, Bus. Wk., Nov. 9, 1992, at 87.

(3) In October, 1992, the SEC amended its proxy regulations to permit much freer communication among institutional investors without fear of being charged with violation of the regulations so long as there was no solicitation of proxies. Anecdotal evidence indicates that executives of corporations in which institutional investors had substantial holdings almost immediately displayed increased sensitivity to the concerns of major shareholders. For example, in July 1993, IBM announced the formation of a new "corporate governance" committee of the board of directors composed entirely of outside directors. About the same time, TIAA/ CREF (a major institutional investor) announced that it planned to open discussion with directors at a number of underperforming portfolio companies. See John A. Byrne, The Best and & Worst Boards: Our New Report Card on Corporate Governance, Business Week, November 25, 1996, 82, 94. By the year 2000, the activity of the traditional active funds—e.g. CalPERS and TIAA—REF—had declined in part because of their prior successes. In 2000, for example, "CalPERS dropped two targets from its '10 company focus list' and withdrew proposals at five others following fruitful talks." Corporate Governance Advisor, September/October 2000, at 20.

(4) Some institutional investors have created monitoring programs for portfolio corporations. Perhaps the most extensive program is by TIAA/CREF, which owns approximately one percent of all equities issued by large publicly held corporations; it directly monitors 25 governance issues (including board independence and conflicts of interest) for 1,500 companies. Specific governance proposals put forth by institutional investors include "de-staggering" boards of directors in order to give shareholders greater voting power (Reebok Corporation), executive compensation (Walt Disney, and others), and the elimination of ineffective chief executive officers and individual directors. See Joann S. Lublin, Irate Shareholders Target Ineffective Board Members, Wall St. J., November 6, 1995, Section B, p. 1, col. 5 (reporting a strong negative vote by institutional investors in Archer–Daniels–Midland Company before the management reorganization that occurred in that company). Some institutional investors show their displeasure at corporate governance policies in specific corporations by withholding their vote for manage-

ment-nominated directors. See Richard H. Koppes, Corporate Governance, Institutional Investors, Now In Control of More Than Half The Shares of U.S. Corporations, Demand More Accountability, The National Law Journal, April 14, 1997, p. b5 (reporting that following a $90 million payout by Walt Disney to former President Michael Ovitz, the holders of 12.5 percent of Disney shares withheld their votes for five directors in protest). It is not a coincidence that the most active institutional investors generally have been pension and retirement funds, since they have long-term interests that require substantial payments in the future to employees; their portfolios are so large that they are unlikely to try to sell shares on a wide scale in protest of corporate governance issues. They are, in short, the epitome of the locked-in long term investor.

For a negative view of institutional investor activity based on a detailed study of one incident, see D. Gordon Smith, Corporate Governance and Managerial Incompetence: Lessons from Kmart, 74 N.C.L.Rev. 1037 (1996). See also Bernard Black, Shareholder Activism and Corporate Governance in the United States, Peter Newman, ed., 3 The New Palsgrave Dictionary of Economics and the Law, (1998), at 460. For a rather negative assessment of whether anyone is overseeing these institutional investor overseers, see Roberta Romano, Public Pension Fund Activism in Corporate Governance Reconsidered, 93 Colum.L.Rev. 795, 796 (1993).

3. NOMINEES, BOOK ENTRY, AND "STREET NAMES"

Most publicly traded shares owned by individual investors today are held in a form of ownership that is best described as "book entry." When an individual purchases securities through a brokerage firm, the broker will register her securities in its name or the name of another "nominee." This practice is referred to as "street name" registration. The brokerage firm will hold the securities and will keep a record in its books of the holdings owned by its customers (the beneficial owners). Under this "book entry" system, the broker must provide the beneficial owner with an account statement listing her holdings with the firm on at least a quarterly and annual basis. One unique consequence of book entry ownership is that a single nominee, Cede & Co. (Cede), has become the record owner of an astonishingly high percentage of all publicly traded shares. Cede and Company is the nominee for the Depository Trust Company (DTC), the central clearing facility for the New York Stock Exchange.[16] In order to understand book entry ownership, some history is required.[17]

From time immemorial, securities transactions involving publicly traded shares have been settled five days after the transaction date by the delivery of certificates, recorded either in street name[18] or in the name of the selling shareholders and suitably indorsed. Wall Street maintained a small army of

---

16. [By the Editors] The other two clearing houses in the United States are the Mid–West Securities Depository Company and the Philadelphia Depository Trust Company.

17. [By the Editors] Much of the information set forth in this text and the following notes is drawn from the Report of Thomas H. Jackson, Special Master dated January 28, 1992, in State of Delaware v. State of New York, 501 U.S. 1228, 111 S.Ct. 2849, 115 L.Ed.2d 1017 (1991).

18. [By the Editors] "Street name" here refers to certificates recorded in the name of a Wall Street brokerage firm and indorsed in blank. Street name certificates were routinely used in New York to close securities transactions since they were essentially bearer securities and could be delivered with a minimum of paperwork.

messengers whose duties were to deliver packages containing indorsed or street name certificates to the offices of various brokerage firms to permit individual transactions to be settled. This system worked adequately until the volume of trading increased dramatically in the late 1960s—volume doubled and even tripled in a relatively short period—and the traditional method of handling securities transfers simply broke down. The back offices of the major New York brokerage firms became awash in uncompleted transactions and share certificates of uncertain ownership; more than 150 brokerage firms failed or were forcibly merged before these problems were straightened out in the early 1970s.[19]

The back office crisis was solved by the creation of a new form of recording share ownership, which has permitted the volume of trading on the New York Stock Exchange to grow from a range of five to ten million shares a day in the early 1960s to more than 1200 million shares a day in 2001. The basic concept is the "immobilization" of share certificates in a clearing house and the recordation of all transfers thereafter to the maximum possible extent through entries on the books of the clearing house and the brokerage firms rather than by transfer of certificates. Brokerage firms that are participants in the clearing house deposit shares owned for their own account as well as for the accounts of their customers with the clearing house, all to be recorded in the name of the nominee, Cede, on the books of each issuing corporation. Certificates are physically deposited and held at DTC's offices in New York or elsewhere. The ownership of securities by individual shareholders is thereafter reflected solely by direct book entries in the records of the brokerage firm, and indirect book entries in the records of the central depository under the name of the brokerage firm. Once this system is set up, most transactions in shares are settled simply by changes in book entries either within the central depository or in the records of brokerage firms, or both, with no movement of certificates at all.

An essential aspect of this plan was the enactment of the Securities Investor Protection Act of 1970,[20] which insures investors against losses from the insolvency of brokerage firms, thereby allowing investors to rely with confidence on monthly statements from brokerage firms showing specified securities in the investors' accounts.

DTC is the principal clearing house in the United States. It holds virtually all U.S. equity securities registered in street name. The "participants" in DTC—the organizations that have securities held by DTC—consist of the major brokerage firms, banks, and other clearing agencies in the United States and Canada.

DTC's primary mission (as is the mission of all clearing houses) is the reduction of costs for securities transactions offered to the public by its

---

19. [By the Editors] For a general description of the back office crisis, see Joel Seligman, The Transformation of Wall Street: A History of the Securities and Exchange Commission and Modern Corporate Finance 340–56 (1982); Study of Unsafe and Unsound Practices of Brokers and Dealers, Report and Recommendations of the SEC, H.R. Doc. No. 92–231, 92nd Cong., 1st Sess. (1971).

20. [By the Editors] 15 U.S.C.A. §§ 78aaa–lll. The Act insures against broker insolvency up to $500,000 for each account, except that the maximum is $100,000 to the extent that a claim is for cash rather than securities. This insurance is provided by the Securities Investor Protection Corporation, which is funded by assessments against its members composed of brokers and dealers registered under the Securities Exchange Act of 1934.

participants. Each participant has a book entry position in securities it has deposited with DTC. When a participant deposits physical certificates with DTC or receives securities via transfer by book entry from other participants, its account balance is credited. As a practical matter, offsetting transactions by each participant are netted each day, and only net changes are reflected by book entry changes at DTC. Thus, in substantial part, settlement of transactions between participants is handled by adjustments to book accounts rather than the movement of certificates.

Today, when a person makes a routine purchase of publicly traded shares through a broker, the purchaser will not receive a certificate for those shares unless special arrangements are made. Rather, his or her ownership will be reflected simply by monthly statements of account from the brokerage firm that show the investor is the owner of a specified number of shares. The brokerage firm, in turn, is normally either a participant in DTC or affiliated with such a participant. As a result, in the modern securities world of book entry, no specific share certificates anywhere can be attributed to any single beneficial owner. There is simply a huge common pool of certificates or master certificates held in the name of Cede and a very large number of beneficial owners who rely entirely on the bookkeeping records of DTC and the brokerage firm to establish ownership.

An investor may specify, of course, that he wishes to receive physical certificates registered in his name, though some brokers may charge a fee for doing so. A subsequent transfer of certificated shares is more complicated than the sale of book entry shares, requiring the physical delivery of the certificate on the settlement date, appropriately indorsed, which may require a trip to a bank or brokerage firm to obtain a guarantee of the signature of the registered owner.

Notes

(1) Because of (a) the historic use of "street names" to facilitate securities transactions, (b) nominee ownership by institutional investors, and (c) the widespread use of the book entry system by all participants in securities trading, the records of share ownership maintained by publicly held issuers shed almost no light on beneficial ownership. Cede & Co. is by far the largest record owner of shares in most publicly held corporations, but there is no way to discover the beneficial ownership of those shares except by examining records of DTC and its members. The ownership of the great bulk of modern American industry is thus hidden today below one or more layers of nominee ownership.

(2) In the book entry system, there are always at least two intermediaries between an individual beneficial owner of shares and the issuer or its transfer agent. This system is largely invisible to the ordinary investor who usually receives both his dividends and voting information on time.

(a) Distributions are handled by wire transfers directly to the accounts of participants in DTC. Each participant allocates the payments to individual investors entitled thereto on the records of the brokerage firm on the same day. The brokerage firm then either credits the appropriate account with the payment, or prepares a check which is mailed or delivered to the owner of the account.

(b) The book entry system creates obvious problems in connection with voting by proxy and the distribution of information in the form of annual reports, proxy statements, and interim financials. The SEC first attacked this problem in 1965 by requiring issuers to deliver to banks, securities dealers, brokers or voting trustees, upon their request, sufficient copies of annual reports and other materials to provide beneficial owners with copies. However, many record owners did not in fact receive such material. One study in 1973, for example, revealed that of the 17 percent of corporate stock then held in street name, as many as 68 percent of the beneficial owners were not receiving annual reports. The Silence Imposed by Street Names, Bus. Wk., Dec. 8, 1973, at 40. In 1974, the SEC significantly revised the rules to improve the transmission of materials to beneficial owners; the rules of securities exchanges and the National Association of Securities Dealers were also amended to require brokers and dealers to obtain and forward such materials to beneficial owners in a timely manner. These rules now primarily appear in 17 C.F.R. §§ 240.14a–3, 240.14b–1, 240.14b–2, and to a lesser extent, 240.14c–7 (2000).

(c) The book entry system has also created problems for issuers in connection with holding meetings, assuring the presence of quorums and so forth. Stephen P. Norman, Shareholder Communications: Direct Registration of Beneficial Shareholders, Insights, Vol. 3, No. 6, at 10, 10–12 (June 1989) (concluding that layered ownership patterns in securities trading contributes to lateness and error in the proxy voting system). For a more current evaluation, see John C. Wilcox, Shareholder Communications: Electronic Communication and Proxy Voting, Insights, vol. 11, No. 3, March 1997, 8.

(3) In 1983, the SEC developed a more direct means of communication between registrants and their beneficial owners. 17 C.F.R. § 240.14b–1(b)(3) (2002) sets forth the basic concept. It requires each broker/dealer to:

> Provide the registrant, upon the registrant's request, with the names, addresses and securities positions, compiled as of a date specified in the registrant's request which is no earlier than five business days after the date the registrant's request is received, of its customers who are beneficial owners of the registrant's securities and who have not objected to disclosure of such information; * * *

(a) The reaction of the brokerage community to the nonobjecting beneficial owner (NOBO) approach was strongly negative. David M. Doret, et al., Carey v. PEI: Voting Shortcuts Cut Short, Insights, Vol. 3, No. 12, at 3, 7 (Dec. 1989) (explaining that many fiduciary institutions, and brokerage firms in particular, strongly disfavored the adoption of procedures which will disclose the identity of the underlying beneficial holders as they fear it creates a shopping list of which their competitors may prey and institutional holders often wish that their positions remain confidential).

(b) Sadler v. NCR Corp., 928 F.2d 48 (2d Cir.1991) holds that a corporation may be required to produce a NOBO list as well as a shareholders list under state law. See also Parsons v. Jefferson–Pilot Corp., 333 N.C. 420, 426 S.E.2d 685 (1993) (common law inspection right includes NOBO list if it is in the corporation's possession, but the corporation cannot be required to compile such a list if it does not use the list in making its own solicitations); Cenergy Corp. v. Bryson Oil & Gas P.L.C., 662 F.Supp. 1144 (D.Nev.1987) (right to inspect corporate records includes right to inspect NOBO list); Nu Med Home Health Care, Inc. v. Hospital Staffing Services, 664 So.2d 353 (Fla.App.1995)(corporation cannot be compelled to create a NOBO list; one judge dissented); Luxottica Group v. U.S. Shoe Corp., 919 F.Supp. 1091 (S.D.Ohio 1995)(disclosure of NOBO list not required at all under Ohio statute).

(4) The "settlement" of a securities transaction involves the payment of the purchase price by the buyer and the delivery of the securities by the seller. After a transaction has been entered into, even though settlement has not occurred, a purchaser of securities carries the economic risk that the securities may decline in value and the economic benefit that the securities may increase in value. Settlement historically occurred five business days after the transaction, colloquially called T + 5. Effective as of June 7, 1995, the SEC reduced the period between the transaction and the settlement from five days to three, from T + 5 to T + 3.[21] At the same time, the SEC proposed the implementation of the Direct Registration System (DRS) which would allow an investor to have securities registered in her name and held on the issuer's books.

(5) The DRS system is described briefly by the SEC in "The SEC Speaks in 2000" (PLI Order No. B0–00GF, March 2000) as follows:

> [The] DRS, as developed by the industry, is a facility that allows investors the ability to hold their securities on the issuer's books, through the issuer's transfer agent, rather than holding in street name or in certificated form. Instructions to create investors' book-entry positions in DRS or to move those positions are transmitted through electronic systems. The DTC currently administers the systems used to facilitate DRS transactions between participating transfer agents and broker-dealers. Securities Exchange Act Release No. 35038, (1994), 59 Fed.Reg. 63652. At the end of 1999, there are eleven participating transfer agents and 291 eligible issues in DRS. In September 1999, the Commission approved a rule change submitted by DTC that requires transfer agents participating in DRS and broker-dealers to use an electronic communication system referred to as the Profile Modification System (Profile). * * * Profile allows a broker-dealer, upon instructions from the broker-dealer's customer, to electronically request that the transfer agent move the customer's DRS positions to the broker-dealer's account at DTC.

According to the SEC, as of November 2003, 600 issuers and 17 transfer agents were participating in DRS. SEC Rel. No. 33–8398, 69 Fed. Reg.12922 (2004).

(6) The book entry system has been superimposed upon state statutes that continue to require action by record owners. It should not be surprising that this combination sometimes creates problems. In Tabbi v. Pollution Control Indus., Inc., 508 A.2d 867 (Del.Ch.1986) "a demand filed by Cede on behalf of Shearson Lehman/American Express, Inc. * * * with respect to 44,500 shares held beneficially" was held to be untimely even though Shearson had prepared the demand letter two days before the meeting and sent it by overnight courier to Cede. (For some reason, the demand letter was delivered one day late and Cede's demand letter to the issuer in turn was received by the issuer one hour and five minutes after the polls were closed). Enstar Corp. v. Senouf, 535 A.2d 1351 (Del.1987) held that a right to appraisal was not validly perfected when the demand for appraisal was made in the name of the beneficial owner and signed by an employee of the brokerage firm but not made in the name of Cede, the record owner. In Alabama By–Products Corp. v. Cede & Co., 657 A.2d 254 (Del.1995), an inadvertent withdrawal of shares from an appraisal proceeding by agents for record owners

---

21. With continued improvements in efficiency a "T + 1" settlement procedure may be practical. The T + 1 settlement procedures would help ensure that the market is prepared for increases in trading volumes. However, under this settlement procedure, investors will have to alter the way they buy and sell securities. Certificates may have to be delivered to brokers before orders are executed. In addition, investors may need to keep funds at the brokerage firm before executing orders.

was held not to be binding on beneficial owners under language of Del. GCL § 262. In Allison v. Preston, 651 A.2d 772 (Del.Ch.1994) the manager of an employee's saving plan that also provided for a "pass through" of voting rights to beneficial owners solicited members with respect to a disputed proxy contest. The manager received proxy forms from both factions in the contest and followed the members' wishes by voting 80,386 shares favorably on one proxy form and 80,386 shares unfavorably on the other. However, since negative votes are not allowed, the inspector of elections proposed to disallow both proxies but the court held that the obvious intent of the shareholders should be respected and only the favorable proxy should be considered.

(7) The Independent Election Corporation of America (IECA) contracts with banks and brokerage houses to disseminate proxy material directly to the beneficial owners of securities. In a contested election situation, IECA tabulates the proxies on behalf of the beneficial shareholders and then executes a "contest voting form" which indicates the beneficial shareholders' votes for each of IECA's clients. See Concord Fin. Group, Inc. v. Tri–State Motor Transit Co. of Delaware, 567 A.2d 1 (Del.Ch.1989) (holding that the proxy [voted by IECA as authorized by Q & R Clearing] overvoted the stock it represented, and since that error could not be corrected by looking at the face of the proxy or the books and records of Tri–State, the proxy should have been disregarded). Following this decision, Delaware amended its General Corporation Law, § 231, to permit inspectors of election to consider "other reliable information for the limited purpose of reconciling proxies and ballots submitted by or on behalf of banks, brokers, their nominees or similar persons which represent more votes than the holder of a proxy is authorized by the record owner to cast or more votes than the stockholder holds of record."

(8) In 2004 the SEC adopted Regulation SHO in order to address the problem of "naked short selling." In traditional short selling, a seller borrows shares and sells them with the requirement that he purchase shares on the market and return them to the lender at some later date. The seller is betting that the share price will drop and he will profit by keeping the difference between his sell price and subsequent purchase price. In naked short selling, however, the seller sells shares of stock he has not borrowed. Often the naked short seller has no intention of ever delivering the shares the buyer thinks she has purchased. The shares the buyer ultimately receives are merely electronic book entry. James W. Christian et al., Naked Short Selling: How Exposed Are Investors?, 43 Houston L. Rev. 1033 (2006).

The practice allows manipulative market participants to flood the market with sales of a company's shares, driving down the price. Id. at 1046. In the release accompanying proposed regulation of naked short selling, the SEC noted some of the problems created by the practice: "the naked short seller unilaterally converts a securities contract (which should settle in three days after the trade date) into an undated futures-type contract, which the buyer might not have agreed to or that would have been priced differently. The seller's failure to deliver securities may also adversely affect certain rights of the buyer, such as the right to vote. More significantly, naked short sellers enjoy greater leverage than if they were required to borrow securities and deliver within a reasonable time period, and they may use this additional leverage to engage in trading activities that deliberately depress the price of a security." SEC Rel. No. 34–48709, 68 Fed. Reg. 62972 (2003).

Regulation SHO requires a broker to have reasonable belief that the security can be borrowed and delivered by the time it is due before executing a short sale order, and requires brokers to document this "locate" prior to executing the short sale. It also requires that orders placed with broker-dealers be marked "long" or "short." Failures to deliver securities within the standard three-day settlement period have declined 20 percent since the adoption of Regulation SHO. Randall Smith, Suits Focus on Street's Role in 'Naked Shorting', Wall St. J., June 28, 2006, at C1.

C. DIRECTORS

ROBERT W. HAMILTON, RELIANCE AND LIABILITY STANDARDS FOR OUTSIDE DIRECTORS
24 Wake Forest L.Rev. 5, 9–12 (1989).

Modern boards of directors have practically nothing to do with the day-to-day business of the corporation. Publicly held corporations are immense economic entities. * * * The internal organization of such large economic entities necessarily involves complex hierarchical structures in which successively higher levels of management are given increasingly broad discretion and responsibility. Indeed, starting at the lowest level of corporate management, such as shop foreman or a similar position, successive layers of broader responsibility can be traced up through several levels of management. By following this process through to its logical conclusion, the highest level reached still would be below the level of the board of directors.

Even this description does not adequately describe the complexity of the internal structure of many publicly held corporations. Many corporations today are so large and are involved in so many diverse lines of business that business decision-making is diversified and diffused. Several largely independent internal hierarchical structures may exist within the lower levels of the corporate bureaucracy, each culminating in a single person or, in rare instances, a small committee that has responsibility for one or more areas of operations. A person may be "President of the Plastics Division" or "Head of the Chemicals Sector" of a large corporation with responsibility for the profitability of a multi-plant business with sales of billions of dollars per year and yet be several hierarchical levels below the highest management level within the corporation itself.

Above these lower level internal hierarchies there is an "umbrella organization," the "corporate headquarters" or "home office" of the publicly held corporation, of which the board of directors loosely forms a part. The "Plastics Division" or "Chemical Sector" in this situation may be structured as a wholly owned subsidiary of the publicly held corporation, or it may be a department or division of the corporation with no separate legal structure. In either event, it may have its own "board of directors," consisting usually of management personnel drawn from the operating components and from corporate headquarters staff, to advise and assist its managers. It may function as a largely autonomous business having wide discretion over research, product development, advertising, sales policies, and other matters. These semi-autonomous businesses within a single corporate structure often are described as "profit centers."

There are centralized levels of bureaucracy in corporate headquarters above these profit centers that have general oversight of the management of each profit center. Corporate headquarters imposes constraints on autonomy by setting profit goals or objectives for each center that are expected to be met—or sought—each year in terms of net profit, return on invested capital, or other similar measures. The operating head of the profit center has the responsibility for meeting these goals and may lose his or her job if the goals are not met. In addition, corporate headquarters usually handles certain core functions for all branches of the business. These functions relate to the processes of evaluation of performance and control over funds, specifically auditing, legal services, management compensation policies, fringe benefits, and accounting. Others are handled centrally because of perceived efficiency. It is not uncommon, for example, for corporate headquarters to handle the investment of excess funds. Under such a system, each profit center is required to turn over all excess funds on a daily basis to headquarters for investment, with the profit center having the privilege of withdrawing funds as needed for operations. Typically, corporate headquarters also has the sole responsibility of raising capital and allocating it among the profit centers. These functions require centralized review and approval of proposed capital investments by profit centers to assure that the corporation divides its limited resources among competing proposals put forth by autonomous profit centers in order to maximize overall return. Despite these restraints by corporate headquarters, many profit centers are sufficiently discrete and independent that they may be sold off by the corporation or be spun off as entirely separate entities without major changes in operating procedures.

Corporate headquarters itself has a hierarchical structure. At the highest levels are a series of executive managers, usually organized on a functional rather than a product basis, who have ultimate authority over broad areas of corporate activities. They have titles, such as "chief legal officer," "chief operations officer," "chief financial officer," and "chief accounting officer," that bear no relationship to the traditional corporate officers of "President," "Secretary," or "Treasurer" referred to in older state corporation statutes. At the ultimate apex is an individual referred to almost universally as the chief executive officer (the "CEO") who has responsibility for the enterprise as a whole. The CEO may have additional titles and roles, such as "President" or "Chairman of the Board of Directors," but many CEOs do not. The CEO has responsibility for the management team that directs the enterprise. If, for example, he loses confidence in the chief financial officer, the CEO must replace him and find a more satisfactory one. In theory, the CEO has power to call the shots in the corporate bureaucracy on narrow issues as well as broad ones, where and when he wishes. Of course, the CEO, as the head of a large bureaucratic organization, cannot hope to run details of the business operations; if he is to be effective, authority over details must be delegated to subordinates, and the CEO must concentrate on the broadest issues relating to the corporation.[24]

---

24. [By the Author] The effect of this delegation of details has been characterized as follows:

[P]ower—having great influence, force, and authority—is slipping through the chief executive's hands, and has been for some time. * * * Now a chief executive hardly ever "runs" anything. * * * Chief executives, many management gurus agree, are less powerful today than they were 10 or 15 years ago. The most significant reason is that their task is much bigger. It's one thing to manage a single operation well. It's another thing to decide that you're no longer in a certain business, to change, cut back, and

Because the CEO has ultimate responsibility for the success or failure of the business, he—and quite possibly he alone—will make the final decision on whether to embark upon a radical change in business strategy that may lead to the loss of his or her job if the change turns out to be disastrous. He may decide, for example, to close fifteen plants in order to redirect the primary emphasis of the corporation, or to develop a new product such as a state-of-the-art airplane or modern computer that will strain the economic resources of the entire entity and may well be unsuccessful; "betting the company" is the slang phrase that describes such fundamental and risky decisions. Such decisions may or may not be reviewed by the board of directors before they are implemented, but it is almost certain that if the CEO wishes to embark on such a course of action, the board of directors will acquiesce in that decision despite the reservations of many, or even all, members.[25]

Where then does the board of directors fit in? It does not have a place in the clearly demarcated hierarchy that leads from shop foreman or steward to CEO. The board is also not part of a direct chain of command above the CEO, since many or most important business decisions do not come before the board at all. Rather, it is somewhere above the CEO, and floating off to one side. Its principal source of power is a cataclysmic one: If it loses confidence in the CEO, it can compel his resignation and the installation of a successor. Obviously, such a power is an extreme one with wide-reaching implications upon the management of the business and is used only rarely and in extreme circumstances. Furthermore, it is not exercised easily. Because of the manner of their selection and the nature of their working relationships with the CEO, directors tend to give the CEO the benefit of the doubt. Even a discussion among directors about the possibility of replacing the CEO is a serious matter fraught with danger and uncertainty.

H.R. LAND, BUILDING A MORE EFFECTIVE BOARD OF DIRECTORS

[An undated promotional brochure published in about 1972 by H.R. Land & Company, Management Consultants, Los Angeles, California.]

The corporate Board of Directors is a topic of increasing concern to Chief Executive Officers. Directors, now keenly aware of their legal liabilities, are pressing for greater participation in corporate affairs and new forms of compensation. In response to this greater interest on the part of their directors, a number of Chief Executives are rethinking the use of their boards and adopting new policies intended to strengthen the director/management relationship.

This report is designed to assist the Chief Executive Officer in dealing with his board. It is based upon independent interviews conducted by H.R. Land & Company with Chief Executives and Directors representing more than 60 corporations active in all segments of the economy. The survey sample purposely included small privately held firms and medium sized regionally traded companies as well as widely traded Fortune 500 corporations.

---

deal with foreign competition. The agenda has been greatly expanded. * * *

John A. Byrne and Laurie Baum, The Limits of Power, Bus. Wk., October 23, 1987, 33–34.

25. [By the Author] A vote on an issue of the nature described in the text is, in effect, a vote of confidence on the stewardship of the CEO. * * *

No attempt has been made to develop statistical tabulations of the findings. Rather, *the emphasis is on policies and techniques which could be of practical value to large numbers of Chief Executive Officers*. Because of the many types of corporations included in the study, not all of the ideas presented are suitable for use in any one firm. Our intent has been to present a number of ideas from which a Chief Executive might select and adopt those which are appropriate for use in his own firm.

The CEO Determines the Board's Effectiveness

The Principal Determinant of the Effectiveness of a Board of Directors is the Chief Executive Officer. His personal convictions on what a board should be will do more to shape the role of his directors than any other single factor. In most instances we found the board to be a mirror image of the CEO's desires and intentions. Exceptions tended to occur only where the board was made up of individuals representing major equity interests or financial institutions who were not necessarily of the CEO's choosing.

The attitude of the CEO is critical; he creates the atmosphere—hopefully one of candor and frankness in which the directors feel their participation is of real value. The ideal CEO/director relationship is one of professional respect and admiration. Friendship is a part of the relationship, but it must remain a "business" friendship rather than a "personal" relationship if the directors' "check and balance" function is to remain intact. The most effective boards seem to share a philosophy in which both the CEO and each director consider themselves as donors and recipients in a mutually beneficial relationship.

Obviously the CEO's actions have a major impact on the board. What he does to select, attract, involve, motivate, compensate and protect his directors is the subject of the remainder of this booklet. Equally important are the personal touches—periodically inviting a director to lunch, remembering his individual likes and dislikes, being cognizant of his other business and personal obligations, letting him know you are thinking of him on special occasions. * * *

How a Potential Director Views Board Membership

* * * In asking directors what motivated them to accept membership on individual boards the most frequent responses centered on (1) existing or potential *personal relationships* with management and the other directors, (2) the *experience and satisfaction* accompanying board membership, and (3) *status and prestige* attached to being a corporate director. Annual retainers and meeting fees were rarely cited as a reason for accepting, although the opportunity for a *capital gain* is obviously a strong motivating factor. In this regard, one professional director told us that he looks for companies whose stock is depressed, whose management has an equity position strong enough to provide him with a "fair" block of stock, and whose circumstances are such that outside help is clearly needed.

Getting Directors Involved

The Key to Making a Director Effective is to Involve Him Personally. A good way to establish the feeling of "our company" is with financial participation. Some publicly traded firms make attractive investment financing available for their directors; in a privately held business financial involvement can be achieved by allowing a director to buy in at book and, when he resigns, to sell at book. * * *

Notes

(1) The author of the foregoing brochure presumably never dreamed that it would find its way into a law school casebook or a set of readings as to the role of directors in corporations. As a result, his point of view is revealing in terms of the relative roles of the CEO and individual directors as of the 1960s. The relationship between CEO and board envisioned by Land was probably reasonably accurate for most corporations of the era: not only did the CEO personally select and approve each director but most boards consisted primarily (or, in some cases, entirely) of inside directors—persons who held lucrative positions with the corporation that were terminable at the will of the CEO. The CEO was almost always the chair of the board of directors, he presided at all meetings, and controlled the agenda. Furthermore, a retiring CEO usually selected his successor. One commentator has described boards of this era as "[l]ittle more than a claque of the CEO's cronies, [who] would quietly nod and smile at their buddy's flip charts and rubber-stamp his agenda for the corporation." John A. Byrne, The Best and Worst Boards: Our New Report Card on Corporate Governance, Bus. Wk., Nov. 25, 1996, 82.

(2) Changes in the relationship between the CEO and board of directors can be traced to the Watergate scandals of the early 1970s. As part of the general disclosures of misconduct during the Nixon era, it was revealed that a large number of publicly held corporations had engaged in a significant amount of illegal or questionable conduct: paying bribes or "commissions" to high-placed officials in friendly countries, making illegal campaign contributions to American politicians, and the like. About four hundred corporations voluntarily admitted such conduct, including such well-known names as Lockheed Aircraft Corporation, Gulf Oil Corporation, Northrop Corporation, and G.D. Searle and Company. A. A. Sommer, the Impact of the SEC on Corporate Governance, reprinted in Deborah A. DeMott, Corporations at the Crossroads, Governance and Reform 200 (1980). A number of individuals and corporations pleaded guilty or nolo contendere to criminal charges based on similar conduct. In some instances, the SEC brought suit to compel changes in the governance of specific corporations, and in other instances, it negotiated plans for impartial investigations of responsibility for misconduct. See Robert W. Hamilton, Corporate Governance in America 1950–2000: Major Changes But Uncertain Benefits, 25 J.Corp.L. 349, 359 (2000) (explaining that one visible result of these scandals was the creation by the American Law Institute of a major project that ultimately led to the publication of an influential study, *Principles of Corporate Governance*, and that the ALI was one among many voices urging major changes in corporate governance). Throughout this period of widespread disclosures, it was apparent that many directors were unaware of the existence of illegal or inappropriate conduct within their own corporations. Indeed, in some instances it was also doubtful that top management knew of the illegal use of fairly large sums of money.

(3) What do boards of directors actually do? They do not manage the business of the corporation—everyone agrees that the CEO and other officers—"the management" of the corporation—do that. MBCA § 8.01(b) provides an unsatisfactory answer when it states that the business and affairs of a corporation may be "managed under the direction of" the board of directors. More light is shed by studies based on what outside directors say they actually do. One such study,

completed in 1971, is Myles L. Mace, Directors: Myth and Reality (1971); a more recent study is Jay W. Lorsch, Pawns or Potentates: The Reality of America's Corporate Boards (1989). Both studies are based on interviews with a large number of persons who serve as directors in publicly held corporations, and a comparison of the two studies' conclusions shows clearly that the role of directors has evolved significantly since the 1970s. See also Paul H. Zalecki, The Corporate Governance Roles of The Inside and Outside Directors, 24 U.Toledo L.Rev. 831 (1993).

According to Mace, (at 178–81) directors at regular meetings where there is no crisis demanding immediate action performed only two basic functions:

(a) They provide advice and counsel to management. They may be a sounding board from which a variety of views on board or difficult questions may be obtained. The views of a director with expertise in an area such as law or finance may be given greater weight with respect to questions arising within his or her area of expertise.

(b) They provide discipline to management, who must appear before them and present information and defend business decisions. Even though the board may not question the management's conclusion, the mere fact that it is a possibility requires an organization of thoughts and points of view and a careful review of work of subordinates. The mere fact that a difficult question *might* be asked ensures that the chief executive officer will prepare carefully for his appearance before the board.

Writing nearly twenty years later, Lorsch (Id. at 75–80) identified two additional roles of directors in "normalcy" situations: consideration of long-term strategic planning, and efforts to make sure that the corporation "does the right thing," that is, assuring that the corporation's affairs are conducted in ethical, legal, and socially responsible ways. Lorsch recognized that many CEOs felt that board involvement in strategic planning could infringe on the CEO's "prerogatives" but participation in that area had become accepted. Concern with "doing the right thing" was largely reflected in the work of the audit committee of the board of directors and the development of compliance programs in various areas by committees of the board. Lorsch also pointed out that the CEO dominance over the board of directors by way of control of the selection process, the agenda, and corporate information in general had waned significantly since Mace's era.

(4) Section 3.02(a) of The Principles of Corporate Governance (1994) lists five mandatory functions of a board of a publicly held corporation:

(1) Select, regularly evaluate, fix the compensation of, and, where appropriate, replace the principal senior executives;

(2) Oversee the conduct of the corporation's business to evaluate whether the business is being properly managed;

(3) Review and, where appropriate, approve the corporation's financial objectives and major corporate plans and activities;

(4) Review and, where appropriate, approve major changes in, and determinations of other major questions of choice respecting, the appropriate auditing and accounting principles and practices to be used in the preparation of the corporation's financial statements;

(5) Perform such other functions as are prescribed by law, or assigned to the board under a standard of the corporation.

Section 3.02(b) lists seven additional functions that "a board of directors also has power" to perform, including initiation of corporate plans, changes in accounting principles, providing advice and counsel to senior executives, and so forth.

(5) A leading source of principles of good corporate practice is the Corporate Directors Guidebook (4th Ed. 2004) prepared and published by the Committee on Corporate Laws, Section of Business Law, American Bar Association. The backbone of the modern view of corporate governance is based on basic concepts: A substantial majority of members of a board of directors should be "independent of management," and the critical oversight committees—audit, compensation, and nominating—should be staffed entirely by "independent" or "nonmanagement" directors. Id., at 26–27. Today the New York Stock Exchange and the Nasdaq Stock Market require a majority of board members to meet their definitions of independence, and require all members of audit committees to meet the criteria for director independence set forth in the Sarbanes–Oxley Act. In light of the growing importance of independent directors, the American Bar Association has published a manual to help independent directors understand the legal and governance issues they face. Bruce F. Davis, Independent Director's Guidebook (2007).

(6) Rather than the CEO leading and the board of directors concurring, the independence of the board of directors has increased to the point that "the CEO is viewed more as a key employee rather than as the ultimate boss of the enterprise." Gilbert Fischsberg, Chief Executives See Their Power Shrink, Wall St.J., March 15, 1993, at B1, col. 3. Many corporations have separated the roles of chairman of the board of directors and CEO or, where the CEO is also the chairman, have appointed a "lead director" to run the board in a time of crisis. Boards also provide institutionally for the periodic review of the performance of the CEO by outside directors. Joann S. Lublin, CEOs Give Up More Clout to Boards: Chiefs Endorse Lead Directors, Performance Reviews, Wall St.J., July 26, 1996, at A10A. CEO firings have become more common over the past few years, with executives from Disney, Boeing, Merck, and other large companies being forced to step aside by unhappy directors. See Alan Murray, Leash Gets Shorter For Beleaguered CEOs, Wall St. J., Aug., 23, 2006, at A2. Independent directors helped oust Hewlett–Packard CEO Carly Fiorina in 2005. Directors also initiated the investigation into the leaking of information from board meetings, which ultimately led to the exit of Ms. Fiorina's successor, Patricia Dunn, amid allegations she approved questionable methods to uncover the sources of the leaks. Recent years have seen a rise in the number of "executive sessions"—meetings of boards of directors outside the presence of top management. The percentage of companies expecting their boards to meet in executive session increased by 20 percent between 2003 and 2005. George Anders, Private Time: As More Boards Meet Without Management Present, It Makes for Franker Talk—And Anxious CEOs, Wall St. J., Oct. 9, 2006, at R4.

(7) The corporate scandals of recent years have raised the personal stakes for corporate directors. In 2005, eleven WorldCom directors settled a shareholder class action suit for $20 million, or 20 percent of their aggregate net worth, rather than relying on D&O insurance. See Daniel Akst, Fining the Directors Misses the Mark, N.Y. Times, Aug. 21, 2005, at Section 3 pg 6. That same year former Enron directors agreed to pay $13 million of their own money to settle a shareholder suit arising from the company's demise. Some argue that increasing the personal risks associated with serving on a corporate board will make it difficult to staff boards with knowledgeable, competent directors. See The Directors' Cut, Wall St. J., Jan. 13, 2005, at A12; Jonathan D. Glater, A Big New Worry For Corporate Directors,

N.Y. Times, Jan. 6, 2005, at C1. For an opposing view, see Lucian Bebchuk, What's $13 Million Among Friends?, N.Y. Times, Jan. 17, 2005, at A17.

D. CORPORATE GOVERNANCE IN 2007

ROBERT W. HAMILTON, CORPORATE GOVERNANCE IN AMERICA 1950–2000: MAJOR CHANGES BUT UNCERTAIN BENEFITS

25 J. Corporate Law 349, 359–73 (1999).[30]

[This combination of factors] * * * (the growth of the institutional investor, the decline of the takeover movement, and the disclosures following the Nixon resignation) led to a surge of interest in proposals for improved corporate governance. These proposals began in the early 1970s and have continued today. * * * Several have come from organizations with close ties to the business community, such as the Business Roundtable, the National Association of Corporate Directors, and the Council of Institutional Investors.

The response of the Business Roundtable was particularly important. That organization is composed of the CEOs of the 200 largest corporations in the United States. It has long been viewed as a bastion of conservatism, successfully opposing many corporate governance proposals put forth by the American Law Institute and other groups. In August 1997, however, it surprised many persons by publishing a "Statement on Corporate Governance," that endorsed principles regarding board and committee independence and an annual review of CEO performance by independent directors.[31] In short, ideas that were anathema in 1950 had become an accepted part of American corporate culture by 1999.

---

1. BUSINESS FAILURES AND CORPORATE SCANDALS

Several related factors contributed to a significant decline in confidence of a rosy and profitable future and led ultimately to the enactment of the Sarbanes–Oxley Act. These developments include:

1. The Collapse of the Dot-coms. The so-called dot-com companies that were created in the flush period of the 1990s often competed directly with existing business establishments. However, rather than having significant competitive advantages, the dot-com development turned out to be somewhat of a fad, and after a great deal of initial interest and enthusiasm (and the

---

30. Copyright 1999 by the University of Iowa (*The Journal of Corporation Law*). Reproduced with permission. ([By the Editors:] Most citations have been omitted.)

31. [By the Author] The Business Roundtable's Statement lists a number of general principles, including recommendations that the board of directors should have a substantial majority of independent directors, that there should be an annual review of the CEO's performance, and that the independent directors should meet at least once a year without representatives of management being present. Busi-

ness Roundtable, Statement on Corporate Governance (last modified Sept. 1, 1997) <http://www.brtable.org/document.cfm/11>. In general terms, the Business Roundtable principles differ from many other proposals put forth by other groups in that they stress general standards and core principles rather than establishing objective criteria. Based on the practical experience of its members, the Business Roundtable recognizes the diversity of practices among its members to achieve common goals and avoids detailed proposals.

investment of significant amounts of money by many individual and corporate investors), most dot-coms discovered that their markets were unprofitable or limited, and they could not effectively compete with traditional established businesses. Most quietly folded their tents and went out of business. A handful have survived: Amazon.com, e-Bay, Autobytel,Inc, Google and perhaps a dozen others, but most of them are gone. The loss to individual investors in failed dot-coms was often substantial; for example, one of my law school colleagues had invested significantly in DrKoop.com, and lost his entire investment when that business collapsed. Fortunately, the loss he suffered was not devastating, but doubtless the same cannot be said for many modest investors, as well as for some substantial ones.[32]

2.   The Collapse of the Telecoms. The collapse of the telecommunications industry was much more devastating economically than the collapse of the dot-coms. The telecommunications industry had been largely deregulated in 1986 when the old AT&T monopoly was broken up.[33] Almost immediately thereafter, money began to pour into the industry as companies rushed to install new fiber optic networks to carry the anticipated growth in electronic communications. A rumor that Internet traffic was expected to double every three months fueled massive investments in new capacity. A Wall Street Journal article[34] graphically describes the consequence:

> The belief that Internet traffic could grow so quickly—if true, it would have meant annual growth of more than 1,000%—led more than a dozen companies to build expensive networks as they rushed to claim a piece of the next gold rush. The statistic sprouted up in reports by industry analysts, journalists and even government agencies * * *. 'Internet traffic,' the Commerce Department said in a 1998 report 'doubles every 100 days.'

> Except that it didn't. Analysts now believe that Internet traffic actually grew at closer to 100% a year, a solid growth rate by most standards but one that was not nearly fast enough to use all of the millions of miles of fiber optic lines that were buried beneath streets and oceans during the late–1990s * * *."

Two new players, WorldCom, Inc. and Global Crossing, Ltd., became active players, acquiring existing telecommunication systems and combining them into huge national systems. By early 2001, it had become evident that the telecom industry was not growing as fast as predicted, and that overcapacity would be a problem for many years. Thousands of skilled workers were laid off, and, as described below, both WorldCom and Global Crossing were forced to make major accounting adjustments.

3.   Winners and Losers in the Telecom Debacle. Reflective of this collapse is the fact that between January and June, 2002, at least 112 telecom companies were required to restate downward prior earnings even though

32.   In January, 2005, the New York Times reported that DrKoop.com shares were still being offered for sale in the "pink sheets" market at a price of one-hundredth of a cent per share. The pink sheets is an informal public market for highly speculative securities.

33.   See Yochi J. Dreazen & Rebecca Blumenstein, Familiar Rings: How Effort to Open Local Phone Markets Helped the Baby Bells, Wall St.J., Feb. 11, 2002, at A1.

34.   Yochi J. Dreason, Telecom Carriers Were Driven by Wildly Optimistic Data on Internet's Growth Rate, Wall St. J., Sept. 26, 2002, at B1.

public accounting firms had previously given clean bills of health to over 93 per cent of them.[35]

4. The Collapse of Enron, November, 2001. Undoubtedly, the most violent initial shock of the post–2000 era was the unexpected collapse of Enron Corporation in November, 2001. Enron had been formed in 1985 by the merger of two interstate pipelines; in less than a decade it had converted itself from being a rather stodgy pipeline operator to a "virtual company," trading in a wide variety of tangible and intangible goods such as natural gas, electricity, and other products or services for present or future delivery. In 2000, Business Week ranked Enron No. 22 of the 100 best American companies, while Kenneth Lay, its CEO was named as one of the top 25 managers in the United States. Enron was publicly described as "a titan in the natural gas industry,"[36] and as "the world's leading integrated natural gas and electricity giant."[37] In 2000, Enron was also named as 25th among "the world's most admired companies."[38]

It is difficult to imagine the shock that was created when, on December 2, 2001, Enron Corporation and 13 of its affiliates unexpectedly filed for Chapter 11 bankruptcy protection in the Southern District of New York. At the time, this was the largest bankruptcy filing in history: the original affiliated entities that filed for bankruptcy listed over $63 billion in assets and debts of nearly $50 billion.[39]

The complex transactions that led to Enron's collapse have been extensively explored and discussed.[40] The disclosures by Sherron Watkins, an Enron employee and a whistle-blower whose name became nationally associated with the Enron collapse, led to a major restatement of earnings: Enron announced that it had overstated earnings by $567 million in the previous year alone, and shortly thereafter filed for bankruptcy protection. Virtually overnight, the value of Enron common shares dropped from $80 to pennies per share. It turned out that the widespread use of "special purpose entities" by Enron had permitted it to hide very substantial liabilities and avoid disclosure of the inherent weaknesses in its business operations over a lengthy period.[41]

Enron's collapse set off a storm of litigation. A portion of this litigation involved a complex transaction involving Nigerian electricity-producing barges that were purchased by Merrill Lynch from Enron. Andrew Fastow, Enron's former finance chief, apparently gave an illicit promise in December 1999 to

---

35. Cf. Dennis K. Berman et al., Telecom Glut Could Linger as Failed Networks are Rescued, Wall St. J., Aug. 14, 2002, at B1.

36. Daniel Southerland, You've Heard of Big Oil. This is the Story of Big Gas * * * and It Begins With Enron Corporation, Which Wants to be No. 1 in World, Washington Post, Feb. 4, 1996, at H1.

37. Erin Davis, Enron: The Power's Back On, Fortune, Apr. 13, 1998.

38. Nicholas Stein, The World's Most Admired Companies, Fortune, Oct. 2, 2000, at 182.

39. About six months later, WorldCom's bankruptcy filing listed $107 billion in assets and $41 billion in debts.

40. Perhaps the most insightful article on the Enron collapse is John R. Kroger, Enron, Fraud, and Securities Reform: An Enron Prosecutor's Perspective, 76 U. Colo.L.Rev. 57 (2005). Mr. Kroger served as a trial attorney with the United States Department of Justice's Enron Task Force from June 2002 to July 2003.

41. See the Report of Investigation by the Special Investigative Committee of the Board of Directors of Enron Corp., William C. Powers (Chair), Dean of the University of Texas School of Law.

Merrill officials concerning the contemplated purchase of the barges and promised to "take Merrill Lynch out of the deal" within six months if Merrill was unable to find a purchaser on its own terms that would make the transaction economically profitable. In 2003, Merrill settled with the Justice Department, accepting responsibility for the role its employees allegedly played in the transaction. In 2004, four Merrill executives were convicted for knowingly entering into a sham transaction with respect to those barges in order to preserve Enron's tax position. Those convictions were overturned by the Fifth Circuit in 2006.

Over thirty former Enron executives were criminally prosecuted, but the trial that garnered the most public attention was that of former CEO Ken Lay and former CEO and COO Jeffrey Skilling. In May 2006, both men were convicted of conspiracy and fraud in connection with the company's collapse. Mr. Lay died just weeks after his conviction. Mr. Skilling was sentenced to 24 years in prison. As of March 2007, Enron's website states that the company is "in the midst of liquidating its remaining operations and distributing its assets to its creditors."[42]

5. The Collapse of Arthur Andersen, L.L.P. The well-known accounting firm, Arthur Andersen, L.L.P., was the auditor for Enron and a substantial number of other important corporations. However, it had engaged in a "cleaning" of Enron files relating to its financial activities shortly before Enron collapsed, and as a result was convicted of obstruction of justice. Like Enron, Arthur Andersen essentially went out of business, though a portion of its business has reorganized and continued under the name Accenture. The collapse of Arthur Anderson reduced the number of major independent auditors to four. In 2005, the United States Supreme Court overturned the firm's criminal conviction. Today the firm employs just 200 people, most of whom are dealing with remaining litigation. At its peak, Andersen employed 28,000 workers. See Jess Bravin, Justices Overturn Criminal Verdict in Andersen Case, Wall St. J., June 1, 2005, at A1.

6. The Collapse of WorldCom, Inc. The original developer of WorldCom was Bernard Ebbers, who began his career as the owner of a small chain of budget hotels. He created a telecommunications company called LDDS Communications, Inc. in 1983 and shortly thereafter begin purchasing other companies in the telecommunications industry using the name WorldCom, Inc. The business grew by the use of the stock of that corporation to pay for its acquisitions. In October, 1997, Ebbers purchased MCI, Inc. for $30 billion in WorldCom stock. By 2000, Ebbers had made some 65 acquisitions and he proudly announced that WorldCom then had more than $107 billion in assets. Shortly thereafter, he announced an offer to purchase Sprint for $129 billion (mostly in the form of WorldCom common stock). However, the Department of Justice nixed this transaction under the antitrust laws.[43]

In April, 2002, WorldCom announced that it was laying off ten percent of its workforce and reducing its revenue projections for the year. On April 30, WorldCom announced that Ebbers had been requested to

---

42. The principal winners in this Enron story were, of course, the lawyers, consultants, accountants and other professionals who earned nearly $1 billion in fees in constructing the ultimate settlement.

43. Sorry, Wrong Number: Endgame, Wall St. J., June 27, 2002, at A12.

resign as CEO by WorldCom's board of directors. A month later it was announced that Scott Sullivan, WorldCom's long time chief financial officer had been dismissed,[44] and that a significant downward restatement of WorldCom's profits would be announced.

In June, 2002, WorldCom announced that it had overstated its previous profits by $3.85 billion by treating a number of expense items as capital investments rather than as expenses. At the time, this was the largest restatement of income ever announced by an American corporation (though as it turned out, it was merely the first of a sequence of profit restatements and fraud charges against this corporation and other telecommunication companies).

In July, 2002, Ebbers and Sullivan were invited to appear before the House Financial Services Committee to testify about Arthur Andersen's relationships with the collapse of WorldCom, but both refused to appear, stating they would invoke the Fifth Amendment. In August, Sullivan and another senior WorldCom executive, David Myers, were arrested and charged with securities fraud, conspiracy to commit securities fraud and making false statements to the SEC. The complaint alleged that the two defendants had directed that funds be transferred wrongfully to retain the appearance of profitability, and that WorldCom's public balance sheet bore no relation to the actual financial condition of the company. It was specifically alleged that in April, 2001, Sullivan had directed Myers to arrange for the transfer of $771 million from "line cost expenses" to the asset account for property, plant and equipment, thereby instantly "converting" an expense to an asset. Apparently, these transactions had been hidden from Arthur Andersen, WorldCom's outside auditor.

On July 11, 2002, WorldCom filed for bankruptcy under Chapter 11. It was not to reappear for two years and after a $30 million further downward restatement of earnings, when it resumed operations under the name MCI, Inc. MCI was later acquired by Verizon Communications, Inc.

The WorldCom debacle ultimately led to a high-profile criminal prosecution. Although he initially vowed to fight any charges against him, Sullivan struck a deal with prosecutors and agreed to plead guilty and testify against Ebbers in exchange for a lighter sentence. In March 2005 Ebbers was convicted of conspiracy and securities fraud and sentenced to 25 years in prison. Sullivan received a five-year sentence.

7. **The Crisis at Adelphia Communications Co.**[45] The early history of Adelphia was in many ways similar to that of WorldCom. John Rigas operated a theater in the small town of Coudersport, Pennsylvania. In 1952, he purchased the local cable franchise, and then acquired additional suburban cable operations as they became available.[46] By the year 2000, Rigas and his two sons Timothy and Michael, had built the company into the nation's sixth-largest cable operation, with major systems in upstate New York and the Los

---

44. Jared Sandberg, et al., WorldCom Admits $3.8 Billion Error in Its Accounting, Wall St. J., June 26, 2002, at A1.

45. Much of this discussion is drawn from Robert W. Hamilton, The Crisis in Corporate

Governance: 2002 Style, 40 Houston L.Rev. 22–24 (2003).

46. Jerry Markon and Robert Frank, Five Adelphia Officials Arrested on Fraud Charges, Wall.St.J. July 25, 2002, at A3.

Angeles areas.[47] By 1999, the number of cable subscribers had doubled to more than five million subscribers.

What followed in 2002 was also very similar to the history of WorldCom and several other companies. On March 27, Adelphia announced that the company had "hidden" $2.3 billion in "off-balance sheet" debt. Shortly thereafter, two new board members resigned, stating that "disclosures of wrongdoing" at Adelphia had made it "impossible to contribute meaningfully to the process."[48] Adelphia announced that Deloitte & Touche, LLP had been dismissed as its auditor "because it was aware of transactions between the company and the family-controlled entities that had not been disclosed." A few days later Adelphia announced that it had overstated revenues and cash-flow over the previous two years by $500 million.

These disclosures led to criminal charges being brought against John Rigas, his two sons, Timothy and Michael, and two non-related officers, the former vice president of finance and the former director of internal reporting. The charges included bank, securities, and wire fraud.[49] In June, 2002, Adelphia filed for bankruptcy protection, listing $18.5 billion in debt. John and Timothy Rigas were convicted of conspiracy and fraud in 2004. In 2006, Deloitte & Touche agreed to pay $210 million to settle lawsuits related to Adelphia.

8.   The Crisis at Qwest Communications International, Inc. Qwest was the dominant local telephone company in fourteen states from Minnesota to the state of Washington. On July 28, 2002 it announced that it would restate its financial results for the period 1999–2001 because it had improperly booked $1.16 billion as current profits rather than as capital investments. It also announced that it was cutting its revenue predictions by approximately $1 billion, and writing down the book value of its good will and intangible assets by $30 billion. Qwest's former CEO, Joseph P. Nacchio, had profited by $230 million by selling Qwest shares shortly after they were awarded to him either in the form of stock options (that he promptly exercised) or actual grants of shares of Qwest stock. These sales apparently had occurred long before the announcements described in the previous paragraph. In 2005 Nacchio was indicted on insider trading charges. The trial had not commenced as of March 2007. One of the lawyers involved in the Ken Lay and Jeffrey Skilling prosecutions is leading the case against Nacchio.

9.   The Collapse of Global Crossing, Ltd. Global Crossing was founded in 1997 by Gary Winnick, a former bond salesman for Drexel Burnham Lambert, Inc. He promptly built a major undersea phone network linking 27 countries and 200 cities. At its peak, Global Crossing had a market capitalization of about $45 million.

When the market for telecom shares collapsed, Global Crossing filed for bankruptcy, stating that it owed $12.4 billion to creditors. Three months later it also admitted to improper shredding of corporate documents. Like Nacchio,

---

47.   Andrew Ross Sorkin, Founder of Adelphia and 2 Sons Arrested, N.Y. Times, July 25, 2002, at C1.

48.   Deborah Solomon, Adelphia Overstated Cash Flow, Revenue Over Past Two years, Wall St. J., June 11, 2002, at B5.

49.   It was also alleged that the Rigases used company money to buy stock, to build a $13 million golf course on land owned by John Rigas, and to provide African safari vacations for family members.

Gary Winnick had received significant grants of stock and options to purchase stock during the high-flying telecommunication period. He sold these shares into the market for a personal gain of about $734 million. However, he used a unique strategy: when Global Crossing shares began to decline in value he purchased "collars" [binding contracts to sell] that locked in their value at or near their high point in price. These collars permitted him to preserve personally a significant part of the original value of the Global Crossing shares.

    10.   The Crisis at Tyco International, Inc. Another example is Tyco International, a company that grew from a sleepy industrial company into one of the world's most aggressive "deal machines" during the period from 1998 to 2002. The driving forces in Tyco were L. Dennis Kozlowski, its CEO, and Mark H. Swartz, its CFO. Between 1998 and 2001, Mr. Kozlowski arranged to acquire hundreds of companies at prices ranging from hundreds of thousands of dollars to one transaction that involved $9.5 billion.[50] Its diverse business interests ranged from its basic product of fire alarm systems to items such as adult diapers, clothes hangers, and water hoses. Tyco's headquarters were in Bermuda but the company operated out of offices in West Windsor, New Jersey.

    In 2002, Tyco admitted that it had made accounting mistakes in the past, overstating revenue by more than two billion dollars, and revised its financials back to 1998. Complex transactions with a major subsidiary, ADT Corporation, were stated to be the principal cause of these restatements. Mr. Kozlowski unexpectedly resigned his CEO post on June 2, 2002, the day before he was indicted for evading more than one million dollars in New York state sales taxes on art purchases. It was alleged that he had avoided sales taxes through false invoices and falsely marking boxes containing art objects that were being shipped to his New Hampshire office as being "empty." Further investigation revealed that Mr. Kozlowski for an extended period had regularly used Tyco funds for personal purchases; for example, he had received a $19 million non-interest bearing loan from Tyco to permit him to complete his purchase of a new home in Florida. Repayment of this loan was later forgiven by Tyco's board of directors but the shareholders were never advised of this transaction. Mr. Kozlowski also arranged to have his former home purchased by Tyco for $4.5 million, about three times its market value. He also billed Tyco for flowers, jewelry, clothing, for his personal use and for his wife. Shortly after these disclosures, Tyco reported a $2.32 billion loss for its fiscal third quarter of 2002. In 2002, Mr. Swartz and Mr. Kozlowski were charged with grand larceny, enterprise corruption, and falsifying business records for diverting up to $600 million from corporate coffers.[51] In September, 2002 Kozlowski and Swartz were jointly indicted on additional charges of stealing more than $170 million from the corporation, mainly through unauthorized compensation paid to corporate officers.

---

50. William C. Symonds, A To-do List for Tyco's CEO, Bus. Wk., Aug. 12, 2002, at 37, states that at this time Tyco's assets were worth approximately $36 billion, with approximately one billion in debt maturing within one year.

51. Chad Bray, Executives on Trial: Belnick's Defense Wants to Use Testimony from First Tyco Case, Wall St. J., May 25, 2004, at C3.

A story in the New York Times on September 25, 2002,[52] stated that Tyco had suffered a significant economic loss when it paid an above-market price for a company but then falsely claimed that the transaction had generated a profit of $79.4 million. It was also alleged that the transaction was used to justify additional bonuses to Messrs. Kozlowski and Swartz. In the subsequent trial, Mr. Swartz testified for nine days on the witness stand. However, the proceeding against Kozlowski and Swartz ultimately ended in a mistrial in 2004 when a juror told presiding Judge Obus that he had received threats that he believed originated from the defendants. After a second trial, Kozlowski and Swartz were convicted on multiple counts of looting the company. They were sentenced to 8⅓ years to 25 years in prison and ordered to pay $240 million in restitution and fines.

Misconduct during this period was not limited to these well-known public corporations. A number of smaller corporations also restated downward their previously announced earnings during this period: e.g. Berlin Metals, Computer Associates, Dynegy, HomeStore, Livent, PNC Financial, Reliant Resources, Sunbeam, Waste Management, and others.

2. THE RESPONSE TO SUBSTANTIAL MISCONDUCT

The numerous events involving fraud and misconduct described in the previous section shocked and angered both the business community and ordinary investors. Investors began to bail out of securities holdings, and a sharp decline in securities prices followed. The attitude of investors was well reflected in comments by Tom Sticke, Chairman of the California Chamber of Commerce: "Until we see a CEO and a General Counsel march off to jail together—for a long, uncomfortable non-country club sentence—capitalism is at risk because people are losing confidence."[53]

The response of the market to these events was quite predictable: securities values dropped precipitously. The Dow Jones Industrial Average declined from above 11,000 to under 10,000, and then dropped to about 4,000 when the full magnitude and extent of corporate misconduct became known. While Enron was the largest and most visible collapse, it was only the first in a combination of events that cumulatively led to a major crisis in corporate governance beginning in July 2002. This crisis atmosphere was augmented by a report issued by the American Bar Association Task Force on Corporate Responsibility in July 2002.[54] The conclusions in this report were stark:

> * * * [T]he system of corporate governance at many public companies has failed dramatically. It is a clear failure of corporate responsibility, for example, if a corporation belatedly and precipitously discloses that the equity on its balance sheet has been overstated by billions of dollars. It is a clear failure of corporate responsibility if employees whose retire-

52. Floyd Norris, Tyco Took Profit on Bad Deal, Then Paid Bonuses to Executives, N.Y. Times, Sept. 25, 2002, at C1.

53. Abraham C. Reich and Michelle T. Wirnter, What Do You Do When Confronted with Fraud? Business Law Today, September/October 2002, at 39. See also the comments of Jonathan Wiseman, Efforts to Restrict Re-

tirement Funds Lose Steam, Wash. Post, Aug. 7, 2002, p. 1, col. 3, stating that the disclosures "initially fueled a wave of indignation among lawmakers in Washington and solemn vows to protect" their constituents in the future.

54. See James Cheek III, et al., Am.Bar Ass'n, Preliminary Report of the American Bar Association Task Force on Corporate Responsibility, 1–7 (2002).

ment amounts are heavily invested in the corporation's stock are assured by management of the corporation's financial prospects and then discover that the value of that stock has promptly vanished as a result of earnings misstatements and self-dealing by corporate officers. It is a clear failure of corporate responsibility if executive officers aware of potential accounting irregularities sell millions of dollars of stock to public investors who are unaware of such information.

President George W. Bush had taken office in January 2001. His first response to the corporate governance crisis was dismissive: the problems arose, he said, because of "a few bad apples" but the economy was still "fundamentally sound." However, this approach had little traction as the economy continued to decline and bad news continued to make headlines. He then changed course dramatically and announced that he would address the current problems when legislation that was then being considered was presented to him for signature. He stated that "[a]t this moment, America's greatest economic need is higher ethical standards, standards enforced by strict laws and upheld by responsible business leaders." He added, "[I]f you're a CEO and you think you can fudge the books in order to make yourselves look better, we're going to find you, we're going to arrest you and we're going to hold you to account."[55]

3. THE ENACTMENT OF THE SARBANES–OXLEY ACT

The only legislation that was in the Congressional pipeline that dealt directly with corporate governance problems was the Sarbanes–Oxley bill, a proposed statute that had been rather hastily cobbled together by Senator Paul Sarbanes of Maryland, with the addition of some provisions developed by Congressman Michael Oxley of Ohio. This bill included ideas and proposals that had been discussed from time to time prior to the corporate governance crisis but had not been seriously considered or studied by corporate scholars. Indeed, until the governance crisis became acute in 2002, enactment of Sarbanes–Oxley seemed quite improbable and as a result had not been seriously considered or reviewed by corporate scholars.[56]

However, in 2002, matters were moving far too fast for affected businesses to gear up and consider, let along significantly affect, the provisions of this proposed legislation. Congressman Oxley introduced his draft bill in the House of Representatives; one day was allocated for the House's consideration of the proposed bill; there was no discussion of the impact of the various provisions on state law and practice. The Senate version, modified by Senator Sarbanes, was debated at some length, but the political environment changed dramatically when the WorldCom scandal was announced on June 26, 2002. There was a media frenzy over WorldCom, the declining stock market, the high profile accounting frauds, and the numerous business failures in the

55. Patricia Wilson, Bush Says Law Means "Hard Time" for Corporate Crooks, Reuters, July 31, 2002.

56. David S. Hizenrath, et al., How Congress Rode a "Storm" to Corporate Reform, Wash.Post, July 28, 2002, at A01, chronicles the sequence of events surrounding the creation and enactment of Sarbanes–Oxley. He notes that "the collaboration between Sarbanes and Oxley resulted in few changes to Sarbanes's original bill." He added, "few people gave Sarbanes much chance of bringing his bill to the Senate floor, much less passing it into law," but the disclosures of WorldCom's accounting misstatements had renewed "public anger over corporate misdeeds that had faded somewhat following Enron's collapse."

middle of an election year. A lobbyist for the Chamber of Commerce (which was opposing the Senate bill) described the situation by saying that "when the WorldCom scandal hit, it became to me, a bit of a—a very different attitude and atmosphere, if not a political tsunami," and we quickly decided that "an unconditional surrender was inevitable."

President Bush announced that he planned to sign the Sarbanes–Oxley bill as soon as it was presented to him. Professor John Coffee wryly commented: "I don't think he [Bush] can claim credit at all. * * * [The Republicans] resisted it until they saw a tidal wave forming. They had the good judgment not to stand in the way of a Tsunami."[57] President Bush signed the new legislation on July 30, 2002, the day after it was presented to him. Predictably he put the best possible "spin" on recent events. He attempted to overcome the very common impression that he valued "big corporations over ordinary Americans," and "strongly" challenged "the perception that his administration was too close to big business." America's greatest need, he said, was "higher ethical standards, standards enforced by strict laws and upheld by responsible business leaders."[58] He also strongly criticized the excesses of the previous few years, commenting that corporate corruption had offended "the conscience of our nation." He later added, there was to be "[n]o more easy money for corporate criminals. Just hard time."[59]

4. THE NEW ERA OPENS

In January, 2003, the SEC began the process of preparing rules and regulations that were necessary to implement Sarbanes–Oxley. A stream of new regulations began shortly thereafter.

On January 22, 2003, the SEC adopted Regulation G requiring disclosure of non-GAAP financial information, including presentation of the most directly comparable GAAP financial rule. On January 23, it issued Rel. No. 33–8177, implementing section 407 of Sarbanes–Oxley, requiring each registered agency to have at least one "financial expert," and if it did not have one, to explain "why it did not."

On January 28, 2003, the SEC issued final rules implementing section 208(a) of the Sarbanes–Oxley Act, designed to establish and ensure the independence of auditors. Rel. 33–8183. These are complex rules, providing for a cooling-off period for former employees of auditors, auditor rotation, pre-approval of non-audit services, and limitations on sources of compensation of audit partners. This regulation is usually referred to as the "Auditor Independence Release." Also on January 28, 2003, the SEC issued final rules under section 401(a) of Sarbanes–Oxley, requiring disclosure of all off-balance sheet arrangements and aggregate contractual obligations and other relationships with unconsolidated entities or persons. Rule 2–06 of Regulation S–X was promulgated at the same time requiring retention of audit records for seven years.

57. Randall Mikkelsem, Bush to Sign Corporate Crackdown Legislation, Reuters, July 30, 2002 (quotation marks omitted).

58. Remarks on Corporate Responsibility in New York City, 38 Weekly Comp. Pres.Doc. 1158 (July 9, 2002).

59. Patricia Wilson, Bush Says Law Means "Hard Time" for Corporate Crooks, Reuters, July 31, 2002.

Additional regulations were adopted In April and May of 2003. Rel. 33–8230 mandated electronic filing and posting on web sites of stock ownership reports under section 16(a). Rel. 33–8220 prohibited the listing of securities if they were not in compliance with audit committee requirements. This regulation, among other things, also required electronic filing and web site postings of reports of beneficial stock ownership.

On November 4, 2003, still another major series of regulations were adopted by the SEC. Rel. 34–48745, providing for funding for the audit committee and its advisers. The release also imposed a number of substantive requirements, including an important requirement that the majority of each board of directors must be independent of management, and that Listed Company Manuals for NYSE and NASDAQ companies must require proxy statements to disclose whether or not a majority of the board of directors are in fact independent. If a company does not utilize a proxy statement, independence must be established by appropriate provisions in its annual report. Other provisions establish standards for independence in a variety of situations and impose mandatory requirements: for example, independent directors must meet at regularly scheduled sessions when management is absent; interested parties must have access to and be able to communicate with independent directors or with a presiding director; each audit committee must be composed entirely of independent directors; the auditors must report solely to the audit committee; and so forth.

A similar pattern continued in 2004. On April 29, 2004, the SEC announced the adoption of another significant set of rules, this time relating to the nominating process for directors. Information must be disclosed whether the corporation has a nominating committee, and if so, the nature of its charter, if any; it also must describe the process by which candidates are nominated and screened. The rules must also establish "the minimum qualifications for a nominating committee-recommended nominee and specify any further skills that the nominating committee believes are necessary or desirable for board members to possess." Rel. Nos. 33–8340, 34–48825. IC–26262, File No. S7–14–03. On May 6, 2004, the SEC announced the adoption of yet another set of rules, this time relating to certification of reports by management, investment companies, and shareholders. These certifications are intended to ensure that shareholders receive accurate information about various corporate activities. These documents are called "Exchange Act Periodic Reporting Forms" and their disclosure is required by Sections 406 and 407 of Sarbanes–Oxley. Rel.No. 34–477262, IC–25914, File Nos. 57–33–02, S7–40–02.

Also in 2004, Congress amended the Sarbanes–Oxley Act to increase penalties for mail fraud (§ 305(5)), to permit private suits to obtain disgorgement of ill-gotten profits (§ 308), and to add a civil penalty to any disgorgement where appropriate (§ 603–21D(6)).

5. THE CAMPAIGN AGAINST FRAUD AND MISCONDUCT FROM 2004–2007

An important aspect of the increased activism of the SEC has been its continued pursuit of wrongdoing across all major commercial areas. For example, in connection with the Enron debacle, the SEC leveled charges against JPMorgan Chase, Citibank, Merrill Lynch, and Canadian Imperial Bank of Commerce, for assisting Enron.

On July 10, 2004, Adelphia Communications Corporation,[60] the nation's fifth-largest cable company, was charged with conspiracy and fraud in connection with payments to members of the Rigas family. James R. Brown, formerly the Vice President of Finance of Adelphia, pleaded guilty to criminal charges and agreed to cooperate with the government as part of his plea bargain. He testified that he specifically discussed the inflation of company data with both Michael and John Rigas and that Assistant Treasurer Michael Mulcahey maintained two sets of books: one to be shown to bank lenders while the other had the "details about things that had been manipulated." Mr. Mulcahey was asked on cross examination whether he owed loyalty to company shareholders. "I really didn't think in terms of the shareholders," he replied, adding "I always felt I had to please my boss for whatever job I was in;" and "I was just doing my job."

On June 17, 2004, four former Adelphia executives, on trial for bank fraud, were sentenced for up to 30 years in prison. The prosecutor had cited examples of how the executives spent Adelphia's cash for personal items such as 17 cars, a golf course, and $6,000 to arrange to have two Christmas trees flown to New York. Other examples of claimed misuse of corporate funds that were cited include Timothy Rigas hiring a golf professional at Adelphia's expense to help clients improve their game, and a $7,000 "junket" to Pebble Beach, California. Another witness testified that he had been hired by an Adelphia executive to deliver eggs, paper towels, toilet paper, and a pair of Christmas trees to John Rigas' daughter in 2000.

In September 2004, the SEC filed fraud charges against Computer Associates and three of its former top executives. The Commission alleged the company prematurely recognized over $2 billion in revenue in fiscal years 2000 and 2001. The company reached a settlement with the government in which it agreed to establish a restitution fund of $225 million to compensate shareholders and to take steps to improve its internal corporate governance.

In January 2005, Nortel Networks announced that a dozen current executives who played no role in earlier stock manipulation would voluntarily repay $8.6 million in bonuses and would return the last two installments of a restricted stock payout that began in 2003. These payments were not mandated by the Sarbanes–Oxley Act because that statute requires forfeiture of bonuses only by chief executives and chief financial officers. In 2003, Nortel had originally announced earnings of $732 million, but upon financial review, the earnings were restated to be $434 million. This revision led to the dismissal of Frank A. Dunn, the CEO, and nine other executives. Civil charges were filed against Mr. Dunn and other former executives in March 2007.

In April 2006, David Wittig, the former CEO of Westar Energy, Inc., was convicted of conspiracy and fraud in connection with the looting of the Kansas energy company. Wittig was sentenced to 18 years in prison. In 2007, the former chairman of Cendant, Walter Forbes was sentenced to 12 years in prison and ordered to pay $3.28 billion in connection with overseeing massive accounting fraud that cost shareholders $14 billion in the 1990s. Despite the government's successes against former executives of Enron, WorldCom, Tyco, and other companies, prosecutors suffered a setback in their aggressive pursuit of corporate criminals in the case of Richard Scrushy, the former CEO

60. The scandals surrounding Adelphia are also discussed in Part 1 of this Section.

of HealthSouth. Employees at HealthSouth engaged in widespread accounting fraud. The cost of the fraud to shareholders was estimated at over $300 million. In June 2005, Scrushy was acquitted on criminal charges that included conspiracy and mail and wire fraud.

2006 saw the emergence of a new scandal relating to the practice of backdating stock options. In backdating, an executive moves the date of a stock option grant to a previous point in time at which the share price was lower, thus generating greater profits when the executive exercises the option. Federal prosecutors brought conspiracy charges against former executives of Comverse Technology, a New York software manufacturer, arising from the alleged backdating of stock options. Charles Forelle & James Bandler, Dating Game—Stock Options Criminal Charge, Wall St. J., Aug. 10, 2006, at A1. Executives of Brocade Communications Systems, a computer hardware company, were charged with fraud relating to backdating for activities that included doctoring board minutes. James Bandler & Charles Forelle, In Internal Probes of Stock Options, Conflicts Abound, Wall St. J., Aug. 11, 2006, at A1. A number of large U.S. corporations, including Apple Computer and Monster Worldwide, Inc., have launched internal investigations into alleged backdating. The bringing of criminal charges against former Comverse and Brocade Systems executives could be an ominous signal for executives at these corporations.

6. ANALYSIS OF THE PROVISIONS OF THE SARBANES–OXLEY ACT

The Sarbanes–Oxley Act was enacted July 30, 2002,[61] in the middle of an election year during a period of a declining stock market and a seemingly endless series of increasingly salient corporate accounting frauds and business failures. The major network evening news coverage during the January–July 2002 period contained 613 stories about business events, 471 of which involved discussion of various corporate scandals.[62]

Given the broad scope of Sarbanes–Oxley and its unprecedented incursion into corporate governance, a traditional domain of state law, the provisions of the law are cursory, and the structure of the statute is skeletal, reflecting the limited legislative consideration given to the Act. From the outset, Sarbanes–Oxley was criticized by corporate governance experts. One commentator described the Act as a "sparsely worded law [that] is both poorly written and hastily put together so there's little to go on when it comes to interpreting some of its murkier provisions."[63] Another commentator asserted that the Act is "a telling example of the law of unintended consequences. It will have wide-ranging effects on securities, derivative and other (private) shareholder lawsuits."[64] Other commentators generally tended to dismiss the legislation on the grounds (1) that it was unnecessary, (2) that the changes it made were at best only incremental, (3) that on balance it was undesirable because it would impose significant new costs on US firms, or (4) that it was probably

61. Pub.L. 107–204, enacted July 30, 2002 (107th Cong.).

62. Roberta Romano, The Sarbanes–Oxley Act and the Making of Quack Corporate Governance (2004), draft, at 141.

63. Renee Deger, New Law Has Corporate Lawyers Scrambling, The Recorder, Aug. 13, 2002, at 1.

64. Gregory P. Joseph, Master Class: Corporate Fraud Act, Nat'l L.J. Aug. 5, 2002, at B9.

unnecessary because modern markets were liquid and quite capable of responding adequately to fraud on their own without additional regulation.

Commentators were also skeptical as to the need for this legislation in the first place. Professor Larry Ribstein opined that the Act "represents a hasty, panicked reaction of an electorate looking for an easy fix to the apparent 'problem' that stock prices go down as well as up. Whether or not the Act has provided some short-term relief, in the long run regulatory responses to corporate frauds are unlikely to be more effective in preventing future frauds than existing regulation has been in preventing the current problem, and have a significant chance of imposing substantial costs * * *."[65]

In an important article, Professor Romano reviewed each of the major provisions of Sarbanes–Oxley and evaluated their desirability from a policy standpoint, emphasizing the extent to which the provisions of the Act conflicted with the best research in finance, economics and the other relevant social sciences.[66]

Beginning in 2004 several of the largest American corporations reported that costs of compliance with the various provisions of Sarbanes–Oxley had increased very significantly. The audit costs imposed by the PCAOB alone on such corporations were estimated to be as much as two million dollars a year. For smaller firms, audit costs had increased by 30% or more over the pre Sarbanes–Oxley period. Perhaps more significantly, the cost of compliance with other new corporate governance provisions imposed by Sarbanes–Oxley for publicly held companies had increased by 100% or more. Furthermore, many of these extra costs did not appear to improve the effectiveness of the statute itself.

A 2004 survey of projected expenditures to meet Sarbanes–Oxley internal controls indicated that companies with annual revenues over $5 billion were projecting annual external consulting, software and additional audit fees of 2.8 million, while companies with annual revenues under $25 million were projecting additional costs in the range of $220,000 per year. The new attestation requirements of section 404 were estimated to have created an additional 38 percent increase in costs. It was also suggested that these additional costs were unexpected and explain the decision by many smaller firms to go "private" following the enactment of Sarbanes–Oxley.

Professor Romano's analysis of the costs involved with the implementation found the following:

1. Section 301 of Sarbanes–Oxley requires all listed companies to have audit committees composed entirely of independent directors (these persons may not accept any 'consulting, advisory or other compensatory fee' nor be an 'affiliated person' of the issuer or a subsidiary). Also there must be disclosure of whether individual directors are "financial experts", and if none, why there were none. Under Sarbanes–Oxley, shareholders do not have the power to

65. Ribstein, Similarly, an unsigned student note in the Duquesne L. Rev., The Sarbanes–Oxley Act: How a Current Model in the Law of Unintended Consequences May Affect Securities Litigation, 42 Duquesne L. Rev. 293 (Winter 2004) argued that Sarbanes–Oxley "is more appropriately characterized as a legisla-

tive backlash to the extraordinary amount of serious financial disclosure and reporting transgressions, as well as corporate governance improprieties, which were publicly disclosed in 2001 and 2002."

66. Romano, *supra* note 67.

hire or fire an outside auditor since such authority is vested solely in the audit committee. These provisions have increased the cost of the audit function since state law permits the full board to grant or retract delegated authority and to select auditors; Sarbanes–Oxley does not. State law also does not mandate the composition of the board of directors or committees, while Sarbanes–Oxley does. State law also does not define what constitutes "independence" while Sarbanes–Oxley does. Professor Romano suggests that these requirements of Sarbanes–Oxley go "far beyond" existing corporate law and increase auditing costs.

2. Since 1999 stock exchanges have listing standards that require audit committees to be comprised of independent directors, but they permit the appointment of non-independent directors and exempt small businesses from the listing requirements. Sarbanes–Oxley does not permit such appointments or exemptions, thereby increasing costs.

3. Many studies in economics and finance show that independent boards of directors do not improve corporate performance. Boards with too many independent persons may actually have a negative impact on performance. Sarbanes–Oxley requires all members of the board of directors to be independent.

4. Studies show that the presence of a single director with financial expertise is of more value for investor protection against accounting fraud than a fully independent audit committee. Sarbanes–Oxley requires the entire committee to be independent. Studies of the relation between audit committee characteristics (director independence) and abnormal accruals in large public corporations[67] show that such abnormal accruals are inversely related to audit committee independence.

5. Section 201 of Sarbanes–Oxley prohibits accounting firms from providing a wide variety of specified non-audit services to firms that they audit: these prohibitions include financial information system design and implementation, appraisal or valuation services, internal auditing services, investment banking services, legal and expert services unrelated to the audit, brokerage services and actuarial services. This provision, Professor Romano observes, is in effect a Congressional judgment as to what services the board or shareholders should purchase from the auditor. However there is no evidence that audits were ever compromised as a result of the provision of non-audit services by auditors.

6. Section 402(a) of Sarbanes–Oxley prohibits corporations from arranging or extending credit to executive officers or directors (with narrow exceptions). This blanket prohibition appears to prohibit standard compensation practices that are clearly desirable in specific situations: advancing indemnification expenses, the purchase of split-life insurance policies (the company advances funds for the premiums and is repaid out of the policy's later payout following retirement or death), the cashless exercise of stock options under incentive compensation plans, and the like. Professor Romano points out that

67. Such accruals are often a proxy for earnings management or manipulation of accounting figures.

while state law on such payments varies, no state forbids absolutely such payments. Moreover, the prohibition in Sarbanes–Oxley may be easily evaded by the simple, but generally undesirable strategy of increasing compensation levels of officers and executives to cover desired expenses. Studies suggest that a blanket prohibition against executive loans was "self-evidently a public policy error."

7.   Section 302 of Sarbanes–Oxley requires the CEO and CFO to certify that the company's periodic reports do not contain any material misstatements or omissions and "fairly present" the firm's financial conditions and results of operations. This is a substantive corporate governance mandate imposing significant responsibility for establishing and maintaining internal controls, and evaluating their effectiveness on the certifying officer. Another provision of Sarbanes–Oxley, section 906(a) establishes criminal penalties for a knowing violation of a similar certification requirement.[68] Professor Romano observes that the impact of this provision has been extensively studied, and that the data appears to be consistent with the view that this provision was more "rhetoric than reform," and does not appear to improve firm performance or reduce accounting improprieties.

8.   Perhaps the most central concern by companies subject to Sarbanes–Oxley is section 404 of Sarbanes–Oxley. This section requires companies to include in their annual reports an acknowledgement of management's obligation to establish internal controls and procedures for financial disclosure; these reports must also contain an assessment by management of the adequacy and effectiveness of both the internal controls and the reporting procedures. In addition, the independent auditor's report on internal control over financial reporting must include the auditor's opinions on (1) whether management's assessment is fairly stated in all material respects (that is, whether the auditor concurs with management's conclusions about the effectiveness of internal control over financial reporting), and (2) the effectiveness if the company's internal control over financial reporting. These requirements are relatively new and were not extensively discussed during the enactment process that led to Sarbanes–Oxley.

Large publicly held companies have reported that compliance with these provisions have proven to be exceptionally costly: One major corporation, for example, estimated compliance costs to be as much as $5 billion for the original assessment of the firm's continuing world-wide operations plus an additional $4.7 million annually thereafter each year for review of the compliance report by the auditor who must formally attest to the continued adequacy and effectiveness of the corporation's internal controls and financial reporting procedures.[69]

68.   Prior to enactment of Sarbanes–Oxley in June 2002, the SEC had imposed a certification requirement on the largest public firms in response to the Enron scandal. This certification requirement was one of the proposals advanced by President Bush in his Ten–Point plan announced on March 7, 2002 in response to the Enron fiasco to make corporate executives more accountable to investors.

69.   This and the following discussion is based on Perspectives for Financial Market Participants: A Resource for Financial Market Participants (December 2004), a report prepared by Deloitte & Touche, LLP, Ernst & Young, LLP, KPMG, LLP, and Pricewaterhouse–Coopers LLP, dated December 2004.

Faced with the costs of complying with Sarbanes–Oxley, a number of large publicly held corporations, particularly foreign firms with shares traded in the U.S. have considered possible ways to avoid Sarbanes–Oxley by deregistering as an "issuer" under sections 3 and 12 of the Securities Exchange Act of 1934.[70] This requires the number of investors to be reduced to less than 300, a result which may be achieved by a reverse triangular merger or by other devices. In a reverse triangular merger, the corporation announces a reclassification of its issued shares, e.g., each certificate for a specified number of old shares or a multiple thereof can be exchanged for one new share, or a multiple thereof. All certificates for less than the specified number of old shares have no continuing value in the corporation but they may be exchanged for cash of a specified amount per share. After the transaction the number of outstanding shares has been greatly reduced. The specified number of shares is determined so that all remaining shareholders after the transaction own at least one new certificate (reflecting the 300 or more shares he owned before that transaction).[71]

The SEC has given small companies with market capitalizations under $75 million until July 2007 to comply with Section 404's internal controls requirements. In 2005 the SEC chartered the Advisory Committee on Small Public Companies to assess the impact of corporate governance regulatory requirements, and of Sarbanes–Oxley in particular, on small companies and to make suggestions for improvements. The Committee concluded that Sarbanes–Oxley disproportionately burdens smaller companies, and recommended creating a new system of scaled regulation for microcap and smallcap companies. The recommendations have been applauded by some, see Bob Greifeld, It's Time to Pull up Our SOX, Wall St. J., Mar. 6, 2006, at A14, and derided by others, see Arthur Levitt, Jr., A Misguided Exemption, Wall St. J., Jan. 27, 2006, at A8.

The best empirical evidence suggests that no justification existed for the principal corporate governance mandates in Sarbanes–Oxley, and that these new mandates will not benefit investors. However, their enactment can be very readily explained by the confluence of significant events in 2002—the Enron scandal, the collapse of Global Crossing, Adelphia Communications, Tyco International, WorldCom, etc. plus a very substantial decline in securities prices that led to widespread losses to investors.

During this period, several Senators explicitly referred to the steep market decline as a rationale for the need for prompt legislative action.[72] Rightly or wrongly, they interpreted the market decline from April through July 2002 as requiring legislative action, particularly with an upcoming election looming. There was need for action but no prior study as to what action was needed.

70. 15 U.S.C. 78l.

71. This device, which permits the corporation to terminate its registration under the Securities Acts is often referred to as "going black."

72. On July 25, 2002, Senator Gramm justified his support of the proposed bill, saying, "If people on Wall Street are listening to the debate and trying to figure out whether they should be concerned about this bill, I think they can rightly feel that this bill could have been much worse. I think that if people had wanted to be irresponsible, this is a bill on which they could have been irresponsible and almost anything would have passed on the floor of the Senate." 148 Cong. Rec. S7354 (July 25, 2002).

The ultimate conclusion of Professor Romano's exhaustive analysis is that the Sarbanes–Oxley provisions were poorly conceived and ineffective as an original matter, and should be treated as default provisions under which smaller companies would be free to opt out of the federal mandates by shareholder vote:

> Congressional repeal of [Sarbanes–Oxley]'s corporate governance mandates is not on the near-term political horizon as the corporate accounting scandals have not receded from view. The alternative of treating [Sarbanes–Oxley] as a set of default rules could be implemented by the SEC under its general exemptive authority but it is improbable that the agency will do so given its current leadership, whose instinct is to move in the wrong direction. It is therefore important to work to educate the media, the public, political leaders and agency personnel regarding the reality that Congress committed a public policy blunder in enacting [Sarbanes–Oxley]'s corporate governance mandates, and that there is a need to rectify the error. Though it is doubtful that this Provision will be implemented.

Notes

(1) The collapse of Enron, the ensuing barrage of corporate scandals, and the enactment of Sarbanes–Oxley sparked an onslaught of criticism and analysis from both business and legal academics alike. See Douglas G. Baird & Robert K. Rasmussen, Four (or Five) Easy Lessons from Enron, 55 Vand. L. Rev. 1787 (2002); Jeffrey N. Gordon, Governance Failures of the Enron Board and the New Information Order of Sarbanes–Oxley, 35 Conn. L. Rev. 1125 (2003); Jill I. Gross, Securities Analysts' Undisclosed Conflicts of Interest: Unfair Dealing or Securities Fraud?, 2002 Colum. Bus. L. Rev. 631 (2002); Claire A. Hill, Rating Agencies Behaving Badly: The Case of Enron, 35 Conn. L. Rev. 1145 (2003); Jonathan R. Macey, A Pox on Both Your Houses: Enron, Sarbanes–Oxley and the Debate Concerning the Relative Efficacy of Mandatory Versus Enabling Rules, 81 Wash. U. L.Q. 329 (2003); David Millon, Enron and the Dark Side of Worker Ownership, 1 Seattle J. for Soc. Just. 113 (2002); Larry E. Ribstein, Bubble Laws, 40 Hous. L. Rev. 77 (2003); Hillary A. Sale, Gatekeepers, Disclosure, and Issuer Choice, 81 Wash. U. L.Q. 403 (2003); Steven L. Schwarcz, Enron and the Use and Abuse of Special Purpose Entities in Corporate Structures, 70 U. Cin. L. Rev. 1309 (2002); and Joseph M. Schwartz, Democracy Against the Free Market: The Enron Crisis and the Politics of Global Deregulation, 35 Conn. L. Rev. 1097 (2003).

(2) The collapse of Arthur Andersen and the SEC's development of minimum standards of professional responsibility for corporate lawyers have generated their own review in the academic literature. See William T. Allen & Arthur Siegel, Threats and Safeguards in the Determination of Auditor Independence, 80 Wash. U. L.Q. 519 (2002); James D. Cox, The Paradoxical Corporate and Securities Law Implications of Counsel Serving on the Client's Board, 80 Wash. U. L.Q. 541 (2002); Theodore Eisenberg & Jonathan R. Macey, 1 J. Empirical Legal Stud. 263 (2004); and Jonathan R. Macey & Hillary A. Sale, Observations on the Role of Commodification, Independence, and Governance in the Accounting Industry, 48 Vill. L. Rev. 1167 (2003).

E. PROXY REGULATION AND DISCLOSURE REQUIREMENTS

1. SCOPE OF REGULATION

SECURITIES EXCHANGE ACT OF 1934 §§ 14(a), 12(a), 12(g)

15 U.S.C.A. §§ 78n, 78*l*.

PROXIES

Section 14. (a) It shall be unlawful for any person, by the use of the mails or by any means or instrumentality of interstate commerce or of any facility of a national securities exchange or otherwise, in contravention of such rules and regulations as the Commission may prescribe as necessary or appropriate in the public interest or for the protection of investors, to solicit or to permit the use of his name to solicit any proxy or consent or authorization in respect of any security (other than an exempted security) registered pursuant to section 12 of this title.

REGISTRATION REQUIREMENTS FOR SECURITIES

Section 12. (a) It shall be unlawful for any member, broker, or dealer to effect any transaction in any security (other than an exempted security) on a national securities exchange unless a registration is effective as to such security for such exchange in accordance with the provisions of this title and the rules and regulations thereunder. * * *

(g)(1) Every issuer which is engaged in interstate commerce, or in a business affecting interstate commerce, or whose securities are traded by use of the mails or any means or instrumentality of interstate commerce shall—

(A) within one hundred and twenty days after the last day of its first fiscal year ended after the effective date[73] of this subsection on which the issuer has total assets exceeding $1,000,000 and a class of equity security (other than an exempted security) held of record by seven hundred and fifty or more persons; and

(B) within one hundred and twenty days after the last day of its first fiscal year ended after two years from the effective date of this subsection on which the issuer has total assets exceeding $1,000,000 and a class of equity security (other than an exempted security) held of record by five hundred or more but less than seven hundred and fifty persons,

register such security by filing with the Commission a registration statement * * *.

(4) Registration of any class of security pursuant to this subsection shall be terminated ninety days, or such shorter period as the Commission may determine, after the issuer files a certification with the Commission that the

---

73. The "effective date" referred to in § 12(g)(1) is July 1, 1964. Pub.Law 88–467 § 13(1), 78 Stat. 565.

number of holders of record of such class of security is reduced to less than three hundred persons. * * *

(5) For the purposes of this subsection the term "class" shall include all securities of an issuer which are of substantially similar character and the holders of which enjoy substantially similar rights and privileges. * * *

Notes

(1) The SEC has adopted the following regulations under § 12(g):

§ 240.12g–1 Exemption from section 12(g).

An issuer shall be exempt from the requirement to register any class of equity securities pursuant to section 12(g)(1) if on the last day of its most recent fiscal year the issuer had total assets not exceeding $10 million * * *

§ 240.12g–4 Certifications of termination of registration under section 12(g).

(a) Termination of registration of a class of securities shall take effect 90 days * * * after the issuer certifies to the Commission * * * that:

(1) Such class of securities is held of record by: (i) Less than 300 persons; or (ii) by less than 500 persons, where the total assets of the issuer have not exceeded $10 million on the last day of each of the issuer's most recent three fiscal years. * * *

17 C.F.R. §§ 240.12g–1, 240.12g–4 (2002). The statutory provision requires registration of corporations with more than $1 million of assets if they meet the number of shareholders requirement. In 1982, the SEC increased the asset requirement from $1 million to $3 million primarily as an "inflation adjustment" to the original statutory criterion established in 1964. The level was increased from $3 million to $5 million in 1986, and from $5 million to $10 million in 1997. The SEC estimated that about 700 issuers were likely to be affected by the increase in the asset requirement from $3 million to $5 million; about 650 more were affected by the increase from $5 million to $10. SEC Rel. No. 34–22483, 50 Fed.Reg. 41162 (1985); SEC Rel. No. 34–37157,61 Fed.Reg. 21354 (1996).

(2) Under § 12(g) and rules 12g–1 and 12g–4, how should the following problems be resolved:

(a) Company A sells securities under § 4(2) of the Securities Act of 1933 every year for three years. It eventually has total assets of $11 million and 450 shareholders. Does Company A have to register under § 12?

(b) Company B sells securities under § 4(2) every year for three years. Eventually it has total assets of $9.8 million and 700 shareholders. Does Company B have to register under § 12?

(c) Company C has been registered under § 12(g) for four years, and has consistently had $9.8 million in total assets and 450 shareholders. May its registration under § 12 be terminated?

(3) A corporation that is required to register a securities issue under § 12 is subject to a significant degree of regulation under various sections of the Securities Exchange Act of 1934 in addition to the regulation of proxy solicitations. Many of these sections are discussed below and in the following chapters. When considering federally imposed requirements under the 1934 Act it is important to ascertain whether the requirements are applicable only to corporations required to

register under § 12, or whether they are more broadly applicable to all corporations using the mails or the facilities of interstate commerce.

(4) Registration of the publicly held securities of an issuer under § 12 of the 1934 Act should be distinguished from the registration of an issue for its public distribution under the 1933 Act described in Chapter 8. Registration under § 12 of the 1934 Act involves the submission of information about the issuer, its organization, its finances, its securities, and similar matters. There is also a requirement for the periodic revision of information; these periodic reports are colloquially referred to as 8–K and 10–K reports. Historically, registration of an issue under the 1933 Act for sale to the public was considered more onerous and difficult than supplying information for registration under § 12. The emphasis on full disclosure at the time an issue is sold publicly under the 1933 Act is partly an historical accident, and a more rational system would doubtless emphasize issuer registration and periodic full disclosure rather than full disclosure only when the issuer wishes to sell securities. In 1982, the SEC achieved essentially this result by regulation through its integrated disclosure program, SEC Rel. No. 33–6383, AS Rel. No. 306, 47 Fed.Reg. 11380 (1982). The general effect of this program is to permit issuers that have filed reports under the 1934 Act for more than three years to incorporate by reference this information in its 1933 Act filing, thereby greatly simplifying the registration process under that Act.

(5) In 1988, the SEC promulgated Rule 19c–4, which prohibited national securities exchanges from listing for trading the securities of corporations that created weighted or unequal voting classifications for classes of common shares, the so-called "one share/one vote" principle. In Business Roundtable v. S.E.C., 905 F.2d 406, 410–11 (D.C.Cir.1990), the Court invalidated this rule on the ground that it exceeded the power granted to the Commission by § 14 of the Securities Exchange Act:

> * * * [A]lthough § 14(a) broadly bars use of the mails (and other means) "to solicit * * * any proxy" in contravention of Commission rules and regulations, it is not seriously disputed that Congress's central concern was with disclosure. See J.I. Case Co. v. Borak, 377 U.S. 426, 431, 84 S.Ct. 1555, 1559, 12 L.Ed.2d 423 (1964) ("The purpose of § 14(a) is to prevent management or others from obtaining authorization for corporate action by means of deceptive or inadequate disclosure in proxy solicitation"); see also Santa Fe Industries, Inc. v. Green, 430 U.S. 462, 477–78, 97 S.Ct. 1292, 1302–04, 51 L.Ed.2d 480 (1977) (emphasizing Exchange Act's philosophy of full disclosure and dismissing the fairness of the terms of the transaction as "at most a tangential concern of the statute" once full and fair disclosure has occurred).

> While the House Report indeed speaks of fair corporate suffrage, it also plainly identifies Congress's target—the solicitation of proxies by well informed insiders "without fairly informing the stockholders of the purposes for which the proxies are to be used." 1934 House Report at 14. The Senate Report contains no vague language about "corporate suffrage," but rather explains the purpose of the proxy protections as ensuring that stockholders have "adequate knowledge" about the "financial condition of the corporation * * * [and] the major questions of policy, which are decided at stockholders' meetings." S.Rep. No. 792, 73d Cong., 2d Sess. 12 (1934) ("1934 Senate Report"). Finally, both reports agree on the power that the proxy sections gave the Commission—"power to control the conditions under which proxies may be solicited." 1934 House Report at 14. See also 1934 Senate Report at 12 (similar language).

That proxy regulation bears almost exclusively on disclosure stems as a matter of necessity from the nature of proxies. Proxy solicitations are, after all, only communications with potential absentee voters. The goal of federal proxy regulation was to improve those communications and thereby to enable proxy voters to control the corporation as effectively as they might have by attending a shareholder meeting. Id. See also S.Rep. No. 1455, 73d Cong., 2d Sess. 74 (1934); Sheldon E. Bernstein and Henry G. Fischer, The Regulation of the Solicitation of Proxies: Some Reflections on Corporate Democracy, 7 U.Chi.L.Rev. 226, 227–28 (1940).

We do not mean to be taken as saying that disclosure is necessarily the sole subject of § 14. See Louis Loss, Fundamentals of Securities Regulation 452–53 (1988) (asserting that § 14 is not limited to ensuring disclosure), quoted in Final Rule, 53 Fed.Reg. at 26,391 n. 163; * * * For example, the Commission's Rule 14a–4(b)(2) requires a proxy to provide some mechanism for a security holder to withhold authority to vote for each nominee individually. * * * It thus bars a kind of electoral tying arrangement, and may be supportable as a control over management's power to set the voting agenda, or, slightly more broadly, voting procedures. * * * But while Rule 14a–4(b)(2) may lie in a murky area between substance and procedure, Rule 19c–4 much more directly interferes with the substance of what the shareholders may enact. It prohibits certain reallocations of voting power and certain capital structures, even if approved by a shareholder vote subject to full disclosure and the most exacting procedural rules.

905 F.2d, at 410. See also Eckstein v. Balcor Film Investors, 8 F.3d 1121, 1130 (7th Cir.1993), where Judge Easterbrook encapsulates the holding of *Business Roundtable* by stating that § 14 does not include "merit regulation." The legislative history of the 1934 Act is fragmentary and the court's reading, at best, is open to serious question. See Jill E. Fisch, From Legitimacy to Logic: Reconstructing Proxy Regulation, 46 Vand.L.Rev. 1129, 1173–89 (1993). However, a judicial opinion by the Seventh Circuit carries more weight than a law review article.

STUDEBAKER CORP. v. GITTLIN

United States Court of Appeals, Second Circuit, 1966.
360 F.2d 692.

FRIENDLY, CIRCUIT JUDGE:

Richard Gittlin, a stockholder of Studebaker Corporation, a Michigan corporation, appeals from an order of the District Court for the Southern District of New York, in an action brought against him by the corporation. The order enjoined the use of other stockholders' authorizations in a New York state court proceeding to obtain inspection of Studebaker's shareholders list, N.Y. Business Corporation Law, McKinney's Consol.Laws, c. 4, § 1315, save after compliance with the Proxy Rules of the Securities and Exchange Commission issued under § 14(a) of the Securities Exchange Act. * * *

Studebaker's resort to the district court was occasioned by the service upon it on March 21 of papers in a proceeding begun by Gittlin in the Supreme Court of New York to inspect the record of the company's shareholders. Gittlin's application to the New York court recited that he was the record owner of 5,000 shares of Studebaker stock and that he was acting on behalf of himself and on written authorization from 42 other shareholders owning in excess of 145,000 shares which constituted more than 5% of the company's stock; that he and his associates had been endeavoring to get the Studebaker management to agree to certain changes in its board of directors and had announced their intention to solicit proxies for the forthcoming annual meeting if the request was not met; and that when these talks had broken down, he had requested access to the stockholders list and had been refused.

Studebaker's affidavit and subsequent complaint allege that Gittlin obtained the authorization from the 42 other stockholders in violation of the Proxy Rules issued by the SEC under § 14(a) of the Securities Exchange Act. Specifically the company contends that Gittlin claimed to be holding the authorizations as early as March 14, and that at that time he had made no filing of proxy material with the SEC. * * *

The contention most heavily pressed is that § 14(a) of the Securities Exchange Act does not include authorizations for the limited purpose of qualifying under a state statute permitting the holders of a given percentage of shares to obtain inspection of a stockholders list. The statute is worded about as broadly as possible, forbidding any person "to solicit any proxy or consent or authorization" in respect of any security therein specified "in contravention of such rules and regulations as the Commission may prescribe as necessary or appropriate in the public interest or for the protection of investors;" the definitions in the Proxy Rules, 14a–1, exhaust the sweep of the power thus conferred. The assistant general counsel of the SEC, which responded to our request for its views with promptness and definitude, stated at the argument that the Commission believes § 14(a) should be construed, in all its literal breadth, to include authorizations to inspect stockholders lists, even in cases where obtaining the authorizations was not a step in a planned solicitation of proxies.[74]

We need not go that far to uphold the order of the district court. In SEC v. Okin, 132 F.2d 784 (2d Cir.1943), this court ruled that a letter which did not request the giving of any authorization was subject to the Proxy Rules if it was part of "a continuous plan" intended to end in solicitation and to prepare the way for success. This was the avowed purpose of Gittlin's demand for inspection of the stockholders list and, necessarily, for his soliciting authorizations sufficient to aggregate the 5% of the stock required by § 1315 of New York's Business Corporation Law. Presumably the stockholders who gave authorizations were told something and, as Judge L. Hand said in *Okin,* "one need only spread the misinformation adequately before beginning to solicit, and the Commission would be powerless to protect shareholders." 132 F.2d at 786. Moreover, the very fact that a copy of the stockholders list is a valuable instrument to a person seeking to gain control is a good reason for insuring that shareholders have full information before they aid its procurement. We

74. [By the Court] The Commission states in a letter to the court:

"Section 14(a) of the Securities Exchange Act of 1934 and the Commission's rules thereunder apply to any proxy, consent, authorization and are not limited to proxies, consents, and authorizations in situations involving elections to office. There is no reason to suppose that Congress intended that the protective provisions of the proxy rules should not reach other situations in which a stockholder is requested to permit another to act for him, whatever may be the purpose of the authorization."

The Proxy Rules [14a–2(b)], exempt solicitation otherwise than on behalf of management where the total number of persons solicited is less than ten.

see no reason why, in such a case, the words of the Act should be denied their literal meaning. * * *

This brings us to Gittlin's claim that Studebaker made no adequate showing of need for injunctive relief in failing to demonstrate "irreparable injury." Recitation of this term generally produces more dust than light. A plaintiff asking an injunction because of the defendant's violation of a statute is not required to show that otherwise rigor mortis will set in forthwith; all that "irreparable injury" means in this context is that unless an injunction is granted, the plaintiff will suffer harm which cannot be repaired. At least that is enough where, as here, the only consequence of an injunction is that the defendant must effect a compliance with the statute which he ought to have done before. To be sure, time is of the essence in proxy contests—at least the participants generally think it to be. But the district court could properly have considered that the public interest in enforcing the Proxy Rules outweighed any inconvenience to Gittlin in having to start again. In this aspect decision rested in the judge's sound discretion; we find no abuse.

Affirmed.

Notes

(1) The question of what constitutes a "solicitation" has also arisen in other contexts, particularly in connection with proxy fights and other struggles for control discussed in Chapter 15. See, e.g., Brown v. Chicago, Rock Island & Pac. R.R. Co., 328 F.2d 122 (7th Cir.1964) (an advertisement directed to "Rock Island Stockholders, Employees, Shippers, and Midwest Communities" is not a "solicitation"); Allen v. Lloyd's of London, 94 F.3d 923 (4th Cir.1996) (settlement offer by Lloyd's to American "Names" that provided each Name the choice of waiving claim against Lloyd's in exchange for partial funding by Lloyd's of Name's liability to Lloyd's is not a solicitation subject to section 14(a)).

(2) The broad definition of "solicitation" approved in *Studebaker* obviously chilled the ability of institutional investors to communicate with each other and present a common front when approaching management of corporations with respect to matters of corporate governance of interest to investors generally. The cost of preparing and filing a proxy statement for this purpose was estimated to exceed $50,000, and the problems of timing might make such an approach impractical in any event. In October 1992, the SEC amended rule 14a–1 to add a "safe harbor":

(2) The terms ["solicit" and "solicitation"] do not apply, however, to:
* * *

(iv) A communication by a security holder who does not otherwise engage in a proxy solicitation (other than a solicitation exempt under § 240.14a–2) stating how the security holder intends to vote and the reasons therefor, provided that the communication:

(A) Is made by means of speeches in public forums, press releases, published or broadcast opinions, statements, or advertisements appearing in a broadcast media, or newspaper, magazine or other bona fide publication disseminated on a regular basis,

(B) Is directed to persons to whom the security holder owes a fiduciary duty in connection with the voting of securities of a registrant held by the security holder, or

(C) Is made in response to unsolicited requests for additional information with respect to a prior communication by the security holder made pursuant to this paragraph (1)(2)(iv).

17 C.F.R. § 240.14a–1(*l*)(2)(2002). In addition, the SEC exempted from the costly proxy statement creation process "[a]ny solicitation by or on behalf of any person who does not, at any time during such solicitation, seek directly or indirectly, either on its own or another's behalf, the power to act as proxy for a security holder and does not furnish or otherwise request, or act on behalf of a person who furnishes or requests, a form of revocation, abstention, consent or authorization." There are ten exceptions to this provision to prevent candidates and others directly involved with the proxy solicitation from using these "free" communications. 17 C.F.R. § 240.14a–2(b)(1)(2000). The SEC must be provided five copies of the communication within three business days after it is distributed. 17 C.F.R. § 240.14a–6(g)(2000). 17 C.F.R. § 240.14a–2(b)(2) (2002) exempts a solicitation "made otherwise than on behalf of the registrant where the total number of persons solicited is not more than 10. 17 C.F.R. § 240.14a–3(f) (2002) permits communications by means of "speeches in public forums, press releases, published or broadcast opinions, statements, or advertisements appearing in a broadcast media, newspaper, magazine or other bona fide publication disseminated on a regular basis" if there is a definitive proxy statement on file with the SEC and no form of proxy or consent is provided to a security holder in connection with the communication." See Comment, The Recent Revisions to Federal Proxy Regulations: Lifting the Ban on Shareholders Communications, 68 Tulane L.Rev. 69 (1993); Carol Goforth, Proxy Reform as a Means of Increasing Shareholder Participation in Corporate Governance: Too Little But Not Too Late, 43 Am. U.L.Rev. 379 (1994); and Roberta Romano, Does Confidential Proxy Voting Matter?, 32 J. Legal Stud. 465 (2003).

(3) These modified regulations (excluding § 240.14a–2(b)(2)) had become effective in October 1992. See Bernard Black, Next Steps in Proxy Reform, 18 J. Corp. L. 1, 3 (1992) (efforts by Business Roundtable to defeat proposed proxy regulations described). During the "proxy season" in the Spring of 1993, numerous institutional investors took advantage of them. For example, Leslie Scism, Midsize Companies No Longer Escape Activists' Ire, Wall St.J., Nov. 3, 1993, at C1, reports that "two top New York City fund executives used computerized databases to identify the largest shareholders [of Cracker Barrel Old Country Store, Inc.], dispatched 300 letters and now are following up with calls" in an effort to persuade Cracker Barrel to adopt a policy prohibiting discrimination against homosexuals. The SEC's position with respect to shareholder proposals dealing with employment discrimination is discussed in Part 4 of this Chapter.

2.   PROXY FORMS, PROXY STATEMENTS, AND ANNUAL REPORTS

The comprehensive federal proxy regulations provide the basic structure for whatever corporate democracy exists in the modern public corporation. The import of these rather lengthy and detailed regulations is difficult to summarize. Further, the sequence in which they are set forth by the SEC is not very logical. It is simpler to discuss them by subject matter rather than numerically even though the result is skipping around the numbers. Most of these regulations are discussed in this Chapter while Chapter 15 deals with proxy fights. The mere listing of the principal areas discussed in this Chapter gives an indication of the scope and importance of these regulations:

(a) The regulations relating to the form of proxy, the proxy statement, and annual reports are discussed immediately below;

(b) The regulation prohibiting false and misleading statements in connection with proxies is discussed in Part (3) of this Section of this Chapter;

(c) The regulation requiring the inclusion of certain shareholder proposals in the proxy solicitation is discussed in Part (4) of this Section of this Chapter; and

(d) The regulation requiring communications to be mailed to securities holders in certain circumstances is discussed in Part (5) of this Section of this Chapter.

a. Form of Proxy. Rule 14a–4 of the proxy regulations contains specific requirements as to the form of proxy documents. The purpose of this rule is to ensure that shareholders have the option to vote to approve or disapprove issues submitted to them, and to vote for or against the directors proposed by the persons soliciting the proxy, usually management. Broad grants of discretionary power to the nominee are prohibited subject to certain exceptions; for example, generally a proxy may not confer power to vote for a person as a director unless he is named in the proxy statement as a nominee. However, a proxy may confer discretion to vote for a person not named to replace a bona fide nominee who is unable to serve or for good cause will not serve. Similarly, a proxy must be for a specified meeting, and undated or post-dated proxies are prohibited (Rule 14a–10).

Generally, it is difficult to given an accurate description of these disclosure documents. The following is an example of a routine proxy that meets SEC requirements.

BARNES & NOBLE, INC.
06/07/00

DIRECTORS
(MARK "X" FOR ONLY ONE BOX)

FOR ALL NOMINEES

WITHHOLD ALL NOMINEES

WITHHOLD AUTHORITY TO VOTE FOR
ANY INDIVIDUAL NOMINEE. WRITE
NUMBER(S) OF NOMINEE(S) BELOW.

SEE NUMBER(S) ONLY

PLEASE INDICATE YOUR PROPOSAL SELECTION BY
FIRMLY PLACING AN "X" IN THE APPROPRIATE
NUMBERED BOX WITH BLUE OR BLACK INK. ONLY.

SEE VOTING INSTRUCTION NO. 1 ON REVERSE

ACCOUNT NO: L4661 51D84115 00

CUSIP: 067774109

CONTROL NO: 7363 5439 1003

CLIENT NO: 161 200

PLACE 'X' HERE IF YOU PLAN TO ATTEND
AND VOTE YOUR SHARES AT THE MEETING

PLEASE CHECK THIS BOX AND INDICATE
ANY COMMENTS ON THE BACK OF FORM

Merrill Lynch
P.O. BOX 45000
NEW BRUNSWICK, N.J. 08945-5000

MLPF& S CUST FPO
ROBERT HAMILTON BASIC
FBO ROBERT HAMILTON
727 E DEAN KEETON ST
AUSTIN TX   78705-3224

120208

DATE

SIGNATURE(S)

FOR   AGAINST   ABSTAIN

DO NOT USE
DO NOT USE
DO NOT USE
DO NOT USE
DO NOT USE
DO NOT USE
DO NOT USE
DO NOT USE
DO NOT USE
DO NOT USE
DO NOT USE
DO NOT USE

3221229064O3   7363543910 P10614

BARNES & NOBLE, INC. ANNUAL MEETING TO BE HELD ON 06/07/00
FOR HOLDERS AS OF 04/18/00
120208   40-0801

AS AN ALTERNATIVE TO COMPLETING THIS FORM, YOU MAY ENTER YOUR VOTE
INSTRUCTION BY TELEPHONE AT 1-800-474-7492, OR VIA THE INTERNET AT
WWW.PROXYVOTE.COM AND FOLLOW THE SIMPLE INSTRUCTIONS.

CUSIP: 067774109

CONTROL NO. 7363 5439 1003

DIRECTORS
DIRECTORS RECOMMEND: A VOTE FOR ELECTION OF THE FOLLOWING NOMINEES
1 - 01-WILLIAM DILLARD II,02-IRENE R. MILLER,03-MICHAEL N. ROSEN

PROPOSAL(S)

DIRECTORS
RECOMMEND

2 - RATIFICATION OF THE APPOINTMENT OF BDO SEIDMAN, LLP, AS THE ----->>>   FOR ----->>>
    INDEPENDENT CERTIFIED PUBLIC ACCOUNTANTS OF THE COMPANY FOR THE
    FISCAL YEAR ENDING FEBRUARY 3, 2001.

NOTE SUCH OTHER BUSINESS AS MAY PROPERLY COME BEFORE THE
MEETING OR ANY ADJOURNMENT THEREOF

TELEPHONE VOTE AT 1-800-474-7492 OR
INTERNET VOTE AT WWW.PROXYVOTE.COM

VIF23H

VOTING INSTRUCTIONS

TO OUR CLIENTS:

WE HAVE BEEN REQUESTED TO FORWARD TO YOU THE ENCLOSED PROXY MATERIAL RELATIVE TO SECURITIES HELD BY US IN YOUR ACCOUNT BUT NOT REGISTERED IN YOUR NAME. SUCH SECURITIES CAN BE VOTED ONLY BY US AS THE HOLDER OF RECORD. WE SHALL BE PLEASED TO VOTE YOUR SECURITIES IN ACCORDANCE WITH YOUR WISHES. IF YOU WILL EXECUTE THE FORM AND RETURN IT TO US PROMPTLY IN THE ENCLOSED BUSINESS REPLY ENVELOPE. IT IS UNDERSTOOD THAT. IF YOU SIGN WITHOUT OTHERWISE MARKING THE FORM. THE SECURITIES WILL BE VOTED AS RECOMMENDED BY THE BOARD OF DIRECTORS ON ALL MATTERS TO BE CONSIDERED AT THE MEETING.

FOR THIS MEETING. THE EXTENT OF OUR AUTHORITY TO VOTE YOUR SECURITIES IN THE ABSENCE OF YOUR INSTRUCTIONS CAN BE DETERMINED BY REFERRING TO THE APPLICABLE VOTING INSTRUCTION NUMBER INDICATED ON THE FACE OF YOUR FORM.

VOTING INSTRUCTION NUMBER 1 -
WE URGE YOU TO SEND IN YOUR INSTRUCTIONS SO THAT WE MAY VOTE YOUR SECURITIES IN ACCORDANCE WITH YOUR WISHES. HOWEVER, THE RULES OF THE NEW YORK STOCK EXCHANGE PROVIDE THAT IF INSTRUCTIONS ARE NOT RECEIVED FROM YOU PRIOR TO THE ISSUANCE OF THE FIRST VOTE. <u>THE PROXY MAY BE GIVEN AT DISCRETION BY THE HOLDER OF RECORD OF THE SECURITIES</u> (ON THE TENTH DAY. IF THE PROXY MATERIAL WAS MAILED AT LEAST 15 DAYS PRIOR TO THE MEETING DATE: ON THE FIFTEENTH DAY IF PROXY MATERIAL WAS MAILED 25 DAYS OR MORE PRIOR TO THE MEETING DATE). IF YOU ARE UNABLE TO COMMUNICATE WITH US BY SUCH DATE. WE WILL NEVERTHELESS FOLLOW YOUR INSTRUCTIONS. EVEN IF OUR DISCRETIONARY VOTE HAS ALREADY BEEN GIVEN, PROVIDED YOUR INSTRUCTIONS ARE RECEIVED PRIOR TO THE MEETING DATE.

VOTING INSTRUCTION NUMBER 2 -
WE WISH TO CALL YOUR ATTENTION TO THE FACT THAT. UNDER THE RULES OF THE NEW YORK STOCK EXCHANGE. <u>WE CANNOT VOTE YOUR SECURITIES ON ONE OR MORE OF THE MATTERS TO BE ACTED UPON AT THE MEETING WITHOUT YOUR SPECIFIC VOTING INSTRUCTIONS.</u>

IF WE DO NOT HEAR FROM YOU PRIOR TO THE ISSUANCE OF THE FIRST VOTE. <u>WE MAY VOTE YOUR SECURITIES IN OUR DISCRETION TO THE EXTENT PERMITTED BY THE RULES OF THE EXCHANGE</u> (ON THE TENTH DAY, IF THE PROXY MATERIAL WAS MAILED AT LEAST 15 DAYS PRIOR TO THE MEETING DATE: ON THE FIFTEENTH DAY IF THE PROXY MATERIAL WAS MAILED 25 DAYS OR MORE PRIOR TO THE MEETING DATE). IF YOU ARE UNABLE TO COMMUNICATE WITH US BY SUCH DATE. WE WILL NEVERTHELESS FOLLOW YOUR VOTING INSTRUCTIONS. EVEN IF OUR DISCRETIONARY VOTE HAS ALREADY BEEN GIVEN. PROVIDED YOUR INSTRUCTIONS ARE RECEIVED PRIOR TO THE MEETING DATE.

VOTING INSTRUCTION NUMBER 3 -
IN ORDER FOR YOUR SECURITIES TO BE REPRESENTED AT THE MEETING. <u>IT WILL BE NECESSARY FOR US TO HAVE YOUR SPECIFIC VOTING INSTRUCTIONS.</u> PLEASE DATE. SIGN AND RETURN YOUR VOTING INSTRUCTIONS TO US PROMPTLY IN THE RETURN ENVELOPE PROVIDED.

VOTING INSTRUCTION NUMBER 4
REMINDER - WE HAVE PREVIOUSLY SENT YOU PROXY SOLICITING MATERIAL PERTAINING TO THE MEETING OF SHAREHOLDERS OF THE COMPANY INDICATED.

ACCORDING TO OUR LATEST RECORDS, WE HAVE NOT AS YET RECEIVED YOUR VOTING INSTRUCTION ON THE MATTERS TO BE CONSIDERED AT THIS MEETING AND THE COMPANY HAS REQUESTED US TO COMMUNICATE WITH YOU IN AN ENDEAVOR TO HAVE YOUR SECURITIES VOTED.

THE VOTING INSTRUCTIONS REQUEST PERTAINS TO SECURITIES CARRIED BY US IN YOUR ACCOUNT BUT NOT REGISTERED IN YOUR NAME. SUCH SECURITIES CAN BE VOTED ONLY BY US AS THE HOLDER OF RECORD OF THE SECURITIES.
PLEASE DATE. SIGN AND RETURN YOUR VOTING INSTRUCTIONS TO US PROMPTLY IN THE RETURN ENVELOPE PROVIDED.

SHOULD YOU WISH TO ATTEND THE MEETING AND <u>VOTE</u> IN PERSON. PLEASE CHECK THE BOX ON THE FRONT OF THE FORM FOR THIS PURPOSE. A LEGAL PROXY COVERING YOUR SECURITIES WILL BE ISSUED TO YOU.

b.   Proxy Statements. Rule 14a–3 requires that a proxy solicitation be accompanied by a proxy statement containing the information set forth in Schedule 14A, 17 C.F.R. § 240.14a–101 (2002). However, for several items, Schedule 14A in turn refers to two more general regulations applicable to public disclosures: Regulation S–X (relating to financial data) and Regulation S–K (relating to non financial data). The type of information required depends of course to some extent on the type of issue to be presented to the shareholders for their vote. The following are the disclosure requirements relating to the annual selection of an independent public accountant:

Item 9. Independent public accountants. If the solicitation is made on behalf of the registrant and relates to: (1) The annual (or special meeting in lieu of annual) meeting of security holders at which directors are to be elected, or a solicitation of consents or authorizations in lieu of such meeting or (2) the election, approval or ratification of the registrant's accountant, furnish the following information describing the registrant's relationship with its independent public accountant:

(a) The name of the principal accountant selected or being recommended to security holders for election, approval or ratification for the current year. If no accountant has been selected or recommended, so state and briefly describe the reasons therefor.

(b) The name of the principal accountant for the fiscal year most recently completed if different from the accountant selected or recommended for the current year or if no accountant has yet been selected or recommended for the current year.

(c) The proxy statement shall indicate: (1) Whether or not representatives of the principal accountant for the current year and for the most recently completed fiscal year are expected to be present at the security holders' meeting, (2) whether or not they will have the opportunity to make a statement if they desire to do so, and (3) whether or not such representatives are expected to be available to respond to appropriate questions.

(d) If during the registrant's two most recent fiscal years or any subsequent interim period, (1) an independent accountant who was previously engaged as the principal accountant to audit the registrant's financial statements, or an independent accountant on whom the principal accountant expressed reliance in its report regarding a significant subsidiary, has resigned (or indicated it has declined to stand for re-election after the completion of the current audit) or was dismissed, or (2) a new independent accountant has been engaged as either the principal accountant to audit the registrant's financial statements or as an independent accountant on whom the principal accountant has expressed or is expected to express reliance in its report regarding a significant subsidiary, then, notwithstanding any previous disclosure, provide the information required by Item 304(a) of Regulation S–K (§ 229.304 of this chapter).[75]

Schedule 14A, Item 9, 17 C.F.R. § 240.14a–101 (2000). The information in the proxy statement must be "clearly presented." Rule 14a–5. Furthermore, there is a procedure by which preliminary copies of certain proxy statements and soliciting material must be submitted to the SEC for review. Prior to 1992, preliminary review was required of virtually all such material, but the October 22, 1992 amendments narrowed sharply the SEC's program of making preliminary reviews of proxy documents. Proxy statements must be

---

75. [By the Editors] Item 304 of Regulation S–K applies only when there has been a change in or disagreement with the independent public accountant within the prior two most recent fiscal years. Item 304 is composed of four densely packed pages of instructions relating to various aspects of the reasons for the change and the nature of the disagreement.

submitted for preliminary review only if out-of-the-ordinary matters are to be considered. Rule 14a–6. Copies of the definitive documents must be filed with the SEC when they are distributed to shareholders.

In 2006, the SEC adopted changes to disclosure requirements that will compel companies to provide information about executive and director compensation, related person transactions, and security ownership of officers and directors in their proxy statements and periodic reports. SEC Rel. No. 33–8732A, 71 Fed. Reg. 53,158 (2006). The amendments require that the information be written in "plain English" to make it comprehensible to the average investor. For example, the disclosures must use the active voice, use short sentences, avoid legalese, and use everyday words.

In early 2007 the SEC adopted new rules allowing the electronic dissemination of proxy materials. An issuer can satisfy the SEC's delivery requirements by posting a copy of its proxy on its website and notifying shareholders of the proxy's electronic availability. The issuer must mail or email the Notice of Internet Availability of Proxy Materials at least 40 days before the shareholder meeting. Issuers may begin using the "notice and access" method July 1, 2007. SEC Rel. No. 34–55146, 72 Fed. Reg. 4148 (2007). This "notice and access" approach may help reduce costs associated with proxy solicitation.

c. Annual Reports. Rule 14a–3 provides that if a solicitation is by management and relates to an annual meeting at which directors are to be elected; the solicitation must be accompanied or preceded by an annual report containing the financial information and other material described in the rule. 17 C.F.R. § 240.14a–3(b) (2002). Many state incorporation statutes do not require the distribution of even such minimal information to shareholders; see, however, MBCA § 16.20. The SEC has long recognized that the annual report is an effective means of communication between management and security holders. In part this was because annual reports are generally readable and avoid legalistic and technical terminology. In its integration of filings under the various securities acts, the SEC broadened the information required to be included in annual reports. It is not practical to provide an example of an annual report, but they are widely available; indeed many issuers treat the annual report as a modest advertising device, using flashy covers and high quality paper and printing, and offering to mail copies free to any person who asks.

d. Management's Discussion of Financial Condition and Results of Operations. 2 Loss & Seligman, Securities Regulation 668 (3d ed. 1989) states that "[o]ften the most important textual disclosure item" in the annual report is formally known as "Management's Discussion and Analysis of Financial Condition and Results of Operations," usually shortened to "MD & A." Codified as Item 303 of Regulation S–K, it is to consist of a discussion of the registrant's "financial condition, changes in financial condition and results of operations," specifically with respect to liquidity and capital resources. It "also shall provide such other information that the registrant believes to be necessary to an understanding of its financial condition, changes in financial condition and results of operations." 17 C.F.R. § 229.303(a) (2000). In the promulgating release, the purpose of the MD & A is somewhat fancifully stated to be "to give the investor an opportunity to look at the company through the eyes of management by providing both a short- and long-term analysis of the business of the company." Concept Release on Management's Discussion and Analysis of Financial Condition and Operations, Sec.Act Rel. 33–6711 (April 17, 1987), at 3. Item 303 must be responded to not only in the annual report, but also whenever financial information must be made public.

In order to appreciate the MD & A, and the problems it creates for issuers, a brief discussion of the SEC's approach toward the disclosure of forward-looking information is helpful. See generally Edmund W. Kitch, The Theory and Practice of Securities Disclosure, 61 Brook.L.Rev. 763 (1995). Historically, the SEC insisted that financial disclosures be limited to historical facts. "Conjecture and speculations as to the future are left by the Act to the investor on the theory that he is as competent as anyone to predict the future from the given facts." Harry Heller, Disclosure Requirements Under Federal Securities Regulation, 16 Bus.Law. 300, 307, n. 31 (1961). This position that full disclosure should be limited to "hard"—that is readily verifiable—historical data and that projections or predictions were "soft"—that is, unverifiable—and therefore inherently misleading—permitted easy administration by the SEC but was unrealistic: investors generally are interested in future predictions rather than past events, investors are certainly less able to make reliable predictions about the future from past data than knowledgeable management, and undue emphasis on historical data leads to long and unreadable prospectuses and proxy statements. Consult Homer Kripke, The SEC and Corporate Disclosure: Regulation in Search of a Purpose (1979).

The SEC decided to permit projections of financial data, discussion of management objectives and goals for future performance, and the assumptions underlying such statements, ("forward looking statements") only after considerable soul-searching and a study by an advisory committee, SEC Rel. No. 33–5993, 43 Fed.Reg. 53251 (1978). In 1979, the SEC adopted a "safe harbor" rule that provided that such statements would not be deemed false or misleading unless they were "made or reaffirmed without a reasonable basis or [were] disclosed other than in good faith." 17 C.F.R. §§ 230.175, 240.3b–6 (1997). The Private Securities Litigation Reform Act of 1995 (discussed in chapter 13) enacted a new section 21E to the Securities Exchange Act of 1934 providing a much broader and more secure "safe harbor" provision while preserving Rule 3b–6. See Edward A. Fallone, Section 10(b) and the Vagaries of Federal Common Law: The Merits of Codifying the Private Cause of Action Under a Structuralist Approach, 1997 U.Ill.L.Rev. 71, 86 (explaining that statements qualifying for the safe harbor cannot give rise to private liability if either of two tests is met: no private liability may be imposed for forward-looking statements made without actual knowledge that the statements were false or misleading and no private liability may be imposed if the forward-looking statement is identified as such when made and is accompanied by meaningful cautionary language identifying important factors that could prevent the statement from becoming accurate).

See Jeanne Calderon and Rachel Kowal, Safe Harbors: Historical and Current Approaches to Future Forecasting, 22 J.Corp.L. 661 (1997). Rather paradoxically, this new section does not appear to have the intended effect since its enactment. Item 10(b) of Regulation S–K encourages but does not require the use of "management's projections of future economic performance" in other financial information filed with the SEC and sets forth extensive guidelines for the use and presentation of projections. 17 C.F.R. § 229.10(b) (2002).

The MD & A requirements in effect often mandate a discussion of forward-looking information in annual reports and other financial documents filed with the SEC. As discussed in 17 C.F.R. § 229.303 (Item 303), Instruction 7, "forward looking information * * * is to be distinguished from presently known data which will impact upon future operating results, such as known future increases in costs of labor or materials. This latter data may be required to be disclosed. Any forward-looking information supplied is expressly covered by the safe harbor rules for projections. See Rule 175 under the Securities Act, 17 C.F.R. 230.175, Rule 3b–6 under the Exchange Act, 17 C.F.R. 240.3b–6, and Securities Act Release, No. 6084."

The following administrative proceeding deals with compliance with Item 303 in two SEC periodic disclosure documents, Forms 10–K and 10–Q, but is "the" SEC statement as to the interpretation of Rule 175 and the MD & A requirement.

IN THE MATTER OF CATERPILLAR, INC.

Administrative Proceeding File No. 3–7692.
SEC Rel. No. 34–30532 (1992).

The Commission deems it appropriate and in the public interest that public administrative proceedings be instituted pursuant to Section 21C of the Securities Exchange Act of 1934 ("Exchange Act") to determine whether Caterpillar Inc. ("Caterpillar") has failed to comply with Section 13(a) of the Exchange Act and Rules 13a–1 and 13a–13 promulgated under the Exchange Act in connection with reports on Form 10–K and Form 10–Q filed with the Commission. Accordingly, such proceedings are hereby instituted.

In anticipation of the institution of these administrative proceedings, Caterpillar has submitted an Offer of Settlement for the purpose of disposing of the issue raised in these proceedings. * * *

On the basis of this Order and the Respondent's Offer of Settlement, the Commission finds the following: * * *

This matter involves Caterpillar's failure in its Form 10–K for the year ended December 31, 1989, and it Form 10–Q for the first quarter of 1990 to comply with Item 303 of Regulation S–K, Management's Discussion and Analysis of Financial Conditions and Results of Operations ("MD & A"). Specifically, the MD & A rules required Caterpillar to disclose information about the 1989 earnings of Caterpillar Brasil, S.A. ("CBSA"), its wholly owned Brazilian subsidiary, and uncertainties about CBSA's 1990 earnings.

1. CBSA's 1989 RESULTS

Caterpillar has had a Brazilian subsidiary since the 1950's. Nineteen eighty-nine was an exceptionally profitable year for CBSA. That year, without accounting for the effect of integration, CBSA accounted for some 23 percent of Caterpillar's net profits of $497 million, although its revenues represented only 5 percent of the parent company's revenues. In 1989, CBSA's operating profit was in line with prior years but a number or nonoperating items contributed to greater than usual overall profit. Those items included currency translation gains, export subsidies, interest income, and Brazilian tax loss carryforwards. Many of these gains were caused by the hyperinflation in Brazil in 1989 and the fact that the dollar-cruzado exchange rate lagged behind inflation.

CBSA's financial results were presented on a consolidated basis with the remainder of Caterpillar's operations. Thus, the impact of CBSA's operations on Caterpillar's overall results was not apparent from the face of Caterpillar's financial statements or the notes thereto.

2. MANAGEMENT'S VIEW OF CBSA

Caterpillar was and is a highly integrated organization. Its various divisions and subsidiaries were, and are, very interdependent. As a consequence, Caterpillar typically viewed and managed the organization on a consolidated basis. While unadjusted profit numbers for subsidiaries and divisions were available to management, they were not viewed by management as reliable indicators of that subsidiary's or division's contribution to the consolidated enterprise. The various divisions and subsidiaries were not viewed as profit centers but rather as cost centers. Profit and results of operations were managed on a consolidated basis. Because of that management perspective, the profit contribution of each subsidiary or division has not historically been used as a basis for personnel, product sourcing or disclosure decisions.

In January of 1990, accounting department personnel began to separately analyze CBSA's 1989 results compared with its 1990 forecast. In the process of that analysis, the various components of CBSA's results were aggregated. The result of that analysis was conveyed to top management and then to the board. By the middle of February 1990—i.e., at least two weeks before Caterpillar filed its 1989 Form 10–K—Caterpillar's top management had recognized that, to adequately understand Caterpillar's 1990 forecast, it was necessary to understand CBSA's 1990 forecast. Management also recognized that CBSA's future performance was exceptionally difficult to predict—particularly in light of anticipated sweeping economic reforms to be instituted by a new administration in Brazil—and that there were substantial uncertainties whether CBSA would repeat its exceptional 1989 earnings in 1990.

The board of directors was told in February 1990 that Brazil was "volatile" and that "the impact of Brazil is so significant to reduced 1990 projected results, [management] felt it was necessary to explain it [to the directors] in some detail."

Minutes of the February 1990 board meeting include the following about Brazil:

> [Management] commented on results of operations in Brazil because of the significant [negative] impact they will have on overall results for 1990. Beginning in February 1990 and continuing through the rest of the year management departed from this usual practice of viewing the company as a whole and provided projections to the board of directors which separated out the impact of Brazil.

During the interim between the February board meeting and the next board meeting, held on April 11, 1990, a new administration took office in Brazil. Fernando Collor de Mello, who had been elected president of Brazil in

December 1989, was inaugurated on March 15, 1990, "putting an end," as one Brazilian business journal put it, "to weeks of intense speculation as to what economic measures he will actually announce." Collor immediately instituted sweeping economic and monetary changes in an effort to bring Brazil's hyperinflation under control. * * *

When the Caterpillar board met on April 11, management gave presentations in which it discussed, among other things, the likely negative effects the Collor plan would have on CBSA's sales and profits:

> At our last meeting, we reviewed the impact that [CBSA] is expected to have on our 1990 results * * *. Brazil is volatile and difficult to predict. Their recently announced economic reforms have made the situation even more uncertain.

> The impact of these reforms is not at all clear, so we have made no attempt to change the forecast. However, it's difficult to see any short-term positives, so there is considerable risk that Brazil's new economic plan could bring additional pressure on our 1990 profit.

> [Management] * * * also noted * * * that the profit in Brazil will be substantially lower than in 1989.

Throughout April and May of 1990 Caterpillar continued to monitor the events in Brazil and their effects on CBSA, including the consequences of the Collor plan on Caterpillar. * * * However, after a review of April and May results, the company concluded the new economic policies would cause CBSA to suffer significant losses in 1990. It also concluded that those losses would not likely be balanced by gains in other parts of the world and consolidated results would be lower than originally anticipated.

At 8:00 a.m. on Monday, June 25, 1990, before the beginning of trading, the company voluntarily issued a press release explaining that the anticipated results for 1990 would be substantially lower than previously projected. * * *

3. PREPARATION AND REVIEW OF CATERPILLAR'S PERIODIC REPORTS

The MD & A sections of the 1989 10–K and 10–Q for the first quarter of 1990 were drafted by employees in Caterpillar's accounting department.[76] Prior to the issuance of those reports, the language of the MD & A was reviewed by the Controller, Financial Vice President, Treasurer, and the company's legal, economic, and public affairs departments. After that, the language of the MD & A was reviewed by the top officers of the Company.

The board of directors reviewed the final draft of the 1989 Form 10–K, including the MD & A, at the February 1990 board meeting. At that time, the board, including top management, who were members of the board, received a written opinion of the company's independent auditor that the financial statements complied with the rules and regulations of the Commission, and also an opinion of the company's General Counsel that the Form 10–K complied with all the rules and regulations of the Commission.

In rendering their opinion on the financial statements contained in Caterpillar's 1989 Form 10–K, the auditor had reviewed the disclosure set

---

76. [By the Commission] The same employees also drafted portions of management's presentations regarding Brazil to the February and April 1990 meetings of the board of directors.

forth in the MD & A for inconsistencies with the financial statements but did not opine on the MD & A. The General Counsel was aware of management's concerns regarding Brazil, however, he disregarded management's statements about Brazil when reviewing and opining upon the MD & A disclosure regarding Brazil.

4. CATERPILLAR'S DISCLOSURE REGARDING CBSA

Neither the 1989 Form 10–K nor the first quarter 1990 Form 10–Q indicated the extent to which CBSA had affected Caterpillar's bottom line in 1989, nor did they indicate that a decline in CBSA's future results could have a material adverse effect on Caterpillar's bottom line in 1990.[77] * * *

Nothing in the MD & A section of the 1989 Form 10–K suggested the disproportionate impact of CBSA's profits on Caterpillar's 1989 overall profitability. Similarly, the 1989 Form 10–K and the Form 10–Q for the first quarter of 1990 did not adequately mention management's uncertainty about CBSA's 1990 performance.

II.   APPLICABLE LAW

* * * *A. Management's Discussion and Analysis as Required by Item 303 of Regulation S–K*

For reports on Form 10–K, Item 303(a) requires the registrant to discuss the liquidity, capital resources, and results of operations of the registrant and to "provide such other information that the registrant believes to be necessary to an understanding of its financial condition, changes in financial condition and results of operations." Item 303(a) also specifically requires

> [W]here in the registrant's judgment a discussion of segment information or of other subdivisions of the registrant's business would be appropriate to an understanding of such business, the discussion shall focus on each

---

77. [By the Commission] The 1989 Form 10–K contained the following statements about Brazil:

Sales Outside the United States

Dealer machine sales rose in most selling areas, with demand especially strong in Europe, Brazil, Australia, and the Far East.

Latin America

Sales rose 14% in 1989, the sixth consecutive year of improvement. The biggest gain was in Brazil, where very high inflation rates increased demand for hard goods, including earth moving equipment. (Given the extraordinarily high rate of inflation in Brazil, many contractors preferred to own hard assets, such as equipment, rather than depreciating cruzados.) Toward year-end, however, sales growth in Brazil moderated as interest rates rose.

Outlook

Latin American countries continue to be plagued with debt problems. However, debt rescheduling; stable profitable commodity prices; and increased privatization should

help business in some countries. Sales in Brazil, however, could be hurt by post-election policies which will likely aim at curbing inflation.

The Form 10–Q for the first quarter of 1990 contained the following statements about Brazil:

Demand also rose in a number of Latin American countries. In Brazil, demand increased over one year ago despite the uncertainty of the Brazilian economy.

The company hasn't changed its outlook from what was stated in its 1989 annual report.

Caterpillar Chairman George Schaefer said:

First-quarter sales were somewhat stronger than anticipated. Nevertheless, the company continues to be concerned about tight monetary policies in major industrial countries; the recent weakening of the Japanese yen; and the uncertainty of the economic situation in Brazil.

relevant, reportable segment or other subdivision of the business and on the registrant as a whole.

In discussing results of operations the registrant is to "[d]escribe any unusual or infrequent events or transactions * * * that materially affected the amount of reported income from continuing operations and in each case, indicate the extent to which income was so affected." Item 303(a)(3)(i). Furthermore, the registrant is to describe other significant components of revenues or expenses that should be described to allow a reader of the company's financial statements to understand the registrant's results of operations. Id.

As a separate component of the discussion of results of operations, the registrant is to discuss "any known trends or uncertainties that have had or that the registrant reasonably expects will have a material favorable or unfavorable impact on net sales or revenues or income from continuing operations." Item 303(a)(3)(ii). "The discussion and analysis shall focus specifically on material events and uncertainties known to management that would cause reported financial information not to be necessarily indicative of future operating results." Instruction 3 to Item 303(a). Registrants are instructed to discuss both new matters which will have an impact on future results, and matters which have previously had an impact on reported operations but which are not expected to have an impact on future operations. Id.

For interim reports such as a Form 10–Q, Item 303(b) requires a discussion and analysis of the results of operations to enable the reader to assess material changes in financial condition and results of operations that have occurred since the end of the preceding fiscal year. Item 303(b). Discussions of material changes in results of operations must identify any significant elements of the registrant's income or loss from continuing operations which do not arise from or are not necessarily representative of the registrant's business. Instruction 4 to Item 303(b).

B.   The MD & A Release

In 1989, the Commission determined that additional interpretive guidance was needed regarding a number of areas of MD & A disclosure and published an interpretive release. Release Nos. 33–6835, 34–26831, IC–16961, FR–36 (May 18, 1989) (hereafter "MD & A Release"). Drawing on earlier releases, the MD & A Release noted the underlying rationale for requiring MD & A disclosure and management's core responsibility in providing that disclosure: The MD & A is needed because, without such a narrative explanation, a company's financial statements and accompanying footnotes may be insufficient for an investor to judge the quality of earnings and the likelihood that past performance is indicative of future performance. MD & A is intended to give the investor an opportunity to look at the company through the eyes of management by providing both a short and long-term analysis of the business of the company.

MD & A Release Par. III.A (quoting Securities Act Release No. 6771 (April 24, 1987)). It is management's responsibility in the MD & A to identify and address those key variables and other qualitative and quantitative factors which are peculiar to and necessary for an understanding and evaluation of the company.[78]

MD & A Release Par. III.A (quoting Securities Act Release No. 6349 (September 28, 1981)). The MD & A Release further notes,

> The MD & A requirements are intentionally flexible and general. Because no two registrants are identical, good MD & A disclosure for one registrant is not necessarily good * * * for another. The same is true for MD & A disclosure of the same registrant in different years.

MD & A Release Par. IV.

As to prospective information, the MD & A Release sets forth the following test for determining when disclosure is required:

Where a trend, demand, commitment, event or uncertainty is known, management must make two assessments:

(1) Is the known trend, demand, commitment, event or uncertainty likely to come to fruition? If management determines that it is not reasonably likely to occur, no disclosure is required.

(2) If management cannot make that determination, it must evaluate objectively the consequences of the known trend, demand, commitment, event or uncertainty, on the assumption that it will come to fruition.

Disclosure is then required unless management determines that a material effect on the registrant's financial condition or results of operations is not reasonably likely to occur.

MD & A Release Par. III.B. Where the test for disclosure is met, "MD & A disclosure of the effects [of the uncertainty,] quantified to the extent reasonably practicable, [is] required."[79] Id. * * *

C. ANALYSIS

Regulation S–K requires disclosure of information necessary to understand the registrant's financial statements. Item 303(a); MD & A Release Par. III.A. Caterpillar's failure to include required information about CBSA in the MD & A left investors with an incomplete picture of Caterpillar's financial condition and results of operations and denied them the opportunity to see the company "through the eyes of management." MD & A Release Par. IV.

Specifically, by failing (i) in its Annual Report on Form 10–K for the year ended December 31, 1989 to provide an adequate discussion and analysis of the impact of CBSA on its 1989 results of operations as contained in its

78. [By the Commission] Although an auditor or other third party may review the MD & A section of a periodic report, the substance of the S–K Item 303 disclosure is the responsibility of management.

79. [By the Commission] The Commission has noted:

"Both required disclosure regarding the future impact of presently known trends, events or uncertainties and optional forward-looking information may involve some prediction or projection. The distinction between the two rests with the nature of the prediction required. Required disclosure is based on currently known trends, events, and uncertainties that are reasonably expected to have material effects * * *. In contrast, optional forward-looking disclosure involves anticipating a future trend or event or anticipating a less predictable impact of a known event, trend or uncertainty."

Securities Act Release No. 6711 (April 24, 1987) (final paragraph of Part III); MD & A Release P III.B. (text at n. 21).

financial statements, and (ii) to adequately disclose in its 1989 Form 10–K and in its Quarterly Report on Form 10–Q for the first quarter of 1990 known uncertainties reasonably likely to have a material effect on Caterpillar's future results of operations, due to CBSA's questionable ability to repeat its 1989 performance, Caterpillar violated Section 13(a) of the Exchange Act and Rules 13a–1 and 13a–13 thereunder.[80] * * *

Given the magnitude of CBSA's contribution to Caterpillar's overall earnings, disclosure of the extent of that contribution was required under the MD & A provisions of Regulation S–K since CBSA's earnings materially affected Caterpillar's reported income from continuing operations. See, Item 303(a)(3)(i). Furthermore, the MD & A should have discussed various factors which contributed to CBSA's earnings including currency translation gains, export subsidies, interest income, and Brazilian tax loss carryforwards since such items were significant components of CBSA's revenues that should have been identified and addressed in order for a reader of the company's financial statements to understand Caterpillar's results of operations. * * *

By the time of the February 14, 1990, board meeting—two weeks before Caterpillar's Form 10–K for 1989 was filed—management could not conclude that lower earnings from CBSA were not reasonably likely to occur, nor could management conclude that a material effect on Caterpillar's results of operations was not reasonably likely to occur due to CBSA's lower earnings. It was at that meeting that management told the company's directors "the impact of Brazil is so significant to reduced 1990 projected results, * * * it was necessary to explain it [to the directors] in some detail."

By the end of the first quarter of 1990, before Caterpillar's Form 10–Q for the first quarter of 1990 was filed, management had concluded that "the profit in Brazil will be substantially lower than in 1989." Therefore, it became even more apparent that management could not conclude that lower earnings from CBSA were not reasonably likely to occur, nor could management conclude that a material effect on Caterpillar's results of operations was not reasonably likely to occur due to CBSA's lower earnings. Thus, discussion of the uncertainties surrounding CBSA's earnings, and possible material future impact on Caterpillar's overall financial condition and results of operations was required. * * *

Caterpillar's MD & A disclosure was deficient in two respects. First, Caterpillar's Annual Report on Form 10–K for the year ended December 31, 1989 should have discussed the impact of CBSA on Caterpillar's overall results of operations. Second, both the Annual Report on Form 10–K for 1989 and the Quarterly Report on Form 10–Q for the first quarter of 1990 should have discussed the future uncertainties regarding CBSA's operations, the possible risk of Caterpillar having materially lower earnings as a result of that risk and, to the extent reasonably practicable, quantified the impact of such risk. MD & A Release Par.III.B. The MD & A disclosure in the 1989 Form 10–K and the Form 10–Q for the first quarter of 1990 failed to adequately disclose the risk of lower earnings and did not attempt to quantify the impact of lower earnings from CBSA on Caterpillar. * * *

80. [By the Commission] During the time period in question, Caterpillar did not have adequate procedures in place designed to en- sure compliance with the MD & A require- ments.

Note

Edmund W. Kitch, The Theory and Practice of Securities Disclosure, 61 Brook.L.Rev. 763, 807–19 (1995):

> The Commission has not been pleased with issuer compliance with Item 303. In Release 33–6835, issued in May 1989, the Commission reported that the staff had undertaken "a special review of the MD & A disclosures to assess the adequacy of disclosure practices and to identify any common areas of deficiencies." Of the 218 registrants reviewed, 206 received letters of comment, many of which related to more than one report. * * * The Commission treated this high level of deficiency as a problem of lack of understanding by registrants, and proceeded to discuss what disclosure was required and to give examples of adequate disclosure. * * * As it turned out the Commission had had enough of preaching. It was time for a test case, and the object of the test case turned out to be the Caterpillar Corporation. * * *

Professor Kitch also pointed out that the SEC's analysis of the economic importance of the Brazil operations to Caterpillar was less than complete, that the issue was not whether the profitability of the operations of Caterpillar in Brazil had declined, but whether the overall profitability of Caterpillar had declined as a result. It was quite possible, he suggests, that the company could have made the forecast of 1990 earnings it did in good faith and did not learn until later that its other operations would not offset the negative events in Brazil. His strongest criticism, however, was directed at the reliance by the SEC on management's communications with the board of directors. He argues that SEC reliance on these discussions in litigation over proxy deficiencies will lead management's communications to become guarded or non-existent, withholding important information from the board and preventing effective board governance.

3.   FALSE OR MISLEADING STATEMENTS IN CONNECTION WITH PROXY SOLICITATIONS

REGULATION 14a. SOLICITATION OF PROXIES
17 C.F.R. § 240.14a–9 (2002).

§ 240.14a–9 FALSE OR MISLEADING STATEMENTS

(a) No solicitation subject to this regulation shall be made by means of any proxy statement, form of proxy, notice of meeting or other communication, written or oral, containing any statement which, at the time and in the light of the circumstances under which it is made, is false or misleading with respect to any material fact, or which omits to state any material fact necessary in order to make the statements therein not false or misleading or necessary to correct any statement in any earlier communication with respect to the solicitation of a proxy for the same meeting or subject matter which has become false or misleading.

(b) The fact that a proxy statement, form of proxy or other soliciting material has been filed with or examined by the Commission shall not be deemed a finding by the Commission that such material is accurate or complete or not false or misleading, or that the Commission has passed upon the merits of or approved any statement contained therein or any matter to be acted upon by security holders. No representation contrary to the foregoing shall be made.

Note: The following are some examples of what, depending upon particular facts and circumstances, may be misleading within the meaning of this section.

(a) Predictions as to specific future market values.

(b) Material which directly or indirectly impugns character, integrity or personal reputation, or directly or indirectly makes charges concerning improper, illegal or immoral conduct or associations, without factual foundation.

(c) Failure to so identify a proxy statement, form of proxy and other soliciting material as to clearly distinguish it from the soliciting material of any other person or persons soliciting for the same meeting or subject matter.

(d) Claims made prior to a meeting regarding the results of a solicitation.

Notes

(1) Is this provision a restatement of common law principles or is it broader? In a pre–1964 case, Bresnick v. Home Title Guar. Co., 175 F.Supp. 723 (S.D.N.Y. 1959), the Court stated that the test at common law "is not compliance with the technical rules, but rather whether the proxy soliciting material was so tainted with fraud that an inequitable result was accomplished." 175 F.Supp. at 725.

(2) The note to rule 14a–9 formerly included, as examples of potentially misleading statements, "predictions as to specific future market values, earnings, or dividends," and was changed to its present form in July 1979 to reflect the SEC policy with respect to forward looking statements described briefly in the prior section. SEC Rel. No. 34–15944, 44 Fed.Reg. 38810 (1979).

J.I. CASE CO. v. BORAK

Supreme Court of the United States, 1964.
377 U.S. 426, 84 S.Ct. 1555, 12 L.Ed.2d 423.

MR. JUSTICE CLARK delivered the opinion of the Court.

This is a civil action brought by respondent, a stockholder of petitioner J.I. Case Company, charging deprivation of the preemptive rights of respondent and other shareholders by reason of a merger between Case and the American Tractor Corporation. It is alleged that the merger was effected through the circulation of a false and misleading proxy statement by those proposing the merger. The complaint was in two counts, the first based on diversity and claiming a breach of the directors' fiduciary duty to the stockholders. The second count alleged a violation of § 14(a) of the Securities Exchange Act of 1934 with reference to the proxy solicitation material. The trial court held that as to this count it had no power to redress the alleged violations of the Act but was limited solely to the granting of declaratory relief thereon under § 27 of the Act.[81] The court held Wis.Stat., 1961, § 180.405(4),

---

81. [By the Court] Section 27 of the Act, provides in part: "The district courts of the United States, the Supreme Court of the District of Columbia, and the United States courts of any Territory or other place subject to the jurisdiction of the United States shall have exclusive jurisdiction of violations of this title or the rules and regulations thereunder, and of all suits in equity and actions at law brought to enforce any liability or duty created by this title or the rules and regulations thereunder. Any criminal proceeding may be brought in the district wherein any act or transaction constituting the violation occurred. Any suit or action to enforce any liability or duty created by this title or rules and regulations thereunder, which requires posting security for expenses in derivative actions,[82] applicable to both counts, except that portion of Count 2 requesting declaratory relief. It ordered the respondent to furnish a bond in the amount of $75,000 thereunder and upon his failure to do so, dismissed the complaint, save that part of Count 2 seeking a declaratory judgment. On interlocutory appeal the Court of Appeals reversed on both counts, holding that the District Court had the power to grant remedial relief and that the Wisconsin statute was not applicable. 317 F.2d 838. We granted certiorari. 375 U.S. 901, 84 S.Ct. 195, 11 L.Ed.2d 143. We consider only the question of whether § 27 of the Act authorizes a federal cause of action for rescission or damages to a corporate stockholder with respect to a consummated merger which was authorized pursuant to the use of a proxy statement alleged to contain false and misleading statements violative of § 14(a) of the Act. This being the sole question raised by petitioners in their petition for certiorari, we will not consider other questions subsequently presented.

I.

Respondent, the owner of 2,000 shares of common stock of Case acquired prior to the merger, brought this suit based on diversity jurisdiction seeking to enjoin a proposed merger between Case and the American Tractor Corporation (ATC) on various grounds, including breach of the fiduciary duties of the Case directors, self-dealing among the management of Case and ATC and misrepresentations contained in the material circulated to obtain proxies. The injunction was denied and the merger was thereafter consummated. Subsequently successive amended complaints were filed and the case was heard on the aforesaid two-count complaint. The claims pertinent to the asserted violation of the Securities Exchange Act were predicated on diversity jurisdiction as well as on § 27 of the Act. They alleged: that petitioners, or their predecessors, solicited or permitted their names to be used in the solicitation of proxies of Case stockholders for use at a special stockholders' meeting at which the proposed merger with ATC was to be voted upon; that the proxy solicitation material so circulated was false and misleading in violation of § 14(a) of the Act and Rule 14a–9 which the Commission had promulgated

---

or to enjoin any violation of such title or rules and regulations, may be brought in any such district or in the district wherein the defendant is found or is an inhabitant or transacts business, and process in such cases may be served in any other district of which the defendant is an inhabitant or wherever the defendant may be found."

82. [By the Editors] Deborah A. DeMott, Shareholder Derivative Actions: Law and Practice § 3:01 (1987) describes "security for expenses" statutes as follows:

Nineteen states have statutes permitting the corporation, and in some instances, other defendants, to demand that the plaintiff in a derivative suit provide security for the expenses, including attorney fees, that may be incurred in the defense of the suit. The amount of security is determined by the court. With few exceptions, these statutes apply *only* to plaintiffs whose stockholdings fall beneath a percentage amount stated in the statute, typically five percent of a class of outstanding stock or $25,000 in market value. Defendants may have recourse to the security if they prevail in the litigation, although some statutes limit recourse to those cases which the court determines were brought without reasonable cause. * * *

Plaintiffs may be able to avoid the security requirements by purchasing more shares themselves or by seeking the intervention as plaintiffs of additional stockholders, so that the aggregate holdings of the plaintiffs and intervenors exceed the amount or percentage provided by the statute. The potential impact of security for expense statutes is also limited by the fact that Congress has never enacted a general security statute applicable to all derivative actions raising federal claims. * * *

Reprinted with permission. Published by Callaghan & Co.

The false
proxy led
to a narrow
vote approving
a merger with
another corp.

Borak argues
that this merger,
which wouldn't
have succeeded
but for the
false proxy,
caused him
damages.

Issues:
Whether
14(a) gives
a private
right of
action to
stockholders

2. Whether
statutes only
provides prospective
relief (e.g.
a restraining
order).

thereunder; that the merger was approved at the meeting by a small margin of votes and was thereafter consummated; that the merger would not have been approved but for the false and misleading statements in the proxy solicitation material; and that Case stockholders were damaged thereby. The respondent sought judgment holding the merger void and damages for himself and all other stockholders similarly situated, as well as such further relief "as equity shall require." The District Court ruled that the Wisconsin security for expenses statute did not apply to Count 2 since it arose under federal law. However, the court found that its jurisdiction was limited to declaratory relief in a private, as opposed to a government, suit alleging violation of § 14(a) of the Act. Since the additional equitable relief and damages prayed for by the respondent would, therefore, be available only under state law, it ruled those claims subject to the security for expenses statute. After setting the amount of security at $75,000 and upon the representation of counsel that the security would not be posted, the court dismissed the complaint, save that portion of Count 2 seeking a declaration that the proxy solicitation material was false and misleading and that the proxies and, hence, the merger were void.

II.

It appears clear that private parties have a right under § 27 to bring suit for violation of § 14(a) of the Act. Indeed, this section specifically grants the appropriate District Court's jurisdiction over "all suits in equity and actions at law brought to enforce any liability or duty created" under the Act. The petitioners make no concessions, however, emphasizing that Congress made no specific reference to a private right of action in § 14(a); that, in any event, the right would not extend to derivative suits and should be limited to prospective relief only. In addition, some of the petitioners argue that the merger can be dissolved only if it was fraudulent or non-beneficial, issues upon which the proxy material would not bear. But the causal relationship of the proxy material and the merger are questions of fact to be resolved at trial, not here. We therefore do not discuss this point further.

III.

While the respondent contends that his Count 2 claim is not a derivative one, we need not embrace that view, for we believe that a right of action exists as to both derivative and direct causes.

The purpose of § 14(a) is to prevent management or others from obtaining authorization for corporate action by means of deceptive or inadequate disclosure in proxy solicitation. The section stemmed from the congressional belief that "[f]air corporate suffrage is an important right that should attach to every equity security bought on a public exchange." H.R.Rep. No. 1383, 73d Cong., 2d Sess., 13. It was intended to "control the conditions under which proxies may be solicited with a view to preventing the recurrence of abuses which * * * [had] frustrated the free exercise of the voting rights of stockholders." Id., at 14. "Too often proxies are solicited without explanation to the stockholder of the real nature of the questions for which authority to cast his vote is sought." S.Rep. No. 792, 73d Cong., 2d Sess., 12. These broad remedial purposes are evidenced in the language of the section which makes it "unlawful for any person * * * to solicit or to permit the use of his name to solicit any proxy or consent or authorization in respect of any security * * * registered on any national securities exchange in contravention of such rules and regulations as the Commission may prescribe as necessary or appropriate in the public interest *or for the protection of investors.*" (Italics supplied.) While this language makes no specific reference to a private right of action, among its chief purposes is "the protection of investors," which certainly implies the availability of judicial relief where necessary to achieve that result.

The injury which a stockholder suffers from corporate action pursuant to a deceptive proxy solicitation ordinarily flows from the damage done the corporation, rather than from the damage inflicted directly upon the stockholder. The damage suffered results not from the deceit practiced on him alone but rather from the deceit practiced on the stockholders as a group. To hold that derivative actions are not within the sweep of the section would therefore be tantamount to a denial of private relief. Private enforcement of the proxy rules provides a necessary supplement to Commission action. As in antitrust treble damage litigation, the possibility of civil damages or injunctive relief serves as a most effective weapon in the enforcement of the proxy requirements. The Commission advises that it examines over 2,000 proxy statements annually and each of them must necessarily be expedited. Time does not permit an independent examination of the facts set out in the proxy material and this results in the Commission's acceptance of the representations contained therein at their face value, unless contrary to other material on file with it. Indeed, on the allegations of respondent's complaint, the proxy material failed to disclose alleged unlawful market manipulation of the stock of ATC, and this unlawful manipulation would not have been apparent to the Commission until after the merger.

We, therefore, believe that under the circumstances here it is the duty of the courts to be alert to provide such remedies as are necessary to make effective the congressional purpose. As was said in Sola Electric Co. v. Jefferson Electric Co., 317 U.S. 173, 176, 63 S.Ct. 172, 174, 87 L.Ed. 165 (1942):

> When a federal statute condemns an act as unlawful, the extent and nature of the legal consequences of the condemnation, though left by the statute to judicial determination, are nevertheless federal questions, the answers to which are to be derived from the statute and the federal policy which it has adopted.

It is for the federal courts "to adjust their remedies so as to grant the necessary relief" where federally secured rights are invaded. "And it is also well settled that where legal rights have been invaded, and a federal statute provides for a general right to sue for such invasion, federal courts may use any available remedy to make good the wrong done." Bell v. Hood, 327 U.S. 678, 684, 66 S.Ct. 773, 777, 90 L.Ed. 939 (1946). Section 27 grants the District Courts jurisdiction "of all suits in equity and actions at law brought to enforce any liability or duty created by this title * * *." In passing on almost identical language found in the Securities Act of 1933, the Court found the words entirely sufficient to fashion a remedy to rescind a fraudulent sale, secure restitution and even to enforce the right to restitution against a third party holding assets of the vendor. Deckert v. Independence Shares Corp., 311 U.S. 282, 61 S.Ct. 229, 85 L.Ed. 189 (1940). This significant language was used:

"The power to *enforce* implies the power to make effective the right of recovery afforded by the Act. And the power to make the right of recovery effective implies the power to utilize any of the procedures or actions normally available to the litigant according to the exigencies of the particular case." At 288 of 311 U.S., at 233 of 61 S.Ct.

Nor do we find merit in the contention that such remedies are limited to prospective relief. This was the position taken in Dann v. Studebaker–Packard Corp., 6 Cir., 288 F.2d 201, where it was held that the "preponderance of questions of state law which would have to be interpreted and applied in order to grant the relief sought * * * is so great that the federal question involved * * * is really negligible in comparison." At 214. But we believe that the overriding federal law applicable here would, where the facts required, control the appropriateness of redress despite the provisions of state corporation law, for it "is not uncommon for federal courts to fashion federal law where federal rights are concerned." Textile Workers Union of America v. Lincoln Mills, 353 U.S. 448, 457, 77 S.Ct. 912, 918, 1 L.Ed.2d 972 (1957). In addition, the fact that questions of state law must be decided does not change the character of the right; it remains federal. As Chief Justice Marshall said in Osborn v. Bank of United States, 9 Wheat. 738, 6 L.Ed. 204 (1824):

> If this were sufficient to withdraw a case from the jurisdiction of the federal Courts, almost every case, although involving the construction of a law, would be withdrawn * * *. At 819–820 of 9 Wheat.

Moreover, if federal jurisdiction were limited to the granting of declaratory relief, victims of deceptive proxy statements would be obliged to go into state courts for remedial relief. And if the law of the State happened to attach no responsibility to the use of misleading proxy statements, the whole purpose of the section might be frustrated. Furthermore, the hurdles that the victim might face (such as separate suits, as contemplated by Dann v. Studebaker–Packard Corp., supra, security for expenses statutes, bringing in all parties necessary for complete relief, etc.) might well prove insuperable to effective relief.

IV.

Our finding that federal courts have the power to grant all necessary remedial relief is not to be construed as any indication of what we believe to be the necessary and appropriate relief in this case. We are concerned here only with a determination that federal jurisdiction for this purpose does exist. Whatever remedy is necessary must await the trial on the merits.

The other contentions of the petitioners are denied.

Affirmed.

Notes

(1) The significant issue in the Borak case, discussed by the Court rather summarily, was whether a private cause of action existed for violations of Rule 14a–9. The same question has arisen under a number of statutes and regulations since 1964, several involving other provisions of the securities acts. It is clear that the Supreme Court no longer follows the rather free-wheeling and broad brush approach used by Justice Clark in *Borak*. In Touche Ross & Co. v. Redington, 442

U.S. 560, 575–78, 99 S.Ct. 2479, 2489–90, 61 L.Ed.2d 82, 95–97 (1979), Justice Rehnquist writing for the court dismissed an argument based on *Borak* by stating "in a series of cases since *Borak* we have adhered to a stricter standard for the implication of private causes of action, and we follow that stricter standard today." Despite the change in attitude about the implication of private causes of action under federal statutes and regulations, the holding in *Borak* itself, that a private cause of action exists under rule 14a–9, has not been seriously questioned.

(2) The private cause of action recognized in the principal case was materially strengthened by the Supreme Court's decision in Mills v. Electric Auto–Lite Co., 396 U.S. 375, 90 S.Ct. 616, 24 L.Ed.2d 593 (1970). This case involved a proxy statement relating to a proposed merger where the misstatement did not go to the value of the transaction itself but to the manner of its approval. The proxy statement had prominently disclosed that Electric Auto–Lite's board of directors had recommended approval of the merger but did not disclose that Auto–Lite's board had in fact been selected by the other party to the merger, Merganthaler Linotype Company, which had owned or controlled about 54 percent of Auto–Lite's shares for several years. Would the failure to disclose this additional information have influenced the decisions of shareholders as to whether or not to vote in favor of the merger? The principal issue before the Supreme Court, however, was not whether the statements made in the proxy statement were materially misleading but rather, assuming that they were, what standard of causation should exist between the materially misleading statement and the transaction in order to set forth a claim under rule 14a–9. Justice Harlan's opinion set forth a rule that is easily applied:

> The decision below, by permitting all liability to be foreclosed on the basis of a finding that the merger was fair, would allow the stockholders to be bypassed, at least where the only legal challenge to the merger is a suit for retrospective relief after the meeting has been held. A judicial appraisal of the merger's merits could be substituted for the actual and informed vote of the stockholders. The result would be to insulate from private redress an entire category of proxy violations—those relating to matters other than the terms of the merger. Even outrageous misrepresentations in a proxy solicitation, if they did not relate to the terms of the transaction, would give rise to no cause of action under § 14(a). Particularly if carried over to enforcement actions by the Securities and Exchange Commission itself, such a result would subvert the congressional purpose of ensuring full and fair disclosure to shareholders.

> Further, recognition of the fairness of the merger as a complete defense would confront small shareholders with an additional obstacle to making a successful challenge to a proposal recommended through a defective proxy statement. The risk that they would be unable to rebut the corporation's evidence of the fairness of the proposal, and thus to establish their cause of action, would be bound to discourage such shareholders from the private enforcement of the proxy rules that "provides a necessary supplement to Commission action." J.I. Case Co. v. Borak, 377 U.S., at 432, 84 S.Ct. at 1560.[83] * * *

83. [By the Court] The Court of Appeals' ruling that "causation" may be negated by proof of the fairness of the merger also rests on a dubious behavioral assumption. There is no justification for presuming that the shareholders of every corporation are willing to accept any and every fair merger offer put before them; yet such a presumption is implicit in the opinion of the Court of Appeals. That court gave no indication of what evidence petitioners might adduce, once respondents had established that the merger proposal was equitable, in order to show that the shareholders would nevertheless have rejected it if the solicitation had not been misleading. * * *

Holding in
Electric-Auto:
Even if
shareholders
got a fair
deal, if an
honest proxy
statement would
have effected
their descision

Where the misstatement or omission in a proxy statement has been shown to be "material," as it was found to be here, that determination itself indubitably embodies a conclusion that the defect was of such a character that it might have been considered important by a reasonable shareholder who was in the process of deciding how to vote.[84] This requirement that the defect have a significant *propensity* to affect the voting process is found in the express terms of Rule 14a–9, and it adequately serves the purpose of ensuring that a cause of action cannot be established by proof of a defect so trivial, or so unrelated to the transaction for which approval is sought, that correction of the defect or imposition of liability would not further the interests protected by § 14(a).

There is no need to supplement this requirement, as did the Court of Appeals, with a requirement of proof of whether the defect actually had a decisive effect on the voting. Where there has been a finding of materiality, a shareholder has made a sufficient showing of causal relationship between the violation and the injury for which he seeks redress if, as here, he proves that the proxy solicitation itself, rather than the particular defect in the solicitation materials, was an essential link in the accomplishment of the transaction. This objective test will avoid the impracticalities of determining how many votes were affected, and, by resolving doubts in favor of those the statute is designed to protect, will effectuate the congressional policy of ensuring that the shareholders are able to make an informed choice when they are consulted on corporate transactions.

396 U.S. at 381–85, 90 S.Ct. at 620–22, 24 L.Ed.2d at 600–02.

(3) Why didn't the plaintiffs in *Mills* seek a temporary restraining order? Not having done so, and the merger having been completed, what remedy can the Court provide? Justice Harlan also considered this question:

Our conclusion that petitioners have established their case by showing that proxies necessary to approval of the merger were obtained by means of a materially misleading solicitation implies nothing about the form of relief to which they may be entitled. We held in *Borak* that upon finding a violation the courts were "to be alert to provide such remedies as are necessary to make effective the congressional purpose," noting specifically that such remedies are not to be limited to prospective relief. 377 U.S., at 433, 434, 84 S.Ct. at 1560. In devising retrospective relief for violation of the proxy rules, the federal courts should consider the same factors that would govern the relief granted for any similar illegality or fraud. One important factor may be the fairness of the terms of the merger. Possible forms of relief will include setting aside the merger or granting other equitable relief, but, as the Court of Appeals below noted, nothing in the statutory policy "requires the court to unscramble a corporate transaction merely because a violation occurred." 403

---

84. [By the Court] In this case, where the misleading aspect of the solicitation involved failure to reveal a serious conflict of interest on the part of the directors, the Court of Appeals concluded that the crucial question in determining materiality was "whether the minority shareholders were sufficiently alerted to the board's relationship to their adversary to be on their guard." 403 F.2d, at 434. An adequate disclosure of this relationship would have warned the stockholders to give more careful scrutiny to the terms of the merger than they might have given to one recommended by an entirely disinterested board. Thus, the failure to make such a disclosure was found to be a material defect "as a matter of law," thwarting the informed decision at which the statute aims, regardless of whether the terms of the merger were such that a reasonable stockholder would have approved the transaction after more careful analysis.

F.2d, at 436. In selecting a remedy, the lower courts should exercise " 'the sound discretion which guides the determinations of courts of equity,' keeping in mind the role of equity as 'the instrument for nice adjustment and reconciliation between the public interest and private needs as well as between competing private claims.' " Hecht Co. v. Bowles, 321 U.S. 321, 329–330, 64 S.Ct. 587, 591–592, 88 L.Ed. 754 (1944), quoting from Meredith v. Winter Haven, 320 U.S. 228, 235, 64 S.Ct. 7, 11, 88 L.Ed. 9 (1943). * * *

Monetary relief will, of course, also be a possibility. Where the defect in the proxy solicitation relates to the specific terms of the merger, the district court might appropriately order an accounting to ensure that the shareholders receive the value that was represented as coming to them. On the other hand, where, as here, the misleading aspect of the solicitation did not relate to terms of the merger, monetary relief might be afforded to the shareholders only if the merger resulted in a reduction of the earnings or earnings potential of their holdings. In short, damages should be recoverable only to the extent that they can be shown. If commingling of the assets and operations of the merged companies makes it impossible to establish direct injury from the merger, relief might be predicated on a determination of the fairness of the terms of the merger at the time it was approved. These questions, of course, are for decision in the first instance by the District Court on remand, and our singling out of some of the possibilities is not intended to exclude others.

396 U.S. at 386–89, 90 S.Ct. at 622–24, 24 L.Ed.2d at 603–04.

(4) In *Mills*, Justice Harlan also concluded that the minority shareholders' attorneys should be entitled to an interim award of attorneys' fees from Auto–Lite (actually from Merganthaler, its successor, since the merger had been completed) on the basis of a partial summary judgment on the issue of liability:

The result would have been, not only that respondents, rather than petitioners, would have borne the costs of the appeal, but also, we think, that petitioners would have been entitled to an interim award of litigation expenses and reasonable attorneys' fees. We agree with the position taken by petitioners, and by the United States as *amicus*, that petitioners, who have established a violation of the securities laws by their corporation and its officials, should be reimbursed by the corporation or its survivor for the costs of establishing the violation.

The absence of express statutory authorization for an award of attorneys' fees in a suit under § 14(a) does not preclude such an award in cases of this type. * * *

While the general American rule is that attorneys' fees are not ordinarily recoverable as costs, both the courts and Congress have developed exceptions to this rule for situations in which overriding considerations indicate the need for such a recovery. A primary judge-created exception has been to award expenses where a plaintiff has successfully maintained a suit, usually on behalf of a class, that benefits a group of others in the same manner as himself. To allow the others to obtain full benefit from the plaintiff's efforts without contributing equally to the litigation expenses would be to enrich the others unjustly at the plaintiff's expense. This suit presents such a situation. The dissemination of misleading proxy solicitations was a "deceit practiced on the stockholders as a group," J.I. Case Co. v. Borak, 377 U.S., at 432, 84 S.Ct., at 1560, and the expenses of petitioners' lawsuit have been incurred for the benefit of the corporation and the other shareholders.

The fact that this suit has not yet produced, and may never produce, a monetary recovery from which the fees could be paid does not preclude an award based on this rationale. * * *

In many suits under § 14(a), particularly where the violation does not relate to the terms of the transaction for which proxies are solicited, it may be impossible to assign monetary value to the benefit. Nevertheless, the stress placed by Congress on the importance of fair and informed corporate suffrage leads to the conclusion that, in vindicating the statutory policy, petitioners have rendered a substantial service to the corporation and its shareholders. Whether petitioners are successful in showing a need for significant relief may be a factor in determining whether a further award should later be made. But regardless of the relief granted, private stockholders' actions of this sort "involve corporate therapeutics," and furnish a benefit to all shareholders by providing an important means of enforcement of the proxy statute. To award attorneys' fees in such a suit to a plaintiff who has succeeded in establishing a cause of action is not to saddle the unsuccessful party with the expenses but to impose them on the class that has benefited from them and that would have had to pay them had it brought the suit.

396 U.S. at 389–92, 396–97, 90 S.Ct. at 624–25, 627–28, 24 L.Ed.2d, at 605–06, 608–09. This last holding was too much for Justice Black, who commented that he did not agree with the holding "that stockholders who hire lawyers to prosecute their claims in such a case can recover attorneys' fees in the absence of a valid contractual agreement so providing or an explicit statute creating such a right of recovery." He added, "The courts are interpreters, not creators, of legal rights to recover and if there is a need for recovery of attorneys' fees to effectuate the policies of the Act here involved, that need should, in my judgment, be met by Congress, not by this Court." 396 U.S. at 397, 90 S.Ct. at 628, 24 L.Ed.2d, at 609. The leading post-*Mills* case involving the shifting of attorneys' fees is Alyeska Pipeline Serv. Co. v. Wilderness Soc'y, 421 U.S. 240, 95 S.Ct. 1612, 44 L.Ed.2d 141 (1975), where the Court held that it was improper to award attorneys' fees to several environmental organizations on the theory that they were acting as a "private attorney general." *Mills* was cited as an example of the "historic power of equity to permit the trustee of a fund or property, or a party preserving or recovering a fund for the benefit of others in addition to himself, to recover his costs, including his attorneys' fees, from the fund or property itself or directly from the other parties enjoying the benefit." 421 U.S. at 257–58, 95 S.Ct. at 1621–22, 44 L.Ed.2d at 153. The dissent argued that *Mills* and other cases simply cannot be reconciled with the majority's argument.

(5) Both the causation holding and the interim award of attorneys' fees in *Mills* undoubtedly encouraged the development of entrepreneurial class and derivative litigation by plaintiffs' attorneys in the securities area. Justice Black's dissent in *Mills* apparently assumed that the individual shareholders who served as plaintiffs in this litigation actually selected their lawyers. The reality, however, is often far different. Consult John C. Coffee, Jr., Understanding the Plaintiff's Attorney: The Implications of Economic Theory for Private Enforcement of Law Through Class and Derivative Actions, 86 Colum.L.Rev. 669, 677–79, 681–84 (1986) (arguing that the American legal system has long accepted, if somewhat uneasily, the concept of the plaintiff's attorney in class and derivative actions as an entrepreneur who performs the socially useful function of deterring undesirable conduct, and thus the attorney may expend more resources to find a violation first and a [nominal] client second). The dynamics with respect to section 14(a) litigation were dramatically changed first in 1995 by the enactment of the Private

Securities Litigation Reform Act of 1995, Pub. Law 104–67, 109 Stat. 737, and second in 1998 by the Securities Litigation Uniform Standards Act, Pub. Law 105–353, 112 Stat. 3235. The background and impact of this legislation is discussed in Chapter 13, section D.

(6) In Mills v. Elec. Auto–Lite Co., 552 F.2d 1239 (7th Cir.1977), cert. denied, 434 U.S. 922, 98 S.Ct. 398, 54 L.Ed.2d 279, the Court reversed the lower court's award of damages of $1,233,918.35 plus interest and, concluding that the merger terms were fair, held that the plaintiffs should recover nothing. The Court further held that the plaintiffs were not entitled to compensation for fees and expenses incurred after their initial victory in the United States Supreme Court, citing *Alyeska*.

TSC INDUS., INC. v. NORTHWAY, INC.

Supreme Court of the United States, 1976.
426 U.S. 438, 96 S.Ct. 2126, 48 L.Ed.2d 757.

JUSTICE MARSHALL delivered the opinion of the Court.

The proxy rules promulgated by the Securities and Exchange Commission under the Securities Exchange Act of 1934 bar the use of proxy statements that are false or misleading with respect to the presentation or omission of material facts. We are called upon to consider the definition of a material fact under those rules, and the appropriateness of resolving the question of materiality by summary judgment in this case.

I

The dispute in this case centers on the acquisition of petitioner TSC Industries, Inc., by petitioner National Industries, Inc. In February 1969 National acquired 34% of TSC's voting securities by purchase from Charles E. Schmidt and his family. Schmidt, who had been TSC's founder and principal shareholder, promptly resigned along with his son from TSC's board of directors. Thereafter, five National nominees were placed on TSC's board; and Stanley R. Yarmuth, National's president and chief executive officer, became chairman of the TSC board, and Charles F. Simonelli, National's executive vice president, became chairman of the TSC executive committee. On October 16, 1969, the TSC board, with the attending National nominees abstaining, approved a proposal to liquidate and sell all of TSC's assets to National. * * * On November 12, 1969, TSC and National issued a joint proxy statement to their shareholders, recommending approval of the proposal. The proxy solicitation was successful, * * * and the exchange of shares was effected.

This is an action brought by respondent Northway, a TSC shareholder, against TSC and National, claiming that their joint proxy statement was incomplete and materially misleading in violation of § 14(a) of the Securities Exchange Act of 1934, and Rules 14a–3 and 14a–9, promulgated thereunder. The basis of Northway's claim under Rule 14a–3 is that TSC and National failed to state in the proxy statement that the transfer of the Schmidt interests in TSC to National had given National control of TSC. The Rule 14a–9 claim, insofar as it concerns us, is that TSC and National omitted from the proxy statement material facts relating to the degree of National's control over TSC and the favorability of the terms of the proposal to TSC shareholders.

* * * [T]he Court of Appeals reversed the District Court's denial of summary judgment to Northway on its Rule 14a–9 claims, holding that certain omissions of fact were material as a matter of law. 512 F.2d 324 (1975).

We granted certiorari because the standard applied by the Court of Appeals in resolving the question of materiality appeared to conflict with the standard applied by other Courts of Appeals. 423 U.S. 820, 96 S.Ct. 33, 46 L.Ed.2d 37 (1975). We now hold that the Court of Appeals erred in ordering that partial summary judgment be granted to Northway.

II

A

As we have noted on more than one occasion, § 14(a) of the Securities Exchange Act "was intended to promote 'the free exercise of the voting rights of stockholders' by ensuring that proxies would be solicited with 'explanation to the stockholder of the real nature of the questions for which authority to cast his vote is sought.' " Mills v. Electric Auto–Lite Co., 396 U.S. 375, 381, 90 S.Ct. 616, 620, 24 L.Ed.2d 593 (1970). See also J.I. Case Co. v. Borak, 377 U.S. 426, 431, 84 S.Ct. 1555, 1559, 12 L.Ed.2d 423 (1964). In *Borak,* the Court held that § 14(a)'s broad remedial purposes required recognition under § 27 of the Securities Exchange Act, of an implied private right of action for violations of the provision. And in *Mills,* we attempted to clarify to some extent the elements of a private cause of action for violation of § 14(a). In a suit challenging the sufficiency under § 14(a) and Rule 14a–9 of a proxy statement soliciting votes in favor of a merger, we held that there was no need to demonstrate that the alleged defect in the proxy statement actually had a decisive effect on the voting. So long as the misstatement or omission was material, the causal relation between violation and injury is sufficiently established, we concluded, if "the proxy solicitation itself * * * was an essential link in the accomplishment of the transaction." 396 U.S., at 385, 90 S.Ct., at 622. After *Mills,* then, the content given to the notion of materiality assumes heightened significance.[85]

B

The question of materiality, it is universally agreed, is an objective one, involving the significance of an omitted or misrepresented fact to a reasonable investor. Variations in the formulation of a general test of materiality occur in the articulation of just how significant a fact must be or, put another way, how certain it must be that the fact would affect a reasonable investor's judgment.

The Court of Appeals in this case concluded that material facts include "all facts which a reasonable shareholder *might* consider important." 512 F.2d, at 330 (emphasis added). This formulation of the test of materiality has been explicitly rejected by at least two courts as setting too low a threshold for the imposition of liability under Rule 14a–9. * * *

---

85. [By the Court] Our cases have not considered, and we have no occasion in this case to consider, what showing of culpability is required to establish the liability under § 14(a) of a corporation issuing a materially misleading proxy statement, or of a person involved in the preparation of a materially misleading proxy statement. See Ernst & Ernst v. Hochfelder, 425 U.S. 185, 209 n. 28, 96 S.Ct. 1375, 1388, 47 L.Ed.2d 668 (1976).

C

In formulating a standard of materiality under Rule 14a–9, we are guided, of course, by the recognition in *Borak* and *Mills* of the Rule's broad remedial purpose. That purpose is not merely to ensure by judicial means that the transaction, when judged by its real terms, is fair and otherwise adequate, but to ensure disclosures by corporate management in order to enable the shareholders to make an informed choice. As an abstract proposition, the most desirable role for a court in a suit of this sort, coming after the consummation of the proposed transaction, would perhaps be to determine whether in fact the proposal would have been favored by the shareholders and consummated in the absence of any misstatement or omission. But as we recognized in *Mills,* supra, at 382 n.5, 90 S.Ct., at 620, such matters are not subject to determination with certainty. Doubts as to the critical nature of information misstated or omitted will be commonplace. And particularly in view of the prophylactic purpose of the Rule and the fact that the content of the proxy statement is within management's control, it is appropriate that these doubts be resolved in favor of those the statute is designed to protect.

We are aware, however, that the disclosure policy embodied in the proxy regulations is not without limit. Some information is of such dubious significance that insistence on its disclosure may accomplish more harm than good. The potential liability for a Rule 14a–9 violation can be great indeed, and if the standard of materiality is unnecessarily low, not only may the corporation and its management be subjected to liability for insignificant omissions or misstatements, but also management's fear of exposing itself to substantial liability may cause it simply to bury the shareholders in an avalanche of trivial information—a result that is hardly conducive to informed decision-making. Precisely these dangers are presented, we think, by the definition of a material fact adopted by the Court of Appeals in this case—a fact which a reasonable shareholder *might* consider important. We agree with Judge Friendly, speaking for the Court of Appeals in *Gerstle,* that the "might" formulation is "too suggestive of mere possibility, however unlikely." 478 F.2d, at 1302.

The general standard of materiality that we think best comports with the policies of Rule 14a–9 is as follows: An omitted fact is material if there is a substantial likelihood that a reasonable shareholder would consider it important in deciding how to vote. This standard is fully consistent with *Mills* general description of materiality as a requirement that "the defect have a significant *propensity* to affect the voting process." It does not require proof of a substantial likelihood that disclosure of the omitted fact would have caused the reasonable investor to change his vote. What the standard does contemplate is a showing of a substantial likelihood that, under all the circumstances, the omitted fact would have assumed actual significance in the deliberations of the reasonable shareholder. Put another way, there must be a substantial likelihood that the disclosure of the omitted fact would have been viewed by the reasonable investor as having significantly altered the "total mix" of information made available.[86]

86. [By the Court] In defining materiality under Rule 14a–9, we are, of course, giving content to a rule promulgated by the SEC pursuant to broad statutory authority to promote "the public interest" and "the protection of investors." Cf. Ernst & Ernst v. Hochfelder,

D

The issue of materiality may be characterized as a mixed question of law and fact, involving as it does the application of a legal standard to a particular set of facts. In considering whether summary judgment on the issue is appropriate, we must bear in mind that the underlying objective facts, which will often be free from dispute, are merely the starting point for the ultimate determination of materiality. The determination requires delicate assessments of the inferences a "reasonable shareholder" would draw from a given set of facts and the significance of those inferences to him, and these assessments are peculiarly ones for the trier of fact. Only if the established omissions are "so obviously important to an investor, that reasonable minds cannot differ on the question of materiality" is the ultimate issue of materiality appropriately resolved "as a matter of law" by summary judgment. * * *

[In Part III of its opinion the Court conducts a careful reexamination of the facts and concludes that none of the claimed omissions were material.]

IV

In summary, none of the omissions claimed to have been in violation of Rule 14a–9 were, so far as the record reveals, materially misleading as a matter of law, and Northway was not entitled to partial summary judgment. The judgment of the Court of Appeals is reversed, and the case is remanded for further proceedings consistent with this opinion.

It is so ordered.

JUSTICE STEVENS took no part in the consideration or decision of this case.

Notes

(1) What are the implications of this decision for the interim recovery of plaintiffs' fees and expenses under *Mills*?

(2) Shidler v. All American Life & Fin. Corp., 775 F.2d 917 (8th Cir.1985) involved a proxy statement for a merger that included a statement that under Iowa law the transaction required the approval of two-thirds of all classes of shares, common and preferred, voting together in a single election. This statement turned out to be incorrect since the Iowa Supreme Court later concluded that Iowa law required a two-thirds vote of each class of shares, voting separately. Shidler v. All American Life & Fin. Corp., 298 N.W.2d 318 (Iowa 1980). This result, however, could hardly have been predicted with certainty since the issue was a novel one under Iowa law. In holding that no claim for relief under Rule 14a–9 was stated, the Court concluded that Rule 14a–9 did not impose strict liability, and that the lower court's conclusion that the corporation and its directors were not negligent in including the incorrect statement was not "clearly erroneous." The Court held, however, that a claim might be stated under Iowa law for damages for conversion or breach of contract. Consult also Nelson v. All American Life & Fin. Corp., 889 F.2d 141 (8th Cir.1989).

425 U.S., at 212–214, 96 S.Ct., at 1390–1391. Under these circumstances, the SEC's view of the proper balance between the need to insure adequate disclosure and the need to avoid the adverse consequences of setting too low a threshold for civil liability is entitled to consideration. The standard we adopt is supported by the SEC.

VIRGINIA BANKSHARES, INC. v. SANDBERG

Supreme Court of the United States, 1991.
501 U.S. 1083, 111 S.Ct. 2749, 115 L.Ed.2d 929.

JUSTICE SOUTER delivered the opinion of the Court.

* * * The questions before us are whether a statement couched in conclusory or qualitative terms purporting to explain directors' reasons for recommending certain corporate action can be materially misleading within the meaning of Rule 14a–9, and whether causation of damages compensable under § 14(a) can be shown by a member of a class of minority shareholders whose votes are not required by law or corporate bylaw to authorize the corporate action subject to the proxy solicitation. We hold that knowingly false statements of reason may be actionable even though conclusory in form, but that respondents have failed to demonstrate the equitable basis required to extend the § 14(a) private action to such shareholders when any indication of congressional intent to do so is lacking.

I

In December 1986, First American Bankshares, Inc., (FABI), a bank holding company, began a "freeze-out" merger,[87] in which the First American Bank of Virginia (Bank) eventually merged into Virginia Bankshares, Inc., (VBI), a wholly owned subsidiary of FABI. VBI owned 85% of the Bank's shares, the remaining 15% being in the hands of some 2,000 minority shareholders. FABI hired the investment banking firm of Keefe, Bruyette & Woods (KBW) to give an opinion on the appropriate price for shares of the minority holders, who would lose their interests in the Bank as a result of the merger. Based on market quotations and unverified information from FABI, KBW gave the Bank's executive committee an opinion that $42 a share would be a fair price for the minority stock. The executive committee approved the merger proposal at that price, and the full board followed suit.

Although Virginia law required only that such a merger proposal be submitted to a vote at a shareholders' meeting, and that the meeting be preceded by circulation of a statement of information to the shareholders, the directors nevertheless solicited proxies for voting on the proposal at the annual meeting set for April 21, 1987.[88] In their solicitation, the directors urged the proposal's adoption and stated they had approved the plan because of its opportunity for the minority shareholders to achieve a "high" value, which they elsewhere described as a "fair" price, for their stock.

Although most minority shareholders gave the proxies requested, respondent Sandberg did not, and after approval of the merger, she sought damages in the United States District Court for the Eastern District of Virginia from VBI, FABI, and the directors of the Bank. She pleaded two counts, one for soliciting proxies in violation of § 14(a) and Rule 14a–9, and the other for

---

87. [By the Editors] In a "freeze-out" merger, minority shareholders (who do not have the power to block the merger with their votes) are required to accept cash in a specified amount for their shares and have no right to a continuing ownership interest in the combined entity. However, if dissatisfied with the offered price, minority shareholders have the statutory right of dissent-and-appraisal that permits them, if they follow prescribed procedures, to have a judicial appraisal of the value of their shares and be paid that appraised value. Freeze-out mergers are discussed in chapters 8 and 9.

88. [By the Court] Had the directors chosen to issue a statement instead of a proxy solicitation, they would have been subject to an SEC antifraud provision analogous to Rule 14a–9. See 17 CFR 240.14c–6 (1990).

breaching fiduciary duties owed to the minority shareholders under state law. Under the first count, Sandberg alleged, among other things, that the directors had not believed that the price offered was high or that the terms of the merger were fair, but had recommended the merger only because they believed they had no alternative if they wished to remain on the board. At trial, Sandberg invoked language from this Court's opinion in *Mills v. Electric Auto–Lite Co.*, 396 U.S. 375, 385, 90 S.Ct. 616, 622, 24 L.Ed.2d 593 (1970), to obtain an instruction that the jury could find for her without a showing of her own reliance on the alleged misstatements, so long as they were material and the proxy solicitation was an "essential link" in the merger process.

The jury's verdicts were for Sandberg on both counts, after finding violations of Rule 14a–9 by all defendants and a breach of fiduciary duties by the Bank's directors. The jury awarded Sandberg $18 a share, having found that she would have received $60 if her stock had been valued adequately. * * *

On appeal, the United States Court of Appeals for the Fourth Circuit affirmed * * *, holding that certain statements in the proxy solicitation were materially misleading for purposes of the Rule, and that respondents could maintain their action even though their votes had not been needed to effectuate the merger. 891 F.2d 1112 (1989).[89] We granted certiorari because of the importance of the issues presented. 495 U.S. 903, 110 S.Ct. 1921, 109 L.Ed.2d 285 (1990).

II

The Court of Appeals affirmed petitioners' liability for two statements found to have been materially misleading in violation of § 14(a) of the Act, one of which was that "The Plan of Merger has been approved by the Board of Directors because it provides an opportunity for the Bank's public shareholders to achieve a high value for their shares." Petitioners argue that statements of opinion or belief incorporating indefinite and unverifiable expressions cannot be actionable as misstatements of material fact within the meaning of Rule 14a–9, and that such a declaration of opinion or belief should never be actionable when placed in a proxy solicitation incorporating statements of fact sufficient to enable readers to draw their own, independent conclusions.

A

We consider first the actionability per se of statements of reasons, opinion or belief. Because such a statement by definition purports to express what is consciously on the speaker's mind, we interpret the jury verdict as finding that the directors' statements of belief and opinion were made with knowledge that the directors did not hold the beliefs or opinions expressed, and we confine our discussion to statements so made. That such statements may be materially significant raises no serious question. * * *

89. [By the Court] The Court of Appeals reversed the District Court, however, on its refusal to certify a class of all minority shareholders in Sandberg's action. Consequently, it ruled that petitioners were liable to all of the Bank's former minority shareholders for $18 per share. 891 F.2d, at 1119.

B

1

But, assuming materiality, the question remains whether statements of reasons, opinions, or beliefs are statements "with respect to * * * material fact[s]" so as to fall within the strictures of the Rule. * * *

* * * [D]irectors' statements of reasons or belief * * * are factual in two senses: as statements that the directors do act for the reasons given or hold the belief stated and as statements about the subject matter of the reason or belief expressed. In neither sense does the proof or disproof of such statements * * * [permit the plaintiff] to manufacture claims of hypothetical action, unconstrained by independent evidence. Reasons for directors' recommendations or statements of belief are * * * characteristically matters of corporate record subject to documentation, to be supported or attacked by evidence of historical fact outside a plaintiff's control. Such evidence would include not only corporate minutes and other statements of the directors themselves, but circumstantial evidence bearing on the facts that would reasonably underlie the reasons claimed and the honesty of any statement that those reasons are the basis for a recommendation or other action, a point that becomes especially clear when the reasons or beliefs go to valuations in dollars and cents.

It is no answer to argue, as petitioners do, that the quoted statement on which liability was predicated did not express a reason in dollars and cents, but focused instead on the "indefinite and unverifiable" term, "high" value, much like the similar claim that the merger's terms were "fair" to shareholders.[90] The objection ignores the fact that such conclusory terms in a commercial context are reasonably understood to rest on a factual basis that justifies them as accurate, the absence of which renders them misleading. Provable facts either furnish good reasons to make a conclusory commercial judgment, or they count against it, and expressions of such judgments can be uttered with knowledge of truth or falsity just like more definite statements, and defended or attacked through the orthodox evidentiary process that either substantiates their underlying justifications or tends to disprove their existence. In addressing the analogous issue in an action for misrepresentation, the court in *Day v. Avery*, 179 U.S.App.D.C. 63, 548 F.2d 1018 (1976), for example, held that a statement by the executive committee of a law firm that no partner would be any "worse off" solely because of an impending merger could be found to be a material misrepresentation. Id., at 70–72, 548 F.2d at 1025–1027. Cf. *Vulcan Metals Co. v. Simmons Mfg. Co.*, 248 F. 853, 856 (C.A.2 1918) (L. Hand, J.) ("An opinion is a fact * * * [w]hen the parties are so

---

90. [By the Court] Petitioners are also wrong to argue that construing the statute to allow recovery for a misleading statement that the merger was "fair" to the minority shareholders is tantamount to assuming federal authority to bar corporate transactions thought to be unfair to some group of shareholders. It is, of course, true that we said in *Santa Fe Industries, Inc. v. Green*, 430 U.S. 462, 479, 97 S.Ct. 1292, 1304, 51 L.Ed.2d 480 (1977), that " '[c]orporations are creatures of state law, and investors commit their funds to corporate directors on the understanding that, except where federal law *expressly* requires certain responsibilities of directors with respect to stockholders, state law will govern the internal affairs of the corporation,' " quoting *Cort v. Ash*, 422 U.S. 66, 84, 95 S.Ct. 2080, 2091, 45 L.Ed.2d 26 (1975). But § 14(a) does impose responsibility for false and misleading proxy statements. Although a corporate transaction's "fairness" is not, as such, a federal concern, a proxy statement's claim of fairness presupposes a factual integrity that federal law is expressly concerned to preserve.

situated that the buyer may reasonably rely upon the expression of the seller's opinion, it is no excuse to give a false one"). In this case, whether $42 was "high," and the proposal "fair" to the minority shareholders depended on whether provable facts about the Bank's assets, and about actual and potential levels of operation, substantiated a value that was above, below, or more or less at the $42 figure, when assessed in accordance with recognized methods of valuation.

Respondents adduced evidence for just such facts in proving that the statement was misleading about its subject matter and a false expression of the directors' reasons. Whereas the proxy statement described the $42 price as offering a premium above both book value and market price, the evidence indicated that a calculation of the book figure based on the appreciated value of the Bank's real estate holdings eliminated any such premium. The evidence on the significance of market price showed that KBW had conceded that the market was closed, thin and dominated by FABI, facts omitted from the statement. There was, indeed, evidence of a "going concern" value for the Bank in excess of $60 per share of common stock, another fact never disclosed. However conclusory the directors' statement may have been, then, it was open to attack by garden-variety evidence, subject neither to a plaintiff's control nor ready manufacture, and there was no undue risk of open-ended liability or uncontrollable litigation in allowing respondents the opportunity for recovery on the allegation that it was misleading to call $42 "high." * * *

2

Under § 14(a), then, a plaintiff is permitted to prove a specific statement of reason knowingly false or misleadingly incomplete, even when stated in conclusory terms. In reaching this conclusion, we have considered statements of reasons of the sort exemplified here, which misstate the speaker's reasons and also mislead about the stated subject matter (e.g., the value of the shares). A statement of belief may be open to objection only in the former respect, however, solely as a misstatement of the psychological fact of the speaker's belief in what he says. In this case, for example, the Court of Appeals alluded to just such limited falsity in observing that "the jury was certainly justified in believing that the directors did not believe a merger at $42 per share was in the minority stockholders' interest but, rather, that they voted as they did for other reasons, e.g., retaining their seats on the board." 891 F.2d, at 1121.

The question arises, then, whether disbelief, or undisclosed belief or motivation, standing alone, should be a sufficient basis to sustain an action under § 14(a), absent proof by the sort of objective evidence described above that the statement also expressly or impliedly asserted something false or misleading about its subject matter. We think that proof of mere disbelief or belief undisclosed should not suffice for liability under § 14(a), and if nothing more had been required or proven in this case we would reverse for that reason. * * *

C

Petitioners' fall-back position assumes the same relationship between a conclusory judgment and its underlying facts that we described in Part II–B–

1, supra. Thus, citing *Radol v. Thomas*, 534 F.Supp. 1302, 1315, 1316 (S.D.Ohio 1982), petitioners argue that even if conclusory statements of reason or belief can be actionable under § 14(a), we should confine liability to instances where the proxy material fails to disclose the offending statement's factual basis. There would be no justification for holding the shareholders entitled to judicial relief, that is, when they were given evidence that a stated reason for a proxy recommendation was misleading, and an opportunity to draw that conclusion themselves.

The answer to this argument rests on the difference between a merely misleading statement and one that is materially so. While a misleading statement will not always lose its deceptive edge simply by joinder with others that are true, the true statements may discredit the other one so obviously that the risk of real deception drops to nil. Since liability under § 14(a) must rest not only on deceptiveness but materiality as well (i.e., it has to be significant enough to be important to a reasonable investor deciding how to vote), petitioners are on perfectly firm ground insofar as they argue that publishing accurate facts in a proxy statement can render a misleading proposition too unimportant to ground liability.

But not every mixture with the true will neutralize the deceptive. If it would take a financial analyst to spot the tension between the one and the other, whatever is misleading will remain materially so, and liability should follow. *Gerstle v. Gamble–Skogmo, Inc.*, 478 F.2d 1281, 1297 (C.A.2 1973) ("[I]t is not sufficient that overtones might have been picked up by the sensitive antennae of investment analysts"). * * * The point of a proxy statement, after all, should be to inform, not to challenge the reader's critical wits. Only when the inconsistency would exhaust the misleading conclusion's capacity to influence the reasonable shareholder would a § 14(a) action fail on the element of materiality.

Suffice it to say that the evidence invoked by petitioners in the instant case fell short of compelling the jury to find the facial materiality of the misleading statement neutralized. The directors claim, for example, to have made an explanatory disclosure of further reasons for their recommendation when they said they would keep their seats following the merger, but they failed to mention what at least one of them admitted in testimony, that they would have had no expectation of doing so without supporting the proposal.[91] And although the proxy statement did speak factually about the merger price in describing it as higher than share prices in recent sales, it failed even to mention the closed market dominated by FABI. None of these disclosures that the directors point to was, then, anything more than a half-truth, and the record shows that another fact statement they invoke was arguably even worse. The claim that the merger price exceeded book value was controverted, as we have seen already, by evidence of a higher book value than the directors

---

91. [By the Court] Petitioners fail to dissuade us from recognizing the significance of omissions such as this by arguing that we effectively require them to accuse themselves of breach of fiduciary duty. Subjection to liability for misleading others does not raise a duty of self-accusation; it enforces a duty to refrain from misleading. We have no occasion to decide whether the directors were obligated to state the reasons for their support of the merger proposal here, but there can be no question that the statement they did make carried with it no option to deceive. Cf. Berg v. First American Bankshares, Inc., 254 U.S.App.D.C. 198, 205, 796 F.2d 489, 496 (1986)("Once the proxy statement purported to disclose the factors considered * * *, there was an obligation to portray them accurately").

conceded, reflecting appreciation in the Bank's real estate portfolio. Finally, the solicitation omitted any mention of the Bank's value as a going concern at more than $60 a share, as against the merger price of $42. There was, in sum, no more of a compelling case for the statement's immateriality than for its accuracy.

III

The second issue before us, left open in *Mills v. Electric Auto–Lite Co.*, is whether causation of damages compensable through the implied private right of action under § 14(a) can be demonstrated by a member of a class of minority shareholders whose votes are not required by law or corporate bylaw to authorize the transaction giving rise to the claim. *J.I. Case Co. v. Borak*, 377 U.S. 426, 84 S.Ct. 1555, 12 L.Ed.2d 423 (1964), did not itself address the requisites of causation, as such, or define the class of plaintiffs eligible to sue under § 14(a). But its general holding, that a private cause of action was available to some shareholder class, acquired greater clarity with a more definite concept of causation in *Mills*, where we addressed the sufficiency of proof that misstatements in a proxy solicitation were responsible for damages claimed from the merger subject to complaint.

* * * The *Mills* Court avoided the evidentiary morass that would have followed from requiring individualized proof that enough minority shareholders had relied upon the misstatements to swing the vote [by holding] that causation of damages by a material proxy misstatement could be established by showing that minority proxies necessary and sufficient to authorize the corporate acts had been given in accordance with the tenor of the solicitation[. The] Court described such a causal relationship by calling the proxy solicitation an "essential link in the accomplishment of the transaction." In the case before it, the Court found the solicitation essential, as contrasted with one addressed to a class of minority shareholders without votes required by law or by-law to authorize the action proposed, and left it for another day to decide whether such a minority shareholder could demonstrate causation.

In this case, respondents address *Mills'* open question by proffering two theories that the proxy solicitation addressed to them was an "essential link" under the *Mills* causation test.[92] They argue, first, that a link existed and was essential simply because VBI and FABI would have been unwilling to proceed with the merger without the approval manifested by the minority shareholders' proxies, which would not have been obtained without the solicitation's express misstatements and misleading omissions. On this reasoning, the causal connection would depend on a desire to avoid bad shareholder or public relations, and the essential character of the causal link would stem not from

---

92. [By the Court] Citing the decision in Schlick v. Penn–Dixie Cement Corp., 507 F.2d 374, 382–383 (C.A.2 1974), petitioners characterize respondents' proffered theories as examples of so-called "sue facts" and "shame facts" theories. "A 'sue fact' is, in general, a fact which is material to a sue decision. A 'sue decision' is a decision by a shareholder whether or not to institute a representative or derivative suit alleging a state-law cause of action." Gelb, Rule 10b–5 and Santa Fe—Herein of Sue Facts, Shame Facts, and Other Matters, 87 W.Va.L.Rev. 189, 198, and n. 52 (1985), quoting Borden, "Sue Fact" Rule Mandates Disclosure to Avoid Litigation in State Courts, 10 SEC § 82, pp. 201, 204–205 (1982). See also Note, Causation and Liability in Private Actions for Proxy Violations, 80 Yale L.J. 107, 116 (1970) (discussing theories of causation). "Shame facts" are said to be facts which, had they been disclosed, would have "shamed" management into abandoning a proposed transaction.

the enforceable terms of the parties' corporate relationship, but from one party's apprehension of the ill will of the other.

In the alternative, respondents argue that the proxy statement was an essential link between the directors' proposal and the merger because it was the means to satisfy a state statutory requirement of minority shareholder approval, as a condition for saving the merger from voidability resulting from a conflict of interest on the part of one of the Bank's directors, Jack Beddow, who voted in favor of the merger while also serving as a director of FABI. Under the terms of [MBCA § 8.31(a)], minority approval after disclosure of the material facts about the transaction and the director's interest was one of three avenues to insulate the merger from later attack for conflict, the two others being ratification by the Bank's directors after like disclosure, and proof that the merger was fair to the corporation. On this theory, causation would depend on the use of the proxy statement for the purpose of obtaining votes sufficient to bar a minority shareholder from commencing proceedings to declare the merger void.[93]

Although respondents have proffered each of these theories as establishing a chain of causal connection in which the proxy statement is claimed to have been an "essential link," neither theory presents the proxy solicitation as essential in the sense of *Mills'* causal sequence, in which the solicitation links a directors' proposal with the votes legally required to authorize the action proposed. As a consequence, each theory would, if adopted, extend the scope of *Borak* actions beyond the ambit of *Mills*, and expand the class of plaintiffs entitled to bring *Borak* actions to include shareholders whose initial authorization of the transaction prompting the proxy solicitation is unnecessary.

Assessing the legitimacy of any such extension or expansion calls for the application of some fundamental principles governing recognition of a right of action implied by a federal statute, the first of which was not, in fact, the considered focus of the *Borak* opinion. The rule that has emerged in the years since *Borak* and *Mills* came down is that recognition of any private right of action for violating a federal statute must ultimately rest on congressional intent to provide a private remedy, *Touche Ross & Co. v. Redington*, 442 U.S. 560, 575, 99 S.Ct. 2479, 2488–2489, 61 L.Ed.2d 82 (1979). From this the corollary follows, that the breadth of the right once recognized should not, as a general matter, grow beyond the scope congressionally intended.

This rule and corollary present respondents with a serious obstacle, for we can find no manifestation of intent to recognize a cause of action (or class of plaintiffs) as broad as respondents' theory of causation would entail. At first blush, it might seem otherwise, for the *Borak* Court certainly did not

---

93. [By the Court] The district court and court of appeals have grounded causation on a further theory, that Virginia law required a solicitation of proxies even from minority shareholders as a condition of consummating the merger. While the provisions of [MBCA §§ 11.03(a),(d),(e)] are said to have required the Bank to solicit minority proxies, they actually compelled no more than submission of the merger to a vote at a shareholders' meeting, [MBCA § 11.03(e)], preceded by issuance of an informational statement, [MBCA § 11.03(d)]. There was thus no need under this statute to solicit proxies, although it is undisputed that the proxy solicitation sufficed to satisfy the statutory obligation to provide a statement of relevant information. On this theory causation would depend on the use of the proxy statement to satisfy a statutory obligation, even though a proxy solicitation was not, as such, required. In this Court, respondents have disclaimed reliance on any such theory.

ignore the matter of intent. Its opinion adverted to the statutory object of "protection of investors" as animating Congress' intent to provide judicial relief where "necessary," *Borak*, 377 U.S., at 432, 84 S.Ct., at 1559–1560, and it quoted evidence for that intent from House and Senate Committee Reports, id., at 431–32, 84 S.Ct., at 1559–1560. *Borak*'s probe of the congressional mind, however, never focused squarely on private rights of action, as distinct from the substantive objects of the legislation, and one member of the *Borak* Court later characterized the "implication" of the private right of action as resting modestly on the Act's "exclusively procedural provision affording access to a federal forum." *Bivens v. Six Unknown Fed. Narcotics Agents*, 403 U.S. 388, 403, n.4, 91 S.Ct. 1999, 2008, n.4, 29 L.Ed.2d 619 (1971) (Harlan, J., concurring in judgment) (internal quotation marks omitted). In fact, the importance of enquiring specifically into intent to authorize a private cause of action became clear only later, see *Cort v. Ash*, 422 U.S., at 78, 95 S.Ct., at 2087–2088, and only later still, in *Touche Ross*, was this intent accorded primacy among the considerations that might be thought to bear on any decision to recognize a private remedy. There, in dealing with a claimed private right under § 17(a) of the Act, we explained that the "central inquiry remains whether Congress intended to create, either expressly or by implication, a private cause of action." 442 U.S., at 575–576, 99 S.Ct., at 2489.

Looking to the Act's text and legislative history mindful of this heightened concern reveals little that would help toward understanding the intended scope of any private right. According to the House report, Congress meant to promote the "free exercise" of stockholders' voting rights, H.R.Rep. No. 1383, 73d Cong., 2d Sess., 14 (1934), and protect "[f]air corporate suffrage," id., at 13, from abuses exemplified by proxy solicitations that concealed what the Senate report called the "real nature" of the issues to be settled by the subsequent votes, S.Rep. No. 792, 73d Cong., 2d Sess., 12 (1934). While it is true that these reports, like the language of the Act itself, carry the clear message that Congress meant to protect investors from misinformation that rendered them unwitting agents of self-inflicted damage, it is just as true that Congress was reticent with indications of how far this protection might depend on self-help by private action. The response to this reticence may be, of course, to claim that § 14(a) cannot be enforced effectively for the sake of its intended beneficiaries without their participation as private litigants. *Borak*, supra, 377 U.S., at 432, 84 S.Ct., at 1559–1560. But the force of this argument for inferred congressional intent depends on the degree of need perceived by Congress, and we would have trouble inferring any congressional urgency to depend on implied private actions to deter violations of § 14(a), when Congress expressly provided private rights of action in §§ 9(e), 16(b) and 18(a) of the same Act.[94]

The congressional silence that is thus a serious obstacle to the expansion of cognizable *Borak* causation is not, however, a necessarily insurmountable barrier. This is not the first effort in recent years to expand the scope of an

---

94. [By the Court] The object of our enquiry does not extend further to question the holding of either *J.I. Case Co. v. Borak*, 377 U.S. 426, 84 S.Ct. 1555, 12 L.Ed.2d 423 (1964), or *Mills v. Electric Auto–Lite Co.*, 396 U.S. 375, 90 S.Ct. 616, 24 L.Ed.2d 593 (1970) at this date, any more than we have done so in the past, see *Touche Ross & Co. v. Redington*, 442 U.S. 560, 577, 99 S.Ct. 2479, 2489–2490, 61 L.Ed.2d 82 (1979). Our point is simply to recognize the hurdle facing any litigant who urges us to enlarge the scope of the action beyond the point reached in *Mills*.

action originally inferred from the Act without "conclusive guidance" from Congress, and we may look to that earlier case for the proper response to such a plea for expansion. There, we accepted the proposition that where a legal structure of private statutory rights has developed without clear indications of congressional intent, the contours of that structure need not be frozen absolutely when the result would be demonstrably inequitable to a class of would-be plaintiffs with claims comparable to those previously recognized. Faced in that case with such a claim for equality in rounding out the scope of an implied private statutory right of action, we looked to policy reasons for deciding where the outer limits of the right should lie. We may do no less here, in the face of respondents' pleas for a private remedy to place them on the same footing as shareholders with votes necessary for initial corporate action.

A

[We reject] respondents' first theory, that a desire to avoid minority shareholders' ill will should suffice to justify recognizing the requisite causality of a proxy statement needed to garner that minority support.

* * * [If this were accepted, c]ausation would turn on inferences about what the corporate directors would have thought and done without the minority shareholder approval unneeded to authorize action. A subsequently dissatisfied minority shareholder would have virtual license to allege that managerial timidity would have doomed corporate action but for the ostensible approval induced by a misleading statement, and opposing claims of hypothetical diffidence and hypothetical boldness on the part of directors would probably provide enough depositions in the usual case to preclude any judicial resolution short of the credibility judgments that can only come after trial. Reliable evidence would seldom exist. Directors would understand the prudence of making a few statements about plans to proceed even without minority endorsement, and discovery would be a quest for recollections of oral conversations at odds with the official pronouncements, in hopes of finding support for ex post facto guesses about how much heat the directors would have stood in the absence of minority approval. The issues would be hazy, their litigation protracted, and their resolution unreliable. Given a choice, we would reject any theory of causation that raised such prospects, and we reject this one.[95]

B

The theory of causal necessity derived from the requirements of Virginia law dealing with postmerger ratification seeks to identify the essential charac-

---

95. [By the Court] In parting company from us on this point, Justice Kennedy emphasizes that respondents in this particular case substantiated a plausible claim that petitioners would not have proceeded without minority approval. FABI's attempted freeze-out merger of a Maryland subsidiary had failed a year before the events in question when the subsidiary's directors rejected the proposal because of inadequate share price, and there was evidence of FABI's desire to avoid any renewal of ad-

verse comment. The issue before us, however, is whether to recognize a theory of causation generally, and our decision against doing so rests on our apprehension that the ensuing litigation would be exemplified by cases far less tractable than this. Respondents' burden to justify recognition of causation beyond the scope of Mills must be addressed not by emphasizing the instant case but by confronting the risk inherent in the cases that could be expected to be characteristic if the causal theory were adopted.

ter of the proxy solicitation from its function in obtaining the minority approval that would preclude a minority suit attacking the merger. Since the link is said to be a step in the process of barring a class of shareholders from resort to a state remedy otherwise available, this theory of causation rests upon the proposition of policy that § 14(a) should provide a federal remedy whenever a false or misleading proxy statement results in the loss under state law of a shareholder plaintiff's state remedy for the enforcement of a state right. Respondents agree with the suggestions of counsel for the SEC and FDIC that causation be recognized, for example, when a minority shareholder has been induced by a misleading proxy statement to forfeit a state-law right to an appraisal remedy by voting to approve a transaction, cf. *Swanson v. American Consumers Industries, Inc.*, 475 F.2d 516, 520–521 (C.A.7 1973), or when such a shareholder has been deterred from obtaining an order enjoining a damaging transaction by a proxy solicitation that misrepresents the facts on which an injunction could properly have been issued. Respondents claim that in this case a predicate for recognizing just such a causal link exists in [MBCA § 8.31(a)(2)], which sets the conditions under which the merger may be insulated from suit by a minority shareholder seeking to void it on account of Beddow's conflict.

This case does not, however, require us to decide whether § 14(a) provides a cause of action for lost state remedies, since there is no indication in the law or facts before us that the proxy solicitation resulted in any such loss. The contrary appears to be the case. Assuming the soundness of respondents' characterization of the proxy statement as materially misleading, the very terms of the Virginia statute indicate that a favorable minority vote induced by the solicitation would not suffice to render the merger invulnerable to later attack on the ground of the conflict. The statute bars a shareholder from seeking to avoid a transaction tainted by a director's conflict if, inter alia, the minority shareholders ratified the transaction following disclosure of the material facts of the transaction and the conflict. [MBCA § 8.31(a)(2), Subchapter F]. Assuming that the material facts about the merger and Beddow's interests were not accurately disclosed, the minority votes were inadequate to ratify the merger under state law, and there was no loss of state remedy to connect the proxy solicitation with harm to minority shareholders irredressable under state law.[96] Nor is there a claim here that the statement misled respondents into entertaining a false belief that they had no chance to upset the merger, until the time for bringing suit had run out.

The judgment of the Court of Appeals is reversed.

It is so ordered.

JUSTICE SCALIA, concurring in part and concurring in the judgment.

I

As I understand the Court's opinion, the statement "In the opinion of the Directors, this is a high value for the shares" would produce liability if in fact

---

96. [By the Court] In his opinion dissenting on this point, Justice Kennedy suggests that materiality under Virginia law might be defined differently from the materiality standard of our own cases, resulting in a denial of state remedy even when a solicitation was materially misleading under federal law. Respondents, however, present nothing to suggest that this might be so.

it was not a high value and the Directors knew that. It would not produce liability if in fact it was not a high value but the Directors honestly believed otherwise. The statement "The Directors voted to accept the proposal because they believe it offers a high value" would not produce liability if in fact the Directors' genuine motive was quite different—except that it would produce liability if the proposal in fact did not offer a high value and the Directors knew that.

I agree with all of this. However, not every sentence that has the word "opinion" in it, or that refers to motivation for Directors' actions, leads us into this psychic thicket. Sometimes such a sentence actually represents facts as facts rather than opinions—and in that event no more need be done than apply the normal rules for § 14(a) liability. I think that is the situation here. In my view, the statement at issue in this case is most fairly read as affirming *separately* both the fact of the Directors' opinion *and* the accuracy of the facts upon which the opinion was assertedly based. It reads as follows:

> The Plan of Merger has been approved by the Board of Directors because it provides an opportunity for the Bank's public shareholders to achieve a high value for their shares. App. to Pet. for Cert. 53a.

Had it read "because *in their estimation* it provides an opportunity, etc." it would have set forth nothing but an opinion. As written, however, it asserts both that the Board of Directors acted for a particular reason *and* that that reason is correct. * * *

If the present case were to proceed, therefore, I think the normal § 14(a) principles governing misrepresentation of fact would apply.

II

I recognize that the Court's disallowance (in Part II–B–2) of an action for misrepresentation of belief is entirely contrary to the modern law of torts, as authorities cited by the Court make plain. I have no problem with departing from modern tort law in this regard, because I think the federal cause of action at issue here was never enacted by Congress, and hence the more narrow we make it (within the bounds of rationality) the more faithful we are to our task. * * *

JUSTICE STEVENS, with whom JUSTICE MARSHALL joins, concurring in part and dissenting in part.

While I agree in substance with Parts I and II of the Court's opinion, I do not agree with the reasoning in Part III. * * *

The case before us today involves a merger that has been found by a jury to be unfair, not fair. The interest in providing a remedy to the injured minority shareholders therefore is stronger, not weaker, than in *Mills*. The interest in avoiding speculative controversy about the actual importance of the proxy solicitation is the same as in *Mills*. Moreover, as in *Mills*, these matters can be taken into account at the remedy stage in appropriate cases. Accordingly, I do not believe that it constitutes an unwarranted extension of the rationale of *Mills* to conclude that because management found it necessary—whether for "legal or practical reasons"—to solicit proxies from minority shareholders to obtain their approval of the merger, that solicitation "was an essential link in the accomplishment of the transaction." In my opinion, shareholders may bring an action for damages under § 14(a) of the Securities Exchange Act of 1934, whenever materially false or misleading statements are made in proxy statements. That the solicitation of proxies is not required by law or by the bylaws of a corporation does not authorize corporate officers, once they have decided for whatever reason to solicit proxies, to avoid the constraints of the statute. I would therefore affirm the judgment of the Court of Appeals.

JUSTICE KENNEDY, with whom JUSTICE MARSHALL, JUSTICE BLACKMUN, and JUSTICE STEVENS join, concurring in part and dissenting in part.

I am in general agreement with Parts I and II of the majority opinion, but do not agree with the views expressed in Part III regarding the proof of causation required to establish a violation of § 14(a). With respect, I dissent from Part III of the Court's opinion. * * *

II

A

The severe limits the Court places upon possible proof of nonvoting causation in a § 14(a) private action are justified neither by our precedents nor any case in the courts of appeals. These limits are said to flow from a shift in our approach to implied causes of action that has occurred since we recognized the § 14(a) implied private action in J.I. Case Co. v. *Borak*, 377 U.S. 426, 84 S.Ct. 1555, 12 L.Ed.2d 423 (1964).

I acknowledge that we should exercise caution in creating implied private rights of action and that we must respect the primacy of congressional intent in that inquiry. Where an implied cause of action is well accepted by our own cases and has become an established part of the securities laws, however, we should enforce it as a meaningful remedy unless we are to eliminate it altogether. As the Court phrases it, we must consider the causation question in light of the underlying "policy reasons for deciding where the outer limits of the right should lie."

According to the Court, acceptance of non-voting causation theories would "extend the scope of *Borak* actions beyond the ambit of *Mills*." But *Mills* did not purport to limit the scope of *Borak* actions, and some courts have applied nonvoting causation theories to *Borak* actions for at least the past 25 years.

To the extent the Court's analysis considers the purposes underlying § 14(a), it does so with the avowed aim to limit the cause of action and with undue emphasis upon fears of "speculative claims and procedural intractability." The result is a sort of guerrilla warfare to restrict a well-established implied right of action. If the analysis adopted by the Court today is any guide, Congress and those charged with enforcement of the securities laws stand forewarned that unresolved questions concerning the scope of those causes of action are likely to be answered by the Court in favor of defendants.

B

The Court seems to assume, based upon the footnote in *Mills* reserving the question, that Sandberg bears a special burden to demonstrate causation because the public shareholders held only 15 percent of the Bank's stock. Justice Stevens is right to reject this theory. Here, First American Bankshares, Inc. (FABI) and Virginia Bankshares, Inc. (VBI) retained the option to back out of the transaction if dissatisfied with the reaction of the minority shareholders, or if concerned that the merger would result in liability for violation of duties to the minority shareholders. The merger agreement was conditioned upon approval by two-thirds of the shareholders, App. 463, and VBI could have voted its shares against the merger if it so decided. To this extent, the Court's distinction between cases where the "minority" shareholders could have voted down the transaction and those where causation must be proved by nonvoting theories is suspect. Minority shareholders are identified only by a post hoc inquiry. The real question ought to be whether an injury was shown by the effect the nondisclosure had on the entire merger process, including the period before votes are cast.

The Court's distinction presumes that a majority shareholder will vote in favor of management's proposal even if proxy disclosure suggests that the transaction is unfair to minority shareholders or that the board of directors or majority shareholder are in breach of fiduciary duties to the minority. If the majority shareholder votes against the transaction in order to comply with its state law duties, or out of fear of liability, or upon concluding that the transaction will injure the reputation of the business, this ought not to be characterized as nonvoting causation. Of course, when the majority shareholder dominates the voting process, as was the case here, it may prefer to avoid the embarrassment of voting against its own proposal and so may cancel the meeting of shareholders at which the vote was to have been taken. For practical purposes, the result is the same: because of full disclosure the transaction does not go forward and the resulting injury to minority shareholders is avoided. The Court's distinction between voting and nonvoting causation does not create clear legal categories. * * *

There is no authority whatsoever for limiting § 14(a) to protecting those minority shareholders whose numerical strength could permit them to vote down a proposal. One of Section 14(a)'s "chief purposes is 'the protection of investors.' " *J.I. Case Co. v. Borak*, 377 U.S., at 432, 1559–1560. Those who lack the strength to vote down a proposal have all the more need of disclosure. The voting process involves not only casting ballots but also the formulation and withdrawal of proposals, the minority's right to block a vote through court action or the threat of adverse consequences, or the negotiation of an increase in price. The proxy rules support this deliberative process. These practicalities can result in causation sufficient to support recovery.

The facts in the case before us prove this point. Sandberg argues that had all the material facts been disclosed, FABI or the Bank likely would have withdrawn or revised the merger proposal. The evidence in the record, and more that might be available upon remand, meets any reasonable requirement of specific and nonspeculative proof.

FABI wanted a "friendly transaction" with a price viewed as "so high that any reasonable shareholder will accept it." Management expressed concern that the transaction result in "no loss of support for the bank out in the community, which was important." Although FABI had the votes to push through any proposal, it wanted a favorable response from the minority shareholders. Because of the "human element involved in a transaction of this nature," FABI attempted to "show those minority shareholders that [it was] being fair."

The theory that FABI would not have pursued the transaction if full disclosure had been provided and the shareholders had realized the inadequacy of the price is supported not only by the trial testimony but also by notes of the meeting of the Bank's board which approved the merger. The inquiry into causation can proceed not by "opposing claims of hypothetical diffidence and hypothetical boldness," but through an examination of evidence of the same type the Court finds acceptable in its determination that directors' statements of reasons can lead to liability. Discussion at the board meeting focused upon matters such as "how to keep PR afloat" and "how to prevent adverse reac[tion]/perception," demonstrating the directors' concern that an unpopular merger proposal could injure the Bank.

Only a year or so before the Virginia merger, FABI had failed in an almost identical transaction, an attempt to freeze out the minority shareholders of its Maryland subsidiary. FABI retained Keefe, Bruyette & Woods (KBW) for that transaction as well, and KBW had given an opinion that FABI's price was fair. The subsidiary's board of directors then retained its own adviser and concluded that the price offered by FABI was inadequate. The Maryland transaction failed when the directors of the Maryland bank refused to proceed; and this was despite the minority's inability to outvote FABI if it had pressed on with the deal.

In the Virginia transaction, FABI again decided to retain KBW. Beddow, who sat on the boards of both FABI and the Bank, discouraged the Bank from hiring its own financial adviser, out of fear that the Maryland experience would be repeated if the Bank received independent advice. Directors of the Bank testified they would not have voted to approve the transaction if the price had been demonstrated unfair to the minority. Further, approval by the Bank's board of directors was facilitated by FABI's representation that the transaction also would be approved by the minority shareholders.

These facts alone suffice to support a finding of causation, but here Sandberg might have had yet more evidence to link the nondisclosure with completion of the merger. FABI executive Robert Altman and Bank Chairman Drewer met on the day before the shareholders meeting when the vote was taken. Notes produced by petitioners suggested that Drewer, who had received some shareholder objections to the $42 price, considered postponing the meeting and obtaining independent advice on valuation. Altman persuaded him to go forward without any of these cautionary measures. This information, which was produced in the course of discovery, was kept from the jury on grounds of privilege. Sandberg attacked the privilege ruling on five grounds in the Court of Appeals. In light of its ruling in favor of Sandberg, however, the panel had no occasion to consider the admissibility of this evidence.

Though I would not require a shareholder to present such evidence of causation, this case itself demonstrates that nonvoting causation theories are quite plausible where the misstatement or omission is material and the damage sustained by minority shareholders is serious. As Professor Loss summarized the holdings of a "substantial number of cases," even if the minority cannot alone vote down a transaction, minority stockholders will be in a better position to protect their interests with full disclosure and * * * an unfavorable minority vote might influence the majority to modify or reconsider the transaction in question. In [*Schlick v. Penn–Dixie Cement Corp.*, 507 F.2d 374, 384 (C.A.2 1974),] where the stockholders had no appraisal rights under state law because the stock was listed on the New York Stock Exchange, the court advanced two additional considerations: (1) the *market* would be informed; and (2) even 'a rapacious controlling management' might modify the terms of a merger because it would not want to 'hang its dirty linen out on the line and thereby expose itself to suit or Securities Commission or other action—in terms of reputation and future takeovers.'

L. Loss, Fundamentals of Securities Regulation at 1119–1120 (footnote omitted).

I conclude that causation is more than plausible; it is likely, even where the public shareholders cannot vote down management's proposal. Causation is established where the proxy statement is an essential link in completing the transaction, even if the minority lacks sufficient votes to defeat a proposal of management. * * *

Notes

(1) Do you agree that a statement that an offer price is higher than "book value" is misleading because the statement would not be true if a recalculated book value—based on current market values for real estate rather than historical cost—was used? Would it be misleading if the disclosure made clear that the comparison was being made with book value "calculated in the traditional manner and without regard to current real estate values"? Would an average investor understand that distinction? Or would the proxy statement have to say what the recalculated book value was if "book value" is referred to at all? After this decision, could the SEC amend rule 14a–9 to make it applicable to proxy solicitations that are not "essential" to the transaction in the sense used by Justice Souter? Or does that require an amendment to § 14(a) of the Securities Exchange Act of 1934?

(2) What do you think of Justice Scalia's approach toward cases involving implied causes of action that because "the federal cause of action at issue here was never enacted by Congress, * * * the more narrow we make it (within the bounds of rationality) the more faithful we are to our task"? What is "the task" that Justice Scalia refers to?

(3) If the protection of rule 14a–9 is removed from minority shareholders by *Virginia Bankshares*, can any statement, no matter how outrageously wrong, be made by management?

(4) One question left open in Justice Souter's opinion is whether a different rule should be applicable if minority shareholders induced to vote in favor of a proposal because of false statements thereby lose state remedies, such as the right of dissent and appraisal or the right to serve as a derivative plaintiff. Two decisions holding that *Virginia Bankshares* does not extend that far are Howing Co. v. Nationwide Corp., 972 F.2d 700 (6th Cir.1992), cert. denied 507 U.S. 1004, 113 S.Ct. 1645, 123 L.Ed.2d 266 (1993), and Wilson v. Great American Indus., Inc. 979 F.2d 924 (2d Cir.1992). But see Roosevelt v. E.I. Du Pont de Nemours & Co., 958 F.2d 416 (D.C.Cir.1992); Scattergood v. Perelman, 945 F.2d 618 (3d Cir.1991). For an analysis of these issues, see Scott Jordan, Loss of State Claims as a Basis for Rule 10b–5 and 14a–9 Actions: The Impact of *Virginia Bankshares*, 49

Bus.Law. 295 (1993); Note, Virginia Bankshares v. Sandberg: Should Minority Approval be Required by Law or Corporate Bylaw? 37 Ariz.L.Rev. 913 (1995).

4. SHAREHOLDER PROPOSALS

REGULATION 14a. SOLICITATION OF PROXIES
17 C.F.R. § 240.14a–8 (2002).

§ 240.14a–8   PROPOSALS OF SECURITY HOLDERS (65 Fed.Reg. 11911)

§ 240.14a–8   Shareholder proposals.

This section addresses when a company must include a shareholder's proposal in its proxy statement and identify the proposal in its form of proxy when the company holds an annual or special meeting of shareholders. In summary, in order to have your shareholder proposal included on a company's proxy card, and included along with any supporting statement in its proxy statement, you must be eligible and follow certain procedures. Under a few specific circumstances, the company is permitted to exclude your proposal, but only after submitting its reasons to the Commission. We structured this section in a question-and-answer format so that it is easier to understand. The references to "you" are to a shareholder seeking to submit the proposal.

(a) *Question 1*: What is a proposal? A shareholder proposal is your recommendation or requirement that the company and/or its board of directors take action, which you intend to present at a meeting of the company's shareholders. Your proposal should state as clearly as possible the course of action that you believe the company should follow. If your proposal is placed on the company's proxy card, the company must also provide in the form of proxy means for shareholders to specify by boxes a choice between approval or disapproval, or abstention. Unless otherwise indicated, the word "proposal" as used in this section refers both to your proposal, and to your corresponding statement in support of your proposal (if any).

(b) *Question 2*: Who is eligible to submit a proposal, and how do I demonstrate to the company that I am eligible?

(1) In order to be eligible to submit a proposal, you must have continuously held at least $2,000 in market value, or 1%, of the company's securities entitled to be voted on the proposal at the meeting for at least one year by the date you submit the proposal. You must continue to hold those securities through the date of the meeting.

(2) If you are the registered holder of your securities, which means that your name appears in the company's records as a shareholder, the company can verify your eligibility on its own, although you will still have to provide the company with a written statement that you intend to continue to hold the securities through the date of the meeting of shareholders. However, if like many shareholders you are not a registered holder, the company likely does not know that you are a shareholder, or how many shares you own. In this case, at the time you submit your proposal, you must prove your eligibility to the company in one of two ways:

(i) The first way is to submit to the company a written state-ment from the "record" holder of your securities (usually a broker or bank) verifying that, at the time you submitted your proposal, you continuously held the securities for at least one year. You must also include your own written statement that you intend to continue to hold the securities through the date of the meeting of shareholders; or

(ii) The second way to prove ownership applies only if you have filed a Schedule 13D (§ 240.13d–101), Schedule 13G (§ 240.13d–102), Form 3 (§ 249.103 of this chapter), Form 4 (§ 249.104 of this chapter) and/or Form 5 (§ 249.105 of this chapter), or amendments to those documents or updated forms, reflecting your ownership of the shares as of or before the date on which the one-year eligibility period begins. If you have filed one of these documents with the SEC, you may demonstrate your eligibility by submitting to the company:

(A) A copy of the schedule and/or form, and any subsequent amendments reporting a change in your ownership level;

(B) Your written statement that you continuously held the required number of shares for the one-year period as of the date of the statement; and

(C) Your written statement that you intend to continue ownership of the shares through the date of the company's annual or special meeting.

(c) *Question 3*: How many proposals may I submit? Each shareholder may submit no more than one proposal to a company for a particular shareholders' meeting.

(d) *Question 4*: How long can my proposal be? The proposal, including any accompanying supporting statement, may not exceed 500 words.

(e) *Question 5*: What is the deadline for submitting a proposal?

(1) If you are submitting your proposal for the company's annual meeting, you can in most cases find the deadline in last year's proxy statement. However, if the company did not hold an annual meeting last year, or has changed the date of its meeting for this year more than 30 days from last year's meeting, you can usually find the deadline in one of the company's quarterly reports on Form 10–Q (§ 249.308a of this chapter) or 10–QSB (§ 249.308b of this chapter), or in shareholder reports of investment companies under § 270.30d–1 of this chapter of the Investment Company Act of 1940. In order to avoid controversy, share-holders should submit their proposals by means, including electronic means, that permit them to prove the date of delivery.

(2) The deadline is calculated in the following manner if the proposal is submitted for a regularly scheduled annual meeting. The proposal must be received at the company's principal executive offices not less than 120 calendar days before the date of the company's proxy statement released to shareholders in connection with the previous year's annual meeting. However, if the company did not hold an annual meeting the previous year, or if the date of this year's annual meeting has been changed by more than 30 days from the date of the previous year's meeting, then the

deadline is a reasonable time before the company begins to print and mail its proxy materials.

(3) If you are submitting your proposal for a meeting of shareholders other than a regularly scheduled annual meeting, the deadline is a reasonable time before the company begins to print and mail its proxy materials.

(f) *Question 6*: What if I fail to follow one of the eligibility or procedural requirements explained in answers to Questions 1 through 4 of this section?

(1) The company may exclude your proposal, but only after it has notified you of the problem, and you have failed adequately to correct it. Within 14 calendar days of receiving your proposal, the company must notify you in writing of any procedural or eligibility deficiencies, as well as of the time frame for your response. Your response must be postmarked, or transmitted electronically, no later than 14 days from the date you received the company's notification. A company need not provide you such notice of a deficiency if the deficiency cannot be remedied, such as if you fail to submit a proposal by the company's properly determined deadline. If the company intends to exclude the proposal, it will later have to make a submission under § 240.14a–8 and provide you with a copy under Question 10 below, § 240.14a–8(j).

(2) If you fail in your promise to hold the required number of securities through the date of the meeting of shareholders, then the company will be permitted to exclude all of your proposals from its proxy materials for any meeting held in the following two calendar years.

(g) *Question 7*: Who has the burden of persuading the Commission or its staff that my proposal can be excluded? Except as otherwise noted, the burden is on the company to demonstrate that it is entitled to exclude a proposal.

(h) *Question 8*: Must I appear personally at the shareholders' meeting to present the proposal?

(1) Either you, or your representative who is qualified under state law to present the proposal on your behalf, must attend the meeting to present the proposal. Whether you attend the meeting yourself or send a qualified representative to the meeting in your place, you should make sure that you, or your representative, follow the proper state law procedures for attending the meeting and/or presenting your proposal.

(2) If the company holds its shareholder meeting in whole or in part via electronic media, and the company permits you or your representative to present your proposal via such media, then you may appear through electronic media rather than traveling to the meeting to appear in person.

(3) If you or your qualified representative fail to appear and present the proposal, without good cause, the company will be permitted to exclude all of your proposals from its proxy materials for any meetings held in the following two calendar years.

(i) *Question 9*: If I have complied with the procedural requirements, on what other bases may a company rely to exclude my proposal?

(1) Improper under state law: If the proposal is not a proper subject for action by shareholders under the laws of the jurisdiction of the company's organization;

> Note to paragraph (i)(1): Depending on the subject matter, some proposals are not considered proper under state law if they would be binding on the company if approved by shareholders. In our experience, most proposals that are cast as recommendations or requests that the board of directors take specified action are proper under state law. Accordingly, we will assume that a proposal drafted as a recommendation or suggestion is proper unless the company demonstrates otherwise.

(2) Violation of law: If the proposal would, if implemented, cause the company to violate any state, federal, or foreign law to which it is subject;

> Note to paragraph (i)(2): We will not apply this basis for exclusion to permit exclusion of a proposal on grounds that it would violate foreign law if compliance with the foreign law would result in a violation of any state or federal law.

(3) Violation of proxy rules: If the proposal or supporting statement is contrary to any of the Commission's proxy rules, including § 240.14a–9, which prohibits materially false or misleading statements in proxy soliciting materials;

(4) Personal grievance; special interest: If the proposal relates to the redress of a personal claim or grievance against the company or any other person, or if it is designed to result in a benefit to you, or to further a personal interest, which is not shared by the other shareholders at large;

(5) Relevance: If the proposal relates to operations which account for less than 5 percent of the company's total assets at the end of its most recent fiscal year, and for less than 5 percent of its net earnings and gross sales for its most recent fiscal year, and is not otherwise significantly related to the company's business;

(6) Absence of power/authority: If the company would lack the power or authority to implement the proposal;

(7) Management functions: If the proposal deals with a matter relating to the company's ordinary business operations;

(8) Relates to election: If the proposal relates to an election for membership on the company's board of directors or analogous governing body;

(9) Conflicts with company's proposal: If the proposal directly conflicts with one of the company's own proposals to be submitted to shareholders at the same meeting;

> Note to paragraph (i)(9): A company's submission to the Commission under this section should specify the points of conflict with the company's proposal.

(10) Substantially implemented: If the company has already substantially implemented the proposal;

(11) Duplication: If the proposal substantially duplicates another proposal previously submitted to the company by another proponent that will be included in the company's proxy materials for the same meeting;

(12) Resubmissions: If the proposal deals with substantially the same subject matter as another proposal or proposals that has or have been previously included in the company's proxy materials within the preceding 5 calendar years, a company may exclude it from its proxy materials for any meeting held within 3 calendar years of the last time it was included if the proposal received:

(i) Less than 3% of the vote if proposed once within the preceding 5 calendar years;

(ii) Less than 6% of the vote on its last submission to shareholders if proposed twice previously within the preceding 5 calendar years; or

(iii) Less than 10% of the vote on its last submission to shareholders if proposed three times or more previously within the preceding 5 calendar years; and

(13) Specific amount of dividends: If the proposal relates to specific amounts of cash or stock dividends.

(j) *Question 10*: What procedures must the company follow if it intends to exclude my proposal?

(1) If the company intends to exclude a proposal from its proxy materials, it must file its reasons with the Commission no later than 80 calendar days before it files its definitive proxy statement and form of proxy with the Commission. The company must simultaneously provide you with a copy of its submission. The Commission staff may permit the company to make its submission later than 80 days before the company files its definitive proxy statement and form of proxy, if the company demonstrates good cause for missing the deadline.

(2) The company must file six paper copies of the following:

(i) The proposal;

(ii) An explanation of why the company believes that it may exclude the proposal, which should, if possible, refer to the most recent applicable authority, such as prior Division letters issued under the rule; and

(iii) A supporting opinion of counsel when such reasons are based on matters of state or foreign law.

(k) *Question 11*: May I submit my own statement to the Commission responding to the company's arguments?

Yes, you may submit a response, but it is not required. You should try to submit any response to us, with a copy to the company, as soon as possible after the company makes its submission. This way, the Commission staff will have time to consider fully your submission before it issues its response. You should submit six paper copies of your response.

(*l*) *Question 12*: If the company includes my shareholder proposal in its proxy materials, what information about me must it include along with the proposal itself?

(1) The company's proxy statement must include your name and address, as well as the number of the company's voting securities that you hold. However, instead of providing that information, the company may instead include a statement that it will provide the information to shareholders promptly upon receiving an oral or written request.

(2) The company is not responsible for the contents of your proposal or supporting statement.

(m) *Question 13*: What can I do if the company includes in its proxy statement reasons why it believes shareholders should not vote in favor of my proposal, and I disagree with some of its statements?

(1) The company may elect to include in its proxy statement reasons why it believes shareholders should vote against your proposal. The company is allowed to make arguments reflecting its own point of view, just as you may express your own point of view in your proposal's supporting statement.

(2) However, if you believe that the company's opposition to your proposal contains materially false or misleading statements that may violate our anti-fraud rule, § 240.14a–9, you should promptly send to the Commission staff and the company a letter explaining the reasons for your view, along with a copy of the company's statements opposing your proposal. To the extent possible, your letter should include specific factual information demonstrating the inaccuracy of the company's claims. Time permitting, you may wish to try to work out your differences with the company by yourself before contacting the Commission staff.

(3) We require the company to send you a copy of its statements opposing your proposal before it mails its proxy materials, so that you may bring to our attention any materially false or misleading statements, under the following timeframes:

(i) If our no-action response requires that you make revisions to your proposal or supporting statement as a condition to requiring the company to include it in its proxy materials, then the company must provide you with a copy of its opposition statements no later than 5 calendar days after the company receives a copy of your revised proposal; or

(ii) In all other cases, the company must provide you with a copy of its opposition statements no later than 30 calendar days before it files definitive copies of its proxy statement and form of proxy under § 240.14a–6.

Notes

(1) Rule 14a–8 has long been viewed by the SEC as a potentially important element of corporate democracy since it in effect permits individual shareholders to place proposals before the body of shareholders through the corporation's proxy statement. Is this right of ballot access based on state law or is it federally

created? See Jill E. Fisch, From Legitimacy to Logic: Reconstructing Proxy Regulation, 46 Vand.L.Rev. 1129, 1143–48 (1993):

> Many of the restrictions in Rule 14a–8 appear both sensible and within the SEC's power to impose. Few commentators would argue with the propriety of permitting management to exclude proposals that are false and misleading or that call for the corporation to violate state or federal law. Only the first basis for exclusion, however, which requires that the proposal deal with a matter that is a proper subject for shareholder action under state law, is strictly true to the SEC's original premise that proper subject is determined by state law.
>
> Moreover, many of the bases for exclusion are not grounded directly in state law. * * * Rule 14a–8(a)(1) imposes minimum ownership requirements and holding period qualifications upon shareholders who seek inclusion of a proposal under Rule 14a–8. No uniform state or common-law principle requires that a shareholder hold one percent or one thousand dollars worth of a corporation's stock for a minimum of one year before making a motion at a shareholders' meeting. No state law bars a shareholder from making the same motion or proposal in successive years, yet Rule 14a–8(c)(12) limits a shareholder's ability to do so. Additionally, state law does not restrict shareholders to dealing with issues concerning more than five percent of the corporation's total assets or extraordinary business matters. The SEC, however, has imposed these limits on shareholder democracy.
>
> Many of the restrictions imposed by the proxy rules can be attributed to a pragmatic effort by the SEC to limit the number of shareholder proposals and to restrict use of the proxy statement to issues of general importance to shareholders. Although such limits may be desirable, they have no foundation in state or common-law restrictions regarding proper subjects to be raised at a shareholders' meeting. The SEC's authority to impose these restrictions on the use of the proxy mechanism is therefore unclear.
>
> Apart from pragmatic concerns, the SEC's restrictions appear to stem primarily from the general principle that state law vests management, rather than shareholders, with the authority to run the corporation. State corporation statutes generally provide that the corporation shall be managed by or under the direction of the board of directors. This common provision suggests that a shareholder proposal affecting the management of the corporation's affairs may improperly interfere with the board's authority.
>
> The absence of modern judicial decisions voiding shareholder action on the basis of these statutes suggests that their limitation on shareholder activity is, at best, minimal. Additionally, it would seem that framing the proposal as a shareholder recommendation rather than an attempt to bind the board would address any limitation the statutes impose. * * *
>
> Accordingly, both in determining appropriate criteria for excluding shareholder proposals and in applying those criteria, the SEC does not replicate passively the annual meeting process by applying state law principles, but creates a federal common law as to what constitutes a proper subject for shareholder action.

(2) The major sources of shareholder proposals today are the members of the Interfaith Center on Corporate Responsibility, a loose organization of nearly 250 Protestant and Roman Catholic denominations, religious communities, agencies,

pension funds,[97] healthcare systems, dioceses, and a few individuals. In 1997 nearly one hundred ICCR-member religious investors sponsored 191 resolutions to 137 companies. Examples include: requesting RJR Nabisco "to adopt a policy ending Joe Camel ads anywhere in the world by the end of 1997;" requesting Anheuser Busch to "revise existing company educational materials and develop all future materials to include in a prominent fashion the definition of moderate drinking found in the Dietary Guidelines * * *;" to General Electric to "no longer seek new nuclear fuel sales abroad, and instead, promote the sale of safer, lower-risk, energy-efficient alternate generating systems to foreign markets;" and to more than 40 companies to endorse the CERES Principles for Public Environmental Accountability. However, many proposals also relate to traditional corporate governance concerns, for example: proposals to Coca–Cola and four other companies to create a Nominating Committee of the board of directors consisting entirely of independent directors; to Texaco and four other companies to declassify the election of directors so that all directors are elected annually; and to more than a dozen companies to make formal review of executive compensation policies. The Corporate Examiner, Vol. 25, No. 7–8, at 8–10, 14 (1997).

(3) The construction of 14a–8(i) in the context of social responsibility issues has a considerable history. The original attitude of the SEC was to permit proposals of this nature to be excluded, but the courts disagreed. The leading case involved an attempt in 1968 by an organization called the Medical Committee for Human Rights, to require Dow Chemical Company to include the following "resolution" in its proxy statement:

> RESOLVED, that the shareholders of the Dow Chemical Company request the Board of Directors, in accordance with the laws of the State of Delaware, and the Composite Certificate of Incorporation of the Dow Chemical Company, to adopt a resolution setting forth an amendment to the Composite Certificate of Incorporation of the Dow Chemical Company that napalm shall not be sold to any buyer unless that buyer gives reasonable assurance that the substance will not be used on or against human beings.

The letter concluded with the following statement:

> Finally, we wish to note that our objections to the sale of this product [are] primarily based on the concerns for human life inherent in our organization's credo. However, we are further informed by our investment advisers that this product is also bad for our company's business as it is being used in the Vietnamese War. It is now clear from company statements and press reports that it is increasingly hard to recruit the highly intelligent, well-motivated, young college men so important for company growth. There is, as well, an adverse impact on our global business, which our advisers indicate, suffers as a result of the public reaction to this product.

In Medical Comm. for Human Rights v. SEC, 432 F.2d 659 (D.C.Cir.1970), vacated as moot 404 U.S. 403, 92 S.Ct. 577, 30 L.Ed.2d 560 (1972), the Court did not hold that this proposal was includable, but strongly intimated that it was, and that rule 14a–8 was an important mechanism for shareholder democracy and control of management. The Supreme Court appeal, incidentally, became moot after the corporation voluntarily submitted the Medical Committee proposal to its

---

97. [By the Editors] Before 1992, Rule 14a–8 was widely used by institutional investors to raise economic issues with individual corporations, often with a considerable degree of success. Today, most of these issues are raised by institutional investors directly with the targeted issuer.

shareholders, where it received the support of less than three percent of the shares voting on the issue.

(4) In SEC Rel. No. 34–12999, 41 Fed. Reg. 52,994, 52,998 (1976), the SEC announced a major change in policy with respect to its view of "ordinary business operations":

> [T]he term "ordinary business operations" has been deemed on occasion to include certain matters which have significant policy, economic or other implications inherent in them. For instance, a proposal that a utility company not construct a proposed nuclear power plant has in the past been considered excludable * * *. In retrospect, however, it seems apparent that the economic and safety considerations attendant to nuclear power plants are of such magnitude that a determination whether to construct one is not an "ordinary" business matter. Accordingly proposals of that nature, as well as others that have major implications, will in the future be considered beyond the realm of an issuer's ordinary business operations, and future interpretive letters of the Commission's staff will reflect that view.

> * * * [W]here proposals involve business matters that are mundane in nature and do not involve any substantial policy or other considerations, the subparagraph may be relied upon to omit them.

Following the 1976 release, the SEC required a number of corporations to include proposals reporting on their compliance with the requirements of equal opportunity and affirmative action. Generally, the SEC considered whether the subject of the reporting related to "day-to-day" employment matters (in which event the proposal was excludable as relating to "ordinary business matters") or whether it raised significant policy considerations.

(5) In March 1991, the SEC's position with respect to employment matters again changed significantly. This new policy was set forth most explicitly in a "no action letter"[98] addressed to Cracker Barrel Old Country Store, Inc. relating to a proposal that Cracker Barrel be required to establish a policy not to discriminate against homosexuals. 1992 WL 289095 (Oct. 13, 1992):

> As a general rule, the staff views proposals directed at a company's employment policies and practices with respect to its non-executive workforce to be uniquely matters relating to the conduct of the company's ordinary business operations. Examples of the categories of proposals that have been deemed to be excludable on this basis are: employee health benefits, general compensation issues not focused on senior executives, management of the workplace, employee supervision, labor-management relations, employee hiring and firing, conditions of employment and employee training and motivation.

> Notwithstanding the general view that employment matters concerning the workforce of the company are excludable as matters involving the conduct of day-to-day business, exceptions have been made in some cases where a proponent based an employment-related proposal on "social policy" concerns. In recent years, however, the line between includable and excludable employment-related proposals based on social policy considerations has become increasingly difficult to draw. The distinctions recognized by the staff are characterized by many as tenuous, without substance and effectively nullify-

98. [By the Editors] A "no action" letter is a letter sent by SEC staff to a corporation stating that "it will not recommend any en- forcement action to the Commission if the proposal is omitted." The legal status of such a letter is discussed in the following text.

ing the application of the ordinary business exclusion to employment related proposals.

The Division has reconsidered the application of Rule 14a–8(c)(7) to employment-related proposals in light of these concerns and the staff's experience with these proposals in recent years. As a result, the Division has determined that the fact that a shareholder proposal concerning a company's employment policies and practices for the general workforce is tied to a social issue will no longer be viewed as removing the proposal from the realm of ordinary business operations of the registrant. Rather, determinations with respect to any such proposals are properly governed by the employment-based nature of the proposal.

* * * [The Division distinguished these "social policy proposals" from proposals relating to the compensation of senior executives and directors, asserting that the latter were inherently outside the scope of "ordinary business of the corporation" as they involved the relationships between shareholders and management.]

Efforts by labor unions to enjoin the implementation of this revised policy relating to employment-related proposals failed essentially on procedural grounds. In 1997 the SEC proposed to reverse its *Cracker Barrel* interpretation:

The Cracker Barrel interpretation has been controversial since it was announced. While the reasons for adopting the Cracker Barrel interpretation continue to have some validity, as well as significant support in the corporate community,[99] we believe that reversal of the position is warranted in light of the broader package of reforms proposed today. Reversal will require companies to include proposals in their proxy materials that some shareholders believe are important to companies and fellow shareholders. In place of the 1992 position, the Division would return to its approach to such proposals prevailing before it adopted the position. That is, employment-related proposals focusing on significant social policy issues could not automatically be excluded under the "ordinary business" exclusion.

Under this proposal, the "bright line" approach for employment-related proposals established by the Cracker Barrel position would be replaced by the case-by-case analysis that prevailed previously. Return to a case-by-case approach should redress the concerns of shareholders interested in submitting for a vote by fellow shareholders employment-related proposals raising significant social issues. While this would be a change in the Commission's interpretation of the rule, we nonetheless request your comments on whether we should reverse the Cracker Barrel interpretation. * * *

Proposed Rule: Amendments to Rules on Shareholder Proposals, SEC Rel. No. 34–39093 (September 25, 1997), at 9–10. The reversal was approved in Exchange Act Rel. 40018 (May 21, 1998). See Note (Patricia R. Uhlenbrock), Roll Out the Barrel: The SEC Reverses Its Stance on Employment–Related Shareholder Proposals Under Rule 14a–8—Again, 25 Del.J.Corp.L. 277, 308 (2000) (arguing that the 1998 reversal has not yet provided a meaningful standard for guidance in an important area of the law and that state law should step in to fill the void).

99. [By the SEC] In response to the Questionnaire, 91% of companies favored excluding employment-related shareholder proposals raising significant social policy issues under the Cracker Barrel interpretation. Eighty-six percent of shareholders thought such proposals should be included.

TIAA–CREF, a large institutional investor which manages pension funds for teachers and college professors, decided to use Rule 14a–8 to try to control what it regarded as the excessive use of stock options as compensation for corporate employees. On October 26, 2001, TIAA–CREF proposed that Synopsys, Inc. include in its proxy solicitation the following proposal:

RESOLVED: That the shareholders request that the Board of Directors submit all equity compensation plans (other than those that would not result in material potential dilution) to shareholders for approval.

The Staff of the Securities and Exchange Commission, Division of Corporate Finance, ruled initially that Synopsys could properly exclude the TIAA–CREF proposal on the grounds that it concerned "ordinary business operations." The Staff based its decision on the fact that the Synopsys stock option plan covered not only senior executive officers and directors, but the entire workforce of the company, and thus related to general employee compensation matters, excludable under SEC Rule 14a–8(i)(7).

TIAA–CREF appealed within the SEC, arguing that their proposal raised fundamental issues of substantial importance, and not ordinary business issues. TIAA–CREF argued that the explosion in the use of stock options had dramatically transformed the compensation structure of U.S. corporations and the relationship between equity owners and employees. At many companies, the value of options granted to executives and employees constituted a significant fraction of earnings and revenues thereby causing serious dilution to shareholders.

On July 12, 2002, the SEC's Division of Corporate Finance reversed the earlier decision of its staff, noting that "the public debate regarding shareholder approval of equity compensation plans has become significant in recent months. Consequently, in view of the widespread public debate regarding shareholder approval of equity compensation plans we are modifying our treatment of proposals relating to this topic." From now on, a public company may not rely on the rule's "ordinary business" provision to omit the following proposals from its proxy statement: "any proposal that focuses on equity compensation plans that potentially would result in material dilution to existing shareholders, regardless of who participates in the plan."

RAUCHMAN v. MOBIL CORP.

United States Court of Appeals, Sixth Circuit, 1984.
739 F.2d 205.

Before ENGEL and KEITH, CIRCUIT JUDGES, and WEICK, SENIOR CIRCUIT JUDGE.

ENGEL, CIRCUIT JUDGE.

The principal issue in this appeal is whether defendant Mobil Corporation properly refused to include in its proxy statement a proposal which would amend Mobil's bylaws to prevent a citizen of an OPEC country from sitting on Mobil's board of directors. The plaintiff's claim is premised upon the existence of an implied private cause of action under section 14(a) of the Securities Exchange Act, and upon Rule 14a–8 promulgated thereunder. Rauchman asserts that Mobil was required to include the proposal in the corporation's proxy statement for the 1982 annual meeting.

I.

The plaintiff, Irvin Rauchman, owns sixty-four voting shares of Mobil stock. In 1981, pursuant to Securities Exchange Commission (SEC or Commission) Rule 14a–8(a), Rauchman submitted a proposed amendment to Mobil's bylaws for inclusion in Mobil's proxy statement for the company's 1982 annual meeting.

The proposal read as follows:

Proposal: It is resolved that the bylaws of the Corporation are amended to read as follows: Citizens of countries belonging to OPEC are not qualified for election to, or membership on, the Corporation's Board of Directors.

Supporting Statement: On October 31, 1980, Mobil's directors appointed a Saudi Arabian citizen to its Board of Directors. This individual reportedly has ties to members of the present Saudi Arabian government. Saudi Arabia, of course, makes harmful political use of its oil supply. Mobil, by appointing a Saudi Arabian to its Board of Directors, is, in effect, also approving of Saudi Arabia's activities.

Other corporations successfully transact business with OPEC countries without appointing citizens of those countries to their boards. Other means are available to obtain a working relationship with OPEC. Mobil has erred by associating with a country that has, for example, provided an abundance of cash and weapons to the Palestine Liberation Organization. A provision in Mobil's bylaws excluding citizens of OPEC countries from its Board of Directors will be a step in the right direction.

The[r]e are qualified American citizens who can contribute to the continued success of Mobil. It is unnecessary for Mobil to prostitute itself to the power of OPEC and become a silent partner to OPEC's destructive activities.

Evidently, Mr. Rauchman's concern with the presence of an OPEC citizen on the Mobil board was caused by the appointment to the board of Suliman S. Olayan, a Saudi Arabian citizen.

After receiving Rauchman's proposal, Mobil wrote to the SEC staff requesting that the staff recommend to the Commission that no action be taken if Mobil did not include Rauchman's proposal in the proxy statement. Mobil maintained in its letter to the SEC that under Rule 14a–8(c)(8), which allows a company to exclude a proposal if it relates to an election to office of the company's board of directors, the proposal need not be included. Mobil took this position because Olayan was eligible for reelection at Mobil's 1982 annual meeting. The SEC staff responded with a letter indicating that it would not recommend any enforcement action to the Commission if Mobil omitted the proposal. In its letter the staff noted that

[t]here appears to be some basis for your opinion that the proposal may be omitted from the Company's proxy material under Rule 14a–8(c)(8), since it relates to the election to office of the Company's Board of Directors. In the staff's view, the proposal and supporting statement call into question the qualifications of Mr. Olayan for reelection and thus the proposal may be deemed an effort to oppose management's solicitation on behalf of the reelection of this person. Under the circumstances, this Division will not recommend any enforcement action to the Commission if the Company omits the proposal from its proxy material.

Following the staff's determination, Rauchman brought suit in the United States District Court for the Southern District of Ohio to force Mobil to include the proposal in the Company's proxy statement. The District Court assumed that Rauchman had a private right of action under section 14(a) of the Securities Exchange Act and Rule 14a–8 promulgated thereunder. The court then found that Mobil properly excluded Rauchman's proposal from its proxy statement because the proposal related to an election to office. The court found that the proposal was related to the reelection of Olayan to Mobil's board of directors because, had the proposal been adopted, Mr. Olayan would have been ineligible to sit on Mobil's board. Thus, the court concluded: "Rauchman's proposal * * * is clearly intended to render Mr. Olayan ineligible to serve as a Mobil director." Based on these findings the district court granted Mobil's motion for summary judgment.

II.

* * * [The Court concludes with "substantial reservations" that a private cause of action exists for violation of Rule 14a–8.]

III.

Turning therefore to the merits of the appeal, we conclude that the district judge did not err in granting Mobil's motion for summary judgment. It was undisputed that Suliman S. Olayan, a Saudi Arabian citizen, was running for reelection to Mobil's board of directors. The election of Olayan to the board would have been forbidden by the proposed bylaw amendment, since the amendment would have made him ineligible to sit on the board. Paragraph one of the proposed comment submitted by Rauchman unmistakably and expressly referred to Olayan, although not by name. In our view, this circumstance sufficiently supports the trial judge's holding that the proposal relates to an election to office and, under the rules of the Commission, was not required to be included.

It is suggested on appeal that the proposal would have only an incidental impact upon Olayan's reelection. We disagree. As the district court noted, "Mobile [sic] stockholders could not vote for Rauchman's proposal and at the same time ratify the nomination of Mr. Olayan." By forcing the shareholders to choose between ratifying the proposal and reelecting Olayan, Rauchman's proposal could clearly be viewed as an "effort to oppose management's solicitation on behalf of" Olayan's reelection. It is a form of electioneering which Mobil was not required to include in its proxy statement.

Plaintiff suggests in his brief that if we conclude that Mr. Olayan's presence on the Mobil board of directors invalidates Rauchman's "otherwise proper proposal," the remedy would be to insert a "grandfather clause" rendering the bylaw inapplicable to Olayan. We are not aware that this suggestion was ever made to the district court or to Mobil until this appeal. We are not disposed to act on that suggestion at this late date and at this level.

Mobil argued that the proposed bylaw would transgress the laws of the state of Mobil's incorporation (Delaware) and of the state of its principal place of business (New York). Mobil also argued that Rauchman's proposal conflicts with the executive agreement of November 7, 1983, 48 Stat. 1826, between the United States and Saudi Arabia. In view of our decision that the proposal relates to an election to office, it is unnecessary for us to consider Mobil's contention that the proposal could be excluded under Rule 14a–8(c)(2) which permits a company to omit any proposal which, if implemented, would "require the issuer to violate any state law or federal law of the United States."

We believe that Mobil was fully within its rights in declining to submit the proposed proxy material, at least in the form proposed by Mr. Rauchman. Affirmed.

Notes

(1) Do not the SEC's rules with respect to the nomination of directors and to voting tend to ensure the election of management candidates and to reduce shareholder effectiveness? See Jill E. Fisch, From Legitimacy to Logic: Reconstructing Proxy Regulation, 46 Vand.L.Rev. 1129, 1162–64 (1993):

* * * In spite of congressional concern in 1934 that corporate insiders controlled the election process, a concern to which the proxy regulations appear to be addressed, insider domination of the election process remains pervasive today. * * * The continued ability of corporate insiders to control director elections can be attributed, in part, to deficiencies in the federal proxy rules. The proxy rules both have failed to provide affirmative access for shareholders to participate in the nomination process and have thwarted shareholder attempts at participation.

The most obvious omission from the federal proxy rules is a mechanism for shareholders to access the nomination process. * * * In 1942, the SEC proposed a rule that would have required corporations to include shareholder nominated director candidates in the corporation's proxy statement.[100] Corporate management criticized the rule on the grounds that it was unworkable; shareholders might nominate unqualified candidates or create ballot confusion by nominating too many candidates. These interferences with effective corporate management could prove costly in connection with the wartime effort. Ultimately the SEC abandoned its efforts to pass the rule. Ironically, the exclusion [of Rule 14a–8] originated with * * * [this] proposal * * *. Subsequently, the SEC amended the text of the Rule to exclude proposals relating to director elections explicitly. * * *

Although the SEC has not interpreted the exclusion to bar general proposals relating to election procedures, such as cumulative voting rights and general qualifications for directors, the provision prevents a shareholder from using Rule 14a–8 to nominate or advocate the election of a particular director. Furthermore, the SEC has allowed management to rely on the exclusion to bar any proposal that could be viewed as interfering with election of existing directors or director slates. * * *

(2) In United Paperworkers International Union v. International Paper Co., 985 F.2d 1190 (2d Cir.1993), the Union filed a Rule 14a–8 request that the company sign and actively implement the "Valdez principles" relating to reducing waste, marketing safe products, and providing redress for environmental damage. The company included the proposal in its proxy statement, and recommended a vote against it, stating that "International Paper is dedicated to safe and environmentally sound products, packaging and operations;" that the Valdez principles are consistent with the company's "long-standing policies on environment, health and safety" and that the company had a "strong environmental compliance

100. [By the Author] Exchange Act Release No. 3347, 1942 SEC LEXIS 44 (Dec. 18, 1942).

program." It turned out that these statements were simply false: the company had been accused of numerous environmental offenses, had pleaded guilty to felonies, had agreed to pay large fines, and had been the target of numerous administrative complaints. The District Court refused to enjoin the meeting and the Valdez proposal was defeated, receiving 5.937 percent of the votes cast. However, the District Court ordered the corporation to resubmit the Valdez proposal at the next annual meeting, and the Court of Appeals directed that a statement "such as the following" should be included:

> (i) that the district court declared the board of directors' March 31, 1992 proxy statement, in responding to the Valdez Proposal, to be materially misleading in violation of federal securities law; (ii) that the district court declared the shareholder vote held May 12, 1992, on the Valdez Resolution null and void; and (iii) that the district court ordered the Company to resubmit the proposal for a new vote of the shareholders.

Id. at 1202. Is that sufficient? Should a court get in the business of writing corrective language for a proxy statement?

(3) Most shareholder proposals are phrased as recommendations or requests for director action and thus fall comfortably within the note to paragraph (i)(1) of question 9. However, not all proposals are so phrased. In 1992, a shareholder of Exxon proposed the creation of a three member shareholder advisory committee to review the management of Exxon's business affairs and to advise the board of directors both of its own views and the views of other shareholders; the advisory committee was to have the power to employ outside advisers and also to include a 2,500 word report and evaluation in the Exxon proxy statement. Large shareholders were to be entitled to nominate advisory committee members who would be elected by the shareholders along with the directors. The critical state law issue raised by this proposal was that it was cast in the form of a proposed amendment to the Exxon bylaws, a matter on which shareholders are entitled to vote under New Jersey law. The SEC staff required the proposal to be included over the arguments (i) that it was excludable as relating to "ordinary business operations" and (ii) that it was not a "proper subject" of shareholder action under New Jersey law since it was inconsistent with the general prescription that the business affairs of the corporation was to be managed by or under the direction of a board of directors. The proposal received the affirmative vote of about 8 percent of Exxon shareholders.

The Exxon decision, however, was not followed in early 1993 when a similar mandatory bylaw proposal was advanced for inclusion in the Pennzoil proxy statement. Pennzoil submitted an opinion by its Delaware counsel that the proposal was contrary to Delaware statutory and case law since it interfered with the discretion of directors. After the staff indicated that it intended to issue a no action letter permitting the proposal to be excluded, the applicant amended the proposal to make it a request addressed to the board of directors. The staff, however, concluded that this proposal also need not be included since it provided that the proposed bylaw could be amended only by shareholders and that was not proper under state law. The history of the Exxon/Pennzoil proposals is discussed in John C. Coffee, Jr., The SEC and the Institutional Investor: a Halftime Report, 15 Cardozo L.Rev. 837, 882–91 (1994); see also Charles F. Richards and Anne C. Foster, Exxon Revisited: The SEC Allows Pennzoil To Exclude Both Mandatory and Precatory Proposals Seeking to Create a Shareholder Advisory Committee, 48 Bus. Law. 1509 (1993); John C. Coffee, Jr., The Bylaw Battlefield: Can Institutions Change the Outcome of Corporate Control Contests, 51 U. Miami L. Rev. 605 (1997).

(4) Shareholder activists have been trying to persuade the SEC to allow shareholders to nominate corporate board members. In October 2003 the Commission proposed rules that would give shareholders the right in some circumstances to nominate directors. The proposals met stiff opposition from groups such as the U.S. Chamber of Commerce and the rules were never adopted. See Phil McCarty, SEC's Proxy Plan Threatened With Suit by Business Chamber, Wall St. J., Mar. 11, 2004, at A6. In September 2006, the U.S. Court of Appeals for the Second Circuit reinvigorated the debate about shareholder access to corporate proxies in its decision in American Federation of State, County & Municipal Employees, Employees Pension Plan v. American International Group, Inc. (AIG), 462 F.3d 121 (2d Cir. 2006). The union, an AIG shareholder, had submitted a proposal to be included in the proxy statement that would amend the bylaws to require that the names of shareholder-nominated candidates to the board of directors be included in proxy materials alongside candidates nominated by the AIG board. AIG excluded the proposal and the union sued. The district court found in favor of the company, citing a 1990 SEC interpretation of Rule 14a–8.

The Second Circuit reversed, finding that the 1990 interpretation was at odds with the Commission's interpretation at the time the Rule was implemented fifteen years earlier. The Court held the original interpretation controlled, and that shareholder proposals that sought to change a corporation's bylaws so as to establish a procedure by which shareholder candidates would be included on the corporate ballot can not be excluded under Rule 14a–8. Therefore the union's proposal should be included in the proxy. In response to the decision, the SEC announced it would convene an open hearing on the topic of shareholder access to proxies in October 2006. Consideration of any amendments to Rule 14a–8 was delayed from October to December 2006. As of early 2007, the outcome of the SEC's renewed interest in enabling shareholder access to proxies was uncertain.

(5) Rule 14a–4 provides that an issuer's proxy materials must disclose matters that it believes will be presented at the meeting, "whether raised by management or shareholders." In 1996, two labor unions targeted ten companies for shareholder proposals and, in an effort to avoid Rule 14a–8 limitations, submitted proposals directly under Rule 14a–4 with a statement that they will be raised by individual shareholders at the meeting and requesting that information about them be included in the company's proxy statement. The Company refused. This "backdoor" approach to avoiding the limitations of Rule 14a–8 was short-circuited when the SEC informally accepted the Company's position on the specific facts presented, but there is obvious tension between Rule 14a–8 and Rule 14a–4.

5.   COMMUNICATING WITH SHAREHOLDERS

REGULATION 14A.   SOLICITATION OF PROXIES
17 C.F.R. § 240.14a–7 (2002).

§ 240.14a–7   OBLIGATIONS OF REGISTRANTS TO PROVIDE A LIST OF, OR MAIL SOLICITING MATERIAL TO, SECURITY HOLDERS

(a) If the registrant has made or intends to make a proxy solicitation in connection with a security holder meeting or action by consent or authorization, upon the written request by any record or beneficial holder of securities of the class entitled to vote at the meeting or to execute a consent or authorization to provide a list of security holders or to mail the requesting security holder's materials, regardless of whether the request references this section, the registrant shall:

(1) Deliver to the requesting security holder within five business days after receipt of the request:

(i) Notification as to whether the registrant has elected to mail the security holder's soliciting materials or provide a security holder list if the election under paragraph (b) of this section is to be made by the registrant;

(ii) A statement of the approximate number of record holders and beneficial holders, separated by type of holder and class, owning securities in the same class or classes as holders which have been or are to be solicited on management's behalf * * *; and

(iii) The estimated cost of mailing a proxy statement, form of proxy or other communication to such holders * * *;

(2) Perform the acts set forth in either paragraphs (a)(2)(i) or (a)(2)(ii) of this section, at the registrant's or requesting security holder's option * * *:

(i) Mail copies of any proxy statement, form of proxy or other soliciting material furnished by the security holder to the record holders, including banks, brokers, and similar entities, designated by the security holder. * * * The registrant shall mail the security holder material with reasonable promptness after tender of the material to be mailed, envelopes or other containers therefor, postage or payment for postage and other reasonable expenses of effecting such mailing. The registrant shall not be responsible for the content of the material; or

(ii) Deliver the following information to the requesting security holder within five business days of receipt of the request: a reasonably current list of the names, addresses and security positions of the record holders, including banks, brokers and similar entities, holding securities in the same class or classes as holders which have been or are to be solicited on management's behalf, or any more limited group of such holders designated by the security holder if available or retrievable under the registrant's or its transfer agent's security holder data systems; the most recent list of names, addresses and security positions of [nonobjecting] beneficial owners * * * in the possession, or which subsequently comes into the possession, of the registrant. All security holder list information shall be in the form requested by the security holder to the extent that such form is available to the registrant without undue burden or expense. The registrant shall furnish the security holder with updated record holder information on a daily basis or, if not available on a daily basis, at the shortest reasonable intervals, *provided, however*, the registrant need not provide beneficial or record holder information more current than the record date for the meeting or action. * * *

(e) The security holder shall reimburse the reasonable expenses incurred by the registrant in performing the acts requested pursuant to paragraph (a) of this rule.

Notes

(1) Omitted portions of this rule provide that the requesting security holder must certify that he will not misuse or disclose the information provided under this rule.

(2) Many institutional investors routinely publish detailed information about their portfolios, and it may be possible to learn the identities of the major beneficial owners of a large, publicly held corporation through this route more simply (and without alerting the registrant) than by invoking rule 14a–7 or seeking to inspect the shareholders list under state law.

6. REGULATION FD

Mandatory public disclosure is the most significant defining characteristic of securities regulation in the United States. However, historically there has been a significant amount of private disclosure of sensitive information by publicly held corporations to securities analysts, securities brokers, and other professionals in the securities industry.[101] It was customary, for example, for a securities analyst to have private conversations with the chief financial officer of a corporation prior to the analyst announcing an estimate of the company's short-term future performance. Such information can obviously be used by the recipient to make substantial profits before it is disclosed publicly and the markets react. While doubtless most of the information so disclosed was not used for private profit, the temptation certainly exists. In 2000, the SEC developed a controversial program designed to "level the playing field" and assure immediate public disclosure of sensitive information that is being made available to professionals (and some shareholders) by an issuer. The disclosure requirement is set forth in Regulation FD, Rel. No. 33–7881 (Aug. 24, 2000), effective October 23, 2000. "FD" stands for "Fair Disclosure."

Regulation FD provides that a company disclosing material, non-public information to specified types of securities market professionals (or shareholders "under circumstances in which it is reasonably foreseeable that the security holder will trade on the basis of the information") must thereafter publicly disclose that information. Such disclosure is called "selective disclosure." If the selective disclosure is "intentional," the company must simultaneously make public disclosure; if "unintentional" the disclosure must be made "promptly" thereafter.[102]

Regulation FD relates to information that is material and not previously available. The following is not material non-public information: "in our most recent earnings report we have given the following guidance" (since the earnings report is publicly available and is not being supplemented or modified by the statement). However, the following may be material non-public information: "we have not changed the guidance given in our most recent earnings report" (since this statement adds the previously undisclosed fact that conditions have not changed since the earnings report). Fed.Sec.L.Rep.

---

101. [By the Editors] Of course, there may also be disclosure by corporate executives to friends, family members, and the like. Such disclosures presumably often lead to unlawful insider trading. See Chapter 12, infra.

102. US Securities and Exchange Commission, Fact Sheet: Regulation Fair Disclosure and New Insider Trading Rules, available at http://www.sec.gov/news/extra/seldsfct.htm (last accessed Mar. 5, 2005).

No. 1947 (11/1/00). However, innocently providing a "snippet" of information that is not itself material to a securities professional is not a violation of Regulation FD even though it may enable the professional to infer material non-public information.

The "public disclosure" requirement may be met by a press release distributed through widely circulated news or wire services, announcements made through press conferences or conference calls that interested members of the public may attend or listen to either in person,[103] by telephonic transmission, or by other electronic transmission, including use of the Internet. The public must be given adequate notice of the conference or call and the means for accessing it. In addition, the public disclosure requirement may be met by filing or furnishing a widely used SEC form, Form 8–K.

Regulation FD states specifically that a failure to make a required disclosure does not of itself constitute securities fraud actionable under Rule 10b–5 (discussed in chapter 13). A plaintiff may not rely on a failure to make a required disclosure under Regulation FD in a law suit under that Rule.

The SEC suffered a setback in its enforcement of Regulation FD in August 2005. A court dismissed the SEC's action against Siebel Systems arising from allegations that in 2003, at two private events, the company's CFO told institutional investors the company's business activities were "good" and "better" and that there were several $5 million deals in the works. The court found the disclosures were neither material nor non-public. In dismissing the case, the judge reprimanded the SEC for enforcing Reg FD in an overly aggressive manner, asserting such actions "cannot effectively encourage full and complete public disclosure of facts reasonably deemed relevant to investment decision making." SEC v. Siebel Systems, Inc., 384 F.Supp.2d 694, 708 (S.D.N.Y. 2005).

A second major development relates to audit committees. In early 1999 a Blue Ribbon Committee on Corporate Audit Committee Effectiveness was formed by the NYSE and the NASD at the suggestion of the Chairman of the SEC, who had often expressed the concern that many audit committees failed to adequately monitor management and work with the outside auditors themselves. His major concern was that the accounting industry was being transformed by significant changes in the structure of the largest accounting firms. The non-audit functions provided by these major firms had increased significantly and the revenues from those services had increased in a similar fashion. The importance of these revenues might have an adverse impact on the independence of the auditing firm. Also, concern was expressed that there was increased mobility of accounting firm employees and dual career families that increased the number of conflicts of interest and improper disclosures arising from the audit.

In 2000, the SEC approved another controversial rule addressing auditor independence in the context of these significant changes within the auditing industry. The rule was proposed in SEC Rel. 33–7870 (July 12, 2000), and modified and promulgated in SEC Rel. 33–7919 (December 5, 2000). Among other things, the rule requires disclosures in the proxy statement of the non-

---

103. [By the Editors] The regulations add that "public disclosure" does not require that members of the general public be given the opportunity to ask questions or make comments.

audit functions being performed by the outside auditor and other matters possibly affecting the independence of the auditor. The SEC received more than 3,000 comment letters on its original proposed rule. The final release, responding to these letters and promulgating a rule establishing new independence standards for auditors, runs hundreds of pages.

The Sarbanes–Oxley Act of 2002 also makes dramatic changes in the legal responsibilities of audit committees, the regulation of the accounting profession, and the relationship between corporations and their auditors. The statute creates a new independent regulatory entity, the Public Company Accounting Oversight Board (PCAOB), consisting of five members to oversee the auditing of publicly traded companies. Under Sarbanes–Oxley, the SEC appoints the chair and other members of the PCAOB, after consultation with the Chairman of the Board of Governors of the Federal Reserve System and the Secretary of the Treasury. The PCAOB is funded by fees assessed against public companies and is broadly charged with responsibility for regulating the accounting profession.

Section 202 of Sarbanes–Oxley imposes significant new responsibilities on audit committees. All audit services must be pre-approved by corporate management and the company's audit committee. Section 201(a) of Sarbanes–Oxley goes significantly beyond the requirements of prior law by making it unlawful for accounting firms that audit public companies simultaneously to provide the company with a variety of non-audit services: book-keeping, services related to accounting records and financial statements, financial information systems design and implementation, fairness opinions, management or human resource functions, legal services, and expert services unrelated to the audit.

In essence, Sarbanes–Oxley requires accounting firms to contract for services with the audit committees of the boards of directors of the companies they propose to audit rather than with management. This major change in the relationship between auditors and audit clients is effectuated by Section 301 of Sarbanes–Oxley, which provides that the audit committee of each issuer "shall be directly responsible for the appointment, compensation, and oversight of the work of any registered public accounting firm employed by the issuer (including resolution of disagreements between management and the auditor regarding financial reporting)."[104]

The power of audit committees is bolstered by provisions in Sarbanes–Oxley that require any accounting firm performing an audit of a public company to timely report to the audit committee: (1) all critical accounting policies and practices; (2) all alternative treatments of financial information within GAAP that have been discussed with management, the "ramifications" of the use of such alternative disclosures and treatments, and the treatment preferred by the accounting firm; and (3) other material written communications between the registered public accounting firm and management of the issuer.[105]

---

104. Public Law 107–204, Section 301, amending Section 10A of the Securities Exchange Act of 1934, (15 U.S.C. Section 78f).

105. Public Law 107–204, Section 204, amending Section 10A of the Securities Exchange Act of 1934, (15 U.S.C. Section 78j–1).

Sarbanes–Oxley also requires the audit committee to set up procedures for handling complaints by "whistleblowers" within the company,[106] and to engage independent legal counsel and other advisors where necessary to carry out its duties.[107]

Perhaps the best-known provisions of Sarbanes–Oxley are the new rules relating to "Corporate Responsibility for Financial Reports."[108] These rules require the principal executive officer (CEO), and the principal financial officer (CFO) of each public company to certify that he/she has reviewed each quarterly or annual report filed with the SEC, that to his or her knowledge the report does not contain any material false statements or omissions, and that it fairly presents, in all material respects, the financial condition and results of operations of the company for the period being reported. CEOs and CFOs also must certify that they have evaluated the effectiveness of the company's internal controls and have presented their conclusions about the effectiveness of such controls.[109] Knowingly false certifications may be punished by fines of up to $1 million and imprisonment not exceeding ten years.[110]

Other provisions of Sarbanes–Oxley are designed to restore the integrity of the public company audit process. They make it unlawful for any person to fraudulently influence, coerce manipulate, or to mislead any accountant performing an audit of the company's financial statements for the purpose of rendering the financial statements materially misleading.[111] Audit firms also are forbidden to perform audit services for a public company if the company's chief executive officer, controller, chief financial officer, chief accounting officer, or similarly situated corporate official has been employed by the accounting firm and participated in the audit of the company during the one-year period prior to the initiation of the audit.[112]

Outside of these requirements, auditors are subject to whistle-blowing provisions of the Private Securities Litigation Reform Act of 1995.[113] They must include as part of their audit process procedures designed to detect illegal acts by their clients and under certain circumstances report such illegal activity to the SEC.

---

106. Public Law 107–204, Section 301(4), amending Section 10A of the Securities Exchange Act of 1934, (15 U.S.C. Section 78f), provides that public company audit committees must establish procedures for:

(A) the receipt, retention, and treatment of complaints received by the issuer regarding accounting, internal accounting controls, or auditing matters; and

(B) the confidential, anonymous submission by employees of the issuer of concerns regarding questionable accounting matters.

Section 806 of the Act provides further protection for whistleblowers by making it illegal to retaliate against or to harass people who assist in an investigation of the company's violations of securities laws.

107. Public Law 107–204, Section 301(6)(B), amending Section 10A of the Securi-

ties Exchange Act of 1934, (15 U.S.C. Section 78f).

108. Public Law 107–204, Section 302.

109. Public Law 107–204, Section 302(a).

110. Public Law 107–204, Section 906 (c)(1), amending Chapter 63 of title, 18, USC, by inserting new material after existing Section 1349. Willful violations are punished even more severely than knowing violations. See Section 906(c)(2), punishing willful violations with fines of up to $5 million, and/or 20 years of imprisonment.

111. Public Law 107–204, Section 303(c).

112. Public Law 107–204, Section 206, amending Section 10A of the Securities Exchange Act of 1934 (15 USC 78j–1).

113. [By the Editors] Section 10A of PSLRA, 15 U.S.C. § 78j–1.

Chapter Eleven

DUTY OF CARE AND THE BUSINESS JUDGMENT RULE

LITWIN v. ALLEN

Supreme Court of New York, 1940.
25 N.Y.S.2d 667.

SHIENTAG, JUSTICE.

[Editors: This was a derivative suit brought on behalf of persons owning 36 shares of the stock of Guaranty Trust Company ("Trust Company") out of 900,000 outstanding against the directors of Guaranty Trust, members of the banking firm of J.P. Morgan & Co., and directors of a subsidiary of the Trust Company called Guaranty Company of New York ("Guaranty Company."). The complaint sought to impose liability on the defendants for losses incurred as a result of four transactions. The Court concluded that no liability existed for three of the transactions. The portions of the opinion set forth below relate to the Justice's general discussion and the fourth transaction on which liability was imposed. The sequence of the paragraphs set forth below has been rearranged.] * * *

II.

THE MISSOURI PACIFIC BOND TRANSACTION

This transaction involves the participation by the Trust Company or Guaranty Company or both, to the extent of $3,000,000, in a purchase of Missouri Pacific convertible debentures on October 16, 1930, through the firm of J.P. Morgan & Co. at par, with an option to the seller, Alleghany Corporation to repurchase them at the same price at any time within six months.

In the fall of 1930, the question of putting Alleghany Corporation in funds to the extent of $10,500,000 was first broached. Alleghany had purchased certain terminal properties in Kansas City and St. Joseph, Missouri, and the balance of the purchase price, amounting to slightly in excess of $10,000,000 and interest, had to be paid by October 16. Alleghany needed money to make this payment. Because of the borrowing limitation in Alleghany's charter (which limitation had been reached or exceeded in October 1930) Alleghany was unable to borrow the money. To overcome this borrowing limitation and solely to enable Alleghany to consummate the purchase of the terminal properties, discussions were commenced concerning the means whereby the necessary money could be raised. It is important that this circumstance be constantly kept in mind, in order that the purpose and pattern of the transaction as it did take place be fully understood.

Not being able to make a loan, the way that Alleghany could raise the necessary funds was by sale of some of the securities that it held. Among them was a large block of about $23,500,000 of Missouri Pacific convertible 5 1/2 debentures. These were unsecured and subordinate to other Missouri Pacific bond issues. They were convertible into common stock at the rate of ten shares for each $1,000 bond. In 1929, Guaranty Company had participated to the extent of $1,500,000 in the underwriting of these bonds at 97 1/2. At one time in 1929, the bonds had sold as high as 124 and had never gone below par except in November 1929 when they sold at 97. Between October 1 and October 10, 1930 Missouri Pacific common stock had dropped from 53 to 44. There was a decline in the bonds from 113 in April 1930 to 107 on October 1, 1930, and thereafter a decline of about two more points to 105 1/2 by the date of the consummation of the transaction we are considering on October 16, 1930.

The Van Sweringens suggested that $10,000,000 of these bonds be sold to J.P. Morgan & Co. for cash at par, the latter to give an option to Alleghany to buy them back within six months for the price paid. If the transaction were carried through on that basis, namely, a sale by Alleghany with an option to them to repurchase at the same price, the same purpose would be accomplished, for Alleghany at any rate, as if a loan had been made.

The defendants testified that they were informed that the Van Sweringens insisted upon the option to repurchase within six months in order that there might be no possibility of their loss of control of Missouri Pacific through Alleghany, since these bonds were convertible and the privilege to do so might be exercised by third parties in the event of a distribution of these bonds in the market; this, despite the fact that the common stock of Missouri Pacific was then quoted in the neighborhood of 44, while the conversion price was 100.

The fact is that the only purpose served by the option was to make the transaction conform as closely as possible to a loan without the usual incidents of a loan transaction. * * *

At or shortly before the time that the Trust Company made its written commitment to J.P. Morgan & Co. to participate in the bond purchase, the Guaranty Company committed itself to the Trust Company to take up the bonds from the Trust Company at the end of the six-months' period, on April 16, 1931, for the same price that the Trust Company paid, that is, par and interest, if Alleghany failed to exercise its option to repurchase. * * *

The decline in the market continued. On October 23, 1930, when the Executive Committee of the Trust Company approved the transaction the Missouri Pacific bonds were at 103 7/8. On November 5, 1930, when the Board of Directors of the Trust Company gave its approval, the bonds sold for 102 7/8, and on November 18, 1930, when the board of the Guaranty Company approved its commitment, the bonds had dropped to 98 5/8. At the end of the six months' period, on April 16, 1931, the bonds sold at 86 high and 81 low (the quotations being for the week ending April 18), and Guaranty

Company took them over from the Trust Company at par and accrued interest and carried them on its books as an investment. * * *

[T]he main transactions attacked in this case * * * took place in October, 1930. There had been a crash in the stock market in October, 1929. In April, 1930, there was an upswing in the market. Shortly thereafter there began a slow but steady decline until October, 1930, when there was another severe break. The real significance of what was taking place was, generally speaking, missed at the time, but is plain in retrospect. Forces were at work which for the most part were unforeseeable. Men who were judging conditions in October, 1930, by what had been the course and the experience of past panics thought that the bottom had been reached and that the worst of the depression was over; that any change would be for the better and that recovery might reasonably be envisaged for the near future. Experience turned out to be fallacious and judgment proved to be erroneous; but that did not become apparent until some time in 1931. In order to judge the transactions complained of, therefore, we must not only hold an inquest on the past but, what is much more difficult, we must attempt to take ourselves back to the time when the events here questioned occurred and try to put ourselves in the position of those who engaged in them. * * *

There is no evidence in this case of any improper influence or domination of the directors or officers of the Trust Company or of the Guaranty Company by J.P. Morgan & Co. When J.P. Morgan & Co. were advised by Shriver that there would be a participation in the purchase to the extent of $5,000,000 the latter was told that such a commitment would be accepted only to the extent of $3,000,000 because the First National Bank of New York would be given a similar amount while Morgan & Co. themselves would participate to the extent of the balance amounting to $4,500,000. Moreover, there is no evidence to indicate that any of the defendants' officers or directors acted in bad faith or profited or attempted to profit or gain personally by reason of any phase of this transaction. * * *

I shall now proceed to consider generally the rules to be applied in determining the liability of directors. It has sometimes been said that directors are trustees. If this means that directors in the performance of their duties stand in a fiduciary relationship to the company, that statement is essentially correct. Bosworth v. Allen, 168 N.Y. 157, 61 N.E. 163, 55 L.R.A. 751, 85 Am.St.Rep. 667. "The directors are bound by all those rules of conscientious fairness, morality, and honesty in purpose which the law imposes as the guides for those who are under the fiduciary obligations and responsibilities. They are held, in official action, to the extreme measure of candor, unselfishness, and good faith. Those principles are rigid, essential, and salutary." Kavanaugh v. Kavanaugh Knitting Co., 226 N.Y. 185, 193, 123 N.E. 148, 151.

It is clear that a director owes loyalty and allegiance to the company—a loyalty that is undivided and an allegiance that is influenced in action by no consideration other than the welfare of the corporation. Any adverse interest of a director will be subjected to a scrutiny rigid and uncompromising. He may not profit at the expense of his corporation and in conflict with its rights; he may not for personal gain divert unto himself the opportunities which in equity and fairness belong to his corporation. He is required to use his independent judgment. In the discharge of his duties a director must, of course, act honestly and in good faith, but that is not enough. He must also exercise some degree of skill and prudence and diligence.

In a leading case the Court of Appeals, in referring to the duties of directors, said: "They should know of and give direction to the general affairs of the institution and its business policy, and have a general knowledge of the manner in which the business is conducted, the character of the investments, and the employment of the resources. No custom or practice can make a directorship a mere position of honor void of responsibility, or cause a name to become a substitute for care and attention. The personnel of a directorate may give confidence and attract custom; it must also afford protection." Kavanaugh v. Gould, 223 N.Y. 103, 106, 119 N.E. 237, 238.

In other words, directors are liable for negligence in the performance of their duties. Not being insurers, directors are not liable for errors of judgment or for mistakes while acting with reasonable skill and prudence. It has been said that a director is required to conduct the business of the corporation with the same degree of fidelity and care as an ordinarily prudent man would exercise in the management of his own affairs of like magnitude and importance. General rules, however, are not altogether helpful. In the last analysis, whether or not a director has discharged his duty, whether or not he has been negligent, depends upon the facts and circumstances of a particular case, the kind of corporation involved, its size and financial resources, the magnitude of the transaction, and the immediacy of the problem presented. A director is called upon "to bestow the care and skill" which the situation demands. New York Cent. Railroad Company v. Lockwood, 17 Wall. 357, 382, 383, 21 L.Ed. 627.

Undoubtedly, a director of a bank is held to stricter accountability than the director of an ordinary business corporation. A director of a bank is entrusted with the funds of depositors, and the stockholders look to him for protection from the imposition of personal liability. Gause v. Commonwealth Trust Co., 196 N.Y. 134, 153–155, 89 N.E. 476, 24 L.R.A., N.S., 967. But clairvoyance is not required even of a bank director. The law recognizes that the most conservative director is not infallible, and that he will make mistakes, but if he uses that degree of care ordinarily exercised by prudent bankers he will be absolved from liability although his opinion may turn out to have been mistaken and his judgment faulty.

Finally, in order to determine whether transactions approved by a director subject him to liability for negligence, we must "look at the facts as they exist at the time of their occurrence, not aided or enlightened by those which subsequently take place". Purdy v. Lynch, 145 N.Y. 462, 475, 40 N.E. 232, 236. "A wisdom developed after an event, and having it and its consequences as a source, is a standard no man should be judged by." Costello v. Costello, 209 N.Y. 252, 262, 103 N.E. 148, 152. * * *

Although * * * there is no case precisely in point, it would seem that if it is against public policy for a bank, anxious to dispose of some of its securities, to agree to buy them back at the same price, it is even more so where a bank purchases securities and gives the seller the option to buy them back at the same price, thereby incurring the entire risk of loss with no possibility of gain other than the interest derived from the securities during the period that the bank holds them. Here, if the market price of the securities should rise, the holder of the repurchase option would exercise it in order to recover his securities from the bank at the lower price at which he sold them to the bank. If the market price should fall, the seller holding the option will not exercise it and the bank will sustain the loss. Thus, any benefit of a sharp rise in the price of the securities is assured the seller and any risk of heavy loss is inevitably assumed by the bank. If such an option agreement as is here involved were sustained, it would force the bank to set aside for six months whatever securities it had purchased. A bank certainly could not free itself from this obligation by engaging in a "short sale". In other words, while a resale option would force a bank to freeze an amount of cash equal to the selling price of the securities sold by it, a repurchase option would force a bank to freeze the securities themselves for the period of the option. In both situations the true financial condition of the bank could not be determined wholly from its books. It would depend upon the fluctuations of the market. In both cases there is a contingent liability which the balance sheet does not show. * * *

Directors are not in the position of trustees of an express trust who, regardless of good faith, are personally liable for losses arising from an infraction of their trust deed. Matter of Smith, 279 N.Y. 479, 489, 18 N.E.2d 666; see Fletcher Cyc. Corp., Perm.Ed., § 847. If liability is to be imposed on these directors it should rest on a more solid foundation. I find liability in this transaction because the entire arrangement was so improvident, so risky, so unusual and unnecessary as to be contrary to fundamental conceptions of prudent banking practice. A bank director when appointed or elected takes oath that he will, so far as the duty devolves on him "diligently and honestly administer the affairs of the bank or trust company." Banking Law, § 117. The oath merely adds solemnity to the obligation which the law itself imposes. Honesty alone does not suffice; the honesty of the directors in this case is unquestioned. But there must be more than honesty—there must be diligence, and that means care and prudence, as well. This transaction, it has been said, was unusual; it was unique, yet there is nothing in the record to indicate that the advice of counsel was sought. It is not surprising that a precedent cannot be found dealing with such a situation.

What sound reason is there for a bank, desiring to make an investment, short term or otherwise, to buy securities under an arrangement whereby any appreciation will inure to the benefit of the seller and any loss will be borne by the bank? The five and one-half point differential is no answer. It does not meet the fundamental objection that whatever loss there is would have to be borne by the Bank and whatever gain would go to the customer. There is more here than a question of business judgment as to which men might well differ. The directors plainly failed in this instance to bestow the care which the situation demanded. Unless we are to do away entirely with the doctrine that directors of a bank are liable for negligence in administering its affairs liability should be imposed in connection with this transaction.

The same result would be reached if we adopted the defendants' version of this transaction, namely, that it was initially a purchase by the Guaranty Company, with an option to the Alleghany Corporation to rebuy at the same price, and that the transaction was financed by the Bank, so that the immediate interest that the Bank had in it was a short term 5 1/2% investment. * * *

Whichever way we look at this transaction, therefore, it was so improvident, so dangerous, so unusual and so contrary to ordinary prudent banking practice as to subject the directors who approved it to liability in a derivative stockholders' action.

The real issue as to damages is whether the directors should be liable for the total loss suffered when the bonds were ultimately sold, approximately an 81% loss, or only for that portion of the loss which accrued within the six months option period, making allowance for a period thereafter during which defendants could make reasonable and diligent efforts to sell the bonds. The record discloses that none of the bonds were sold until October 8, 1931, about six months after the Alleghany option had expired, and that they were not completely disposed of until December 28, 1937. The Missouri Pacific Railroad went into receivership in April, 1933, and between August 2 and September 25, 1933, $126,000 more of the bonds were purchased by the Company in an attempt to reduce the loss. A total loss was sustained on the bonds of approximately $2,250,000.

I believe that as to the decline of the bonds after April 16, 1931, there is no causal connection with the option which had expired on that date. A director is not liable for loss or damage other than what was proximately caused by his own acts or omissions in breach of his duty. The portion of the present transaction which is tainted with improvidence and negligence is the repurchase option. Once the option had expired, there was nothing to prevent the directors of the Company, which had taken over the bonds in accordance with its agreement, from selling them. Any loss on the bonds which was incurred after the option had expired on April 16, 1931, was occasioned as a result of the directors' independent business judgment in holding them thereafter. The further loss should not be laid at the door of the improper but already expired repurchase option.

Therefore, defendants are only liable for the loss attributable to the improper repurchase option itself, and this option ceased to be the motivating cause of the loss within a reasonable time after April 16, 1931. The price of the bonds for the week ending April 18, 1931, was 86 high and 81 low and closing. The matter will be referred to a Referee for assessment of damages to determine what price could have been obtained for these bonds if defendants had proceeded to sell them after April 16, 1931.

Defendants Charged With Liability

The next question to consider is: Against what defendants has liability been established?

1. All of the directors who were present and voted at the meetings of the Executive Committee of the Trust Company on October 23, 1930, and the meeting of the Board of Directors of the Trust Company on November 5, 1930, are liable. * * * [R]atification by directors of a transaction already consummated by the officers or by themselves acting as officers imposes liability upon the directors, since the ratification is equivalent to prior acquiescence. Fletcher, Cyc.Corp., Perm.Ed., § 782, and cases there collected. Ratification of the officer's acts was essential in order completely to bind the

Bank and the Company, and in any case such ratification vitiated a possible later rescission on the ground that it was not authorized by the directors.

2. Mr. Swan is liable even though he did not actually vote on the transaction as a director. His active participation and acquiescence are sufficient.

3. The defendants Kimball, Shriver and Stephenson while not directors are liable as officers who actively participated in the transaction.

4. No director of the Guaranty Company, as such, except Walker, is liable. He admittedly knew of the transaction, but there is nothing in the record to show that the repurchase option was brought to the attention of the directors at the meeting of the Executive Committee or of the Board of Directors of Guaranty Company. * * *

Note

Patricia A. McCoy, The Notional Business Judgment Rule in Banking, 44 Cath.U.L.Rev. 1031, 1038–40 (1995):

> The one aspect of judicial substantive bank regulation that the corporate law literature has probed consists of a handful of cases, notably Hun v. Cary[1] and Litwin v. Allen, that struck down bank decisions for lack of "minimum rationality." These cases earned the sobriquet "minimum rationality" because they sought to stamp out transactions that were patently irrational from the bank's or depositors' point of view: i.e., transactions with no apparent profit potential on their face. * * *

> In the half century since *Litwin*, its soundness on the facts has been rightly challenged. True, the directors signed away the right to potential market appreciation for six months while retaining the risk of loss. But the matter did not end there. Even without a put,[2] the transaction might have been potentially profitable if the directors had bargained for some other consideration, such as higher interest or a collateral financial benefit. And in fact, they did: after all, Guaranty Trust was entitled to 5% interest. * * *

> These uncertainties are testament to the fact that it is no easy thing to pinpoint lack of profit potential from the bench, even with the benefit of hindsight. For this reason, later courts shied away from this type of financial analysis in banking cases, leaving *Hun* and *Litwin* in splendid isolation. * * * The fact that courts do not even ask if overdrafts are potentially profitable shows how moribund the "minimum rationality" test has become.

SHLENSKY v. WRIGLEY

Appellate Court of Illinois, 1968.
95 Ill.App.2d 173, 237 N.E.2d 776.

SULLIVAN, JUSTICE.

This is an appeal from a dismissal of plaintiff's amended complaint on motion of the defendants. The action was a stockholders' derivative suit

---

1. [By the Author] 82 N.Y. 65 (N.Y. 1880).

2. [By the Editors] A "put" is a type of option that gives the holder the contractual right, but not the obligation, to sell a security at a fixed price for a stated period. A put option protects the owner of the option against downturns in the price of the underlying security.

Paul Luzzi

against the directors for negligence and mismanagement. The corporation was also made a defendant. Plaintiff sought damages and an order that defendants cause the installation of lights in Wrigley Field and the scheduling of night baseball games.

Plaintiff is a minority stockholder of defendant corporation, Chicago National League Ball Club (Inc.), a Delaware corporation with its principal place of business in Chicago, Illinois. Defendant corporation owns and operates the major league professional baseball team known as the Chicago Cubs. The corporation also engages in the operation of Wrigley Field, the Cubs' home park, the concessionaire sales during Cubs' home games, television and radio broadcasts of Cubs' home games, the leasing of the field for football games and other events and receives its share, as visiting team, of admission moneys from games played in other National League stadia. The individual defendants are directors of the Cubs and have served for varying periods of years. Defendant Philip K. Wrigley is also president of the corporation and owner of approximately 80% of the stock therein.

Plaintiff alleges that since night baseball was first played in 1935 nineteen of the twenty major league teams have scheduled night games. In 1966, out of a total of 1620 games in the major leagues, 932 were played at night. Plaintiff alleges that every member of the major leagues, other than the Cubs, scheduled substantially all of its home games in 1966 at night, exclusive of opening days, Saturdays, Sundays, holidays and days prohibited by league rules. Allegedly this has been done for the specific purpose of maximizing attendance and thereby maximizing revenue and income.

The Cubs, in the years 1961–65, sustained operating losses from its direct baseball operations. Plaintiff attributes those losses to inadequate attendance at Cubs' home games. He concludes that if the directors continue to refuse to install lights at Wrigley Field and schedule night baseball games, the Cubs will continue to sustain comparable losses and its financial condition will continue to deteriorate.

Plaintiff alleges that, except for the year 1963, attendance at Cubs' home games has been substantially below that at their road games, many of which were played at night.

Plaintiff compares attendance at Cubs' games with that of the Chicago White Sox, an American League club, whose weekday games were generally played at night. The weekend attendance figures for the two teams was similar; however, the White Sox week-night games drew many more patrons than did the Cubs' weekday games.

Plaintiff alleges that the funds for the installation of lights can be readily obtained through financing and the cost of installation would be far more than offset and recaptured by increased revenues and incomes resulting from the increased attendance.

Plaintiff further alleges that defendant Wrigley has refused to install lights, not because of interest in the welfare of the corporation but because of his personal opinions "that baseball is a 'daytime sport' and that the installation of lights and night baseball games will have a deteriorating effect upon the surrounding neighborhood." It is alleged that he has admitted that he is not interested in whether the Cubs would benefit financially from such action because of his concern for the neighborhood, and that he would be willing for the team to play night games if a new stadium were built in Chicago.

Plaintiff alleges that the other defendant directors, with full knowledge of the foregoing matters, have acquiesced in the policy laid down by Wrigley and have permitted him to dominate the board of directors in matters involving the installation of lights and scheduling of night games, even though they knew he was not motivated by a good faith concern as to the best interests of defendant corporation, but solely by his personal views set forth above. It is charged that the directors are acting for a reason or reasons contrary and wholly unrelated to the business interests of the corporation; that such arbitrary and capricious acts constitute mismanagement and waste of corporate assets, and that the directors have been negligent in failing to exercise reasonable care and prudence in the management of the corporate affairs.

The question on appeal is whether plaintiff's amended complaint states a cause of action. It is plaintiff's position that fraud, illegality and conflict of interest are not the only bases for a stockholder's derivative action against the directors. Contrariwise, defendants argue that the courts will not step in and interfere with honest business judgment of the directors unless there is a showing of fraud, illegality or conflict of interest.

The cases in this area are numerous and each differs from the others on a factual basis. However, the courts have pronounced certain ground rules which appear in all cases and which are then applied to the given factual situation. The court in Wheeler v. Pullman Iron and Steel Company, 143 Ill. 197, 207, 32 N.E. 420, 423, said:

> It is, however, fundamental in the law of corporations, that the majority of its stockholders shall control the policy of the corporation, and regulate and govern the lawful exercise of its franchise and business. * * * Every one purchasing or subscribing for stock in a corporation impliedly agrees that he will be bound by the acts and proceedings done or sanctioned by a majority of the shareholders, or by the agents of the corporation duly chosen by such majority, within the scope of the powers conferred by the charter, and courts of equity will not undertake to control the policy or business methods of a corporation, although it may be seen that a wiser policy might be adopted and the business more successful if other methods were pursued. The majority of shares of its stock, or the agents by the holders thereof lawfully chosen, must be permitted to control the business of the corporation in their discretion, when not in violation of its charter or some public law, or corruptly and fraudulently subversive of the rights and interests of the corporation or of a shareholder.

The standards set in Delaware are also clearly stated in the cases. In Davis v. Louisville Gas & Electric Co., 16 Del.Ch. 157, 142 A. 654, a minority shareholder sought to have the directors enjoined from amending the certificate of incorporation. The court said on page 659:

> We have then a conflict in view between the responsible managers of a corporation and an overwhelming majority of its stockholders on the one hand and a dissenting minority on the other—a conflict touching matters of business policy, such as has occasioned innumerable applications to courts to intervene and determine which of the two conflicting views should prevail. The response which courts make to such applications is

that it is not their function to resolve for corporations questions of policy and business management. The directors are chosen to pass upon such questions and their judgment *unless shown to be tainted with fraud* is accepted as final. The judgment of the directors of corporations enjoys the benefit of a presumption that it was formed in good faith and was designed to promote the best interests of the corporation they serve. (Emphasis supplied) * * *

Plaintiff argues that the allegations of his amended complaint are sufficient to set forth a cause of action under the principles set out in Dodge v. Ford Motor Co., 204 Mich. 459, 170 N.W. 668. In that case plaintiff, owner of about 10% of the outstanding stock, brought suit against the directors seeking payment of additional dividends and the enjoining of further business expansion. In ruling on the request for dividends the court indicated that the motives of Ford in keeping so much money in the corporation for expansion and security were to benefit the public generally and spread the profits out by means of more jobs, etc. The court felt that these were not only far from related to the good of the stockholders, but amounted to a change in the ends of the corporation and that this was not a purpose contemplated or allowed by the corporate charter. The court relied on language found in Hunter v. Roberts, Throp & Co., 83 Mich. 63, 47 N.W. 131, 134, wherein it was said:

Courts of equity will not interfere in the management of the directors unless it is clearly made to appear that they are guilty of fraud or misappropriation of the corporate funds, or refuse to declare a dividend when the corporation has a surplus of net profits which it can, without detriment to its business, divide among its stockholders, and when a refusal to do so would amount to such an abuse of discretion as would constitute a fraud or breach of that good faith which they are bound to exercise toward the stockholders.

From the authority relied upon in that case it is clear that the court felt that there must be fraud or a breach of that good faith which directors are bound to exercise toward the stockholders in order to justify the courts entering into the internal affairs of corporations. This is made clear when the court refused to interfere with the directors' decision to expand the business. The following appears on page 684 of 170 N.W.:

We are not, however, persuaded that we should interfere with the proposed expansion of the business of the Ford Motor Company. In view of the fact that the selling price of products may be increased at any time, the ultimate results of the larger business cannot be certainly estimated. *The judges are not business experts.* It is recognized that plans must often be made for a long future, for expected competition, for a continuing as well as an immediately profitable venture. * * * We are not satisfied that the alleged motives of the directors, in so far as they are reflected in the conduct of business, menace the interests of the shareholders. (Emphasis supplied)

Plaintiff in the instant case argues that the directors are acting for reasons unrelated to the financial interest and welfare of the Cubs. However, we are not satisfied that the motives assigned to Philip K. Wrigley, and through him to the other directors, are contrary to the best interests of the corporation and the stockholders. For example, it appears to us that the effect on the surrounding neighborhood might well be considered by a director who was considering the patrons who would or would not attend the games if the park were in a poor neighborhood. Furthermore, the long run interest of the corporation in its property value at Wrigley Field might demand all efforts to keep the neighborhood from deteriorating. By these thoughts we do not mean to say that we have decided that the decision of the directors was a correct one. That is beyond our jurisdiction and ability. We are merely saying that the decision is one properly before directors and the motives alleged in the amended complaint showed no fraud, illegality or conflict of interest in their making of that decision.

While all the courts do not insist that one or more of the three elements must be present for a stockholder's derivative action to lie, nevertheless we feel that unless the conduct of the defendants at least borders on one of the elements, the courts should not interfere. The trial court in the instant case acted properly in dismissing plaintiff's amended complaint.

We feel that plaintiff's amended complaint was also defective in failing to allege damage to the corporation. * * *

There is no allegation that the night games played by the other nineteen teams enhanced their financial position or that the profits, if any, of those teams were directly related to the number of night games scheduled. There is an allegation that the installation of lights and scheduling of night games in Wrigley Field would have resulted in large amounts of additional revenues and incomes from increased attendance and related sources of income. Further, the cost of installation of lights, funds for which are allegedly readily available by financing, would be more than offset and recaptured by increased revenues. However, no allegation is made that there will be a net benefit to the corporation from such action, considering all increased costs.

Plaintiff claims that the losses of defendant corporation are due to poor attendance at home games. However, it appears from the amended complaint, taken as a whole, that factors other than attendance affect the net earnings or losses. For example, in 1962, attendance at home and road games decreased appreciably as compared with 1961, and yet the loss from direct baseball operation and of the whole corporation was considerably less.

The record shows that plaintiff did not feel he could allege that the increased revenues would be sufficient to cure the corporate deficit. The only cost plaintiff was at all concerned with was that of installation of lights. No mention was made of operation and maintenance of the lights or other possible increases in operating costs of night games and we cannot speculate as to what other factors might influence the increase or decrease of profits if the Cubs were to play night home games. * * *

Finally, we do not agree with plaintiff's contention that failure to follow the example of the other major league clubs in scheduling night games constituted negligence. Plaintiff made no allegation that these teams' night schedules were profitable or that the purpose for which night baseball had been undertaken was fulfilled. Furthermore, it cannot be said that directors, even those of corporations that are losing money, must follow the lead of the other corporations in the field. Directors are elected for their business capabilities and judgment and the courts cannot require them to forego their judgment because of the decisions of directors of other companies. Courts may not decide these questions in the absence of a clear showing of dereliction of duty on the part of the specific directors and mere failure to "follow the crowd" is not such a dereliction.

For the foregoing reasons the order of dismissal entered by the trial court is affirmed.

Affirmed.

Notes

(1) It is easy to say that corporate directors have a fiduciary duty of care. A perennial problem in corporate law has been articulating that duty with a sufficient level of precision to provide an effective guide for directors and for the lawyers who advise them. Consider MBCA § 8.30(a). The language of this section was revised in 1998. Prior to that time, § 8.30(a), as approved in 1984, read as follows:

"(a) A director shall discharge his duties as a director, including his duties as a member of a committee:

(1) in good faith;

(2) with the care an ordinarily prudent person in a like position would exercise under similar circumstances; and

(3) in a manner he reasonably believes to be in the best interests of the corporation."

This simple section was by far the most contentious issue that arose during the 1984 recodification, and at the time was marked for reconsideration. Why was paragraph (a)(2) of old § 8.30 so controversial? Should not directors always act as "ordinarily prudent persons" when making decisions with respect to their corporation? The Official Comment to the present section explains the reason for the change:

The use of the phrase "ordinarily prudent person" in a basic guideline for director conduct, suggesting caution or circumspection vis-á-vis danger or risk, has long been problematic given the fact that risk-taking decisions are central to the directors' role. When coupled with the exercise of "care" the prior text had a familiar resonance long associated with the field of tort law. * * * The further coupling with the verb "shall discharge" added to the inference that former section 8.30(a)'s standard of conduct involved a negligence standard, with resultant confusion.

Clearly, "risk taking is central to the directors' role" when making decisions on behalf of the corporation. What then is wrong with a "negligence standard" or "the ordinarily prudent person" test in this context? However, aren't the risks involved in director-made decisions usually different from ordinary negligence? Consider, for example, the question whether an electronics company should invest the bulk of its resources in a novel computer language; that is presumably a high risk decision that may have either spectacular or disastrous consequences. Can such a decision be judged on an "ordinarily prudent person" standard? On the other hand, don't we also want some degree of preliminary investigation and consideration by directors before the making of such decisions?

(2) Revised MBCA § 8.30(b) requires directors, "when becoming informed in connection with their decision-making function or devoting attention to their oversight function," to exercise the care "that a person in a like position would

reasonably believe appropriate in similar circumstances." There are two fundamentally important insights about corporate law packed into this short statutory provision. First, "Section 8.30 sets forth the standards of conduct for directors by focusing on the manner in which the directors perform their duties, not the correctness of the decisions made." Does that make sense? Second, the legal regime that governs directors operates when directors are performing two functions that are separate and distinct from one another. What are the two directorial functions described in MBCA § 8.30(b)? Which of these functions was involved in Litwin v. Allen? Which was involved in Shlensky v. Wrigley?

(3) The Official Comment to revised § 8.30(a) states that it "establishes the basic standards of conduct for all directors. Its command is to be understood as peremptory—its obligations are to be observed by every director—and at the core of the subsection's mandate is the requirement that, when performing directors' duties, a director shall act in good faith coupled with conduct reasonably believed to be in the best interests of the corporation. This mandate governs all aspects of directors' duties: the duty of care, the duty to become informed, the duty of inquiry, the duty of informed judgment, the duty of attention, the duty of loyalty, the duty of fair dealing and, finally, the broad concept of fiduciary duty that the courts often use as a frame of reference when evaluating a director's conduct."

(4) Consider also the revised MBCA § 8.31. Should there be a different test for the imposition of liability on directors than for determining whether appropriate care was exercised? The Official Comment to this section describes the relationship between new MBCA §§ 8.30 and 8.31 as follows:

"Section 8.30(b)'s standard of conduct is frequently referred to as a director's duty of care. * * * Although some decisions turn out to be unwise or the result of a mistake of judgment, it is not reasonable to reexamine an unsuccessful decision with the benefit of hindsight. * * * Therefore, as a general rule, a director is not exposed to personal liability for injury or damage caused by an unwise decision. * * * [A] director[, however,] can be held liable for misfeasance or nonfeasance in performing the duties of a director."

(5) The American Law Institute, Principles of Corporate Governance: Analysis and Recommendations, § 4.01:[3]

(a) A director or officer has a duty to the corporation to perform the director's or officer's functions in good faith, in a manner that he or she reasonably believes to be in the best interests of the corporation, and with the care that an ordinarily prudent person would reasonably be expected to exercise in a like position and under similar circumstances. This Subsection (a) is subject to the provisions of Subsection (c) (the business judgment rule) where applicable. * * *

(c) A director or officer who makes a business judgment in good faith fulfills the duty under this Section if the director or officer:

(1) is not interested in the subject of the business judgment;

(2) is informed with respect to the subject of the business judgment to the extent the director or officer reasonably believes to be appropriate under the circumstances; and

(3) rationally believes that the business judgment is in the best interests of the corporation.

Does this reach essentially the same result as the revised MBCA provisions discussed in the previous note?

(6) Section 4.01(d) of the Principles of Corporate Governance reads as follows:

> (d) A person challenging the conduct of a director or officer under this Section has the burden of proving a breach of the duty of care, including the inapplicability of the provisions as to the fulfillment of duty under Subsection (b) or (c), and, in a damage action, the burden of proving that the breach was the legal cause of damage suffered by the corporation.

Section 7.18 of the *Principles* states that "legal cause" of loss exists where the plaintiff proves "that (i) satisfaction of the applicable standard would have been a substantial factor in averting the loss, and (ii) the likelihood of injury would have been foreseeable to an ordinarily prudent person in like position to that of the defendant and in similar circumstances. It is not a defense to liability in such cases that damage to the corporation would not have resulted but for the acts or omissions of other individuals."

(7) The justification for the "business judgment rule" is set forth by Charles Hansen, The ALI Corporate Governance Project: Of the Duty of Due Care and the Business Judgment Rule, 41 Bus.Law. 1237, 1238–42, 1247 (1986):[4]

> The foundation stone of the American law of corporate governance is currently enunciated in the holdings (not the dicta) of the leading corporate law states: there must be a minimum of interference by the courts in internal corporate affairs. Except in the egregious case of bad judgment or when there is evidence of bad faith, courts have made no attempt to second-guess directors on the substantive soundness of decisions reached. * * *

> * * * Under [the business judgment rule], as long as a director acts in good faith and with due care in the process sense, the director will not be found liable even though the decision itself was not that of the "ordinarily prudent person." The process due care test will be met if the director takes appropriate steps to become informed. Thus, the description of the duty in section 4.01(a) [of the ALI Corporate Governance Project] as "the care that an ordinarily prudent person would reasonably be expected to exercise in a like position and under similar circumstances" is misleading.

> * * * *Cramer v. General Telephone & Electronics Corp.*, for example, states the appropriate principle of law: "Absent bad faith or some other corrupt motive, directors are normally not liable to the corporation for mistakes of judgment. * * * "[5]

> A careful reading of the cases illustrates the substantial difference between applying the due care test in tort law and the standard actually employed by the courts in reaching decisions under corporate law. * * *

> * * * [U]nder corporate law, the standard of due care is met if two tests are satisfied: (i) due care must be used in "ascertaining relevant facts and law

---

4. Copyright 1986 by the American Bar Association. All rights reserved. Reprinted with the permission of the American Bar Association and its Section of Corporation, Banking and Business Law.

5. [By the Author] 582 F.2d 259, 274 (3d Cir.1978).

before making the decision," and (ii) the decision must be made after reasonable deliberation. * * * Thus, the due care standard in corporate law is applied to the decision-making process and not to its result. * * *

The one possible exception to applying the standard of due care to process, rather than to content or result, concerns egregious conduct. * * *

(8) Should the standard of care and the business judgment rule as codified in revised MBCA §§ 8.30 and 8.31 be applicable to all corporations without regard to the nature of the business of the corporation? In *Litwin,* Justice Shientag comments that a higher standard of care is required of bank directors than of directors of general business corporations. Certainly the legal development has been entirely different. See, A. McCoy, A Political Economy of the Business Judgment Rule In Banking: Implications for Corporate Law, 47 Case Wes. Res.L.Rev. 1 (1996).

(9) In the Financial Institutions Reform, Recovery, and Enforcement Act of 1989 (FIRREA), 12 U.S.C.A. § 1821(k), Congress attempted to clarify the standard of care for directors of financial institutions:

A director or officer of an insured depository institution may be held personally liable for monetary damages in any civil action by, on behalf of, or at the request or direction of the [RTC] * * * for gross negligence, including any similar conduct or conduct that demonstrates a greater disregard of a duty of care (than gross negligence) including intentional tortious conduct, as such terms are defined and determined under applicable State law. Nothing in this paragraph shall impair or affect any right of the [RTC] under other applicable law.

In Atherton v. F.D.I.C, 519 U.S. 213, 117 S.Ct. 666, 136 L.Ed.2d 656 (1997), the Supreme Court held that the early federal law of bank director liability had disappeared with Erie R. Co. v. Tompkins, 304 U.S. 64, 58 S.Ct. 817, 82 L.Ed. 1188 (1938) and that state law defined the duty of directors of both federal and state-chartered institutions, subject to § 1821(k), which the court construed to mean "the statute's 'gross negligence' standard provides only a floor—a guarantee that officers and directors must meet at least a gross negligence standard. It does not stand in the way of a stricter standard that the laws of some States provide." 117 S.Ct., at 674.

(10) The legal literature relating to the business judgment rule is voluminous and growing steadily, reflecting its importance and controversial nature. "The" definitive book is Dennis J. Block, Nancy E. Barton, and Stephen A. Radin, The Business Judgment Rule: Fiduciary Duties of Corporate Directors, Fifth Edition (1998), consisting of two volumes aggregating 2,496 pages, and a 2002 Supplement. Articles published since 1996 include Melvin Aron Eisenberg, The Director's Duty of Care in Negotiated Dispositions, 51 U. Miami L.Rev. 579 (1997); Mathew Taylor, Tender Offers and the Business Judgment Rule, 7 U.Miami L.Rev. 1171 (1998); A. Gilchrist Sparks, III, et al. Special Committee of Directors: When Does the Business Judgment Rule Apply and to What Extent are Committee Proceedings Confidential? SE ALI–ABA 275 (1999); Real Estate Law Report, Condominiums: Business Judgment Rule Applies to Directors, 29–Nov Real Est. L.Rep. 3 (1999); Jeffrey Selman, Applying the Business Judgment Rule to the Franchise Relationship, 19 WTR Franchise L.J. 111 (2000); Lyman Johnson, The Modest Business Judgment Rule, 55 Bus.Law. 625 (2000); Kenneth B. Davis, Once More, The Business Judgment Rule, 2000 Wis. L.Rev. 573 (2000); Peter V. Letsou, Implications of Shareholder Diversification on Corporate Law and Organization: The Case Of The Business Judgment Rule, 77 Chi.-Kent L. Rev. 179 (2001); Robin

E. Phelan, et al., If Their Business Judgment Was So Good How Come They're In Bankruptcy and Other Perplexing Mysteries Of The Business Judgment Rule: Corporate Governance Issues For The Financially Troubled Company, 10 J. Bankr. L. & Prac. 471 (2001); Paula J. Dalley, To Whom It May Concern: Fiduciary Duties and Business Associations, 26 Del. J. Corp. L. 515 (2001); Norm Gregory Scott Crespi, Rethinking Corporate Fiduciary Duties: The Inefficiency of The Shareholder Primacy, 55 SMU L. Rev. 141 (2002).

SMITH v. VAN GORKOM

Supreme Court of Delaware, 1985.
488 A.2d 858.

Before HERRMANN, C.J., and McNEILLY, HORSEY, MOORE and CHRISTIE, JJ., constituting the Court en banc.

HORSEY, JUSTICE (for the majority):

This appeal from the Court of Chancery involves a class action brought by shareholders of the defendant Trans Union Corporation ("Trans Union" or "the Company"), originally seeking rescission of a cash-out merger of Trans Union into the defendant New T Company ("New T"), a wholly-owned subsidiary of the defendant, Marmon Group, Inc. ("Marmon"). Alternate relief in the form of damages is sought against the defendant members of the Board of Directors of Trans Union * * *.

Following trial, the former Chancellor granted judgment for the defendant directors by unreported letter opinion dated July 6, 1982. Judgment was based on [the finding that] that the Board of Directors had acted in an informed manner so as to be entitled to protection of the business judgment rule in approving the cash-out merger * * *. The plaintiffs appeal.

Speaking for the majority of the Court, we conclude that [the ruling] of the Court of Chancery [is] clearly erroneous. Therefore, we reverse and direct that judgment be entered in favor of the plaintiffs and against the defendant directors for the fair value of the plaintiffs' stockholdings in Trans Union, in accordance with Weinberger v. UOP, Inc., Del.Supr., 457 A.2d 701 (1983).[6]

We hold * * * that the Board's decision, reached September 20, 1980, to approve the proposed cash-out merger was not the product of an informed business judgment * * *.

I.

The nature of this case requires a detailed factual statement. The following facts are essentially uncontradicted:

–A–

Trans Union was a publicly-traded, diversified holding company, the principal earnings of which were generated by its railcar leasing business. During the period here involved, the Company had a cash flow of hundreds of millions of dollars annually. However, the Company had difficulty in generating sufficient taxable income to offset increasingly large investment tax

6. [By the Court] It has been stipulated that plaintiffs sue on behalf of a class consisting of 10,537 shareholders (out of a total of 12,844) and that the class owned 12,734,404 out of 13,357,758 shares of Trans Union outstanding.

credits (ITCs).[7] Accelerated depreciation deductions had decreased available taxable income against which to offset accumulating ITCs. The Company took these deductions, despite their effect on usable ITCs, because the rental price in the railcar leasing market had already impounded the purported tax savings.

In the late 1970's, together with other capital-intensive firms, Trans Union lobbied in Congress to have ITCs refundable in cash to firms which could not fully utilize the credit. During the summer of 1980, defendant Jerome W. Van Gorkom, Trans Union's Chairman and Chief Executive Officer, testified and lobbied in Congress for refundability of ITCs and against further accelerated depreciation. By the end of August, Van Gorkom was convinced that Congress would neither accept the refundability concept nor curtail further accelerated depreciation.

Beginning in the late 1960's, and continuing through the 1970's, Trans Union pursued a program of acquiring small companies in order to increase available taxable income. In July 1980, Trans Union Management prepared the annual revision of the Company's Five Year Forecast. This report was presented to the Board of Directors at its July, 1980 meeting. The report projected an annual income growth of about 20%. The report also concluded that Trans Union would have about $195 million in spare cash between 1980 and 1985, "with the surplus growing rapidly from 1982 onward." The report referred to the ITC situation as a "nagging problem" and, given that problem, the leasing company "would still appear to be constrained to a tax breakeven." The report then listed four alternative uses of the projected 1982–1985 equity surplus: (1) stock repurchase; (2) dividend increases; (3) a major acquisition program; and (4) combinations of the above. The sale of Trans Union was not among the alternatives. The report emphasized that, despite the overall surplus, the operation of the Company would consume all available equity for the next several years, and concluded: "As a result, we have sufficient time to fully develop our course of action."

–B–

On August 27, 1980, Van Gorkom met with Senior Management of Trans Union. Van Gorkom reported on his lobbying efforts in Washington and his desire to find a solution to the tax credit problem more permanent than a continued program of acquisitions. Various alternatives were suggested and discussed preliminarily, including the sale of Trans Union to a company with a large amount of taxable income.

Donald Romans, Chief Financial Officer of Trans Union, stated that his department had done a "very brief bit of work on the possibility of a leveraged buy-out."[8] This work had been prompted by a media article which Romans had seen regarding a leveraged buy-out by management. The work consisted of a "preliminary study" of the cash which could be generated by the

---

7. [By the Editors] Investment tax credits are subsidies (since repealed) equal to a portion of the cost of depreciable personal property designed to induce taxpayers to invest in that property, thereby stimulating business demand for capital goods. See generally Allaire Urban Karzon and Charles H. Coffin, 1982 Extension of the At–Risk Concept to the In-

vestment Tax Credit: A Shotgun Approach to the Tax Shelter Problem, 1982 Duke L.J. 847.

8. [By the Editors] A "leveraged buy-out" of a corporation is a sale of the corporation in which at least part of the purchase price is obtained through debt assumed by the corporation.

Company if it participated in a leveraged buy-out. As Romans stated, this analysis "was very first and rough cut at seeing whether a cash flow would support what might be considered a high price for this type of transaction."

On September 5, at another Senior Management meeting which Van Gorkom attended, Romans again brought up the idea of a leveraged buy-out as a "possible strategic alternative" to the Company's acquisition program. Romans and Bruce S. Chelberg, President and Chief Operating Officer of Trans Union, had been working on the matter in preparation for the meeting. According to Romans: They did not "come up" with a price for the Company. They merely "ran the numbers" at $50 a share and at $60 a share with the "rough form" of their cash figures at the time. Their "figures indicated that $50 would be very easy to do but $60 would be very difficult to do under those figures." This work did not purport to establish a fair price for either the Company or 100% of the stock. It was intended to determine the cash flow needed to service the debt that would "probably" be incurred in a leveraged buyout, based on "rough calculations" without "any benefit of experts to identify what the limits were to that, and so forth." These computations were not considered extensive and no conclusion was reached.

At this meeting, Van Gorkom stated that he would be willing to take $55 per share for his own 75,000 shares. He vetoed the suggestion of a leveraged buy-out by Management, however, as involving a potential conflict of interest for Management. Van Gorkom, a certified public accountant and lawyer, had been an officer of Trans Union for 24 years, its Chief Executive Officer for more than 17 years, and Chairman of its Board for 2 years. It is noteworthy in this connection that he was then approaching 65 years of age and mandatory retirement.

For several days following the September 5 meeting, Van Gorkom pondered the idea of a sale. He had participated in many acquisitions as a manager and director of Trans Union and as a director of other companies. He was familiar with acquisition procedures, valuation methods, and negotiations; and he privately considered the pros and cons of whether Trans Union should seek a privately or publicly-held purchaser.

Van Gorkom decided to meet with Jay A. Pritzker, a well-known corporate takeover specialist and a social acquaintance. However, rather than approaching Pritzker simply to determine his interest in acquiring Trans Union, Van Gorkom assembled a proposed per share price for sale of the Company and a financing structure by which to accomplish the sale. Van Gorkom did so without consulting either his Board or any members of Senior Management except one: Carl Peterson, Trans Union's Controller. Telling Peterson that he wanted no other person on his staff to know what he was doing, but without telling him why, Van Gorkom directed Peterson to calculate the feasibility of a leveraged buy-out at an assumed price per share of $55. Apart from the Company's historic stock market price,[9] and Van Gorkom's long association with Trans Union, the record is devoid of any compe-

---

9. [By the Court] The common stock of Trans Union was traded on the New York Stock Exchange. Over the five year period from 1975 through 1979, Trans Union's stock had traded within a range of a high of $39 1/2 and a low of $24 1/4. Its high and low range for 1980 through September 19 (the last trading day before announcement of the merger) was $38 1/4–$29 1/2.

tent evidence that $55 represented the per share intrinsic value of the Company.

Having thus chosen the $55 figure, based solely on the availability of a leveraged buy-out, Van Gorkom multiplied the price per share by the number of shares outstanding to reach a total value of the Company of $690 million. Van Gorkom told Peterson to use this $690 million figure and to assume a $200 million equity contribution by the buyer. Based on these assumptions, Van Gorkom directed Peterson to determine whether the debt portion of the purchase price could be paid off in five years or less if financed by Trans Union's cash flow as projected in the Five Year Forecast, and by the sale of certain weaker divisions identified in a study done for Trans Union by the Boston Consulting Group ("BCG study"). Peterson reported that, of the purchase price, approximately $50–80 million would remain outstanding after five years. Van Gorkom was disappointed, but decided to meet with Pritzker nevertheless.

Van Gorkom arranged a meeting with Pritzker at the latter's home on Saturday, September 13, 1980. Van Gorkom prefaced his presentation by stating to Pritzker: "Now as far as you are concerned, I can, I think, show how you can pay a substantial premium over the present stock price and pay off most of the loan in the first five years. * * * If you could pay $55 for this Company, here is a way in which I think it can be financed."

Van Gorkom then reviewed with Pritzker his calculations based upon his proposed price of $55 per share. Although Pritzker mentioned $50 as a more attractive figure, no other price was mentioned. However, Van Gorkom stated that to be sure that $55 was the best price obtainable, Trans Union should be free to accept any better offer. Pritzker demurred, stating that his organization would serve as a "stalking horse" for an "auction contest" only if Trans Union would permit Pritzker to buy 1,750,000 shares of Trans Union stock at market price which Pritzker could then sell to any higher bidder. After further discussion on this point, Pritzker told Van Gorkom that he would give him a more definite reaction soon.

On Monday, September 15, Pritzker advised Van Gorkom that he was interested in the $55 cash-out merger proposal and requested more information on Trans Union. Van Gorkom agreed to meet privately with Pritzker, accompanied by Peterson, Chelberg, and Michael Carpenter, Trans Union's consultant from the Boston Consulting Group. The meetings took place on September 16 and 17. Van Gorkom was "astounded that events were moving with such amazing rapidity."

On Thursday, September 18, Van Gorkom met again with Pritzker. At that time, Van Gorkom knew that Pritzker intended to make a cash-out merger offer at Van Gorkom's proposed $55 per share. Pritzker instructed his attorney, a merger and acquisition specialist, to begin drafting merger documents. There was no further discussion of the $55 price. However, the number of shares of Trans Union's treasury stock to be offered to Pritzker was negotiated down to one million shares; the price was set at $38–75 cents above the per share price at the close of the market on September 19. At this point, Pritzker insisted that the Trans Union Board act on his merger proposal within the next three days, stating to Van Gorkom: "We have to have a decision by no later than Sunday [evening, September 21] before the opening of the English stock exchange on Monday morning." Pritzker's lawyer was then instructed to draft the merger documents, to be reviewed by Van Gorkom's lawyer, "sometimes with discussion and sometimes not, in the haste to get it finished."

On Friday, September 19, Van Gorkom, Chelberg, and Pritzker consulted with Trans Union's lead bank regarding the financing of Pritzker's purchase of Trans Union. The bank indicated that it could form a syndicate of banks that would finance the transaction. On the same day, Van Gorkom retained James Brennan, Esquire, to advise Trans Union on the legal aspects of the merger. Van Gorkom did not consult with William Browder, a Vice-President and director of Trans Union and former head of its legal department, or with William Moore, then the head of Trans Union's legal staff.

On Friday, September 19, Van Gorkom called a special meeting of the Trans Union Board for noon the following day. He also called a meeting of the Company's Senior Management to convene at 11:00 a.m., prior to the meeting of the Board. No one, except Chelberg and Peterson, was told the purpose of the meetings. Van Gorkom did not invite Trans Union's investment banker, Salomon Brothers or its Chicago-based partner, to attend.

Of those present at the Senior Management meeting on September 20, only Chelberg and Peterson had prior knowledge of Pritzker's offer. Van Gorkom disclosed the offer and described its terms, but he furnished no copies of the proposed Merger Agreement. Romans announced that his department had done a second study which showed that, for a leveraged buy-out, the price range for Trans Union stock was between $55 and $65 per share. Van Gorkom neither saw the study nor asked Romans to make it available for the Board meeting.

Senior Management's reaction to the Pritzker proposal was completely negative. No member of Management, except Chelberg and Peterson, supported the proposal. Romans objected to the price as being too low;[10] he was critical of the timing and suggested that consideration should be given to the adverse tax consequences of an all-cash deal for low-basis shareholders; and he took the position that the agreement to sell Pritzker one million newly-issued shares at market price would inhibit other offers, as would the prohibitions against soliciting bids and furnishing inside information to other bidders. Romans argued that the Pritzker proposal was a "lock up" and amounted to "an agreed merger as opposed to an offer." Nevertheless, Van Gorkom proceeded to the Board meeting as scheduled without further delay.

Ten directors served on the Trans Union Board, five inside (defendants Bonser, O'Boyle, Browder, Chelberg, and Van Gorkom) and five outside (defendants Wallis, Johnson, Lanterman, Morgan and Reneker). All directors were present at the meeting, except O'Boyle who was ill. Of the outside directors, four were corporate chief executive officers and one was the former Dean of the University of Chicago Business School. None was an investment banker or trained financial analyst. All members of the Board were well informed about the Company and its operations as a going concern. They

---

10. [By the Court] Van Gorkom asked Romans to express his opinion as to the $55 price. Romans stated that he "thought the price was too low in relation to what he could derive for the company in a cash sale, particularly one which enabled us to realize the values of certain subsidiaries and independent entities."

were familiar with the current financial condition of the Company, as well as operating and earnings projections reported in the recent Five Year Forecast. The Board generally received regular and detailed reports and was kept abreast of the accumulated investment tax credit and accelerated depreciation problem.

Van Gorkom began the Special Meeting of the Board with a twenty-minute oral presentation. Copies of the proposed Merger Agreement were delivered too late for study before or during the meeting.[11] He reviewed the Company's ITC and depreciation problems and the efforts theretofore made to solve them. He discussed his initial meeting with Pritzker and his motivation in arranging that meeting. Van Gorkom did not disclose to the Board, however, the methodology by which he alone had arrived at the $55 figure, or the fact that he first proposed the $55 price in his negotiations with Pritzker.

Van Gorkom outlined the terms of the Pritzker offer as follows: Pritzker would pay $55 in cash for all outstanding shares of Trans Union stock upon completion of which Trans Union would be merged into New T Company, a subsidiary wholly-owned by Pritzker and formed to implement the merger; for a period of 90 days, Trans Union could receive, but could not actively solicit, competing offers; the offer had to be acted on by the next evening, Sunday, September 21; Trans Union could only furnish to competing bidders published information, and not proprietary information; the offer was subject to Pritzker obtaining the necessary financing by October 10, 1980; if the financing contingency were met or waived by Pritzker, Trans Union was required to sell to Pritzker one million newly-issued shares of Trans Union at $38 per share.

Van Gorkom took the position that putting Trans Union "up for auction" through a 90–day market test would validate a decision by the Board that $55 was a fair price. He told the Board that the "free market will have an opportunity to judge whether $55 is a fair price." Van Gorkom framed the decision before the Board not as whether $55 per share was the highest price that could be obtained, but as whether the $55 price was a fair price that the stockholders should be given the opportunity to accept or reject.[12]

Attorney Brennan advised the members of the Board that they might be sued if they failed to accept the offer and that a fairness opinion was not required as a matter of law.

Romans attended the meeting as chief financial officer of the Company. He told the Board that he had not been involved in the negotiations with Pritzker and knew nothing about the merger proposal until the morning of the meeting; that his studies did not indicate either a fair price for the stock or a valuation of the Company; that he did not see his role as directly addressing the fairness issue; and that he and his people "were trying to search for ways to justify a price in connection with such a [leveraged buy-out] transaction, rather than to say what the shares are worth." Romans testified:

---

11. [By the Court] The record is not clear as to the terms of the Merger Agreement. The Agreement, as originally presented to the Board on September 20, was never produced by defendants despite demands by the plaintiffs. Nor is it clear that the directors were given an opportunity to study the Merger Agreement before voting on it. All that can be said is that Brennan had the Agreement before him during the meeting.

12. [By the Court] In Van Gorkom's words: The "real decision" is whether to "let the stockholders decide it" which is "all you are being asked to decide today."

I told the Board that the study ran the numbers at 50 and 60, and then the subsequent study at 55 and 65, and that was not the same thing as saying that I have a valuation of the company at X dollars. But it was a way—a first step towards reaching that conclusion.

Romans told the Board that, in his opinion, $55 was "in the range of a fair price," but "at the beginning of the range."

Chelberg, Trans Union's President, supported Van Gorkom's presentation and representations. He testified that he "participated to make sure that the Board members collectively were clear on the details of the agreement or offer from Pritzker;" that he "participated in the discussion with Mr. Brennan, inquiring of him about the necessity for valuation opinions in spite of the way in which this particular offer was couched;" and that he was otherwise actively involved in supporting the positions being taken by Van Gorkom before the Board about "the necessity to act immediately on this offer," and about "the adequacy of the $55 and the question of how that would be tested."

The Board meeting of September 20 lasted about two hours. Based solely upon Van Gorkom's oral presentation, Chelberg's supporting representations, Romans' oral statement, Brennan's legal advice, and their knowledge of the market history of the Company's stock,[13] the directors approved the proposed Merger Agreement. * * *

The Merger Agreement was executed by Van Gorkom during the evening of September 20 at a formal social event that he hosted for the opening of the Chicago Lyric Opera. Neither he nor any other director read the agreement prior to its signing and delivery to Pritzker. * * *

[Following the approval of the Pritzker proposal, Trans Union retained Salomon Brothers to actively seek other possible offers. This search produced two other possible purchasers, one at $60 per share and the other at $2 to $5 above the $55 price. However, one potential bidder withdrew when Pritzker refused to rescind its merger agreement with Trans Union and the other withdrew when an executive in an important Trans Union subsidiary declined to join the buying group. Van Gorkom made no effort to assist either of these potential offerors and may have affirmatively discouraged them.]

On December 19, this litigation was commenced and, within four weeks, the plaintiffs had deposed eight of the ten directors of Trans Union, including Van Gorkom, Chelberg and Romans, its Chief Financial Officer. On January 21, Management's Proxy Statement for the February 10 shareholder meeting was mailed to Trans Union's stockholders. On January 26, Trans Union's Board met and, after a lengthy meeting, voted to proceed with the Pritzker merger. The Board also approved for mailing, "on or about January 27," a Supplement to its Proxy Statement. The Supplement purportedly set forth all

---

13. [By the Court] The Trial Court stated the premium relationship of the $55 price to the market history of the Company's stock as follows:

* * * [T]he merger price offered to the stockholders of Trans Union represented a premium of 62% over the average of the high and low prices at which Trans Union stock had traded in 1980, a premium of 48% over the last closing price, and a premium of 39% over the highest price at which the stock of Trans Union had traded any time during the prior six years.

information relevant to the Pritzker Merger Agreement, which had not been divulged in the first Proxy Statement. * * *

On February 10, the stockholders of Trans Union approved the Pritzker merger proposal. Of the outstanding shares, 69.9% were voted in favor of the merger; 7.25% were voted against the merger; and 22.85% were not voted.

II.

We turn to the issue of the application of the business judgment rule to the September 20 meeting of the Board.

The Court of Chancery concluded from the evidence that the Board of Directors' approval of the Pritzker merger proposal fell within the protection of the business judgment rule. The Court found that the Board had given sufficient time and attention to the transaction, since the directors had considered the Pritzker proposal on three different occasions, on September 20, and on October 8, 1980 and finally on January 26, 1981. On that basis, the Court reasoned that the Board had acquired, over the four-month period, sufficient information to reach an informed business judgment on the cash-out merger proposal. The Court ruled:

> * * * that given the market value of Trans Union's stock, the business acumen of the members of the board of Trans Union, the substantial premium over market offered by the Pritzkers and the ultimate effect on the merger price provided by the prospect of other bids for the stock in question, that the board of directors of Trans Union did not act recklessly or improvidently in determining on a course of action which they believed to be in the best interest of the stockholders of Trans Union.

> [W]e conclude that the Court's ultimate finding that the Board's conduct was not "reckless or imprudent" is contrary to the record and not the product of a logical and deductive reasoning process.

* * * [The Court reviews the Delaware law relating to the duty of care and the business judgment rule and concludes that "the proper standard for determining whether a business judgment is an informed one in Delaware is predicated upon concepts of gross negligence."]

III.

* * * The issue of whether the directors reached an informed decision to "sell" the Company on September 20, 1980 must be determined only upon the basis of the information then reasonably available to the directors and relevant to their decision to accept the Pritzker merger proposal. This is not to say that the directors were precluded from altering their original plan of action, had they done so in an informed manner. What we do say is that the question of whether the directors reached an informed business judgment in agreeing to sell the Company, pursuant to the terms of the September 20 Agreement presents, in reality, two questions: (A) whether the directors reached an informed business judgment on September 20, 1980; and (B) if they did not, whether the directors' actions taken subsequent to September 20 were adequate to cure any infirmity in their action taken on September 20. We first consider the directors' September 20 action in terms of their reaching an informed business judgment.

–A–

On the record before us, we must conclude that the Board of Directors did not reach an informed business judgment on September 20, 1980 in voting to "sell" the Company for $55 per share pursuant to the Pritzker cash-out merger proposal. * * * [The Court stated that a simple comparison of the current market price of Trans Union with the $55 offer was not an informed business judgment because there had been no study of the "intrinsic value" of Trans Union as a going concern, no valuation study, and no attempt to document the $55 price as a measure of the fair value of Trans Union as a going concern. The Court specifically criticized the failure of directors to request a valuation based on the cash flow of Trans Union.]

We do not imply that an outside valuation study is essential to support an informed business judgment; nor do we state that fairness opinions by independent investment bankers are required as a matter of law. Often insiders familiar with the business of a going concern are in a better position than are outsiders to gather relevant information; and under appropriate circumstances, such directors may be fully protected in relying in good faith upon the valuation reports of their management. See 8 Del.C. § 141(e).

Here, the record establishes that the Board did not request its Chief Financial Officer, Romans, to make any valuation study or review of the proposal to determine the adequacy of $55 per share for sale of the Company. On the record before us: The Board rested on Romans' elicited response that the $55 figure was within a "fair price range" within the context of a leveraged buy-out. No director sought any further information from Romans. No director asked him why he put $55 at the bottom of his range. No director asked Romans for any details as to his study, the reason why it had been undertaken or its depth. No director asked to see the study; and no director asked Romans whether Trans Union's finance department could do a fairness study within the remaining 36–hour period available under the Pritzker offer. * * *

The record also establishes that the Board accepted without scrutiny Van Gorkom's representation as to the fairness of the $55 price per share for sale of the Company—a subject that the Board had never previously considered. The Board thereby failed to discover that Van Gorkom had suggested the $55 price to Pritzker and, most crucially, that Van Gorkom had arrived at the $55 figure based on calculations designed solely to determine the feasibility of a leveraged buy-out.[14] No questions were raised either as to the tax implications of a cash-out merger or how the price for the one million share option granted Pritzker was calculated.

We do not say that the Board of Directors was not entitled to give some credence to Van Gorkom's representation that $55 was an adequate or fair

14. [By the Court] As of September 20 the directors did not know: that Van Gorkom had arrived at the $55 figure alone, and subjectively, as the figure to be used by Controller Peterson in creating a feasible structure for a leveraged buy-out by a prospective purchaser; that Van Gorkom had not sought advice, information or assistance from either inside or outside Trans Union directors as to the value of the Company as an entity or the fair price per share for 100% of its stock; that Van Gorkom had not consulted with the Company's investment bankers or other financial analysts; that Van Gorkom had not consulted with or confided in any officer or director of the Company except Chelberg; and that Van Gorkom had deliberately chosen to ignore the advice and opinion of the members of his Senior Management group regarding the adequacy of the $55 price.

price. Under § 141(e), the directors were entitled to rely upon their chairman's opinion of value and adequacy, provided that such opinion was reached on a sound basis. Here, the issue is whether the directors informed themselves as to all information that was reasonably available to them. Had they done so, they would have learned of the source and derivation of the $55 price and could not reasonably have relied thereupon in good faith. * * *

Thus, the record compels the conclusion that on September 20 the Board lacked valuation information adequate to reach an informed business judgment as to the fairness of $55 per share for sale of the Company. * * *

(2)

* * * [The court concludes in this portion of the opinion that there was not a "post-September 20 market test" of the $55 price sufficient to confirm the reasonableness of the board's decision.]

(3)

* * * [In this portion of the opinion The court rejects the argument that the Board's "collective experience and sophistication" was a sufficient basis for finding that it reached its September 20 decision with informed, reasonable deliberation.][15]

(4)

Part of the defense is based on a claim that the directors relied on legal advice rendered at the September 20 meeting by James Brennan, Esquire, who was present at Van Gorkom's request. Unfortunately, Brennan did not appear and testify at trial even though his firm participated in the defense of this action. There is no contemporaneous evidence of the advice given by Brennan on September 20, only the later deposition and trial testimony of certain directors as to their recollections or understanding of what was said at the meeting. Since counsel did not testify, and the advice attributed to Brennan is hearsay received by the Trial Court over the plaintiffs' objections, we consider it only in the context of the directors' present claims. In fairness to counsel, we make no findings that the advice attributed to him was in fact given. We focus solely on the efficacy of the defendants' claims, made months and years later, in an effort to extricate themselves from liability.

Several defendants testified that Brennan advised them that Delaware law did not require a fairness opinion or an outside valuation of the Company before the Board could act on the Pritzker proposal. If given, the advice was correct. However, that did not end the matter. Unless the directors had before them adequate information regarding the intrinsic value of the Company, upon which a proper exercise of business judgment could be made, mere

---

15. [By the Court] Trans Union's five "inside" directors had backgrounds in law and accounting, 116 years of collective employment by the Company and 68 years of combined experience on its Board. Trans Union's five "outside" directors included four chief executives of major corporations and an economist who was a former dean of a major school of business and chancellor of a university. The "outside" directors had 78 years of combined experience as chief executive officers of major corporations and 50 years of cumulative experience as directors of Trans Union. Thus, defendants argue that the Board was eminently qualified to reach an informed judgment on the proposed "sale" of Trans Union notwithstanding their lack of any advance notice of the proposal, the shortness of their deliberation, and their determination not to consult with their investment banker or to obtain a fairness opinion.

advice of this type is meaningless; and, given this record of the defendants' failures, it constitutes no defense here.[16] * * *

We conclude that Trans Union's Board was grossly negligent in that it failed to act with informed reasonable deliberation in agreeing to the Pritzker merger proposal on September 20; and we further conclude that the Trial Court erred as a matter of law in failing to address that question before determining whether the directors' later conduct was sufficient to cure its initial error. * * *

IV.

Whether the directors of Trans Union should be treated as one or individually in terms of invoking the protection of the business judgment rule and the applicability of 8 Del.C. § 141(c) are questions which were not originally addressed by the parties in their briefing of this case. This resulted in a supplemental briefing and a second rehearing en banc on two basic questions: (a) whether one or more of the directors were deprived of the protection of the business judgment rule by evidence of an absence of good faith; and (b) whether one or more of the outside directors were entitled to invoke the protection of 8 Del.C. § 141(e) by evidence of a reasonable, good faith reliance on "reports," including legal advice, rendered the Board by certain inside directors and the Board's special counsel, Brennan.

The parties' response, including reargument, has led the majority of the Court to conclude: (1) that since all of the defendant directors, outside as well as inside, take a unified position, we are required to treat all of the directors as one as to whether they are entitled to the protection of the business judgment rule; and (2) that considerations of good faith, including the presumption that the directors acted in good faith, are irrelevant in determining the threshold issue of whether the directors as a Board exercised an informed business judgment. For the same reason, we must reject defense counsel's *ad hominem* argument for affirmance: that reversal may result in a multi-million dollar class award against the defendants for having made an allegedly uninformed business judgment in a transaction not involving any personal gain, self-dealing or claim of bad faith.[17]

In their brief, the defendants similarly mistake the business judgment rule's application to this case by erroneously invoking presumptions of good faith and "wide discretion":

This is a case in which plaintiff challenged the exercise of business judgment by an independent Board of Directors. There were no allega-

---

16. [By the Court] Nonetheless, we are satisfied that in an appropriate factual context a proper exercise of business judgment may include, as one of its aspects, reasonable reliance upon the advice of counsel. This is wholly outside the statutory protections of 8 Del.C. § 141(e) involving reliance upon reports of officers, certain experts and books and records of the company.

17. [By the Editors] In the petition for rehearing that was ultimately denied in this case, the Court quotes the beginning of the

oral argument made by counsel for the individual defendants as follows:

> COUNSEL: I'll make the argument on behalf of the nine individual defendants against whom the plaintiffs seek more than $100,000,000 in damages. That is the ultimate issue in this case, whether or not nine honest, experienced businessmen should be subject to damages in a case where—

At this point counsel was interrupted by the Court with a question and never returned to the beginning point.

tions and no proof of fraud, bad faith, or self-dealing by the directors.
* * *

The business judgment rule, which was properly applied by the Chancellor, allows directors wide discretion in the matter of valuation and affords room for honest differences of opinion. In order to prevail, plaintiffs had the heavy burden of proving that the merger price was so grossly inadequate as to display itself as a badge of fraud. That is a burden which plaintiffs have not met.

However, plaintiffs have not claimed, nor did the Trial Court decide, that $55 was a grossly inadequate price per share for sale of the Company. That being so, the presumption that a board's judgment as to adequacy of price represents an honest exercise of business judgment (absent proof that the sale price was grossly inadequate) is irrelevant to the threshold question of whether an informed judgment was reached.

* * * We hold, therefore, that the Trial Court committed reversible error in applying the business judgment rule in favor of the director defendants in this case.

On remand, the Court of Chancery shall conduct an evidentiary hearing to determine the fair value of the shares represented by the plaintiffs' class, based on the intrinsic value of Trans Union on September 20, 1980. * * * Thereafter, an award of damages may be entered to the extent that the fair value of Trans Union exceeds $55 per share. * * *

REVERSED and REMANDED for proceedings consistent herewith.

McNEILLY, JUSTICE, dissenting:

The majority opinion reads like an advocate's closing address to a hostile jury. And I say that not lightly. Throughout the opinion great emphasis is directed only to the negative, with nothing more than lip service granted the positive aspects of this case. In my opinion Chancellor Marvel (retired) should have been affirmed. The Chancellor's opinion was the product of well reasoned conclusions, based upon a sound deductive process, clearly supported by the evidence and entitled to deference in this appeal. Because of my diametrical opposition to all evidentiary conclusions of the majority, I respectfully dissent.

It would serve no useful purpose, particularly at this late date, for me to dissent at great length. I restrain myself from doing so, but feel compelled to at least point out what I consider to be the most glaring deficiencies in the majority opinion. The majority has spoken and has effectively said that Trans Union's Directors have been the victims of a "fast shuffle" by Van Gorkom and Pritzker. That is the beginning of the majority's comedy of errors. The first and most important error made is the majority's assessment of the directors' knowledge of the affairs of Trans Union and their combined ability to act in this situation under the protection of the business judgment rule.

Trans Union's Board of Directors consisted of ten men, five of whom were "inside" directors and five of whom were "outside" directors. The "inside" directors were Van Gorkom, Chelberg, Bonser, William B. Browder, Senior Vice–President–Law, and Thomas P. O'Boyle, Senior Vice–President–Administration. At the time the merger was proposed the inside five directors had collectively been employed by the Company for 116 years and had 68 years of combined experience as directors. The "outside" directors were A.W. Wallis, William B. Johnson, Joseph B. Lanterman, Graham J. Morgan and Robert W. Reneker. With the exception of Wallis, these were all chief executive officers of Chicago based corporations that were at least as large as Trans Union. The five "outside" directors had 78 years of combined experience as chief executive officers, and 53 years cumulative service as Trans Union directors.

The inside directors wear their badge of expertise in the corporate affairs of Trans Union on their sleeves. But what about the outsiders? Dr. Wallis is or was an economist and math statistician, a professor of economics at Yale University, dean of the graduate school of business at the University of Chicago, and Chancellor of the University of Rochester. Dr. Wallis had been on the Board of Trans Union since 1962. He also was on the Board of Bausch & Lomb, Kodak, Metropolitan Life Insurance Company, Standard Oil and others.

William B. Johnson is a University of Pennsylvania law graduate, President of Railway Express until 1966, Chairman and Chief Executive of I.C. Industries Holding Company, and member of Trans Union's Board since 1968.

Joseph Lanterman, a Certified Public Accountant, is or was President and Chief Executive of American Steel, on the Board of International Harvester, Peoples Energy, Illinois Bell Telephone, Harris Bank and Trust Company, Kemper Insurance Company and a director of Trans Union for four years.

Graham Morgan is a chemist, was Chairman and Chief Executive Officer of U.S. Gypsum, and in the 17 and 18 years prior to the Trans Union transaction had been involved in 31 or 32 corporate takeovers.

Robert Reneker attended University of Chicago and Harvard Business Schools. He was President and Chief Executive of Swift and Company, director of Trans Union since 1971, and member of the Boards of seven other corporations including U.S. Gypsum and the Chicago Tribune.

Directors of this caliber are not ordinarily taken in by a "fast shuffle". I submit they were not taken into this multi-million dollar corporate transaction without being fully informed and aware of the state of the art as it pertained to the entire corporate panorama of Trans Union. True, even directors such as these, with their business acumen, interest and expertise, can go astray. I do not believe that to be the case here. These men knew Trans Union like the back of their hands and were more than well qualified to make on the spot informed business judgments concerning the affairs of Trans Union including a 100% sale of the corporation. Lest we forget, the corporate world of then and now operates on what is so aptly referred to as "the fast track". These men were at the time an integral part of that world, all professional business men, not intellectual figureheads. * * *

Notes

(1) The response of the corporate bar to *Van Gorkom* was one of shocked incredulity. "The Delaware Supreme Court * * * exploded a bomb. Stated minimally, the Court * * * pierced the Business Judgment Rule and imposed liability on independent (even eminent) outside directors of Trans Union Corporation * * * because (roughly) the Court thought they had not been careful enough, and had not enquired enough, before deciding to accept and recommend to Trans

Union's shareholders a cash-out merger at a per share price that was less than the 'intrinsic value' of the shares. * * * The corporate bar generally views the decision as atrocious and predicts the most dire consequences as directors come to realize how exposed they have become." Bayless Manning, in a newsletter to his clients. Professor Richard Buxbaum, in a CLE newsletter for California Bar subscribers, headlined his analysis of the case "Summer Lightning Out of Delaware." Subsequent commentary also has not been kind to this decision, though some have found a silver lining. "[W]hile on a professional level, I'd be inclined to endorse Dan Fischel's assessment of *Van Gorkom* as the worst case in corporate law history, I have to say that I think it was an important political and social success. * * * *Van Gorkom* exploded on the world of corporate directors. People most definitely took notice of its stern message. From an ex-ante perspective, it almost certainly has had a positive effect on corporate governance." Former Chancellor William Allen, Symposium on the Next Century of Corporate Law, 25 Delaware J. Corporate Law, 76 (2000). Almost 20 years after the decision, lawyers who regularly advise corporate directors observed "I have never been in a boardroom where I couldn't get a director's attention by saying 'Remember Van Gorkom' ". Remark of Ira Millstein, at a Roundtable on "The Legacy of Smith v. Van Gorkom" 24 Directors and Boards, 28 (2000).

(2) Leo Herzel and Leo Katz argue that court's decision "seems misguided and Trans Union's actions entirely proper." Both Van Gorkom and the board knew a good deal when they saw one. Further, the only effect of the decision will be to create more formalism and transaction costs (lawyers, investment bankers, accountants) for a board when executing a deal. Leo Herzel & Leo Katz, Smith v. Van Gorkom: The Business of Judging Business Judgment, 41 Bus.Law. 1187, 1188–89, 1191 (1986).[18]

(3) Robert Hamilton argues that one of the most immediate effects of *Van Gorkom* was to make finding outside directors much more difficult. The risk of liability outweighed the benefits of an outside director position. Further, *Van Gorkom* created new costs of compliance in the form of financial experts and cumbersome record keeping. Robert W. Hamilton, Reliance and Liability Standards for Outside Directors, 24 Wake Forest L.Rev. 5, 28–29 (1989).

(4) The response of the Delaware legislature to Smith v. Van Gorkom was both swift and decisive. A new paragraph (7) was promptly added to § 102(b) of the Delaware GCL.

DEL. GEN. CORP. LAW
§ 102(b)(7).

§ 102 CONTENTS OF CERTIFICATE OF INCORPORATION

* * * (b) In addition to the matters required to be set forth in the certificate of incorporation by subsection (a) of this section, the certificate of incorporation may also contain any or all of the following matters: * * *

(7) A provision eliminating or limiting the personal liability of a director to the corporation or its stockholders for monetary damages for breach of fiduciary duty as a director, provided that such provision shall not eliminate or limit the liability of a director (i) for any breach of the director's duty of

---

18. Copyright 1986 by the American Bar Association. All rights reserved. Reprinted with the permission of the American Bar Association and its Section of Corporation, Banking and Business Law.

loyalty to the corporation or its stockholders, (ii) for acts or omissions not in good faith or which involve intentional misconduct or a knowing violation of law, (iii) under section 174 of this Title,[19] or (iv) for any transaction from which the director derived an improper personal benefit. No such provision shall eliminate or limit the liability of a director for any act or omission occurring prior to the date when such provision becomes effective. * * *

Notes

(1) Consider also MBCA § 2.02(b)(4), a subsection added in 1990. As of 2004, 43 states had adopted statutes similar either to this section or to Del. GCL § 102(b)(7). These statutory provisions have since become known as "raincoat" provisions, because of the protections they provide to corporate directors.

(2) The Official Comment to § 2.02(b)(4) states:

> Developments in the mid-and late 1980s highlighted the need to permit reasonable protection from exposure to personal liability, in addition to indemnification, so that directors would not be discouraged from fully and freely carrying out their duties, including responsible entrepreneurial risk-taking. These developments included increased costs and reduced availability of director and officer liability insurance, the decision of the Delaware Supreme Court in *Smith v. Van Gorkom* * * *, and the resulting reluctance of qualified individuals to serve as directors.

> So long as any such liability-limitation provision does not extend to liability to third parties, shareholders should be permitted—except when important societal values are at stake—to decide how to allocate the economic risk of the directors' conduct between the corporation and the directors. * * * In addition, it follows the path of virtually all the states that have adopted charter option statutes and is applicable only to money damages and not to equitable relief.

(3) Cede & Co., Cinerama, Inc. v. Technicolor, Inc., 634 A.2d 345 (Del.1993) involved a merger negotiated in 1982 (two years before Smith v. Van Gorkom was decided) under circumstances roughly comparable to those that occurred in *Van Gorkom*. In a suit brought by an individual shareholder, the Court of Chancery refused to impose personal liability on the directors, despite a finding of gross negligence, unless the plaintiff could establish not only that it suffered a loss but also that the loss was caused by the grossly negligent conduct of the directors. The rule of *Van Gorkom* would lead to "draconian results," Chancellor Allen stated, unless modified to require this proof of causation. The Delaware Supreme Court reversed, holding that to require the plaintiff to show a causal connection between the defendants' gross negligence and the damage or loss suffered by the plaintiff "would lead to most unfortunate results, detrimental to goals of heightened and enlightened standards for corporate governance of Delaware corporations." Once the controlling principles of *Van Gorkom* become applicable and the requirements of the business judgment rule are not met, the defendants may avoid liability only if they can establish the entire fairness of the transaction. Tort principles of causation or proximate cause "have no place in a business judgment rule standard of review analysis." Subsequently, Chancellor Allen concluded that no liability existed because the transaction was in all respects fair to shareholders and this

---

19. [By the Editors] Section 174 refers to the liability of directors for unlawful dividends   and stock repurchases or redemptions.

opinion was promptly affirmed. 663 A.2d 1134 (Del.Ch.1994), aff'd 663 A.2d 1156 (Del.1995). The Technicolor decision has been criticized by scholars and practitioners for its use of an "entire fairness" standard to evaluate directors' conduct in a duty of care case. Prior to this case, it had been generally thought that transactions should only be evaluated under an "entire fairness" standard in cases involving violations of the duty of loyalty, not the duty of care. Professor Allen and Vice Chancellors Jack B. Jacobs and Leo E. Strine, Jr., wrote an article that characterized Technicolor as a "surprise" to "corporate practitioners and scholars alike" and observed that the court "cited no precedent, nor offered any explanation, for why on policy grounds duty of care claims should receive the same searching substantive review that traditionally is reserved for duty of loyalty claims." William T. Allen, Jack B. Jacobs & Leo E. Strine, Jr., Function Over Form: A Reassessment of Standards of Review in Delaware Corporation Law, 56 Bus. Law. 1287, 1302–03 (2001).

(4) The issue of how the "raincoat" provisions contained in section 102(b)(7) work from a mechanical perspective has been the subject of considerable controversy in Delaware. Understandably, when directors are sued, they want to know precisely when they can invoke the protections promised by the statute: "[T]he usefulness of director protection statutes turns in large measure upon the ability of directors to rely upon charter provisions adopted in accordance with these statutes in the context of motions to dismiss filed at the outset of litigation and before discovery. Requiring directors to defend such litigation beyond the motion to dismiss stage eviscerates the protection provided by director protection statutes and thus undermines the policy behind the statutes." Stephen A. Radin, Business and Securities Litigator, Director Protection Statutes After Malpiede And Emerald Partners, February, 2002.

(5) Emerald Partners v. Berlin, 787 A.2d 85 (Del.2001) arose out of a merger between May Petroleum Company and 13 corporations owned by Craig Hall, Emerald's Chairman and CEO. Article 15 of May's corporate charter contained an exculpatory clause based on § 102(b)(7). Shareholders sued claiming that the merger was unfair to the minority shareholders because the prices paid for the companies were too high, and because there were flaws in the negotiation that led to the merger. While Hall, the CEO, could not claim the protections of § 102(b)(7) [because he was on both sides of the challenged transaction], the other defendant-directors relied on § 102(b)(7) as an affirmative defense. The Delaware Court of Chancery entered judgment in favor of these directors after finding that (i) they had received no benefit from the merger (except in their capacity as shareholders in May Petroleum Corporation), (ii) were not affiliated with May, and (iii) had acted independently of management. Since the most that could be said about the directors was that they had violated a fiduciary duty of care, the Court found that it was unnecessary to delve further into the transaction. Judgment was entered in favor of the defendant directors: "It cannot be argued that the Court, having found that the directors are exculpated, must nonetheless undertake an entire fairness analysis in order to negate a claim that the defendants breached their fiduciary duty of loyalty." 2001 WL 115340, at *28 (Del.Ch. Feb. 7, 2001).

The Chancery Court's decision was reversed by the Delaware Supreme Court. The Delaware Supreme Court held that, "when entire fairness is the applicable standard of judicial review (as it is whenever a plaintiff/shareholder can show a violation of the directors' duty of care, the duty of loyalty, or the duty to act in good faith) a determination that the director defendants are exculpated from paying monetary damages can be made only after the basis for their liability has been decided. * * * [P]ost-trial judicial scrutiny pursuant to the entire fairness standard of review therefore cannot be avoided by asserting a Section 102(b)(7) provision as a defense to the payment of monetary damages, before a finding of unfairness had been made with a rationale for that determination." Berlin, 787 A.2d at 94. The Supreme Court added that "[i]f the Court of Chancery determines that the transaction was entirely fair, the director defendants have no liability for monetary damages." Id., at 98. However, the Supreme Court also held that if the Court of Chancery determines that the transaction was *not* entirely fair, then the Court of Chancery should examine the directors' Section 102(b)(7) request for exculpation "in the context of the completed judicial analysis that resulted in a finding of unfairness." Id. At that point, directors avoid personal liability for monetary damages "only if they have established that their failure to withstand an entire fairness analysis is exclusively attributable to a violation of the duty of care." Id. On remand, the Chancery Court found that the directors had satisfied the entire fairness analysis. 2003 WL 21003437, at *1 (Del.Ch. Apr. 28, 2003).

Emerald Partners has had a dramatic effect on the way that litigation is conducted. Once a shareholder/plaintiff overcomes the presumption of the business judgment rule with allegations that, if true, would establish a breach of duty of loyalty or good faith, a director's section 102(b)(7) request for exculpation will be examined only "in the context of the completed judicial analysis that resulted in a finding of unfairness"—i.e., after discovery, after a trial, and after a finding that the challenged decision was unfair to shareholders. Section 102(b)(7) no longer results in automatic, instantaneous dismissal of claims against individual directors. Radin, *supra*.

(6) For differing perspectives on the benefits and drawbacks of the corporate governance principles articulated in Smith v. Van Gorkom, see, Professor Mark Roe, in Corporate Law's Limits 31 J. Legal Studies 233 (2002); Lawrence A. Hamermesh, Why I Do Not Teach *Van Gorkom*, 34 Ga.L.Rev. 477 (2000); Jonathan R. Macey, Smith v. Van Gorkom: Insights About CEO's, Corporate Law Rules, and the Jurisdictional competition for Corporate Charters, 96 Nw. U. L. Rev. 607 (2002); David Rosenberg, Making Sense of Good Faith in Delaware Corporate Fiduciary Law: A Contractarian Approach, 29 Del. J. Corp. L. 491 (2004).

IN RE CAREMARK INTERN. INC. DERIVATIVE LITIGATION

Court of Chancery of Delaware, 1996.
698 A.2d 959.

[By the Editors: Caremark was a substantial, publicly held corporation with shares traded on the New York Stock Exchange. It was involved in two main health care business areas, (1) patient care and (2) managed care services. Its patient care business (which accounted for the majority of its revenues) involved alternative site health care services, including infusion therapy, growth hormone therapy, HIV/AIDS-related treatments and hemophilia therapy. Its managed care services included prescription drug programs and the operation of multi-specialty group practices. Caremark had approximately 7,000 employees and ninety branch operations. It also had a decentralized management structure.

A substantial part of the revenues generated by Caremark's businesses was derived from third party payments, insurers, and Medicare and Medicaid reimbursement programs. The latter source of payments was subject to the terms of the Anti–Referral Payments Law ("ARPL"), 42 U.S.C.A. § 1395nn (1989), a federal statute that prohibits health care providers from paying any form of remuneration to induce the referral of Medicare or Medicaid patients. From its inception, Caremark entered into a variety of agreements with hospitals, physicians, and health care providers for advice and services, as well as distribution agreements with drug suppliers. Caremark also entered into contracts for services (e.g., consultation agreements and research grants) with physicians at least some of whom prescribed or recommended services or products that Caremark provided to Medicare recipients and other patients. Such contracts were not prohibited by ARPL but they raised a possibility of unlawful "kickbacks." Caremark repeatedly stated that it was not in violation of ARPL, though it also stated that there was a scarcity of court decisions interpreting ARPL and that there was uncertainty concerning Caremark's interpretation of the law.

In August 1991, the HHS Office of the Inspector General ("OIG") initiated an investigation of Caremark. Caremark was served with a subpoena requiring the production of documents, including Quality Service Agreements ("QSAs") between Caremark and physicians. Under the QSAs, Caremark appears to have paid physicians fees for monitoring patients under Caremark's care, including Medicare and Medicaid recipients. Sometimes apparently those monitoring patients were referring physicians, which raised ARPL concerns. In March 1992, the Department of Justice ("DOJ") joined the OIG investigation and separate investigations were commenced by several additional federal and state agencies.

In 1994 Caremark was charged in an indictment with multiple felonies. It began settlement negotiations with federal and state government entities in May 1995. In return for a guilty plea to a single count of mail fraud by the corporation, the payment of a criminal fine and substantial civil damages, and an agreement to cooperate with further federal investigations on matters relating to the OIG investigation, the government entities agreed to negotiate a settlement that would permit Caremark to continue participating in Medicare and Medicaid programs. On June 15, 1995, Caremark's board approved a settlement ("Government Settlement Agreement") with the DOJ, OIG, other federal agencies, and related state agencies in all fifty states and the District of Columbia.

In all, Caremark paid approximately $250 million to settle all claims against it. No senior officers or directors of Caremark were charged with wrongdoing in the Government Settlement Agreement or in any of the prior indictments. Subsequently, Caremark also agreed to make reimbursements to various private and public parties.

The present derivative suit was filed in 1994, seeking to recover on behalf of the company damages for all losses suffered by Caremark. The defendants were the individual members of the board of directors of Caremark. A proposed settlement was negotiated and a hearing held on its terms following notice to shareholders. The proposed settlement did not require any monetary payment or relinquishment of stock options by the defendants. Rather, the principal provisions of the settlement required Caremark (1) to take steps to assure that no future violations of ARPL occurred, (2) to advise patients in writing of any financial relationship between Caremark and a health care professional or provider who made the referral, and (3) to create a Compliance and Ethics Committee composed of four directors, including two non-management directors to monitor future conduct.

The opinion below dealt with the motion to approve the proposed settlement as fair and reasonable.]

ALLEN, CHANCELLOR.

* * * A motion of this type requires the court to assess the strengths and weaknesses of the claims asserted in light of the discovery record and to evaluate the fairness and adequacy of the consideration offered to the corporation in exchange for the release of all claims made or arising from the facts alleged. The ultimate issue then is whether the proposed settlement appears to be fair to the corporation and its absent shareholders. * * * Legally, evaluation of the central claim made entails consideration of the legal standard governing a board of directors' obligation to supervise or monitor corporate performance. For the reasons set forth below I conclude * * * that there is a very low probability that it would be determined that the directors of Caremark breached any duty to appropriately monitor and supervise the enterprise. Indeed the record tends to show an active consideration by Caremark management and its Board of the Caremark structures and programs that ultimately led to the company's indictment and to the large financial losses incurred in the settlement of those claims.[20] It does not tend to show knowing or intentional violation of law. Neither the fact that the Board, although advised by lawyers and accountants, did not accurately predict the severe consequences to the company that would ultimately follow from the deployment by the company of the strategies and practices that ultimately led to this liability, nor the scale of the liability, gives rise to an inference of breach of any duty imposed by corporation law upon the directors of Caremark. * * *

A. Principles Governing Settlements of Derivative Claims. As noted at the outset of this opinion, this Court is now required to exercise an informed judgment whether the proposed settlement is fair and reasonable in the light of all relevant factors. Polk v. Good, Del.Supr., 507 A.2d 531 (1986). On an application of this kind, this Court attempts to protect the best interests of the corporation and its absent shareholders all of whom will be barred from future litigation on these claims if the settlement is approved. The parties proposing the settlement bear the burden of persuading the court that it is in fact fair and reasonable. Fins v. Pearlman, Del.Supr., 424 A.2d 305 (1980).

B. Directors' Duties to Monitor Corporate Operations. The complaint charges the director defendants with breach of their duty of attention or care in connection with the on-going operation of the corporation's business. The claim is that the directors allowed a situation to develop and continue which exposed the corporation to enormous legal liability and that in so doing they violated a duty to be active monitors of corporate performance.

---

20. [By the Editors] For example, an omitted portion of Chancellor Allen's opinion states: "As early as 1989, Caremark's predecessor issued an internal 'Guide to Contractual Relationships' * * * to govern its employees in entering into contracts with physicians and hospitals. The Guide tended to be reviewed annually by lawyers and updated. Each version of the Guide stated as Caremark's and its predecessor's policy that no payments would me made in exchange for or to induce patient referrals. * * *"

The complaint thus does not charge either director self-dealing or the more difficult loyalty-type problems arising from cases of suspect director motivation, such as entrenchment or sale of control contexts.[21] The theory here advanced is possibly the most difficult theory in corporation law upon which a plaintiff might hope to win a judgment. * * *

1. Potential liability for directoral decisions: Director liability for a breach of the duty to exercise appropriate attention may, in theory, arise in two distinct contexts. First, such liability may be said to follow from a board decision that results in a loss because that decision was ill advised or "negligent". Second, liability to the corporation for a loss may be said to arise from an unconsidered failure of the board to act in circumstances in which due attention would, arguably, have prevented the loss. See generally Veasey & Seitz, The Business Judgment Rule in the Revised Model Act, 63 Texas L.Rev. 1483 (1985). The first class of cases will typically be subject to review under the director-protective business judgment rule, assuming the decision made was the product of a process that was either deliberately considered in good faith or was otherwise rational. See Aronson v. Lewis, Del.Supr., 473 A.2d 805 (1984); Gagliardi v. TriFoods Int'l, Inc., Del.Ch., 683 A.2d 1049 (1996). What should be understood, but may not widely be understood by courts or commentators who are not often required to face such questions,[22] is that compliance with a director's duty of care can never appropriately be judicially determined by reference to the content of the board decision that leads to a corporate loss, apart from consideration of the good faith or rationality of the process employed. That is, whether a judge or jury considering the matter after the fact, believes a decision substantively wrong, or degrees of wrong extending through "stupid" to "egregious" or "irrational," provides no ground for director liability, so long as the court determines that the process employed was either rational or employed in a good faith effort to advance corporate interests. To employ a different rule—one that permitted an "objective" evaluation of the decision—would expose directors to substantive second guessing by ill-equipped judges or juries, which would, in the long-run, be injurious to investor interests.[23] Thus, the business judgment rule is

21. [By the Court] See Weinberger v. UOP, Inc., Del.Supr., 457 A.2d 701, 711 (1983) (entire fairness test when financial conflict of interest involved); Unitrin, Inc. v. American General Corp., Del.Supr., 651 A.2d 1361, 1372 (1995) (intermediate standard of review when "defensive" acts taken); Paramount Communications, Inc. v. QVC Network, Del.Supr., 637 A.2d 34, 45 (1994) (intermediate test when corporate control transferred).

22. [By the Court] See American Law Institute, Principles of Corporate Governance § 4.01(c) (to qualify for business judgment treatment a director must "rationally" believe that the decision is in the best interests of the corporation).

23. [By the Court] The vocabulary of negligence while often employed, e.g., Aronson v. Lewis, Del.Supr., 473 A.2d 805 (1984) is not well-suited to judicial review of board attentiveness, see, e.g. Joy v. North, 692 F.2d 880,

885–6 (2d Cir.1982), especially if one attempts to look to the substance of the decision as any evidence of possible "negligence." Where review of board functioning is involved, courts leave behind as a relevant point of reference the decisions of the hypothetical "reasonable person", who typically supplies the test for negligence liability. It is doubtful that we want business men and women to be encouraged to make decisions as hypothetical persons of ordinary judgment and prudence might. The corporate form gets its utility in large part from its ability to allow diversified investors to accept greater investment risk. If those in charge of the corporation are to be adjudged personally liable for losses on the basis of a substantive judgment based upon what an persons of ordinary or average judgment and average risk assessment talent regard as "prudent" "sensible" or even "rational", such persons will have a strong incentive at the margin to authorize less risky investment projects.

process oriented and informed by a deep respect for all good faith board decisions.

Indeed, one wonders on what moral basis might shareholders attack a good faith business decision of a director as "unreasonable" or "irrational." Where a director in fact exercises a good faith effort to be informed and to exercise appropriate judgment, he or she should be deemed to satisfy fully the duty of attention. If the shareholders thought themselves entitled to some other quality of judgment than such a director produces in the good faith exercise of the powers of office, then the shareholders should have elected other directors. Judge Learned Hand made the point rather better than can I. In speaking of the passive director defendant Mr. Andrews in Barnes v. Andrews, Judge Hand said:

> True, he was not very suited by experience for the job he had undertaken, but I cannot hold him on that account. After all it is the same corporation that chose him that now seeks to charge him * * *. Directors are not specialists like lawyers or doctors * * *. They are the general advisors of the business and if they faithfully give such ability as they have to their charge, it would not be lawful to hold them liable. Must a director guarantee that his judgment is good? Can a shareholder call him to account for deficiencies that their votes assured him did not disqualify him for his office? While he may not have been the Cromwell for that Civil War, Andrews did not engage to play any such role. [298 F. 614, 618 (S.D.N.Y.1924)].

In this formulation Learned Hand correctly identifies, in my opinion, the core element of any corporate law duty of care inquiry: whether there was good faith effort to be informed and exercise judgment.

2. *Liability for failure to monitor:* The second class of cases in which director liability for inattention is theoretically possible entail circumstances in which a loss eventuates not from a decision but, from unconsidered inaction. Most of the decisions that a corporation, acting through its human agents, makes are, of course, not the subject of director attention. Legally, the board itself will be required only to authorize the most significant corporate acts or transactions: mergers, changes in capital structure, fundamental changes in business, appointment and compensation of the CEO, etc. As the facts of this case graphically demonstrate, ordinary business decisions that are made by officers and employees deeper in the interior of the organization can, however, vitally affect the welfare of the corporation and its ability to achieve its various strategic and financial goals. * * * [W]hat is the board's responsibility with respect to the organization and monitoring of the enterprise to assure that the corporation functions within the law to achieve its purposes?

Modernly this question has been given special importance by an increasing tendency, especially under federal law, to employ the criminal law to assure corporate compliance with external legal requirements, including environmental, financial, employee and product safety as well as assorted other health and safety regulations. In 1991, pursuant to the Sentencing Reform Act of 1984,[24] the United States Sentencing Commission adopted Organizational Sentencing Guidelines which impact importantly on the prospective

---

24. [By the Court] Pub.L. 98–473, Title II, § 212(a)(2)(1984); 18 U.S.C.A. §§ 3551–3686.

effect these criminal sanctions might have on business corporations. The Guidelines set forth a uniform sentencing structure for organizations to be sentenced for violation of federal criminal statutes and provide for penalties that equal or often massively exceed those previously imposed on corporations.[25] The Guidelines offer powerful incentives for corporations today to have in place compliance programs to detect violations of law, promptly to report violations to appropriate public officials when discovered, and to take prompt, voluntary remedial efforts.

In 1963, the Delaware Supreme Court in Graham v. Allis–Chalmers Mfg. Co.,[26] addressed the question of potential liability of board members for losses experienced by the corporation as a result of the corporation having violated the anti-trust laws of the United States. There was no claim in that case that the directors knew about the behavior of subordinate employees of the corporation that had resulted in the liability. Rather, as in this case, the claim asserted was that the directors ought to have known of it and if they had known they would have been under a duty to bring the corporation into compliance with the law and thus save the corporation from the loss. The Delaware Supreme Court concluded that, under the facts as they appeared, there was no basis to find that the directors had breached a duty to be informed of the ongoing operations of the firm. In notably colorful terms, the court stated that "absent cause for suspicion there is no duty upon the directors to install and operate a corporate system of espionage to ferret out wrongdoing which they have no reason to suspect exists."[27] The Court found that there were no grounds for suspicion in that case and, thus, concluded that the directors were blamelessly unaware of the conduct leading to the corporate liability.[28]

How does one generalize this holding today? Can it be said today that, absent some ground giving rise to suspicion of violation of law, that corporate directors have no duty to assure that a corporate information gathering and reporting systems exists which represents a good faith attempt to provide senior management and the Board with information respecting material acts, events or conditions within the corporation, including compliance with applicable statutes and regulations? I certainly do not believe so. I doubt that such a broad generalization of the *Graham* holding would have been accepted by the Supreme Court in 1963. The case can be more narrowly interpreted as standing for the proposition that, absent grounds to suspect deception, neither corporate boards nor senior officers can be charged with wrongdoing simply for assuming the integrity of employees and the honesty of their dealings on the company's behalf.

A broader interpretation of Graham v. Allis–Chalmers—that it means that a corporate board has no responsibility to assure that appropriate information and reporting systems are established by management—would not, in any event, be accepted by the Delaware Supreme Court in 1996, in my

25. [By the Court] See United States Sentencing Commission, Guidelines Manuel, Chapter 8 (U.S. Government Printing Office November 1994).

26. [By the Court] Del.Supr., 41 Del.Ch. 78, 188 A.2d 125 (1963).

27. [By the Court] Id. 188 A.2d at 130.

28. [By the Court] Recently, the *Graham* standard was applied by the Delaware Chancery in a case involving Baxter. In Re Baxter International, Inc. Shareholders Litig., Del.Ch., 654 A.2d 1268, 1270 (1995).

opinion. In stating the basis for this view, I start with the recognition that in recent years the Delaware Supreme Court has made it clear—especially in its jurisprudence concerning takeovers, from Smith v. Van Gorkom through Paramount Communications v. QVC[29]—the seriousness with which the corporation law views the role of the corporate board. Secondly, I note the elementary fact that relevant and timely information is an essential predicate for satisfaction of the board's supervisory and monitoring role under Section 141 of the Delaware General Corporation Law. Thirdly, I note the potential impact of the federal organizational sentencing guidelines on any business organization. Any rational person attempting in good faith to meet an organizational governance responsibility would be bound to take into account this development and the enhanced penalties and the opportunities for reduced sanctions that it offers.

In light of these developments, it would, in my opinion, be a mistake to conclude that our Supreme Court's statement in *Graham* concerning "espionage" means that corporate boards may satisfy their obligation to be reasonably informed concerning the corporation, without assuring themselves that information and reporting systems exist in the organization that are reasonably designed to provide to senior management and to the board itself timely, accurate information sufficient to allow management and the board, each within its scope, to reach informed judgments concerning both the corporation's compliance with law and its business performance.

Obviously the level of detail that is appropriate for such an information system is a question of business judgment. And obviously too, no rationally designed information and reporting system will remove the possibility that the corporation will violate laws or regulations, or that senior officers or directors may nevertheless sometimes be misled or otherwise fail reasonably to detect acts material to the corporation's compliance with the law. But it is important that the board exercise a good faith judgment that the corporation's information and reporting system is in concept and design adequate to assure the board that appropriate information will come to its attention in a timely manner as a matter of ordinary operations, so that it may satisfy its responsibility.

Thus, I am of the view that a director's obligation includes a duty to attempt in good faith to assure that a corporate information and reporting system, which the board concludes is adequate, exists, and that failure to do so under some circumstances may, in theory at least, render a director liable for losses caused by non-compliance with applicable legal standards[30]. I now turn to an analysis of the claims asserted with this concept of the directors duty of care, as a duty satisfied in part by assurance of adequate information flows to the board, in mind.

29. [By the Court] Smith v. Van Gorkom, Del.Supr., 488 A.2d 858 (1985); Paramount Communications v. QVC Network, Del.Supr., 637 A.2d 34 (1994).

30. [By the Court] Any action seeking recovery for losses would logically entail a judicial determination of proximate cause, since, for reasons that I take to be obvious, it could never be assumed that an adequate information system would be a system that would prevent all losses. I need not touch upon the burden allocation with respect to a proximate cause issue in such a suit. See Cede & Co. v. Technicolor, Inc., Del.Supr., 636 A.2d 956 (1994); Cinerama, Inc. v. Technicolor, Inc., Del. Ch., 663 A.2d 1134 (1994), aff'd, Del.Supr., 663 A.2d 1156 (1995). Moreover, questions of waiver of liability under certificate provisions authorized by 8 Del.C. § 102(b)(7) may also be faced.

III. ANALYSIS OF THIRD AMENDED COMPLAINT AND SETTLEMENT

A. *The Claims*

On balance, after reviewing an extensive record in this case, including numerous documents and three depositions, I conclude that this settlement is fair and reasonable. In light of the fact that the Caremark Board already has a functioning committee charged with overseeing corporate compliance, the changes in corporate practice that are presented as consideration for the settlement do not impress one as very significant. Nonetheless, that consideration appears fully adequate to support dismissal of the derivative claims of director fault asserted, because those claims find no substantial evidentiary support in the record and quite likely were susceptible to a motion to dismiss in all events.[31]

In order to show that the Caremark directors breached their duty of care by failing adequately to control Caremark's employees, plaintiffs would have to show either (1) that the directors knew or (2) should have known that violations of law were occurring and, in either event, (3) that the directors took no steps in a good faith effort to prevent or remedy that situation, and (4) that such failure proximately resulted in the losses complained of, although under Cede & Co. v. Technicolor, Inc., Del.Supr., 636 A.2d 956 (1994) this last element may be thought to constitute an affirmative defense.

1. Knowing violation of statute: Concerning the possibility that the Caremark directors knew of violations of law, none of the documents submitted for review, nor any of the deposition transcripts appear to provide evidence of it. Certainly the Board understood that the company had entered into a variety of contracts with physicians, researchers, and health care providers and it was understood that some of these contracts were with persons who had prescribed treatments that Caremark participated in providing. The board was informed that the company's reimbursement for patient care was frequently from government funded sources and that such services were subject to the ARPL. But the Board appears to have been informed by experts that the company's practices while contestable, were lawful. There is no evidence that reliance on such reports was not reasonable. Thus, this case presents no occasion to apply a principle to the effect that knowingly causing the corporation to violate a criminal statute constitutes a breach of a director's fiduciary duty. See Roth v. Robertson, N.Y.Sup.Ct., 64 Misc. 343, 118 N.Y.S. 351 (1909); Miller v. American Tel. & Tel. Co., 507 F.2d 759 (3d Cir.1974). It is not clear that the Board knew the detail found, for example, in the indictments arising from the Company's payments. But, of course, the duty to act in good faith to be informed cannot be thought to require directors to possess detailed information about all aspects of the operation of the enterprise. Such a requirement would simply be inconsistent with the scale and scope of efficient organization size in this technological age.

2. Failure to monitor: Since it does appear that the Board was to some extent unaware of the activities that led to liability, I turn to a

---

31. [By the Court] See In Re Baxter International, Inc. Shareholders Litig., Del.Ch., 654 A.2d 1268, 1270 (1995). A claim in some respects similar to that here made was dismissed. The court relied, in part, on the fact that the Baxter certificate of incorporation contained a provision as authorized by section 102(B)(7) of the Delaware General Corporation Law, waiving director liability for due care violations. That fact was thought to require pre-suit demand on the board in that case.

consideration of the other potential avenue to director liability that the pleadings take: director inattention or "negligence." Generally where a claim of directorial liability for corporate loss is predicated upon ignorance of liability creating activities within the corporation, as in *Graham* or in this case, in my opinion only a sustained or systematic failure of the board to exercise oversight—such as an utter failure to attempt to assure a reasonable information and reporting system exits—will establish the lack of good faith that is a necessary condition to liability. Such a test of liability—lack of good faith as evidenced by sustained or systematic failure of a director to exercise reasonable oversight—is quite high. But, a demanding test of liability in the oversight context is probably beneficial to corporate shareholders as a class, as it is in the board decision context, since it makes board service by qualified persons more likely, while continuing to act as a stimulus to good faith performance of duty by such directors.

Here the record supplies essentially no evidence that the director defendants were guilty of a sustained failure to exercise their oversight function. To the contrary, insofar as I am able to tell on this record, the corporation's information systems appear to have represented a good faith attempt to be informed of relevant facts. If the directors did not know the specifics of the activities that lead to the indictments, they cannot be faulted.

The liability that eventuated in this instance was huge. But the fact that it resulted from a violation of criminal law alone does not create a breach of fiduciary duty by directors. The record at this stage does not support the conclusion that the defendants either lacked good faith in the exercise of their monitoring responsibilities or conscientiously permitted a known violation of law by the corporation to occur. The claims asserted against them must be viewed at this stage as extremely weak. * * *

B. The Consideration For Release of Claim

The proposed settlement provides very modest benefits. Under the settlement agreement, plaintiffs have been given express assurances that Caremark will have a more centralized, active supervisory system in the future. Specifically, the settlement mandates duties to be performed by the newly named Compliance and Ethics Committee on an ongoing basis and increases the responsibility for monitoring compliance with the law at the lower levels of management. In adopting the resolutions required under the settlement, Caremark has further clarified its policies concerning the prohibition of providing remuneration for referrals. These appear to be positive consequences of the settlement of the claims brought by the plaintiffs, even if they are not highly significant. Nonetheless, given the weakness of the plaintiffs' claims the proposed settlement appears to be an adequate, reasonable, and beneficial outcome for all of the parties. Thus, the proposed settlement will be approved. * * *

[Chancellor Allen finally considered the request of the attorneys for plaintiffs for an award of attorneys' fees for negotiating the settlement. [He stated,] "in awarding attorneys' fees, this Court considers an array of relevant factors, * * * [including], most importantly, the financial value of the benefit that the lawyers work produced; the strength of the claims (because substantial settlement value may sometimes be produced even though the litigation added little value—i.e., perhaps any lawyer could have settled this claim for this substantial value or more); the amount of complexity of the legal services; the fee customarily charged for such services; and the contingent nature of the undertaking. In this case no factor points to a substantial fee, other than the amount and sophistication of the lawyer services required. There is only a modest substantive benefit produced; in the particular circumstances of the government activity there was realistically a very slight contingency faced by the attorneys at the time they expended. The services rendered required a high degree of sophistication and expertise. I am told that at normal hourly billing rates approximately $710,000 of time was expended by the attorneys. * * * In these circumstances, I conclude that an award of a fee determined by reference to the time expended at normal hourly rates plus a premium of 15% of that amount to reflect the limited degree of real contingency in the undertaking, is fair. Thus I will award a fee of $816,000 plus $53,000 of expenses advanced by counsel."[32]

Notes

(1) The *Caremark* opinion brought into focus the responsibility of the board of directors to monitor corporate operations. The collapse of Enron Corporation in November, 2001, followed shortly thereafter by a spate of cases also involving inappropriate management conduct in other corporations, provides classic illustrations of the potential consequences of a failure by a board of directors to monitor the performance of management as contemplated in Chancellor Allen's classic opinion. Because of these developments, the responsibility of directors to monitor managers is receiving renewed attention by regulators, academics, and lawyers. See Note, Earnings Management, the SEC and Corporate Governance: Director Liability Arising From the Audit Committee Report, 102 Colum.L.Rev. 168 (2002). *Caremark* is the leading case describing and defining this oversight responsibility, and Enron Corporation is the principal current example of the consequences of a virtually total failure to monitor managers.

(2) It seems clear that the board of directors of Enron Corporation failed to meet the monitoring obligation described in *Caremark*. What should the consequence of that failure be? Should all members of the board of directors of Enron be personally liable for their collective failure to monitor? Since the ultimate losses from the collapse of Enron were in the billions of dollars, that would be a catastrophic blow. However, consider the reality of their position. As a member of the board of directors, if you get a clear negative answer to a specific question from an apparently responsible senior executive such as Andrew Fastow, shouldn't you be able to rely on that? If your answer is that they should have inquired further, how much would be enough? In a major corporation with transactions in the billions of dollars one could probably search indefinitely.

(3) In every large corporation, many if not most major decisions (in the sense of being important as an economic matter), are made by executives and employees who are not members of the board of directors. The board of directors may not be aware of specific decisions until many months later. In other words, the typical board of directors is involved only with the most sensitive or significant acts or transactions, despite the fact that "ordinary business decisions" made by officers

---

32. [By the Court] The court has been informed by letter of counsel that after the fairness of the proposed settlement had been submitted to the court, Caremark was involved in a merger in which its stock was canceled and the holders of its stock became entitled to shares of stock of the acquiring corporation. * * *

and employees may vitally affect the welfare of the corporation. Indeed, it is likely that directors will first become aware that damaging decisions have been made only when they are sued by shareholders.

(4) Historically, Post-*Caremark* decisions indicate that shareholder litigation against directors and officers continues to be a tough road. For example, in Salsitz v. Nasser, 208 F.R.D. 589 (E.D.Mich.2002) the directors of the Ford Motor Company were sued for making three unfortunate business decisions. One was the decision to install inadequate tires for Ford Explorers. Second, was a decision to put an ignition system in a location which sometimes caused the motor to quit unexpectedly or the ignition system to fail. The third issue related to the excessive purchases of palladium, a precious metal, that led Ford to take costly write-downs when the excess palladium was resold. A motion by the defendants to dismiss for failure to state a claim was granted.

(5) There are two older cases in which liability was imposed on directors for failure to pay attention or for breach of the duty to be informed with respect to the business of the corporation.

In Bates v. Dresser, 251 U.S. 524, 40 S.Ct. 247, 64 L.Ed. 388 (1920), a bank president who was also a director was held personally liable for the amount stolen by one Coleman, a young bookkeeper at the bank. He was made aware of the missing deposits. He was further told that the Coleman was the likely culprit. Even with these warnings the president still did nothing. The other directors were not held liable, since they reasonably relied on bank examinations and the president.

In Francis v. United Jersey Bank, 87 N.J. 15, 432 A.2d 814 (1981), the sons of the founder of a corporation, an "insurance reinsurance" business, siphoned large sums of money from the corporation in the form of "shareholder loans" and other improper payments to family members. As a result of these transactions, the corporation became insolvent; the bankruptcy trustee brought suit against Mrs. Pritchard, the widow of the founder for more than $10,000,000, representing funds transferred unlawfully from the firm to the family members while she was a director of the company. Mrs. Pritchard literally did nothing in her role as a director. Instead, she began to drink heavily after her husband's death and had nothing to do with direction of the business. The court found that Mrs. Pritchard was grossly negligent in her duties as a director. Most importantly, the court found that Mrs. Pritchard's negligence was a proximate cause of the misappropriations by her two, co-director sons.

(6) The judicial ground of director liability may be shifting in a Post–Enron, Tyco, and WorldCom world. Courts, especially in Delaware, seem more receptive to suits which charge breach of good faith and loyalty by board members. Such claims basically charge that board members *should have* made some decision rather than questioning a real decision. Such claims are also troubling to board members because a breach of good faith voids exculpation clauses such as those permitted by section 102(b)(7) of Delaware Corporate Law. Such exculpation clauses shield directors and officers from personal liability for decisions made on the job. Without such protection personal liability can be astronomical. For a look into this shifting ground of director liability see In re Abbott Laboratories Derivative S'holders Litig., 293 F.3d 378 (7th Cir.2002) (holding that the Abbott board, because of their inattention to costly problems, breached their duty of good faith thus barring the application of the exculpation provision); Pereira v. Cogan, 294 B.R. 449 (S.D.N.Y.2003) (finding that a duty of care was violated by board members thus barring the application of the exculpation provision); In re Walt

Disney Co. Derivative Litig., 825 A.2d 275 (Del.Ch.2003) (evidence that Disney's board breached its duty of good faith by consciously and deliberately ignoring its responsibilities, bars the application of the exculpation provision); Guttman v. Huang, 823 A.2d 492 (Del.Ch.2003).

STONE v. RITTER

Supreme Court of Delaware, 2006.
911 A.2d 362.

Before STEELE, C.J., HOLLAND, BERGER, JACOBS, and RIDGELY, J.J., constituting the Court en Banc.

HOLLAND, Justice.

[Editors: AmSouth Bancorporation (AmSouth) and a subsidiary paid $40 million in fines and $10 million in civil penalties arising from the failure of bank employees to file reports required under the Bank Secrecy Act (BSA) and anti-money laundering (AML) regulations. Plaintiff shareholders filed a derivative suit without making a demand on the company's board of directors, alleging demand futility. The shareholders claimed that AmSouth directors breached their fiduciary duty of oversight. The Chancery Court dismissed the derivative complaint.]

* * * [T]he plaintiffs concede that "[t]he standards for determining demand futility in the absence of a business decision" are set forth in *Rales v. Blasband*. To excuse demand under *Rales*, "a court must determine whether or not the particularized factual allegations of a derivative stockholder complaint create a reasonable doubt that, as of the time the complaint is filed, the board of directors could have properly exercised its independent and disinterested business judgment in responding to a demand." The plaintiffs attempt to satisfy the *Rales* test in this proceeding by asserting that the incumbent defendant directors "face a substantial likelihood of liability" that renders them "personally interested in the outcome of the decision on whether to pursue the claims asserted in the complaint," and are therefore not disinterested or independent.

Critical to this demand excused argument is the fact that the directors' potential personal liability depends upon whether or not their conduct can be exculpated by the section 102(b)(7) provision contained in the AmSouth certificate of incorporation. Such a provision can exculpate directors from monetary liability for a breach of the duty of care, but not for conduct that is not in good faith or a breach of the duty of loyalty. * * *

It is important * * * to clarify a doctrinal issue that is critical to understanding fiduciary liability under *Caremark* as we construe that case. The phraseology used in *Caremark* and that we employ here—describing the lack of good faith as a "necessary condition to liability"—is deliberate. The purpose of that formulation is to communicate that a failure to act in good faith is not conduct that results, *ipso facto*, in the direct imposition of fiduciary liability. The failure to act in good faith may result in liability because the requirement to act in good faith "is a subsidiary element[,]" i.e., a condition, "of the fundamental duty of loyalty." It follows that because a showing of bad faith conduct * * * is essential to establish director oversight liability, the fiduciary duty violated by that conduct is the duty of loyalty.

This view of a failure to act in good faith results in two additional doctrinal consequences. First, although good faith may be described colloquially as part of a "triad" of fiduciary duties that includes the duties of care and loyalty, the obligation to act in good faith does not establish an independent fiduciary duty that stands on the same footing as the duties of care and loyalty. Only the latter two duties, where violated, may directly result in liability, whereas a failure to act in good faith may do so, but indirectly. The second doctrinal consequence is that the fiduciary duty of loyalty is not limited to cases involving a financial or other cognizable fiduciary conflict of interest. It also encompasses cases where the fiduciary fails to act in good faith. * * *

We hold that *Caremark* articulates the necessary conditions predicate for director oversight liability: (a) the directors utterly failed to implement any reporting or information system or controls; *or* (b) having implemented such a system or controls, consciously failed to monitor or oversee its operations thus disabling themselves from being informed of risks or problems requiring their attention. In either case, imposition of liability requires a showing that the directors knew that they were not discharging their fiduciary obligations. Where directors fail to act in the face of a known duty to act, thereby demonstrating a conscious disregard for their responsibilities, they breach their duty of loyalty by failing to discharge that fiduciary obligation in good faith.

The plaintiffs contend that demand is excused under Rule 23.1 because AmSouth's directors breached their oversight duty and, as a result, face a "substantial likelihood of liability" as a result of their "utter failure" to act in good faith to put into place policies and procedures to ensure compliance with BSA and AML obligations. The Court of Chancery found that the plaintiffs did not plead the existence of "red flags"—"facts showing that the board ever was aware that AmSouth's internal controls were inadequate, that these inadequacies would result in illegal activity, and that the board chose to do nothing about problems it allegedly knew existed." In dismissing the derivative complaint in this action, the Court of Chancery concluded:

> This case is not about a board's failure to carefully consider a material corporate decision that was presented to the board. This is a case where information was not reaching the board because of ineffective internal controls. * * *

This Court reviews *de novo* a Court of Chancery's decision to dismiss a derivative suit under Rule 23.1.

Reasonable Reporting System Existed

The KPMG Report evaluated the various components of AmSouth's longstanding BSA/AML compliance program. The KPMG Report reflects that AmSouth's Board dedicated considerable resources to the BSA/AML compliance program and put into place numerous procedures and systems to attempt to ensure compliance. According to KPMG, the program's various components exhibited between a low and high degree of compliance with applicable laws and regulations. * * *

The KPMG Report reflects that the directors not only discharged their oversight responsibility to establish an information and reporting system, but also proved that the system was designed to permit the directors to periodically monitor AmSouth's compliance with BSA and AML regulations. For example, as KPMG noted in 2004, AmSouth's designated BSA Officer "has made annual high-level presentations to the Board of Directors in each of the last five years." Further, the Board's Audit and Community Responsibility Committee (the "Audit Committee") oversaw AmSouth's BSA/AML compliance program on a quarterly basis. The KPMG Report states that "the BSA Officer presents BSA/AML training to the Board of Directors annually," and the "Corporate Security training is also presented to the Board of Directors."

The KPMG Report shows that AmSouth's Board at various times enacted written policies and procedures designed to ensure compliance with the BSA and AML regulations. * * *

* * * KPMG's findings reflect that the Board received and approved relevant policies and procedures, delegated to certain employees and departments the responsibility for filing SARs and monitoring compliance, and exercised oversight by relying on periodic reports from them. Although there ultimately may have been failures by employees to report deficiencies to the Board, there is no basis for an oversight claim seeking to hold the directors personally liable for such failures by the employees. * * *

* * * In the absence of red flags, good faith in the context of oversight must be measured by the directors' actions "to assure a reasonable information and reporting system exists" and not by second-guessing after the occurrence of employee conduct that results in an unintended adverse outcome. Accordingly, we hold that the Court of Chancery properly applied *Caremark* and dismissed the plaintiffs' derivative complaint for failure to excuse demand by alleging particularized facts that created reason to doubt whether the directors had acted in good faith in exercising their oversight responsibilities.

Notes

(1) In affirming the Chancery Court's decision in *Stone*, the Delaware Supreme Court affirmed that the *Caremark* is the law in Delaware. *Stone* also puts to rest the question whether directors have a duty of good faith that is separate from their other fiduciary duties. The Court found that good faith is not a distinct duty but rather a component of the duty of loyalty.

(2) After *Stone*, plaintiffs seeking to hold directors liable for failure to monitor will have to show that "(a) the directors utterly failed to implement any reporting or information system or controls; *or* (b) having implemented such a system or controls, consciously failed to monitor or oversee its operations thus disabling themselves from being informed of risks or problems." Does the Court in *Stone* set the bar too high for proving director oversight liability?

MALONE v. BRINCAT

Supreme Court of Delaware, 1998.
722 A.2d 5.

HOLLAND, JUSTICE (en banc).

Doran Malone, Joseph P. Danielle, and Adrienne M. Danielle, the plaintiffs-appellants, filed this individual and class action in the Court of Chancery.

The complaint alleged that the directors of Mercury Finance Company ("Mercury"), a Delaware corporation, breached their fiduciary duty of disclosure. * * * The complaint also alleged that the defendant-appellee, KPMG Peat Marwick LLP ("KPMG") aided and abetted the Mercury directors' breaches of fiduciary duty. The Court of Chancery dismissed the complaint with prejudice pursuant to Chancery Rule 12(b)(6) for failure to state a claim upon which relief may be granted.

The complaint alleged that the director defendants intentionally overstated the financial condition of Mercury on repeated occasions throughout a four-year period in disclosures to Mercury's shareholders. Plaintiffs contend that the complaint states a claim upon which relief can be granted for a breach of the fiduciary duty of disclosure. Plaintiffs also contend that, because the director defendants breached their fiduciary duty of disclosure to the Mercury shareholders, the Court of Chancery erroneously dismissed the aiding and abetting claim against KPMG.

This Court has concluded that the Court of Chancery properly granted the defendants' motions to dismiss the complaint. That dismissal, however, should have been without prejudice. Plaintiffs are entitled to file an amended complaint. Therefore, the judgment of the Court of Chancery is affirmed in part, reversed in part, and remanded for further proceedings consistent with this opinion. * * *

Mercury is a publicly-traded company engaged primarily in purchasing installment sales contracts from automobile dealers and providing short-term installment loans directly to consumers. This action was filed on behalf of the named plaintiffs and all persons (excluding defendants) who owned common stock of Mercury from 1993 through the present and their successors in interest, heirs and assigns (the "putative class"). The complaint alleged that the directors "knowingly and intentionally breached their fiduciary duty of disclosure because the SEC filings made by the directors and every communication from the company to the shareholders since 1994 was materially false" and that "as a direct result of the false disclosures . . . the Company has lost all or virtually all of its value (about $2 billion)." The complaint also alleged that KPMG knowingly participated in the directors' breaches of their fiduciary duty of disclosure.

According to plaintiffs, since 1994, the director defendants caused Mercury to disseminate information containing overstatements of Mercury's earnings, financial performance and shareholders' equity. Mercury's earnings for 1996 were actually only $56.7 million, or $.33 a share, rather than the $120.7 million, or $.70 a share, as reported by the director defendants. * * * [Similar false statements, though smaller in absolute amounts, were also alleged for each of the years 1993–1995.] Shareholders' equity on December 31, 1996 was disclosed by the director defendants as $353 million, but was only $263 million or less. The complaint alleged that all of the foregoing inaccurate information was included or referenced in virtually every filing Mercury made with the SEC and every communication Mercury's directors made to the shareholders during this period of time.

Having alleged these violations of fiduciary duty, which (if true) are egregious, plaintiffs alleged that as "a direct result of [these] false disclosures * * * the company has lost all or virtually all its value (about $2 billion)," and seeks class action status to pursue damages against the directors and KPMG for the individual plaintiffs and common stockholders. The individual director defendants filed a motion to dismiss, contending that they owed no fiduciary duty of disclosure under the circumstances alleged in the complaint. KPMG also filed a motion to dismiss the aiding and abetting claim asserted against it.

After briefing and oral argument, the Court of Chancery granted both of the motions to dismiss with prejudice. The Court of Chancery held that directors have no fiduciary duty of disclosure under Delaware law in the absence of a request for shareholder action. In so holding, the Court stated:

> The federal securities laws ensure the timely release of accurate information into the marketplace. The federal power to regulate should not be duplicated or impliedly usurped by Delaware. When a shareholder is damaged merely as a result of the release of inaccurate information into the marketplace, unconnected with any Delaware corporate governance issue, that shareholder must seek a remedy under federal law. [1997 WL 697940, at *2 (Oct. 30, 1997).]

We disagree, and although we hold that the Complaint as drafted should have been dismissed, our rationale is different. * * *

This Court has held that a board of directors is under a fiduciary duty to disclose material information when seeking shareholder action[33]:

> It is well-established that the duty of disclosure "represents nothing more than the well-recognized proposition that directors of Delaware corporations are under a fiduciary duty to disclose fully and fairly all material information within the board's control when it seeks shareholder action."[34]

The majority of opinions from the Court of Chancery have held that there may be a cause of action for disclosure violations only where directors seek shareholder action.[35] The present appeal requires this Court to decide whether a director's fiduciary duty arising out of misdisclosure is implicated in the absence of a request for shareholder action. We hold that directors who knowingly disseminate false information that results in corporate injury or damage to an individual stockholder violate their fiduciary duty, and may be held accountable in a manner appropriate to the circumstances.

An underlying premise for the imposition of fiduciary duties is a separation of legal control from beneficial ownership. Equitable principles act in those circumstances to protect the beneficiaries who are not in a position to protect themselves. See McMahon v. New Castle Associates, Del. Ch., 532

---

33. [By the Court] See Loudon v. Archer–Daniels–Midland Co., Del.Supr., 700 A.2d 135, 137–38 (1997)(" * * * Delaware law of the fiduciary duties of directors * * * establishes a general duty to disclose to stockholders all material information reasonably available when seeking stockholder action ... But there is no per se doctrine imposing liability * * *."); Arnold v. Society for Savings Bancorp, Inc., Del.Supr., 650 A.2d 1270, 1277 (1994)(a fiduciary disclosure obligation "attaches to proxy statements and any other disclosures in contemplation of shareholder action."); Stroud v. Grace, Del.Supr., 606 A.2d 75, 84 (1992)("directors of Delaware corpora-

tions are under a fiduciary duty to disclose fully and fairly all material information within the board's control when it seeks shareholder action.").

34. [By the Court] Zirn v. VLI Corp., Del. Supr., 681 A.2d 1050, 1056 (1996) quoting Stroud v. Grace, 606 A.2d at 84 (emphasis added).

35. [By the Court] Kahn v. Roberts, Del. Supr., 679 A.2d 460, 467 (1996) (collecting cases). Cf. Ciro, Inc. v. Gold, D. Del., 816 F.Supp. 253, 267 (1993).

A.2d 601, 604 (1987). One of the fundamental tenets of Delaware corporate law provides for a separation of control and ownership. The board of directors has the legal responsibility to manage the business of a corporation for the benefit of its shareholder owners. 8 Del. C. § 141(a). Accordingly, fiduciary duties are imposed on the directors of Delaware corporations to regulate their conduct when they discharge that function. Mills Acquisition Co. v. Macmillan, Inc., Del.Supr., 559 A.2d 1261, 1280 (1989).

The directors of Delaware corporations stand in a fiduciary relationship not only to the stockholders but also to the corporations upon whose boards they serve.[36] The director's fiduciary duty to both the corporation and its shareholders has been characterized by this Court as a triad: due care, good faith, and loyalty. Cede & Co. v. Technicolor, Inc., Del.Supr., 634 A.2d 345, 361 (1993). That tripartite fiduciary duty does not operate intermittently but is the constant compass by which all director actions for the corporation and interactions with its shareholders must be guided.

Although the fiduciary duty of a Delaware director is unremitting, the exact course of conduct that must be charted to properly discharge that responsibility will change in the specific context of the action the director is taking with regard to either the corporation or its shareholders. Mills Acquisition Co. v. Macmillan, Inc., 559 A.2d at 1280. This Court has endeavored to provide the directors with clear signal beacons and brightly lined-channel markers as they navigate with due care, good faith, and loyalty on behalf of a Delaware corporation and its shareholders.[37] This Court has also endeavored to mark the safe harbors clearly.[38]

The shareholder constituents of a Delaware corporation are entitled to rely upon their elected directors to discharge their fiduciary duties at all times. Whenever directors communicate publicly or directly with shareholders about the corporation's affairs, with or without a request for shareholder action, directors have a fiduciary duty to shareholders to exercise due care, good faith and loyalty. It follows a fortiori that when directors communicate publicly or directly with shareholders about corporate matters the sine qua non of directors' fiduciary duty to shareholders is honesty.[39]

According to the appellants, the focus of the fiduciary duty of disclosure is to protect shareholders as the "beneficiaries" of all material information

---

36. [By the Court] Guth v. Loft, Del.Supr., 5 A.2d 503, 510 (1939). See David A. Drexler et al., Delaware Corporation Law § 15.02 (Matthew Bender 1988).

37. [By the Court] See, e.g., Unocal Corp. v. Mesa Petroleum Co., Del.Supr., 493 A.2d 946, 954 (1985) (directors have an "enhanced duty" in the context of a threatened takeover because of the "omnipresent specter that a board may be acting primarily in its own interests, rather than those of the corporation and its shareholders * * *."); Revlon, Inc. v. MacAndrews Forbes Holdings, Inc., Del.Supr., 506 A.2d 173, 182 (1985)(when sale of the company becomes inevitable, the director's duties are "significantly altered").

38. [By the Court] See Broz v. Cellular Information Systems, Inc., Del.Supr., 673 A.2d

148, 157 (1996); In re Tri–Star Pictures, Inc., Litig., 634 A.2d at 333; Rabkin v. Philip A. Hunt Chemical Corp., 498 A.2d at 1106. Compare Veasey & Manning, Codified Standard, Safe Harbor or Unchartered Reef, 35 Bus. Law. 919 (1980), with Arsht & Hinsey, Codified Standard—Safe Harbor but Chartered Channel, 35 Bus. Law. ix (1980).

39. [By the Court] Marhart, Inc. v. Calmat Co., Del. Ch., CA. No. 11820, Berger, V.C., 1992 WL 212587 (Apr. 22, 1992), slip op. at 6 (reported in 18 Del. J. Corp. L. 330 (1993)) ("Delaware directors are fiduciaries and are held to a high standard of conduct * * *. It is entirely consistent with this settled principle of law that fiduciaries, who undertake the responsibility of informing shareholders about corporate affairs, be required to do so honestly.").

disseminated by the directors. The duty of disclosure is, and always has been, a specific application of the general fiduciary duty owed by directors. The duty of disclosure obligates directors to provide the stockholders with accurate and complete information material to a transaction or other corporate event that is being presented to them for action.

The issue in this case is not whether Mercury's directors breached their duty of disclosure. It is whether they breached their more general fiduciary duty of loyalty and good faith by knowingly disseminating to the stockholders false information about the financial condition of the company. The directors' fiduciary duties include the duty to deal with their stockholders honestly.

Shareholders are entitled to rely upon the truthfulness of all information disseminated to them by the directors they elect to manage the corporate enterprise. Delaware directors disseminate information in at least three contexts: public statements made to the market, including shareholders; statements informing shareholders about the affairs of the corporation without a request for shareholder action; and, statements to shareholders in conjunction with a request for shareholder action. Inaccurate information in these contexts may be the result of a violation of the fiduciary duties of care, loyalty or good faith. We will examine the remedies that are available to shareholders for misrepresentations in each of these three contexts by the directors of a Delaware corporation. * * *

In the absence of a request for stockholder action, the Delaware General Corporation Law does not require directors to provide shareholders with information concerning the finances or affairs of the corporation.[40] Even when shareholder action is sought, the provisions in the General Corporation Law requiring notice to the shareholders of the proposed action do not require the directors to convey substantive information beyond a statutory minimum.[41] Consequently, in the context of a request for shareholder action, the protection afforded by Delaware law is a judicially recognized equitable cause of action by shareholders against directors.

The fiduciary duty of directors in connection with disclosure violations in Delaware jurisprudence was restated in Lynch v. Vickers Energy Corp., Del.Supr., 383 A.2d 278 (1978). In *Lynch*, this Court held that, in making a tender offer to acquire the stock of the minority stockholders, a majority stockholder "owed a fiduciary duty * * * which required 'complete candor' in disclosing fully 'all the facts and circumstances surrounding the' tender offer."[42] In *Stroud v. Grace,* we noted that the language of our jurisprudence should be clarified to the extent that "candor" requires no more than the

40. [By the Court] See David A. Drexler et al., Delaware Corporation Law § 15.07A (Matthew Bender 1998).

41. [By the Court] See Stroud v. Grace, 606 A.2d at 85 (discussing 8 Del. C. § 222(a) and 242(b)(1)).

42. [By the Court] Lynch v. Vickers Energy Corp., Del.Supr., 383 A.2d 278, 279 (1977) quoting Lynch v. Vickers Energy Corp., Del. Ch., 351 A.2d 570, 573 (1976); accord Shell Petroleum, Inc. v. Smith, Del.Supr., 606 A.2d 112, 114–15 (1992) (majority stockholder bears

burden of showing full disclosure of all facts within its knowledge that are material to stockholder action). The fiduciary duty of disclosure is also applicable to directors of a Delaware corporation, In re Anderson, Clayton Shareholders Litig., Del. Ch., 519 A.2d 680, 688–90 (1986); Smith v. Van Gorkom, Del. Supr., 488 A.2d 858, 890 (1985) and to less-than-majority shareholders who control or affirmatively attempt to mandate the destiny of the corporation.In re Tri–Star Pictures, Inc. Litig., 634 A.2d at 328–29.

duty to disclose all material facts when seeking stockholder action.[43] An article by Professor Lawrence Hamermesh[44] includes an excellent historical summary of the content, context, and parameters of the law of disclosure, as it has been developed in a series of decisions during the last two decades.[45]

The duty of directors to observe proper disclosure requirements derives from the combination of the fiduciary duties of care, loyalty and good faith.[46] The plaintiffs contend that, because directors' fiduciary responsibilities are not "intermittent duties," there is no reason why the duty of disclosure should not be implicated in every public communication by a corporate board of directors. The directors of a Delaware corporation are required to disclose fully and fairly all material information within the board's control when it seeks shareholder action.[47] When the directors disseminate information to stockholders when no stockholder action is sought, the fiduciary duties of care, loyalty and good faith apply. Dissemination of false information could violate one or more of those duties.

An action for a breach of fiduciary duty arising out of disclosure violations in connection with a request for stockholder action does not include the elements of reliance, causation and actual quantifiable monetary damages.[48] Instead, such actions require the challenged disclosure to have a connection to the request for shareholder action. The essential inquiry in such an action is whether the alleged omission or misrepresentation is material. Stroud v. Grace, 606 A.2d at 85. Materiality is determined with respect to the shareholder action being sought.[49]

The directors' duty to disclose all available material information in connection with a request for shareholder action must be balanced against its concomitant duty to protect the corporate enterprise, in particular, by keeping certain financial information confidential. Stroud v. Grace, 606 A.2d at 89. Directors are required to provide shareholders with all information that is material to the action being requested and to provide a balanced, truthful

---

43. [By the Court] Stroud v. Grace, 606 A.2d at 84.

44. [By the Court] Lawrence A. Hamermesh, Calling Off the Lynch Mob: A Corporate Director's Fiduciary Disclosure Duty, 49 Vand. L.Rev. 1087, 1174 n. 394 (1996).

45. [By the Court] See, e.g., Zirn v. VLI Corp., 681 A.2d at 1056; see also Arnold v. Society for Savings Bancorp, 650 A.2d at 1276–77; In re Tri–Star Pictures, Inc., Litig., 634 A.2d at 331–32, 334; Cede & Co. v. Technicolor, Inc., 634 A.2d at 372–73; Zirn v. VLI Corp., Del.Supr., 621 A.2d 773, 778 (1993); Stroud v. Grace, 606 A.2d at 84–88; Bershad v. Curtiss–Wright Corp., Del.Supr., 535 A.2d 840, 846 (1987); Rosenblatt v. Getty Oil Co., Del.Supr., 493 A.2d 929, 936, 944–45 (1985); Smith v. Van Gorkom, 488 A.2d at 889–93; Weinberger v. UOP, Inc., Del.Supr., 457 A.2d 701, 710–12 (1983).

46. [By the Court] See Cinerama, Inc. v. Technicolor, Inc., Del. Supr, 663 A.2d 1156, 1160 (1995); Zirn v. VLI Corp., 621 A.2d at 778.

47. [By the Court] Loudon v. Archer–Daniels–Midland Company, 700 A.2d at 141–44; Zirn v. VLI Corp., 681 A.2d at 1056; Arnold v. Society for Savings Bancorp, 650 A.2d at 1276–77; Stroud v. Grace, 606 A.2d at 84. Rosenblatt v. Getty Oil Co., 493 A.2d at 944–45; Smith v. Van Gorkom, 488 A.2d at 889–90; Lynch v. Vickers Energy Corp., 383 A.2d at 279, 281.

48. [By the Court] See Cinerama, Inc. v. Technicolor, Inc., 663 A.2d at 1163; In re Tri–Star Pictures, Inc., Litig., 634 A.2d at 327 n. 10 and 333. Loudon v. Archer–Daniels–Midland Co., 700 A.2d at 142 ("where directors have breached their disclosure duties in a corporate transaction * * * there must at least be an award of nominal damages.").

49. [By the Court] In Rosenblatt v. Getty Oil Co., 493 A.2d at 944, this Court adopted the materiality standard set forth by the United States Supreme Court in TSC Industries, Inc. v. Northway, Inc., 426 U.S. 438, 449, 96 S.Ct. 2126, 48 L.Ed.2d 757 (1976).

account of all matters disclosed in the communications with shareholders.[50] Accordingly, directors have definitive guidance in discharging their fiduciary duty by an analysis of the factual circumstances relating to the specific shareholder action being requested and an inquiry into the potential for deception or misinformation.[51] * * *

When corporate directors impart information they must comport with the obligations imposed by both the Delaware law and the federal statutes and regulations of the United States Securities and Exchange Commission * * *. Historically, federal law has regulated disclosures by corporate directors into the general interstate market.[52] This Court has noted that "in observing its congressional mandate the SEC has adopted a 'basic philosophy of disclosure.' "[53] Accordingly, this Court has held that there is "no legitimate basis to create a new cause of action which would replicate, by state decisional law, the provisions of * * * the 1934 Act." Arnold v. Society for Savings Bancorp, Inc., Del.Supr., 678 A.2d 533, 539 (1996). In deference to the panoply of federal protections that are available to investors in connection with the purchase or sale of securities of Delaware corporations, this Court has decided not to recognize a state common law cause of action against the directors of Delaware corporations for "fraud on the market."[54] Here, it is to be noted, the claim appears to be made by those who did not sell and, therefore, would not implicate federal securities laws which relate to the purchase or sale of securities.

The historic roles played by state and federal law in regulating corporate disclosures have been not only compatible but complementary.[55] That symbiotic relationship has been perpetuated by the recently enacted federal Securities Litigation Uniform Standards Act of 1998.[56] Although that statute by its terms does not apply to this case, the new statute will require securities class actions involving the purchase or sale of nationally traded securities, based upon false or misleading statements, to be brought exclusively in federal court under federal law. The 1998 Act, however, contains two important excep-

---

50. [By the Court] Zirn v. VLI Corp., 681 A.2d at 1056. In *Zirn II,* this Court held, "in addition to the traditional duty to disclose all facts material to the proffered transaction, directors are under a fiduciary obligation to avoid misleading partial disclosures. The law of partial disclosure is likewise clear: Once defendants travel down the road of partial disclosure they have an obligation to provide the stockholders with an accurate, full and fair characterization of those historic events." [internal quotations omitted].

51. [By the Court] See Zirn v. VLI Corp., 681 A.2d at 1062 ("a good faith erroneous judgment as to the proper scope or content of required disclosure implicates the duty of care rather than the duty of loyalty."); Arnold v. Society for Savings Bancorp, 650 A.2d at 1287–88 & n. 36.

52. [By the Court]. See Roger J. Dennis and Patrick J. Ryan, State Corporate and Federal Securities Law: Dual Regulation in a Federal System, 22 Publius: The J. of Federalism 21 (Winter 1992).

53. [By the Court]. Stroud v. Grace, Del. Supr., 606 A.2d 75, 86 (1992). See, e.g., Randall

S. Thomas & Catherine T. Dixon, Aranow & Einhorn on Proxy Contests for Corporation Control, § 21.02 (3d ed.1998).

54. [By the Court]. Gaffin v. Teledyne, Inc., Del.Supr., 611 A.2d 467, 472 (1992). See Basic Incorporated v. Levinson, 485 U.S. 224, 241–42, 108 S.Ct. 978, 99 L.Ed.2d 194 (1988) (discussing the theory of fraud on the market).

55. [By the Court] See Santa Fe Industries, Inc. v. Green, 430 U.S. 462, 474–80, 97 S.Ct. 1292, 51 L.Ed.2d 480 (1977) (discussing state corporation law and the purpose of disclosure in federal securities law). Cf. Roberta Romano, Empowering Investors: A Market Approach to Securities Regulation 107 Yale L.J. 2359 (1998) ("advocating fundamental reform of the current strategy toward securities regulation by implementing a regulatory approach of competitive federalism.").

56. [By the Court] Securities Litigation Uniform Standards Act of 1998, Pub.L. No. 105–353, 112 Stat. 3227 (1998). [Editor: SLUSA is discussed in Chapter 14.]

tions:[57] the first provides that an "exclusively derivative action brought by one or more shareholders on behalf of a corporation" is not preempted; the second preserves the availability of state court class actions, where state law already provides that corporate directors have fiduciary disclosure obligations to shareholders.[58] These exceptions have become known as the "Delaware carve-outs."[59]

We need not decide at this time, however, whether this new Act will have any effect on this litigation if plaintiffs elect to replead. See Section (c) of the Act:

> (c) Applicability.—The amendments made by this section shall not affect or apply to any action commenced before and pending on the date of enactment of this Act.

* * * Delaware law also protects shareholders who receive false communications from directors even in the absence of a request for shareholder action. When the directors are not seeking shareholder action, but are deliberately misinforming shareholders about the business of the corporation, either directly or by a public statement, there is a violation of fiduciary duty. That violation may result in a derivative claim on behalf of the corporation or a cause of action for damages. See Zirn v. VLI Corp., 681 A.2d at 1060–61. There may also be a basis for equitable relief to remedy the violation.

Here the complaint alleges (if true) an egregious violation of fiduciary duty by the directors in knowingly disseminating materially false information. Then it alleges that the corporation lost about $2 billion in value as a result. Then it merely claims that the action is brought on behalf of the named plaintiffs and the putative class. It is a non sequitur rather than a syllogism.

---

57. [By the Court] Section 16(d) of the Act provides: * * *

(d) Preservation of Certain Actions.—(1) Actions under state law of state of incorporation.—

(A) Actions preserved.—Notwithstanding subsection (b) or (c), a covered class action described in subparagraph (B) of this paragraph that is based upon the statutory or common law of the State in which the issuer is incorporated (in the case of a corporation) or organized (in the case of any other entity) may be maintained in a State or Federal court by a private party.

(B) Permissible actions.—A covered class action is described in this subparagraph if it involves—

(i) the purchase or sale of securities by the issuer or an affiliate of the issuer exclusively from or to holders of equity securities of the issuer; or

(ii) any recommendation, position, or other communication with respect to the sale of securities of the issuer that—

(I) is made by or on behalf of the issuer or an affiliate of the issuer to holders of equity securities of the issuer; and

(II) concerns decisions of those equity holders with respect to voting their securi-

ties, acting in response to a tender or exchange offer, or exercising dissenters' or appraisal rights. Securities Litigation Uniform Standards Act of 1998, Pub.L. No. 105–353, § 16(d) 112 Stat. 3227 (1998).

58. [By the Court] See, e.g., Zirn v. VLI Corp., 621 A.2d 773; Zirn v. VLI Corp., 681 A.2d at 1060–61. See also Michael A. Perino, Fraud and Federalism: Preempting Private State Securities Fraud Causes of Action, 50 Stan. L.Rev. 273 (1998).

59. [By the Court] The Senate Committee Report on the Act is instructive. It states, in part:

> The Committee is keenly aware of the importance of state corporate law, specifically those states that have laws that establish a fiduciary duty of disclosure. It is not the intent of the Committee in adopting this legislation to interfere with state law regarding the duties and performance of an issuer's directors or officers in connection with a purchase or sale of securities by the issuer or an affiliate from current shareholders or communicating with existing shareholders with respect to voting their shares, acting in response to a tender or exchange offer, or exercising dissenters' or appraisal rights.

S. Rep. No. 105–182, at 11–12 (May 4, 1998).

The allegation in paragraph 3 that the false disclosures resulted in the corporation losing virtually all its equity seems obliquely to claim an injury to the corporation. The plaintiffs, however, never expressly assert a derivative claim on behalf of the corporation or allege compliance with Court of Chancery Rule 23.1, which requires pre-suit demand or cognizable and particularized allegations that demand is excused.[60] If the plaintiffs intend to assert a derivative claim,[61] they should be permitted to replead to assert such a claim and any damage or equitable remedy sought on behalf of the corporation.[62] Likewise, the plaintiffs should have the opportunity to replead to assert any individual cause of action and articulate a remedy that is appropriate on behalf of the named plaintiffs individually, or a properly recognizable class consistent with Court of Chancery Rule 23, and our decision in Gaffin.[63]

The Court of Chancery properly dismissed the complaint before it against the individual director defendants, in the absence of well-pleaded allegations stating a derivative, class or individual cause of action and properly assertable remedy. Without a well-pleaded allegation in the complaint for a breach of fiduciary duty, there can be no claim for aiding and abetting such a breach.[64] Accordingly, the plaintiffs' aiding and abetting claim against KPMG was also properly dismissed.

Nevertheless, we disagree with the Court of Chancery's holding that such a claim cannot be articulated on these facts. The plaintiffs should have been permitted to amend their complaint, if possible, to state a properly cognizable cause of action against the individual defendants and KPMG. Consequently, the Court of Chancery should have dismissed the complaint without prejudice.

The judgment of the Court of Chancery to dismiss the complaint is affirmed. The judgment to dismiss the complaint with prejudice is reversed. This matter is remanded for further proceedings in accordance with this opinion.

---

60. [By the Court] It seems that plaintiffs have attempted to allege the basis for demand excusal by the very nature of the central claim that the directors knowingly misstated the company's financial condition, thus seemingly taking this case out of the business judgment rule because all the directors are alleged to be implicated in the wrongdoing.

61. [By the Court] This will require an articulation of the classic "direct v. derivative" theory. See Grimes v. Donald, Del.Supr., 673 A.2d 1207 (1996) (distinguishing individual and derivative actions).

62. [By the Court] We express no opinion whether equitable remedies such as injunctive relief, judicial removal of directors or disqualification from directorship could be asserted here. No such equitable relief has been sought in the current complaint. See Randall S. Thomas & Catherine T. Dixon, Aranow & Einhorn on Proxy Contests for Corporate Control, § 19.01 (3d ed.1998).

63. [By the Court] Gaffin v. Teledyne, Inc., 611 A.2d 467, 474 (1992) ("A class action may not be maintained in a purely common law or equitable fraud case since individual questions of law or fact, particularly as to the element of justifiable reliance, will inevitably predominate over common questions of law or fact."). See Barnes v. American Tobacco Co., 3rd Cir., 161 F.3d 127 (1998). Broussard v. Meineke Discount Muffler Shops, Inc., 4th Cir., 155 F.3d 331 (1998). Cimino v. Raymark Industries, Inc., 5th Cir., 151 F.3d 297 (1998). Amchem Products, Inc. v. Windsor, 521 U.S. 591, 117 S.Ct. 2231, 138 L.Ed.2d 689 (1997). See also Donald J. Wolfe and Michael A. Pittenger, Corporate and Commercial Practice in the Delaware Court of Chancery § 9–3 (1998).

64. [By the Court] In re Santa Fe Pacific Corp. Shareholder Litig., Del. Supr., 669 A.2d 59 (1995). Cf. Lewis B. Lowenfels and Alan R. Bromberg, Liabilities of Lawyers and Accountants Under Rule 10(b)–5, 53 Bus. Law. 1157 (1998).

Notes

(1) *Caremark* and *Malone* broaden to some extent long-accepted obligations of directors of publicly held Delaware corporations. Should these obligations be extended to closely held as well as publicly held corporations? See Mary Siegel, Fiduciary Myths in Close Corporate Law, 29 Del. J. Corp. L. 377 (2004).

(2) Is it appropriate for Delaware courts to impose new obligations on these types on directors? Should that not be the role of the Delaware legislature? Jill E. Fisch, The Peculiar Role of the Delaware Courts in the Competition for Corporate Charters, 68 U. Cincinnati L.Rev. 1061, 1071 (2000) comments that "[a] substantial portion of Delaware's corporate law is made by the courts, but the Delaware courts make law in a manner traditionally associated with legislative rather than judicial lawmaking." She concludes that "Delaware's unusual lawmaking structure enhances firm value and perhaps explains the widespread preference for Delaware incorporation." Id., at 1081.

(3) In *Malone,* the Delaware Supreme Court stated that it has "endeavored to provide the directors with clear signal beacons and brightly lined channel markers as they navigate with due care, good faith, and loyalty * * *." Has the court succeeded? One of the issues that remain open after *Malone* is what the standard will be for showing that nondisclosures in the absence of a request for shareholder action are material. Another important issue is how the liability shield in Section 102(b)(7) will operate in the context of a violation of the disclosure requirements in Delaware, particularly when the false or misleading disclosures arise outside of the context of a request for shareholder action, See Note, Fiduciary Duties and Disclosure Obligations: Resolving Questions After Malone v. Brincat, 26 Del. J. Corp. L. 563 (2001).

GALL v. EXXON CORP.

United States District Court, Southern District of New York, 1976.
418 F.Supp. 508.

ROBERT L. CARTER, DISTRICT JUDGE.

Defendants have moved, pursuant to Rule 56, F.R.Civ.P., for summary judgment dismissing plaintiff's complaint on the grounds that the Special Committee on Litigation ("Special Committee"), acting as the Board of Directors of Exxon Corporation ("Exxon"), has determined in the good faith exercise of its sound business judgment that it is contrary to the interests of Exxon to institute suit on the basis of any matters raised in plaintiff's complaint. Defendants' motion is hereby denied without prejudice to its renewal after plaintiff has conducted relevant discovery. * * *

Plaintiff's complaint arises out of the alleged payment by Exxon Corporation of some $59 million in corporate funds as bribes or political payments, which were improperly contributed to Italian political parties and others during the period 1963–1974, in order to secure special political favors as well as other allegedly illegal commitments. * * *

On September 24, 1975, Exxon's Board of Directors unanimously resolved, pursuant to Article III, Section 1, of Exxon's By–Laws to establish a Special Committee on Litigation, composed of Exxon directors Jack F. Bennett, Richard P. Dobson and Edward G. Harness,[65] and refer to the Special

---

65. [By the Court] * * * According to the affidavits submitted, each of the members of the Special Committee has confirmed that he has not been in any way connected or involved

Committee for the determination of Exxon's action the matters raised in this and several other pending actions relating to the Italian expenditures. * * *

On January 23, 1976, after an investigation of approximately four months, including interviews with over 100 witnesses, the Special Committee issued the "Determination and Report of the Special Committee on Litigation" ("Report"), an 82–page document summarizing the Committee's findings and recommendations. The facts as uncovered by the Special Committee may be briefly summarized as follows. * * *

[Editor: The Committee report described a pattern of secret payments made for various purposes between 1963 and 1972 and political contributions to Italian political parties during the same period. The secret payments, totaling about 39 million dollars, were made through secret bank accounts not reflected on the books of Exxon's Italian subsidiary, Esso Italiana. The political contributions, totaling about 20 million dollars, were channeled through newspaper and public relations firms connected with Italian political parties; these payments were reflected by fictitious invoices purportedly for services rendered. Several of the Exxon directors named as defendants in this suit were aware of the existence of at least the political payments in Italy prior to their termination in 1972. Some of the defendants had simply been advised of the existence of the payments; others, in positions of responsibility within corporate management urged that the contributions be phased out as promptly as possible. Some of the defendant-directors were also aware of the payments made through the secret bank accounts, but apparently the knowledge of these payments was more limited than the knowledge about the political contributions.]

After careful review, analysis and investigation, and with the advice and concurrence of Special Counsel,[66] the Special Committee unanimously determined on January 23, 1976, that it would be contrary to the interests of Exxon and its shareholders for Exxon, or anyone on its behalf, to institute or maintain a legal action against any present or former Exxon director or officer.[67] The Committee further resolved to direct and authorize the proper officers of Exxon and its General Counsel to oppose and seek dismissal of all shareholder derivative actions relating to payments made by or on behalf of Esso Italiana S.p.A., which had been filed against any present or former Exxon director or officer.

DISCUSSION

There is no question that the rights sought to be vindicated in this lawsuit are those of Exxon and not those of the plaintiff suing derivatively on

with the matters relating to the Italian expenditures referred to in this action or in the other related actions and none has been named as a defendant in any of the pending actions. Indeed, none of the members of the Committee was elected to the Exxon Board until long after the Italian expenditures complained of were terminated and Exxon had taken steps to ensure that such expenditures would not be resumed.

66. [By the Court] At its second meeting on October 29, 1975, the Special Committee appointed Justice Joseph Weintraub, former Chief Justice of the New Jersey Supreme Court, as its Special Counsel.

67. [By the Court] Among the factors cited by the Special Committee in reaching its decision were the unfavorable prospects for success of the litigation, the cost of conducting the litigation, interruption of corporate business affairs and the undermining of personnel morale.

the corporation's behalf. Since it is the interests of the corporation which are at stake, it is the responsibility of the directors of the corporation to determine, in the first instance, whether an action should be brought on the corporation's behalf. It follows that the decision of corporate directors whether or not to assert a cause of action held by the corporation rests within the sound business judgment of the management. See, e.g., United Copper Securities Co. v. Amalgamated Copper Co., 244 U.S. 261, 263–4, 37 S.Ct. 509, 61 L.Ed. 1119 (1917).

This principle, which has come to be known as the business judgment rule, was articulated by Mr. Justice Brandeis speaking for a unanimous Court in United Copper Securities Co. v. Amalgamated Copper Co., supra, 244 U.S. at 263–64, 37 S.Ct. at 510. In that case the directors of a corporation chose not to bring an antitrust action against a third party. Mr. Justice Brandeis said:

> Whether or not a corporation shall seek to enforce in the courts a cause of action for damages is, like other business questions, ordinarily a matter of internal management, and is left to the discretion of the directors, in the absence of instruction by vote of the stockholders. Courts interfere seldom to control such discretion intra vires the corporation, except where the directors are guilty of misconduct equivalent to a breach of trust, or where they stand in a dual relation which prevents an unprejudiced exercise of judgment. * * *

It is clear that absent allegations of fraud, collusion, self-interest, dishonesty or other misconduct of a breach of trust nature, and absent allegations that the business judgment exercised was grossly unsound, the court should not at the instigation of a single shareholder interfere with the judgment of the corporate officers. * * *

In recent months, the legality and morality of foreign political contributions, bribes and other payments by American corporations has been widely debated. The issue before me for decision, however, is not whether the payments made by Esso Italiana to Italian political parties and other unauthorized payments were proper or improper. Were the court to frame the issue in this way, it would necessarily involve itself in the business decisions of every corporation, and be required to mediate between the judgment of the directors and the judgment of the shareholders with regard to particular corporate actions. As Mr. Justice Brandeis said in his concurring opinion in Ashwander v. Tennessee Valley Authority, 297 U.S. [288,] at 343, 56 S.Ct. [466,] at 481, "[i]f a stockholder could compel the officers to enforce every legal right, courts instead of chosen officers, would be the arbiters of the corporation's fate." Rather, the issue is whether the Special Committee, acting as Exxon's Board of Directors and in the sound exercise of their business judgment, may determine that a suit against any present or former director or officer would be contrary to the best interests of the corporation. * * *

Plaintiff also calls into question the disinterestedness and bona fides of the Special Committee, suggesting that the members of the Special Committee may have been personally involved in the transactions in question, or, at the least, interested in the alleged wrongdoing "in a way calculated to impair their exercise of business judgment on behalf of the corporation." Klotz v. Consolidated Edison of New York, Inc., supra, 386 F.Supp. at 581.[68]

With the foregoing in mind, I am constrained to conclude that it is premature at this stage of the lawsuit to grant summary judgment. Plaintiff must be given an opportunity to test the bona fides and independence of the Special Committee through discovery and, if necessary, at a plenary hearing. Issues of intent, motivation, and good faith are particularly inappropriate for summary disposition.

Accordingly, defendants' motion for summary judgment is hereby denied without prejudice to its renewal after plaintiff has conducted relevant discovery. * * *

Notes

(1) *Gall* involved a decision by presumably independent directors not to pursue a derivative suit in which other directors were the ultimate target. In invoking the business judgment rule, Judge Carter relied on *United Copper Securities Co.,* a case involving a decision by directors not to sue an unrelated third party. Are these situations really comparable?

(2) The litigation committee device adopted by Exxon to seek dismissal of the Gall suit has become the standard response of publicly held corporations to derivative suits brought or threatened by shareholders which the corporation does not desire to have pursued. In effect it transmutes a discussion of the merits of the plaintiffs' suit into a discussion of the *bona fides* of the business judgment of a special committee of the board to discontinue inconvenient litigation.

(3) The development of the independent litigation committee has produced a torrent of law review commentary. For a sampling of this literature see the following: Michael P. Dooley and E. Norman Veasey, The Role of the Board in Derivative Litigation: Delaware Law and the Current ALI Proposals Compared, 44 Bus.Law. 503, 521–22 (1989) (arguing for the economic and management benefits of special litigation committees)[69]; James D. Cox, Searching for the Corporation's Voice in Derivative Suit Litigation: A Critique of *Zapata* and the ALI Project, 1982 Duke L.J. 959, 960 (1982) (arguing that special litigation committees limit waste of valuable corporate resources); Comment, The Propriety of Judicial Deference to Corporate Boards of Directors, 96 Harv.L.Rev. 1894, 1896, 1906–08 (1983) (arguing that corporate boards produce structural biases which make dismissal much more likely).[70] For an even stronger statement that directors have a "structural bias" in favor of dismissing all derivative litigation, see James D. Cox & Henry C. Munsinger, Bias in the Boardroom: Psychological Foundations and Legal Implications of Corporation Cohesion, 48 Law & Contem.Probs. 83 (Summer 1985).

---

68. [By the Court] * * * At a hearing held on February 27, 1976, plaintiff, for the first time, questioned the independence and bona fides of the members of the Special Committee. Subsequently, on March 2, 1976, plaintiff submitted to the court a statement * * * challenging defendants' assertion that the resolution of the Special Committee was made in the independent, disinterested and good faith exercise of their business judgment. Rule 56, F.R.Civ.P., requires that the moving party demonstrate, on the basis of admissible evidence adduced from persons with personal knowledge of the facts, that "there is no genuine issue as to any material fact." Where this initial showing is not made, summary judgment will be denied, even though the party opposing the motion has submitted no probative evidence to support its position or to establish that there is a genuine issue for trial.

69. Reprinted with permission from the American Bar Association.

70. Copyright © 1983 by the Harvard Law Review Association.

Many corporate lawyers reject the underlying premise of this argument, which is also not accepted by some commentators familiar with the underlying social science research. See Robert J. Haft, Business Decisions by the New Board: Behavioral Science and Corporate Law, 80 Mich.L.Rev. 1 (1981); Charles W. Murdock, Corporate Governance: The Role of Special Litigation Committees, 68 Wash.L.Rev. 79, 101–20 (1993); Renier Kraakman, Hyun Park, and Steven Shavell, When Are Shareholder Suits in Shareholder Interests?, 82 Geo.L.J. 1733 (1994)(attempts to evaluate the fundamental relationship between shareholder suits and shareholder welfare).

(4) One practical question involving the procedure followed in *Gall* is how independent must a "litigation committee" be? If you were attorney for a plaintiff faced with the prospect of a *Gall*-type defense, might you consider naming all the directors as defendants? Could a director without direct involvement in a transaction be sufficiently independent to satisfy the *Gall* principle, if named a nominal defendant? Assume the corporation appoints or elects two new directors and names them as the litigation committee. Do you have any basis for naming them as defendants? What about bringing or threatening a derivative suit claiming that a decision by an independent committee was itself a violation of fiduciary duty? Even if the prospects for success of such a suit are slim, could it be used to disqualify directors from serving on the "litigation committee?" Could the corporation appoint yet another litigation committee in order to consider dismissing that suit?

ZAPATA CORP. v. MALDONADO

Supreme Court of Delaware, 1981.
430 A.2d 779.

[By the Editors] The Delaware Chancery Court described the underlying controversy involved in this case as follows:

The relevant facts, construed most favorably to Maldonado, show that in 1970 Zapata's board of directors adopted a stock option plan under which certain of Zapata's officers and directors were granted options to purchase Zapata common stock at $12.15 per share. The plan provided for the exercise of the options in five separate installments, the last of which was to occur on July 14, 1974. In 1971 this plan was ratified by Zapata's stockholders. As the date for the exercise of the final options grew near, however, Zapata was planning a tender offer for 2,300,000 of its own shares. Announcement of the tender offer was expected to be made just prior to July 14, 1974, and it was predicted that the effect of the announcement would be to increase the then market price of Zapata stock from $18–$19 per share to near the tender offer price of $25 per share.

Zapata's directors, most of whom were optionees under the 1970 plan, were aware that the optionees would incur substantial additional federal income tax liability if the options were exercised after the date of the tender offer announcement and that this additional liability could be avoided if the options were exercised prior to the announcement. This was so because the amount of capital gain for federal income tax purposes to the optionees would have been an amount equal to the difference between the $12.15 option price and the price on the date of the exercise of the option: $18–$19 if the options were exercised prior to the tender offer announcement, or nearly $25 if the options were exercised immediately after the announcement.

In order to reduce the amount of federal income tax liability the optionees would incur in exercising their options, Zapata's directors accelerated the date on which the options could be exercised to July 2, 1974. On that day the optionees exercised their options and the directors requested the New York Stock Exchange to suspend trading in Zapata shares pending "an important announcement". On July 8, 1974 Zapata announced the tender offer. The market price of Zapata stock promptly rose to $24.50.

413 A.2d 1251, 1254–5.

Before Duffy, Quillen and Horsey, JJ.

Quillen, Justice:

This is an interlocutory appeal from an order entered on April 9, 1980, by the Court of Chancery denying appellant-defendant Zapata Corporation's (Zapata) alternative motions to dismiss the complaint or for summary judgment. The issue to be addressed has reached this Court by way of a rather convoluted path.

In June, 1975, William Maldonado, a stockholder of Zapata, instituted a derivative action in the Court of Chancery on behalf of Zapata against ten officers and/or directors of Zapata, alleging, essentially, breaches of fiduciary duty. Maldonado did not first demand that the board bring this action, stating instead such demand's futility because all directors were named as defendants and allegedly participated in the acts specified.[71] * * *

By June, 1979, four of the defendant-directors were no longer on the board, and the remaining directors appointed two new outside directors to the board. The board then created an "Independent Investigation Committee" (Committee), composed solely of the two new directors, to investigate Maldonado's actions, as well as a similar derivative action then pending in Texas, and to determine whether the corporation should continue any or all of the litigation. The Committee's determination was stated to be "final, * * * not * * * subject to review by the Board of Directors and * * * in all respects * * * binding upon the Corporation."

Following an investigation, the Committee concluded, in September, 1979, that each action should "be dismissed forthwith as their continued maintenance is inimical to the Company's best interests * * *." Consequently, Zapata moved for dismissal or summary judgment * * *.

On March 18, 1980, the Court of Chancery, in a reported opinion, the basis for the order of April 9, 1980, denied Zapata's motions, holding that Delaware law does not sanction this means of dismissal. More specifically, it held that the "business judgment" rule is not a grant of authority to dismiss derivative actions and that a stockholder has an individual right to maintain derivative actions in certain instances. Maldonado v. Flynn, Del.Ch., 413 A.2d

---

71. [By the Court] Court of Chancery Rule 23.1 states in part: "The complaint shall also allege with particularity the efforts, if any, made by the plaintiff to obtain the action he desires from the directors or comparable authority and the reasons for his failure to obtain the action or for not making the effort."

1251 (1980). * * * We limit our review in this interlocutory appeal to whether the Committee has the power to cause the present action to be dismissed.

We begin with an examination of the carefully considered opinion of the Vice Chancellor which states, in part, that the "business judgment" rule does not confer power "to a corporate board of directors to terminate a derivative suit," 413 A.2d at 1257. His conclusion is particularly pertinent because several federal courts, applying Delaware law, have held that the business judgment rule enables boards (or their committees) to terminate derivative suits * * *.

As the term is most commonly used, and given the disposition below, we can understand the Vice Chancellor's comment that "the business judgment rule is irrelevant to the question of whether the Committee has the authority to compel the dismissal of this suit". 413 A.2d at 1257. Corporations, existing because of legislative grace, possess authority as granted by the legislature. Directors of Delaware corporations derive their managerial decision making power, which encompasses decisions whether to initiate, or refrain from entering, litigation,[72] from 8 Del.C. § 141(a).[73] This statute is the fount of directorial powers. The "business judgment" rule is a judicial creation that presumes propriety, under certain circumstances, in a board's decision.[74] Viewed defensively, it does not create authority. In this sense the "business judgment" rule is not relevant in corporate decision making until after a decision is made. It is generally used as a defense to an attack on the decision's soundness. The board's managerial decision making power, however, comes from § 141(a). The judicial creation and legislative grant are related because the "business judgment" rule evolved to give recognition and deference to directors' business expertise when exercising their managerial power under § 141(a).

In the case before us, although the corporation's decision to move to dismiss or for summary judgment was, literally, a decision resulting from an exercise of the directors' (as delegated to the Committee) business judgment, the question of "business judgment", in a defensive sense, would not become relevant until and unless the decision to seek termination of the derivative lawsuit was attacked as improper. This question was not reached by the Vice Chancellor because he determined that the stockholder had an individual right to maintain this derivative action.

Thus, the focus in this case is on the power to speak for the corporation as to whether the lawsuit should be continued or terminated. As we see it, this issue in the current appellate posture of this case has three aspects: the conclusions of the Court below concerning the continuing right of a stockholder to maintain a derivative action; the corporate power under Delaware law of an authorized board committee to cause dismissal of litigation instituted for

---

72. [By the Court] See Dent, The Power of Directors to Terminate Shareholder Litigation: The Death of the Derivative Suit? 75 Nw. U.L.Rev. 96, 98 & n. 14 (1980); Comment, The Demand and Standing Requirements in Stockholder Derivative Actions, 44 U.Chi.L.Rev. 168, 192 & nn. 153–54 (1976) (herein Stockholder Derivative Actions).

73. [By the Court] 8 Del.C. § 141(a) states:

The business and affairs of every corporation organized under this chapter shall be managed by or under the direction of a board of directors.

74. [By the Court] See Arsht, The Business Judgment Rule Revisited, 8 Hofstra L.Rev. 93, 97, 130–33 (1979).

the benefit of the corporation; and the role of the Court of Chancery in resolving conflicts between the stockholder and the committee.

Accordingly, we turn first to the Court of Chancery's conclusions concerning the right of a plaintiff stockholder in a derivative action. We find that its determination that a stockholder, once demand is made and refused, possesses an independent, individual right to continue a derivative suit for breaches of fiduciary duty over objection by the corporation, as an absolute rule, is erroneous. * * * McKee v. Rogers, Del.Ch. 156 A. 191 (1931), stated "as a general rule" that "a stockholder cannot be permitted * * * to invade the discretionary field committed to the judgment of the directors and sue in the corporation's behalf when the managing body refuses. This rule is a well settled one." 156 A. at 193.

The *McKee* rule, of course, should not be read so broadly that the board's refusal will be determinative in every instance. Board members, owing a well-established fiduciary duty to the corporation, will not be allowed to cause a derivative suit to be dismissed when it would be a breach of their fiduciary duty. Generally disputes pertaining to control of the suit arise in two contexts.

Consistent with the purpose of requiring a demand, a board decision to cause a derivative suit to be dismissed as detrimental to the company, after demand has been made and refused, will be respected unless it was wrongful.[75] See, e.g., United Copper Securities Co. v. Amalgamated Copper Co., 244 U.S. 261, 263–64, 37 S.Ct. 509, 510, 61 L.Ed. 1119, 1124 (1917). A claim of a wrongful decision not to sue is thus the first exception and the first context of dispute. Absent a wrongful refusal, the stockholder in such a situation simply lacks legal managerial power.

But it cannot be implied that, absent a wrongful board refusal, a stockholder can never have an individual right to initiate an action. For, as is stated in *McKee,* a "well settled" exception exists to the general rule.

> [A] stockholder may sue in equity in his derivative right to assert a cause of action in behalf of the corporation, *without prior demand* upon the directors to sue, when it is apparent that a demand would be futile, that the officers are under an influence that sterilizes discretion and could not be proper persons to conduct the litigation.

156 A. at 193 (emphasis added). This exception, the second context for dispute, is consistent with the Court of Chancery's statement below, that "[t]he stockholders' individual right to bring the action does not ripen, however, * * * unless he can show a demand to be futile."

These comments in *McKee* and in the opinion below make obvious sense. A demand, when required and refused (if not wrongful), terminates a stockholder's legal ability to initiate a derivative action.[76] But where demand is

---

75. [By the Court] In other words, when stockholders, after making demand and having their suit rejected, attack the board's decision as improper, the board's decision falls under the "business judgment" rule and will be respected if the requirements of the rule are met. See Dent, * * * 75 Nw.U.L.Rev. at 100–01 & nn. 24–25. That situation should be distinguished from the instant case, where demand was not made, and the power of the board to seek a dismissal, due to disqualification, presents a threshold issue. For examples of what has been held to be a wrongful decision not to sue, see Stockholder Derivative Actions, supra note 23, 44 U.Chi.L.Rev. at 193–98. We recognize that the two contexts can overlap in practice.

76. [By the Court] Even in this situation it may take litigation to determine the stockholder's lack of power, i.e., standing.

properly excused, the stockholder does possess the ability to initiate the action on his corporation's behalf.

These conclusions, however, do not determine the question before us. Rather, they merely bring us to the question to be decided. It is here that we part company with the Court below. Derivative suits enforce corporate rights and any recovery obtained goes to the corporation. "The right of a stockholder to file a bill to litigate corporate rights is, therefore, solely for the purpose of preventing injustice where it is apparent that material corporate rights would not otherwise be protected." We see no inherent reason why the "two phases" of a derivative suit, the stockholder's suit to compel the corporation to sue and the corporation's suit should automatically result in the placement in the hands of the litigating stockholder sole control of the corporate right throughout the litigation. To the contrary, it seems to us that such an inflexible rule would recognize the interest of one person or group to the exclusion of all others within the corporate entity. Thus, we reject the view of the Vice Chancellor as to the first aspect of the issue on appeal.

The question to be decided becomes: When, if at all, should an authorized board committee be permitted to cause litigation, properly initiated by a derivative stockholder in his own right, to be dismissed? As noted above, a board has the power to choose not to pursue litigation when demand is made upon it, so long as the decision is not wrongful. If the board determines that a suit would be detrimental to the company, the board's determination prevails. Even when demand is excusable, circumstances may arise when continuation of the litigation would not be in the corporation's best interests. Our inquiry is whether, under such circumstances, there is a permissible procedure under § 141(a) by which a corporation can rid itself of detrimental litigation. If there is not, a single stockholder in an extreme case might control the destiny of the entire corporation. This concern was bluntly expressed by the Ninth Circuit in Lewis v. Anderson, 615 F.2d 778, 783 (9th Cir.1979), cert. denied, 449 U.S. 869, 101 S.Ct. 206, 66 L.Ed.2d 89 (1980): "To allow one shareholder to incapacitate an entire board of directors merely by leveling charges against them gives too much leverage to dissident shareholders." But, when examining the means, including the committee mechanism examined in this case, potentials for abuse must be recognized. This takes us to the second and third aspects of the issue on appeal.

Before we pass to equitable considerations as to the mechanism at issue here, it must be clear that an independent committee possesses the corporate power to seek the termination of a derivative suit. Section 141(c) allows a board to delegate all of its authority to a committee. Accordingly, a committee with properly delegated authority would have the power to move for dismissal or summary judgment if the entire board did.

Even though demand was not made in this case and the initial decision of whether to litigate was not placed before the board, Zapata's board, it seems to us, retained all of its corporate power concerning litigation decisions. If Maldonado had made demand on the board in this case, it could have refused to bring suit. Maldonado could then have asserted that the decision not to sue was wrongful and, if correct, would have been allowed to maintain the suit. The board, however, never would have lost its statutory managerial authority. The demand requirement itself evidences that the managerial power is retained by the board. When a derivative plaintiff is allowed to bring suit after a wrongful refusal, the board's authority to choose whether to pursue the litigation is not challenged although its conclusion—reached through the exercise of that authority—is not respected since it is wrongful. Similarly, Rule 23.1, by excusing demand in certain instances, does not strip the board of its corporate power. It merely saves the plaintiff the expense and delay of making a futile demand resulting in a probable tainted exercise of that authority in a refusal by the board or in giving control of litigation to the opposing side. But the board entity remains empowered under § 141(a) to make decisions regarding corporate litigation. The problem is one of member disqualification, not the absence of power in the board.

The corporate power inquiry then focuses on whether the board, tainted by the self-interest of a majority of its members, can legally delegate its authority to a committee of two disinterested directors. We find our statute clearly requires an affirmative answer to this question. As has been noted, under an express provision of the statute, § 141(c), a committee can exercise all of the authority of the board to the extent provided in the resolution of the board. Moreover, at [least] by analogy to our statutory section on interested directors, 8 Del.C. § 141, it seems clear that the Delaware statute is designed to permit disinterested directors to act for the board.[77]

We do not think that the interest taint of the board majority is per se a legal bar to the delegation of the board's power to an independent committee composed of disinterested board members. The committee can properly act for the corporation to move to dismiss derivative litigation that is believed to be detrimental to the corporation's best interest.

Our focus now switches to the Court of Chancery which is faced with a stockholder assertion that a derivative suit, properly instituted, should continue for the benefit of the corporation and a corporate assertion, properly made by a board committee acting with board authority, that the same derivative suit should be dismissed as inimical to the best interests of the corporation.

At the risk of stating the obvious, the problem is relatively simple. If, on the one hand, corporations can consistently wrest bona fide derivative actions

---

77. [By the Court] 8 Del.C. § 144 [Interested directors; quorum] states:

(a) No contract or transaction between a corporation and 1 or more of its directors or officers, or between a corporation and any other corporation, partnership, association, or other organization in which 1 or more of its directors or officers are directors or officers, or have a financial interest, shall be void or voidable solely for this reason, or solely because the director or officer is present at or participates in the meeting of the board or committee which authorizes the contract or transaction, or solely because his or their votes are counted for such purpose, if:

(1) The material facts as to his relationship or interest and as to the contract or transaction are disclosed or are known to the board of directors or the committee, and the board or committee in good faith authorizes the contract or transaction by the affirmative

votes of a majority of the disinterested directors, even though the disinterested directors be less than a quorum; or

(2) The material facts as to his relationship or interest and as to the contract or transaction are disclosed or are known to the shareholders entitled to vote thereon, and the contract or transaction is specifically approved in good faith by vote of the shareholders; or

(3) The contract or transaction is fair to the corporation as of the time it is authorized, approved or ratified, by the board of directors, a committee, or the shareholders.

(b) Common or interested directors may be counted in determining the presence of a quorum at a meeting of the board of directors or of a committee which authorizes the contract or transaction.

away from well-meaning derivative plaintiffs through the use of the committee mechanism, the derivative suit will lose much, if not all, of its generally-recognized effectiveness as an intra-corporate means of policing boards of directors. If, on the other hand, corporations are unable to rid themselves of meritless or harmful litigation and strike suits, the derivative action, created to benefit the corporation, will produce the opposite, unintended result. * * * It thus appears desirable to us to find a balancing point where bona fide stockholder power to bring corporate causes of action cannot be unfairly trampled on by the board of directors, but the corporation can rid itself of detrimental litigation.

As we noted, the question has been treated by other courts as one of the "business judgment" of the board committee. If a "committee, composed of independent and disinterested directors, conducted a proper review of the matters before it, considered a variety of factors and reached, in good faith, a business judgment that [the] action was not in the best interest of [the corporation]," the action must be dismissed. The issues become solely independence, good faith, and reasonable investigation. The ultimate conclusion of the committee, under that view, is not subject to judicial review.

We are not satisfied, however, that acceptance of the "business judgment" rationale at this stage of derivative litigation is a proper balancing point. While we admit an analogy with a normal case respecting board judgment, it seems to us that there is sufficient risk in the realities of a situation like the one presented in this case to justify caution beyond adherence to the theory of business judgment.

The context here is a suit against directors where demand on the board is excused. We think some tribute must be paid to the fact that the lawsuit was properly initiated. It is not a board refusal case. Moreover, this complaint was filed in June of 1975 and, while the parties undoubtedly would take differing views on the degree of litigation activity, we have to be concerned about the creation of an "Independent Investigation Committee" four years later, after the election of two new outside directors. Situations could develop where such motions could be filed after years of vigorous litigation for reasons unconnected with the merits of the lawsuit.

Moreover, notwithstanding our conviction that Delaware law entrusts the corporate power to a properly authorized committee, we must be mindful that directors are passing judgment on fellow directors in the same corporation and fellow directors, in this instance, who designated them to serve both as directors and committee members. The question naturally arises whether a "there but for the grace of God go I" empathy might not play a role. And the further question arises whether inquiry as to independence, good faith and reasonable investigation is sufficient safeguard against abuse, perhaps subconscious abuse.

There is another line of exploration besides the factual context of this litigation which we find helpful. The nature of this motion finds no ready pigeonhole, as perhaps illustrated by its being set forth in the alternative. It is perhaps best considered as a hybrid summary judgment motion for dismissal because the stockholder plaintiff's standing to maintain the suit has been lost. But it does not fit neatly into a category described in Rule 12(b) of the Court of Chancery Rules nor does it correspond directly with Rule 56 since the question of genuine issues of fact on the merits of the stockholder's claim are not reached. * * *

Whether the Court of Chancery will be persuaded by the exercise of a committee power resulting in a summary motion for dismissal of a derivative action, where a demand has not been initially made, should rest, in our judgment, in the independent discretion of the Court of Chancery. We thus steer a middle course between those cases which yield to the independent business judgment of a board committee and this case as determined below which would yield to unbridled plaintiff stockholder control. In pursuit of the course, we recognize that "[t]he final substantive judgment whether a particular lawsuit should be maintained requires a balance of many factors— ethical, commercial, promotional, public relations, employee relations, fiscal as well as legal." But we are content that such factors are not "beyond the judicial reach" of the Court of Chancery which regularly and competently deals with fiduciary relationships, disposition of trust property, approval of settlements and scores of similar problems. We recognize the danger of judicial overreaching but the alternatives seem to us to be outweighed by the fresh view of a judicial outsider. Moreover, if we failed to balance all the interests involved, we would in the name of practicality and judicial economy foreclose a judicial decision on the merits. At this point, we are not convinced that is necessary or desirable.

After an objective and thorough investigation of a derivative suit, an independent committee may cause its corporation to file a pretrial motion to dismiss in the Court of Chancery. The basis of the motion is the best interests of the corporation, as determined by the committee. The motion should include a thorough written record of the investigation and its findings and recommendations. Under appropriate Court supervision, akin to proceedings on summary judgment, each side should have an opportunity to make a record on the motion. As to the limited issues presented by the motion noted below, the moving party should be prepared to meet the normal burden under Rule 56 that there is no genuine issue as to any material fact and that the moving party is entitled to dismiss as a matter of law.[78] The Court should apply a two-step test to the motion.

First, the Court should inquire into the independence and good faith of the committee and the bases supporting its conclusions. Limited discovery may be ordered to facilitate such inquiries. The corporation should have the burden of proving independence, good faith and a reasonable investigation, rather than presuming independence, good faith and reasonableness.[79] If the Court determines either that the committee is not independent or has not shown reasonable bases for its conclusions, or, if the Court is not satisfied for other reasons relating to the process, including but not limited to the good

---

78. [By the Court] We do not foreclose a discretionary trial of factual issues but that issue is not presented in this appeal. See Lewis v. Anderson, supra, 615 F.2d at 780. Nor do we foreclose the possibility that other motions may proceed or be joined with such a pretrial summary judgment motion to dismiss, e.g., a partial motion for summary judgment on the merits.

79. [By the Court] Compare Auerbach v. Bennett, 47 N.Y.2d 619, 419 N.Y.S.2d 920, 928–29, 393 N.E.2d 994 (1979). Our approach here is analogous to and consistent with the Delaware approach to "interested director" transactions, where the directors, once the transaction is attacked, have the burden of establishing its "intrinsic fairness" to a court's careful scrutiny. See, e.g., Sterling v. Mayflower Hotel Corp., Del.Supr., 93 A.2d 107 (1952).

faith of the committee, the Court shall deny the corporation's motion. If, however, the Court is satisfied under Rule 56 standards that the committee was independent and showed reasonable bases for good faith findings and recommendations, the Court may proceed, in its discretion, to the next step.

The second step provides, we believe, the essential key in striking the balance between legitimate corporate claims as expressed in a derivative stockholder suit and a corporation's best interests as expressed by an independent investigating committee. The Court should determine, applying its own independent business judgment, whether the motion should be granted.[80] This means, of course, that instances could arise where a committee can establish its independence and sound bases for its good faith decisions and still have the corporation's motion denied. The second step is intended to thwart instances where corporate actions meet the criteria of step one, but the result does not appear to satisfy its spirit, or where corporate actions would simply prematurely terminate a stockholder grievance deserving of further consideration in the corporation's interest. The Court of Chancery of course must carefully consider and weigh how compelling the corporate interest in dismissal is when faced with a non-frivolous lawsuit. The Court of Chancery should, when appropriate, give special consideration to matters of law and public policy in addition to the corporation's best interests.

If the Court's independent business judgment is satisfied, the Court may proceed to grant the motion, subject, of course, to any equitable terms or conditions the Court finds necessary or desirable.

The interlocutory order of the Court of Chancery is reversed and the cause is remanded for further proceedings consistent with this opinion.

Note

Following this decision, several courts refused to give decisions by litigation committees the finality that appeared to be required under pre-Zapata decisions. Among these cases are Joy v. North, 692 F.2d 880 (2d Cir.1982), cert. denied sub nom. Citytrust v. Joy, 460 U.S. 1051, 103 S.Ct. 1498, 75 L.Ed.2d 930 (1983) (nominally decided under Connecticut law); Hasan v. CleveTrust Realty Investors, 729 F.2d 372 (6th Cir.1984) (no presumption of regularity or good faith to support litigation committee decision); In Matter of Continental Illinois Sec. Litig., 732 F.2d 1302 (7th Cir.1984). While there were dissents in some of these cases, the majority opinions generally reflect skepticism about the wisdom of uncritical acceptance of the principle that plaintiffs attacking a corporate transaction should be remitted only to an attack on the independence and good faith of the litigation committee. However, the development of Delaware law was not complete.

ARONSON v. LEWIS

Supreme Court of Delaware, 1984.
473 A.2d 805.

Before McNEILLY, MOORE and CHRISTIE, JJ.

MOORE, JUSTICE:

In the wake of Zapata Corp. v. Maldonado, Del.Supr., 430 A.2d 779 (1981), this Court left a crucial issue unanswered: when is a stockholder's

---

80. [By the Court] This step shares some of the same spirit and philosophy of the statement by the Vice Chancellor: "Under our system of law, courts and not litigants should decide the merits of litigation." 413 A.2d at 1263.

demand upon a board of directors, to redress an alleged wrong to the corporation, excused as futile prior to the filing of a derivative suit? We granted this interlocutory appeal to the defendants, Meyers Parking System, Inc. (Meyers), a Delaware corporation, and its directors, to review the Court of Chancery's denial of their motion to dismiss this action, pursuant to Chancery Rule 23.1, for the plaintiff's failure to make such a demand or otherwise demonstrate its futility. The Vice Chancellor ruled that plaintiff's allegations raised a "reasonable inference" that the directors' action was unprotected by the business judgment rule. Thus, the board could not have impartially considered and acted upon the demand. See Lewis v. Aronson, Del.Ch., 466 A.2d 375, 381 (1983).

We cannot agree with this formulation of the concept of demand futility. In our view demand can only be excused where facts are alleged with particularity which create a reasonable doubt that the directors' action was entitled to the protections of the business judgment rule. Because the plaintiff failed to make a demand, and to allege facts with particularity indicating that such demand would be futile, we reverse the Court of Chancery and remand with instructions that plaintiff be granted leave to amend the complaint. * * *

The issues of demand futility rest upon the allegations of the complaint. The plaintiff, Harry Lewis, is a stockholder of Meyers. The defendants are Meyers and its ten directors, some of whom are also company officers.

In 1979, Prudential Building Maintenance Corp. (Prudential) spun off its shares of Meyers to Prudential's stockholders. Prior thereto Meyers was a wholly owned subsidiary of Prudential. Meyers provides parking lot facilities and related services throughout the country. Its stock is actively traded over-the-counter.

This suit challenges certain transactions between Meyers and one of its directors, Leo Fink, who owns 47% of its outstanding stock. Plaintiff claims that these transactions were approved only because Fink personally selected each director and officer of Meyers.[81]

Prior to January 1, 1981, Fink had an employment agreement with Prudential which provided that upon retirement he was to become a consultant to that company for ten years. This provision became operable when Fink retired in April 1980. Thereafter, Meyers agreed with Prudential to share Fink's consulting services and reimburse Prudential for 25% of the fees paid Fink. Under this arrangement Meyers paid Prudential $48,332 in 1980 and $45,832 in 1981.

On January 1, 1981, the defendants approved an employment agreement between Meyers and Fink for a five year term with provision for automatic renewal each year thereafter, indefinitely. Meyers agreed to pay Fink $150,000 per year, plus a bonus of 5% of its pre-tax profits over $2,400,000. Fink could terminate the contract at any time, but Meyers could do so only upon six months' notice. At termination, Fink was to become a consultant to

---

81. [By the Court] The Court of Chancery stated that Fink had been chief executive offi- cer of Prudential prior to the spinoff and there- after became chairman of Meyers' board.

Meyers and be paid $150,000 per year for the first three years, $125,000 for the next three years, and $100,000 thereafter for life. Death benefits were also included. Fink agreed to devote his best efforts and substantially his entire business time to advancing Meyers' interests. The agreement also provided that Fink's compensation was not to be affected by any inability to perform services on Meyers' behalf. Fink was 75 years old when his employment agreement with Meyers was approved by the directors. There is no claim that he was, or is, in poor health.

Additionally, the Meyers board approved and made interest-free loans to Fink totaling $225,000. These loans were unpaid and outstanding as of August 1982 when the complaint was filed. At oral argument defendants' counsel represented that these loans had been repaid in full.

The complaint charges that these transactions had "no valid business purpose", and were a "waste of corporate assets" because the amounts to be paid are "grossly excessive", that Fink performs "no or little services", and because of his "advanced age" cannot be "expected to perform any such services." The plaintiff also charges that the existence of the Prudential consulting agreement with Fink prevents him from providing his "best efforts" on Meyers' behalf. Finally, it is alleged that the loans to Fink were in reality "additional compensation" without any "consideration" or "benefit" to Meyers.

The complaint alleged that no demand had been made on the Meyers board because:

13.   * * * such attempt would be futile for the following reasons:

(a) All of the directors in office are named as defendants herein and they have participated in, expressly approved and/or acquiesced in, and are personally liable for, the wrongs complained of herein.

(b) Defendant Fink, having selected each director, controls and dominates every member of the Board and every officer of Meyers.

(c) Institution of this action by present directors would require the defendant-directors to sue themselves, thereby placing the conduct of this action in hostile hands and preventing its effective prosecution.

The relief sought included the cancellation of the Meyers–Fink employment contract and an accounting by the directors, including Fink, for all damage sustained by Meyers and for all profits derived by the directors and Fink. * * *

A cardinal precept of the General Corporation Law of the State of Delaware is that directors, rather than shareholders, manage the business and affairs of the corporation. 8 Del.C. § 141(a). * * * The existence and exercise of this power carries with it certain fundamental fiduciary obligations to the corporation and its shareholders.[82] Loft, Inc. v. Guth, Del.Ch., 2 A.2d 225

---

82. [By the Court] The broad question of structuring the modern corporation in order to satisfy the twin objectives of managerial freedom of action and responsibility to shareholders has been extensively debated by commentators. See, e.g., Fischel, The Corporate Governance Movement, 35 Vand.L.Rev. 1259 (1982); Dickstein, Corporate Governance and the Shareholders' Derivative Action: Rules and Remedies for Implementing the Monitoring Model, 3 Cardozo L.Rev. 627 (1982); Haft, Business Decisions by the New Board: Behavioral Science and Corporate Law, 80 Mich. L.Rev. 1 (1981); Dent, The Revolution in Cor-

(1938), aff'd, Del.Supr., 5 A.2d 503 (1939). Moreover, a stockholder is not powerless to challenge director action which results in harm to the corporation. The machinery of corporate democracy and the derivative suit are potent tools to redress the conduct of a torpid or unfaithful management. The derivative action developed in equity to enable shareholders to sue in the corporation's name where those in control of the company refused to assert a claim belonging to it. The nature of the action is two-fold. First, it is the equivalent of a suit by the shareholders to compel the corporation to sue. Second, it is a suit by the corporation, asserted by the shareholders on its behalf, against those liable to it.

By its very nature the derivative action impinges on the managerial freedom of directors.[83] Hence, the demand requirement of Chancery Rule 23.1 exists at the threshold, first to ensure that a stockholder exhausts his intracorporate remedies, and then to provide a safeguard against strike suits. Thus, by promoting this form of alternate dispute resolution, rather than immediate recourse to litigation, the demand requirement is a recognition of the fundamental precept that directors manage the business and affairs of corporations.

In our view the entire question of demand futility is inextricably bound to issues of business judgment and the standards of that doctrine's applicability. The business judgment rule is an acknowledgment of the managerial prerogatives of Delaware directors under Section 141(a). See Zapata Corp. v. Maldonado, 430 A.2d at 782. It is a presumption that in making a business decision the directors of a corporation acted on an informed basis, in good faith and in the honest belief that the action taken was in the best interests of the company. Kaplan v. Centex Corp., Del.Ch., 284 A.2d 119, 124 (1971); Robinson v. Pittsburgh Oil Refinery Corp., Del.Ch., 126 A. 46 (1924). Absent an abuse of discretion, that judgment will be respected by the courts. The burden is on the party challenging the decision to establish facts rebutting the presumption. See Puma v. Marriott, Del.Ch., 283 A.2d 693, 695 (1971).

The function of the business judgment rule is of paramount significance in the context of a derivative action. It comes into play in several ways—in addressing a demand, in the determination of demand futility, in efforts by independent disinterested directors to dismiss the action as inimical to the corporation's best interests, and generally, as a defense to the merits of the

porate Governance, The Monitoring Board, and The Director's Duty of Care, 61 B.U.L.Rev. 623 (1981); Moore, Corporate Officer & Director Liability: Is Corporate Behavior Beyond the Control of Our Legal System? 16 Capital U.L.Rev. 69 (1980); Jones, Corporate Governance: Who Controls the Large Corporation? 30 Hastings L.J. 1261 (1979); Small, The Evolving Role of the Director in Corporate Governance, 30 Hastings L.J. 1353 (1979).

83. [By the Court] Like the broader question of corporate governance, the derivative suit, its value, and the methods employed by corporate boards to deal with it have received much attention by commentators. See, e.g., Brown, Shareholder Derivative Litigation and the Special Litigation Committee, 43 U.Pitt.L.Rev. 601 (1982); Coffee and Schwartz, The Survival of the Derivative Suit: An Evaluation and a Proposal for Legislative Reform, 81 Colum.L.Rev. 261 (1981); Shnell, A Procedural Treatment of Derivative Suit Dismissals by Minority Directors, 69 Calif.L.Rev. 885 (1981); Dent, The Power of Directors to Terminate Shareholder Litigation: The Death of the Derivative Suit? 75 N.W.U.L.Rev. 96 (1980); Jones, An Empirical Examination of the Incidence of Shareholder Derivative and Class Action Lawsuits, 1971–1978, 60 B.U.L.Rev. 306 (1980); Comment, The Demand and Standing Requirements in Stockholder Derivative Actions, 44 U.Chi.L.Rev. 168 (1976); Dykstra, The Revival of the Derivative Suit, 116 U.Pa. L.Rev. 74 (1967); Note, Demand on Directors and Shareholders as a Prerequisite to a Derivative Suit, 73 Harv.L.Rev. 729 (1960).

suit. However, in each of these circumstances there are certain common principles governing the application and operation of the rule.

First, its protections can only be claimed by disinterested directors whose conduct otherwise meets the tests of business judgment. From the standpoint of interest, this means that directors can neither appear on both sides of a transaction nor expect to derive any personal financial benefit from it in the sense of self-dealing, as opposed to a benefit which devolves upon the corporation or all stockholders generally. Sinclair Oil Corp. v. Levien, Del. Supr., 280 A.2d 717, 720 (1971); Cheff v. Mathes, Del.Supr., 199 A.2d 548, 554 (1964). See also 8 Del.C. § 144. Thus, if such director interest is present, and the transaction is not approved by a majority consisting of the disinterested directors, then the business judgment rule has no application whatever in determining demand futility.

Second, to invoke the rule's protection directors have a duty to inform themselves, prior to making a business decision, of all material information reasonably available to them. Having become so informed, they must then act with requisite care in the discharge of their duties. While the Delaware cases use a variety of terms to describe the applicable standard of care, our analysis satisfies us that under the business judgment rule director liability is predicated upon concepts of gross negligence.[84] See Veasey & Manning, Codified Standard—Safe Harbor or Uncharted Reef? 35 Bus.Law. 919, 928 (1980).

However, it should be noted that the business judgment rule operates only in the context of director action. Technically speaking, it has no role where directors have either abdicated their functions, or absent a conscious decision, failed to act.[85] But it also follows that under applicable principles, a conscious decision to refrain from acting may nonetheless be a valid exercise of business judgment and enjoy the protections of the rule.

The gap in our law, which we address today, arises from this Court's decision in *Zapata Corp. v. Maldonado*. There, the Court defined the limits of a board's managerial power granted by Section 141(a) and restricted application of the business judgment rule in a factual context similar to this action. Zapata Corp. v. Maldonado, 430 A.2d at 782–86, rev'g, Maldonado v. Flynn, Del.Ch., 413 A.2d 1251 (1980).

By way of background, this Court's review in *Zapata* was limited to whether an independent investigation committee of disinterested directors

---

84. [By the Court] While the Delaware cases have not been precise in articulating the standard by which the exercise of business judgment is governed, a long line of Delaware cases holds that director liability is predicated on a standard which is less exacting than simple negligence. Sinclair Oil Corp. v. Levien, Del.Supr., 280 A.2d 717, 722 (1971), rev'g, Del. Ch., 261 A.2d 911 (1969) ("fraud or gross overreaching"); Getty Oil Co. v. Skelly Oil Co., Del.Supr., 267 A.2d 883, 887 (1970), rev'g, Del. Ch., 255 A.2d 717 (1969) ("gross and palpable overreaching"); Warshaw v. Calhoun, Del. Supr., 221 A.2d 487, 492–93 (1966) ("bad faith * * * or a gross abuse of discretion"); Moskowitz v. Bantrell, Del.Supr., 190 A.2d 749, 750 (1963) ("fraud or gross abuse of discretion");

Penn Mart Realty Co. v. Becker, Del.Ch., 298 A.2d 349, 351 (1972) ("directors may breach their fiduciary duty * * * by being grossly negligent"); Kors v. Carey, Del.Ch., 158 A.2d 136, 140 (1960) ("fraud, misconduct or abuse of discretion"); Allaun v. Consolidated Oil Co., Del.Ch., 147 A. 257, 261 (1929) ("reckless indifference to or a deliberate disregard of the stockholders").

85. [By the Court] Although questions of director liability in such cases have been adjudicated upon concepts of business judgment, they do not in actuality present issues of business judgment. See Arsht, Fiduciary Responsibilities of Directors, Officers & Key Employees, 4 Del.J.Corp.L. 652, 659 (1979).

had the *power* to cause the derivative action to be dismissed. Preliminarily, it was noted in *Zapata* that "[d]irectors of Delaware corporations derive their managerial decision making power, which encompasses decisions whether to initiate, or refrain from entering, litigation, from 8 Del.C. § 141(a)." In that context, this Court observed that the business judgment rule has no relevance to corporate decision making until *after a decision has been made*. In *Zapata*, we stated that a shareholder does not possess an independent individual right to continue a derivative action. Moreover, where demand on a board has been made and refused, we apply the business judgment rule in reviewing the board's refusal to act pursuant to a stockholder's demand. Unless the business judgment rule does not protect the refusal to sue, the shareholder lacks the legal managerial power to continue the derivative action, since that power is terminated by the refusal. We also concluded that where demand is excused a shareholder possesses the ability to initiate a derivative action, but the right to prosecute it may be terminated upon the exercise of applicable standards of business judgment. The thrust of *Zapata* is that in either the demand-refused or the demand-excused case, the board still retains its Section 141(a) managerial authority to make decisions regarding corporate litigation. Moreover, the board may delegate its managerial authority to a committee of independent disinterested directors. See 8 Del.C. § 141(c). Thus, even in a demand-excused case, a board has the power to appoint a committee of one or more independent disinterested directors to determine whether the derivative action should be pursued or dismissal sought. Under *Zapata*, the Court of Chancery, in passing on a committee's motion to dismiss a derivative action in a demand excused case, must apply a two-step test. First, the court must inquire into the independence and good faith of the committee and review the reasonableness and good faith of the committee's investigation. Second, the court must apply its own independent business judgment to decide whether the motion to dismiss should be granted.

After *Zapata* numerous derivative suits were filed without prior demand upon boards of directors. The complaints in such actions all alleged that demand was excused because of board interest, approval or acquiescence in the wrongdoing. In any event, the *Zapata* demand-excused/demand-refused bifurcation, has left a crucial issue unanswered: when is demand futile and, therefore, excused? * * *

The trial court correctly recognized that demand futility is inextricably bound to issues of business judgment, but stated the test to be based on allegations of fact, which, if true, "show that there is a reasonable inference" the business judgment rule is not applicable for purposes of a pre-suit demand.

The problem with this formulation is the concept of reasonable inferences to be drawn against a board of directors based on allegations in a complaint. As is clear from this case, and the conclusory allegations upon which the Vice Chancellor relied, demand futility becomes virtually automatic under such a test. Bearing in mind the presumptions with which director action is cloaked, we believe that the matter must be approached in a more balanced way.

Our view is that in determining demand futility the Court of Chancery in the proper exercise of its discretion must decide whether, under the particularized facts alleged, a reasonable doubt is created that: (1) the directors are disinterested and independent and (2) the challenged transaction was otherwise the product of a valid exercise of business judgment. Hence, the Court of Chancery must make two inquiries, one into the independence and disinterestedness of the directors and the other into the substantive nature of the challenged transaction and the board's approval thereof. As to the latter inquiry the court does not assume that the transaction is a wrong to the corporation requiring corrective steps by the board. Rather, the alleged wrong is substantively reviewed against the factual background alleged in the complaint. As to the former inquiry, directorial independence and disinterestedness, the court reviews the factual allegations to decide whether they raise a reasonable doubt, as a threshold matter, that the protections of the business judgment rule are available to the board. Certainly, if this is an "interested" director transaction, such that the business judgment rule is inapplicable to the board majority approving the transaction, then the inquiry ceases. In that event futility of demand has been established by any objective or subjective standard.[86] See, e.g., Bergstein v. Texas Internat'l Co., Del.Ch., 453 A.2d 467, 471 (1982) (because five of nine directors approved stock appreciation rights plan likely to benefit them, board was interested for demand purposes and demand held futile). This includes situations involving self-dealing directors. See Sinclair Oil Corp. v. Levien, Del.Supr., 280 A.2d 717 (1971).

However, the mere threat of personal liability for approving a questioned transaction, standing alone, is insufficient to challenge either the independence or disinterestedness of directors, although in rare cases a transaction may be so egregious on its face that board approval cannot meet the test of business judgment, and a substantial likelihood of director liability therefore exists. See Gimbel v. Signal Cos., Inc., Del.Ch., 316 A.2d 599, aff'd, Del.Supr., 316 A.2d 619 (1974). In sum the entire review is factual in nature. The Court of Chancery in the exercise of its sound discretion must be satisfied that a plaintiff has alleged facts with particularity which, taken as true, support a reasonable doubt that the challenged transaction was the product of a valid exercise of business judgment. Only in that context is demand excused. * * *

Having outlined the legal framework within which these issues are to be determined, we consider plaintiff's claims of futility here: Fink's domination and control of the directors, board approval of the Fink–Meyers employment agreement, and board hostility to the plaintiff's derivative action due to the directors' status as defendants.

Plaintiff's claim that Fink dominates and controls the Meyers' board is based on: (1) Fink's 47% ownership of Meyers' outstanding stock, and (2) that he "personally selected" each Meyers director. Plaintiff also alleges that mere approval of the employment agreement illustrates Fink's domination and control of the board. In addition, plaintiff argued on appeal that 47% stock ownership, though less than a majority, constituted control given the large number of shares outstanding, 1,245,745.

---

86. [By the Court] We recognize that drawing the line at a majority of the board may be an arguably arbitrary dividing point. Critics will charge that we are ignoring the structural bias common to corporate boards throughout America, as well as the other unseen socialization processes cutting against independent discussion and decisionmaking in the boardroom. The difficulty with structural bias in a demand futile case is simply one of establishing it in the complaint for purposes of Rule 23.1. We are satisfied that discretionary review by the Court of Chancery of complaints alleging specific facts pointing to bias on a particular board will be sufficient for determining demand futility.

Such contentions do not support any claim under Delaware law that these directors lack independence. In Kaplan v. Centex Corp., Del.Ch., 284 A.2d 119 (1971), the Court of Chancery stated that "[s]tock ownership alone, at least when it amounts to less than a majority, is not sufficient proof of domination or control". Id. at 123. Moreover, in the demand context even proof of majority ownership of a company does not strip the directors of the presumptions of independence, and that their acts have been taken in good faith and in the best interests of the corporation. There must be coupled with the allegation of control such facts as would demonstrate that through personal or other relationships the directors are beholden to the controlling person. See Mayer v. Adams, Del.Ch., 167 A.2d 729, 732, aff'd, Del.Supr., 174 A.2d 313 (1961). To date the principal decisions dealing with the issue of control or domination arose only after a full trial on the merits. Thus, they are distinguishable in the demand context unless similar particularized facts are alleged to meet the test of Chancery Rule 23.1.

The requirement of director independence inheres in the conception and rationale of the business judgment rule. The presumption of propriety that flows from an exercise of business judgment is based in part on this unyielding precept. Independence means that a director's decision is based on the corporate merits of the subject before the board rather than extraneous considerations or influences. While directors may confer, debate, and resolve their differences through compromise, or by reasonable reliance upon the expertise of their colleagues and other qualified persons, the end result, nonetheless, must be that each director has brought his or her own informed business judgment to bear with specificity upon the corporate merits of the issues without regard for or succumbing to influences which convert an otherwise valid business decision into a faithless act.

Thus, it is not enough to charge that a director was nominated by or elected at the behest of those controlling the outcome of a corporate election. That is the usual way a person becomes a corporate director. It is the care, attention and sense of individual responsibility to the performance of one's duties, not the method of election, that generally touches on independence.

We conclude that in the demand-futile context a plaintiff charging domination and control of one or more directors must allege particularized facts manifesting "a direction of corporate conduct in such a way as to comport with the wishes or interests of the corporation (or persons) doing the controlling". Kaplan, 284 A.2d at 123. The shorthand shibboleth of "dominated and controlled directors" is insufficient. In recognizing that *Kaplan* was decided after trial and full discovery, we stress that the plaintiff need only allege specific facts; he need not plead evidence. * * *

Here, plaintiff has not alleged any facts sufficient to support a claim of control. The personal-selection-of-directors allegation stands alone, unsupported. At best it is a conclusion devoid of factual support. The causal link between Fink's control and approval of the employment agreement is alluded to, but nowhere specified. The director's approval, alone, does not establish control, even in the face of Fink's 47% stock ownership. See Kaplan v. Centex Corp., 284 A.2d at 122, 123. The claim that Fink is unlikely to perform any services under the agreement, because of his age, and his conflicting consultant work with Prudential, adds nothing to the control claim. Therefore, we cannot conclude that the complaint factually particularizes any circumstances of control and domination to overcome the presumption of board independence, and thus render the demand futile. * * *

Turning to the board's approval of the Meyers–Fink employment agreement, plaintiff's argument is simple: all of the Meyers directors are named defendants, because they approved the wasteful agreement; if plaintiff prevails on the merits all the directors will be jointly and severally liable; therefore, the directors' interests in avoiding personal liability automatically and absolutely disqualifies them from passing on a shareholder's demand.

Such allegations are conclusory at best. * * * The complaint does not allege particularized facts indicating that the agreement is a waste of corporate assets. Indeed, the complaint as now drafted may not even state a cause of action, given the directors' broad corporate power to fix the compensation of officers.

In essence, the plaintiff alleged a lack of consideration flowing from Fink to Meyers, since the employment agreement provided that compensation was not contingent on Fink's ability to perform any services. The bare assertion that Fink performed "little or no services" was plaintiff's conclusion based solely on Fink's age and the existence of the Fink–Prudential employment agreement. As for Meyers' loans to Fink, beyond the bare allegation that they were made, the complaint does not allege facts indicating the wastefulness of such arrangements. Again, the mere existence of such loans, given the broad corporate powers conferred by Delaware law, does not even state a claim.[87]

In sustaining plaintiff's claim of demand futility the trial court relied on Fidanque v. American Maracaibo Co., Del.Ch., 92 A.2d 311, 321 (1952), which held that a contract providing for payment of consulting fees to a retired president/director was a waste of corporate assets. In *Fidanque,* the court found after trial that the contract and payments were in reality compensation for past services. This was based upon facts not present here: the former president/director was a 70 year old stroke victim, neither the agreement nor the record spelled out his consulting duties at all, the consulting salary equaled the individual's salary when he was president and general manager of the corporation, and the contract was silent as to continued employment in the event that the retired president/director again became incapacitated and unable to perform his duties. Contrasting the facts of *Fidanque* with the complaint here, it is apparent that plaintiff has not alleged facts sufficient to render demand futile on a charge of corporate waste, and thus create a reasonable doubt that the board's action is protected by the business judgment rule. * * *

Plaintiff's final argument is the incantation that demand is excused because the directors otherwise would have to sue themselves, thereby placing the conduct of the litigation in hostile hands and preventing its effective prosecution. This bootstrap argument has been made to and dismissed by other courts. See, e.g., Lewis v. Graves, 701 F.2d 245, 248–49 (2d Cir.1983). Its acceptance would effectively abrogate Rule 23.1 and weaken the manageri-

---

87. [By the Court] Plaintiff's allegation ignores 8 Del.C. § 143 which expressly authorizes interest-free loans to "any officer or employee of the corporation * * * whenever, in the judgment of the directors, such loan * * * may reasonably be expected to benefit the corporation." 8 Del.C. § 143.

al power of directors. Unless facts are alleged with particularity to overcome the presumptions of independence and a proper exercise of business judgment, in which case the directors could not be expected to sue themselves, a bare claim of this sort raises no legally cognizable issue under Delaware corporate law. * * *

In sum, we conclude that the plaintiff has failed to allege facts with particularity indicating that the Meyers directors were tainted by interest, lacked independence, or took action contrary to Meyers' best interests in order to create a reasonable doubt as to the applicability of the business judgment rule. Only in the presence of such a reasonable doubt may a demand be deemed futile. Hence, we reverse the Court of Chancery's denial of the motion to dismiss, and remand with instructions that plaintiff be granted leave to amend his complaint to bring it into compliance with Rule 23.1 based on the principles we have announced today. * * *

Reversed and Remanded.

Notes

(1) Dennis J. Block & H. Adam Prussin, Termination of Derivative Suits Against Directors on Business Judgment Grounds: From *Zapata* to *Aronson*, 39 Bus.Law. 1503, 1505–06 (Aug. 1984):[88]

> *Aronson* makes it clear that demand will almost always be required unless a majority of the Board is so directly self-interested in the challenged transaction that there is serious doubt that the business judgment rule would protect that transaction. Self-interest, for these purposes, is defined in terms of direct financial interest in the challenged transaction: the fact that a majority of directors voted to approve the transaction—and are therefore named as defendants in the action—does *not* constitute the requisite self-interest and will not excuse demand. After *Aronson* there should be relatively few demand-excused cases, and therefore relatively few cases where the *Zapata* two-step test will be applied. Thus, in run-of-the-mill cases the test actually applied will be the same under Delaware and New York law, the business judgment rule.

(2) The practical and tactical problems faced by a plaintiff under the complex Delaware structure of rules set forth in *Zapata* and *Aronson* were further complicated by four additional holdings.

(a) Spiegel v. Buntrock, 571 A.2d 767, 775 (Del.1990), holds that where a shareholder makes a demand, he thereby "tacitly acknowledges the absence of facts to support a finding of futility," thus placing his case in the hands of the board of directors under the business judgment rule. As a result of this "waiver" rule, plaintiffs today seldom make demand in Delaware, but instead litigate the issue whether demand was excused and futile. See John C. Coffee, Jr., New Myths and Old Realities: The American Law Institute Faces the Derivative Action, 48 Bus. Law. 1407, 1414 (1993).

(b) In Levine v. Smith, 591 A.2d 194 (Del.1991), a case involving General Motors' buy-out of Ross Perot, Levine made a demand on the directors which was unanimously refused. Levine then filed an amended complaint arguing that the

88. Copyright 1984 by the American Bar Association. All rights reserved. Reprinted with the permission of the American Bar Association and its Section of Corporation, Banking and Business Law.

refusal of the demand by the board of directors was not a proper exercise of business judgment. He sought the right to institute limited discovery in an effort to establish that the refusal was wrongful. The Court held that discovery should not be permitted following a refused demand, and to obtain judicial review of the claim of wrongful refusal, the plaintiff must allege particularized facts that create reasonable doubt that the refusal was a proper exercise of business judgment. In other words judicial review of a decision rejecting a demand was subject to the same pleading standard established in *Aronson* to determine whether demand was excused.

(c) In Scattered Corporation v. Chicago Stock Exchange, 701 A.2d 70 (Del. 1997), the court stated that in determining whether a demand was wrongfully refused, the plaintiff may use the "tools at hand" to obtain information about the basis of the decision. These "tools" include the statutory right of inspection of books, records, and minutes of meetings, but not discovery or production of records through a writ of mandamus.

(d) In re Walt Disney Co. Derivative Litigation, 825 A.2d 275 (Del.Ch.2003) began with a suit which claimed demand futility. The plaintiffs charged that the directors violated their duty of care and good faith by allowing the extravagant compensation package of former President, Michael Ovitz. The Delaware Supreme Court did not excuse demand but they allowed the plaintiffs to amend their original complaint. The plaintiffs, in line with the court's suggestion, requested an inspection of Disney's books and records in order to find evidence of their claim. The plaintiffs were excused demand with their amended complaint in the Court of Chancery.

(3) In virtually every case in which derivative litigation has been considered by a litigation committee or by the board of directors since 1984, the determination has been that pursuit of the litigation is not in the best interest of the corporation. Does this not lend credence to the objection that there is in fact "structural bias" in this decisional process? Or should this datum be explained on the basis that virtually all derivative litigation filed today is without merit? For such a thesis, see Roberta Romano, The Shareholder Suit: Litigation without Foundation?, 7 J.L. Econ. & Org. 56 (1991); Daniel R. Fischel & Michael Bradley, The Role of Liability Rules and the Derivative Suit in Corporate Law: A Theoretical and Empirical Analysis, 71 Cornell L.Rev. 261 (1986); Richard W. Duesenberg, The Business Judgment Rule and Shareholder Derivative Suits: A View From the Inside, 60 Wash. U. L.Q. 311 (1982). Whatever the explanation, certainly one consequence of the use of litigation committees during this period is that control of derivative litigation has largely passed to the board of directors.

(4) The rules established in Delaware are complex and interconnected. They have been criticized on the ground that they prolong litigation by encouraging sparring over the preliminary question whether a demand was required. Judge Easterbrook, in a concurring opinion in Starrels v. First Nat'l Bank of Chicago, 870 F.2d 1168, 1172–76 (7th Cir.1989), offers a negative assessment of the Delaware rules and argues that a rule of universal demand would be more rational. See also John C. Coffee, Jr., New Myths and Old Realities: The American Law Institute Faces the Derivative Action, 48 Bus. Law. 1407, 1414 (1993):[89]

Delaware's demand rule also results in a substantial amount of collateral litigation and sometimes can be a trap for the unwary. * * *

89. Copyright (1993) by the American Bar Association. All rights reserved. Reprinted with permission of the American Bar Association and its Section of Corporation, Banking and Business Law.

[Further,] the shareholder plaintiff usually faces an unattractive choice: either (i) not make a demand and thereby accept the burden of convincing the court that seemingly respectable directors should be deemed too biased even to deserve an opportunity to respond to demand, or (ii) make demand and thereby acknowledge the applicability of the business judgment rule to the directors' decision whether or not to reject demand (and, for most practical purposes, concede the outcome of the case).

(5) Given these criticisms, it is not surprising that mandatory demand in all cases has become the corner-stone of alternative systems in other states for resolving derivative litigation in the corporate context.

IN RE ORACLE CORP. DERIVATIVE LITIGATION

Court of Chancery of Delaware, 2003.
824 A.2d 917.

STRINE, VICE CHANCELLOR.

[Editors: Plaintiff shareholders brought a derivative suit alleging insider trading by four members of Oracle's board of directors—Lawrence Ellison, the company's Chairman and CEO; Jeffrey Henley, the company's CFO; Donald Lucas; and Michael Boskin. In response, Oracle formed a special litigation committee (SLC) to investigate the merits of the claims and to determine whether the company should take any action. Directors Hector Garcia-Molina and Joseph Grundfest were appointed to the SLC. Both men were professors at Stanford University and had obtained their graduate degrees from Stanford. Upon conclusion of its investigation, the SLC recommended no action be taken. Plaintiffs challenged the independence of the SLC. The Court concluded that Garcia-Molina and Grundfest were not independent due to their affiliation with Stanford University. The portions of the opinion set forth below relate to the Vice Chancellor's discussion of how the independence of SLC members should be assessed.]

The SLC's investigation was, by any objective measure, extensive. The SLC reviewed an enormous amount of paper and electronic records. SLC counsel interviewed seventy witnesses, some of them twice. SLC members participated in several key interviews, including the interviews of the Trading Defendants. * * *

In the end, the SLC produced an extremely lengthy Report totaling 1,110 pages (excluding appendices and exhibits) that concluded that Oracle should not pursue the plaintiffs' claims against the Trading Defendants or any of the other Oracle directors serving during the 3Q FY 2001. * * *

In order to prevail on its motion to terminate the Delaware Derivative Action, the SLC must persuade me that: (1) its members were independent; (2) that they acted in good faith; and (3) that they had reasonable bases for their recommendations. * * *

[The court noted that in its report, the SLC asserted that its members were independent.]

Noticeably absent from the SLC Report was any disclosure of several significant ties between Oracle or the Trading Defendants and Stanford

University, the university that employs both members of the SLC. In the Report, it was only disclosed that:

- defendant Boskin was a Stanford professor;

- the SLC members were aware that Lucas had made certain donations to Stanford; and

- among the contributions was a donation of $ 50,000 worth of stock that Lucas donated to Stanford Law School after Grundfest delivered a speech to a venture capital fund meeting in response to Lucas's request. It happens that Lucas's son is a partner in the fund and that approximately half the donation was allocated for use by Grundfest in his personal research.

In view of the modesty of these disclosed ties, it was with some shock that a series of other ties among Stanford, Oracle, and the Trading Defendants emerged during discovery. Although the plaintiffs have embellished these ties considerably beyond what is reasonable, the plain facts are a striking departure from the picture presented in the Report. * * *

1. Boskin

Defendant Michael J. Boskin is the T.M. Friedman Professor of Economics at Stanford University. * * *

During the 1970s, Boskin taught Grundfest when Grundfest was a Ph.D. candidate. Although Boskin was not Grundfest's advisor and although they do not socialize, the two have remained in contact over the years, speaking occasionally about matters of public policy.

Furthermore, both Boskin and Grundfest are senior fellows and steering committee members at the Stanford Institute for Economic Policy Research, which was previously defined as "SIEPR." * * *

2. Lucas

As noted in the SLC Report, the SLC members admitted knowing that Lucas was a contributor to Stanford. They also acknowledged that he had donated $ 50,000 to Stanford Law School in appreciation for Grundfest having given a speech at his request. About half of the proceeds were allocated for use by Grundfest in his research.

But Lucas's ties with Stanford are far, far richer than the SLC Report lets on. To begin, Lucas is a Stanford alumnus, having obtained both his undergraduate and graduate degrees there. By any measure, he has been a very loyal alumnus.

In showing that this is so, I start with a matter of some jousting between the SLC and the plaintiffs. Lucas's brother, Richard, died of cancer and by way of his will established a foundation. Lucas became Chairman of the Foundation and serves as a director along with his son, a couple of other family members, and some non-family members. A principal object of the Foundation's beneficence has been Stanford. The Richard M. Lucas Foundation has given $11.7 million to Stanford since its 1981 founding. Among its notable contributions, the Foundation funded the establishment of the Richard M. Lucas Center for Magnetic Resonance Spectroscopy and Imaging at

Stanford's Medical School. Donald Lucas was a founding member and lead director of the Center. * * *

Lucas's connections with Stanford as a contributor go beyond the Foundation, however. From his own personal funds, Lucas has contributed $4.1 million to Stanford, a substantial percentage of which has been donated within the last half-decade. Notably, Lucas has, among other things, donated $424,000 to SIEPR and approximately $149,000 to Stanford Law School. Indeed, Lucas is not only a major contributor to SIEPR, he is the Chair of its Advisory Board. At SIEPR's facility at Stanford, the conference center is named the Donald L. Lucas Conference Center. * * *

3. Ellison

There can be little doubt that Ellison is a major figure in the community in which Stanford is located. The so-called Silicon Valley has generated many success stories, among the greatest of which is that of Oracle and its leader, Ellison. One of the wealthiest men in America, Ellison is a major figure in the nation's increasingly important information technology industry. Given his wealth, Ellison is also in a position to make—and, in fact, he has made—major charitable contributions.

Some of the largest of these contributions have been made through the Ellison Medical Foundation, which makes grants to universities and laboratories to support biomedical research relating to aging and infectious diseases. Ellison is the sole director of the Foundation. * * *

* * * Stanford has * * * been the beneficiary of grants from the Ellison Medical Foundation—to the tune of nearly $10 million in paid or pledged funds. * * *

During the time Ellison has been CEO of Oracle, the company itself has also made over $300,000 in donations to Stanford. Not only that, when Oracle established a generously endowed educational foundation—the Oracle Help Us Help Foundation—to help further the deployment of educational technology in schools serving disadvantaged populations, it named Stanford as the "appointing authority," which gave Stanford the right to name four of the Foundation's seven directors. * * *

Beginning in the year 2000 and continuing well into 2001—the same year that Ellison made the trades the plaintiffs contend were suspicious and the same year the SLC members were asked to join the Oracle board—Ellison and Stanford discussed a much more lucrative donation. The idea Stanford proposed for discussion was the creation of an Ellison Scholars Program modeled on the Rhodes Scholarship at Oxford. The proposed budget for Stanford's answer to Oxford: $170 million. The Ellison Scholars were to be drawn from around the world and were to come to Stanford to take a two-year interdisciplinary graduate program in economics, political science, and computer technology. During the summer between the two academic years, participants would work in internships at, among other companies, Oracle.

The SLC contends that even together, these facts regarding the ties among Oracle, the Trading Defendants, Stanford, and the SLC members do not impair the SLC's independence. In so arguing, the SLC places great weight on the fact that none of the Trading Defendants have the practical ability to deprive either Grundfest or Garcia-Molina of their current positions at Stanford. Nor, given their tenure, does Stanford itself have any practical ability to punish them for taking action adverse to Boskin, Lucas, or Ellison—each of whom, as we have seen, has contributed (in one way or another) great value to Stanford as an institution. As important, neither Garcia-Molina nor Grundfest are part of the official fundraising apparatus at Stanford; thus, it is not their on-the-job duty to be solicitous of contributors, and fundraising success does not factor into their treatment as professors. * * *

* * * According to the SLC, its members are independent unless they are essentially subservient to the Trading Defendants—*i.e.*, they are under the "domination and control" of the interested parties. * * *

But, in my view, an emphasis on "domination and control" would serve only to fetishize much-parroted language, at the cost of denuding the independence inquiry of its intellectual integrity. * * *

* * * Delaware law should not be based on a reductionist view of human nature that simplifies human motivations on the lines of the least sophisticated notions of the law and economics movement. *Homo sapiens* is not merely *homo economicus*. We may be thankful that an array of other motivations exist that influence human behavior; not all are any better than greed or avarice, think of envy, to name just one. But also think of motives like love, friendship, and collegiality, think of those among us who direct their behavior as best they can on a guiding creed or set of moral values.

Nor should our law ignore the social nature of humans. To be direct, corporate directors are generally the sort of people deeply enmeshed in social institutions. Such institutions have norms, expectations that, explicitly and implicitly, influence and channel the behavior of those who participate in their operation. Some things are "just not done," or only at a cost, which might not be so severe as a loss of position, but may involve a loss of standing in the institution. In being appropriately sensitive to this factor, our law also cannot assume—absent some proof of the point—that corporate directors are, as a general matter, persons of unusual social bravery, who operate heedless to the inhibitions that social norms generate for ordinary folk. * * *

* * * I conclude that the SLC has not met its burden to show the absence of a material factual question about its independence. I find this to be the case because the ties among the SLC, the Trading Defendants, and Stanford are so substantial that they cause reasonable doubt about the SLC's ability to impartially consider whether the Trading Defendants should face suit. * * *

As SLC members, Grundfest and Garcia-Molina were already being asked to consider whether the company should level extremely serious accusations of wrongdoing against fellow board members. As to Boskin, both SLC members faced another layer of complexity: the determination of whether to have Oracle press insider trading claims against a fellow professor at their university. * * * To accuse a fellow professor—whom one might see at the faculty club or at inter-disciplinary presentations of academic papers—of insider trading cannot be a small thing—even for the most callous of academics.

As to Boskin, Grundfest faced an even more complex challenge than Garcia-Molina. Boskin was a professor who had taught him and with whom he had maintained contact over the years. Their areas of academic interest intersected, putting Grundfest in contact if not directly with Boskin, then regularly with Boskin's colleagues. * * * Having these ties, Grundfest (I infer) would have more difficulty objectively determining whether Boskin engaged in improper insider trading than would a person who was not a fellow professor, had not been a student of Boskin, had not kept in touch with Boskin over the years, and who was not a senior fellow and steering committee member at SIEPR. * * *

The same concerns also exist as to Lucas. For Grundfest to vote to accuse Lucas of insider trading would require him to accuse SIEPR's Advisory Board Chair and major benefactor of serious wrongdoing—of conduct that violates federal securities laws. Such action would also require Grundfest to make charges against a man who recently donated $ 50,000 to Stanford Law School after Grundfest made a speech at his request.

And, for both Grundfest and Garcia-Molina, service on the SLC demanded that they consider whether an extremely generous and influential Stanford alumnus should be sued by Oracle for insider trading. Although they were not responsible for fundraising, as sophisticated professors they undoubtedly are aware of how important large contributors are to Stanford, and they share in the benefits that come from serving at a university with a rich endowment. A reasonable professor giving any thought to the matter would obviously consider the effect his decision might have on the University's relationship with Lucas, it being (one hopes) sensible to infer that a professor of reasonable collegiality and loyalty cares about the well-being of the institution he serves. * * *

* * * Ellison's relationship to Stanford itself contributes to my overall doubt, when heaped on top of the ties involving Boskin and Lucas. During the period when Grundfest and Garcia-Molina were being added to the Oracle board, Ellison was publicly considering making extremely large contributions to Stanford. * * *

* * * [T]he SLC contends that neither SLC member was aware of Ellison's relationship with Stanford until after the Report was completed. Thus, this relationship, in its various facets, could not have compromised their independence. Again, I find this argument from ignorance to be unavailing. An inquiry into Ellison's connections with Stanford should have been conducted before the SLC was finally formed and, at the very least, should have been undertaken in connection with the Report. In any event, given how public Ellison was about his possible donations it is difficult not to harbor troublesome doubt about whether the SLC members were conscious of the possibility that Ellison was pondering a large contribution to Stanford. * * *

It seems to me that the connections outlined in this opinion would weigh on the mind of a reasonable special litigation committee member deciding whether to level the serious charge of insider trading against the Trading Defendants. As indicated before, this does not mean that the SLC would be less inclined to find such charges meritorious, only that the connections identified would be on the mind of the SLC members in a way that generates an unacceptable risk of bias. That is, these connections generate a reasonable doubt about the SLC's impartiality because they suggest that material considerations other than the best interests of Oracle could have influenced the SLC's inquiry and judgments.

Notes

(1) The *Oracle* Court's consideration of the social and institutional connections between SLC members and management in analyzing director independence was a departure from the traditional independence inquiry, which focused on directors' financial interests. The Court emphasized the ways in which social ties can have a subconscious influence on directors' judgment. It may be true that social connections could make it awkward for a director on an SLC to vote to proceed with a lawsuit against managers. On the other hand, the fact that individuals must be nominated to boards of directors means there will always be some kind of pre-existing relationship between management and directors. How should companies assess SLC independence going forward? Should a director's social or institutional ties be given as much weight as financial entanglements with management?

(2) The approach to assessing director independence articulated in *Oracle* has been followed by courts outside of Delaware. *See, e.g.*, Klein v. FPL Group, Inc., 2003 WL 22768424 (S.D. Fla. Sept. 26, 2003); Demoulas v. Demoulas Super Markets, Inc, 2004 WL 1895052 (Mass. Super. Ct. Aug. 2, 2004). The rule in *Oracle* was pronounced in a case evaluating the independence of SLC members, but several courts have already applied it beyond that scope. *See* Official Committee of Unsecured Creditors of Integrated Health Services, Inc. v. Elkins, 2004 WL 1949290 (Del. Ch. Aug. 24, 2004) (plaintiffs alleged directors subordinated the best interests of the company to their loyalty to the former president and the court noted that domination and control are not tested by economics alone); Atlantic Coast Airlines Holdings, Inc. v. Mesa Air Group, Inc., 295 F.Supp.2d 75 (D.D.C. 2003) (examining allegations that preexisting business or social relationships rendered individuals unfit to serve as company directors).

(3) For further discussion of *Oracle* and director independence, see Mark J. Loewenstein, The Quiet Transformation of Corporate Law, 57 SMU L. Rev. 353 (2004); Comment, In re Oracle Corp. Derivative Litigation: Death of Special Litigation Committees?, 3 DePaul Bus. & Com. L.J. 617 (2005); Comment, In re Oracle Corporation Derivative Litigation: Has a New Species of Director Independence Been Uncovered, 29 Del. J. Corp. L. 849 (2004).

CUKER v. MIKALAUSKAS

Supreme Court of Pennsylvania, 1997.
547 Pa. 600, 692 A.2d 1042.

Before FLAHERTY, C.J., and ZAPPALA, CAPPY, CASTILLE, NIGRO, and NEWMAN, JJ.

FLAHERTY, C.J.

PECO Energy Company filed a motion for summary judgment seeking termination of minority shareholder derivative actions. When the motion was denied by the court of common pleas, PECO sought extraordinary relief in this court pursuant to Pa.R.A.P. 3309. We granted the petition, limited to the issue of "whether the 'business judgment rule' permits the board of directors of a Pennsylvania corporation to terminate derivative lawsuits brought by minority shareholders."

PECO is a publicly regulated utility incorporated in Pennsylvania which sells electricity and gas to residential, commercial, and industrial customers in

Philadelphia and four surrounding counties. PECO is required to conform to PUC regulations which govern the provision of service to residential customers, including opening, billing, and terminating accounts. PECO is required to report regularly to the PUC on a wide variety of statistical and performance information regarding its compliance with the regulations as interpreted by the PUC. Like other utilities, PECO is required to undergo a comprehensive management audit at the direction of the PUC approximately every ten years. The most recent audit was conducted by Ernst & Young. The report issued in 1991 recommended changes in twenty-two areas, including criticisms and recommendations regarding PECO's credit and collection function.

* * * [Following the PUC report, one set of minority shareholders filed a demand on PECO (the Katzman demand)], alleging wrongdoing by some PECO directors and officers. This Katzman demand, made in May, 1993, asserted that the delinquent officers had damaged PECO by mismanaging the credit and collection function, particularly as to the collection of overdue accounts. The shareholders demanded that PECO authorize litigation against the wrongdoers to recover monetary damages sustained by PECO. At its meeting of June 28, 1993, PECO's board responded by creating a special litigation committee to investigate the Katzman allegations.

Less than a month later, a second group of minority shareholders filed a complaint against PECO officers and directors. Cuker v. Mikalauskas, July Term, 1998, No. 3470 (C.P.Phila.). The Cuker complaint * * * made the same allegations as those in the Katzman demand * * *. The Cuker complaint was filed before the special litigation committee had begun its substantive work of investigating and evaluating the Katzman demand, so the committee's work encompassed both the Katzman and Cuker matters. Only the twelve nondefendant members of the PECO board acted to create the special committee, which consisted of three outside directors who had never been employed by PECO and who were not named in the Katzman demand or the Cuker complaint.

The work of the special committee was aided by the law firm of Dilworth, Paxson, Kalish & Kauffman, as well as PECO's regular outside auditor, Coopers & Lybrand, selected to assist in accounting matters because Coopers was knowledgeable about the utility industry and was familiar with PECO's accounting practices. The special committee conducted an extensive investigation over many months while maintaining a separate existence from PECO and its board of directors and keeping its deliberations confidential. The special committee held its final meeting on January 26, 1994, whereupon it reached its conclusions and prepared its report.

The report of the special committee concluded that there was no evidence of bad faith, self-dealing, concealment, or other breaches of the duty of loyalty by any of the defendant officers. It also concluded that the defendant officers "exercised sound business judgment in managing the affairs of the company" and that their actions "were reasonably calculated to further the best interests of the company." The three-hundred-page report identified numerous factors underlying the conclusions of the special committee. Significant considerations included the utility's efforts before the PUC to raise electricity rates in consequence of the expense of new nuclear generating plants. Other factors were the impact of PUC regulations limiting wintertime termination of residential service and other limitations on the use of collection techniques such as terminations of overdue customers, particularly with a large population of poverty level users among PECO's customer base. These considerations were supported by PUC documents which criticized PECO for aggressive and excessive terminations in recent years. The report of the special litigation committee also described how PECO's management had been attentive to the credit and collection function, with constant efforts to improve performance in that area. According to the report, limiting the use of terminations as a collection technique was a sound business judgment, reducing antagonism between the PUC and PECO and resulting in rate increases which produced revenue far in excess of the losses attributed to nonaggressive collection tactics. The report concluded that proceeding with a derivative suit based largely on findings of the Ernst & Young audit would not be in the best interests of PECO.

When it received the report of the special litigation committee with appendices containing the documents and interviews underlying the report, the board debated the recommendations at two meetings early in 1994. The twelve nondefendant members of the PECO board voted unanimously on March 14, 1994 to reject the Katzman demand and to terminate the Cuker action.

In the Cuker action, the court of common pleas rejected PECO's motion for summary judgment. The court stated that "the 'business judgment rule' [has been] adopted in some states but never previously employed in Pennsylvania." The court held that as a matter of Pennsylvania public policy, a corporation lacks power to terminate pending derivative litigation. * * * PECO sought extraordinary relief in this court under our King's Bench powers, which we granted.

* * * [The Court concludes that the business judgment rule permits the board of directors of a Pennsylvania corporation to terminate derivative lawsuits brought by minority shareholders.] Ironically, this court has never used the term "business judgment rule" in a corporate context nor has it explicitly adopted the business judgment rule. Nevertheless a review of Pennsylvania decisions establishes that the business judgment doctrine or rule is the law of Pennsylvania. * * *

The * * * practical effect of [our] holding needs elaboration. Assuming that an independent board of directors may terminate shareholder derivative actions, what is needed is a procedural mechanism for implementation and judicial review of the board's decision. Without considering the merits of the action, a court should determine the validity of the board's decision to terminate the litigation; if that decision was made in accordance with the appropriate standards, then the court should dismiss the derivative action prior to litigation on the merits.

The business judgment rule should insulate officers and directors from judicial intervention in the absence of fraud or self-dealing, if challenged decisions were within the scope of the directors' authority, if they exercised reasonable diligence, and if they honestly and rationally believed their decisions were in the best interests of the company. It is obvious that a court must examine the circumstances surrounding the decisions in order to determine if the conditions warrant application of the business judgment rule. If they do, the court will never proceed to an examination of the merits of the challenged decisions, for that is precisely what the business judgment rule prohibits. In order to make the business judgment rule meaningful, the preliminary examination should be limited and precise so as to minimize judicial involvement when application of the business judgment rule is warranted.

To achieve these goals, a court might stay the derivative action while it determines the propriety of the board's decision. The court might order limited discovery or an evidentiary hearing to resolve issues respecting the board's decision. Factors bearing on the board's decision will include whether the board or its special litigation committee was disinterested, whether it was assisted by counsel, whether it prepared a written report, whether it was independent, whether it conducted an adequate investigation, and whether it rationally believed its decision was in the best interests of the corporation (i.e., acted in good faith). If all of these criteria are satisfied,[90] the business judgment rule applies and the court should dismiss the action.

These considerations and procedures are all encompassed in Part VII, chapter 1 of the ALI Principles (relating to the derivative action), which provides a comprehensive mechanism to address shareholder derivative actions. A number of its provisions are implicated in the action at bar. Sections 7.02 (standing), 7.03 (the demand rule), 7.04 (procedure in derivative action), 7.05 (board authority in derivative action), 7.06 (judicial stay of derivative action), 7.07, 7.08, and 7.09 (dismissal of derivative action), 7.10 (standard of judicial review), and 7.13 (judicial procedures) are specifically applicable to this case.[91] These sections set forth guidance which is consistent with Pennsylvania law and precedent, which furthers the policies inherent in the business judgment rule, and which provides an appropriate degree of specificity to guide the trial court in controlling the proceedings in this litigation.

We specifically adopt §§ 7.02–7.10, and § 7.13 of the ALI Principles.[92] In doing so we have weighed many considerations. First, the opinion of the trial court, the questions certified to the Superior Court, and the inability of PECO to obtain a definitive ruling from the lower courts all demonstrate the need for specific guidance from this court on how such litigation should be managed; the ALI principles provide such guidance in specific terms which will simplify this litigation. Second, we have often found ALI guidance helpful

---

90. [By the Court] It should be noted that respondents contest all of these criteria * * *. Until factual determinations are made in regard to these disputed issues, a trial court cannot conclude whether or not the business judgment rule requires dismissal of the action.

91. [By the Court] ALI Principles §§ 4.01, 4.02, and 4.03 (duties of directors and officers; the business judgment rule; reliance on committees and other persons) are similar but not identical to the statutory standards found in 15 Pa.C.S. §§ 512, 513, 515, 1712, 1713, and 1715. The statutory standards, of course, control the duties of directors and the application of the business judgment rule in Pennsylvania.

92. [By the Court] The full text of these sections is set forth in the appendix to this opinion. * * * Our adoption of these sections is not a rejection of other sections not cited. We have identified and studied the sections which apply to this case and have adopted those which appear most relevant. The entire publication, all seven parts, is a comprehensive, cohesive work more than a decade in preparation. Additional sections of the publication, particularly procedural ones due to their interlocking character, may be adopted in the future. Issues in future cases or, perhaps, further proceedings in this case might implicate additional sections of the ALI Principles. Courts of the Commonwealth are free to consider other parts of the work and utilize them if they are helpful and appear to be consistent with Pennsylvania law.

in the past, most frequently in adopting or citing sections of various Restatements; the scholarship reflected in work of the American Law Institute has been consistently reliable and useful. Third, the principles set forth by the ALI are generally consistent with Pennsylvania precedent. Fourth, although the ALI Principles incorporate much of the law of New York and Delaware, other states with extensive corporate jurisprudence, the ALI Principles better serve the needs of Pennsylvania. Although New York law parallels Pennsylvania law in many respects, it does not set forth any procedures to govern the review of corporate decisions relating to derivative litigation, and this omission would fail to satisfy the needs evident in this case. Delaware law permits a court in some cases ("demand excused" cases) to apply its own business judgment in the review process when deciding to honor the directors' decision to terminate derivative litigation. In our view, this is a defect which could eviscerate the business judgment rule and contradict a long line of Pennsylvania precedents. Delaware law also fails to provide a procedural framework for judicial review of corporate decisions under the business judgment rule.

Accordingly, we adopt the specified sections of the ALI Principles, reverse the orders of the court of common pleas, and remand the matter for further proceedings consistent with this opinion.

Orders reversed and case remanded.

APPENDIX

2 ALI, Principles of Corporate Governance: Analysis and Recommendations (1994).

§ 7.02 Standing to Commence and Maintain a Derivative Action

(a) A holder of an equity security has standing to commence and maintain a derivative action if the holder:

(1) Acquired the equity security either (A) before the material facts relating to the alleged wrong were publicly disclosed or were known by, or specifically communicated to, the holder, or (B) by devolution of law, directly or indirectly, from a prior holder who acquired the security as described in the preceding clause (A);

(2) Continues to hold the equity security until the time of judgment, unless the failure to do so is the result of corporate action in which the holder did not acquiesce, and either (A) the derivative action was commenced prior to the corporate action terminating the holder's status, or (B) the court finds that the holder is better able to represent the interests of the shareholders than any other holder who has brought suit;

(3) Has complied with the demand requirement of § 7.03 (Exhaustion of Intracorporate Remedies; The Demand Rule) or was excused by its terms; and

(4) Is able to represent fairly and adequately the interests of the shareholders.

(b) On a timely motion, a holder of an equity security should be permitted to intervene in a derivative action, unless the court finds that the interests to be represented by the intervenor are already fairly and adequately represented or that the intervenor is unable to represent fairly and adequately the interests of the shareholders.

(c) A director of a corporation has standing to commence and maintain a derivative action unless the court finds that the director is unable to represent fairly and adequately the interest of the shareholders.

§ 7.03   Exhaustion of Intracorporate Remedies: The Demand Rule

(a) Before commencing a derivative action, a holder or a director should be required to make a written demand upon the board of directors of the corporation, requesting it to prosecute the action or take suitable corrective measures, unless demand is excused under § 7.03(b). The demand should give notice to the board, with reasonable specificity, of the essential facts relied upon to support each of the claims made therein.

(b) Demand on the board should be excused only if the plaintiff makes a specific showing that irreparable injury to the corporation would otherwise result, and in such instances demand should be made promptly after commencement of the action.

(c) Demand on shareholders should not be required.

(d) Except as provided in § 7.03(b), the court should dismiss a derivative action that is commenced prior to the response of the board or a committee thereof to the demand required by § 7.03(a), unless the board or committee fails to respond within a reasonable time.

§ 7.04   Pleading, Demand Rejection, Procedure, and Costs in a Derivative Action

The legal standards applicable to a derivative action should provide that:

(a) Particularity; Demand Rejection.

(1) In General. The complaint shall plead with particularity facts that, if true, raise a significant prospect that the transaction or conduct complained of did not meet the applicable requirements of Parts IV (Duty of Care and the Business Judgment Rule), V (Duty of Fair Dealing), or VI (Role of Directors and Shareholders in Transactions in Control and Tender Offers), in light of any approvals of the transaction or conduct communicated to the plaintiff by the corporation.

(2) Demand Rejection. If the corporation rejects the demand made on the board pursuant to § 7.03, and if, at or following the rejection, the corporation delivers to the plaintiff a written reply to the demand which states that the demand was rejected by directors who were not interested in the transaction or conduct described in and forming the basis for the demand and that those directors constituted a majority of the entire board and were capable as a group of objective judgment in the circumstances, and which provides specific reasons for those statements, then the complaint shall also plead with particularity facts that, if true, raise a significant prospect that either:

(A) The statements in the reply are not correct;

(B) If Part IV, V, or VI provides that the underlying transaction or conduct would be reviewed under a standard other than the business judgment rule, either (i) that the disinterested directors who rejected the demand did not satisfy the good faith and informational requirements (§ 4.01(c)(2)) of the business judgment rule or (ii) that disinterested directors could not reasonably have determined that rejection of the demand was in the best interests of the corporation.

If the complaint fails to set forth sufficiently such particularized facts, defendants shall be entitled to dismissal of the complaint prior to discovery.

(b) Attorney's Certification. Each party's attorney of record shall sign every pleading, motion, and other paper filed on behalf of the party, and such signature shall constitute the attorney's certification that (i) to the best of the attorney's knowledge, information, and belief, formed after reasonable inquiry, the pleading, motion, or other paper is well grounded in fact and is warranted by existing law or by a good faith argument for the extension, modification, or reversal of existing law, and (ii) the pleading, motion, or other paper is not interposed for any improper purpose, such as to harass or to cause unnecessary delay or needless increase in the cost of litigation.

(c) Security for Expenses. Except as authorized by statute or judicial rule applicable to civil actions generally, no bond, undertaking, or other security for expenses shall be required.

(d) Award of Costs. The court may award applicable costs, including reasonable attorney's fees and expenses, against a party, or a party's counsel:

(1) At any time, if the court finds that any specific claim for relief or defense was asserted or any pleading, motion, request for discovery, or other action was made or taken in bad faith or without reasonable cause; or

(2) Upon final judgment, if the court finds, in light of all the evidence, and considering both the state and trend of the substantive law, that the action taken as a whole was brought, prosecuted, or defended in bad faith or in an unreasonable manner.

§ 7.05   Board or Committee Authority in Regard to a Derivative Action

(a) The board of a corporation in whose name or right a derivative action is brought has standing on behalf of the corporation to:

(1) Move to dismiss the action on account of the plaintiff's lack of standing under § 7.02 (Standing to Commence and Maintain a Derivative Action) or the plaintiff's failure to comply with § 7.03 (Exhaustion of Intracorporate Remedies: The Demand Rule) or § 7.04(a) or (b) (Pleading, Demand Rejection, Procedure, and Costs in a Derivative Action) or move for dismissal of the complaint or for summary judgment;

(2) Move for a stay of the action, including discovery, as provided by § 7.06 (Authority of Court to Stay a Derivative Action);

(3) Move to dismiss the action as contrary to the best interests of the corporation, as provided in §§ 7.07–7.12 (dismissal of a derivative action based on a motion requesting dismissal by the board, a board committee, the shareholders, or a special panel);

(4) Oppose injunctive or other relief materially affecting the corporation's interests;

(5) Adopt or pursue the action in the corporation's right;

(6) Comment on, object to, or recommend any proposed settlement, discontinuance, compromise, or voluntary dismissal by agreement between the plaintiff and any defendant under § 7.14 (Settlement of a Derivative Action by Agreement Between the Plaintiff and a Defendant), or any award of attorney's fees and other expenses under § 7.17 (Plaintiff's attorney's Fees and Expenses); and

(7) Seek to settle the action without agreement of the plaintiff under § 7.15 (Settlement of a Derivative Action Without the Agreement of the Plaintiff).

Except as provided above, the corporation may not otherwise defend the action in the place of, or raise defenses on behalf of, other defendants.

(b) The board of a corporation in whose name or right a derivative action is brought may:

(1) Delegate its authority to take any action specified in § 7.05(a) to a committee of directors; or

(2) Request the court to appoint a special panel in lieu of a committee of directors, or a special member of a committee, under § 7.12 (Special Panel or Special Committee Members).

§ 7.06 Authority of Court to Stay a Derivative Action

In the absence of special circumstances, the court should stay discovery and all further proceedings by the plaintiff in a derivative action on the motion of the corporation and upon such conditions as the court deems appropriate pending the court's determination of any motion made by the corporation under § 7.04(a)(2) and the completion within a reasonable period of any review and evaluation undertaken and diligently pursued pursuant to § 7.09 (Procedures for Requesting Dismissal of a Derivative Action). On the same basis the court may stay discovery and further proceedings pending (a) the resolution of a related action or (b) such other event or development as the interests of justice may require.

§ 7.07 Dismissal of a Derivative Action Based on a Motion Requesting Dismissal by the Board or a Committee: General Statement

(a) The court having jurisdiction over a derivative action should dismiss the action as against one or more of the defendants based on a motion by the board or a properly delegated committee requesting dismissal of the action as in the best interests of the corporation, if:

(1) In the case of an action against a person other than a director, senior executive, or person in control of the corporation, or an associate of any such person, the determinations of the board or committee underlying the motion satisfy the requirements of the business judgment rule as specified in § 4.01;

(2) In the case of an action against a director, senior executive, or person in control of the corporation, or an associate of any such person, the conditions specified in § 7.08 (Dismissal of a Derivative Action Against Directors, Senior Executives, Controlling Persons, or Associates

Based on a Motion Requesting Dismissal by the Board or a Committee) are satisfied; or

(3) In any case, the shareholders approve a resolution requesting dismissal of the action in the manner provided in § 7.11 (Dismissal of a Derivative Action Based Upon Action by the Shareholders).

(b) Regardless of whether a corporation chooses to proceed under § 7.08 or § 7.11, it is free to make any other motion available to it under the law, including a motion to dismiss the complaint or for summary judgment.

§ 7.08 Dismissal of a Derivative Action Against Directors, Senior Executives, Controlling Persons, or Associates Based on a Motion Requesting Dismissal by the Board or a Committee

The court should, subject to the provisions of § 7.10(b) (retention of significant improper benefit), dismiss a derivative action against a defendant who is a director, a senior executive, or a person in control of the corporation, or an associate of any such person, if:

(a) The board of directors or a properly delegated committee thereof (either in response to a demand or following commencement of the action) has determined that the action is contrary to the best interests of the corporation and has requested dismissal of the action;

(b) The procedures specified in § 7.09 (Procedures for Requesting Dismissal of a Derivative Action) for the conduct of a review and evaluation of the action were substantially complied with (either in response to a demand or following commencement of the action), or any material departures therefrom were justified under the circumstances; and

(c) The determinations of the board or committee satisfy the applicable standard of review set forth in § 7.10(a) (Standard of Judicial Review with Regard to a Board of Committee Motion Requesting Dismissal of a Derivative Action Under § 7.08).

§ 7.09 Procedures for Requesting Dismissal of a Derivative Action

(a) The following procedural standards should apply to the review and evaluation of a derivative action by the board or committee under § 7.08 (Dismissal of a Derivative Action Against Directors, Senior Executives, Controlling Persons, or Associates Based on a Motion Requesting Dismissal by the Board or a Committee) or § 7.11 (Dismissal of a Derivative Action Based Upon Action by the Shareholders):

(1) The board or a committee should be composed of two or more persons, no participating member of which was interested in the action, and should as a group be capable of objective judgment in the circumstances;

(2) The board or committee should be assisted by counsel of its choice and such other agents as it reasonably considers necessary;

(3) The determinations of the board or committee should be based upon a review and evaluation that was sufficiently informed to satisfy the standards applicable under § 7.10(a); and

(4) If the board or committee determines to request dismissal of the derivative action, it shall prepare and file with the court a report or other written submission setting forth its determinations in a manner sufficient to enable the court to conduct the review required under § 7.10 (Standard of Judicial Review with Regard to a Board or Committee Motion Requesting Dismissal of a Derivative Action Under § 7.08).

(b) If the court is unwilling to grant a motion to dismiss under § 7.08 or § 7.11 because the procedures followed by the board or committee departed materially from the standards specified in § 7.09(a), the court should permit the board or committee to supplement its procedures, and make such further reports or other written submissions, as will satisfy the standards specified in § 7.09(a), unless the court decides that (i) the board or committee did not act on the basis of a good faith belief that its procedures and report were justified in the circumstances; (ii) unreasonable delay or prejudice would result; or (iii) there is no reasonable prospect that such further steps would support dismissal of the action.

§ 7.10 Standard of Judicial Review with Regard to a Board or Committee Motion Requesting Dismissal of a Derivative Action Under § 7.08

(a) Standard of Review. In deciding whether an action should be dismissed under § 7.08 (Dismissal of a Derivative Action Against Directors, Senior Executives, Controlling Persons, or Associates Based on a Motion Requesting Dismissal by the Board or a Committee), the court should apply the following standards of review:

(1) If the gravamen of the claim is that the defendant violated a duty set forth in Part IV (Duty of Care and the Business Judgment Rule), other than by committing a knowing and culpable violation of law that is alleged with particularity, or if the underlying transaction or conduct would be reviewed under the business judgment rule under § 5.03, § 5.04, § 5.05, § 5.06, § 5.08, or § 6.02, the court should dismiss the claim unless it finds that the board's or committee's determinations fail to satisfy the requirements of the business judgment rule as specified in § 4.01(c).

(2) In other cases governed by Part V (Duty of Fair Dealing) or Part VI (Role of Directors and Shareholders in Transactions in Control and Tender Offers), or to which the business judgment rule is not applicable, including cases in which the gravamen of the claim is that defendant committed a knowing and culpable violation of law in breach of Part IV, the court should dismiss the action if the court finds, in light of the applicable standards under Part IV, V, or VI that the board or committee was adequately informed under the circumstances and reasonably determined that dismissal was in the best interests of the corporation, based on grounds that the court deems to warrant reliance.

(3) In cases arising under either Subsection (a)(1) or (a)(2), the court may substantively review and determine any issue of law.

(b) Retention of Significant Improper Benefit. The court shall not dismiss an action if the plaintiff establishes that dismissal would permit a defendant, or an associate, to retain a significant improper benefit where:

(1) The defendant, either alone or collectively with others who are also found to have received a significant improper benefit arising out of the same transaction, possesses control of the corporation; or

(2) Such benefit was obtained:

(A) As the result of a knowing and material misrepresentation or omission or other fraudulent act; or

(B) Without advance authorization or the requisite ratification of such benefit by disinterested directors (or, in the case of a nondirector senior executive, advance authorization by a disinterested superior), or authorization or ratification by disinterested shareholders, and in breach of § 5.02 (Transactions with the Corporation) or § 5.04 (Use by a Director or Senior Executive of Corporate Property, Material Non–Public Corporate Information, or Corporate Position); unless the court determines, in light of specific reasons advanced by the board or committee, that the likely injury to the corporation from continuation of the action convincingly outweighs any adverse impact on the public interest from dismissal of the action.

(c) Subsequent Developments. In determining whether the standards of § 7.10(a) are satisfied or whether § 7.10(b) or any of the exceptions set forth therein are applicable, the court may take into account considerations set forth by the board or committee (or otherwise brought to the court's attention) that reflect material developments subsequent to the time of the underlying transaction or conduct or to the time of the motion by the board or committee requesting dismissal.

§ 7.13 Judicial Procedures on Motions to Dismiss a Derivative Action Under § 7.08 or § 7.11

(a) Filing of Report or Other Written Submission. Upon a motion to dismiss an action under § 7.08 (Dismissal of a Derivative Action Against Directors, Senior Executives, Controlling Persons, or Associates Based on a Motion Requesting Dismissal by the Board or a Committee) or § 7.11 (Dismissal of a Derivative Action Based Upon Action by the Shareholders), the corporation shall file with the court a report or other written submission setting forth the procedures and determinations of the board or committee, or the resolution of the shareholders. A copy of the report or other written submission, including any supporting documentation filed by the corporation, shall be given to the plaintiff's counsel.

(b) Protective Order. The court may issue a protective order concerning such materials, where appropriate.

(c) Discovery. Subject to § 7.06 (Authority of Court to Stay a Derivative Action), if the plaintiff has demonstrated that a substantial issue exists whether the applicable standards of § 7.08, § 7.09, § 7.10, § 7.11, or § 7.12 have been satisfied and if the plaintiff is unable without undue hardship to obtain the information by other means, the court may order such limited discovery or limited evidentiary hearing, as to issues specified by the court, as the court finds to be (i) necessary to enable it to render a decision on the motion under the applicable standards of § 7.08, § 7.09, § 7.10, § 7.11, or § 7.12, and (ii) consistent with an expedited resolution of the motion. In the absence of special circumstances, the court should limit on a similar basis any discovery that is sought by the plaintiff in response to a motion for summary judgment by the corporation or any defendant to those facts likely to be in dispute. The results of any such discovery may be made subject to a protective order on the same basis as under § 7.13(b).

(d) Burdens of Proof. The plaintiff has the burden of proof in the case of a motion (1) under § 7.08 where the standard of judicial review is determined under § 7.10(a)(1) because the basis of the claim involves a breach of a duty set forth in Part IV (Duty of Care and the Business Judgment Rule) or because the underlying transaction would be reviewed under the business judgment rule, or (2) under § 7.07(a)(1) (suits against third parties and lesser corporate officials). The corporation has the burden of proof in the case of a motion under § 7.08 where the standard of judicial review is determined under § 7.10(a)(2) because the underlying transaction would be reviewed under a standard other than the business judgment rule, except that the plaintiff retains the burden of proof in all cases to show (i) that a defendant's conduct involved a knowing and culpable violation of law, (ii) that the board or committee as a group was not capable of objective judgment in the circumstances as required by § 7.09(a)(a), and (iii) that dismissal of the action would permit a defendant or an associate thereof to retain a significant improper benefit under § 7.10(b). The corporation shall also have the burden of proving under § 7.10(b) that the likely injury to the corporation from continuation of the action convincingly outweighs any adverse impact on the public interest from dismissal of the action. In the case of a motion under § 7.11 (Dismissal of a Derivative Action Based Upon Action by the Shareholders), the plaintiff has the burden of proof with respect to § 7.11(b), (c), and (d), and the corporation has the burden of proof with respect to § 7.11(a).

(e) Privilege. The plaintiff's counsel should be furnished a copy of related legal opinions received by the board or committee if any opinion is tendered to the court under § 7.13(a). Subject to that requirement, communications, both oral and written, between the board or committee and its counsel with respect to the subject matter of the action do not forfeit their privileged character, and documents, memoranda, or other material qualifying as attorney's work product do not become subject to discovery, on the grounds that the action is derivative or that the privilege was waived by the production to the plaintiff or the filing with the court of a report, other written submission, or supporting documents pursuant to § 7.13.

Notes

(1) The ALI's Principles of Corporate Governance is not a statute intended for adoption by individual states. Rather, it is a statement of "black letter" principles (several of which are quoted by the Court in its appendix) followed by a plain text explanation of the operation of the "black letter" principles. In this respect it is similar to the various Restatements with which all law students are familiar. Of the various sections quoted by the Court in *Cuker*, by far the most controversial is § 7.10, which was developed and approved only after exhaustive discussion and negotiation. This section was explained as "a mechanism for judicial review of the board's power to dismiss a derivative action [which] is necessary if fiduciary duties are to remain meaningful legal obligations." Com-

ment to § 7.10, The American Law Institute, Principles of Corporate Governance: Analysis and Recommendations.[93] However, much of the controversy arose because of the Reporters' plain text explanation of the operation of this section:

> At the other end of the spectrum from the [simple] due care case is the case involving a substantial duty of loyalty issue, such as one, for example, when a majority of the board personally benefited from the transaction and then expanded the board's size to appoint new directors to staff a litigation committee, which later recommended dismissal of the action. Here, close judicial scrutiny of the justifications offered for dismissal is obviously appropriate. Under *Zapata*, if a majority received a pecuniary benefit, the Delaware courts would excuse demand and permit the trial court to use its own "independent business judgment." Section 7.10 avoids the use of the potentially misleading phrase "independent business judgment." Rather, § 7.10 contemplates that heightened judicial scrutiny should be reserved for a limited number of instances and that, overall, the degree of judicial scrutiny should relate to the legal standards [applicable to the conduct in question]. Thus, for example, if * * * the transaction was one in which the burden of proving fairness remained on the director or senior executive, the reviewing court should be mindful that in this instance Part V invites close judicial scrutiny. Therefore, less deference to the justifications asserted for dismissal by the board or committee would be warranted.

> Put simply, the court should review the board's or committee's determinations in a manner that is consistent with the standards of review and burdens of proof established by [other parts of these principles]. This does not mean, however, that § 7.10 specifies a uniform standard of review for all duty of loyalty cases. The closest review will be in those cases in which the defendant has the burden of proving fairness. For example, such a standard would apply in the case of a corporate opportunity when the corporate rejection of the opportunity was not by a disinterested majority of the board, with the result that * * * the defendant must prove the fairness of the defendant's conduct. Conversely, if a disinterested board had earlier rejected the corporate opportunity after appropriate disclosure, then the board's decision is protected by the business judgment rule * * * and correspondingly a motion to dismiss is to be reviewed under the similar standard * * *. An intermediate case [occurs when] a self interested transaction is approved in advance by disinterested directors or a disinterested superior, the court should determine whether the directors or senior executive "could reasonably have concluded that the transaction was fair to the corporation," even when there has been full disclosure and disinterested approval. In such a case, the standard of review * * * should be less exacting than in a case in which the defendant is required to prove the fairness of the transaction, but more searching than in a case in which the business judgment rule is applicable. * * *

> * * * In some circumstances, disputed factual issues may make it necessary for the court to hold a limited evidentiary hearing, or to delay its decision for additional discovery, before it rules on the motion. However, the importance of an expedited decision should normally lead the court to constrain discovery * * * and seek an early resolution of the motion.

---

93. Copyright (1994) by The American Law Institute. Reprinted with the permission of   The American Law Institute.

This formulation was bitterly attacked, particularly by members who were familiar with the Delaware structure for resolving derivative litigation, as "departing dramatically from well settled principles" established in many cases and as accepting a "litigation model" of corporate governance. Michael Dooley & E. Norman Veasey, The Role of the Board in Derivative Litigation Delaware Law and the Current ALI Proposals Compared, 44 Bus. Law. 503 (1989); Dennis J. Block, et al., Derivative Litigation: Current Law Versus the American Law Institute, 48 Bus. Law. 1443 (1993). Every suggestion of even superficial judicial review of the merits of a litigation committee decision in the "demand required" context is systematically referred to by Dooley and Veasey as "judicially intrusive review." The Block article also accuses the reporters of seeking to undermine a compromise negotiated at an earlier plenary session of the Institute. Id. at 1470, 1474. For a spirited defense, see John C. Coffee, Jr., New Myths and Old Realities: The American Law Institute Faces the Derivative Action, 48 Bus. Law. 1407 (1993). See also Carol B. Swanson, Juggling Shareholder Rights and Strike Suits in Derivative Litigation: The ALI Drops the Ball, 77 Minn. L.Rev. 1339 (1993).

(2) The Committee on Corporate Laws created its own solution to the derivative litigation issue in 1989 when it approved Subchapter D of chapter 7 of the MBCA, §§ 7.40 et seq. The critical sections are § 7.42, relating to demand, and § 7.44 relating to the dismissal of derivative suits. The Official Comment to § 7.42 explains the demand requirement:[94]

> Section 7.42 requires a written demand on the corporation in all cases. The demand must be made at least 90 days before commencement of suit unless irreparable injury to the corporation would result. This approach has been adopted for two reasons. First, even though no director may be independent, the demand will give the board of directors the opportunity to reexamine the act complained of in the light of a potential lawsuit and take corrective action. Secondly, the provision eliminates the time and expense of the litigants and the court involved in litigating the question whether demand is required. * * *

The more critical and controversial section is § 7.44, dealing with the finality of committee and/or board of directors determinations. The Official Comment elaborates upon the language of § 7.44(a):[95]

> Section 7.44(a) requires that the determination be made by the appropriate persons in good faith after conducting a reasonable inquiry upon which their conclusions are based. The word "inquiry" rather than "investigation" has been used to make it clear that the scope of the inquiry will depend upon the issues raised and the knowledge of the group making the determination with respect to the issues. In some cases, the issues may be so simple or the knowledge of the group so extensive that little additional inquiry is required. In other cases, the group may need to engage counsel and other professionals to make an investigation and assist the group in its evaluation of the issues. * * *

As of 1998, eleven states are listed as having in substance adopted section 7.44 of Subchapter D.

(3) The Delaware litigation committee procedures are of course of central importance primarily because of the very large number of publicly held corpora-

94. Reprinted from *Model Business Corporation Act Annotated* with the permission of Prentice Hall Law & Business.

95. Reprinted from *Model Business Corporation Act Annotated* with the permission of Prentice Hall Law & Business.

tions incorporated in that state. The two alternative solutions—one put forth by the ALI, the other by the Committee on Corporate Laws—also deal with the core issue whether a court should simply defer to the business judgment of a litigation committee or board of directors, without more, or whether it should make some kind of substantive review of the apparent merits of that decision. Several state courts have had an opportunity to consider this aspect of the litigation committee device in the absence of statute with mixed results.

(a) A number of states appear to give the committee decision at least the same degree of deference that it is given in Delaware. Dennis J. Block et al., Derivative Litigation: Current Law Versus The American Law Institute, 48 Bus. Law. 1443, 1443–44, 1447 (1993) states that since 1984, "the courts both in and out of Delaware have ruled with near unanimity" that the business judgment rule is the appropriate standard of judicial review.

(b) Basically accepting the "structural bias" argument, the Court in Miller v. Register & Tribune Syndicate, Inc., 336 N.W.2d 709 (Iowa 1983), held that the board of directors was unable to delegate the power to bind the corporation to an independent litigation committee if the board of directors was itself unable to act because a majority was interested in the transaction; the Court suggested that a committee might be appointed by judicial order in this situation.

(c) In Alford v. Shaw, 318 N.C. 289, 349 S.E.2d 41 (1986), the North Carolina Supreme Court uncritically adopted the *Gall* approach in a case involving charges of fraud and self-dealing by a majority of the board of directors; defendant directors participated in the selection of new directors to serve as the special litigation committee. See Deborah DeMott, The Corporate Fox and the Shareholders' Hen House: Reflections on Alford v. Shaw, 65 N.C.L.Rev. 569 (1987). The North Carolina Court then granted a petition for rehearing, and significantly modified—indeed, virtually rejected the underlying premises of—its earlier opinion. 320 N.C. 465, 358 S.E.2d 323 (1987).

(d) In Houle v. Low, 407 Mass. 810, 824, 556 N.E.2d 51, 59 (1990), the Court states that a reviewing court should determine whether the committee (i) was independent and disinterested and (ii) "reached a reasonable and principled decision." Lewis v. Boyd, 838 S.W.2d 215, 224 (Tenn.App.1992), adopts the same test.

(e) Michigan amended its corporation statute in 1989 to authorize a court to appoint one or more "disinterested persons" at the request of the corporation to make findings with respect to a derivative suit. Mich. B.C.A. § 450.1495(1). See Joel Seligman, The Disinterested Person: An Alternative Approach to Shareholder Derivative Litigation, 55 Law & Contemp. Probs. 357 (Autumn 1992). If the determination is made by incumbent directors, the burden shifts to the corporation to establish that the determination was made in good faith and the investigation was reasonable unless all independent disinterested directors agree with the determination.

(f) North Carolina has a similar statute, which provides that upon motion by the corporation, a court may appoint a committee composed of two or more disinterested directors or other disinterested persons acceptable to the corporation; after considering the report and other relevant evidence, "the Court shall determine whether the proceeding should be continued or not." N.C. Bus. Corp. Act § 55–7–40(c). See also MBCA § 7.44(f).

(g) In PSE & G Shareholder Litigation, 173 N.J. 258, 801 A.2d 295 (2002) the New Jersey Supreme Court decided not to follow Delaware or the Model Act.

Instead, it created its own, specialized jurisprudence, despite its admitted lack of experience in dealing with these issues. First, like the North Carolina Court in Alford v. Shaw discussed above, the New Jersey Court held that it would apply a single standard of review in both demand-made and demand-excused cases. The court announced that it would apply a modified business judgment rule that imposes an initial burden on the corporation to demonstrate that in deciding to reject or terminate a shareholder's suit the members of the board: (1) were independent and disinterested, (2) acted in good faith and with due care in their investigation of the shareholders' allegations, and that (3) the board's decision was reasonable. The court also noted that shareholders must be given access to corporate documents and other discovery limited to the narrow issue of what steps the directors took to inform themselves of the shareholder demand and the reasonableness of its decision. 801 A.2d at 312.

(4) Most of the concern about derivative suits, litigation committees and the like relate to publicly held corporations. The elaborate procedures of the ALI Principles of Corporate Governance are not suitable for closely held corporations with relatively few shareholders. Section 7.01(d) of the Principles sets forth a simple and practical solution for derivative litigation within such corporations:

> In the case of a closely held corporation, the court in its discretion may treat an action raising derivative claims as a direct action, exempt it from those restrictions and defenses applicable only to derivative actions, and order an individual recovery, if it finds that to do so will not (i) unfairly expose the corporation or the defendants to a multiplicity of actions, (ii) materially prejudice the interests of creditors of the corporation, or (iii) interfere with a fair distribution of the recovery among all interested persons.

For a case adopting this approach, see Barth v. Barth, 659 N.E.2d 559, 562–63 (Ind.1995).

(5) Since 1996, several other states—Arkansas, Connecticut, Indiana, Minnesota, North Carolina, Oregon, Pennsylvania, Utah, and Virginia , among others— have cited § 7.01 of the Principles in connection with disputes within closely held corporations.

Chapter Twelve

DUTY OF LOYALTY AND CONFLICT OF INTEREST

A. SELF–DEALING

MARCIANO v. NAKASH

Supreme Court of Delaware, 1987.
535 A.2d 400.

Before Horsey, Moore and Walsh, JJ.

Walsh, Justice.

This is an appeal from a decision of the Court of Chancery which validated a claim in liquidation of Gasoline, Ltd. ("Gasoline"), a Delaware corporation, placed in custodial status pursuant to 8 *Del.C.* § 226 by reason of a deadlock among its board of directors. Fifty percent of Gasoline is owned by Ari, Joe, and Ralph Nakash (the "Nakashes") and fifty percent by Georges, Maurice, Armand and Paul Marciano (the "Marcianos"). The Vice Chancellor ruled that $2.5 million in loans made by the Nakashes faction to Gasoline were valid and enforceable debts of the corporation, notwithstanding their origin in self-dealing transactions. The Marcianos argue that the disputed debt is voidable as a matter of law but, in any event, the Nakashes failed to meet their burden of establishing full fairness. We conclude that the Vice Chancellor applied the proper standard for review of self-dealing transactions and the finding of full fairness is supported by the record. Accordingly, we affirm. * * *

The parties agree that the loans made by the Nakashes to Gasoline were interested transactions. The Nakashes as officers of Gasoline executed the various documents which supported the loans and at the same time guaranteed those loans extended through their wholly owned entities. It is also not disputed that, given the control deadlock, the questioned transactions did not receive majority approval of Gasoline's directors or shareholders. The Marcianos argue that the loan transaction is voidable at the option of the corporation notwithstanding its fairness or the good faith of its participants. A review of this contention, rejected by the Court of Chancery, requires analysis of the concept of director self-dealing under Delaware law.

It is a long-established principle of Delaware corporate law that the fiduciary relationship between directors and the corporation imposes fundamental limitations on the extent to which a director may benefit from dealings with the corporation he serves. *Guth v. Loft, Inc.,* Del.Supr., 5 A.2d 503 (1939). Thus, the "voting [for] and taking" of compensation may be deemed "constructively fraudulent" in the absence of shareholder ratification, or statutory or bylaw authorization. *Cahall v. Lofland,* Del.Ch., 114 A. 224, 232 (1921). Perhaps the strongest condemnation of interested director conduct appears in *Potter v. Sanitary Co. of America,* Del.Ch., 194 A. 87 (1937), a decision which the Marcianos advance as definitive of the rule of per se voidability. In *Potter* the Court of Chancery characterized transactions between corporations having common directors and officers "constructively fraudulent," absent shareholder ratification.

Support can also be found for the per se rule of voidability in this Court's decision in *Kerbs v. California Eastern Airways Inc.,* Del.Supr., 90 A.2d 652 (1952). The *Kerbs* court, in considering the validity of a profit sharing plan, ruled that the self-interest of the directors who voted on the plan caused the transaction to be voidable. The court concluded that the profit sharing plan was voidable based on the common law rule that the vote of an interested director will not be counted in determining whether the challenged action received the affirmative vote of a majority of the board of directors. *Id.* at 658 (*citing Bovay v. H.M. Byllesby & Co.,* Del.Supr., 38 A.2d 808 (1944)).

The principle of per se voidability for interested transactions, which is sometimes characterized as the common law rule, was significantly ameliorated by the 1967 enactment of Section 144 of the Delaware General Corporation Law.[1] The Marcianos argue that section 144(a) provides the only basis for immunizing self-interested transactions and since none of the statute's component tests are satisfied the stricture of the common law per se rule applies. The Vice Chancellor agreed that the disputed loans did not withstand a section 144(a) analysis but ruled that the common law rule did not invalidate transactions determined to be intrinsically fair. We agree that section 144(a) does not provide the only validation standard for interested transactions.

It overstates the common law rule to conclude that relationship, alone, is the controlling factor in interested transactions. Although the application of the per se voidability rule in early Delaware cases resulted in the invalidation of interested transactions, the result was not dictated simply by a tainted relationship. Thus in *Potter,* the Court, while adopting the rule of voidability, emphasized that interested transactions should be subject to close scrutiny. Where the undisputed evidence tended to show that the transaction would advance the personal interests of the directors at the expense of stockholders, the stockholders, upon discovery, are entitled to disavow the transaction.

Further, the court examined the motives of the defendant directors and the effect the transaction had on the corporation and its shareholders.

In other Delaware cases, decided before the enactment of section 144, interested director transactions were deemed voidable only after an examination of the fairness of a particular transaction *vis-a-vis* the nonparticipating shareholders and a determination of whether the disputed conduct received the approval of a noninterested majority of directors or shareholders. *Keenan*

---

1. [By the Editors] Section 144 of Title 8 *Del.C.* is set forth in footnote 77, p. 721 supra.

v. Eshleman, Del.Supr., 2 A.2d 904, 908 (1938); *Blish v. Thompson Automatic Arms Corp.,* Del.Supr., 64 A.2d 581, 602 (1948). The latter test is now crystallized in the ratification criteria of section 144(a), although the nonquorum restriction of *Kerbs* has been superseded by the language of subparagraph (b) of section 144.

The Marcianos view compliance with section 144 as the sole basis for avoiding the per se rule of voidability. The Court of Chancery rejected this contention and we agree that it is not consonant with Delaware corporate law. This Court in *Fliegler v. Lawrence,* Del.Supr., 361 A.2d 218 (1976), a postsection 144 decision, refused to view section 144 as either completely preemptive of the common law duty of director fidelity or as constituting a grant of broad immunity. As we stated in *Fliegler:* "It merely removes an 'interested director' cloud when its terms are met and provides against invalidation of an agreement 'solely' because such a director or officer is involved." *Id.* at 222. In *Fliegler* this Court applied a two-tiered analysis: application of section 144 coupled with an intrinsic fairness test.

If section 144 validation of interested director transactions is not deemed exclusive, as *Fliegler* clearly holds, the continued viability of the intrinsic fairness test is mandated not only by fact situations, such as here present, where shareholder deadlock prevents ratification but also where shareholder control by interested directors precludes independent review. Indeed, if an independent committee of the board, contemplated by section 144(a)(1) is unavailable, the sole forum for demonstrating intrinsic fairness may be a judicial one. In such situations the intrinsic fairness test furnishes the substantive standard against which the evidential burden of the interested directors is applied. * * *

This case illustrates the limitation inherent in viewing section 144 as the touchstone for testing interested director transactions. Because of the shareholder deadlock, even if the Nakashes had attempted to invoke section 144, it was realistically unavailable. The ratification process contemplated by section 144 presupposes the functioning of corporate constituencies capable of providing assents. Just as the statute cannot "sanction unfairness" neither can it invalidate fairness if, upon judicial review, the transaction withstands close scrutiny of its intrinsic elements.[2]

[The Marcianos claimed that the Nakashes had not proved that the costs of the loans were fair to the corporation and also that some of the proceeds of the loans had been used to pay invoices from companies controlled by the Nakashes. The Court held, however, that the Chancellor's conclusion that the terms of the loans met the "intrinsic fairness standard" was supported by the record and was the product of a logical deductive process. The Court conclud-

---

2. [By the Court] Although in this case none of the curative steps afforded under section 144(a) were available because of the director-shareholder deadlock, a non-disclosing director seeking to remove the cloud of interestedness would appear to have the same burden under section 144(a)(3), as under prior case law, of proving the intrinsic fairness of a questioned transaction which had been approved or ratified by the directors or share-holders. Folk, *The Delaware General Corp. Law: A Commentary and Analysis,* 86 (1972). On the other hand, approval by fully-informed disinterested directors under section 144(a)(1), or disinterested stockholders under section 144(a)(2), permits invocation of the business judgment rule and limits judicial review to issues of gift or waste with the burden of proof upon the party attacking the transaction.

ed that the possible misuse of the proceeds of the loans should be litigated in a derivative proceeding brought by the Marcianos which was then pending.]

We hold, therefore, that the Court of Chancery properly applied the intrinsic fairness test in determining the validity of the interested director transactions and its finding of full fairness is clearly supported by the record. Accordingly, the decision is Affirmed.

Notes

(1) Consider the general problem of a director who enters into a business transaction with the corporation—for example, the purchase of property from, or the sale of property to, the corporation. Such transactions can take many forms but they have one element in common. There is an obvious risk that the transaction will be skewed in favor of the director and as a result will be harmful to the corporation. Such a risk, of course, is increased if the interested director owns sufficient shares so that he or she can elect or remove a majority of the directors. What position should the law take with respect to such transactions? The position taken during the last part of the nineteenth century was that all such transactions were voidable at the instance of the corporation or its shareholders without regard to the fairness or unfairness of the transaction. This absolute position now appears to be totally rejected, in part because it is clear that many such transactions are beneficial to the corporation and are entered into by the director to assist rather than to harm the corporation.

(2) The problem with self dealing transactions is deciding what tests should be applied to sort out the harmful transaction from the harmless or desirable one. Several possible tests have received some degree of modern judicial approval in the absence of statute:

(a) Such a transaction is voidable if it is not approved or ratified by a disinterested majority of the directors or by the shareholders without regard to its fairness;

(b) Such a transaction is *not* voidable if the interested director can show that the transaction is fair to the corporation;

(c) Such a transaction is voidable if the plaintiff shows that the transaction is unfair to the corporation;

(d) Such a transaction is voidable only if the plaintiff shows that the transaction constitutes fraud, waste, or serious overreaching;

(e) Such a transaction is *not* voidable if it has been approved or ratified by a disinterested majority of the directors, and no further inquiry need be made into its fairness;

(f) Such a transaction is *not* voidable if it has been approved or ratified by a majority of the disinterested shareholders and no further inquiry need be made into its fairness;

(g) Such a transaction is always voidable if the vote of the interested director is necessary to approve the transaction or his presence is necessary to form a quorum;

(h) Such a transaction is always voidable if the interested director participates in the decision-making process, urging approval of the transaction, but does not vote.

Thought will reveal that these alternatives (and there may be others not mentioned) are not mutually exclusive, since some relate to the *procedures* by which the transaction was approved while others (particularly (b), (c), and (d)) relate to the *substance*—the effect of the transaction on the corporation—and it is possible to combine them. For example, one might establish a rule that such a transaction is voidable if it is unfair (alternative (c)) or constitutes waste (alternative (d)) but the disinterested shareholders may ratify the transaction (alternative (f)). Would that rule be desirable? Or, one might establish the rule that a transaction that is voidable under alternative (a) may be made not voidable if the director can establish fairness (alternative (b)). Would that rule be desirable? Of course, at the extreme, there probably is no reason to consider setting aside a transaction approved by *all* the shareholders, no matter how damaging to the corporation, though one can imagine situations involving injury to creditors or senior interests.

(3) While many transactions between directors and their corporation have been held to be valid in the absence of a controlling statute, considerable confusion exists in the case law as to the circumstances which may validate such transactions. If one examines the results of cases (as contrasted with statements in the opinions), the following comments accurately reflect most of the decisions:

(a) If the Court feels the transaction to be fair to the corporation, it will be upheld;

(b) If the Court feels that the transaction involves fraud, undue over-reaching or waste of corporate assets (e.g., a director using corporate assets for personal purposes without paying for them), the transaction will be set aside; and

(c) If the Court feels that the transaction does not involve fraud, undue overreaching or waste of corporate assets, but is not convinced that the transaction is fair, the transaction will be upheld only where the interested director can convincingly show that the transaction was approved (or ratified) by a truly disinterested majority of the board of directors without participation by the interested director or by a majority of the disinterested shareholders, after full disclosure of all relevant facts.

(4) Perhaps the most famous example of director approval of a conflict of interest transaction was the approval by the Enron Corporation's board of directors of transactions between Enron and a variety of partnerships and other special purpose entities (SPEs) controlled by Andrew Fastow, Enron's Chief Financial Officer. Enron is an Oregon corporation, and Oregon has a statutory provision, ORS § 60.361 (2002), similar to Delaware GCL § 144. Even if the directors are shown to have been disinterested, if they were not fully informed, then they will have the difficult burden of showing that transactions in which Enron purchased significant assets from these entities at very high prices were fair to Enron.

(5) Today, the treatment of conflict of interest transactions is largely controlled by statute. Virtually all states have statutes dealing with such transactions. Most of these statutes are similar in structure to Del. GCL § 144 though there are significant variations in language. Most of these statutes were enacted after 1975 and there is little or no case law under them.

(6) In December 1988, the Committee on Corporate Laws approved a new treatment of conflict-of-interest transactions, now codified as §§ 8.60–8.63 of the MBCA. The new subchapter F, as it is usually called, is a much more ambitious undertaking than earlier conflict-of-interest statutes or § 8.31. This new treat-

ment of conflict-of-interest transactions has not been widely adopted: As of January 1, 1999, 12 states had adopted all, or significant portions of Subchapter F. A further reconsideration of Subchapter F by the Committee on Corporate Laws is likely.

(7) Subchapter F is structured similarly to § 8.31: a conflict of interest transaction is not voidable by the corporation if (a) it has been approved by disinterested directors or shareholders, or (b) the interested director establishes the fairness of the transaction. Unlike § 8.31, however, subchapter F is designed to create a series of "bright line" principles that increase predictability and enhance practical administrability.

(8) Abstractly, self-dealing transactions have two attributes that make a substantial degree of judicial oversight desirable: (1) they are voluntary transactions on the part of the self-dealing director and (2) they provide an opportunity for direct pecuniary enrichment at the expense of the corporation by the self-dealing director. Indeed, most commentary on directors' duties recognizes that breaches of the duty of loyalty raise serious problems that merit continuing judicial scrutiny. For example, in Kenneth E. Scott, Corporation Law and the American Law Institute Corporate Governance Project, 35 Stan.L.Rev. 927 (1983), the author urged (long before the Trans Union case) that liability for violations of the duty of care should be entirely eliminated but that judicial vigilance over violations of the duty of loyalty should be vigorously encouraged. Does subchapter F go against the grain of this analysis by withdrawing (or appearing to withdraw) all judicial scrutiny from conflict of interest cases, relying instead on the vote of "qualified directors" to protect the corporation and minority shareholders against overreaching transactions?

(9) Frank Easterbrook and Daniel Fischel have argued that there is no clear distinction between the duty of care and the duty of loyalty. Both duties are supposed to reduced agency costs. It is, therefore, difficult to understand why the legal treatment of violations of the duty of care is more deferential than the treatment of violations of the duty of loyalty. Easterbrook and Fischel attribute the difference in part to the fact that duty of loyalty problems often involve one-shot, large-scale appropriations of corporate funds in which subsequent market penalties are inadequate. In such cases the duty of loyalty supplements market penalties. But this analysis fails to consider that many duty of loyalty cases like *Marciano* do not involve spectacular, one-shot appropriations. Duty of loyalty problems are likely to arise in the context of common situations such as determining executive compensation where the executives are also directors. In addition, duty of care cases sometimes involve one-shot appropriations of enormous sums of money. For a prime example see the excerpts from *Brehm v. Eisner infra*. While it may be the case that markets do not provide adequate remedies for violations of the duty of loyalty, they do not provide remedies for many duty of care problems, such as managerial inattention or laziness. What other explanations could account for the differing treatment of duty of loyalty and duty of care violations?

(10) The Sarbanes–Oxley Act, passed in response to Enron and the other corporate scandals, contains a special provision entitled "Enhanced Conflict of Interest Provisions" that imposes new prohibitions on personal loans to corporate executives. The provision, section 402 of Sarbanes–Oxley, makes it unlawful for any public company to extend credit or to arrange for the extension of credit in the form of a personal loan to any director, or executive officer of the company. There are a variety of narrow exceptions for such things as extensions of credit associated with the use of credit cards (presumably to permit corporate entertain-

ment to continue unabated), and loans that are part of the ordinary business of the issuer, and made on terms no more favorable than those offered to the public.

(11) What about the status of indemnification agreements for corporate officers under section 402 of Sarbanes–Oxley? In one sense an indemnification agreement is like a personal extension of credit prohibited under section 402. But advances for legal fees incurred in the service of the corporation are not like the misappropriated personal loans which section 402 sought to prohibit. The SEC and the courts have yet to give clear guidance on this point.

HELLER v. BOYLAN

Supreme Court of New York, 1941.
29 N.Y.S.2d 653.

[Editors: Only the portions of this opinion dealing with the incentive compensation plan are included.]

COLLINS, JUSTICE.

In this derivative action 7 out of a total of 62,000 stockholders—holding under 1,000 out of a total of 5,074,076 shares—of the American Tobacco Company, seek recovery for the corporation from the Company's directors for alleged improper payments to certain of the Company's officers.

The suit derives from an incentive compensation by-law of the Company, known as Article XII, virtually unanimously adopted by the stockholders in March, 1912. Thereunder 10 percent of the annual profits over the earnings of the corresponding properties in 1910 are to be distributed, 2 1/2 percent to the president and 1 1/2 percent to each of the five vice-presidents "in addition to the fixed salary of each of said officers."

The profits, and consequently the bonuses, undulated with the years; but at all times they were quite lush. By virtue of this by-law, the officers have received from and including 1929 to and including 1939—in addition to $3,784,999.69 in salaries—bonuses aggregating $11,672,920.27, or total compensation during that eleven-year period of $15,457,919.69. The president alone, George W. Hill, Sr., received $592,370 in 1929; $1,010,508 in 1930; $1,051,570 in 1931; $825,537.49 in 1932. The other payments to him during such period were obese, the thinnest being $137,042.65, in 1938, and the average around $400,000. The other officers likewise received handsome compensation though not as huge.

The plaintiffs maintain that these large bonus payments bore no relation to the value of the services for which they were given, that, consequently, they were in reality a gift in part, and that the majority stockholders committed waste and spoliation in thus giving away corporate property against the protest of the minority. Rogers v. Hill, 289 U.S. 582, 590–592, 53 S.Ct. 731, 77 L.Ed. 1385, 88 A.L.R. 744.

The validity of the by-law is not challenged. Indeed, its legality has been sustained. Rogers v. Hill, supra. Nor do plaintiffs impugn the principle of incentive compensation. Rather, they regard it "a legitimate means of accomplishing a desired result," and do not question "that the extra effort, spurred by the promise of extra compensation, may have been an important factor in the prosperity of the Company." That the Company has been singularly prosperous is indubitable. Its growth has been prodigious, its record for earnings is an enviable one, the management has been extraordinarily efficient, and the stockholders, as well as the officers, have been the beneficiaries of this immensely capable organization. The Company has made money even in direful times. Its capital investment is $265,000,000. It produces more than 200,000,000 cigarettes a day. In 1939 the Company's sales amounted to $262,416,000, its most popular brand—"Lucky Strike"—yielding $218,542,749. The Company is one of the world's giant industrial enterprises. Its activities are farflung, if not worldwide. Nevertheless, charge the plaintiffs, the payments to the officers have become "so large as in substance and effect to amount to spoliation or waste of corporate property." Rogers v. Hill, supra.

This is not the first time some of these payments have been attacked. An earlier assault was made by another stockholder, Richard Reid Rogers, and from that litigation stems several of the issues involved in the present suit. It is the principle evoked by the Rogers case which mainly supplies the pattern for this one. * * *

[In] Rogers v. Hill, 289 U.S. 582, 53 S.Ct. 731, 735, 77 L.Ed. 1385, 88 A.L.R. 744, Butler, J., for the unanimous Court, enunciated the principle * * * thus:

It follows from what has been shown that when adopted the by-law was valid. But plaintiff alleges that the measure of compensation fixed by it is not now equitable or fair. And he prays that the court fix and determine the fair and reasonable compensation of the individual defendants, respectively, for each of the years in question. The allegations of the complaint are not sufficient to permit consideration by the court of the validity or reasonableness of any of the payments on account of fixed salaries or of special credits or of the allotments of stock therein mentioned. Indeed, plaintiff alleges that other proceedings have been instituted for the restoration of special credits, and his suits to invalidate the stock allotments were recently considered here. Rogers v. Guaranty Trust Co., 288 U.S. 123, 53 S.Ct. 295, 77 L.Ed. 652 [89 A.L.R. 720]. The only payments that plaintiff by this suit seeks to have restored to the company are the payments made to the individual defendants under the by-law.

We come to consider whether these amounts are subject to examination and revision in the District Court. As the amounts payable depend upon the gains of the business, the specified percentages are not per se unreasonable. The by-law was adopted in 1912 by an almost unanimous vote of the shares represented at the annual meeting and presumably the stockholders supporting the measure acted in good faith and according to their best judgment. The tabular statement in the margin shows the payments to individual defendants under the by-law. Plaintiff does not complain of any made prior to 1921. Regard is to be had to the enormous increase of the company's profits in recent years. The 2 1/2 percent yielded President Hill $447,870.30 in 1929 and $842,507.72 in 1930. The 1 1/2 percent yielded to each of the vice presidents, Neiley and Riggio, $115,141.86 in 1929 and $409,495.25 in 1930 and for these years payments under the by-law were in addition to the cash credits and fixed salaries shown in the statement.

While the amounts produced by the application of the prescribed percentages give rise to no inference of actual or constructive fraud, the payments under the by-law have by reason of increase of profits become so large as to warrant investigation in equity in the interest of the company. Much weight is to be given to the action of the stockholders, and the by-law is supported by the presumption of regularity and continuity. But the rule prescribed by it cannot, against the protest of a shareholder, be used to justify payments of sums as salaries so large as in substance and effect to amount to spoliation or waste of corporate property. The dissenting opinion of Judge Swan indicates the applicable rule: 'If a bonus payment has no relation to the value of services for which it is given, it is in reality a gift in part, and the majority stockholders have no power to give away corporate property against the protest of the minority.' 60 F.2d 109, 113. The facts alleged by plaintiff are sufficient to require that the District Court, upon a consideration of all the relevant facts brought forward by the parties, determine whether and to what extent payments to the individual defendants under the by-laws constitute misuse and waste of the money of the corporation [citing cases].

Following Rogers' victory in the Supreme Court, and before the "investigation in equity" was launched, negotiations for adjustment were started. These eventuated in a settlement, from which the Company benefited—at the time of the settlement in July, 1933—by $6,200,000 and a further saving of about $2,250,000 by March, 1940. Many more millions were saved—inasmuch as the settlement reduced the bonus base and the employee's stock subscription plan was revised. In addition, Rogers was paid a fee of $525,000, the net being $263,000, and the income tax thereon exhausting the remaining $262,000. Thus ended the Rogers campaign.

But the echoes therefrom persisted. Seven stockholders, including three of the plaintiffs in this action (Heller, Wile and Mandelkor), and represented by most of the attorneys who appear for the plaintiffs here, assailed the settlement and sought to have it cancelled on the ground that the huge fee to Rogers was in the nature of a bribe. * * *

The Perplexities of the Case

Quite obviously, this case carries a number of perplexities. A few of them will be noted:

1. The general reluctance of the Courts to interfere with the internal management of a corporation. Pragmatism by the Courts—interference or meddling with free and lawful enterprise honestly conducted—is repugnant to our concept of government. Of course the hesitancy is overcome if fraud or bad faith or over—reaching appears—if the fiduciaries have been faithless to their trust.

2. Though this is a derivative stockholders' action, only 7 out of 62,000 stockholders have joined the onslaught; these 7 holding less than 1,000 out of a total of 5,074,076 shares of the Company. This factor, though significant, bears only on the equities; it is by no means decisive. Tyranny over the minority by the majority is abhorrent and will not be tolerated. The majority cannot, save by due legal process, make that which is illegal, legal, nor can it confiscate the company's assets or dispense them as unearned bounties. Majority rule does not license subjugation or immunize spoliation. The

possession of power does not authorize or excuse its abuse. Power is not a franchise to do wrong. The majority cannot any more than the minority violate the law with impunity.

3.   This case differs from most stockholders suits in that in those cases it is the conduct of directors which forms the basis of the complaint, whereas here not only is the by-law a creature of the stockholders, but on at least two other occasions, one in April, 1933, and again in April, 1940, the stockholders, by almost unanimous vote, ratified many of the payments involved in this suit. To be sure, "the majority stockholders have no power to give away corporate property against the protest of the minority." Rogers v. Hill, supra [60 F.2d 114].

4.   The fact that the by-law has been in existence since 1912 and has been held valid.

5.   The embarrassment which some of the defendants might experience in refunding even a part of what they received, especially since taxes were paid thereon.

6.   The language of finality contained in paragraph 4 of the by-law.[3]

7.   The paucity of apposite precedents.

Let it be emphasized, however, that the above are alluded to only as difficulties; they enter into the equities, but do not constitute a bar. * * *

Now, even a high-bracketer would deem [the stipends involved in this case] munificent. To the person of moderate income they would be princely— perhaps as something unattainable; to the wage-earner ekeing out an existence, they would be fabulous, and the unemployed might regard them as fantastic, if not criminal. To others they would seem immoral, inexcusably unequal, and an indictment of our economic system. The opinion of Judge Swan has been unfairly paraphrased as announcing that "no man can be worth $1,000,000 a year". But see George T. Washington, of the Cornell Law School, The Corporation Executive's living wage, Harvard Law Review, March, 1941, Vol. LIV. 759. Many economists advocate a ceiling for compensation.

At the stockholders meeting on April 3, 1941, a holder of 80 shares of common stock—who thought the compensation grandiose—offered a resolution to restrict the president's bonus to a maximum of $100,000 and to impose other limitations. But the resolution was defeated by 2,193,418 votes to 74,571. Harvard Law Review, supra 747.

Let it be boldly marked that the particular business before this Court is not the revamping of the social or economic order—*justiciable* disputes confront it. * * *

Here, the plaintiffs proffered no testimony whatever in support of their charge of waste. The figures, they reason, speak for themselves, and the

---

3. [By the Editors] Paragraph 4 reads as follows:

The declaration of the Treasurer as to the amount of net profits for the year and the sum due anyone hereunder shall be binding and conclusive on all parties, and no one claiming hereunder shall have the right to question the said declaration, or to any examination of the books or accounts of the Company, and nothing herein contained shall give any incumbent of any office any right to claim to continue therein, or any other right except as herein specifically expressed.

defendants must justify them. The figures do speak, but just what do they say as a matter of equity? They are immense, staggeringly so. Even so, is that enough to compel the substitution of the Court's judgment for that of the stockholders? Larger compensation has been judicially approved. * * *

Assuming, arguendo, that the compensation should be revised, what yardstick is to be employed? Who or what is to supply the measuring-rod? The conscience of equity? Equity is but another name for human being temporarily judicially robed. He is not omnipotent or omniscient. Can equity be so arrogant as to hold that it knows more about managing this corporation than its stockholders?

Yes, the Court possesses the *power* to prune these payments, but openness forces the confession that the pruning would be synthetic and artificial rather than analytic or scientific. Whether or not it would be fair and just, is highly dubious. Yet, merely because the problem is perplexing is no reason for eschewing it. It is not timidity, however, which perturbs me. It is finding a rational or just gauge for revising these figures were I inclined to do so. No blueprints are furnished. The elements to be weighed are incalculable; the imponderables, manifold. To act out of whimsy or caprice or arbitrariness would be more than inexact—it would be the precise antithesis of justice; it would be a farce.

If comparisons are to be made, with whose compensation are they to be made—executives? Those connected with the motion picture industry? Radio artists? Justices of the Supreme Court of the United States? The President of the United States? Manifestly, the material at hand is not of adequate plasticity for fashioning into a pattern or standard. Many instances of positive underpayment will come to mind, just as instances of apparent rank overpayment abound. Haplessly, intrinsic worth is not always the criterion. A classic might perhaps produce trifling compensation for its author, whereas a popular novel might yield a titanic fortune. Merit is not always commensurately rewarded, whilst mediocrity sometimes unjustly brings incredibly lavish returns. Nothing is so divergent and contentious and inexplicable as values.

Courts are ill-equipped to solve or even to grapple with these entangled economic problems. Indeed, their solution is not within the juridical province. Courts are concerned that corporations be honestly and fairly operated by its directors, with the observance of the formal requirements of the law; but what is reasonable compensation for its officers is primarily for the stockholders. This does not mean that fiduciaries are to commit waste, or misuse or abuse trust property, with impunity. A just cause will find the Courts at guard and implemented to grant redress. But the stockholder must project a less amorphous plaint than is here presented.

On this branch of the case, I find for the defendants. Yet it does not follow that I affirmatively approve these huge payments. It means that I cannot by any reliable standard find them to be waste or spoliation; it means that I find no valid ground for disapproving what the great majority of stockholders have approved. In the circumstances, if a ceiling for these bonuses is to be erected, the stockholders who built and are responsible for the present structure must be the architects. Finally, it is not amiss to accent the antiseptic policy stressed by Judge Liebell in Winkelman et al. v. General Motors Corporation, D.C.S.D.N.Y. decided August 14, 1940, 39 F.Supp. 826, that: "The duty of the director executives participating in the bonus seems plain—they should be the first to consider unselfishly whether under all the circumstances their bonus allowances are fair and reasonable".

BREHM v. EISNER

Supreme Court of Delaware, 2000.
746 A.2d 244.

VEASEY, CHIEF JUSTICE. [In this shareholder derivative action, the Court of Chancery dismissed Plaintiffs' Complaint which stated that Defendants, the Board of Directors, had breached its fiduciary duty. This court affirms the decision as set forth in the following opinion.]

The claims before us are that: (a) the board of directors of The Walt Disney Company ("Disney") as it was constituted in 1995 (the "Old Board") breached its fiduciary duty in approving an extravagant and wasteful Employment Agreement of Michael S. Ovitz as president of Disney; (b) the Disney board of directors as it was constituted in 1996 (the "New Board") breached its fiduciary duty in agreeing to a non-fault termination of the Ovitz Employment Agreement, a decision that was extravagant and wasteful; and (c) the directors were not disinterested and independent.

This is potentially a very troubling case on the merits. On the one hand, it appears from the Complaint that: (a) the compensation and termination payout for Ovitz were exceedingly lucrative, if not luxurious, compared to Ovitz' value to the Company; and (b) the processes of the boards of directors in dealing with the approval and termination of the Ovitz Employment Agreement were casual, if not sloppy and perfunctory. On the other hand, the Complaint is so inartfully drafted that it was properly dismissed under our pleading standards for derivative suits. * * * Therefore, both as to the processes of the two Boards and the waste test, this is a close case.

A. The 1995 Ovitz Employment Agreement

By an agreement dated October 1, 1995, Disney hired Ovitz as its president.* * * Although he lacked experience managing a diversified public company, other companies with entertainment operations had been interested in hiring him for high-level executive positions. The Employment Agreement was unilaterally negotiated by [Disney Chairman and CEO Michael] Eisner and approved by the Old Board. Their judgment was that Ovitz was a valuable person to hire as president of Disney, and they agreed ultimately with Eisner's recommendation in awarding him an extraordinarily lucrative contract.

Ovitz' Employment Agreement had an initial term of five years and required that Ovitz "devote his full time and best efforts exclusively to the Company," with exceptions for volunteer work, service on the board of another company, and managing his passive investments. In return, Disney agreed to give Ovitz a base salary of $1 million per year, a discretionary bonus, and two sets of stock options (the "A" options and the "B" options) that collectively would enable Ovitz to purchase 5 million shares of Disney common stock.

[The employment contract provided Ovitz $1 million in annual salary plus a discretionary bonus and options to buy Disney common stock that added up to 5 million shares. A termination clause provided that if Ovitz left Disney's employment and it was not his fault he would receive a compensation package. A lump sum of $10 million plus his remaining salary and an amount representing the probable unpaid installments of the bonus would be awarded if he left before 2002. Things did not work out well and 14 months later the arrangement was terminated on a non-fault basis, and Ovitz left with about $140 million as consolation.] * * *

The Complaint * * * alleges that the Old Board failed properly to inform itself about the total costs and incentives of the Ovitz Employment Agreement, especially the severance package. This is the key allegation related to this issue on appeal. Specifically, plaintiffs allege that the Board failed to realize that the contract gave Ovitz an incentive to find a way to exit the Company via a non-fault termination as soon as possible because doing so would permit him to earn more than he could by fulfilling his contract. The Complaint alleges, however, that the Old Board had been advised by a corporate compensation expert, Graef Crystal, in connection with its decision to approve the Ovitz Employment Agreement. Two public statements by Crystal form the basis of the allegation that the Old Board failed to consider the incentives and the total cost of the severance provisions.* * *

* * * [One] article appears first to paraphrase Crystal: "With no one expecting failure, the sleeper clauses in Ovitz's contract seemed innocuous, Crystal says, explaining that no one added up the total cost of the severance package." The article then quotes Crystal as saying that the amount of Ovitz' severance was "shocking" and that "nobody quantified this and I wish we had." One of the charging paragraphs of the Complaint concludes:

57. As has been conceded by Graef Crystal, the executive compensation consultant who advised the Old Board with respect to the Ovitz Employment Agreement, the Old Board never considered the costs that would be incurred by Disney in the event Ovitz was terminated from the Company for a reason other than cause prior to the natural expiration of the Ovitz Employment Agreement.

B. The New Board's Actions in Approving the Non–Fault Termination

Soon after Ovitz began work, problems surfaced and the situation continued to deteriorate during the first year of his employment. * * * The Complaint uses these reports to suggest that the New Board had reason to believe that Ovitz' performance and lack of commitment met the gross negligence or malfeasance standards of the termination-for-cause provisions of the contract.

The deteriorating situation, according to the Complaint, led Ovitz to begin seeking alternative employment and to send Eisner a letter in September 1996 that the Complaint paraphrases as stating his dissatisfaction with his role and expressing his desire to leave the Company.* * *

On December 11, 1996, Eisner and Ovitz agreed to arrange for Ovitz to leave Disney on the non-fault basis provided for in the 1995 Employment Agreement. Eisner then "caused" the New Board "to rubber-stamp his decision (by 'mutual consent')." This decision was implemented by a December 27, 1996 letter to Ovitz from defendant Sanford M. Litvack, an officer and director of Disney. That letter stated:

"This will confirm the terms of your agreement with the Company as follows:

1. The Term of your employment under your existing Employment Agreement with The Walt Disney Company will end at the close of business today * * *.

2. This letter will for all purposes of the Employment Agreement be treated as a 'Non–Fault Termination.' By our mutual agreement, the total amount payable to you under your Employment Agreement, including the amount payable under Section 11(c) in the event of a 'Non–Fault Termination,' is $38,888,230.77, net of withholding required by law or authorized by you * * *.

3. This letter will further confirm that the option to purchase 3,000,000 shares of the Company's Common Stock granted to you pursuant to Option A described in your Employment Agreement will vest as of today and will expire in accordance with its terms on September 30, 2002."

Although the non-fault termination left Ovitz with what essentially was a very lucrative severance agreement, it is important to note that Ovitz and Disney had negotiated for that severance payment at the time they initially contracted in 1995, and in the end the payout to Ovitz did not exceed the 1995 contractual benefits. * * *

The Complaint charges the New Board with waste, computing the value of the severance package agreed to by the Board at over $140 million, consisting of cash payments of about $39 million and the value of the immediately vesting "A" options of over $101 million. * * *

The allegation of waste is based on the inference most favorable to plaintiffs that Disney owed Ovitz nothing, either because he had resigned (de facto) or because he was unarguably subject to firing for cause. These allegations must be juxtaposed with the presumption that the New Board exercised its business judgment in deciding how to resolve the potentially litigable issues of whether Ovitz had actually resigned or had definitely breached his contract.* * *

Principles of Corporation Law Compared with Good Corporate Governance Practices

All good corporate governance practices include compliance with statutory law and case law establishing fiduciary duties. But the law of corporate fiduciary duties and remedies for violation of those duties are distinct from the aspirational goals of ideal corporate governance practices. Aspirational ideals of good corporate governance practices for boards of directors that go beyond the minimal legal requirements of the corporation law are highly desirable, often tend to benefit stockholders, sometimes reduce litigation and can usually help directors avoid liability. But they are not required by the corporation law and do not define standards of liability. * * *

* * * The sole issue that this Court must determine is whether the particularized facts alleged in this Complaint provide a reason to believe that

the conduct of the Old Board in 1995 and the New Board in 1996 constituted a violation of their fiduciary duties.

Independence of the Disney Board

* * * Plaintiffs' allegation that Eisner was interested in maximizing his compensation at the expense of Disney and its shareholders cannot reasonably be inferred from the facts alleged in Plaintiffs' amended complaint. At all times material to this litigation, Eisner owned several million options to purchase Disney stock. Therefore, it would not be in Eisner's economic interest to cause the Company to issue millions of additional options unnecessarily and at considerable cost. Such a gesture would not, as Plaintiffs suggest, "maximize" Eisner's own compensation package. Rather, it would dilute the value of Eisner's own very substantial holdings. * * * Nothing alleged by Plaintiffs generates a reasonable inference that Eisner would benefit personally from allowing Ovitz to leave Disney without good cause. * * *

Analytical Framework for the Informational Component of Directorial Decisionmaking

* * * The question is whether the trial court's formulation is consistent with our objective test of reasonableness, the test of materiality and concepts of gross negligence. We agree with the Court of Chancery that the standard for judging the informational component of the directors' decisionmaking does not mean that the Board must be informed of every fact. The Board is responsible for considering only material facts that are reasonably available, not those that are immaterial or out of the Board's reasonable reach. * * *

Plaintiffs' Contention that the Old Board Violated the Process Duty of Care in Approving the Ovitz Employment Agreement

Certainly in this case the economic exposure of the corporation to the payout scenarios of the Ovitz contract was material, particularly given its large size, for purposes of the directors' decisionmaking process. And those dollar exposure numbers were reasonably available because the logical inference from plaintiffs' allegations is that Crystal or the New Board could have calculated the numbers. Thus, the objective tests of reasonable availability and materiality were satisfied by this Complaint. But that is not the end of the inquiry for liability purposes.

The fact that Crystal did not quantify the potential severance benefits to Ovitz for terminating early without cause (under the terms of the Employment Agreement) does not create a reasonable inference that the Board failed to consider the potential cost to Disney in the event that they decided to terminate Ovitz without cause. But, even if the Board did fail to calculate the potential cost to Disney, I nevertheless think that this allegation fails to create a reasonable doubt that the former Board exercised due care. * * * Merely because Crystal now regrets not having calculated the package is not reason enough to overturn the judgment of the Board then. It is the essence of the business judgment rule that a court will not apply 20/20 hindsight to second guess a board's decision, except "in rare cases [where] a transaction may be so egregious on its face that the board approval cannot meet the test of business judgment." Because the Board's reliance on Crystal and his decision not to fully calculate the amount of severance lack "egregiousness," this is not that rare case. I think it a correct statement of law that the duty of care is still fulfilled even if a Board does not know the exact amount of a severance payout but nonetheless is fully informed about the manner in which such a payout would be calculated. A board is not required to be informed of every fact, but rather is required to be reasonably informed. * * *

The Complaint, fairly construed, admits that the directors were advised by Crystal as an expert and that they relied on his expertise. Accordingly, the question here is whether the directors are to be "fully protected" (i.e., not held liable) on the basis that they relied in good faith on a qualified expert under Section 141(e) of the Delaware General Corporation Law.[4] The Old Board is entitled to the presumption that it exercised proper business judgment, including proper reliance on the expert.

Although the Court of Chancery did not expressly predicate its decision on Section 141(e), Crystal is presumed to be an expert on whom the Board was entitled to rely in good faith under Section 141(e) in order to be "fully protected." Plaintiffs must rebut the presumption that the directors properly exercised their business judgment, including their good faith reliance on Crystal's expertise. * * *

To survive a Rule 23.1 motion to dismiss in a due care case where an expert has advised the board in its decisionmaking process, the complaint must allege particularized facts (not conclusions) that, if proved, would show, for example, that: (a) the directors did not in fact rely on the expert; (b) their reliance was not in good faith; (c) they did not reasonably believe that the expert's advice was within the expert's professional competence; (d) the expert was not selected with reasonable care by or on behalf of the corporation, and the faulty selection process was attributable to the directors; (e) the subject matter (in this case the cost calculation) that was material and reasonably available was so obvious that the board's failure to consider it was grossly negligent regardless of the expert's advice or lack of advice; or (f) that the decision of the Board was so unconscionable as to constitute waste or fraud.

Plaintiffs' Contention that the Old Board Violated "Substantive Due Care" Requirements and Committed Waste Ab Initio with Ovitz' Employment Agreement

* * * Plaintiffs' principal theory is that the 1995 Ovitz Employment Agreement was a "wasteful transaction for Disney ab initio" because it was structured to "incentivize" Ovitz to seek an early non-fault termination. The Court of Chancery correctly dismissed this theory as failing to meet the stringent requirements of the waste test, i.e., " 'an exchange that is so one sided that no business person of ordinary, sound judgment could conclude that the corporation has received adequate consideration.' " Moreover, the

---

4. [By the Court] Section 141(e) provides: A member of the board of directors, or a member of any committee designated by the board of directors, shall, in the performance of such member's duties, be fully protected in relying in good faith upon the records of the corporation and upon such information, opinions, reports or statements presented to the corporation by any of the corporation's officers or employees, or committees of the board of directors, or by any other person as to matters the member reasonably believes are within such other person's professional or expert competence and who has been selected with reasonable care by or on behalf of the corporation. 8 Del. C. § 141(e).

Court concluded that a board's decision on executive compensation is entitled to great deference. It is the essence of business judgment for a board to determine if "a 'particular individual warrant[s] large amounts of money, whether in the form of current salary or severance provisions.'"

Specifically, the Court of Chancery inferred from a reading of the Complaint that the Board determined it had to offer an expensive compensation package to attract Ovitz and that they determined he would be valuable to the Company. The Court also concluded that the vesting schedule of the options actually was a disincentive for Ovitz to leave Disney.* * *

* * * We agree with the analysis of the Court of Chancery that the size and structure of executive compensation are inherently matters of judgment. As former Chancellor Allen stated in Vogelstein:

* * * Roughly, a waste entails an exchange of corporate assets for consideration so disproportionately small as to lie beyond the range at which any reasonable person might be willing to trade. * * * If, however, there is any substantial consideration received by the corporation, and if there is a good faith judgment that in the circumstances the transaction is worthwhile, there should be no finding of waste, even if the fact finder would conclude ex post that the transaction was unreasonably risky. * * *

To be sure, there are outer limits, but they are confined to unconscionable cases where directors irrationally squander or give away corporate assets. Here, however, we find no error in the decision of the Court of Chancery on the waste test.

As for the plaintiffs' contention that the directors failed to exercise "substantive due care," we should note that such a concept is foreign to the business judgment rule. Courts do not measure, weigh or quantify directors' judgments. We do not even decide if they are reasonable in this context. Due care in the decisionmaking context is process due care only. Irrationality is the outer limit of the business judgment rule. Irrationality may be the functional equivalent of the waste test or it may tend to show that the decision is not made in good faith, which is a key ingredient of the business judgment rule.

Plaintiffs' Contention that the New Board Committed Waste in Its Decision That Ovitz' Contract Should be Terminated on a "Non–Fault" Basis

* * * The terms of the Employment Agreement limit "good cause" for terminating Ovitz's employment to gross negligence or malfeasance, or a voluntary resignation without the consent of the Company. * * * None of Plaintiffs' allegations rise to the level of gross negligence or malfeasance. * * *

* * * But the Complaint fails on its face to meet the waste test because it does not allege with particularity facts tending to show that no reasonable business person would have made the decision that the New Board made under these circumstances. * * *

BREHM v. EISNER

Supreme Court of Delaware, 2006.
906 A.2d 27.

Before STEELE, C.J., HOLLAND, BERGER, JACOBS, and RIDGELEY, J.J., constituting the Court en Banc.

JACOBS, JUSTICE.

[Editors: After this court remanded the case to the Court of Chancery and granted plaintiffs leave to replead in Brehm v. Eisner, 746 A.2d 244 (Del. 2000), the plaintiffs filed their second amended complaint in January 2002. In August 2005, the Court of Chancery entered judgment in favor of all defendants. This court affirms the decision.]

The appellants * * * challenge the Chancellor's determination that although the compensation committee's decision-making process fell far short of corporate governance "best practices," the committee members breached no duty of care in considering and approving the [No Fault Termination (NFT)] terms of the [Ovitz Employment Agreement (OEA)]. That conclusion is reversible error, the appellants claim, because the record establishes that the compensation committee members did not properly inform themselves of the material facts and, hence, were grossly negligent in approving the NFT provisions of the OEA. * * *

* * * In a "best case" scenario, all committee members would have received, before or at the committee's first meeting on September 26, 1995, a spreadsheet or similar document prepared by (or with the assistance of) a compensation expert (in this case, Graef Crystal). Making different, alternative assumptions, the spreadsheet would disclose the amounts that Ovitz could receive under the OEA in each circumstance that might foreseeably arise. One variable in that matrix of possibilities would be the cost to Disney of a non-fault termination for each of the five years of the initial term of the OEA. The contents of the spreadsheet would be explained to the committee members, either by the expert who prepared it or by a fellow committee member similarly knowledgeable about the subject. * * *

Had that scenario been followed, there would be no dispute (and no basis for litigation) over what information was furnished to the committee members or when it was furnished. Regrettably, the committee's informational and decisionmaking process used here was not so tidy. * * *

The Disney compensation committee met twice: on September 26 and October 16, 1995. The minutes of the September 26 meeting reflect that the committee approved the terms of the OEA (at that time embodied in the form of a letter agreement), except for the option grants, which were not approved until October 16—after the Disney stock incentive plan had been amended to provide for those options. At the September 26 meeting, the compensation committee considered a "term sheet" which, in summarizing the material terms of the OEA, relevantly disclosed that in the event of a non-fault termination, Ovitz would receive: (i) the present value of his salary ($1 million per year) for the balance of the contract term, (ii) the present value of his annual bonus payments (computed at $7.5 million) for the balance of the contract term, (iii) a $10 million termination fee, and (iv) the acceleration of his options for 3 million shares, which would become immediately exercisable at market price.

* * * [T]he issue may be framed as whether the compensation committee members knew, at the time they approved the OEA, that the value of the option component of the severance package could reach the $92 million order of magnitude if they terminated Ovitz without cause after one year. The evidentiary record shows that the committee members were so informed. * * *

The compensation committee members derived their information about the potential magnitude of an NFT payout from two sources. The first was the value of the "benchmark" options previously granted to Eisner and Wells and the valuations by Watson of the proposed Ovitz options. * * *

The committee's second source of information was the amount of "downside protection" that Ovitz was demanding. Ovitz required financial protection from the risk of leaving a very lucrative and secure position at CAA, of which he was a controlling partner, to join a publicly held corporation to which Ovitz was a stranger, and that had a very different culture and an environment which prevented him from completely controlling his destiny. The committee members knew that by leaving CAA and coming to Disney, Ovitz would be sacrificing "booked" CAA commissions of $150 to $200 million—an amount that Ovitz demanded as protection against the risk that his employment relationship with Disney might not work out. * * *

The OEA was specifically structured to compensate Ovitz for walking away from $150 million to $200 million of anticipated commissions from CAA over the five-year OEA contract term. This meant that if Ovitz was terminated without cause, the earlier in the contract term the termination occurred the larger the severance amount would be to replace the lost commissions. * * *

* * * [T]he appellants contend that [directors] Poitier and Lozano did not review the spreadsheets generated by Watson at the September 26 meeting. The short answer is that even if Poitier and Lozano did not review the spreadsheets themselves, Russell and Watson adequately informed them of the spreadsheets' contents. * * *

For these reasons, we uphold the Chancellor's determination that the compensation committee members did not breach their fiduciary duty of care in approving the OEA.

(e) HOLDING THAT THE REMAINING DISNEY DIRECTORS DID NOT FAIL TO EXERCISE DUE CARE IN APPROVING THE HIRING OF OVITZ AS THE PRESIDENT OF DISNEY

The Court of Chancery held that the business judgment rule presumptions protected the decisions of the compensation committee and the remaining Disney directors, not only because they had acted with due care but also because they had not acted in bad faith. That latter ruling, the appellants claim, was reversible error because the Chancellor formulated and then applied an incorrect definition of bad faith.

In its Opinion the Court of Chancery defined bad faith as follows:

Upon long and careful consideration, I am of the opinion that the concept of *intentional dereliction of duty*, a *conscious disregard for one's responsibilities*, is an appropriate (although not the only) standard for determining whether fiduciaries have acted in good faith. Deliberate indifference and inaction *in the face of a duty to act* is, in my mind, conduct that is clearly disloyal to the corporation. It is the epitome of faithless conduct.

* * * This case [. . .] is one in which the duty to act in good faith has played a prominent role, yet to date is not a well-developed area of our corporate fiduciary law. * * * [T]he duty to act in good faith is, up to this point relatively uncharted. Because of the increased recognition of the importance of good faith, some conceptual guidance to the corporate community may be helpful. * * *

The precise question is whether the Chancellor's articulated standard for bad faith corporate fiduciary conduct-intentional dereliction of duty, a conscious disregard for one's responsibilities-is legally correct. In approaching that question, we note that the Chancellor characterized that definition as "*an* appropriate (*although not the only*) standard for determining whether fiduciaries have acted in good faith." That observation is accurate and helpful, because as a matter of simple logic, at least three different categories of fiduciary behavior are candidates for the "bad faith" pejorative label.

The first category involves so-called "subjective bad faith," that is, fiduciary conduct motivated by an actual intent to do harm. * * * We need not dwell further on this category, because no such conduct is claimed to have occurred, or did occur, in this case.

The second category of conduct, which is at the opposite end of the spectrum, involves lack of due care—that is, fiduciary action taken solely by reason of gross negligence and without any malevolent intent. In this case, appellants assert claims of gross negligence to establish breaches not only of director due care but also of the directors' duty to act in good faith. Although the Chancellor found, and we agree, that the appellants failed to establish gross negligence, to afford guidance we address the issue of whether gross negligence (including a failure to inform one's self of available material facts), without more, can also constitute bad faith. The answer is clearly no.

* * * Both our legislative history and our common law jurisprudence distinguish sharply between the duties to exercise due care and to act in good faith, and highly significant consequences flow from that distinction.

The Delaware General Assembly has addressed the distinction between bad faith and a failure to exercise due care (*i.e.*, gross negligence) in two separate contexts. The first is Section 102(b)(7) of the DGCL, which authorizes Delaware corporations, by a provision in the certificate of incorporation, to exculpate their directors from monetary damage liability for a breach of the duty of care. That exculpatory provision affords significant protection to directors of Delaware corporations. The statute carves out several exceptions, however, including most relevantly, "for acts or omissions not in good faith. . . ." Thus, a corporation can exculpate its directors from monetary liability for a breach of the duty of care, but not for conduct that is not in good faith. To adopt a definition of bad faith that would cause a violation of the duty of care automatically to become an act or omission "not in good faith," would eviscerate the protections accorded to directors by the General Assembly's adoption of Section 102(b)(7).

A second legislative recognition of the distinction between fiduciary conduct that is grossly negligent and conduct that is not in good faith, is Delaware's indemnification statute, found at 8 *Del. C.* § 145. To oversimplify, subsections (a) and (b) of that statute permit a corporation to indemnify (*inter alia*) any person who is or was a director, officer, employee or agent of the corporation against expenses (including attorneys' fees), judgments, fines and amounts paid in settlement of specified actions, suits or proceedings, where (among other things): (i) that person is, was, or is threatened to be made a party to that action, suit or proceeding, and (ii) that person "acted in good faith and in a manner the person reasonably believed to be in or not opposed to the best interests of the corporation...." Thus, under Delaware statutory law a director or officer of a corporation can be indemnified for liability (and litigation expenses) incurred by reason of a violation of the duty of care, but not for a violation of the duty to act in good faith. * * *

That leaves the third category of fiduciary conduct. * * * This third category is what the Chancellor's definition of bad faith—intentional dereliction of duty, a conscious disregard for one's responsibilities—is intended to capture. The question is whether such misconduct is properly treated as a non-exculpable, non-indemnifiable violation of the fiduciary duty to act in good faith. In our view it must be, for at least two reasons.

First, the universe of fiduciary misconduct is not limited to either disloyalty in the classic sense (*i.e.*, preferring the adverse self-interest of the fiduciary or of a related person to the interest of the corporation) or gross negligence. Cases have arisen where corporate directors have no conflicting self-interest in a decision, yet engage in misconduct that is more culpable than simple inattention or failure to be informed of all facts material to the decision. To protect the interests of the corporation and its shareholders, fiduciary conduct of this kind, which does not involve disloyalty (as traditionally defined) but is qualitatively more culpable than gross negligence, should be proscribed. * * *

Second, the legislature has also recognized this intermediate category of fiduciary misconduct, which ranks between conduct involving subjective bad faith and gross negligence. Section 102(b)(7)(ii) of the DGCL expressly denies money damage exculpation for "acts or omissions not in good faith or which involve intentional misconduct or a knowing violation of law." By its very terms that provision distinguishes between "intentional misconduct" and a "knowing violation of law" (both examples of subjective bad faith) on the one hand, and "acts ... not in good faith," on the other. Because the statute exculpates directors only for conduct amounting to gross negligence, the statutory denial of exculpation for "acts ... not in good faith" must encompass the intermediate category of misconduct captured by the Chancellor's definition of bad faith.

For these reasons, we uphold the Court of Chancery's definition as a legally appropriate, although not the exclusive, definition of fiduciary bad faith. * * *

The appellants' final claim is that even if the approval of the OEA was protected by the business judgment rule presumptions, the payment of the severance amount to Ovitz constituted waste. This claim is rooted in the doctrine that a plaintiff who fails to rebut the business judgment rule presumptions is not entitled to any remedy unless the transaction constitutes waste. * * *

To recover on a claim of corporate waste, the plaintiffs must shoulder the burden of proving that the exchange was "so one sided that no business person of ordinary, sound judgment could conclude that the corporation has received adequate consideration." A claim of waste will arise only in the rare, "unconscionable case where directors irrationally squander or give away corporate assets." This onerous standard for waste is a corollary of the proposition that where business judgment presumptions are applicable, the board's decision will be upheld unless it cannot be "attributed to any rational business purpose."

The claim that the payment of the NFT amount to Ovitz, without more, constituted waste is meritless on its face, because at the time the NFT amounts were paid, Disney was contractually obligated to pay them. The payment of a contractually obligated amount cannot constitute waste, unless the contractual obligation is itself wasteful. Accordingly, the proper focus of a waste analysis must be whether the amounts required to be paid in the event of an NFT were wasteful *ex ante*.

Appellants claim that the NFT provisions of the OEA were wasteful because they incentivized Ovitz to perform poorly in order to obtain payment of the NFT provisions. The Chancellor found that the record did not support that contention. * * *

That ruling is erroneous, the appellants argue, because the NFT provisions of the OEA were wasteful in their very design. Specifically, the OEA gave Ovitz every incentive to leave the Company before serving out the full term of his contract. The appellants urge that although the OEA may have induced Ovitz to join Disney as President, no contractual safeguards were in place to retain him in that position. In essence, appellants claim that the NFT provisions of the OEA created an irrational incentive for Ovitz to get himself fired.

That claim does not come close to satisfying the high hurdle required to establish waste. The approval of the NFT provisions in the OEA had a rational business purpose: to induce Ovitz to leave CAA, at what would otherwise be a considerable cost to him, in order to join Disney. * * * Ovitz had no control over whether or not he would be fired, either with or without cause. To suggest that at the time he entered into the OEA Ovitz would engineer an early departure at the cost of his extraordinary reputation in the entertainment industry and his historical friendship with Eisner, is not only fanciful but also without proof in the record. Indeed, the Chancellor found that it was "patently unreasonable to assume that Ovitz intended to perform just poorly enough to be fired quickly, but not so poorly that he could be terminated for cause."

We agree. Because the appellants have failed to show that the approval of the NFT terms of the OEA was not a rational business decision, their waste claim must fail.

Notes

(1) Executive compensation is like the weather: everybody talks about it, but nobody ever seems to do anything about it. Why is there reluctance to set aside "huge," "staggering," "munificent," or "quite lush" payments of salary to corporate officers?

(2) U.S. executives earn many times what line workers do in total remuneration. In 2004, for example, executives' average pay was 431 times the average pay of production workers. See Jeanne Sahadi, CEO Pay: Sky High Gets Even Higher, Aug. 30, 2005, www.money.cnn.com/2005/08/26/news/economy/ceo_pay. The presidents and CEOs of the very largest companies far outrun these figures, however, and are light-years distant from the ordinary wage-earner.

(3) The *exercise* of stock options following run-ups in market price of the stock accounts for a major component of massive increases in executive compensation: from 72% of total compensation in 1997 to 80% in 1998. Jennifer Reingold and Ronald Grover, Executive Pay: Special Report, Business Week, April 19, 1999, at 74. While it is quite possible that an economic downturn will at least temporarily reverse this pattern, such payments in fact increased until the 2002 collapse.

(4) There is general acceptance today of the idea that compensation of CEOs should be partially performance based, that is executive compensation should be tied to improvements in shareholder wealth. The most common devices are grants of stock options and sales of restricted stock to executives at favorable prices. Both apparently link the level of executive compensation directly with the share price. The examples given above of extremely high levels of compensation are all based on significant increases in the market value of stock. However, several well-known devices permit recipients of options or restricted stock to indirectly obtain their current value immediately and without regard to the subsequent performance of the stock. For example, a recipient of restricted stock options may immediately thereafter sell shares from his portfolio, or may exercise options granted previously and sell the stock so obtained.

(5) Is there any chance of attacking high-levels of executive compensation as "self-dealing" or as "spoilation or waste" under Rogers v. Hill? Presumably if a CEO actually "writes his own ticket," without review by independent directors or shareholders, a test of "fairness" or "intrinsic fairness" might be applicable. However, it is not at all clear whether a court would apply that test, or if it does, whether such a test would effectively limit CEO compensation. How could a court apply a fairness test except by comparing a CEO's income with the incomes of other CEOs? Might this not lead to putting the "fair" label on compensation levels in the millions or tens of millions of dollars? In any event the "spoilation or waste" standard of Rogers v. Hill apparently has never been invoked to attack modern levels of executive compensation.

(6) In publicly held corporations today, of course, the CEO does not typically "write his own ticket." Rather, there is a compensation committee that is composed of outside directors to pass on levels of executive compensation. Presumably if this committee approves a compensation plan for the CEO the test will shift from "fairness" to "lack of business judgment." However, compensation committees may act in a reactive role, screening management proposals rather than implementing their own compensation policies.

(7) Executive compensation was the target of regulatory actions in the early 1990s that have the potential of increasing scrutiny of that sensitive subject.

(a) *Disclosure of Executive Compensation*. In October 1992, the SEC adopted major amendments to its rules governing disclosure of executive compensation. SEC Rel. No. 33–6962, 57 Fed. Reg. 48,126 (Oct. 16, 1992); rev'd SEC Rel. No. 33–7032, 58 Fed.Reg. 63010–01 (Nov. 29, 1993).

(b) *Revenue Reconciliation Act of 1993*. This Act added a new § 162(m) to the Internal Revenue Code, disallowing corporate deductions for executive compensation for 1994 and later years to the extent that the compensation for an executive exceeds $1 million per year.

Certainly § 162(m) has had an effect on current compensation practices: Long-term compensation plans have been modified so that they are based on "performance goals" that comply with § 162(m) and the regulations; compensation arrangements have been shifted toward deferred compensation plans; and the membership of compensation committees have been revised to make sure that the members are all "outside" directors as defined in the regulations. However, not all companies have made these adjustments. Since the only effect of noncompliance with § 162(m) is the disallowance of a portion of a corporate deduction, many corporations have simply continued to pay executives in excess of $1.0 million per year and foregone the tax deduction, even though that increases somewhat their total tax bills.

(8) There are many many views on the subject of executive compensation. Charles Elson led a roundtable of academics, attorneys, and corporate officers to explore the problems with executive compensation. To read a transcript of this roundtable, see, Charles Elson, What's Wrong with Executive Compensation, Harv. Bus. Rev., Jan. 2002.

SINCLAIR OIL CORP. v. LEVIEN

Supreme Court of Delaware, 1971.
280 A.2d 717.

WOLCOTT, CHIEF JUSTICE.

This is an appeal by the defendant, Sinclair Oil Corporation (hereafter Sinclair), from an order of the Court of Chancery, 261 A.2d 911 in a derivative action requiring Sinclair to account for damages sustained by its subsidiary, Sinclair Venezuelan Oil Company (hereafter Sinven), organized by Sinclair for the purpose of operating in Venezuela, as a result of dividends paid by Sinven, the denial to Sinven of industrial development, and a breach of contract between Sinclair's wholly-owned subsidiary, Sinclair International Oil Company, and Sinven.

Sinclair, operating primarily as a holding company, is in the business of exploring for oil and of producing and marketing crude oil and oil products. At all times relevant to this litigation, it owned about 97% of Sinven's stock. The plaintiff owns about 3000 of 120,000 publicly held shares of Sinven. Sinven, incorporated in 1922, has been engaged in petroleum operations primarily in Venezuela and since 1959 has operated exclusively in Venezuela.

Sinclair nominates all members of Sinven's board of directors. The Chancellor found as a fact that the directors were not independent of Sinclair. Almost without exception, they were officers, directors, or employees of corporations in the Sinclair complex. By reason of Sinclair's domination, it is clear that Sinclair owed Sinven a fiduciary duty. Sinclair concedes this.

The Chancellor held that because of Sinclair's fiduciary duty and its control over Sinven, its relationship with Sinven must meet the test of intrinsic fairness. The standard of intrinsic fairness involves both a high degree of fairness and a shift in the burden of proof. Under this standard the burden is on Sinclair to prove, subject to careful judicial scrutiny, that its transactions with Sinven were objectively fair. Guth v. Loft, Inc., 23 Del.Ch. 255, 5 A.2d 503 (1939).

Sinclair argues that the transactions between it and Sinven should be tested, not by the test of intrinsic fairness with the accompanying shift of the burden of proof, but by the business judgment rule under which a court will not interfere with the judgment of a board of directors unless there is a showing of gross and palpable overreaching. Meyerson v. El Paso Natural Gas Co., 246 A.2d 789 (Del.Ch.1967). A board of directors enjoys a presumption of sound business judgment, and its decisions will not be disturbed if they can be attributed to any rational business purpose. A court under such circumstances will not substitute its own notions of what is or is not sound business judgment.

We think, however, that Sinclair's argument in this respect is misconceived. When the situation involves a parent and a subsidiary, with the parent controlling the transaction and fixing the terms, the test of intrinsic fairness, with its resulting shifting of the burden of proof, is applied. The basic situation for the application of the rule is the one in which the parent has received a benefit to the exclusion and at the expense of the subsidiary.

Recently, this court dealt with the question of fairness in parent-subsidiary dealings in Getty Oil Co. v. Skelly Oil Co., [267 A.2d 883 (Del.Sup.) 1970]. In that case, both parent and subsidiary were in the business of refining and marketing crude oil and crude oil products. The Oil Import Board ruled that the subsidiary, because it was controlled by the parent, was no longer entitled to a separate allocation of imported crude oil. The subsidiary then contended that it had a right to share the quota of crude oil allotted to the parent. We ruled that the business judgment standard should be applied to determine this contention. Although the subsidiary suffered a loss through the administration of the oil import quotas, the parent gained nothing. The parent's quota was derived solely from its own past use. The past use of the subsidiary did not cause an increase in the parent's quota. Nor did the parent usurp a quota of the subsidiary. Since the parent received nothing from the subsidiary to the exclusion of the minority stockholders of the subsidiary, there was no self-dealing. Therefore, the business judgment standard was properly applied.

A parent does indeed owe a fiduciary duty to its subsidiary when there are parent-subsidiary dealings. However, this alone will not evoke the intrinsic fairness standard. This standard will be applied only when the fiduciary duty is accompanied by self-dealing—the situation when a parent is on both sides of a transaction with its subsidiary. Self-dealing occurs when the parent, by virtue of its domination of the subsidiary, causes the subsidiary to act in such a way that the parent receives something from the subsidiary to the exclusion of, and detriment to, the minority stockholders of the subsidiary.

We turn now to the facts. The plaintiff argues that, from 1960 through 1966, Sinclair caused Sinven to pay out such excessive dividends that the industrial development of Sinven was effectively prevented, and it became in reality a corporation in dissolution.

From 1960 through 1966, Sinven paid out $108,000,000 in dividends ($38,000,000 in excess of Sinven's earnings during the same period). The Chancellor held that Sinclair caused these dividends to be paid during a period when it had a need for large amounts of cash. Although the dividends paid exceeded earnings, the plaintiff concedes that the payments were made in compliance with 8 Del.C. § 170, authorizing payment of dividends out of surplus or net profits. However, the plaintiff attacks these dividends on the ground that they resulted from an improper motive—Sinclair's need for cash. The Chancellor, applying the intrinsic fairness standard, held that Sinclair did not sustain its burden of proving that these dividends were intrinsically fair to the minority stockholders of Sinven.

Since it is admitted that the dividends were paid in strict compliance with 8 Del.C. § 170, the alleged excessiveness of the payments alone would not state a cause of action. Nevertheless, compliance with the applicable statute may not, under all circumstances, justify all dividend payments. If a plaintiff can meet his burden of proving that a dividend cannot be grounded on any reasonable business objective, then the courts can and will interfere with the board's decision to pay the dividend.

Sinclair contends that it is improper to apply the intrinsic fairness standard to dividend payments even when the board which voted for the dividends is completely dominated. In support of this contention, Sinclair relies heavily on American District Telegraph Co. [ADT] v. Grinnell Corp., (N.Y.Sup.Ct.1969) aff'd. 33 A.D.2d 769, 306 N.Y.S.2d 209 (1969). Plaintiffs were minority stockholders of ADT, a subsidiary of Grinnell. The plaintiffs alleged that Grinnell, realizing that it would soon have to sell its ADT stock because of a pending anti-trust action, caused ADT to pay excessive dividends. Because the dividend payments conformed with applicable statutory law, and the plaintiffs could not prove an abuse of discretion, the court ruled that the complaint did not state a cause of action. Other decisions seem to support Sinclair's contention. In Metropolitan Casualty Ins. Co. v. First State Bank of Temple, 54 S.W.2d 358 (Tex.Civ.App.1932), rev'd. on other grounds, 79 S.W.2d 835 (Sup.Ct.1935), the court held that a majority of interested directors does not void a declaration of dividends because all directors, by necessity, are interested in and benefited by a dividend declaration.

We do not accept the argument that the intrinsic fairness test can never be applied to a dividend declaration by a dominated board, although a dividend declaration by a dominated board will not inevitably demand the application of the intrinsic fairness standard. Moskowitz v. Bantrell, 41 Del.Ch. 177, 190 A.2d 749 (Del.Supr.1963). If such a dividend is in essence self-dealing by the parent, then the intrinsic fairness standard is the proper standard. For example, suppose a parent dominates a subsidiary and its board of directors. The subsidiary has outstanding two classes of stock, X and Y. Class X is owned by the parent and Class Y is owned by minority stockholders of the subsidiary. If the subsidiary, at the direction of the parent, declares a dividend on its Class X stock only, this might well be self-dealing by the parent. It would be receiving something from the subsidiary to the exclusion of and detrimental to its minority stockholders. This self-dealing, coupled with the parent's fiduciary duty, would make intrinsic fairness the proper standard by which to evaluate the dividend payments.

Consequently it must be determined whether the dividend payments by Sinven were, in essence, self-dealing by Sinclair. The dividends resulted in great sums of money being transferred from Sinven to Sinclair. However, a proportionate share of this money was received by the minority shareholders of Sinven. Sinclair received nothing from Sinven to the exclusion of its minority stockholders. As such, these dividends were not self-dealing. We hold therefore that the Chancellor erred in applying the intrinsic fairness test as to these dividend payments. The business judgment standard should have been applied.

We conclude that the facts demonstrate that the dividend payments complied with the business judgment standard and with 8 Del.C. § 170. The motives for causing the declaration of dividends are immaterial unless the plaintiff can show that the dividend payments resulted from improper motives and amounted to waste. The plaintiff contends only that the dividend payments drained Sinven of cash to such an extent that it was prevented from expanding.

The plaintiff proved no business opportunities which came to Sinven independently and which Sinclair either took to itself or denied to Sinven. As a matter of fact, with two minor exceptions which resulted in losses, all of Sinven's operations have been conducted in Venezuela, and Sinclair had a policy of exploiting its oil properties located in different countries by subsidiaries located in the particular countries.

From 1960 to 1966 Sinclair purchased or developed oil fields in Alaska, Canada, Paraguay, and other places around the world. The plaintiff contends that these were all opportunities which could have been taken by Sinven. The Chancellor concluded that Sinclair had not proved that its denial of expansion opportunities to Sinven was intrinsically fair. He based this conclusion on the following findings of fact. Sinclair made no real effort to expand Sinven. The excessive dividends paid by Sinven resulted in so great a cash drain as to effectively deny to Sinven any ability to expand. During this same period Sinclair actively pursued a company-wide policy of developing through its subsidiaries new sources of revenue, but Sinven was not permitted to participate and was confined in its activities to Venezuela.

However, the plaintiff could point to no opportunities which came to Sinven. Therefore, Sinclair usurped no business opportunity belonging to Sinven. Since Sinclair received nothing from Sinven to the exclusion of and detriment to Sinven's minority stockholders, there was no self-dealing. Therefore, business judgment is the proper standard by which to evaluate Sinclair's expansion policies.

Since there is no proof of self-dealing on the part of Sinclair, it follows that the expansion policy of Sinclair and the methods used to achieve the desired result must, as far as Sinclair's treatment of Sinven is concerned, be tested by the standards of the business judgment rule. Accordingly, Sinclair's decision, absent fraud or gross overreaching, to achieve expansion through the medium of its subsidiaries, other than Sinven, must be upheld.

Even if Sinclair was wrong in developing these opportunities as it did, the question arises, with which subsidiaries should these opportunities have been shared? No evidence indicates a unique need or ability of Sinven to develop these opportunities. The decision of which subsidiaries would be used to implement Sinclair's expansion policy was one of business judgment with which a court will not interfere absent a showing of gross and palpable overreaching. No such showing has been made here.

Next, Sinclair argues that the Chancellor committed error when he held it liable to Sinven for breach of contract.

In 1961 Sinclair created Sinclair International Oil Company (hereafter International), a wholly owned subsidiary used for the purpose of coordinating all of Sinclair's foreign operations. All crude purchases by Sinclair were made thereafter through International.

On September 28, 1961, Sinclair caused Sinven to contract with International whereby Sinven agreed to sell all of its crude oil and refined products to International at specified prices. The contract provided for minimum and maximum quantities and prices. The plaintiff contends that Sinclair caused this contract to be breached in two respects. Although the contract called for payment on receipt, International's payments lagged as much as 30 days after receipt. Also, the contract required International to purchase at least a fixed minimum amount of crude and refined products from Sinven. International did not comply with this requirement.

Clearly, Sinclair's act of contracting with its dominated subsidiary was self-dealing. Under the contract Sinclair received the products produced by Sinven, and of course the minority shareholders of Sinven were not able to share in the receipt of these products. If the contract was breached, then Sinclair received these products to the detriment of Sinven's minority shareholders. We agree with the Chancellor's finding that the contract was breached by Sinclair, both as to the time of payments and the amounts purchased.

Although a parent need not bind itself by a contract with its dominated subsidiary, Sinclair chose to operate in this manner. As Sinclair has received the benefits of this contract, so must it comply with the contractual duties.

Under the intrinsic fairness standard, Sinclair must prove that its causing Sinven not to enforce the contract was intrinsically fair to the minority shareholders of Sinven. Sinclair has failed to meet this burden. Late payments were clearly breaches for which Sinven should have sought and received adequate damages. As to the quantities purchased, Sinclair argues that it purchased all the products produced by Sinven. This, however, does not satisfy the standard of intrinsic fairness. Sinclair has failed to prove that Sinven could not possibly have produced or some way have obtained the contract minimums. As such, Sinclair must account on this claim.

Finally, Sinclair argues that the Chancellor committed error in refusing to allow it a credit or setoff of all benefits provided by it to Sinven with respect to all the alleged damages. The Chancellor held that setoff should be allowed on specific transactions, e.g., benefits to Sinven under the contract with International, but denied an overall setoff against all damages claimed. We agree with the Chancellor, although the point may well be moot in view of our holding that Sinclair is not required to account for the alleged excessiveness of the dividend payments.

We will therefore reverse that part of the Chancellor's order that requires Sinclair to account to Sinven for damages sustained as a result of dividends paid between 1960 and 1966, and by reason of the denial to Sinven of expansion during that period. We will affirm the remaining portion of that order and remand the cause for further proceedings.

Notes

(1) Serious problems can arise in a number of areas whenever there are minority shareholders in a corporate subsidiary. For example, the Internal Revenue Code permits a corporation to file a "consolidated return" with subsidiaries that are at least 80 percent owned. The effect of consolidation is that a single return is filed covering the income or loss of all the corporations as a group, and the result may be that a valuable tax loss owned by a subsidiary may be utilized to offset income of the parent or of other subsidiaries within the group. Today, problems created by consolidated returns within parent/subsidiary groups are usually handled by formal written agreements, known as tax allocation or tax sharing agreements. These agreements typically provide that the parent corporation will compensate the subsidiary in cash for the net tax benefits actually obtained by the parent as a result of the consolidation. For a case involving such an agreement (after the subsidiary was sold by the parent to an outside third party), see Summit Nat'l Life Ins. Co. v. Cargill, Inc., 807 F.Supp. 363 (E.D.Pa. 1992), affirmed 981 F.2d 1248 (3d Cir.1992).

(2) While a clause in the subsidiary's articles of incorporation that attempts to validate all transactions between subsidiary and parent will not provide total protection, it may be given some effect by shifting the burden of proving unfairness or "exonerating" the arrangement from "adverse inferences." See Spiegel v. Beacon Participations, Inc., 297 Mass. 398, 417, 8 N.E.2d 895, 907 (1937). Such clauses also usually cover transactions between corporations with common directors (interlocking directors) but with no ownership of securities of one corporation by the other.

(3) Problems such as those involved in the principal case can be avoided by the elimination of the minority shareholders. How can this be done? A negotiated buy-out? What if the minority is unwilling to sell at a reasonable price? Could Sinclair create a wholly owned subsidiary, "X Corporation," transfer its holdings of Sinven to it, and then merge Sinven into X Corporation, requiring the minority shareholders to accept cash rather than X Corporation stock? Compare MBCA §§ 11.01(b)(3) (particularly the phrase "or into cash or other property in whole or in part,") 11.04. What protection does the minority have? See MBCA § 13.02(a) and, generally, MBCA ch. 13.

(4) See John K. Wells, Multiple Directorships: The Fiduciary Duties and Conflicts of Interest That Arise When One Individual Serves More Than One Corporation, 33 John Marshall L.Rev. 561 (2000).

(5) Consider the case of California Public Employees' Retirement System v. Coulter, 2002 WL 31888343 at *1 (Del.Ch. Dec. 18, 2002). Coulter founded the successful Lone Star Steakhouses and took it public in 1992. He subsequently sat as CEO and Chairman of the Board. During his tenure he pushed through the sale of his privately owned, Coulter Enterprises, to Lone Star with biased valuations and misinformation. Further, all three members special committee of Lone Star's

board which approved the sale were, in some way, under the supervision of Coulter at the time of the transaction.

WEINBERGER v. UOP, INC.

Supreme Court of Delaware, 1983.
457 A.2d 701.

Before HERRMANN, C.J., McNEILLY, QUILLEN, HORSEY and MOORE, JJ., constituting the Court en Banc.

MOORE, JUSTICE:

This post-trial appeal was reheard en banc from a decision of the Court of Chancery. It was brought by the class action plaintiff below, a former shareholder of UOP, Inc., who challenged the elimination of UOP's minority shareholders by a cash-out merger between UOP and its majority owner, The Signal Companies, Inc. * * * [T]he defendants in this action were Signal, UOP, [and] certain officers and directors of those companies * * *. The present Chancellor held that the terms of the merger were fair to the plaintiff and the other minority shareholders of UOP. Accordingly, he entered judgment in favor of the defendants.

Numerous points were raised by the parties, but we address only the following questions presented by the trial court's opinion:

(1) The plaintiff's duty to plead sufficient facts demonstrating the unfairness of the challenged merger;

(2) The burden of proof upon the parties where the merger has been approved by the purportedly informed vote of a majority of the minority shareholders;

(3) The fairness of the merger in terms of adequacy of the defendants' disclosures to the minority shareholders;

(4) The fairness of the merger in terms of adequacy of the price paid for the minority shares and the remedy appropriate to that issue; and

(5) The continued force and effect of Singer v. Magnavox Co., Del.Supr., 380 A.2d 969, 980 (1977), and its progeny. * * *

I.

The facts found by the trial court, pertinent to the issues before us, are supported by the record, and we draw from them as set out in the Chancellor's opinion.

Signal is a diversified, technically based company operating through various subsidiaries. Its stock is publicly traded on the New York, Philadelphia and Pacific Stock Exchanges. UOP, formerly known as Universal Oil Products Company, was a diversified industrial company engaged in various lines of business, including petroleum and petrochemical services and related products, construction, fabricated metal products, transportation equipment products, chemicals and plastics, and other products and services including land development, lumber products and waste disposal. Its stock was publicly held and listed on the New York Stock Exchange.

In 1974 Signal sold one of its wholly-owned subsidiaries for $420,000,000 in cash. See Gimbel v. Signal Companies, Inc., Del.Ch., 316 A.2d 599, aff'd, Del.Supr., 316 A.2d 619 (1974). While looking to invest this cash surplus, Signal became interested in UOP as a possible acquisition. Friendly negotiations ensued, and Signal proposed to acquire a controlling interest in UOP at a price of $19 per share. UOP's representatives sought $25 per share. In the arm's length bargaining that followed, an understanding was reached whereby Signal agreed to purchase from UOP 1,500,000 shares of UOP's authorized but unissued stock at $21 per share.

This purchase was contingent upon Signal making a successful cash tender offer for 4,300,000 publicly held shares of UOP, also at a price of $21 per share. This combined method of acquisition permitted Signal to acquire 5,800,000 shares of stock, representing 50.5% of UOP's outstanding shares. The UOP board of directors advised the company's shareholders that it had no objection to Signal's tender offer at that price. Immediately before the announcement of the tender offer, UOP's common stock had been trading on the New York Stock Exchange at a fraction under $14 per share.

The negotiations between Signal and UOP occurred during April 1975, and the resulting tender offer was greatly oversubscribed. However, Signal limited its total purchase of the tendered shares so that, when coupled with the stock bought from UOP, it had achieved its goal of becoming a 50.5% shareholder of UOP.

Although UOP's board consisted of thirteen directors, Signal nominated and elected only six. Of these, five were either directors or employees of Signal. The sixth, a partner in the banking firm of Lazard Freres & Co., had been one of Signal's representatives in the negotiations and bargaining with UOP concerning the tender offer and purchase price of the UOP shares.

However, the president and chief executive officer of UOP retired during 1975, and Signal caused him to be replaced by James V. Crawford, a long-time employee and senior executive vice president of one of Signal's wholly-owned subsidiaries. Crawford succeeded his predecessor on UOP's board of directors and also was made a director of Signal.

By the end of 1977 Signal basically was unsuccessful in finding other suitable investment candidates for its excess cash, and by February 1978 considered that it had no other realistic acquisitions available to it on a friendly basis. Once again its attention turned to UOP.

The trial court found that at the instigation of certain Signal management personnel, including William W. Walkup, its board chairman, and Forrest N. Shumway, its president, a feasibility study was made concerning the possible acquisition of the balance of UOP's outstanding shares. This study was performed by two Signal officers, Charles S. Arledge, vice president (director of planning), and Andrew J. Chitiea, senior vice president (chief financial officer). Messrs. Walkup, Shumway, Arledge and Chitiea were all directors of UOP in addition to their membership on the Signal board.

Arledge and Chitiea concluded that it would be a good investment for Signal to acquire the remaining 49.5% of UOP shares at any price up to $24 each. Their report was discussed between Walkup and Shumway who, along with Arledge, Chitiea and Brewster L. Arms, internal counsel for Signal, constituted Signal's senior management. In particular, they talked about the proper price to be paid if the acquisition was pursued, purportedly keeping in mind that as UOP's majority shareholder, Signal owed a fiduciary responsibility to both its own stockholders as well as to UOP's minority. It was ultimately agreed that a meeting of Signal's executive committee would be called to propose that Signal acquire the remaining outstanding stock of UOP through a cash-out merger in the range of $20 to $21 per share.

The executive committee meeting was set for February 28, 1978. As a courtesy, UOP's president, Crawford, was invited to attend, although he was not a member of Signal's executive committee. On his arrival, and prior to the meeting, Crawford was asked to meet privately with Walkup and Shumway. He was then told of Signal's plan to acquire full ownership of UOP and was asked for his reaction to the proposed price range of $20 to $21 per share. Crawford said he thought such a price would be "generous," and that it was certainly one which should be submitted to UOP's minority shareholders for their ultimate consideration. He stated, however, that Signal's 100% ownership could cause internal problems at UOP. He believed that employees would have to be given some assurance of their future place in a fully-owned Signal subsidiary. Otherwise, he feared the departure of essential personnel. Also, many of UOP's key employees had stock option incentive programs which would be wiped out by a merger. Crawford therefore urged that some adjustment would have to be made, such as providing a comparable incentive in Signal's shares, if after the merger he was to maintain his quality of personnel and efficiency at UOP.

Thus, Crawford voiced no objection to the $20 to $21 price range, nor did he suggest that Signal should consider paying more than $21 per share for the minority interests. Later, at the executive committee meeting the same factors were discussed, with Crawford repeating the position he earlier took with Walkup and Shumway. Also considered was the 1975 tender offer and the fact that it had been greatly oversubscribed at $21 per share. For many reasons, Signal's management concluded that the acquisition of UOP's minority shares provided the solution to a number of its business problems.

Thus, it was the consensus that a price of $20 to $21 per share would be fair to both Signal and the minority shareholders of UOP. Signal's executive committee authorized its management "to negotiate" with UOP "for a cash acquisition of the minority ownership in UOP, Inc., with the intention of presenting a proposal to [Signal's] board of directors * * * on March 6, 1978". Immediately after this February 28, 1978 meeting, Signal issued a press release stating:

> The Signal Companies, Inc. and UOP, Inc. are conducting negotiations for the acquisition for cash by Signal of the 49.5 percent of UOP which it does not presently own, announced Forrest N. Shumway, president and chief executive officer of Signal, and James V. Crawford, UOP president.

> Price and other terms of the proposed transaction have not yet been finalized and would be subject to approval of the boards of directors of Signal and UOP, scheduled to meet early next week, the stockholders of UOP and certain federal agencies.

The announcement also referred to the fact that the closing price of UOP's common stock on that day was $14.50 per share.

Two days later, on March 2, 1978, Signal issued a second press release stating that its management would recommend a price in the range of $20 to $21 per share for UOP's 49.5% minority interest. This announcement referred to Signal's earlier statement that "negotiations" were being conducted for the acquisition of the minority shares.

Between Tuesday, February 28, 1978 and Monday, March 6, 1978, a total of four business days, Crawford spoke by telephone with all of UOP's non-Signal, i.e., outside, directors. Also during that period, Crawford retained Lehman Brothers to render a fairness opinion as to the price offered the minority for its stock. He gave two reasons for this choice. First, the time schedule between the announcement and the board meetings was short (by then only three business days) and since Lehman Brothers had been acting as UOP's investment banker for many years, Crawford felt that it would be in the best position to respond on such brief notice. Second, James W. Glanville, a long-time director of UOP and a partner in Lehman Brothers, had acted as a financial advisor to UOP for many years. Crawford believed that Glanville's familiarity with UOP, as a member of its board, would also be of assistance in enabling Lehman Brothers to render a fairness opinion within the existing time constraints.

Crawford telephoned Glanville, who gave his assurance that Lehman Brothers had no conflicts that would prevent it from accepting the task. Glanville's immediate personal reaction was that a price of $20 to $21 would certainly be fair, since it represented almost a 50% premium over UOP's market price. Glanville sought a $250,000 fee for Lehman Brothers' services, but Crawford thought this too much. After further discussions Glanville finally agreed that Lehman Brothers would render its fairness opinion for $150,000.

During this period Crawford also had several telephone contacts with Signal officials. In only one of them, however, was the price of the shares discussed. In a conversation with Walkup, Crawford advised that as a result of his communications with UOP's non-Signal directors, it was his feeling that the price would have to be the top of the proposed range, or $21 per share, if the approval of UOP's outside directors was to be obtained. But again, he did not seek any price higher than $21.

Glanville assembled a three-man Lehman Brothers team to do the work on the fairness opinion. These persons examined relevant documents and information concerning UOP, including its annual reports and its Securities and Exchange Commission filings from 1973 through 1976, as well as its audited financial statements for 1977, its interim reports to shareholders, and its recent and historical market prices and trading volumes. In addition, on Friday, March 3, 1978, two members of the Lehman Brothers team flew to UOP's headquarters in Des Plaines, Illinois, to perform a "due diligence" visit, during the course of which they interviewed Crawford as well as UOP's general counsel, its chief financial officer, and other key executives and personnel.

As a result, the Lehman Brothers team concluded that "the price of either $20 or $21 would be a fair price for the remaining shares of UOP".

They telephoned this impression to Glanville, who was spending the weekend in Vermont.

On Monday morning, March 6, 1978, Glanville and the senior member of the Lehman Brothers team flew to Des Plaines to attend the scheduled UOP directors meeting. Glanville looked over the assembled information during the flight. The two had with them the draft of a "fairness opinion letter" in which the price had been left blank. Either during or immediately prior to the directors' meeting, the two-page "fairness opinion letter" was typed in final form and the price of $21 per share was inserted.

On March 6, 1978, both the Signal and UOP boards were convened to consider the proposed merger. Telephone communications were maintained between the two meetings. Walkup, Signal's board chairman, and also a UOP director, attended UOP's meeting with Crawford in order to present Signal's position and answer any questions that UOP's non-Signal directors might have. Arledge and Chitiea, along with Signal's other designees on UOP's board, participated by conference telephone. All of UOP's outside directors attended the meeting either in person or by conference telephone.

First, Signal's board unanimously adopted a resolution authorizing Signal to propose to UOP a cash merger of $21 per share as outlined in a certain merger agreement and other supporting documents. This proposal required that the merger be approved by a majority of UOP's outstanding minority shares voting at the stockholders meeting at which the merger would be considered, and that the minority shares voting in favor of the merger, when coupled with Signal's 50.5% interest would have to comprise at least two-thirds of all UOP shares. Otherwise the proposed merger would be deemed disapproved.

UOP's board then considered the proposal. Copies of the agreement were delivered to the directors in attendance, and other copies had been forwarded earlier to the directors participating by telephone. They also had before them UOP financial data for 1974–1977, UOP's most recent financial statements, market price information, and budget projections for 1978. In addition they had Lehman Brothers' hurriedly prepared fairness opinion letter finding the price of $21 to be fair. Glanville, the Lehman Brothers partner, and UOP director, commented on the information that had gone into preparation of the letter. * * *

After consideration of Signal's proposal, Walkup and Crawford left the meeting to permit a free and uninhibited exchange between UOP's non-Signal directors. Upon their return a resolution to accept Signal's offer was then proposed and adopted. While Signal's men on UOP's board participated in various aspects of the meeting, they abstained from voting. However, the minutes show that each of them "if voting would have voted yes."

On March 7, 1978, UOP sent a letter to its shareholders advising them of the action taken by UOP's board with respect to Signal's offer. This document pointed out, among other things, that on February 28, 1978 "both companies had announced negotiations were being conducted."

Despite the swift board action of the two companies, the merger was not submitted to UOP's shareholders until their annual meeting on May 26, 1978. In the notice of that meeting and proxy statement sent to shareholders in

May, UOP's management and board urged that the merger be approved. The proxy statement also advised:

> The price was determined after *discussions* between James V. Crawford, a director of Signal and Chief Executive Officer of UOP, and officers of Signal which took place during meetings on February 28, 1978, and in the course of several subsequent telephone conversations. (Emphasis added.)

In the original draft of the proxy statement the word "negotiations" had been used rather than "discussions". However, when the Securities and Exchange Commission sought details of the "negotiations" as part of its review of these materials, the term was deleted and the word "discussions" was substituted. The proxy statement indicated that the vote of UOP's board in approving the merger had been unanimous. It also advised the shareholders that Lehman Brothers had given its opinion that the merger price of $21 per share was fair to UOP's minority. However, it did not disclose the hurried method by which this conclusion was reached.

As of the record date of UOP's annual meeting, there were 11,488,302 shares of UOP common stock outstanding, 5,688,302 of which were owned by the minority. At the meeting only 56%, or 3,208,652, of the minority shares were voted. Of these, 2,953,812, or 51.9% of the total minority, voted for the merger, and 254,840 voted against it. When Signal's stock was added to the minority shares voting in favor, a total of 76.2% of UOP's outstanding shares approved the merger while only 2.2% opposed it.

By its terms the merger became effective on May 26, 1978, and each share of UOP's stock held by the minority was automatically converted into a right to receive $21 cash.

II.

A.

A primary issue mandating reversal is the preparation by two UOP directors, Arledge and Chitiea, of their feasibility study for the exclusive use and benefit of Signal. This document was of obvious significance to both Signal and UOP. Using UOP data, it described the advantages to Signal of ousting the minority at a price range of $21–$24 per share. Mr. Arledge, one of the authors, outlined the benefits to Signal:[5]

Purpose of the Merger

    (1) Provides an outstanding investment opportunity for Signal— (Better than any recent acquisition we have seen).

    (2) Increases Signal's earnings.

    (3) Facilitates the flow of resources between Signal and its subsidiaries. (Big factor works both ways).

    (4) Provides cost savings potential for Signal and UOP.

    (5) Improves the percentage of Signal's 'operating earnings' as opposed to 'holding company earnings'.

    (6) Simplifies the understanding of Signal.

---

5. [By the Court] The parentheses indicate certain handwritten comments of Mr. Arledge.

(7) Facilitates technological exchange among Signal's subsidiaries.

(8) Eliminates potential conflicts of interest.

Having written those words, solely for the use of Signal, it is clear from the record that neither Arledge nor Chitiea shared this report with their fellow directors of UOP. We are satisfied that no one else did either. This conduct hardly meets the fiduciary standards applicable to such a transaction. * * *

The Arledge–Chitiea report speaks for itself in supporting the Chancellor's finding that a price of up to $24 was a "good investment" for Signal. It shows that a return on the investment at $21 would be 15.7% versus 15.5% at $24 per share. This was a difference of only two-tenths of one percent, while it meant over $17,000,000 to the minority. Under such circumstances, paying UOP's minority shareholders $24 would have had relatively little long-term effect on Signal, and the Chancellor's findings concerning the benefit to Signal, even at a price of $24, were obviously correct.

Certainly, this was a matter of material significance to UOP and its shareholders. Since the study was prepared by two UOP directors, using UOP information for the exclusive benefit of Signal, and nothing whatever was done to disclose it to the outside UOP directors or the minority shareholders, a question of breach of fiduciary duty arises. This problem occurs because there were common Signal–UOP directors participating, at least to some extent, in the UOP board's decision-making processes without full disclosure of the conflicts they faced.[6]

B.

In assessing this situation, the Court of Chancery was required to:

[E]xamine what information defendants had and to measure it against what they gave to the minority stockholders, in a context in which 'complete candor' is required. In other words, the limited function of the Court was to determine whether defendants had disclosed all information in their possession germane to the transaction in issue. And by 'germane' we mean, for present purposes, information such as a reasonable shareholder would consider important in deciding whether to sell or retain stock.

* * * Completeness, not adequacy, is both the norm and the mandate under present circumstances.

Lynch v. Vickers Energy Corp., Del.Supr., 383 A.2d 278, 281 (1977) (*Lynch I*). This is merely stating in another way the long-existing principle of Delaware law that these Signal designated directors on UOP's board still

---

6. [By the Court] Although perfection is not possible, or expected, the result here could have been entirely different if UOP had appointed an independent negotiating committee of its outside directors to deal with Signal at arm's length. See, e.g., Harriman v. E.I. Du Pont de Nemours & Co., 411 F.Supp. 133 (D.Del.1975). Since fairness in this context can be equated to conduct by a theoretical, wholly independent, board of directors acting upon the matter before them, it is unfortunate that this course apparently was neither considered nor pursued. Johnston v. Greene, Del.Supr., 121 A.2d 919, 925 (1956). Particularly in a parent-subsidiary context, a showing that the action taken was as though each of the contending parties had in fact exerted its bargaining power against the other at arm's length is strong evidence that the transaction meets the test of fairness. Getty Oil Co. v. Skelly Oil Co., Del.Supr., 267 A.2d 883, 886 (1970).

owed UOP and its shareholders an uncompromising duty of loyalty. The classic language of Guth v. Loft, Inc., Del.Supr., 5 A.2d 503, 510 (1939), requires no embellishment:

> A public policy, existing through the years, and derived from a profound knowledge of human characteristics and motives, has established a rule that demands of a corporate officer or director, peremptorily and inexorably, the most scrupulous observance of his duty, not only affirmatively to protect the interests of the corporation committed to his charge, but also to refrain from doing anything that would work injury to the corporation, or to deprive it of profit or advantage which his skill and ability might properly bring to it, or to enable it to make in the reasonable and lawful exercise of its powers. The rule that requires an undivided and unselfish loyalty to the corporation demands that there shall be no conflict between duty and self-interest.

Given the absence of any attempt to structure this transaction on an arm's length basis, Signal cannot escape the effects of the conflicts it faced, particularly when its designees on UOP's board did not totally abstain from participation in the matter. There is no "safe harbor" for such divided loyalties in Delaware. When directors of a Delaware corporation are on both sides of a transaction, they are required to demonstrate their utmost good faith and the most scrupulous inherent fairness of the bargain. Gottlieb v. Heyden Chemical Corp., Del.Supr., 91 A.2d 57, 57–58 (1952). The requirement of fairness is unflinching in its demand that where one stands on both sides of a transaction, he has the burden of establishing its entire fairness, sufficient to pass the test of careful scrutiny by the courts. Sterling v. Mayflower Hotel Corp., Del.Super., 93 A.2d 107, 110 (1952).

There is no dilution of this obligation where one holds dual or multiple directorships, as in a parent-subsidiary context. Levien v. Sinclair Oil Corp., Del.Ch., 261 A.2d 911, 915 (1969). Thus, individuals who act in a dual capacity as directors of two corporations, one of whom is parent and the other subsidiary, owe the same duty of good management to both corporations, and in the absence of an independent negotiating structure (see note [6], page 789, supra), or the directors' total abstention from any participation in the matter, this duty is to be exercised in light of what is best for both companies. Warshaw v. Calhoun, Del.Supr., 221 A.2d 487, 492 (1966). The record demonstrates that Signal has not met this obligation.

C.

The concept of fairness has two basic aspects: fair dealing and fair price. The former embraces questions of when the transaction was timed, how it was initiated, structured, negotiated, disclosed to the directors, and how the approvals of the directors and the stockholders were obtained. The latter aspect of fairness relates to the economic and financial considerations of the proposed merger, including all relevant factors: assets, market value, earnings, future prospects, and any other elements that affect the intrinsic or inherent value of a company's stock. Moore, The "Interested" Director or Officer Transaction, 4 Del.J.Corp.L. 674, 676 (1979). See Tri–Continental Corp. v. Battye, Del.Supr., 74 A.2d 71, 72 (1950); 8 Del.C. § 262(h). However, the test for fairness is not a bifurcated one as between fair dealing and price. All aspects of the issue must be examined as a whole since the question is one of entire fairness. However, in a non-fraudulent transaction we recognize that price may be the preponderant consideration outweighing other features of the merger. Here, we address the two basic aspects of fairness separately because we find reversible error as to both.

D.

Part of fair dealing is the obvious duty of candor required by *Lynch I,* supra. Moreover, one possessing superior knowledge may not mislead any stockholder by use of corporate information to which the latter is not privy. Lank v. Steiner, Del.Supr., 224 A.2d 242, 244 (1966). Delaware has long imposed this duty even upon persons who are not corporate officers or directors, but who nonetheless are privy to matters of interest or significance to their company. Brophy v. Cities Service Co., Del.Ch., 70 A.2d 5, 7 (1949). With the well-established Delaware law on the subject, and the Court of Chancery's findings of fact here, it is inevitable that the obvious conflicts posed by Arledge and Chitiea's preparation of their "feasibility study", derived from UOP information, for the sole use and benefit of Signal, cannot pass muster.

The Arledge–Chitiea report is but one aspect of the element of fair dealing. How did this merger evolve? It is clear that it was entirely initiated by Signal. The serious time constraints under which the principals acted were all set by Signal. It had not found a suitable outlet for its excess cash and considered UOP a desirable investment, particularly since it was now in a position to acquire the whole company for itself. For whatever reasons, and they were only Signal's, the entire transaction was presented to and approved by UOP's board within four business days. Standing alone, this is not necessarily indicative of any lack of fairness by a majority shareholder. It was what occurred, or more properly, what did not occur, during this brief period that makes the time constraints imposed by Signal relevant to the issue of fairness.

The structure of the transaction, again, was Signal's doing. So far as negotiations were concerned, it is clear that they were modest at best. Crawford, Signal's man at UOP, never really talked price with Signal, except to accede to its management's statements on the subject, and to convey to Signal the UOP outside directors' view that as between the $20–$21 range under consideration, it would have to be $21. The latter is not a surprising outcome, but hardly arm's length negotiations. Only the protection of benefits for UOP's key employees and the issue of Lehman Brothers' fee approached any concept of bargaining.

As we have noted, the matter of disclosure to the UOP directors was wholly flawed by the conflicts of interest raised by the Arledge–Chitiea report. All of those conflicts were resolved by Signal in its own favor without divulging any aspect of them to UOP.

This cannot but undermine a conclusion that this merger meets any reasonable test of fairness. The outside UOP directors lacked one material piece of information generated by two of their colleagues, but shared only with Signal. True, the UOP board had the Lehman Brothers' fairness opinion, but that firm has been blamed by the plaintiff for the hurried task it performed, when more properly the responsibility for this lies with Signal.

There was no disclosure of the circumstances surrounding the rather cursory preparation of the Lehman Brothers' fairness opinion. Instead, the impression was given UOP's minority that a careful study had been made, when in fact speed was the hallmark, and Mr. Glanville, Lehman's partner in charge of the matter, and also a UOP director, having spent the weekend in Vermont, brought a draft of the "fairness opinion letter" to the UOP directors' meeting on March 6, 1978 with the price left blank. We can only conclude from the record that the rush imposed on Lehman Brothers by Signal's timetable contributed to the difficulties under which this investment banking firm attempted to perform its responsibilities. Yet, none of this was disclosed to UOP's minority.

Finally, the minority stockholders were denied the critical information that Signal considered a price of $24 to be a good investment. Since this would have meant over $17,000,000 more to the minority, we cannot conclude that the shareholder vote was an informed one. Under the circumstances, an approval by a majority of the minority was meaningless. Lynch I, 383 A.2d at 279, 281.

Given these particulars and the Delaware law on the subject, the record does not establish that this transaction satisfies any reasonable concept of fair dealing, and the Chancellor's findings in that regard must be reversed.

Turning to the matter of price, plaintiff also challenges its fairness. His evidence was that on the date the merger was approved the stock was worth at least $26 per share. In support, he offered the testimony of a chartered investment analyst who used two basic approaches to valuation: a comparative analysis of the premium paid over market in ten other tender offer-merger combinations, and a discounted cash flow analysis.

In this breach of fiduciary duty case, the Chancellor perceived that the approach to valuation was the same as that in an appraisal proceeding. Consistent with precedent, he rejected plaintiff's method of proof and accepted defendants' evidence of value as being in accord with practice under prior case law. This means that the so-called "Delaware block" or weighted average method was employed wherein the elements of value, i.e., assets, market price, earnings, etc., were assigned a particular weight and the resulting amounts added to determine the value per share. This procedure has been in use for decades. See In re General Realty & Utilities Corp., Del.Ch., 52 A.2d 6, 14–15 (1947). However, to the extent it excludes other generally accepted techniques used in the financial community and the courts, it is now clearly outmoded. It is time we recognize this in appraisal and other stock valuation proceedings and bring our law current on the subject.

While the Chancellor rejected plaintiff's discounted cash flow method of valuing UOP's stock, as not corresponding with "either logic or the existing law," it is significant that this was essentially the focus, i.e., earnings potential of UOP, of Messrs. Arledge and Chitiea in their evaluation of the merger. Accordingly, the standard "Delaware block" or weighted average method of valuation, formerly employed in appraisal and other stock valuation cases, shall no longer exclusively control such proceedings. We believe that a more liberal approach must include proof of value by any techniques or methods which are generally considered acceptable in the financial community and otherwise admissible in court, subject only to our interpretation of 8

Del.C. § 262(h), infra. This will obviate the very structured and mechanistic procedure that has heretofore governed such matters. See Jacques Coe & Co. v. Minneapolis–Moline Co., Del.Ch., 75 A.2d 244, 247 (1950); Tri–Continental Corp. v. Battye, Del.Ch., 66 A.2d 910, 917–18 (1949).

Fair price obviously requires consideration of all relevant factors involving the value of a company. * * *

Although the Chancellor received the plaintiff's evidence, his opinion indicates that the use of it was precluded because of past Delaware practice. While we do not suggest a monetary result one way or the other, we do think the plaintiff's evidence should be part of the factual mix and weighed as such. Until the $21 price is measured on remand by the valuation standards mandated by Delaware law, there can be no finding at the present stage of these proceedings that the price is fair. Given the lack of any candid disclosure of the material facts surrounding establishment of the $21 price, the majority of the minority vote, approving the merger, is meaningless.

The plaintiff has not sought an appraisal, but rescissory damages of the type contemplated by Lynch v. Vickers Energy Corp., Del., 429 A.2d 497, 505–06 (1981) (*Lynch II*).[7] In view of the approach to valuation that we announce today, we see no basis in our law for *Lynch II*'s exclusive monetary formula for relief. On remand the plaintiff will be permitted to test the fairness of the $21 price by the standards we herein establish, in conformity with the principle applicable to an appraisal—that fair value be determined by taking "into account all relevant factors" [see 8 Del.C. § 262(h), supra]. In our view this includes the elements of rescissory damages if the Chancellor considers them susceptible of proof and a remedy appropriate to all the issues of fairness before him. To the extent that Lynch II, 429 A.2d at 505–06, purports to limit the Chancellor's discretion to a single remedial formula for monetary damages in a cash-out merger, it is overruled.

While a plaintiff's monetary remedy ordinarily should be confined to the more liberalized appraisal proceeding herein established, we do not intend any limitation on the historic powers of the Chancellor to grant such other relief as the facts of a particular case may dictate. The appraisal remedy we approve may not be adequate in certain cases, particularly where fraud, misrepresentation, self-dealing, deliberate waste of corporate assets, or gross and palpable overreaching are involved. Cole v. National Cash Credit Association, Del.Ch., 156 A. 183, 187 (1931). Under such circumstances, the Chancellor's powers are complete to fashion any form of equitable and monetary relief as may be appropriate, including rescissory damages. Since it is apparent that this long completed transaction is too involved to undo, and in view of the Chancellor's discretion, the award, if any, should be in the form of monetary damages based upon entire fairness standards, i.e., fair dealing and fair price.

---

7. [By the Editors] Rescissory damages are defined in *Lynch* as "damages which are the monetary equivalent of rescission and which will, in effect, equal the increment in value that [the defendant] enjoyed as a result of acquiring and holding the * * * stock in issue. That is consistent with the basis for liability which is the law of the case, and it is a norm applied when the equitable remedy of rescission is impractical." 429 A.2d at 501. When calculating rescissory damages, the principle of mitigation of damages is inapplicable, i.e., damages are not reduced by amounts the plaintiff could have saved by making an investment in the security in question at some later time. However, damages are reduced by any amount received by the plaintiff in connection with the wrongful transaction that gave rise to the right to rescissory damages. Id. at 505–06.

Obviously, there are other litigants, like the plaintiff, who abjured an appraisal and whose rights to challenge the element of fair value must be preserved.[8] Accordingly, the quasi-appraisal remedy we grant the plaintiff here will apply only to: (1) this case; (2) any case now pending on appeal to this Court; (3) any case now pending in the Court of Chancery which has not yet been appealed but which may be eligible for direct appeal to this Court; (4) any case challenging a cash-out merger, the effective date of which is on or before February 1, 1983; and (5) any proposed merger to be presented at a shareholders' meeting, the notification of which is mailed to the stockholders on or before February 23, 1983. Thereafter, the provisions of 8 Del.C. § 262, as herein construed, respecting the scope of an appraisal and the means for perfecting the same, shall govern the financial remedy available to minority shareholders in a cash-out merger. Thus, we return to the well established principles of Stauffer v. Standard Brands Inc., Del.Supr., 187 A.2d 78 (1962) and David J. Greene & Co. v. Schenley Industries, Inc., Del.Ch., 281 A.2d 30 (1971), mandating a stockholder's recourse to the basic remedy of an appraisal.

III.

Finally, we address the matter of business purpose. The defendants contend that the purpose of this merger was not a proper subject of inquiry by the trial court. The plaintiff says that no valid purpose existed—the entire transaction was a mere subterfuge designed to eliminate the minority. The Chancellor ruled otherwise, but in so doing he clearly circumscribed the thrust and effect of *Singer*. This has led to the thoroughly sound observation that the business purpose test "may be * * * virtually interpreted out of existence, as it was in *Weinberger*."

The requirement of a business purpose is new to our law of mergers and was a departure from prior case law. In view of the fairness test which has long been applicable to parent-subsidiary mergers, Sterling v. Mayflower Hotel Corp., Del.Supr., 93 A.2d 107, 109–10 (1952), the expanded appraisal remedy now available to shareholders, and the broad discretion of the Chancellor to fashion such relief as the facts of a given case may dictate, we do not believe that any additional meaningful protection is afforded minority shareholders by the business purpose requirement of the trilogy of *Singer, Tanzer* [v. International General Industries, Inc., 379 A.2d 1121 (Del.1977)], [Roland International Corp. v.] *Najjar* [407 A.2d 1032 (Del.1979)], and their progeny. Accordingly, such requirement shall no longer be of any force or effect.

The judgment of the Court of Chancery, finding both the circumstances of the merger and the price paid the minority shareholders to be fair, is reversed. The matter is remanded for further proceedings consistent herewith. Upon remand the plaintiff's post-trial motion to enlarge the class should be granted. * * *

Reversed and Remanded.

---

8. [By the Court] Under 8 Del.C. § 262(a), (d) & (e), a stockholder is required to act within certain time periods to perfect the right to an appraisal.

Notes

(1) In a "cash out" merger a parent corporation owning more than 50 percent of the stock of a subsidiary corporation may compel the minority share-holders of the subsidiary to accept cash for their shares in an amount determined by the parent, subject, however, to the appraisal rights provided in Chapter 13 of the MBCA. The process by which this is accomplished is a merger in which minority shareholders in the subsidiary corporation are required to accept cash rather than shares in the continuing corporation, as permitted by § 11.01(a)(3) of the MBCA. In the modern law of corporations it is important to recognize that a "merger" is not limited to the intuitive notion of two independent corporations agreeing to fuse together with shareholders of both corporations having a continuing interest in the fused enterprise.

(2) There are at least five problems with the appraisal remedy, at least in its traditional form: (1) The shareholders must litigate with the corporation as to the fair value issue; the corporation usually has extensive resources and intimate knowledge of where the skeletons are while the shareholder does not. (2) The shareholder receives nothing until the litigation establishing fair value, including appeals, is exhausted; as a result he or she may receive nothing for five years or so (while a person accepting the transaction receives immediate payment), and an ultimate award of statutory interest is not likely to be viewed as adequate compensation for the loss of the use of the proceeds for a long period. (3) The shareholder must bear his or her own litigation expenses, which may be substantial, particularly if asset valuations are involved. (4) The method of valuation routinely used in most states, the "Delaware block" approach discussed in *Weinberger,* may not yield a valuation that is realistic. (5) The payment of interest on the award is discretionary with the Court, so that no interest at all may be awarded, or interest may be calculated on a simple interest basis rather than on a compound interest basis, as occurred, for example, in In the Matter of the Appraisal of Shell Oil Co., 607 A.2d 1213 (Del.1992).

(3) Actual experience in Delaware with the "business purpose" test revealed that it apparently did not help to separate abusive transactions from proper ones. In Tanzer v. International Gen. Indus., Inc., 379 A.2d 1121 (Del.1977), for example, the Court held that the parent corporation's actions should be measured by reference to its status and interest as a shareholder, including its own corporate concerns, and therefore a purpose "to facilitate long term debt financing" of the parent was a proper business purpose. Id. at 1124–25. Some courts, however, have required a business purpose (as well as meeting the *Weinberger* standards). In Alpert v. 28 Williams St. Corp., 63 N.Y.2d 557, 483 N.Y.S.2d 667, 473 N.E.2d 19 (1984), for example, the New York Court of Appeals stated that in addition to fair dealing and fair price, the directors must justify the variant treatment between the majority and the minority by showing some business purpose for the transaction.

(4) It has become customary in Delaware cash-out transactions to structure the procedure so that "independent" directors of the subsidiary negotiate the terms of the transaction with representatives of the parent, and that approval of the transaction is conditional upon an affirmative vote of a majority of the minority shareholders. One consequence is that it has become standard practice to place outside persons on the board of directors of subsidiaries that have publicly-held minority shares. Cases discussing these procedural requirements include Rosenblatt v. Getty Oil Co., 493 A.2d 929 (Del.1985).

(5) The reason to have an independent committee when negotiating a cash-out is to replicate arm's length bargaining and thereby shift this burden of proof

in a shareholder suit to the plaintiff. In many cases this allocation of the burden of proof is outcome determinative. In Kahn v. Lynch Communication Systems, Inc., 638 A.2d 1110 (Del.1994), a properly constituted and appropriately functioning special committee was created, but the defendants were not able to show that the bargaining process replicated a truly arms-length bargaining process. Hence the burden of proof did not shift to the plaintiff. On remand, the defendants were able to persuade the court that there had been full disclosure and the price was entirely fair so that the transaction was upheld. The Supreme Court accepted this conclusion. Kahn v. Lynch Communication Systems, Inc., 669 A.2d 79 (Del.1995). In Kahn v. Tremont Corporation, 694 A.2d 422 (Del.1997), the Court held (in an unusual 2–1–2 decision) that the burden did not shift where the chairman of the independent committee had close associations with the corporation and in fact dominated the negotiation process while the other two members of the committee were passive. As a result, arms length bargaining was not replicated.

(6) In all of these cases, the Delaware courts have emphasized the importance of full disclosure to the minority shareholders, and have not hesitated to enjoin cash out transactions when such disclosure was lacking. E.g., Joseph v. Shell Oil Co., 482 A.2d 335 (Del.Ch.1984), holding affirmed in connected case, Selfe v. Joseph, 501 A.2d 409 (Del.1985). Similarly, the Delaware courts have set aside transactions where there appears to have been manipulation of the transaction to minimize the financial rights of minority shareholders (e.g., Rabkin v. Philip A. Hunt Chem. Corp., 498 A.2d 1099 (Del.1985)), or the use of unfair or abusive tactics (e.g., Sealy Mattress Co. of N.J. v. Sealy, Inc., 532 A.2d 1324, 1335 (Del.Ch.1987)).

(7) Decisions since *Weinberger* have made it easier for plaintiffs to bring cases using the entire fairness test. In Cede & Co. v. Technicolor, 634 A.2d 345 (Del. 1993), the Delaware Supreme Court held that unfair dealing is compensable even in the absence of an unfair price. The Court of Chancery had found the board of directors had breached its duty of care but dismissed the suit because plaintiffs had not proven an injury resulting from the breach. In rejecting the Chancellor's proximate cause test, the Delaware Supreme Court suggested that unfair dealing alone could be a compensable harm, thus expanding the kinds of harm that fall under the procedural prong of the entire fairness test. In In re Tri-Star Pictures, Inc., Litig., 634 A.2d 319 (Del. 1993), shareholders challenged a transaction that gave Coca-Cola an eighty percent interest in Tri-Star in exchange for Coca-Cola's Entertainment Sector. The Court confronted the difficulty minority shareholders can face in gaining standing because their injuries often sound like derivative claims rather than individualized harms. In *Tri-Star* the Court found that dilution of voting power, equity dilution, and interference with a shareholder's right to cast an informed vote supported individual causes of action against a controlling shareholder when only minority shareholders were harmed.

(8) "Fairness opinions," such as the one provided by Lehman Brothers in connection with the UOP buyout, are virtually standard operating procedures in transactions involving corporate control and cash out transactions. They state that the price is "fair from a financial point of view," and thereby provide assurance to the directors. Valuation of a minority interest in a large corporation is subjective to some extent in many circumstances, and there is a good chance that independent valuations of the same business might vary considerably. Hence, it is certainly not a coincidence that the overwhelming bulk of fairness opinions come in very close to the figure desired by the board of directors authorizing the opinion. There apparently has been no recent example of liability being imposed on an investment banker for an inaccurate fairness opinion.

(9) Rule 13e–3, 17 C.F.R. § 240.13e–3 (2004), promulgated under the Securities Exchange Act of 1934, is applicable to ''going private'' transactions which involve the solicitation of public shareholders in cash-out transactions. This rule and the accompanying schedules require the issuer or affiliate to make extensive disclosures in considerable detail about the source of any fairness opinion, the relationship between the preparer of the opinion and the issuer, and the analyses underlying the opinion, including specific values or ranges of values derived from such analyses. These disclosure requirements probably result in considerably greater care being taken in the preparation of a fairness opinion. The SEC staff also requires similar disclosures in connection with outside opinions or appraisals obtained in connection with control transactions that do not involve the elimination of public shareholders and which therefore are not subject to rule 13e–3.

B.   CORPORATE OPPORTUNITY

NORTHEAST HARBOR GOLF CLUB, INC. v. HARRIS

Supreme Judicial Court of Maine, 1995.
661 A.2d 1146.

Before WATHEN, C.J., and ROBERTS, GLASSMAN, DANA, AND LIPEZ, JJ.

ROBERTS, JUSTICE.

Northeast Harbor Golf Club, Inc., appeals from a judgment entered in the Superior Court (Hancock County, Atwood, J.) following a nonjury trial. The Club maintains that the trial court erred in finding that Nancy Harris did not breach her fiduciary duty as president of the Club by purchasing and developing property abutting the golf course. Because we today adopt principles different from those applied by the trial court in determining that Harris's activities did not constitute a breach of the corporate opportunity doctrine, we vacate the judgment.

I.

THE FACTS

Nancy Harris was the president of the Northeast Harbor Golf Club, a Maine corporation, from 1971 until she was asked to resign in 1990. The Club also had a board of directors that was responsible for making or approving significant policy decisions. The Club's only major asset was a golf course in Mount Desert. During Harris's tenure as president, the board occasionally discussed the possibility of developing some of the Club's real estate in order to raise money. Although Harris was generally in favor of tasteful development, the board always ''shied away'' from that type of activity.

In 1979, Robert Suminsby informed Harris that he was the listing broker for the Gilpin property, which comprised three noncontiguous parcels located among the fairways of the golf course. The property included an unused right-of-way on which the Club's parking lot and clubhouse were located. It was also encumbered by an easement in favor of the Club allowing foot traffic from the green of one hole to the next tee. Suminsby testified that he contacted Harris because she was the president of the Club and he believed that the Club would be interested in buying the property in order to prevent development.

Harris immediately agreed to purchase the Gilpin property in her own name for the asking price of $45,000. She did not disclose her plans to purchase the property to the Club's board prior to the purchase. She informed the board at its annual August meeting that she had purchased the property, that she intended to hold it in her own name, and that the Club would be "protected." The board took no action in response to the Harris purchase. She testified that at the time of the purchase she had no plans to develop the property and that no such plans took shape until 1988.

In 1984, while playing golf with the postmaster of Northeast Harbor, Harris learned that a parcel of land owned by the heirs of the Smallidge family might be available for purchase. The Smallidge parcel was surrounded on three sides by the golf course and on the fourth side by a house lot. It had no access to the road. With the ultimate goal of acquiring the property, Harris instructed her lawyer to locate the Smallidge heirs. Harris testified that she told a number of individual board members about her attempt to acquire the Smallidge parcel. At a board meeting in August 1985, Harris formally disclosed to the board that she had purchased the Smallidge property.[9] The minutes of that meeting show that she told the board she had no present plans to develop the Smallidge parcel. Harris testified that at the time of the purchase of the Smallidge property she nonetheless thought it might be nice to have some houses there. Again, the board took no formal action as a result of Harris's purchase. Harris acquired the Smallidge property from ten heirs, paying a total of $60,000. In 1990, Harris paid $275,000 for the lot and building separating the Smallidge parcel from the road in order to gain access to the otherwise landlocked parcel.

The trial court expressly found that the Club would have been unable to purchase either the Gilpin or Smallidge properties for itself, relying on testimony that the Club continually experienced financial difficulties, operated annually at a deficit, and depended on contributions from the directors to pay its bills. On the other hand, there was evidence that the Club had occasionally engaged in successful fund-raising, including a two-year period shortly after the Gilpin purchase during which the Club raised $115,000. The Club had $90,000 in a capital investment fund at the time of the Smallidge purchase.

In 1987 or 1988, Harris divided the real estate into 41 small lots, 14 on the Smallidge property and 27 on the Gilpin property. Apparently as part of her estate plan, Harris conveyed noncontiguous lots among the 41 to her children and retained others for herself. In 1991, Harris and her children exchanged deeds to reassemble the small lots into larger parcels. At the time the Club filed this suit, the property was divided into 11 lots, some owned by Harris and others by her children who are also defendants in this case. Harris estimated the value of all the real estate at the time of the trial to be $1,550,000.

In 1988, Harris, who was still president of the Club, and her children began the process of obtaining approval for a five-lot subdivision known as Bushwood on the lower Gilpin property. Even when the board learned of the

9. [By the Court] In fact, it appears that Harris did not take title to the property until October 26, 1985. She had only signed a purchase and sale agreement at the time of the August board meeting.

proposed subdivision, a majority failed to take any action. A group of directors formed a separate organization in order to oppose the subdivision on the basis that it violated the local zoning ordinance. After Harris's resignation as president, the Club also sought unsuccessfully to challenge the subdivision. See Northeast Harbor Golf Club, Inc. v. Town of Mount Desert, 618 A.2d 225 (Me.1992). Plans of Harris and her family for development of the other parcels are unclear, but the local zoning ordinance would permit construction of up to 11 houses on the land as currently divided.

After Harris's plans to develop Bushwood became apparent, the board grew increasingly divided concerning the propriety of development near the golf course. At least two directors, Henri Agnese and Nick Ludington, testified that they trusted Harris to act in the best interests of the Club and that they had no problem with the development plans for Bushwood. Other directors disagreed.

In particular, John Schafer, a Washington, D.C., lawyer and long-time member of the board, took issue with Harris's conduct. He testified that he had relied on Harris's representations at the time she acquired the properties that she would not develop them. According to Schafer, matters came to a head in August 1990 when a number of directors concluded that Harris's development plans irreconcilably conflicted with the Club's interests. As a result, Schafer and two other directors asked Harris to resign as president. In April 1991, after a substantial change in the board's membership, the board authorized the instant lawsuit against Harris for the breach of her fiduciary duty to act in the best interests of the corporation. The board simultaneously resolved that the proposed housing development was contrary to the best interests of the corporation.

The Club filed a complaint against Harris, her sons John and Shepard, and her daughter-in-law Melissa Harris. As amended, the complaint alleged that during her term as president Harris breached her fiduciary duty by purchasing the lots without providing notice and an opportunity for the Club to purchase the property and by subdividing the lots for future development. The Club sought an injunction to prevent development and also sought to impose a constructive trust on the property in question for the benefit of the Club.

The trial court found that Harris had not usurped a corporate opportunity because the acquisition of real estate was not in the Club's line of business. Moreover, it found that the corporation lacked the financial ability to purchase the real estate at issue. Finally, the court placed great emphasis on Harris's good faith. It noted her long and dedicated history of service to the Club, her personal oversight of the Club's growth, and her frequent financial contributions to the Club. The court found that her development activities were "generally * * * compatible with the corporation's business." This appeal followed.

II.

THE CORPORATE OPPORTUNITY DOCTRINE

Corporate officers and directors bear a duty of loyalty to the corporations they serve. As Justice Cardozo explained the fiduciary duty in Meinhard v. Salmon, 249 N.Y. 458, 164 N.E. 545, 546 (1928): * * * Maine has embraced this "unbending and inveterate" tradition. Corporate fiduciaries in Maine must discharge their duties in good faith with a view toward furthering the interests of the corporation. They must disclose and not withhold relevant information concerning any potential conflict of interest with the corporation, and they must refrain from using their position, influence, or knowledge of the affairs of the corporation to gain personal advantage. See Rosenthal v. Rosenthal, 543 A.2d 348, 352 (Me.1988); 13–A M.R.S.A. § 716 (Supp.1994).

Despite the general acceptance of the proposition that corporate fiduciaries owe a duty of loyalty to their corporations, there has been much confusion about the specific extent of that duty when, as here, it is contended that a fiduciary takes for herself a corporate opportunity. See, e.g., Victor Brudney & Robert C. Clark, A New Look at Corporate Opportunities, 94 Harv.L.Rev. 998, 998 (1981) ("Not only are the common formulations vague, but the courts have articulated no theory that would serve as a blueprint for constructing meaningful rules."). This case requires us for the first time to define the scope of the corporate opportunity doctrine in Maine.

Various courts have embraced different versions of the corporate opportunity doctrine. The test applied by the trial court and embraced by Harris is generally known as the "line of business" test. The seminal case applying the line of business test is Guth v. Loft, Inc., 5 A.2d 503 (Del.1939). In Guth, the Delaware Supreme Court adopted an intensely factual test stated in general terms as follows:

> [I]f there is presented to a corporate officer or director a business opportunity which the corporation is financially able to undertake, is, from its nature, in the line of the corporation's business and is of practical advantage to it, is one in which the corporation has an interest or a reasonable expectancy, and, by embracing the opportunity, the self-interest of the officer or director will be brought into conflict with that of his corporation, the law will not permit him to seize the opportunity for himself.

Id. at 511. The "real issue" under this test is whether the opportunity "was so closely associated with the existing business activities * * * as to bring the transaction within that class of cases where the acquisition of the property would throw the corporate officer purchasing it into competition with his company." Id. at 513. The Delaware court described that inquiry as "a factual question to be decided by reasonable inferences from objective facts." Id.

The line of business test suffers from some significant weaknesses. First, the question whether a particular activity is within a corporation's line of business is conceptually difficult to answer. The facts of the instant case demonstrate that difficulty. The Club is in the business of running a golf course. It is not in the business of developing real estate. In the traditional sense, therefore, the trial court correctly observed that the opportunity in this case was not a corporate opportunity within the meaning of the Guth test. Nevertheless, the record would support a finding that the Club had made the policy judgment that development of surrounding real estate was detrimental to the best interests of the Club. The acquisition of land adjacent to the golf course for the purpose of preventing future development would have enhanced the ability of the Club to implement that policy. The record also shows that the Club had occasionally considered reversing that policy and expanding its operations to include the development of surrounding real estate. Harris's activities effectively foreclosed the Club from pursuing that option with respect to prime locations adjacent to the golf course.

Second, the Guth test includes as an element the financial ability of the corporation to take advantage of the opportunity. The court in this case relied on the Club's supposed financial incapacity as a basis for excusing Harris's conduct. Often, the injection of financial ability into the equation will unduly favor the inside director or executive who has command of the facts relating to the finances of the corporation. Reliance on financial ability will also act as a disincentive to corporate executives to solve corporate financing and other problems. In addition, the Club could have prevented development without spending $275,000 to acquire the property Harris needed to obtain access to the road.

The Massachusetts Supreme Judicial Court adopted a different test in Durfee v. Durfee & Canning, Inc., 323 Mass. 187, 80 N.E.2d 522 (1948). The Durfee test has since come to be known as the "fairness test." According to Durfee, the

> true basis of governing doctrine rests on the unfairness in the particular circumstances of a director, whose relation to the corporation is fiduciary, taking advantage of an opportunity [for her personal profit] when the interest of the corporation justly call[s] for protection. This calls for application of ethical standards of what is fair and equitable * * * in particular sets of facts.

Id. at 529 (quoting Ballantine on Corporations 204–05 (rev. ed. 1946)). As with the Guth test, the Durfee test calls for a broad-ranging, intensely factual inquiry. The Durfee test suffers even more than the Guth test from a lack of principled content. It provides little or no practical guidance to the corporate officer or director seeking to measure her obligations.

The Minnesota Supreme Court elected "to combine the 'line of business' test with the 'fairness' test." Miller v. Miller, 301 Minn. 207, 222 N.W.2d 71, 81 (1974). It engaged in a two-step analysis, first determining whether a particular opportunity was within the corporation's line of business, then scrutinizing "the equitable considerations existing prior to, at the time of, and following the officer's acquisition." Id. The Miller court hoped by adopting this approach "to ameliorate the often-expressed criticism that the [corporate opportunity] doctrine is vague and subjects today's corporate management to the danger of unpredictable liability." Id. In fact, the test adopted in Miller merely piles the uncertainty and vagueness of the fairness test on top of the weaknesses in the line of business test.

Despite the weaknesses of each of these approaches to the corporate opportunity doctrine, they nonetheless rest on a single fundamental policy. At bottom, the corporate opportunity doctrine recognizes that a corporate fiduciary should not serve both corporate and personal interests at the same time. As we observed in Camden Land Co. v. Lewis, 101 Me. 78, 97, 63 A. 523, 531 (1905), corporate fiduciaries "owe their whole duty to the corporation, and they are not to be permitted to act when duty conflicts with interest. They cannot serve themselves and the corporation at the same time." The various formulations of the test are merely attempts to moderate the potentially harsh consequences of strict adherence to that policy. It is important to preserve some ability for corporate fiduciaries to pursue personal business interests that present no real threat to their duty of loyalty.

III.

THE AMERICAN LAW INSTITUTE APPROACH

In an attempt to protect the duty of loyalty while at the same time providing long-needed clarity and guidance for corporate decisionmakers, the American Law Institute has offered the most recently developed version of the corporate opportunity doctrine. PRINCIPLES OF CORPORATE GOVERNANCE § 5.05 (May 13, 1992), provides as follows:

§ 5.05 Taking of Corporate Opportunities by Directors or Senior Executives

(a) General Rule. A director [§ 1.13] or senior executive [§ 1.33] may not take advantage of a corporate opportunity unless:

(1) The director or senior executive first offers the corporate opportunity to the corporation and makes disclosure concerning the conflict of interest [§ 1.14(a)] and the corporate opportunity [§ 1.14(b)];

(2) The corporate opportunity is rejected by the corporation; and

(3) Either:

(A) The rejection of the opportunity is fair to the corporation;

(B) The opportunity is rejected in advance, following such disclosure, by disinterested directors [§ 1.15], or, in the case of a senior executive who is not a director, by a disinterested superior, in a manner that satisfies the standards of the business judgment rule [§ 4.01(c)]; or

(C) The rejection is authorized in advance or ratified, following such disclosure, by disinterested shareholders [§ 1.16], and the rejection is not equivalent to a waste of corporate assets [§ 1.42].

(b) Definition of a Corporate Opportunity. For purposes of this Section, a corporate opportunity means:

(1) Any opportunity to engage in a business activity of which a director or senior executive becomes aware, either:

(A) In connection with the performance of functions as a director or senior executive, or under circumstances that should reasonably lead the director or senior executive to believe that the person offering the opportunity expects it to be offered to the corporation; or

(B) Through the use of corporate information or property, if the resulting opportunity is one that the director or senior executive should reasonably be expected to believe would be of interest to the corporation; or

(2) Any opportunity to engage in a business activity of which a senior executive becomes aware and knows is closely related to a business in which the corporation is engaged or expects to engage.

(c) Burden of Proof. A party who challenges the taking of a corporate opportunity has the burden of proof, except that if such party establishes that the requirements of Subsection (a)(3)(B) or (C) are not met, the director or the senior executive has the burden of proving that the rejection and the taking of the opportunity were fair to the corporation.

(d) Ratification of Defective Disclosure. A good faith but defective disclosure of the facts concerning the corporate opportunity may be cured if at any time (but no later than a reasonable time after suit is filed challenging the taking of the corporate opportunity) the original rejection of the corporate opportunity is ratified, following the required disclosure, by the board, the shareholders, or the corporate decisionmaker who initially approved the rejection of the corporate opportunity, or such decisionmaker's successor.

(e) Special Rule Concerning Delayed Offering of Corporate Opportunities. Relief based solely on failure to first offer an opportunity to the corporation under Subsection (a)(1) is not available if: (1) such failure resulted from a good faith belief that the business activity did not constitute a corporate opportunity, and (2) not later than a reasonable time after suit is filed challenging the taking of the corporate opportunity, the corporate opportunity is to the extent possible offered to the corporation and rejected in a manner that satisfies the standards of Subsection (a).

The central feature of the ALI test is the strict requirement of full disclosure prior to taking advantage of any corporate opportunity. Id., § 5.05(a)(1). "If the opportunity is not offered to the corporation, the director or senior executive will not have satisfied § 5.05(a)." Id., cmt. to § 5.05(a). The corporation must then formally reject the opportunity. Id., § 505(a)(2). The ALI test is discussed at length and ultimately applied by the Oregon Supreme Court in Klinicki v. Lundgren, 298 Or. 662, 695 P.2d 906 (1985). As Klinicki describes the test, "full disclosure to the appropriate corporate body is * * * an absolute condition precedent to the validity of any forthcoming rejection as well as to the availability to the director or principal senior executive of the defense of fairness." Id. at 920. A "good faith but defective disclosure" by the corporate officer may be ratified after the fact only by an affirmative vote of the disinterested directors or shareholders. Principles of Corporate Governance § 5.05(d).

The ALI test defines "corporate opportunity" broadly. It includes opportunities "closely related to a business in which the corporation is engaged." Id., § 5.05(b). It also encompasses any opportunities that accrue to the fiduciary as a result of her position within the corporation. Id. This concept is most clearly illustrated by the testimony of Suminsby, the listing broker for the Gilpin property, which, if believed by the factfinder, would support a finding that the Gilpin property was offered to Harris specifically in her capacity as president of the Club. If the factfinder reached that conclusion, then at least the opportunity to acquire the Gilpin property would be a corporate opportunity. The state of the record concerning the Smallidge purchase precludes us from intimating any opinion whether that too would be a corporate opportunity.

Under the ALI standard, once the Club shows that the opportunity is a corporate opportunity, it must show either that Harris did not offer the opportunity to the Club or that the Club did not reject it properly. If the Club shows that the board did not reject the opportunity by a vote of the disinterested directors after full disclosure, then Harris may defend her actions on the basis that the taking of the opportunity was fair to the corporation. Id., § 5.05(c). If Harris failed to offer the opportunity at all, however, then she may not defend on the basis that the failure to offer the opportunity was fair. Id., cmt. to § 5.05(c).

The Klinicki court viewed the ALI test as an opportunity to bring some clarity to a murky area of the law. Klinicki, 695 P.2d at 915. We agree, and today we follow the ALI test. The disclosure-oriented approach provides a clear procedure whereby a corporate officer may insulate herself through prompt and complete disclosure from the possibility of a legal challenge. The requirement of disclosure recognizes the paramount importance of the corporate fiduciary's duty of loyalty. At the same time it protects the fiduciary's ability pursuant to the proper procedure to pursue her own business ventures free from the possibility of a lawsuit.

The importance of disclosure is familiar to the law of corporations in Maine. Pursuant to 13–A M.R.S.A. § 717 (1981), a corporate officer or director may enter into a transaction with the corporation in which she has a personal or adverse interest only if she discloses her interest in the transaction and secures ratification by a majority of the disinterested directors or shareholders.[10] * * * Like the ALI rule, section 717 was designed to "eliminate the inequities and uncertainties caused by the existing rules." Model Business Corp. Act § 41, ¶ 2, at 844 (1971).

IV.

CONCLUSION

The question remains how our adoption of the rule affects the result in the instant case. The trial court made a number of factual findings based on an extensive record.[11] The court made those findings, however, in the light of legal principles that are different from the principles that we today announce. Similarly, the parties did not have the opportunity to develop the record in this case with knowledge of the applicable legal standard. In these circumstances, fairness requires that we remand the case for further proceedings. Those further proceedings may include, at the trial court's discretion, the taking of further evidence. * * *

---

10. [By the Court] Unlike the ALI rule, 13–A M.R.S.A. § 717(1)(C) permits the director to defend on the ground of fairness even in the absence of disclosure. We are not troubled by this difference because the nature of the transactions covered by section 717 is such that the board will necessarily be aware of the transaction. It may therefore act to protect the interests of the corporation even if it is not aware of the interest of the fiduciary. In the case of a usurpation of a corporate opportunity, the corporation is defenseless unless the director discloses.

11. [By the Court] Harris raised the defense of laches and the statute of limitations but the court made no findings on those issues. We do not intimate what result the application of either doctrine would produce in this case. * * *

Judgment vacated [and remanded] for further proceedings consistent with the opinion herein.

All concurring.

Notes

(1) On a subsequent appeal, Northeast Harbor Golf Club v. Harris, 725 A.2d 1018 (Me.1999), the Maine Supreme Court held that while Harris had usurped corporate opportunities, the 6–year Maine statute of limitations had run on the bulk of Ms. Harris' acquisitions. The doctrine of laches was applied with respect to one small tract, and these two doctrines together barred entirely the Club's recovery. In the principal case, the Supreme Court of Maine rejects the traditional notion that an executive can usurp a corporate opportunity only if it is shown that the corporation had the financial ability to pursue the opportunity itself. What reasons does the Court give for doing this? Is the rationale unique to the facts of this case? While most courts refuse to allow financial inability to justify the pursuit of a financial opportunity by a fiduciary, Delaware recently affirmed the view that in order to plead usurpation of corporate opportunity, "the plaintiff must plead (*inter alia*) facts that demonstrate that the company had the financial means to take advantage of the alleged opportunity." Gibralt Capital Corp. v. Smith, 2001 WL 647837 (Del.Ch. May. 9, 2001).

(2) The complicating factor of corporate opportunity doctrine is that its application cannot be determined by simple hard and fast rules. Rather, it requires a particularized analysis of the circumstances. As a result, courts may readily disagree whether a specific opportunity should be viewed as a corporate opportunity. Section 5.05 seems to be a reasonable effort to encapsulate tests for this difficult, fact-sensitive area.

(3) The earliest test for corporate opportunities has been described as the "interest or expectancy" test. Professor Richard A. Epstein analyzes this test in the context of a contractual approach toward corporation law in Contract and Trust in Corporate Law: The Case of Corporate Opportunity, 21 Del.J.Corp.L. 5, 14–15 (1996).

(4) The most widely cited common law test is the "seminal" holding in Guth v. Loft, discussed in the principal case. In addition to the criticisms of this test in the principal opinion, Professor Pat K. Chew complains that it is much too favorable to the corporation. Professor Chew argues that this test actually restrains beneficial competition by preventing competition to established corporations. Professor Chew argues strongly that the corporate opportunity doctrine is warped in favor of the corporation and that as a result, it is a serious "restraint on individuals' freedom to compete [which] is contrary to society's long-standing goal of promoting competition." Pat K. Chew, Competing Interests in the Corporate Opportunity Doctrine, 67 N.C.L.Rev. 435, 456–58 (1989).

Not surprisingly, a significant number of corporate opportunity cases arise in Delaware. While *Guth* is always cited as the controlling case, Delaware courts have in fact moved toward the fairness test both in holding and in dicta. In Johnston v. Greene, 35 Del.Ch. 479, 121 A.2d 919, 923 (Supr.1956), for example, the court stated that the test in every corporate opportunity case was "whether or not the director had appropriated something to himself *that in all fairness should belong to his corporation.*" (Emphasis added) This language was quoted approvingly in a recent Delaware corporate opportunity case, Broz v. Cellular Information Systems, Inc., 673 A.2d 148 (Del. 1996), which added that *Guth* provided "guidelines * * * in balancing the equities."

(5) One of the allegations in a derivative suit against Martha Stewart, and other corporate officers and directors of Martha Stewart Living Omnimedia, was usurping of a corporate opportunity. The complaint alleged that Stewart and other officers had usurped a corporate opportunity by selling shares of their stock. The judge used the test in *Broz* to dismiss the allegation:

> [A] corporate officer or director may not take a business opportunity for his own if: (1) the corporation is financially able to exploit the opportunity; (2) the opportunity is within the corporation's line of business; (3) the corporation has an interest or expectancy in the opportunity; and (4) by taking the opportunity for his own, the corporate fiduciary will thereby be placed in a position [inimical] to his duties to the corporation. Broz, 673 A.2d at 155.

In short, the stock was not in the corporation's line of business, the corporation did not have an interest or expectancy in the stock, and the sale of stock did not make Stewart and others inimical to the corporation. See Beam v. Stewart, 833 A.2d 961, 972 (Del.Ch.2003).

(6) May a corporation renounce an opportunity voluntarily in order to enable an officer, director, or shareholder to take advantage of the opportunity? In 2000, Delaware added § 122(17) to its GCL that expressly authorizes such a renunciation. While such a renunciation when minority shareholders exist would seem clearly to implicate fiduciary duties, a renunciation before any minority interests are created presumably would not.

(7) Academic interest in the corporate opportunity doctrine has, if anything, increased since 1990. But Eric Talley, Turning Service Opportunities to Gold: A Strategic Analysis of the Corporate Opportunity Doctrine, 108 Yale L.J. 277 (1998) comments that "repeated endeavors by litigants, judges, and legal scholars to clarify the doctrine have generated a panoply of tests, variations, and hybrids. But the end product of this collective effort appears—by virtually all accounts—more tautologous than diagnostic, replete with exceptions and indecipherable distinctions that provide little guidance either to theorists or to practitioners." Professor Talley proposes a "normative account of the [corporate opportunity doctrine] that emerges from the economic theory of contract."

C. DUTIES TO CORPORATE CONSTITUENCIES OTHER THAN COMMON SHAREHOLDERS

The foregoing materials make clear that the principal duties owed by corporate officers and directors run to holders of the common stock. However, limited duties also exist with respect to preferred shareholders and to creditors. It has also been argued that duties should be extended to a wide array of other non-shareholder constituencies.

(1) *Preferred shareholders.* In Jedwab v. MGM Grand Hotels, Inc., 509 A.2d 584, 594 (Del.Ch.1986), the Court stated:

> [W]ith respect to matters relating to preferences or limitations that distinguish preferred stock from common, the duty of the corporation and its directors is essentially contractual and the scope of the duty is appropriately defined by reference to the specific words evidencing that contract; where however the right asserted is not to a preference as

against the common stock but rather a right shared equally with the common, the existence of such right and the scope of the correlative duty may be measured by equitable [i.e. fiduciary] as well as legal standards.

Whatever the merits of the *Jedwab* distinction, Delaware courts have also recognized fiduciary duties running to preferred shareholders on questions such as whether the proceeds of a merger were being fairly divided between preferred and common shareholders. In re FLS Holdings, Inc. Shareholders Litigation, 1993 WL 104562 (Del.Ch. Apr. 21, 1993). However, in HB Korenvaes Inv., L.P. v. Marriott Corp., 1993 WL 205040, Fed.Sec.L.Rep. ¶ 97,728 (Del.Ch. June 9, 1993), the Court refused to consider a plausible fiduciary duty claim that a special dividend of stock to the common shareholders was designed to reorganize Marriott into two corporations in order to permit the resumption of dividends on the common shares without honoring the preferreds' priority right. The Court accepted the argument that since the certificate of incorporation contained a provision relating to the payment of special dividends, that provision was necessarily controlling. See Robert B. Robbins & Barton Clark, The Board's Fiduciary Duty to Preferred Stockholders, Insights, Vol. 7, No. 11 at 18 (Nov. 1993).

(2) *Holders of Convertible Securities.* Holders of convertible securities have the right to convert those securities (usually bonds) into another type of securities, usually preferred or common stock. Owners of these sorts of convertible securities have argued, unsuccessfully, that they are entitled to fiduciary duties where other creditors are not, because they have an interest or expectancy in the underlying common stock. The same argument would seem to apply to holders of "call" options, which give the owners the right, but not the obligation to purchase equity in the company. Courts have refused to recognize the existence of fiduciary duties in this context on the grounds that, until the security is converted into stock the owner of the convertible security "has no equitable interest, and remains a creditor of the corporation whose interests are protected by the contractual terms of the indenture." Simons v. Cogan, 549 A.2d 300 (Del.1988).

Sometimes, convertible securities have "call features" which permit the issuer of the securities to repurchase them at a contractually agreed upon price. Call features give issuers the ability to refinance their outstanding indebtedness when their credit ratings improve, or when interest rates drop. Generally, when securities are called for redemption, holders have the option of converting into common shares instead of allowing the issuer to redeem them. The corporation has a duty to provide the holders of those securities with accurate information about the desirability of each alternative. Zahn v. Transamerica Corporation, 162 F.2d 36 (3d Cir.1947); Speed v. Transamerica Corporation, 235 F.2d 369 (3d Cir.1956) [Transamerica violated its fiduciary duty by calling the preferred for redemption without advising preferred shareholders that an unrealized appreciation in tobacco inventory made the conversion option more attractive than redemption]. Since these early decisions, the usual practice of corporations is to give notice and precise information as to which course is most desirable for preferred shareholders under the circumstances. Van Gemert v. Boeing Co., 520 F.2d 1373 (2d Cir.1975), cert. denied 423 U.S. 947, 96 S.Ct. 364, 46 L.Ed.2d 282 (1975), is an example of an inadequate notice. The facts of this case were summarized as follows in a subsequent Supreme Court decision affirming the allowance of plaintiffs' counsel fees:

> In March 1966, The Boeing Company called for the redemption of certain convertible debentures. Boeing announced the call through newspaper notices and mailings to investors who had registered their debentures. The notices, given in accordance with the indenture agreement, recited that each $100 amount of principal could be redeemed for $103.25 or converted into two shares of the Company's common stock. They set March 29 as the deadline for the exercise of conversion rights. Two shares of the Company's common stock on that date were worth $316.25. When the deadline expired, the holders of debentures with a face value of $1,544,300 had not answered the call. These investors were left with the right to redeem their debentures for slightly more than face value.

Boeing Co. v. Van Gemert, 444 U.S. 472, 474, 100 S.Ct. 745, 747, 62 L.Ed.2d 676 (1980).

Boeing's literal compliance with the notice requirements of the indenture and the requirements of the New York Stock Exchange was not enough under the circumstances. The Second Circuit held that publishing the notice in fine print and at the last moment did not fulfill notice requirements. 520 F.2d at 1383. "[A]lmost all" of the newspaper notices actually published "were in fine print, buried in the multitude of information and data published about the financial markets and scarcely of a kind to attract the eye of the average lay investor or debenture holder." Id. at 1379. For an essentially inconsistent decision, see Meckel v. Continental Resources Co., 758 F.2d 811 (2d Cir.1985).

(3) *Creditors.* As a general rule, directors do not owe fiduciary duties to creditors—whether they are short-term trade creditors, long-term bondholders, or holders of debt securities convertible into common shares. Simons v. Cogan, 549 A.2d 300 (Del.1988); Geyer v. Ingersoll Publications Co., 621 A.2d 784 (Del.Ch.1992). This is because the rights of holders of debt securities are defined exclusively by the contractual terms of their obligations, not by an open-ended fiduciary duty. There are, of course, non-contractual doctrines that protect creditors to some extent, such as fraud, deceit, fraudulent conveyance principles, and rules against illegal distributions, but there is no general fiduciary duty owed to creditors. During the 1980s and early 1990s, a number of leveraged buyouts involved the addition of large amounts of debt to the balance sheets of target corporations, thereby reducing outstanding investment-quality bonds or debentures previously issued by the corporation to the category of "junk bonds." When these transactions occurred, the holders of outstanding debt securities suffered very substantial capital losses. Since the specific transactions were not prohibited by the trust indentures, however, courts refused to intervene. See generally Morey W. McDaniel, Stockholders and Stakeholders, 21 Stetson L.Rev. 121 (1991); David M.W. Harvey, Bondholders' Rights and the Case for a Fiduciary Duty, 65 St. John's L.Rev. 1023 (1991); George S. Corey et al., Are Bondholders Owed a Fiduciary Duty?, 18 Fla. St. U. L.Rev. 971 (1991); Morey W. McDaniel, Bondholders and Stockholders, 13 J. Corp. L. 205 (1988); W. Morey McDaniel, Bondholders and Corporate Governance, 41 Bus. Law. 413 (1986).

When a corporation is insolvent and the shareholders have no viable economic interest in the enterprise but the corporation is not in federal

bankruptcy proceedings, the directors' primary duty shifts from the shareholders to the creditors to preserve the value of the corporate assets for
eventual distribution to them. Clarkson Co. Ltd. v. Shaheen, 660 F.2d 506 (2d
Cir.1981). In Credit Lyonnais Bank Nederland, N.V. v. Pathe Communications Corp., 1991 WL 277613, 17 Del.J.Corp.L. 1099 (Del.Ch. Dec. 30, 1991),
Chancellor Allen suggested that this duty should shift once the corporation
enters "the vicinity of insolvency." Directors then owe their duty to "the
corporate enterprise," predominantly the interests of creditors and employees.
Is this a practical standard? Insolvency itself is not always a clear concept; is
not "the vicinity of insolvency" even less clear in marking the time this major
shift in the focus of the duties of directors occurs? Also, is there anything
wrong if a board of directors of a corporation in "the vicinity of insolvency"
takes aggressive and risky steps to save the corporation, even though the
unsecured creditors carry most of the risk and receive little of the benefit?

(4) To whom does a director's loyalty go when a company is nearly
insolvent? Consider the case of Blackmore Partners v. Link Energy L.L.C.,
864 A.2d 80 (Del.Ch.2004). Shareholders sued Link Energy and its directors
for breach of fiduciary duty. At the time of the sale Link Energy was highly
leveraged and their business was declining. But Link was not fully insolvent.
The directors decided that selling the company's assets made the most
business sense. Plaintiffs claimed that the directors violated their fiduciary
duty by selling their assets to creditors in excess of their liability. Plaintiffs
did not make any charges of self-interest or lack of independence. Instead,
Plaintiffs argue that the sale was unwarranted and the price too low. In
rejecting the defendant's motion to dismiss the judge implied that there is still
a duty of care to the shareholders, and not only the creditors, when a
corporation is near insolvency.

But now consider the doctrine of "deepening insolvency." This doctrine
holds that directors and officers should not prolong the life of an insolvent or,
more interestingly, a nearly insolvent corporation to the detriment of creditors. In short, the loyalties of directors and officers of insolvent or nearly
insolvent corporations must shift to creditors and the protection of their
assets. If not, the creditors have a cause of action against the corporation
under the doctrine of "deepening insolvency." How does this doctrine square
with the *Blackmore* decision? When should the loyalty shift?

(5) *Other constituencies.* There remains a heterogeneous group of persons
who may have an interest in the continued well-being of a corporation:
present or retired employees, suppliers, customers, creditors, the local community in which the principal corporate facility is located, and so forth. As
described later, more than 30 states have enacted statutes that authorize
corporate directors to consider, in addition to the long-and short-term interests of the corporation, these various groups. Statutes usually also provide
that that directors cannot be held liable if they fail to elevate the interests of
shareholders over these disparate groups. These statutes were enacted in
response to the takeover movement of the 1980s discussed in chapter 15, and
were designed to provide a defensible position of "just saying no" to takeover
bids.

Despite the fact that these statutes have been very controversial, see
Committee on Corporate Laws, Other Constituencies Statutes: Potential for

Confusion 45 Bus. Law. 2253 (1990), their net effect in all areas has been zero or very close to zero. See Lynda J. Oswald, Shareholders v. Stakeholders: Evaluating Corporate Constituency States Under the Takings Clause, 24 J.Corp.L. 1 (1998); Jonathan D. Springer, Corporate Constituency Statutes: Hollow Hopes and False Fears, 1999 Annual Survey of American Law 85. One reason that these statutes has had such little effect is that most of them simply "allow" the directors to take the interests of nonshareholder constituencies into account when considering the best interest of the corporation. As such, the statutes do not "allow" the directors to do anything that is inconsistent with their fiduciary duties to shareholders. However, one of the statutes, (Connecticut) requires directors to consider other constituencies in certain circumstances such as mergers. The impact of this statute is not clear. One pair of commentators observed that the distinction between statutes that allow directors to take other constituencies into account and statutes that require directors to take other constituencies into account when making decisions, "probably makes little practical difference although the mandatory nature of these statutes (Connecticut and Maine [Maine repealed in 2003]) does create the theoretical possibility that employees or other nonshareholder groups might seek to enforce the directors' statutory obligation to consider their interests." Mark Sargent and Dennis Honabach, Nonshareholder Constituency Statutes, D & O Liability Handbook, Chapter I (2002).

Chapter Thirteen

TRANSACTIONS IN SHARES: RULE 10b–5, INSIDER TRADING AND SECURITIES FRAUD

A. THE DEVELOPMENT OF A FEDERAL REMEDY: RULE 10b–5

The foundational rule against insider trading (and other fraudulent activities) is SEC Rule 10b–5 promulgated by the Securities and Exchange Commission pursuant to authority granted by Congress in Section 10(b) of the Securities Exchange Act of 1934. Rule 10b–5 is, by a considerable margin, the most famous rule in securities law and probably in all of business law. The notes following the statute tell the story of how the rule came to be enacted in response to a particular case of insider trading that the existing rules didn't appear to cover.

SECURITIES EXCHANGE ACT OF 1934
15 U.S.C.A. § 78j (1981).

Section 10. It shall be unlawful for any person, directly or indirectly, by the use of any means or instrumentality of interstate commerce or of the mails, or of any facility of any national securities exchange—* * *

(b) To use or employ, in connection with the purchase or sale of any security registered on a national securities exchange or any security not so registered, any manipulative or deceptive device or contrivance in contravention of such rules and regulations as the Commission may prescribe as necessary or appropriate in the public interest or for the protection of investors.

RULE 10b–5: EMPLOYMENT OF MANIPULATIVE AND DECEPTIVE DEVICES
17 C.F.R. § 240.10b–5 (2000).

It shall be unlawful for any person, directly or indirectly, by the use of any means or instrumentality of interstate commerce, or of the mails or of any facility of any national securities exchange,

(a) to employ any device, scheme, or artifice to defraud,

(b) to make any untrue statement of a material fact or to omit to state a material fact necessary in order to make the statements made, in the light of the circumstances under which they were made, not misleading, or

(c) to engage in any act, practice, or course of business which operates or would operate as a fraud or deceit upon any person, in connection with the purchase or sale of any security.

Notes

(1) A variety of factors contributed to the original growth of Rule 10b–5. A major factor was that the state law of securities fraud was embryonic. There was little question that if A sold shares of stock to B on the basis of a misrepresentation, B could sue A for fraud under state law. Some state blue sky laws also provided a limited remedy against fraud in the sale of registered securities by issuers, but there appeared to be no practical state remedy against many perceived abuses in the markets for publicly traded securities. An early effort to bring a private action against a corporate officer who had engaged in insider trading was unsuccessful because of the lack of an affirmative misstatement by the defendant, and no duty was owed by a corporate officer to an individual shareholder. Goodwin v. Agassiz, 283 Mass. 358, 186 N.E. 659 (1933). Where, however, managers dealt personally with the shareholders or hid their identities by the use of intermediaries, concepts of fraud, misrepresentation and reliance were developed that form part of the basis of the modern state law of securities fraud and influenced developments under Rule 10b–5. This is well-illustrated by two famous cases: 1. Strong v. Repide, 213 U.S. 419, 29 S.Ct. 521, 53 L.Ed. 853 (1909)(holding for the plaintiff because a director used "special information" to buy undervalued stock from shareholders), and 2. Hotchkiss v. Fischer, 136 Kan. 530, 16 P.2d 531 (1932)(holding for the plaintiff shareholder because she was told to sell her stock because a dividend was not going to be declared even though the president of the company intended to declare a dividend).

(2) There were differing standards for insider trading before Federal Securities Laws. See Blazer v. Black, 196 F.2d 139 (10th Cir.1952); Amen v. Black, 234 F.2d 12 (10th Cir.1956); Delano v. Kitch, 542 F.2d 550 (10th Cir.1976), cert. denied, 456 U.S. 946, 102 S.Ct. 2012, 72 L.Ed.2d 468 (1982). Bailey v. Vaughan, 178 W.Va. 371, 375–77, 359 S.E.2d 599, 603–05 (1987) summarizes these differing state law developments.

(3) The first significant step in the development of Rule 10b–5 was the holding by Judge Kirkpatrick in 1947 that Rule 10b–5 could be the basis of a private suit to rescind a securities transaction. Kardon v. National Gypsum Co., 73 F.Supp. 798 (E.D.Pa.1947). The facts of this case, as set forth by Judge Kirkpatrick, were as follows:

> The plaintiffs, Morris and Eugene B. Kardon (father and son), and the defendants, Leon A. Slavin and William Slavin (brothers), owned all the capital stock of Western Board and Paper Co. and Michigan Paper Stock Co., its affiliate, each of the four holding one fourth. Western was engaged in manufacturing paper board and other paper products, having its plant located at Kalamazoo, and Michigan was a purchasing agent dealing chiefly in waste paper and similar materials for Western. All four were officers and together constituted the entire board of directors[.] * * *

Prior to March 18, 1946, Leon Slavin had agreed for the corporation, by written instrument, considered by the parties to it to be binding, to sell to National Gypsum, the plant and equipment of Western for the sum of $1,500,000. * * * The agreement was signed by Leon Slavin in his capacity as Executive Vice President of Western.

On March 18, 1946, the Slavins purchased all the stock of the Kardons in the two corporations, Western and Michigan, for $504,000. At that time the Kardons knew nothing whatever about the negotiations with National Gypsum, and the Slavins did not disclose any of the facts relating to them[.] * * *

Having acquired the plaintiffs' stock, the Slavins proceeded to consummate the transaction with National Gypsum. * * *

73 F.Supp. at 800.

On the critical question whether Rule 10b–5 might be used as the basis for a private cause of action in federal court, the judge simply stated that while the statute and rule "does not even provide in express terms for a remedy, * * * the existence of a remedy is implicit under general principles of the law." Id. at 802. Is this not a simple, garden-variety fraud case of little national or federal interest? Why should such litigation be in the federal courts in the absence of diversity? Rather surprisingly, various limiting doctrines for Rule 10b–5 later developed by the Supreme Court do not affect at all the availability of that rule for plaintiffs in *Kardon*-type cases, and such cases may continue to be freely brought in federal courts under the federal cause of action provided by Rule 10b–5. See, e.g., Glick v. Campagna, 613 F.2d 31 (3d Cir.1979). Indeed, one possible doctrine that might deflect many of these garden-variety fraud cases back to state court—the so-called "sale of business" doctrine—was expressly rejected by the United States Supreme Court in Landreth Timber Co. v. Landreth, 471 U.S. 681, 105 S.Ct. 2297, 85 L.Ed.2d 692 (1985).

(4) Rule 10b–5 quickly became the provision routinely relied upon in all cases involving not only claims of improper trading by insiders, but also claims of securities fraud, deception, or trading in securities on the basis of undisclosed information in both publicly held and closely held corporations. The language of the Rule was broad, flexible, and not hedged with qualifications or limiting doctrine. Plaintiffs came to prefer the federal forum with its Rule 10b–5 precedents rather than the limited or nonexistent case law in the state courts. Rule 10b–5 flourished, and the state law tended to atrophy.

(5) The decisions of the United States Supreme Court relating to Rule 10b–5 before 1975, while not numerous, undoubtedly contributed to this trend. The first case reaching the Supreme Court, Securities and Exch. Comm'n v. National Sec., Inc., 393 U.S. 453, 89 S.Ct. 564, 21 L.Ed.2d 668 (1969), illustrates the initial attitude of the Court to this rule. The basic claim by the SEC in this case was that two insurance companies had been merged by the use of a proxy statement that contained false and misleading statements; § 14 did not apply because the case arose before the 1964 amendments to § 12 of the Securities Exchange Act of 1934. The Court, through Justice Marshall, stated:

Although § 10(b) and Rule 10b–5 may well be the most litigated provisions in the federal securities laws, this is the first time this Court has found it necessary to interpret them. * * * They arise in an area where glib generalizations and unthinking abstractions are major occupational hazards. With this in mind, we turn to respondents' particular contentions. * * *

According to the amended complaint, Producers' shareholders were misled in various material respects prior to their approval of a merger. The deception furthered a scheme which resulted in their losing their status as shareholders in Producers and becoming shareholders in a new company. Moreover, by voting in favor of the merger, each approving shareholder individually lost any right under Arizona law to obtain an appraisal of his stock and payment for it in cash. Ariz.Rev.Stat.Ann. § 10–347 (1956). Whatever the terms "purchase" and "sale" may mean in other contexts, here an alleged deception has affected individual shareholders' decisions in a way not at all unlike that involved in a typical cash sale or share exchange. The broad antifraud purposes of the statute and the Rule would clearly be furthered by their application to this type of situation. Therefore we conclude that Producers' shareholders "purchased" shares in the new company by exchanging them for their old stock. * * *

Respondents' alternative argument that Rule 10b–5 does not cover misrepresentations which occur in connection with proxy solicitations can be dismissed rather quickly. Section 14 of the 1934 Act, and the rules adopted pursuant to that section, set up a complex regulatory scheme covering proxy solicitations. * * * The two sections of the Act apply to different sets of situations. Section 10(b) applies to all proscribed conduct in connection with a purchase or sale of any security; § 14 applies to all proxy solicitations, whether or not in connection with a purchase or sale. The fact that there may well be some overlap is neither unusual nor unfortunate. * * *

393 U.S. at 465–68, 89 S.Ct. at 571–73, 21 L.Ed.2d at 679–81. This rather free-wheeling approach toward Rule 10b–5 moved Justice Harlan, with whom Justice Stewart joined, to dissent:

I am at a loss to understand why the Court finds it necessary to * * * construe Rule 10b–5 promulgated under § 10(b) of the Securities Exchange Act of 1934. The Court of Appeals did not reach this question * * *. The Government's petition for certiorari is similarly limited. * * * When the respondents' brief on the merits argued that Rule 10b–5 did not apply to the present case, the Solicitor General did not even attempt to present the Government's position on that score because he quite properly believed that "the question is not appropriately before this Court for decision."

Despite the fact that we have not heard the views of the Securities and Exchange Commission, the Court chooses this case as a vehicle to construe for the first time one of the most important and elusive provisions of the securities laws. Moreover, the decision has far-reaching radiations, despite the fact that the precise issue presented is a narrow one. Courts and commentators have long debated whether Rule 10b–5 should be read as a sweeping prohibition against fraud in the securities industry when this results in rendering nullities of the other antifraud provisions of more limited scope which can be found in the statute books. * * * Even those who take an extremely broad view of the scope of the Rule have recognized that it could well be argued that the courts should not rush in to apply § 10(b) to regulate proxy solicitations where Congress has refused to permit the Commission to intervene under § 14. * * * Nevertheless, the majority believes it can answer this question "rather quickly," without any real recognition of the basic principles which hang in the balance. * * *

I am unwilling to decide these fundamental matters without full-dress argument. Indeed, if the courts of appeals are not to be permitted to develop the law in this area on a case-by-case basis, I think it much wiser for us to consider the basic issues in a case which squarely raises them rather than in one which is of marginal importance.

393 U.S. at 469–72, 89 S.Ct. at 573–74, 21 L.Ed.2d at 681–83. Two other Supreme Court decisions that reflect expansive readings of Rule 10b–5 are Superintendent of Insurance of New York v. Bankers Life and Casualty Co., 404 U.S. 6, 92 S.Ct. 165, 30 L.Ed.2d 128 (1971), and Affiliated Ute Citizens of Utah v. United States, 406 U.S. 128, 92 S.Ct. 1456, 31 L.Ed.2d 741 (1972).

(6) Procedural advantages also encouraged the use of Rule 10b–5. The federal forum was viewed as superior for several reasons: nationwide service of process under § 27 of the Securities Exchange Act of 1934, liberal venue provisions, and generous discovery rules. The doctrine of pendent jurisdiction permits a federal court to hear both the Rule 10b–5 claim and the state claim in a single proceeding, while a state court cannot hear the Rule 10b–5 claim.

(7) Is there likely to be a problem meeting the jurisdictional requirements of Rule 10b–5 and § 10(b)? Section 3(a)(17) of the Securities Exchange Act of 1934, as amended in 1975, states that the term "interstate commerce" includes "intrastate use of (A) any facility of a national securities exchange or of a telephone or other interstate means of communication or (B) any other interstate instrumentality." 15 U.S.C.A. § 78c(a)(17) (1981).

(8) The private cause of action for violations of Rule 10b–5, judicially created in Kardon v. National Gypsum Co., has received legislative recognition in federal statutes. In Musick, Peeler & Garrett v. Employers Ins. of Wausau, 508 U.S. 286, 292, 113 S.Ct. 2085, 2089, 124 L.Ed.2d 194, 202 (1993), the Court referred to these statutory references and commented that "[w]e infer from these references an acknowledgment of the 10b–5 action without any further expression of legislative intent to define it."

————

Beginning in 1975, changes in the composition and philosophical orientation of the Supreme Court resulted in a significant change in approach toward Rule 10b–5. In a word, the period of unlimited growth and the use of Rule 10b–5 as a sort of universal solvent to resolve all securities problems ended. Three decisions outline the modern contours of Rule 10b–5.

(1) *Blue Chip Stamps v. Manor Drug Stores,* 421 U.S. 723, 95 S.Ct. 1917, 44 L.Ed.2d 539 (1975). In this case, the Court was faced with a claim by a person who was offered an opportunity to purchase securities but failed to do so because of materially misleading and overly pessimistic statements in the prospectus. An earlier decision by the Second Circuit, Birnbaum v. Newport Steel Corp., 193 F.2d 461 (2d Cir.), certiorari denied, 343 U.S. 956, 72 S.Ct. 1051, 96 L.Ed. 1356 (1952), had held that private plaintiffs in Rule 10b–5 suits should be limited to actual purchasers or sellers of securities. Over the dissent of Justices Blackmun, Douglas and Brennan—the then liberal wing of the Court—Justice Rehnquist approved of the *Birnbaum* rule in an opinion that reflected profound skepticism about the growth of Rule 10b–5. The opinion starts with a brief outline of the provisions of the Securities Act of 1933, the Securities Exchange Act of 1934, and Rule 10b–5. The Court then launched into a discussion of the scope of Rule 10b–5:

Having said all this, we would by no means be understood as suggesting that we are able to divine from the language of § 10(b) the express "intent of Congress" as to the contours of a private cause of action under Rule 10b–5. When we deal with private actions under Rule 10b–5, we deal with a judicial oak which has grown from little more than a legislative acorn. Such growth may be quite consistent with the congressional enactment and with the role of the federal judiciary in interpreting it, see J.I. Case v. Borak, supra, but it would be disingenuous to suggest that either Congress in 1934 or the Securities and Exchange Commission in 1942 foreordained the present state of the law with respect to Rule 10b–5. It is therefore proper that we consider, in addition to the factors already discussed, what may be described as policy considerations when we come to flesh out the portions of the law with respect to which neither the congressional enactment nor the administrative regulations offer conclusive guidance. * * *

A great majority of the many commentators on the issue before us have taken the view that the *Birnbaum* limitation on the plaintiff class in a Rule 10b–5 action for damages is an arbitrary restriction which unreasonably prevents some deserving plaintiffs from recovering damages which have in fact been caused by violations of Rule 10b–5. See, e.g., Lowenfels, The Demise of the *Birnbaum* Doctrine: A New Era for Rule 10b–5, 54 Va.L.Rev. 268 (1968). The Securities and Exchange Commission has filed an *amicus* brief in this case espousing that same view. We have no doubt that this is indeed a disadvantage of the *Birnbaum* rule,[1] and if it had no countervailing advantages it would be undesirable as a matter of policy, however much it might be supported by precedent and legislative history. But we are of the opinion that there are countervailing advantages to the *Birnbaum* rule, purely as a matter of policy, although those advantages are more difficult to articulate than is the disadvantage.

We believe that the concern expressed for the danger of vexatious litigation which could result from a widely expanded class of plaintiffs under Rule 10b–5 is founded in something more substantial than the common complaint of the many defendants who would prefer avoiding lawsuits entirely to either settling them or trying them. These concerns have two largely separate grounds.

The first of these concerns is that in the field of federal securities laws governing disclosure of information even a complaint which by objective standards may have very little chance of success at trial has a settlement value to the plaintiff out of any proportion to its prospect of success at trial so long as he may prevent the suit from being resolved against him by dismissal or summary judgment. * * *

The potential for possible abuse of the liberal discovery provisions of the Federal Rules of Civil Procedure may likewise exist in this type of case to a greater extent than they do in other litigation * * * [T]o the

---

1. [By the Court] Obviously this disadvantage is attenuated to the extent that remedies are available to nonpurchasers and nonsellers under state law. Thus for example in *Birnbaum* itself, while the plaintiffs found themselves without federal remedies, the conduct alleged as the gravamen of the federal complaint later provided the basis for recovery in a cause of action based on state law. And in the immediate case, respondent has filed a state court class action held in abeyance pending the outcome of this suit.

extent that it permits a plaintiff with a largely groundless claim to simply take up the time of a number of other people, with the right to do so representing an *in terrorem* increment of the settlement value, rather than a reasonably founded hope that the process will reveal relevant evidence, it is a social cost rather than a benefit.

Without the *Birnbaum* rule, an action under Rule 10b–5 will turn largely on which oral version of a series of occurrences the jury may decide to credit, and therefore no matter how improbable the allegations of the plaintiff, the case will be virtually impossible to dispose of prior to trial other than by settlement. * * *

The *Birnbaum* rule, on the other hand, permits exclusion prior to trial of those plaintiffs who were not themselves purchasers or sellers of the stock in question. The fact of purchase of stock and the fact of sale of stock are generally matters which are verifiable by documentation, and do not depend upon oral recollection. * * *

The second ground for fear of vexatious litigation is based on the concern that, given the generalized contours of liability, the abolition of the *Birnbaum* rule would throw open to the trier of fact many rather hazy issues of historical fact the proof of which depended almost entirely on oral testimony. * * * The Securities and Exchange Commission, while opposing the adoption of the *Birnbaum* rule by this Court, states that it agrees with petitioners "that the effect, if any, of a deceptive practice on someone who has neither purchased nor sold securities may be more difficult to demonstrate than is the effect on a purchaser or seller." * * * The Commission suggests that in particular cases additional requirements of corroboration of testimony and more limited measure of damages would correct the dangers of an expanded class of plaintiffs.

But the very necessity, or at least the desirability, of fashioning unique rules of corroboration and damages as a correlative to the abolition of the *Birnbaum* rule suggests that the rule itself may have something to be said for it. * * *

In today's universe of transactions governed by the 1934 Act, privity of dealing or even personal contact between potential defendant and potential plaintiff is the exception and not the rule. The stock of issuers is listed on financial exchanges utilized by tens of millions of investors and corporate representations reach a potential audience, encompassing not only the diligent few who peruse filed corporate reports or the sizeable number of subscribers to financial journals, but the readership of the Nation's daily newspapers. Obviously neither the fact that issuers or other potential defendants under Rule 10b–5 reach a large number of potential investors, or the fact that they are required by law to make their disclosures conform to certain standards, should in any way absolve them from liability for misconduct which is proscribed by Rule 10b–5.

But in the absence of the *Birnbaum* rule, it would be sufficient for a plaintiff to prove that he had failed to purchase or sell stock by reason of a defendant's violation of Rule 10b–5. * * * The very real risk in permitting those in respondent's position to sue under Rule 10b–5 is that the door will be open to recovery of substantial damages on the part of one who offers only his own testimony to prove that he ever consulted a prospectus of the issuer, that he paid any attention to it, or that the representations contained in it damaged him.[2] * * *

We quite agree that if Congress had legislated the elements of a private cause of action for damages, the duty of the Judicial Branch would be to administer the law which Congress enacted. * * * We are dealing with a private cause of action which has been judicially found to exist, and which will have to be judicially delimited one way or another unless and until Congress addresses the question. Given the peculiar blend of legislative, administrative, and judicial history which now surrounds Rule 10b–5, we believe that practical factors to which we have adverted, and to which other courts have referred, are entitled to a good deal of weight.

Thus we conclude that what may be called considerations of policy, which we are free to weigh in deciding this case, are by no means entirely on one side of the scale. Taken together with the precedential support for the *Birnbaum* rule over a period of more than 20 years, and the consistency of that rule with what we can glean from the intent of Congress, they lead us to conclude that it is a sound rule and should be followed. * * *

Notes

(1) One issue discussed in *Blue Chip* was whether Rule 10b–5 might apply to transactions that also fall within express liability provisions of other federal securities laws. This issue was definitively answered in Herman & MacLean v. Huddleston, 459 U.S. 375, 103 S.Ct. 683, 74 L.Ed.2d 548 (1983), where the Court unanimously held that a cause of action may be maintained under Rule 10b–5 for fraudulent misrepresentations and omissions in a 1933 Act prospectus even though that conduct might also be actionable under § 11 of the 1933 Act.

(2) The *Birnbaum* principle involves a qualifying test for *plaintiffs* in Rule 10b–5 suits. As will appear below, a *defendant* may readily violate Rule 10b–5 even though it is not a purchaser or seller of securities, e.g., by influencing the market by a false press release or preparing a prospectus that contains false statements. Further, the issuer itself may be a nonselling defendant in Rule 10b–5 cases.

---

(2) Ernst & Ernst v. Hochfelder, 425 U.S. 185, 96 S.Ct. 1375, 47 L.Ed.2d 668 (1976) limited the scope of Rule 10b–5 by holding that the Rule applies

2. [By the Court] The SEC, recognizing the necessity for limitations on nonpurchaser, non-seller plaintiffs in the absence of the *Birnbaum* rule, suggests two such limitations to mitigate the practical adverse effects flowing from abolition of the rule. First it suggests requiring some corroborative evidence in addition to oral testimony tending to show that the investment decision of a plaintiff was affected by an omission or misrepresentation. Apparently ownership of stock or receipt of a prospectus or press release would be sufficient corroborative evidence in the view of the SEC to reach the jury. We do not believe that such a requirement would adequately respond to the concerns in part underlying the *Birnbaum* rule. Ownership of stock or receipt of a prospectus says little about whether a plaintiff's investment decision was affected by a violation of Rule 10b–5 or whether a decision was even made. Second, the SEC would limit the vicarious liability of corporate issuers to nonpurchasers and nonsellers to situations where the corporate issuer has been unjustly enriched by a violation. We have no occasion to pass upon the compatibility of this limitation with § 20(a) of the 1934 Act. We do not believe that this proposed limitation is relevant to the concerns underlying in part the *Birnbaum* rule as we have expressed them. * * *

only to activities that involve scienter. Later, the accounting profession was given even greater insulation from liability arising from Rule 10b–5 by the holding that it does not apply to claims based on aiding and abetting. Central Bank of Denver, N.A. v. First Interstate Bank of Denver, N.A., 511 U.S. 164, 114 S.Ct. 1439, 128 L.Ed.2d 119 (1994). Ernst & Ernst v. Hochfelder involved a claim against an accounting firm for failing to have discovered a major fraud in a securities firm under the following circumstances:

> Petitioner, Ernst & Ernst, is an accounting firm. From 1946 through 1967 it was retained by First Securities Company of Chicago (First Securities) * * * to perform periodic audits of the firm's books and records. In connection with these audits Ernst & Ernst prepared for filing with the Securities and Exchange Commission (Commission) the annual reports required of First Securities under § 17(a) of the 1934 Act.[3] It also prepared for First Securities responses to the financial questionnaires of the Midwest Stock Exchange (Exchange).

> Respondents were customers of First Securities who invested in a fraudulent securities scheme perpetrated by Leston B. Nay, president of the firm and owner of 92% of its stock. Nay induced the respondents to invest funds in "escrow" accounts that he represented would yield a high rate of return. Respondents did so from 1942 through 1966, with the majority of the transactions occurring in the 1950's. In fact, there were no escrow accounts as Nay converted respondents' funds to his own use immediately upon receipt. These transactions were not in the customary form of dealings between First Securities and its customers. The respondents drew their personal checks payable to Nay or a designated bank for his account. No such escrow accounts were reflected on the books and records of First Securities, and none was shown on its periodic accounting to respondents in connection with their other investments. Nor were they included in First Securities' filings with the Commission or the Exchange.

> This fraud came to light in 1968 when Nay committed suicide, leaving a note that described First Securities as bankrupt and the escrow accounts as "spurious." Respondents subsequently filed this action for damages against Ernst & Ernst in the United States District Court for the Northern District of Illinois under § 10(b) of the 1934 Act. The complaint charged that Nay's escrow scheme violated § 10(b) and Commission Rule 10b–5,[4] and that Ernst & Ernst had "aided and abetted"

3. [By the Court] Section 17(a) requires that securities brokers or dealers "make * * * and preserve * * * such accounts * * * books, and other records, and make such reports, as the Commission by its rules and regulations may prescribe as necessary or appropriate in the public interest or for the protection of investors." During the period relevant here, Commission Rule 17a–5, 17 CFR § 240.17a–5 (1975), required that First Securities file an annual report of its financial condition that included a certificate stating "clearly the opinion of the accountant with respect to the financial statement covered by the certificate and the accounting principles and practices reflected therein." The rule required Ernst & Ernst to state in its certificate, *inter alia,*

"whether the audit was made in accordance with generally accepted auditing standards applicable in the circumstances" and provided that nothing in the Rule should "be construed to imply authority for the omission of any procedure which independent accountants would ordinarily employ in the course of an audit for the purpose of expressing the opinions required" by the rule.

4. [By the Court] Immediately after Nay's suicide the Commission commenced receivership proceedings against First Securities. In those proceedings all of the respondents except two asserted claims based on the fraudulent escrow accounts. These claims ultimately were allowed in SEC v. First Securities Co., 463 F.2d

Nay's violations by its "failure" to conduct proper audits of First Securities. As revealed through discovery, respondents' cause of action rested on a theory of negligent nonfeasance. The premise was that Ernst & Ernst had failed to utilize "appropriate auditing procedures" in its audits of First Securities, thereby failing to discover internal practices of the firm said to prevent an effective audit. The practice principally relied on was Nay's rule that only he could open mail addressed to him at First Securities or addressed to First Securities to his attention, even if it arrived in his absence. Respondents contended that if Ernst & Ernst had conducted a proper audit, it would have discovered this "mail rule." The existence of the rule then would have been disclosed in reports to the Exchange and to the Commission by Ernst & Ernst as an irregular procedure that prevented an effective audit. This would have led to an investigation of Nay that would have revealed the fraudulent scheme. Respondents specifically disclaimed the existence of fraud or intentional misconduct on the part of Ernst & Ernst.[5] * * *

As in *Blue Chip*, the court approached the issue of whether scienter was required as an element of a Rule 10b–5 violation in a narrow fashion:

> * * * Courts and commentators long have differed with regard to whether scienter is a necessary element of such a cause of action, or whether negligent conduct alone is sufficient. In addressing this question, we turn first to the language of § 10(b), for "[t]he starting point in every case involving construction of a statute is the language itself."[6]

> Section 10(b) makes unlawful the use or employment of "any manipulative or deceptive device or contrivance" in contravention of Commission rules. The words "manipulative or deceptive" used in conjunction with "device or contrivance" strongly suggest that § 10(b) was intended to proscribe knowing or intentional misconduct. * * * [Their use makes] unmistakable a congressional intent to proscribe a type of conduct quite different from negligence.[7] Use of the word "manipulative" is especially significant. It is and was virtually a term of art when used in connection with securities markets. It connotes intentional or willful conduct designed to deceive or defraud investors by controlling or artificially affecting the price of securities.[8] * * *

> * * * The Commission contends * * * that subsections (b) and (c) of Rule 10b–5 are cast in language which—if standing alone—could encompass both intentional and negligent behavior. * * * Viewed in isolation the language of subsection (b), and arguably that of subsection (c), could be read as proscribing, respectively, any type of material misstatement or omission, and any course of conduct, that has the effect of defrauding investors, whether the wrongdoing was intentional or not.

981, 986 (CA7), cert. denied, 409 U.S. 880, 93 S.Ct. 85, 34 L.Ed.2d 134 (1972), where the court held that Nay's conduct violated § 10(b) and Rule 10b–5, and that First Securities was liable for Nay's fraud as an aider and abettor. The question of Ernst & Ernst's liability was not considered in that case.

5. [By the Court] In their response to interrogatories in the District Court respondents conceded that they did "not accuse Ernst &

Ernst of deliberate, intentional fraud," merely with "inexcusable negligence."

6. [By the Editors] The court cites for this proposition the opinion of Justice Powell, concurring, in *Blue Chip*.

7. [footnote omitted]

8. [footnote omitted]

We note first that such a reading cannot be harmonized with the administrative history of the rule, a history making clear that when the Commission adopted the rule it was intended to apply only to activities that involved scienter.[9] More importantly, Rule 10b–5 was adopted pursuant to authority granted the Commission under § 10(b). The rulemaking power granted to an administrative agency charged with the administration of a federal statute is not the power to make law. Rather, it is " 'the power to adopt regulations to carry into effect the will of Congress as expressed by the statute.' " Dixon v. United States, 381 U.S. 68, 74, 85 S.Ct. 1301, 1305, 14 L.Ed.2d 223, 228 (1965). Thus, despite the broad view of the Rule advanced by the Commission in this case, its scope cannot exceed the power granted the Commission by Congress under § 10(b). * * * When a statute speaks so specifically in terms of manipulation and deception, and of implementing devices and contrivances—the commonly understood terminology of intentional wrongdoing—and when its history reflects no more expansive intent, we are quite unwilling to extend the scope of the statute to negligent conduct.[10] * * *

Notes

(1) The question whether scienter should be required in SEC enforcement actions seeking injunctive relief was definitely resolved in Aaron v. Securities and Exch. Comm'n, 446 U.S. 680, 100 S.Ct. 1945, 64 L.Ed.2d 611 (1980), where the Court held that scienter was a critical ingredient of all rule 10b–5 cases.

9. [By the Court] Apparently the rule was a hastily drafted response to a situation clearly involving intentional misconduct. * * * See Conference on Codification of the Federal Securities Laws, 22 Bus.Law. 793, 922 (1967) (remarks of Milton Freeman, one of the rule's co-drafters). * * * There is no indication in the administrative history of the Rule that any of the subsections was intended to proscribe conduct not involving scienter. Indeed the Commission's release issued contemporaneously with the rule explained:

"The Securities and Exchange Commission today announced the adoption of a rule prohibiting fraud by any person in connection with the purchase of securities. The previously existing rules against fraud in the purchase of securities applied only to brokers and dealers. The new rule closes a loophole in the protections against fraud administered by the Commission by prohibiting individuals or companies from buying securities if they engage in fraud in their purchase." SEC Release No. 3230 (May 21, 1942).

That same year, in its Annual Report, the Commission again stated that the purpose of the rule was to protect investors against "fraud":

"During the fiscal year the Commission adopted Rule X–10B–5 as an additional protection to investors. The new rule prohibits fraud by any person in connection with the purchase of securities, while the previously existing rules against fraud in the purchase of securities applied only to brokers and dealers." 1942 Annual Report of the Securities Exchange Commission 10.

10. [By the Court] As we find the language and history of § 10(b) dispositive of the appropriate standard of liability, there is no occasion to examine the additional considerations of "policy," set forth by the parties, that may have influenced the lawmakers in their formulation of the statute. We do note that the standard urged by respondents would significantly broaden the class of plaintiffs who may seek to impose liability upon accountants and other experts who perform services or express opinions with respect to matters under the Acts * * *.

This case, on its facts, illustrates the extreme reach of the standard urged by respondents. As investors in transactions initiated by Nay, not First Securities, they were not foreseeable users of the financial statements prepared by Ernst & Ernst. Respondents conceded that they did not rely on either these financial statements or Ernst & Ernst's certificates of opinion. The class of persons eligible to benefit from such a standard, though small in this case, could be numbered in the thousands in other cases. Acceptance of respondents' view would extend to new frontiers the "hazards" of rendering expert advice under the Acts, raising serious policy questions not yet addressed by Congress.

(2) Virtually all lower courts addressing the question whether "reckless disregard" might constitute "scienter" since *Hochfelder* have concluded that a rule 10b–5 violation may be grounded on "recklessness" or "reckless disregard of the truth" and that knowing, intentional misconduct is not a necessary ingredient of establishing liability. See, e.g., First Interstate Bank of Denver, N.A. v. Pring, 969 F.2d 891, 901 (10th Cir.1992), stating that "[t]he established rule is that recklessness is sufficient scienter for a primary violation of § 10(b) and Rule 10b–5." The Supreme Court granted certiorari in this case and reversed it on the grounds that rule 10b–5 does not permit claims based on aiding and abetting.

(3) Santa Fe Indus., Inc. v. Green, 430 U.S. 462, 97 S.Ct. 1292, 51 L.Ed.2d 480 (1977). This case involved the question whether Rule 10b–5 could be applied to a Delaware short-form cash-out merger when the transaction was unfair to the minority shareholders but the effect of the transaction was fully disclosed.[11] The Court of Appeals held that although Rule 10b–5 clearly reaches material misrepresentations and nondisclosures in connection with the purchase or sale of securities, neither misrepresentation nor nondisclosure was an essential element of a Rule 10b–5 action. Rather, the rule also reached "breaches of fiduciary duty by a majority against minority shareholders without any charge of misrepresentation or lack of disclosure."[12] The Court of Appeals held:

> "We hold that a complaint alleges a claim under Rule 10b–5 when it charges, in connection with a Delaware short-form merger, that the majority has committed a breach of its fiduciary duty to deal fairly with minority shareholders by effecting the merger without any justifiable business purpose. The minority shareholders are given no prior notice of the merger, thus having no opportunity to apply for injunctive relief, and the proposed price to be paid is substantially lower than the appraised value reflected in the Information Statement." Id., at 1291.

The Supreme Court reversed in an opinion by Justice White:

> *Ernst & Ernst* makes clear that in deciding whether a complaint states a cause of action for "fraud" under Rule 10b–5, "we turn first to the language of § 10(b), for '[t]he starting point in every case involving construction of a statute is the language itself.' " * * *
>
> To the extent that the Court of Appeals would rely on the use of the term "fraud" in Rule 10b–5 to bring within the ambit of the rule all breaches of fiduciary duty in connection with a securities transaction, its interpretation would, like the interpretation rejected by the Court in *Ernst & Ernst,* "add a gloss to the operative language of the statute quite different from its commonly accepted meaning." Id., at 199. But as the Court there held, the language of the statute must control the interpreta-

---

11. [By the Editors] The Delaware appraisal procedure was available to dissenting shareholders on the facts of this case, but that remedy was unattractive because the case antedated by several years the *Weinberger* liberalization of the rules surrounding this state-created remedy. See p. 785, supra.

12. [By the Court] Id., at 1287. The court concluded its discussion thus:

"Whether full disclosure has been made is not the crucial inquiry since it is the merger and the undervaluation which constituted the fraud, and not whether or not the majority determines to lay bare their real motives. If there is no valid corporate purpose for the merger, then even the most brazen disclosure of that fact to the minority shareholders in no way mitigates the fraudulent conduct."
533 F.2d, at 1292.

tion of the rule.[13] * * * Thus the claim of fraud and fiduciary breach in this complaint states a cause of action under any part of Rule 10b–5 only if the conduct alleged can be fairly viewed as "manipulative or deceptive" within the meaning of the statute.

It is our judgment that the transaction, if carried out as alleged in the complaint, was neither deceptive nor manipulative and therefore did not violate either § 10(b) of the Act or Rule 10b–5. * * * [T]he cases do not support the proposition, adopted by the Court of Appeals below and urged by respondents here, that a breach of fiduciary duty by majority stockholders, without any deception, misrepresentation, or nondisclosure, violates the statute and the Rule.

It is also readily apparent that the conduct alleged in the complaint was not "manipulative" within the meaning of the statute. "Manipulation" is "virtually a term of art when used in connection with securities markets." Ernst & Ernst, 425 U.S., at 199, 96 S.Ct., at 1384. The term refers generally to practices, such as wash sales, matched orders, or rigged prices, that are intended to mislead investors by artificially affecting market activity. * * * Indeed, nondisclosure is usually essential to the success of a manipulative scheme. * * * But we do not think it would have chosen this "term of art" if it had meant to bring within the scope of § 10(b) instances of corporate mismanagement such as this, in which the essence of the complaint is that shareholders were treated unfairly by a fiduciary. * * *

The language of the statute is, we think, "sufficiently clear in its context" to be dispositive here, Ernst & Ernst, 425 U.S., at 201, 96 S.Ct., at 1385; but even if it were not, there are additional considerations that weigh heavily against permitting a cause of action under Rule 10b–5 for the breach of corporate fiduciary duty alleged in this complaint. Congress did not expressly provide a private cause of action for violations of § 10(b). Although we have recognized an implied cause of action under that section in some circumstances, Superintendent of Insurance v. Bankers Life & Cas. Co., supra, we have also recognized that a private cause of action under the antifraud provisions of the Securities Exchange Act should not be implied where it is "unnecessary to ensure the fulfillment of Congress' purposes" in adopting the Act. Piper v. Chris–Craft Industries, 430 U.S., at 41, 97 S.Ct., at 949 (1977). As we noted earlier, the Court repeatedly has described the "fundamental purpose" of the Act as implementing a "philosophy of full disclosure"; once full and fair disclosure has occurred, the fairness of the terms of the transaction is at most a tangential concern of the statute. As in Cort v. Ash, 422 U.S. 66, 78, 80, 95 S.Ct. 2080, 2087, 2090, 45 L.Ed.2d 26 (1975), we are reluctant to recognize a cause of action here to serve what is "at best a subsidiary purpose" of the federal legislation.

---

13. [By the Court] The case for adhering to the language of the statute is even stronger here than in Ernst & Ernst, where the interpretation of Rule 10b–5 rejected by the Court was strongly urged by the Commission. See also Piper v. Chris–Craft Industries, Inc., 430 U.S. 1, 97 S.Ct. 926, 51 L.Ed.2d 124 (1977), and Blue Chip Stamps v. Manor Drug Stores, 421 U.S. 723, 95 S.Ct. 1917, 44 L.Ed.2d 539 (1975) (rejecting interpretations of Rule 10b–5 urged by the SEC as amicus curiae). * * *

A second factor in determining whether Congress intended to create a federal cause of action in these circumstances is "whether 'the cause of action [is] one traditionally relegated to state law. * * *'" Piper v. Chris–Craft Industries, Inc., 430 U.S., at 40, 97 S.Ct., at 949, quoting Cort v. Ash, 422 U.S., at 78, 95 S.Ct., at 2087. The Delaware Legislature has supplied minority shareholders with a cause of action in the Delaware Court of Chancery to recover the fair value of shares allegedly undervalued in a short-form merger. Of course, the existence of a particular state law remedy is not dispositive of the question whether Congress meant to provide a similar federal remedy, but as in Cort and Piper, we conclude that "it is entirely appropriate in this instance to relegate respondent and others in his situation to whatever remedy is created by state law." 422 U.S., at 84, 95 S.Ct., at 2091; 430 U.S., at 41, 97 S.Ct., at 949.

The reasoning behind a holding that the complaint in this case alleged fraud under Rule 10b–5 could not be easily contained. * * * The result would be to bring within the Rule a wide variety of corporate conduct traditionally left to state regulation. In addition to posing a "danger of vexatious litigation which could result from a widely expanded class of plaintiffs under Rule 10b–5," Blue Chip Stamps v. Manor Drug Stores, 421 U.S., at 740, 95 S.Ct., at 1927 (1975), this extension of the federal securities laws would overlap and quite possibly interfere with state corporate law.[14] * * * Absent a clear indication of congressional intent, we are reluctant to federalize the substantial portion of the law of corporations that deals with transactions in securities, particularly where established state policies of corporate regulation would be overridden. As the Court stated in Cort v. Ash, supra, "Corporations are creatures of state law, and investors commit their funds to corporate directors on the understanding that, except where federal law *expressly* requires certain responsibilities of directors with respect to stockholders, state law will govern the internal affairs of the corporation." 422 U.S., at 84, 95 S.Ct., at 2091.

The practical effect of the Supreme Court's decision in this case was to focus attention on state law as the regulator of transactions that literally followed state statute but were or might be unfair to defenseless interests. Six years following the decision in *Santa Fe,* the Delaware Supreme Court imposed duties of "intrinsic fairness" or "fiduciary duties" as a matter of state law to protect such interests. See Weinberger v. UOP, Inc., supra page 785 and the cases cited in the notes following that case.

---

(3) *Miscellaneous Issues.* The United States Supreme Court resolved three significant Rule 10b–5 issues in the 1990s, involving the relevant statute of limitations, the doctrine of aiding and abetting, and the right to contribution among defendants. They reveal the continuing controversial nature of the private cause of action under Rule 10b–5 and the continuing intent of the Supreme Court to contain or limit the scope of the Rule 10b–5 implied cause of action.

14. [Footnote omitted]

(a) *The Statute of Limitations.* Because there is no express statute of limitation in Rule 10b–5, courts have struggled with what statute of limitations should be applicable in such cases. The generally accepted view was that a statute of limitations should be "borrowed" from the applicable state law. Fischman v. Raytheon Mfg. Co., 188 F.2d 783 (2d Cir.1951). However, this was more complex than might first appear, since states have several different statutes of limitations that arguably might be "borrowed." In practice, the borrowing doctrine gave plaintiffs a field day for forum shopping for the most beneficial statute of limitations since the venue and service of process provisions of the Securities Exchange Act usually permitted suit to be brought in virtually any district.

On June 20, 1991, the United States Supreme Court massively roiled the waters of Rule 10b–5 litigation when it handed down Lampf, Pleva, Lipkind, Prupis & Petigrow v. Gilbertson, 501 U.S. 350, 111 S.Ct. 2773, 115 L.Ed.2d 321 (1991). Rather than borrowing a state statute of limitations, the majority concluded that courts should look to the statute from which the federal cause of action was implied to determine whether a uniform period of limitations was imposed in similar suits. The majority also concluded that the appropriate statute for application to all Rule 10b–5 cases was that suits must be "brought within one year after the discovery of the facts constituting the cause of action and within three years after such cause of action accrued." 15 U.S.C.A. § 78r(c) (1981). Under this statute there is no tolling or delayed accrual dates. See generally Alan R. Bromberg and Lewis D. Lowenfels, SEC Rule 10b–5 and Its New Statute of Limitations: The Circuits Defy the Supreme Court, 51 Bus. Law. 1 (1996). Section 804(a) of the Sarbanes–Oxley Act of 2002 extends the statute of limitations for private securities fraud claims to the earlier of two years after discovery of the facts constituting the violation or five years after the violation. The new statute of limitations applies to proceedings commenced after July 30, 2002.

(b) *"Aiding and Abetting."* Prior to 1993, many Federal District Courts and Courts of Appeal had recognized that claims against aiders and abettors could be pursued under Rule 10b–5. Indeed, the issue seemed so clearly to be settled that the original petition for writ of certiorari in Central Bank of Denver, N.A. v. First Interstate Bank of Denver, N.A., (a suit against an aider or abettor) did not present the question as one for review.[15] However, the Supreme Court on its own motion directed the parties to brief and argue the issue, 508 U.S. 959, 113 S.Ct. 2927, 124 L.Ed.2d 678 (1993), and then, in a sharply divided 5–4 set of opinions, adopted a literalistic interpretation of § 10(b) and Rule 10b–5 and concluded that claims based on aiding and abetting were not authorized under that Rule. 511 U.S. 164, 114 S.Ct. 1439, 128 L.Ed.2d 119 (1994). Though the Court made clear that its holding was limited to aiding and abetting:

> The absence of § 10(b) aiding and abetting liability does not mean that secondary actors in the securities markets are always free from liability under the securities acts. Any person or entity, including a

---

15. [By the Editors] However, the aiding and abetting issue had been specifically reserved in both *Hochfelder* and Herman & Mac- Lean v. Huddleston, 459 U.S. 375, 103 S.Ct. 683, 74 L.Ed.2d 548 (1983).

lawyer, accountant, or bank, who employs a manipulative device or makes a material misstatement (or omission) on which a purchaser or seller of securities relies may be liable as a primary violator under 10b–5, assuming all of the requirements for primary liability under Rule 10b–5 are met.

511 U.S., at 191, 114 S.Ct., at 1455.

In the Private Securities Litigation Reform Act of 1995, Congress restored the remedy against knowing aiders or abettors but only in connection with suits brought by the SEC. Securities Exchange Act of 1934, § 20, as amended by Pub. Law 104–67, 109 Stat. 737, § 104. See generally Robert S. De Leon, The Fault Lines Between Primary Liability and Aiding and Abetting Claims Under Rule 10b–5, 22 J.Corp.L. 723 (1997). The Private Securities Litigation Reform Act is discussed in Part D of this Chapter.

(c) *Right of Contribution.* In Musick, Peeler & Garrett v. Employers Ins. of Wausau, 508 U.S. 286, 113 S.Ct. 2085, 124 L.Ed.2d 194 (1993), the Supreme Court held that there is an implied right of contribution among defendants in § 10 and rule 10b–5 cases, Justices Scalia and Thomas dissenting. The court relied on analogous express liability provisions in the securities acts, and on the nearly uniform acceptance of the right of contribution by lower federal courts. On the surface, this opinion seems inconsistent in principle with the holding in *Central Bank.* In the Private Securities Litigation Reform Act of 1995, Congress substituted a complex scheme of proportionate liability for the joint and several liability among defendants that previously existed under Rule 10b–5 (and that gave rise to the right of contribution). Securities Exchange Act of 1934, § 21D(g), added by Pub. Law 104–67, 109 Stat. 737, § 201. Section 21D(g)(8) preserves the right of contribution among persons who are found liable for the same damages, but in proportion to their relative responsibility.

(d) *Bad Faith Breach of Contract.* In Wharf (Holdings) Ltd. v. United International Holdings, Inc., 532 U.S. 588, 121 S.Ct. 1776, 149 L.Ed.2d 845 (2001), Wharf orally granted United an option to purchase 10 percent of the stock of Wharf's Hong Kong cable system if United provided specified services. United provided the services, but Wharf refused to recognize the existence of a binding option contract. However, internal Wharf documents subsequently revealed that Wharf had agreed to, but never intended to honor, the option agreement. Following a trial, the jury awarded United compensatory damages of $67 million and punitive damages of $58.5 million in light of "circumstances of fraud, malice, or willful and wanton conduct" by Wharf. Judgment was entered on this verdict and upheld by the Court of Appeals. The Supreme Court of the United States unanimously upheld this award under Rule 10b–5. Justice Breyer stated that the "security" involved in this case was the option to purchase stock in Wharf and not the stock that was itself the subject of the option, and that the failure of Wharf to disclose its intention not to recognize the binding effect of the option was itself a fraudulent misrepresentation of a security in violation of Rule 10b–5.

IN RE ENRON CORPORATION SECURITIES, DERIVATIVE & ERISA LITIGATION

United States District Court for the Southern District of Texas, 2002.
235 F.Supp.2d 549.

HARMON, DISTRICT JUDGE:

The above referenced putative class action, brought on behalf of purchasers of Enron Corporation's publicly traded equity and debt securities during a proposed federal Class Period from October 19, 1998 through November 27, 2001, alleges * * * that: (1) Canadian Imperial Bank of Commerce ("CIBC") (2) CitiGroup Inc. (3) J.P. Morgan Chase & Co.; (4) Vinson & Elkins L.L.P.; (5) Arthur Andersen LLP ; (6) Barclays PLC; (7) Credit Suisse First Boston; (8) Kirkland & Ellis; (9) Bank of America Corporation; (10) Merrill Lynch & Co.; (11) Lehman Brothers Holdings Inc.; and (12) Deutsche Bank AG, and other named Defendants, "are liable for (i) making false statements, or failing to disclose adverse facts while selling Enron securities and/or (ii) participating in a scheme to defraud and/or a course of business that operated as a fraud or deceit on purchasers of Enron's public securities during the Class Period."
* * *

c.   *Central Bank* and Primary Violations

Of substantial relevance to the motions this Court now reviews is the Supreme Court's holding in a 5–4 decision in *Central Bank of Denver, N.A. v. First Interstate Bank of Denver, N.A.,* 511 U.S. 164, 114 S.Ct. 1439, 128 L.Ed.2d 119 (1994), based on the language and legislative history of the statute, that a private plaintiff may not bring an aiding and abetting claim under § 10(b) and Rule 10b–5. The high court construed the general anti-fraud provision as prohibiting only the making of a material misstatement or a material omission or the commission of a manipulative act; therefore it does not prohibit giving aid to another, who then commits a primary § 10(b) violation. It further emphasized that none of the express private causes of action in both the Securities Act of 1933 and the 1934 Exchange Act imposes liability on one who aids or abets such primary violators.

[handwritten margin note: – Reaffirm no claim against aiders, und 10(b)-5]

Nevertheless, the Supreme Court did not conclude that secondary actors such as lawyers, accountants, banks, and underwriters were therefore always shielded from § 10(b) and Rule 10b–5 liability:

> * * * Any person or entity, including a lawyer, accountant, or bank, who employs a manipulative device or makes a material misstatement (or omission) on which a purchaser or seller of securities relies may be liable as a primary violator under 10b–5, assuming *all* of the requirements for primary liability under Rule 10b–5 are met. * * *

[handwritten margin note: ← Secondary actors may have primary liability]

The SEC proposes * * * the following rule for primary liability of a secondary party under § 10(b): "when a person, acting alone or with others, creates a misrepresentation [on which the investor-plaintiffs relied], the person can be liable as a primary violator * * * if * * * he acts with the requisite scienter. * * * Moreover it would not be necessary for a person to be the initiator of a misrepresentation in order to be a primary violator. Provided that a plaintiff can plead and prove scienter, a person can be a primary

[handwritten margin note: – Accounts, lawyers, etc must have scienter]

violator if he or she writes misrepresentations for inclusion in a document to be given to investors, even if the idea for those misrepresentations came from someone else." * * *

Because § 10(b) expressly delegated rule-making authority to the agency, which it exercised *inter alia* in promulgating Rule 10b–5, this Court accords considerable weight to the SEC's construction of the statute since the Court finds that construction is not arbitrary, capricious or manifestly contrary to the statute. * * * *Chevron, U.S.A., Inc. v. Natural Resources Defense Council,* 467 U.S. 837, 842–44, 104 S.Ct. 2778, 81 L.Ed.2d 694 (1984) ("considerable weight should be accorded to an executive department's construction of a statutory scheme it is entrusted to administer" * * *).

Thus * * * to survive a motion to dismiss, a complaint alleging that more than one defendant participated in a "scheme" to defraud must allege a primary violation of § 10(b) by each defendant.

1. Attorneys

The issue of attorney liability involving a duty to disclose nonmisleading information to nonclients and third parties is a thorny one, complicated by tension between the need to provide remedy to parties suffering monetary loss because of a lawyer's conduct and the attorney-client relationship with its attendant confidentiality, loyalty and zealous representation requirements and policy concerns. * * *

Pursuant to ABA Model Rule of Professional Conduct 1.2(d) an attorney "shall not counsel a client to engage, or assist a client in, conduct that the lawyer knows is criminal or fraudulent * * *, but the attorney may discuss the legal consequences of any proposed conduct and help the client make a good faith effort to determine the application of the law to that proposed conduct. However, a lawyer may not knowingly assist a client in criminal or fraudulent conduct. There is a critical distinction between presenting an analysis of legal aspects of questionable conduct and recommending the means by which a crime or fraud might be committed with impunity." * * *

This Court concludes that professionals, including lawyers and accountants, when they take the affirmative step of speaking out, whether individually or as essentially an author or co-author in a statement or report, whether identified or not, about their client's financial condition, do have a duty to third parties not in privity not to knowingly or with severe recklessness issue materially misleading statements on which they intend or have reason to expect that those third parties will rely.

2. Accountant/Auditor

There is no accountant/client privilege analogous to that accorded to lawyers. The United States Supreme Court has held, "[b]y certifying the public reports that collectively depict a corporation's financial status, the independent auditor assumes a public responsibility transcending any employment relationship with the client. The independent public accountant performing this special function owes ultimate allegiance to the corporation's creditors and stockholders, as well as to the investing public." *United States v. Arthur Young & Co.,* 465 U.S. 805, 817–18, 104 S.Ct. 1495, 79 L.Ed.2d 826 (1984). * * *

III. Lead Plaintiff's Allegations in Consolidated Complaint

A. The Scheme, Generally

Lead Plaintiff asserts that Defendants participated in "an enormous Ponzi scheme, the largest in history," involving illusory profits "generated by phony, non-arm's-length transactions with Enron-controlled entities and improper accounting tricks" in order to inflate Enron's reported revenues and profits, conceal its growing debts, maintain its artificially high stock prices and investment grade credit rating, as well as allow individual defendants to personally enrich themselves by looting the corporation, while continuing to raise money from public offerings of Enron or related entities' securities to sustain the scheme and to postpone the collapse of the corporation, a scenario characterized by Lead Plaintiff as "a hall of mirrors inside a house of cards." The consolidated complaint sets out an elaborate scheme of off-the-books, illicit partnerships, secretly controlled by Enron and established at times critical for requisite financial disclosures by Enron in order to conceal its actual financial status. These Enron-controlled entities typically would buy troubled assets from Enron, which Enron would have had difficulty selling in an arm's length transaction to an independent entity and which otherwise would have to be reported on Enron's balance sheet, by means of sham swaps, hedges, and transfers, to record phony profits and conceal debt on Enron's balance sheet. Lead Plaintiff further paints a picture of participation in the scheme by Enron's accountants, outside law firms, and banks, which all were the beneficiaries of such enormous fees and increasing business, as well as investment opportunities for personal enrichment, with the result that their opinions were rubber stamps that deceived investors and the public. * * *

[T]he consolidated complaint charges that Defendants caused Enron to violate GAAP (Generally Accepted Accounting Principles) and SEC rules in order to overstate Enron's assets, shareholders' equity, net income and earnings per share, and to understate its debt. Defendants also caused Enron to present materially misleading statements in Enron's financial statements (including press releases and SEC filings, such as Form 10–Qs for interim results and Form 10–Ks for annual results), which were incorporated into Registration Statements and Prospectuses (filed during the Class Period). Enron also made misrepresentations about Defendants' manipulations, all concealed by the following numerous, improper accounting ploys: not consolidating illicit SPEs (Special Purpose Entities) into Enron's financial statements to properly reflect reduced earnings and debt on Enron's balance sheet; improperly accounting for common stock issued to a related-party entity that should have been treated as a reduction in shareholders' equity, but was identified as a note receivable; improperly accounting for broadband transactions; abusing mark-to-market accounting; characterizing loans as forward contracts to conceal Enron's debt; improperly accounting for long-term contracts; failing to record required write-downs for impairment in value of Enron's investments, long-term assets, and its broadband and technology investments in a timely manner; failing to record an aggregate of $92 million in proposed audit adjustments from 1997 until the end of the Class period; failing to disclose related-party transactions; and misstating Enron's debt-to-equity ratio (measured as debt to total capitalization, a figure which rating agencies use to determine a company's credit rating) and ratio of earnings to fixed charges. Even while demonstrating the contrast between Enron's original financial statements and its restatement results, the consolidated complaint notes that many of Defendants' manipulations are not included in the restatement, such as the effects of Enron's abuse of accounting techniques.

B. Defendant–Specific Allegations

1. The Banks

Lead Plaintiff alleges that the banks participated in the Ponzi scheme for personal enrichment and for continuing business generating spectacular fees (such as the "long gravy train" of lucrative underwriting of Enron stock and bond offerings). Moreover, according to the complaint, once they were involved, their continued participation was also to limit their exposure to risk, salvage their financial investments, and save their reputations.

The charges against the banks are a blend of repetitive, conclusory, cookie-cutter contentions and of assertions that are unique or limited to only a few Defendants. In the former group, the consolidated complaint alleges that the banks advanced funds [to the SPEs] at key times to allow them and Enron to complete bogus transactions just before year-or quarter-end in order to create fake profits and to conceal billions of dollars of Enron debt that should have been reported on its balance sheet. Aware of Enron's financial fragility, the banks further made loans to Enron to insure its liquidity and continuing operations, while simultaneously aiding Enron in selling securities to public investors so that Enron could continue to pay down its short-term commercial paper and bank debt and keep the fraudulent Ponzi scheme afloat. The banks were central players in inflating and supporting the price of Enron stock through issuance of glowing research reports with misleading information about Enron.

JP Morgan, CitiGroup, and Credit Suisse First Boston also concealed billions of dollars in loans to Enron that were disguised as sales transactions. * * *

b. CitiGroup

The complaint asserts that * * * CitiGroup enjoyed huge underwriting, advisory and transactional fees, interest, and commitment charges, and that some of its executives were given the opportunity to invest and did invest $15 million in LJM2 for lucrative returns. Its senior executives also allegedly interacted nearly daily with top executives at Enron, discussing its business in detail. It participated in the fraudulent course of conduct and business through loans to Enron of over $4 billion during the Class Period, helping Enron raise over $2 billion from the investing public through the sale of securities during the Class Period; it helped to structure and finance one or more of the illicit partnerships or SPEs that Enron used to inflate its earnings and conceal its debt; and it engaged in disguised loans to Enron that allowed Enron to falsify its financial situation.

CitiGroup purportedly also made false and misleading statements in the Registration Statements and Prospectuses for Enron securities sales for which it was an underwriter, including false interim and annual financial statements and statements regarding the structure of and Enron's relationship to SPEs and related parties. The complaint asserts that CitiGroup is liable for its participation as lead underwriter in the resale of the Enron zero coupon convertible notes on or after 7/18/01.

Lead Plaintiff further complains that CitiGroup issued numerous analysts' reports on Enron that contained false and misleading statements about Enron's financial condition, * * * all serving to artificially inflate the price of Enron's publicly traded securities.

2. Law Firms

The consolidated complaint claims that Vinson & Elkins, Enron's outside general counsel during the Class Period, * * * participated in writing, reviewing, and approving Enron's SEC filings, shareholder reports and financial press releases, and in creating Chewco, JEDI, LJM1, LJM2, and nearly all the related SPEs' transactions. They knew that LJM2's principal purpose was to engage in transactions with Enron and that Enron insiders Fastow, Kopper and Glisan were operating on both sides of the transactions, to virtually insure lucrative returns for the entities' partners.

a. Vinson & Elkins L.L.P.

Enron was Vinson & Elkins' largest client, accounting for more than 7% of the firm's revenues. Over the years more than twenty Vinson & Elkins lawyers have left the firm and joined Enron's in-house legal department.

The complaint recites a long history of alleged improprieties by Vinson & Elkins as part of the elaborate Ponzi scheme.

The complaint asserts that Vinson & Elkins participated in the negotiations for, prepared the transactions for, participated in the structuring of, and approved the illicit partnerships and the SPEs with knowledge that they were manipulative devices, not independent third parties and not valid SPEs, designed to move debt off Enron's books, inflate its earnings, and falsify Enron's reported financial results and financial condition at crucial times. Vinson & Elkins repeatedly provided "true sale"[16] and other opinions that were false and were indispensable for the sham deals to close and the fraudulent scheme to continue. * * *

Specifically, the complaint asserts that Vinson & Elkins provided advice in structuring virtually every Enron off-balance sheet transaction and prepared the transaction documents, * * * Vinson & Elkins allegedly had to know about and joined in the fraudulent Ponzi scheme because of its continuing, intimate involvement in the formation of and transactions with these blatantly fraudulent entities, created solely to cook Enron's books. * * *

The complaint * * * asserts that common to all Enron related-party disclosures, drafted and approved by Vinson & Elkins, was concealment of the following material matters known to Vinson & Elkins: (1) that the transactions were not true commercial, economic transactions comparable to those with independent third-parties; (2) the "disclosures" concealed the real substance and effect of the transactions on Enron and on its financial statements, e.g., that the transactions should have been consolidated on Enron's financial

---

16. [By the Court:] The complaint explains, "[T]rue sales opinions are letters that law firms write vouching for the fact that the business transactions meet particular legal requirements." Complaint at 404.

statements; and (3) they failed to disclose Fastow's actual financial interest in or compensation from the LJM partnerships. Instead the disclosures in SEC filings through the Class Period gave the impression that each transaction was fair to the company, not contrived, but made at arm's length as it would have been if made with an independent third party. In actuality the transactions, which were controlled only by Enron, Fastow or Kopper * * * were bogus, contrived to enrich individual Defendants, and, according to the special investigative committee [led by Dean William Powers], designed "to accomplish financial results, not achieve *bona fide* economic objectives or to transfer risk." * * *

The complaint points out that although [Enron employee and whistleblower] Sherron Watkins' August 2001 letter to Ken Lay represented that Vinson & Elkins had been involved in the fraud and had a clear conflict of interest, Lay still turned to top Vinson & Elkins partners to find out how to cover up the allegations. Furthermore, Vinson & Elkins despite this obvious conflict, agreed to conduct an investigation into the charges and to issue a letter or report dismissing the allegations of fraud that Vinson & Elkins knew were true. Vinson & Elkins also agreed not to "second guess" the accounting work or judgments of Arthur Andersen and to limit its inquiry to top level executives at Enron. Vinson & Elkins' review took place between August 15 and October 15, 2001.

During its investigation, according to the complaint, Vinson & Elkins only interviewed top level executives that Vinson & Elkins knew were involved in the fraud and would deny it. On October 15, 2001 the law firm issued a letter to Enron dismissing all of Sherron Watkins' allegations even though Vinson & Elkins knew they were true from its own involvement. The letter is quoted in part in the complaint:

You requested that Vinson & Elkins L.L.P. ("V & E") conduct an investigation into certain allegations initially made on an *anonymous* basis by an employee of Enron Corp. ("Enron"). Those allegations question the propriety of Enron's accounting treatment and public disclosures. * * * The anonymous employee later identified herself as Sherron Watkins, who met with Kenneth L. Lay, Chairman and Chief Executive Officer of Enron, for approximately one hour to express her concerns and provided him with materials to supplement her initial anonymous letter. * * *

In general, the scope of V & E's undertaking was to review the allegations raised by Ms. Watkins' anonymous letter and supplemental materials to conduct an investigation to determine whether the facts she has raised warrant further independent legal or accounting review.

In preliminary discussions with you, it was decided that our initial approach would not involve the second guessing of the accounting advice and treatment provided by AA, that there would be no detailed analysis of each and every transaction and that there would be no full scale discovery style inquiry. Instead the inquiry would be confined to a determination whether the anonymous letter and supplemental materials raised new factual information that would warrant a broader investigation. * * *

Interviews were also conducted with various Enron personnel. * * * Interviews were also conducted with David B. Duncan and Debra A. Cash, both partners with AA assigned to the Enron audit engagement. * * *

[N]one of the individuals interviewed could identify any transaction between Enron and LJM that was not reasonable from Enron's standpoint or that was contrary to Enron's best interests. * * *

The concern with adequacy of disclosures is that one can always argue in hindsight that disclosures contained in proxy solicitations, management's discussion and analysis and financial footnotes could be more detailed. In this regard, it is our understanding that Enron's practice is to provide its financial statements and disclosure statements to V & E with a relatively short time frame with which to respond with comments. * * *

The complaint recites that although Lay wanted to fire Watkins, he and Vinson & Elkins agreed that discharge would be a mistake and would lead to a wrongful termination suit, disclosing Watkins' allegations about transactions at Enron. So she was shifted to another position at Enron where she would have less exposure to information damaging to Enron.

3. The Accountant/Auditor: Arthur Andersen LLP

Noting that an independent auditor is supposed to be the "investing public's watch dog," the complaint at 447 quotes the United States Supreme Court in *United States v. Arthur Young & Co.,* 465 U.S. 805, 817–18 (1984):

By certifying the public reports that collectively depict a corporation's financial status, the independent auditor assumes a public responsibility transcending any employment relationship with the client. The independent public accountant performing this special function owes ultimate allegiance to the corporation's creditors and stockholders, as well as to the investing public. This "public watchdog" function demands that the accountant maintain total independence from the client at all times and requires complete fidelity to the public trust.

The complaint charges that Arthur Andersen abandoned its responsibilities to Enron investors and to the investing public and violated professional standards in perpetrating a massive accounting fraud.

The consolidated complaint maintains that Arthur Andersen was not independent of its client. Enron was Arthur Andersen's second largest client and Arthur Andersen was economically dependent on Enron, which generated approximately $50 million in fees annually for Arthur Andersen and expectations for more in the future. Indeed Arthur Andersen estimated internally that its fees for services for Enron could increase to $100 million per year. To generate even more fees, Arthur Andersen pressured, and provided incentive compensation to, its audit partners to solicit and market non-audit consulting services, which were far more lucrative, from Enron as well as other clients. David Duncan in the Houston office was earning as much as $2 million a year based largely on the level of fees he "controlled" or sold to his clients. The complaint asserts that the pressures on partners to generate more fees created a conflict of interest for auditors on the Enron engagement and were a substantial factor in Arthur Andersen's abandonment of its independence,

objectivity, and integrity on the Enron financial statement audits and reviews.
* * *

Arthur Andersen knew that the critical factor to increasing its fees was to maintain Enron's investment-grade credit rating, requiring a careful balance between creating outside entities to hold assets and the debt Enron was incurring to finance them and making it appear that Enron was not controlling these entities to avoid consolidation of their assets and debts into Enron's financial statements under GAAP. Aware of the risk, in a meeting on February 2001 about Enron's accounting issues, top level Arthur Andersen partners from the Houston and Chicago offices decided that the potential for doubling its fees to $100 million a year justified retaining Enron as a client. Furthermore when partner Carl Bass objected to and opposed the improper accounting practices used at Enron in 1999–2000, and thereby upset Enron management, top level Arthur Andersen partners removed him from his oversight role on the Enron audits.

Arthur Andersen operated its consulting services in a manner that revealed its lack of independence in audits and reviews.

Arthur Andersen was fully aware of Enron's unusually complex organization because it helped structure hundreds of complicated partnerships, many with no business purpose other than to conceal debt and losses. The number of related-party transactions was enormous, and in many Enron maintained control over the entities and deliberately and improperly did not consolidate them. Andersen knew that Enron utilized at least 600 offshore tax haven entities to shift income, minimize taxation, circumvent United States laws, and maintain secrecy. * * * Even Arthur Andersen's tax and consulting departments knew that Enron's use of such entities was excessive and that many had no business justification. * * *

A number of surviving Arthur Andersen documents reveal that Arthur Andersen knew, was concerned about, yet covered up or ignored fraudulent accounting practices by Enron. * * *

During a meeting on February 5, 2001, top Arthur Andersen executives from the Chicago headquarters participated in a teleconference with top Houston and Gulf Coast partners assigned to the Enron engagement about whether to retain Enron as a client. * * * The minutes of the meeting reflect a discussion, and therefore the participants' knowledge, of the accounting issues that ultimately caused Enron's collapse, including significant related-party transactions with LJM, the materiality of such amounts to Enron's income statement, and the amount retained "off balance sheet"; Fastow's conflict of interest in serving as CFO of Enron and LJM fund manager; Fastow's compensation for his services and participation in LJM; disclosures of transactions in the financial footnotes; Enron's mark-to-market earnings, described as "intelligent gambling;" Enron's reliance on its credit rating to maintain solvency; and Enron's aggressive transaction structuring. They decided to keep Enron as a client despite the red flags because of the potential $100 million fee they could receive, and a few weeks later Arthur Andersen issued a "clean" audit opinion on Enron's 2000 financial statements. * * *

In its audits of Enron's financial statements in 1997, Arthur Andersen identified $51 million of adjustments where the accounting was improper. Arthur Andersen knew these adjustments altogether constituted almost 50%

of Enron's $105 million net income for that year and were therefore clearly material to the financial statements and needed to be made if those statements were not to be misleading. Nevertheless, Enron informed Arthur Andersen it did not want to make those adjustments, which would radically reduce the net income that management wanted to report to the public. Arthur Andersen acquiesced in order to retain its lucrative client, and it abandoned its role as a public watch dog and violated GAAS. To justify not making such large adjustments, Arthur Andersen obfuscated the information by calculating the $51 million as an immaterial 8% of a contrived figure that it denominated as "normalized earnings," requiring no adjustment, instead of as a very material 51% of Enron's net income for 1997, which would require an adjustment. The complaint asserts that in 2001, too late for thousands of investors who lost billions of dollars because they relied on earlier years' financial statements, Enron restated its financial statements for 1997–2000 and Arthur Andersen commented that the audit reports covering the year-end financial statements for 1997–2000 "should not be relied upon."

III.   Motions to Dismiss and the Court's Rulings

A.   Defendants' Common Objections

A number of Defendants argue that Lead Plaintiff's allegations that Defendants knew of the Ponzi scheme and yet poured millions of dollars into it or risked their reputations to conceal the scheme merely for fees, payments and profits, and subsequently, once caught in the scheme, shored it up in order to limit their exposure to liability and obtain what payments they could on Enron's debts to them, are inherently irrational, implausible, and/or illogical and the alleged actions are against Defendants' own self-interest. This Court notes that what may have been implausible two or three years ago is hardly so today, in light of a plethora of revelations, investigations, evidence, indictments, guilty pleas, and confessions of widespread corporate corruption and fraud by companies, auditors, brokerage houses, and banks. Lining one's pockets with gold, at the expense of investors, employees, and the public, appears too often to be a dominating ambition, and public skepticism about the market is very prevalent.

The third-party entities have objected with justification to the undifferentiated, boiler-plate allegations repetitively applied to all or many defendants or with generalized references. * * * They also criticize claims of misconduct based on what are common, legitimate business actions or practices (e.g., loans, commodity swaps, passive investments, underwriting securities offerings, regular working relationships with a company's executives, issuance of analyst reports, and desire to earn profits) that are not inherently improper or fraudulent. This Court responds that the activities must be viewed in context, i.e., within the totality of surrounding circumstances, to determine whether they are merely ordinary and legitimate acts or contrivances and deceptive devices used to defraud. * * *

B.   Section 10(b) Claims Against Defendants Individually

Rather than focusing upon deficiencies in the complaint, especially conclusory or boiler plate allegations, of which the Court agrees that there are many, the Court examines what Lead Plaintiff has specifically and successfully pled in this complaint against each Defendant to determine whether it adequately states a claim with specificity under § 10(b) and raises a strong inference of the requisite scienter that warrants denial of its motion to dismiss.

1. Legal Standards

As a factor common to all, the Court initially finds that the scienter pleading requirement is partially satisfied by allegations of a regular pattern of related and repeated conduct involving the creation of unlawful, Enron-controlled SPEs, sale of unwanted Enron assets to these entities in clearly non-arm's length transactions and often with guarantees of no risk, in order to shift debt off Enron's balance sheet and sham profits onto its books at critical times when quarterly or year-end reports to the SEC, and by extension the public, were due, followed in many cases by the undoing of these very deals once the reports had been made. These transactions were not isolated, * * * but deliberate, repeated actions with shared characteristics that were part of an alleged common scheme through which Defendants all profited handsomely, many exorbitantly. The very pattern that is alleged undermines claims of unintentional or negligent behavior and supports allegations of intent to defraud. * * *

Moreover, Lead Plaintiff has pleaded effectively the common motive of, fixation on, and obsession with monetary gain. It has not only alleged that extraordinary fees, interest rates, etc., were pocketed by the secondary actor Defendants, which only inflated with the expanding mirage of corporate success that they allegedly fraudulently created. * * *

Similarly, conclusory allegations asserted against all or most of the secondary actor Defendants, such as the long-term, continuous, intimate and extensive relationships with Enron and daily interaction with Enron's top executives, necessarily raise the specter of potential and unusual opportunities to learn about and take an active role in Enron's financial affairs, open access to nonpublic information about Enron, intimacy blending into complicity fueled by financial interests, and involvement in formulating, funding, drafting, and decision-making about key aspects of Enron's business, including the structuring and financing of Enron's secretly controlled partnerships with no economic purpose other than to defraud. In addition, the provision of both commercial banking and investment banking services to Enron raises the possibility of conflicts of interest and the standard mandatory in-depth credit analyses required of borrowers by lenders, etc., which should have raised red flags, are all background factors to be considered. * * *

Defendants have complained that they are being targeted for performing the normal functions of their businesses, e.g., lending money, underwriting stocks, accounting and auditing, or drafting legal documents. Obviously, regular business conduct within the bounds of the law would not support a claim of securities law violation; instead the allegations must demonstrate that they knowingly or with reckless disregard stepped outside the boundary of legitimate and professionally acceptable activities in performing material acts to defraud the public. * * *

a.   The Banks

Viewing the specific allegations together, the Court finds that plaintiff has stated a claim against Citigroup [and several other banks] as a primary violator under § 10(b) and Rule 10b–5 [because it] knowingly, or at least with severe recklessness, [made] a material misrepresentation * * * or engaged in an act, practice or course of business that operated as a fraud or deceit upon Enron investors. * * * Citigroup, through its Cayman Island subsidiary, also allegedly participated in a repeated pattern of * * * disguised large loans to Enron totaling $2.4 billion that were never disclosed on its balance sheet, through the [so-called] Delta transactions, at interest rates nearly double the normal borrowing rate, providing Citigroup with nearly $70 million annually for its participation in the Ponzi scheme.

b.   The Law Firms

Contrary to Vinson & Elkins' contention, the situation alleged in the consolidated complaint is not one in which Vinson & Elkins merely represented and kept confidential the interests of its client, which has the final authority to control the contents of the registration statement, other filing, or prospectus. Instead, the complaint alleges that the two were in league, with others, participating in a plan, with each participant making material misrepresentations or omissions or employing a device, scheme or artifice to defraud, or engaging in an act, practice or course of business that operated as a fraud, in order to establish and perpetuate a Ponzi scheme that was making them all very rich. * * *

Among the complaint's specific allegations of acts in furtherance of the scheme are that the firm's involvement in negotiation and structuring of the illicit partnerships and off-the-books SPEs, whose formation documentation it drafted, as well as that of the subsequent transactions of these entities. * * * In other words, it "effected the very" deceptive devices and contrivances that were the heart of the alleged Ponzi scheme. *SEC v. U.S. Environmental,* 155 F.3d at 112. According to the allegations in the complaint, Vinson & Elkins chose to engage in illegal activity for and with its client in return for lucrative fees. Contrary to the Rules of Professional Conduct, it did not resign and thereby violated its professional principles and ethics. Nevertheless, had Vinson & Elkins remained silent publicly, the attorney/client relationship and the traditional rule of privity for suit against lawyers might protect Vinson & Elkins from liability to nonclients for such alleged actions on its client's (and its own) behalf.

But the complaint goes into great detail to demonstrate that Vinson & Elkins did not remain silent, but chose not once, but frequently, to make statements to the public about Enron's business and financial situation. Moreover in light of its alleged voluntary, essential, material, and deep involvement as a primary violator in the ongoing Ponzi scheme, Vinson & Elkins was not merely a drafter, but essentially a co-author of the documents it created for public consumption concealing its own and other participants' actions. Vinson & Elkins made the alleged fraudulent misrepresentations to potential investors, credit agencies, and banks, whose support was essential to the Ponzi scheme, and Vinson & Elkins deliberately or with severe recklessness directed those public statements toward them in order to influence those investors to purchase more securities, credit agencies to keep Enron's credit high, and banks to continue providing loans to keep the Ponzi scheme afloat. Therefore Vinson & Elkins had a duty to be accurate and truthful. Lead Plaintiff has alleged numerous inadequate disclosures by Vinson & Elkins that breached that duty.

Vinson & Elkins protests that its purported "whitewash" investigation and report in the wake of Sherron Watkins' August 1999 memorandum were not disclosed to the public until after Enron waived the attorney/client privilege and produced the report for Congressional hearings in 2002, after the Class Period ended, and thus cannot be the basis of a § 10(b) misrepresentation claim by the investors. Nevertheless the investigation and report can serve as the basis of a § 10(b) and Rule 10b–5(a) or (c) claim alleging use of a device, scheme or artifice to defraud or engagement in an act, practice or course of business that operated as a fraud in the perpetuation of the Ponzi scheme.

For these reasons the Court finds that Lead Plaintiff has stated claims under § 10(b) against Vinson & Elkins.

b.   The Accountant/Auditor: Arthur Andersen

Lead Plaintiff has alleged specific facts giving rise to a strong inference of scienter. Arthur Andersen's comprehensive accounting, auditing, and consulting services to Enron necessarily made it intimately privy to the smallest details of Enron's alleged fraudulent activity. Lead Plaintiff has described several similar prior fraudulent audits of other companies, establishing a pattern of such conduct, and the SEC's and courts' repeated imposition of penalties on Arthur Andersen and its employees, including the consent decree and injunction from the Waste Management fraud which was in effect at the time Lead Plaintiff alleges that Arthur Andersen violated § 10(b) in auditing Enron. Lead Plaintiff has also alleged details of the February 5, 2001 teleconference meeting of senior Arthur Andersen partners * * * from Chicago and Houston and the Gulf Coast when they discussed material concerns at the heart of the consolidated complaint: related-party transactions with LJM, Fastow's conflicts of interest, disclosures of transactions in financial footnotes, Enron's mark-to-market earnings, and Enron's aggressive transaction structuring, in essence the risk of continuing fraudulent accounting for Enron and retaining it as a client. They decided to continue because Enron's business was so lucrative, and a few weeks later they issued a clean audit opinion on the 2000 financial statements. Moreover, it has described e-mails and internal memoranda between and among Arthur Andersen employees * * * before the '99 financial statements were issued that reflect Arthur Andersen's knowledge and intent to continue in the fraudulent scheme. * * *

Because Lead Plaintiff has alleged numerous violations of GAAP and GAAS and pleaded facts giving rise to a strong inference of scienter, he has pleaded a securities fraud claim against Arthur Andersen.

Notes

(1) Judge Harmon allowed the plaintiffs to use circumstantial evidence to create an inference that the defendants acted with the requisite scienter to

support a cause of action for a violation of the securities laws. The circumstantial evidence used in this case was the active and intimate involvement of Enron's lawyers, accountants and bankers in structuring the deals that misled investors and regulators. Doesn't this eviscerate the holding in Central Bank of Denver v. First Interstate Bank of Denver that the securities laws do not prohibit giving aid to another, who then commits a primary § 10(b) violation? If Judge Harmon's approach is correct, won't it always be possible to infer that advisers had knowledge of the misrepresentations and omissions of the primary actor?

(2) Note also the last two sentences in the Vinson & Elkins letter reporting on its investigation of Sherron Watkins' concerns about Enron's accounting practices: "[t]he concern with adequacy of disclosures is that one can always argue in hindsight that disclosures contained in proxy solicitations, management's discussion and analysis and financial footnotes could be more detailed. In this regard, it is our understanding that Enron's practice is to provide its financial statements and disclosure statements to V & E with a relatively short time frame with which to respond with comments." Whose interests were these sentences intended to serve?

(3) In high profile criminal proceedings, Kenneth Lay, Enron's former CEO, Jeffrey Skilling, alternately COO and CEO of Enron, and Richard Causey, Enron's Chief accounting auditor, were charged individually and indicted by a grand jury on charges of multiple securities law violations, including violations of Rule 10b–5. Indictment in United States v. Causey, Cr. No. H–04–25 (S–2) (S.D. Tex.), filed July 7, 2004. Among other things, the three defendants were accused of misleading the public about Enron's true financial situation right up until the company's collapse in 2001. Causey ultimately pled guilty, while Skilling and Lay were convicted by a jury in early 2006. Skilling was sentenced to 24 years and 4 months in prison for his role in the debacle, while Causey received a sentence of 5 ½ years. Lay's conviction was vacated after his sudden death in July, 2006, prior to sentencing, from heart disease. United States v. Lay, 456 F.Supp.2d 869 (S.D. Tex. 2006).

B. INSIDER TRADING

The first statement that trading on the basis of inside information in the anonymous securities markets might violate Rule 10b–5 appeared in In the Matter of Cady, Roberts & Co., 40 SEC 907 (1961). This was an administrative proceeding by the SEC to discipline a broker who learned from a director of Curtiss–Wright Corporation that Curtiss–Wright planned to reduce its dividend and who then sold Curtiss–Wright common stock (and entered into several short sales of that stock) before the announcement of the dividend cut was made. Chairman Cary's opinion for the Commission broadly stated that insider trading violated Rule 10b–5:

> We have already noted that the anti-fraud provisions are phrased in terms of "any person" and that a special obligation has been traditionally required of corporate insiders, e.g., officers, directors and controlling stockholders. These three groups, however, do not exhaust the classes of persons upon whom there is such an obligation. Analytically, the obligation rests on two principal elements: first, the existence of a relationship giving access, directly or indirectly, to information intended to be available only for a corporate purpose and not for the personal benefit of anyone; and second, the inherent unfairness involved where a party takes

advantage of such information knowing it is unavailable to those with whom he is dealing. In considering these elements under the broad language of the anti-fraud provisions we are not to be circumscribed by fine distinctions and rigid classifications. Thus our task here is to identify those persons who are in a special relationship with a company and privy to its internal affairs, and thereby suffer correlative duties in trading in its securities. Intimacy demands restraint lest the uninformed be exploited.

40 SEC at 912. Chairman Cary also rejected arguments that an insider's responsibility was limited to existing shareholders, that there was no prohibition against selling shares to members of the general public, and that Rule 10b–5 was only applicable to face-to-face transactions or cases of misrepresentation or manipulation.

While this holding received attention at the time, its full implication did not sink in for nearly eight years.

SECURITIES AND EXCHANGE COMM'N v. TEXAS GULF SULPHUR CO.

United States Court of Appeals, Second Circuit, 1968.
401 F.2d 833, cert. denied, 394 U.S. 976, 89 S.Ct. 1454, 22 L.Ed.2d 756 (1969).

Before LUMBARD, CHIEF JUDGE, and WATERMAN, MOORE, FRIENDLY, SMITH, KAUFMAN, HAYS, ANDERSON and FEINBERG, CIRCUIT JUDGES.

WATERMAN, CIRCUIT JUDGE:

This action was commenced in the United States District Court for the Southern District of New York by the Securities and Exchange Commission (the SEC) pursuant to Sec. 21(e) of the Securities Exchange Act of 1934 (the Act), against Texas Gulf Sulphur Company (TGS) and several of its officers, directors and employees, to enjoin certain conduct by TGS and the individual defendants said to violate Section 10(b) of the Act, and Rule 10b–5 (the Rule) promulgated thereunder, and to compel the rescission by the individual defendants of securities transactions assertedly conducted contrary to law. * * *

THE FACTUAL SETTING

This action derives from the exploratory activities of TGS begun in 1957 on the Canadian Shield in eastern Canada. In March of 1959, aerial geophysical surveys were conducted over more than 15,000 square miles of this area by a group led by defendant Mollison, a mining engineer and a Vice President of TGS. The group included defendant Holyk, TGS's chief geologist, defendant Clayton, an electrical engineer and geophysicist, and defendant Darke, a geologist. These operations resulted in the detection of numerous anomalies, i.e., extraordinary variations in the conductivity of rocks, one of which was on the Kidd 55 segment of land located near Timmins, Ontario.

On October 29 and 30, 1963, Clayton conducted a ground geophysical survey on the northeast portion of the Kidd 55 segment which confirmed the presence of an anomaly and indicated the necessity of diamond core drilling for further evaluation. Drilling of the initial hole, K–55–1, at the strongest part of the anomaly was commenced on November 8, and terminated on

November 12 at a depth of 655 feet. Visual estimates by Holyk of the core of K–55–1 indicated an average copper content of 1.15% and an average zinc content of 8.64% over a length of 599 feet. This visual estimate convinced TGS that it was desirable to acquire the remainder of the Kidd 55 segment, and in order to facilitate this acquisition TGS President Stephens instructed the exploration group to keep the results of K–55–1 confidential and undisclosed even as to other officers, directors, and employees of TGS. The hole was concealed and a barren core was intentionally drilled off the anomaly. Meanwhile, the core of K–55–1 had been shipped to Utah for chemical assay which, when received in early December, revealed an average mineral content of 1.18% copper, 8.26% zinc, and 3.94% ounces of silver per ton over a length of 602 feet. These results were so remarkable that neither Clayton, an experienced geophysicist, nor four other TGS expert witnesses, had ever seen or heard of a comparable initial exploratory drill hole in a base metal deposit. So, the trial court concluded, "There is no doubt that the drill core of K–55–1 was unusually good and that it excited the interest and speculation of those who knew about it." [258 F.Supp.] at 282. By March 27, 1964, TGS decided that the land acquisition program had advanced to such a point that the company might well resume drilling, and drilling was resumed on March 31.

During this period, from November 12, 1963 when K–55–1 was completed, to March 31, 1964 when drilling was resumed, certain of the individual defendants[17] and persons[18] said to have received "tips" from them, purchased

17. [By the Court] The purchases by the parties during this record were:

18. [By the Court]. The purchases made by "tippees" during this period were:

Purchase Date	Purchaser	Shares Number	Shares Price	Calls Number	Calls Price
1964					
Nov. 12	Fogarty	300	17¾–18		
15	Clayton	200	17¾		
15	Fogarty	700	17⅝–17⅞		
15	Mollison	100	17⅞		
19	Fogarty	500	18⅛		
26	Fogarty	200	17¾		
29	Holyk (Mrs.)	50	18		

Chemical Assays of Drill Core of K–55–1 Received December 9–13, 1963

Purchase Date	Purchaser	Shares Number	Shares Price	Calls Number	Calls Price
1963					
Dec. 10	Holyk (Mrs.)	100	20⅜		
12	Holyk (or wife)			200	21
13	Mollison	100	21⅛		
30	Fogarty	200	22		
31	Fogarty	100	23¼		
1964					
Jan.	Holyk (or wife)			100	23⅝
	Murray			400	23¼
24	Holyk (or wife)			200	22¼–22⅜
Feb. 10	Fogarty	300	22⅛–22¼		
20	Darke	300	24⅛		
24	Clayton	400	23⅞		
24	Holyk (or wife)			200	24⅛
26	Holyk (or wife)			200	23⅜
26	Huntington	50	23¼		
Feb. 27	Darke (Moran as nominee)			1000	22⅝–22¾
Mar.	Holyk (Mrs.)	200	22⅜		
3	Clayton	100	22¼		
16	Huntington			100	22⅜
16	Holyk (or wife)			300	23¼

TGS stock or calls[19] thereon. Prior to these transactions these persons had owned 1135 shares of TGS stock and possessed no calls; thereafter they owned a total of 8235 shares and possessed 12,300 calls.

Date	Purchaser	Shares Number	Price	Calls Number	Price
17	Holyk (Mrs.)	100	23⅞		
23	Darke			1000	24¾
26	Clayton	200	25		
Land Acquisition Completed March 27, 1964					
Mar. 30	Darke			1000	25½
30	Holyk (Mrs.)	100	25⅞		
Core Drilling of Kidd Segment Resumed March 31, 1964					
April 1	Clayton	60	26½		
1	Fogarty	400	26½		
2	Clayton	100	26⅞		
6	Fogarty	400	28⅛–28⅞		
8	Mollison (Mrs.)	100	28⅛		

Date	Purchaser	Shares Number	Price	Calls Number	Price
First Press Release Issued April 12, 1964					
April 15	Clayton	600	30⅛–30¼		
Second Press Release Issued 10:00–10:10 or 10:15 A.M., April 16, 1964					
April 16 (app. 10:20 A.M.)					
	Coates (for family trusts)	2000	31–31⅝		

19. [By the Court] A "call" is a negotiable option contract by which the bearer has the right to buy from the writer of the contract a certain number of shares of a particular stock at a fixed price on or before a certain agreed-upon date.

Purchase Date	Purchaser	Shares Number	Price	Calls Number	Price
Chemicals Assays of K–55–1 Received Dec. 9–13, 1963					
1963					
Dec. 30	Caskey (Darke)			300	22 ¼
1964					
Jan. 16	Westreich (Darke)	2000	21 ¼–21 ¾		
Feb. 17	Atkinson (Darke)	50	23 ¼	200	23 1/8
17	Westreich (Darke)	50	23 ¼	1000	23 ¼–23 3/8
24	Miller (Darke)			200	23 ¾
25	Miller (Darke)			300	23 3/8–23 ½
Mar. 3	E. W. Darke (Darke)			500	22 ½–22 5/8
17	E. W. Darke (Darke)			200	23 3/8
Land Acquisition Completed Mar. 27, 1964					
1964					
Mar. 30	Atkinson (Darke)			400	25 ¾–25 7/8
	Caskey (Darke)	100	25 7/8		
	E. W. Darke (Darke)			1000	25 ¾–25 7/8
	Miller (Darke)			200	25 ½
	Westreich (Darke)	500	25 ¾		
30–31	Klotz (Darke)			2000	25 ½–26 1/8
Second Press Release Issued April 16, 1964 (Reported over Dow Jones tape at 10:54 A.M.)					
April 16 (from 10:31 A.M.)					
	Haemisegger (Coates)	1500	31 ¼–35		

In this connection, we point out that, though several of the Holyk purchases of shares and calls made between November 29, 1963 and March 30, 1964 were in the name of Mrs. Holyk or were in the names of both spouses, we have treated these purchases as if made in the name of defendant Holyk alone.

Defendant Mollison purchased 100 shares on November 15 in his name only and on April 8 100 shares were purchased in the name of Mrs. Mollison. We have made no distinction between those purchases.

Defendant Crawford ordered 300 shares about midnight on April 15 and 300 more shares the following morning, to be purchased for himself, and his wife, and these purchases are treated as having been made by the defendant Crawford.

In these particulars we have followed the lead of the court below. * * * It would be unrealistic to include any of these purchases as having been made by other than the defendants, and unrealistic to include them as hav-

On February 20, 1964, also during this period, TGS issued stock options to 26 of its officers and employees whose salaries exceeded a specified amount, five of whom were the individual defendants Stephens, Fogarty, Mollison, Holyk, and Kline. Of these, only Kline was unaware of the detailed results of K–55–1, but he, too, knew that a hole containing favorable bodies of copper and zinc ore had been drilled in Timmins. At this time, neither the TGS Stock Option Committee nor its Board of Directors had been informed of the results of K–55–1, presumably because of the pending land acquisition program which required confidentiality. All of the foregoing defendants accepted the options granted them. * * *

[Editor: Texas Gulf had discovered one of the largest copper/zinc deposits in North America. As drilling explorations continued at the site to determine the size of the deposit, Texas Gulf also sought to acquire land or mineral rights in the area. Rumors leaked out that Texas Gulf had made a major mineral discovery. On April 12, Texas Gulf issued a press release downplaying the importance of the exploration activity, but issued a corrective release four days later confirming the scope of the discovery.]

During the period of drilling in Timmins, the market price of TGS stock fluctuated but steadily gained overall. On Friday, November 8, when the drilling began, the stock closed at 17 3/8; on Friday, November 15, after K–55–1 had been completed, it closed at 18. After a slight decline to 16 3/8 by Friday, November 22, the price rose to 20 7/8 by December 13, when the chemical assay results of K–55–1 were received, and closed at a high of 24 1/8 on February 21, the day after the stock options had been issued. It had reached a price of 26 by March 31, after the land acquisition program had been completed and drilling had been resumed, and continued to ascend to 30 1/8 by the close of trading on April 10, at which time the drilling progress up to then was evaluated for the April 12th press release. On April 13, the day on which the April 12 release was disseminated, TGS opened at 30 1/8, rose immediately to a high of 32 and gradually tapered off to close at 30 7/8. It closed at 30 1/4 the next day, and at 29 3/8 on April 15. On April 16, the day of the official announcement of the Timmins discovery, the price climbed to a high of 37 and closed at 36 3/8. By May 15, TGS stock was selling at 58 1/4.

I. The Individual Defendants

A. *Introductory*

Rule 10b–5, on which this action is predicated, * * * was promulgated * * * to prevent inequitable and unfair practices and to insure fairness in securities transactions generally, whether conducted face-to-face, over the counter, or on exchanges, see 3 Loss, Securities Regulation 1455–56 (2d ed. 1961). The Act and the Rule apply to the transactions here, all of which were consummated on exchanges. Whether predicated on traditional fiduciary concepts, see, e.g., Hotchkiss v. Fischer, 136 Kan. 530, 16 P.2d 531 (Kan. 1932), or on the "special facts" doctrine, see, e.g., Strong v. Repide, 213 U.S. 419, 29 S.Ct. 521, 53 L.Ed. 853 (1909), the Rule is based in policy on the justifiable expectation of the securities marketplace that all investors trading on impersonal exchanges have relatively equal access to material information. The essence of the Rule is that anyone who, trading for his own account in

ing been made by members of the general public receiving "tips" from insiders.

the securities of a corporation has "access, directly or indirectly, to information intended to be available only for a corporate purpose and not for the personal benefit of anyone" may not take "advantage of such information knowing it is unavailable to those with whom he is dealing," i.e., the investing public. Matter of Cady, Roberts & Co., 40 SEC 907, 912 (1961). Insiders, as directors or management officers are, of course, by this Rule, precluded from so unfairly dealing, but the Rule is also applicable to one possessing the information who may not be strictly termed an "insider" within the meaning of Sec. 16(b) of the Act. Thus, anyone in possession of material inside information must either disclose it to the investing public, or if he is disabled from disclosing it in order to protect a corporate confidence, or he chooses not to do so, must abstain from trading in or recommending the securities concerned while such inside information remains undisclosed. So, it is here no justification for insider activity that disclosure was forbidden by the legitimate corporate objective of acquiring options to purchase the land surrounding the exploration site; if the information was, as the SEC contends, material,[20] its possessors should have kept out of the market until disclosure was accomplished. Cady, Roberts, supra at 911.

B. Material Inside Information

[Editor: The Court concludes that K–55–1 constituted "material" information, an issue now controlled by the test of TSC Industries v. Northway, supra. In the course of this discussion, the Court included observations about insider trading that are relevant today:]

An insider is not, of course, always foreclosed from investing in his own company merely because he may be more familiar with company operations than are outside investors. An insider's duty to disclose information or his duty to abstain from dealing in his company's securities arises only in "those situations which are essentially extraordinary in nature and which are reasonably certain to have a substantial effect on the market price of the security if [the extraordinary situation is] disclosed." Fleischer, Securities Trading and Corporate Information Practices: The Implications of the Texas Gulf Sulphur Proceeding, 51 Va.L.Rev. 1271, 1289.

Nor is an insider obligated to confer upon outside investors the benefit of his superior financial or other expert analysis by disclosing his educated guesses or predictions. 3 Loss, op. cit. supra at 1463. The only regulatory objective is that access to material information be enjoyed equally, but this objective requires nothing more than the disclosure of basic facts so that outsiders may draw upon their own evaluative expertise in reaching their own investment decisions with knowledge equal to that of the insiders. * * *

The speculators and chartists of Wall and Bay Streets are also "reasonable" investors entitled to the same legal protection afforded conservative traders. * * *

Our survey of the facts found below conclusively establishes that knowledge of the results of the discovery hole, K–55–1, would have been important

---

20. [By the Court] Congress intended by the Exchange Act to eliminate the idea that the use of inside information for personal ad- vantage was a normal emolument of corporate office. See Sections 2 and 16 of the Act.

to a reasonable investor and might have affected the price of the stock.[21] * * *

[A] major factor in determining whether the K–55–1 discovery was a material fact is the importance attached to the drilling results by those who knew about it. In view of other unrelated recent developments favorably affecting TGS, participation by an informed person in a regular stock—purchase program, or even sporadic trading by an informed person, might lend only nominal support to the inference of the materiality of the K–55–1 discovery; nevertheless, the timing by those who knew [of their stock purchases] and their purchases of *short-term calls*—purchases in some cases by individuals who had never before purchased calls or even TGS stock—virtually compels the inference that the insiders were influenced by the drilling results. This insider trading activity, * * * surely constitutes highly pertinent evidence and the only truly objective evidence of the materiality of the K–55–1 discovery. * * *

Our decision to expand the limited protection afforded outside investors * * * is not at all shaken by fears that the elimination of insider trading benefits will deplete the ranks of capable corporate managers by taking away an incentive to accept such employment. Such benefits, in essence, are forms of secret corporate compensation, see Cary, Corporate Standards and Legal Rules, 50 Calif.L.Rev. 408, 409–10 (1962). * * * Moreover, adequate incentives for corporate officers may be provided by properly administered stock options and employee purchase plans of which there are many in existence. In any event, the normal motivation induced by stock ownership, i.e., the identification of an individual with corporate progress, is ill-promoted by condoning the sort of speculative insider activity which occurred here[.]* * *

The core of Rule 10b–5 is the implementation of the Congressional purpose that all investors should have equal access to the rewards of participation in securities transactions. * * * The insiders here were not trading on an equal footing with the outside investors. They alone were in a position to evaluate the probability and magnitude of what seemed from the outset to be a major ore strike; they alone could invest safely, secure in the expectation that the price of TGS stock would rise substantially in the event such a major strike should materialize, but would decline little, if at all, in the event of failure, for the public, ignorant at the outset of the favorable probabilities would likewise be unaware of the unproductive exploration, and the additional exploration costs would not significantly affect TGS market prices. Such inequities based upon unequal access to knowledge should not be shrugged off as inevitable in our way of life, or in view of the congressional concern in the area, remain uncorrected.

We hold, therefore, that all transactions in TGS stock or calls by individuals apprised of the drilling results of K–55–1 were made in violation of Rule

---

21. [By the Court] We do not suggest that material facts must be disclosed immediately; the timing of disclosure is a matter for the business judgment of the corporate officers entrusted with the management of the corporation within the affirmative disclosure requirements promulgated by the exchanges and by the SEC. Here, a valuable corporate purpose was served by delaying the publication of the K–55–1 discovery. We do intend to convey, however, that where a corporate purpose is thus served by withholding the news of a material fact, those persons who are thus quite properly true to their corporate trust must not during the period of non-disclosure deal personally in the corporation's securities or give to outsiders confidential information not generally available to all the corporations' stockholders and to the public at large.

10b–5. Inasmuch as the visual evaluation of that drill core (a generally reliable estimate though less accurate than a chemical assay) constituted material information, those advised of the results of the visual evaluation as well as those informed of the chemical assay traded in violation of law. The geologist Darke possessed undisclosed material information and traded in TGS securities. Therefore we reverse the dismissal of the action as to him and his personal transactions. The trial court also found that Darke, after the drilling of K–55–1 had been completed and with detailed knowledge of the results thereof, told certain outside individuals that TGS "was a good buy." These individuals thereafter acquired TGS stock and calls. The trial court also found that later, as of March 30, 1964, Darke not only used his material knowledge for his own purchases but that the substantial amounts of TGS stock and calls purchased by these outside individuals on that day, was "strong circumstantial evidence that Darke must have passed the word to one or more of his 'tippees' that drilling on the Kidd 55 segment was about to be resumed." 258 F.Supp. at 284. Obviously if such a resumption were to have any meaning to such "tippees," they must have previously been told of K–55–1.

Unfortunately, however, there was no definitive resolution below of Darke's liability in these premises for the trial court held as to him, as it held as to all the other individual defendants, that this "undisclosed information" never became material until April 9. As it is our holding that the information acquired after the drilling of K–55–1 was material, we, on the basis of the findings of direct and circumstantial evidence on the issue that the trial court has already expressed, hold that Darke violated Rule 10b–5(3) and Section 10(b) by "tipping" and we remand, pursuant to the agreement of the parties, for a determination of the appropriate remedy. As Darke's "tippees" are not defendants in this action, we need not decide whether, if they acted with actual or constructive knowledge that the material information was undisclosed, their conduct is as equally violative of the Rule as the conduct of their insider source, though we note that it certainly could be equally reprehensible. * * *

C.   When May Insiders Act?

Appellant Crawford, who ordered[22] the purchase of TGS stock shortly before the TGS April 16 official announcement, and defendant Coates, who placed orders with and communicated the news to his broker immediately after the official announcement was read at the TGS-called press conference, concede that they were in possession of material information. They contend, however, that their purchases were not proscribed purchases for the news had already been effectively disclosed. We disagree.

Crawford telephoned his orders to his Chicago broker about midnight on April 15 and again at 8:30 in the morning of the 16th, with instructions to buy at the opening of the Midwest Stock Exchange that morning. The trial court's finding that "he sought to, and did, 'beat the news,' " 258 F.Supp. at

---

22. [By the Court] The effective protection of the public from insider exploitation of advance notice of material information requires that the time that an insider places an order, rather than the time of its ultimate execution, be determinative for Rule 10b–5 purposes. Otherwise, insiders would be able to "beat the news," cf. Fleischer, supra, 51 Va.L.Rev. at 1291, by requesting in advance that their orders be executed immediately after the dissemination of a major news release but before outsiders could act on the release. * * *

287, is well documented by the record. The rumors of a major ore strike which had been circulated in Canada and, to a lesser extent, in New York, had been disclaimed by the TGS press release of April 12, which significantly promised the public an official detailed announcement when possibilities had ripened into actualities. The abbreviated announcement to the Canadian press at 9:40 A.M. on the 16th by the Ontario Minister of Mines and the report carried by The Northern Miner, parts of which had sporadically reached New York on the morning of the 16th through reports from Canadian affiliates to a few New York investment firms, are assuredly not the equivalent of the official 10–15 minute announcement which was not released to the American financial press until after 10:00 A.M. Crawford's orders had been placed before that. Before insiders may act upon material information, such information must have been effectively disclosed in a manner sufficient to insure its availability to the investing public. * * *

Coates was absolved by the court below because his telephone order was placed shortly before 10:20 A.M. on April 16, which was after the announcement had been made even though the news could not be considered already a matter of public information. This result seems to have been predicated upon a misinterpretation of dicta in *Cady, Roberts,* where the SEC instructed insiders to "keep out of the market until the established procedures for public release of the information are *carried out* instead of hastening to execute transactions in advance of, and in frustration of, the objectives of the release," 40 SEC at 915 (emphasis supplied). This reading of a news release, which prompted Coates into action, is merely the first step in the process of dissemination required for compliance with the regulatory objective of providing all investors with an equal opportunity to make informed investment judgments. Assuming that the contents of the official release could instantaneously be acted upon,[23] at the minimum Coates should have waited until the news could reasonably have been expected to appear over the media of widest circulation, the Dow Jones broad tape, rather than hastening to insure an advantage to himself and his broker son-in-law.[24] * * *

E. May Insiders Accept Stock Options Without Disclosing Material Information to the Issuer?

On February 20, 1964, defendants Stephens, Fogarty, Mollison, Holyk and Kline accepted stock options issued to them and a number of other top

---

23. [By the Court] Although the only insider who acted after the news appeared over the Dow Jones broad tape is not an appellant and therefore we need not discuss the necessity of considering the advisability of a "reasonable waiting period" during which outsiders may absorb and evaluate disclosures, we note in passing that, where the news is of a sort which is not readily translatable into investment action, insiders may not take advantage of their advance opportunity to evaluate the information by acting immediately upon dissemination. In any event, the permissible timing of insider transactions after disclosures of various sorts is one of the many areas of expertise for appropriate exercise of the SEC's rulemaking power, which we hope will be utilized in the future to provide some predictability of certainty for the business community.

24. [By the Court] The record reveals that news usually appears on the Dow Jones broad tape 2–3 minutes after the reporter completes dictation.

Here, assuming that the Dow Jones reporter left the press conference as early as possible, 10:10 A.M., the 10–15 minute release (which took at least that long to dictate) could not have appeared on the wire before 10:22, and for other reasons unknown to us did not appear until 10:54. Indeed, even the abbreviated version of the release reported by Merrill Lynch over its private wire did not appear until 10:29. Coates, however, placed his call no later than 10:20.

officers of TGS, although not one of them had informed the Stock Option Committee of the Board of Directors or the Board of the results of K–55–1, which information we have held was then material. The SEC sought rescission of these options. The trial court, in addition to finding the knowledge of the results of the K–55 discovery to be immaterial, held that Kline had no detailed knowledge of the drilling progress and that Holyk and Mollison could reasonably assume that their superiors, Stephens and Fogarty, who were directors of the corporation, would report the results if that was advisable; indeed all employees had been instructed not to divulge this information pending completion of the land acquisition program. Therefore, the court below concluded that only directors Stephens and Fogarty, of the top management, would have violated the Rule by accepting stock options without disclosure, but it also found that they had not acted improperly as the information in their possession was not material. In view of our conclusion as to materiality we hold that Stephens and Fogarty violated the Rule by accepting them. However, as they have surrendered the options and the corporation has canceled them, we find it unnecessary to order that the injunctions prayed for be actually issued. We point out, nevertheless, that the surrender of these options after the SEC commenced the case is not a satisfaction of the SEC claim, and a determination as to whether the issuance of injunctions against Stephens and Fogarty is advisable in order to prevent or deter future violations of regulatory provisions is remanded for the exercise of discretion by the trial court.

Contrary to the belief of the trial court that Kline had no duty to disclose his knowledge of the Kidd project before accepting the stock option offered him, we believe that he, a vice president, who had become the general counsel of TGS in January 1964, but who had been secretary of the corporation since January 1961, and was present in that capacity when the options were granted, and who was in charge of the mechanics of issuance and acceptance of the options, was a member of top management and under a duty before accepting his option to disclose any material information he may have possessed, and, as he did not disclose such information to the Option Committee we direct rescission of the option he received.[25] As to Holyk and Mollison, the SEC has not appealed the holding below that they, not being then

---

25. [By the Court] The options granted on February 20, 1964 to Mollison, Holyk, and Kline were ratified by the Texas Gulf directors on July 15, 1965 after there had been, of course, a full disclosure and after this action had been commenced. However, the ratification is irrelevant here, for we would hold with the district court that a member of top management, as was Kline, is required, before accepting a stock option, to disclose material inside information which, if disclosed, might affect the price of the stock during the period when the accepted option could be exercised. Kline had known since November 1962 that K–55–1 had been drilled, that the drilling had intersected a sulphide body containing copper and zinc, and that TGS desired to acquire adjacent property.

Of course, if any of the five knowledgeable defendants had rejected his option there might

well have been speculation as to the reason for the rejection. Therefore, in a case where disclosure to the grantors of an option would seriously jeopardize corporate security, it could well be desirable, in order to protect a corporation from selling securities to insiders who are in a position to appreciate their true worth at a price which may not accurately reflect the true value of the securities and at the same time to preserve when necessary the secrecy of corporate activity, not to require that an insider possessed of undisclosed material information reject the offer of a stock option, but only to require that he abstain from exercising it until such time as there shall have been a full disclosure and, after the full disclosure, a ratification such as was voted here. However, as this suggestion was not presented to us, we do not consider it or make any determination with reference to it.

members of top management (although Mollison was a vice president) had no duty to disclose their knowledge of the drilling before accepting their options. Therefore, the issue of whether, by accepting, they violated the Act, is not before us, and the holding below is undisturbed. * * *

CONCLUSION

In summary, therefore, we affirm the finding of the court below that appellants Richard H. Clayton and David M. Crawford have violated [§ 10b] and Rule 10b–5; we reverse the judgment order entered below dismissing the complaint against appellees Charles F. Fogarty, Richard H. Clayton, Richard D. Mollison, Walter Holyk, Kenneth H. Darke, Earl L. Huntington, and Francis G. Coates, as we find that they have violated [§ 10b] and Rule 10b–5. As to these eight individuals we remand so that in accordance with the agreement between the parties the Commission may notice a hearing before the court below to determine the remedies to be applied against them. We reverse the judgment order dismissing the complaint against Claude O. Stephens, Charles F. Fogarty, and Harold B. Kline as recipients of stock options, direct the district court to consider in its discretion whether to issue injunction orders against Stephens and Fogarty, and direct that an order issue rescinding the option granted Kline and that such further remedy be applied against him as may be proper by way of an order of restitution. * * *

FRIENDLY, CIRCUIT JUDGE (concurring):

Agreeing with the result reached by the majority and with most of Judge Waterman's searching opinion, I take a rather different approach to * * * a situation that will not often arise, involving as it does the acceptance of stock options during a period when inside information likely to produce a rapid and substantial increase in the price of the stock was known to some of the grantees but unknown to those in charge of the granting. I suppose it would be clear, under Ruckle v. Roto American Corp., 339 F.2d 24 (2 Cir.1964),[26] that if a corporate officer having such knowledge persuaded an unknowing board of directors to grant him an option at a price approximating the current market, the option would be rescindable in an action under Rule 10b–5. It would seem, by the same token, that if, to make the pill easier to swallow, he urged the directors to include others lacking the knowledge he possessed, he would be liable for all the resulting damage. The novel problem in the instant case is to define the responsibility of officers when a directors' committee administering a stock option plan proposes of its own initiative to make options available to them and others at a time when they know that the option price, geared to the market value of the stock, did not reflect a substantial increment likely to be realized in short order and was therefore unfair to the corporation.

A rule requiring a minor officer to reject an option so tendered would not comport with the realities either of human nature or of corporate life. If the SEC had appealed the ruling dismissing this portion of the complaint as to Holyk and Mollison, I would have upheld the dismissal quite apart from the

---

26. [By the Judge] * * * If we were writing on a clean slate, I would have some doubt whether the framers of the Securities Exchange Act intended § 10b to provide a remedy for an evil that had long been effectively handled by derivative actions for waste of corporate assets under state law simply because in a particular case the waste took the form of a sale of securities. * * *

special circumstance that a refusal on their part could well have broken the wall of secrecy it was important for TGS to preserve. Whatever they knew or didn't know about Timmins, they were entitled to believe their superiors had reported the facts to the Option Committee unless they had information to the contrary. Stephens, Fogarty and Kline stand on an altogether different basis; as senior officers they had an obligation to inform the Committee that this was not the right time to grant options at 95% of the current price. Silence, when there is a duty to speak, can itself be a fraud. I am unimpressed with the argument that Stephens, Fogarty and Kline could not perform this duty on the peculiar facts of this case, because of the corporate need for secrecy during the land acquisition program. Non-management directors would not normally challenge a recommendation for postponement of an option plan from the President, the Executive Vice President, and the Vice President and General Counsel. Moreover, it should be possible for officers to communicate with directors, of all people, without fearing a breach of confidence. Hence, as one of the foregoing hypotheticals suggests, I am not at all sure that a company in the position of TGS might not have a claim against top officers who breached their duty of disclosure for the entire damage suffered as a result of the untimely issuance of options, rather than merely one for rescission of the options issued to them.[27] Since that issue is not before us, I merely make the reservation of my position clear. * * *

[Concurring opinions of JUDGES IRVING R. KAUFMAN, HAYS, and ANDERSON, and a dissenting opinion of JUDGE MOORE (with whom CHIEF JUDGE LUMBARD concurs) are omitted.]

Notes

(1) On remand, the District Court required Darke to pay to TGS the profits which he and his tippees made on TGS stock prior to April 17, 1964, and required Holyk, Huntington, and Clayton to pay to TGS the profits which each of them made on the TGS stock prior to April 17, 1964. The order stated that the payments were to be held in escrow in an interest-bearing account for a period of five years, subject to disposition in such manner as the Court might direct upon application by the SEC or other interested person, or on the Court's own motion. At the end of the five years, any money remaining would become the property of TGS. To protect these defendants against double liability, any private judgments against them arising out of the events of this case were to be paid from this fund. This order was affirmed in its entirety by a panel consisting of Judges Friendly, Waterman, and Hays. 446 F.2d 1301 (2d Cir.1971), cert. denied, 404 U.S. 1005, 92 S.Ct. 561, 30 L.Ed.2d 558 (1971). The Court specifically rejected the argument that the required restitution constituted a penalty:

> Restitution of the profits on these transactions merely deprives the appellants of the gains of their wrongful conduct. Nor does restitution impose

27. [By the Judge] Though the Board of Directors of TGS ratified the issuance of the options after the Timmins discovery had been fully publicized, it obviously was of the belief that Kline had committed no serious wrong in remaining silent. Throughout this litigation TGS has supported the legality of the actions of all the defendants—the company's counsel having represented, among others, Stephens, Fogarty and Kline. Consequently, I agree with the majority in giving the Board's action no weight here. If a fraud of this kind may ever be cured by ratification, compare Continental Securities Co. v. Belmont, 206 N.Y. 7, 99 N.E. 138, 51 L.R.A., N.S., 112 (1912), with Claman v. Robertson, 164 Ohio St. 61, 128 N.E.2d 429 (1955); that cannot be done without an appreciation of the illegality of the conduct proposed to be excused.

a hardship in this case. The lowest purchase price of any of the transactions here was $17.75 per share paid by Clayton on November 15, 1963. * * * By May 15, 1964, the stock was selling at $58.25 per share. * * * It would severely defeat the purposes of the Act if a violator of Rule 10b–5 were allowed to retain the profits from his violation. * * *

As to the requirement that Darke make restitution for the profits derived by his tippees, admittedly more of a hardship is imposed. However, without such a remedy, insiders could easily evade their duty to refrain from trading on the basis of inside information. Either the transactions so traded could be concluded by a relative or an acquaintance of the insider, or implied understandings could arise under which reciprocal tips between insiders in different corporations could be given.

446 F.2d at 1308. Later cases recognize that full "disgorgement" or restitution may be sought from tippees as well as from insiders themselves. See, e.g., SEC v. Lund, 570 F.Supp. 1397 (C.D.Cal.1983). Presumably, Darke's tippees could have been required to restore the profits they made if they had been named as parties in the original suit by the SEC.

(2) What kind of trading strategy should an officer or director adopt to eliminate or minimize exposure under Rule 10b–5 as applied in *TGS*? The New York Stock Exchange Listed Company Manual § 309.00, discusses this problem and offers the following analysis:

Shareholders have indicated however that they want directors and officers to have a meaningful investment in the companies they manage. So, in the interest of promoting better shareholder relationships, some general rules under which corporate officials may properly buy or sell stock in their company may be helpful. One appropriate method of purchase might be a periodic investment program where the directors or officers make regular purchases under an established program administered by a broker and where the timing of purchases is outside the control of the individual. It would also seem appropriate for officials to buy or sell stock in their companies for a 30–day period commencing one week after the annual report has been mailed to shareholders and otherwise broadly circulated (provided, of course, that the annual report has adequately covered important corporate developments and that no new major undisclosed developments occur within that period).

Transactions may also be appropriate under the following circumstances, provided that prior to making a purchase or sale a director or officer contacts the chief executive officer of the company to be sure there are no important developments pending which need to be made public before an insider could properly participate in the market:

● Following a release of quarterly results, which includes adequate comment on new developments during the period. This timing of transactions might be even more appropriate where the report has been mailed to shareholders.

● Following the wide dissemination of information on the status of the company and current results. For example, transactions may be appropriate after a proxy statement or prospectus which gives such information in connection with a merger or new financing.

● At those times when there is relative stability in the company's operations and the market for its securities. Under these circumstances, timing of transactions may be relatively less important. Of course such periods of relative stability will vary greatly from time to time and will also depend to a large extent on the nature of the industry or the company.

Where a development of major importance is expected to reach the appropriate time for announcement within the next few months, transactions by directors and officers should be avoided.

Corporate officials should wait until after the release of earnings, dividends, or other important developments have appeared in the press before making a purchase or sale. This permits the news to be widely disseminated and negates the inference that officials had an inside advantage. Similarly, transactions just prior to important press releases should be avoided.

In granting stock options to directors and key officers, the same philosophy that relates to purchases and sales may well apply. Where an established pattern or formula is part of a plan specifically approved by shareholders, the question of timing may not arise. In taking up an option, the timing of a purchase is not usually critical as the price is set at the time the option is granted. The reasoning relating to stock options might also apply to employee stock purchase plans in which directors and officers may be entitled to participate.

The considerations that affect director and officer transactions in stock of their own company may be pertinent to transactions in the shares of other companies with which discussions of merger, acquisition, important contracts, etc., are being considered or carried on. The same considerations apply to the families or close associates of directors and officers who are often presumed to have preferential access to information. As far as the public is concerned, they also are insiders. While this assumption may be unjustified in many cases, it is a fact of life which those in positions of leadership and responsibility cannot ignore.

Some companies have adopted policies for the guidance of their personnel relating to transactions in the company's stock, as well as other areas where conflicts of interest could arise. Such policies can be very helpful to employees who have access to important confidential information, as well as to the directors and officers.

In the final analysis, directors and officers must be guided by a sense of fairness to all segments of the investing public. * * *

DENNIS W. CARLTON & DANIEL R. FISCHEL, THE REGULATION OF INSIDER TRADING

35 Stan.L.Rev. 857, 857–58, 866, 868 (1983).

Imagine two firms, A and B, which are identical in all respects except that, in its charter, firm A prohibits the trading of its shares based on inside (nonpublic) information. The firm requires insiders (employees) to report their trades, which a special committee or an independent accounting firm then checks to ensure compliance with the charter provision. Firm B, by contrast, neither prohibits insider trading nor requires reporting. Insiders openly trade shares of firm B and regularly earn positive abnormal returns. In competitive capital markets, which charter provision will survive?

Despite the deceptive simplicity of this question, it has no obvious answer. The consensus, to the extent that any exists, appears to be that firm

A's charter will survive because it eliminates various perceived harmful effects of insider trading. Thus, investors would pay less for shares in B. The managers of B, in order to maximize the value of B shares, would have to adopt a similar charter provision.

As for these harmful effects, many believe that insider trading is "unfair" and undermines public confidence in capital markets. Other critics have argued that insider trading creates perverse incentives by allowing corporate managers to profit on bad news as well as good, encourages managers to invest in risky projects, impedes corporate decisionmaking, and tempts managers to delay public disclosure of valuable information. Some also have argued that insider trading is an inefficient compensation scheme because, in effect, it compensates risk-averse managers with a benefit akin to lottery tickets. Still others have claimed that insider trading allows insiders to divert part of the firm's earnings that would otherwise go to shareholders and therefore raises the firm's cost of capital. Under this "insider trading is harmful to investors" hypothesis, competitive capital markets would force firm B to prohibit insider trading.

The difficulty with this hypothesis is that it appears to be contradicted by the actions of firms. * * *

A. Information Effects

The social gains from efficient capital markets are well known. The more accurately prices reflect information, the better prices guide capital investment in the economy. * * *

Since the firm's shareholders value the ability to control information that flows to the stock market, they may also value insider trading because it gives the firm an additional method of communicating and controlling information. If insiders trade, the share price will move closer to what it would have been had the information been disclosed. How close will depend on the amount of "noise" surrounding the trade. The greater the ability of market participants to identify insider trading, the more information such trading will convey. * * *

Several reasons explain why communicating information through insider trading may be of value to the firm. Through insider trading, a firm can convey information it could not feasibly announce publicly because an announcement would destroy the value of the information, would be too expensive, not believable, or—owing to the uncertainty of the information—would subject the firm to massive damage liability if it turned out ex post to be incorrect. Conversely, firms also could use insider trading to limit the amount of information to be reflected in price. Controlling the number of traders who have access to information may be easier than controlling how much information gets announced over time. In other words, announcement of information need not be continuous, while trading on inside information can be. Thus, insider trading gives firms a tool either to increase or to decrease the amount of information that is contained in share prices.

Notes

(1) In the year prior to the bankruptcy of Enron, Kenneth Lay, the Company's then-chairman, sold $70 million in stock. During the period December 1999 through the bankruptcy in December 2001, Enron insiders sold a stunning total of $1,190,479,472 in Enron stock, totaling 51% of the shares held by insiders. Bill Lerach, a partner in Milberg Weiss Bershad Hynes & Lerach, LLP, the law firm that is leading the securities litigation against Enron, described the Enron transactions as "one of the worst instances of illegal insider trading we've ever encountered." Steven Taub, Enron and On it Goes: More Investigations, Suits, http://www.cfo.com/article/ (accessed November 7, 2002). Is the existence of such trading consistent with the thesis put forward by Carlton and Fischel?

(2) An early justification for permitting insider trading appeared in a provocative book by Professor Henry G. Manne entitled "Insider Trading and the Stock Market" (1966). Professor Manne argued that insider trading is essential to the survival of our economic system because without it, in his view, truly creative, risk-taking entrepreneurs would shun the corporate world. The authors refer to Professor Manne's path-breaking book as "brilliant" and state that it is the "starting point for anyone interested in the subject." 35 Stan.L.Rev. 857, n. 1 (1983). Following similar economic reasoning, the authors also suggest that corporations may prefer to permit insiders to trade on inside information because it "allows a manager to alter his compensation package in light of new knowledge, thereby avoiding continual renegotiation," and it "provides firms with valuable information concerning prospective managers." Id. at 870, 871.

(3) Many economics scholars have questioned the Manne thesis. See, e.g., Mark Klock, Mainstream Economics and the Case for Prohibiting Inside Trading, 10 Ga.St.L.J. 297 (1994). Professor Klock, an economist and not a lawyer by training, concludes that allocational economic analysis justifies a ban on inside trading, with a possible exception based on the cost of enforcing such a ban. See also, Boyd Kimball Dyer, Economic Analysis, Insider Trading, and Game Markets, 1992 Utah L.Rev. 1, 6 (1992). More recently, law and finance scholars have looked at the social consequences of insider trading by examining whether countries with capital markets that fail to enforce vigorously the applicable legal prohibitions on insider trading must pay higher capital costs. These studies show that, while passing laws that regulate insider trading don't lower the cost of capital, enforcing the laws that are on the books does improve the operation of the capital markets by lowering the costs of raising capital. See Utpal Bhattacharya and Hazem Daouk, The World Price of Insider Trading, 57 Journal of Finance 75 (2002).

(4) For an argument that some anonymous investor is inevitably harmed by insider trading, see William K.S. Wang, Trading on Material Nonpublic Information on Impersonal Stock Markets: Who is Harmed, and Who Can Sue Whom Under SEC Rule 10b–5?, 54 S.Cal.L.Rev. 1217 (1981). For a further articulation of this argument, see William K.S. Wang and Marc I. Steinberg, Insider Trading, Chs. 2–3 (1996). Professor Wang's argument that someone always loses as a result of insider trading seems logically unassailable. However, should that make trading on nonpublic information unlawful or even criminal? Should not one also consider possible benefits as an offset?

(5) Professors Carleton and Fischel respond to the intuitive argument that trading on inside information—a sure thing—is fundamentally and obviously unfair and immoral as follows:

We have left for last the most common argument against insider trading—that it is unfair or immoral. * * *

* * * A more powerful response to the argument that insiders profit at the expense of outsiders is that if insider trading is a desirable compensation scheme, it benefits insiders and outsiders alike. Nobody would argue seriously that salaries, options, bonuses, and other compensation devices allow insiders to profit at the expense of outsiders because these sums otherwise would have gone to shareholders. Compensating managers in this fashion increases the size of the pie, and thus outsiders as well as insiders profit from the incentives managers are given to increase the value of the firm. Insider trading does not come "at the expense of" outsiders for precisely the same reason.

Contrary to popular sentiment with respect to insider trading, therefore, there is no tension between considerations of fairness and of efficiency. To say that insider trading is a desirable method of compensating corporate managers is to say that shareholders would voluntarily enter into contractual arrangements with insiders giving them property rights in valuable information. If insider trading is efficient, no independent notions of fairness suggest that it should be prohibited.

Dennis W. Carlton & Daniel R. Fischel, The Regulation of Insider Trading, 35 Stan.L.Rev. 857, 880–82 (1983).

(6) Despite complaints and arguments by some law and economics scholars that insider trading is harmless and may be beneficial, the SEC has continued to enforce vigorously the prohibition against such trading. However, insider trading law is made primarily by courts, particularly the Supreme Court of the United States.

CHIARELLA v. UNITED STATES

Supreme Court of the United States, 1980.
445 U.S. 222, 100 S.Ct. 1108, 63 L.Ed.2d 348.

Justice Powell delivered the opinion of the Court.

The question in this case is whether a person who learns from the confidential documents of one corporation that it is planning an attempt to secure control of a second corporation violates § 10(b) of the Securities Exchange Act of 1934 if he fails to disclose the impending takeover before trading in the target company's securities.

I

Petitioner is a printer by trade. In 1975 and 1976, he worked as a "markup man" in the New York composing room of Pandick Press, a financial printer. Among documents that petitioner handled were five announcements of corporate takeover bids. When these documents were delivered to the printer, the identities of the acquiring and target corporations were concealed by blank spaces or false names. The true names were sent to the printer on the night of the final printing.

The petitioner, however, was able to deduce the names of the target companies before the final printing from other information contained in the documents. Without disclosing his knowledge, petitioner purchased stock in the target companies and sold the shares immediately after the takeover attempts were made public. By this method, petitioner realized a gain of slightly more than $30,000 in the course of 14 months. Subsequently, the Securities and Exchange Commission (Commission or SEC) began an investigation of his trading activities. In May 1977, petitioner entered into a consent decree with the Commission in which he agreed to return his profits to the sellers of the shares. On the same day, he was discharged by Pandick Press.

In January 1978, petitioner was indicted on 17 counts of violating § 10(b) of the Securities Exchange Act of 1934 (1934 Act) and SEC Rule 10b–5.[28] After petitioner unsuccessfully moved to dismiss the indictment, he was brought to trial and convicted on all counts.

The Court of Appeals for the Second Circuit affirmed petitioner's conviction. 588 F.2d 1358 (1978). We granted certiorari, 441 U.S. 942, 99 S.Ct. 2158, 60 L.Ed.2d 1043 (1979), and we now reverse.

II

* * * This case concerns the legal effect of the petitioner's silence. The District Court's charge permitted the jury to convict the petitioner if it found that he willfully failed to inform sellers of target company securities that he knew of a forthcoming takeover bid that would make their shares more valuable. In order to decide whether silence in such circumstances violates § 10(b), it is necessary to review the language and legislative history of that statute as well as its interpretation by the Commission and the federal courts.

Although the starting point of our inquiry is the language of the statute, Ernst & Ernst v. Hochfelder, 425 U.S. 185, 197, 96 S.Ct. 1375, 1382, 47 L.Ed.2d 668 (1976), § 10(b) does not state whether silence may constitute a manipulative or deceptive device. Section 10(b) was designed as a catch-all clause to prevent fraudulent practices. But neither the legislative history nor the statute itself affords specific guidance for the resolution of this case. When Rule 10b–5 was promulgated in 1942, the SEC did not discuss the possibility that failure to provide information might run afoul of § 10(b).

The SEC took an important step in the development of § 10(b) when it held that a broker-dealer and his firm violated that section by selling securities on the basis of undisclosed information obtained from a director of the issuer corporation who was also a registered representative of the brokerage firm. In Cady, Roberts & Co., 40 SEC 907 (1961), the Commission decided that a corporate insider must abstain from trading in the shares of his corporation unless he has first disclosed all material inside information known to him. The obligation to disclose or abstain derives from

> [a]n affirmative duty to disclose material information[,] [which] has been traditionally imposed on corporate 'insiders,' particular officers, directors, or controlling stockholders. We, and the courts have consistently held that insiders must disclose material facts which are known to them by virtue of their position but which are not known to persons with whom

---

28. [By the Court] Only Rules 10b–5(a) and (c) are at issue here. Rule 10b–5(b) provides that it shall be unlawful "[t]o make any untrue statement of a material fact or to omit to state a material fact necessary in order to make the statements made, in the light of the circum-stances under which they were made, not misleading." The portion of the indictment based on this provision was dismissed because the petitioner made no statements at all in connection with the purchase of stock.

they deal and which, if known, would affect their investment judgment. Id., at 911.

The Commission emphasized that the duty arose from (i) the existence of a relationship affording access to inside information intended to be available only for a corporate purpose, and (ii) the unfairness of allowing a corporate insider to take advantage of that information by trading without disclosure.[29]

That the relationship between a corporate insider and the stockholders of his corporation gives rise to a disclosure obligation is not a novel twist of the law. At common law, misrepresentation made for the purpose of inducing reliance upon the false statement is fraudulent. But one who fails to disclose material information prior to the consummation of a transaction commits fraud only when he is under a duty to do so. And the duty to disclose arises when one party has information "that the other [party] is entitled to know because of a fiduciary or other similar relation of trust and confidence between them." In its *Cady, Roberts* decision, the Commission recognized a relationship of trust and confidence between the shareholders of a corporation and those insiders who have obtained confidential information by reason of their position with that corporation.[30] This relationship gives rise to a duty to disclose because of the "necessity of preventing a corporate insider from * * * [taking] unfair advantage of the uninformed minority stockholders." Speed v. Transamerica Corp., 99 F.Supp. 808, 829 (D.Del.1951).

The federal courts have found violations of § 10(b) where corporate insiders used undisclosed information for their own benefit. E.g., SEC v. Texas Gulf Sulphur Co., 401 F.2d 833 (C.A.2 1968), cert. denied, 404 U.S. 1005, 92 S.Ct. 561, 30 L.Ed.2d 558 (1971). The cases also have emphasized, in accordance with the common-law rule, that "[t]he party charged with failing to disclose market information must be under a duty to disclose it." Frigitemp Corp. v. Financial Dynamics Fund, Inc., 524 F.2d 275, 282 (C.A.2 1975). Accordingly, a purchaser of stock who has no duty to a prospective seller because he is neither an insider nor a fiduciary has been held to have no obligation to reveal material facts. * * *

---

29. [By the Court] In *Cady, Roberts*, the broker-dealer was liable under § 10(b) because it received nonpublic information from a corporate insider of the issuer. Since the insider could not use the information, neither could the partners in the brokerage firm with which he was associated. The transaction of *Cady, Roberts* involved sale of stock to persons who previously may not have been shareholders in the corporation. The Commission embraced the reasoning of Judge Learned Hand that "the director or officer assumed a fiduciary relation to the buyer by the very sale; for it would be a sorry distinction to allow him to use the advantage of his position to induce the buyer into the position of a beneficiary although he was forbidden to do so once the buyer had become one." Id., at 914, n. 23, quoting *Gratz v. Claughton*, 187 F.2d 46, 49 (CA2), cert. denied, 341 U.S. 920, 71 S.Ct. 741, 95 L.Ed. 1353 (1951).

30. [By the Court] The dissent of Mr. Justice Blackmun suggests that the "special facts" doctrine may be applied to find that silence constitutes fraud where one party has superior information to another. This Court has never so held. In Strong v. Repide, 213 U.S. 419, 431–434, 29 S.Ct. 521, 525, 526, 53 L.Ed. 853 (1909), this Court applied the special facts doctrine to conclude that a corporate insider had a duty to disclose to a shareholder. In that case, the majority shareholder of a corporation secretly purchased the stock of another shareholder without revealing that the corporation, under the insider's direction, was about to sell corporate assets at a price that would greatly enhance the value of the stock. The decision in Strong v. Repide was premised upon the fiduciary duty between the corporate insider and the shareholder. See Pepper v. Litton, 308 U.S. 295, 307, n. 15, 60 S.Ct. 238, 245, n. 15, 84 L.Ed. 281 (1939).

Thus, administrative and judicial interpretations have established that silence in connection with the purchase or sale of securities may operate as a fraud actionable under § 10(b) despite the absence of statutory language or legislative history specifically addressing the legality of nondisclosure. But such liability is premised upon a duty to disclose arising from a relationship of trust and confidence between parties to a transaction. Application of a duty to disclose prior to trading guarantees that corporate insiders, who have an obligation to place the shareholder's welfare before their own, will not benefit personally through fraudulent use of material nonpublic information.[31]

III

In this case, the petitioner was convicted of violating § 10(b) although he was not a corporate insider and he received no confidential information from the target company. Moreover, the "market information" upon which he relied did not concern the earning power or operations of the target company, but only the plans of the acquiring company. Petitioner's use of that information was not a fraud under § 10(b) unless he was subject to an affirmative duty to disclose it before trading. In this case, the jury instructions failed to specify any such duty. In effect, the trial court instructed the jury that petitioner owed a duty to everyone; to all sellers, indeed, to the market as a whole. The jury simply was told to decide whether petitioner used material, nonpublic information at a time when "he knew other people trading in the securities market did not have access to the same information."

The Court of Appeals affirmed the conviction by holding that "[a]nyone— corporate insider or not—who regularly receives material nonpublic information may not use that information to trade in securities without incurring an affirmative duty to disclose." Although the court said that its test would include only persons who regularly receive material nonpublic information, its rationale for that limitation is unrelated to the existence of a duty to disclose.[32] The Court of Appeals, like the trial court, failed to identify a

31. [By the Court] "Tippees" of corporate insiders have been held liable under § 10(b) because they have a duty not to profit from the use of inside information that they know is confidential and know or should know came from a corporate insider, Shapiro v. Merrill Lynch, Pierce, Fenner & Smith, 495 F.2d 228, 237–238 (C.A.2 1974). The tippee's obligation has been viewed as arising from his role as a participant after the fact in the insider's breach of a fiduciary duty. Subcommittees of American Bar Association Section of Corporation, Banking, and Business Law, Comment Letter on Material, Non–Public Information (Oct. 15, 1973) reprinted in BNA, Securities Regulation & Law Report No. 233, at D–1, D–2 (Jan. 2, 1974).

32. [By the Court] The Court of Appeals said that its "regular access to market information" test would create a workable rule embracing "those who occupy * * * strategic places in the market mechanism." 588 F.2d, at 1365. These considerations are insufficient to support a duty to disclose. A duty arises from the relationship between parties, and not

merely from one's ability to acquire information because of his position in the market.

The Court of Appeals also suggested that the acquiring corporation itself would not be a "market insider" because a tender offeror creates, rather than receives, information and takes a substantial economic risk that its offer will be unsuccessful. Again, the Court of Appeals departed from the analysis appropriate to recognition of a duty. The Court of Appeals for the Second Circuit previously held, in a manner consistent with our analysis here, that a tender offeror does not violate § 10(b) when it makes preannouncement purchases precisely because there is no relationship between the offeror and the seller: "We know of no rule of law * * * that a purchaser of stock, who was not an 'insider' and had no fiduciary relation to a prospective seller, had any obligation to reveal circumstances that might raise a seller's demands and thus abort the sale." General Time Corp. v. Talley Industries, 403 F.2d 159, 164 (1968), cert. denied, 393 U.S. 1026, 89 S.Ct. 631, 21 L.Ed.2d 570 (1969).

relationship between petitioner and the sellers that could give rise to a duty. Its decision thus rested solely upon its belief that the federal securities laws have "created a system providing equal access to information necessary for reasoned and intelligent investment decisions." The use by anyone of material information not generally available is fraudulent, this theory suggests, because such information gives certain buyers or sellers an unfair advantage over less informed buyers and sellers.

This reasoning suffers from two defects. First not every instance of financial unfairness constitutes fraudulent activity under § 10(b). See Santa Fe Industries, Inc. v. Green, 430 U.S. 462, 474–477, 97 S.Ct. 1292, 1301–1303, 51 L.Ed.2d 480 (1977). Second, the element required to make silence fraudulent—a duty to disclose—is absent in this case. No duty could arise from petitioner's relationship with the sellers of the target company's securities, for petitioner had no prior dealings with them. He was not their agent, he was not a fiduciary, he was not a person in whom the sellers had placed their trust and confidence. He was, in fact, a complete stranger who dealt with the sellers only through impersonal market transactions.

We cannot affirm petitioner's conviction without recognizing a general duty between all participants in market transactions to forgo actions based on material, nonpublic information. Formulation of such a broad duty, which departs radically from the established doctrine that duty arises from a specific relationship between two parties, should not be undertaken absent some explicit evidence of congressional intent.

As we have seen, no such evidence emerges from the language or legislative history of § 10(b). Moreover, neither the Congress nor the Commission ever has adopted a parity-of-information rule. * * *

We see no basis for applying such a new and different theory of liability in this case. As we have emphasized before, the 1934 Act cannot be read " 'more broadly than its language and the statutory scheme reasonably permit.' " Touche Ross & Co. v. Redington, 442 U.S. 560, 578, 99 S.Ct. 2479, 2490, 61 L.Ed.2d 82 (1979). Section 10(b) is aptly described as a catch-all provision, but what it catches must be fraud. When an allegation of fraud is based upon nondisclosure, there can be no fraud absent a duty to speak. We hold that a duty to disclose under § 10(b) does not arise from the mere possession of nonpublic market information. The contrary result is without support in the legislative history of § 10(b) and would be inconsistent with the careful plan that Congress has enacted for regulation of the securities markets. Cf. Santa Fe Industries, Inc. v. Green, 430 U.S., at 479, 97 S.Ct., at 1304.[33]

33. [By the Court] Mr. Justice Blackmun's dissent would establish the following standard for imposing criminal and civil liability under § 10(b) and Rule 10b–5:

"[P]ersons having access to confidential material information that is not legally available to others generally are prohibited * * * from engaging in schemes to exploit their structural information advantage through trading in affected securities."

This view is not substantially different from the Court of Appeals theory that anyone "who regularly receives material nonpublic information may not use that information to trade in securities without incurring an affirmative duty to disclose," and must be rejected for the reasons stated in Part III. Additionally, a judicial holding that certain undefined activities "generally are prohibited" by § 10(b) would raise questions whether either criminal or civil defendants would be given fair notice that they have engaged in illegal activity.

It is worth noting that this is apparently the first case in which criminal liability has been

IV

In its brief to this Court, the United States offers an alternative theory to support petitioner's conviction. It argues that petitioner breached a duty to the acquiring corporation when he acted upon information that he obtained by virtue of his position as an employee of a printer employed by the corporation. The breach of this duty is said to support a conviction under § 10(b) for fraud perpetrated upon both the acquiring corporation and the sellers.

We need not decide whether this theory has merit for it was not submitted to the jury. * * *

The jury instructions demonstrate that petitioner was convicted merely because of his failure to disclose material, nonpublic information to sellers from whom he bought the stock of target corporations. The jury was not instructed on the nature or elements of a duty owed by petitioner to anyone other than the sellers. Because we cannot affirm a criminal conviction on the basis of a theory not presented to the jury, we will not speculate upon whether such a duty exists, whether it has been breached, or whether such a breach constitutes a violation of § 10(b).

The judgment of the Court of Appeals is reversed.

[The separate opinions of JUSTICE STEVENS, concurring in the majority opinion and judgment, and JUSTICE BRENNAN, concurring in the judgment, are omitted.]

CHIEF JUSTICE BURGER, dissenting.

I believe that the jury instructions in this case properly charged a violation of § 10(b) and Rule 10b–5, and I would affirm the conviction.

I

As a general rule, neither party to an arm's length business transaction has an obligation to disclose information to the other unless the parties stand in some confidential or fiduciary relation. See Prosser, Law of Torts § 106 (2d ed.1955). This rule permits a businessman to capitalize on his experience and skill in securing and evaluating relevant information; it provides incentive for hard work, careful analysis, and astute forecasting. But the policies that underlie the rule also should limit its scope. In particular, the rule should give way when an informational advantage is obtained, not by superior experience, foresight, or industry, but by some unlawful means. * * * I would read § 10(b) and Rule 10b–5 to encompass and build on this principle: to mean that a person who has misappropriated nonpublic information has an absolute duty to disclose that information or to refrain from trading.

The language of § 10(b) and of Rule 10b–5 plainly support such a reading. By their terms, these provisions reach *any* person engaged in *any* fraudulent scheme. This broad language negates the suggestion that congressional concern was limited to trading by "corporate insiders" or to deceptive practices related to "corporate information."[34] Just as surely Congress cannot

imposed upon a purchaser for § 10(b) nondisclosure. Petitioner was sentenced to a year in prison, suspended except for one month, and a five-year term of probation.

34. [By the Chief Justice] Academic writing

have intended one standard of fair dealing for "white collar" insiders and another for the "blue collar" level. The very language of § 10(b) and Rule 10b–5 "by repeated use of the word 'any' [was] obviously meant to be inclusive." Affiliated Ute Citizens v. United States, 406 U.S. 128, 151, 92 S.Ct. 1456, 1471, 31 L.Ed.2d 741 (1972).

The history of the statute and of the rule also supports this reading. * * *

II

The Court's opinion, as I read it, leaves open the question whether § 10(b) and Rule 10b–5 prohibit trading on misappropriated nonpublic information.[35] Instead, the Court apparently concludes that this theory of the case was not submitted to the jury. In the Court's view, the instructions given the jury were premised on the erroneous notion that the mere failure to disclose nonpublic information, however acquired, is a deceptive practice. And because of this premise, the jury was not instructed that the means by which Chiarella acquired his informational advantage—by violating a duty owed to the acquiring companies—was an element of the offense.

The Court's reading of the District Court's charge is unduly restrictive. * * * In sum, the evidence shows beyond all doubt that Chiarella, working literally in the shadows of the warning signs in the printshop, misappropriated—stole to put it bluntly—valuable nonpublic information entrusted to him in the utmost confidence. He then exploited his ill-gotten informational advantage by purchasing securities in the market. In my view, such conduct plainly violates § 10(b) and Rule 10b–5. Accordingly, I would affirm the judgment of the Court of Appeals.

JUSTICE BLACKMUN, with whom JUSTICE MARSHALL joins, dissenting.

Although I agree with much of what is said in Part I of the dissenting opinion of The Chief Justice, I write separately because, in my view, it is unnecessary to rest petitioner's conviction on a "misappropriation" theory. The fact that petitioner Chiarella purloined, or, to use The Chief Justice's word, "stole," information concerning pending tender offers certainly is the most dramatic evidence that petitioner was guilty of fraud. He has conceded that he knew it was wrong, and he and his co-workers in the print shop were specifically warned by their employer that actions of this kind were improper and forbidden. But I also would find petitioner's conduct fraudulent within the meaning of § 10(b) [and] Rule 10b–5, even if he had obtained the blessing of his employer's principals before embarking on his profiteering scheme.

---

in recent years has distinguished between "corporate information"—information which comes from within the corporation and reflects on expected earnings or assets—and "market information." See, e.g., Fleischer, Mundheim & Murphy, An Initial Inquiry into the Responsibility to Disclose Market Information, 121 U.Pa.L.Rev. 798, 799 (1973). It is clear that the § 10(b) and Rule 10b–5 by their terms and by their history make no such distinction. See Brudney, Insiders, Outsiders, and Informational Advantages Under the Federal Securities Laws, 93 Harv.L.Rev. 322, 329–333 (1979).

35. [By the Chief Justice] There is some language in the Court's opinion to suggest that only "a relationship between petitioner and the sellers * * * could give rise to a duty [to disclose]." The Court's holding, however, is much more limited, namely that mere possession of material nonpublic information is insufficient to create a duty to disclose or to refrain from trading. Accordingly, it is my understanding that the Court has not rejected the view, advanced above, that an absolute duty to disclose or refrain arises from the very act of misappropriating nonpublic information.

Indeed, I think petitioner's brand of manipulative trading, with or without such approval, lies close to the heart of what the securities laws are intended to prohibit.

The Court continues to pursue a course, charted in certain recent decisions, designed to transform § 10(b) from an intentionally elastic "catch-all" provision to one that catches relatively little of the misbehavior that all too often makes investment in securities a needlessly risky business for the uninitiated investor. See, e.g., Ernst & Ernst v. Hochfelder, 425 U.S. 185, 96 S.Ct. 1375, 47 L.Ed.2d 668 (1976); Blue Chip Stamps v. Manor Drug Stores, 421 U.S. 723, 95 S.Ct. 1917, 44 L.Ed.2d 539 (1975). Such confinement in this case is now achieved by imposition of a requirement of a "special relationship" akin to fiduciary duty before the statute gives rise to a duty to disclose or to abstain from trading upon material nonpublic information.[36] * * *

Whatever the outer limits of the Rule, petitioner Chiarella's case fits neatly near the center of its analytical framework. He occupied a relationship to the takeover companies giving him intimate access to concededly material information that was sedulously guarded from public access. The information, in the words of Cady, Roberts & Co., 40 SEC, at 912, was "intended to be available only for a corporate purpose and not for the personal benefit of anyone." Petitioner, moreover, knew that the information was unavailable to those with whom he dealt. And he took full, virtually riskless advantage of this artificial information gap by selling the stocks shortly after each takeover bid was announced. By any reasonable definition, his trading was "inherent[ly] unfai[r]." This misuse of confidential information was clearly placed before the jury. Petitioner's conviction, therefore, should be upheld and I dissent from the Court's upsetting that conviction.

Notes

(1) Would the Court's construction of Rule 10b–5 reach the following persons:

(a) The secretary or messenger who overhears snippets of conversations from his superiors, infers that a favorable development is about to occur, and buys shares of his employer? *—Yes. Fiduciary relationship between secretary and corp.*

(b) The person sitting in a restaurant who overhears conversations at the next table from which she infers that a favorable development is about to occur with respect to XX Company, and buys shares in XX Company? *No fiduciary duty*

(c) The reporter who attends a press conference at which a favorable development is announced, and then, immediately after the conference and before the news appears on the ticker services, telephones his broker and places an order to purchase? *Misappropriation theory → Liability*

(d) A subtippee who believes his tippee has "connections" with employees of the corporation but is not himself employed by the corporation? *No liability under Chiarella, maybe under Dirk*

(2) Vincent Chiarella was apparently the first person against whom criminal charges were filed for violation of Rule 10b–5. The press noted at the time that he

36. [By the Justice] The Court fails to specify whether the obligations of a special relationship must fall directly upon the person engaging in an allegedly fraudulent transaction, or whether the derivative obligations of "tippees" that lower courts long have recognized, are encompassed by its rule.

was a "blue collar" worker and commented that it seemed unfair to apply the criminal process only against persons in lower economic classes.

(3) The criminalization of insider trading reached a new level in Carpenter v. United States, 484 U.S. 19, 108 S.Ct. 316, 98 L.Ed.2d 275 (1987), where the court upheld a conviction under the mail and wire fraud statute, 18 U.S.C.A. §§ 1341, 1343,[37] of Kenneth Felis and R. Foster Winans under the following circumstances:

In 1981, Winans became a reporter for the Wall Street Journal (the Journal) and in the summer of 1982 became one of the two writers of a daily column, "Heard on the Street." That column discussed selected stocks or groups of stocks, giving positive and negative information about those stocks and taking "a point of view with respect to investment in the stocks that it reviews." Winans regularly interviewed corporate executives to put together interesting perspectives on the stocks that would be highlighted in upcoming columns, but, at least for the columns at issue here, none contained corporate inside information or any "hold for release" information. Because of the "Heard" column's perceived quality and integrity, it had the potential of affecting the price of the stocks which it examined. The District Court concluded on the basis of testimony presented at trial that the "Heard" column "does have an impact on the market, difficult though it may be to quantify in any particular case."

The official policy and practice at the Journal was that prior to publication, the contents of the column were the Journal's confidential information. Despite the rule, with which Winans was familiar, he entered into a scheme in October 1983 with Peter Brant and petitioner Felis, both connected with the Kidder Peabody brokerage firm in New York City, to give them advance information as to the timing and contents of the "Heard" column. This permitted Brant and Felis and another conspirator, David Clark, a client of Brant, to buy or sell based on the probable impact of the column on the market. Profits were to be shared. The conspirators agreed that the scheme would not affect the journalistic purity of the "Heard" column, and the District Court did not find that the contents of any of the articles were altered to further the profit potential of petitioners' stock-trading scheme. Over a four-month period, the brokers made prepublication trades on the basis of information given them by Winans about the contents of some 27 Heard columns. The net profits from these trades were about $690,000.

37. [By the Editors] Section 1341 provides:

Whoever, having devised or intending to devise any scheme or artifice to defraud, or for obtaining money or property by means of false or fraudulent pretenses, representations, or promises, or to sell, dispose of, loan, exchange, alter, give away, distribute, supply, or furnish or procure for unlawful use any counterfeit or spurious coin, obligation, security, or other article, or anything represented to be or intimated or held out to be such counterfeit or spurious article, for the purpose of executing such scheme or artifice or attempting so to do, places in any post office or authorized depository for mail matter, any matter or thing whatever to be sent or delivered by the Postal Service, or takes or receives therefrom, any such matter or thing, or knowingly causes to be delivered by mail according to the direction thereon, or at the place at which it is directed to be delivered by the person to whom it is addressed, any such matter or thing, shall be fined not more than $1,000 or imprisoned not more than five years, or both.

Section 1343 provides:

Whoever, having devised or intending to devise any scheme or artifice to defraud, or for obtaining money or property by means of false or fraudulent pretenses, representations, or promises, transmits or causes to be transmitted by means of wire, radio, or television communication in interstate or foreign commerce, any writings, signs, signals, pictures, or sounds for the purpose of executing such scheme or artifice, shall be fined not more than $1,000 or imprisoned not more than five years, or both.

In November 1983, correlations between the "Heard" articles and trading in the Clark and Felis accounts were noted at Kidder Peabody and inquiries began. Brant and Felis denied knowing anyone at the Journal and took steps to conceal the trades. Later, the Securities and Exchange Commission began an investigation. Questions were met by denials both by the brokers at Kidder Peabody and by Winans at the Journal. As the investigation progressed, the conspirators quarreled, and on March 29, 1984, Winans and Carpenter went to the SEC and revealed the entire scheme. This indictment and a bench trial followed. Brant, who had pled guilty under a plea agreement, was a witness for the Government.

In addition, Felis and Winans were convicted of conspiracy under 18 U.S.C.A. § 371,[38] and David Carpenter, Winans' roommate, was convicted of aiding and abetting. The defendants were also charged with criminal violations of § 10(b) and Rule 10b–5 under the theory set forth in Chief Justice Burger's dissent, an issue on which the Justices were evenly divided and therefore did not address. The convictions under the mail and wire fraud statutes, however, were unanimously affirmed:

> We have little trouble in holding that the conspiracy here to trade on the Journal's confidential information is not outside the reach of the mail and wire fraud statutes, provided the other elements of the offenses are satisfied. The Journal's business information that it intended to be kept confidential was its property; the declaration to that effect in the employee manual merely removed any doubts on that score and made the finding of specific intent to defraud that much easier. Winans continued in the employ of the Journal, appropriating its confidential business information for his own use, all the while pretending to perform his duty of safeguarding it. * * * Furthermore, the District Court's conclusion that each of the petitioners acted with the required specific intent to defraud is strongly supported by the evidence.

> Lastly, we reject the submission that using the wires and the mail to print and send the Journal to its customers did not satisfy the requirement that those mediums be used to execute the scheme at issue. The courts below were quite right in observing that circulation of the "Heard" column was not only anticipated but an essential part of the scheme. Had the column not been made available to Journal customers, there would have been no effect on stock prices and no likelihood of profiting from the information leaked by Winans.

The federal mail and wire fraud statute, 18 U.S.C.A. § 1341, is widely used by federal prosecutors in white collar crime cases. A U.S. attorney has written that it is "our Stradivarius, our Colt 45, our Louisville Slugger, our Cuinsinart—and our true love." Jed S. Rakoff, The Federal Mail Fraud Statute (Part 1), 18 Duq. L.Rev. 771 (1980).

(4) The theory of liability set forth in Chief Justice Burger's dissenting opinion in *Chiarella* (and which evenly divided the Justices in *Carpenter*) is called the "misappropriation" theory. Basically, it provides that an insider trading violation may be based on a breach of fiduciary duty by the trader, regardless of

---

38. [By the Editors] Section 371 provides:
If two or more persons conspire either to commit any offense against the United States, or to defraud the United States, or any agency thereof in any manner or for any purpose, and one or more of such persons do any act to effect the object of the conspiracy, each shall be fined not more than $10,000 or imprisoned not more than five years, or both.

whether that duty runs to the issuer of the securities involved or to other parties. See page 868, infra.

(5) If Chiarella is guilty under Rule 10b–5 under the misappropriation theory, have we not simply criminalized violations by employees of employer work rules? Is there any public harm to the securities markets or securities trading if Chiarella disobeys the signs posted by his employer? For a negative evaluation of *Carpenter* on the grounds that it "overcriminalizes" what should essentially be a matter for the civil law and that it tends to "trivialize" the mail and wire fraud case of *McNally,* see John C. Coffee, Jr., Hush! The Criminal Status of Confidential Information after *McNally* and *Carpenter* and the Enduring Problem of Overcriminalization, 26 Am.Crim.L.Rev. 121 (1988). For the perspective of an official of the Department of Justice on the *Carpenter* decision and background on the mail and wire fraud statute, see Michael R. Dreeben, Insider Trading and Intangible Rights: The Redefinition of the Mail Fraud Statute, 26 Am.Crim.L.Rev. 181 (1988). See generally, Charles C. Cox & Kevin S. Fogarty, Bases of Insider Trading Law, 49 Ohio St.L.Rev. 353 (1988); Lawrence E. Mitchell, The Jurisprudence of the Misappropriation Theory and the New Insider Trading Legislation: From Fairness to Efficiency and Back, 52 Alb.L.Rev. 775 (1988).

(6) Approximately four months after *Chiarella* was decided, the SEC adopted Rule 14e–3 pursuant to §§ 14(e) and 23 of the Securities Exchange Act. SEC Rel. No. 34–17120, 45 Fed.Reg. 60410 (1980). These sections of the Exchange Act are part of the Williams Act (described in chapter 8), relating to takeover bids and cash tender offers. The SEC release describes the purpose and scope of this rule as follows:

The rule pertains to trading by persons in securities which may be the subject of a tender offer as well as tipping of material, nonpublic information relating to a contemplated tender offer. It should be noted that the rule applies only in the context of tender offers. * * *

II. Synopsis of Rule

* * * Rule 14e–3(a) imposes a duty of disclosure under Section 14(e) on any person who trades in securities which will be sought or are being sought in a tender offer while that person is in possession of material information which he knows or has reason to know is nonpublic and has been acquired directly or indirectly from the offering person, from the issuer or from an officer, director, partner or employee or any other person acting on behalf of the offering person or the issuer. Since no duty to disclose would arise if a person subject to the rule does not purchase or sell or cause the purchase or sale of such securities while in possession of such information, the rule establishes a specific duty to "disclose or abstain from trading" under Section 14(e). The "disclose or abstain from trading" framework of Rule 14e–3(a) is similar to the approach taken in *Texas Gulf* and *Cady, Roberts* which the *Chiarella* Court cited with approval. In the Commission's view this framework is the least restrictive method of regulating this abusive practice. * * *

The operation of Rule 14e–3(a) may be illustrated by examples. It should be emphasized that these examples are not exclusive and do not constitute the only situations in which the duty under Rule 14e–3(a) would arise:

(1) If an offering person tells another person that the offering person will make a tender offer which information is nonpublic, the other person has acquired material, nonpublic information directly from the offering person and has a duty under Rule 14e–3(a). * * *

(3) If the offering person sends a nonpublic letter to a subject company notifying the subject company of a proposed tender offer at a specified price and upon specified terms and the management of the subject company learns the contents of the letter, the management of the subject company has acquired material, nonpublic information directly from the offering person. An individual member of such management will violate Rule 14e–3(a) if he purchases or sells or causes the purchase or sale of the securities to be sought in the tender offer.

(4) If, under the facts in the preceding example, the management of the subject company also tells other persons not affiliated with management of the letter, then those other persons have acquired material, nonpublic information indirectly from the offering person and are under a duty to disclose or abstain from trading under Rule 14e–3(a). * * *

(6) If a person steals, converts or otherwise misappropriates material, nonpublic information relating to a tender offer from an offering person, such person will have acquired the information directly from the offering person and has a duty under Rule 14e–3(a).

(7) If an offering person tells another person of his intention to make a tender offer, and such other person subsequently tells a third person that a tender offer will be made and this third person knows or has reason to know that this non-public information came indirectly from the offering person, then this third person has a duty under Rule 14e–3(a).

45 Fed.Reg. 60410–60414. The validity of Rule 14e–3 remained in some doubt until the following decision by the Supreme Court.

UNITED STATES v. O'HAGAN

Supreme Court of the United States, 1997.
521 U.S. 642, 117 S.Ct. 2199, 138 L.Ed.2d 724.

JUSTICE GINSBURG delivered the opinion of the Court.

This case concerns the interpretation and enforcement of § 10(b) and § 14(e) of the Securities Exchange Act of 1934, and rules made by the Securities and Exchange Commission pursuant to these provisions, Rule 10b–5 and Rule 14e–3(a). Two prime questions are presented. The first relates to the misappropriation of material, nonpublic information for securities trading; the second concerns fraudulent practices in the tender offer setting. In particular, we address and resolve these issues: (1) Is a person who trades in securities for personal profit, using confidential information misappropriated in breach of a fiduciary duty to the source of the information, guilty of violating § 10(b) and Rule 10b–5? (2) Did the Commission exceed its rulemaking authority by adopting Rule 14e–3(a), which proscribes trading on undisclosed information in the tender offer setting, even in the absence of a duty to disclose? Our answer to the first question is yes, and to the second question, viewed in the context of this case, no.

I

Respondent James Herman O'Hagan was a partner in the law firm of Dorsey & Whitney in Minneapolis, Minnesota. In July 1988, Grand Metropolitan PLC (Grand Met), a company based in London, England, retained Dorsey & Whitney as local counsel to represent Grand Met regarding a potential tender offer for the common stock of the Pillsbury Company, headquartered in Minneapolis. Both Grand Met and Dorsey & Whitney took precautions to protect the confidentiality of Grand Met's tender offer plans. O'Hagan did no work on the Grand Met representation. Dorsey & Whitney withdrew from representing Grand Met on September 9, 1988. Less than a month later, on October 4, 1988, Grand Met publicly announced its tender offer for Pillsbury stock.

On August 18, 1988, while Dorsey & Whitney was still representing Grand Met, O'Hagan began purchasing call options for Pillsbury stock. Each option gave him the right to purchase 100 shares of Pillsbury stock by a specified date in September 1988. Later in August and in September, O'Hagan made additional purchases of Pillsbury call options. By the end of September, he owned 2,500 unexpired Pillsbury options, apparently more than any other individual investor. O'Hagan also purchased, in September 1988, some 5,000 shares of Pillsbury common stock, at a price just under $39 per share. When Grand Met announced its tender offer in October, the price of Pillsbury stock rose to nearly $60 per share. O'Hagan then sold his Pillsbury call options and common stock, making a profit of more than $4.3 million.

The Securities and Exchange Commission (SEC or Commission) initiated an investigation into O'Hagan's transactions, culminating in a 57–count indictment. The indictment alleged that O'Hagan defrauded his law firm and its client, Grand Met, by using for his own trading purposes material, nonpublic information regarding Grand Met's planned tender offer.[39] According to the indictment, O'Hagan used the profits he gained through this trading to conceal his previous embezzlement and conversion of unrelated client trust funds.[40] O'Hagan was charged with 20 counts of mail fraud, in violation of 18 U.S.C. § 1341; 17 counts of securities fraud, in violation of § 10(b) of the Securities Exchange Act of 1934, and SEC Rule 10b–5; 17 counts of fraudulent trading in connection with a tender offer, in violation of § 14(e) of the Exchange Act and SEC Rule 14e–3(a); and 3 counts of violating federal money laundering statutes, 18 U.S.C. §§ 1956(a)(1)(B)(i), 1957. A jury convicted O'Hagan on all 57 counts, and he was sentenced to a 41–month term of imprisonment.

A divided panel of the Court of Appeals for the Eighth Circuit reversed all of O'Hagan's convictions. 92 F.3d 612 (1996). Liability under § 10(b) and Rule 10b–5, the Eighth Circuit held, may not be grounded on the "misappropriation theory" of securities fraud on which the prosecution relied. The Court of Appeals also held that Rule 14e–3(a)—which prohibits trading while

---

39. [By the Court] As evidence that O'Hagan traded on the basis of nonpublic information misappropriated from his law firm, the Government relied on a conversation between O'Hagan and the Dorsey & Whitney partner heading the firm's Grand Met representation. That conversation allegedly took place shortly before August 26, 1988. O'Hagan urges that the Government's evidence does not show he traded on the basis of nonpublic information. O'Hagan points to news reports on August 18 and 22, 1988, that Grand Met was interested in acquiring Pillsbury, and to an earlier, August

12, 1988, news report that Grand Met had put up its hotel chain for auction to raise funds for an acquisition. O'Hagan's challenge to the sufficiency of the evidence remains open for consideration on remand.

40. [By the Court] O'Hagan was convicted of theft in state court, sentenced to 30 months' imprisonment, and fined. See State v. O'Hagan, 474 N.W.2d 613, 615, 623 (Minn.App. 1991). The Supreme Court of Minnesota disbarred O'Hagan from the practice of law. See In re O'Hagan, 450 N.W.2d 571 (Minn.1990).

in possession of material, nonpublic information relating to a tender offer—exceeds the SEC's § 14(e) rulemaking authority because the rule contains no breach of fiduciary duty requirement. The Eighth Circuit further concluded that O'Hagan's mail fraud and money laundering convictions rested on violations of the securities laws, and therefore could not stand once the securities fraud convictions were reversed. Judge Fagg, dissenting, stated that he would recognize and enforce the misappropriation theory, and would hold that the SEC did not exceed its rulemaking authority when it adopted Rule 14e–3(a) without requiring proof of a breach of fiduciary duty.

Decisions of the Courts of Appeals are in conflict on the propriety of the misappropriation theory under § 10(b) and Rule 10b–5, and on the legitimacy of Rule 14e–3(a) under § 14(e). We granted certiorari, 519 U.S 1087, 117 S.Ct. 759, 136 L.Ed.2d 695 (1997), and now reverse the Eighth Circuit's judgment.

II

We address first the Court of Appeals' reversal of O'Hagan's convictions under § 10(b) and Rule 10b–5. Following the Fourth Circuit's lead, see United States v. Bryan, 58 F.3d 933, 943–959 (1995), the Eighth Circuit rejected the misappropriation theory as a basis for § 10(b) liability. We hold, in accord with several other Courts of Appeals, that criminal liability under § 10(b) may be predicated on the misappropriation theory.[41] * * *

A

* * * [Section] 10(b) of the Exchange Act * * * proscribes (1) using any deceptive device (2) in connection with the purchase or sale of securities, in contravention of rules prescribed by the Commission. The provision, as written, does not confine its coverage to deception of a purchaser or seller of securities, see United States v. Newman, 664 F.2d 12, 17 (C.A.2 1981); rather, the statute reaches any deceptive device used "in connection with the purchase or sale of any security."

Pursuant to its § 10(b) rulemaking authority, the Commission has adopted Rule 10b–5 * * *. Liability under Rule 10b–5, our precedent indicates, does not extend beyond conduct encompassed by § 10(b)'s prohibition. See Ernst & Ernst v. Hochfelder, 425 U.S. 185, 214, 96 S.Ct. 1375, 1391, 47 L.Ed.2d 668 (1976) (scope of Rule 10b–5 cannot exceed power Congress granted Commission under § 10(b)); see also Central Bank of Denver, N.A. v. First Interstate Bank of Denver, N.A., 511 U.S. 164, 173, 114 S.Ct. 1439, 1446, 128 L.Ed.2d 119 (1994) ("We have refused to allow [private] 10b–5 challenges to conduct not prohibited by the text of the statute.").

Under the "traditional" or "classical theory" of insider trading liability, § 10(b) and Rule 10b–5 are violated when a corporate insider trades in the

---

41. [By the Court] Twice before we have been presented with the question whether criminal liability for violation of § 10(b) may be based on a misappropriation theory. In Chiarella v. United States * * * the jury had received no misappropriation theory instructions, so we declined to address the question. In Carpenter v. United States, * * * the Court divided evenly on whether, under the circumstances of that case, convictions resting on the misappropriation theory should be affirmed. See Barbara B. Aldave, The Misappropriation Theory: Carpenter and Its Aftermath, 49 Ohio St. L.J. 373, 375 (1988) (observing that "Carpenter was, by any reckoning, an unusual case," for the information there misappropriated belonged not to a company preparing to engage in securities transactions, e.g., a bidder in a corporate acquisition, but to the Wall Street Journal).

securities of his corporation on the basis of material, nonpublic information. Trading on such information qualifies as a "deceptive device" under § 10(b), we have affirmed, because "a relationship of trust and confidence [exists] between the shareholders of a corporation and those insiders who have obtained confidential information by reason of their position with that corporation." Chiarella v. United States, 445 U.S. 222, 228, 100 S.Ct. 1108, 1114, 63 L.Ed.2d 348 (1980). That relationship, we recognized, "gives rise to a duty to disclose [or to abstain from trading] because of the 'necessity of preventing a corporate insider from * * * tak[ing] unfair advantage of * * * uninformed * * * stockholders.' " Id., at 228–229, 100 S.Ct., at 1115 (citation omitted). The classical theory applies not only to officers, directors, and other permanent insiders of a corporation, but also to attorneys, accountants, consultants, and others who temporarily become fiduciaries of a corporation. See Dirks v. SEC, 463 U.S. 646, 655, n. 14, 103 S.Ct. 3255, 3262, 77 L.Ed.2d 911 (1983).

The "misappropriation theory" holds that a person commits fraud "in connection with" a securities transaction, and thereby violates § 10(b) and Rule 10b–5, when he misappropriates confidential information for securities trading purposes, in breach of a duty owed to the source of the information. Under this theory, a fiduciary's undisclosed, self-serving use of a principal's information to purchase or sell securities, in breach of a duty of loyalty and confidentiality, defrauds the principal of the exclusive use of that information. In lieu of premising liability on a fiduciary relationship between company insider and purchaser or seller of the company's stock, the misappropriation theory premises liability on a fiduciary-turned-trader's deception of those who entrusted him with access to confidential information.

The two theories are complementary, each addressing efforts to capitalize on nonpublic information through the purchase or sale of securities. The classical theory targets a corporate insider's breach of duty to shareholders with whom the insider transacts; the misappropriation theory outlaws trading on the basis of nonpublic information by a corporate "outsider" in breach of a duty owed not to a trading party, but to the source of the information. The misappropriation theory is thus designed to "protec[t] the integrity of the securities markets against abuses by 'outsiders' to a corporation who have access to confidential information that will affect th[e] corporation's security price when revealed, but who owe no fiduciary or other duty to that corporation's shareholders." Ibid.

In this case, the indictment alleged that O'Hagan, in breach of a duty of trust and confidence he owed to his law firm, Dorsey & Whitney, and to its client, Grand Met, traded on the basis of nonpublic information regarding Grand Met's planned tender offer for Pillsbury common stock. This conduct, the Government charged, constituted a fraudulent device in connection with the purchase and sale of securities.[42]

42. [By the Court] The Government could not have prosecuted O'Hagan under the classical theory, for O'Hagan was not an "insider" of Pillsbury, the corporation in whose stock he traded. Although an "outsider" with respect to Pillsbury, O'Hagan had an intimate association with, and was found to have traded on confidential information from, Dorsey & Whitney, counsel to tender offeror Grand Met. Under the misappropriation theory, O'Hagan's securities trading does not escape Exchange Act sanction, as it would under the dissent's reasoning, simply because he was associated with, and gained nonpublic information from, the bidder, rather than the target.

B

We agree with the Government that misappropriation, as just defined, satisfies § 10(b)'s requirement that chargeable conduct involve a "deceptive device or contrivance" used "in connection with" the purchase or sale of securities. We observe, first, that misappropriators, as the Government describes them, deal in deception. A fiduciary who "[pretends] loyalty to the principal while secretly converting the principal's information for personal gain," Brief for United States 17, "dupes" or defrauds the principal. See Aldave, Misappropriation: A General Theory of Liability for Trading on Nonpublic Information, 13 Hofstra L.Rev. 101, 119 (1984).

We addressed fraud of the same species in Carpenter v. United States, 484 U.S. 19, 108 S.Ct. 316, 98 L.Ed.2d 275 (1987), which involved the mail fraud statute's proscription of "any scheme or artifice to defraud," 18 U.S.C. § 1341. Affirming convictions under that statute, we said in *Carpenter* that an employee's undertaking not to reveal his employer's confidential information "became a sham" when the employee provided the information to his co-conspirators in a scheme to obtain trading profits. 484 U.S., at 27, 108 S.Ct., at 321. A company's confidential information, we recognized in *Carpenter*, qualifies as property to which the company has a right of exclusive use. The undisclosed misappropriation of such information, in violation of a fiduciary duty, the Court said in *Carpenter*, constitutes fraud akin to embezzlement " 'the fraudulent appropriation to one's own use of the money or goods entrusted to one's care by another.' " Id., at 27, 108 S.Ct., at 317 (quoting Grin v. Shine, 187 U.S. 181, 189, 23 S.Ct. 98, 101–102, 47 L.Ed. 130 (1902)); see Aldave, 13 Hofstra L.Rev., at 119. Carpenter's discussion of the fraudulent misuse of confidential information, the Government notes, "is a particularly apt source of guidance here, because [the mail fraud statute] (like Section 10(b)) has long been held to require deception, not merely the breach of a fiduciary duty."

Deception through nondisclosure is central to the theory of liability for which the Government seeks recognition. As counsel for the Government stated in explanation of the theory at oral argument: "To satisfy the common law rule that a trustee may not use the property that [has] been entrusted [to] him, there would have to be consent. To satisfy the requirement of the Securities Act that there be no deception, there would only have to be disclosure." [S]ee generally Restatement (Second) of Agency §§ 390, 395 (1958) (agent's disclosure obligation regarding use of confidential information).[43]

The misappropriation theory advanced by the Government is consistent with Santa Fe Industries, Inc. v. Green, 430 U.S. 462, 97 S.Ct. 1292, 51 L.Ed.2d 480 (1977), a decision underscoring that § 10(b) is not an all-purpose breach of fiduciary duty ban; rather, it trains on conduct involving manipulation or deception. In contrast to the Government's allegations in this case,

---

43. [By the Court] Under the misappropriation theory urged in this case, the disclosure obligation runs to the source of the information, here, Dorsey & Whitney and Grand Met. Chief Justice Burger, dissenting in Chiarella, advanced a broader reading of § 10(b) and Rule 10b–5; the disclosure obligation, as he envisioned it, ran to those with whom the misappropriator trades ("a person who has misappropriated nonpublic information has an absolute duty to disclose that information or to refrain from trading") * * *. The Government does not propose that we adopt a misappropriation theory of that breadth.

in *Santa Fe Industries*, all pertinent facts were disclosed by the persons charged with violating § 10(b) and Rule 10b–5; therefore, there was no deception through nondisclosure to which liability under those provisions could attach. Similarly, full disclosure forecloses liability under the misappropriation theory: Because the deception essential to the misappropriation theory involves feigning fidelity to the source of information, if the fiduciary discloses to the source that he plans to trade on the nonpublic information, there is no "deceptive device" and thus no § 10(b) violation—although the fiduciary-turned-trader may remain liable under state law for breach of a duty of loyalty.[44]

We turn next to the § 10(b) requirement that the misappropriator's deceptive use of information be "in connection with the purchase or sale of [a] security." This element is satisfied because the fiduciary's fraud is consummated, not when the fiduciary gains the confidential information, but when, without disclosure to his principal, he uses the information to purchase or sell securities. The securities transaction and the breach of duty thus coincide. This is so even though the person or entity defrauded is not the other party to the trade, but is, instead, the source of the nonpublic information. See Aldave, 13 Hofstra L.Rev., at 120 ("a fraud or deceit can be practiced on one person, with resultant harm to another person or group of persons"). A misappropriator who trades on the basis of material, nonpublic information, in short, gains his advantageous market position through deception; he deceives the source of the information and simultaneously harms members of the investing public.

The misappropriation theory targets information of a sort that misappropriators ordinarily capitalize upon to gain no-risk profits through the purchase or sale of securities. Should a misappropriator put such information to other use, the statute's prohibition would not be implicated. The theory does not catch all conceivable forms of fraud involving confidential information; rather, it catches fraudulent means of capitalizing on such information through securities transactions.

The Government notes another limitation on the forms of fraud § 10(b) reaches: "The misappropriation theory would not * * * apply to a case in which a person defrauded a bank into giving him a loan or embezzled cash from another, and then used the proceeds of the misdeed to purchase securities." In such a case, the Government states, "the proceeds would have value to the malefactor apart from their use in a securities transaction, and the fraud would be complete as soon as the money was obtained." In other words, money can buy, if not anything, then at least many things; its misappropriation may thus be viewed as sufficiently detached from a subsequent securities transaction that § 10(b)'s "in connection with" requirement would not be met.

The dissent's charge that the misappropriation theory is incoherent because information, like funds, can be put to multiple uses misses the point. The Exchange Act was enacted in part "to insure the maintenance of fair and honest markets," and there is no question that fraudulent uses of confidential

---

44. [By the Court] Where, however, a person trading on the basis of material, nonpublic information owes a duty of loyalty and confidentiality to two entities or persons—for example, a law firm and its client—but makes disclosure to only one, the trader may still be liable under the misappropriation theory.

information fall within § 10(b)'s prohibition if the fraud is "in connection with" a securities transaction. It is hardly remarkable that a rule suitably applied to the fraudulent uses of certain kinds of information would be stretched beyond reason were it applied to the fraudulent use of money.

The dissent does catch the Government in overstatement. Observing that money can be used for all manner of purposes and purchases, the Government urges that confidential information of the kind at issue derives its value *only* from its utility in securities trading. See Brief for United States 10, 21 (several times emphasizing the word "only"). Substitute "ordinarily" for "only," and the Government is on the mark.[45] * * *

The misappropriation theory comports with § 10(b)'s language, which requires deception "in connection with the purchase or sale of any security," not deception of an identifiable purchaser or seller. The theory is also well-tuned to an animating purpose of the Exchange Act: to insure honest securities markets and thereby promote investor confidence. See 45 Fed.Reg. 60412 (1980) (trading on misappropriated information "undermines the integrity of, and investor confidence in, the securities markets"). Although informational disparity is inevitable in the securities markets, investors likely would hesitate to venture their capital in a market where trading based on misappropriated nonpublic information is unchecked by law. An investor's informational disadvantage vis-a-vis a misappropriator with material, nonpublic information stems from contrivance, not luck; it is a disadvantage that cannot be overcome with research or skill. See Brudney, Insiders, Outsiders, and Informational Advantages Under the Federal Securities Laws, 93 Harv. L.Rev. 322, 356 (1979) ("If the market is thought to be systematically populated with * * * transactors [trading on the basis of misappropriated information] some investors will refrain from dealing altogether, and others will incur costs to avoid dealing with such transactors or corruptly to overcome their unerodable informational advantages."); Aldave, 13 Hofstra L.Rev., at 122–123.

In sum, considering the inhibiting impact on market participation of trading on misappropriated information, and the congressional purposes underlying § 10(b), it makes scant sense to hold a lawyer like O'Hagan a § 10(b) violator if he works for a law firm representing the target of a tender offer, but not if he works for a law firm representing the bidder. The text of the statute requires no such result.[46] The misappropriation at issue here was

45. [By the Court] The dissent's evident struggle to invent other uses to which O'Hagan plausibly might have put the nonpublic information is telling. It is imaginative to suggest that a trade journal would have paid O'Hagan dollars in the millions to publish his information. Counsel for O'Hagan hypothesized, as a nontrading use, that O'Hagan could have "misappropriat[ed] this information of [his] law firm and its client, deliver[ed] it to [Pillsbury], and suggest[ed] that [Pillsbury] in the future * * * might find it very desirable to use [O'Hagan] for legal work." But Pillsbury might well have had large doubts about engaging for its legal work a lawyer who so stunningly displayed his readiness to betray a client's confidence. Nor is the Commission's theory "inco-

herent" or "inconsistent," for failing to inhibit use of confidential information for "personal amusement * * * in a fantasy stock trading game."

46. [By the Court] As noted earlier, however, the textual requirement of deception precludes § 10(b) liability when a person trading on the basis of nonpublic information has disclosed his trading plans to, or obtained authorization from, the principal—even though such conduct may affect the securities markets in the same manner as the conduct reached by the misappropriation theory. Contrary to the dissent's suggestion, the fact that § 10(b) is only a partial antidote to the problems it was designed to alleviate does not call into question

properly made the subject of a § 10(b) charge because it meets the statutory requirement that there be "deceptive" conduct "in connection with" securities transactions.

C

The Court of Appeals rejected the misappropriation theory primarily on two grounds. First, as the Eighth Circuit comprehended the theory, it requires neither misrepresentation nor nondisclosure. * * * Second and "more obvious," the Court of Appeals said, the misappropriation theory is not moored to § 10(b)'s requirement that "the fraud be 'in connection with the purchase or sale of any security.'" * * * * "[O]nly a breach of a duty to parties to the securities transaction," the Court of Appeals concluded, "or, at the most, to other market participants such as investors, will be sufficient to give rise to § 10(b) liability." 92 F.3d, at 618. We read the statute and our precedent differently, and note again that § 10(b) refers to "the purchase or sale of any security," not to identifiable purchasers or sellers of securities. * * * [A discussion of earlier Supreme Court decisions is omitted.]

In sum, the misappropriation theory, as we have examined and explained it in this opinion, is both consistent with the statute and with our precedent. Vital to our decision that criminal liability may be sustained under the misappropriation theory, we emphasize, are two sturdy safeguards Congress has provided regarding scienter. To establish a criminal violation of Rule 10b–5, the Government must prove that a person "willfully" violated the provision. Furthermore, a defendant may not be imprisoned for violating Rule 10b–5 if he proves that he had no knowledge of the rule.[47] O'Hagan's charge that the misappropriation theory is too indefinite to permit the imposition of criminal liability, thus fails not only because the theory is limited to those who breach a recognized duty. In addition, the statute's "requirement of the presence of culpable intent as a necessary element of the offense does much to destroy any force in the argument that application of the [statute]" in circumstances such as O'Hagan's is unjust.

III

We consider next the ground on which the Court of Appeals reversed O'Hagan's convictions for fraudulent trading in connection with a tender offer, in violation of § 14(e) of the Exchange Act and SEC Rule 14e–3(a). A sole question is before us as to these convictions: Did the Commission, as the Court of Appeals held, exceed its rulemaking authority under § 14(e) when it adopted Rule 14e–3(a) without requiring a showing that the trading at issue entailed a breach of fiduciary duty? We hold that the Commission, in this regard and to the extent relevant to this case, did not exceed its authority.

The governing statutory provision, § 14(e) of the Exchange Act, reads in relevant part:

its prohibition of conduct that falls within its textual proscription. Moreover, once a disloyal agent discloses his imminent breach of duty, his principal may seek appropriate equitable relief under state law. Furthermore, in the context of a tender offer, the principal who authorizes an agent's trading on confidential information may, in the Commission's view, incur liability for an Exchange Act violation under Rule 14e–3(a).

47. [By the Court] The statute provides no such defense to imposition of monetary fines.

It shall be unlawful for any person * * * to engage in any fraudulent, deceptive, or manipulative acts or practices, in connection with any tender offer. * * * The [SEC] shall, for the purposes of this subsection, by rules and regulations define, and prescribe means reasonably designed to prevent, such acts and practices as are fraudulent, deceptive, or manipulative.

Section 14(e)'s first sentence prohibits fraudulent acts in connection with a tender offer. This self-operating proscription was one of several provisions added to the Exchange Act in 1968 by the Williams Act. The section's second sentence delegates definitional and prophylactic rulemaking authority to the Commission. Congress added this rulemaking delegation to § 14(e) in 1970 amendments to the Williams Act.

Through § 14(e) and other provisions on disclosure in the Williams Act, Congress sought to ensure that shareholders "confronted by a cash tender offer for their stock [would] not be required to respond without adequate information." Rondeau v. Mosinee Paper Corp., 422 U.S. 49, 58, 95 S.Ct. 2069, 2076, 45 L.Ed.2d 12 (1975). As we recognized in Schreiber v. Burlington Northern, Inc., 472 U.S. 1, 105 S.Ct. 2458, 86 L.Ed.2d 1 (1985), Congress designed the Williams Act to make "disclosure, rather than court imposed principles of 'fairness' or 'artificiality,' * * * the preferred method of market regulation." we explained, "supplements the more precise disclosure provisions found elsewhere in the Williams Act, while requiring disclosure more explicitly addressed to the tender offer context than that required by § 10(b)." [472 U.S.], at 10–11, 105 S.Ct., at 2464.

Relying on § 14(e)'s rulemaking authorization, the Commission, in 1980, promulgated Rule 14e–3(a). * * * As characterized by the Commission, Rule 14e–3(a) is a "disclose or abstain from trading" requirement. 45 Fed.Reg. 60410 (1980).[48] The Second Circuit concisely described the rule's thrust:

"One violates Rule 14e–3(a) if he trades on the basis of material nonpublic information concerning a pending tender offer that he knows or has reason to know has been acquired 'directly or indirectly' from an insider of the offeror or issuer, or someone working on their behalf. Rule 14e–3(a) is a disclosure provision. It creates a duty in those traders who fall within its ambit to abstain or disclose, *without regard to whether the trader owes a pre-existing fiduciary duty* to respect the confidentiality of the information." United States v. Chestman, 947 F.2d 551, 557 (1991) (en banc) (emphasis added), cert. denied, 503 U.S. 1004, 112 S.Ct. 1759, 118 L.Ed.2d 422 (1992).

* * * [The Court holds that this Rule does not exceed the SEC's powers under § 14(e) of the Securities Exchange Act.]

We need not resolve in this case whether the Commission's authority under § 14(e) to "define * * * such acts and practices as are fraudulent" is broader than the Commission's fraud-defining authority under § 10(b), for we agree with the United States that Rule 14e–3(a), as applied to cases of this genre, qualifies under § 14(e) as a "means reasonably designed to prevent"

---

48. [By the Court] The rule thus adopts for the tender offer context a requirement resembling the one Chief Justice Burger would have adopted in Chiarella for misappropriators under § 10(b).

fraudulent trading on material, nonpublic information in the tender offer context. * * * We hold * * * that under § 14(e), the Commission may prohibit acts, not themselves fraudulent under the common law or § 10(b), if the prohibition is "reasonably designed to prevent * * * acts and practices [that] are fraudulent."[49]

Because Congress has authorized the Commission, in § 14(e), to prescribe legislative rules, we owe the Commission's judgment "more than mere deference or weight." Batterton v. Francis, 432 U.S. 416, 424–426, 97 S.Ct. 2399, 2406, 53 L.Ed.2d 448 (1977). Therefore, in determining whether Rule 14e–3(a)'s "disclose or abstain from trading" requirement is reasonably designed to prevent fraudulent acts, we must accord the Commission's assessment "controlling weight unless [it is] arbitrary, capricious, or manifestly contrary to the statute." Chevron U.S.A., Inc. v. Natural Resources Defense Council, Inc., 467 U.S. 837, 844, 104 S.Ct. 2778, 2782, 81 L.Ed.2d 694 (1984). In this case, we conclude, the Commission's assessment is none of these. * * *

IV

Based on its dispositions of the securities fraud convictions, the Court of Appeals also reversed O'Hagan's convictions, under 18 U.S.C. § 1341, for mail fraud. Reversal of the securities convictions, the Court of Appeals recognized, "d[id] not as a matter of law require that the mail fraud convictions likewise be reversed." (citing Carpenter * * *). But in this case, the Court of Appeals said, the indictment was so structured that the mail fraud charges could not be disassociated from the securities fraud charges, and absent any securities fraud, "there was no fraud upon which to base the mail fraud charges." 92 F.3d, at 627–628.

The United States urges that the Court of Appeals' position is irreconcilable with Carpenter: Just as in Carpenter, so here, the "mail fraud charges are independent of [the] securities fraud charges, even [though] both rest on the same set of facts." We need not linger over this matter, for our rulings on the securities fraud issues require that we reverse the Court of Appeals judgment on the mail fraud counts as well.[50]

O'Hagan, we note, attacked the mail fraud convictions in the Court of Appeals on alternate grounds; his other arguments, not yet addressed by the Eighth Circuit, remain open for consideration on remand.

The judgment of the Court of Appeals for the Eighth Circuit is reversed, and the case is remanded for further proceedings consistent with this opinion.

It is so ordered.

JUSTICE SCALIA, concurring in part and dissenting in part.

49. [By the Court] The Commission's power under § 10(b) is more limited. * * * Rule 10b–5 may proscribe only conduct that § 10(b) prohibits.

50. [By the Court] The dissent finds O'Hagan's convictions on the mail fraud counts, but not on the securities fraud counts, sustainable. Under the dissent's view, securities traders like O'Hagan would escape SEC civil actions and federal prosecutions under legislation targeting securities fraud, only to be caught for their trading activities in the broad mail fraud net. If misappropriation theory cases could proceed only under the federal mail and wire fraud statutes, practical consequences for individual defendants might not be large; however, "proportionally more persons accused of insider trading [might] be pursued by a U.S. Attorney, and proportionally fewer by the SEC," Our decision, of course, does not rest on such enforcement policy considerations.

I join Parts I, III, and IV of the Court's opinion. I do not agree, however, with Part II of the Court's opinion, containing its analysis of respondent's convictions under § 10(b) and Rule 10b–5.

I do not entirely agree with Justice Thomas's analysis of those convictions either, principally because it seems to me irrelevant whether the Government's theory of why respondent's acts were covered is "coherent and consistent." It is true that with respect to matters over which an agency has been accorded adjudicative authority or policymaking discretion, the agency's action must be supported by the reasons that the agency sets forth, SEC v. Chenery Corp., 318 U.S. 80, 94, 63 S.Ct. 454, 462, 87 L.Ed. 626 (1943); see also SEC v. Chenery Corp., 332 U.S. 194, 196, 67 S.Ct. 1575, 91 L.Ed. 1995 (1947), but I do not think an agency's unadorned application of the law need be, at least where (as here) no Chevron deference is being given to the agency's interpretation. In point of fact, respondent's actions either violated § 10(b) and Rule 10b–5, or they did not—regardless of the reasons the Government gave. And it is for us to decide.

While the Court's explanation of the scope of § 10(b) and Rule 10b–5 would be entirely reasonable in some other context, it does not seem to accord with the principle of lenity we apply to criminal statutes (which cannot be mitigated here by the Rule, which is no less ambiguous than the statute). * * * In light of that principle, it seems to me that the unelaborated statutory language: "[t]o use or employ in connection with the purchase or sale of any security * * * any manipulative or deceptive device or contrivance," § 10(b), must be construed to require the manipulation or deception of a party to a securities transaction.

Justice Thomas, with whom The Chief Justice joins, concurring in the judgment in part and dissenting in part.

Today the majority upholds respondent's convictions for violating § 10(b) of the Securities Exchange Act of 1934, and Rule 10b–5 promulgated thereunder, based upon the Securities and Exchange Commission's "misappropriation theory." Central to the majority's holding is the need to interpret § 10(b)'s requirement that a deceptive device be "use[d] or employ[ed], in connection with the purchase or sale of any security." Because the Commission's misappropriation theory fails to provide a coherent and consistent interpretation of this essential requirement for liability under § 10(b), I dissent.

The majority also sustains respondent's convictions under § 14(e) of the Securities Exchange Act, and Rule 14e–3(a) promulgated thereunder, regardless of whether respondent violated a fiduciary duty to anybody. I dissent too from that holding because, while § 14(e) does allow regulations prohibiting nonfraudulent acts as a prophylactic against certain fraudulent acts, neither the majority nor the Commission identifies any relevant underlying fraud against which Rule 14e–3(a) reasonably provides prophylaxis. With regard to the respondent's mail fraud convictions, however, I concur in the judgment of the Court.

I

I do not take issue with the majority's determination that the undisclosed misappropriation of confidential information by a fiduciary can constitute a "deceptive device" within the meaning of § 10(b). Nondisclosure where there is a pre-existing duty to disclose satisfies our definitions of fraud and deceit for purposes of the securities laws.

Unlike the majority, however, I cannot accept the Commission's interpretation of when a deceptive device is "use[d] * * * in connection with" a securities transaction. Although the Commission and the majority at points seem to suggest that any relation to a securities transaction satisfies the "in connection with" requirement of § 10(b), both ultimately reject such an overly expansive construction and require a more integral connection between the fraud and the securities transaction. The majority states, for example, that the misappropriation theory applies to undisclosed misappropriation of confidential information "for securities trading purposes," thus seeming to require a particular intent by the misappropriator in order to satisfy the "in connection with" language. * * * The Commission goes further, and argues that the misappropriation theory satisfies the "in connection with" requirement because it "depends on an inherent connection between the deceptive conduct and the purchase or sale of a security." * * *

The Commission's construction of the relevant language in § 10(b), and the incoherence of that construction, become evident as the majority attempts to describe why the fraudulent theft of information falls under the Commission's misappropriation theory, but the fraudulent theft of money does not. * * * And when the majority seeks to distinguish the embezzlement of funds from the embezzlement of information, it becomes clear that neither the Commission nor the majority has a coherent theory regarding § 10(b)'s "in connection with" requirement. * * *

Notes

(1) Justice Thomas' dissent (only a small portion of which is reprinted above) points out logical problems in the position of the majority (and the SEC) with respect to the "in connection with" requirement. Accepting for purposes of argument that it is not entirely logical, is that a justification for rejecting the misappropriation doctrine? Consider the consequences of rejecting that doctrine. If an attorney represents the aggressor in a takeover attempt, he does not violate Rule 10b–5 if he capitalizes on that information and buys stock (or options on stock) of the target. However, if he represents the target, he commits a serious crime if he makes the same purchases. Isn't that even more illogical? Perhaps the answer is that Rule 14e–3 should have been upheld and the misappropriation doctrine rejected? Might there be other situations in a non-takeover context in which similar irrational results would arise?

(2) During the course of the oral argument in *O'Hagan*, the Government conceded that on the facts of Carpenter v. United States, if Winans had gone to the Wall Street Journal and said, "look, you know, you're not paying me very much; I'd like to make a little bit more money by buying stock, particularly the stocks that are going to appear in my Heard on the Street column," and the Wall Street Journal had said, "that's fine," there would have been no deception of the Wall Street Journal, and no violation of Rule 10b–5. Do you agree? If not, what possible theory is available, given the language of § 10(b) and Rule 10b–5?

(3) *O'Hagan* was, of course, a major victory for the SEC. However, it did not resolve all problems. For one thing, Justice Ginsburg's opinion consistently refers to O'Hagan trading "on the basis of" insider information. The phrase preferred by

the SEC is "trading while in possession of" insider information. Does Justice Ginsburg's formulation mean that a person may possess insider information but trade "on the basis of" other factors (such as the mistaken belief that the information has been released publicly) without violating Rule 10b–5? See United States v. Teicher, 987 F.2d 112, 120–1 (2d Cir.1993), where the Court held that the appropriate standard of causation was "knowing possession" of insider information at the time of the trade ("As a matter of policy then, a requirement of a causal connection between the information and the trade could frustrate attempts to distinguish between legitimate trades and those conducted in connection with inside information. * * * Unlike a loaded weapon which may stand ready but unused, material information can not lay idle in the human brain").

(4) The SEC resolved the "use-possession" debate about whether insiders who possess but do not use non-public information are guilty of insider trading by adopting Rule 10b–5–1, SEC Rel. 34–43154 (August 24, 2000). This rule establishes the test of liability to be trading "on the basis of" material nonpublic information, a test that is satisfied if the person "was aware of the material nonpublic information when the person made the purchase or sale."

This provision defines what is included in trading based on material nonpublic information in insider trading cases under Section 10–b. The importance of Rule 10b–5–1 from the standpoint of insiders subject to the inside trading prohibition cannot be overstated. Before the adoption of this Rule, there could never be complete certainty as to whether an insider's securities transaction might run afoul of Rule 10b–5. Now certainty can be obtained simply by full compliance with Rule 10b–5–1, which is an absolute safe harbor that insiders can rely on for their trades. If speculation arises in the press that certain trades made in strict conformity with Rule 10b–5–1 may have been based on inside information, the insider can simply respond that they were pursuant to a qualified preplanned program. Many brokerage and securities firms have urged their executives and employees to create qualified "contracts, instructions, or plans" for the benefit of themselves and their families. A Rule 10b–5–1 plan may provide, for example, for specified periodic sales of shares to provide a steady family income. At the same time, the SEC created a "safe harbor" or "affirmative defense" for purchases or sales of shares pursuant to "binding contracts, instructions, or written plans" that meet the standards set forth below:

> (1) The person demonstrates that before becoming aware of the information, he or she had entered into a binding contract to purchase or sell the security, provided instructions to another person to execute the trade for the instructing person's account, or adopted a written plan for trading securities.

> (2) The person demonstrates that the contract, instructions or plan either (i) expressly specified the amount, price and date; (ii) provided a written formula or algorithm, or computer program, for determining amounts, prices and dates; or (iii) did not permit the person to exercise any subsequent influence over, how, when or whether to effect purchases of sales; and

> (3) The person demonstrates that the purchase or sale that occurred was pursuant to the prior contract, instruction, or plan. A purchase or sale is not pursuant to a contract, instruction, or plan if, among other things, the person who entered into the contract, instruction, or plan altered or deviated from the contract, instruction, or plan or entered into or altered a corresponding or hedging transaction or position with respect to those securities.

(5) There was considerable unhappiness about the loss of the opportunity to argue that the "use" test should be applied in Rule 10b–5 cases by persons not eligible for (or not taking advantage of) the safe harbor. Indeed, the substitution of the "knowing possession" test significantly increases the risk of Rule 10b–5 violations in many situations. Might an argument be made that the SEC did not have authority to promulgate Rule 10b–5–1 given the admitted fact that the whole doctrine has been judicially created out of whole cloth?

(6) While plans complying with Rule 10b–5–1 can be amended from time to time, they cannot be amended to take advantage of material nonpublic information. Rule 10b–5–1 also provides protection only under the antifraud rules. Transactions that involve violations of other sections of the securities acts are not immunized by the Rule.

DIRKS v. SEC

Supreme Court of the United States, 1983.
463 U.S. 646, 103 S.Ct. 3255, 77 L.Ed.2d 911.

JUSTICE POWELL delivered the opinion of the Court.

Petitioner Raymond Dirks received material nonpublic information from "insiders" of a corporation with which he had no connection. He disclosed this information to investors who relied on it in trading in the shares of the corporation. The question is whether Dirks violated the antifraud provisions of the federal securities laws by this disclosure.

I.

In 1973, Dirks was an officer of a New York broker-dealer firm who specialized in providing investment analysis of insurance company securities to institutional investors. On March 6, Dirks received information from Ronald Secrist, a former officer of Equity Funding of America. Secrist alleged that the assets of Equity Funding, a diversified corporation primarily engaged in selling life insurance and mutual funds, were vastly overstated as the result of fraudulent corporate practices. Secrist also stated that various regulatory agencies had failed to act on similar charges made by Equity Funding employees. He urged Dirks to verify the fraud and disclose it publicly.

Dirks decided to investigate the allegations. He visited Equity Funding's headquarters in Los Angeles and interviewed several officers and employees of the corporation. The senior management denied any wrongdoing, but certain corporation employees corroborated the charges of fraud. Neither Dirks nor his firm owned or traded any Equity Funding stock, but throughout his investigation he openly discussed the information he had obtained with a number of clients and investors. Some of these persons sold their holdings of Equity Funding securities, including five investment advisers who liquidated holdings of more than $16 million.[51]

---

51. [By the Court] Dirks received from his firm a salary plus a commission for securities transactions above a certain amount that his clients directed through his firm. But "[i]t is not clear how many of those with whom Dirks spoke promised to direct some brokerage business through [Dirks' firm] to compensate Dirks, or how many actually did so." The Boston Company Institutional Investors, Inc., promised Dirks about $25,000 in commissions, but it is unclear whether Boston actually generated any brokerage business for his firm.

While Dirks was in Los Angeles, he was in touch regularly with William Blundell, The *Wall Street Journal's* Los Angeles bureau chief. Dirks urged Blundell to write a story on the fraud allegations. Blundell did not believe, however, that such a massive fraud could go undetected and declined to write the story. He feared that publishing such damaging hearsay might be libelous.

During the two-week period in which Dirks pursued his investigation and spread word of Secrist's charges, the price of Equity Funding stock fell from $26 per share to less than $15 per share. This led the New York Stock Exchange to halt trading on March 27. Shortly thereafter California insurance authorities impounded Equity Funding's records and uncovered evidence of the fraud. Only then did the Securities and Exchange Commission (SEC) file a complaint against Equity Funding[52] and only then, on April 2, did the *Wall Street Journal* publish a front-page story based largely on information assembled by Dirks. Equity Funding immediately went into receivership.[53]

The SEC began an investigation into Dirks' role in the exposure of the fraud. After a hearing by an administrative law judge, the SEC found that Dirks had aided and abetted violations of § 17(a) of the Securities Act of 1933,[54] § 10(b) of the Securities Exchange Act of 1934, and SEC Rule 10b–5, by repeating the allegations of fraud to members of the investment community who later sold their Equity Funding stock. The SEC concluded: "Where 'tippees'—regardless of their motivation or occupation—come into possession of material 'information that they know is confidential and know or should know came from a corporate insider,' they must either publicly disclose that information or refrain from trading." Recognizing, however, that Dirks "played an important role in bringing [Equity Funding's] massive fraud to light," the SEC only censured him.

Dirks sought review in the Court of Appeals for the District of Columbia Circuit. The court entered judgment against Dirks "for the reasons stated by the Commission in its opinion." * * *

In view of the importance to the SEC and to the securities industry of the question presented by this case, we granted a writ of certiorari. 459 U.S. 1014, 103 S.Ct. 371, 74 L.Ed.2d 506 (1982). We now reverse. * * *

52. [By the Court] As early as 1971, the SEC had received allegations of fraudulent accounting practices at Equity Funding. Moreover, on March 9, 1973, an official of the California Insurance Department informed the SEC's regional office in Los Angeles of Secrist's charges of fraud. Dirks himself voluntarily presented his information at the SEC's regional office beginning on March 27.

53. [By the Court] A federal grand jury in Los Angeles subsequently returned a 105–count indictment against 22 persons, including many of Equity Funding's officers and directors. All defendants were found guilty of one or more counts, either by a plea of guilty or a conviction after trial.

54. [By the Editors] Section 17(a) of the Securities Act of 1933, 15 U.S.C.A. § 77q(a) (1981), provides:

It shall be unlawful for any person in the offer or sale of any securities by the use of any means or instruments of transportation or communication in interstate commerce or by the use of the mails, directly or indirectly—

(1) to employ any device, scheme, or artifice to defraud, or

(2) to obtain money or property by means of any untrue statement of a material fact or any omission to state a material fact necessary in order to make the statements made, in the light of the circumstances under which they were made, not misleading, or

(3) to engage in any transaction, practice, or course of business which operates or would operate as a fraud or deceit upon the purchaser.

III.

We were explicit in *Chiarella* in saying that there can be no duty to disclose where the person who has traded on inside information "was not [the corporation's] agent, * * * was not a fiduciary, [or] was not a person in whom the sellers [of the securities] had placed their trust and confidence." 445 U.S., at 232, 100 S.Ct., at 1116. Not to require such a fiduciary relationship, we recognized, would "depar[t] radically from the established doctrine that duty arises from a specific relationship between two parties" and would amount to "recognizing a general duty between all participants in market transactions to forgo actions based on material, nonpublic information." Id., at 232, 233, 100 S.Ct., at 1116, 1117. This requirement of a specific relationship between the shareholders and the individual trading on inside information has created analytical difficulties for the SEC and courts in policing tippees who trade on inside information. Unlike insiders who have independent fiduciary duties to both the corporation and its shareholders, the typical tippee has no such relationships.[55] In view of this absence, it has been unclear how a tippee acquires the *Cady, Roberts* duty to refrain from trading on inside information.

A.

The SEC's position, as stated in its opinion in this case, is that a tippee "inherits" the *Cady, Roberts* obligation to shareholders whenever he receives inside information from an insider:

> "In tipping potential traders, Dirks breached a duty which he had assumed as a result of knowingly receiving confidential information from [Equity Funding] insiders. Tippees such as Dirks who receive non-public material information from insiders become 'subject to the same duty as [the] insiders.' Shapiro v. Merrill Lynch, Pierce, Fenner & Smith, Inc. [495 F.2d 228, 237 (C.A.2 1974) (quoting Ross v. Licht, 263 F.Supp. 395, 410 (S.D.N.Y.1967))]. Such a tippee breaches the fiduciary duty which he assumes from the insider when the tippee knowingly transmits the information to someone who will probably trade on the basis thereof. * * * Presumably, Dirks' informants were entitled to disclose the [Equity Funding] fraud in order to bring it to light and its perpetrators to justice. However, Dirks—standing in their shoes—committed a breach of the fiduciary duty which he had assumed in dealing with them, when he passed the information on to traders." 21 SEC Docket, at 1410, n. 42.

This view differs little from the view that we rejected as inconsistent with congressional intent in *Chiarella*. In that case, the Court of Appeals agreed with the SEC and affirmed Chiarella's conviction, holding that " '[a]nyone—

---

55. [By the Editors: This famous footnote is number 14 in the original opinion.] Under certain circumstances, such as where corporate information is revealed legitimately to an underwriter, accountant, lawyer, or consultant working for the corporation, these outsiders may become fiduciaries of the shareholders. The basis for recognizing this fiduciary duty is not simply that such persons acquire nonpublic corporate information, but rather that they have entered into a special confidential relationship in the conduct of the business of the enterprise and are given access to information solely for corporate purposes. When such a person breaches his fiduciary relationship, he may be treated more properly as a tipper than a tippee. See Shapiro v. Merrill Lynch, Pierce, Fenner & Smith, Inc., 495 F.2d 228, 237 (C.A.2 1974) (investment banker had access to material information when working on a proposed public offering for the corporation). For such a duty to be imposed, however, the corporation must expect the outsider to keep the disclosed nonpublic information confidential, and the relationship at least must imply such a duty.

corporate insider or not—who regularly receives material nonpublic information may not use that information to trade in securities without incurring an affirmative duty to disclose.' " United States v. Chiarella, 588 F.2d 1358, 1365 (C.A.2 1978) (emphasis in original). Here, the SEC maintains that anyone who knowingly receives nonpublic material information from an insider has a fiduciary duty to disclose before trading.[56]

In effect, the SEC's theory of tippee liability in both cases appears rooted in the idea that the antifraud provisions require equal information among all traders. This conflicts with the principle set forth in *Chiarella* that only some persons, under some circumstances, will be barred from trading while in possession of material nonpublic information. * * * We reaffirm today that "[a] duty [to disclose] arises from the relationship between parties * * * and not merely from one's ability to acquire information because of his position in the market." 445 U.S., at 232–233, n. 14, 100 S.Ct., at 1116–17, n. 14.

Imposing a duty to disclose or abstain solely because a person knowingly receives material nonpublic information from an insider and trades on it could have an inhibiting influence on the role of market analysts, which the SEC itself recognizes is necessary to the preservation of a healthy market.[57] It is commonplace for analysts to "ferret out and analyze information," 21 SEC, at 1406,[58] and this often is done by meeting with and questioning corporate officers and others who are insiders. And information that the analysts obtain normally may be the basis for judgments as to the market worth of a

---

56. [By the Court] Apparently, the SEC believes this case differs from *Chiarella* in that Dirks' receipt of inside information from Secrist, an insider, carried Secrist's duties with it, while Chiarella received the information without the direct involvement of an insider and thus inherited no duty to disclose or abstain. The SEC fails to explain, however, why the receipt of nonpublic information from an insider automatically carries with it the fiduciary duty of the insider. As we emphasized in *Chiarella,* mere possession of nonpublic information does not give rise to a duty to disclose or abstain; only a specific relationship does that. And we do not believe that the mere receipt of information from an insider creates such a special relationship between the tippee and the corporation's shareholders.

Apparently recognizing the weakness of its argument in light of *Chiarella,* the SEC attempts to distinguish that case factually as involving not "inside" information, but rather "market" information, i.e., "information generated within the company relating to its assets or earnings." This Court drew no such distinction in *Chiarella* and, as The Chief Justice noted, "[i]t is clear that § 10(b) and Rule 10b–5 by their terms and by their history make no such distinction." 445 U.S., at 241, n. 1, 100 S.Ct., at 1121, n. 1 (dissenting opinion).

57. [By the Court] The SEC expressly recognized that "[t]he value to the entire market of [analysts'] efforts cannot be gainsaid; market efficiency in pricing is significantly enhanced by [their] initiatives to ferret out and analyze information, and thus the analyst's

work redounds to the benefit of all investors." 21 S.E.C., at 1406. The SEC asserts that analysts remain free to obtain from management corporate information for purposes of "filling in the 'interstices in analysis'. * * * " But this rule is inherently imprecise, and imprecision prevents parties from ordering their actions in accord with legal requirements. Unless the parties have some guidance as to where the line is between permissible and impermissible disclosures and uses, neither corporate insiders nor analysts can be sure when the line is crossed.

58. [By the Court] On its facts, this case is the unusual one. Dirks is an analyst in a broker-dealer firm, and he did interview management in the course of his investigation. He uncovered, however, startling information that required no analysis or exercise of judgment as to its market relevance. Nonetheless, the principle at issue here extends beyond these facts. The SEC's rule—applicable without regard to any breach by an insider—could have serious ramifications on reporting by analysts of investment views.

Despite the unusualness of Dirks' "find," the central role that he played in uncovering the fraud at Equity Funding, and that analysts in general can play in revealing information that corporations may have reason to withhold from the public, is an important one. Dirks' careful investigation brought to light a massive fraud at the corporation. And until the Equity Funding fraud was exposed, the information in the trading market was grossly inaccurate. But for Dirks' efforts, the fraud might well have gone undetected longer.

corporation's securities. The analyst's judgment in this respect is made available in market letters or otherwise to clients of the firm. It is the nature of this type of information, and indeed of the markets themselves, that such information cannot be made simultaneously available to all of the corporation's stockholders or the public generally.

B.

The conclusion that recipients of inside information do not invariably acquire a duty to disclose or abstain does not mean that such tippees always are free to trade on the information. The need for a ban on some tippee trading is clear. Not only are insiders forbidden by their fiduciary relationship from personally using undisclosed corporate information to their advantage, but they may not give such information to an outsider for the same improper purpose of exploiting the information for their personal gain. * * * Similarly, the transactions of those who knowingly participate with the fiduciary in such a breach are "as forbidden" as transactions "on behalf of the trustee himself." Mosser v. Darrow, 341 U.S. 267, 272, 71 S.Ct. 680, 682 (1951). As the Court explained in *Mosser,* a contrary rule "would open up opportunities for devious dealings in the name of the others that the trustee could not conduct in his own." 341 U.S., at 271, 71 S.Ct., at 682. See SEC v. Texas Gulf Sulphur Co., 446 F.2d 1301, 1308 (CA2), cert. denied, 404 U.S. 1005, 92 S.Ct. 561, (1971). Thus, the tippee's duty to disclose or abstain is derivative from that of the insider's duty. As we noted in *Chiarella,* "[t]he tippee's obligation has been viewed as arising from his role as a participant after the fact in the insider's breach of a fiduciary duty." 445 U.S., at 230, n. 12, 100 S.Ct., at 1115, n. 12.

Thus, some tippees must assume an insider's duty to the shareholders not because they receive inside information, but rather because it has been made available to them *improperly.* And for rule 10b–5 purposes, the insider's disclosure is improper only where it would violate his *Cady, Roberts* duty. Thus, a tippee assumes a fiduciary duty to the shareholders of a corporation not to trade on material nonpublic information only when the insider has breached his fiduciary duty to the shareholders by disclosing the information to the tippee and the tippee knows or should know that there has been a breach. As Commissioner Smith perceptively observed in *Investors Management Co.:* "[T]ippee responsibility must be related back to insider responsibility by a necessary finding that the tippee knew the information was given to him in breach of a duty by a person having a special relationship to the issuer not to disclose the information * * *." 44 SEC, at 651 (concurring in the result). Tipping thus properly is viewed only as a means of indirectly violating the *Cady, Roberts* disclose-or-abstain rule.[59]

---

59. [By the Court] We do not suggest that knowingly trading on inside information is ever "socially desirable or even that it is devoid of moral considerations." Dooley, Enforcement of Insider Trading Restrictions, 66 Va.L.Rev. 1, 55 (1980). Nor do we imply an absence of responsibility to disclose promptly indications of illegal actions by a corporation to the proper authorities—typically the SEC and exchange authorities in cases involving securities. Depending on the circumstances, and even where permitted by law, one's trading on material nonpublic information is behavior that may fall below ethical standards of conduct. But in a statutory area of the law such as securities regulation, where legal principles of general application must be applied, there may be "significant distinctions between actual legal obligations and ethical ideals." SEC, Report of the Special Study of Securities Markets, H.R.Doc. No. 95, 88th Cong., 1st Sess., pt. 1, pp. 237–238

C.

In determining whether a tippee is under an obligation to disclose or abstain, it thus is necessary to determine whether the insider's "tip" constituted a breach of the insider's fiduciary duty. All disclosures of confidential corporate information are not inconsistent with the duty insiders owe to shareholders. In contrast to the extraordinary facts of this case, the more typical situation in which there will be a question whether disclosure violates the insider's *Cady, Roberts* duty is when insiders disclose information to analysts. In some situations the insider will act consistently with his fiduciary duty to shareholders, and yet release of the information may affect the market. For example, it may not be clear—either to the corporate insider or to the recipient analyst—whether the information will be viewed as material nonpublic information. Corporate officials may mistakenly think the information already has been disclosed or that it is not material enough to affect the market. Whether disclosure is a breach of duty therefore depends in large part on the purpose of the disclosure. This standard was identified by the SEC itself in *Cady, Roberts:* a purpose of the securities laws was to eliminate "use of inside information for personal advantage." 40 SEC, at 912, n. 15. Thus, the test is whether the insider personally will benefit, directly or indirectly, from his disclosure. Absent some personal gain, there has been no breach of duty to stockholders. And absent a breach by the insider, there is no derivative breach. As Commissioner Smith stated in *Investors Management Co.:* "It is important in this type of case to focus on policing insiders and what they do * * * rather than on policing information *per se* and its possession. * * * " 44 SEC, at 648 (concurring in the result).

The SEC argues that, if inside-trading liability does not exist when the information is transmitted for a proper purpose but is used for trading, it would be a rare situation when the parties could not fabricate some ostensibly legitimate business justification for transmitting the information. We think the SEC is unduly concerned. In determining whether the insider's purpose in making a particular disclosure is fraudulent, the SEC and the courts are not required to read the parties' minds. Scienter in some cases is relevant in determining whether the tipper has violated his *Cady, Roberts* duty.[60] But to determine whether the disclosure itself "deceive[s], manipulate[s], or defraud[s]" shareholders, Aaron v. SEC, 446 U.S. 680, 686, 100 S.Ct. 1945, 1950

(1963). The SEC recognizes this. At oral argument, the following exchange took place:

"QUESTION: So, it would not have satisfied his obligation under the law to go to the SEC first?

"[SEC's counsel]: That is correct. That an insider has to observe what has come to be known as the abstain or disclosure rule. Either the information has to be disclosed to the market if it is inside information * * * or the insider must abstain."

Thus, it is clear that Rule 10b–5 does not impose any obligations simply to tell the SEC about the fraud before trading.

60. [By the Court] *Scienter*—"a mental state embracing intent to deceive, manipulate, or defraud," Ernst & Ernst v. Hochfelder, 425

U.S. 185, 193, n. 12, 96 S.Ct. 1375, 1381, n. 12 (1976)—is an independent element of a Rule 10b–5 violation. See Aaron v. SEC, 446 U.S. 680, 695, 100 S.Ct. 1945, 1955, (1980). * * * It is not enough that an insider's conduct results in harm to investors; rather, a violation may be found only where there is "intentional or willful conduct designed to deceive or defraud investors by controlling or artificially affecting the price of securities." Ernst & Ernst v. Hochfelder, supra, at 199, 96 S.Ct., at 1383. The issue in this case, however, is not whether Secrist or Dirks acted with *scienter*, but rather whether there was any deceptive or fraudulent conduct at all, i.e., whether Secrist's disclosure constituted a breach of his fiduciary duty and thereby caused injury to shareholders. Only if there was such a breach did Dirks, a tippee, acquire a fiduciary duty to disclose or abstain.

(1980), the initial inquiry is whether there has been a breach of duty by the insider. This requires courts to focus on objective criteria, i.e., whether the insider receives a direct or indirect personal benefit from the disclosure, such as a pecuniary gain or a reputational benefit that will translate into future earnings. Cf. 40 SEC, at 912, n. 15; Brudney, Insiders, Outsiders, and Informational Advantages Under the Federal Securities Laws, 93 Harv.L.Rev. 324, 348 (1979) ("The theory * * * is that the insider, by giving the information out selectively, is in effect selling the information to its recipient for cash, reciprocal information, or other things of value for himself. * * * "). There are objective facts and circumstances that often justify such an inference. For example, there may be a relationship between the insider and the recipient that suggests a *quid pro quo* from the latter, or an intention to benefit the particular recipient. The elements of fiduciary duty and exploitation of non-public information also exist when an insider makes a gift of confidential information to a trading relative or friend. The tip and trade resemble trading by the insider himself followed by a gift of the profits to the recipient.

Determining whether an insider personally benefits from a particular disclosure, a question of fact, will not always be easy for courts. But it is essential, we think, to have a guiding principle for those whose daily activities must be limited and instructed by the SEC's inside-trading rules, and we believe that there must be a breach of the insider's fiduciary duty before the tippee inherits the duty to disclose or abstain. In contrast, the rule adopted by the SEC in this case would have no limiting principle.[61]

IV.

Under the inside-trading and tipping rules set forth above, we find that there was no actionable violation by Dirks. It is undisputed that Dirks himself was a stranger to Equity Funding, with no pre-existing fiduciary duty to its shareholders. He took no action, directly or indirectly, that induced the shareholders or officers of Equity Funding to repose trust or confidence in him. There was no expectation by Dirks' sources that he would keep their information in confidence. Nor did Dirks misappropriate or illegally obtain the information about Equity Funding. Unless the insiders breached their *Cady, Roberts* duty to shareholders in disclosing the nonpublic information to Dirks, he breached no duty when he passed it on to investors as well as to the *Wall Street Journal.*

It is clear that neither Secrist nor the other Equity Funding employees violated their *Cady, Roberts* duty to the corporation's shareholders by providing information to Dirks.[62] The tippers received no monetary or personal

61. [By the Court] Without legal limitations, market participants are forced to rely on the reasonableness of the SEC's litigation strategy, but that can be hazardous, as the facts of this case make plain. * * *

62. [By the Court] In this Court, the SEC appears to contend that an insider invariably violates a fiduciary duty to the corporation's shareholders by transmitting nonpublic corporate information to an outsider when he has reason to believe that the outsider may use it to the disadvantage of the shareholders. "Thus, regardless of any ultimate motive to

bring to public attention the derelictions at Equity Funding, Secrist breached his duty to Equity Funding shareholders." Brief for Respondent 31. This perceived "duty" differs markedly from the one that the SEC identified in Cady, Roberts and that has been the basis for federal tippee-trading rules to date. In fact, the SEC did not charge Secrist with any wrongdoing, and we do not understand the SEC to have relied on any theory of a breach of duty by Secrist in finding that Dirks breached his duty to Equity Funding's shareholders. * * *

benefit for revealing Equity Funding's secrets, nor was their purpose to make a gift of valuable information to Dirks. As the facts of this case clearly indicate, the tippers were motivated by a desire to expose the fraud. In the absence of a breach of duty to shareholders by the insiders, there was no derivative breach by Dirks. Dirks therefore could not have been "a participant after the fact in [an] insider's breach of a fiduciary duty." Chiarella, 445 U.S., at 230, n.12, 100 S.Ct., at 1115, n.12.

V.

We conclude that Dirks, in the circumstances of this case, had no duty to abstain from use of the inside information that he obtained. The judgment of the Court of Appeals therefore is

Reversed.

JUSTICE BLACKMUN, with whom JUSTICE BRENNAN and JUSTICE MARSHALL join, dissenting. * * * [The dissenting opinion is omitted.]

Notes

(1) Academic commentary on the "benefit" requirement imposed by *Dirks* has been generally negative: "This benefit requirement is a curious and largely unnecessary wrinkle; if there is one clear understanding in the common law of fiduciary responsibility, it is that an intent to benefit is not a necessary element." Donald Langevoort, Commentary—The Insider Trading Sanctions Act of 1984 and its Effect on Existing Law, 37 Vand.L.Rev. 1273, 1292 (1984). On the other hand, the SEC appears to have little problem in finding a "benefit" in order to meet this requirement. In United States v. Reed, 601 F.Supp. 685 (S.D.N.Y.1985), the Court refused to dismiss an indictment of a tippee who was the son of the tipper, even though there was no evidence that the father intended to benefit his son by the disclosure. See also SEC v. Gaspar, 1985 WL 521 (CBM) (S.D.N.Y.1985) (tipper received an "enhanced professional relationship" from tippee).

(2) In SEC v. Switzer, 590 F.Supp. 756 (W.D.Okla.1984), Barry Switzer, then coach of the University of Oklahoma football team, was attending his son's high school track meet when he unintentionally overheard a Mr. Platt discussing business problems. Switzer traded profitably on the information he thereby learned, but was absolved of liability under the Dirks standard since Switzer was basically an eavesdropper and the information was not disclosed by Mr. Platt for his own benefit.

(3) One important issue in insider trading law is the extent to which prosecutors can pursue remote tippees, persons who indirectly acquire partial

Chiarella made it explicitly clear there is no general duty to forgo market transactions "based on material, nonpublic information." 455 U.S., at 233, 100 S.Ct., at 1117. Such a duty would "depar[t] radically from the established doctrine that duty arises from a specific relationship between two parties."

Moreover, to constitute a violation of Rule 10b–5, there must be fraud. See Ernst & Ernst v. Hochfelder, 425 U.S. 185, 199, 96 S.Ct. 1375, 1383, 47 L.Ed.2d 668 (1976) (statutory words "manipulative," "device," and "contrivance * * * connot[e] intentional or willful conduct

designed to deceive or defraud investors by controlling or artificially affecting the price of securities") (emphasis added). There is no evidence that Secrist's disclosure was intended to or did in fact "deceive or defraud" anyone. Secrist certainly intended to convey relevant information that management was unlawfully concealing, and—so far as the record shows—he believed that persuading Dirks to investigate was the best way to disclose the fraud. Other efforts had proved fruitless. Under any objective standard, Secrist received no direct or indirect personal benefit from the disclosure.

information about developments that have not been publicly disclosed. This issue was graphically raised by the ImClone litigation in 2002. ImClone, Inc. is a publicly held pharmaceutical company, the founder of which was Dr. Samuel Waksal. ImClone's most promising drug was Erbitux, an anti-cancer drug. ImClone had filed a new drug application with the Food and Drug Administration ("FDA") that was pending. In December, 2001, ImClone common stock was trading in the $60 range. On December 25, 2001, Dr. Waksal learned indirectly that the FDA had determined not to complete the review of ImClone's Erbitrux application because clinical studies had not adequately established its effectiveness. Dr. Waksal learned of this decision through a conversation with an officer of Bristol–Myers Squibb, Co., who was apparently unaware that the FDA decision on Erbitux had not been formally announced. The FDA decision was not formally announced until December 28, 2001.

Almost immediately after learning of this decision, Dr. Waksal began to sell his shares of ImClone. Dr. Waksal also advised friends and his immediate family members, many of whom owned ImClone shares, that he was selling his ImClone stock but apparently did not tell them the reason. The consequence of this disclosure was that there were numerous sales of ImClone stock over the next few days. Following the formal FDA announcement on December, 28, the price of ImClone common stock declined from about $60 per share to between $10 and $15 per share. Assuming that Dr. Waksal told family and friends that he was selling his ImClone shares, but did not disclose the reason why nor directly recommend that they also sell their shares, have the family members and friends that sold their ImClone shares before December 28 violated Rule 10b–5?

The loss avoided by Dr. Waksal and his family and friends exceeded $9 million.[63] In June, 2002, Dr. Waksal was arrested and charged with insider trading in connection with the sale of his own stock and providing "tips" to family and friends. Dr. Waksal subsequently pleaded guilty to six charges of insider trading, bank fraud, perjury and insider trading. To date, friends and family members who sold ImClone shares in the period from December 25 through December 28, 2001, have not been indicted.

(4) One of Dr. Waksal's close friends was Ms. Martha Stewart, the CEO and Chair of Martha Stewart Omnimedia, Inc., a publicly held corporation that was widely known for its television presence and sales of home products through K–Mart. Ms. Stewart owned several thousand shares of ImClone, which she sold on December 27, 2001, one day before the announcement of the FDA decision. She has strenuously argued that she had no inside information, and that her sale of ImClone shares was authorized by a standing instruction she had given to her brokers at Merrill Lynch to sell her ImClone shares if the market price dropped below $60 per share. If this statement is true, it is clear that Ms. Stewart has done nothing improper.

The major problem facing Ms. Stewart was that Merrill Lynch, and the brokers involved, particularly her close friend and stockbroker, Peter Bacanovic has been unable to verify receipt of such an instruction. Bacanovic's former assistant, Douglas Faneuil initially confirmed Ms. Stewart's story and later testified in the criminal trail against Stewart and Bacnovic. The following is the gist of Faneuil's story which contradicts Stewart's story of a prearranged agreement to sell her ImClone stock. On December 26, 2001 Martha Stewart was flying to a Mexican beach resort. While the plane was refueling in Texas on its way from New York to Cancun, Ms. Stewart called her office, and a call from Peter

---

63. Wall Street Journal, June 13, 2002, p. A1, col. 8.

Bacanovic was forwarded to her. Apparently during this call Bacanovic told Ms. Stewart that ImClone shares were trading downward. Two minutes later, Merrill Lynch sold Ms. Stewart's ImClone shares. Peter Bacanovic has filed an affidavit which states:

> Stewart, however, was unreachable. She was on a private plane, on her way from Connecticut to San Antonio, Texas. As they waited for Stewart's plane to land, Bacanovic * * * and Fanneuil swapped e-mails. At 1:17 p.m. Bacanovic wrote [to Faneuill] "Has news come out yet? Let me know." * * * When Stewart's plane landed at 1:30 p.m., she called her office, where her assistant had earlier noted in the message long: "Peter thinks ImClone is going to start trading downward." Almost immediately, Stewart called Bacanovic's office and 11 minutes later, the broker was selling all of Stewart's ImClone stock. Fanneuil wrote: "Dear Ms. Stewart, You sold your remaining (3,928 imcl) shares at an average price of $58.43(25). As always, feel free to call me with any questions." * * *

In addition to Stewart's criminal prosecution, the SEC has also filed a civil suit on June 4, 2003, against Martha Stewart and Peter Baconovic for insider trading. The SEC is seeking disgorgement of $43,673, which is the amount of loss avoided by Stewart from selling her ImClone stock, and civil penalties.

In 2004 Martha Stewart and Peter Beconovic were both convicted of criminal charges stemming from the sale of ImClone stock. Interestingly enough, none of Stewart's or Baconovic's convictions involved charges of securities fraud. They were both convicted of making misleading statements, perjury, and conspiracy. For a more detailed account see, United States v. Stewart, 305 F.Supp.2d 368 (S.D.N.Y. 2004).

(5) Courts have readily accepted the idea set forth in footnote 55 (footnote number 14 in Justice Powell's original opinion) that a person may become a "temporary insider." See SEC v. Lund, 570 F.Supp. 1397 (C.D.Cal.1983) (a confidant of a corporate officer); SEC v. Musella, 578 F.Supp. 425 (S.D.N.Y.1984) (the manager of office services of Sullivan and Cromwell); SEC v. Tome, 638 F.Supp. 596 (S.D.N.Y.1986) (social friend and adviser to CEO).

(6) The opinion in *Dirks* was a victory for securities markets analysts and a defeat for the SEC. The *Dirks* opinion appeared to permit corporate executives to provide sensitive information to favored securities analysts prior to the public release of the information so long as the executives making the disclosures did not receive any personal benefit. In the 1990s, the SEC became increasing concerned about such "selective disclosure."

(7) Regulation FD, discussed in chapter 10, section F, supra, provided the desired weapon against selective disclosure. Regulation FD in effect limits or prohibits selective disclosure by requiring companies and executives that provide material, non-public information to market professionals (such as securities analysts and money managers) to publish this information immediately if the disclosure was intentional, and within 24 hours if the disclosure was unintentional. A violation of Regulation FD does not give rise to liability for securities fraud but may give rise to an SEC enforcement action. Regulation FD also exempts ordinary, business-related communication between corporations and their customers or suppliers, and for communications with members of the press if analysts are not present.

(8) The purpose of Regulation FD in this respect is laudable in theory since it directly relates to the policies behind the prohibition against insider trading. It

raises, however, some serious practical problems. For example, it is often difficult for companies to know whether or not a particular disclosure will be viewed as "material," a term that is not defined in SEC regulations. There is also concern that corporate officials may elect not to disclose information to outsiders in order to make sure that they do not run afoul of Regulation FD. See also Goshen and Parchomovsky, On Insider Trading, Markets, and "Negative Property Rights in Information," 87 Virginia L.Rev. 1229, 1270 (2002) [Regulation FD may have negative impact "on small companies with low liquidity, companies that fail to attract analysts' coverage"]. The prior practice, according to Goshen and Parchomovsky, permitted analysts covering small companies to give informational benefits or rewards in exchange for covering the company, but this practice appears to be prohibited by Regulation FD.

UNITED STATES v. CHESTMAN

United States Court of Appeals, Second Circuit, 1991.
947 F.2d 551, cert. denied, 503 U.S. 1004, 112 S.Ct. 1759, 118 L.Ed.2d 422 (1992).

Before OAKES, CHIEF JUDGE, FEINBERG,[64] MESKILL, NEWMAN, KEARSE, CARDAMONE, WINTER, PRATT, MINER, ALTIMARI, MAHONEY and MCLAUGHLIN, CIRCUIT JUDGES.

ON REHEARING EN BANC

MESKILL, CIRCUIT JUDGE, joined by CARDAMONE, PRATT, MINER and ALTIMARI, CIRCUIT JUDGES: * * *

[Ira Waldbaum was the controlling shareholder of Waldbaum, Inc., a corporation that owned a large supermarket chain. In 1986, Ira agreed to sell the corporation to A & P. Ira told his sister, Shirley Witkin, three of his children, and a nephew, about the pending sale, admonished them to keep the news quiet and confidential until after a public announcement, and offered to tender their shares, along with his controlling block, to enable them to avoid the administrative difficulties of tendering after the public announcement. Shirley nevertheless told her daughter, Susan Loeb, who in turn told her husband, Keith Loeb. The circumstances under which these disclosures occurred are described in the dissenting opinion below. Keith Loeb telephoned Robert Chestman, a broker used by the junior members of the family, and told him that Waldbaum, Inc. was going to be sold at a "substantially higher" price than the market price. Chestman knew that Susan Loeb was a granddaughter of the Waldbaums. That morning Chestman executed several purchases of Waldbaum stock both for his own account and for the discretionary accounts of several customers, including Keith Loeb. After the SEC investigation began, Keith agreed to cooperate with the government, disgorging a profit of $25,000 and paying a $25,000 fine. Chestman was indicted and convicted on 31 counts of violation of Rule 10b–5, mail fraud, violation of Rule 14e–3(a), and one count of perjury. A panel of the Second Circuit set aside this conviction in its entirety, 903 F.2d 75 (2d Cir.1990).] * * *

B. RULE 10b–5

Chestman's Rule 10b–5 convictions were based on the misappropriation theory, which provides that "one who misappropriates nonpublic information

---

64. [By the Court] Judge Feinberg participated in the decision to rehear the appeal *in banc* and heard oral argument. He subsequently retired from regular active service, however, and thus did not vote in the *en banc* decision. *See* 28 U.S.C. § 46(c); *United States v. American–Foreign S.S. Corp.*, 363 U.S. 685, 80 S.Ct. 1336, 4 L.Ed.2d 1491 (1960).

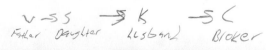

in breach of a fiduciary duty and trades on that information to his own advantage violates Section 10(b) and Rule 10b–5." *SEC v. Materia*, 745 F.2d 197, 203 (2d Cir.1984), *cert. denied*, 471 U.S. 1053, 105 S.Ct. 2112, 85 L.Ed.2d 477 (1985). With respect to the shares Chestman purchased on behalf of Keith Loeb, Chestman was convicted of aiding and abetting Loeb's misappropriation of nonpublic information in breach of a duty Loeb owed to the Waldbaum family and to his wife Susan. As to the shares Chestman purchased for himself and his other clients, Chestman was convicted as a "tippee" of that same misappropriated information. Thus, while Chestman is the defendant in this case, the alleged misappropriator was Keith Loeb. The government agrees that Chestman's convictions cannot be sustained unless there was sufficient evidence to show that (1) Keith Loeb breached a duty owed to the Waldbaum family or Susan Loeb based on a fiduciary or similar relationship of trust and confidence, and (2) Chestman knew that Loeb had done so. We have heretofore never applied the misappropriation theory—and its predicate requirement of a fiduciary breach—in the context of family relationships. * * *

3. Fiduciary Duties and Their Functional Equivalent

* * * [W]e turn to our central inquiry—what constitutes a fiduciary or similar relationship of trust and confidence in the context of Rule 10b–5 criminal liability? We begin by noting two factors that do not themselves create the necessary relationship.

First, a fiduciary duty cannot be imposed unilaterally by entrusting a person with confidential information. *Walton v. Morgan Stanley & Co.*, 623 F.2d 796, 799 (2d Cir.1980) (applying Delaware law). *Walton* concerned the conduct of an investment bank, Morgan Stanley. While investigating possible takeover targets for one of its clients, Morgan Stanley obtained unpublished material information (internal earnings reports) on a confidential basis from a prospective target, Olinkraft. After its client abandoned the planned takeover, Morgan Stanley was charged with trading in Olinkraft's stock on the basis of the confidential information. Observing that the parties had bargained at "arm's length" and that there had not been a pre-existing agreement of confidentiality between Morgan Stanley and Olinkraft, we rejected the argument that

> Morgan Stanley became a fiduciary of Olinkraft by virtue of the receipt of the confidential information * * *. [T]he fact that the information was confidential did nothing, in and of itself, to change the relationship between Morgan Stanley and Olinkraft's management. Put bluntly, although, according to the complaint, Olinkraft's management placed its confidence in Morgan Stanley not to disclose the information, Morgan Stanley owed no duty to observe that confidence.

Walton, 623 F.2d at 799. *See also Dirks*, 463 U.S. at 662 n. 22, 103 S.Ct. at 3265 n. 22 (citing *Walton* approvingly as "a case turning on the court's determination that the disclosure did not impose any fiduciary duties on the recipient of the inside information"). Reposing confidential information in another, then, does not by itself create a fiduciary relationship.

Second, marriage does not, without more, create a fiduciary relationship. " '[M]ere kinship does not of itself establish a confidential relation.' * * * Rather, the existence of a confidential relationship must be determined independently of a preexisting family relationship." *Reed*, 601 F.Supp. at 706. Although spouses certainly may by their conduct become fiduciaries, the marriage relationship alone does not impose fiduciary status. In sum, more than the gratuitous reposal of a secret to another who happens to be a family member is required to establish a fiduciary or similar relationship of trust and confidence.

We take our cues as to what *is* required to create the requisite relationship from the securities fraud precedents and the common law. *See Chiarella*, 445 U.S. at 227–30, 100 S.Ct. at 1114–16. * * * [I]t is clear that the relationships involved in this case—those between Keith and Susan Loeb and between Keith Loeb and the Waldbaum family—were not traditional fiduciary relationships.

That does not end our inquiry, however. The misappropriation theory requires us to consider not only whether there exists a fiduciary relationship but also whether there exists a "similar relationship of trust and confidence." * * *

A fiduciary relationship involves discretionary authority and dependency: One person depends on another—the fiduciary—to serve his interests. In relying on a fiduciary to act for his benefit, the beneficiary of the relation may entrust the fiduciary with custody over property of one sort or another. Because the fiduciary obtains access to this property to serve the ends of the fiduciary relationship, he becomes duty-bound not to appropriate the property for his own use. What has been said of an agent's duty of confidentiality applies with equal force to other fiduciary relations: "an agent is subject to a duty to the principal not to use or to communicate information confidentially given him by the principal or acquired by him during the course of or on account of his agency." Restatement (Second) of Agency § 395 (1958). These characteristics represent the measure of the paradigmatic fiduciary relationship. A similar relationship of trust and confidence consequently must share these qualities.

In *Reed*, 601 F.Supp. 685, the district court confronted the question whether these principal characteristics of a fiduciary relationship—dependency and influence—were necessary factual prerequisites to a similar relationship of trust and confidence. There a member of the board of directors of Amax, Gordon Reed, disclosed to his son on several occasions confidential information concerning a proposed tender offer for Amax. Allegedly relying on this information, the son purchased Amax stock call options. The son was subsequently indicted for violating, among other things, Rule 10b–5 based on breach of a fiduciary duty arising between the father and son. The son then moved to dismiss the indictment, contending that he did not breach a fiduciary duty to his father. The district court sustained the indictment.

Both the government and Chestman rely on *Reed*. The government draws on *Reed*'s application of the misappropriation theory in the family context and its expansive construction of relationships of trust and confidence. Chestman, without challenging the holding in *Reed*, argues that *Reed* cannot sustain his Rule 10b–5 convictions because, unlike *Reed* senior and junior, Keith and Susan Loeb did not customarily repose confidential business information in one another. Neither party challenges the holding of *Reed*. And we decline to do so *sua sponte*. To remain consistent with our interpretation of a "similar relationship of trust and confidence," however, we limit *Reed* to its essential holding: the repeated disclosure of business secrets between family members may substitute for a factual finding of dependence and influence and thereby sustain a finding of the functional equivalent of a fiduciary relationship. We note, in this regard, that *Reed* repeatedly emphasized that the father and son "frequently discussed business affairs." * * *

We have little trouble finding the evidence insufficient to establish a fiduciary relationship or its functional equivalent between Keith Loeb and the Waldbaum family. The government presented only two pieces of evidence on this point. The first was that Keith was an extended member of the Waldbaum family, specifically the family patriarch's (Ira Waldbaum's) "nephew-in-law." The second piece of evidence concerned Ira's discussions of the business with family members. "My children," Ira Waldbaum testified, "have always been involved with me and my family and they know we never speak about business outside of the family." His earlier testimony indicates that the "family" to which he referred were his "three children who were involved in the business."

Lending this evidence the reasonable inferences to which it is entitled, it falls short of establishing the relationship necessary for fiduciary obligations. Kinship alone does not create the necessary relationship. The government proffered nothing more to establish a fiduciary-like association. It did not show that Keith Loeb had been brought into the family's inner circle, whose members, it appears, discussed confidential business information either because they were kin or because they worked together with Ira Waldbaum. Keith was not an employee of Waldbaum and there was no showing that he participated in confidential communications regarding the business. The critical information was gratuitously communicated to him. The disclosure did not serve the interests of Ira Waldbaum, his children or the Waldbaum company. Nor was there any evidence that the alleged relationship was characterized by influence or reliance of any sort. Measured against the principles of fiduciary relations, the evidence does not support a finding that Keith Loeb and the Waldbaum family shared either a fiduciary relation or its functional equivalent. * * *

Keith's status as Susan's husband could not itself establish fiduciary status. Nor, absent a pre-existing fiduciary relation or an express agreement of confidentiality, could the coda—"Don't tell." That leaves the unremarkable testimony that Keith and Susan had shared and maintained generic confidences before. The jury was not told the nature of these past disclosures and therefore it could not reasonably find a relationship that inspired fiduciary, rather than normal marital, obligations.

In the absence of evidence of an explicit acceptance by Keith of a duty of confidentiality, the context of the disclosure takes on special import. While acceptance may be implied, it must be implied from a pre-existing fiduciary-like relationship between the parties. Here the government presented the jury with insufficient evidence from which to draw a rational inference of implied acceptance. Susan's disclosure of the information to Keith served no purpose, business or otherwise. The disclosure also was unprompted. Keith did not induce her to convey the information through misrepresentation or subterfuge. Superiority and reliance, moreover, did not mark this relationship either before or after the disclosure of the confidential information. Nor did Susan's dependence on Keith to act in her interests for some purpose inspire the disclosure. The government failed even to establish a pattern of sharing business confidences between the couple. The government, therefore, failed to offer sufficient evidence to establish the functional equivalent of a fiduciary relation.

In sum, because Keith owed neither Susan nor the Waldbaum family a fiduciary duty or its functional equivalent, he did not defraud them by disclosing news of the pending tender offer to Chestman. Absent a predicate act of fraud by Keith Loeb, the alleged misappropriator, Chestman could not be derivatively liable as Loeb's tippee or as an aider and abettor. Therefore, Chestman's Rule 10b–5 convictions must be reversed. * * *

C. MAIL FRAUD

[The court held that "whatever ethical obligation Loeb may have owed the Waldbaum family or Susan Loeb, it was too ethereal to be protected by either the securities or mail fraud statutes."]

Accordingly, we affirm the Rule 14e–3(a) convictions and reverse the Rule 10b–5 and mail fraud convictions. The reversal of these convictions does not warrant reconsideration of the sentence since the sentences on the Rule 10b–5 and mail fraud convictions are concurrent with the sentences in the Rule 14(e)–3(a) counts. The panel's reversal of the perjury conviction remains intact.

WINTER, CIRCUIT JUDGE (joined by OAKES, CHIEF JUDGE, NEWMAN, KEARSE, and MCLAUGHLIN, CIRCUIT JUDGES), concurring in part and dissenting in part:

I concur in the decision to affirm Chestman's convictions under Section 14(e) of the Securities Exchange Act of 1934, and under Rule 14e–3. I respectfully dissent, however, from the reversals of his convictions under Section 10(b) and under the mail fraud statute.

a) Insider Trading

The difficulty this court finds in resolving the issues raised by this appeal stems largely from the history of the development of the law concerning insider trading. * * *

Notwithstanding the ambiguities surrounding Section 10(b)'s impact on insider trading—including its very definition—Congress has increased the penalties for violations of that prohibition. The SEC in turn has failed to promulgate rules outside the area of tender offers but its decisions have continued to march, in the eyes of one commentator, to the beat of its own drummer.

It is hardly surprising that disagreement exists within an [e]n banc court of appeals as to the import of present caselaw. Nor is it surprising that the lower courts have added to the *Dirks* breach of duty doctrine a misappropriation of information doctrine, which prohibits trading in securities based on material, nonpublic information acquired in violation of a duty to any owner of such information, whether or not the owner is the corporation whose shares are traded.

b) Property Rights in Inside Information

One commentator has attempted to explain the Supreme Court decisions in terms of the business-property rationale for banning insider trading mentioned in *Cady, Roberts & Co. See* Easterbrook, [*Insider Trading, Secret Agents, Evidentiary Privileges and the Production of Information*, 1981 Sup. Ct.Rev. 309], at 309–39. That rationale may be summarized as follows. Information is perhaps the most precious commodity in commercial markets. It is expensive to produce, and, because it involves facts and ideas that can be easily photocopied or carried in one's head, there is a ubiquitous risk that those who pay to produce information will see others reap the profit from it. Where the profit from an activity is likely to be diverted, investment in that activity will decline. If the law fails to protect property rights in commercial information, therefore, less will be invested in generating such information.

For example, mining companies whose investments in geological surveys have revealed valuable deposits do not want word of the strike to get out until they have secured rights to the land. If word does get out, the price of the land not only will go up, but other mining companies may also secure the rights. In either case, the mining company that invested in geological surveys (including the inevitably sizeable number of unsuccessful drillings) will see profits from that investment enjoyed by others. If mining companies are unable to keep the results of such surveys confidential, less will be invested in them. * * *

Insider trading may reduce the return on information in two ways. First, it creates incentives for insiders to generate or disclose information that may disregard the welfare of the corporation. That risk is not implicated by the facts in the present case, and no further discussion is presently required.

Second, insider trading creates a risk that information will be prematurely disclosed by such trading, and the corporation will lose part or all of its property in that information. Although trades by an insider may rarely affect market price, others who know of the insider's trading may notice that a trader is unusually successful, or simply perceive unusual activity in a stock and guess the information and/or make piggyback trades.[65] A broker who executes a trade for a geologist or for a financial printer may well draw relevant conclusions. Or, as in the instant matter, the trader, Loeb, may tell his or her broker about the inside information, who may then trade on his or her account, on clients' accounts, or may tell friends and relatives. One inside trader has publicly attributed his exposure in part to the fact that the bank through which he made trades piggybacked on the trades, as did the broker who made the trades for the bank. *See* Levine, *The Inside Story of An Inside Trader*, Fortune, May 21, 1990, at 80. Once activity in a stock reaches an unusual stage, others may guess the reason for the trading—the corporate secret. Insider trading thus increases the risk that confidential information

---

65. [By the Judge] Section 16(a) of the '34 Act requires insiders to report trades in a corporation's stock (i) at the time of a new issue, (ii) when they become an insider, and (iii) each month thereafter in which trades occur. Where insiders are able to avoid "profits" as defined in Section 16(b) and trade heavily—e.g., a series of purchases that cannot be matched with sales during the six months at either end of the activity—other traders may well draw accurate inferences. In that respect, federal law causes the information on which insiders are trading to become known.

acquired at a cost may be disclosed. If so, the owner of the information may lose its investment.

This analysis provides a policy rationale for prohibiting insider trading when the property rights of a corporation in information are violated by traders. However, the rationale stops well short of prohibiting all trading on material nonpublic information. Efficient capital markets depend on the protection of property rights in information. However, they also require that persons who acquire and act on information about companies be able to profit from the information they generate so long as the method by which the information is acquired does not amount to a form of theft. A rule commanding equal access would result in a securities market governed by relative degrees of ignorance because the profit motive for independently generating information about companies would be substantially diminished. Easterbrook, *supra*, at 313–14. Under such circumstances, the pricing of securities would be less accurate than in circumstances in which the production of information is encouraged by legal protection.

One may speculate that it was for these reasons that the Supreme Court declined in *Chiarella* to adopt a broad ban on trading on material nonpublic information[66] and then imposed in *Dirks* a breach of fiduciary duty requirement—not running to those with whom the trader buys or sells. Under the *Dirks* rule, insider trading is illegal only where the trader has received the information as a result of the trader's or tipper's breach of a duty to keep information confidential.

The misappropriation theory * * * fits within this rationale. Misappropriation also involves the misuse of confidential information in a way that risks making information public in a fashion similar to trading by corporate insiders. In *U.S. v. Carpenter*, for example, where the information belonged to the *Wall Street Journal* rather than to the corporations whose shares were traded, the misuse of information created an incentive on the part of the traders to create false information that might affect the efficiency of the market's pricing of the corporations' stock. Moreover, the potential for piggybacking would add to that inefficiency. * * *

c) The Instant Case

When this analysis is applied to a family-controlled corporation such as that involved in the instant case, I believe that family members who have benefitted from the family's control of the corporation are under a duty not to disclose confidential corporate information that comes to them in the ordinary course of family affairs. In the case of family-controlled corporations, family and business affairs are necessarily intertwined, and it is inevitable that from

---

66. [By the Judge] Comprehensive protection of those who trade with insiders is unattainable because the most common form of insider trading by far is failing to trade. An insider possessing nonpublic information may purchase or sell other securities or borrow instead of trading in the corporation's stock. Such trading seems virtually undiscoverable and unregulable, however, although it is functionally indistinguishable from insider trading so far as those who deal with the trader are concerned.

Under the business property rationale, not-trading because of inside information is not the functional equivalent of trading because not-trading creates at most a negligible risk of disclosure of corporate secrets. Unlike trading, not-trading does not involve persons other than the trader, such as brokers, and does not create an unusual volume. *But see* Easterbrook, *supra*, at 336–37 (discussing signals sent to such parties by *not* trading).

time to time normal familial interactions will lead to the revelation of confidential corporate matters to various family members. Indeed, the very nature of familial relationships may cause the disclosure of corporate matters to avoid misunderstandings among family members or suggestions that a family member is unworthy of trust.

Keith Loeb learned of the pending acquisition of Waldbaum's by A & P through precisely such interactions. His wife Susan was asked one day by her sister to take carpool responsibilities for their children. When Susan inquired as to why this was necessary, the sister was vague and said that she had to take their mother somewhere. After further inquiry, the sister flatly declined to tell Susan what was going on. Susan did not say, "Gee, confidential corporate information must be involved, and I have no right to such information." Instead, concerned about her mother's ongoing health problems, Susan made direct inquiry of her mother, who revealed that Susan's sister took her to get stock certificates to give to Ira Waldbaum for the initial phase of the A & P acquisition. The mother swore Susan to secrecy, telling Susan that the acquisition would be very profitable to the family and premature disclosure could ruin the deal. Susan then asked whether she could tell her husband Keith. Instead of saying, "No, Keith may be your husband but you are to button your lips in his presence," her mother assented but warned against disclosure to anyone else.

Susan and Keith Loeb jointly owned a large number of Waldbaum shares at that time, all of which had been a gift from her mother. The Loebs' children also owned shares received as a gift from their grandmother. Susan told Keith about the A & P acquisition in the course of discussing the financial benefits they and their children would receive as a result of that transaction. She stressed the need for absolute secrecy. Susan testified that she and her husband had shared confidences in the past and that on each such occasion they had indicated to each other that the confidences would be respected. Thereafter, Keith Loeb informed Chestman about the A & P acquisition in the hope of making a profit.

I have little difficulty in concluding that Chestman's convictions can be affirmed on either the *Dirks* rule or on a misappropriation theory. The disclosure of information concerning the A & P acquisition among Ira Waldbaum's extended family was the result of ordinary familial interactions that can be expected in the case of family-controlled corporations. Members of a family who receive such information are placed in a position in which their trading on the information risks financial injury to the corporation, its public shareholders and other family members. When members of a family have benefitted from the family's control of a corporation and are in a position to acquire such information in the ordinary course of family interactions, that position carries with it a duty not to disclose. * * * Such a duty is of course based on mutual understandings among family members—quite explicit in this case—and owed to the family. However, the duty originates in the corporation and is ultimately intended to protect the corporation and its public shareholders. The duty is thus also owed to the corporation, to a degree sufficient in my view to trigger the *Dirks* rule. Because trading on inside information so acquired by family members amounts to theft, the misappropriation theory also applies.

Under my colleagues' theory, the disclosure of family corporate information can be avoided only by family members extracting formal, express promises of confidentiality or by elderly mothers in poor health refusing to tell their daughters about mysterious travels. If disclosure is made, daughters may not disclose their mother's doings or potential financial benefits to the daughters' husbands without a formal, express promise of confidentiality. If, for example, Susan had earlier shared with Keith her concerns about her mother's mysterious travels before learning of their purpose, she would not have been able to tell him what she later learned about those travels no matter how persistently he asked. For my colleagues in the majority, the critical gap in the government's case was that Susan did not testify either that on this occasion Keith agreed not to disclose the pending acquisition by A & P or that prior confidential communications between her and her husband had involved the Waldbaum's corporation.

I have no lack of sympathy with my colleagues' concern about the difficulty of drawing lines in this area. Nevertheless, the line they draw seems very unrealistic in that it expects family members to behave like strangers toward each other. It also leads to the perverse and circular result that where family business interests are concerned, family members must act as if there are no mutual obligations of trust and confidence because the law does not recognize such obligations. Under such a regime, parents and children must conceal their comings and goings, family members must cease to speak when a son-in-law enters a room, and offended members of the family must understand that such conduct is always related only to business.

I thus believe that a family member (i) who has received or expects (e.g., through inheritance) benefits from family control of a corporation, here gifts of stock, (ii) who is in a position to learn confidential corporate information through ordinary family interactions, and (iii) who knows that under the circumstances both the corporation and the family desire confidentiality, has a duty not to use information so obtained for personal profit where the use risks disclosure. The receipt or expectation of benefits increases the interest of such family members in corporate affairs and thus increases the chance that they will learn confidential information. Disclosure in the present case occurred in the course of a discussion that included, *inter alia*, an examination of the benefits of the A & P acquisition to Susan, Keith and their children. Susan's warning to Keith about secrecy was clearly intended to protect the corporation as well as the family and clearly had originated with Ira Waldbaum. In such circumstances, Susan's saying "Don't tell" is enough for me. Not to have such a rule means that a family-controlled corporation with public shareholders is subject to greater risk of disclosure of confidential information than is a corporation that is entirely publicly owned.

I see no room for argument over whether there was sufficient evidence for the jury to find that Chestman knew Keith Loeb was violating an obligation. The record fairly brims with Chestman's consciousness that Keith Loeb was behaving improperly. * * *

MINER, CIRCUIT JUDGE, concurring:

I concur in the comprehensive opinion of Judge Meskill * * *. I write only to comment upon the "familial relationship" rule of insider trading proposed by Judge Winter in his partially dissenting opinion.

The rule urged upon us would impose a duty of nondisclosure upon "a family member (i) who has received or expects (e.g., through inheritance) benefits from family control of a corporation, here gifts of stock, (ii) who is in a position to learn confidential corporate information through ordinary family interactions, and (iii) who knows that under the circumstances both the corporation and the family desire confidentiality." The duty is said to consist of an obligation "not to use information so obtained for personal profit where the use risks disclosure." *Id.*

The rationale for the proposed rule apparently is rooted in the notion that family members would be encouraged to speak freely on all matters pertaining to the family, knowing that the lips of those who receive confidential corporate information in the course of ongoing family interchanges would be sealed. Thus, in this case, so the argument goes, Ira Waldbaum could reveal the pending stock sale to his sister, Shirley Witkin, who could reveal it to her daughter, Susan Loeb, who could reveal it to her husband, Keith Loeb, all with the understanding that a duty imposed by law on each family member would protect against use of the confidential information for profit. Without the rule, it is maintained, family members in this case would have been inhibited from discussing such matters as the reason for Shirley Witkin's unusual absence from her home, because such a discussion inevitably would lead to disclosure of the confidential information regarding the sale of Waldbaum stock to A & P.

It seems to me, however, that family discourse would be inhibited, rather than promoted, by a rule that would automatically assure confidentiality on the part of a family member receiving non-public corporate information. What speaker, secure in the knowledge that a relative could be prosecuted for insider trading, would reveal to that relative anything remotely connected with corporate dealings? Given the uncertainties surrounding the definition of insider trading, a term as yet unclarified by Congress, what family members would want to receive any information whatsoever that might bear on the family business? How could family news be disseminated freely in an atmosphere where the members must be ultra-sensitive to whether "both the corporation and the family" are seeking some measure of confidentiality "under the circumstances."

The difficulty of identifying those who would be covered by the proposed familial rule adds an additional element of uncertainty to what already are uncertain crimes. It is not clear just who would be subject to the duty of confidentiality: family members "who ha[ve] received or expect[] * * * benefits from family control of a corporation" belong to a very broad category indeed. Here, those who have received gifts of stock are included. But does the category include those who have received only small amounts of stock? Does it matter what proportion the stock bears to the total issued and outstanding shares? Does the category include one who expects to receive stock through inheritance but never receives any? Does it include grandchildren who expect ultimately to inherit assets purchased with the proceeds of the sale of the family-controlled corporation? The net would be spread wider than appropriate in a criminal context. * * *

In the same vein, it is conceivable that minor children could find themselves "in a position to learn confidential corporate information through ordinary family interactions." If they came into the possession of such information and somehow acquired the knowledge "that under the circumstances both the corporation and the family desire[d] confidentiality," would they become tippers who would expose other family members to criminal liability as tippees when they passed the information along?

It is important to note that in the case at bar we deal with an attenuated trail of family confidences in which information was received without any assurance of confidentiality by the receiver and without any prior sharing of business information within the family. Neither Shirley Witkin nor her daughter nor her son-in-law were involved in any way in the operation of the Waldbaum business or privy to any of its past secrets. Family relationships being what they are, it makes little sense under the circumstances to imply assurances that confidentiality would be maintained. Of course, a different situation obtains where the giver of business confidences, in addition to having a family relationship with the receiver, also has a history of reposing such confidences in the receiver. *See United States v. Reed*, 601 F.Supp. 685, 712, 717 (S.D.N.Y.), *rev'd on other grounds*, 773 F.2d 477 (2d Cir.1985) (son of corporate director as receiver of non-public corporate information). Under those circumstances, the duty of confidentiality is implied from the business relationship coupled with the family one.

Finally, to further extend the concept of confidential duty would be to take the courts into an area of securities regulation not yet entered by Congress. It would give the wrong signal to prosecutors in their continuing efforts to push against existing boundaries in the prosecution of securities fraud cases. "[P]rosecutors can often claim that some confidential relationship was abused—whether between lovers, family members, longtime friends, or simply that well-known confidential relationship between bartender and drunk. Such a test inherently creates legal uncertainty and invites selective prosecutions." Coffee, *Outsider Trading, That New Crime*, Wall St.J., Nov. 14, 1990, at 16, col. 4. I would await further instructions from Congress before sailing into this unchartered area.

[The opinion of MAHONEY, CIRCUIT JUDGE, concurring in part and dissenting in part, is omitted.]

Notes

(1) As well illustrated by the principal case, another unsettled issue in insider trading law has been under what circumstances certain non-business relationships, such as family and personal relationships, may provide the duty of trust or confidence required under the misappropriation theory. See Ray J. Grzebielski, *Friends, Family, Fiduciaries, Personal Relationships as a Basis for Insider Trading Violations*, Cath. U. L. Rev. 467 (2002).

(2) In 2001, a federal judge in San Francisco dismissed criminal charges against a corporate outsider who, through his membership in an exclusive club for corporate officers, learned about merger talks between two companies and traded on that information. The government unsuccessfully alleged that he violated the insider trading prohibitions of federal securities laws because the information was confidential. United States v. Kim, 184 F.Supp.2d 1006 (N.D. Cal. 2002).

(3) In 2000, the SEC promulgated two new rules: Rule 10b–5–1, intended to clarify the definition of insider trading, and Rule 10b–5–2, designed to provide

more of a bright-line test for certain enumerated close family relationships. SEC Rel. No. 34–43154 (Aug. 24, 2000). Rule 10b–5–1 addressed conflicts among courts over whether a person can be found guilty of insider trading merely by a showing that the person traded *while in knowing possession* of insider information, or whether a showing that the person actually *used* such insider information was necessary. Rule 10b–5–1 reveals that a standard closer to "knowing possession" rather than "use" is appropriate and states that a person is guilty of insider trading when he or she makes a trade while aware of material, nonpublic information. The Rule does, however, contain a safe harbor for certain pre-planned trades where the person making the trade was not in possession of material, non-public information at the time the trade was planned.

The second new provision, Rule 10b–5–2, sets forth a non-exclusive list of three situations in which a person has a duty of trust or confidence for purposes of the misappropriation theory: (1) where a person agrees to maintain information in confidence; (2) when two people have a history, pattern, or practice of sharing confidences such that the recipient of the information knows or reasonably should know that the person communicating the material nonpublic information expects that the recipient will maintain is confidentiality; or (3) a "bright line" rule that states that a duty of trust or confidence exists when a person receives or obtains material nonpublic information from spouses, parents, children, or siblings. It may be noted that an automatic relationship of trust or confidence is not created between unmarried domestic partners, step-parents, or step-children (though such a relationship might arises under alternatives (1) or (2)).

(4) In United States v. Cassese, 273 F.Supp.2d 481 (S.D.N.Y. 2003), the defendant was charged with insider trading under the misappropriation doctrine. Cassese was told by an arms length business contact that his company was merging with another company. Cassese then executed an order for the company's stock and subsequently sold the stock for a handsome profit. The court dismissed all charges against Cassese due to an absence of a fiduciary duty between the tipper and recipient of non-public information required under the misappropriation doctrine.

SECURITIES EXCHANGE ACT OF 1934
15 U.S.C.A. § 78u–1 (1997).

Section 21A. Civil Penalties for Insider Trading

(a) AUTHORITY TO IMPOSE CIVIL PENALTIES

(1) *Judicial actions by Commission authorized.* Whenever it shall appear to the Commission that any person has violated any provision of this chapter or the rules or regulations thereunder by purchasing or selling a security while in possession of material, nonpublic information in, or has violated any such provision by communicating such information in connection with, a transaction on or through the facilities of a national securities exchange or from or through a broker or dealer, and which is not part of a public offering by an issuer of securities other than standardized options, the Commission—

(A) may bring an action in a United States district court to seek, and the court shall have jurisdiction to impose, a civil penalty to be paid by the person who committed such violation; and

(B) may, subject to subsection (b)(1) of this Section, bring an action in a United States district court to seek, and the court shall have jurisdiction to impose, a civil penalty to be paid by a person who, at the time of the violation, directly or indirectly controlled the person who committed such violation.

(2) *Amount of penalty for person who committed violation.* The amount of the penalty which may be imposed on the person who committed such violation shall be determined by the court in light of the facts and circumstances, but shall not exceed three times the profit gained or loss avoided as a result of such unlawful purchase, sale, or communication.

(3) *Amount of penalty for controlling person.* The amount of the penalty which may be imposed on any person who, at the time of the violation, directly or indirectly controlled the person who committed such violation, shall be determined by the court in light of the facts and circumstances, but shall not exceed the greater of $1,000,000, or three times the amount of the profit gained or loss avoided as a result of such controlled person's violation. If such controlled person's violation was a violation by communication, the profit gained or loss avoided as a result of the violation shall, for purposes of this paragraph only, be deemed to be limited to the profit gained or loss avoided by the person or persons to whom the controlled person directed such communication.

(b) LIMITATIONS ON LIABILITY

(1) *Liability of controlling persons.* No controlling person shall be subject to a penalty under subsection (a)(1)(B) of this section unless the Commission establishes that—

(A) such controlling person knew or recklessly disregarded the fact that such controlled person was likely to engage in the act or acts constituting the violation and failed to take appropriate steps to prevent such act or acts before they occurred; or

(B) such controlling person knowingly or recklessly failed to establish, maintain, or enforce any policy or procedure required under section 15(f) of this title[67] or section 204A of the Investment Advisers Act of 1940 and such failure substantially contributed to or permitted the occurrence of the act or acts constituting the violation.

(2) *Additional restrictions on liability.* No person shall be subject to a penalty under subsection (a) of this section solely by reason of employing another person who is subject to a penalty under such subsection, unless such employing person is liable as a controlling person under paragraph (1) of this subsection. Section 20(a) of this title[68] shall not apply to actions under subsection (a) of this section.

67. [By the Editors] The referenced section 15(b) provides:

"Every registered broker or dealer shall establish, maintain and enforce written policies and procedures reasonably designed, taking into consideration the nature of such broker's or dealer's business, to prevent the misuse in violation of this title, or the rules or regulations thereunder, of material, nonpublic information by such broker or dealer or any person associated with such broker or dealer." The Commission, as it deems necessary or appropri-ate in the public interest or for the protection of investors, shall adopt rules or regulations to require specific policies or procedures reasonably designed to prevent misuse in violation of this title (or the rules or regulations thereunder) of material, nonpublic information.

68. [By the Editors] Section 20(a) provides:

"Every person who, directly or indirectly, controls any person liable under any provision of this title or of any rule or regulation thereunder shall also be liable jointly and

(c) AUTHORITY OF COMMISSION

The Commission, by such rules, regulations, and orders as it considers necessary or appropriate in the public interest or for the protection of investors, may exempt, in whole or in part, either unconditionally or upon specific terms and conditions, any person or transaction or class of persons or transactions from this section.

(d) PROCEDURES FOR COLLECTION

(1) *Payment of penalty to treasury.* A penalty imposed under this section shall (subject to subsection (e) of this section) be payable into the Treasury of the United States. * * *

(e) AUTHORITY TO AWARD BOUNTIES TO INFORMANTS

Notwithstanding the provisions of subsection (d)(1) of this section, there shall be paid from amounts imposed as a penalty under this section and recovered by the Commission or the Attorney General, such sums, not to exceed 10 percent of such amounts, as the Commission deems appropriate, to the person or persons who provide information leading to the imposition of such penalty. Any determinations under this subsection, including whether, to whom, or in what amount to make payments, shall be in the sole discretion of the Commission, except that no such payment shall be made to any member, officer, or employee of any appropriate regulatory agency, the Department of Justice, or a self-regulatory organization. Any such determination shall be final and not subject to judicial review.

(f) DEFINITION

For purposes of this section, "profit gained" or "loss avoided" is the difference between the purchase or sale price of the security and the value of that security as measured by the trading price of the security a reasonable period after public dissemination of the nonpublic information.

Notes

(1) Section 21A was enacted as part of the Insider Trading Sanctions Act of 1984, Pub.L.No. 98–376, 98 Stat. 1264 (ITSA). The power to impose civil penalties greatly increases the risk of insider trading, since the penalty is added to the disgorgement of profit, and the inside trader ends up much worse off than if he had never traded at all. Courts have consistently added substantial civil penalties to the disgorgement of insider trading profits.

(2) A second statute, the Insider Trading and Securities Fraud Enforcement Act of 1988, Pub.L.No. 100–704, 102 Stat. 4677 (codified in scattered sections of 15 U.S.C.) (ITSFEA) increased the criminal penalties for willful violation of the Securities Acts or regulations issued thereunder from $100,000 and five years to $1,000,000 and ten years for individuals, and a fine of up to $2,500,000 when the defendant is a "person other than a natural person." ITSFEA, § 4.

(3) Given these draconian penalties, it is surprising that cases continue to arise involving lawyers or sophisticated persons "who should have known better."

severally with and to the same extent as such controlled person to any person to whom such controlled person is liable, unless the controlling person acted in good faith and did not directly or indirectly induce the act or acts constituting the violation or cause of action."

These usually are high profile cases involving lawyers or corporate executives, and prison sentences are quite common.

(4) The SEC has adopted a zero-tolerance approach to insider trading cases. In effect, it pursues small cases as well as large ones. Many of the defendants might be categorized as "ordinary Joes" rather than sophisticated insiders. The following anecdotal sampling of cases indicates the willingness of the SEC and the Department of Justice to invest prosecutorial resources to pursue persons with modest means:

(a) In 1996, Cameron, a "close friend" of Donald Tyson, a former chairman of Tyson Foods Inc. settled charges that he had purchased Tyson stock based on a possible merger that he had heard about from his friend. Cameron agreed to disgorge $46,125 in unlawful profits, pay $18,153.43 in prejudgment interest, and a $46,125 civil penalty. Tyson also agreed to pay a $46,125 civil penalty to dismiss the suit.

(b) A typesetting supervisor for Applied Graphics Technology, Inc., a printing company where *Business Week* is published, agreed to pay $46,000 (about the amount that he, his girlfriend, and his girlfriend's family made on 43 securities transactions over six months), based on advance knowledge of stories that later appeared in *Business Week*.

(c) A general counsel of a small Atlanta-based medical services company agreed to disgorge $8,450, plus $1,183.27 in prejudgment interest, and a civil penalty of $8,450, in order to settle claims brought by the SEC that she gave non-public information to other individuals.

(5) A word of warning to readers: since the SEC pursues with vigor law firm partners, associates, paralegals, employees and others who engage in insider trading, one must assume that even modest profits based on inside information, will, if discovered, be prosecuted. It is unlikely that a law firm would provide any assistance to, or retain, a partner, associate, or staff employee charged with insider trading—rather, the most likely response is immediate dismissal. The prohibitions against insider trading are therefore of particular concern to partners and employees of law firms where non-public information may be openly discussed. The temptation to engage in even a discreet amount of trading on inside information obtained from one's work should be sternly resisted.

(6) Consider section 21A(a)(1)(B) (page 903 supra) which was added by ITSFEA in 1988. Under these provisions, would Texas Gulf Sulphur, Inc. have been liable for the insider trading transactions of Darke (the geologist)? Would Pandick Press have been liable for Chiarella's transactions? As a result of this provision, a wide variety of employers whose employees may have access to valuable inside information have found it necessary to establish policies or procedures designed to prevent the misuse of information: issuers, accounting firms, financial printing companies, and the like. Furthermore, the policies or procedures must go much deeper down into the organization than merely the officers, directors, partners, and top-level personnel. It is likely that most readers of this note will have firsthand experience with these procedures, either by being subject to them personally or by creating and applying such policies on behalf of clients, or both.

(7) Might a law firm whose office manager engaged in inside trading be liable as a controlling person? The same question might be asked of Sullivan and Cromwell or of Skadden, Arps, Slate, Meagher and Flom for the actions of Garvey, a paralegal, or Cleary Gottlieb for the trading of Craig Spradling. See ABA

Subcommittee on Civil Litigation and SEC Enforcement Matters, Law Firm Policies Regarding Insider Trading and Confidentiality, 47 Bus. Law. 235 (1991)[69]:

> Notwithstanding the Commission's hortatory urgings, considerable differences of view exist whether, and to what extent, and under what circumstances, law firms can be vicariously liable for the trading activities of firm members and/or employees. In this context, although a large number of law firms have resorted to formal, written, statements of policy regarding insider trading and client confidentiality, it must be borne in mind that no court has held that law firms must have in place a formal statement of policy or procedures in order to avoid vicarious liability for the errant acts of misguided employees or members. Indeed, as then SEC Commissioner Philip R. Lochner, Jr., recently wrote, "[i]n some cases, depending on the size of the firm and the nature of its practice, the best procedure [for a law firm to adopt] may be no procedure."

> Nonetheless, because so many law firms appear to have decided, on their own, to adopt these policies, the Subcommittee on Civil Litigation and Enforcement Matters (the "Subcommittee") of the American Bar Association's Section of Business Law Federal Securities Law Committee undertook a survey of existing law firm confidentiality and/or securities trading policies, in the hope that, by setting forth a variety of examples, those firms that deemed it appropriate to adopt such policies might have some guidance on the types of provisions that might be included.[70]

See also Peter M.O. Wong, Insider Trading Regulation of Law Firms: Expanding ITSFEA's Policy and Procedures Requirement, 44 Hastings L.J. 1159 (1993).

(8) Assume that you overhear a colleague talking about or appearing to execute a transaction that sounds suspiciously like insider trading. May you turn him or her in and claim a "bounty" for doing so? See § 21A(e) (page 904, supra). Senator D'Amato described the objective of this provision as follows on the floor of the United States Senate:

> To those who oppose bounty I ask that they put themselves in the place of an employee or coworker of an insider trader. What incentive is there to blow the whistle that can counteract the clear risk to profession and livelihood? They may answer that civic duty is enough, and one would hope they were right. But I disagree. Bounty is a positive incentive we can offer and I see no real cost in doing so.

134 Cong.Rec. S17219 (Oct. 21, 1988). The SEC has issued regulations describing the procedures for applying for, and obtaining, bounties under this section. 17 C.F.R. § 201.61 (2000).

---

69. Copyright (1991) by the American Bar Association. All rights reserved. Reprinted with permission of the American Bar Association and its Section of Corporation, Banking and Business Law.

70. [By the Subcommittee] Upon reviewing a draft of this report, SEC Chairman Richard C. Breeden noted his concern that attorneys are still being implicated in insider trading cases. Although Chairman Breeden declined to provide specific comments on the draft or the kinds of procedures he believes a particular law firm should consider adopting, he did state that law firms would be "well-advised to revisit the issue of protecting client confidences and to consider what measures may be required to prevent violations of the federal securities laws." *See* Letter from Richard C. Breeden to Harvey L. Pitt (May 20, 1991), on file with *The Business Lawyer*.

SECURITIES EXCHANGE ACT OF 1934

15 U.S.C.A. § 78t–1 (2000).

Section 20A. Liability to contemporaneous traders for insider trading

(a) PRIVATE RIGHTS OF ACTION BASED ON CONTEMPORANEOUS TRADING

Any person who violates any provision of this chapter or the rules or regulations thereunder by purchasing or selling a security while in possession of material, nonpublic information shall be liable in an action in any court of competent jurisdiction to any person who, contemporaneously with the purchase or sale of securities that is the subject of such violation, has purchased (where such violation is based on a sale of securities) or sold (where such violation is based on a purchase of securities) securities of the same class.

(b) LIMITATIONS ON LIABILITY

(1) *Contemporaneous trading actions limited to profit gained or loss avoided.* The total amount of damages imposed under subsection (a) of this section shall not exceed the profit gained or loss avoided in the transaction or transactions that are the subject of the violation.

(2) *Offsetting disgorgements against liability.* The total amount of damages imposed against any person under subsection (a) of this section shall be diminished by the amounts, if any, that such person may be required to disgorge, pursuant to a court order obtained at the instance of the Commission, in a proceeding brought * * * relating to the same transaction or transactions.

(3) *Controlling person liability.* No person shall be liable under this section solely by reason of employing another person who is liable under this section, but the liability of a controlling person under this section shall be subject to section 20(a) of this title.

(4) *Statute of limitations.* No action may be brought under this section more than 5 years after the date of the last transaction that is the subject of the violation.

(c) JOINT AND SEVERAL LIABILITY FOR COMMUNICATING

Any person who violates any provision of this title or the rules or regulations thereunder by communicating material, nonpublic information shall be jointly and severally liable under subsection (a) of this section with, and to the same extent as, any person or persons liable under subsection (a) of this section to whom the communication was directed.

(d) AUTHORITY NOT TO RESTRICT OTHER EXPRESS OR IMPLIED RIGHTS OF ACTION

Nothing in this section shall be construed to limit or condition the right of any person to bring an action to enforce a requirement of this title or the availability of any cause of action implied from a provision of this chapter.

(e) PROVISIONS NOT TO AFFECT PUBLIC PROSECUTIONS

This section shall not be construed to bar or limit in any manner any action by the Commission or the Attorney General under any other provision of this chapter, nor shall it bar or limit in any manner any action to recover penalties, or to seek any other order regarding penalties.

Notes

(1) Prior to enactment of this section, the question whether private actions may be maintained against persons trading on inside information had arisen in a number of cases; the leading cases in which such suits were permitted are Elkind v. Liggett & Myers, Inc., 635 F.2d 156 (2d Cir.1980), and Shapiro v. Merrill Lynch, Pierce, Fenner & Smith, Inc., 495 F.2d 228 (2d Cir.1974). A majority of courts, however, did not permit such suits, in part dismayed by the complex and erratic consequences of such litigation, particularly in the computation of damages. See Fridrich v. Bradford, 542 F.2d 307 (6th Cir.1976), cert. denied 429 U.S. 1053, 97 S.Ct. 767, 50 L.Ed.2d 769 (1977) (defendants did not purchase shares from plaintiffs and their trading in no way affected the plaintiffs' decision to sell; private civil liability does not need to be coextensive with the reach of the SEC); Moss v. Morgan Stanley Inc., 719 F.2d 5 (2d Cir.1983), cert. denied sub nom. Moss v. Newman, 465 U.S. 1025, 104 S.Ct. 1280, 79 L.Ed.2d 684 (1984) (defendants were tippees of aggressor in proposed tender offer and traded in the target's stock; the Court held that the tippees owed no duty to the plaintiffs on an impersonal market).

(2) Plaintiffs have not had much greater success under § 20A, which was added by ITSFEA in 1988. Most (though not all) complaints have been dismissed or summary judgments for defendants have been entered before trial. Major issues have been how contemporaneous must "contemporaneous trading" be and how particularized allegations must be that the defendants in fact possessed material nonpublic information at the time of trading. Simon v. American Power Conversion Corp., 945 F.Supp. 416 (D.R.I.1996) held that trading that occurred during the same week was "contemporaneous" and refused to grant a motion to dismiss, while In re AST Research Securities Litigation, 887 F.Supp. 231 (C.D.Cal.1995) took the position that trading must occur on the same day if it is to meet the "contemporaneous trading" requirement. While some cases have suggested that a five-or six-day period is "contemporaneous," In re MicroStrategy, Inc. Securities Litigation, 115 F.Supp.2d 620 (E.D.Va.2000) holds that a purchase of stock three days after an officer's sale at a higher price was not "contemporaneous." Other § 20A cases in which defendants obtained dismissal of complaints or summary judgments include In re VeriFone Securities Litigation, 11 F.3d 865 (9th Cir.1993) (plaintiffs traded before any trades by insiders); Fujisawa Pharmaceutical Co., Ltd. v. Kapoor, 932 F.Supp. 208 (N.D.Ill.1996) (§ 20A does not apply to direct face-to-face transactions between insiders); Clay v. Riverwood Int'l Corp., 964 F.Supp. 1559 (N.D.Ga.1997) (exercise of stock appreciation right cannot be matched with open market purchase of stock). Obviously, the broader the period that is deemed to be "contemporaneous" the greater the exposure of the defendant, though abstractly it is difficult to explain why a person who traded on an impersonal stock exchange four days after the defendant's trade should have a cause of action while one who traded one week later does not. In neither case is the confluence of the two trades based on more than chance. See William K.S. Wang, Trading on Material Nonpublic Information on Impersonal Stock Markets: Who is Harmed, and Who Can Sue Whom Under SEC Rule 10b–5? 54 S.Cal.L.Rev. 1217, 1274–84 (1981).

(3) Should a person who receives a false tip and loses money by trading on it have a claim against his tipper? Of course, if the information had been accurate, the tippee would have himself violated rule 10b–5, and a plausible argument may be made that he has unclean hands and should not be permitted to maintain a

suit against his tipper. Several lower courts split on the issue whether the *in pari delicto* defense should be applied in such a case, but the United States Supreme Court firmly resolved the disagreement in Bateman Eichler, Hill Richards, Inc. v. Berner, 472 U.S. 299, 105 S.Ct. 2622, 86 L.Ed.2d 215 (1985). The Court stated that a plaintiff should be barred in these circumstances only where "(1) as a direct result of his own actions, the plaintiff bears at least substantially equal responsibility for the violations he seeks to redress, and (2) preclusion of suit would not significantly interfere with the effective enforcement of the securities laws and protection of the investing public." 472 U.S. at 310–11, 105 S.Ct. at 2629, 86 L.Ed.2d at 224.

SECURITIES EXCHANGE ACT OF 1934

48 Stat. 896 (1934), 15 U.S.C.A. § 78p (1997).

Section 16. Directors, officers, and principal stockholders

(a) Every person who is directly or indirectly the beneficial owner of more than 10 percent of any class of any equity security (other than an exempted security) which is registered pursuant to section 12 of this title, or who is a director or an officer of the issuer of such security, shall file, at the time of the registration of such security on a national securities exchange or by the effective date of a registration statement filed pursuant to section 12(g) of this title, or within ten days after he becomes such beneficial owner, director, or officer, a statement with the Commission (and, if such security is registered on a national securities exchange, also with the exchange) of the amount of all equity securities of such issuer of which he is the beneficial owner, and within ten days after the close of each calendar month thereafter, if there has been a change in such ownership during such month, shall file with the Commission (and if such security is registered on a national securities exchange, shall also file with the exchange), a statement indicating his ownership at the close of the calendar month and such changes in his ownership as have occurred during such calendar month.

(b) For the purpose of preventing the unfair use of information which may have been obtained by such beneficial owner, director, or officer by reason of his relationship to the issuer, any profit realized by him from any purchase and sale, or any sale and purchase, of any equity security of such issuer (other than an exempted security) within any period of less than six months, unless such security was acquired in good faith in connection with a debt previously contracted, shall inure to and be recoverable by the issuer, irrespective of any intention on the part of such beneficial owner, director, or officer in entering into such transaction of holding the security purchased or of not repurchasing the security sold for a period exceeding six months. Suit to recover such profit may be instituted at law or in equity in any court of competent jurisdiction by the issuer, or by the owner of any security of the issuer in the name and in behalf of the issuer if the issuer shall fail or refuse to bring such suit within sixty days after request or shall fail diligently to prosecute the same thereafter; but no such suit shall be brought more than two years after the date such profit was realized. This subsection shall not be construed to cover any transaction where such beneficial owner was not such both at the time of the purchase and sale, or the sale and purchase, of the security involved, or any transaction or transactions which the Commission by rules and regulations may exempt as not comprehended within the purpose of this subsection.

Notes

(1) Section 16(b), enacted as part of the original 1934 Exchange Act, is probably the most quirky provision of Federal securities law. Read § 16(b) again, carefully. From the first, the courts have held that this section establishes a "crude rule of thumb" and that it is no defense to argue that the offsetting transactions were entered into for innocent reasons unconnected with inside information about the corporation's affairs. If a purchase and sale (or sale and purchase) by an officer, director, or 10% shareholder takes place within a six-month period, the "profit" is automatically recoverable by the corporation. Section 16(b) states that its purpose is to prevent "the unfair use of information which may have been obtained by [the] beneficial owner, director, or officer by reason of his relationship to the issuer." The conventional reading of this statement of purpose is rather literal, that it prevents an insider from trading on nonpublic information and then restoring his or her securities position after that information has become public. However, § 16(b) is almost completely ineffective to achieve this purpose since most persons trading on nonpublic information are willing to hold securities for more than six months in order to capitalize on that information. A more rational explanation of § 16(b) is that its true purpose is to prevent manipulation of market prices by insiders. Dennis W. Carlton & Daniel R. Fischel, The Regulation of Insider Trading, 35 Stan. L.Rev. 857, 892 (1983); Frank H. Easterbrook & Daniel R. Fischel, The Economic Structure of Corporate Law 273–74 (1991). Based on original research into the background and origins of § 16(b), other related explanations have been put forth. Steve Thel, The Genius of Section 16: Regulating the Management of Publicly Held Companies, 42 Hastings L.J. 391 (1991) (purpose was to discourage manipulation of corporate affairs to create opportunities to trade corporate stock profitably since insiders must invest for the long term); Karl Shumpei Okamoto, Rereading Section 16(b) of the Securities Exchange Act, 27 Ga. L.Rev. 183 (1992) (purpose was to deter insiders from sending false signals that artificially affect prices when in fact there was no inside information at all).

(2) How are violations discovered? Nothing could be easier, since the reports required by § 16(a) are promptly made publicly available by the SEC. It is simply a matter of comparing transactions.

(3) Is there any incentive to find violations given the fact that the recovery inures to the corporation? Again from the first, the courts recognized that attorneys for plaintiff shareholders who locate § 16(b) violations, bring them to the attention of the corporation, and if necessary, bring suit on them (as contemplated by § 16(b)) are entitled to attorneys' fees. Further, "[s]ince in many cases such as this the possibility of recovering attorney's fees will provide the sole stimulus for the enforcement of § 16(b), the allowance must not be too niggardly." Smolowe v. Delendo Corp., 136 F.2d 231, 241 (2d Cir.1943), cert. denied, 320 U.S. 751, 64 S.Ct. 56, 88 L.Ed. 446 (1943). Finally, it is not necessary to actually resort to litigation in order to earn the fee. Gilson v. Chock Full O'Nuts Corp., 326 F.2d 246 (2d Cir.1964). It is enough to find violations and report them to the corporation if they lead to payment to the corporation.

(4) How difficult is it to find a plaintiff in whose name a suit may be brought to recover for a § 16(b) violation? Not difficult at all, since there is no requirement that the plaintiff be a shareholder at the time of either the purchase or sale,

and the ownership of a single share purchased specifically for bringing the suit is sufficient. See generally 9 Louis Loss & Joel Seligman, Securities Regulation 4286–89 (3d ed. 1992). In a word, it is legalized champerty.

(5) How are profits computed if there is a series of transactions? In a word, punitively. "The only rule whereby all possible profits can surely be recovered is that of lowest price in, highest price out within six months." Smolowe v. Delendo Corp., supra note (910), at 239, Gratz v. Claughton, 187 F.2d 46 (2d Cir.1951), cert. denied, 341 U.S. 920, 71 S.Ct. 741, 95 L.Ed. 1353 (1951). To illustrate:

Assume that an insider enters into the following transactions, which are grouped together for simplicity of analysis:

(1)	7/1/75	Buys 100 shares	@	115
(2)	5/15/76	Sells 100 shares	@	93
(3)	5/18/76	Buys 100 shares	@	90
(4)	5/21/76	Buys 100 shares	@	95
(5)	5/23/76	Sells 100 shares	@	97
(6)	5/26/76	Buys 100 shares	@	105
(7)	5/29/76	Sells 100 shares	@	108
(8)	8/10/76	Sells 100 shares	@	115

A businessman examining this sequence of transactions would probably conclude that the insider made a profit of $300 on transactions (2) and (3), $200 on (4) and (5), $300 on (6) and (7), and $0 on (1) and (8), closing the account, for a total trading profit of $800. However, by matching lowest price in with highest price out, the following tabulation is made:

Purchases	Sales	Profit
100 @ 90 (trans. (3))	100 @ 115 (trans. (8))	2500
100 @ 95 (trans. (4))	100 @ 108 (trans. (7))	1300
100 @ 105 (trans. (6))	100 @ 97 (trans. (5))	0

Thus there is a total § 16(b) profit of $3,800. In this computation, all transactions which yield losses are to be ignored. The Supreme Court has not had occasion to consider specifically the propriety of this method of calculating "profits." See Andrew Chin, Accurate Calculation of Short Swing Profits Under Section 16(b) of the Securities Exchange Act of 1934, 22 Del.J.Corp.L. 587, 588 (1997) [The lowest-in, highest-out "algorithm * * * originated from an erroneous 1943 analysis that cannot be defended in today's complex, computerized environment."].

(6) An officer, director or ten percent shareholder, subject to § 16(b), must accommodate his or her securities transactions to the requirements of that section, whether or not the transactions are motivated by nonpublic information. In order to avoid application of that section, a covered person who purchases or sells securities of the corporation must avoid entering into an offsetting transaction—a sale if the other transaction was a purchase, or a purchase if the other transaction was a sale—for a period that begins six months before the transaction in question and ends six months after the transaction. In effect, in-and-out trading is proscribed for a one-year period surrounding every transaction. Of course, § 16(b) is not violated if there are either a succession of purchase transactions or a succession of sale transactions without any offsetting transac-

tions, no matter how much nonpublic information is used. Further, there is no "profit" to return to the corporation if the highest sale price during every possible six-month period is below the lowest purchase price during every possible six-month period surrounding the transaction; however, as illustrated in note (5) above, transactions are matched in such a way that a single purchase at a lower price than any sale price will always generate § 16(b) profits no matter what the net profit or loss in the account was over the same or a different period.

(7) Section 16(b), in short, is an *in terrorem* provision that appears to combine an effective enforcement system with virtually no loopholes for a violator. Since avoidance of the section is relatively easy—spacing offsetting transaction six months and one day apart provides complete protection—one might assume that violations are rather rare, the product of ignorance, carelessness or inattention. The history is far different. Before about 1980 the federal reports fairly bristle with cases in which § 16(b) was applied. In addition to reported cases, there were numerous instances in which officers and directors voluntarily repaid § 16(b) profits to the issuer because they had no plausible defense; certainly, in many of these transaction nonpublic information was not involved. Why were there so many inadvertent violations? In a few instances, persons clearly covered by § 16(b) violated the section because they were unaware of the section's existence, careless in calculating the six month period, or because they relied on uninformed or erroneous advice. However, many cases also arose because of uncertainty as to the applicability of § 16(b): Should a conversion of convertible preferred into common be viewed as a "sale" of the convertible or a "purchase" of the common, or both? Is a receipt of an option to purchase a "purchase?" Or does the "purchase" occur when the option is exercised? Is the writing of a call a "sale" or the writing of a put a "purchase"? Is a person who was not an officer or director at the time of the first transaction but was at the time of the second transaction covered by the section? What about a person who was an officer or director at the time of the first transaction but not at the time of the second? Is a "vice president" an "officer"? It is fair to say that in most of the reported cases during this era, the transactions did not in fact appear to involve the use of nonpublic information but liability was imposed because § 16(b) was an automatic liability section. Karl Shumpei Okamoto, Oversimplification and the SEC's Treatment of Derivative Securities Trading by Corporate Insiders, 1993 Wisc.L.Rev. 1287, 1289–90[71] accurately summarized the law of § 16(b) when he wrote:

> It is difficult to accommodate the broad goal of deterring insider trading within this narrow prohibition of short-swing trading. There is no necessary correlation between the simple fact of a purchase and sale or a sale and purchase within six months and the abuse of inside information. Inside information can be abused with but one trade, and matched trades are not ineluctably motivated by inside information. Therefore, courts have been forced to struggle with the innocent insider whose activity fits within the literal prohibition, as well as with the clearly culpable insider whose antics do not. Cohesive rules of application have evaded the courts as they seek to apply the basic statute to a purpose it was not well suited to achieve.

(8) The number of reported § 16(b) cases has declined significantly in the last two decades. One factor is improved distribution of information about the dangers of inadvertent violations. General counsel of issuers of registered securities regularly distribute cautionary memoranda to directors, officers, large sharehold-

---

71. Copyright 1994 by the Board of Regents of the University of Wisconsin System;   Reprinted by permission of the Wisconsin Law Review.

ers, and employees who are subject to § 16(b). Since 1988, these memoranda have been virtually required by ITSFEA, but even before the enactment of that statute, they were widely used.

A second important factor are the exemptive regulations promulgated by the SEC in 1991 and 1996, that go a long way toward rationalizing the coverage of § 16(b). The last sentence of § 16(b) grants the SEC power to exempt transactions from that section if they are "not comprehended within the purpose of this subsection." Prior to 1991, the SEC had exercised this power of exemption sparingly and unsystematically. Perhaps the most important exemptions were § 240.16b–3 (relating to employee benefit plans and stock appreciation rights), and § 240.16b–6 (relating to the exercise of long-term options). In 1991, however, the SEC adopted new regulations that significantly reduce areas of uncertainty about the application of § 16(b) and modify to some extent policies previously adopted by the SEC; in 1996 the SEC returned to the task and smoothed out additional "rough edges," particularly in the director and officer compensation area. 17 C.F.R. § 240.16a–1 (1997), et seq.; Rel.No. 34–28869, 56 Fed. Reg. 7241 (Feb. 8, 1991), Rel.No. 34–37260 (June 14, 1996). These regulations constitute more than 15 densely packed pages of the Code of Federal Regulations and deal with a number of significant issues under § 16(b):

(a) The definition of "officers" is narrowed to include only the issuer's president, principal financial officer, principal accounting officer, any vice president in charge of a principal business unit, division, or function, and other persons performing policy-making functions for the issuer. Any executive officer identified as such in an issuer's 10–K Annual Report is presumed to be an "officer" for purposes of § 16.

(b) The definitions of "beneficial owner" and "equity security" are made more objective, defining direct and indirect pecuniary interests, but excluding ownership of derivatives such as options or warrants.

(c) The treatment of derivative securities—warrants, options, puts, and calls—are treated quite differently than before. Previously, acquiring an option or a call to purchase securities was not a § 16(b) purchase; the purchase occurred when the option or call was exercised. Under the regulations, the acquisition of an option is a § 16(b) purchase and its exercise is not. 16 C.F.R. §§ 240.16a–4, 240.16b–6 (1997). Previously, a covered person might speculate on inside information by matching the acquisition of a derivative with the purchase or sale of the underlying security without incurring § 16(b) liability. This is now prevented, but a covered person may now exercise a stock option and immediately sell the acquired shares without incurring § 16(b) liability. See Marc I. Steinberg & Daryl L. Landsdale, The Judicial and Regulatory Constriction of Section 16(b) of the Securities Exchange Act of 1934, 68 Notre Dame L. Rev. 33, 60–69 (1992); Karl Shumpei Okamoto, Oversimplification and the SEC's Treatment of Derivative Securities Trading by Corporate Insiders, 1993 Wisc.L.Rev. 1287.

(d) Purchases or sales made before a person becomes an officer or director need not be reported and therefore may not be matched with sales or purchases after the person becomes an officer or director. 17 C.F.R. § 240.16a–2(a) (1997). Steinberg & Landsdale criticize this change as giving away a "crown jewel" of the prohibitions against insider trading. Steinberg & Landsdale, supra at 69–78.

(e) The rules with respect to employee benefit plans were substantially reorganized and supplemented in 1991 and then completely revised in 1996 to meet criticisms and complaints about the complexity of the 1991 regulations. 17 C.F.R. § 240.16b–3 (1997). Basically, the 1996 regulations work from the premise that transactions between an issuer and its officers and directors who owe state law fiduciary duties to the issuer and its shareholders do not present the possibility of insider trading. The revised regulations completely exempt compensation and stock purchase plans that are qualified for favorable tax treatment. They also provide guidelines for the application of § 16(b) to "discretionary decisions" by participants in these plans. See Ronald O. Mueller, SEC Adopts Final, Section 16 Rule Revisions, Insights, Vol. 10, No. 8, at 2 (August 1996).

(f) The 1996 regulations also make numerous changes designed to simplify the reporting requirements for specific transactions under § 16(a).

(9) The 10 percent shareholder provision of § 16(b) makes the section potentially applicable in takeover situations wherever an aggressor acquires more than 10 percent of the target's shares but fails to acquire control of the target and thereafter disposes of the purchased shares within six months. That disposition may be to the target by private sale at a premium (greenmail), to a successful competitor for control, or on the open market by a series of sales, usually to risk arbitrageurs or conceivably to long-term investors who are not seeking control of the target. Since takeover disputes rarely extend for long periods, the probability is relatively high that offsetting transactions will occur within six months of the failed takeover bid. The United States Supreme Court addressed this issue in a series of opinions during the 1970s, and like the lower federal courts, became trapped by the irreconcilable tensions between § 16(b) as an objective crude rule of thumb, on the one hand, and the unjust or irrational results often reached when that objective standard was literally applied on the other. The Court reached plausible results through a process of inconsistent interpretation:

(a) In Reliance Elect. Co. v. Emerson Elect. Co., 404 U.S. 418, 92 S.Ct. 596, 30 L.Ed.2d 575 (1972), an aggressor purchased 13.2 percent of the target's stock in an unsuccessful takeover attempt; when it was clear the battle was lost, the aggressor sold its shares to the successful purchaser in two sales, the first that reduced its holding to 9.6 percent, and the second the balance of its holding. In a 4–3 decision, the Supreme Court held that § 16(b) applied to the first sale but not to the second, since the seller was no longer a 10 percent shareholder.

(b) In Kern County Land Co. v. Occidental Petroleum Corp., 411 U.S. 582, 93 S.Ct. 1736, 36 L.Ed.2d 503 (1973), Occidental purchased more than 10 percent of Kern County shares in a takeover attempt, but was blocked by a defensive merger between Kern County and Tenneco. As a result of the merger Occidental received Tenneco preferred shares. Occidental requested the SEC to exempt the exchange, but the SEC refused. Occidental thereafter granted Tenneco the option to purchase its preference shares exercisable exactly six months and one-day after the Tenneco tender offer expired. In a 6–3 decision, the Supreme Court held that the exchange transaction and the grant of the option was not within § 16(b) because they did not lend themselves to the evil against which § 16(b) was directed—the utilization of confidential information.

(c) In Foremost–McKesson, Inc. v. Provident Sec. Co., 423 U.S. 232, 96 S.Ct. 508, 46 L.Ed.2d 464 (1976) the Court finally solved most § 16(b) problems in the takeover context by holding that the transaction by which a person becomes a 10 percent shareholder is not itself a purchase that may be matched with subsequent sales. On the perhaps debatable assumption that the aggressor who accepts cash tenders from tens or hundreds of thousands of shareholders does so in a single transaction, most of the problems of applying § 16(b) to takeover situations disappeared. Of course, all purchases after the one that increases the holding to above ten percent continue to be subject to § 16(b).

(10) Do you think that § 16(b) is now obsolete and should be repealed given the growth of rule 10b–5, the enactment by Congress of ITSA and ITSFEA during the 1980s, and the development of the 1991 and 1996 regulations? For a strong argument supporting that suggestion see Michael H. Dessent, Weapons to Fight Insider Trading in the 21st Century: A Call for the Repeal of Section 16(B), 33 Akron L.Rev. 481 (2000). Professor Dessent suggests Rule 10b–5, including the misappropriation doctrine approved in *O'Hagan*, provides more rational application of the prohibition against insider trading than § 16(b). Alternatively, Professor Dessent also suggests that it might be sensible to limit enforcement of § 16(b) actions to the SEC.

(11) Section 16(b) still prevents in-and-out trading by officers, directors, and large shareholders within a six month period. Is that a sufficient justification to retain this section, despite its quirky and erratic nature and the inequities and champertous litigation that it generates? The SEC has considered proposals to recommend the repeal of this section, but has never actually supported such a proposal.

C. JUDICIAL DEVELOPMENT OF LIABILITY FOR SECURITIES FRAUD

BASIC INC. v. LEVINSON

Supreme Court of the United States, 1988.
485 U.S. 224, 108 S.Ct. 978, 99 L.Ed.2d 194.

JUSTICE BLACKMUN delivered the opinion of the Court.

This case requires us to apply the materiality requirement of § 10(b) of the Securities Exchange Act of 1934, and the Securities and Exchange Commission's Rule 10b–5, in the context of preliminary corporate merger discussions. We must also determine whether a person who traded a corporation's shares on a securities exchange after the issuance of a materially misleading statement by the corporation may invoke a rebuttable presumption that, in trading, he relied on the integrity of the price set by the market.

I

Prior to December 20, 1978, Basic Incorporated was a publicly traded company primarily engaged in the business of manufacturing chemical refractories for the steel industry. As early as 1965 or 1966, Combustion Engineering, Inc., a company producing mostly alumina-based refractories, expressed some interest in acquiring Basic, but was deterred from pursuing this inclination seriously because of antitrust concerns it then entertained. In 1976, however, regulatory action opened the way to a renewal of Combustion's interest. The "Strategic Plan," dated October 25, 1976, for Combustion's Industrial Products Group included the objective: "Acquire Basic Inc. $30 million."

Beginning in September 1976, Combustion representatives had meetings and telephone conversations with Basic officers and directors,[72] * * * concerning the possibility of a merger.[73] During 1977 and 1978, Basic made three

---

72. [By the Court] In addition to Basic itself, petitioners are individuals who had been members of its board of directors prior to 1979. * * *

73. [By the Court] In light of our disposi-

public statements denying that it was engaged in merger negotiations.[74] On December 18, 1978, Basic asked the New York Stock Exchange to suspend trading in its shares and issued a release stating that it had been "approached" by another company concerning a merger. On December 19, Basic's board endorsed Combustion's offer of $46 per share for its common stock, and on the following day publicly announced its approval of Combustion's tender offer for all outstanding shares.

Respondents are former Basic shareholders who sold their stock after Basic's first public statement of October 21, 1977, and before the suspension of trading in December 1978. Respondents brought a class action against Basic and its directors, asserting that the defendants issued three false or misleading public statements and thereby were in violation of § 10(b) of the 1934 Act and of Rule 10b–5. Respondents alleged that they were injured by selling Basic shares at artificially depressed prices in a market affected by petitioners' misleading statements and in reliance thereon.

The District Court adopted a presumption of reliance by members of the plaintiff class upon petitioners' public statements that enabled the court to conclude that common questions of fact or law predominated over particular questions pertaining to individual plaintiffs. See Fed.Rule Civ.Proc. 23(b)(3). The District Court therefore certified respondents' class. On the merits, however, the District Court granted summary judgment for the defendants. It held that, as a matter of law, any misstatements were immaterial: there were no negotiations ongoing at the time of the first statement, and although negotiations were taking place when the second and third statements were issued, those negotiations were not "destined, with reasonable certainty, to become a merger agreement in principle."

The United States Court of Appeals for the Sixth Circuit affirmed the class certification, but reversed the District Court's summary judgment, and remanded the case. 786 F.2d 741 (1986). The court reasoned that while petitioners were under no general duty to disclose their discussions with Combustion, any statement the company voluntarily released could not be " 'so incomplete as to mislead.' " *Id.*, at 746, quoting *SEC v. Texas Gulf Sulphur Co.*, 401 F.2d 833, 862 (C.A.2 1968) (en banc), cert. denied *sub nom. Coates v. SEC*, 394 U.S. 976, 89 S.Ct. 1454, 22 L.Ed.2d 756 (1969). In the

tion of this case, any further characterization of these discussions must await application, on remand, of the materiality standard adopted today.

74. [By the Court] On October 21, 1977, after heavy trading and a new high in Basic stock, the following news item appeared in the Cleveland Plain Dealer:

"[Basic] President Max Muller said the company knew no reason for the stock's activity and that no negotiations were under way with any company for a merger. He said Flintkote recently denied Wall Street rumors that it would make a tender offer of $25 a share for control of the Cleveland-based maker of refractories for the steel industry."

On September 25, 1978, in reply to an inquiry from the New York Stock Exchange, Basic issued a release concerning increased activity in its stock and stated that

"management is unaware of any present or pending company development that would result in the abnormally heavy trading activity and price fluctuation in company shares that have been experienced in the past few days."

On November 6, 1978, Basic issued to its shareholders a "Nine Months Report 1978." This Report stated:

"With regard to the stock market activity in the Company's shares we remain unaware of any present or pending developments which would account for the high volume of trading and price fluctuations in recent months."

Court of Appeals' view, Basic's statements that no negotiations were taking place, and that it knew of no corporate developments to account for the heavy trading activity, were misleading. With respect to materiality, the court rejected the argument that preliminary merger discussions are immaterial as a matter of law, and held that "once a statement is made denying the existence of any discussions, even discussions that might not have been material in absence of the denial are material because they make the statement made untrue." 786 F.2d, at 749.

The Court of Appeals joined a number of other circuits in accepting the "fraud-on-the-market theory" to create a rebuttable presumption that respondents relied on petitioners' material misrepresentations, noting that without the presumption it would be impractical to certify a class under Fed.Rule Civ.Proc. 23(b)(3).

We granted certiorari, 479 U.S. 1083, 107 S.Ct. 1284, 94 L.Ed.2d 142 (1987), to resolve the split, among the Courts of Appeals as to the standard of materiality applicable to preliminary merger discussions, and to determine whether the courts below properly applied a presumption of reliance in certifying the class, rather than requiring each class member to show direct reliance on Basic's statements.

II

The 1934 Act was designed to protect investors against manipulation of stock prices. Underlying the adoption of extensive disclosure requirements was a legislative philosophy: "There cannot be honest markets without honest publicity. Manipulation and dishonest practices of the market place thrive upon mystery and secrecy." H.R.Rep. No. 1383, 73d Cong., 2d Sess., 11 (1934). This Court "repeatedly has described the 'fundamental purpose' of the Act as implementing a 'philosophy of full disclosure.'" *Santa Fe Industries, Inc. v. Green,* 430 U.S. 462, 477–478, 97 S.Ct. 1292, 1303, 51 L.Ed.2d 480 (1977), quoting *SEC v. Capital Gains Research Bureau, Inc.,* 375 U.S. 180, 186, 84 S.Ct. 275, 280, 11 L.Ed.2d 237 (1963).

Pursuant to its authority under § 10(b) of the 1934 Act, the Securities and Exchange Commission promulgated Rule 10b–5. Judicial interpretation and application, legislative acquiescence, and the passage of time have removed any doubt that a private cause of action exists for a violation of § 10(b) and Rule 10b–5, and constitutes an essential tool for enforcement of the 1934 Act's requirements.

The Court previously has addressed various positive and common-law requirements for a violation of § 10(b) or of Rule 10b–5. The Court also explicitly has defined a standard of materiality under the securities law, see *TSC Industries, Inc. v. Northway, Inc.,* 426 U.S. 438, 96 S.Ct. 2126, 48 L.Ed.2d 757 (1976), concluding in the proxy-solicitation context that "[a]n omitted fact is material if there is a substantial likelihood that a reasonable shareholder would consider it important in deciding how to vote." *Id.,* at 449, 96 S.Ct., at 2132. Acknowledging that certain information concerning corporate developments could well be of "dubious significance," *Id.,* at 448, 96 S.Ct., at 2132, the Court was careful not to set too low a standard of materiality; it was concerned that a minimal standard might bring an overabundance of information within its reach, and lead management "simply to bury the shareholders in an avalanche of trivial information—a result that is hardly conducive to informed decisionmaking." *Id.*, at 448–449, 96 S.Ct., at 2132. It further explained that to fulfill the materiality requirement "there must be a substantial likelihood that the disclosure of the omitted fact would have been viewed by the reasonable investor as having significantly altered the 'total mix' of information made available." We now expressly adopt the *TSC Industries* standard of materiality for the § 10(b) and Rule 10b–5 context.

III

The application of this materiality standard to preliminary merger discussions is not self-evident. Where the impact of the corporate development on the target's fortune is certain and clear, the *TSC Industries* materiality definition admits straightforward application. Where, on the other hand, the event is contingent or speculative in nature, it is difficult to ascertain whether the "reasonable investor" would have considered the omitted information significant at the time. Merger negotiations, because of the ever-present possibility that the contemplated transaction will not be effectuated, fall into the latter category.

A

Petitioners urge upon us a Third Circuit test for resolving this difficulty. Under this approach, preliminary merger discussions do not become material until "agreement-in-principle" as to the price and structure of the transaction has been reached between the would-be merger partners. See *Greenfield v. Heublein, Inc.,* 742 F.2d 751, 757 (C.A.3 1984), cert. denied, 469 U.S. 1215 (1985). By definition, then, information concerning any negotiations not yet at the agreement-in-principle stage could be withheld or even misrepresented without a violation of Rule 10b–5.

Three rationales have been offered in support of the "agreement-in-principle" test. The first derives from the concern expressed in *TSC Industries* that an investor not be overwhelmed by excessively detailed and trivial information, and focuses on the substantial risk that preliminary merger discussions may collapse: because such discussions are inherently tentative, disclosure of their existence itself could mislead investors and foster false optimism. The other two justifications for the agreement-in-principle standard are based on management concerns: because the requirement of "agreement-in-principle" limits the scope of disclosure obligations, it helps preserve the confidentiality of merger discussions where earlier disclosure might prejudice the negotiations; and the test also provides a usable, brightline rule for determining when disclosure must be made.

None of these policy-based rationales, however, purports to explain why drawing the line at agreement-in-principle reflects the significance of the information upon the investor's decision. The first rationale, and the only one connected to the concerns expressed in *TSC Industries,* stands soundly rejected, even by a Court of Appeals that otherwise has accepted the wisdom of the agreement-in-principle test. "It assumes that investors are nitwits, unable to appreciate—even when told—that mergers are risky propositions up until the closing." *Flamm v. Eberstadt,* 814 F.2d [1169], at 1175, [(7th Cir.) cert. denied 484 U.S. 853 (1987)]. Disclosure, and not paternalistic withhold-

ing of accurate information, is the policy chosen and expressed by Congress.
* * *

The second rationale, the importance of secrecy during the early stages of merger discussions, also seems irrelevant to an assessment whether their existence is significant to the trading decision of a reasonable investor. To avoid a "bidding war" over its target, an acquiring firm often will insist that negotiations remain confidential, and at least one Court of Appeals has stated that "silence pending settlement of the price and structure of a deal is beneficial to most investors, most of the time." *Flamm v. Eberstadt,* 814 F.2d, at 1177.[75]

We need not ascertain, however, whether secrecy necessarily maximizes shareholder wealth—although we note that the proposition is at least disputed as a matter of theory and empirical research[76]—for this case does not concern the *timing* of a disclosure; it concerns only its accuracy and completeness. * * *

The final justification offered in support of the agreement-in-principle test seems to be directed solely at the comfort of corporate managers. A bright-line rule indeed is easier to follow than a standard that requires the exercise of judgment in the light of all the circumstances. But ease of application alone is not an excuse for ignoring the purposes of the securities acts and Congress' policy decisions. Any approach that designates a single fact or occurrence as always determinative of an inherently fact-specific finding such as materiality, must necessarily be over-inclusive or under-inclusive. In *TSC Industries* this Court explained: "The determination [of materiality] requires delicate assessments of the inferences a 'reasonable shareholder' would draw from a given set of facts and the significance of those inferences to him * * *." 426 U.S., at 450. After much study, the Advisory Committee on Corporate Disclosure cautioned the SEC against administratively confining materiality to a rigid formula.[77] Courts also would do well to heed this advice.

We therefore find no valid justification for artificially excluding from the definition of materiality information concerning merger discussions, which would otherwise be considered significant to the trading decision of a reasonable investor, merely because agreement-in-principle as to price and structure has not yet been reached by the parties or their representatives. * * *

---

75. [By the Court] Reasoning backwards from a goal of economic efficiency, that Court of Appeals stated: "Rule 10b–5 is about *fraud,* after all, and it is not fraudulent to conduct business in a way that makes investors better off * * *." Flamm v. Eberstadt, 814 F.2d, at 1177.

76. [By the Court] See Flamm v. Eberstadt, 814 F.2d, at 1177, n. 2 (citing scholarly debate). See also In re Carnation Co., Exchange Act Release No. 22214, 33 S.E.C. Docket 1025, 1030 (1985) ("The importance of accurate and complete issuer disclosure to the integrity of the securities markets cannot be overemphasized. To the extent that investors cannot rely upon the accuracy and completeness of issuer statements, they will be less likely to invest, thereby reducing the liquidity of the securities

markets to the detriment of investors and issuers alike").

77. [By the Court] "Although the Committee believes that ideally it would be desirable to have absolute certainty in the application of the materiality concept, it is its view that such a goal is illusory and unrealistic. The materiality concept is judgmental in nature and it is not possible to translate this into a numerical formula. The Committee's advice to the [SEC] is to avoid this quest for certainty and to continue consideration of materiality on a case-by-case basis as problems are identified." Report of the Advisory Committee on Corporate Disclosure to the Securities and Exchange Commission 327 (House Committee on Interstate and Foreign Commerce, 95th Cong., 1st Sess.) (Comm. Print) (1977).

C

Even before this Court's decision in *TSC Industries,* the Second Circuit had explained the role of the materiality requirement of Rule 10b–5, with respect to contingent or speculative information or events, in a manner that gave that term meaning that is independent of the other provisions of the Rule. Under such circumstances, materiality "will depend at any given time upon a balancing of both the indicated probability that the event will occur and the anticipated magnitude of the event in light of the totality of the company activity." *SEC v. Texas Gulf Sulphur Co.,* 401 F.2d [833, 849 (2d Cir.1968)]. Interestingly, neither the Third Circuit decision adopting the agreement-in-principle test nor petitioners here take issue with this general standard. Rather, they suggest that with respect to preliminary merger discussions, there are good reasons to draw a line at agreement on price and structure.

In a subsequent decision, the late Judge Friendly, writing for a Second Circuit panel, applied the *Texas Gulf Sulphur* probability/magnitude approach in the specific context of preliminary merger negotiations. After acknowledging that materiality is something to be determined on the basis of the particular facts of each case, he stated:

> Since a merger in which it is bought out is the most important event that can occur in a small corporation's life, to wit, its death, we think that inside information, as regards a merger of this sort, can become material at an earlier stage than would be the case as regards lesser transactions— and this even though the mortality rate of mergers in such formative stages is doubtless high. *SEC v. Geon Industries, Inc.,* 531 F.2d 39, 47–48 (1976).

We agree with that analysis.[78]

Whether merger discussions in any particular case are material therefore depends on the facts. Generally, in order to assess the probability that the event will occur, a factfinder will need to look to indicia of interest in the transaction at the highest corporate levels. Without attempting to catalog all such possible factors, we note by way of example that board resolutions, instructions to investment bankers, and actual negotiations between principals or their intermediaries may serve as indicia of interest. To assess the magnitude of the transaction to the issuer of the securities allegedly manipulated, a factfinder will need to consider such facts as the size of the two corporate entities and of the potential premiums over market value. No particular event or factor short of closing the transaction need be either necessary or sufficient by itself to render merger discussions material.[79]

78. [By the Court] The SEC in the present case endorses the highly fact-dependent probability/magnitude balancing approach of *Texas Gulf Sulphur.* It explains: "The *possibility* of a merger may have an immediate importance to investors in the company's securities even if no merger ultimately takes place." The SEC's insights are helpful, and we accord them due deference.

79. [By the Court] To be actionable, of course, a statement must also be misleading. Silence, absent a duty to disclose, is not mis-leading under Rule 10b–5. "No comment" statements are generally the functional equivalent of silence. * * * See New York Stock Exchange Listed Company Manual § 202.01 (premature public announcement may properly be delayed for valid business purpose and where adequate security can be maintained). It has been suggested that given current market practices, a "no comment" statement is tantamount to an admission that merger discussions are underway. See *Flamm v. Eberstadt,* 814 F.2d, at 1178. That may well hold true to the

As we clarify today, materiality depends on the significance the reasonable investor would place on the withheld or misrepresented information.[80] The fact-specific inquiry we endorse here is consistent with the approach a number of courts have taken in assessing the materiality of merger negotiations.[81] Because the standard of materiality we have adopted differs from that used by both courts below, we remand the case for reconsideration of the question whether a grant of summary judgment is appropriate on this record.

IV

A

We turn to the question of reliance and the fraud-on-the-market theory. Succinctly put:

> The fraud on the market theory is based on the hypothesis that, in an open and developed securities market, the price of a company's stock is determined by the available material information regarding the company and its business. * * * Misleading statements will therefore defraud purchasers of stock even if the purchasers do not directly rely on the misstatements. * * * The causal connection between the defendants' fraud and the plaintiffs' purchase of stock in such a case is no less significant than in a case of direct reliance on misrepresentations. *Peil v. Speiser,* 806 F.2d 1154, 1160–1161 (C.A.3 1986).

Our task, of course, is not to assess the general validity of the theory, but to consider whether it was proper for the courts below to apply a rebuttable presumption of reliance, supported in part by the fraud-on-the-market theory.

extent that issuers adopt a policy of truthfully denying merger rumors when no discussions are underway, and of issuing "no comment" statements when they are in the midst of negotiations. There are, of course, other statement policies firms could adopt; we need not now advise issuers as to what kind of practice to follow, within the range permitted by law. Perhaps more importantly, we think that creating an exception to a regulatory scheme founded on a prodisclosure legislative philosophy, because complying with the regulation might be "bad for business," is a role for Congress, not this Court.

80. [By the Court] We find no authority in the statute, the legislative history, or our previous decisions for varying the standard of materiality depending on who brings the action or whether insiders are alleged to have profited. See, *e.g., Pavlidis v. New England Patriots Football Club, Inc.,* 737 F.2d 1227, 1231 (C.A.1 1984) ("A fact does not become more material to the shareholder's decision because it is withheld by an insider, or because the insider might profit by withholding it").

We recognize that trading (and profit making) by insiders can serve as *an* indication of materiality, see *SEC v. Texas Gulf Sulphur Co.,* 401 F.2d, at 851. We are not prepared to agree, however, that "[i]n cases of the disclosure of inside information to a favored few, determination of materiality has a different aspect than when the issue is, for example, an

inaccuracy in a publicly disseminated press release." SEC v. Geon Industries, Inc., 531 F.2d 39, 48 (C.A.2 1976). Devising two different standards of materiality, one for situations where insiders have traded in abrogation of their duty to disclose or abstain (or for that matter when any disclosure duty has been breached), and another covering affirmative misrepresentations by those under no duty to disclose (but under the ever-present duty not to mislead), would effectively collapse the materiality requirement into the analysis of defendant's disclosure duties.

81. [By the Court] See, e.g., SEC v. Shapiro, 494 F.2d 1301, 1306–1307 (C.A.2 1974) (in light of projected very substantial increase in earnings per share, negotiations material, although merger still less than probable); Holmes v. Bateson, 583 F.2d 542, 558 (C.A.1 1978) (merger negotiations material although they had not yet reached point of discussing terms); SEC v. Gaspar, CCH Fed.Sec.L.Rep. (1984–1985 Transfer Binder) ¶ 92,004, pp. 90,-977–90,978 (SDNY 1985) (merger negotiations material although they did not proceed to actual tender offer); Dungan v. Colt Industries, Inc., 532 F.Supp. 832, 837 (N.D.Ill.1982) (fact that defendants were seriously exploring the sale of their company was material); American General Ins. Co. v. Equitable General Corp., 493 F.Supp. 721, 744–745 (E.D.Va.1980) (merger negotiations material four months before agreement-in-principle reached).

This case required resolution of several common questions of law and fact concerning the falsity or misleading nature of the three public statements made by Basic, the presence or absence of scienter, and the materiality of the misrepresentations, if any. In their amended complaint, the named plaintiffs alleged that in reliance on Basic's statements they sold their shares of Basic stock in the depressed market created by petitioners. Requiring proof of individualized reliance from each member of the proposed plaintiff class effectively would have prevented respondents from proceeding with a class action, since individual issues then would have overwhelmed the common ones. The District Court found that the presumption of reliance created by the fraud-on-the-market theory provided "a practical resolution to the problem of balancing the substantive requirement of proof of reliance in securities cases against the procedural requisites of [Federal Rule of Civil Procedure] 23." The District Court thus concluded that with reference to each public statement and its impact upon the open market for Basic shares, common questions predominated over individual questions, as required by Federal Rule of Civil Procedure 23(a)(2) and (b)(3).

Petitioners and their *amici* complain that the fraud-on-the-market theory effectively eliminates the requirement that a plaintiff asserting a claim under Rule 10b–5 prove reliance. They note that reliance is and long has been an element of common-law fraud, see *e.g.*, Restatement (Second) of Torts § 525 (1977), and argue that because the analogous express right of action includes a reliance requirement, see, *e.g.*, § 18(a) of the 1934 Act, as amended, so too must an action implied under § 10(b).

We agree that reliance is an element of a Rule 10b–5 cause of action. Reliance provides the requisite causal connection between a defendant's misrepresentation and a plaintiff's injury. There is, however, more than one way to demonstrate the causal connection. Indeed, we previously have dispensed with a requirement of positive proof of reliance, where a duty to disclose material information had been breached, concluding that the necessary nexus between the plaintiffs' injury and the defendant's wrongful conduct had been established. Similarly, we did not require proof that material omissions or misstatements in a proxy statement decisively affected voting, because the proxy solicitation itself, rather than the defect in the solicitation materials, served as an essential link in the transaction. See *Mills v. Electric Auto–Lite Co.*, 396 U.S. 375, 384–385 (1970).

The modern securities markets, literally involving millions of shares changing hands daily, differ from the face-to-face transactions contemplated by early fraud cases, and our understanding of Rule 10b–5's reliance requirement must encompass these differences.

> In face-to-face transactions, the inquiry into an investor's reliance upon information is into the subjective pricing of that information by that investor. With the presence of a market, the market is interposed between seller and buyer and, ideally, transmits information to the investor in the processed form of a market price. Thus the market is performing a substantial part of the valuation process performed by the investor in a face-to-face transaction. The market is acting as the unpaid agent of the investor, informing him that given all the information available to it, the

value of the stock is worth the market price. *In re LTV Securities Litigation,* 88 F.R.D. 134, 143 (N.D.Tex.1980).

Accord, *e.g., Peil v. Speiser,* 806 F.2d, at 1161 ("In an open and developed market, the dissemination of material misrepresentations or withholding of material information typically affects the price of the stock, and purchasers generally rely on the price of the stock as a reflection of its value"); *Blackie v. Barrack,* 524 F.2d 891, 908 (C.A.9 1975) ("[T]he same causal nexus can be adequately established indirectly, by proof of materiality coupled with the common sense that a stock purchaser does not ordinarily seek to purchase a loss in the form of artificially inflated stock"), cert. denied, 429 U.S. 816 (1976).

B

Presumptions typically serve to assist courts in managing circumstances in which direct proof, for one reason or another, is rendered difficult. See, *e.g.,* 1 D. Louisell & C. Mueller, Federal Evidence 541–542 (1977). The courts below accepted a presumption, created by the fraud-on-the-market theory and subject to rebuttal by petitioners, that persons who had traded Basic shares had done so in reliance on the integrity of the price set by the market, but because of petitioners' material misrepresentations that price had been fraudulently depressed. Requiring a plaintiff to show a speculative state of facts, *i.e.,* how he would have acted if omitted material information had been disclosed, or if the misrepresentation had not been made, would place an unnecessarily unrealistic evidentiary burden on the Rule 10b–5 plaintiff who has traded on an impersonal market.

Arising out of considerations of fairness, public policy, and probability, as well as judicial economy, presumptions are also useful devices for allocating the burdens of proof between parties. The presumption of reliance employed in this case is consistent with, and, by facilitating Rule 10b–5 litigation, supports, the congressional policy embodied in the 1934 Act. In drafting that Act, Congress expressly relied on the premise that securities markets are affected by information, and enacted legislation to facilitate an investor's reliance on the integrity of those markets:

> No investor, no speculator, can safely buy and sell securities upon the exchanges without having an intelligent basis for forming his judgment as to the value of the securities he buys or sells. The idea of a free and open public market is built upon the theory that competing judgments of buyers and sellers as to the fair price of a security brings *[sic]* about a situation where the market price reflects as nearly as possible a just price. Just as artificial manipulation tends to upset the true function of an open market, so the hiding and secreting of important information obstructs the operation of the markets as indices of real value. H.R.Rep. No. 1383, at 11.[82]

The presumption is also supported by common sense and probability. Recent empirical studies have tended to confirm Congress' premise that the

---

82. [By the Court] Contrary to the dissent's suggestion, the incentive for investors to "pay attention" to issuers' disclosures comes from their motivation to make a profit, not their attempt to preserve a cause of action under Rule 10b–5. Facilitating an investor's reliance on the market, consistently with Congress' expectations, hardly calls for "dismantling the federal scheme which mandates disclosure."

market price of shares traded on well-developed markets reflects all publicly available information, and, hence, any material misrepresentations.[83] It has been noted that "it is hard to imagine that there ever is a buyer or seller who does not rely on market integrity. Who would knowingly roll the dice in a crooked crap game?" *Schlanger v. Four–Phase Systems Inc.*, 555 F.Supp. 535, 538 (S.D.N.Y.1982). Indeed, nearly every court that has considered the proposition has concluded that where materially misleading statements have been disseminated into an impersonal, well-developed market for securities, the reliance of individual plaintiffs on the integrity of the market price may be presumed.[84] Commentators generally have applauded the adoption of one variation or another of the fraud-on-the-market theory.[85] An investor who buys or sells stock at the price set by the market does so in reliance on the integrity of that price. Because most publicly available information is reflected in market price, an investor's reliance on any public material misrepresentations, therefore, may be presumed for purposes of a Rule 10b–5 action.

C

The Court of Appeals found that petitioners "made public, material misrepresentations and [respondents] sold Basic stock in an impersonal, efficient market. Thus the class, as defined by the district court, has established the threshold facts for proving their loss." 786 F.2d, at 751. The court acknowledged that petitioners may rebut proof of the elements giving rise to the presumption, or show that the misrepresentation in fact did not lead to a distortion of price or that an individual plaintiff traded or would have traded despite his knowing the statement was false.

Any showing that severs the link between the alleged misrepresentation and either the price received (or paid) by the plaintiff, or his decision to trade at a fair market price, will be sufficient to rebut the presumption of reliance. For example, if petitioners could show that the "market makers" were privy to the truth about the merger discussions here with Combustion, and thus that the market price would not have been affected by their misrepresentations, the causal connection could be broken: the basis for finding that the fraud had been transmitted through market price would be gone.[86] Similarly, if, despite petitioners' allegedly fraudulent attempt to manipulate market price, news of the merger discussions credibly entered the market and dissipated the effects of the misstatements, those who traded Basic shares after the corrective statements would have no direct or indirect connection

---

83. [By the Court] See *In re LTV Securities Litigation,* 88 F.R.D. 134, 144 (N.D.Tex.1980) (citing studies); Fischel, Use of Modern Finance Theory in Securities Fraud Cases Involving Actively Traded Securities, 38 Bus.Law. 1, 4, n. 9 (1982) (citing literature on efficient-capital-market theory). We need not determine by adjudication what economists and social scientists have debated through the use of sophisticated statistical analysis and the application of economic theory. For purposes of accepting the presumption of reliance in this case, we need only believe that market professionals generally consider most publicly announced material statements about companies, thereby affecting stock market prices.

84. [By the Editors] The Court cites seven appellate decisions, all after 1978.

85. [By the Court] See, *e.g.,* Black, Fraud on the Market: A Criticism of Dispensing with Reliance Requirements in Certain Open Market Transactions, 62 N.C.L.Rev. 435 (1984).

86. [By the Court] By accepting this rebuttable presumption, we do not intend conclusively to adopt any particular theory of how quickly and completely publicly available information is reflected in market price. Furthermore, our decision today is not to be interpreted as addressing the proper measure of damages in litigation of this kind.

with the fraud.[87] Petitioners also could rebut the presumption of reliance as to plaintiffs who would have divested themselves of their Basic shares without relying on the integrity of the market. For example, a plaintiff who believed that Basic's statements were false and that Basic was indeed engaged in merger discussions, and who consequently believed that Basic stock was artificially underpriced, but sold his shares nevertheless because of other unrelated concerns, *e.g.*, potential antitrust problems, or political pressures to divest from shares of certain businesses, could not be said to have relied on the integrity of a price he knew had been manipulated. * * *

The judgment of the Court of Appeals is vacated, and the case is remanded to that court for further proceedings consistent with this opinion.

It is so ordered.

THE CHIEF JUSTICE, JUSTICE SCALIA, and JUSTICE KENNEDY took no part in the consideration or decision of this case.

JUSTICE WHITE, with whom JUSTICE O'CONNOR joins, concurring in part and dissenting in part.

I join Parts I–III of the Court's opinion, as I agree that the standard of materiality we set forth in *TSC Industries, Inc. v. Northway, Inc.,* 426 U.S. 438, 449 (1976), should be applied to actions under § 10(b) and Rule 10b–5. But I dissent from the remainder of the Court's holding because I do not agree that the "fraud-on-the-market" theory should be applied in this case.

I

Even when compared to the relatively youthful private cause-of-action under § 10(b), see *Kardon v. National Gypsum Co.,* 69 F.Supp. 512 (E.D.Pa. 1946), the fraud-on-the-market theory is a mere babe.[88] Yet today, the Court embraces this theory with the sweeping confidence usually reserved for more mature legal doctrines. In so doing, I fear that the Court's decision may have many adverse, unintended effects as it is applied and interpreted in the years to come.

A

At the outset, I note that there are portions of the Court's fraud-on-the-market holding with which I am in agreement. Most importantly, the Court rejects the version of that theory, heretofore adopted by some courts, which equates "causation" with "reliance," and permits recovery by a plaintiff who claims merely to have been *harmed* by a material misrepresentation which altered a market price, notwithstanding proof that the plaintiff did not in any way *rely* on that price. I agree with the Court that if Rule 10b–5's reliance

---

87. [By the Court] We note there may be a certain incongruity between the assumption that Basic shares are traded on a well-developed, efficient, and information-hungry market, and the allegation that such a market could remain misinformed, and its valuation of Basic shares depressed, for 14 months, on the basis of the three public statements. Proof of that sort is a matter for trial, throughout which the District Court retains the authority to amend the certification order as may be appropriate. Thus, we see no need to engage in the kind of factual analysis the dissent suggests that manifests the "oddities" of applying a rebuttable presumption of reliance in this case.

88. [By the Justice] The earliest Court of Appeals case adopting this theory cited by the Court is *Blackie v. Barrack,* 524 F.2d 891 (C.A.9 1975), cert. denied, 429 U.S. 816 (1976). Moreover, widespread acceptance of the fraud-on-the-market theory in the Courts of Appeals cannot be placed any earlier than five or six years ago.

requirement is to be left with any content at all, the fraud-on-the-market presumption must be capable of being rebutted by a showing that a plaintiff did not "rely" on the market price. For example, a plaintiff who decides, months in advance of an alleged misrepresentation, to purchase a stock; one who buys or sells a stock for reasons unrelated to its price; one who actually sells a stock "short" days before the misrepresentation is made-surely none of these people can state a valid claim under Rule 10b–5. Yet, some federal courts have allowed such claims to stand under one variety or another of the fraud-on-the-market theory.[89]

Happily, the majority puts to rest the prospect of recovery under such circumstances. A nonrebuttable presumption of reliance—or even worse, allowing recovery in the face of "affirmative evidence of nonreliance," *Zweig v. Hearst Corp.,* 594 F.2d 1261, 1272 (C.A.9 1979) (Ely, J., dissenting)—would effectively convert Rule 10b–5 into "a scheme of investor's insurance." *Shores v. Sklar,* 647 F.2d 462, 469, n. 5 (C.A.5 1981) (en banc), cert. denied, 459 U.S. 1102 (1983). There is no support in the Securities [Exchange] Act, the Rule, or our cases for such a result.

B

But even as the Court attempts to limit the fraud-on-the-market theory it endorses today, the pitfalls in its approach are revealed by previous uses by the lower courts of the broader versions of the theory. Confusion and contradiction in court rulings are inevitable when traditional legal analysis is replaced with economic theorization by the federal courts.

In general, the case law developed in this Court with respect to § 10(b) and Rule 10b–5 has been based on doctrines with which we, as judges, are familiar: common-law doctrines of fraud and deceit. Even when we have extended civil liability under Rule 10b–5 to a broader reach than the common law had previously permitted, we have retained familiar legal principles as our guideposts. The federal courts have proved adept at developing an evolving jurisprudence of Rule 10b–5 in such a manner. But with no staff economists, no experts schooled in the "efficient-capital-market hypothesis," no ability to test the validity of empirical market studies, we are not well equipped to embrace novel constructions of a statute based on contemporary microeconomic theory.[90]

---

89. [By the Justice] *Abrams v. Johns–Manville Corp.,* [1981–1982] CCH Fed.Sec.L.Rep. ¶ 98,348, p. 92,157 (SDNY 1981) * * *.

The *Abrams* decision illustrates the particular pliability of the fraud-on-the-market presumption. In *Abrams,* the plaintiff represented a class of purchasers of defendant's stock who were allegedly misled by defendant's misrepresentations in annual reports. But in a deposition taken shortly after the plaintiff filed suit, she testified that she had bought defendant's stock primarily because she thought that favorable changes in the federal tax code would boost sales of its product (insulation).

Two years later, after the defendant moved for summary judgment based on the plaintiff's failure to prove reliance on the alleged misrepresentations, the plaintiff resuscitated her case by executing an affidavit which stated that she "certainly [had] assumed that the market price of Johns–Manville stock was an accurate reflection of the worth of the company" and would not have paid the then-going price if she had known otherwise. Based on this affidavit, the District Court permitted the plaintiff to proceed on her fraud-on-the-market theory.

Thus, *Abrams* demonstrates how easily a *post hoc* statement will enable a plaintiff to bring a fraud-on-the-market action—even in the rare case where a plaintiff is frank or foolhardy enough to admit initially that a factor other than price led her to the decision to purchase a particular stock.

90. [By the Justice] This view was put well by two commentators who wrote a few years ago:

Of all recent developments in financial economics, the efficient capital market hy-

* * * [T]he Court today ventures into this area beyond its expertise, beyond—by its own admission—the confines of our previous fraud cases. Even if I agreed with the Court that "modern securities markets * * * involving millions of shares changing hands daily" require that the "understanding of Rule 10b–5's reliance requirement" be changed, I prefer that such changes come from Congress in amending § 10(b). The Congress, with its superior resources and expertise, is far better equipped than the federal courts for the task of determining how modern economic theory and global financial markets require that established legal notions of fraud be modified. In choosing to make these decisions itself, the Court, I fear, embarks on a course that it does not genuinely understand, giving rise to consequences it cannot foresee.[91]

For while the economists' theories which underpin the fraud-on-the-market presumption may have the appeal of mathematical exactitude and scientific certainty, they are—in the end—nothing more than theories which may or may not prove accurate upon further consideration. Even the most earnest advocates of economic analysis of the law recognize this. Thus, while the majority states that, for purposes of reaching its result it need only make modest assumptions about the way in which "market professionals generally" do their jobs, and how the conduct of market professionals affects stock prices, I doubt that we are in much of a position to assess which theories aptly describe the functioning of the securities industry.

Consequently, I cannot join the Court in its effort to reconfigure the securities laws, based on recent economic theories, to better fit what it perceives to be the new realities of financial markets. I would leave this task to others more equipped for the job than we.

C

At the bottom of the Court's conclusion that the fraud-on-the-market theory sustains a presumption of reliance is the assumption that individuals rely "on the integrity of the market price" when buying or selling stock in "impersonal, well-developed market[s] for securities." Even if I was prepared to accept (as a matter of common sense or general understanding) the assumption that most persons buying or selling stock do so in response to the market price, the fraud-on-the-market theory goes further. For in adopting a "presumption of reliance," the Court *also* assumes that buyers and sellers

pothesis ('ECMH') has achieved the widest acceptance by the legal culture.* * * Yet the legal culture's remarkably rapid and broad acceptance of an economic concept that did not exist twenty years ago is not matched by an equivalent degree of understanding.
Gilson & Kraakman, The Mechanisms of Market Efficiency, 70 Va.L.Rev. 549, 549–550 (1984) (footnotes omitted; emphasis added).

While the fraud-on-the-market theory has gained even broader acceptance since 1984, I doubt that it has achieved any greater understanding.

91. [By the Justice] For example, Judge Posner in his Economic Analysis of Law § 15.8, pp. 423–424 (3d ed. 1986), submits that

the fraud-on-the-market theory produces the "economically correct result" in Rule 10b–5 cases but observes that the question of damages under the theory is quite problematic. Notwithstanding the fact that "[a]t first blush it might seem obvious," the proper calculation of damages when the fraud-on-the-market theory is applied must rest on several "assumptions" about "social costs" which are "difficult to quantify." Ibid. Of course, answers to the question of the proper measure of damages in a fraud-on-the-market case are essential for proper implementation of the fraud-on-the-market presumption. Not surprisingly, the difficult damages question is one the Court expressly declines to address today.

rely—not just on the market price—but on the *"integrity"* of that price. It is this aspect of the fraud-on-the-market hypothesis which most mystifies me.

To define the term "integrity of the market price," the majority quotes approvingly from cases which suggest that investors are entitled to " 'rely on the price of a stock as a reflection of its value' " (quoting *Peil v. Speiser,* 806 F.2d 1154, 1161 (C.A.3 1986)). But the meaning of this phrase eludes me, for it implicitly suggests that stocks have some "true value" that is measurable by a standard other than their market price. While the Scholastics of Medieval times professed a means to make such a valuation of a commodity's "worth," I doubt that the federal courts of our day are similarly equipped.

Even if securities had some "value"—knowable and distinct from the market price of a stock—investors do not always share the Court's presumption that a stock's price is a "reflection of [this] value." Indeed, "many investors purchase or sell stock because they believe the price *inaccurately* reflects the corporation's worth." See Black, Fraud on the Market: A Criticism of Dispensing with Reliance Requirements in Certain Open Market Transactions, 62 N.C.L.Rev. 435, 455 (1984) (emphasis added). If investors really believed that stock prices reflected a stock's "value," many sellers would never sell, and many buyers never buy (given the time and cost associated with executing a stock transaction). As we recognized just a few years ago: "[I]nvestors act on inevitably incomplete or inaccurate information, [consequently] there are always winners and losers; but those who have 'lost' have not necessarily been defrauded." *Dirks v. SEC,* 463 U.S. 646, 667, n. 27 (1983). Yet today, the Court allows investors to recover who can show little more than that they sold stock at a lower price than what might have been.[92]

I do not propose that the law retreat from the many protections that § 10(b) and Rule 10b–5, as interpreted in our prior cases, provide to investors. But any extension of these laws, to approach something closer to an investor insurance scheme, should come from Congress, and not from the courts. * * *

III

Finally, the particular facts of this case make it an exceedingly poor candidate for the Court's fraud-on-the-market theory, and illustrate the illogic achieved by that theory's application in many cases.

Respondents here are a class of sellers who sold Basic stock between October 1977 and December 1978, a 14–month period. At the time the class period began, Basic's stock was trading at $20 a share (at the time, an all-time high); the last members of the class to sell their Basic stock got a price of just over $30 a share. It is indisputable that virtually every member of the class made money from his or her sale of Basic stock.

---

92. [By the Justice] This is what the Court's rule boils down to in practical terms. For while, in theory, the Court allows for rebuttal of its "presumption of reliance"—a proviso with which I agree—in practice the Court must realize, as other courts applying the fraud-on-the-market theory have, that such rebuttal is virtually impossible in all but the most extraordinary case.

Consequently, while the Court considers it significant that the fraud-on-the-market presumption it endorses is a rebuttable one, the majority's implicit rejection of the "pure causation" fraud-on-the-market theory rings hollow. In most cases, the Court's theory will operate just as the causation theory would, creating a nonrebuttable presumption of "reliance" in future Rule 10b–5 actions.

The oddities of applying the fraud-on-the-market theory in this case are manifest. First, there are the facts that the plaintiffs are sellers and the class period is so lengthy—both are virtually without precedent in prior fraud-on-the-market cases. * * * [T]hese two facts render this case less apt to application of the fraud-on-the-market hypothesis.

Second, there is the fact that in this case, there is no evidence that petitioner's officials made the troublesome misstatements for the purpose of manipulating stock prices, or with any intent to engage in underhanded trading of Basic stock. Indeed, during the class period, petitioners do not appear to have purchased or sold *any* Basic stock whatsoever. I agree with *amicus* who argues that "[i]mposition of damages liability under Rule 10b–5 makes little sense * * * where a defendant is neither a purchaser nor a seller of securities." In fact, in previous cases, we had recognized that Rule 10b–5 is concerned primarily with cases where the fraud is committed by one trading the security at issue. And it is difficult to square liability in this case with § 10(b)'s express provision that it prohibits fraud *"in connection with* the purchase or sale of any security."

Third, there are the peculiarities of what kinds of investors will be able to recover in this case. As I read the District Court's class certification order, there are potentially many persons who did not purchase Basic stock until *after* the first false statement (October 1977), but who nonetheless *will* be able to recover under the Court's fraud-on-the-market theory. Thus, it is possible that a person who heard the first corporate misstatement and *disbelieved* it—*i.e.,* someone who purchased Basic stock thinking that petitioners' statement was false—may still be included in the plaintiff-class on remand. How a person who undertook such a speculative stock-investing strategy—and made $10 a share doing so (if he bought on October 22, 1977, and sold on December 15, 1978)—can say that he was "defrauded" by virtue of his reliance on the "integrity" of the market price is beyond me.[93] And such speculators may not be uncommon, at least in this case.

Indeed, the facts of this case lead a casual observer to the almost inescapable conclusion that many of those who bought or sold Basic stock during the period in question flatly disbelieved the statements which are alleged to have been "materially misleading." Despite three statements denying that merger negotiations were underway, Basic stock hit record-high after record-high during the 14–month class period. It seems quite possible that, like Casca's knowing disbelief of Caesar's "thrice refusal" of the Crown,[94] clever investors were skeptical of petitioners' three denials that merger talks were going on. Yet such investors, the savviest of the savvy, will be able to recover under the Court's opinion, as long as they now claim that they believed in the "integrity of the market price" when they sold their stock (between September and December 1978). Thus, persons who bought after hearing and relying on the *falsity* of petitioners' statements may be able to prevail and recover money damages on remand.

93. [By the Justice] The Court recognizes that a person who sold his Basic shares believing petitioners' statements to be false may not be entitled to recovery. Yet it seems just as clear to me that one who bought Basic stock under this same belief—hoping to profit from the uncertainty over Basic's merger plans—should not be permitted to recover either.

94. [By the Justice] See W. Shakespeare, Julius Caesar, Act I, Scene II.

And who will pay the judgments won in such actions? I suspect that all too often the majority's rule will "lead to large judgments, payable in the last analysis by innocent investors, for the benefit of speculators and their lawyers." Cf. *SEC v. Texas Gulf Sulphur Co.,* 401 F.2d 833, 867 (C.A.2 1968) (en banc) (Friendly, J., concurring), cert. denied, 394 U.S. 976 (1969). This Court and others have previously recognized that "inexorably broadening * * * the class of plaintiff[s] who may sue in this area of the law will ultimately result in more harm than good." *Blue Chip Stamps v. Manor Drug Stores, supra,* at 747–748. See also *Ultramares Corp. v. Touche,* 255 N.Y. 170, 179–180, 174 N.E. 441, 444–445 (1931) (Cardozo, C.J.). Yet such a bitter harvest is likely to be reaped from the seeds sewn by the Court's decision today. * * *

Notes

(1) Two preliminary aspects of this case should be noted. First, Justice Blackmun's opinion is a plurality opinion. Five of the nine sitting Justices did not sign this opinion, either by disqualification or dissent. Second, assuming that the various issues remanded by Justice Blackmun are resolved in favor of the plaintiffs, the defendants may be held liable for damages to all members of a class of plaintiffs who traded in Basic stock over a relatively long period. Depending on the number of members of the class and how damages are computed, the monetary liability of the defendants may be very substantial. May the defendants who are directors take advantage of Del.Gen.Corp.Law § 102(b)(7)? Two of the three false statements denying that merger negotiations were taking place were made by press releases. The third was made in a public statement by Max Muller, the President of Basic Incorporated, which appeared as a news item in the Cleveland Plain Dealer. No officer or director of Basic was accused of actually trading in Basic stock or otherwise personally benefiting from the violations. In both *Chiarella* and *Dirks,* discussed earlier in this chapter, the Supreme Court went out of its way to emphasize that there must be a breach of a fiduciary duty in order for there to be a violation of Rule 10b–5. Where was the breach of fiduciary duty in *Basic?* For a discussion of this issue, see Jonathan Macey and Geoffrey Miller, Good Finance, Bad Economics: An Analysis of the Fraud on the Market Theory, 42 Stan. L. Rev. 1059 (1990).

(2) A controversial aspect of *Basic* is Justice White's stinging criticism of the "fraud on the market" thesis. For a strong defense of the "fraud on the market" thesis, see Daniel R. Fischel, Use of Modern Finance Theory in Securities Fraud Cases Involving Actively Traded Securities, 38 Bus.Law. 1 (1982). Professors Carney and Fischel are both strongly identified with the "Chicago school" of law and economics. On the other hand, some post-*Basic* legal literature expresses serious reservations about the broad validity of the efficient capital market hypothesis and the desirability of the fraud on the market doctrine. See Donald C. Langevoort, Theories, Assumptions, and Securities Regulation: Market Efficiency Revisited, 140 U. Pa. L.Rev. 851, 853–54 (1992) ("In the 1980s, using more sophisticated data sets and computer technology, a number of economists began to question the accuracy of the tests that were thought to validate the efficiency model. * * * [T]he idea of strong capital market efficiency [is now] a legitimately debatable issue"); Carol Goforth, The Efficient Capital Market Hypothesis—An Inadequate Justification for the Fraud–on–the–Market Presumption, 27 Wake Forest L.Rev. 895, 897 (1992) ("While substantial empirical data supports certain

aspects of the ECMH, much of the data is anomalous, and numerous aspects of the theory have not been researched adequately'').

(3) Liability may be avoided, of course, if the defendants can establish that the misrepresented or undisclosed information was not material. The information in *Basic* dealt with merger negotiations; is there any chance at all of the defendants establishing lack of materiality of such an important development? Consider the comments of Judge Easterbrook in Flamm v. Eberstadt, 814 F.2d 1169, 1174 (7th Cir.1987):

> From one perspective this conclusion [that merger negotiations were not material] is simply another cause for wonderment at the legal mind. Investors were looking at potential prices from $11.75 (if Microdot had defeated all bids) to $17 (if General Cable's bid had succeeded) to $21 (under Northwest's bid), and maybe more if a better bid were available. This is almost a 100% range. Only an addlepated investor would consider a 100% difference in price unimportant in deciding what to do.

Does this reasoning make all preliminary merger inquiries at attractive prices material? What about extremely preliminary or tentative inquiries? Might premature disclosure "chill" other possible bidders? Or might it attract competing offers? To handle these types of problems, Justice Blackmun substitutes a "fact-specific" inquiry into the significance the reasonable investor would place on the withheld or misrepresented information for the more mechanical "agreement in principle" test adopted by the lower court. Can you see any practical problems with the test applied by Justice Blackmun? Assume you are the general counsel of a corporation that receives a "feeler" from a third party; what do you have the corporation say and when should it say it? For a more detailed explication of this problem see, Dennis J. Karjala, A Coherent Approach to Misleading Corporate Announcements, Fraud, and Rule 10b–5, 52 Alb. L.Rev. 957, 977 (1988).

Given these problems, is not the only sensible approach to say "no comment" in response to all inquiries? And, thus, is not the practical consequence of Justice Blackmun's opinion to choke off rather than improve the flow of information into the market?

(4) Rule 10b–5 is described in the leading Supreme Court decisions of the 1970s as being an "antifraud" provision. See, for example, Ernst & Ernst v. Hochfelder, p. 820 supra. Though, Justice Blackmun emphasizes the "fundamental purpose" of the securities acts as "full disclosure" of material facts. "Antifraud" and "full disclosure" are related but distinguishable concepts. See, for example, Roeder v. Alpha Indus., Inc., 814 F.2d 22 (1st Cir.1987) (fact that corporation and its managers would probably be indicted for paying a bribe was "material" information for investors but failure to disclose that information was not actionable under rule 10b–5 since that rule is an antifraud provision and there is no duty to disclose material information in absence of inaccurate, incomplete, or misleading prior disclosures). The language of Rule 10b–5(b) that refers to an omission "to state a material fact necessary in order to make the statements made, in the light of the circumstances under which they were made, not misleading" has been construed to require affirmative disclosure in only limited situations:

(a) Disclosure is required if undisclosed information renders previous public statements by the corporation misleading.

(b) Disclosure is required if the corporation has reason to believe that individuals are engaged in trading in the securities markets on the basis of the information that has not been disclosed.

(c) Disclosure is required if there are rumors swirling through the brokerage community that are generally (though incorrectly) being attributed to the issuer.

On the other hand, one should not make too much of the distinction between "antifraud" and "full disclosure." Registration under § 12 of the 1934 Act carries with it substantial affirmative disclosure obligations. A failure to disclose merger negotiations or other major developments may render statements in these disclosure documents misleading or, equally likely, the affirmative disclosure requirements will themselves require prompt disclosure. For a discussion of the limited obligation to make affirmative disclosures under rule 10b–5 see Symposium, Affirmative Disclosure Obligations under the Securities Laws, 46 Md.L.Rev. 907 (1987).

(5) Except to the extent required by the MD & A, disclosure of projections remains voluntary rather than mandatory,[95] and many issuers routinely do not make public their projections of future earnings or cash flow, though such information may be disclosed to securities analysts and others. In In re Lyondell Petrochemical Co. Sec. Litig., 984 F.2d 1050, 1052–53 (9th Cir.1993), the Court held that forward-looking statements that had been made to a lender did not have to be disclosed to the general public. See generally Harvey L. Pitt & Matt T. Morley, Through a Glass Starkly: A Practical Guide for Management's Forward–Looking Disclosures, Insights, Vol. 7, No. 6, at 3 (June 1993).

(6) New York Stock Exchange Listed Company Manual, §§ 202.03–202.06 has well-established disclosure policies for NYSE-listed companies:

202.03   Dealing With Rumors or Unusual Market Activity

The market activity of a company's securities should be closely watched at a time when consideration is being given to significant corporate matters. If rumors or unusual market activity indicate that information on impending developments has leaked out, a frank and explicit announcement is clearly required. If rumors are in fact false or inaccurate, they should be promptly denied or clarified. A statement to the effect that the company knows of no corporate developments to account for the unusual market activity can have a salutary effect. It is obvious that if such a public statement is contemplated, management should be checked prior to any public comment so as to avoid any embarrassment or potential criticism. If rumors are correct or there are developments, an immediate candid statement to the public as to the state of negotiations or of development of corporate plans in the rumored area must be made directly and openly. Such statements are essential despite the business inconvenience which may be caused and even though the matter may not as yet have been presented to the company's Board of Directors for consideration. * * *

202.04   Exchange Market Surveillance

---

95. [By the Editors] The question whether a failure to disclose projections constitutes a violation of SEC regulations has arisen in a significant number of cases and various courts of appeals have adopted quite different approaches. Before the SEC changed its policy to encourage projections, courts faced with this question uniformly answered this question in the negative; since then, however, several courts of appeals have found an obligation to disclose projections in specific circumstances. See, e.g., Flynn v. Bass Bros. Enter., Inc., 744 F.2d 978 (3d Cir.1984). Other courts have disagreed, though under different circumstances.

The Exchange maintains a continuous market surveillance program through its Market Surveillance and Evaluation Division. An "on-line" computer system has been developed which monitors the price movement of every listed stock—on a trade-to-trade basis—throughout the trading session. * * * If the price movement of a stock exceeds a predetermined guideline, it is immediately "flagged" and review of the situation is immediately undertaken to seek the causes of the exceptional activity. Under these circumstances, the company may be called by its Exchange representative to inquire about any company developments which have not been publicly announced but which could be responsible for unusual market activity. Where the market appears to reflect undisclosed information, the company will normally be requested to make the information public immediately. Occasionally it may be necessary to carry out a review of the trading after the fact, and the Exchange may request such information from the company as may be necessary to complete the inquiry.

The Listing Agreement provides that a company must furnish the Exchange with such information concerning the company as the Exchange may reasonably require. * * *

202.05   Timely Disclosure of Material News Developments

A listed company is expected to release quickly to the public any news or information which might reasonably be expected to materially affect the market for its securities. This is one of the most important and fundamental purposes of the listing agreement which the company enters into with the Exchange.

A listed company should also act promptly to dispel unfounded rumors which result in unusual market activity or price variations.

202.06   Procedure for Public Release of Information

(A) Immediate Release Policy

The normal method of publication of important corporate data is by means of a press release. This may be either by telephone or in written form. Any release of information that could reasonably be expected to have an impact on the market for a company's securities should be given to the wire services and the press *"For Immediate Release."* * * *

It should be a company's primary concern to assure that news will be handled in proper perspective. This necessitates appropriate restraint, good judgment, and careful adherence to the facts. Any projections of financial data, for instance, should be soundly based, appropriately qualified, conservative, and factual. Excessive or misleading conservatism should be avoided. Likewise, the repetitive release of essentially the same information is to be avoided. * * *

(B) Telephone Alert to the Exchange

When the announcement of news of a material event or a statement dealing with a rumor which calls for immediate release is made shortly before the opening or during market hours (presently 9:30 A.M. to 5:00 P.M., New York time), it is recommended that the company's Exchange representative be notified by telephone at least ten minutes prior to release of the announcement to the news media. If the Exchange receives such notification in time, it will be in a position to consider whether, in the opinion of the Exchange, trading in the security should be temporarily halted. A delay in trading after

934 **TRANSACTIONS IN SHARES** Ch. 13

the appearance of the news on the Dow Jones, Reuters or Bloomberg news wires provides a period of calm for public evaluation of the announcement. * * * A longer delay in trading may be necessary if there is an unusual influx of orders. The Exchange attempts to keep such interruptions in the continuous auction market to a minimum. However, where events transpire during market hours, the overall importance of fairness to all those participating in the market demands that these procedures be followed.

(C) Release to Newspapers and News Wire Services

News which ought to be the subject of immediate publicity must be released by the fastest available means. The fastest available means may vary in individual cases and according to the time of day. Ordinarily, this requires a release to the public press by telephone, telegraph, or hand delivery, or some combination of such methods. Transmittal of such a release to the press solely by mail is not considered satisfactory. Similarly, release of such news exclusively to local press would not be sufficient for adequate and prompt disclosure to the investing public.

To insure adequate coverage, releases requiring immediate publicity should be given to Dow Jones & Company, Inc., Reuters Economic Services, and Bloomberg Business News.

Companies are also encouraged to promptly distribute their releases to Associated Press and United Press International as well as to newspapers in New York City and in cities where the company is headquartered or has plants or other major facilities. * * *

In 1970, the SEC issued a general release entitled "Timely Disclosure of Material Corporate Developments," SEC Rel. No. 8995, 35 Fed.Reg. 16733 (Oct. 15, 1970), to much the same effect.

(7) Consider the "truth on the market" defense in securities fraud claims. A securities action based on the "fraud on the market" theory contends that the defendant made material misrepresentations which distorted the free flow of information to which every investor is entitled. In a "truth on the market" defense, the defendant argues misrepresentations are immaterial if they are already widely known to the public. Therefore, even if the defendant did make misrepresentations they are not actionable if such misrepresentations are counterbalanced by public information. For a good illustration of the "truth on the market" defense see, White v. H & R Block, Inc., 2004 WL 1698628 (S.D.N.Y. July 28, 2004).

D. LIABILITY FOR SECURITIES FRAUD: STATUTORY REGULATION

As a result of the *Basic* decision, the number of class action lawsuits alleging securities fraud increased in the federal courts (though other factors, including the development of law firms specializing in plaintiff securities fraud litigation, undoubtedly also contributed to this increase). Much of this new-breed litigation was viewed as the product of entrepreneurial lawyers brought primarily for their own personal benefit. The result was the enactment of the Private Securities Litigation Reform Act of 1995, Pub.Law 104–67, 109 Stat. 737,[96] probably the most significant securities-related legislation

---

96. [By the Editors] Legislation dealing with securities fraud cases was part of the Republican "Contract with America." President Clinton vetoed this legislation but his veto was promptly overridden by Congress.

since the original enactment of the classic statutes in the early 1930s. This Act is referred to as "PSLRA" or the "Reform Act" in the subsequent materials. Unanticipated consequences of PSLRA in turn led to enactment of the Securities Litigation Uniform Standards Act, Pub.L. 105–353, 112 Stat. 3227 (1998), referred to here as "SLUSA" or the "Standards Act."

RICHARD M. PHILLIPS AND GILBERT C. MILLER, THE PRIVATE SECURITIES LITIGATION REFORM ACT OF 1995: REBALANCING LITIGATION RISKS AND REWARDS FOR CLASS ACTION PLAINTIFFS, DEFENDANTS AND LAWYERS[97]

51 Bus. Law. 1009, 1009–15 (1996).

The Reform Act came into being because sizeable bipartisan majorities of both houses of Congress became persuaded that the private securities litigation system was seriously out of balance. A properly balanced system would give appropriate weight to two competing interests: the interest in deterring securities fraud and remedying it when it occurs, and the interest in assuring that the litigation process is not used for abusive purposes and does not unfairly target defendants who are guilty of no wrongdoing.

The evidence presented in many months of congressional hearings strongly suggested that the second of these interests was not receiving adequate protection. The principal culprit was identified as the speculative securities class action lawsuit—a strike suit initiated not because plaintiffs or their class action lawyers had any persuasive evidence of fraudulent conduct on the part of the defendants but primarily as an *in terrorem* device for extracting settlements from the defendants irrespective of the merits of the underlying claims. * * * [U]nwarranted settlements could be extracted because plaintiffs and their counsel, at relatively little cost and risk to themselves, were able to impose enormous discovery costs and the risks of astronomical damage awards on defendants.

Securities class action complaints are almost invariably predicated on the antifraud provisions of section 10(b) of the Exchange Act and Rule 10b–5 thereunder * * *. Most securities complaints are filed in federal court because, if Exchange Act claims are involved, federal courts have exclusive jurisdiction. The defendants in these suits almost always include some combination of the issuer, officers and directors (including outside directors) of the issuer, underwriters (if the case involves a public offering), and independent accountants (if the issuer's financials are claimed to be fraudulent).

Securities class action claims often are instituted after there has been a sudden, large decline in the price of a company's stock following a disappointing earnings announcement or other negative news about the company's operations. The typical fraud complaint alleges that the defendant company's public disclosures have been overly optimistic in light of negative information that management knew or was reckless in not knowing. Relying on the fraud-

97. [By the Editors] Many footnotes in this excerpt have been omitted.

on-the-market theory that false or misleading public statements artificially inflate market prices, the suits allege that if the company had revealed the information sooner, the stock price would have been lower and all persons purchasing during the period that the negative news was not disclosed would have paid less. The claimed damages can be astronomical because millions of shares may have changed hands during the time the allegedly false information was influencing the price. Even if each share only loses a small amount of its value, the total loss for all affected shares can be immense.

The class action mechanism makes it feasible for a broad group of investors who have small individual claims to maintain an action for damages. Because of the limited stakes that most investors have in such class action suits, however, they have tended to be sponsored and controlled not by aggrieved investors, but by a relatively small number of entrepreneurial law firms that specialize in this field. These firms typically do not have traditional client relationships with the named plaintiffs.[98] Prior to the Reform Act, these named plaintiffs often were called "professional plaintiffs," individuals who lent their names to the actions simply to accommodate plaintiffs' counsel and, in some cases, receive bonuses for their limited efforts. * * *

Because the lawyers who filed the first complaint often controlled the class litigation from the plaintiffs' side, there developed a "race to the courthouse" mentality that discouraged the plaintiffs' counsel from conducting reasonable factual investigations before initiating a class suit. Complaints frequently were filed within days or even hours of a stock price drop precipitated by an unexpected earnings decline or other negative news about the company's operations.[99] * * *

A high percentage of securities class action lawsuits have involved high-tech or other growth-oriented companies. * * * Such companies have been natural targets for class action securities suits because of the volatility of their stock prices. * * *

In the course of the Reform Act hearings, Congress became persuaded that speculative securities class action suits served to discredit the credibility of the private securities litigation system and operated to the general detriment of investors, corporations and the economy as a whole. * * *

Expert witnesses testified that the shareholders themselves, on whose behalves the suits ostensibly were instituted, were often indirect victims of class action litigation. Even if included within the class, shareholders generally recovered only a small fraction of their losses from the settlement process. Moreover, if they still held shares of the defendant companies, the value of their shares were diminished by the losses the companies suffered, directly and indirectly, as a consequence of the litigation. Congress came to understand that the only "winners" of these speculative lawsuits were the class action lawyers themselves whom Congress perceived to be richly rewarded,

---

98. [By the Author] One plaintiffs' class action lawyer rather famously observed: "I have the greatest practice * * * in the world. * * * I have no clients." William P. Barret, I have No Clients." Forbes, Oct. 11, 1993, at 32.

99. [By the Author] Evidence adduced at the Senate hearings indicated that more than one in five actions was filed within 48 hours of negative news. * * * Melvyn Weiss, a noted

securities litigator who frequently represents plaintiffs in securities class actions, provided information that, over a period three years, out of 229 Rule 10b–5 actions filed by his firm, 157 were filed within 10 days of a major adverse disclosure to the market by the defendant corporation.

without commensurate risk, for their efforts at the expense of other participants in the system. * * *

Congress saw that speculative class action suits were able to thrive because talented and motivated class action lawyers were able to exploit the litigation system. Liberal notice pleading requirements under the Federal Rules made it relatively easy to frame fraud complaints with little if any supporting evidence. This was especially true in the case of forward-looking statements such as earnings projections that, by their very nature as prognostications, were prone to being erroneous. While Rule 9(b) of the Federal Rules requires fraud to be pled with particularity, it proved only partially successful in weeding out speculative class suits because many courts allowed the element of scienter to be pled generally, without any facts to support a charge that defendants knew or were reckless in not knowing that their statements were false or misleading. Moreover, many courts were generally reluctant to grant motions to dismiss unless complaints appeared frivolous on their face, in part, because Rule 12(b)(6) of the Federal Rules itself imposed rigorous standards for granting such motions and, in part, because the securities fraud allegations of the complaints normally turned on complex mixed issues of law and fact that were difficult to dispose of by pretrial motions.

Even before a court ruled on defendants' motions to dismiss, plaintiffs' counsel could begin blanketing defendants with discovery demands. Counsel knew, of course, that a major pressure point for defendants was the enormous costs and burdens that discovery entailed. Many courts, moreover, were unwilling to stay discovery even when a motion to dismiss was pending and the plaintiffs' case appeared weak. * * * Although courts had authority under Rule 11 of the Federal Rules [of Civil Procedure] to impose sanctions on counsel for instituting meritless class suits, they seldom did so, often to avoid creating additional contentious issues for resolution by an already overburdened federal judiciary.

From the perspective of plaintiffs' lawyers, there were no compelling reasons not to initiate speculative class action lawsuits. * * * The downside risks were small compared to the potential rewards because once the suits were filed, and motions to dismiss had been averted, settlements almost always could be achieved that compensated plaintiffs' lawyers handsomely quite irrespective of any lack of merit in the underlying claims.

By contrast, from the perspective of defendants, the legal terrain appeared much less hospitable. Defendant issuers realized that they could be exposed to huge damage claims regardless of the lack of evidence to support a complaint's allegations of fraud. * * *

Individual defendants in class action suits were particularly risk averse and prone to settle. For them, going to trial, even with a strong defense, ran the risk, however slight, of a personally ruinous damage award. This risk was greatly exacerbated by the rule of joint and several liability. * * * [A] defendant who had only peripheral responsibility for an allegedly fraudulent misstatement or omission, and who had no intent to commit a knowing fraud, could be forced to pay 100 percent of the class action damages. Insurance coverage available in settlements could be jeopardized if a defendant went to trial and lost on the merits. Moreover, the securities laws have been construed to prohibit defendants from enforcing indemnity contracts after an adjudication of fraud under Rule 10b–5.[100] Thus, in order to preserve the ability to use insurance or indemnity agreements to defray all or part of their losses, individual defendants were strongly disposed to settle with no admission of liability rather than run any risk of losing at trial.

Note

While the battle in Congress was pending, Professor Joseph A. Grundfest, an SEC commissioner from 1985 to 1990, proposed that the SEC "disimply" some aspects of the implied cause of action created under Rule 10b–5. Joseph A. Grundfest, Disimplying Private Rights of Action Under the Federal Securities Laws: The Commissions's Authority, 107 Harv.L.Rev. 963 (1994). Professor Joel Seligman, The Merits Do Matter, 108 Harv.L.Rev. 438 (1994) responded that there was "insufficient evidence to justify significant rule or legislative changes that would further burden private securities litigation." 108 Harv.L.Rev., at 439. Professor Grundfest responded in "Why Disimply," 108 Harv.L.Rev. 727 (1994), pointing out that the SEC had issued a concept release, Safe Harbor for Forward–Looking Statements, Exchange Act Rel. No. 33–7107 (Oct. 13, 1994). Any possibility of administrative reform of securities litigation rules disappeared as Congress proceeded to enact the PSLRA over President Clinton's veto.

EDWARD A. FALLONE, SECTION 10(b) AND THE VAGARIES OF FEDERAL COMMON LAW: THE MERITS OF CODIFYING THE PRIVATE CAUSE OF ACTION UNDER A STRUCTURALIST APPROACH[101]

1997 U.Ill.L.Rev.71, 81–88 (1997).[102]

The [Private Securities Litigation Reform] Act, as originally drafted, was intended to revolutionize the manner in which private actions are brought under Rule 10b–5. Early drafts of the legislation contained many procedural reforms, some of them novel in character, intended to discourage the filing of meritless claims. * * *

However, the final legislation, as it developed in congressional subcommittees and eventually in conference committee, largely confines itself to procedural reforms and avoids questions relating to the definition of fraudulent conduct. As it relates to the Securities Exchange Act, the law contains eight general reforms to private litigation.[103] Few of the reforms relate in any meaningful way to the actual scope of liability to be imposed under Rule 10b–5.

---

100. [By the Editors] See the excerpt from Monteleone & McCarrick in Chapter 14, p. 964 infra.

101. [By the Editors] Many footnotes in this excerpt have been omitted.

102. Reprinted with permission of the University of Illinois Law Review. Copyright held by The Board of Trustees of the University of Illinois.

103. [By the Author] The following discussion is limited to those aspects of the new law that directly affect securities fraud actions under the Securities Exchange Act. The Private Securities Litigation Reform Act also modifies the Securities Act of 1933 in several similar respects and contains an important modification to the Racketeer Influenced and Corrupt Organizations Act (RICO).

1. CLASS ACTION PROCEDURES

The Act contains procedural provisions designed to reduce the ability of the plaintiffs' bar to serve as the instigator of class action filings and to diminish the likelihood that owners of a small economic stake in the defendant corporation will become the class representative in a suit brought under Rule 10b–5. In furtherance of this goal, the Act requires all plaintiffs seeking to serve as representatives in class actions under the Securities Exchange Act to file sworn certifications stating, among other things, that they have reviewed the complaints, that they did not purchase stock at the direction of counsel in order to qualify as class representatives, and that they will not accept any payment for serving as class representatives.[104] The Act also contains new procedures for the appointment of lead plaintiff in a securities class action and requires courts to presume that the plaintiff with the "largest financial stake in the relief sought" is the most appropriate lead plaintiff.[105] In addition, Section 21D(a)(3) of the Act also provides that the lead plaintiff appointed under these procedures will be responsible for selecting and retaining lead counsel, and it contains provisions limiting the capacity of any person to serve as a lead plaintiff more than five times over any three-year period. All of these provisions serve to enhance the independence of the lead plaintiff from the attorney for the class.

The class action attorney's influence and control over the course of the litigation is further diminished by provisions in the Act that limit the lead plaintiff's recovery to a pro rata share of the final judgment, thereby reducing the prospect of the lead plaintiff being co-opted by class counsel. A provision that bars the filing of settlements under seal without "good cause" operates to discourage self-serving settlements on the part of counsel.[106] All proposed and final settlements now must be disseminated to the members of the class in a new format designed to include all of the information deemed necessary to permit the class to evaluate the settlement. In addition, the lead attorney's fees are capped at a "reasonable percentage" of the amount of damages and interest actually paid to the class, thus tying the attorney's compensation more closely to the interests of the class.

2. DELAY OF FACT DISCOVERY

The Act contains provisions designed to delay the onset of litigation costs associated with fact discovery until after the defendant has had the opportunity to bring a motion to dismiss. * * *

104. [By the Author] * * * For ease of reference, this article will use the citation "Securities Exchange Act § ___" to denote the Securities Exchange Act as amended by the Private Securities Litigation Reform Act of 1995

105. [By the Author] Securities Exchange Act § 21D(a)(3). See generally Joseph A. Grundfest & Michael A. Perino, The Pentium Papers: A Case Study of Collective Institutional Investor Activism in Litigation, 38 Ariz. L. Rev. 559 (1996). In July 1996, the State of Wisconsin Investment Board asserted its rights

as a class action member under this provision and successfully filed a motion seeking to replace class counsel with counsel of its own choosing. See Dean Starkman, Fund Displaces Law Firm to Lead CellStar Lawsuit, Wall St. J., Oct. 2, 1996, at B9. The Wisconsin Investment Board is among the largest institutional investors to date to utilize this new statutory provision. See Keith Johnson, Deployment of Institutions in the Securities Class Action Wars, 38 Ariz. L. Rev. 627, 631 (1996).

106. [By the Author] See id. § 21D(a)(5).

3. Imposition of Proportionate Liability

The Act alters the present system of joint and several liability in order to limit the circumstances under which one defendant is required to pay for injuries caused by the conduct of another defendant. A new system of "fair share" proportionate liability is instituted whereby, under certain circumstances, a particular defendant may be held liable solely for the portion of the judgment for which he is adjudged responsible. * * *

4. Strengthening Rule 11

The Act strengthens the application of Rule 11 of the Federal Rules of Civil Procedure to private securities actions in order to better deter frivolous filings.[107] The law now requires the court, upon final adjudication of the action, to enter findings in the record concerning each attorney's compliance with his or her obligations under Rule 11 in connection with the lawsuit.[108] * * *

5. Heightened Pleading Requirements

The Act heightens the pleading standards necessary in any complaint under the Securities Exchange Act that requires an allegation of the defendant's state of mind. The goal of the Act is to "establish uniform and more stringent pleading requirements to curtail the filing of meritless lawsuits."[109] Wherever liability is dependent upon the defendant having acted with a particular state of mind, the complaint must contain particularized facts that give rise to a "strong inference" that the defendant possessed the requisite scienter.[110] * * *

6. New Measure of Damages

The Act introduces a new method for calculating damages once liability has been ascertained in a case alleging securities fraud. * * * Congress feared that the use of the market price in calculating damages often leads to an overestimation of the plaintiff's damages, due to the possibility that the price at the time of disclosure resulted from market conditions unconnected to the fraud. Therefore, the Act contains provisions that no damage award based on the market price of a security may exceed the difference between the purchase (or sale) price of the security and the mean trading price at which the security traded within the ninety-day period immediately following the disclosure of corrective information.[111]

7. New Statutory Duties for Auditors

The Act imposes explicit new duties on corporate auditors to identify and report suspected illegal conduct. These duties include obligations to investigate possible illegalities that come to the attention of the auditor during its engagement, obligations to report instances of illegal conduct to the appropriate level of management and to the board of directors, and obligations, under

107. [By the Author] See H.R. Conf. Rep. No. 104–369, at 738; see, e.g., Katz v. Household Int'l, Inc., 91 F.3d 1036 (7th Cir.1996).

108. [By the Author] See Securities Exchange Act § 21D(c).

109. [By the Author] H.R. Conf. Rep. No. 104–369, at 740.

110. [By the Author] Securities Exchange Act § 21D(b)(2).

111. [By the Author] See Securities Exchange Act, § 21D(e).

certain circumstances, to report instances of illegal conduct to the Securities and Exchange Commission.

8. New Safe Harbor for Forward–Looking Information * * * [Editor] This material is described at pp. 600–601, supra.

D. WHAT THE REFORM ACT DOES NOT DO

The Act is actually change on a modest scale.[112] Its most significant reforms are reforms of the procedural limitations placed on the class action plaintiff and her attorney in a securities fraud lawsuit. The primary goals of the legislation are transparent: to allow more claims to be dismissed at the pleading stage, to place greater control over litigation in the hands of large shareholder plaintiffs (as opposed to the owners of single shares and their "strike suit" lawyers), and to enact penalties for filing a lawsuit without an adequate factual investigation of the asserted claims. * * *

Despite the passage of the Act, it is readily apparent that most of the preexisting judge-made law concerning the scope of the Rule 10b–5 cause of action remains untouched. The Act does touch upon the scope of liability in the following ways: (1) the previously recognized existence of loss causation as a separate element of the plaintiff's case is reaffirmed; (2) the measure of damages and the application of proportionate liability are modified for certain cases; and (3) one change to existing standards of liability is effectuated through the creation of a safe harbor for forward-looking statements.

The Act purposefully avoids defining the state of mind required for imposition of liability for securities fraud. It leaves for another day the issues raised by the "fraud on the market" theory. The sole meaningful change to the scope of conduct giving rise to liability is the creation of a new safe harbor of limited availability, which may act to foreclose liability under some circumstances where the judicially created "bespeaks caution" doctrine does not.[113]

By failing to do little more than fiddle with the elements of the cause of action as currently defined, the Act avoids the fundamental question underlying recent Supreme Court jurisprudence in this area: What types of conduct should give rise to a private cause of action under Section 10(b) and Rule 10b–5? Although the new legislation will make it more difficult for certain types of "professional plaintiffs" and their attorneys to assert claims, it will have little effect on the ability of plaintiffs in general to recover under a law whose boundaries are currently uncertain.[114] Even after Congress's recent effort to reassert itself in the arena of securities fraud, the primary expositor of the scope of conduct that constitutes a violation of Section 10(b) remains the federal judiciary. It is therefore appropriate to review the history of the judiciary's interpretation of the private cause of action.

---

112. [By the Author] In the wake of the Reform Act's passage, one attorney observer has noted that new securities fraud filings in federal court have not slowed significantly and "to a large extent, it's business as usual." Phyllis Diamond, California Initiative Could Undermine Reform Legislation, Lawyers Warn, 28 Sec. Reg. & Law Rep. (BNA) 971, 972 (Aug. 9, 1996); see also Dean Starkman, Securities Class–Action Suits Seem Immune to Effects of a New Law, Wall St. J., Nov. 12, 1996, at B7.

But see Stephen F. Black et al., The Private Securities Litigation Reform Act of 1995: A Preliminary Analysis, 24 Sec. Reg. L.J. 117, 141 (1996) ("The Reform Act is an ambitious effort to curb the costs and burdens imposed by private federal securities litigation on issuers and others.").

113. [Footnote omitted]

114. [Footnote omitted]

Notes

(1) Valuable information about the impact of PSLRA on actual litigation, some of which is contained in these notes, is available from the Stanford Securities Class Action Clearinghouse website (http://securities.stanford.edu).

(2) The effects of PSLRA can be best described as an example of the law of unintended consequences in action. As Professor Joe Grundfest observed, "the data indicate that there has been no material decrease in the volume of litigation activity since passage of the Private Securities Litigation Reform Act of 1995. Plaintiffs continue to have powerful economic incentives to sue companies for large sums of money. Whether these claims have merit is an entirely different issue." March 15, 2002, Press Release, Stanford Law School Securities Class Action Clearinghouse. And while the total number of federal securities class actions has decreased since the peak of 327 filings in 2001, the average number of annual filings is still above pre-PSLRA levels. In 2004, 212 federal securities class actions were filed.

(3) By far the most dramatic (and unexpected) consequence of the enactment of PSLRA was an increase in the number of securities fraud class action suits filed in state courts. Before PSLRA, relatively few of these class action suits were brought in state court; however, from January 1, 1996 through June 30, 1997, 92 companies were sued in state court.[115] Of this number, 54 were sued only in state court while 38 were sued simultaneously in both federal and state courts. The written testimony of Michael A. Perino, before the Subcommittee on Securities of the Committee on Banking, Housing, and Urban Affairs, United States Senate, July 24, 1997 (posted on the Stanford website) comments on this development:

> The level of class action securities fraud litigation declined by about a third in federal courts, but there has been an almost equal increase in the level of state court activity, largely as a result of a "substitution effect" whereby plaintiffs resort to state court to avoid the new, more stringent requirements of federal cases. There has also been an increase in parallel litigation between state and federal courts in an apparent effort to avoid the federal discovery stay or other provisions of the Act. This increase in state activity has the potential not only to undermine the intent of the Act, but to increase the overall cost of litigation to the extent that the Act encourages the filing of parallel claims.

THE SECURITIES LITIGATION UNIFORM STANDARDS ACT OF 1998: THE SUN SETS ON CALIFORNIA'S BLUE SKY LAWS

David M. Levine and Adam C. Pritchard.
54 Bus. Law. 1, 2 (1998).

It is often said that California sets the pace for changes in America's tastes. * * * The most recent trend to emerge from California, instead of catching on in the rest of the country, has been stopped dead in its tracks by a legislative rebuke from Washington, D.C. California's latest, albeit short-lived, contribution to the nation was a migration of securities fraud class actions from federal to state court.

This migration had its origin in Washington, D.C., not Los Angeles. Less than three years ago, Congress passed the Private Securities Litigation

---

115. [By the Editors] Since federal jurisdiction over Rule 10b–5 cases is exclusive, these cases have been brought under state blue sky or anti-fraud statutes.

Reform Act of 1995 * * *. The corporate lobby and professionals who serve corporations persuaded Congress that companies and their managers were being harassed by class action lawyers more concerned with a case's settlement value (and potential attorneys' fees) than its merits. In response to that perceived abuse, Congress enacted the Reform Act, a series of primarily procedural measures making it more difficult to bring securities fraud class actions.

Three years after its passage, the Act has greatly altered the course of securities litigation; however, its effect on capital formation and investor protection remains uncertain. * * * Class action lawyers sought to avoid the restrictions imposed by the Reform Act by resorting to state law actions brought in state court. The majority of the state class actions filed since passage of the Reform Act have been filed in California. * * *[116]

The rise of state court class actions led California-based issuers, particularly high-technology companies located in Silicon Valley, to Washington seeking further legislation restricting such suits. Shifting securities fraud litigation to state court, they argued, would undermine the effectiveness of the Reform Act. Congress once again responded by * * * passing the Securities Litigation Uniform Standards Act of 1998, which preempts most securities fraud class actions brought in state court. The President signed the Uniform Standards Act into law on November 3, 1998.

* * * The most problematic aspect of the migration has been the filing of parallel lawsuits, one at the state level and a second at the federal level. Discovery obtained in the state case may then be used in the federal case where it would otherwise be unavailable due to the federal discovery stay. * * * These parallel lawsuits are difficult to justify: they create wasteful duplication and undermine Congress' purposes in enacting the discovery stay. * * * [A] number of issuers reported that defending on two fronts has made securities litigation more expensive than ever. * * * A second problem raised by the migration to state court involves the Reform Act's safe harbor for forward-looking statements. Issuers have complained that they cannot take full advantage of the safe harbor provided by the Reform Act because they remain exposed to liability in state court. * * *

[SLUSA preempts only "covered class actions." SLUSA defines the term "covered class action"] * * * as follows:

(i) any single lawsuit in which (I) damages are sought on behalf of more than 50 persons or prospective class members, and questions of law or fact common to those persons or members of the prospective class, without reference to issues of individualized reliance on an alleged misstatement or omission, predominate over any questions affecting only individual persons or members; or (II) one or more named parties seek to recover damages on a representative basis on behalf of themselves and other unnamed parties similarly situated, and questions of law or fact common to those persons or members of the prospective class predomi-

---

116. [By the Editors] The authors assess the impact of this shift as follows: "[We] conclude that claims regarding the magnitude of migration to state court were overblown, but that parallel state and federal cases were a serious problem for corporate issuers forced to defend such dual-track litigation and that state liability concerns threatened to undermine the Reform Act's safe harbor for forward-looking statements." Id., at 1.

nate over any questions affecting only individual persons or members; or (ii) any group of lawsuits filed in or pending in the same court and involving common questions of law or fact, in which—(I) damages are sought on behalf of more than 50 persons; and (II) the lawsuits are joined, consolidated, or otherwise proceed as a single action for any purpose. [Securities Act § 16(f)(2)(A), codified as 15 U.S. § 77p(f)(2)(A)]

* * * The preemption of the Uniform Standards Act is limited in another important way—it reaches only "covered securities" * * *: Securities "listed, or authorized for listing, on the [NYSE], or the [AMEX], or listed on the [NASDAQ]" or "a security of the same issuer that is equal in seniority or that is a senior security" of the same issuer who has a security listed on the NYSE, AMEX or NASDAQ. * * * If the issuer has any securities listed on a national trading market, all of its securities equal or senior to that listed security are exempt from state anti-fraud class actions. This captures debt within the scope of preemption. For example, if a company has its stock listed for trading on the NYSE, its unlisted debt would also be exempt. Issuers whose securities are not listed on national markets, however—primarily micro-cap and penny stock issuers—remain subject to state actions. * * * In response to a criticism by Professor John Coffee that the covered security definition was potentially overbroad, the Uniform Standards Act also excludes debt securities issued in a private placement from the definition. Professor Coffee pointed out that these securities issuances are governed by private placement agreements containing numerous warranties and covenants, the breach of which gives rise to a contract claim. * * *

A related carve-out further limits the preemptive reach of the Uniform Standards Act. In response to another concern raised by Professor Coffee, the Uniform Standards Act excludes from its reach any class action "that seeks to enforce a contractual agreement between an issuer and an indenture trustee" if brought by "a party to the agreement or a successor to such party." Such claims sound more in contract than in fraud, even if misstatements are alleged, and state courts are the appropriate forum for these contractual claims.

The Delaware Carve–Out

Another change to the bills in response to concerns of the SEC and others was the so-called "Delaware carve-out."[117] The original bills would have had the unintended effect of preempting a substantial body of state corporate law. * * * The overall definition of class action was revised to explicitly exclude "an exclusively derivative action brought by 1 or more shareholders on behalf of a corporation."[118] Derivative actions, of course, are the primary enforcement vehicle available for most corporate law duties, traditionally the province of state courts.

Other corporate law duties, however, required a more carefully tailored carve-out. Under state corporate law, issuers and their officers and directors generally owe a duty of disclosure to their shareholders as one element of their fiduciary duties. That duty of disclosure requires the issuer and its managers to speak truthfully when soliciting action by shareholders. Even

---

117. [By the Editors] Securities Act § 16(d)(1), codified as 15 U.S.C. 78bb(f)(3)(C).

118. [By the Editors] Securities § 16(d)(1) codified at 15 USC § 77p(d)(1).

though the corporate law duty of disclosure significantly overlaps with the coverage of federal securities law, actions based on corporate duty of disclosure were not considered to be part of the problem that the Uniform Standards Act was intended to address. Claims based on the breach of this duty typically arise out of mergers, tender offers, and other extraordinary corporate transactions. These claims are either individual, rather than derivative, or both because they involve the voting rights of shareholders or other rights of the individual, even though they may have an effect on the corporation as a whole. These claims are routinely litigated in state courts, most notably the Delaware * * * Chancery Court. The Chancery Court, with its steady diet of corporate claims, has developed expertise in this area that the federal courts are unlikely to match. In addition, the Delaware courts can resolve these claims within days rather than months, an important consideration if a merger is pending.

In order to preserve these advantages of state law, a provision was drafted by an ad hoc committee led by then—SEC General Counsel Richard H. Walker and consisting of certain members of the American Bar Association's Task Force on Securities Reform and the Delaware bar, as well as academics and SEC staff. This effort had widespread support, including that of corporate issuers, who were interested in maintaining the predictability offered by Delaware corporate law. The preliminary approach taken was to limit the scope of preemption to transactions effected over national markets. This approach would have excluded mergers, stock buybacks, and tender offers, as these transactions are typically completed through the force of state law or an escrow agent. Such an approach also would have excluded most public offerings, however, which proponents deemed essential to preemption. Accordingly, a carve-out from the general scope of preemption was adopted instead. The carve-out contains two prongs. Subsection (A) preserves state jurisdiction for breach of fiduciary duty claims arising from transactions taking place between the issuer and its security holders. These include: (i) repurchases of securities by the issuer from its security holders, i.e., "buybacks"; (ii) reorganizations, such as the exchange by the issuer of one class of securities for another; and (iii) offerings of additional securities solely to existing shareholders, i.e., "rights offerings." Subsection (B) preserves state jurisdiction for breach of fiduciary duty claims arising from an issuer's recommendation, position, or other communication concerning three other types of corporate transactions: (i) mergers and other corporate transactions requiring shareholder approval; (ii) tender offers; and (iii) situations where majority shareholders force minority shareholders to relinquish their shares, i.e., "freeze-outs." Both prongs extend to misstatements made by affiliates, so issuers cannot insulate themselves from liability by directing misleading disclosure through its parent, subsidiary, controlling shareholder, or an underwriter.

Both provisions are limited to actions "based upon the statutory or common law of the State in which the issuer is incorporated * * * or organized." This limitation gives the issuer control over its litigation exposure because of its ability to choose its state of incorporation. The Senate legislative history suggests plaintiffs are expected to file these cases in the defendant's state of incorporation and the Conference Committee Report repeats the suggestion. Limiting claims against Delaware corporations to the Chancery Court would help maintain the uniformity and predictability of Delaware corporate law. * * *

MDCM HOLDINGS, INC. v. CREDIT SUISSE FIRST BOSTON CORPORATION

United States District Court, S.D. New York, 2002.
216 F.Supp.2d 251.

Opinion and Order

Scheindlin, District Judge.

This is a class action brought against Credit Suisse First Boston Corporation ("Credit Suisse" or "CSFB") on behalf of internet-related and high technology companies that hired Credit Suisse to underwrite their initial public offering of stock ("IPO"). Plaintiffs' four causes of action are state law claims related to underwriting contracts that they entered into with Credit Suisse. Three of these claims assert that Credit Suisse breached the expressed terms of the contracts as well as the implied covenants and the fiduciary duties arising under those contracts.

Credit Suisse now moves to dismiss the Complaint in its entirety or in part. *See infra* Part III.C. For the reasons discussed below, this motion is denied. * * *

A. Allegations

Out of a desire to raise new capital, corporations often decide to sell ownership of the company to the public by issuing stock. The first step in this process requires a company to find an investment bank that will agree to underwrite its IPO. Agreements between the company issuing the stock ("issuer") and the investment bank underwriting the IPO ("underwriter") are executed in a contract commonly referred to as an underwriting agreement.

As with most contracts between sophisticated parties, representatives of the company and the investment bank discuss many topics before signing on the bottom line. The parties generally negotiate the amount of capital that the company seeks to raise, the type of security to be issued, the price and any special features of the security, and the underwriter's compensation. For example, the contract may "obligate the underwriter to acquire the IPO securities from the issuer at a [discounted] fixed price, and then resell the IPO securities to the public in accordance with the terms, and at a fixed offering price." (citation omitted). The difference between these two prices is typically 7% of the IPO proceeds. The investment bank's profit in selling the issuer's stock to the public is intended to serve as compensation for its services.

Mortgage.com, a company that specialized in providing online mortgage services, was one of the many internet-related and high technology companies that went public in the late 1990s. In July 1999, Mortgage.com's Board of Directors authorized the corporation to enter into an underwriting agreement with Credit Suisse, one of the nation's leading underwriters. On August 11, 1999, Mortgage.com and Credit Suisse executed the underwriting agreement. The same day, shares in Mortgage.com were issued to the public and began trading on the NASDAQ National Market under the ticker symbol "MDCM".

Pursuant to the underwriting agreement, Mortgage.com sold 7,062,500 shares of common stock to Credit Suisse for $7.44 per share, exactly 7% less than the public offering price of $8.00 per share. In addition, Credit Suisse exercised an option under the underwriting agreement and acquired 379,375 additional shares for the same price. *See id.* As a result, Mortgage.com's IPO generated gross proceeds of approximately $59.5 million. The compensation for Credit Suisse's service was $4,167,450.

Two weeks after the IPO, Mortgage.com's stock had almost doubled in value. Such an increase was not unusual during the late 1990s: Mortgage.com was one of many issuers whose shares dramatically increased in value after being issued to the public.

The complaint alleges that Credit Suisse used this phenomenon to enrich itself by requiring that customers who wanted to purchase IPO shares pay it the prospectus price plus, directly or indirectly, a share of profits that the customers realized.[119] Moreover, the Complaint asserts that Credit Suisse purposely under priced certain securities in order to guarantee that those shares would rise in value once issued to the public. From the issuers' perspective, there was "money left on the table" because of this under pricing. For example, if Mortgage.com's original offering price had been somewhere between the high and low price of August 26, 1999, the company would have realized additional gross proceeds of $54 million to $109 million.

B. MDCM's Class Action

On May 25, 2001, the corporation formerly known as Mortgage.com, now called MDCM Holdings, Inc. sued Credit Suisse on behalf of issuers that had used the investment bank to underwrite their IPOs from January 1, 1998, to October 31, 2000. The putative class is limited to companies whose securities increased in value 15% or more above their original offering price within 30 days following the IPO.[120]

Count I of the Complaint alleges that Credit Suisse breached the explicit terms of the underwriting agreements in two ways. *First*, Credit Suisse did not sell the IPO shares to the public as the contract requires, but instead directed shares to favored customers. *Second*, Credit Suisse did not sell the IPO shares for the price provided in the prospectus, but instead required purchasers to pay a higher price.[121]

* * *

119. [By the Court] "These payments frequently took the form of direct sharing in their clients' profits who quickly sold (or 'flipped') the particular IPO stock at issue to other investors in the aftermarket * * *." Am. Compl. ¶ 29. * * *

120. [By the Court] Like many other internet and high technology companies of the late 1990s, Mortgage.com was not successful and eventually ceased operations.

121. [By the Court] The contract between Credit Suisse and Mortgage.com states in pertinent part:

3. *Purchase, Sale and Delivery of Offered Securities.* On the basis of the representations, warranties and agreements herein contained, but subject to the terms and conditions herein set forth, the Company agrees to sell to the Underwriters, and the Underwriters agree, severally and not jointly, to purchase from the Company, at a purchase price of $7.44 per share, the respective numbers [sic] of shares of Firm Securities set forth opposite the names of the Underwriters in Schedule A hereto.

Count II alleges that Credit Suisse violated implied covenants of good faith and fair dealing that accompanied its performance of the underwriting agreements. Credit Suisse allegedly violated these covenants by under pricing the IPO shares so that it could allocate undervalued shares to favored clients and receive additional compensation. As a result, the issuers received deficient and overpriced underwriting services. *See id.*

Count III alleges that Credit Suisse owed fiduciary duties of loyalty, due care and fair dealing to the issuers. These duties arose because Credit Suisse was the underwriter of the IPOs and had superior knowledge and expertise, receipt of confidential information, and acted as an agent and advisor to the issuers. According to the Complaint, Credit Suisse violated those duties by allocating shares to favored customers and sharing in the profits made by those customers.

Count IV asserts a claim of unjust enrichment against Credit Suisse on the ground that the issuers conferred benefits upon Defendant in connection with their IPOs which, in the circumstances * * * would be inequitable for Defendant to retain. Count IV further alleges that the profit-sharing compensation from favored customers unjustly enriched Credit Suisse.

C. Credit Suisse's Motion to Dismiss

Credit Suisse argues that MDCM's complaint should be dismissed, in its entirety or in part, [because, *inter alia*], MDCM's state law claims are barred by the Securities Litigation Uniform Standards Act of 1998 ("SLUSA"), 15 U.S.C. §§ 77p, 78bb(f).

IV. SLUSA does not Bar This Class Action

A. Statutory Framework and Purpose

When Congress enacted the Private Securities Litigation Reform Act of 1995 ("PSLRA"), it sought to raise the bar for bringing class actions under the Securities Act of 1933 and Securities Exchange Act of 1934. Among other things, the PSLRA heightened pleading standards, generally required courts to stay discovery pending resolution of a motion to dismiss, and placed limits on recovery. *See* 15 U.S.C. § 77z–1 to–2 (Securities Act of 1933). In the aftermath of the PSLRA, plaintiffs increasingly filed securities class actions in state courts under state law theories of liability.

Congress responded in 1998 by enacting SLUSA, which aims to "prevent plaintiffs from seeking to evade the protections that Federal law provides against abusive litigation by filing suit in State court, rather than Federal court." H.R.Rep. No, 105–803 (1998). The purpose of SLUSA was to make federal court the exclusive venue, and federal law the exclusive remedy, for most securities class actions. SLUSA provides in pertinent part:

No covered class action based upon the statutory or common law of any State or subdivision thereof may be maintained in any State or Federal court by any party alleging—

(1) an untrue statement or omission of a material fact in connection with the purchase or sale of a covered security; or

(2) that the defendant used or employed any manipulative or deceptive device or contrivance in connection with the purchase or sale of a covered security. 15 U.S.C. § 77bb (f)(1).

SLUSA thus provides for federal preemption of any claim that meets four prerequisites. The lawsuit must be: (1) a "covered class action," (2) based on state law; (3) in which the plaintiff has alleged either a "misrepresentation or omission of a material fact" or "any manipulative or deceptive device or contrivance;" (4) "in connection with the purchase or sale of a covered security." Because plaintiffs do not allege the third element of SLUSA—misrepresentations or omissions—the statute does not preempt their class action.

B. MDCM's Complaint Does Not Allege Any Misrepresentations or Omissions

When determining whether SLUSA preempts a lawsuit, a court is directed to look at what the "private party" [is] alleging. MDCM only alleges * * * that Credit Suisse signed numerous contracts in which it promised to do one thing but then did another. "The failure to carry out a promise made in connection with a securities transaction is normally a breach of contract. It does not constitute fraud unless, when the promise was made, the defendant secretly intended not to perform or knew that he could not perform." MDCM has now alleged that Credit Suisse had such an intent and, to prevail on its breach of contract claims, MDCM need not offer any evidence about Credit Suisse's mental state. Under its current claims, it only needs to prove that Credit Suisse did not satisfy the requirements laid out in the underwriting agreements. Therefore, the contract claims do not involve allegations of misrepresentation or omissions by Credit Suisse.

Credit Suisse argues that "court[s] * * * have disregarded state law labels and dismissed [such] claims under SLUSA." (citation omitted). The cases relied on by Credit Suisse, however, involve plaintiffs who made *explicit* allegations of misrepresentation or material omission. In none of those cases was it necessary for the court to speculate about the defendant's intent at the time it signed a contract.

Here, it would be inappropriate to transform MDCM's contract claims into fraud claims because New York law would require dismissal of such claims. "Under New York law, a fraud claim is precluded where it relates to a breach of contract." *Trepel v. Abdoulaye*, 185 F.Supp.2d 308, 310 (S.D.N.Y. 2002) (applying New York law). "[A] simple breach of contract is not to be considered a tort unless a legal duty *independent* of the contract itself has been violated." With and dependent upon the contract. * * *

VI. Conclusion

For the reasons given above, Credit Suisse's motion to dismiss is denied. A conference is scheduled * * *.

Notes

(1) In Xpedior Creditor Trust v. Credit Suisse First Boston, 341 F. Supp. 2d 258 (S.D.N.Y.2004), the plaintiff class essentially made the same breach of

contract claims against CSFB as in MDCM v. Credit Suisse First Boston. CSFB tried to remove the class action to federal court arguing that the SLUSA preempted New York state law. According to the carve out exceptions in the SLUSA, normal contract claims are not preempted by federal law. But a mere pleading of breach of contract is not enough to keep a case out of federal court. Xpedior makes clear that a class action contract claim, brought under state law, cannot include substantial elements of fraud if it is to avoid preemption by the SLUSA. Judge Scheindlin, often citing the controlling case of Spielman v. Merrill Lynch, Pierce, Fenner & Smith, Inc., 332 F.3d 116 (2d Cir.2003), wrote:

> Thus, under the necessary component test, a complaint is preempted under SLUSA only when it asserts (1) an explicit claim of fraud (e.g., common law fraud or fraudulent inducement), or (2) other garden-variety state law claims that "sound in fraud."[122] But SLUSA does not preempt claims "which do not have as a necessary component misrepresentation[s], untrue statements, or omissions of material facts"[123] made in connection with the purchase or sale of a security.

Xpedior, 341 F.Supp.2d at 266.

CSFB's motion to remove the class action to federal court was denied because the plaintiff's complaint did not "sound in fraud" but was a normal breach of contract claim. Plaintiffs can no longer simply plead contract violations under state law to avoid preemption by the SLUSA under the "necessary component test."

(2) More federal preemption? The Class Action Fairness Act (CAFA) was signed into law on February 18, 2005. Unlike the PSLRA and the SLUSA, the CAFA affects all class actions. It will surely affect the procedural postures of both plaintiffs and defendants. The most interesting aspect of the CAFA is the grant of original jurisdiction to federal courts over all class actions which exceed five million dollars and where any of the defendants and plaintiffs are from different states. All class actions where less than one-third of the plaintiffs are from the same state will also stay in federal court. State courts automatically have jurisdiction only when more than two-thirds of a plaintiff class is from the state or if the class is less than one hundred. To complicate matters even more, there are provisions which exempt certain class actions:

> (1) a claim concerning a covered security as defined under section 16(f)(3) of the Securities Act of 1933 (15 U.S.C. 78p(f)(3)) and section 28(f)(5)(E) of the Securities Exchange Act of 1934 (15 U.S.C. 78bb(f)(5)(E)); (2) a claim that relates to the internal affairs or governance of a corporation or other form of business enterprise and arises under or by virtue of the laws of the State in which such corporation or business enterprise is incorporated or organized; or(3) a claim that relates to the rights, duties (including fiduciary duties), and obligations relating to or created by or pursuant to any security (as defined under section 2(a)(1) of the Securities Act of 1933 (15 U.S.C. 77b(a)(1)) and the regulations issued thereunder).

Class Action Fairness Act, Pub. L. No. 109–002, § 5(d) (2005).

Even though these exemptions may seem clear on paper they undoubtedly will be litigated by both the defense and plaintiff bars.

---

122. Rombach v. Chang, 355 F.3d 164 (2d Cir.2004)

123. McEachern v. Equitable Life Assur. Soc., 2001 WL 747320, at *2 (N.D.Ala.2001).

Chapter Fourteen

INDEMNIFICATION AND INSURANCE

A. A. Sommer, Jr., Review of Olson and Hatch, Director and Officer Liability: Indemnification and Insurance, 47 Bus. Law. 355, 355–56 (1991),[1] captures the importance of the principles discussed in this Chapter:

> Before the onset of * * * litigation, directors are usually unconcerned with the mundane details of the corporation's indemnification provisions, the limitations upon indemnification permitted under state law or the terms of the corporation's directors' and officers' liability policy ("lawyer stuff!", they say). Let the complaint be filed naming him (or her), and here this reviewer speaks from personal experience as a director, and then those matters assume consuming importance, for on them may depend the prosperity of the director's future and the comfort of his or her retirement years. At that point limits on the ability of the corporation to indemnify, or even to advance expenses (most important given the costs of litigation and the increasing insistence by lawyers upon ongoing payments), and the exclusionary clauses of the D & O policy are examined with all the attention and devotion, and parsed as carefully for every nuance, as were once youthful love letters.

MERRITT–CHAPMAN & SCOTT CORP. v. WOLFSON

Superior Court of Delaware, 1974.
321 A.2d 138.

BALICK, JUDGE.

These actions arise over claims of Louis Wolfson, Elkin Gerbert, Joseph Kosow and Marshal Staub (claimants) for indemnification by Merritt–Chapman & Scott Corporation (MCS) against expenses incurred in a criminal action. All parties seek summary judgment.

Claimants were charged by indictment with participation in a plan to cause MCS to secretly purchase hundreds of thousands of shares of its own common stock. Count one charged all claimants with conspiracy to violate federal securities laws. Count two charged Wolfson and count three charged Gerbert with perjury before the * * * SEC. Counts four and five charged

1. Copyright (1991) by the American Bar Association. All rights reserved. Reprinted with permission of the American Bar Association and its Section of Corporation, Banking and Business Law.

Wolfson, Gerbert, and Staub with filing false annual reports for 1962 and 1963 respectively with the SEC and New York Stock Exchange.

At the first trial the court dismissed part of the conspiracy count but the jury returned guilty verdicts on all charges against all claimants. At that stage this court held that Wolfson, Gerbert, and Kosow were not entitled to partial indemnification. Merritt–Chapman & Scott v. Wolfson, 264 A.2d 358 (Del.Super.1970). Thereafter the convictions were reversed. United States v. Wolfson, 437 F.2d 862 (2d Cir.1970).

There were two retrials of the perjury and filing false annual report charges against Wolfson and Gerbert. At the first retrial the court entered a judgment of acquittal on count four at the end of the State's case, and the jury could not agree on the other counts. At the second retrial the jury returned a guilty verdict on count three, but could not agree further.

The charges were then settled as follows: Wolfson entered a plea of *nolo contendere* to count five and the other charges against him were dropped. He was fined $10,000 and given a suspended sentence of eighteen months. Gerbert agreed not to appeal his conviction of count three, on which he was fined $2,000 and given a suspended sentence of eighteen months, and the other charges against him were dropped. The prosecution also dropped the charges against Kosow and Staub.

Indemnification of corporate agents involved in litigation is the subject of legislation in Delaware. Title 8 Delaware Code § 145. Subsection (a), which permits indemnification, and subsection (c), which requires indemnification, provide as follows:

> (a) A corporation may indemnify any person who was or is a party or is threatened to be made a party to any threatened, pending or completed action, suit or proceeding, whether civil, criminal, administrative or investigative (other than an action by or in the right of the corporation) by reason of the fact that he is or was a director, officer, employee or agent of the corporation, or is or was serving at the request of the corporation as a director, officer, employee or agent of another corporation, partnership, joint venture, trust or other enterprise, against expenses (including attorneys' fees), judgments, fines and amounts paid in settlement actually and reasonably incurred by him in connection with such action, suit or proceeding if he acted in good faith and in a manner he reasonably believed to be in or not opposed to the best interests of the corporation, and, with respect to any criminal action or proceeding, had no reasonable cause to believe his conduct was unlawful. The termination of any action, suit or proceeding by judgment, order, settlement, conviction, or upon a plea of *nolo contendere* or its equivalent, shall not, of itself, create a presumption that the person did not act in good faith and in a manner which he reasonably believed to be in or not opposed to the best interests of the corporation, and, with respect to any criminal action or proceeding, had reasonable cause to believe that his conduct was unlawful. * * *

> (c) To the extent that a director, officer, employee or agent of a corporation has been successful on the merits or otherwise in defense of any action, suit or proceeding referred to in [subsection (a)], or in defense of any claim, issue or matter therein, he shall be indemnified against

expenses (including attorneys' fees) actually and reasonably incurred by him in connection therewith.

The policy of the statute and its predecessor has been described as follows, Folk, The Delaware General Corporation Law, 98 (1972):

The invariant policy of Delaware legislation on indemnification is to "promote the desirable end that corporate officials will resist what they consider" unjustified suits and claims, "secure in the knowledge that their reasonable expenses will be borne by the corporation they have served if they are vindicated." Beyond that, its larger purpose is "to encourage capable men to serve as corporate directors, secure in the knowledge that expenses incurred by them in upholding their honesty and integrity as directors will be borne by the corporation they serve."

MCS argues that the statute and sound public policy require indemnification only where there has been vindication by a finding or concession of innocence. It contends that the charges against claimants were dropped for practical reasons, not because of their innocence, and that in light of the conspiracy charged in the indictment, the judgment of acquittal on count four alone is not vindication.

The statute requires indemnification to the extent that the claimant "has been successful on the merits or otherwise." Success is vindication. In a criminal action, any result other than conviction must be considered success. Going behind the result, as MCS attempts, is neither authorized by subsection (c) nor consistent with the presumption of innocence.

The statute does not require complete success. It provides for indemnification to the extent of success "in defense of any claim, issue or matter" in an action. Claimants are therefore entitled to partial indemnification if successful on a count of an indictment, which is an independent criminal charge, even if unsuccessful on another, related count. * * *

Wolfson was sentenced upon a plea of *nolo contendere* to count five of the indictment * * * [while] Gerbert was sentenced upon a guilty verdict on count three, * * *. Conviction of these offenses establishes that Wolfson and Gerbert were adjudged to have been derelict in the performance of their duty as director or officer, and they are therefore not entitled to indemnification against expenses incurred in connection with counts three and five. * * *

Notes

(1) In its opinion in the earlier proceeding, 264 A.2d 358, 360 (Del.Super.1970), the Court described the purpose of § 145 as follows:

Indemnification statutes were enacted in Delaware, and elsewhere, to induce capable and responsible businessmen to accept positions in corporate management. [§ 145] is a new statute, enacted to clarify its predecessor, and to give vindicated directors and others involved in corporate affairs a judicially enforcible (sic) right to indemnification.

It would be anomalous, indeed, and diametrically opposed to the spirit and purpose of the statute and sound public policy to extend the benefits of indemnification to these defendants under the circumstances of this case. * * *

Yes; nolo
contendo
or a judgment
is not itself
determinative
as to whether
director failed
to act in
good faith
or against
the interest
of corp.

If the corporation had wished to do so, could it have indemnified Wolfson and Gerbert for the expenses incurred in connection with claims three and five? See MBCA § 8.51(c).

(2) While fees paid to directors may seem relatively generous, they do not begin to cover the out-of-pocket costs incurred by a director who is named as a defendant in any major litigation. The decision by the Delaware Supreme Court in *Van Gorkom* (p. 674 supra) doubtless contributed to the concern of directors about personal liability generally and the need for iron-clad indemnification rights against the corporation in particular.

(3) The need for indemnification to attract directors seems clearest in the case of litigation that ultimately vindicates the actions of the director on the merits. However, reflection should also indicate that a test requiring complete vindication on the merits is too narrow. For example, should directors be entitled to indemnification for costs if a settlement is available that involves a relatively nominal payment to the plaintiffs and their attorneys? Should not the corporation and the defendant directors be able to settle nuisance suits by nominal payments to or on behalf of the plaintiffs without shifting litigation costs from the corporation back to the defendant directors? Can one distinguish such settlements from situations where directors settle because the probability that they will lose is high? Should there be indemnification in such cases? Questions such as these raise the fundamental issue of what should be the outside limits of the power of indemnification.

(4) One court has held that a director who settles an administrative proceeding by voluntarily paying a fine has conclusively established that he lacked the requisite good faith necessary to be entitled to indemnification even though indemnification was apparently authorized by a broadly phrased by-law provision. Waltuch v. Conticommodity Services, Inc., 88 F.3d 87 (2d Cir.1996). The *Waltuch* court also held that success "on the merits or otherwise" means not being required to pay anything; the fact that other similarly situated defendants did make payments in a settlement was not relevant.

(5) In VonFeldt v. Stifel Financial Corp., 714 A.2d 79 (Del.1998), the Delaware Supreme Court held that a person elected to be a director of a wholly owned subsidiary by the parent corporation was serving "at the request of" the parent corporation and was therefore entitled to indemnification from the parent corporation. The court went to some lengths to warn against "hyper-technical readings" of § 145. See Micah John Schreurs, VonFeldt v. Stifel Financial Corporation: Clarifying the Scope of Delaware Corporate Indemnification Law, 25 J.Corp.L. 161 (1999). In *Waltuch*, the Second Circuit had narrowly read the scope of indemnification permitted under § 145 of Delaware law. Consult Kurt A. Mayr, II, Indemnification of Directors and Officers: The "Double Whammy" of Mandatory Indemnification under Delaware Law in Waltuch v. Conticommodity Services, 42 Vill.L.Rev. 223 (1997).

(6) When a corporation files for bankruptcy, the corporation's indemnification obligations become lumped in with the corporation's other obligations to creditors. Creditors frequently argue that payments to officers and directors should come after the corporation's obligations to third-party creditors are satisfied. The risk of bankruptcy provides yet another reason why officers and directors should require corporations they serve to purchase directors' and officers' liability insurance.

(7) Subchapter E of Chapter 8 of the MBCA (§§ 8.50–8.59) defines the scope of permissible indemnification. See § 8.59. Subchapter E was significantly amend-

ed in 1994 to integrate it with MBCA § 2.02(b)(4), authorizing a corporation to limit the liability of directors by charter amendments. Both liability limitation and indemnification effectively shift the economic cost for the director's acts or omissions from the director to the corporation. Both liability limitations and indemnification, therefore, raise the issue whether it is appropriate to shift this cost to the corporation in the specific case.

(8) The policy considerations underlying the MBCA indemnification provisions are described in part as follows:

> * * * Today, * * * it would be difficult to persuade responsible persons to serve as directors if they were compelled to bear personally the cost of vindicating the propriety of their conduct in every instance in which it might be challenged. * * *

> * * * If permitted too broadly, however, indemnification may violate equally basic tenets of public policy. It is inappropriate to permit management to use corporate funds to avoid the consequences of certain conduct. For example, a director who intentionally inflicts harm on the corporation should not expect to receive assistance from the corporation for legal or other expenses and should be required to satisfy from his personal assets not only any adverse judgment but also expenses incurred in connection with the proceeding. * * *

> A further policy issue is raised in connection with indemnification against liabilities or sanctions imposed under state or federal civil or criminal statutes. * * *

> The fundamental issue that must be addressed by an indemnification statute is the establishment of policies consistent with these broad principles: to ensure that indemnification is permitted only where it will further accepted corporate policies and to prohibit indemnification where it might protect or encourage wrongful or improper conduct. * * *

Introductory Comment to Subchapter E.[2]

(9) What about indemnification of directors in derivative suits brought by shareholders in the name of the corporation? See MBCA § 8.51(d)(1), added in 1994. See also James J. Hanks, Jr., Evaluating Recent State Legislation on Director and Officer Liability Limitation and Indemnification, 43 Bus.Law. 1207, 1221, 1240 (1988):

> At least ten states * * * have enacted statutes expanding the right of corporations to indemnify their directors for expenses, settlements, and adverse judgments in derivative suits. * * *

> In the absence of any applicable liability limitation, the disadvantage of permitting indemnification against settlements and adverse judgments and derivative suits is its circularity. Any money recovered from the director or officer is paid, less the stockholders' attorneys' fees, by the individual to the corporation, which then returns the money, together with reimbursement for the individual's legal expenses, to the individual as indemnification. Although the individual is made whole, the corporation winds up paying not only the amount of the loss but also the stockholders' and individual's attorneys' fees

2. Reprinted from *Model Business Corpora-* *tion Act Annotated* (Third Edition) with the permission of Prentice Hall Law & Business.

and costs. * * * The real beneficiaries of circular indemnification are the stockholders' lawyers.

Moreover, while statutes may permit a corporation to indemnify a director or officer held liable for negligence in a derivative suit, they do not * * * require indemnification. Thus, unless the charter or by-laws require indemnification in such circumstances, the individual is left in a state of uncertainty as to whether indemnification will actually be authorized in his particular case. This type of uncertainty has caused many directors to leave corporate boards. While expanded indemnifiability helps directors and officers by giving them at least one source of reimbursement (assuming the corporation can afford to pay at the time of the loss), it will not provide any relief for the insurance carriers.

Mr. Hanks was discussing developments in indemnification that occurred essentially between 1984 and 1988. These four years were tumultuous times for directors, with widely publicized cases imposing liability on directors, the "drying up" of liability insurance, and the enactment of state statutes limiting the monetary liability of directors.

DIANE H. MAZUR, INDEMNIFICATION OF DIRECTORS IN ACTIONS DIRECTLY BY THE CORPORATION: MUST THE CORPORATION FINANCE ITS OPPONENT'S DEFENSE?

19 J.Corp.L. 201, 202–05 (1994).

Anyone outside the world of corporate law might not believe it. To Public Service Company of New Mexico, the largest public corporation in the state, it was all too serious. Public Service Company of New Mexico, commonly known as "PNM" within the state, had sued three of its former executives, including its former president and chairman of the board of directors, for breach of their duties of loyalty to the corporation. The company alleged that the former executives had diverted approximately five million dollars of corporate funds for their personal benefit in the form of improper bonuses, personal consulting contracts, and retirement benefits.

However, six months after the company filed suit, the state district court hearing the case ruled that the company would have to pay dearly for the opportunity to recover the money. Under the court's interpretation of New Mexico statutory law, the company's bylaws, and the executives' contracts with the company, PNM would have to pay all attorneys' fees and expenses for all the defendants, in addition to its own. The defendants would not even have to "run a tab" for reimbursement at a later date; the company was ordered to pay all legal bills submitted by the defendants' three law firms on a monthly basis, within two days of demand.

Although the company filed suit against its former executives in 1991, the suit arose out of prior litigation that began almost two years earlier. PNM is a utility company providing electric, gas, and water service throughout New Mexico. In early 1989, a class-action group of shareholders sued PNM for securities law violations, alleging that PNM either misrepresented or failed to disclose material facts in its public documents, resulting in an artificially inflated value of PNM stock. The alleged misrepresentations and omissions largely fell in two areas: PNM's excess electric generating capacity and PNM's investments in real estate and other non-utility businesses.

PNM anticipated that shareholder derivative suits alleging mismanagement in the same two areas were soon to come, and as a result, the company appointed a "special litigation committee" (SLC) to investigate the potential claims.[3] * * *

[I]n the process of investigating the non-utility investment claims, the SLC also reviewed the compensation paid to senior executives, an issue which the shareholders had not raised. The SLC concluded that several executives had steered corporate funds to themselves through improper bonuses, personal consulting contracts, and retirement benefits. The committee directed PNM to file its own suit for recovery.

In response to the suit that charged them with improper personal benefit, the executives demanded that PNM begin to finance their defense. They contended that PNM was obligated to pay all attorneys' fees needed to defend the action, and that PNM was obligated to pay those fees as soon as they were incurred. The former executives relied on New Mexico law, PNM's bylaws, and separate contracts they had with PNM in support of their demands.

Although New Mexico statutory law gives corporations the power to indemnify if they choose, the law does not obligate corporations to indemnify. However, corporations are free to grant stronger indemnification rights to directors through corporate bylaws or separate contracts. In the case of PNM, the corporation had granted further indemnification rights to its executives by both methods.[4]

---

3. [By the Author] Report of the Special Litigation Committee of the Board of Directors of Public Service Company of New Mexico at 5, Kaplan v. Geist, No. CIV–89–1033JC (D.N.M. filed January 31, 1991) (hereinafter SLC Report).

4. [PNM's] indemnification bylaw was standard, obligating PNM to indemnify "to the full extent of the authority of the Company to so indemnify as authorized by the law of New Mexico." * * * The separate indemnification contracts executed by PNM were more specific, granting a number of special procedural protections:

"2. Basic Indemnification Arrangement.

"(a) In the event Indemnitee was, is or becomes a party to * * * a Claim * * * the Company shall indemnify Indemnitee to the fullest extent permitted by law as soon as practicable but in any event no later than thirty days after written demand is presented to the Company, against any and all Expenses, judgments, fines, penalties and amounts paid in settlement * * * of such Claim. If so requested by Indemnitee, the Company shall advance (within two business days of such request) any and all Expenses to Indemnitee (an 'Expense Advance').

"(b) Notwithstanding the foregoing, * * * the obligations of the Company * * * shall be subject to the condition that the Review-

ing Party shall not have determined * * * that Indemnitee would not be permitted to be indemnified under applicable law * * * provided, however, that if Indemnitee has commenced or thereafter commences legal proceedings * * * to secure a determination that Indemnitee should be indemnified under applicable law, any determination made by the Reviewing Party * * * shall not be binding and Indemnitee shall not be required to reimburse the Company for any Expense Advance until a final judicial determination is made with respect thereto (as to which all rights of appeal therefrom have been exhausted or lapsed). If there has not been a Change in Control, the Reviewing Party shall be selected by the Board of Directors, and if there has been such a Change in Control * * * the Reviewing Party shall be the Independent Legal Counsel * * * If there has been no determination by the Reviewing Party or if the Reviewing Party determines that Indemnitee substantively would not be permitted to be indemnified * * * under applicable law, Indemnitee shall have the right to commence litigation * * * seeking an initial determination by the Court or challenging any such determination by the Reviewing Party * * * including the legal and factual bases therefor. * * *

"6. Burden of Proof. In connection with any determination by the Reviewing Party or

The defendants argued that all three sources of indemnification rights— New Mexico law, PNM bylaw, and contract—entitled them to payment of all attorneys' fees on demand. The corporation balked at paying defense costs under these circumstances. It was not that PNM considered the statutes, bylaws, or contracts unenforceable. In fact, PNM had paid defense costs incurred by the individual defendants in the numerous class action and derivative suits. However, in those actions, financing the individual costs of defense was an appropriate use of corporate funds.

* * * To PNM, the suit to recover corporate funds that had been improperly diverted for personal benefit was another story entirely. The corporation had brought those claims only after a long investigation, and it believed that the directors had forfeited any right to indemnification because they had failed to serve PNM in good faith. Certainly they were not entitled to payment of attorneys' fees in advance of trial because "the facts then known" to PNM showed a clear lack of good faith.

The court disagreed. It ruled that under New Mexico law, PNM's bylaws, and the separate contracts, PNM had no right to deny immediate payment to the defendants' attorneys, no matter what the circumstances. PNM could not deny attorneys' fees on the basis of its investigation into wrongful conduct; it had to pay the defense lawyers until the defendants' conduct was proved wrongful. Even if PNM prevailed at trial, it would have to continue to pay all defense costs until the verdict was upheld on appeal. In essence, by finding that PNM was obligated to pay the attorneys for all parties, PNM would be forced to finance an action both for and against itself if it hoped to recover any improperly paid compensation.

According to The New Mexico Lawyer, the court's ruling that the company had to finance every party to its lawsuit was "the turning point" in the case:[5]

> As a practical matter, the ruling meant that the trio of defendants could now litigate almost endlessly, because they were tapped directly into PNM's coffers to pay their legal bills. Because they paid no money out of pocket, there would also be little incentive for them to settle on unfavorable terms.

otherwise as to whether Indemnitee is entitled to be indemnified hereunder, the burden of proof shall be on the Company to establish that Indemnitee is not so entitled.

"7. No Presumptions * * * (N)either the failure of the Reviewing Party to have made a determination as to whether Indemnitee has met any particular standard of conduct or had any particular belief, nor an actual determination by the Reviewing Party that Indemnitee has not met such standard of conduct or did not have such belief, prior to the commencement of legal proceedings by Indemnitee to secure a judicial determination that Indemnitee should be indemnified under applicable law shall be a defense to Indemnitee's claim or create a presumption that Indemnitee has not met any particular standard of conduct or did not have any particular belief."

All PNM directors received the same form of indemnification contract, which had been drafted by the New York law firm of Skadden, Arps, Slate, Meagher & Flom. The contract provides several common procedural protections that, in general, raise no public policy concerns: 1) time limits on the corporation's response to an indemnification demand; 2) a wide choice of persons who can make the indemnification decision on behalf of the corporation (the "Reviewing Party"); and 3) the option for a de novo evaluation of conduct by a court. * * * [Under the contract, a Reviewing Party can be "any appropriate person or body" who is not a party to the litigation.]

5. [By the Author] Michael Haederle, PNM Settlement Began with Legal Gamble, N.M. Law., June 1992, at 5.

The case was settled within four months of the ruling on attorneys' fees. * * *

[S]ome of these procedural protections are so extreme and so skewed in favor of the director that they, in practice, undermine substantive statutory restrictions. * * * For example, the contract requires PNM to make expense advances within two days of demand. To the extent that a two-day time limit makes any reasonable evaluation of conduct impossible, the provision allows the corporation to ignore the conduct standard and is not enforcible (sic).

Second, all presumptions and burdens of proof for entitlement to indemnification under the contract are in favor of the director. If those presumptions and burdens of proof allow the corporation to grant indemnification by default, instead of on the basis of a conduct evaluation, they violate public policy.

Third, if the Reviewing Party concludes that a director's conduct fails to meet the required standard, the contract essentially silences the corporation on that issue until the end of the litigation. If the Reviewing Party decides against the director, as it did in the PNM case, the contract states that the Reviewing Party's finding "shall not be binding" and cannot be used by the corporation as a defense to the director's claim for indemnification. The contract goes on to provide that the director "shall not be required to reimburse the Company for any Expense Advance until a final judicial determination is made with respect thereto," including all rights of appeal. This contractual right can be read (as it apparently was by the PNM court) to require the corporation to make expense advances throughout trial and appeal even though the corporation's investigation found that the director breached a fiduciary duty. * * *

Notes

(1) There are obviously two sides to the advancement of expenses issue. Consider the position of a director who has been named as a defendant and must incur expenses to prepare her defense. These initial expenditures may be very substantial and absolutely essential if the director is to be vindicated. On the other hand, as PNM's unfortunate experience graphically demonstrates, advances for expenses may dramatically change the dynamics of litigation, possibly to such an extent as to make meritorious litigation impractical.

(2) An optional provision authorizing advances of expenses is satisfactory as a practical matter only if management of the corporation remains friendly to the defendant director. If there has been a change in control there is a real risk that the new board of directors may decline to advance expenses to a defeated adversary if the provision is optional. Thus, as a practical matter, an optional provision authorizing advances is likely to provide no protection at all when it is needed the most. Recognizing this, sophisticated directors insist that advances should be made mandatory to the maximum extent possible and such provisions are very common in modern articles of incorporation and bylaws. Statutes generally make these provisions enforceable. See MBCA § 8.58(a). Indeed, the last sentence of this section goes a step further and routinely ties mandatory advances of expenses to agreements to provide mandatory indemnification to the "fullest extent permitted by law." Is this wise? The Official Comment to § 8.58 warns of the potential PNM problem as follows:

Also, a corporation should consider whether obligatory expense advance is intended for direct suits by the corporation as well as for derivative suits by shareholders in the right of the corporation. In the former case, assuming compliance with subsections (a) and (b) of section 8.53, the corporation could be required to fund the defense of a defendant director even where the board of directors has already concluded that he has engaged in significant wrongdoing.

Is this warning sufficient? Or was the problem in PNM an apparent unthinking acceptance of procedural requirements that were clearly drafted to make mandatory advances automatically available in all circumstances?

(3) In Fidelity Fed. Sav. & Loan Ass'n v. Felicetti, 830 F.Supp. 262 (E.D.Pa. 1993), the court found a conflict between the fiduciary obligation of directors to act only in the corporation's best interest and a bylaw provision that mandated advancement of expenses in all events. The court concluded that "the only reasonable interpretation requires that the directors abide by their fiduciary obligations to act only as they believe is in the best interest of the corporation. Accordingly, [the corporation] is not required to advance the funds necessary for Felicetti and Scarcia to defend themselves in this action. * * * " 830 F.Supp. at 269. Most courts, however, have rejected this approach in which preliminary judgments are made about the merits. See Ridder v. CityFed Financial Corp., 47 F.3d 85 (3d Cir.1995).

(4) Where advancement of expenses is not mandatory, the decision by the board of directors is to be judged by the standards of the business judgment rule. In this respect, an evaluation (1) of the likelihood the defendants will be able to satisfy their commitments to reimburse the corporation if they are found not eligible for indemnification and (2) whether ultimately the advancement would on balance be likely to promote the corporation's interests, are required. Advanced Mining Systems v. Fricke, 623 A.2d 82, 84 (Del.Ch.1992). In Havens v. Attar, 1997 WL 55957 (Del.Ch. Jan. 30, 1997), the Court held that a decision to advance expenses to a majority of the board of directors without considering the financial abilities of the individuals was not protected by the business judgment rule.

(5) What about the status of indemnification agreements for corporate officers under section 402 of Sarbanes–Oxley? In one sense an indemnification agreement is like a personal extension of credit prohibited under section 402. But advances for legal fees incurred in the service of the corporation are not like the misappropriated personal loans which section 402 sought to prohibit. The SEC and the courts have yet to give clear guidance on this point.

———

Consider MBCA § 8.57. Even in states without express authorization, the purchase of D & O insurance may be implicit in other corporate powers relating to the compensation of officers and directors. Is such insurance erosive of the public policy underlying the securities acts and other rules providing for liability? Of course, § 8.57 is only enabling, and significant express exceptions and exclusions appear in all such policies.

McCULLOUGH v. FIDELITY & DEPOSIT CO.

United States Court of Appeals, Fifth Circuit, 1993.
2 F.3d 110.

Before GOLDBERG, HIGGINBOTHAM, AND DAVIS, CIRCUIT JUDGES.

W. EUGENE DAVIS, CIRCUIT JUDGE:

The Federal Deposit Insurance Corporation (FDIC) filed a declaratory judgment action against Fidelity and Deposit Company of Maryland (F & D) to determine whether F & D provided coverage under a directors' and officers' liability policy. The district court found no coverage under F & D's policy and granted summary judgment to F & D. Because the insured failed to give F & D adequate notice to trigger coverage under the "claims made" insurance policy, we affirm.

I.

F & D issued four directors' and officers' (D & O) liability policies to four affiliate banks, including Harris County Bankshares, Inc. and three of its subsidiaries (banks). The policy covers claims made against the insured officers and directors if the required notice is given to the insurer during the policy period. This coverage is expanded by Section 6(a) of the policy to cover claims made after expiration of the policy term if the insured gives F & D certain written notice during the policy period of potential claims. Section 6 of the policy provides, in pertinent part:

(a) If during the policy period, or during the extended discovery period * * * the Bank or the Directors and Officers shall:

(1) receive written or oral notice from any party that it is the intention of such party to hold the Directors and Officers, or any of them, responsible for a specified Wrongful Act; or

(2) become aware of any *act, error, or omission* which *may subsequently give rise to a claim* being made against the Directors and Officers, or any of them, for a *specified Wrongful Act*;

and shall during such period give written notice thereof to the Company as soon as practicable and prior to the date of termination of the policy, then any claim which may subsequently be made against the Directors and Officers arising out of such Wrongful Act shall, for the purpose of this policy, be treated as a claim made during the Policy Year or the extended discovery period in which such notice was first given. (emphasis added).

The summary judgment evidence focused on information the banks furnished F & D about their lending activities. The parties disagreed about whether that information was adequate to put F & D on notice of a potential claim under § 6 of the policy.

As requested by F & D, the banks provided F & D with June 1984—March 1985 Call Reports[6] that described increasing loan losses and delinquencies. In conjunction with the 1985 renewal of the policies, the banks provided

---

6. [By the Court] A Call Report is a quarterly report of financial condition that each insured institution is required to furnish its primary regulator.

F & D a 1984 annual report. Footnote M of that report referred to the issuance of a cease and desist order to one of the subsidiaries by its primary regulator, the Office of the Comptroller of the Currency (OCC). The bank did not send the order itself.

F & D continued to express concern about the banks' financial condition and continued to request Call Reports and other information. In one of F & D's letters, they expressed concern about the banks' "problem with the Feds." In September 1985, in response to the increasing loan losses, F & D informed the banks that it intended to cancel their policies mid-term, effective October 9.

After a merger of the subsidiary banks, the OCC declared the bank insolvent in February 1988 and declared the FDIC as Receiver. FDIC sued the banks' directors and officers for improperly or illegally making, administering, or collecting loans. F & D denied coverage to the officers and directors under the D & O policies. FDIC then filed its declaratory judgment action against F & D, seeking a determination that F & D provided coverage under the D & O liability policies.

In the declaratory judgment action, * * * [t]he court found that FDIC had failed to show that F & D received written notice of a potential claim under § 6(a)(2) of the policy, and on reconsideration it entered final judgment for F & D. FDIC timely appealed.

II.

FDIC * * * [argues] that a genuine issue of fact exists regarding whether, pursuant to § 6(a)(2) of the "claims made" policy, they provided F & D sufficient written notice of potential claims during the policy period. * * *

A.

The parties first contest the type of notice the policy requires the banks to give to F & D. F & D contends that the policy requires the bank to notify it of "specified Wrongful Acts" of directors and officers having claim potential. FDIC argues that the notice can be in the broader form of "any act, error or omission" which may give rise to a claim for specified wrongful acts.

We agree with F & D that the policy requires the insured to give notice of specified wrongful acts of officers and directors. First, the plain language supports F & D's argument. § 6 of the policy provides that coverage will be provided if the Bank notifies the insurer of:

> any act, error, or omission which may subsequently give rise to a claim being made against Directors and Officers, or any of them, for a specified Wrongful Act * * *

F & D contends, and this court agrees, that "specified" modifies "Wrongful Act" and not "claim." The word "specified" is meaningless if it is read to modify "claim"; we cannot envision an *unspecified* claim. The policy language thus makes sense only if we read it to require notice of specified wrongful acts, errors, or omissions that may give rise to a claim.

Notice, as provided in the policy, is required in a claims made policy to trigger coverage. Notice in a claims made policy therefore serves a very different function than prejudice-preventing notice required under an "occurrence" policy. If the policy requirement for notice of specified wrongful acts is relaxed, then policy coverage actually expands. For example, if notice that an insured attorney has a poor docket control system is accepted as coverage triggering notice of the attorney's wrongful act, the attorney's malpractice coverage would be triggered for any number of suits predicated on missed deadlines.[7] For all of the above reasons, we are persuaded that the policy requires the insured to give the insurer notice of specified wrongful acts to trigger coverage.

B.

We next must determine whether the insureds gave adequate notice of specified wrongful acts. FDIC argues that even if notice of specified wrongful acts is required, a genuine issue of fact exists regarding whether it provided this notice. FDIC contends that reference to the cease and desist order and the reports of the banks' deteriorating financial condition put F & D on notice of acts or omissions of directors and officers which could later give rise to claims for specified wrongful acts. They argue that the policies define "wrongful act" to include a breach of duty, and the information they furnished F & D was adequate to inform F & D that the insureds breached their duty to properly supervise the banks' lending operations.

Critically, the banks did not furnish F & D with a copy of the cease and desist order. The banks' annual report simply referred to it. But even if we assume that notice of the issuance of a cease and desist order informs the insurer that the bank is having some difficulty, the issuance of such an order does not identify specified wrongful acts. The banks gave F & D no notice of the particular subsidiary involved, the particular agents, officers, or directors involved, the time period during which the events occurred, the identity of potential claimants, and the specific unsound practices made the basis of the order.

We agree with the district court that the insureds failed to give F & D adequate notice of specific wrongful acts to trigger coverage under § 6(a). Notice of an institution's worsening financial condition is not notice of an officer's or director's act, error, or omission. See *American Casualty Co. v. FDIC*, 944 F.2d 455, 460 (8th Cir.1991) and *California Union Ins. Co. v. American Diversified Savings Bank*, 914 F.2d 1271, 1277–78 (9th Cir.1990), cert. denied, 498 U.S. 1088, 111 S.Ct. 966, 112 L.Ed.2d 1052 (1991). Rising delinquencies and bad loan portfolios, especially in light of falling real estate prices, are insufficient to constitute such notice. The district court correctly granted summary judgment. * * *

AFFIRMED.

Notes

(1) Do you understand the difference between a "claims made" policy and an "occurrence" policy? The former provides coverage for claims first made against an insured during the policy period, while the latter provides coverage for injuries that take place during the policy period regardless of when the claim is asserted.

---

7. [By the Court] See *Hirsch v. Texas Lawyers' Ins. Exchange*, 808 S.W.2d 561, 565 (Tex. Ct.App.1991) (court reluctant to permit expansion of "claims made" coverage through relaxation of coverage-triggering notice requirements).

Originally, D & O policies were occurrence-based, but the practical difficulties created by the possibility that claims may be asserted many years later caused all companies to shift to claims made policies. For example, it is reported that many of the problems of Lloyds of London arose because of the issuance of occurrence policies covering asbestos liability and similar long-term events. Claims under these policies were asserted years after the close of the year for which the insurance was purchased.

(2) Claims made insurance open up the possibility that an insured who retires or leaves an employer may not have any insurance in force (or may be insured by an entirely different insurer) at the time a claim arising out of an earlier period is first asserted. For example, a claim that arose from conduct in 1997 may first be asserted in 1999; such a claim is covered only by the 1999 claims made policy. An employee who was covered in 1997 but has retired may not have any coverage in 1999.

JOSEPH P. MONTELEONE & JOHN F. McCARRICK, DIRECTORS' AND OFFICERS' LIABILITY, A D & O POLICY ROAD MAP: THE COVERAGE EXCLUSIONS

Insights, Vol. 7, No. 7, at 8 (July 1993).[8]

A discussion of exclusions typically contained in directors' and officers' liability (D & O) policies may seem a curious place to begin an evaluation of D & O coverage. However, the unique nature of D & O policies and the potentially broad scope of this coverage suggest that it may be easier to identify what is not covered than to spell out what *is* covered.

At the outset, an analysis of exclusions in a D & O policy cannot be limited to a review of the "Exclusions" section of the policy. Coverage limitations that, as a practical matter, constitute exclusions exist throughout the policy form. They may be found in the insuring agreement, in various policy definitions, and even in the policy application.

It is also important to recognize that, unlike general liability policies which typically are derived from common industry wording developed by the Insurance Services Office (ISO), D & O policies largely have developed through each D & O insurer's loss experience. Therefore, the coverage distinctions between various D & O policies may be significant. Further, different policy forms reflect the exposure risks to the niche markets being underwritten. For example, to the extent D & O coverage is available to a biotechnology or high-technology public company (generally perceived as high-risk D & O exposures), the policy terms, conditions and exclusions are likely to be more restrictive than those contained in a policy issued to a *Fortune 100* company. * * *

There are generally three categories of exclusions in D & O policies. "Conduct" exclusions seek to eliminate coverage for certain conduct which is deemed to be sufficiently self-serving or egregious that insurance protection is considered inappropriate. The personal profit and advantage, dishonesty, remuneration, and § 16(b) exclusions are examples. The "other insurance" category of exclusions implements the concept that the D & O policy is the

8. Reprinted from *Insights,* July 1993, Volume 7, Number 7, with the permission of Pren-   tice Hall Law & Business.

ultimate "backstop" protection for directors and officers. If a corporation can purchase another type of insurance to cover a specific D & O risk, the D & O insurer expects that other insurance to be purchased and therefore the D & O policy will not cover that risk. Examples of exclusions in this category include the exclusions for bodily injury/property damage, ERISA, libel and slander, notice under a prior policy and (at least historically) pollution. Finally, the "laser" exclusions are intended to address specific risks unique to the insured corporation which the insurer has identified as inconsistent with its underwriting principles. * * *

In light of the "claims made" nature of D & O policies, policy applications typically inquire whether any claims against directors and officers currently are pending, or whether any director or officer has knowledge of facts or circumstances which might give rise to a claim in the future. If, however, the insurer simply is offering renewal terms, these questions likely will not be asked unless the insureds are seeking a higher limit of liability or otherwise are seeking to expand their coverage.

As a general rule, material misrepresentations made by an insured on the policy application may provide grounds for the insurer to subsequently rescind and treat the policy as void *ab initio*.[9] However, the question inquiring whether any director or officer has knowledge of facts or circumstances which might subsequently give rise to a claim is usually followed by a statement to the effect that if any insureds have such knowledge or such information exists, then any resulting claim will be excluded from coverage. This exclusion differs from the rescission remedy in that a rescission of the policy voids coverage for all claims regardless of whether or not any claim arises from the materially misrepresented facts. The application exclusion, on the other hand, excludes coverage only for those claims arising from the known or existing facts or circumstances. * * *

By limiting the scope of defined terms, insurers also may limit the scope of coverage under D & O policies. For example, the term "loss" typically is defined to exclude penalties imposed by law or matters uninsurable under the law pursuant to which the policy is construed. Also, depending upon the policy form, the definition of "loss" may exclude: (1) punitive or exemplary damages; (2) treble damages; (3) taxes; (4) amounts for which the directors and officers are not personally liable (*i.e.*, nonrecourse settlements); (5) amounts incurred by a special committee in the investigation or evaluation of a claim by or on behalf of the corporation; (6) the multiple portion of any multiplied damages award; or (7) any costs, charges or expenses incurred in connection with a grand jury or criminal proceeding. * * *

The term "wrongful act" typically is defined to exclude claims brought against an insured director or officer in an uninsured capacity. For example, if a lawsuit includes allegations against a director who also performs some outside function (*e.g.*, outside counsel), coverage may not be available for that director to the extent the claim does not relate to his or her position solely as a director. * * *

---

9. [By the Author] *See, e.g., Shapiro v. American Home Assurance Co.*, 584 F.Supp. 1245 (D.Mass.1984) (a material misrepresentation by a company's president in an application for D & O insurance invalidated the D & O policy as to all insureds, innocent and otherwise); *accord INA Underwriters Ins. Co. v. D.H. Forde & Co.*, 630 F.Supp. 76 (W.D.N.Y. 1985).

In the early days of D & O policies, D & O coverage was afforded under two separate policies: one policy which insured the corporation for its indemnification obligations to its directors and officers (often referred to as "corporate reimbursement" coverage), and a second policy ensuring the directors and officers in those instances where the corporation either would not or could not provide indemnification (often referred to as "D & O" or "direct" coverage). Because the various state indemnification statutes were understood to prohibit indemnification of inappropriate conduct, including dishonesty and unentitled personal profit, there was no perceived need to apply exclusions relating to such conduct to the corporate reimbursement coverage. However, since the policies offering direct coverage contained no such underlying protection, exclusions relating to such conduct as "unentitled personal profit" and "dishonesty" were added to the direct policies. Eventually, the two separate policies evolved into a single policy with alternative insuring agreements. Some policy forms still retain the distinction and apply these so-called "conduct" exclusions only to the direct insuring agreement. Most policy forms, however, ignore the historical distinction and apply all exclusions to both insuring agreements.

Some of the more common exclusions found in the exclusions section of D & O policies include the following.

Personal profit or advantage exclusion. Most D & O policies exclude claims based upon or attributable to directors or officers gaining any personal profit or advantage to which they were not legally entitled. Some policy forms require that the personal profiting be established "in fact"[;] other policy forms require an adjudication of unentitled personal profit in the underlying litigation.

Dishonesty exclusion. Given the liberal pleading requirements in virtually every federal and state court, the dishonesty exclusion has potential applicability to virtually all D & O claims and, therefore, is frequently identified in insurers' reservation of rights letters as a potential coverage defense. First, the scope of the exclusion varies among different D & O policy forms in several respects. The conduct falling within the exclusion also may vary. Some policy forms exclude claims brought about or contributed to by the "dishonest" or the "fraudulent, dishonest or criminal" acts of the insureds. Other forms exclude "deliberately fraudulent" or "deliberately dishonest" conduct or a "willful violation of any statute, rule or regulation."

Second, the triggering conditions for the applicability of dishonesty exclusions vary. Some policy forms require a judgment or other final adjudication which establishes that "acts of active and deliberate dishonesty" were committed "with actual dishonest purpose and intent." Other forms simply require the requisite conduct to have occurred "in fact," while yet other forms have no expressed triggering condition. As to policy forms requiring a final adjudication, courts have consistently held that the adjudication must occur in the underlying D & O proceeding (and cannot be established in separate coverage litigation) and, therefore, the exclusion is inapplicable if the underlying D & O litigation is settled prior to a final adjudication. If the exclusion does not expressly require an adjudication, the exclusion has potential applicability even where the underlying lawsuit is settled.

Bodily injury/property damage exclusion. All D & O policies exclude coverage with respect to claims for bodily injury, sickness, disease or death, or property damage. More recent policy forms also may exclude emotional or mental distress, violation of a person's right of privacy, wrongful entry, eviction, false arrest and assault and battery, as well as libel, slander and defamation.

ERISA exclusion. Almost all D & O policy forms exclude claims arising under ERISA or a similar federal or state law. Given this wording, the D & O insurers' intent with respect to this exclusion appears to be to avoid providing overlapping coverage with that typically provided by fiduciary liability insurance. The exclusion may also be deemed sufficiently broad to apply to a claim for benefits in connection with a wrongful termination claim whether or not the claim for benefits is explicitly based on an alleged violation of ERISA.

Section 16(b) ("short-swing profit") exclusion. * * * Since the issue of intent or conduct is not relevant in determining whether liability should be imposed, D & O insurers typically separately exclude claims arising under Section 16(b) regardless of whether or not the trading constituted "personal profit" or "dishonesty."

Return of illegal remuneration exclusion. This exclusion was developed in response to D & O insurers' concerns that if a director or officer is forced to return to the corporation profits or excessive compensation, insureds might seek to obtain those funds under a D & O policy. Like the "short-swing profit" exclusion, it is not necessary that there be a factual finding or adjudication of "personal profit" or "dishonesty" in order for the D & O insurer to invoke this exclusion. Recent policies combine this exclusion with the "personal profit" exclusion.

Pollution exclusion. Virtually every D & O insurance policy contains a "broad form" pollution exclusion, although substantial variations in exclusionary wording exist among policy forms. The intent of most insurers is to exclude coverage for any type of direct or indirect pollution or environmental exposure. Some exclusions are drafted to be more comprehensive than others. Under the most commonly used "broad form" pollution exclusions, coverage is excluded not only for claims by parties seeking recovery for pollution damages, but also for secondary suits, such as shareholder derivative and nondisclosure suits against directors and officers arising out of environment-related losses incurred by the corporation.

In some instances, insureds may be able to obtain an exception to this exclusion through negotiation with D & O insurers and obtain coverage for non-indemnifiable secondary pollution suits.

Insured v. insured exclusion. Prior to the mid–1980s, most D & O policies did not exclude claims brought by the corporation or by some directors and officers against other directors and officers. However, in light of suits brought by corporations against their directors and officers under circumstances which created an appearance that the entities simply were converting their D & O policies to cash by suing their own directors and officers, virtually all D & O policy forms now exclude claims brought against directors and officers by other directors and officers or by the company. Most newer policy forms incorporate this exclusion into the Exclusions section of the policy. Older policy forms generally add this exclusion by endorsement.

The "insured v. insured" exclusion varies significantly from policy to policy, with the primary differences relating to which claims are excepted from the exclusion (and are therefore covered). Almost all policy forms contain an exception to the "insured v. insured" exclusion to provide coverage for derivative lawsuits brought without the solicitation, assistance or participation of an insured. Other exceptions to the "insured v. insured" exclusion may preserve coverage for claims for wrongful termination and claims for contribution or indemnity.

In recent years, the "insured v. insured" exclusion has been frequently litigated in the context of claims brought by the regulatory banking agencies against directors and officers of failed financial institutions. Courts have reached different results as to whether the "insured v. insured" exclusion applies to these claims. * * *

D & O policies typically exclude coverage for claims which may be covered under other insurance policies. This exclusion may be found in the exclusions section of the policy in some policy forms, or in separate provisions in other forms. Some policy forms apply this exclusion only to the extent of actual payments under other policies; others limit the exclusion to other "valid" or "valid and collectible" insurance. In virtually all policies, the exclusion applies only to the amount of such other insurance, with the D & O insurance policy affording coverage in excess of such other insurance.

Endorsements

In addition to policy exclusions contained in standardized policy forms, D & O insurers may add further exclusions to the policy by endorsement and thus tailor the policy coverage to a specific risk or industry. The following are some commonly found endorsement exclusions.

Pending/prior litigation exclusion. When an insurer first issues a D & O policy to a corporation, an exclusion is frequently included which eliminates coverage for claims arising from pending or prior litigation or from any facts or circumstances involved in such litigation. In this way, the insurer's intent is to avoid exposure for a claim already in progress or which is likely to arise from existing litigation. The "pending/prior litigation" exclusion typically will reference a date frequently the inception date of the policy which is used to determine whether the litigation is "pending or prior." In evaluating different policy forms, one important inquiry should be which party is the subject of the pending or prior litigation. Some forms of this exclusion limit the scope of the exclusion to litigation, claims, demands, or proceedings *against* the insured directors and officers and, in some forms, the corporation. Other forms apply the exclusion to *any* pending or prior litigation, claims, demands or proceedings whether or not the corporation or any insured is a party or even knows of the existence of the matter.

Depending upon the specific wording, the "pending/prior litigation" exclusion may broadly apply and, therefore, may create inadvertent coverage gaps. For example, if the prior litigation asserts claims against only the corporation (or under the broader form of this exclusion, against only a third party), and insured directors and officers subsequently are named as defendants in the litigation or are subsequently subject to separate litigation based upon the same matters as alleged in the pending litigation, it is likely that no coverage will exist under the newly-issued policy. Thus, unless a notice of circumstances referencing the matters alleged in the prior litigation was submitted to the prior D & O insurer, if any, the defendant directors and officers may well be without any D & O coverage for such claims.

Regulatory exclusion. Although potentially applicable to any corporation subject to regulation by a governmental agency, this exclusion is most commonly endorsed onto D & O policies issued to financial institutions—and particularly where there are concerns that the institution may be taken over by regulators. Beginning in the late 1980s, some courts ruled that this exclusion was unenforceable as being ambiguous and against public policy because it frustrated the broad powers and duties bestowed upon financial institution regulators. During the past two years, however, courts have almost unanimously upheld the enforceability of this exclusion.[10] * * *

Notes

(1) According to a survey taken in 2002 by management consultants Tillinghast–Towers Perrin, D & O premiums rose 20% in 2001 and were on track to increase by an additional 30% in 2002. Premiums for the largest companies, those with market capitalizations of $5 billion or more, are increasing even more rapidly: by some reports as much as 70% in 2004. Premiums for these companies average around 10–15% of the coverage amounts. There are at least three reasons for the dramatic increase in the cost of D & O insurance. First, of course, the large number of high-profile corporate scandals since 2001 have increased the perceived liability risks of corporate directors and officers. Second, even before these scandals hit, there had been a steady increase in the average dollar amount of settlements in class action lawsuits against directors and officers. Research that examines the amount of settlements as a percentage of the estimated damages in cases shows that settlements now average about five percent of the estimated damages in cases, up from around 2 percent five years ago. Third, the recent passage of Sarbanes–Oxley has significantly increased the duties and obligations of corporate officers and directors, thereby increasing potential liability. Some of the changes, such as the extension of the statutes of limitations in securities fraud actions and the creation of new securities fraud causes of action (such as having an "improper influence over a corporate audit"), have obvious implications for insurers' potential liability.

(2) In a modern D & O policy, advancements of expenses to defend insureds usually reduce the available coverage by the amount of the payment. As a result, extended litigation may deplete the policy and limit the protection available to insureds. Not all policies are structured in this fashion.

(3) As the Monteleone–McCarrick article makes clear, material misrepresentations made by an insured on a policy application give the insurance company the right to rescind insurance coverage. Of particular concern are questions on many insurance forms that ask companies to disclose "any fact and circumstances that might give rise to a claim in the future." When a lawsuit is filed, the insurance

---

10. [By the Author] Indeed, the only four federal circuit courts that have addressed the issue have agreed that the regulatory exclusion is enforceable. *See FDIC v. American Casualty Co.*, [995 F.2d 471] (4th Cir.1993); *Fidelity & Deposit Co. of Maryland v. Conner*, 973 F.2d 1236 (5th Cir.1992); *St. Paul Fire and Marine Ins. Co. v. FDIC*, 968 F.2d 695 (8th Cir.1992); *American Casualty Co. v. FDIC*, 944 F.2d 455 (8th Cir.1991); *FDIC v. American Casualty Co.*, 975 F.2d 677 (10th Cir.1992).

company can claim that it has the right to rescind on the grounds that the company failed to disclose the facts and circumstances that might have given rise to the claim being asserted. An issue that sometimes arises is whether a corporation's fraudulent failure to disclose material facts gives the insurance company the right to deny coverage to officers or directors who were unaware that a misrepresentation had been made. With this in mind, lawyers reviewing insurance policies for officers and directors often insist on "severability clauses." One such clause provides that a corporation's misrepresentations or failure to disclose acts or circumstances that might give rise to a claim "shall not be imputed, for the purpose of rescission of this Policy, to any other insured Persons who are not aware" of the fraud.

(4) Significant problems arise when litigation involves claims brought simultaneously against directors and officers who are insured and persons who are not insured: corporate agents and employees, directors of subsidiaries or affiliated corporations, and the corporation itself. (Traditional policies covered only the indemnification obligations of the corporation itself and not its direct liability; some new policies now insure the corporation itself as well as directors and officers.) If a settlement is reached, the insurer must allocate the settlement payment among the insureds and the uninsureds based on relative fault or culpability. Not surprisingly, litigation has arisen over the propriety of specific allocations. See Caterpillar v. Great American Ins. Co., 62 F.3d 955 (7th Cir.1995); Safeway Stores v. National Union Fire Ins. Co., 64 F.3d 1282 (9th Cir.1995). Somewhat similar issues arise when the corporation is insolvent and settlement is proposed for some but not all the defendants. See Joseph P. Monteleone and John F. McCarrick, Settlement Issues in Securities Litigation Involving Officers and Directors, Insights, Vol. 7, No. 9, Sept. 1996, at 7.

As mentioned earlier in this chapter, in situations where a corporation is not required by law to advance the attorney fees of its officers or directors, the corporation generally may still choose to contractually promise to advance the costs of defending a suit. As you have seen, courts typically attach significant weight to a corporation's promises to advance fees, and will enforce contracts and bylaw provisions in a wide variety of circumstances. Even if there is no contractual or bylaw provision providing for advancement, however, a corporation may still voluntarily choose to advance the fees of officers and directors. Recently, federal prosecutors have challenged this practice by taking it as a sign that a corporation accused of wrongdoing is seeking to construct a "wall of silence" to prevent cooperation with government prosecutors.

In June 2006, Judge Lewis Kaplan, a Federal District Court judge overseeing a criminal tax shelter case against top KPMG officials, attacked a government prosecutorial tactic which interprets the Thompson Memorandum, a 2003 DOJ document, to mean that companies under investigation can gain favor with prosecutors by cutting off legal fee support to employees caught up in criminal investigations. The Judge agreed with the defendants that KPMG was improperly pressured to cut legal fees of indicted former employees, saying that this violated the employees' 5th Amendment right to a fair trail and 6th Amendment right to an attorney. Lynnley Browning, U.S. Tactic on KPMG Questioned, N.Y. Times, June 28, 2006 at C1. In September, 2006 the DOJ responded to criticisms that these tactics were being used to force companies into cooperation by defending such tactics as a needed response in the wake of Enron. Lynnley Browning, Justice Department is Reviewing Corporate Prosecution Guidelines, N.Y. Times, Sept. 15, 2006, at C3.

MEMORANDUM

TO: Heads of Department Components

United States Attorneys

FROM: Larry D. Thompson

Deputy Attorney General

SUBJECT: Principles of Federal Prosecution of Business Organizations

As the Corporate Fraud Task Force has advanced in its mission, we have confronted certain issues in the principles for the federal prosecution of business organizations that require revision in order to enhance our efforts against corporate fraud. While it will be a minority of cases in which a corporation or partnership is itself subjected to criminal charges, prosecutors and investigators in every matter involving business crimes must assess the merits of seeking the conviction of the business entity itself.

Attached to this memorandum are a revised set of principles to guide Department prosecutors as they make the decision whether to seek charges against a business organization. These revisions draw heavily on the combined efforts of the Corporate Fraud Task Force and the Attorney General's Advisory Committee to put the results of more than three years of experience with the principles into practice.

The main focus of the revisions is increased emphasis on and scrutiny of the authenticity of a corporation's cooperation. Too often business organizations, while purporting to cooperate with a Department investigation, in fact take steps to impede the quick and effective exposure of the complete scope of wrongdoing under investigation. The revisions make clear that such conduct should weigh in favor of a corporate prosecution. The revisions also address the efficacy of the corporate governance mechanisms in place within a corporation, to ensure that these measures are truly effective rather than mere paper programs.

Further experience with these principles may lead to additional adjustments. I look forward to hearing comments about their operation in practice. * * *

* * *

VI.   Charging a Corporation: Cooperation and Voluntary Disclosure

* * *

Another factor to be weighed by the prosecutor is whether the corporation appears to be protecting its culpable employees and agents. Thus, while cases will differ depending on the circumstances, a corporation's promise of support to culpable employees and agents, either through the advancing of attorneys fees,[1] through retaining the employees without sanction for their misconduct, or through providing information to the employees about the government's investigation pursuant to a joint defense agreement, may be considered by the prosecutor in weighing the extent and value of a corporation's cooperation. By the same token, the prosecutor should be wary of attempts to shield corporate officers and employees from liability by a willingness of the corporation to plead guilty.

(5) Nevertheless, the DOJ updated the Thompson Memorandum with the McNulty Memorandum in December, 2006. The McNulty Memorandum states that companies that advance the legal fees of employees charged with crimes may no longer be considered uncooperative:

---

1. Some states require corporations to pay the legal fees of officers under investigation prior to a formal determination of their guilt. Obviously, a corporation's compliance with governing law should not be considered a failure to cooperate.

MEMORANDUM

TO: Heads of Department Components

United States Attorneys

FROM: Paul J. McNulty

Deputy Attorney General

SUBJECT: <u>Principles of Federal Prosecution of Business Organizations</u>

The Department experienced unprecedented success in prosecuting corporate fraud during the last four years. We have aggressively rooted out corruption in financial markets and corporate board rooms across the country. Federal prosecutors should be justifiably proud that the information used by our nation's financial markets is more reliable, our retirement plans are more secure, and the investing public is better protected as a result of our efforts. The most significant result of this enforcement initiative is that corporations increasingly recognize the need for self-policing, self-reporting, and cooperation with law enforcement. Through their self-regulation efforts, fraud undoubtedly is being prevented, sparing shareholders from the financial harm accompanying corporate corruption. The Department must continue to encourage these efforts.

Though much has been accomplished, the work of protecting the integrity of the marketplace continues. As we press forward in our enforcement duties, it is appropriate that we consider carefully proposals which could make our efforts more effective. I remain convinced that the fundamental principles that have guided our enforcement practices are sound. In particular, our corporate charging principles are not only familiar, but they are welcomed by most corporations in our country because good corporate leadership shares many of our goals. Like federal prosecutors, corporate leaders must take action to protect shareholders, preserve corporate value, and promote honesty and fair dealing with the investing public.

We have heard from responsible corporate officials recently about the challenges they face in discharging their duties to the corporation while responding in a meaningful way to a government investigation. Many of those associated with the corporate legal community have expressed concern that our practices may be discouraging full and candid communications between corporate employees and legal counsel. To the extent this is happening, it was never the intention of the Department for our corporate charging principles to cause such a result.

Therefore, I have decided to adjust certain aspects of our policy in ways that will further promote public confidence in the Department, encourage corporate fraud prevention efforts, and clarify our goals without sacrificing our ability to prosecute these important cases effectively. The new language expands upon the Department's long-standing policies concerning how we evaluate the authenticity of a corporation's cooperation with a government investigation.

This memorandum supersedes and replaces guidance contained in the Memorandum from Deputy Attorney General Larry D. Thompson entitled Principles of Federal Prosecution of Business Organizations (January 20, 2003) (the "Thompson Memorandum") and the Memorandum from the Acting Deputy Attorney General Robert D. McCallum, Jr. entitled Waiver of Corporate Attorney–Client and Work Product Protections (October 21, 2005)(the "McCallum Memorandum").

* * *

VII.   Charging a Corporation: The Value of Cooperation

* * *

3.   Shielding Culpable Employees and Agents

Another factor to be weighed by the prosecutor is whether the corporation appears to be protecting its culpable employees and agents. Thus, while cases will differ depending on the circumstances, a corporation's promise of support to culpable employees and agents, *e.g.*, through retaining the employees without sanction for their misconduct or through providing information to the employees about the government's investigation pursuant to a joint defense agreement, may be considered by the prosecutor in weighing the extent and value of a corporation's cooperation.

Prosecutors generally should not take into account whether a corporation is advancing attorneys' fees to employees or agents under investigation and indictment. Many state indemnification statutes grant corporations the power to advance the legal fees of officers under investigation prior to a formal determination of guilt. As a consequence, many corporations enter into contractual obligations to advance attorneys' fees through provisions contained in their corporate charters, bylaws or employment agreements. Therefore, a corporation's compliance with governing state law and its contractual obligations cannot be considered a failure to cooperate.[2] This prohibition is not meant to prevent a prosecutor from asking questions about an attorney's representation of a corporation or its employees.[3]

---

2. In extremely rare cases, the advancement of attorneys' fees may be taken into account when the totality of the circumstances show that it was intended to impede a criminal investigation. In these cases, fee advancement is considered with many other telling facts to make a determination that the corporation is acting improperly to shield itself and its culpable employees from government scrutiny. *See discussion in* Brief of Appellant–United States, *United States v. Smith and Watson*, No. 06–3999–cr (2d Cir. Nov. 6, 2006). Where these circumstances exist, approval must be obtained from the Deputy Attorney General before prosecutors may consider this factor in their charging decisions. Prosecutors should follow the authorization process established for waiver requests of Category II information (see section V1I–2, *infra*).

3. Routine questions regarding the representation status of a corporation and its employees, including how and by whom attorneys' fees are paid, frequently arise in the course of an investigation. They may be necessary to assess other issues, such as conflict-of-interest. Such questions are appropriate and this guidance is not intended to prohibit such inquiry.

Chapter Fifteen

TAKEOVERS

We live in an era in which publicly-held corporations are objects of commerce. Even the largest U.S. publicly-held corporation can become the target of a hostile acquisition attempt. This era began sometime in the late 1960s. Takeovers appear to come in waves. There was a strong wave in the 1980s, followed by a short pause in the early 1990s. A new wave began in the mid–1990s and has continued into the Twenty-first Century.

In the earlier period that began in the late 1960s and ended in approximately 1990, large publicly-held corporations were (1) bought and sold, (2) bought, recapitalized, and then reintroduced to the public markets as new and quite different publicly held corporations, (3) bought, broken up and individual components sold, or (4) bought and retained by the purchaser as wholly-owned subsidiaries or divisions of the purchaser. The potential acquirer is usually called the "aggressor" and the sought-after corporation the "target." In the 1980s, two or more aggressors often competed simultaneously against each other to acquire the target. These immense and widely-publicized contests during the 1980s impressed their image on the decade in much the same way as the flappers impressed their image on the 1920s.

Before the pause in the early 1990s, the takeover movement largely involved aggressors seeking to acquire controlling interests in targets over the opposition and resistance of the target's incumbent management. While we still observe hostile takeovers, they have become less common in recent years. Defensive strategies have become so durable and effective that at some point, hostile takeover bids in the modern period end up either abandoned or negotiated directly with incumbent management. While from the outside these deals look like consensual transactions rather than the brutal, no-holds-barred battles that occurred during the earlier period, they are often highly competitive. While fending off other potential bidders, the aggressor seeks to acquire a target as well as a target management team that prefers either to remain independent or to negotiate with another, more congenial acquirer. Defensive strategies today usually permit incumbent management to defeat even attractive takeover bids if they are sufficiently motivated. Once a company becomes an acquisition target, however, it rarely remains independent because it usually is acquired by some outsider or other.

The power of management to defeat takeover bids raises serious policy questions about whether the interests of shareholders or the interests of management are paramount. It should be apparent that these two interests are usually in direct conflict: shareholders prefer to sell their shares to would-be acquirers at attractive prices considerably above the former market price, while management prefers to retain lucrative positions managing the enterprise. Similar questions about whether the interests of shareholders are being served by takeovers arise from the observation that, while shareholders of companies that are targets of hostile takeovers enjoy significant gains in the form of a high sales price, shareholders of the acquiring companies almost always fare less well. Indeed, the share prices of target firms usually increase dramatically when there is an outside bid, but the shares of the firms making the bids usually slightly decline in price.

A. THE BEGINNINGS OF THE TAKEOVER MOVEMENT

WILLIAM ALLEN, U.S. CORPORATE GOVERNANCE IN A POST–MANAGERIAL AGE

Text of speech given as the Fifth Distinguished Lecture in International
Business and Trade Law, University of Toronto Faculty of Laws.
Pp. 6–12 (Oct. 20, 1993).

* * * [John Kenneth Galbraith, in his influential book, *The New Industrial State,* written in the 1960s,] saw the social landscape dominated by huge, virtually autonomous business institutions, under the control of an elite corps of professional managers. These corporations—or what, in this view, amounted to the same thing, these senior managers—had largely freed themselves from the constraints imposed by * * * capital markets by internally generating required funds. Berle and Means had long since shown that the modern U.S. corporation was managed free of constraint from shareholders, who— widely dispersed and diversified—could be counted upon to affirm any proposal that management offered. The picture of autonomous management was completed by reference to long-term labor contracts in which management entered into peace treaties with labor and by the co-opting of the regulatory processes of government through revolving door employment practices. Atop these large and powerful institutions, of course, sat self-perpetuating hierarchies of senior management.

Galbraith saw these powerful corporations of * * * [this era]—General Motors, IBM, the Pennsylvania Railroad, U.S. Steel, etc.—as impervious, nearly governmental in nature and nearly permanent. We now know that this vision badly underestimated the power of markets, but at the time it reflected what I take to have been a widely held perception.

Businessmen * * *, I feel sure, never felt control over their environment to the degree that Mr. Galbraith posited. But the view of the corporation as a quasi-public institution was quite consistent with the dominant view among managers. If they did not view the public corporation as impervious to markets, business leaders did see the large-scale business enterprise as a quasi-public institution. This was the dogma of managerialism. It was one of managerial authority and managerial responsibility. It implied, of course, that corporations did not exist in a brutally competitive world. * * *

But changes began to undermine the secure suppositions of the managerialist ideology. Those changes included innovation and growth in credit markets and the evolution of takeover entrepreneurs; the explosive growth of pension funds and other institutional shareholders and the striking emergence of a global market place. These forces came together by the early 1980s to trigger a period of significant restructuring in the private sector of the U.S. economy. In that process the premises of the managerialist vision of the corporation were directly challenged by a device that might have come straight out of a neo-classical economics textbook: the hostile cash tender offer.

Historically, legal devices have long existed by which inefficient or dishonest corporate managers could be removed from office. In a few instances, individual shareholders or families owned sufficient shares to influence directly the decisions of boards of directors. Palace coups in which a majority of the directors determined secretly to oust incumbent management and replace them with more competent persons were also a possibility. In some instances, the management of publicly held corporations in dire financial straits voluntarily agreed to be taken over by more successful entities. An aggressor rebuffed by management of a target might obtain voting control over the target by going over the heads of incumbent management and the board of directors and approaching shareholders of the target with a proposal to exchange shares issued by the aggressor for the target's voting shares. Such an offer is a public offering of securities by the aggressor that requires registration under the Securities Act of 1933 and historically has been viewed as a high risk strategy that was unlikely to be successful.

1. PROXY FIGHTS

The most important traditional device used to oust incumbent managers who insisted on remaining independent—a device much more talked about than actually used—was the proxy fight. Since they are often used today, sometimes alone[1] but more often in connection with other takeover devices, a brief discussion of them is appropriate.

A traditional proxy fight was a struggle for control of a public corporation in which most of the high cards were held by management. The nonmanagement group owning a small minority of shares often recently acquired—the "insurgents"—competed with management in an effort to obtain sufficient proxy votes to elect a majority (or all) of the board of directors, and thereby take over control of the corporation. The insurgent group usually made some open market purchases of shares before publicly announcing its intentions, and in some instances assembled a substantial block of shares before management became aware that someone was accumulating shares. In order to solicit proxies successfully, the insurgents had to obtain a list of shareholders, which usually involved a trip to the courthouse and certainly warned incumbent management that an unfriendly proxy solicitation was being contemplated by someone.

After a proxy contest was announced by insurgents, proxies were actively solicited by both incumbent management and insurgents. Proxies were solicited by mailings, by personal contact, and by newspaper and radio commer-

---

1. [By the Editors] In 1998, a pure proxy fight conducted by TIAA/CREF ousted the entire board of directors of Furr's/Bishop, Inc. a struggling publicly held restaurant chain. This apparently was the first modern instance of the use of a proxy fight by an institutional investor to effect a change in management of a substantial publicly held corporation.

cials. Even though institutional investors did not have the holdings they do today, they were often individually courted. Specialized proxy solicitation firms assisted both the insurgents and management in what was essentially a political campaign for control of the corporation, somewhat similar to an election for public office.

Proxy fights obviously were expensive if the number of shareholders was large. The accepted view was that such fights were not feasible at all in very large corporations with hundreds of thousands of shareholders since the costs of solicitation were prohibitive. Furthermore, incumbent management could have the corporation assume most (or all) of its costs while the insurgents had to finance their campaign entirely out of their own pockets. The expenses of an unsuccessful proxy fight by insurgents were likely to be sunk costs that were simply lost if the proxy fight failed, so that the insurgents had much more to lose than management. And, in addition, insurgents seeking proxy solicitations from numerous shareholders had the burden of persuading them that they would be better off if new (and often unknown) management were substituted for incumbent management. These burdens alone meant that proxy fights were likely to be successful only if the corporation's recent economic performance had been weak.

Is there any problem with management charging expenses of a proxy fight to the corporation even though the fight is basically designed to preserve their positions in the corporation? Is there any problem with insurgents, if successful, charging their expenses to the corporation after they take it over? Since the ousted management will have used corporate funds to finance their defense while they were in office, the usual result where the insurgents won was that the corporation paid the expenses of both sides. Is there anything wrong with that? There is a fair amount of law on the appropriateness of charging proxy contest expenses to the corporation. Delaware has adopted a "policy/personality" distinction that permits management to charge expenses relating to the development of policy issues but prohibits them from doing so when the issue is purely a personality contest. Palumbo v. Deposit Bank, 758 F.2d 113 (3d Cir.1985); Levin v. Metro–Goldwyn–Mayer, Inc., 264 F.Supp. 797 (S.D.N.Y.1967). Can one draw a meaningful distinction between "policy" and "personality"? Cannot all personality disputes be formulated in terms of a policy disagreement? New York narrowly avoided adopting an even more stringent test in Rosenfeld v. Fairchild Engine & Airplane Corp., 309 N.Y. 168, 128 N.E.2d 291 (1955). So far as the insurgents are concerned, the rule clearly is "no reimbursement" if the insurgents are unsuccessful (certainly it is highly unlikely that successful incumbent management will volunteer to pay the losing faction's expenses). If they are successful insurgents may argue that they should be reimbursed by the corporation because of the benefit conferred by the change in management. Academic commentary suggested that the usual result where insurgents are successful (that the corporation in effect pays the expenses of both sides) was less than optimal, but there was little movement to try to change this result. Lucian Arye Bebchuk & Marcel Kahan, A Framework for Analyzing Legal Policy Towards Proxy Contests, 78 Cal. L.Rev. 1071 (1990); Franklin C. Latcham & Frank D. Emerson, Proxy Contest Expenses and Shareholder Democracy, 4 Western Res. L.Rev. 5 (1952). Should reimbursement of unsuccessful insurgents be required if their campaign leads to beneficial changes in policy? What kinds of restrictions or limitations might be built into such a plan to eliminate the risk that publicity seekers, cranks, and the like might institute hopeless proxy fights?

SEC proxy regulations contain detailed rules relating to disclosure requirements in connection with proxy solicitations. 17 C.F.R. §§ 240.14a–4—14a–6, 240.14a–12—14a–15, 240.14a–101 (2002). These regulations require "participants" other than management in a proxy contest to file specified information with the SEC and securities exchanges at least five days before a solicitation begins. "Participant" is defined so as to include anyone who contributes more than $500 for the purpose of financing the contest. The information that must be disclosed relates to the identity and background of the participants, their interests in securities of the corporation, when they were acquired, financing arrangements, participation in other proxy contests, and understandings with respect to future employment with the corporation. The solicitation of majority consents is also subject to these third-party proxy solicitation rules, as is a solicitation by an institutional investor to more than ten other institutional investors to act in concert on a matter relating to shareholder voting.

The general philosophy of these contested proxy regulations is described by Judge Clark as follows:

> Appellants' fundamental complaint appears to be that stockholder disputes should be viewed in the eyes of the law just as are political contests, with each side free to hurl charges with comparative unrestraint, the assumption being that the opposing side is then at liberty to refute and thus effectively deflate the "campaign oratory" of its adversary. Such, however, was not the policy of Congress as enacted in the Securities Exchange Act. There Congress has clearly entrusted to the Commission the duty of protecting the investing public against misleading statements made in the course of a struggle for corporate control.

Securities and Exch. Comm'n v. May, 229 F.2d 123, 124 (2d Cir.1956).

The number of proxy fights subject to SEC jurisdiction historically was rather small. For example, only thirty-seven companies were involved in proxy contests for the election of directors in fiscal 1977. Control was involved in twenty-six instances; in eight of these, management retained control, three were settled by negotiation, five were won by nonmanagement factions, and ten were pending at the end of the year. In eleven instances, representation, not control, was sought; management retained all places on the board in six contests and opposition candidates won places on the board in five cases. 1977 S.E.C. Annual Report, at 107. Similar SEC data are not available for more recent years.

The proxy fight was largely eclipsed as a takeover mechanism by the cash tender offer that evolved in the 1960s and is discussed in the following section.[2] During the late 1980s, however, there was a brief resurgence of

---

2. [By the Editors] Sophisticated defensive techniques developed against cash tender offers described in Parts B and C, *infra,* are routinely used to defeat outside proxy solicitations. See generally Randall Thomas, Judicial Review of Defensive Tactics in Proxy Contests: When Is Using a Rights Plan Right?, 46 Vand. L.Rev. 503 (1993); Irvin H. Warren & Kevin G. Abrams, Evolving Standards of Judicial Review of Procedural Defenses in Proxy Contests, 47 Bus. Law. 647 (1992); Mark A. Stach, An Overview of Legal and Tactical Considerations in Proxy Contests: The Primary Means of Effect-

contested proxy campaigns in connection with purchase-type takeover attempts. During the period between October 1984 and September 1990, there were 165 proxy contests seeking full or partial control of the board of directors. Joseph A. Grundfest, Just Vote No: A Minimalist Strategy for Dealing with Barbarians Inside the Gates, 45 Stan. L. Rev. 857, 862 n. 17 (1993). In some instances, the target was simply too big for the aggressor to finance the purchase of a majority of the shares. If the aggressor had financial resources to acquire only fifteen or twenty percent of the outstanding shares, a proxy fight might be instituted in an effort to attract sufficient additional votes to oust incumbent management without purchasing an outright majority of the voting stock or, at least, mount a viable threat to encourage the target to negotiate. A well-known example of this strategy was Carl Icahn's proxy fight against the incumbent management of Texaco, Inc. in 1986. In other instances, takeover defenses proved to be impregnable against an outside cash tender offer, and the aggressor attempted an end run by launching a proxy fight in order to compel the removal of the defenses. See Christopher Power, Why the Proxy Fight is Back, Bus. Wk., Mar. 7, 1988, at 32; Judith Dobrzynski, et al., Whose Company Is It Anyway? Proxy Fights Are Spreading as Shareholders Seek More Power, Bus. Wk., Apr. 25, 1988, at 60. In yet another type of case, proxy fights were launched in an effort to persuade a target corporation to enter into a recapitalization or financial restructuring that involved an extraordinary distribution to shareholders. In about 50 percent of these situations, the insurgents were wholly or partially successful.[3] Grundfest, supra at 863 n. 17. In 1990, financing for all-cash takeovers began to dry up, and there was a spurt of more than a dozen proxy fights instituted against major corporations. This trend, however, did not last. The number of proxy fights again declined markedly by 1993.[4]

2. CASH TENDER OFFERS

ROBERT W. HAMILTON AND RICHARD BOOTH, CORPORATION FINANCE: CASES AND MATERIALS (3rd Ed., 2001)
Pp. 763–66.

Prior to the 1960s, most contests for corporate control took the form of a proxy fight. * * * There is, of course, a more direct way to gain the votes necessary to unseat the incumbent board. A bidder may simply buy up the shares of the target company either on the open market or [by] making an offer to the public shareholders (or both). Prior to the 1960s, most such offers took the form of exchange offers in which the bidder would offer its own stock or other securities to the stockholders of the target company. Such an offer is,

---

ing Fundamental Corporate Change in the 1990s, 13 George Mason U.L.Rev. 745 (1991).

3. [By the Editors] The major successful proxy fight during this period was won by a group headed by Robert Gintel, who began with a 21.6 percent voting interest in Xtra Corporation, and obtained sufficient proxy votes to oust the incumbent management. See Randall Smith, Storming the Barricades with a Proxy: Takeover Defenses Prove to be Flimsy,

Wall St. J., May 10, 1990, at C1. In the situations where proxy fights were not directly successful, the target often felt the pressure of this tactic in its negotiations with the insurgents or with other possible aggressors.

4. [By the Editors] By 1992, the number of proxy fights had shrunk to less than half of the 1989 peak. Id.

of course, a public offering of securities and is therefore subject to registration under the 1933 Act. * * *

Cash is not a security, and there is no need to register an offer of cash in exchange for target company stock. Thus, cash tender offers were largely unregulated up to and through most of the 1960s. Essentially, a cash tender offer is a public invitation to the shareholders of the target corporation to *tender* their shares to the bidder for purchase for cash. As developed during the 1960s, the offering price was set usually 15 to 20 per cent in excess of the then current market price. The bidder sought enough shares to gain control of the target corporation, although sometimes the bidder sought a higher percentage or all of the outstanding shares. The bidder usually made a public offer or invitation for tenders of shares under which it was not obligated to purchase any shares unless the required amount was tendered. If an excess was tendered, the bidder could, at its option, purchase the excess shares or purchase the required amount only on a pro rata or first-come first-served basis. The tender offer was usually made by an advertisement in the financial press, and copies were often mailed to all shareholders as well. The offer usually provided for a generous commission to brokers who persuaded customers to tender shares.

* * * Initially, the probability of success of a tender offer appeared to be greater than a proxy fight in part because of the element of surprise. During this period it was not uncommon for management of target companies to learn of the offer only when the Wall Street Journal blossomed with a full page ad announcing the offer. Offers often remained open for a brief period so that little time was available to incumbent management to respond and shareholders were panicked into tendering quickly lest they lose out on the offer entirely. Indeed, the phrase *Saturday Night Special,* was coined to describe an offer after the close of the market on Friday and expiring at midnight on Sunday. Such an offer had the advantage (from the bidder's point of view) of denying target shareholders any information as to the reaction of the market. After all, if the offer was a low ball, the market might actually react by bidding up the price of the shares over the offer price in anticipation of a higher offer to come, in which case the shareholders would have no reason to tender. They could sell in the market for more.

Another factor favoring the tender offer over the proxy fight is that in a cash tender offer, the individual shareholder's decision tends to be a simple investment decision rather than a choice between competing factions for control. In a proxy contest, the shareholder's choice is between competing factions for the right to run the corporation in which the shareholder will have a continuing interest.

When a cash tender offer was made, the open market price for the shares usually increased dramatically. (Whether it equaled or exceeded the tender offer price depended on a complex variety of factors, including the probability that a competing offer at a higher price might be made, whether the offer was likely to be over-subscribed, whether it was on a first-come first-served basis, and so forth.) Persons owning shares thus had the choice of selling their shares in the open market, retaining them, or tendering them. Most shares sold on the open market ultimately were tendered. A group of speculators, known as arbitrageurs, or simply arbs, purchased shares in the open market at prices below the tender offer price in order to tender them and profit by the difference between the two prices. In many tender offers, the arbs came to control enough shares to dictate the outcome of the offer.

This classic picture of the tender offer was significantly modified by the 1968 enactment of the Williams Act, which technically was an amendment to sections 13 and 14 of the Securities Exchange Act of 1934. The Williams Act does essentially two things. First, it provides for disclosures by the bidder. Unlike the 1933 Act or the proxy rules under the 1934 Act, however, these disclosures need not be made or filed in advance of the offer. In other words, the element of surprise is preserved under the Williams Act, although the act does require that anyone who acquires five percent or more of the stock of a registered company (or thereafter increases his or her holdings) must disclose the acquisition and notify the issuer within ten days. Second, the Williams Act provides a set of bidding rules to govern the conduct of tender offers. These rules have been modified somewhat over the years by the SEC, but in essence they provide (1) that there is a minimum period during which a tender offer must remain open (currently 20 business days), (2) that a tendering shareholder has the right during the offer to withdraw shares tendered, (3) that all tendering shareholders must receive the highest price paid in the offer, and (4) that if the offer is over-subscribed then all shareholders may have their shares purchased pro rata in proportion to the number of shares they tendered. In general, the Williams Act applies only to companies that are registered under the 1934 Act, although the catch-all anti-fraud rules adopted thereunder apply in connection with all tender offers in interstate commerce.

The central idea behind the Williams Act was not to stop tender offers altogether, but rather (1) to slow down the process, and give shareholders information about the offer, and give target management a chance to respond, and (2) to assure that the shareholders would be treated equally and get the highest possible price, in part by increasing the chances for a competing bid to arise. Whether these goals are worthy and whether the Williams Act achieves them are separate questions.

Numerous devices were designed to avoid or minimize the impact of the Williams Act bidding rules. For example, a bidder might launch a front end loaded two tier tender offer, offering an attractive premium for 51 percent of the shares in the front end tender offer and announcing that the remaining 49 percent of the shares will be cashed out in a later merger at the pre tender offer market price. The idea is to induce shareholders to tender their shares even if they might prefer to hold out for a higher price. Or a bidder might announce an offer for a bare controlling interest and say nothing about what might happen to the remaining minority interest if the bid was successful, raising the possibility that the bidder might loot the target after a successful bid and that the minority shares would end up worth even less than the pre bid market price. Target management argued that such bids were coercive and that greater leeway should be allowed under principles of fiduciary duty in resisting such offers. Some also argued that such bids violated the spirit of the Williams Act and perhaps even its letter in that they were designed to manipulate the price at which the offer would succeed. Some even argued that the United States should adopt the United Kingdom rule that any offer for 30 percent or more of target shares must be an offer for all of the shares.

Although neither of these fixes came to pass, the courts did allow target management considerable flexibility in defending against coercive offers. Moreover, the SEC promulgated regulations designed to modify or eliminate some tactics, and the states enacted statutes designed to limit others. The overall result of these developments has been the creation of a regulatory scheme for tender offers of increasing, and sometimes bewildering, complexity. Ultimately, however, two tier and partial offers probably evolved away because of competitive forces. Given the choice, target shareholders would presumably favor an all cash offer for any and all shares over any other sort of offer. Thus, anyone who made a two tier or partial offer would likely find that another bidder would emerge offering the same price in cash for more of the shares, assuming, of course, that the cash was available.

During the late 1980s, both the size and number of transactions increased dramatically. The previously little known securities firms of Drexel Burnham Lambert and Kohlberg Kravis Roberts & Co. became major players with access to billions of dollars for the purchase of large publicly owned corporations. Multi-billion dollar all-cash transactions became commonplace, culminating in the $24.8 billion leveraged buyout of RJR Nabisco, Inc. by KKR at the end of 1988, a year in which there were also about 85 hostile takeovers. According to Securities Data Company, there were 4239 priced deals valued at $5 million or more in 1990 of which 177 were leveraged buyouts. The peak year for leveraged buyouts was 1989 in which there were 293 such transactions valued at $75.5 billion or about 24 percent of the $317 billion in aggregate deal value that year. During the 1980s as whole, 30 percent of the Fortune 500 companies were the target of a hostile offer. See John C. Coates IV, Measuring the Domain of Mediating Hierarchy: How Contestable Are U.S. Public Corporations?, 24 J. Corp. L. 837, 851 (1999).

Notes

(1) Not all tender offers are hostile. In some cases, it may make more sense for a friendly bidder to use a tender offer rather than some other device. For example, a company that desires to purchase a large stake in another company for strategic or investment purposes may find that there are fewer legal risks in a tender offer than in a negotiated purchase of stock and that it is cheaper to purchase stock from existing shareholders. Or it may be that the bidder also wants to reduce the public float of the target company and possibly raise the market price in the bargain. Moreover, bids that start out hostile may evolve into friendly deals and *vice versa*.

(2) The Williams Act also governs tender offers by an issuer for its own shares. The rules relating to such self tender offers are roughly the same as those relating to third-party tender offers, although it is common for a self tender offer to take the form of a Dutch Auction[5] in which the shareholders specify the price within a range at which they are willing to sell. In this type of auction, bidding starts high and declines until a buyer claims the item. When multiple items are auctioned, more bidders claim the items as the price decreases, therefore the first winner pays more than subsequent winners. However, if two buyers want the

---

5. [By the Editors] The purchaser in a Dutch auction determines how many shares he wishes to buy and accepts all bids at (or below) the price that yields the desired quantity he wishes to buy.

item at the initial suggested price, the buyers bid against each other until only one bidder is left to purchase at the final bid price.

(3) A variation of the cash tender offer is the "exchange offer," in which the aggressor offers to exchange a package of its own securities for the shares of the target. The package usually consists of both debt and equity interests, and might include highly-speculative warrants or options to acquire further equity interests in the aggressor. Such interests sometimes receive the derogatory label "funny money." In any event, cash tender offers and public exchange offers can be utilized by different aggressors seeking control of a single target corporation. For example, in the fight for Armour & Co. in the late 1960s, a cash tender offer by Greyhound Lines, Inc. was met with a public exchange offer by General Host Corporation.

In a broad sense, public exchange offers can be viewed as a type of financing device by aggressors. An aggressor might sell its own securities to create a pool of capital in order to make offers to shareholders of a target corporation to buy shares for cash. Alternatively, the aggressor might offer its own securities directly to the target shareholders in a public exchange offer, eliminating the cash-raising step and making the target shareholders the source of capital for the takeover.

(4) Premiums in hostile deals tend to be somewhat higher than premiums in friendly deals. During the period from 1974–85, the average premium was around 75% over the pre-bid market price. *See* Nathan & O'Keefe, The Rise in Takeover Premiums: An Exploratory Study, 23 J. Fin. Econ. 101, 101 (1989). According to Securities Data Company, the average premium for the year ended March 31, 1999 was 34.6 percent over the day-before-announcement price.

(5) In a recent article, Guhan Subramanian suggests that, in the case of freezeouts, both mergers and tender offers are flawed tools for majorities to use to buy out minority interests. Guhan Subramanian, Fixing Freezouts, 115 Yale L.J. 2 (2005). Professor Subramanian explains:

> On August 2, 2004, Barbara Cox Anthony and Anne Cox Chambers, who together owned a 62% equity interest and a 73% voting interest in Cox Communications, announced that they would offer $32 cash per share in a "freezeout" of the Cox minority shareholders. The offer represented a 16% premium over the preannouncement trading price for Cox, or $7.9 billion in total value. Cox formed a special committee (SC) of three independent directors to review the offer and negotiate with the Cox sisters' representatives. Minority shareholders sued alleging that the offer price was unfair. Over the following four months, the SC bargained hard: counteroffering at $38 per share, walking away from the table at several points, and finally agreeing to a deal at $34.75 per share, representing a 26% premium over the pre-offer price. The deal closed on December 8, 2004.

> One month later, on January 10, 2005, News Corporation, controlled by publishing magnate Rupert Murdoch, announced a freezeout exchange offer for the 18% of Fox Entertainment Group that it did not already own. The proposed ratio of 1.9 News shares for each Fox share represented a 7.4% premium over the preannouncement trading price for Fox, or $6.0 billion in total value. As in the Cox freezeout, Fox formed an SC of independent directors to review the offer, and plaintiffs' counsel filed suit alleging that the offer price was unfair to the minority. However, in contrast to the Cox freezeout, News stated that it might go forward with the transaction even if the Fox SC did not approve the offer. On January 24, the Fox SC issued a statement taking no position on the News offer, explaining that it needed

more time. On March 4, News raised its offer to 2.04 News shares per Fox share, or a 17.6% premium over the preannouncement trading price for Fox. On March 7, the SC approved the revised offer, and the deal closed on March 22, 2005.

As the Cox Communications and Fox Entertainment Group examples illustrate, freezeouts are back. Due at least in part to the stock market decline of 2000 and the additional costs imposed on public companies under the Sarbanes–Oxley Act of 2002, freezeout activity in the United States has increased to more than twice its historical levels: 128 announced transactions in the four years between July 2001 and July 2005 (32 per year, on average), compared to 154 freezeouts during the ten years between 1987 and 1996 (15 per year, on average). At the same time that freezeout activity has been increasing, the Delaware courts have established different standards of judicial review for the two ways of freezing out minority shareholders. The traditional route, known as a statutory merger freezeout, mandates an SC with veto power over the deal, followed by stringent "entire fairness" review by the courts. The Cox sisters (or, more accurately, their legal advisors) chose this transactional form for the Cox Communications freezeout. The new route, known as a tender offer freezeout, does not give the SC veto power and, at least as of mid–2001, is subject only to deferential business judgment review by the courts. News Corporation chose this transactional form for the Fox Entertainment freezeout.

These procedural differences have substantive implications. Examining the outcomes of all freezeouts in the current doctrinal regime, I find that minority shareholders received less in tender offer freezeouts than in merger freezeouts, as measured by premiums over preannouncement stock prices. This finding is illustrated dramatically by the Cox and Fox examples above: If the Fox minority shareholders had received the same 26.0% premium that the Cox minority shareholders received (rather than their actual 17.6%), they would have achieved an additional $504 million in total consideration from News Corporation.

Commentators have debated the wisdom of doctrinal contours that create procedural and substantive differences based on choice of transactional form, and several have advocated convergence toward a single judicial approach to freezeouts. The need for change has nevertheless remained unclear because of the possibility for adjustments in ex ante pricing of a minority stake. This Article makes the case for change by identifying two social welfare costs of the current regime. First, the tender-offer-freezeout mechanism facilitates some inefficient (value-destroying) transactions by allowing the controller to exploit asymmetric information against the minority. Second, the merger freezeout mechanism deters some efficient (value-increasing) transactions because of the SC's power to veto the deal. Tender-offer-freezeout doctrine goes too far, and merger-freezeout doctrine does not go far enough, in facilitating freezeouts. Put another way, some companies that should not "go private" do, while others that should do not. As a result, there is a suboptimal distribution of companies between public and private status.

After identifying this efficiency loss, this Article proposes specific doctrinal adjustments that would fix freezeouts. Rather than propose a patchwork solution, this Article advocates a return to first principles of corporate law in the freezeout context. The objective is to replicate the elements of an armslength negotiation—namely, disinterested board approval and disinterested shareholder approval—in the freezeout context. Translating the arms-length standard to the freezeout arena requires, first, meaningful approval by an SC of independent directors; and second, approval by a majority of the minority shareholders. When both of these procedural protections are provided, this Article proposes that courts should apply deferential business judgment review to assess the transaction. If either or both of these protections are absent, this Article proposes that courts should step in to scrutinize the transaction under the entire fairness standard. The result of this re-grounding would be convergence in standards of judicial review for freezeouts and elimination of the efficiency loss inherent in the existing doctrine.

If, as Professor Subramanian suggests, tender offers are always cheaper for the majority, why do majorities ever use mergers instead? What solution would you propose to the problems Professor Subramanian identifies?

3. LEVERAGED BUYOUTS

The leveraged buyout (LBO) of the 1980s initially appeared to be a new and irresistible business form. An LBO involved an aggressor (an existing management, another corporation, or a corporate raider) who purchased all or most of the outstanding stock of the target for a substantial premium over market price. The acquisition was financed through loans that initially might involve short-term "mezzanine" or "bridge" loans (short-term financing with payment of only interest until the whole balance is due) plus low-grade high-interest debt instruments—noninvestment-grade junk bonds. The transaction was structured so that the repayment of this newly-created debt ultimately became the obligation of the target corporation. It was a classic bootstrap transaction: the proceeds of the debt assumed by the target were used to purchase the publicly-held shares of the target. Funds to pay the debt assumed by the target were to be obtained by the sale of components of the target's business or by use of the target's subsequent cash flow. This cash flow was increased by tax savings arising from the deductions for interest payments made on the new debt. In making the financial calculations to see how much debt a target can carry, the standard measure is "EBIT"—net "earnings before interest and taxes"—because the tax obligation is eliminated by the interest deductions for payments on the new debt. When the debt was paid down sufficiently, the target could again become a publicly-held corporation through the sale of shares to the general public. In the best of all worlds, everyone benefited. In the worst, the corporation was unable to carry the load of the new debt and went into bankruptcy; at that point, the issue became whether the LBO transaction itself could be attacked as a fraudulent conveyance.

ROBERT W. HAMILTON AND RICHARD A. BOOTH, BUSINESS BASICS FOR LAW STUDENTS: ESSENTIAL TERMS AND CONCEPTS[6]
Pp. 355, 360–61 (1997).

It is important to recognize that even if the bidder acquires over 50 percent of the outstanding shares and replaces the target's board of directors

---

6. Reprinted with permission of Aspen Law   pen Publishers, Inc.
& Business/Panel Publishers, a division of As-

and management, it does not have a free hand with respect to the target's assets. The target is still a publicly owned company with the public owning 49.9 percent; the presence of this minority interest sharply circumscribes and limits what the bidder can do with the target's assets. For example, the bidder may not simply distribute to itself * * * $50,000,000 in excess cash or combine a manufacturing division owned by the target with a similar division owned by the bidder. Transactions of these types would almost certainly be viewed as in breach of the fiduciary duty new management has assumed to the former target company and would likely give rise to immediate shareholder derivative suits. Transactions between the bidder and its new partially owned subsidiary must be made at arms-length and, even then, there is a substantial opportunity for distracting litigation brought by minority shareholders of the target. * * *

* * * However, it is not possible, as a practical matter, to acquire 100 percent of the shares of a publicly held corporation by a tender offer. Even in an irresistibly attractive tender offer for all shares, a few shareholders always fail to tender by reason of inadvertence or inattention, and there always are a few small shareholders who hold out and refuse to accept an offer at any price. A follow-up transaction to eliminate the remaining shareholders is an essential step where 100 percent ownership is desired. These follow-up transactions, often called back-end or mop-up transactions, are statutory [cash-out] mergers [in which minority shares are converted into a specified amount of cash]. A back-end transaction is not necessary if the bidder is willing to accept the status of a majority shareholder in a publicly held corporation with minority shareholders.

In a public cash tender offer, the bidder may make the back-end transaction an affirmative weapon. The bidder may make a partial tender offer, seeking to acquire a controlling interest but less than all of the target's outstanding shares, and at the same time announce, as part of its takeover strategy, the terms of the back-end merger that will eliminate all of the remaining outstanding shares if the original partial offer is successful. Such an offer is known as a two-step offer or two-tier offer. The terms of the back-end part of the two-step offer, moreover, may be [considerably] less attractive than the terms of the original cash tender offer, thereby encouraging (or coercing) all shareholders to tender promptly to avoid the less attractive terms of the follow-up transaction. Such an offer is known as a front-end loaded offer and is sometimes referred to as a coercive offer (although coercion comes in many forms). Many states have enacted statutes restricting back-end transactions.

ROBERT W. HAMILTON, CORPORATE MERGERS AND ACQUISITIONS

The Guide to American Law Yearbook.
Pp. 66, 72–75 (1990).

Most acquisition transactions since 1985 have involved all-cash purchases of the stock of the target corporation. * * * Even transactions involving little-known companies routinely involve all-cash transactions of hundreds of millions of dollars. The amounts involved in these transactions are so large as to have been almost unimaginable in a private transaction just two decades ago. An important question * * * [is] where [is] all the money * * * coming from[?]

In one sense, the answer is very simple: Most of the capital that goes into modern takeover attempts is borrowed. Borrowed money is what makes the modern takeover world go round; if that source of funding disappeared, the present takeover movement would stop instantly. It is true that aggressors such as Conoco and Texaco have immense operations of their own and can accumulate large amounts of cash, but even companies of that size cannot readily finance a multibillion dollar takeover entirely from internal sources. * * *

Loans from commercial banks are the source of most of the borrowed capital in large takeover bids, but other sources of high-risk financing also exist. During the 1980s, a market for high-risk, below-investment-grade debt instruments or "bonds," usually called "junk bonds," was largely created by Drexel Burnham Lambert, Inc. This market has grown to the point that it is able to absorb several billion dollars of high-risk debt to finance specific takeover bids. Many institutional investors are active in this market because junk bonds pay interest at rates considerably higher than can be obtained from the less risky "investment-grade" bonds.

In addition, a major source of equity capital has been created by takeover firms such as KKR, which has attracted takeover funds from sophisticated investors, including many institutional investors. The proposed financing by KKR of its purchase of RJR Nabisco illustrates the operation of these modern financing sources. KKR needed $20.1 billion in cash to purchase RJR. (The remaining $4.8 billion was represented by the debt securities being issued to tendering RJR shareholders.) KKR raised the $20.1 billion from the following sources:

    1. Bank loans were obtained from a large consortium of domestic and foreign (largely Japanese) banks—$13.3 billion.

    2. Five billion dollars in "bridge financing" was provided by the brokerage houses of Drexel Burnham Lambert, Inc. ($3.5 billion) and Merrill Lynch & Company ($1.5 billion). This bridge financing was to be refinanced within a year by the sale of junk bonds to investors.

    3. KKR limited partners put up $1.5 billion in equity capital. KKR itself put up only $15 million, or 1 percent of the entire risk capital and a tiny fraction of the total purchase price. Altogether, KKR raised $25.7 billion to cover the purchase price and expenses but invested only about $15 million of its own capital in order to acquire the nation's nineteenth largest commercial enterprise!

Why do banks and others agree to make such large loans to fund buyouts? For one thing, the return is good—interest rates on both takeover—directed bank loans and junk bonds are well above those available from other alternative investments. For another thing, fees for making loan commitments are earned whether or not the sale actually occurs. In the RJR Nabisco transaction, Merrill Lynch & Company and Drexel Burnham Lambert, Inc., received fees of about $200 million for their commitment to invest $5 billion, while the banks received a somewhat larger amount in commitment fees for making their much larger commitments. These fees are earned and paid when the commitment is made and are not dependent on the success of the bid.

Yet when all is said and done, commitment fees and high interest rates alone do not explain the attractiveness of these loans. One does not make money even from large loan commitment fees and high interest rates if the loans are so risky that they are unlikely to be repaid. These transactions are attractive because the risks are not as great as they first appear. An essential attribute of the ability of KKR and other takeover firms to raise immense amounts of capital is that these loans are in effect secured by the assets and cash flow of the target corporation itself. Such transactions are called "leveraged buyouts" or "bootstrap transactions." Approximately one-half of the recent takeover transactions were of this type. The banks were willing to lend more than $13 billion to KKR to purchase RJR Nabisco common stock because they were assured that, if the transaction succeeded, the assets and cash flow of RJR Nabisco would be used to pay the interest on and secure the repayment of the loans and junk bonds used to finance the purchase.

Of course, RJR Nabisco already had some indebtedness on its books. The new debt was simply added onto this existing debt and it is expected to repay the entire amount. Needless to say, Nabisco's existing creditors were not happy at these new obligations being assumed by RJR Nabisco. Since the proceeds of the new loans were used to pay shareholders, they did not benefit RJR Nabisco, and loans owed to existing creditors now were less secure and considerably more risky. But there was not very much they could do about the transaction.

After a leveraged buyout, the target may find that its total debt obligations greatly exceed its ability to repay them if business is continued as usual. Such a corporation may find it necessary to make Herculean efforts to reduce costs and increase cash flow. It may be compelled to sell portions of its business to third parties in order to liquidate at least a portion of the new indebtedness and permit the corporation to remain solvent. Transactions in which such later sales of components of the original business are contemplated at the time of the offer are called "bust-up transactions" or "bust-up acquisitions." Improvements in earnings and cash flow may also be achieved from the savings inherent in not being a reporting publicly-held corporation, from the immense tax deductions arising from the interest payments on its debt, from the elimination of dividends, and from economic improvements to the target's business. Indeed, the disciplinary effect of the increase in debt has been cited by some observers as a major benefit arising from leveraged transactions since it encourages increased efficiency and control of costs.

Many established businesses that have been acquired in leveraged buyouts have proven that they are able to carry large increases of indebtedness during periods of high economic activity. However, the recent spate of multibillion dollar leveraged buyouts, bust-up transactions, and junk bond financing because of the immense sums of money involved has caused concern among regulatory agencies, legislators, and the general public. The principal concern that has been expressed about the growth of such leveraged transactions generally is whether most of these debt-burdened businesses can survive when there is an economic downturn. Since there was no significant downturn during the 1980s, no one really knows the answer to this question. A secondary concern that has sometimes been expressed is whether the large investments by commercial banks and institutional investors in leveraged buyout loans and investments may harm the public's confidence in the nation's financial institutions during an economic downturn. If such a downturn occurs, the future of the spectacular mergers and acquisitions examined here will be in grave doubt. * * *

Corporate law firms thrived during the late 1980s as never before. Lawyers were close to the center of the takeover movement, charting strategy, devising defenses, and documenting and effectuating the transactions as they occurred. Immense acquisition transactions required structuring, the production of legal documents, of legal opinions, of tax analysis, and so forth. Securities and banking lawyers also played key roles in negotiating the financing of major transactions: the suppliers of huge amounts of capital required legal teams whose size rivaled those of the target and the aggressor. And finally there was the litigation that surrounded virtually every major takeover. Suits were often simultaneously pending in Delaware and six or seven other states as the target attempted to evade the grasp of the aggressor.

The largest takeover transaction ever attempted—the 1988 leveraged buyout of RJR–Nabisco, Inc. by the KKR firm * * * reflected both the high point and culmination of a movement that had shaken large American enterprise to its roots.

Note

Is all this only of historical interest? Not entirely. In 2000, there were fifteen leveraged buyout firms each with assets in excess of three billion dollars. The largest LBO firm, KKR, had assets in excess of eight billion dollars. See Return of the LBO: It May Not Be the Glory Years, But Buyout Shops Are Back, Raising Billions—and Heading Into Uncharted Waters, Business Week, October 16, 2000, at 130. Leveraged buyouts were on the rise in 2001 and 2002, fueled in part by historically low share prices. The largest leveraged transaction in 2001 was the $7+ billion purchase of Qwest's directory unit by Carson, Anderson & Stowe.

B. DEFENSES: STATE LEGISLATION

CTS CORP. v. DYNAMICS CORP. OF AMERICA

Supreme Court of the United States, 1987.
481 U.S. 69, 107 S.Ct. 1637, 95 L.Ed.2d 67.

JUSTICE POWELL delivered the opinion of the Court.

This case presents the questions whether the Control Share Acquisitions Chapter of the Indiana Business Corporation Law, Ind.Code § 23–1–42–1 *et seq.* (Supp.1986), is preempted by the Williams Act or violates the Commerce Clause of the Federal Constitution, Art. I, § 8, cl. 3.

I

A

On March 4, 1986, the Governor of Indiana signed a revised Indiana Business Corporation Law, Ind.Code § 23–1–17–1 *et seq.* (Supp.1986). That law included the Control Share Acquisitions Chapter (Indiana Act or Act). Beginning on August 1, 1987, the Act will apply to any corporation incorporated in Indiana, § 23–1–17–3(a), unless the corporation amends its articles or incorporation or bylaws to opt out of the Act, § 23–1–42–5. Before that date, any Indiana corporation can opt into the Act by resolution of its board of directors. § 23–1–17–3(b). The Act applies only to "issuing public corporations." The term "corporation" includes only businesses incorporated in Indiana. See § 23–1–20–5. An "issuing public corporation" is defined as:

"a corporation that has:

"(1) one hundred (100) or more shareholders;

"(2) its principal place of business, its principal office, or substantial assets within Indiana; and

"(3) either:

"(A) more than ten percent (10%) of its shareholders resident in Indiana;

"(B) more than ten percent (10%) of its shares owned by Indiana residents; or

"(C) ten thousand (10,000) shareholders resident in Indiana." § 23–1–42–4(a).[7]

The Act focuses on the acquisition of "control shares" in an issuing public corporation. Under the Act, an entity acquires "control shares" whenever it acquires shares that, but for the operation of the Act, would bring its voting power in the corporation to or above any of three thresholds: 20%, 33 1/3%, or 50%. § 23–1–42–1. An entity that acquires control shares does not necessarily acquire voting rights. Rather, it gains those rights only "to the extent granted by resolution approved by the shareholders of the issuing public corporation." § 23–1–42–9(a). Section 23–1–42–9(b) requires a majority vote of all disinterested[8] shareholders holding each class of stock for passage of such a resolution. The practical effect of this requirement is to condition acquisition of control of a corporation on approval of a majority of the pre-existing disinterested shareholders.

7. [By the Court] These thresholds are much higher than the 5% threshold acquisition requirement that brings a tender offer under the coverage of the Williams Act.

8. [By the Court] "Interested shares" are shares with respect to which the acquiror, an officer, or an inside director of the corporation "may exercise or direct the exercise of the voting power of the corporation in the election of directors." § 23–1–42–3. If the record date passes before the acquiror purchases shares pursuant to the tender offer, the purchased shares will not be "interested shares" within the meaning of the Act; although the acquiror may own the shares on the date of the meeting, it will not "exercise * * * the voting power" of the shares.

As a practical matter, the record date usually will pass before shares change hands. Under Securities and Exchange Commission (SEC) regulations, the shares cannot be purchased

until 20 business days after the offer commences. 17 CFR § 240.14e–1(a) (1986). If the acquiror seeks an early resolution of the issue—as most acquirors will—the meeting required by the Act must be held no more than 50 calendar days after the offer commences, about three weeks after the earliest date on which the shares could be purchased. See § 23–1–42–7. The Act requires management to give notice of the meeting "as promptly as reasonably practicable * * * to all shareholders of record as of the record date set for the meeting." § 23–1–42–8(a). It seems likely that management of the target corporation would violate this obligation if it delayed setting the record date and sending notice until after 20 business days had passed. Thus, we assume that the record date usually will be set before the date on which federal law first permits purchase of the shares.

The shareholders decide whether to confer rights on the control shares at the next regularly scheduled meeting of the shareholders, or at a specially scheduled meeting. The acquiror can require management of the corporation to hold such a special meeting within 50 days if it files an "acquiring person statement,"[9] requests the meeting, and agrees to pay the expenses of the meeting. See § 23–1–42–7. If the shareholders do not vote to restore voting rights to the shares, the corporation may redeem the control shares from the acquiror at fair market value, but it is not required to do so. § 23–1–42–10(b). Similarly, if the acquiror does not file an acquiring person statement with the corporation, the corporation may, if its bylaws or articles of incorporation so provide, redeem the shares at any time after 60 days after the acquiror's last acquisition. § 23–1–42–10(a).

B

On March 10, 1986, appellee Dynamics Corporation of America (Dynamics) owned 9.6% of the common stock of appellant CTS Corporation, an Indiana corporation. On that day, six days after the Act went into effect, Dynamics announced a tender offer for another million shares in CTS; purchase of those shares would have brought Dynamics' ownership interest in CTS to 27.5%. Also on March 10, Dynamics filed suit in the United States District Court for the Northern District of Illinois, alleging that CTS had violated the federal securities laws in a number of respects no longer relevant to these proceedings. On March 27, the board of directors of CTS, an Indiana corporation, elected to be governed by the provisions of the Act, see § 23–1–17–3.

Four days later, on March 31, Dynamics moved for leave to amend its complaint to allege that the Act is preempted by the Williams Act, and violates the Commerce Clause, Art. I, § 8, cl. 3. Dynamics sought a temporary restraining order, a preliminary injunction, and declaratory relief against CTS' use of the Act. On April 9, the District Court ruled that the Williams Act preempts the Indiana Act and granted Dynamics' motion for declaratory relief. 637 F.Supp. 389 (N.D.Ill.1986). Relying on Justice White's plurality opinion in *Edgar v. MITE Corp.*, 457 U.S. 624 (1982), the court concluded that the Act "wholly frustrates the purpose and objective of Congress in striking a balance between the investor, management, and the takeover bidder in takeover contests." 637 F.Supp., at 399. A week later, on April 17, the District Court issued an opinion accepting Dynamics' claim that the Act violates the Commerce Clause. This holding rested on the court's conclusion that "the substantial interference with interstate commerce created by the [Act] outweighs the articulated local benefits so as to create an impermissible indirect burden on interstate commerce." *Id.*, at 406. The District Court certified its decisions on the Williams Act and Commerce Clause claims as final under Federal Rule of Civil Procedure 54(b). Ibid.

CTS appealed the District Court's holdings on these claims to the Court of Appeals for the Seventh Circuit. Because of the imminence of CTS' annual meeting, the Court of Appeals consolidated and expedited the two appeals. On April 23rd—23 days after Dynamics first contested application of the Act in

---

9. [By the Court] An "acquiring person statement" is an information statement describing, *inter alia*, the identity of the acquir ing person and the terms and extent of the proposed acquisition. See § 23–1–42–6.

the District Court—the Court of Appeals issued an order affirming the judgment of the District Court. The opinion followed on May 28. 794 F.2d 250 (C.A.7 1986).

After disposing of a variety of questions not relevant to this appeal, the Court of Appeals examined Dynamics' claim that the Williams Act preempts the Indiana Act. The court looked first to the plurality opinion in *Edgar v. MITE Corp., supra,* in which three Justices found that the Williams Act preempts state statutes that upset the balance between target management and a tender offeror. The court noted that some commentators had disputed this view of the Williams Act, concluding instead that the Williams Act was "an anti-takeover statute, expressing a view, however benighted, that hostile takeovers are bad." 794 F.2d, at 262. It also noted:

> [I]t is a big leap from saying that the Williams Act does not itself exhibit much hostility to tender offers to saying that it implicitly forbids states to adopt more hostile regulations * * *. But whatever doubts of the Williams' Act preemptive intent we might entertain as an original matter are stilled by the weight of precedent. *Ibid.*

Once the court had decided to apply the analysis of the *MITE* plurality, it found the case straightforward:

> Very few tender offers could run the gauntlet that Indiana has set up. In any event, if the Williams Act is to be taken as a congressional determination that a month (roughly) is enough time to force a tender offer to be kept open, 50 days is too much; and 50 days is the minimum under the Indiana act if the target corporation so chooses. *Id.,* at 263.

The court next addressed Dynamic's Commerce Clause challenge to the Act. Applying the balancing test articulated in *Pike v. Bruce Church, Inc.,* 397 U.S. 137 (1970), the court found the Act unconstitutional:

> Unlike a state's blue sky law the Indiana statute is calculated to impede transactions between residents of other states. For the sake of trivial or even negative benefits to its residents Indiana is depriving nonresidents of the valued opportunity to accept tender offers from other nonresidents.

> * * * Even if a corporation's tangible assets are immovable, the efficiency with which they are employed and the proportions in which the earnings they generate are divided between management and shareholders depends on the market for corporate control—an interstate, indeed international, market that the State of Indiana is not authorized to opt out of, as in effect it has done in this statute. 794 F.2d, at 264.

Finally, the court addressed the "internal affairs" doctrine, a "principle of conflict of laws * * * designed to make sure that the law of only one state shall govern the internal affairs of a corporation or other association." It stated:

> We may assume without having to decide that Indiana has a broad latitude in regulating those affairs, even when the consequence may be to make it harder to take over an Indiana corporation. * * * But in this case the effect on the interstate market in securities and corporate control is direct, intended, and substantial. * * * [T]hat the mode of regulation

involves jiggering with voting rights cannot take it outside the scope of judicial review under the commerce clause. *Ibid.*

Accordingly, the court affirmed the judgment of the District Court.

Both Indiana and CTS filed jurisdictional statements. We noted probable jurisdiction and now reverse. * * *

II

The first question in these cases is whether the Williams Act preempts the Indiana Act. As we have stated frequently, absent an explicit indication by Congress of an intent to preempt state law, a state statute is preempted only

'where compliance with both federal and state regulations is a physical impossibility.* * *,' *Florida Lime & Avocado Growers, Inc. v. Paul,* 373 U.S. 132, 142–143 (1963), or where the state 'law stands as an obstacle to the accomplishment and execution of the full purposes and objectives of Congress.' *Hines v. Davidowitz,* 312 U.S. 52, 67 (1941). * * * *Ray v. Atlantic Richfield Co.,* 435 U.S. 151, 158, (1978).

Because it is entirely possible for entities to comply with both the Williams Act and the Indiana Act, the state statute can be preempted only if it frustrates the purposes of the federal law.

A

Our discussion begins with a brief summary of the structure and purposes of the Williams Act. * * *

B

The Indiana Act differs in major respects from the Illinois statute that the Court considered in *Edgar v. MITE Corp.,* 457 U.S. 624 (1982). After reviewing the legislative history of the Williams Act, Justice White, joined by Chief Justice Burger and Justice Blackmun (the plurality), concluded that the Williams Act struck a careful balance between the interests of offerors and target companies, and that any state statute that "upset" this balance was preempted. *Id.,* at 632–634.

The plurality then identified three offending features of the Illinois statute. Justice White's opinion first noted that the Illinois statute provided for a 20–day precommencement period. During this time, management could disseminate its views on the upcoming offer to shareholders, but offerors could not publish their offers. The plurality found that this provision gave management "a powerful tool to combat tender offers." *Id.,* at 635. This contrasted dramatically with the Williams Act; Congress had deleted express precommencement notice provisions from the Williams Act. According to the plurality, Congress had determined that the potentially adverse consequences of such a provision on shareholders should be avoided. Thus, the plurality concluded that the Illinois provision "frustrate[d] the objectives of the Williams Act." *Ibid.* The second criticized feature of the Illinois statute was a provision for a hearing on a tender offer that, because it set no deadline, allowed management " 'to stymie indefinitely a takeover,' " *id.,* at 637. * * * The plurality noted that " 'delay can seriously impede a tender offer,' " 457 U.S., at 637 (quoting *Great Western United Corp. v. Kidwell,* 577 F.2d 1256, 1277 (C.A.5 1978) (Wisdom, J.)), and that "Congress anticipated that investors and the takeover offeror would be free to go forward without unreasonable delay," 457 U.S., at 639. Accordingly, the plurality concluded that this provision conflicted with the Williams Act. The third troublesome feature of the Illinois statute was its requirement that the fairness of tender offers would be reviewed by the Illinois Secretary of State. Noting that "Congress intended for investors to be free to make their own decisions," the plurality concluded that " '[t]he state thus offers investor protection at the expense of investor autonomy—an approach quite in conflict with that adopted by Congress.' " *Id.,* at 639–640 (quoting *MITE Corp. v. Dixon, supra,* at 494).

C

As the plurality opinion in *MITE* did not represent the views of a majority of the Court, we are not bound by its reasoning. We need not question that reasoning, however, because we believe the Indiana Act passes muster even under the broad interpretation of the Williams Act articulated by Justice White in *MITE*. As is apparent from our summary of its reasoning, the overriding concern of the *MITE* plurality was that the Illinois statute considered in that case operated to favor management against offerors, to the detriment of shareholders. By contrast, the statute now before the Court protects the independent shareholder against both of the contending parties. Thus, the Act furthers a basic purpose of the Williams Act, " 'plac[ing] investors on an equal footing with the takeover bidder,' " *Piper v. Chris–Craft Industries,* 430 U.S., at 30, (quoting the Senate Report accompanying the Williams Act, S.Rep. No. 550, 90th Cong., 1st Sess., 4 (1967)).[10]

The Indiana Act operates on the assumption, implicit in the Williams Act, that independent shareholders faced with tender offers often are at a disadvantage. By allowing such shareholders to vote as a group, the Act protects them from the coercive aspects of some tender offers. If, for example, shareholders believe that a successful tender offer will be followed by a purchase of nontendering shares at a depressed price, individual shareholders may tender their shares—even if they doubt the tender offer is in the corporation's best interest—to protect themselves from being forced to sell their shares at a depressed price. As the SEC explains: "The alternative of not accepting the tender offer is virtual assurance that, if the offer is successful, the shares will have to be sold in the lower priced, second step." Two–Tier Tender Offer Pricing and Non–Tender Offer Purchase Programs, SEC Exchange Act Rel. No. 21079 (June 21, 1984) (hereinafter SEC Release No. 21079). See Lowenstein, Pruning Deadwood in Hostile Takeovers: A Proposal for Legislation, 83 Colum.L.Rev. 249, 307–309 (1983). In such a situation

---

10. [By the Court] Dynamics finds evidence of an intent to favor management in several features of the Act. * * *

The Act * * * imposes some added expenses on the offeror, requiring it, *inter alia,* to pay the costs of special shareholder meetings to vote on the transfer of voting rights, see § 23–1–42–7(a). In our view, the expenses of such a meeting fairly are charged to the offeror. A corporation pays the costs of annual meetings that it holds to discuss its affairs. If an offeror—who has no official position with the corporation—desires a special meeting solely to discuss the voting rights of the offeror, it is not unreasonable to have the offeror pay for the meeting.

Of course, by regulating tender offers, the Act makes them more expensive and thus deters them somewhat, but this type of reasonable regulation does not alter the balance between management and offeror in any significant way. The principal result of the Act is to grant shareholders the power to deliberate collectively about the merits of tender offers. This result is fully in accord with the purposes of the Williams Act.

under the Indiana Act, the shareholders as a group, acting in the corporation's best interest, could reject the offer, although individual shareholders might be inclined to accept it. The desire of the Indiana Legislature to protect shareholders of Indiana corporations from this type of coercive offer does not conflict with the Williams Act. Rather, it furthers the federal policy of investor protection.

In implementing its goal, the Indiana Act avoids the problems the plurality discussed in *MITE*. Unlike the *MITE* statute, the Indiana Act does not give either management or the offeror an advantage in communicating with the shareholders about the impending offer. The Act also does not impose an indefinite delay on tender offers. Nothing in the Act prohibits an offeror from consummating an offer on the 20th business day, the earliest day permitted under applicable federal regulations. Nor does the Act allow the state government to interpose its views of fairness between willing buyers and sellers of shares of the target company. Rather, the Act allows *shareholders* to evaluate the fairness of the offer collectively.

D

The Court of Appeals based its finding of pre-emption on its view that the practical effect of the Indiana Act is to delay consummation of tender offers until 50 days after the commencement of the offer. 794 F.2d, at 263. As did the Court of Appeals, Dynamics reasons that no rational offeror will purchase shares until it gains assurance that those shares will carry voting rights. Because it is possible that voting rights will not be conferred until a shareholder meeting 50 days after commencement of the offer, Dynamics concludes that the Act imposes a 50–day delay. This, it argues, conflicts with the shorter 20–business–day period established by the SEC as the minimum period for which a tender offer may be held open. We find the alleged conflict illusory. * * *

Finally, we note that the Williams Act would preempt a variety of state corporate laws of hitherto unquestioned validity if it were construed to preempt any state statute that may limit or delay the free exercise of power after a successful tender offer. State corporate laws commonly permit corporations to stagger the terms of their directors. See Model Business Corp. Act § 37 (1969 draft) in 3 Model Business Corp. Act Ann. (2d ed. 1971) (hereinafter MBCA); American Bar Foundation, Revised Model Business Corp. Act § 8.06 (1984 draft) (1985) (hereinafter RMBCA).[11] By staggering the terms of directors, and thus having annual elections for only one class of directors each year, corporations may delay the time when a successful offeror gains control of the board of directors. Similarly, state corporation laws commonly provide for cumulative voting. See MBCA § 33, par. 4; RMBCA § 7.28. By enabling minority shareholders to assure themselves of representation in each class of directors, cumulative voting provisions can delay further the ability of offerors to gain untrammeled authority over the affairs of the target corporation. See Hochman & Folger, Deflecting Takeovers: Charter and By–Law Techniques, 34 Bus.Law. 537, 538–539 (1979).

---

11. [By the Court] Every State except Arkansas and California allows classification of directors to stagger their terms of office. See 2 Model Business Corp. Act Ann. § 8.06, p. 830 (3d ed., Supp.1986).

In our view, the possibility that the Indiana Act will delay some tender offers is insufficient to require a conclusion that the Williams Act preempts the Act. The longstanding prevalence of state regulation in this area suggests that, if Congress had intended to preempt all state laws that delay the acquisition of voting control following a tender offer, it would have said so explicitly. The regulatory conditions that the Act places on tender offers are consistent with the text and the purposes of the Williams Act. Accordingly, we hold that the Williams Act does not preempt the Indiana Act.

III

As an alternative basis for its decision, the Court of Appeals held that the Act violates the Commerce Clause of the Federal Constitution. We now address this holding. * * * [The Court concludes that the Indiana Act does not discriminate against interstate commerce nor does it adversely affect interstate commerce by subjecting activities to inconsistent regulations.]

C

The Court of Appeals * * * [found] the Act unconstitutional * * * [because of] its view of the Act's potential to hinder tender offers. We think the Court of Appeals failed to appreciate the significance for Commerce Clause analysis of the fact that state regulation of corporate governance is regulation of entities whose very existence and attributes are a product of state law. As Chief Justice Marshall explained:

> A corporation is an artificial being, invisible, intangible, and existing only in contemplation of law. Being the mere creature of law, it possesses only those properties which the charter of its creation confers upon it, either expressly, or as incidental to its very existence. These are such as are supposed best calculated to effect the object for which it was created. *Trustees of Dartmouth College v. Woodward,* 4 Wheat. 518, 636, 4 L.Ed. 629 (1819).

Every State in this country has enacted laws regulating corporate governance. By prohibiting certain transactions, and regulating others, such laws necessarily affect certain aspects of interstate commerce. This necessarily is true with respect to corporations with shareholders in States other than the State of incorporation. Large corporations that are listed on national exchanges, or even regional exchanges, will have shareholders in many States and shares that are traded frequently. The markets that facilitate this national and international participation in ownership of corporations are essential for providing capital not only for new enterprises but also for established companies that need to expand their businesses. This beneficial free market system depends at its core upon the fact that a corporation—except in the rarest situations—is organized under, and governed by, the law of a single jurisdiction, traditionally the corporate law of the State of its incorporation.

These regulatory laws may affect directly a variety of corporate transactions. Mergers are a typical example. In view of the substantial effect that a merger may have on the shareholders' interests in a corporation, many States require supermajority votes to approve mergers. See, *e.g.,* MBCA * * * 11.03 (requiring approval of a merger by a majority of all shares, rather than simply a majority of votes cast) * * * By requiring a greater vote for mergers than is required for other transactions, these laws make it more difficult for corporations to merge. State laws also may provide for "dissenters' rights" under which minority shareholders who disagree with corporate decisions to take particular actions are entitled to sell their shares to the corporation at fair market value. See, *e.g.,* MBCA § 13.02. By requiring the corporation to purchase the shares of dissenting shareholders, these laws may inhibit a corporation from engaging in the specified transactions.[12]

It thus is an accepted part of the business landscape in this country for States to create corporations, to prescribe their powers, and to define the rights that are acquired by purchasing their shares. A State has an interest in promoting stable relationships among parties involved in the corporations it charters, as well as in ensuring that investors in such corporations have an effective voice in corporate affairs.

There can be no doubt that the Act reflects these concerns. The primary purpose of the Act is to protect the shareholders of Indiana corporations. It does this by affording shareholders, when a takeover offer is made, an opportunity to decide collectively whether the resulting change in voting control of the corporation, as they perceive it, would be desirable. A change of management may have important effects on the shareholders' interests; it is well within the State's role as overseer of corporate governance to offer this opportunity. The autonomy provided by allowing shareholders collectively to determine whether the takeover is advantageous to their interests may be especially beneficial where a hostile tender offer may coerce shareholders into tendering their shares.

Appellee Dynamics responds to this concern by arguing that the prospect of coercive tender offers is illusory, and that tender offers generally should be favored because they reallocate corporate assets into the hands of management who can use them most effectively.[13] See generally Easterbrook & Fischel, The Proper Role of a Target's Management in Responding to a

12. [By the Court] Numerous other common regulations may affect both nonresident and resident shareholders of a corporation. Specified votes may be required for the sale of all of the corporation's assets. See MBCA § 12.02. The election of directors may be staggered over a period of years to prevent abrupt changes in management. See MBCA § 8.06. Various classes of stock may be created with differences in voting rights as to dividends and on liquidation. See MBCA § 6.01(c). Provisions may be made for cumulative voting. See MBCA § 7.28. Corporations may adopt restrictions on payment of dividends to ensure that specified ratios of assets to liabilities are maintained for the benefit of the holders of corporate bonds or notes. See MBCA * * * 6.40 (noting that a corporation's articles of incorporation can restrict payment of dividends) * * *. Where the shares of a corporation are held in States other than that of incorporation, actions taken pursuant to these and similar provisions of state law will affect all shareholders alike wherever they reside or are domiciled.

Nor is it unusual for partnership law to restrict certain transactions. For example, a purchaser of a partnership interest generally can gain a right to control the business only with the consent of other owners. See Uniform Partnership Act § 27, Revised Uniform Limited Partnership Act §§ 702, 704. These provisions—in force in the great majority of the States—bear a striking resemblance to the Act at issue in this case.

13. [By the Court] It is appropriate to note when discussing the merits and demerits of tender offers that generalizations usually require qualification. No one doubts that some successful tender offers will provide more effective management or other benefits such as needed diversification. But there is no reason to assume that the type of conglomerate corporation that may result from repetitive takeovers necessarily will result in more effective management or otherwise be beneficial to shareholders. The divergent views in the literature—and even now being debated in the Congress—reflect the reality that the type and utility of tender offers vary widely. Of course, in many situations the offer to shareholders is simply a cash price substantially higher than the market price prior to the offer.

Tender Offer, 94 Harv.L.Rev. 1161 (1981). * * * Indiana's concern with tender offers is not groundless. Indeed, the potentially coercive aspects of tender offers have been recognized by the SEC, see SEC Release No. 21079, and by a number of scholarly commentators, see, *e.g.,* Bradley & Rosenzweig, Defensive Stock Repurchases, 99 Harv.L.Rev. 1377, 1412–1413 (1986). * * * The Constitution does not require the States to subscribe to any particular economic theory. We are not inclined "to second-guess the empirical judgments of lawmakers concerning the utility of legislation," *Kassel v. Consolidated Freightways Corp.,* 450 U.S., at 679, 101 S.Ct., at 1321 (Brennan, J., concurring in judgment). In our view, the possibility of coercion in some takeover bids offers additional justification for Indiana's decision to promote the autonomy of independent shareholders.

Dynamics argues in any event that the State has " 'no legitimate interest in protecting the nonresident shareholders.' " Dynamics relies heavily on the statement by the *MITE* Court that "[i]nsofar as the * * * law burdens out-of-state transactions, there is nothing to be weighed in the balance to sustain the law." 457 U.S., at 644, 102 S.Ct., at 2641. But that comment was made in reference to an Illinois law that applied as well to out-of-state corporations as to in-state corporations. We agree that Indiana has no interest in protecting nonresident shareholders *of nonresident corporations.* But this Act applies only to corporations incorporated in Indiana. We reject the contention that Indiana has no interest in providing for the shareholders of its corporations the voting autonomy granted by the Act. Indiana has a substantial interest in preventing the corporate form from becoming a shield for unfair business dealing. Moreover, unlike the Illinois statute invalidated in *MITE,* the Indiana Act applies only to corporations that have a substantial number of shareholders in Indiana. See Ind.Code § 23–1–42–4(a)(3) (Supp.1986). Thus, every application of the Indiana Act will affect a substantial number of Indiana residents, whom Indiana indisputably has an interest in protecting.

D

Dynamics' argument that the Act is unconstitutional ultimately rests on its contention that the Act will limit the number of successful tender offers. There is little evidence that this will occur. But even if true, this result would not substantially affect our Commerce Clause analysis. We reiterate that this Act does not prohibit any entity—resident or nonresident—from offering to purchase, or from purchasing, shares in Indiana corporations, or from attempting thereby to gain control. It only provides regulatory procedures designed for the better protection of the corporations' shareholders. We have rejected the "notion that the Commerce Clause protects the particular structure or methods of operation in a * * * market." *Exxon Corp. v. Governor of Maryland,* 437 U.S., at 127, 98 S.Ct., at 2215. The very commodity that is traded in the securities market is one whose characteristics are defined by state law. Similarly, the very commodity that is traded in the "market for corporate control"—the corporation—is one that owes its existence and attributes to state law. Indiana need not define these commodities as other States do; it need only provide that residents and nonresidents have equal access to them. This Indiana has done. Accordingly, even if the Act should decrease the number of successful tender offers for Indiana corporations, this would not offend the Commerce Clause.

IV

On its face, the Indiana Control Share Acquisitions Chapter evenhanded-ly determines the voting rights of shares of Indiana corporations. The Act does not conflict with the provisions or purposes of the Williams Act. To the limited extent that the Act affects interstate commerce, this is justified by the State's interests in defining the attributes of shares in its corporations and in protecting shareholders. Congress has never questioned the need for state regulation of these matters. Nor do we think such regulation offends the Constitution. Accordingly, we reverse the judgment of the Court of Appeals.

It is so ordered.

JUSTICE SCALIA, concurring in part and concurring in the judgment.

* * * [H]aving found * * * that the Indiana Control Share Acquisitions Chapter neither "discriminates against interstate commerce," nor "create[s] an impermissible risk of inconsistent regulation by different States," I would conclude without further analysis that it is not invalid under the dormant Commerce Clause. * * * Whether the control shares statute "protects share-holders of Indiana corporations," or protects incumbent management seems to me a highly debatable question, but it is extraordinary to think that the constitutionality of the Act should depend on the answer. Nothing in the Constitution says that the protection of entrenched management is any less important a "putative local benefit" than the protection of entrenched share-holders, and I do not know what qualifies us to make that judgment—or the related judgment as to how effective the present statute is in achieving one or the other objective—or the ultimate (and most ineffable) judgment as to whether, given importance-level x, and effectiveness-level y, the worth of the statute is "outweighed" by impact-on-commerce. * * *

I also agree with the Court that the Indiana Control Shares Act is not preempted by the Williams Act, but I reach that conclusion without entering into the debate over the purposes of the two statutes. The Williams Act is governed by the antipreemption provision of the Securities Exchange Act of 1934, 15 U.S.C. § 78bb(a), which provides that nothing it contains "shall affect the jurisdiction of the securities commission (or any agency or officer performing like functions) of any State over any security or any person insofar as it does not conflict with the provisions of this chapter or the rules and regulations thereunder." Unless it serves no function, that language forecloses preemption on the basis of conflicting "purpose" as opposed to conflicting "provision." Even if it does not have literal application to the present case (because, perhaps, the Indiana agency responsible for securities matters has no enforcement responsibility with regard to this legislation), it nonetheless refutes the proposition that Congress meant the Williams Act to displace *all* state laws with conflicting purpose. And if any are to survive, surely the States' corporation codes are among them. It would be peculiar to hold that Indiana could have pursued the purpose at issue here through its blue-sky laws, but cannot pursue it through the State's even more sacrosanct authority over the structure of domestic corporations. Prescribing voting rights for the governance of state-chartered companies is a traditional state function with which the Federal Congress has never, to my knowledge, intentionally interfered. I would require far more evidence than is available here to find implicit preemption of that function by a federal statute whose provisions concededly do not conflict with the state law.

I do not share the Court's apparent high estimation of the beneficence of the state statute at issue here. But a law can be both economic folly and constitutional. The Indiana Control Share Acquisitions Chapter is at least the latter. I therefore concur in the judgment of the Court.

JUSTICE WHITE, with whom JUSTICE BLACKMUN and JUSTICE STEVENS join as to Part II, dissenting.

The majority today upholds Indiana's Control Share Acquisitions Chapter, a statute which will predictably foreclose completely some tender offers for stock in Indiana corporations. I disagree with the conclusion that the Chapter is neither preempted by the Williams Act nor in conflict with the Commerce Clause. The Chapter undermines the policy of the Williams Act by effectively preventing minority shareholders, in some circumstances, from acting in their own best interests by selling their stock. In addition, the Chapter will substantially burden the interstate market in corporate ownership, particularly if other States follow Indiana's lead as many already have done. The Chapter, therefore, directly inhibits interstate commerce, the very economic consequences the Commerce Clause was intended to prevent. The opinion of the Court of Appeals is far more persuasive than that of the majority today, and the judgment of that court should be affirmed. * * *

Given the impact of the Control Share Acquisitions Chapter, it is clear that Indiana is directly regulating the purchase and sale of shares of stock in interstate commerce. Appellant CTS' stock is traded on the New York Stock Exchange, and people from all over the country buy and sell CTS' shares daily. Yet, under Indiana's scheme, any prospective purchaser will be effectively precluded from purchasing CTS' shares if the purchaser crosses one of the Chapter's threshold ownership levels and a majority of CTS' shareholders refuse to give the purchaser voting rights. This Court should not countenance such a restraint on interstate trade. * * *

Notes

(1) Prior to the decision in the principal case, and based largely on language in the plurality opinion in *MITE,* a number of academic scholars of the Chicago "law and economics school" argued that an interstate market for corporate control existed and that states were powerless to regulate it. Under this approach, state statutes regulating tender offers seemed clearly unconstitutional, and perhaps even traditional state corporation law provisions could be invalidated if they unreasonably restricted or interfered with the market for corporate control. This type of argument was accepted by Judge Posner in the opinion reversed by the Supreme Court in the principal case. The "market for corporate control" idea appealed to economists but troubled many lawyers because, to the extent it applied to publicly held corporations, this "market" seemed to be a "slippery slope" that could federalize much of the state law of corporations. The CTS opinion is of major importance in the corporate area because of its dicta about the relative rules of federal and state law in this area.

(2) Pennsylvania's anti-takeover law, the most restrictive of any state's, took effect on April 27, 1990 but gave companies until July 27, 1990 to exempt

themselves (opt-out) of the law. BCL Section 2541–2548. Section 25E of the statute requires a person who acquires 20 percent or more of the voting power of a target company pay in cash the "fair value" for the shares of other shareholders who object to the transaction. This provision creates a form of dissenters' appraisal rights applicable to acquirors rather than to issuers. Corporations may opt-out of Section 25E but not the rest of the statute.

In addition, Pennsylvania has a strong "shareholder constituency" statute that expressly permits Pennsylvania companies that are the targets of hostile takeovers to take into consideration the interests of employees and communities affected by a takeover when deciding how to respond.

NORMAN VEASEY, ET AL., THE DELAWARE TAKE-OVER LAW: SOME ISSUES, STRATEGIES AND COMPARISONS[14]

43 Bus.Law. 865, 866–69 (1988).

Some states have followed the Indiana model, while others adopted different approaches. For example, New York in 1986 and New Jersey in 1987 adopted statutes prohibiting an acquiror from accomplishing a second-step "business combination"—such as a merger—with the target for a period of five years. Concern was raised that states were trying to outdo each other in their attempts to regulate tender offers of corporations domiciled in other states (notably Delaware), thus leading to a worrisome balkanization of state tender offer statutes. In *TLX Acquisition Corp. v. Telex Corp.*, the federal district court sitting in Oklahoma held that an Oklahoma statute that purported to regulate the tender offer process and thus the internal affairs of a Delaware corporation was unconstitutional even though there were substantial contacts with Oklahoma.[15] * * *

The major question in that national puzzle was whether Delaware would adopt any legislation and, if so, how far it would go. Delaware, of course, is the principal architect and steward of a "national corporation law" since it is the domicile of over 180,000 corporations, many of which are major, national public corporations with no substantial operations in Delaware. Indeed, over half of the Fortune 500 companies are Delaware corporations. As at least one commentator has noted, Delaware has always been wary of antitakeover legislation for at least three reasons: doubts about constitutionality (at least pre–*CTS*); concerns over preemption; and the fact that such statutes simply don't fit comfortably into the mold of a state enabling statute governing internal corporate affairs.[16]

---

14. Copyright 1988 by the American Bar Association. All rights reserved. Reprinted with permission of the ABA and its Section of Business Law.

15. [By the Author] TLX Acquisition Corp. v. Telex Corp., 679 F.Supp. 1022 (W.D.Okla. 1987).

16. [By the Author] See Black, Why Delaware Is Wary of Anti–Takeover Law, Wall St. J., July 10, 1987, at 18, col. 3:

Although Delaware prides itself on being a leader in corporation law, it has always been

wary of laws regulating tender offers. For one thing, such laws have never fit well in corporation statutes. For another, they don't work. Efforts to regulate tender offers at the federal level under the Williams Act have distorted the process. Since the Williams Act was enacted in 1968, the Securities and Exchange Commission (and the states, through such acts as the now-validated Indiana law) has played an endless game of catch up, adopting rules that seem to fix one problem only to give rise to another.

Nevertheless, there was an expectation following *CTS* that Delaware would do something, and it did. After a lengthy "on-again, off-again" process stretching from May 1987 through January 1988, the Delaware State Bar Association proposed a new takeover statute,[17] which was adopted in late January substantially in *haec verba* by the Delaware General Assembly. It became effective with the signature of Governor Castle on February 2, 1988. The statute is codified as new section 203 of the Delaware General Corporation Law. Section 203 is a modified "business combination" statute based on the concept, adopted in New York and New Jersey,[18] of regulating second-step transactions between acquirors and the corporation rather than regulating the initial acquisition of stock or voting rights.

With the enactment of section 203, Delaware became the twenty-eighth state to enact a post-*MITE* takeover statute. About half of these statutes were adopted in the wake of the Supreme Court opinion in *CTS*. California is the only major state (in terms of the number of incorporations) without a takeover law.

OPERATION OF SECTION 203

Section 203 is not an enabling (or "opt-in") provision * * *. Rather, section 203 is an "opt-out" statute. It automatically applies (with certain exceptions) to every public corporation formed under the laws of Delaware unless (i) the corporation's original charter contains a provision opting out of the protection of the statute, or (ii) within ninety days of the effective date of the statute (February 2, 1988), the board of directors adopts a by-law opting out of the statute. In addition, the holders of a majority of shares entitled to vote can opt out by amending the certificate or the by-laws. Although such an amendment can be adopted at any time, it will not become effective for twelve months and will not apply to a business combination with a person who was an interested stockholder at or prior to the time of the amendment.

---

17. [By the Author] The Delaware statute is the product of a lengthy study by the Corporation Law Section of the Delaware State Bar Association. In June 1987, following the *CTS* decision, the Section studied and sought national comment on a draft control share acquisition statute of the type upheld by the Supreme Court in that case. CTS Corp. v. Dynamics Corp. of America, 107 S.Ct. 1637 (1987). There were many uncertainties regarding the operation and effect of such legislation, including concern that it may, ironically, help put "in play" corporations which might not otherwise become takeover targets. Accordingly, the Section determined that it would not be appropriate to propose such a statute for Delaware. Nevertheless, because of continued interest in takeover legislation, the Council of the Section began a new study in the late summer of 1987. An exposure draft of a "business combination statute" was released for public comment in November. Over 150 comment letters were received from corporations, lawyers, Commissioners of the Securities and Exchange Commission and the Federal Trade Commission, executives, institutional investors, academics, and many others. Some comments were based on broad policy grounds, some made narrower policy suggestions, and still others recommended drafting changes. During the bar association debate and the legislative process, some law firms represented specific clients and took positions as a firm. Richards, Layton & Finger [the firm in which the authors are partners] did not take a position as a firm and would not accept representation by a client to lobby for or against the bill. Each lawyer in the firm had the freedom to express his or her own personal view since the clients of the firm had divergent views. Some members of the firm fully supported the statute; others supported it with a few specific reservations (for example whether 85% should be 80% and whether the grandfather date should be the effective date); others opposed it on broad policy grounds. Governor Castle strongly supported the legislation, but he said that the issue is "neither black nor white, but gray."

18. [By the Author] New York Bus.Corp. Law § 912 (McKinney 1986); N.J.Stat.Ann. § 14A:10A (West Supp.1987), as amended by 1988 N.J.Laws 380 (effective Jan. 8, 1988).

Assuming the statute is applicable and the corporation has not opted out, its operative effect can be briefly summarized as follows. If a person acquires fifteen percent or more of a corporation's voting stock (thereby becoming an "interested stockholder"), he may not engage in a wide range of transactions with the corporation [for three years], unless the board has approved the transaction or exempted the stockholder before he reaches the fifteen-percent threshold or unless one of two exceptions is satisfied: (i) Upon consummation of the transaction which resulted in such person becoming an interested stockholder, the interested stockholder owned at least eighty-five percent of the corporation's voting stock outstanding at the time the transaction commenced (excluding shares owned by officer-directors and shares owned by employee stock plans in which participants do not have the right to determine confidentially whether shares will be tendered in a tender or exchange offer); or (ii) after the acquiror becomes an interested stockholder, the business combination is approved by the board of directors and authorized by the affirmative vote (at an annual or special meeting, and not by written consent) of at least two-thirds of the outstanding voting stock excluding that owned by the interested stockholder.[19] * * *

Notes

(1) Suits attacking the constitutionality of § 203 were unsuccessful. Black & Decker Corp. v. American Standard Inc., 679 F.Supp. 1183 (D.Del.1988); SWT Acquisition Corp. v. TW Services, Inc., 700 F.Supp. 1323 (D.Del.1988).

(2) Wisconsin has a business combination statute that is even more restrictive than Delaware's. Under this statute, no Wisconsin corporation having its headquarters, substantial operations, 10 percent of its shares, or 10 percent of its shareholders in Wisconsin may enter into a "business combination" with an interested shareholder (defined as one with a 10 percent interest in the corporation) for a period of three years after the interested shareholder acquires his or her stock, unless the board of directors has approved the business combination before acquisition. In Amanda Acquisition Corp. v. Universal Foods Corp., 877 F.2d 496 (7th Cir.1989), cert. denied, 493 U.S. 955, 110 S.Ct. 367, 107 L.Ed.2d 353 (1989), the Court, per Easterbrook, C.J., upheld this statute despite the "almost hermetic separation of bidder and target for three years after the bidder obtains 10 percent of the stock—unless the target's board consented before then. No matter how popular the offer, the ban applies: obtaining 85% (even 100%) of the stock held by non-management shareholders won't allow the bidder to engage in a business combination, as it would under Delaware law." 877 F.2d at 498. After expressing his distaste for the economics and policies that Wisconsin has apparently embraced, Judge Easterbrook concluded that the Wisconsin law is constitutional under *CTS*.

(3) In addition to controlling share acquisition statutes of the Indiana type and restrictions on "second step" transactions of the Delaware/New York/New Jersey type, States continue to experiment with statutes. The most popular of these "other" statutes are "fair price" and "supermajority voting" requirements

---

19. [By the Editors] A more candid statement of the intent and effect of this statute is that it makes a bidder either negotiate with management or make an offer so attractive that it garners virtually all of the target shares. Many (indeed probably most) legal scholars were critical of laws designed to protect target companies from takeover and were therefore critical of the Delaware statute. See, e.g., Easterbrook & Fischel, The Proper Role of a Target's Management in Responding to a Tender Offer, 94 Harv.L.Rev. 1161 (1981).

for second-step transactions with interested shareholders patterned after the Maryland statute (Md.Corps. & Ass'ns Code Ann. §§ 3–601 to 3–603) and adopted by about fifteen states. Other statutes provide for an appraisal-type "cash out" privilege for minority shareholders upon the acquisition of a specified percentage of the corporation's shares. See, e.g., Pa.Bus.Corp.L. §§ 2542–2548 (acquisition of 20 percent or more of voting shares [subject to certain exceptions] triggers buyout right).

C. DEFENSES: POISON PILLS

The "ultimate" in defensive tactics is the "shareholder rights plan," more commonly called a "poison pill." Here the preliminary question is not whether these potent anti-takeover devices are constitutional, but whether they are consistent with existing state corporate law for allocating rights and responsibilities within the corporation.

MORAN v. HOUSEHOLD INT'L, INC.

Supreme Court of Delaware, 1985.
500 A.2d 1346.

McNEILLY, JUSTICE.

This case presents to this Court for review the most recent defensive mechanism in the arsenal of corporate takeover weaponry—the Preferred Share Purchase Rights Plan ("Rights Plan" or "Plan"). The validity of this mechanism has attracted national attention. *Amici curiae* briefs have been filed in support of appellants by the Security and Exchange Commission ("SEC")[20] and the Investment Company Institute. An *amicus curiae* brief has been filed in support of appellees ("Household") by the United Food and Commercial Workers International Union.

In a detailed opinion, the Court of Chancery upheld the Rights Plan as a legitimate exercise of business judgment by Household. Moran v. Household International, Inc., Del.Ch., 490 A.2d 1059 (1985). We agree, and therefore, affirm the judgment below.

I

* * * A review of the basic facts is necessary for a complete understanding of the issues.

On August 14, 1984, the Board of Directors of Household International, Inc. adopted the Rights Plan by a fourteen to two vote.[21] The intricacies of the Rights Plan are contained in a 48–page document entitled "Rights Agreement". Basically, the Plan provides that Household common stockholders are entitled to the issuance of one Right per common share under certain triggering conditions. There are two triggering events that can activate the

---

20. [By the Court] The SEC split 3B2 on whether to intervene in this case. The two dissenting Commissioners have publicly disagreed with the other three as to the merits of the Rights Plan. 17 Securities Regulation & Law Report 400; The Wall Street Journal, March 20, 1985, at 6.

21. [By the Court] Household's Board has ten outside directors and six who are members of management. Messrs. Moran (appellant) and Whitehead voted against the Plan. The record reflects that Whitehead voted against the Plan not on its substance but because he thought it was novel and would bring unwanted publicity to Household.

Rights. The first is the announcement of a tender offer for 30 percent of Household's shares ("30% trigger") and the second is the acquisition of 20 percent of Household's shares by any single entity or group ("20% trigger").

If an announcement of a tender offer for 30 percent of Household's shares is made, the Rights are issued and are immediately exercisable to purchase 1/100 share of new preferred stock for $100 and are redeemable by the Board for $0.50 per Right. If 20 percent of Household's shares are acquired by anyone, the Rights are issued and become non-redeemable and are exercisable to purchase 1/100 of a share of preferred. If a Right is not exercised for preferred, and thereafter, a merger or consolidation occurs, the Rights holder can exercise each Right to purchase $200 of the common stock of the tender offeror for $100.[22] This "flip-over" provision of the Rights Plan is at the heart of this controversy. * * *

Household did not adopt its Rights Plan during a battle with a corporate raider, but as a preventive mechanism to ward off future advances. The Vice–Chancellor found that as early as February 1984, Household's management became concerned about the company's vulnerability as a takeover target and began considering amending its charter to render a takeover more difficult. After considering the matter, Household decided not to pursue a fair price amendment.

In the meantime, appellant Moran, one of Household's own Directors and also Chairman of the Dyson–Kissner–Moran Corporation, ("D–K–M") which is the largest single stockholder of Household, began discussions concerning a possible leveraged buy-out of Household by D–K–M. D–K–M's financial studies showed that Household's stock was significantly undervalued in relation to the company's break-up value. It is uncontradicted that Moran's suggestion of a leveraged buy-out never progressed beyond the discussion stage.

Concerned about Household's vulnerability to a raider in light of the current takeover climate, Household secured the services of Wachtell, Lipton, Rosen and Katz ("Watchell, Lipton") and Goldman, Sachs & Co. ("Goldman, Sachs") to formulate a takeover policy for recommendation to the Household Board at its August 14 meeting. After a July 31 meeting with a Household Board member and a pre-meeting distribution of material on the potential takeover problem and the proposed Rights Plan, the Board met on August 14, 1984.

22. [By the Editors] In other words, each Household shareholder receives one "right" for each Household share of stock held. If a triggering event occurs, this right authorizes the holder to purchase $200 of the common stock of the offeror or purchaser for $100, thereby causing massive dilution of the value of the aggressor's shares. Prior to the triggering event, the right is automatically fixed (or, figuratively "stapled") to the shares and cannot be traded separately from the shares. Hence the rights may remain in existence indefinitely without interfering with normal business transactions of Household. The option to purchase a fractional interest in a preferred share of Household was "window dressing" designed to assure that the "rights" would always be tied to Household shares; it was never intended that anyone would ever exercise that option, as indicated by the very high price for a very small fractional interest in a share of very limited value.

Before rights are triggered, Household may cancel them; if they have been triggered, Household may elect to redeem the rights at a nominal price. The power to cancel or redeem these rights at any time was thought to give Household flexibility to negotiate a voluntary merger or sale with the aggressor or some other corporation or entity.

In Leonard Loventhal Account v. Hilton Hotels Corp., 2000 WL 1528909 (Del.Ch. Oct. 10, 2000) the court held that poison pills attach automatically to all outstanding shares and cannot be rejected by a major shareholder.

Representatives of Wachtell, Lipton and Goldman, Sachs attended the August 14 meeting. The minutes reflect that Mr. Lipton explained to the Board that his recommendation of the Plan was based on his understanding that the Board was concerned about the increasing frequency of "bust-up" takeovers, the increasing takeover activity in the financial service industry, such as Leucadia's attempt to take over Arco, and the possible adverse effect this type of activity could have on employees and others concerned with and vital to the continuing successful operation of Household even in the absence of any actual bust-up takeover attempt. Against this factual background, the Plan was approved.

Thereafter, Moran and the company of which he is Chairman, D–K–M, filed this suit. * * * The trial was held, and the Court of Chancery ruled in favor of Household. Appellants now appeal from that ruling to this Court.

II

The primary issue here is the applicability of the business judgment rule as the standard by which the adoption of the Rights Plan should be reviewed. Much of this issue has been decided by our recent decision in Unocal Corp. v. Mesa Petroleum Co. [493 A.2d 946 (Del.1985).] * * *. In *Unocal,* we applied the business judgment rule to analyze Unocal's discriminatory self-tender. We explained:

> When a board addresses a pending takeover bid it has an obligation to determine whether the offer is in the best interests of the corporation and its shareholders. In that respect a board's duty is no different from any other responsibility it shoulders, and its decisions should be no less entitled to the respect they otherwise would be accorded in the realm of business judgment.

* * * Other jurisdictions have also applied the business judgment rule to actions by which target companies have sought to forestall takeover activity they considered undesirable. * * * [The court cites ten cases, including Gearhart Industries, Inc. v. Smith International, 5th Cir., 741 F.2d 707 (1984) (sale of discounted subordinate debentures containing springing warrants); Treco, Inc. v. Land of Lincoln Savings and Loan, 7th Cir., 749 F.2d 374 (1984) (amendment to by-laws); Panter v. Marshall Field, 7th Cir., 646 F.2d 271 (1981) (acquisitions to create antitrust problems); Johnson v. Trueblood, 3d Cir., 629 F.2d 287 (1980), cert. denied, 450 U.S. 999, 101 S.Ct. 1704, 68 L.Ed.2d 200 (1981) (refusal to tender); and Crouse–Hinds Co. v. InterNorth, Inc., 2d Cir., 634 F.2d 690 (1980) (sale of stock to favored party).]

This case is distinguishable from the ones cited, since here we have a defensive mechanism adopted to ward off possible future advances and not a mechanism adopted in reaction to a specific threat. This distinguishing factor does not result in the Directors losing the protection of the business judgment rule. To the contrary, pre-planning for the contingency of a hostile takeover might reduce the risk that, under the pressure of a takeover bid, management will fail to exercise reasonable judgment. Therefore, in reviewing a pre-planned defensive mechanism it seems even more appropriate to apply the business judgment rule. * * *

Of course, the business judgment rule can only sustain corporate decision making or transactions that are within the power or authority of the Board.

Therefore, before the business judgment rule can be applied it must be determined whether the Directors were authorized to adopt the Rights Plan.

III

Appellants vehemently contend that the Board of Directors was unauthorized to adopt the Rights Plan. First, appellants contend that no provision of the Delaware General Corporation Law authorizes the issuance of such Rights. Secondly, appellants, along with the SEC, contend that the Board is unauthorized to usurp stockholders' rights to receive hostile tender offers. Third, appellants and the SEC also contend that the Board is unauthorized to fundamentally restrict stockholders' rights to conduct a proxy contest. We address each of these contentions in turn.

A.

While appellants contend that no provision of the Delaware General Corporation Law authorizes the Rights Plan, Household contends that the Rights Plan was issued pursuant to 8 *Del.C.* §§ 151(g) and 157. It explains that the Rights are authorized by § 157[23] and the issue of preferred stock underlying the Rights is authorized by § 151.[24] Appellants respond by making several attacks upon the authority to issue the Rights pursuant to § 157.

Appellants begin by contending that § 157 cannot authorize the Rights Plan since § 157 has never served the purpose of authorizing a takeover defense. Appellants contend that § 157 is a corporate financing statute, and that nothing in its legislative history suggests a purpose that has anything to do with corporate control or a takeover defense. Appellants are unable to demonstrate that the legislature, in its adoption of § 157, meant to limit the applicability of § 157 to only the issuance of Rights for the purposes of corporate financing. Without such affirmative evidence, we decline to impose such a limitation upon the section that the legislature has not. Compare Providence & Worchester Co. v. Baker, Del.Supr., 378 A.2d 121, 124 (1977) (refusal to read a bar to protective voting provisions into 8 *Del.C.* § 212(a)).

As we noted in *Unocal:*

> [O]ur corporate law is not static. It must grow and develop in response to, indeed in anticipation of, evolving concepts and needs. Merely because the

---

23. [By the Court] The power to issue rights to purchase shares is conferred by 8 *Del.C.* § 157 which provides in relevant part:

Subject to any provisions in the certificate of incorporation, every corporation may create and issue, whether or not in connection with the issue and sale of any shares of stock or other securities of the corporation, rights or options entitling the holders thereof to purchase from the corporation any shares of its capital stock of any class or classes, such rights or options to be evidenced by or in such instrument or instruments as shall be approved by the board of directors.

24. [By the Court] 8 Del.C. § 151(g) provides in relevant part:

When any corporation desires to issue any shares of stock of any class or of any series of any class of which the voting powers,

designations, preferences and relative, participating, optional or other rights, if any, or the qualifications, limitations or restrictions thereof, if any, shall not have been set forth in the certificate of incorporation or in any amendment thereto but shall be provided for in a resolution or resolutions adopted by the board of directors pursuant to authority expressly vested in it by the provisions of the certificate of incorporation or any amendment thereto, a certificate setting forth a copy of such resolution or resolutions and the number of shares of stock of such class or series shall be executed, acknowledged, filed, recorded, and shall become effective, in accordance with § 103 of this title.

General Corporation Law is silent as to a specific matter does not mean that it is prohibited. * * * 493 A.2d at 957.

Secondly, appellants contend that § 157 does not authorize the issuance of sham rights such as the Rights Plan. They contend that the Rights were designed never to be exercised, and that the Plan has no economic value. In addition, they contend the preferred stock made subject to the Rights is also illusory, citing *Telvest, Inc. v. Olson,* Del.Ch., C.A. No. 5798, Brown, V.C. (March 8, 1979).

Appellants' sham contention fails in both regards. As to the Rights, they can and will be exercised upon the happening of a triggering mechanism, as we have observed during the current struggle of Sir James Goldsmith to take control of Crown Zellerbach. See Wall Street Journal, July 26, 1985, at 3, 12. As to the preferred shares, we agree with the Court of Chancery that they are distinguishable from sham securities invalidated in *Telvest,* supra. The Household preferred, issuable upon the happening of a triggering event, have superior dividend and liquidation rights. * * *

[Next], appellants contend that if § 157 authorizes the Rights Plan it would be unconstitutional pursuant to the Commerce Clause and Supremacy Clause of the United States Constitution * * * since it is an obstacle to the accomplishment of the policies underlying the Williams Act. Appellants put heavy emphasis upon the case of Edgar v. MITE Corp., 457 U.S. 624, 102 S.Ct. 2629, 73 L.Ed.2d 269 (1982), in which the United States Supreme Court held that the Illinois Business Takeover Act was unconstitutional, in that it unduly burdened interstate commerce in violation of the Commerce Clause. We do not read the analysis in *Edgar* as applicable to the actions of private parties. The fact that directors of a corporation act pursuant to a state statute provides an insufficient nexus to the state for there to be state action which may violate the Commerce Clause or Supremacy Clause. * * *

Having concluded that sufficient authority for the Rights Plan exists in 8 *Del.C.* § 157, we note the inherent powers of the Board conferred by 8 *Del.C.* § 141(a), concerning the management of the corporation's "business and *affairs*" (emphasis added), also provides the Board additional authority upon which to enact the Rights Plan.

B.

Appellants contend that the Board is unauthorized to usurp stockholders' rights to receive tender offers by changing Household's fundamental structure. We conclude that the Rights Plan does not prevent stockholders from receiving tender offers, and that the change of Household's structure was less than that which results from the implementation of other defensive mechanisms upheld by various courts.

Appellants' contention that stockholders will lose their right to receive and accept tender offers seems to be premised upon an understanding of the Rights Plan which is illustrated by the SEC *amicus* brief which states: "The Chancery Court's decision seriously understates the impact of this plan. In fact, as we discuss below, the Rights Plan will deter not only two-tier offers, but virtually all hostile tender offers."

The fallacy of that contention is apparent when we look at the recent takeover of Crown Zellerbach, which has a similar Rights Plan, by Sir James

Goldsmith. Wall Street Journal, July 26, 1985, at 3, 12. The evidence at trial also evidenced many methods around the Plan ranging from tendering with a condition that the Board redeem the Rights, tendering with a high minimum condition of shares and Rights, tendering and soliciting consents to remove the Board and redeem the Rights, to acquiring 50% of the shares and causing Household to self-tender for the Rights. One could also form a group of up to 19.9% and solicit proxies for consents to remove the Board and redeem the Rights. These are but a few of the methods by which Household can still be acquired by a hostile tender offer.

In addition, the Rights Plan is not absolute. When the Household Board of Directors is faced with a tender offer and a request to redeem the Rights, they will not be able to arbitrarily reject the offer. They will be held to the same fiduciary standards any other board of directors would be held to in deciding to adopt a defensive mechanism, the same standard as they were held to in originally approving the Rights Plan.

In addition, appellants contend that the deterrence of tender offers will be accomplished by what they label "a fundamental transfer of power from the stockholders to the directors." They contend that this transfer of power, in itself, is unauthorized.

The Rights Plan will result in no more of a structural change than any other defensive mechanism adopted by a board of directors. The Rights Plan does not destroy the assets of the corporation. The implementation of the Plan neither results in any outflow of money from the corporation nor impairs its financial flexibility. It does not dilute earnings per share and does not have any adverse tax consequences for the corporation or its stockholders. The Plan has not adversely affected the market price of Household's stock.

Comparing the Rights Plan with other defensive mechanisms, it does less harm to the value structure of the corporation than do the other mechanisms. Other mechanisms result in increased debt of the corporation. See Whittaker Corp. v. Edgar, supra (sale of "prize asset"), Cheff v. Mathes, supra, (paying greenmail to eliminate a threat), Unocal Corp. v. Mesa Petroleum Co., supra, (discriminatory self-tender).

There is little change in the governance structure as a result of the adoption of the Rights Plan. The Board does not now have unfettered discretion in refusing to redeem the Rights. The Board has no more discretion in refusing to redeem the Rights than it does in enacting any defensive mechanism.

The contention that the Rights Plan alters the structure more than do other defensive mechanisms because it is so effective as to make the corporation completely safe from hostile tender offers is likewise without merit. As explained above, there are numerous methods to successfully launch a hostile tender offer.

C.

Appellants' third contention is that the Board was unauthorized to fundamentally restrict stockholders' rights to conduct a proxy contest. Appellants contend that the "20% trigger" effectively prevents any stockholder from first acquiring 20% or more shares before conducting a proxy contest and further, it prevents stockholders from banding together into a group to solicit proxies if, collectively, they own 20% or more of the stock.[25] In addition, at trial, appellants contended that read literally, the Rights Agreement triggers the Rights upon the mere acquisition of the right to vote 20% or more of the shares through a proxy solicitation, and thereby precludes any proxy contest from being waged.[26]

Appellants seem to have conceded this last contention in light of Household's response that the receipt of a proxy does not make the recipient the "beneficial owner" of the shares involved which would trigger the Rights. In essence, the Rights Agreement provides that the Rights are triggered when someone becomes the "beneficial owner" of 20% or more of Household stock. Although a literal reading of the Rights Agreement definition of "beneficial owner" would seem to include those shares which one has the right to vote, it has long been recognized that the relationship between grantor and recipient of a proxy is one of agency, and the agency is revocable by the grantor at any time. Henn, *Corporations* § 196, at 518. Therefore, the holder of a proxy is not the "beneficial owner" of the stock. As a result, the mere acquisition of the right to vote 20% of the shares does not trigger the Rights.

The issue, then, is whether the restriction upon individuals or groups from first acquiring 20% of shares before waging a proxy contest fundamentally restricts stockholders' right to conduct a proxy contest. Regarding this issue the Court of Chancery found:

> Thus, while the Rights Plan does deter the formation of proxy efforts of a certain magnitude, it does not limit the voting power of individual shares. On the evidence presented it is highly conjectural to assume that a particular effort to assert shareholder views in the election of directors or revisions of corporate policy will be frustrated by the proxy feature of the Plan. Household's witnesses, Troubh and Higgins described recent corporate takeover battles in which insurgents holding less than 10% stock ownership were able to secure corporate control through a proxy contest or the threat of one.

490 A.2d at 1080.

We conclude that there was sufficient evidence at trial to support the Vice–Chancellor's finding that the effect upon proxy contests will be minimal. Evidence at trial established that many proxy contests are won with an insurgent ownership of less than 20%, and that very large holdings are no guarantee of success. There was also testimony that the key variable in proxy contest success is the merit of an insurgent's issues, not the size of his holdings.

IV

Having concluded that the adoption of the Rights Plan was within the authority of the Directors, we now look to whether the Directors have met their burden under the business judgment rule.

---

25. [By the Court] Appellants explain that the acquisition of 20% of the shares trigger the Rights, making them non-redeemable, and thereby would prevent even a future friendly offer for the ten year life of the Rights.

26. [By the Court] The SEC still contends that the mere acquisition of the right to vote 20% of the shares through a proxy solicitation triggers the rights. We do not interpret the Rights Agreement in that manner.

The business judgment rule is a "presumption that in making a business decision the directors of a corporation acted on an informed basis, in good faith and in the honest belief that the action taken was in the best interests of the company." Aronson v. Lewis, Del.Supr., 473 A.2d 805, 812 (1984) (citations omitted). Notwithstanding, in *Unocal* we held that when the business judgment rule applies to adoption of a defensive mechanism, the initial burden will lie with the directors. The "directors must show that they had reasonable grounds for believing that a danger to corporate policy and effectiveness existed. * * * [T]hey satisfy that burden 'by showing good faith and reasonable investigation * * *'" *Unocal*, 493 A.2d at 955 (citing Cheff v. Mathes, 199 A.2d at 554–55). In addition, the directors must show that the defensive mechanism was "reasonable in relation to the threat posed." *Unocal*, 493 A.2d at 955. Moreover, that proof is materially enhanced, as we noted in *Unocal*, where, as here, a majority of the board favoring the proposal consisted of outside independent directors who have acted in accordance with the foregoing standards. *Unocal*, 493 A.2d at 955; *Aronson*, 473 A.2d at 815. Then, the burden shifts back to the plaintiffs who have the ultimate burden of persuasion to show a breach of the directors' fiduciary duties. *Unocal*, 493 A.2d at 958.

There are no allegations here of any bad faith on the part of the Directors' action in the adoption of the Rights Plan. There is no allegation that the Directors' action was taken for entrenchment purposes. Household has adequately demonstrated, as explained above, that the adoption of the Rights Plan was in reaction to what it perceived to be the threat in the market place of coercive two-tier tender offers. Appellants do contend, however, that the Board did not exercise informed business judgment in its adoption of the Plan. * * * Appellants contend the Delaware counsel did not express an opinion on the flip-over provision of the Rights, rather only that the Rights would constitute validly issued and outstanding rights to subscribe to the preferred stock of the company.

To determine whether a business judgment reached by a board of directors was an informed one, we determine whether the directors were grossly negligent. Smith v. Van Gorkom, Del.Supr., 488 A.2d 858, 873 (1985). Upon a review of this record, we conclude the Directors were not grossly negligent. The information supplied to the Board on August 14 provided the essentials of the Plan. The Directors were given beforehand a notebook which included a three-page summary of the Plan along with articles on the current takeover environment. The extended discussion between the Board and representatives of Wachtell, Lipton and Goldman, Sachs before approval of the Plan reflected a full and candid evaluation of the Plan. Moran's expression of his views at the meeting served to place before the Board a knowledgeable critique of the Plan. The factual happenings here are clearly distinguishable from the actions of the directors of Trans Union Corporation who displayed gross negligence in approving a cash-out merger.

In addition, to meet their burden, the Directors must show that the defensive mechanism was "reasonable in relation to the threat posed". The record reflects a concern on the part of the Directors over the increasing frequency in the financial services industry of "boot-strap" and "bust-up" takeovers. The Directors were also concerned that such takeovers may take the form of two-tier offers.[27] In addition, on August 14, the Household Board was aware of Moran's overture on behalf of D–K–M. In sum, the Directors reasonably believed Household was vulnerable to coercive acquisition techniques and adopted a reasonable defensive mechanism to protect itself.

V

* * * While we conclude for present purposes that the Household Directors are protected by the business judgment rule, that does not end the matter. The ultimate response to an actual takeover bid must be judged by the Directors' actions at that time, and nothing we say here relieves them of their basic fundamental duties to the corporation and its stockholders. Smith v. Van Gorkom, 488 A.2d at 872–73. Their use of the Plan will be evaluated when and if the issue arises.

Affirmed.

Notes

(1) The "Rights Plan" approved in *Moran* was the first "poison pill." "Innovations" and "improvements" quickly followed. See Julian Velasco, The Enduring Illegitimacy of the Poison Pill, 27 J. Corp. 381 (2002).

(2) One federal district court case arising under Delaware law, Moore Corp., Ltd. v. Wallace Computer Services, Inc., 907 F.Supp. 1545 (D.Del. 1995), comes close to accepting the proposition that "management can do no wrong" and may "just say no" under Delaware law. The court refused to order a poison pill withdrawn even though 73 percent of Wallace's shareholders had accepted the aggressor's (Moore's) offer, and even though Wallace made no effort to find a more friendly bidder or make a share buyback offer (as in *Unitrin*). Furthermore, Wallace had a staggered Board of Directors, so that for Moore to have elected a majority of the directors of Wallace, proxy fights in two successive years would have been necessary. Following this decision, Moore withdrew its bid. See Andrew R. Brownstein, Face-off on Poison Pills, 11 Insights, No. 1, January 1997, 12, 15.

(3) Faced with an apparently unbreakable poison pill and an obdurate management, a few bidders sought to obtain a majority of the Board of Directors through a proxy fight. If successful, they could withdraw or redeem the poison pill, allowing the takeover to succeed. The response of incumbent management was immediate: poison pills were revised to provide that they could be withdrawn only by the vote of "continuing directors"—those who originally authorized the pill or persons nominated by those directors. Thus the "dead hand" pill was born. Bank of New York v. Irving Bank Corp., 139 Misc.2d 665, 528 N.Y.S.2d 482 (Sup.Ct. 1988), invalidated such a poison pill on the grounds that it improperly intruded on the power of boards of directors to manage the company, and was an attempt by one Board of Directors to limit improperly the powers of future Boards. However, in Invacare Corp. v. Healthdyne Technologies, Inc., 968 F.Supp. 1578 (N.D.Ga. 1997) a similar shareholder rights plan was upheld under Ga. Code Ann. § 14–2–624(c) that authorized terms of options and similar rights to be set in the "sole discretion" of the Board of Directors.

---

27. [By the Court] We have discussed the coercive nature of two-tier tender offers in Unocal, 493 A.2d at 956, n. 12. We explained in *Unocal* that a discriminatory self-tender was reasonably related to the threat of two-tier tender offers and possible greenmail.

MENTOR GRAPHICS CORPORATION v. QUICKTURN DESIGN SYSTEMS, INC.

Court of Chancery of Delaware, 1998.
728 A.2d 25.

JACOBS, VICE CHANCELLOR.

In the ever-evolving field of corporate takeover jurisprudence, the defensive mechanism that has mutated more rapidly than others, and has prompted the most widespread debate, is the "poison pill" rights plan. Since making its legal debut in 1985, the story of the poison pill has been a work-in-progress, with each variation and innovation generating new litigation and occasions for judicial opinion writing. This case involves the pill's most recent incarnation—a "no hand" poison pill of limited duration and scope.[28] It marks the latest (but by no means the last) chapter of that work-in-progress.

To put this case into context, in Carmody v. Toll Brothers, Inc. ("Toll Brothers"),[29] this Court, in denying a Rule 12(b)(6) motion to dismiss a complaint attacking a so-called "dead hand" poison pill,[30] ruled that that form of rights plan was subject to legal challenge under the Delaware General Corporation Law ("DGCL") and Delaware corporate fiduciary principles. The Toll Brothers dead hand poison pill plan provided that if there were a change of control of the board of directors, then for the entire lifetime of the pill only the "continuing directors" would be empowered to redeem the rights to facilitate an acquisition by a hostile bidder.

The "no hand" poison pill being challenged here is a variation of, and operates in a different manner from, the "dead hand" pill addressed in Toll Brothers. The pill in Toll Brothers created two classes of directors. One would have the power to redeem and the other would not. That limitation would last the entire lifetime of the pill. In contrast, the "no hand" pill in this case would create no classes. It would evenhandedly prevent all members of a newly elected target board, whose majority is nominated or supported by the hostile bidder, from redeeming the rights to facilitate an acquisition by the bidder. The duration of this "no hand" pill would be for six months after the new directors take office. Those nuanced distinctions and their legal effect, none of which were addressed in Toll Brothers, are what this lawsuit is about.

The dispute that underlies these actions for declarative and injunctive relief arises out of an ongoing effort by Mentor Graphics Corporation ("Mentor"), a hostile bidder, to acquire Quickturn Design Systems, Inc. ("Quick-

---

28. [By the Court] Some practitioners of the art have described this iteration as a "slow hand" poison pill.

29. [By the Court] Del.Ch., C.A. No. 15983, Jacobs, V.C., 723 A.2d 1180 (July 24, 1998, revised, July 27, 28, and Aug. 4, 1998).

30. [By the Court] A "dead hand" rights plan permits only the directors in office at the time the rights plan was adopted or their designated successors ("continuing directors") to redeem the rights. Thus, if the continuing directors are ousted from office in a proxy con-

test waged by a bidder making a hostile tender offer, the bidder's newly-elected board nominees could not redeem the rights to permit the bidder from acquiring the stock tendered to it. Only the previous incumbent directors (or their designated successors) could do so. See Toll Brothers, supra note 37; Jeffrey N. Gordon, "Just Say Never?" Poison Pills, Dead Hand Pills, and Shareholder Adopted Bylaws: An Essay for Warren Buffet, 19 Cardozo L. Rev. 511, 523, 531–32 (1997).

turn"), the target company. The plaintiffs are Mentor[31] and an unaffiliated stockholder of Quickturn; the named defendants are Quickturn and its directors. The plaintiffs challenge the validity, on Delaware fiduciary and statutory grounds, of a "no hand" rights plan of limited duration (the "Delayed Redemption Provision" or "DRP") that the target company board adopted in response to the hostile bidder's tender offer and proxy contest to replace that board as part of the bidder's larger effort to acquire the target company. In response to that hostile bid, the board also amended the company's by-laws to delay the holding of any special stockholders meeting requested by stockholders, for 90 to 100 days after the validity of the request is determined (the "Amendment" or "By–Law Amendment"). The plaintiffs also challenge the legality of that By–Law Amendment.

This is the Opinion of the Court, after trial on the merits. For the reasons discussed below, the Court determines that the DRP is invalid on fiduciary duty grounds, and that the By–Law Amendment is valid and will be upheld. * * *

I. STATEMENT OF FACTS

* * * [Both Mentor (an Oregon corporation) and Quickturn (a Delaware corporation) are publicly held corporations engaged in the electronics business with securities traded on NASDAQ. Mentor sold a certain emulation product to Quickturn in 1992. Later, Mentor re-entered the emulation business when it acquired a French company called Meta Systems ("Meta"), and began to market Meta's products in the United States in December 1995. Quickturn reacted by commencing a proceeding before the International Trade Commission ("ITC") claiming that Meta and Mentor were infringing Quickturn's patents. Quickturn was ultimately successful in this litigation, and Mentor was barred from competing with Quickturn in the United States emulation market.]

After it became clear that these legal barriers prevented Mentor from competing effectively against Quickturn, Mentor began exploring the possibility of acquiring Quickturn. If Mentor owned Quickturn, it would also own the patents, and be in a position to "unenforce" them by seeking to vacate Quickturn's injunctive orders against Mentor in the patent litigation.[32]

The exploration process began when Mr. Bernd Braune, a Mentor senior executive, retained Arthur Andersen ("Andersen") to advise Mentor how it could successfully compete in the emulation market. The result was a report Andersen issued in October 1997, entitled "PROJECT VELOCITY" and "Strategic Alternatives Analysis." The Andersen report identified several advantages and benefits Mentor would enjoy if it acquired Quickturn.[33]

31. [By the Court] Mentor and MGZ Corp., a wholly owned Mentor subsidiary specially created as a vehicle to acquire Quickturn, are referred to collectively as "Mentor." Unless otherwise indicated, Mentor and Howard Shapiro, the shareholder plaintiffs * * * are referred to collectively as "plaintiffs."

32. [By the Court] Mentor assiduously denies that obtaining ownership of the patents, which effectively would enable Mentor to reenter the United States market, was a motivating factor for making its hostile bid. I conclude, however, that was the primary, if not sole, motivation for Mentor's takeover bid, and reject * * * contrary testimony on this subject as lacking credibility.

33. [By the Court] These included: (i) eliminating the time and expense associated with litigation; (ii) creating synergy from combining two companies with complementary core competencies; (iii) reducing customer confusion over product availability, which in turn would

The Andersen report also analyzed whether Mentor would create more value by selling Meta or by purchasing Quickturn. Andersen concluded that selling Meta would eliminate (for Mentor) Meta's forecasted 1998 loss of $3.4 million and would possibly bring $50 million in a sale. Acquiring Quickturn, on the other hand, would enable Mentor to sell its Meta products worldwide; obtain Quickturn's product line, manufacturing facilities, and sales force; and ultimately provide Mentor $610–$640 million of value. Lastly, Andersen concluded that Mentor could pay $300 to $320 million—about $16.80 to $17.90 per share—to acquire Quickturn and still create an additional $290–$320 million in synergistic value for Mentor.

Six weeks later, in December 1997, Mentor retained Salomon Smith Barney ("Salomon") to act as its financial advisor in connection with a possible acquisition of Quickturn. [Salomon's study made in early 1998 concluded that the market price of Quickturn was so high that a takeover bid was not feasible. Later that year, however, Quickturn's stock price declined, and Mentor decided to make a public bid to purchase Quickturn.]

On August 11, 1998, the evening before Mentor launched its bid, Dr. Rhines [Chairman of Mentor's board of directors] scheduled a dinner with Glen Antle, Quickturn's board chairman. After dinner Dr. Rhines informed Mr. Antle that Mentor would be launching a hostile tender offer for the outstanding shares of Quickturn the next morning. Dr. Rhines then handed Mr. Antle a previously prepared letter to that effect. At no time during the three month planning period did Mentor ever attempt to contact Quickturn's management or its board to negotiate a consensual deal.[34]

The next morning, on August 12, 1998, Mentor announced an unsolicited cash tender offer for all outstanding common shares of Quickturn at $12.125 per share—a price representing an approximate 50% premium over Quickturn's immediate pre-offer price, and a 20% discount from Quickturn's February 1998 stock price levels. Mentor's tender offer, once consummated, would be followed by a second step merger in which Quickturn's nontendering stockholders would receive, in cash, the same $12.125 per share tender offer price. Mentor also announced its intent to solicit proxies to replace the board at a special meeting. Relying upon Quickturn's then-applicable by-law provision governing the call of special stockholders meetings, Mentor began soliciting agent designations from Quickturn stockholders to satisfy the by-law's stock ownership requirements to call such a meeting.[35] * * *

accelerate sales; and (iv) eliminating the threat of a large competitor moving into the emulation market. Mentor has utilized these reasons in public statements in which it attempted to explain why its bid made sense.

34. [By the Court] What Dr. Rhines did not disclose to Mr. Antle at that dinner was that Mentor had already prepared two complaints, which Mentor planned to file the next day, naming Mr. Antle and the other Quickturn board members as defendants. Dr. Rhines claims that he did not disclose this because the subject "just didn't come up." Dr. Rhines also refused Mr. Antle's requests that Quickturn be given time to consider Mentor's offer and per-

haps proceed on a friendly basis, because it was "too late."

35. [By the Court] The applicable by-law (Article II, § 2.3) authorized a call of a special stockholders meeting by shareholders holding at least 10% of Quickturn's shares. In their agent solicitation, Mentor informed Quickturn stockholders that Mentor intended to call a special meeting approximately 45 days after it received sufficient agent designations to satisfy the 10% requirement under the original by-law. The solicitation also disclosed Mentor's intent to set the date for the special meeting, and to set the record date and give formal notice of that meeting.

[After three board meetings to discuss Mentor's proposal,] the Quickturn board concluded that Mentor's offer was inadequate, and decided to recommend that Quickturn shareholders reject Mentor's offer. * * * At the August 21 board meeting, the Quickturn board adopted two defensive measures in response to Mentor's hostile takeover bid.

First, the board amended Article II, § 2.3 of Quickturn's by-laws, which permitted stockholders holding 10% or more of Quickturn's stock to call a special stockholders meeting. The By–Law Amendment provides that if any such special meeting is requested by shareholders, the corporation (Quickturn) would fix the record date for, and determine the time and place of, that special meeting, which must take place not less than 90 days nor more than 100 days after the receipt and determination of the validity of the shareholders' request.

Second, the board amended Quickturn's shareholder rights plan ("Rights Plan") by eliminating its "dead hand" feature and replacing it with the Deferred Redemption Plan ("DRP"), under which no newly elected board could redeem the Rights Plan for six months after taking office, if the purpose or effect of the redemption would be to facilitate a transaction with an "Interested Person" (one who proposed, nominated or financially supported the election of the new directors to the board).[36] Mentor would be an Interested Person.

The effect of the By–Law Amendment would be to delay a shareholder-called special meeting for at least three months. The effect of the DRP would be to delay the ability of a newly-elected, Mentor-nominated board to redeem the poison pill for six months in any transaction with an Interested Person. Thus, the combined effect of the two defensive measures would be to delay any acquisition of Quickturn by Mentor for at least nine months. * * *

Mentor filed this action on August 12, 1998 [sic], seeking (i) a declaratory judgment that Quickturn's newly adopted takeover defenses are invalid, and (ii) an injunction requiring the Quickturn board to dismantle those defenses. After expedited discovery, the defendants moved for summary judgment. Following extensive briefing and oral argument, the Court denied defendants' motion * * * [and] a trial was held on October 19, 20, 23, 26, and 28, 1998, during which the parties amassed a voluminous record; thereafter, the parties submitted extensive post trial briefs on an expedited schedule.

During the course of the litigation, the Quickturn board, relying upon the By–Law Amendment, noticed the special meeting requested by Mentor from January 8, 1999—71 days after the October 1, 1998 meeting date originally noticed by Mentor. After the trial, Mentor announced in Amendments to its Schedule 14A–1 that were filed with the S.E.C., that it had received tenders of

---

36. [By the Court] The amended Rights Plan pertinently provides that: "[I]n the event that a majority of the Board of Directors of the Company is elected by stockholder action at an annual or special meeting of stockholders, then until the 180th day following the effectiveness of such election (including any postponement or adjournment thereof), the Rights shall not be redeemed if such redemption is reasonably likely to have the purpose or effect of facilitating a Transaction with an Interested Person."

An "Interested Person" is defined under the amended Rights Plan as "any Person who (i) is or will become an Acquiring Person if such Transaction were to be consummated or an Affiliate or Associate of such a Person, and (ii) is, or directly or indirectly proposed, nominated or financially supported, a director of [Quickturn] in office at the time of consideration of such Transaction who was elected at an annual or special meeting of stockholders."

Quickturn shares which, together with the shares that Mentor already owned, represent over 51% of Quickturn's outstanding stock.

* * * [The court concluded that the bylaw amendment was valid, but it invalidated the DRP on the following analysis:]

At the time Mentor commenced its bid, Quickturn had in place a Rights Plan that contained a so-called "dead hand" provision. That provision had a limited "continuing director" feature that became operative only if an insurgent that owned more than 15% of Quickturn's common stock successfully waged a proxy contest to replace a majority of the board. In that event, only the "continuing directors" (those directors in office at the time the poison pill was adopted) could redeem the rights. During the same August 21, 1998 meeting at which it amended the special meeting by-law, the Quickturn board also amended the Rights Plan to eliminate its "continuing director" feature, and to substitute a "no hand" or "delayed redemption" rights plan.

The DRP provides that, if a majority of the directors are replaced by stockholder action, the newly elected board cannot redeem the rights for six months if the purpose or effect of the redemption would be to facilitate a transaction with an "Interested Person." * * * The plaintiffs attack the DRP on * * * [the ground that it] was a disproportionate response to any threat reasonably perceived by the Mentor bid and, therefore, violated the fiduciary principles articulated in Unocal and Unitrin. The plaintiffs contend, specifically, that the Quickturn board has failed to establish that (i) the Mentor offer and proxy contest constituted a legally cognizable threat, (ii) the DRP is not coercive or preclusive, and that (iii) the DRP falls within a range of reasonable potential responses to Mentor's hostile takeover efforts.[37] * * *

The Court concludes that, in adopting the DRP, the Quickturn board, even though motivated by a good faith belief that their actions were in the company's best interests, nonetheless transgressed their fiduciary duties under Unocal and Unitrin.[38] * * *

* * * Decisions made by a board of directors are normally subject to the business judgment form of review, which is a "presumption that in making a business decision, the directors of a corporation acted on an informed basis, in good faith and in the honest belief that the action was taken in the best interest of the Company."[39] Under that form of review, the burden to rebut that presumption rests on the party that challenges the board's decision, and a court will not substitute its judgment for that of the board if the decision is attributable to a "rational business purpose."[40] But where a board of a Delaware corporation takes action to resist or defend against a hostile bid for

---

37. [By the Editors] The plaintiff also alleged that the plan (1) violated the board's fiduciary duties to Quickturn and its shareholders, and (2) the plan was invalid because it impermissibly deprived a newly board of its core authority to manage the corporation. The court did not find it necessary to address either of these contentions.

38. [By the Court] The Court acknowledges that a disposition of this issue on fiduciary, rather than upon statutory, grounds may appear counterintuitive. In this case, however, the statutory argument—which appears as the last in the sequence of arguments in Mentor's

brief, and went virtually unanswered in the defendants' briefs—was not adequately developed by the parties. Because the briefing focused almost entirely upon the fiduciary claims, the Court rests its DRP ruling on those grounds as well.

39. [By the Court] Unitrin, 651 A.2d at 1373 (quoting Aronson v. Lewis, 473 A.2d 805, 812 (1984)).

40. [By the Court] Id. (citing Sinclair Oil Corp. v. Levien, Del.Supr., 280 A.2d 717, 720 (1971)).

control, the review standard is quite different. In that case the target company board's defensive actions are subjected to "enhanced" judicial scrutiny, because of the "omnipresent specter" that the board may be acting in its own interests rather than the interests of the corporation or its unaffiliated stockholders.[41] For a target board's actions to be entitled to business judgment rule protection, the target board must first establish that (i) it had reasonable grounds to believe that the hostile bid constituted a threat to corporate policy and effectiveness, and (ii) that the defensive measures adopted were "proportionate," that is, reasonable in relation to the threat that the board reasonably perceived. The DRP is reviewed under that standard.[42]

The parties first dispute whether the Quickturn board has established the existence of a legally cognizable threat. On that issue, the board may satisfy its burden by showing that it conducted a reasonable investigation and took defensive action in good faith. That proof is enhanced if a majority of the board that approved the defensive measures were outside independent directors. Although Mentor contends that its offer did not pose a legally cognizable threat, I conclude otherwise * * *.

A major point of contention (and confusion) concerns what precisely the Quickturn board perceived to be the threat posed by Mentor's hostile bid. Our Supreme Court has recognized that three categories of threats normally arise in the corporate takeover context: (i) opportunity loss * * * [where] a hostile offer might deprive target shareholders of the opportunity to select a superior alternative offered by target management [or, we would add, offered by another bidder]; (ii) structural coercion, * * * the risk that disparate treatment of non-tendering shareholders might distort shareholders' tender decisions; and * * * (iii) substantive coercion, * * * the risk that shareholders will mistakenly accept an underpriced offer because they disbelieve management's representations of intrinsic value.[43] * * *

Despite the defendants' diverse characterizations of the threat, the evidence, viewed as a whole, shows that the perceived threat that led the Quickturn board to adopt the DRP, was the concern that Quickturn shareholders might mistakenly, in ignorance of Quickturn's true value, accept Mentor's inadequate offer, and elect a new board that would prematurely sell the company before the new board could adequately inform itself of Quickturn's fair value and before the shareholders could consider other options. In so finding, I reject the effort by Quickturn's attorneys to characterize the threat differently in their briefs. * * *

Having concluded that the board reasonably perceived a cognizable threat, the issue then becomes whether the board's response—the DRP—was reasonable in relation to that threat. * * * A board " 'does not have unbridled discretion to defeat any perceived threat by any Draconian means available.' "[44] Accordingly, our law requires that Quickturn's board establish that the DRP was proportional to the threat posed by Mentor's offer.

---

41. [By the Court] Id. (quoting Unocal, 493 A.2d at 954).

42. [By the Court] Unocal, 493 A.2d at 955; see also Unitrin, 651 A.2d at 1372 (1995); Paramount Communications, Inc. v. Time Inc., Del.Supr., 571 A.2d 1140, 1152 (1989) ("Time").

43. [By the Court] Unitrin, 651 A.2d at 1384; see also Ronald J. Gilson & Reinier Kraakman, Delaware's Intermediate Standard for Defensive Tactics: Is There Substance to Proportionality Review?, 44 Bus. Law. 247, 267 (1989).

44. [By the Court] Unitrin, 651 A.2d at 1387 (quoting Unocal, 493 A.2d at 955).

For the reasons next discussed, the Court concludes that the DRP was disproportionate, because although the DRP is neither coercive nor preclusive in these particular circumstances, it does fall outside the range of reasonable responses to Mentor's hostile bid. * * *

The record establishes, and I therefore find, that the board's justification or rationale for adopting the DRP was to force any newly elected board (as distinguished from only a Mentor-nominated board) to take sufficient time to become familiar with Quickturn and its value, and to provide shareholders the opportunity to consider alternatives, before selling Quickturn to any acquiror.

Unfortunately, that justification renders the DRP a disproportionate response, because the justification is at war with how the DRP, as adopted by the board, would actually operate. The DRP does not create a six month pill redemption delay in all cases where a newly elected, Mentor-nominated board seeks to sell the company to any bidder. It creates such a delay only if a newly elected board seeks to sell Quickturn to an "Interested Person," which in this case is Mentor. It is undisputed that under the terms of the DRP, a new board could sell the company to anyone other than Mentor on its very first day in office, or at any time during the six month nonredemption period. An example of the inconsistency between the theory (the directors' justification for the DRP) and the reality (how the DRP would actually operate) makes the point. Suppose that the day after the new Mentor-nominated board takes office, a third party makes a $14 per share offer, which tops Mentor's $12.125 bid. An auction then ensues. Mentor decides to increase its offer to $15, and becomes the high bidder. Under the DRP, the new board could redeem the pill and accept the $14 bid immediately, but could not accept Mentor's $15 bid for six months. There is no evidence that when it decided to adopt that defensive measure the board considered that the DRP could operate in this way. Because the operative terms of the DRP cannot be reconciled with the directors' stated justification for adopting it, the board has not carried its burden of demonstrating that the DRP is reasonable in relation to the perceived threat.

The defendants have also failed to carry their burden because they are unable to articulate a cogent reason why a six month delay period is reasonable. The board did discuss alternate time periods, but it ultimately settled on six months because that period was "reasonable" and the "minimum" time a newly elected board would need to become sufficiently informed about Quickturn, based upon their own experience as to how long they, as directors, needed to learn about the company. * * * [However,] the board has offered no justification that is anchored to any objective fact or criterion for adopting the six month nonredemption period in the DRP.

Finally, the DRP cannot pass the proportionality test because its articulated purpose—to give a newly elected board time to inform itself of Quickturn's value—would already have been achieved by the conclusion of the three month delay period imposed by the By–Law Amendment. The purpose of the Amendment is to give shareholders 90 to 100 days' time to make an informed decision about which slate to vote for. The DRP would protract the delay by another six months, purportedly to enable the newly elected board to educate itself about Quickturn's value before committing to a sale of the company.

The problem with this rationale is that the subject matter about which the shareholders would be informing themselves during the By–Law Amendment 90 to 100 day delay period, and the subject about which a new board would be informing itself during the six month DRP nonredemption period, is the same: should the company be sold and, if so, when and at what price? If three months is an adequate time for shareholders to become informed, why should a new board require six months? More fundamentally, why would the Mentor director nominees be unable to inform themselves on that issue (as the Quickturn shareholders must) during the three month period imposed by the Amended By–Law? * * * The conclusion that must be drawn is that the board has failed to show why the additional six month delay imposed by the DRP is necessary to achieve the board's stated purpose for its adoption.

For these reasons the DRP cannot survive scrutiny under Unocal and must be declared invalid.[45]

Notes

(1) On an expedited appeal, the Supreme Court of Delaware affirmed this decision, but on significantly broader grounds than that used by Chancellor Jacobs. See Quickturn Design Systems, Inc. v. Shapiro, 721 A.2d 1281, 1290–99 (Del.1998).

(2) Is it a fair inference from this holding that all dead-hand, slow-hand, and no-hand poison pills are invalid in Delaware? See Peter Letsou, Are Dead Hand (And No Hand) Poison Pills Really Dead?, 68 U. Cincinnati L.Rev. 1101 (2000).

(3) Another commentator made the cautious suggestion that "these decisions represent the first real shift in Delaware takeover law after more than a decade of decisions that all seemed to favor targets." Paul T. Schnell, From the Editor: A Good Year for Bidders in Delaware, 3 Glasser LegalWorks, No. 6, 2 (1999). This certainly does not intimate that a seismic change was underway in Delaware.

(4) If the principal case really does mean that current boards of directors cannot restrict the power of their successors (following a successful purchase

---

45. [By the Court] By way of postscript, this Court is mindful that higher level issues lurk behind the factual shadows of this dispute, issues that are not addressed in this Opinion. In this ever-changing area of the law where there is a potential (and, perhaps, also the need) to afford guidance to the corporate bar in the form of bright-line standards, for a Court to adjudicate the validity of an innovative takeover defense on the basis of equitable and fiduciary principles that by their nature are highly fact specific and particularized, is admittedly unsatisfying. That there are underlying policy issues is inevitable, given the tension between the directors' acknowledged authority to manage the affairs of the corporation, and the shareholders' independent right and authority to choose the corporation's ultimate destiny, whether by approving or disapproving a fundamental transaction or by electing a new board committed to a direction the shareholders think desirable. In a contest for corporate control where the incumbent board adopts a poison pill and an insurgent slate of board candidates vow to redeem it, should the target company shareholders have the final word on whether or not the pill should be redeemed? To express the question in fiduciary terms, should a proxy contest in this setting be viewed as a referendum on whether the company should be sold, and if so, should the board of directors be allowed to delay the effect of that referendum? To pose the issue in statutory terms, should a delayed redemption provision be found invalid under 8 Del. C. § 141(a) because it temporarily deprives a newly elected insurgent board of a portion of its core authority that the board arguably may need (or have a fiduciary duty) to exercise during the period of deprivation? * * * To craft a principle, or "bright line" test, that will readily enable a court to determine the validity of a limited duration "no hand" poison pill, would require a court to address issues of this kind. This Opinion does not meet that challenge * * *.

offer), is there danger that publicly-held corporations might migrate to states more hospitable than their state of incorporation? Maryland, for example, made minor changes in language to its statutes to make clear that Maryland Board of Directors had complete freedom to bind subsequent boards.

Maryland was the first state specifically to validate a slow-hand provision in rights plans following the *Quickturn* decision. The Maryland statute, it may be noted, leaves open the measuring time for the beginning of the 180 day period. It also apparently gives the "stockholder rights plan" unlimited discretion to define "future director." Is there any room within these Maryland statutes for a judicial decision such as the Delaware Supreme Court's decision in Quickturn?

INTERNATIONAL BROTHERHOOD OF TEAMSTER v. FLEMING COMPANIES

Supreme Court of Oklahoma, 1999.
975 P.2d 907.

SIMMS, J. THE UNITED STATES COURT OF APPEALS, TENTH CIRCUIT, JOHN C. PORFILIO, PRESIDING JUDGE, * * * certified to the Oklahoma Supreme Court the following question of law:

> Does Oklahoma law [A] restrict the authority to create and implement shareholder rights plans exclusively to the board of directors, or [B] may shareholders propose resolutions requiring that shareholder rights plans be submitted to the shareholders for vote at the succeeding annual meeting?

We answer the first part of the question in the negative and the second part affirmatively. We hold under Oklahoma law there is no exclusive authority granted boards of directors to create and implement shareholder rights plans, where shareholder objection is brought and passed through official channels of corporate governance. We find no Oklahoma law which gives exclusive authority to a corporation's board of directors for the formulation of shareholder rights plans and no authority which precludes shareholders from proposing resolutions or bylaw amendments regarding shareholder rights plans. We hold shareholders may propose bylaws which restrict board implementation of shareholder rights plans, assuming the certificate of incorporation does not provide otherwise.

The International Brotherhood of the Teamsters General Fund [Teamsters] owns sixty-five shares of Fleming Companies, Inc. * * * In 1986, Fleming implemented a shareholder's rights plan with the term of the plan to expire in 1996. The rights plan implemented by Fleming is an anti-takeover mechanism. Such plans give boards of directors authority to adopt and execute discriminatory shareholder rights upon the occurrence of some triggering event, usually when a certain percentage of shares has been amassed by a single shareholder. A board can place "restrictions or conditions on the exercise, transfer or receipt of" shareholder rights which can severely dilute the shareholding power of one seeking control of a company.[46] The defensive plans usually result in entrenching existing management, making a takeover without the approval of incumbent management more difficult. These rights

---

46. John H. Matheson & Brent A. Olson, Shareholder Rights and Legislative Wrongs; Toward Balanced Takeover Legislation, 59 Geo.Wash.L.Rev. 1425, 1450 (1990).

plans can make it far more expensive to effect a takeover. Because the rights plans make the merger of companies more painful for the suitor and assist incumbent management in maintaining control, the plans are often called "poison pill rights plans" or "poison pills."

From a target company's perspective, rights plans can often buy valuable time to implement merger strategy or even secure more lucrative offers from other suitors. In this context, a rights plan might serve not only the protectionist objectives of an existing management, but also the company's overall interests in the event of takeover, including the interests of shareholders.

However, rights plans can often stifle mergers, causing some shareholder groups to view them with increasing skepticism, because, company mergers can be financially lucrative for shareholders who own stock in a target company. A poison pill not only makes many mergers cost prohibitive and therefore might prevent a merger altogether, but it can decrease the profits in those mergers which do ultimately occur. As a result, poison pills have the ability to strip shareholders of financial benefit which might normally be associated with a takeover.

The stock market has had a long history of shareholder passivity, but this is likely a thing of the past. The rise of the institutional investor and the increased knowledge of stockholders as a whole is forcing an increased accountability to shareholders for many boards of directors. As a result, the demands of the Teamsters in its case against Fleming is something courts may encounter with increasing frequency in the years to come.

The trial court, which ruled in the Teamsters' (shareholders) favor, expressed concern with Fleming's position, stating that it effectively removed corporate authority regarding share marketability from the shareholders and vested it exclusively in a board of directors, which might view the situation from the most self-interested point of view. Teamsters were critical of Fleming's rights plan, seeing it as a means of entrenching the current Fleming board of directors in the event Fleming became the target of a takeover. In 1996, the Teamsters organized and introduced a non-binding resolution for the annual shareholders meeting. The 1996 resolution called on the Fleming board to redeem the existing rights plan. The then current rights plan had been in effect since 1986 and was scheduled for renewal. The Teamsters proposal was met with apparent hostility from Fleming's board and the rights plan remained intact, despite a majority shareholder vote in agreement with the Teamsters' resolution to redeem it.

The following year, 1997, Teamsters mounted a more organized effort to change the continued implementation of the rights plan. Teamsters prepared a proxy statement for inclusion in the proxy materials for the 1997 annual shareholder's meeting. With the proxy effort, the Teamsters proposed an amendment to the company's bylaws which would require any rights plan implemented by the board of directors to be put to the shareholders for a majority vote.[47] The proposal was essentially a ratification procedure wherein

47. [By the Court] The 1997 proxy proposal provided:

"Resolved, That shareholders hereby exercise their right under 18 O.S.A. Sec. 1013 to amend the bylaws of Fleming Companies, Inc. to add the following Article:

"Article X Poison Pills (Shareholder Rights Plans)

the shareholders would force the board to formulate a rights plan both the board and shareholders could agree on or do away with such a plan altogether.

Fleming refused to include the resolution in its 1997 proxy statement, declaring the proposal was not a subject for shareholder action under Oklahoma law. Teamsters then brought an action in the Federal District Court for the Western District of Oklahoma. The district court ruled in favor of the Teamsters, the court finding that "shareholders, through the device of by-laws, have a right of review." Fleming appealed to the 10th Circuit Court of Appeals, which submitted the certified question to this Court.

Fleming sought to postpone any shareholder vote on the 1997 proxy issue until after the resolution of this case. But the U.S. District Court and later the 10th Circuit denied Fleming's motion to suspend the injunction. Fleming was then forced to allow its shareholders to vote on the Teamsters' proxy. The Teamsters' resolution passed with approximately 60% of the voted shares.

Fleming's position is that 18 O.S.1991 § 1038[48] gives the board of directors authority to create and issue shareholder rights plans, subject only to limits which might exist in the corporation's certificate of incorporation; and that shareholders cannot through bylaws restrict the board's powers to implement a rights plan. The Teamsters' position is that 18 O.S.1991 s 1013 gives shareholders of a publicly traded corporation, such as Fleming, the authority to adopt bylaws addressing a broad range of topics from a corporation's business, corporate affairs, and rights and powers of shareholders and directors.[49] It is this apparent conflict which brings this federal certified question to this Court.

This is a case of first impression in Oklahoma and there is little guidance from other states. Oklahoma and Delaware have substantially similar corporation acts, especially with regard to Title 18, §§ 1013 & 1038 which are of primary concern here. 8 Del.C. § 109(a) & (b); 8 Del.C. § 157. However, a

"A. The Corporation shall not adopt or maintain a poison pill, shareholder rights plan, rights agreement or any other form of 'poison pill' which is designed to or has the effect of making acquisition of large holdings of the Corporation's shares of stock more difficult or expensive (such as the 1986 'Rights Agreement'), unless such plan is first approved by a majority shareholder vote. The Company shall redeem any such rights now in effect. The affirmative vote of a majority of shares voted shall suffice to approve such a plan.

"B. This article shall be effective immediately and automatically as of the date it is approved by the affirmative vote of the holders of a majority of the shares, present, in person or by proxy at a regular or special meeting of shareholders.

"C. Notwithstanding any other provision of these bylaws, this Article may not be amended, altered, deleted or modified in any way by the Board of Directors without prior shareholder approval."

48. [By the Court] 18 O.S.1991 § 1038, Rights and options respecting stock: "Subject

to any provisions in the certificate of incorporation, every corporation may create and issue, whether or not in connection with the issue and sale of any shares of stock or other securities of the corporation, rights or options entitling the holders thereof to purchase from the corporation any shares of its capital stock of any instrument or instruments as shall be approved by the board of directors. * * * "

49. [By the Court] 18 O.S.1991 § 1038(A) & (B), Bylaws: " * * * After a corporation has received any payment for any of its stock, the power to adopt, amend or repeal bylaws shall be in the shareholders entitled to vote * * *; provided, however, any corporation, in its certificate of incorporation, may confer the power to adopt, amend or repeal bylaws upon the directors * * *. The fact that such power has been so conferred upon the directors or governing body, as the case may be, shall not divest the shareholders or members of the power, nor limit their power to adopt, amend or repeal bylaws."

review of Delaware decisions revealed no comparable case from that state. The 10th Circuit's question is ultimately one of corporate governance and what degree of control shareholders can exact upon the corporations in which they own stock.

In the scheme of corporate governance the role of shareholders has been purposefully indirect. Shareholders' direct authority is limited. * * * This is true for obvious reasons. Large corporations with perhaps thousands of stockholders could not function if the daily running of the corporation was subject to the approval of so many relatively attenuated people. However, the authority given a board of directors under the Oklahoma General Corporation Act, is not without shareholder oversight. * * *

Fleming's argument relies on this passage [from] 18 O.S.1991 § 1038: "Subject to any provisions in the certificate of incorporation, every *corporation* may create and issue * * * rights or options entitling the holders thereof to purchase from the corporation any shares of its capital stock of any class or classes, such rights or options to be evidenced by or in such instrument or instruments as shall be approved by the *board of directors*. [Emphasis added] In making its argument, Fleming asserts that the word 'corporation' is synonymous with 'board of directors' as the term is used in 18 § 1038. Therefore, according to Fleming, 'every corporation may create and issue * * * rights and options[.]', can actually be read to say '[every corporation's board of directors] may create and issue * * * rights and options[.]' However, * * * this assertion is flawed. * * * [T]he former Business Corporation Act, 18 § 1.2(1) and (23), defines 'corporation' and 'director' differently. The statutes indicate our legislature has an understanding of the distinct definitions it assigns to these terms, and we find it unlikely the legislature would interchange them as Fleming contends. While this Court would agree with Fleming that a corporation may create and issue rights and options within the grant of authority given it in 18 § 1038, it does not automatically translate that the board of directors of that corporation has in itself the same breadth of authority."

A shareholder rights plan is essentially a variety of stock option plan. Its use as an anti-takeover mechanism does not change its essential character. While shareholder ratification of poison pills has not been tested in the courts, the same cannot be said for stock option plans as a whole. There is authority supporting shareholder ratification of stock option plans. * * * For example, in Michelson v. Duncan, 407 A.2d 211, 218–20 (Del.1979), shareholders ratified a stock option package, curing a voidable act of the corporation's board of directors. Unlike the instant case, Michelson does not focus on whether shareholders have the authority to ratify the stock option plan, but rather explains that shareholder approval can cure the invalidity of an otherwise voidable act of the company's board. Despite this distinction, however, the case does reveal that stock option plans themselves can be subject to shareholder approval. * * *

We find nothing in the Oklahoma General Corporation Act * * * or existing case law which indicates the shareholder rights plan is somehow exempt from shareholder adopted bylaws. Fleming argues that only the certificate of incorporation can limit the board's authority to implement such a plan * * *. While this Court might agree that a certificate of incorporation, which somehow precludes bylaw amendments directed at shareholder rights plans, could preclude the Teamsters from seeking the bylaw changes which are proposed in this case, neither party has indicated Fleming's certificate speaks in any way to the board's authority or shareholder constraints regarding shareholder rights plans. We find no authority to support the contention that a certificate of incorporation which is silent with regard to shareholder rights plans precludes shareholder enacted bylaws regarding the implementation of rights plans.

A number of states have taken affirmative steps to ensure their domestic corporations, and in many instances the board of directors itself, are able to implement shareholder rights plans to protect the company from takeover. The legislation is typically called a shareholders rights plan endorsement statute. However, the Oklahoma legislature has not passed such legislation. There are at least twenty-four states with these share rights plan endorsement statutes.[50]

* * * [The Idaho statute illustrates] how a board of directors can operate with relative autonomy when a rights plan endorsement statute applies. This does not suggest the absence of a share rights plan endorsement statute in Oklahoma precludes the implementation of such a takeover defense. We merely find that without the authority granted in such an endorsement statute, the board may well be subject to the general procedures of corporate governance, including the enactment of bylaws which limit the board's authority to implement shareholder rights plans.

This Court understands much of the reasoning behind the enactment of rights plan endorsement statutes and why so many state legislatures are inclined to facilitate this takeover protection for their domestic corporations. In addition, we understand Fleming's desire to have a rights plan available for quick, and more effective, implementation. However, if, as in this case, the certificate of incorporation does not offer directors this broad authority to protect against mergers and takeover, corporations must look to Oklahoma's legislature, not this Court, which is more properly vested with the means to offer boards such authority.

In answering this certified question, we do not suggest all shareholder rights plans are required to submit to shareholder approval, ratification or review; this is not the question presented to us. Instead, we find shareholders may, through the proper channels of corporate governance, restrict the board of directors authority to implement shareholder rights plans.

---

50. [By the Court] John H. Matheson & Brent A. Olson, Shareholder Rights and Legislative Wrongs: Toward Balanced Takeover Legislation, 59 Geo. Wash. L.Rev. 1425, 1554–58 (August 1991). * * * [S]tates with shareholder rights plan endorsement statutes are Colorado, Georgia, Hawaii, Idaho, Illinois, Indiana, Iowa, Kentucky, Massachusetts, Michigan, Nevada, New Jersey, New York, North Carolina, Ohio, Oregon, Pennsylvania, Rhode Island, South Dakota, Tennessee, Utah, Virginia, Wyoming, [and] Wisconsin. * * * [An example] of [a] shareholders rights plan endorsement statute[] which give explicit authority to directors of the corporation reads as follows: "Nothing contained in this chapter is intended or shall be construed in any way to limit, modify or restrict an issuing public corporation's authority to take any action which the directors may appropriately determine to be in furtherance of the protection of the interests of the corporation and its shareholders, including without limitation the authority to adopt or enter into plans, arrangements or instruments that deny rights, privileges, power or authority to the holder or holders of at least a specified number of shares or percentage of share ownership or voting power in certain circumstances." [Idaho] St. § 30–1706(1).

SUMMERS, C.J., HARGRAVE, V.C.J., LAVENDER, OPALA, WILSON, KAUGER, and WATT, JJ., concur. HODGES, J., no vote.

Notes

(1) Some institutional investors that oppose poison pills have had success as proponents of nonbinding precatory shareholder proposals under Rule 14a–8 to redeem the poison pill. See also MBCA § 10.21, which provides explicitly for the primacy of shareholder-approved by-laws over directorial action.

(2) This issue has given rise to a substantial amount of law review commentary supporting the validity of shareholder rights bylaws. See e.g. Lawrence Hamermesh, Corporate Democracy and Stockholder Adopted Bylaws: Taking Back the Street?, 73 Tulane L.Rev. 409 (1998); Jonathan R. Macey, The Legality and Utility of the Shareholder Rights Bylaw, 26 Hofstra L.Rev. 835 (1998) ["concern about its legality is misplaced"]; Robert Thompson, Preemption and Federalism in Corporate Governance: Protecting Shareholder Rights to Vote, Sell, and Sue, 62 Law & Contemp. Prob. 215 (1999); E. Norman Veasey, An Economic Rationale for Judicial Decisionmaking in Corporate Law, 53 Bus.Law. 681 (1998).

D.   TAKEOVER DEFENSES AND JUDICIAL REVIEW

Assuming that a takeover offer—either all cash or cash and marketable securities—is made, does incumbent management have a duty to oppose it? To support it? To remain neutral and neither support nor oppose it? These questions raise fundamental issues about the roles of shareholders and management that are at the center of the modern debate over takeovers. If, as will normally be the case, the aggressor has the financial strength to carry out the contemplated offer, shareholders of the target corporation will almost certainly realize more for their shares if the offer succeeds than if it fails. If one accepts the basic proposition that the sole goal of management should be to maximize shareholder wealth, does it not follow that management certainly should not be permitted to actively oppose an offer, and that it should further have an affirmative obligation either to support the offer or seek even more favorable offers from other sources?

On the other hand, the underlying justification for the many state statutes that authorize consideration of non-shareholder constituencies (see Chapter 12, Section C) is to liberate management from the chains of this apparently-compelling theoretical argument that it has a duty always to maximize the financial interests of the shareholders. It is also clear that acceptance of a takeover bid is often not value-maximizing from the standpoint of incumbent management. These individuals face the loss of prestigious positions, six- or seven-figure salaries, desirable "perks," lucrative fringe benefits, and the loss of power to control a large enterprise. Thus, it is not surprising that management usually feels it is a matter of the highest urgency to defeat uninvited takeover bids at all costs.

The derogatory term "entrenchment" usually describes defensive tactics that are designed solely to defeat an offer in order to preserve management's position. Entrenchment is a breach of the fiduciary duty of loyalty (since the tactics are not for a corporate purpose but to preserve the position of the managers). Open descriptions of one's motive to entrench and preserve one's position are clear losers, therefore other justifications to defeat the offer must be developed. Examples include (1) the offered price is too low and does not reflect the "true" value of the corporation's business; (2) the aggressor's reputation for sound fiscal management is not good; (3) the aggressor is assuming debt obligations which it probably cannot meet without using the target's assets, thereby injuring remaining shareholders or senior security or debt holders; (4) it is simply in the best long-run interests of the shareholders for the corporation to remain independent (the "just say no" defense); (5) management has already embarked on long-range plans to improve the corporation's profits and stock price, and the decision to pursue those plans is protected by the business judgment rule; (6) the proposed transaction would result in the violation of the antitrust laws or some other federal or state statute; or (7) the offer is a partial one and is structured in a way that makes it unfair to shareholders by "coercing" them to tender. Whether or not such arguments are persuasive or even plausible obviously depends on the facts of the particular takeover. If one accepts the premise that takeovers occur primarily to weed out less efficient managers, the conclusions that management should be sharply restricted in the defensive tactics it may employ and that basic economic forces should decide the outcome are considerably strengthened.

The economic stakes in a takeover battle are so great that litigation to test the validity of any defenses employed by management—at least in the 1980s—was a virtual certainty. This litigation was traditionally in the form of suits for equitable relief based either on violations of the Williams Act or on breaches of the duty of care or loyalty by management, or both. However, where management effectively defeated a tender offer without providing an offsetting management buyout or leveraged recapitalization to replace some or all of the lost value to shareholders, there inevitably was a precipitous decline in the market price of the target stock, and litigation commenced on the theory that the directors should be held personally liable for the losses since they opposed the takeover in order to preserve their positions with the corporation.

Suits by shareholders against the directors and officers first foundered on the business judgment rule in its most permissive form. The leading case was Panter v. Marshall Field & Co., 646 F.2d 271 (7th Cir.1981), cert. denied, 454 U.S. 1092, 102 S.Ct. 658, 70 L.Ed.2d 631 (1981), where Marshall Field successfully fended off an unwanted takeover bid from Carter Hawley Hale (CHH), a national retail chain that operated Nieman–Marcus and other stores. Marshall Field adopted and vigorously pursued a policy to preserve its independence; among other things, it adopted an expansion program that led to Marshall Field stores coming into direct competition with Nieman–Marcus in several markets. When CHH withdrew its bid in part because of antitrust complications, the price of Marshall Field common stock precipitously declined from about $34 per share to $19 per share. The Court absolved the defendants of liability under the business judgment rule and the presumption of good faith that protects directors: "The plaintiffs also contend that the 'defensive acquisitions' of the five Liberty House stores and the Galleria were imprudent, and designed to make Field's less attractive as an acquisition, as well as to exacerbate any antitrust problems created by the CHH merger. It is precisely this sort of Monday-morning-quarterbacking that the business judgment rule was intended to prevent." 646 F.2d at 297.

This approach was too much for Judge Cudahy:

> Unfortunately, the majority here has moved one giant step closer to shredding whatever constraints still remain upon the ability of corporate directors to place self-interest before shareholder interest in resisting a hostile tender offer for control of the corporation. There is abundant evidence in this case to go to the jury on the state claims for breach of fiduciary duty. I emphatically disagree that the business judgment rule should clothe directors, battling blindly to fend off a threat to their control, with an almost irrebuttable presumption of sound business judgment, prevailing over everything but the elusive hobgoblins of fraud, bad faith or abuse of discretion. * * *

> Addressing first the state law claims of breach of fiduciary duty by the Board, the majority has adopted an approach which would virtually immunize a target company's board of directors against liability to shareholders, provided a sufficiently prestigious (and expensive) array of legal and financial talent were retained to furnish *post hoc* rationales for fixed and immutable policies of resistance to takeover. Relying on several recent decisions interpreting the Delaware business judgment rule, the majority fails to make the important distinction between the activity of a corporation in managing a business enterprise and its function as a vehicle for collecting and using capital and distributing profits and losses. The former involves corporate functioning in competitive business affairs in which judicial interference may be undesirable. *The latter involves only the corporation-shareholder relationship, in which the courts may more justifiably intervene to insist on equitable behavior. Note, Protection for Shareholder Interests in Recapitalizations of Publicly Held Companies,* 58 Colum.L.Rev. 1030, 1066 (1958) (emphasis supplied).

> The theoretical justification for the "hands off" precept of the business judgment rule is that courts should be reluctant to review the acts of directors in situations where the expertise of the directors is likely to be greater than that of the courts. But, where the directors are afflicted with a conflict of interest, relative expertise is no longer crucial. Instead, the great danger becomes the channeling of the directors' expertise along the lines of their personal advantage—sometimes at the expense of the corporation and its stockholders. Here courts have no rational choice but to subject challenged conduct of directors and questioned corporate transactions to their own disinterested scrutiny. Of course, the self-protective bias of interested directors may be entirely devoid of corrupt motivation, but it may nonetheless constitute a serious threat to stockholder welfare. * * *

> Directors of a New York Stock Exchange-listed company are, at the very least, "interested" in their own positions of power, prestige and prominence (and in their not inconsequential perquisites). They are "interested" in defending against outside attack the management which they have, in fact, installed or maintained in power—"their" management (to which, in many cases, they owe their directorships). And they are "interested" in maintaining the public reputation of their own

leadership and stewardship against the claims of "raiders" who say that they can do better. Thus, regardless of their technical "independence," directors of a target corporation are in a very special position, where the slavish application of the majority's version of the good faith presumption is particularly disturbing.

646 F.2d, at 299–300.

It is debatable whether or not Panter v. Marshall Field involved a proper application of the business judgment rule. To some extent the decision may have been influenced by the threatened imposition of immense liabilities on outside directors who did not materially benefit from the transaction.[51] In any event, the development of numerous sophisticated and powerful defensive tactics caused the Delaware courts to reject the almost simplistic application of the business judgment rule of *Panter*, and to seek a "more balanced" analysis of the equities of the situation. These defenses often work in tandem with each other, while others are freestanding.

(1) Among the most common (and effective) are three-tier plans that include (a) a classification of the board of directors into three groups, with one group being elected each year, (b) a prohibition against removing directors except for cause, and (c) a provision that prohibited certain designated types of amendments to the articles of incorporation or bylaws (which could result in a change of control) unless approved by a supermajority (*e.g.* 80 percent) of the directors. The cumulative effect of these provisions is to prevent an aggressor that acquired even 100 percent of the shares from replacing a majority of the board of directors for two years. Compare MBCA §§ 7.27, 8.06, 8.24(a) and (c), 10.21. Delaware's statute is similar to these provisions except that Del. Gen. Corp. Law § 141(d) authorizes the staggering of elections to the board of directors without regard to the privilege of voting cumulatively. Consider also New York Bus. Corp. Law § 616(c), which requires a two-thirds vote to adopt a supermajority amendment to the articles of incorporation and also requires a conspicuous reference to such a provision on each share certificate. Do such provisions provide adequate protection to the shareholders or to the public against possible misuse of these entrenchment provisions?

(2) Poison pills and state takeover legislation discussed in the previous sections.

(3) A requirement that 80 percent or more of the shareholders approve certain transactions (*e.g.*, mergers) between the corporation and persons that own more than 10 percent of the corporate shares—adopted by Southwest Airlines and others.

(4) A requirement that a majority of the shares other than shares owned by a party to a proposed transaction approve the proposed transaction—adopted by Baldor Electric, Inc. and others.

(5) A requirement that 95 percent approval of certain transactions between the corporation and large shareholders be obtained unless the transac-

---

51. This type of litigation against directors for damages is probably not precluded by Del. Gen.Corp.L. § 102(b)(7) (discussed at page 687, supra) because it involves an arguable breach of the duty of loyalty or the receipt of an improper, personal benefit. It may be barred by some statutes enacted after *Van Gorkom*, p. 674, supra.

tion meets certain precise price and other substantive terms set forth in the articles or bylaws—adopted by Anchor Hocking Corporation and others.

(6) A provision that allows minority shareholders to redeem their shares for cash from the corporation at a price set forth in the articles or bylaws for a limited period following any transaction in which a person acquires a majority of the outstanding shares or a majority shareholder increases his holdings—adopted by Rubbermaid Corporation and others.

(7) A provision creating special classes of preferred shares to be held by a limited number of holders and requiring approval of that class of shares of certain classes of transactions—*e.g.*, Outdoor Sports Industries, Inc.

(8) Fair price amendments to articles of incorporation which mandate that shareholders receive equivalent consideration (both in terms of amount and form) on both ends of a two-tiered bid—adopted by numerous corporations.

(9) Anti-greenmail provisions: amendments to articles of incorporation prohibiting the repurchase by the company of stock at a premium from a three percent or greater holder unless the repurchase is approved by a majority vote of the shareholders—adopted by International Minerals & Chemical Corporation and others.

Notes

(1) Staggered terms for corporate boards of directors are an increasingly popular defensive device available to management. Only 34% of U.S. companies that went public in 1990 had staggered boards; by 2001, over 71% of companies going public had such boards, and 59% of all publicly held companies had such boards. A 'staggered board' is a board of directors that is usually divided into three groups with one group being elected each year. In a staggered board only a minority of directors are elected each year and directors stand for election only every third year. See Lucian Bebchuk, John Coates, and Guhan Subramanian, The Powerful Antitakeover Force of Staggered Boards: Theory, Evidence and Policy, 54 Stan. L. Rev. 887, 895 (2002). Staggered boards have defensive characteristics because they prevent a hostile acquirer from gaining control of the company in a single election.

(2) Other popular defensive devices include fair-price charter amendments that require (1) all shareholders be paid the same price, (2) a supermajority vote for proposed mergers, (3) dual class capitalization plans with different classes of voting shares, (4) cumulative voting, (5) provisions limiting the power of shareholders to act by written consent without a shareholders' meeting, (6) charter amendments limiting the power of shareholders to call special shareholders' meetings, (7) charter amendments discouraging greenmail, (8) provisions that acquire secret ballots, and (9) proposals specifically authorizing directors to consider the interests of other constituencies when evaluating outside acquisition attempts. Of course, many companies adopt several of these devices. In some states, these defensive devices, are automatically in effect by reason of statute.

(3) Dual class capitalization plans led to major legal battles during the 1980s. A dual class capitalization plan builds on the basic notion that a corporation is totally takeover-proof if a majority of its voting shares are held by a single person, entity, or family group. During the 1980s, a number of publicly held corporations seriously considered the creation of "supervoting stock" as the ultimate antitake-

over device. Supervoting stock gives holders of a class the right to cast multiple votes for each share owned. In other words, Class A stock might have five votes per share while Class B stock had one vote per share.

(4) Supervoting shares ran afoul of a rule that existed on the New York Stock Exchange (but not on other exchanges or NASDAQ) that prohibited a registered corporation from having classes of shares with different voting rights. However, when General Motors proposed the creation of classes with different voting rights, the NYSE abandoned its one-share-one-vote rule in 1984 to assure that GM would remain listed on the NYSE.

In 1988, the SEC adopted Rule 19c–4, which not only replaced the NYSE's one-share-one-vote rule, but also expanded the rule to cover all publicly-traded securities. The rule prevented the NASD or the exchanges to bar the listing of a domestic corporation's securities if that company issued securities or took any other action that nullified, restricted or disparately reduced the per share voting rights of the common stockholders. However, the U.S. Court of Appeals for the D.C. Circuit, in Business Roundtable v. SEC, 905 F.2d 406 (D.C.Cir.1990), nullified Rule 19c–4 on the grounds that the SEC does not have the statutory authority to adopt rules of corporate governance. The adoption of corporate governance rules is the province of state law, unless there is a clear expression of intent by Congress to permit an administrative agency to enter this field. In the words of the court, giving the SEC the power to adopt rules concerning the internal corporate governance of firms would "overturn or at least impinge severely on the tradition of state regulation of corporate law." 905 F.2d 406, 411. This ruling, as Roberta Karmel recently pointed out in an excellent article on this subject, "did not put an end to the voting rights rule story." The exchanges and the NASD, knowing where their bread was buttered, "voluntarily" adopted rules that were "modified versions of former SEC Rule 19c–4." See Roberta Karmel, The Future of Corporate Governance Listing Requirements, 54 SMU L. Rev. 325 (2001).

There are three leading—but essentially inconsistent—cases involving takeover defenses in Delaware.

I.

Unocal Corporation v. Mesa Petroleum Co., 493 A.2d 946 (Del.1985). In this case, Mesa launched a takeover fight against Unocal, a major oil company. Mesa offered $54 per share for 64,000,000 shares, just enough to bring its ownership to 50 percent. The bulk of the $3.4 billion purchase price was to be borrowed in the form of junk bonds. At the same time, Mesa announced that if it were successful in the tender offer, it would thereafter purchase the balance of the Unocal stock it did not already own through a second-step merger in which the holders would receive "highly subordinated securities" (presumably subordinated to the borrowings needed to raise the initial $3.4 billion) with a value that the Delaware Supreme Court stated was "purportedly" also $54 per share. Unocal's ultimate defense was a flatly discriminatory proposal: an "exchange offer" that provided that if Mesa bought the 64,000,000 shares it sought, the remaining Unocal shareholders could exchange all of their remaining shares for debt securities worth $72 per share that would be senior to Mesa's junk bond financing. The exchange offer expressly provided that Mesa and persons affiliated with Mesa were not eligible to participate in the offer. The effect of the "Mesa exclusion"—the provision allowing Unocal to offer debt securities to all of its shareholders other than Mesa—devastated Mesa's financing. If it completed its tender offer and obtained control of Unocal, the remaining Unocal shareholders would swap their shares for senior Unocal debt, and Mesa would end up owning virtually 100 percent of a corporation that was awash in debt. Indeed, this defense involves such strong medicine and is so devastatingly effective that it seems ill-matched with the very permissive business judgment rule. The Delaware Supreme Court evolved a new standard for evaluating such proposals:

> In the board's exercise of corporate power to forestall a takeover bid our analysis begins with the basic principle that corporate directors have a fiduciary duty to act in the best interests of the corporation's stockholders. Guth v. Loft, Inc., Del.Supr., 5 A.2d 503, 510 (1939). As we have noted, their duty of care extends to protecting the corporation and its owners from perceived harm whether a threat originates from third parties or other shareholders.[52] But such powers are not absolute. A corporation does not have unbridled discretion to defeat any perceived threat by any Draconian means available.

> The restriction placed upon a selective stock repurchase is that the directors may not have acted solely or primarily out of a desire to perpetuate themselves in office. See Cheff v. Mathes, 199 A.2d 548, 556 (1964).

> Of course, to this is added the further caveat that inequitable action may not be taken under the guise of law. Schnell v. Chris–Craft Industries, Inc., Del.Supr., 285 A.2d 437, 439 (1971).[53] The standard of proof established in Cheff v. Mathes * * * is designed to ensure that a defensive measure to thwart or impede a takeover is indeed motivated by a good faith concern for the welfare of the corporation and its stockholders, which in all circumstances must be free of any fraud or other misconduct. Cheff v. Mathes, 199 A.2d at 554–55. However, this does not end the inquiry.

> A further aspect is the element of balance. If a defensive measure is to come within the ambit of the business judgment rule, it must be reasonable in relation to the threat posed. This entails an analysis by the directors of the nature of the takeover bid and its effect on the corporate enterprise. Examples of such concerns may include: inadequacy of the price offered, nature and timing of the offer, questions of illegality, the impact on "constituencies" other than shareholders (i.e., creditors, customers, employees, and perhaps even the community generally), the risk of nonconsummation, and the quality of securities being offered in the exchange. 40 Bus.Law. 1403 (1985). While not a controlling factor, it also seems to us that a board may reasonably consider the basic stockholder

52. [By the Court]. It has been suggested that a board's response to a takeover threat should be a passive one. Easterbrook & Fischel, 36 Bus.Law. at 1750. However, that clearly is not the law of Delaware, and as the proponents of this rule of passivity readily con-cede, it has not been adopted either by courts or state legislatures. Easterbrook & Fischel, supra, 94 Harv.L.Rev. at 1194.

53. [By the Editors] The facts of *Schnell* are discussed in the notes following this excerpt.

interests at stake, including those of short term speculators, whose actions may have fueled the coercive aspect of the offer at the expense of the long term investor.[54] Here, the threat posed was viewed by the Unocal board as a grossly inadequate two-tier coercive tender offer coupled with the threat of greenmail. * * *

In adopting the selective exchange offer, the board stated that its objective was either to defeat the inadequate Mesa offer or, should the offer still succeed, provide the 49% of its stockholders, who would otherwise be forced to accept "junk bonds", with $72 worth of senior debt. We find that both purposes are valid.

However, such efforts would have been thwarted by Mesa's participation in the exchange offer. First, if Mesa could tender its shares, Unocal would effectively be subsidizing the former's continuing effort to buy Unocal stock at $54 per share. Second, Mesa could not, by definition, fit within the class of shareholders being protected from its own coercive and inadequate tender offer.

Thus, we are satisfied that the selective exchange offer is reasonably related to the threats posed. It is consistent with the principle that "the minority stockholder shall receive the substantial equivalent in value of what he had before." Sterling v. Mayflower Hotel Corp., Del.Supr., 93 A.2d 107, 114 (1952). This concept of fairness, while stated in the merger context, is also relevant in the area of tender offer law. Thus, the board's decision to offer what it determined to be the fair value of the corporation to the 49% of its shareholders, who would otherwise be forced to accept highly subordinated "junk bonds", is reasonable and consistent with the directors' duty to ensure that the minority stockholders receive equal value for their shares.

Notes

(1) Shortly after the Delaware Supreme Court's opinion in *Unocal,* the SEC adopted Rule 14d–10, 17 C.F.R. § 240.14d–10 (1989), 51 Fed.Reg. 25,882 (1986), popularly known as the "All Holders Rule," which required that an offer be open to all security holders of the same class of securities. It is clear that the purpose of this rule was to eliminate the *Unocal* strategy, though the SEC explained its purpose as follows:

A major aspect of the legislative effort to protect investors was to avoid favoring either management or the takeover bidder. In implementing this policy of neutrality, the Commission has administered the Williams Act in an even-handed

---

54. [By the Court] There has been much debate respecting such stockholder interests. One rather impressive study indicates that the stock of over 50 percent of target companies, who resisted hostile takeovers, later traded at higher market prices than the rejected offer price, or were acquired after the tender offer was defeated by another company at a price higher than the offer price. See Lipton, 35 Bus.Law. at 106–109, 132–133. Moreover, an update by Kidder Peabody & Company of this study, involving the stock prices of target companies that have defeated hostile tender offers during the period from 1973 to 1982 demonstrates that in a majority of cases the target's shareholders benefited from the defeat. The stock of 81% of the targets studied has, since the tender offer, sold at prices higher than tender offer price. When adjusted for the time value of money, the figure is 64%. The thesis being that this strongly supports application of the business judgment rule in response to takeover threats. There is, however, a rather vehement contrary view. See Easterbrook & Fischel, supra 36 Bus.Law. at 1739–1745.

fashion favoring neither side in a contest. Also implicit in these provisions, and necessary for the functioning of the Williams Act are the requirements that a bidder make a tender offer to all security holders of the class of securities which is the subject of the offer and that the offer made to all holders on the same terms.

The investor protection purposes of the Exchange Act would not be achieved without these requirements because tender offers could be extended to some security holders but not to others or to all security holders but on different terms.
* * *

SEC Rel. No. 34–22,198, 50 Fed.Reg. 27,976, 27,977 (1985).

Is the all holders rule really neutral as between the aggressor and management?

(2) In Polaroid Corp. v. Disney, 862 F.2d 987 (3d Cir.1988), the Court upheld the all-holders rule on the theory that it broadly related to disclosure. The Court also held that disadvantaged shareholders had standing to enjoin violations of the all-holders rule by a third party but that the issuer did not have standing to sue on its own behalf.

(3) From a relatively early time, courts have indicated that more or less brazen attempts to perpetuate incumbent management in office would be enjoined. The leading case is Schnell v. Chris–Craft Industries, Inc., 285 A.2d 430 (Del.Ch.1971), reversed, 285 A.2d 437 (Del.1971), discussed in *Unocal*. Later cases have struggled with the *Schnell* principle in the takeover context. Aprahamian v. HBO & Co., 531 A.2d 1204 (Del.Ch.1987), for example, enjoined a change of the date of the annual meeting after directors learned that a dissident shareholder had successfully obtained a large number of proxies. Blasius Indus., Inc. v. Atlas Corp., 564 A.2d 651 (Del.Ch.1988), enjoined the addition of two new persons to a staggered board that had the effect of making impractical a transaction that was being proposed in a pending consent solicitation. In both of these cases, the enjoined actions would clearly have been protected by the business judgment rule in the absence of pending shareholder action on the same subject and an intention to defeat the shareholder-initiated action. On the other hand, Stroud v. Grace, 606 A.2d 75 (Del.1992), declined to apply the *Schnell* principle in a situation where the board of directors was not under a threat.

(4) *Stroud* and several other Delaware cases involve bylaw amendments that require names of potential board of director candidates to be submitted to the management in advance of the meeting date. Nomad Acquisition Corp. v. Damon Corp., 1988 WL 383667, 14 Del.J.Corp.L. 814 (Del.Ch. Sept. 20, 1988), holds that such a provision is not invalid on its face, but it is clear from Lerman v. Diagnostic Data, 421 A.2d 906 (Del.Ch.1980), and Hubbard v. Hollywood Park Realty Enter., Inc., 1991 WL 3151, 17 Del. J. Corp. L. 238 (Del.Ch. Jan. 14, 1991), that such a provision cannot be applied inequitably in the heat of a takeover contest.

II.

Revlon, Inc. v. MacAndrews & Forbes Holdings, Inc., 506 A.2d 173 *(Del.1985).* This litigation arose after Pantry Pride, Inc. made a hostile tender offer for any and all shares of Revlon, Inc. for $47.50 per share. Viewing this price as inadequate, considering the value of Revlon's assets, and receiving information that Pantry Pride planned to break up and sell off Revlon's component businesses, Revlon management instituted a series of defensive tactics, particularly an offer to purchase 10,000,000 of its own shares in part for promissory notes that contained poison pill provisions.

Pantry Pride then increased its offer in a series of steps, first to $50 per share, then to $53, and then to $56.25, contingent in each case on Pantry Pride waiving the poison pill features of the notes. Faced with this steady pressure, Revlon decided to seek a more friendly purchaser, a "white knight." One potential white knight was Forstmann Little & Co. After some negotiations with Forstmann (during which Forstmann was given access to financial information about Revlon that had been denied to Pantry Pride), Forstmann and Revlon management agreed to a leveraged buyout transaction at a price of $57.25 per share. A critical aspect of the Forstmann agreement was that Forstmann received "a lock-up option[55] to purchase Revlon's Vision Care and National Health Laboratories divisions for $525 million, some $100–$175 million below the value ascribed to them by Lazard Freres, if another acquiror got 40% of Revlon's shares."

Pantry Pride then raised its price to $58 per share contingent upon removal not only of the poison pill provisions but also the Forstmann lock-up. When Revlon management decided to go through with the Forstmann sale (apparently in large part because Forstmann promised to support the price of the notes issued earlier by Revlon to create poison pill protection), the decision moved into the Delaware courts.

The Delaware Supreme Court upheld Revlon's actions to fight off Pantry Pride's initial "inadequate" offers but then enunciated a new legal principle:

> However, when Pantry Pride increased its offer to $50 per share, and then to $53, it became apparent to all that the break-up of the company was inevitable. The Revlon board's authorization permitting management to negotiate a merger or buyout with a third party was a recognition that the company was for sale. The duty of the board had thus changed from the preservation of Revlon as a corporate entity to the maximization of the company's value at a sale for the stockholders' benefit. This significantly altered the board's responsibilities under the *Unocal* standards. It no longer faced threats to corporate policy and effectiveness, or to the stockholders' interests, from a grossly inadequate bid. The whole question of defensive measures became moot. The directors' role changed from defenders of the corporate bastion to auctioneers charged with getting the best price for the stockholders at a sale of the company. * * *

> The original threat posed by Pantry Pride—the break-up of the company—had become a reality which even the directors embraced. Selective dealing to fend off a hostile but determined bidder was no longer a proper objective. Instead, obtaining the highest price for the benefit of the stockholders should have been the central theme guiding director action. Thus, the Revlon board could not make the requisite showing of good faith by preferring the noteholders and ignoring its duty of loyalty to the shareholders. * * *

> The Revlon board argued that it acted in good faith in protecting the noteholders because *Unocal* permits consideration of other corporate constituencies. Although such considerations may be permissible, there

---

55. [By the Editors] "Lock-ups" are discussed on page 1041 of this Chapter.

are fundamental limitations upon that prerogative. A board may have regard for various constituencies in discharging its responsibilities, provided there are rationally related benefits accruing to the stockholders. *Unocal,* 493 A.2d at 955. However, such concern for non-stockholder interests is inappropriate when an auction among active bidders is in progress, and the object no longer is to protect or maintain the corporate enterprise but to sell it to the highest bidder. * * *

While Forstmann's $57.25 offer was objectively higher than Pantry Pride's $56.25 bid, the margin of superiority is less when the Forstmann price is adjusted for the time value of money. In reality, the Revlon board ended the auction in return for very little actual improvement in the final bid. The principal benefit went to the directors, who avoided personal liability to a class of creditors to whom the board owed no further duty under the circumstances. Thus, when a board ends an intense bidding contest on an insubstantial basis, and where a significant by-product of that action is to protect the directors against a perceived threat of personal liability for consequences stemming from the adoption of previous defensive measures, the action cannot withstand the enhanced scrutiny which *Unocal* requires of director conduct. * * *

* * * [I]n granting an asset option lock-up to Forstmann, we must conclude that under all the circumstances the directors allowed considerations other than the maximization of shareholder profit to affect their judgment, and followed a course that ended the auction for Revlon, absent court intervention, to the ultimate detriment of its shareholders. No such defensive measure can be sustained when it represents a breach of the directors' fundamental duty of care. See Smith v. Van Gorkom, Del.Supr., 488 A.2d 858, 874 (1985). In that context the board's action is not entitled to the deference accorded it by the business judgment rule. * * *

Notes

(1) The Revlon decision permits management to justify poison pills and other defensive tactics if they slow down an initial offeror and lead to an auction involving additional bidders. The theory is that an auction should produce a better price for shareholders than a sale to the first serious bidder. [For a case in which a poison pill in fact led to this result, see CRTF Corp. v. Federated Dep't Stores, Inc., 683 F.Supp. 422 (S.D.N.Y.1988).] Even though poison pills permit management to negotiate with potential aggressors, once the decision to sell the company has been made under the *Revlon* principle, the role of management shifts to obtaining the best price for shareholders.

(2) See John C. Coffee, Jr., Securities Law: Defining 'Sale' Is Paramount Concern, Nat'l L. J., Nov. 8, 1993, at 18, 20. As Professor Coffee indicates, the *Revlon* principle is easily stated, but its application in practice is difficult. For example, what is a "sale"? A management buyout? What about a merger between companies roughly equal in size? Further, how should an auction be conducted? When may the board of directors decide that it is concluded? What should the board of directors do if it receives "out of the blue" an unexpected offer at an attractive price? May it simply take that offer or should it publicly announce its intention, seek additional bids, and conduct an auction? What if a board of

directors enters into a contract to be acquired by an offeror, but then a second bidder unexpectedly arrives? Does not the board of directors commit a breach of contract if it then decides to conduct a *Revlon* auction? Should it therefore have included an "out" clause in the initial contract to guard against this possibility? What if it didn't?

(3) Subsequent Delaware Supreme Court cases nicely illustrate the difficulty of determining the relationship between the *Revlon* and *Unocal* principles. See, for example, Paramount Communications, Inc. v. Time Inc. 571 A.2d 1140 (Del.1989) (*Revlon* duty was not triggered when a cash tender offer was substituted for a merger transaction involving an exchange of shares in a strategic combination); and Paramount Communications v. QVC Network Inc., 637 A.2d 34 (Del.1994) (*Revlon* duty was triggered when a cash tender offer was substituted for a merger transaction involving an exchange of cash for shares).

However, the consistency of these two decisions is not intuitively obvious and the decisions have been criticized, both individually and collectively. See Alan E. Garfield, *Paramount*: The Mixed Merits of Mush, 17 Del. J. Corp. L. 33 (1992) [the Court in *Paramount* "took a decisive turn in takeover jurisprudence in favor of management" and "left no clear standards in its wake"]; Marc I. Steinberg, Nightmare On Main Street: The *Paramount* Picture Horror Show, 16 Del. J. Corp. L. 1 (1991) [author was a "wishful thinker" when he earlier expressed the view that shareholders were protected in Delaware]; John C. Coffee, Jr., The Battle to Control Paramount is Over, But the Legal and Strategic Questions Raised by This Epic Corporate Struggle May Have Just Begun, Nat'l L. J., Mar. 28, 1994, at B5. Professor Coffee suggests that "*Paramount* represents a half-step retreat from the Delaware Supreme Court's apparent position * * * that only a breakup or liquidation of the company triggers a duty to auction." The focus of when the *Revlon* duty is triggered, he states, appears to be whether the transaction involves the acquisition of control by a new controlling shareholder but a number of questions remain unanswered.

(4) Consider if there is real inconsistency between the Delaware decisions that trust shareholders to make voting decisions in the hostile takeover context and those decisions that insist that the board of directors rather than the shareholders decide whether the corporation should be sold. See Robert B. Thompson, Shareholders As Grown–Ups: Voting, Selling, and Limits on the Board's Power to "Just Say No", 67 U. Cincinnati L.Rev. 999 (1999).

———

III.

Unitrin, Inc. v. American General Corp. The activism of the Delaware Supreme Court in reviewing defensive tactics was tempered by its decision in Unitrin, Inc. v. American General Corp., 651 A.2d 1361 (Del.1995). The target corporation, Unitrin, initiated a major share repurchase plan in the face of an unwanted all-cash tender offer and proxy contest. The Delaware Chancery Court enjoined this maneuver on the ground that it was a disproportionate response to the threat posed by American General's "inadequate" tender offer, but the Supreme Court reversed, applying the following analysis to a defensive tactic:

>   This Court has recognized "the prerogative of a board of directors to resist a third party's unsolicited acquisition proposal or offer." Para-

mount Communications, Inc. v. QVC Network Inc., Del.Supr., 637 A.2d 34, 43 n. 13 (1994). The Unitrin Board did not have unlimited discretion to defeat the threat it perceived from the American General Offer by any draconian[56] means available. Pursuant to the Unocal proportionality test, the nature of the threat associated with a particular hostile offer sets the parameters for the range of permissible defensive tactics. Accordingly, the purpose of enhanced judicial scrutiny is to determine whether the Board acted reasonably in "relation * * * to the threat which a particular bid allegedly poses to stockholder interests." Mills Acquisition Co. v. Macmillan, Inc., Del.Supr., 559 A.2d 1261, 1288 (1989).

* * * Courts, commentators and litigators have attempted to catalogue the threats posed by hostile tender offers. Commentators have categorized three types of threats: (i) opportunity loss ... [where] a hostile offer might deprive target shareholders of the opportunity to select a superior alternative offered by target management [or, we would add, offered by another bidder]; (ii) structural coercion, * * * the risk that disparate treatment of non-tendering shareholders might distort shareholders' tender decisions; and (iii) substantive coercion, * * * the risk that shareholders will mistakenly accept an underpriced offer because they disbelieve management's representations of intrinsic value. * * *

* * * As common law applications of Unocal's proportionality standard have evolved, at least two characteristics of draconian defensive measures taken by a board of directors in responding to a threat have been brought into focus through enhanced judicial scrutiny. In the modern takeover lexicon, it is now clear that since Unocal, this Court has consistently recognized that defensive measures which are either preclusive or coercive are included within the common law definition of draconian.

If a defensive measure is not draconian, however, because it is not either coercive or preclusive, the Unocal proportionality test requires the focus of enhanced judicial scrutiny to shift to "the range of reasonableness." Paramount Communications, Inc. v. QVC Network Inc., Del.Supr., 637 A.2d 34, 45–46 (1994). Proper and proportionate defensive responses are intended and permitted to thwart perceived threats. When a corporation is not for sale, the board of directors is the defender of the metaphorical medieval corporate bastion and the protector of the corporation's shareholders. The fact that a defensive action must not be coercive or preclusive does not prevent a board from responding defensively before a bidder is at the corporate bastion's gate.[57]

---

56. [By the Court] Draconian, adj. of or pert. to Draco, an archon and member of the Athenian eupatridae, or the code of laws which is said to have been framed about 621 B.C. by him as thesmothete. In them the penalty for most offenses was death, and to a later age they seemed so severe that they were said to be written in blood. Hence, barbarously severe; harsh; cruel. Webster's New International Dictionary 780 (2d ed. 1951).

57. [By the Court] This Court's choice of the term draconian in Unocal was a recognition that the law affords boards of directors substantial latitude in defending the perimeter of the corporate bastion against perceived threats. Thus, continuing with the medieval metaphor, if a board reasonably perceives that a threat is on the horizon, it has broad authority to respond with a panoply of individual or combined defensive precautions, e.g., staffing the barbican, raising the drawbridge, and low-

The ratio decidendi for the "range of reasonableness" standard is a need of the board of directors for latitude in discharging its fiduciary duties to the corporation and its shareholders when defending against perceived threats. The concomitant requirement is for judicial restraint. Consequently, if the board of directors' defensive response is not draconian (preclusive or coercive) and is within a "range of reasonableness," a court must not substitute its judgment for the board's. * * *

In this case, the Court of Chancery erred by substituting its judgment, that the Repurchase Program was unnecessary, for that of the Board. The Unitrin Board had the power and the duty, upon reasonable investigation, to protect Unitrin's shareholders from what it perceived to be the threat from American General's inadequate all-cash for all-shares Offer. The adoption of the poison pill and the limited Repurchase Program was not coercive and the Repurchase Program may not be preclusive. Although each made a takeover more difficult, individually and collectively, if they were not coercive or preclusive the Court of Chancery must determine whether they were within the range of reasonable defensive measures available to the Board.

If the Court of Chancery concludes that individually and collectively the poison pill and the Repurchase Program were proportionate to the threat the Board believed American General posed, the Unitrin Board's adoption of the Repurchase Program and the poison pill is entitled to review under the traditional business judgment rule. The burden will then shift "back to the plaintiffs who have the ultimate burden of persuasion [in a preliminary injunction proceeding] to show a breach of the directors' fiduciary duties." In order to rebut the protection of the business judgment rule, the burden on the plaintiffs will be to demonstrate, "by a preponderance of the evidence that the directors' decisions were primarily based on [(1)] perpetuating themselves in office or [(2)] some other breach of fiduciary duty such as fraud, overreaching, lack of good faith, or [(3)] being uninformed." Unocal, 493 A.2d at 958 (emphasis added).

E.   THE VIEW FROM THE YEAR 2003

As noted above, takeovers come in waves. The development of new legal strategies affects the supply of takeovers, as do credit conditions. Public sentiment also has an effect. The insider trading scandals, many of which involved privileged information about mergers or hostile takeovers caused a decline in takeover activity during the 1990s according to Professor Joseph Grundfest. See Joseph A. Grundfest, Just Vote No: A Minimalist Strategy for Dealing with Barbarians Inside the Gates, 45 Stan. L.Rev. 857, 858 (1993).

When the market turns down, buyers sometimes look for ways to withdraw from previously-agreed-upon merger agreements. And there can be litigation in friendly deals as well as in hostile transactions. While buyers

---

ering the portcullis. Stated more directly, depending upon the circumstances, the board may respond to a reasonably perceived threat by adopting individually or sometimes in combination: advance notice by-laws, supermajority voting provisions, shareholder rights plans, repurchase programs, etc.

perform significant amounts of due diligence before consummating a friendly merger transaction, there often still are surprises. In 2001, IBP, Inc., the nation's number one beef distributor sued Tyson Foods, Inc., the nation's leading chicken distributor for specific enforcement of the IBP–Tyson merger agreement. In the litigation, the court concluded that merger partners can obtain specific enforcement of merger agreements. At issue was whether the standard "MAC" or Material Adverse Change in the merger agreement had been violated. One of the key issues in the case was the accounting problem in DFG, an IBP subsidiary. However, the court found that the Merger Agreement specifically allocated certain risks to Tyson, including the risk of any losses or financial effects from the accounting improprieties at DFG. Thus the court concluded that these risks cannot serve as a basis for Tyson to terminate the merger and ordered specific performance of the merger agreement. In re IBP, Inc. Shareholders Litigation, 789 A.2d 14 (Del.Ch.2001).

The takeovers in the 1990s appeared to differ significantly from those of the 1980s. Charles V. Bagli, A New Breed of Wolf at the Corporate Door, N.Y. Times, Mar. 19, 1997, at c1, col. 3:[58]

What a difference a decade makes. In the 1980s, takeover battles were like Wild West shootouts, and descriptions of the strife relied on the imagery of violence: greenmailers and raiders with their bear hugs and Saturday night specials were pitted against white knights and corporate managers who fended off their attackers with poison pills and shark repellent. There was even a "Predators' Ball" to celebrate the mayhem.

Today, a new respectability reigns in the takeover game. No longer do the likes of Mr. Pickens, Ronald O. Perelman and Carl C. Icahn begin raids with high-risk junk bonds only to carve up their acquisitions and sell off the pieces for a quick profit. Instead, corporations seek to forge "strategic alliances" that will enable them to grow and prosper in an increasingly competitive marketplace. And the lexicon of even the most hostile endeavors is filled with sober phrases like synergy, the global marketplace and accretion to earnings.

And almost everybody, it seems is doing it.

The 1980s was a period of finance-oriented transactions; the transactions in the 1990s were focused more on operational improvements involving firms in the same or complementary lines of business. In other words, by the year 2003, the justification for most transactions was economic, grounded in the business interests of the parties. The purchaser was ordinarily an operating corporation or a private equity firm interested in improving operating results. LBO specialists and raiders planning to acquire control in order to sell off components of the acquired business still existed, but they were no longer the dominant players in the mergers and acquisitions market. Premiums over pre-transaction stock prices of target corporations were also significantly lower: about 28 percent in the 1990s compared to 50 percent or higher in the 1980s. In the technology sector, declining share prices have forced premiums even lower. For example, when the communications-chip maker GlobeSpan announced in October, 2002 that it was buying rival Virata for $1.3 billion in stock, the price represented a valuation of Virata of $9.22 a share, 7.6 percent less than the company's closing price the day before the merger announce-

---

58. Copyright © 1997 by the New York Times Co. Reprinted by permission.

ment and 78 percent below its prior 52–week high. Acquisitions like this have been referred to as "takeunders," and reflect the desperation of target companies such as Virata.

Undoubtedly, less doubt about the enforceability of defensive tactics over time contributed to the change in legal environment. This assertion is borne out by the fact that only 66% of hostile bids succeed today as compared with almost 80% as recently as 1999.

Two other trends are worth noting. First, in the 1980s and 1990s, virtually all of the mergers and acquisitions activity in the world occurred in the U.S. and Great Britain. By 2002, significant merger and acquisition activity was appearing on the European continent. The introduction of the Euro as common European currency doubtless fueled this trend, but globalization was also a major contributing factor. In 2002, global industries such as banking and finance, telecommunications, natural resources, and global brands led an increase in merger and acquisition activity of 11 percent in the US, 37 percent in Australia, and 100 percent in Europe.

F. LOCKUPS

MICHAEL G. HATCH, CLEARLY DEFINING PRECLUSIVE CORPORATE LOCK–UPS: A BRIGHT LINE TEST FOR LOCK–UP PROVISIONS IN DELAWARE

75 Wash.L.Rev. 1267–76 (2000).

Record-breaking merger and acquisition volume in each of the previous four years has placed the United States in the midst of an unprecedented merger phenomenon. Ten of the largest transactions in history[59] were announced in 1998 and 1999. Fueling this merger boom is the fact that the merger, offering a quick solution for businesses seeking greater competitiveness, resources, market share, and new technology, has become the preferred tool for strategic and corporate development. This current wave of megamergers, coupled with the intense competition for merger partners, has resulted in merger battles with fiercely contested auctions[60] for control of corporations.

Merging corporations often seek to defend their deals from subsequent bidders with defensive measures known as lock-up provisions. Lock-ups are promises by a target company's board of directors to compensate the prospective acquirer if the target breaches or does not consummate the merger agreement. Lock-ups are designed to protect the negotiated deal by compensating the prospective acquirer and by imposing the threat of additional costs on other competitors who might decide to make offers. Under certain circumstances, courts must enjoin lock-ups that preclude shareholders the opportunity to receive other potentially higher offers in the merger transaction. However, courts are unable to make this determination accurately because it

---

59. [By the Author] Transactions are measured by equity value.

60. [By the Author] An auction occurs when directors decide to sell the corporation to the highest bidder. In an auction, the target corporation will solicit bids and the highest bidder will obtain control of the corporation. * * *

involves evaluating competing bids, an increasingly complex calculation in the current merger environment. As a result, the size and scope of defensive measures have skyrocketed as both courts and corporations have been unsure how to determine the validity of lock-ups.

In the 1990s, large corporations began to use mergers to gain advantage within their industries.[61] This phenomenon, combined with rapidly increasing stock market values, has greatly increased the price paid in recent mergers. As a result, corporations seeking merger partners have faced increasing transaction costs. In addition, large corporations are no longer content to sit by as competitors enter strategic mergers. Large corporations are willing to compete for targets[62] by making unsolicited bids after a competitor has announced a merger agreement. In partial response to these increased costs and competition, the size and scope of deal-protecting lock-up provisions have skyrocketed. * * *

A. THE STRATEGIC MERGER

Corporations are increasingly using strategic mergers to gain advantages within their industries.[63] Intense foreign competition has focused many corporations' strategic goals on increasing efficiency and dominating their markets.[64] While efficiency increases shareholder value by reducing overhead, corporations appear to have concluded that a short-term increase in shareholder value may result from boosting market share either by eliminating competitors or acquiring an important supplier that competitors need. Typically, strategic mergers are negotiated deals focusing on long-term growth and increasing efficiency, either between former competitors or between a supplier and a producer.[65] The merging corporations are often of similar size, and stockholders of the respective corporations own approximately an equal amount of the post-merger corporation.

A prospective acquirer must incur substantial costs in identifying and consummating a strategic merger. Initially, it may be expensive for the prospective acquirer to perform the research necessary to identify the target as a profitable opportunity.[66] Once it identifies the target, the acquirer incurs additional costs negotiating the agreement and ensuring that the target is truthfully representing itself. These costly and time-consuming steps require expert analysis, due diligence reports[67] by lawyers, and fairness opinions[68] by

61. [By the Author] See Richard G. Parker and David A. Balto, The Merger Wave: Tenders in Merger Enforcement and Litigation, 55 Bus. Law. 351, 356 (1999).

62. [By the Author] The target is the corporation that is to be acquired in a merger or acquisition. * * *

63. [By the Author] See John C. Coffee, Jr., Under the "Merger of Equals" Doctrine, Can a Target Board Always Favor a Friendly Suitor When a Second Bidder Makes a Higher Unsolicited Offer?, Nat'l L.J. Mar. 30, 1998, at B5.

64. [By the Author] * * * For example, Unilever recently acquired Bestfoods to become the world's second largest foodmaker. * * * Through the acquisition Unilever hopes to increase efficiency and regain dominance in the food producing industry.

65. [By the Author] See Nathan A. Treu, Exxon Mobil, Can the Merger of Equals Doctrine Save the Proposed Marriage of Two Oil

Giants?, 36 Hous.L.Rev. 989, 993 (1999).

66. [By the Author] See Stephen Bainbridge, Exclusive Merger Agreements and Lock–Ups in Negotiated Corporate Acquisitions, 75 Minn.L.Rev. 239, 242 (1990).

67. [By the Author] Due diligence refers to the legal audit performed on the target company. In a due diligence investigation, lawyers investigate the books and records of the target company, check the accuracy of factual representations, and look for potential problems. See Dale A. Oesterle, The Law of Mergers and Acquisitions 270 (1999). The due diligence investigation precedes the signing of the final acquisition agreement in order to give the acquirer a high level of confidence in the accuracy and completeness of the target's representations and warranties in the acquisition agreement.

68. [By the Author] Fairness opinions are reports by investment bankers confirming that

investment bankers. All of these costs and efforts are expended to determine the core issue in the merger: that the price to be paid for the target is fair in the eyes of both parties.

Although the fair value of the target is the core issue in a merger, considerable uncertainty surrounds the determination of that value. Valuation begins with the determination of how much the target is worth as it stands alone, and then focuses on how much its value will increase when combined with the acquirer. To assist in the valuation, both sets of corporate directors will retain the services of investment bankers to determine a "fair" price for the target. However, valuation is a very inexact inquiry, and often involves a range of values rather than a specific price. Although valuation studies or fairness opinions may be important, a contested auction will often lead to prices that substantially exceed any fair price determination, a price that a board of directors cannot know without an auction. In addition, the current trend of "deal-jumping" followed by hotly contested bidding wars has further widened the disparity between a fair price determined by an investment banker and a price obtained through competitive bidding at an auction for a company.

B. THE THREAT OF "DEAL-JUMPING"

Hostile takeovers, or "deal-jumping," by competitors represent the most serious threat to negotiated strategic mergers. According to one study, deal-jumpers or second bidders prevail in a "substantial majority" of contests.[69] In a strategic merger, the acquirer and target will negotiate an initial offer; however, competitors within the industry may attempt to jump the deal by making unsolicited bids for the target corporation. In this situation, the initial prospective acquirer is at a disadvantage. Its initial bid may provide insights into the financial viability and long-term prospects of the target as well as a signal that existing management is amenable to a sale. This allows the deal-jumper to avoid incurring identification and research costs.[70] The deal-jumper is then able to use the money saved on research costs in its attempt to top the initial bid. Absent a large lock-up, a bidding war may result where the original acquirer must compete with other bidders for control of the target corporation. Even if the initial bidder ultimately prevails, competition will likely force the final price much higher than the initial bid. For example, 1999 witnessed a number of high profile jumped deals: AT & T's successful $58 billion hostile takeover of MediaOne, which had previously agreed to a $53 billion merger with Comcast; Vodafone's successful $60 billion takeover of Airtouch, topping Bell Atlantic's original bid of $45 billion; and Pfizer's $90.27 billion hostile takeover of Warner–Lambert, dwarfing the original $72 billion bid by American Home Products. Given the deal-jumper's competitive advantage, acquiring

the acquisition price is within a range of fair prices that adequately compensates the target's shareholders.

69. [By the Author] Bainbridge, supra, n. 100, at 242 * * *.

70. [By the Author] See Frank H. Easterbrook & Daniel R. Fischel, Auctions and Sunk Costs in Tender Offers, 35 Stan.L.Rev. 1, 2 (1982).

corporations use a number of lock-up devices in an attempt to protect their negotiated deals.

C. Lock-Up Provisions in General

The current wave of mega-mergers, coupled with the growing threat of deal-jumping, has dramatically increased the size and scope of lock-up provisions as directors attempt to protect their merger costs and expected profits. An acquiring corporation will often demand some form of lock-up provision,[71] such as a stock option, termination fee or other device, in the merger agreement to protect itself from deal-jumping as well as to guarantee some benefit in the event the merger is not consummated. The Supreme Court of Delaware, in its first evaluation of a lock-up, recognized that lock-ups may be necessary to facilitate mergers because they provide incentives to merging corporations to enter and complete the transaction.[72] However, lock-ups may also be excessive, deterring other, possibly better, offers.

D. Types of Lock-Up Provisions

Lock-ups are promises by a target's board of directors to compensate the prospective acquirer in some fashion if the target breaches or does not consummate the merger agreement.[73] Lock-ups are designed both to compensate the prospective acquirer in case of a breach and to protect the negotiated deal by imposing additional costs on other competitors who might decide to make offers. The acquirer may ask the target's board of directors to grant a number of lock-up provisions including: (1) an irrevocable stock option, (2) an asset option, (3) a "topping" fee, (4) an expense reimbursement provision, and (5) a termination or "break-up" fee.

The most common lock-up provision involves an irrevocable stock option by which the target corporation usually grants the acquirer the right to purchase ten to twenty percent[74] of the target's stock at a favorable price.[75] The right to exercise the option is usually conditioned upon the defeat of the favored bidder's attempt to acquire the target corporation. In addition, use of the stock option by the original bidder may preclude an intervening third party from using "pooling of interests" accounting,[76] a significant deterrent itself.

---

71. [By the Author] Delaware courts have tended to define the term "lock-up" expansively. See Vincent F. Garrity, Jr. & Mark A. Morton, Would the CSX/Conrail Express Have Derailed in Delaware? A Comparative Analysis of Lock–Up Provisions Under Delaware and Pennsylvania Law, 51 U. Miami L.Rev. 677, 678, n.4 (1997). Although the narrow interpretation of lock-ups only includes asset and stock options, for purpose of this Comment, such measures as termination fees and no shop provisions are also lock-up devices.

72. [By the Author] See Revlon, Inc. v. MacAndrews & Forbes Holdings, Inc., 506 A.2d 173, 183 (Del.1985); see also Garrity & Morton, supra, at 69 (noting that Delaware courts recognize benefits of lock-ups to shareholders).

73. [By the Author] See Stephen Fraidin & Jon D. Hanson, Toward Unlocking Lockups, 103 Yale L.J. 1739, 1742 (1994).

74. [By the Author] See, e.g., Paramount Communications, Inc. v. QVC Network Inc., 637 A.2d 34, 39 (Del.1994); see also Dennis J. Block et al., Defensive Measures in Anticipation of and in Response to Unsolicited Takeover Proposals, 51 U. Miami L. Rev. 623, 654 (1997) (noting that target will typically grant acquirer option to purchase from 10 to 20% of target's outstanding voting stock).

75. [By the Author] Typically the price of the stock option is market price before the bid. * * *

76. [By the Author] See Linda Vincent, Equity Valuation Implications of Purchase Versus Pooling Accounting, J. Fin. Statement Analysis, Summer 1997, at 5. Pooling of interests accounting is a favorable accounting method under which the asset and liability accounts of the bidder and target are combined at book

In an asset option or "crown jewel" defense, the target grants the acquirer the option to purchase a particularly desirable asset of the target at a negotiated price.[77] If the deal is not consummated, this option compensates the prospective acquirer, because it will still acquire the desirable asset at a price below fair market value. In addition, an asset option may deter bidders as they may be unwilling to suffer the loss from a sale of the asset at below fair market value. Furthermore, regardless of the price, other bidders often lose interest once they cannot acquire the truly vital asset of the target.

Topping fees are a type of lock-up where the target must pay a fee to the initial bidder if the target accepts another bidder's offer. The fee is based on a percentage of the amount by which the accepted bid exceeds the initial bid. For example, in In re KDI Corp. Shareholders Litigation,[78] the parties agreed to a topping fee or "override" equal to one-half of the difference between the stock price and any other future offer.

A fourth type of lock-up is an expense-reimbursement provision, which is similar to a liquidated-damages provision although not subject to the same analysis. In an expense-reimbursement provision, if the target accepts another bid, then the target reimburses the initial prospective acquirer for any costs incurred during the initial merger effort. The reimbursement covers any actual or estimated out-of-pocket expenses such as research or legal fees incurred by the prospective acquirer in its unsuccessful attempt to merge with the target. For example, in Kahn v. Dairy Mart Convenience Stores, Inc.,[79] Dairy Mart agreed to reimburse the acquirer for expenses up to $2.25 million if the merger failed for any reason other than a breach of warranty or representation by the acquirer.

Finally, an acquirer may negotiate for a termination or "break-up" fee. In the event the target terminates the merger, this provision requires the target to pay the acquirer often as much as three percent of the value of the transaction.[80] For example, in 1995 the Supreme Court of Delaware approved a termination fee of $550 million designed to protect the $28 billion merger of Bell Atlantic and NYNEX.[81] Recently, Warner–Lambert agreed to a record-breaking $1.8 billion termination fee to American Home Products as protection for their original merger agreement valued at $72 billion. * * *

E.   Lock–Ups Under the Business Judgment Rule

Depending on the form of the transaction, Delaware courts apply a doctrinal framework that contains three different standards used to deter-

---

value as though the two firms had always been a single enterprise. See id. at 7. This method allows corporations to record their combined assets at historical values and the surviving entity to avoid recording goodwill. See id. Not recording goodwill results in greater annual earnings on paper and is the preferred method of accounting for business combinations. See Phillip J. Azzollini, Note, The Wake of Paramount v. QVC: Can a Majority Shareholder Avoid Triggering the Auction Duty During a Merger and Retain a Significant Equity Interest? Suggestion: A Pooling of Interests, 63 Fordham L. Rev. 573, 596 (1994).

77. [By the Author] See e.g. Revlon, Inc. v. MacAndrews & Forbes Holdings, Inc., 506 A.2d 173, 178–79 (Del.1985) (noting Revlon granted lock-up option for key division at price below market value).

78. [By the Author] 1990 WL 201385 (Del. Ch.1990).

79. [By the Author] 1996 WL 159628 (Del. Ch.1996).

80. [By the Author] See * * * Dennis J. Block & Stephen A. Raidin, Termination Provisions After Bell Atlantic, 11 Insights, Aug. 1997, at 2, 2.

81. [By the Author] See Brazen v. Bell Atl. Corp., 695 A.2d 43, 49 (Del.1997).

mine the validity of a lock-up. The central inquiry in the doctrinal framework is whether the lock-up is preclusive. If the lock-up is not preclusive and if the transaction does not involve a change of control, the business judgment rule will protect the lock-up from court invalidation, provided the decision to grant the lock-up was reached in an informed manner. If the transaction involves a change of corporate control, under Revlon, Inc. v. MacAndrews & Forbes Holdings, Inc.[82] the validity of a lock-up provision depends on whether it facilitates receipt by target-company shareholders of a maximum value for their shares.[83] If the lock-up was intended solely as a defensive measure against a subsequent hostile threat and the merger involves no change of control, the lock-up's validity, under Unocal Corp. v. Mesa Petroleum Co.,[84] depends on whether the lock-up is a balanced response to the threat posed by the future bidder. * * *

A non-preclusive lock-up in a transaction that does not involve a change of control is protected by the business judgment rule and will not be disturbed provided it was reached in an informed manner. Following the business judgment rule, courts generally presume that "in making a business decision the directors of a corporation acted on an informed basis, in good faith and in an honest belief that the action was taken in the best interests of the company."[85] Any party challenging the applicability of the presumption has the burden of establishing facts rebutting the presumption. * * * A court's inquiry under the business judgment rule focuses on the process by which the board reached a decision, not the merits of the decision itself. Accordingly, a Delaware court will not interfere with the board's substantive decision to grant lock-up provisions provided there is any rational business purpose and the decision was reached in an informed manner.

F. THE LIMITED APPLICATION OF REVLON DUTIES TO LOCK–UPS IN TRANSACTIONS INVOLVING A CHANGE OF CONTROL OR BREAK–UP OF THE TARGET

Under Revlon and its progeny,[86] if a transaction involves a change of control the validity of the lock-up depends on whether it facilitates receipt by target-company shareholders of a maximum value for their shares. If it does not, then the lock-up is preclusive and should be enjoined. In *Revlon*, the Supreme Court of Delaware found that Revlon's directors effectively had put the company up for sale and granted lock-ups[87] that precluded further bids offering a higher value to Revlon's shareholders.[88] According to the *Revlon* court, the critical inquiry for lock-up provisions involves distinguishing "those lock-ups which draw bidders into the battle" from those that "end an active

---

82. [By the Author] 506 A.2d 173 (Del. 1985).

83. [By the Author] Id. at 185.

84. [By the Author] 493 A.2d 946 (Del. 1985).

85. [By the Author] Aronson v. Lewis, 473 A.2d 805, 812 (Del.1984)

86. [By the Author] See e.g. Paramount Communications v. QVC Network Inc., 637 A.2d 34 (Del.1994); Mills Acquisition Co. v. Macmillan, Inc., 559 A.2d 1261 (Del.1989).

87. [By the Author] Revlon's directors agreed to a $25 million termination fee and an

asset lock-up option allowing Forstmann Little to acquire certain key Revlon divisions at $100–$175 million below market value. * * * Revlon, Inc. v. MacAndrews & Forbes Holdings, Inc., 506 A.2d 173, 183 (Del.1985).

88. [By the Author] * * * According to the court, when the directors put the company up for sale, their "role changed from defenders of the corporate bastion to auctioneers charged with getting the best price for the stockholders at a sale of the company." [506 A.2d,] at 183,

auction and foreclose further bidding."[89] Therefore, in a sale of a corporation implicating *Revlon* duties, courts must enjoin preclusive lock-ups that prevent the target corporation's shareholders from obtaining the maximum value for their shares. * * *

Notes

(1) A theoretical debate has long continued over whether lock-ups should be permitted at all. Frank H. Easterbrook & Daniel R. Fischel, The Proper Role of a Target's Management in Responding to a Tender Offer, 94 Harv.L.Rev. 1161, 1164 (1981) believed that all lock-ups ultimately decreased shareholder wealth and therefore no defensive tactics should be permitted. Once it was realized that some lock-ups increased shareholder wealth, the issue became how desirable lock-ups should be distinguished from undesirable ones. Professor Bainbridge suggested a bright-line rule: invalidate all lock-ups equal to more than ten percent of the value of the favored bidder's proposal. Stephen Bainbridge, Exclusive Merger Agreements and Lock–Ups in Negotiated Corporate Acquisitions, 75 Minn.L.Rev. 239 (1990). The author of the above Comment suggested a bright line drawn at three percent of the bidder's proposal. 75 Wash. Law Rev., at 1292.

(2) The negotiation of a "deal" to acquire another business entity is costly. The potential purchaser naturally wishes to preserve its investment and will seek provisions designed to protect the deal from other suitors. The result is a variety of "no shop" clauses, lock-ups, termination fees, stock options, and the like. Is there anything wrong with that?

(3) Brazen v. Bell Atlantic Corp., 695 A.2d 43 (Del.1997), involved the merger between Bell Atlantic and NYNEX. The merger was viewed as a merger of equals. The parties negotiated an agreement under which Bell Atlantic agreed to pay NYNEX $200 million if Bell Atlantic withdrew. Furthermore, if Bell Atlantic was merged with another entity within 18 months, Bell Atlantic agreed to pay NYNEX and additional $350 million. The two payments together constituted approximately 2 percent of Bell Atlantic's net worth. The payments were defined in the Agreement to be liquidated damages for breach of contract and not a termination fee. The Delaware Supreme Court accepted this characterization of the payments and held that they were not a penalty and therefore enforceable.

G. RECENT FUNDAMENTAL CHANGES IN THE MBCA

The MBCA provisions relating to mergers, takeovers, and the appraisal remedy were significantly revised in 1999. *See* 54 Bus.Law. 209 (1998); 54 Bus.Law. 685 (1999); 55 Bus.Law. 405 (1999). These provisions diverge to some extent from the law of Delaware and other states. However, the net effect or spirit of these MBCA provisions is generally consistent with the way the law works in Delaware and elsewhere. Moreover, these provisions are much more detailed and precise and far better organized than the statutes of most states. However, potential problems with the revised MBCA are that new sections sometimes contain too much detail and are not phrased in traditional statutory language. In addition, the amendments deal primarily with publicly-traded corporations while most states that closely track the

---

89. [By the Author] *Id*. at 183.

MBCA in their corporation statutes have relatively few publicly-traded corporations. Nevertheless, the current MBCA is definitely a logical construct, and its innovations should be seriously considered by important commercial states.

1. Section 6.21(f). The new § 6.21(f) requires a shareholder vote on every transaction by a corporation that involves the issuance of shares (other than shares issued for cash) that carry more than 20 percent of the voting power in the corporation as measured before the issuance. Thus, shareholders of a surviving corporation must vote on significant share-for-share mergers whether or not they are structured as triangular mergers.

2. Section 11.02(a). The MBCA states that "one or more domestic corporations may merge with a domestic or foreign corporation or other entity pursuant to a plan of merger." Thus, a corporation may merge into a partnership, LLC, or other non-corporate entity (provided that the other entity is allowed under its governing statute to merge with a corporation). The surviving entity may be either the corporation or the non-corporate entity. This is an important option, particularly in light of the extraordinary growth of non-corporate entities in recent years. However, there are usually significant tax costs if a corporation is merged into a non-corporate entity since the IRS views such a transaction as a dissolution of the corporation and immediately taxes of all unrealized appreciation in the value of the corporation's assets. This tax is avoided if the corporation is the surviving entity, but then the surviving entity is not eligible for Subchapter K taxation. Moreover, if any kind of entity has ownership interests that are publicly-traded, it is taxed as a C corporation no matter what its legal form is.

3. Section 11.04(e). The MBCA reduces the required vote to approve a merger or similar transaction from a majority of all shares eligible to vote to a majority of eligible shares present at a meeting at which a quorum is present. Thus, a merger or other similar transaction may in theory be approved by as few as 25 percent plus one of the shares. If class voting is required, each class must meet this "majority of a majority" requirement.

4. Section 11.04(g). The shareholders of a corporation that is a party to a merger are not entitled to vote on the merger at all (i) if the corporation will be a surviving corporation or "is an acquiring corporation in a share exchange," (ii) its articles of incorporation will not changed except for amendments permitted by section 10.05, (iii) its shareholders' rights and preferences will not changed, and (iv) a vote is not required by § 6.21(f).

5. Section 12.02. The standards for determining what constitutes a sale of assets requiring a shareholder vote are significantly revised. In earlier versions of the MBCA, only a disposition of "all or substantially all" of the assets of a corporation triggered a mandatory shareholder vote. Section 12.02 now provides that a vote is required whenever the transaction would leave the corporation without a "significant continuing business activity," which in turn is defined as a situation where "continuing business activity represented at least 25 percent of the total assets and 25 percent of either income from continuing operations before income taxes or revenues from continuing operation." The older "all or substantially all" test continues to appear in virtually all corporate statutes. In practice, however, courts applying this older test use language somewhat comparable to that embodied in 12.02(a). For example, in

Gimbel v. Signal Cos., 316 A.2d 599 (Del.Ch.1974), aff'd, 316 A.2d 619 (Del.1974), the court stated, "While it is true that [the 'all or substantially all'] test does not lend itself to a strict mathematical standard to be applied in every case, the qualitative factor can be defined to some degree * * *. If the sale is of assets quantitatively vital to the operation of the corporation and is out of the ordinary [course] and substantially affects the existence and purpose of the corporation then it is beyond the power of the Board of Directors." The court added, "The need for shareholder * * * approval is to be measured not by the size of a sale alone, but also by its qualitative effect upon the corporation. Thus, it is relevant to ask whether a transaction 'is out of the ordinary' and substantially affects the existence and purpose of the corporation." 316 A.2d, at 606.

In determining whether a disposition would leave a corporation without a significant continuing business activity, the term "the corporation" includes subsidiaries that are or should be consolidated with the parent under generally accepted accounting principles.

The 25% safe harbor embodied in section 12.02(a) obviously represents a policy judgment that more certainty than is provided by interpretations of the current case law is desirable .

6. Chapter 13, Dissenters' Rights. This subchapter was also substantially revised in 1999; it provides for a significant degree of private ordering (see section 13.02(a)(5)) and as a result, the scope of the statutory appraisal remedy in the revised Act is somewhat narrower than that provided in the 1984 Act. In general, the right of appraisal under the MBCA is available only for corporate actions that will result in a fundamental change in the shares to be affected by the action and then only when uncertainty concerning the fair value of the affected shares may cause reasonable differences about the fairness of the terms of the corporate action. There are several types of transactions that satisfy these criteria:

(1) *A merger pursuant to section 11.04 or a short-form merger pursuant to section 11.05.* Holders of any class or series that is to be exchanged or converted in connection with a merger under sections 11.04 or 11.05 are entitled both to a vote under section 11.04(f) and to appraisal under section 13.02(a)(1). Although shareholders of a subsidiary that is a party to a merger under section 11.05 may not be entitled to vote on the merger, they are entitled to appraisal under 13.02(a)(1) because their interests will be extinguished by the merger. Section 13.02(a)(1)(i), however, denies appraisal rights to any class or series of shares in the surviving corporation if such class or series remains outstanding after the transaction.

(2) *A share exchange under section 11.03 if the corporation is a party whose shares are being acquired in the exchange.* Consistent with the treatment in § 13.02(a)(1) of mergers requiring shareholder approval, an appraisal remedy is available only for holders of shares that will be exchanged.

(3) *Shareholders who are entitled to vote on a matter requiring the approval of shareholders.* Holders of classes or series of shares who are entitled to vote on transactions requiring shareholder approval are also generally entitled to assert appraisal rights with respect to these transactions. Section 13.02(a)(1). The form of the transaction disposing of the corporation's assets determines whether shares of a class or series that do not have general

voting rights will be entitled to vote on an asset disposition (and thus become entitled to appraisal rights). In a typical transaction governed by chapter 12, the acquirer purchases substantially all of the assets and assumes substantially all of the liabilities of the corporation. The selling corporation then liquidates pursuant to a plan of dissolution approved by the shareholders as part of the transaction and distributes to its shareholders the consideration received from the acquirer.

If the transaction protects the liquidation preference of a non-voting class of preferred, that class is entitled neither to vote nor to appraisal rights. However, if the preferred shares are required in order to accept any consideration different from its liquidation the transaction triggers both voting by voting group and appraisal rights on behalf of the class.

(4) *Reverse stock splits.* Appraisal rights are available in connection with amendments to the articles of incorporation that effectuate a reverse stock split that reduces the number of shares a shareholder owns to a fractional share if the corporation has the obligation or right to repurchase the fractional share so created. Section 13.02(a)(4). The reason for granting appraisal rights in this situation is similar to the reasons for granting such rights in all cases of cash-out mergers that compel affected shareholders to accept cash for their investment in an amount established by the corporation.

(5) *Voluntary appraisal rights.* Section 13.02(a)(5) provides that a corporation may voluntarily authorize appraisal rights with respect to a merger, share exchange, disposition of assets, or amendment to the articles of incorporation. Such an authorization may be by provision in the articles of incorporation, bylaws, or by a resolution of the board of directors. The theory is that a corporation may wish to grant appraisal rights in connection with important transactions even though the MBCA does not provide for them. A voluntary grant of appraisal rights may satisfy unhappy shareholders who otherwise might seek other remedies. Further, if the existence of the appraisal right is itself in dispute, a voluntary offer of an appraisal right may avoid litigation. An express grant of voluntary appraisal right under section 13.02(a)(5) overrides the exceptions to the availability of appraisal rights in section 13.02(a) and automatically makes all provisions of chapter 13 applicable to the corporation and its holders.

7. Market exception to Appraisal Rights. Section 13.02(b) creates a market exception to appraisal rights. If a liquid and reliable market exists, shareholders do not have an appraisal right and they may either accept the consideration offered in the transaction or sell their shares at the market price. This provision assumes that an efficient market exists and the market price will therefore be an adequate proxy for the appraised value of the corporation's shares. This market exception reflects a judgment that the uncertainty, costs, and time commitment involved in appraisal proceedings are unwarranted where an efficient, fair, and liquid market exists. Approximately half of the states have similar market exceptions in their appraisal statutes. However, the 1999 amendments eliminating appraisal rights for publicly traded corporations in some circumstances is not new: a similar exception was added to the MBCA in the 1960s, diluted in the 1970s, and eliminated entirely in the 1984 MBCA.

Section 13.02(a) is unusual in that it defines in great detail when a market is "liquid" and when the appraisal right is therefore not available. Liquidity is present if the class or series is either listed on the New York Stock Exchange or the American Stock Exchange or is designated as a national market system security on an interdealer quotation system by the National Association of Securities Dealers, Inc. Liquidity is also present in other markets if the class or series has at least 2,000 record or beneficial shareholders and the outstanding class or series also has a market value of at least $20 million, excluding the value of shares held by the corporation's subsidiaries, senior executives, directors, and beneficial shareholders owning more than 10 percent of the class or series.

Section 13.02(b) contains in even greater detail a series of exceptions to the exception: circumstances in which an appraisal right remains available even though a liquid market as defined in § 13.02(a) exists. For example, the market exception is inapplicable if the transaction requires shareholders to accept anything other than cash or securities that meet the liquidity tests of section 13.02(b)(1). Thus, shareholders are assured of receiving either appraisal rights, cash from the transaction, liquid shares, or other proprietary interests in the survivor entity. Other exceptions to the exception include transactions involving persons who were directors or officers of the corporation within the previous year, or who are receiving a financial benefit not generally available to all shareholders. Appraisal rights are also preserved in certain types of transactions, including conflicting interest transactions such as management buyouts and cashout mergers.

Section 13.02(c) permits the corporation to eliminate or limit appraisal rights for the holders of series or classes of preferred shares. Such a provision may initially appear in the corporation's articles of incorporation. If added thereafter by amendment, the provision does not become effective for one year with respect to outstanding shares or shares which the corporation is or may be required to issue or sell at some later date. Section 13.02 apparently does not permit the corporation to eliminate or limit appraisal rights with respect to common shares in similar situations.

Section 13.02(d) provides that, with two exceptions, appraisal is the exclusive remedy for a corporate action that has been completed even though litigation with other shareholders may be unresolved. The theory is that when a majority of shareholders have approved a change, the corporation should be permitted to proceed even if a minority disagrees. Even though a subsequent judicial test of the fairness of the appraisal may yield a higher valuation, no inference should be drawn that the original judgment of the majority accepting the proffered amount was in error or that additional compensation should now be paid to those shareholders. While an exclusivity principle is usually justified, there may be exceptional circumstances where the process by which the corporate action was originally approved was so flawed that relief should be provided to all shareholders. Section 13.02(d) permits challenges if there are serious procedural defects in approving the original action—including a failure to obtain the votes required by statute or by the corporation's own documents, fraud, or material misrepresentation that affected the shareholder vote. A complaint based solely on adequacy of consideration is not actionable unless accompanied by credible allegations of wrongdoing. Since section 13.02(d) is concerned only with challenges to the corporate action, it does not address remedies that shareholders might have against directors or other persons as a result of the corporate action.

8. Section 13.02(a)(4). The 1999 amendments also provide for appraisal rights in connection with amendments to the articles of incorporation if they effect a cashout via a reverse stock split.

Notes

(1) Under the MBCA as amended in 1999, appraisal rights are available generally only if the shareholder is entitled to vote on the transaction (except in the case of a short form merger) and only if the shares owned by the shareholder will not remain outstanding after the transaction. Thus, because voting rights have been eliminated for the shareholders of the surviving corporation, those shareholders have no appraisal rights. In most jurisdictions, the surviving corporation can avoid a vote of its own shareholders as well as appraisal rights if the transaction is structured as a triangular merger or a purchase of assets. But the law of most states provides for a vote and appraisal rights for the shareholders of the surviving corporation in a plain-vanilla merger. In other words, the MBCA departs from the law of most states, and it remains to be seen how many states will follow its lead in this area. In a merger of equals, it is certainly arguable that the surviving corporation undergoes as significant a change as the nonsurviving corporation.

(2) As the Official Comment to § 13.01 notes, the 1999 revisions to the MBCA eliminate the right of shareholders to an appraisal in connection with amendments to the articles of incorporation in the absence of a merger, share exchange, or disposition of assets requiring a shareholder vote. Prior to the 1999 revisions, appraisal was available to a class of shares if an amendment *materially and adversely* affected the rights of that class of shares. (Under § 10.04, however, a class of shares is entitled to vote as a class on any amendment that changes the rights of that class in any way.) Appraisal remains available in connection with an amendment effecting a reverse stock split that has the effect of cashing out some of the shares of a class or series. The 1999 revisions also eliminate appraisal rights for classes of shares entitled to vote as a class in connection with a merger, share exchange, or disposition of assets, if the change will not alter the rights of the class or series.

(3) The 1999 amendments to the MBCA include an exception to the stock market exception for conflicting interest transactions. This provision is described as applying to transactions in which there is a likelihood that the price being offered to the shareholders is on the low side. The provision is similar to many state anti-takeover statutes and may allow a target company in a hostile takeover to maintain an appraisal action in lieu of, or in addition to, litigation.

(4) As described above, appraisal rights for preferred shares may be limited or eliminated in some circumstances. *See* MBCA § 13.02(c). It is interesting to note that this apparently is the only provision in the MBCA that assumes that the phrase "preferred stock" has a generally-accepted meaning.

(5) Section 13.01(4) of the MBCA, as amended in 1999, defines fair value for appraisal purposes to mean "the value of the corporation's shares determined: (i) immediately before the effectuation of the corporate action to which the shareholder objects; (ii) using customary and current valuation concepts and techniques generally employed for similar businesses in the context of the transaction requiring appraisal; and (iii) without discounting for lack of marketability or

minority status except, if appropriate, for amendments to the articles pursuant to section 13.02(a)(5)." A lengthy Official Comment expands upon this definition.

Chapter Sixteen

CORPORATE BOOKS AND RECORDS

Chapter 16 of the MBCA attempts to provide guidelines for certain issues relating to corporate books and records. Most older corporation statutes are silent on these issues, dealing only with the inspection rights of shareholders. Of course, in addition to the rules, lawyers advising corporations also need to be aware of regulatory guidelines concerning record-keeping promulgated by administrative agencies, such as the Securities and Exchange Commission, the Food and Drug Administration, and the Federal Trade Commission. For example, in December 2002, five prominent securities firms—Deutsche Bank Securities, Goldman Sachs, Morgan Stanley, Salomon Smith Barney, and U.S. Bancorp Piper Jaffray—each paid fines of $1.65 million to the SEC for failing to preserve internal e-mail communications as required by the securities laws.

MBCA Section 16.01(a) requires every corporation to "keep as permanent records" a minimum set of core documents that reflect decisions made by the directors and shareholders of the corporation. In addition, § 16.01(e) requires every corporation to "keep a copy" of specified basic corporate documents at the principal office of the corporation. These documents must be made available for routine inspection by any shareholder during regular business hours. MBCA § 16.02(a).

Section 16.01(b) requires every corporation to "maintain appropriate accounting records." The word "maintain" should be contrasted with the word "keep" in § 16.01(a) and (e); "keep" means permanent retention while "maintain" refers to current records only and does not address the question of how long financial and other records should be kept. Thus, the retention and destruction of all records other than the limited records the corporation is directed to "keep" by the MBCA, is dictated by considerations or rules independent of the MBCA. In part, specific record retention rules may be established by state or federal tax or regulatory statutes, or perhaps by general state statutes. Many corporations have established internal policies that permit the destruction of records after some suitably-long period of time, taking into account statutes of limitations and the possibility that products liability claims may arise long after the records relating to those products were generated.

The word "appropriate" with respect to accounting records in MBCA § 16.01(b) reflects a general recognition of the fact that the nature and size of the business largely determines its accounting system, which in turn largely determines its accounting records. The Official Comment suggests that "appropriate" records are "generally records that permit financial statements to be prepared which fairly present the financial position and transactions of the corporation. In some very small businesses operating on a cash basis, however, 'appropriate' accounting records may consist only of a check register, vouchers, and receipts." Today most accounting and financial records are maintained electronically, a development recognized in MBCA § 16.01(d).

MBCA § 16.01(c) requires every corporation to "maintain" a record of its shareholders. In larger corporations, records of shareholders are usually maintained electronically; this function is often delegated to transfer agents that have the responsibility of recording transfers of securities. In closely held corporations, the record may consist only of the filled-in stubs of stock certificates previously issued, if that.

Publicly-held corporations registered under the Securities Exchange Act of 1934 are required to prepare detailed financial statements that are distributed to shareholders and to the public. See Chapter 10. Historically, state statutes did not contain an analogous requirement, so that shareholders of closely held or unregistered corporations did not have the right to receive routine financial statements from the corporation. However, this is gradually changing. The MBCA first introduced such a requirement in 1979. The current provision, MBCA § 16.20, is carefully constructed so as not to impose onerous requirements on very small corporations and yet to require larger corporations that have financial statements professionally prepared to distribute those statements to shareholders. Every corporation under this provision must furnish at the minimum a balance sheet, an income statement, and a statement of changes in shareholders' equity for the year. Financial statements require accounting principles to be established for their preparation; § 16.20 does not require the use of generally-accepted accounting principles (GAAP) or any specific set of accounting principles, but if financial statements are prepared for the corporation on the basis of GAAP, the annual financial statements must likewise be prepared on a GAAP basis. Section 16.20(b) sets forth general principles for disclosing the "basis of preparation" of financial statements and whether the system used was consistent with that of the preceding year.

Under most state statutes, there are few mandatory disclosure requirements, though some states require the filing of annual reports or tax statements that may be available for inspection by shareholders or the public. See MBCA § 16.20.

One issue that is more or less addressed in all state corporation statutes is the extent to which shareholders are entitled to inspect corporate books and records. Shareholders, as ultimate owners of the enterprise, enjoyed qualified rights at common law to inspect the corporate books and records, including shareholder lists, contracts, correspondence, tax returns, and other documents. Harry G. Henn & John R. Alexander, Laws of Corporations and Other Business Enterprises § 199 (3rd ed. 1983). As described below, this qualified common-law right continues to exist under the MBCA and in many states. In addition, many states supplement the common-law right with a statutory right.

At one time, most inspection cases revolved around the list of shareholders required to be maintained by the corporation. This list, of course, is a list of record shareholders only. Most statutes permit a virtually automatic-right of inspection of the list of record shareholders entitled to vote at a scheduled shareholders' meeting shortly before and during the meeting itself. See MBCA § 7.20. At other times, a list of shareholders may be inspected only if the shareholder qualifies under the general shareholder inspection statutes. See MBCA § 16.02.

Shareholders continue to request shareholder lists in connection with proxy fights or takeover bids for publicly held corporations. However, access to this list by an insurgent or by outside bidders has become less important than it was twenty or thirty years ago. This shift is a result of the widespread use of nominees as record holders (thus limiting the usefulness of the list itself), and the growth of institutional investors, many of whom make information about their entire portfolios available as a matter of public record. Of course, access to a current shareholders' list may still be essential in situations involving closely held corporations or publicly held corporations with shares widely held of record by individuals rather than institutional investors.

THOMAS & BETTS CORPORATION v. LEVITON MANUFACTURING CO., INC.

Supreme Court of Delaware, 1996.
681 A.2d 1026.

Before VEASEY, C.J., WALSH and BERGER, JJ.

VEASEY, CHIEF JUSTICE:

In this appeal we affirm the order of the Court of Chancery denying in part and limiting a stockholder's entitlement to inspection of books and records. In doing so, we rest our decision on the fact that the trial court's determination of the stockholder's failure to show a proper purpose turned on legal and credibility assessments well within the proper burden placed on a stockholder seeking an inspection. Such a stockholder has the burden of showing, by a preponderance of the evidence, a proper purpose entitling the stockholder to an inspection of every item sought. Here, the Court of Chancery overstated the burden on the stockholder as a "greater-than-normal evidentiary burden." The burden on the stockholder is a normal burden and this stockholder failed to adduce sufficient evidence to meet that burden.

I. FACTS

Plaintiff below—appellant, Thomas & Betts Corporation ("Thomas & Betts" or "plaintiff"), appeals from a decision of the Court of Chancery granting in part and denying in part its request for inspection of certain books and records of defendant below—appellee, Leviton Manufacturing Co., Inc. ("Leviton" or "defendant").

Leviton is a closely held Delaware corporation engaged in the business of manufacturing electronic components and residential wiring devices. Thomas & Betts is a publicly traded New Jersey corporation engaged in the electronics business. Thomas & Betts and Leviton are not considered to be in competition with one another. This is due, in large part, to Leviton's focus on the residential market. For a number of years, Thomas & Betts has expressed an interest either in acquiring Leviton or engaging in some form of joint venture.

During the summer of 1993, Thomas & Betts and Leviton engaged in preliminary negotiations concerning a possible union of the two companies, but no agreement was ever reached. To date, Leviton has not expressed any interest in participating in a change-of-control or joint venture transaction with Thomas & Betts.

Leviton's President and CEO, Harold Leviton, is also the company's majority stockholder. Harold Leviton and his wife control a voting trust which represents 76.45 percent of Leviton's Class A voting stock. He and the other Leviton insiders are members of the Leviton family and most bear some relationship to the company's founder. By all accounts, Harold Leviton is the dominant figure in the corporation, deciding the company's strategy, operations and future goals.

Thomas & Betts decided to seek a minority position in Leviton in order to force a sale of the company to Thomas & Betts. In April of 1994, without the knowledge of Harold Leviton, Thomas & Betts began negotiations with Leviton's former Group Vice President, Thomas Blumberg ("Blumberg"). Blumberg and his wife, who is Harold Leviton's niece, owned approximately 29.1 percent of Leviton's outstanding shares. Negotiations for the sale of the Blumberg stock to Thomas & Betts were clandestine. In furtherance of the transaction, Blumberg provided Thomas & Betts with confidential internal Leviton documents and disclosed various facets of Leviton's internal strategies and accounting figures. Ultimately, Thomas & Betts paid Blumberg $50 million for his Leviton stake, with a promise of up to an additional $20 million if Thomas & Betts were to accomplish its desired acquisition of Leviton. Thomas & Betts indemnified Blumberg against, inter alia, litigation by Leviton, and also agreed to pay up to $7.5 million to Blumberg, in equal quarterly installments, if the sale of his shares were enjoined. At the time of sale, Thomas & Betts was fully aware that Leviton did not pay dividends and that Leviton's accounting practices did not follow Generally Accepted Accounting Principles ("GAAP").

The sale of the Blumberg shares was consummated on July 12, 1994, and Harold Leviton was informed of the sale the following day. Harold Leviton immediately fired Blumberg, only to hire him back and fire him again days later, along with his children and their secretaries. Harold Leviton rebuffed overtures from Thomas & Betts to establish an amicable relationship. Instead, Harold Leviton sought to buy out the interest of Thomas & Betts. From July 1994 to February of 1995, various representatives of Thomas & Betts met with Leviton insiders in an attempt to cultivate a working relationship. On October 6, 1994, Kevin Dunnigan ("Dunnigan"), the CEO of Thomas & Betts, reported to the board of Thomas & Betts on his strategy:

> On the Leviton front, we are moving to the next phase. I will write to Harold Leviton next week to give him a rationale on why it is in everyone's best interests to start a dialogue. We will follow this up with a legal request to review all the books and records of Leviton which will start either a dialogue or a lawsuit.

Harold Leviton, however, remained obstinate in his opposition to Thomas & Betts' ownership position. Although some concessions were made and Thomas & Betts was allowed limited access to Leviton's books and records, by

February 1995 it was abundantly clear that Harold Leviton intended to thwart any acquisition of Leviton by Thomas & Betts.

On February 8, 1995, Thomas & Betts served Leviton with a formal demand seeking inspection of the following documents:

1. Leviton's stockholder list,

2. Minutes of Leviton shareholder and directors meetings as well as written consents,

3. Audited financial statements for Leviton and its subsidiaries,

4. Internal financial statements for the current fiscal year provided on a monthly basis,

5. Tax returns filed for Leviton and its subsidiaries,

6. Organizational charts for Leviton and its subsidiaries,

7. Documents relating to interested party transactions between Leviton or its subsidiaries and its shareholders, directors or officers,

8. Documents relating to "key man" life insurance policies taken out by Leviton,

9. Material contracts between Leviton and its subsidiaries,

10. Documents relating to Leviton leases for real estate or equipment.

On February 16, 1995, Dunnigan wrote to Harold Leviton and offered to purchase the balance of Leviton's stock for $250 million, net of expenses. Dunnigan's letter threatened litigation if this final offer were rebuffed:

> You are forcing us down a road where given a choice, I am sure neither of us wants to go. Often, once this process gets started, it ends up with consequences that were never intended. Watch! It won't be long before the lawyers, the government and the courts are completely in charge, and in the end neither you nor I will have much say in the outcome. There will be only victims, but it won't be the lawyers.

On February 17, 1995, Leviton formally refused both Thomas & Betts' acquisition offer and its inspection demand.

On February 27, 1995, Thomas & Betts filed this action in the Court of Chancery seeking to compel inspection of Leviton's books and records pursuant to 8 Del.C. § 220. After a four-day trial, the Court of Chancery determined that: (1) plaintiff's demand was not motivated by its stated purposes of investigating waste and mismanagement, * * * and valuation of those shares; (2) plaintiff's actual motivation was to gain leverage in its efforts to acquire Leviton; (3) this motive was antithetical to the interests of Leviton; (4) despite the initially improper purpose of its demand, Thomas & Betts was entitled to limited inspection so it could value its Leviton shares since a fundamental change of circumstances had occurred; and (5) this inspection should be narrowly circumscribed. From this decision, Thomas & Betts appeals. Leviton has not cross-appealed.

II. PROPER PURPOSE

Thomas & Betts' Demand Letter purported to state [two] separate purposes for its requested inspection of Leviton's books and records. Specifically, plaintiff asserted that the books and records were necessary: (1) to investigate possible waste and mismanagement; * * * and (2) to assist in the valuation of Thomas & Betts' Leviton shares. After trial, the Court of Chancery concluded that plaintiff's articulated purposes were not its actual purposes and that plaintiff's actual purpose was improper.[1] Specifically, the trial court held that Thomas & Betts was attempting to use the Section 220 proceeding as leverage in its efforts to acquire Leviton. The trial court concluded, however, that Thomas & Betts should be allowed to inspect those books and records necessary to value its investment in Leviton in view of the fact that there had been a change in circumstances.

Thomas & Betts now asserts that the * * * [purpose] for inspection not credited by the trial court—investigation of waste and mismanagement—constituted [a] proper purpose under Section 220 and that the trial court erred in refusing inspection of books and records relevant to [this purpose]. These contentions are addressed seriatim below.

"The question of a 'proper purpose' under Section 220(b) of our General Corporation Law is an issue of law and equity which this Court reviews de novo." Compaq Computer Corp. v. Horton, Del.Supr., 631 A.2d 1, 3 (1993) (citing Oberly v. Kirby, Del.Supr., 592 A.2d 445, 462 (1991)); Western Air Lines, Inc. v. Kerkorian, Del.Supr., 254 A.2d 240 (1969) (court reviewed proper purpose determination in stocklist case de novo). "The determination of whether [plaintiff's] * * * stated purpose for the inspection was its primary purpose, is a question of fact warranting deference to the trial court's credibility assessments." State ex rel. Scattered Corp., Del.Supr., No. 444, 1995, Veasey, C.J., 1996 WL 191023 (April 4, 1996) (ORDER); accord CM & M Group, Inc. v. Carroll, Del.Supr., 453 A.2d 788, 793 (1982).

III. PLAINTIFF'S CLAIMS OF WASTE AND MISMANAGEMENT

As found by the Court of Chancery, plaintiff's claims of waste and mismanagement are grounded on Leviton's purportedly substandard financial performance, the company's failure to pay dividends, Leviton's poor cash flow and the company's higher than average expenses. As specific instances of misconduct, plaintiff asserted that: "(a) Leviton has paid for the Leviton family's personal expenses, including use of the company's accounting firm for tax and estate planning purposes; (b) Leviton has been overcompensating its officers and directors at the shareholders' expense; and (c) Leviton's lease agreements with members of the Leviton family are self-dealing transac-

---

1. [By the Court] See, e.g., BBC Acquisition Corp. v. Durr–Fillauer Medical, Inc., Del.Ch., 623 A.2d 85, 88 (1992):

[W]hen seeking inspection of books and records other than the corporate stock ledger or stock list, a shareholder has the burden of proving that his purpose is proper. Since such a shareholder will often have more than one purpose, that requirement has been construed to mean that the shareholder's primary purpose must be proper; any secondary purpose, whether proper or not, is irrelevant. CM & M Group, Inc. v. Carroll, Del.Supr., 453 A.2d 788, 792 (1982); Helmsman Man-

agement Services, Inc. v. A & S Consultants, Inc., Del.Ch., 525 A.2d 160, 164 (1987).

See also Ostrow v. Bonney Forge Corp., Del. Ch., C.A. No. 13270, Allen, C., mem. op., 1994 WL 114807 (April 6, 1994) ("Once a shareholder has established a proper purpose for the demanded inspection, any secondary purpose he or she may have is generally considered to be irrelevant. * * * The primary purpose may not, however, be adverse to the corporation's best interests.") (citing CM & M Group, Inc. v. Carroll, Del.Supr., 453 A.2d 788, 792 (1982); Skoglund v. Ormand Indus., Inc., Del.Ch., 372 A.2d 204, 207 (1976)).

tions." The trial court found, however, that these claims "are so lacking in record support" that inspection could not be justified.

Plaintiff contends that the Court of Chancery applied an incorrect legal standard in determining that plaintiff's stated purpose lacked adequate record support. Specifically, Thomas & Betts points to portions of the trial court's holding which appear to impose on plaintiff "a greater-than-normal evidentiary burden," to "adduce evidence from which a credible possibility of mismanagement and waste may be inferred" and to "adduce specific evidence of waste and mismanagement."

The Court of Chancery incorrectly articulated the governing legal standard. It is well established that investigation of waste and mismanagement is a proper purpose for a Section 220 books and records inspection. Nodana Petroleum Corp. v. State, Del.Supr., 123 A.2d 243, 246 (1956). When a stockholder seeks inspection of books and records, the burden of proof is on the stockholder to demonstrate that his purpose is proper. CM & M Group, 453 A.2d at 792.[2] In order to meet that burden of proof, a stockholder must present some credible basis from which the court can infer that waste or mismanagement may have occurred. Skouras v. Admiralty Enters., Inc., Del.Ch., 386 A.2d 674, 678 (1978) ("more than a general statement is required in order for the Court to determine the propriety of a demand"); Helmsman Management Servs., Inc. v. A & S Consultants, Inc., Del.Ch., 525 A.2d 160, 166 (1987) ("A mere statement of a purpose to investigate possible general mismanagement, without more, will not entitle a shareholder to broad '220 inspection relief. There must be some evidence of possible mismanagement as would warrant further investigation of the matter."); Neely v. Oklahoma Publishing Co., Del.Ch., C.A. No. 5293, Brown, V.C. (Aug. 15, 1977); Everett v. Hollywood Park, Inc., Del.Ch., C.A. No. 14556, Jacobs, V.C., mem. op., 1996 WL 32171 (Jan. 19, 1996) ("Where, as here, the plaintiff's purpose is to investigate possible waste or mismanagement, she must also adduce evidence of potential mismanagement sufficient to support her suspicions and to warrant going forward."). While stockholders have the burden of coming forward with specific and credible allegations sufficient to warrant a suspicion of waste and mismanagement, they are not required to prove by a preponderance of the evidence that waste and management are actually occurring.[3]

A general standard that a stockholder seeking inspection of books and records bears "a greater-than-normal evidentiary burden" is unclear and could be interpreted as placing an unduly difficult obstacle in the path of stockholders seeking to investigate waste and mismanagement. Viewed in

2. [By the Court] While a stockholder has the burden to show a proper purpose for an inspection of books and records, the corporation has the burden of showing an improper purpose when a stockholder seeks only to inspect the stockholder list. 8 Del.C. § 220(c). The trial court held that plaintiff "has established a proper purpose for seeking inspection of Leviton's shareholder list," and the corporation failed to meet its burden that plaintiff's purpose was improper.

3. [By the Court] The Revised Model Business Corporation Act requires that a stockholder "describe with reasonable particularity his purpose and the records he desires to inspect." Revised Model Business Corp. Act § 16.02(c). See Grimes v. Donald, 673 A.2d 1207, 1217 (1996), for an analogous discussion of the reasonable doubt, or reason to believe, standard in the context of a derivative suit. * * * Contrary to plaintiff's assertion in the instant case, this Court in Grimes did not suggest that its reference to a Section 220 demand as one of the "tools at hand" was intended to eviscerate or modify the need for a stockholder to show a proper purpose under Section 220. Id. at 1216 n. 11 (noting that Section 220 can be used to secure information to support demand futility).

context, however, the articulation in dispute here accurately describes a stockholder's position in cases such as the one at bar, where substantial evidence supports a finding that plaintiff's primary motives for the inspection are improper.

In the final analysis, the decision of the trial court did not turn solely on a legal conclusion that Thomas & Betts had failed to meet an elevated evidentiary burden. As discussed further, infra, the trial court's determination turned, in large part, on the Vice Chancellor's determination that plaintiff's witnesses were not credible. According appropriate deference to the factual findings of the Court of Chancery, we conclude that plaintiff failed to satisfy the appropriate standard for inspection of the books and records with regard to the claim of waste and mismanagement. Levitt v. Bouvier, Del.Supr., 287 A.2d 671, 673 (1972) ("When the determination of facts turns on a question of credibility and the acceptance or rejection of 'live' testimony by the trial judge, his findings will be approved upon review."); State ex rel. Scattered Corp., Del.Supr., No. 444, 1995, Veasey, C.J. (April 4, 1996) (ORDER) ("The determination of whether Scattered's stated purpose for the inspection was its primary purpose, is a question of fact warranting deference to the trial court's credibility assessments.") * * *

More significantly, the trial court did not exclude this testimony. Rather, the Vice Chancellor heard the testimony and found it unworthy of belief. In this posture, plaintiff's evidentiary objections carry little weight. Similarly, Thomas & Betts' citation to Skoglund v. Ormand Industries is unavailing. Skoglund, 372 A.2d at 208, 211–13. As in the case at bar, the Skoglund court allowed hearsay testimony regarding statements made by a corporate insider. Unlike the instant case, however, the trial court in Skoglund chose to credit that testimony as worthy of belief.

Finally, plaintiff's arguments ignore the underlying posture of this case. Unlike the cases relied on by plaintiff, this case does not involve a typical uninformed stockholder seeking to protect his or her investment. Thomas & Betts acquired its shares in Leviton with the acknowledged purpose of acquiring the company. Moreover, Thomas & Betts did so with full knowledge that Leviton's CEO would likely oppose any such transaction. Thomas & Betts first praised Harold Leviton for his expert management of the company, seeking an amicable union of the two corporations. When Thomas & Betts' friendly overtures proved unavailing, it filed an inspection demand to create leverage. Its self-avowed acquisition motives cast serious doubt on the genuineness of its claim that it seeks the books and records to investigate waste and mismanagement.

These facts were properly before the Court of Chancery. See, e.g., Helmsman Management Servs., 525 A.2d at 164 ("The propriety of a demanding shareholder's purpose must be determined from the facts in each case, and the burden of proving a proper purpose is upon the shareholder."). The Court of Chancery concluded that "Thomas & Betts' initial primary purpose in seeking a books and records inspection was * * * to exert pressure on Harold Leviton to negotiate a sale of his controlling interest or, alternatively, the entire company." Ultimately, the Court of Chancery found Thomas & Betts' articulated purpose to be "highly opportunistic" and unworthy of belief.

Thomas & Betts has provided no reason for this Court to revisit those factual determinations and credibility assessments. * * *

V. THE SCOPE OF THE INSPECTION

After trial, the Court of Chancery found that Thomas & Betts had failed to meet its burden of establishing that it sought inspection in furtherance of its concerns regarding * * * mismanagement. The trial court found that Thomas & Betts' primary purpose for inspection was to further its plans for acquiring Leviton and that this interest was antithetical to the interests of the corporation. Despite Thomas & Betts' initially improper motives, the Court acknowledged that Thomas & Betts had experienced a fundamental change of circumstances. The court reasoned that, owing to Harold Leviton's unwillingness to negotiate a change-of-control transaction, Thomas & Betts was now in the unenviable position of a "locked-in" minority stockholder. Based on this fact, the trial court allowed inspection of certain Leviton books and records, but limited the scope of that inspection to those documents which are "essential and sufficient" to Thomas & Betts' valuation purpose. Thomas & Betts now contends that the Court of Chancery abused its discretion in limiting the scope of its inspection of Leviton's books and records.

Absent any apparent error of law, this Court reviews for abuse of discretion the decision of the trial court regarding the scope of a stockholder's inspection of books and records. 8 Del.C. § 220(c); CM & M Group, 453 A.2d at 794. The plaintiff bears the burden of proving that each category of books and records is essential to accomplishment of the stockholder's articulated purpose for the inspection. Helmsman Management Servs., 525 A.2d at 168.

The plain language of 8 Del.C. § 220(c) provides that "[t]he Court may, *in its discretion*, prescribe any limitations or conditions with reference to the inspection." (emphasis supplied). The responsibility of the trial court to narrowly tailor the inspection right to a stockholder's stated purpose is well established. See BBC Acquisition Corp., 623 A.2d at 88–89 (entitlement is restricted to those books and records needed to perform the task). In discharging this responsibility, the trial court has wide latitude in determining the proper scope of inspection. Undergirding this discretion is a recognition that the interests of the corporation must be harmonized with those of the inspecting stockholder.

Here, the trial court has found that Thomas & Betts' primary purpose for inspection is at odds with the interests of the corporation. In this posture, it was entirely appropriate for the Court of Chancery to limit plaintiff's inspection to those documents which are essential and sufficient to its valuation purpose.

Moreover, even in a case where no improper purpose has been attributed to the inspecting stockholder, the burden of proof is always on the party seeking inspection to establish that each category of the books and records requested is essential and sufficient to the stockholder's stated purpose. Helmsman Management Servs., 525 A.2d at 167. The trial court specifically found that Thomas & Betts had not met its burden of proof as to certain of the books and records of Leviton. This finding is supported by the record and is the product of an orderly and logical deductive process. Accordingly, the finding of the Court of Chancery and its concomitant decision to limit inspection will not be disturbed on appeal. * * *

We AFFIRM the order of the Court of Chancery.

Notes

(1) Why should a shareholder's right of inspection be so limited? If a shareholder suspects that improper conduct may have occurred, should he not have the right to make a general search of corporate records and documents to see if his suspicions are justified? In a word, the answer is "no." The right of inspection reflects a balancing between the shareholder's right to have information about his investment and the fealty of "his" agents in managing the affairs of the corporation (on the one hand, see Shaw v. Agri–Mark, Inc., 663 A.2d 464, 467 (Del.1995), and the competing interest of the corporation to be free from harassment by unhappy investors) on the other, see Randall S. Thomas, Improving Shareholder Monitoring and Corporate Management by Statutory Access to Information, 38 Ariz.L.Rev. 331, 334 (1996)).

(2) Even if generalized purposes for an inspection are not acceptable, many cases state that a "proper purpose" is to examine financial records in order to determine the value of one's own shares. See, e.g., CM & M Group, Inc. v. Carroll, 453 A.2d 788 (Del.1982).

(3) All states adopt a "proper purpose" or similar test for shareholder inspection of records. Hundreds of cases have classified specific purposes as set forth in trial testimony or deposition as "proper" or "not proper." In resolving these disputes, as in the principal case, courts tend to look beyond the formal statements of purpose put forth and inquire into the shareholder's motive and relationship with the corporation. For a good example in the publicly-held corporation context, see State ex rel. Pillsbury v. Honeywell, Inc., 291 Minn. 322, 191 N.W.2d 406 (1971).

(4) Of course the right of inspection is only one avenue to the information. See MBCA § 16.02(e)(1). In modern litigation, broad discovery rights exist and these rights appear to be independent of the statutory or common law inspection right of shareholders.

SAITO v. McKESSON HBOC, INC.

Supreme Court of Delaware, 2002.
806 A.2d 113.

BERGER, JUSTICE.

In this appeal, we consider the limitations on a stockholder's statutory right to inspect corporate books and records. The statute, 8 *Del.C.* § 220, enables stockholders to investigate matters "reasonably related to [their] interest as [stockholders]" including, among other things, possible corporate wrongdoing. It does not open the door to the wide ranging discovery that would be available in support of litigation. For this statutory tool to be meaningful, however, it cannot be read narrowly to deprive a stockholder of necessary documents solely because the documents were prepared by third parties or because the documents predate the stockholder's first investment in the corporation. A stockholder who demands inspection for a proper purpose should be given access to all of the documents in the corporation's possession, custody or control, that are necessary to satisfy that proper purpose. Thus, where a § 220 claim is based on alleged corporate wrongdoing, and assuming the allegation is meritorious, the stockholder should be given enough information to effectively address the problem, either through derivative litigation or through direct contact with the corporation's directors and/or stockholders.

A. THE STANDING LIMITATION

[Under 8 Del. C. § 327], stockholders who bring derivative suits must allege that they were stockholders of the corporation "at the time of the transaction of which such stockholder complains * * *." The Court of Chancery decided that this limitation on Saito's ability to maintain a derivative suit controlled the scope of his inspection rights. As a result, the court held that Saito was "effectively limited to examining conduct of McKesson and McKesson HBOC's boards *following* the negotiation and public announcement of the merger agreement."

Although we recognize that there may be some interplay between the two statutes, we do not read § 327 as defining the temporal scope of a stockholder's inspection rights under § 220. The books and records statute requires that a stockholder's purpose be one that is "reasonably related" to his or her interest as a stockholder. The standing statute, § 327, bars a stockholder from bringing a derivative action unless the stockholder owned the corporation's stock at the time of the alleged wrong. If a stockholder wanted to investigate alleged wrongdoing that substantially predated his or her stock ownership, there could be a question as to whether the stockholder's purpose was reasonably related to his or her interest as a stockholder, especially if the stockholder's only purpose was to institute derivative litigation. But stockholders may use information about corporate mismanagement in other ways, as well. They may seek an audience with the board to discuss proposed reforms or, failing in that, they may prepare a stockholder resolution for the next annual meeting, or mount a proxy fight to elect new directors. None of those activities would be prohibited by § 327.

Even where a stockholder's only purpose is to gather information for a derivative suit, the date of his or her stock purchase should not be used as an automatic "cut-off" date in a § 220 action. First, the potential derivative claim may involve a continuing wrong that both predates and postdates the stockholder's purchase date. In such a case, books and records from the inception of the alleged wrongdoing could be necessary and essential to the stockholder's purpose. Second, the alleged post-purchase date wrongs may have their foundation in events that transpired earlier. In this case, for example, Saito wants to investigate McKesson's apparent failure to learn of HBOC's accounting irregularities until months after the merger was consummated. Due diligence documents generated before the merger agreement was signed may be essential to that investigation. In sum, the date on which a stockholder first acquired the corporation's stock does not control the scope of records available under § 220. If activities that occurred before the purchase date are "reasonably related" to the stockholder's interest as a stockholder, then the stockholder should be given access to records necessary to an understanding of those activities.[4]

---

4. [By the Court] [A] Section 220 proceeding does not open the door to wide ranging discovery. See Brehm v. Eisner, 746 A.2d 244, 266–67 (Del.2000) (Plaintiffs "bear the burden

B.   THE FINANCIAL ADVISORS' DOCUMENTS

The Court of Chancery denied Saito access to documents in McKesson–HBOC's possession that the corporation obtained from financial and accounting advisors, on the ground that Saito could not use § 220 to develop potential claims against third parties. On appeal, Saito argues that he is seeking third party documents for the same reason he is seeking McKesson HBOC documents—to investigate possible wrongdoing by McKesson and McKesson HBOC. Since the trial court found that to be a proper purpose, Saito argues that he should not be precluded from seeing documents that are necessary to his purpose, and in McKesson HBOC's possession, simply because the documents were prepared by third party advisors.

We agree that, generally, the source of the documents in a corporation's possession should not control a stockholder's right to inspection under § 220. It is not entirely clear, however, that the trial court restricted Saito's access on that basis. The Court of Chancery decided that Saito's interest in pursuing claims against McKesson HBOC's advisors was not a proper purpose. It recognized that a secondary improper purpose usually is irrelevant if the stockholder establishes his need for the same documents to support a proper purpose. But the court apparently concluded that the categories of third party documents that Saito demanded did not support the proper purpose of investigating possible wrongdoing by McKesson and McKesson HBOC.

We cannot determine from the present record whether the Court of Chancery intended to exclude all third party documents, but such a blanket exclusion would be improper. The source of the documents and the manner in which they were obtained by the corporation have little or no bearing on a stockholder's inspection rights. The issue is whether the documents are necessary and essential to satisfy the stockholder's proper purpose. In this case, Saito wants to investigate possible wrongdoing relating to McKesson and McKesson HBOC's failure to discover HBOC's accounting irregularities. Since McKesson and McKesson HBOC relied on financial and accounting advisors to evaluate HBOC's financial condition and reporting, those advisors' reports and correspondence would be critical to Saito's investigation.

C.   HBOC DOCUMENTS

Finally, the Court of Chancery held that Saito was not entitled to any HBOC documents because he was not a stockholder of HBOC before or after the merger. Although Saito is a stockholder of HBOC's parent, McKesson HBOC, stockholders of a parent corporation are not entitled to inspect a subsidiary's books and records, "[a]bsent a showing of a fraud or that a subsidiary is in fact the mere alter ego of the parent * * *." (citations omitted). The Court of Chancery found no basis to disregard HBOC's separate existence and, therefore, denied access to its records.

We reaffirm this settled principle, which applies to those HBOC books and records that were never provided to McKesson or McKesson HBOC. But

---

of showing a proper purpose and [must] make specific and discrete identification, with rifled precision * * * [to] establish that each category of books and records is essential to the accomplishment of their articulated purpose * * *."); Security First Corp. v. U.S. Die Casting and Dev. Co., 687 A.2d 563, 568, 570 (Del. 1997) ("mere curiosity or desire for a fishing expedition" is insufficient.)

it does not apply to relevant documents that HBOC gave to McKesson before the merger, or to McKesson HBOC after the merger. We assume that HBOC provided financial and accounting information to its proposed merger partner and, later, to its parent company. As with the third party advisors' documents, Saito would need access to relevant HBOC documents in order to understand what his company's directors knew and why they failed to recognize HBOC's accounting irregularities.

Conclusion

Based on the foregoing, the decision of the Court of Chancery is AFFIRMED in part and REVERSED in part, and this matter is REMANDED for further action in accordance with this decision.

Notes

(1) The accounting irregularities in Saito evoke images of Enron, WorldCom, and the other corporate scandals that prompted passage of the Sarbanes–Oxley Act of 2002. Among the Act's reforms are new obstruction-of-justice crimes and enhanced criminal penalties related to document destruction. Provisions such as Section 802 of the Act (18 U.S.C. § 1519) in Sarbanes–Oxley fill gaps in other federal obstruction of justice statutes. Section 802 covers *anticipated matters or cases*, not just pending proceedings which are covered under 18 U.S.C. § 1505, or official proceedings, which are covered under 18 U.S.C. § 1512(b). See also Sarbanes–Oxley § 1102, 18 U.S.C. § 1512(c).

(2) In some instances, a dissident director rather than a shareholder may seek to inspect records of the corporation. This may occur, for example, in closely held corporations in which cumulative voting is mandatory and a minority faction has sufficient voting power to elect one or more directors. Does a director have inspection rights greater than those of a shareholder? It depends on the jurisdiction. See Pilat v. Broach Systems, Inc., 108 N.J.Super. 88, 260 A.2d 13 (1969), at 16–18, for a discussion of the rules in various jurisdictions.

(3) Consider the case of Cohen v. El Paso Corp., 2004 WL 2340046, at *1 (Del.Ch. Oct. 18, 2004). Cohen, a shareholder in the El Paso Corporation (El Paso), proceeded in an action to inspect the company books under Section 220 of the Delaware General Corporations Law. El Paso, also a defendant in a federal securities class action, argued that a stay of discovery in the federal case prevented Cohen from inspecting the corporate books and records. The Delaware court rejected El Paso's argument. The judge held that the Private Securities Litigation Act and the Securities Litigation Standards Act, which allowed for the stay of discovery, only applied to federal class action cases. Because Cohen's demand had nothing to do with the federal class action his action to inspect the company's books and records is allowed under Section 220.

(4) A demand for corporate books and records can also be helpful to a shareholder who wants to commence a derivative suit. In order to get past the initial motion to dismiss, a derivative plaintiff must plead sufficient facts to excuse pre-suit demand on the corporation's board. Two Delaware cases illustrate how a demand for corporate books and records can make the excuse of demand more likely.

In Beam v. Stewart, 845 A.2d 1040 (Del. 2004), the court affirmed the dismissal of several claims in a derivative suit due to a lack of sufficient facts to excuse demand. Though the court was perplexed as to why the plaintiff did not first request to inspect the corporate books and records under Section 220: "[F]ailure to seek a books and records inspection that may have uncovered the facts necessary to support a reasonable doubt of independence has resulted in substantial cost to the parties and the judiciary." 845 A.2d at 1057. In short, a request to inspect books and records can only help the plaintiff, will reduce litigation costs for both parties, and will save the judiciary unnecessary work.

In Brehm v. Eisner, 746 A.2d 244 (Del.2000), the court affirmed the lower court's dismissal of a derivative action against Disney. The derivative action stemmed from the extravagant compensation package given to Disney's former President, Michael Ovitz. The original complaint alleged that the board breached its fiduciary duty by agreeing to the terms of Ovitz's employment. In an unusual move, the court allowed the plaintiffs to amend their complaint. And in line with the court's advice, the plaintiff shareholders made a books-and-records request under Section 220. Plaintiffs filed an amended complaint with new facts backing up their claim that the board breached its fiduciary duty. The court denied Disney's motion to dismiss based upon the amended complaint.

(5) Over time, Section 220 of the Delaware General Corporation Law has become a powerful tool, allowing both owners of record and beneficial owners of stock to inspect a company's books and records for "any proper purpose." Del. Code Ann. Tit. 8, § 220(b). The powers granted to shareholders under this section are sometimes referred to as "tools at hand," and represent a crucial element of many derivative and other shareholder-initiated suits. Indeed, it is precisely these tools at hand that allow shareholders in many cases to plead with the particularity necessary to reach a trial on the merits. As evidenced by the cases discussed in Note 4, the Delaware courts have made a concerted effort to encourage shareholders to take advantage of Section 220's tools at hand, and shareholders who do not take advantage of these rights may find themselves in the unsavory position of the plaintiffs in *Beam*. See Tara L. Dunn, The Developing Theory of Good Faith in Director Conduct: Are Delaware Courts Ready to Force Corporate Directors to Go Out-of-Pocket After Disney IV?, 83 Denv. U. L. Rev. 531 (2005), S. Mark Hurd & Lisa Whittaker, Books and Records Demands and Litigation: Recent Trends and Their Implications for Corporate Governance, 9 Del. L. Rev. 1 (2006), Stephen Radin, The New Stage of Corporate Governance Litigation: Section 220 Demands, 26 Cardozo L. Rev. 1595 (2005).

PARSONS v. JEFFERSON–PILOT CORP.

Supreme Court of North Carolina, 1993.
333 N.C. 420, 426 S.E.2d 685.

MITCHELL, JUSTICE.

Louise Price Parsons, a shareholder in Jefferson–Pilot Corporation, initiated this action by filing a complaint and motion for preliminary injunction seeking to compel the defendant corporation to allow her to inspect, *inter alia*, its accounting records and records of shareholder and director action. The defendant answered and filed a motion for summary judgment and for sanctions under Rule 11 of the North Carolina Rules of Civil Procedure.

The evidence introduced at a hearing on the defendant's motion tended to show the following. The plaintiff, Louise Price Parsons, is a shareholder of Jefferson–Pilot Corporation and owns 300,000 shares of its stock, which are worth several million dollars. On 14 February 1991, the plaintiff sent a letter to the defendant corporation requesting that it allow her to inspect and copy designated corporate records that would enable her to communicate with its other shareholders. The defendant allowed the plaintiff to inspect and copy certain records. However, the defendant refused to provide the plaintiff with a list of beneficial owners of its stock, stating that it did not possess such information or maintain such a list. In her letter of 14 February 1991, the plaintiff also requested that the defendant allow her to inspect and copy certain "accounting records" so that she could determine "any possible mismanagement of the company or any possible misappropriation of the company's assets." In refusing the plaintiff's request, the defendant stated that such records "are not within the scope of N.C.G.S. § 55–16–02(b)."[5] On 4

5. [By the Editors] North Carolina has adopted MBCA § 16.02 with modifications. As of the time this case was decided, § 55–16–02 of the North Carolina Business Corporation Act was virtually identical to MBCA § 16.02 with the exception of amendments made to § 16.02(a), (b), (c), and the addition of new subsections (g) and (h). Set forth below is § 55–16–02 with the additions to § 16.02 italicized and language in MBCA § 16.02 that does not appear in § 55–16–02 marked through:

(a) Subject to section 16.03, a qualified shareholder of a corporation is entitled to inspect and copy, during regular business hours at the corporation's principal office, any of the records of the corporation described in section 16.01(0) G.S. 55–16–01(e) if he gives the corporation written notice of his demand at least five business days before the date on which he wishes to inspect and copy.

(b) A qualified shareholder of a corporation is entitled to inspect and copy, during regular business hours at a reasonable location specified by the corporation, any of the following records of the corporation if the shareholder meets the requirements of subsection (c) and gives the corporation written notice of his demand at least five business days before the date on which he wishes to inspect and copy:

(1) excerpts from minutes of any meeting of the board of directors, records of any final action taken with or without a meeting by the board of directors, or by of a committee of the board of directors while acting in place of the board of directors on behalf of the corporation, minutes of any meeting of the shareholders, and records of action taken by the shareholders or board of directors without a meeting, to the extent not subject to inspection under section 16.02(a) G.S. 55–16–02(a);

(2) Accounting records of the corporation; and

(3) The record of shareholders;

provided that a shareholder of a public corporation shall not be entitled to inspect or copy any accounting records of the corporation or any records of the corporation with respect to any matter which the corporation determines in good faith may, if disclosed,

adversely affect the corporation in the conduct of its business or may constitute material nonpublic information at the time the shareholder's notice of demand to inspect is received by the corporation.

(c) A qualified shareholder may inspect and copy the records identified described in subsection (b) only if:

(1) his demand is made in good faith and for a proper purpose;

(2) he describes with reasonable particularity his purpose and the records he desires to inspect; and

(3) the records are directly connected with his purpose.

(d) The right of inspection granted by this section many not be abolished or limited by a corporation's articles of incorporation or bylaws.

(e) This section does not affect:

(1) the right of a shareholder to inspect records under section 7.20 G.S.55–7–20 or, if the shareholder is in litigation with the corporation, to the same extent as any other litigant;

(2) the power of a court, independently of this Act, to compel the production of corporate records for examination.

(f) For purposes of this section "shareholder" includes a beneficial owner whose shares are held in a voting trust or by a nominee on his behalf and whose beneficial ownership is certified to the corporation by that voting trust or nominee.

(g) For purposes of this section, a "qualified shareholder" of a corporation is a person who shall have been a shareholder in the corporation for at least six months immediately preceding his demand or who shall be the holder of at least five percent (5%) of the corporation's outstanding shares of any class.

(h) A qualified shareholder of a corporation that has the power to elect, appoint, or designate a majority of the directors of another domestic or foreign corporation or of a domestic or foreign nonprofit corporation, shall have the inspection rights provided in this section

March 1991, the plaintiff sent another letter to the defendant narrowing her request for accounting records to those dealing with "compensation paid to, perquisites made available to and relationships with only the executive officers and directors of the company, their family members and companions." The defendant still refused to allow the plaintiff to inspect and copy any "accounting records." As a result, on 6 May 1991, the plaintiff filed a motion for preliminary injunction seeking, among other things, an order directing the defendant to give her access to its accounting records and to give her a list of beneficial owners of its stock.

At the conclusion of the hearing, Judge Allen entered an order denying the defendant's motion for summary judgment and Rule 11 sanctions, concluding that the defendant must permit the plaintiff to inspect its accounting records and records of shareholder and director action. Judge Allen also found that the defendant, Jefferson–Pilot Corporation, did not have the names of the non-objecting beneficial owners of its stock in its possession and, therefore, that the plaintiff was not entitled to an order requiring that the defendant provide her with a list of such individuals. Both parties appealed to the Court of Appeals.

The Court of Appeals affirmed the trial court's order to the extent that the order indicated that the plaintiff was not entitled to require the defendant corporation to obtain the names of non-objecting beneficial owners of the defendant's shares or to provide the plaintiff with a list of such non-objecting beneficial owners (NOBO list), where the defendant had neither the names nor a list of such individuals in its possession. The Court of Appeals also affirmed that part of the trial court's order which had concluded that the plaintiff's written demands to inspect other corporate records described her purpose and the records she sought with "reasonable particularity." However, the Court of Appeals reversed that part of the trial court's order which had concluded that the plaintiff had the right to inspect the defendant's accounting records. The Court of Appeals remanded the case to the trial court for its determination of whether the records the plaintiff sought were "directly connected" to her described purpose in seeking them and for a determination as to whether certain records sought by the plaintiff were in fact "accounting records." This Court allowed both the plaintiff's and the defendant's petitions for discretionary review on 3 September 1992.

I.

By her first assignment of error, the plaintiff contends that the Court of Appeals erroneously concluded that N.C.G.S. § 55–16–02(b) abrogated a shareholder's common law right to inspect the accounting records of a public corporation. The statute provides, in pertinent part, that a qualified shareholder of any corporation is entitled to inspect and copy accounting records of the corporation if she gives the corporation written notice of her demand at least five days before the date on which she wishes to inspect and copy such records. This right as guaranteed by the statute is limited, however, by its proviso that a shareholder of a public corporation[6] shall not be entitled to

with respect to the records of that other corporation.

6. [By the Court] The term "public corporation" as used in the North Carolina Business Corporation Act "means any corporation that

inspect or copy any accounting records of the corporation. The Court of Appeals concluded that this proviso restricts a shareholder's statutory right *and abrogates any common law right* to inspect a public corporation's accounting records. We disagree.

Under common law, a shareholder of a corporation has a right to make reasonable inspection of its books and records. *White v. Smith*, 256 N.C. 218, 123 S.E.2d 628 (1962); *Carter v. Wilson Construction Co.*, 83 N.C.App. 61, 348 S.E.2d 830 (1986). This Court has expressly recognized that the shareholders of a corporation have a common law right to make a reasonable inspection of its books to assure themselves of efficient management. We have also noted that the rationale behind the common law right of inspection is that those in charge of the corporation are merely agents of the shareholders, and a shareholder's right to inspect a corporation's books and records is only the right to inspect and examine that which is his own. *Cooke v. Outland*, 265 N.C. 601, 610, 144 S.E.2d 835, 841 (1965).

In light of the controlling case law, it is clear that a common law right to inspect the accounting records of a corporation existed in 1990 when the North Carolina Business Corporation Act, 1989 N.C.Sess.Laws ch. 265, took effect. The issue to be resolved here, then, is whether that common law right to inspect accounting records has been abrogated by N.C.G.S. § 55–16–02(b) or, to the contrary, has been preserved by N.C.G.S. § 55–16–02(e)(2), which provides that section 16–02 does not affect "the power of a court, independently of this Chapter, to compel the production of corporate records for examination."

The North Carolina Business Corporation Act, *inter alia*, provides shareholders certain rights of inspection of corporate records which did not exist under the common law. For example, the Act provides shareholders of corporations other than "public corporations" a new right to an *expedited inspection* of a corporation's accounting records *within five business days* after making a proper demand. N.C.G.S. § 55–16–02(b) (Supp.1992). There seems to be general agreement, however, that the General Assembly did not intend the granting of such new or expanded rights of inspection under the Act to abrogate shareholders' rights of inspection already existing at common law; instead, it intended that N.C.G.S. § 55–16–02(e)(2) preserve all existing common law rights of inspection of corporate records. In this regard, one leading commentator has correctly noted:

> The North Carolina Business Corporation Act * * * prescribes statutory inspection rights in detail. Those statutory rights are nonexclusive because the present Act expressly provides that they do not affect the power of a court, independent of the Act, to compel the production of corporate records for examination; they also do not affect discovery rights in litigation.

Robinson [on North Carolina Corporation Law (4th ed. 1990)] § 10.1, at 174 (footnotes omitted) (citing N.C.G.S. § 55–16–02(e)(1) and (2)). Both the Official Comment and the North Carolina Commentary to N.C.G.S. § 55–16–02 concur in this view. * * *

has a class of shares registered under Section 12 of the Securities Exchange Act of 1934, as amended (15 U.S.C. § 781)." N.C.G.S. § 55–1–40(18a) (Supp.1992).

N.C.G.S. § 55–16–02(e)(2) expressly provides that "this section" (section 16–02) does not affect "the power of a court, independently of this Chapter, to compel the production of corporate records for examination." The Official Comment states that "Section 16.02(e) provides that the right of inspection granted by section 16.02 is an independent right of inspection that is not a substitute for or in derogation of rights of inspection that may exist * * * as a 'common law' right of inspection, if any is found to exist by a court, to examine corporate records. Section 16.02(e) simply preserves whatever independent right of inspection exists * * *." N.C.G.S. § 55–16–02 official cmt. 4 (1990). * * *

We conclude that N.C.G.S. § 55–16–02(e)(2) preserves a shareholder's common law rights of inspection, including the right to make reasonable inspections of the accounting records of a public corporation for proper purposes. *Cooke*, 265 N.C. at 610, 144 S.E.2d at 841. Further, a shareholder who seeks to exercise her common law right—as opposed to a statutory right—to examine corporate records for a proper purpose also has a common law right to utilize the mandamus power of the courts to compel a reluctant corporation to disclose its corporate records pertinent to that purpose. *State ex rel. Lillie v. Cosgriff Co.*, 240 Neb. 387, 482 N.W.2d 555 (1992). Therefore, we reverse that part of the Court of Appeals' opinion which concluded that the plaintiff in the present case did not retain these common law rights after the adoption of the North Carolina Business Corporation Act.

II.

By her next assignment of error, the plaintiff shareholder contends that the Court of Appeals erred in failing to compel the defendant corporation to provide her with a NOBO list for inspection. A NOBO list is a list of beneficial owners of a corporation's stock who do not object to the disclosure of their names and addresses by the registered owner of the stock (typically, a stock broker or a bank) to the corporation itself for the limited purpose of allowing direct communication on corporate matters. Only recently have NOBO lists been recognized under federal law. When creating the rules requiring banks, stock brokers and dealers to create such lists upon requests by issuing corporations, the Securities and Exchange Commission reviewed the question of whether a corporation's shareholders should themselves be granted the right to compel the production of a NOBO list on the same terms as the issuer of the shares. See Exchange Act Release No. 34–22533, 50 Fed.Reg. 42, 672 (Oct. 22, 1985). However, the Commission has not promulgated any rule providing shareholders with such a right.

A qualified shareholder has a statutory right to inspect a "record of shareholders." N.C.G.S. § 55–16–02(b)(3) (1990). The plaintiff contends that the record of shareholders made available by this statute includes a NOBO list. Our Court of Appeals concluded in the present case that the defendant corporation does not have to provide the plaintiff shareholder with a NOBO list, because the defendant corporation does not have the information needed to create such a list and does not use such a list in communicating with shareholders. We agree.

Other courts have held that where a corporation has obtained a NOBO list and is or will be using it to solicit shareholders, a shareholder should be allowed the same channel of communication. *E.g., Shamrock Associates v.*

Texas American Energy, 517 A.2d 658 (Del.Ch.1986); *Bohrer v. International Banknote Co.*, 150 A.D.2d 196, 540 N.Y.S.2d 445 (1989). However, there is a paucity of cases addressing the issue before us in the present case—whether a corporation must provide a shareholder a NOBO list even though the corporation does not have in its possession the names of its non-objecting beneficial owners and does not use such information to solicit shareholders. * * *

We believe that the legislative intent embodied in N.C.G.S. § 55–16–02(b)(3) is that shareholders be entitled to the information concerning the identity of shareholders which is *possessed by the corporation* in order that they may have the same opportunity as the corporation to communicate with the other shareholders. In order to effectuate that legislative goal, it is necessary that shareholders have access to NOBO lists or other information which the corporation itself has in its possession; however, a shareholder is not granted a right under the statute to require a corporation to obtain NOBO lists or the information necessary to compile NOBO lists when the corporation does not possess or use such information. Since the defendant corporation does not have in its possession a NOBO list or the information needed to compile a NOBO list, it is not required to obtain that information simply because the plaintiff shareholder has requested that it do so for an otherwise proper purpose. Therefore, we affirm that part of the opinion of the Court of Appeals which affirmed the trial court's holding that the defendant corporation was not required to provide the plaintiff with a NOBO list.

III.

In its sole assignment of error, the defendant contends that the Court of Appeals erred in concluding that the plaintiff had satisfied the "reasonable particularity" requirement of N.C.G.S. § 55–16–02(c)(2). This statute provides that a "qualified shareholder may inspect and copy the records described in subsection (b) only if" she describes with reasonable particularity her purpose and the records she desires to inspect. N.C.G.S. § 55–16–02(c)(2) (1990). In her demand, the plaintiff requested:

> For the purpose of determining any possible mismanagement of the Company or any possible misappropriation, misapplication or improper use of any property or asset of the Company, all records of any final action taken, with or without a meeting, by the Board of Directors of the Company, or by a committee of the Board of Directors of the Company while acting in place of the Board of Directors of the Company on behalf of the Company, minutes of any meeting of the shareholders of the Company and records of action taken by the shareholders of the Company without a meeting.

Since no court has yet construed the "reasonable particularity" requirement of N.C.G.S. § 55–16–02(c)(2), we find it helpful to consider the interpretation placed upon the "reasonable particularity" requirement contained in Rule 34(b) of the Federal Rules of Civil Procedure. In determining whether the "reasonable particularity" requirement of this federal rule governing document production has been satisfied, it has been recognized:

> The test must be a relative one, turning on the degree of knowledge that a movant in a particular case has about the documents he requests. In some cases he has such exact and definite knowledge that he can

designate, identify, and enumerate with precision the documents to be produced. This is the ideal designation, since it permits the party responding to go at once to his files and without difficulty produce the document for inspection. But the ideal is not always attainable and Rule 34 does not require the impossible. Even a generalized designation should be sufficient when the party seeking discovery cannot give a more particular description and the party from whom discovery is sought will have no difficulty in understanding what is wanted. The goal is that the designation be sufficient to apprise a man of ordinary intelligence what documents are required.

Charles A. Wright & Arthur R. Miller, *Federal Practice and Procedure* § 2211, at 628–31 (1970). This test is in line with the Official Comment to N.C.G.S. § 55–16–02(c)(2), which provides that under the "reasonable particularity" requirement, a shareholder should make more meaningful statements of purpose and the desired records when "feasible." Whether a shareholder has described his purpose or the desired records with reasonable particularity necessarily depends upon the facts and circumstances of each case.

In the present case, the record does not show that the plaintiff had any specific knowledge of corporate mismanagement or of any improper use of corporate assets at the time that she made the demand. The record shows only that the plaintiff was dissatisfied with the return on her investment in the defendant corporation. In light of the plaintiff's actual knowledge at the time of the demand, it would not have been feasible to state her purpose with any greater particularity. In addition, the plaintiff specifically described the desired records in her demand. The plaintiff sought "all records of any final action taken by the Board or by a committee of the Board, the minutes of any meeting of the shareholders, and records of action taken by the shareholders of the Company without a meeting." Although the plaintiff's demand was broad, we agree with the Court of Appeals' determination that there is nothing in this record to show that the plaintiff could have described the desired records with any greater particularity than she did, and the defendant company should not have had any trouble understanding what the plaintiff desired. Assuming *arguendo* that N.C.G.S. § 55–16–02(c) controls situations in which a shareholder exercises a common law right of inspection, as well as situations in which the statutory right is being exercised, we conclude that the plaintiff described both her purpose and the desired records with the "reasonable particularity" required by that statute. This assignment of error is overruled. * * *

Affirmed in part; reversed in part; and remanded.

Notes

(1) *Parsons* was decided on March 12, 1993. On October 1, 1993, North Carolina added the following new paragraph (i) to § 55–16–02:

(i) Notwithstanding the provisions of this section, or any other provisions of this Chapter or interpretations thereof to the contrary, a shareholder of a public corporation shall have no common law rights to inspect or copy any accounting records of the corporation or any other records of the corporation that may not be inspected or copied by a shareholder of a public corporation as provided in G.S. 55–16–02(b).

Do you believe that the addition of this section is desirable? As a result of this amendment, may a shareholder ever obtain more complete information about a public corporation's financial affairs than provided in the SEC-required disclosures?

(2) NOBOs are discussed in Chapter 10, Section B(3). See also Randall S. Thomas, Improving Shareholder Monitoring and Corporate Management by Expanding Statutory Access to Information, 38 Ariz.L.Rev. 331, 332, n. 8 (1996).

(3) Enforcement of inspection rights has long been a problem. Prior to the enactment of statutes dealing specifically with shareholder inspection rights, the normal reaction of management to an inspection request was to refuse to provide anything, which required the shareholder to go to court. In an effort to make the inspection right more meaningful and less costly to shareholders, a variety of statutory inspection rights were created. Some placed the burden of showing an improper purpose on the corporation while others imposed penalties on corporate officers that failed to accord inspection rights without reasonable cause. Some statutes required the corporation to pay a successful shareholder's expenses. The MBCA now addresses the enforcement problem in MBCA § 16.04.

(4) A related problem arises with respect to the scope of the inspection itself. An inspection is not very useful to a shareholder if, for example, the corporation produces a list of 26,000 shareholders of record at the corporation's principal office, but then refuses a request that a copy be provided and refuses a further request that the shareholder be permitted to make a xerographic copy of the list. An inspection right is also of limited usefulness if the corporation refuses to permit the shareholder to be accompanied by his attorney and accountant when inspecting the records. MBCA § 16.03 is intended to provide comprehensive answers to such problems.

(5) Many states adopting streamlined inspection rights limited them to "eligible" shareholders, usually defining eligible shareholders as those holding a specified number of shares or holding a number of shares for some period of time. The Model Act did not include these restrictions on the theory that they were not effective, but North Carolina retained these restrictions through its definition of "qualified shareholder" in § 55–16–02(g). Do you think that the drafters of the Model Act should have retained these restrictions?

Index

References are to Pages

WHISTLEBLOWERS
Sarbanes-Oxley Act protections, 115, 658

WILLIAMS ACT
  Generally, 981
  Preemption of state antitakeover laws, 989

†